IMPORTANT:

HERE IS YOUR REGISTRATION CODE TO ACCESS YOUR PREMIUM McGRAW-HILL RYERSON ONLINE RESOURCES.*

For key premium online resources you need THIS CODE to gain access. Once the code is entered, you will be able to use the Web resources for a period of six months.

Access is provided if you have purchased a new book. If you purchased a used book, the registration code may have expired, or been previously accessed. If the registration code is invalid, the registration screen on our Website will tell you how to purchase a new code.

Registering for McGraw-Hill Ryerson Online Resources

To gain access to your McGraw-Hill web resources simply follow the steps below:

1. USE YOUR WEB BROWSER TO GO TO: **http://www.mcgrawhill.ca/college/nickels**, CHOOSING THE HYPERLINK TO 5TH EDITION.
2. CLICK ON **FIRST TIME USER**.
3. CLICK ON **I AM A STUDENT**.
4. CLICK ON **I HAVE A REGISTRATION CODE**.
5. ENTER THE REGISTRATION CODE* PRINTED ON THE RED SECTION ON THE RIGHT.
6. AFTER YOU HAVE ENTERED YOUR REGISTRATION CODE, CLICK **CONTINUE**.
7. FOLLOW THE INSTRUCTIONS TO SET-UP YOUR PERSONAL UserID AND PASSWORD.
8. WRITE YOUR UserID AND PASSWORD DOWN FOR FUTURE REFERENCE. KEEP IT IN A SAFE PLACE.

Thank you, and welcome to your McGraw-Hill Ryerson online Resources!

McGraw-Hill Ryerson

MCGRAW-HILL RYERSON
ONLINE RESOURCES

REGISTRATION CODE

QXFT-UTNV-63JQ-GQ7G-JBPQ

McGraw-Hill Ryerson

0-07-092199-7 NICKELS: UNDERSTANDING CANADIAN BUSINESS, 5/E

Edition 5

Understanding Canadian Business

WILLIAM G. NICKELS

University of Maryland

JAMES M. McHUGH

St. Louis Community College at Forest Park

SUSAN M. McHUGH

Applied Learning Systems

PAUL D. BERMAN

Retired Chartered Accountant and Professor of Business

RITA COSSA

McMaster University

McGraw-Hill Ryerson

Toronto Montréal Boston Burr Ridge, IL Dubuque, IA Madison, WI New York
San Francisco St. Louis Bangkok Bogotá Caracas Kuala Lumpur Lisbon London Madrid
Mexico City Milan New Delhi Santiago Seoul Singapore Sydney Taipei

The *McGraw·Hill* Companies

McGraw-Hill
Ryerson

UNDERSTANDING CANADIAN BUSINESS
Fifth Edition

ISBN: 0-07-092199-7

2 3 4 5 6 7 8 9 10 QP 0 9 8 7 6

Printed and bound in the U.S.

Statistics Canada information is used with the permission of the Minister of Industry, as Minister responsible for Statistics Canada. Information on the availability of the wide range of data from Statistics Canada can be obtained from Statistics Canada's Regional Offices, its World Wide Web site at http://www.statcan.ca, and its toll-free access number 1-800-263-1136.

Vice President, Editorial and Media Technology: *Pat Ferrier*
Sponsoring Editor: *Kim Brewster*
Senior Marketing Manager: *Kelly Smyth*
Developmental Editors: *Tracey Haggert/Lori McLellan*
Production Coordinator: *Paula Brown*
Supervising Editor: *Anne Nellis*
Copy Editor: *Kelli Howey*
Cover Design: *Greg Devitt*
Interior Designer: *Diane Beasley*
Cover Image Credit: *Douglas E. Walker/Masterfile*
Permissions Researcher: *Christina Beamish*
Composition: *SR Nova Pvt Ltd, Bangalore, India*
Printer: *Quebecor Printing, Dubuque*

Library and Archives Canada Cataloguing in Publication

Understanding Canadian business / William G. Nickels ... [et al.]. — 5th ed.

Includes bibliographical references and index.
ISBN 0-07-092199-7

1. Industrial management. 2. Business. I. Nickels, William G.
HD31.U5135 2004   650   C2004-905849-5

Credit for profile on page 125:
Sources: "Notes for an address by Sheila Fraser" (8 May 2002), Toronto: Certified General Accountants Association of Canada. Retrieved from the World Wide Web: http://www.cga-canada.org/eng/news/economic_lunch_may02.pdf; "IGNORING THE FISCAL WATCHDOG: Auditor-General's reports of gov't waste fail to spur reforms," (March 2003), Ottawa: Canadian Centre for Policy Alternatives. Retrieved from the World Wide Web: http://www.policyalternatives.ca/publications /articles/article362.html; "Guarding the Public Purse" (2003), Toronto: The Institute of Chartered Accountants of Ontario. Retrieved from the World Wide Web: http://www.icao.on.ca/index.cfm/ci_id/416.htm; Ed Finn; "About the Auditor General" (June 2003), Ottawa: Office of the Auditor General of Canada. Retrieved from the World Wide Web: http://www.oag-bvg.gc.ca/domino/other.nsf/html/ 00agbio_e.html; Les Whittington, "At war with waste and corruption," Toronto Star, 11 October, 2003, sec. H, p. 4; www.oag-bvg.gc.ca, November 23, 2003; Auditor General's Report 2004 (11 February 2004), Ottawa: CBC News. Retrieved 25 May 2004 from http://www.cbc.ca/news/background/auditorgeneral/report2004.html.

Dedication

To my husband, Stephen, for his love and support.

Rita Cossa.

To my thousands of students of varying cultures, ages, interests, and abilities—who

taught me so much. And to all other students who, I hope, will find this text useful in

their studies and when thinking about their future careers.

Paul D. Berman.

Brief Contents

Contents

PART 3

Leadership, Organization, and Production to Satisfy Customers

CHAPTER 8

Management and Leadership 216

CHAPTER 9

Adapting Organizations to Today's Markets 248

PART 6

Accounting Information and Financial Activities

CHAPTER 16

Understanding Accounting and Financial Information 484

CHAPTER 17

Financial Management 520

About the Authors

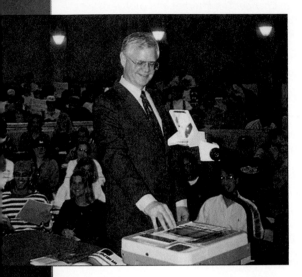

BILL NICKELS is an associate professor of business at The University of Maryland, College Park. With over 30 years of teaching experience, he teaches introduction to business in large sections (250 students) every semester. He teaches smaller sections in the summer. He also teaches the marketing principles course to large sections (500 students). Bill has won the Outstanding Teacher on Campus Award four times. He received his M.B.A. degree from Western Reserve University and his Ph.D. from The Ohio State University. He has written a marketing communications text and two marketing principles texts in addition to many articles in business publications. He believes in living a balanced life and wrote a book called *Win the Happiness Game* to share his secrets with others. Bill gives marketing and general business lectures to a variety of business and nonprofit organizations. Bill and his wife, Marsha, proudly anticipate the impending graduation of their son, Joel, who will become the third Dr. Nickels in the family.

JIM McHUGH is an associate professor of business at St. Louis Community College/Forest Park. He holds an M.B.A. degree from Lindenwood University and has broad experience in education, business, and government. In addition to teaching several sections of introduction to business each semester for 20 years, Jim maintains an adjunct professorship at Lindenwood University, teaching in the marketing and management areas at both the undergraduate and graduate levels. Jim has conducted numerous seminars in business, and maintains several consulting positions with small and large business enterprises. He is also actively involved in the public service sector.

SUSAN McHUGH is a learning specialist with extensive training and experience in adult learning and curriculum development. She holds a M.Ed. degree from the University of Missouri and has completed her course work for a Ph.D. in education administration with a specialty in adult learning theory. As a professional curriculum developer, she has directed numerous curriculum projects and educator training programs. She has worked in the public and private sector as a consultant in training and employee development. While Jim and Susan treasure their participation in the *UCB* project, their greatest accomplishment is their collaboration on their three children, Casey, Molly, and Michael, who have all grown up regarding *UCB* as a fourth sibling. Casey was a fervent user of the 4th edition, Molly eagerly anticipates using this edition, and Michael will have to wait for the next edition.

PAUL D. BERMAN founded a firm of chartered accountants and was actively engaged in the fields of management consulting, auditing, and taxation for 35 years. These activities involved considerable time overseas. He then went on to John Abbott College near Montreal, where he taught a variety of business courses for more than two decades. After a decade of teaching International Business Policy at McGill University, Paul retired in 1999.

Paul's academic work has also taken him overseas. He has taken students to Denmark and the former East Germany to study these countries' education systems and how they do business. In the late 1980s Paul spent considerable time in China, under a CIDA program, teaching, lecturing, and doing management consulting. This led to a special award from China's highest economic body, the State Economic Commission. Paul has also spent time in Japan, where he engaged in a joint research project with Japanese colleagues, and he has conducted seminars in several countries. Paul has also written a book on small business and entrepreneurship.

RITA COSSA has been teaching in the DeGroote School of Business at McMaster University since 1999. She teaches two of the larger undergraduate courses, which are Business Environment & Organization and Introduction to Marketing. Rita has also taught Marketing Concepts and Applications (M.B.A.-level) and Marketing in the Non-Profit Sector. Prior to teaching, Rita held several management positions in the financial services industry. Upon completion of her M.B.A., she began her academic career, where she has since been nominated for several teaching awards. A co-author on the previous edition, Rita is now the sole Canadian author for this edition. When she is not working, Rita enjoys spending time with her husband, Stephen, and their daughter, Mattia.

Preface

As authors, it is thrilling to see the results of the work we love be embraced by colleagues in colleges and universities across Canada. *Understanding Canadian Business* has been designed to introduce students to the exciting topic of business. It also provides insight into career choices and opportunities, as well as a look at the ethical dilemmas businesses and managers face.

This book marks the fifth Canadian edition of the most popular introductory business text in Canada. This edition has undergone major revisions to reflect the marketplace today. Most of the examples cited are Canadian companies or transnational companies operating in Canada. The number of chapters, 18, was decided on after careful thought and discussion. This number takes into consideration the limitations of the 13- to 15-week semester or term commonly found in Canada, and students' capacity to absorb information.

Faculty who teach the course and students who have used the book and its supplements were formally involved in various stages of our research and writing of this edition. Prior to writing this edition, we held various close-to-the-customer focus groups in several cities across the country. Discussions with instructors and students in these sessions helped us define, clarify, and test the needs of the diverse group who teach and take this course.

Additionally, more than 36 instructors provided us with in-depth evaluations of the fifth edition. Their insights for improvements are reflected on every page of this edition. Once the first draft was written, another group of instructors critiqued our initial effort, which led to many more important refinements. While this is an extensive product development process, we consider this talking about and sharing of ideas with colleagues and students critical if we are to produce a book that reflects what students should be learning about business in Canada and around the world.

Below are a few of the changes and improvements made in response to the recommendations from some dedicated educators and reviewers.

KEEPING UP WITH WHAT'S NEW

Users of *Understanding Canadian Business* have always appreciated the currency of the material and the large number of examples from companies of all sizes and industries (e.g., service, manufacturing, profit and nonprofit) in Canada and around the world. Accordingly, this edition features the latest business practices and other developments affecting business, including

- privacy and security issues with information technology;
- corporate scandals;
- the latest changes in the Euro;
- e-commerce's impact on the role of intermediaries;
- the most recent population trends;
- the relevance of business law;
- online banking and smart cards;

- issues regarding the World Bank and IMF;
- the latest quality standards;
- storing and mining data;

and much, much more.

NEW ADDITIONS

Chapter 18: The Financial Services Industry in Canada   Money, banking, investing, insurance, financing, and financial planning are just some of the areas represented by the financial services industry in Canada. Given its importance to our economy and its relevance to our daily lives, reviewers felt that a chapter dedicated to this topic would add depth to their students' education.

Appendix A: Using Technology to Manage Information   The use of the Internet as a business tool has resulted in the rethinking and restructuring of traditional business relationships. Such changes are introduced in each chapter so that students can see how these new developments are impacting every aspect of business. In response to reviewer feedback that some programs cover this topic in a separate course, we created this appendix to provide a background for those that required it.

Appendix B: Working within the Legal Environment of Business   Laws are an essential part of a civilized nation. They are created and enforced to protect consumers, as well as to promote fair and competitive business practices. This appendix provides a foundation for students in understanding the importance of laws to the Canadian marketplace.

Dealing With Change   One of the major themes in this text is managing change. In response, we have integrated new focus boxes, called "Dealing With Change," throughout the text that discuss the rapidly changing business environment and the need to adjust to these changes. In addition, we continue to feature boxes titled "Spotlight on Small Business," "Making Ethical Decisions," and "Reaching Beyond Our Borders" throughout the text.

Online Learning Centre: Managing Personal Finances to Achieve Financial Security   Building on Chapter 18, this supplement will, on a more personal note, review how students can control their assets. They will be introduced to ways they can build a financial base, buy the appropriate insurance, and develop a strategy for retiring with enough money to last a lifetime.

We firmly believe that no course in school is more important than the introduction to business course. That's why we are willing to spend so much time helping others make this the best course on campus. We are proud of the text and the integrated teaching and testing system that you have helped us develop over the years. We thank the many text and supplements users who have supported us through the years and welcome new instructors to the team. We look forward to a continuing relationship with all of you and to sharing what we consider the most rewarding classroom experience possible: teaching introduction to business.

Acknowledgements

Many friends, colleagues, academics, entrepreneurs, managers, and students have made important contributions, in different ways, to *Understanding Canadian Business*. There are too many to be able to thank them all individually. We would like to single out the reviewers and focus group participants from several cities who, on several occasions, took the time to review and discuss different versions of the manuscript for the fifth edition and made invaluable suggestions to improve its quality, coverage, and supplements package. We would like to extend our deepest thanks to all of these people, some of whose names are listed below:

Bob Sproule, University of Waterloo

Carson Rappell, Dawson College

Christopher Gadsby, British Columbia Institute of Technology

David Fleming, George Brown College

Diane Gauvin, Dawson College

Don Haidey, Mount Royal College

Ed Leach, Dalhousie University

Erica Morrill, Fanshawe College

Helen Stavaris, Dawson College

Jane Forbes, Seneca College

Jenny Yang, Seneca College

Jim Ridler, Queen's University

John Cavaliere, Sault College

Kate Muller, Humber College

Keith Hebblewhite, Seneca College

Laura Allan, Wilfrid Laurier University

Les Miscampbell, Centennial College

Lydia Dragunas, Champlain College

Michael LeRoy, University of British Columbia

Peter Mombourquette, Mount Saint Vincent University

Richard Powers, University of Toronto

Ted Brown, Langara College

Terry Wu, University of Ontario Institute of Technology

Thomas McKaig, Ryerson University

Victoria Digby, Fanshawe College

Wendy Rotenberg, University of Toronto

Will Thurber, Brock University

We would also like to thank Ray Klapstein of Dalhousie University, who contributed Appendix B, "Working within the Legal Environment of Business."

Focus Group Participants

Carson Rappell, Dawson College

Christine Tomchak, Humber College

Debra Warren, Centennial College

Diane Gauvin, Dawson College

Elaine Daigle, George Brown College

Erica Morrill, Fanshawe College

Helen Stavaris, Dawson College

Jane Forbes, Seneca College

Jenny Yang, Seneca College

Kate Muller, Humber College

Lydia Dragunas, Champlain College

Michael Hockenstein, Vanier College

Orrin Benn, Seneca College

Thomas McKaig, Ryerson University

Many thanks are also due to the following McGraw-Hill Ryerson staff who worked hard to make this book a reality: Kim Brewster, Sponsoring Editor; Tracey Haggert and Lori McLellan, Developmental Editors; Anne Nellis, Supervising Editor; Kelly Dickson, Manager, Editorial Services and Design; Kelli Howey, Copy Editor; Christina Beamish, Photos and Permissions; Greg Devitt, Designer; and Paula Brown, Production Coordinator.

Paul would like to "extend many thanks to my children, Victor, David, Joanne, Judith, and Rae. I owe them a great deal for their patience and co-operation as I plied them with questions and requests relating to their various fields of expertise. I would also like to thank my three grandsons—Eric, Jamie, and Michel—for their help in giving me incisive comments on the current thinking of undergraduate and graduate students as well as young entrepreneurs. Finally, I would like to express my deep appreciation to my wife, Esther Berman, whose patience, direct and indirect assistance in so many ways, and critical comments over an extended period of time really made this book possible."

Rita would like to "extend my deepest appreciation to all the business professionals who allowed me to highlight their company practices as well as their own business careers. With this information, students can take a peek into different businesses and they can start to consider the many options that are open to them. A special thank you is extended to Dr. Maureen Hupfer for sharing her insight into western Canada; your articles, company, and entrepreneur suggestions were most appreciated."

Paul D. Berman

Rita Cossa

Presenting a
Special Visual Tour of

Understanding Canadian Business

5th edition

Before students can begin to understand today's business world, you'll have to provide them the most up-to-date and relevant material. With help from reviews and focus groups, *Understanding Canadian Business* provides a unified collection of educational tools. This combination of text and visual media works together to teach students everything they should know before entering the real world of business.

This special walkthrough section was developed to highlight the new and retained features that have made this text the clear market leader. After reading through this material, if you still have questions, please contact your local McGraw-Hill Ryerson *i*-Learning Sales Specialist.

"the most up-to-date and
relevant material"

Integration of Important Concepts throughout the Text

Based on research and the preferences expressed by both users and nonusers of *Understanding Canadian Business*, the following key topics are incorporated as themes throughout the text:

- Constant change
- Small business and entrepreneurship
- Global business
- Technology and change
- Pleasing customers
- Ethics and social responsibility
- Teams
- Quality
- E-commerce
- Cultural diversity

These themes reflect a strong consensus among introduction to business instructors that certain topics deserve and need special emphasis. Among these, they encouraged us to add particular focus in the areas of small business/entrepreneurship, ethics, global business, and e-commerce. In response, this edition includes many small business, global, and Internet examples throughout. It continues to feature boxes titled "Spotlight on Small Business," "Making Ethical Decisions," and "Reaching Beyond Our Borders" in every chapter. And…

…A NEW box has been added called "Dealing With Change." This feature emphasizes the importance of the dynamic nature of business.

Learning Business Skills That Will Last a Lifetime

To help your students connect what they learn in class to the world outside, it is important that they understand five key workplace competencies:

1. Resource skills
2. Interpersonal skills
3. Information ability
4. Systems understanding
5. Technology ability

Throughout the fifth edition of *Understanding Canadian Business*, several pedagogical devices are used to help students master these skills.

Learning Goals

Tied directly to the summaries at the end of the chapter and to the test questions, the Learning Goals help students preview what they should know after reading the chapter, and then test that knowledge by answering the questions in the summary.

Developing Workplace Skills

The Developing Workplace Skills section has activities designed to increase student involvement in the learning process. Some of these miniprojects require library or Internet searches, while others can be used as team activities either in or out of the classroom.

Cross-Reference System

This system, unique to this text, refers students back to the primary discussion and examples of key concepts. A specific page reference appears when a key concept occurs in a chapter subsequent to its original discussion, which eliminates the need to continuously revisit and restate key concepts, thus reducing overall text length.

Getting to Know Business Professionals

Each chapter begins with a profile of a person whose career relates closely to the material covered in the chapter. Not all the personalities are famous, since many of them work in small businesses and nonprofit organizations. Getting to know these business professionals provides the perfect transition to the text material.

"increase student involvement in the learning process"

Video Cases  CBC ◉

Video cases are provided for each chapter. They feature companies, processes, practices, and managers that highlight and bring to life the key concepts, and especially the themes, of the fifth edition.

Practising Management Decisions

Each chapter concludes with a case to allow students to practise managerial decision making. They are intentionally brief and meant to be discussion starters rather than comprehensive cases that could require the entire class period.

Photo and Illustration Essays

More and more students have expressed that they are visually oriented learners; therefore, this increased emphasis on the pedagogical value of the illustrations is essential. Each photo and illustration in the text is accompanied by a short essay that highlights the relevance of the visuals to the material in the text.

We are seeing more examples of co-branding. For example, Tim Hortons kiosks can be found in numerous Esso Tiger Express outlets in Canada. As well, there are Tim Hortons/Wendy's combo stores. These combo units have their own separate counter, kitchen, and drive-through, but they share the dining area. Have you seen examples of this in your area?

distributing a good or service, or both, to achieve a maximum market impact with a minimum investment.

Some people develop ideas and build a winning good or service that they attempt to exploit through a franchise agreement. A **franchise agreement** is an arrangement whereby someone with a good idea for a business (the **franchisor**) sells to another (the **franchisee**) the rights to use the business name and sell a product in a given territory. As you might suspect, both franchisors and franchisees have a stake in the success of the **franchise.**

So what looks like a chain of stores—Canadian Tire, Quizno's Sub, Buck or Two—is usually a franchise operation with each unit owned by a different person or company; they are all part of a franchise operation, as explained in the previous paragraph. Sometimes one person or group m...

franchise agreement
An arrangement whereby someone with a good idea for a business sells the rights to use the business name and sell its products in a given territory.

franchisor
A company that d...

Progress Assessments

If students are not understanding and retaining the material, Progress Assessments will stop them and show them that they need to review before proceeding. The Progress Assessment is a proven learning tool that helps students comprehend and retain the material.

Taking It to the Net Exercises

Each chapter contains Taking It to the Net exercises that allow students to research topics and issues on the Web and make decisions based on their research.

Critical Thinking Questions

Found in each chapter, Critical Thinking Questions ask students to pause and think about how the material they are reading applies to their own lives.

Interactive Summaries

The end-of-chapter summaries are directly tied with the learning goals and are written in a question-and-answer format.

The Latest in Technology

Perhaps the fastest-changing and most dynamic element of business today is the use of the Internet. Many new e-businesses have already come and gone, but even in failure they have left in their wake a new way of doing business. Although the business-to-business market is in a state of flux, use of the Internet as a dynamic business tool has resulted in the rethinking and restructuring of traditional business relationships, redesign of supply chains, and many other new ways of conducting and facilitating customer interaction.

The fifth edition of *Understanding Canadian Business* integrates Web material throughout the text along with useful components that work flawlessly with the text.

Online Learning Centre

www.mcgrawhill.ca/college/nickels

The McGraw-Hill Online Learning Centre is an interactive site that includes such features as links to professional resources and other exciting instructor support tools as well as Web-based projects. Some student features include video streaming; Student Success Tool Kit for concept mastery; crossword puzzles that help review key terms; additional chapter quizzes; and conceptual assessment questions.

Primis Online

McGraw-Hill's Primis Online gives you access to the most abundant resource at your fingertips—literally. With a few mouse clicks, you can create customized learning tools simply and affordably. McGraw-Hill Ryerson has included many of our market-leading textbooks within Primis Online for eBook and print customization as well as many licensed readings and cases.

Business Plan Software and Manual

For those who include business planning as part of their course, this business planning CD is available for optional packaging with the text along with a user manual. This new manual includes exercises based on the modules in the software, as well as a semester-long project. The new Business Mentor leads students through the sections of the feasibility and business plans.

Team Learning Assistant

Team Learning Assistant (TLA) is an interactive online resource that monitors team members' participation in a peer review. The program is designed to maximize the students' team learning experience, and to save professors and students valuable time. (Available as an optional package.)

Intro to Business Simulations

Mike's Bikes:
Ask your *i*-Learning Sales Specialist about our next-generation interactive business simulations, designed specifically for an Intro to Business course.

PowerWeb Helps Keep Your Course Up to Date

PowerWeb provides the easiest way to integrate current real-world content with this latest edition of *Understanding Canadian Business*. Experienced instructors have culled articles and essays from a wide range of periodicals including *Canadian Business, The Globe and Mail, BusinessWeek, Forbes*, and many others.

Now you can access PowerWeb articles and updates specifically created to accompany *Understanding Canadian Business* through the text's Online Learning Centre (www.mcgrawhill.ca/college/nickels) and see firsthand what PowerWeb can mean to your course. (Available as an optional package.)

PowerWeb to Go is new and allows you to download PowerWeb content to your PDA for a minimal price.

Create an Online Course Today!

If you are interested in educating students online, McGraw-Hill Ryerson offers *Understanding Canadian Business* content for complete online courses. We have joined forces with the most popular delivery platforms available, such as WebCT and Blackboard. These platforms have been designed for instructors who want complete control over course content and how it is presented to their students. You can customize the *Understanding Canadian Business* Online Learning Centre content or author your own course materials—it's entirely up to you. Remember, the content of *Understanding Canadian Business* is flexible enough to use with any platform currently available (and it's free). If your department or school is already using a platform, we can certainly help.

PageOut is the easiest way to create a Website for your introductory business course. There's no need for HTML coding, graphic design, or a thick how-to book. Just fill in a series of boxes and click on one of our professional designs. In no time at all, your course is online.

If you need assistance in preparing your course Website, our team of product specialists is ready to help you take your course materials and build a custom Website. Simply contact your McGraw-Hill Ryerson *i*-Learning Sales Specialist to start the process. Best of all, PageOut is free when you adopt *Understanding Canadian Business*! To learn more, please visit www.pageout.net.

The Best Instructional Materials

All the supplements that are available with the fifth edition of *Understanding Canadian Business* were originally developed by the authors to help instructors use their class time more effectively and make this course more practical and interesting for students. Users say that no introductory business text package is as market responsive, easy to use, and fully integrated as this one.

Preparation

Instructor's Manual

All material in the Instructor's Manual (IM) is easy to use and has been widely praised by new instructors and experienced educators alike. Many instructors tell us that the IM is a valuable time-saver. Lecture outlines contain supplementary cases, Critical Thinking exercises, and more.

Online Learning Centre

www.mcgrawhill.ca/college/nickels
Your interactive instructor site features downloadable supplements, additional cases, and more.

Instructor's Presentation CD-ROM

ISBN: 0-07-093778-8
The Instructor's Manual, the PowerPoint slides, and Test Bank, are compiled in electronic format on a CD for your convenience in customizing multimedia lectures.

The Integrator

The Integrator is your road map to all the elements of your text's support package. Keyed to the chapters and topics of *Understanding Canadian Business,* the Integrator ties together all of the elements in your resource package, guiding you to where you'll find corresponding coverage in each of the related support package components.

Testing

Computerized Test Bank

The *Understanding Canadian Business* Test Bank is designed to test three levels of learning:

1. Knowledge of key terms.
2. Understanding of concepts and principles.
3. Application of principles.

A rationale for the correct answer and the corresponding text page add to the uniqueness of the 3,000+ question Test Bank, as does the fact that the Test Bank asks questions about the boxed material in the text. It comes in a computerized version that allows users to add and edit questions; save and reload multiple test versions; select questions based on type, difficulty, or key word; and utilize password protection.

Presentation Tools

Videos CBC ⚛

Most segments are 8 to 15 minutes in length and are suitable for classroom, home, or lab viewing. The video package is available on VHS tapes, on-line streaming, or in DVD format for those professors who have access to a DVD player in the classroom. This allows for easy selection of the video you'd like to watch through a simple menu.

PowerPoint

Over 500 slides keyed to the text are available and include many additional slides that support and expand the text discussion. These slides can be modified with PowerPoint and are also available on the Instructor's CD and the Online Learning Centre.

eInstruction's Classroom Performance System (CPS)

Bring interactivity into the classroom or lecture hall.

CPS is a student response system using wireless connectivity. It gives instructors and students immediate feedback from the entire class. The response pads are remotes that are easy to use and engage students.

- **CPS** helps you to increase **student preparation, interactivity, and active learning** so you can receive immediate feedback and know what students understand.
- **CPS** allows you to administer quizzes and tests, and provide **immediate grading.**
- With **CPS** you can create lecture questions that can be multiple-choice, true/false, and subjective. You can even create questions on-the-fly as well as conduct group activities.
- **CPS** not only allows you to **evaluate classroom attendance, activity, and grading** for your course as a whole, but CPSOnline allows you to provide students with an immediate study guide. All results and scores can easily be imported into Excel and can be used with various classroom management systems.

CPS-ready content is available for use with *Understanding Canadian Business*. Please contact your *i*-Learning Sales Specialist for more information on how you can integrate CPS into your introduction to business classroom.

"easy to use, and fully integrated"

Online Learning Centre for Concept Mastery and Student Success

This student website contains quizzes, Internet exercises, crossword puzzles, video streaming, and a new Student Success Toolkit for concept mastery. This toolkit, with free access provided with each new copy of the text, adds another dimension to the text's lessons for students.

Approximately 25 additional practice exam questions for every chapter, modelled on but not taken from the Test Bank, are included. The presented assessment questions test students' ability to apply the concepts they've learned in the chapter to different situations.

To help many of our ESL students understand the key term definitions, the Toolkit contains glossary translations in Spanish, in Russian, and in both Traditional and Simplified Mandarin Chinese.

Student Assessment and Learning Aid

ISBN: 007093834-2

The Student Assessment and Learning Aid contains various forms of open-ended questions, key term review, practice test and answers, and Internet exercises to help students be successful in the introduction to business course.

Study to Go

Study to Go is a fun new PDA feature. Students can download (for free) digital content from the *Understanding Canadian Business* Website onto their Pocket PC or PDA. There they'll have mobile access to flashcards, quizzes, and key terms from the book. With Study to Go students can study anytime, anywhere.

E-STAT   Σ-STAT

E-STAT is Statistics Canada's education resource that allows instructors and students to view socio-economic and demographic data in charts, graphs, and maps. Access to E-STAT and the CANSIM II database is made available from the student Online Learning Centre.

Superior Service

Service takes on a whole new meaning with McGraw-Hill Ryerson and *Understanding Canadian Business*. More than just bringing you the textbook, we have consistently raised the bar in terms of innovation and educational research—both in introduction to business and in education in general. These investments in learning and the education community have helped us to understand the needs of students and educators across the country, and allowed us to foster the growth of truly innovative, integrated learning.

Integrated Learning

Your Integrated Learning Sales Specialist is a McGraw-Hill Ryerson representative who has the experience, product knowledge, training, and support to help you assess and integrate any of our products, technology, and services into your course for optimum teaching and learning performance. Whether it's using our test bank software, helping your students improve their grades, or putting your entire course online, your *i*-Learning Sales Specialist is there to help you do it. Contact your local *i*-Learning Sales Specialist today to learn how to maximize all of McGraw-Hill Ryerson's resources!

i-Learning Services Program

McGraw-Hill Ryerson offers a unique *i*Services package designed for Canadian faculty. Our mission is to equip providers of higher education with superior tools and resources required for excellence in teaching. For additional information, visit www.mcgrawhill.ca/highereducation/iservices.

Teaching, Technology & Learning Conference Series

The educational environment has changed tremendously in recent years, and McGraw-Hill Ryerson continues to be committed to helping you acquire the skills you need to succeed in this new milieu. Our innovative Teaching, Technology & Learning Conference Series brings faculty together from across Canada with 3M Teaching Excellence award winners to share teaching and learning best practices in a collaborative and stimulating environment. Preconference workshops on general topics, such as teaching large classes and technology integration, will also be offered. We will also work with you at your own institution to customize workshops that best suit the needs of your faculty at your institution.

Research Reports into Mobile Learning and Student Success

These landmark reports, undertaken in conjunction with academic and private-sector advisory boards, are the result of research studies into the challenges professors face in helping students succeed and the opportunities that new technology presents to impact teaching and learning. Please contact your local *i*-Learning Sales Specialist to obtain copies, or visit www.mcgrawhill.ca/highereducation/eservices.

PART 1

Chapter 1

Managing within the Dynamic Business Environment

Learning Goals

After you have read and studied this chapter, you should be able to

1 Describe the relationship of businesses' profit to risk assumption.

2 Discuss the groups that are considered stakeholders and indicate which stakeholders are most important to a business.

3 Explain the importance of entrepreneurship to the wealth of an economy.

4 Review the six elements that make up the business environment and explain why the business environment is important to organizations.

5 Identify various ways in which businesses can meet and beat competition.

6 Understand how the service sector has replaced manufacturing as the principal provider of jobs, but why manufacturing remains vital for Canada.

Getting to Know Meg Whitman from eBay

Going, going, gone! Meg Whitman, president and chief executive officer (CEO) of eBay Inc., has turned an online auction site into one of the world's biggest dot-com success stories. When she took over eBay, it had $6 million in revenues. Today, it is closer to $476 million. This is based on trades of about $14 billion a year.

How did Whitman get to such a lofty position? She began her career in product management at Procter & Gamble. That experience led to 10 years in consulting with Bain & Company. From there, Whitman went to Disney, where, among her other accomplishments, she opened the first Disney store in Japan. She then moved on to Stride Rite, where she added to her reputation by revising the Keds brand. Her successes led to her becoming the CEO of Florists' Transworld Delivery (FTD) and launching FTD's Internet strategy. That experience proved invaluable to her long-term career. In the interim, she went to Hasbro's Playskool division—which you may know as the maker of Mr. Potato Head.

With such a successful career, not to mention two children, Whitman did not need any new challenges. When eBay asked her to come to California, she hesitated. But the potential was too much to deny, so she moved her family and took up the daunting task of running eBay.

eBay began as an Internet auction company that resembled an online garage sale. The process involved bidding for items—mostly used goods—and waiting to see if others outbid you. It turned out to be a wonderful way of selling stuff that was cluttering up the house. It also became a great way to find collectors' items and goods of all kinds. Suddenly people had a way of buying and selling used goods as well as new but unneeded items they received for weddings, birthdays, and other events. Today customers are so devoted to the site that they don't consider themselves "bidding" for items as much as "winning" them. But just how did Meg Whitman turn an online auction process into a profitable business?

First, because some people wanted to buy items outright and not get involved in a bidding war, Whitman bought a company that bought and sold goods at set prices. Now Whitman can offer all kinds of goods at fixed prices. But what kinds of goods? eBay has more than 50,000 categories of saleable items. They range from garage-sale-type items to more expensive goods such as homes, antiques, and cars. The question becomes, Where does it stop? Should the company get more involved in business-to-business (B2B) sales? How will it expand overseas? Whitman's goal is to make overseas sales reach half of eBay's total sales.

eBay has operations in 28 countries, including Canada, which is now its fourth-largest market. Burnaby, B.C., is the site of a new customer support centre; it was chosen because eBay wanted to have a culturally diverse and technologically savvy workforce capable of communicating with users in Canada, Australia, and the United States.

The Canadian site, eBay.ca, was launched in April 2000. Since its launch, eBay.ca has continued to show impressive growth. According to comScore Media Metrix, eBay was visited by more than 10.5 million unique Canadian visitors in February 2004. In the same month, eBay.ca was visited by one in two Canadians online. eBay.ca is the most visited Canadian retail site, and also number one for total time spent on any retail site, at an average of 45.2 minutes per user.

You can see that eBay faces all kinds of environmental challenges: technological, competitive, economic, social, and political. For example, the technological system can fail, and has. The company was once offline for 20 hours. Whitman immediately responded by refunding fees and making sure customers were satisfied with any adjustments they had to make. Competition is also a major issue. Amazon.com, Yahoo, and Lycos have all tried to capture the same market. Whitman has successfully maintained her leadership position but must constantly adapt her offerings to stay ahead of the competition. The idea is to monitor changes and adapt accordingly. Expanding overseas, as Whitman has been doing, is difficult because eBay has to respond to the political, social, and economic differences in each country.

The purpose of this text is to introduce you to the exciting and challenging world of business. Each chapter will begin with a story like this one. You will meet more successful businesspeople like Meg Whitman, and entrepreneurs who have started businesses of all kinds. You will learn about all aspects of business. Let us begin by looking at some key terms.

Sources: Hilary Johnson, "Meg Whitman," *Worth,* June 2002, pp. 60–61; Melanie Wells, "D-Day for eBay," *Business 2.0,* June 2002, pp. 68–70; Alynda Wheat and Matthew Schuerman, "The Power," *Fortune,* October 14, 2002, p. 107; Annie Groer, "Furnishing the eBay Way," *The Washington Post,* March 27, 2003, pp. H1 & H6; David Kirkpatrick, "Tech: Where the Action Is," *Fortune,* May 12, 2003, pp. 78–84; Peter Kennedy, "Whitman a Winner with eBay," *The Globe and Mail,* August 18, 2003, p. B4; and eBay.ca, May 20, 2004.

BUSINESS AND ENTREPRENEURSHIP: REVENUES, PROFITS, AND LOSSES

Many business students are interested in learning how to be successful when they graduate from their program. Part of this process requires that you are aware of what is happening in the business world. Near the end of this chapter, we will explore some of the significant trends that are evident in Canadian business today. During your program, you will learn new terms and skills that will help you in your quest; before proceeding, let us review some of the terms that you will hear throughout this textbook.

One of the ways to become a success in Canada, or almost anywhere else in the world, is to start a business. A **business** is any activity that seeks to provide goods and services to others while operating at a profit. **Profit** is the amount a business earns above and beyond what it spends for salaries and other expenses.

Since not all businesses make a profit, starting a business can be a risky proposition. An **entrepreneur** is a person who risks time and money to start and manage a business. Once an entrepreneur has started a business, there is usually a need for good managers and other workers to keep the business going. Not all entrepreneurs are skilled at being managers.

Businesses provide people with the opportunity to become wealthy. There are about 497 billionaires in the world today, with at least 30 of them in Canada.[1] Figure 1.1 lists Canada's top billionaires. Another well-known billionaire is Bill Gates, who started Microsoft—he is said to be worth about $36 billion, making him among the richest people in the world. The number of millionaires is also increasing. There are about 11 million millionaires in the world, and that number is expected to be about 30 million in 2025.[2] Maybe someday you will be one!

Businesses don't make money just for entrepreneurs. Businesses provide us all with necessities such as food, clothing, housing, medical care, and transportation, as well as other goods and services that make our lives easier and better.

Matching Risk with Profit

Profit, remember, is the amount of money a business earns *above and beyond* what it pays out for salaries and other expenses. For example, if you were to start a business selling hot dogs in the summer, you would have to pay for the

business
Any activity that seeks to provide goods and services to others while operating at a profit.

profit
The amount a business earns above and beyond what it spends for salaries and other expenses.

entrepreneur
A person who risks time and money to start and manage a business.

FIGURE 1.1

CANADA'S WEALTHIEST CITIZENS

Canadian Business (www.canadianbusiness.com) tracks the fortunes of Canada's wealthiest citizens. This is an excerpt from the Rich 100 2003–2004 edition that lists those that fall under the first five rankings.

RANK	NAME	WORTH ($ BILLIONS CAD)	COMPANY
1	Kenneth Thomson and Family	$21.67	Thomson Corp., Woodbridge Co. Ltd.
2	Galen Weston	$9.27	George Weston Ltd., Loblaw Cos. Ltd.
3	Jeff Skoll	$4.63	eBay Inc.
4	James, Arthur, and John Irving	$3.88	Irving Oil Ltd., J.D. Irving Ltd.
5	Bernard Sherman	$3.24	Apotex Group

Source: www.canadianbusiness.com/rich100/wholeList.asp, August 24, 2004.

cart rental, for the hot dogs and other materials, and for someone to run the cart while you were away. After you paid your employee and yourself, paid for the food and materials you used, paid the rent on the cart, and paid your taxes, any money left over would be profit. Keep in mind that profit is over and above the money you pay yourself in salary. You could use any profit you make to rent or buy a second cart and hire other employees. After a few summers, you might have a dozen carts employing dozens of workers.

Revenue is the total amount of money a business takes in during a given period by selling goods and services. A **loss** occurs when a business's expenses are more than its revenues. If a business loses money over time, it will likely have to close, putting its employees out of work. Most business failures are due to poor management or problems associated with cash flow (which we discuss later in this book). You will learn more about terms such as *revenue* and *expenses* when you read the accounting chapter (Chapter 16).

Starting a business involves risk. **Risk** is the chance an entrepreneur takes of losing time and money on a business that may not prove profitable. Even among companies that do make a profit, not all make the same amount. Those companies that take the most risk may make the most profit. There is a lot of risk involved, for example, in making a movie. Even one James Bond film, *Casino Royale*, lost money. Of course, some movies make a huge profit. *My Big Fat Greek Wedding*, for example, cost only $5 million to make and brought in about US$210 million.[3]

As a potential business owner, you need to do research (e.g., talk to other businesspeople, read business publications) to find the right balance between risk and profit for you. Different people have different tolerances for risk. To decide which is the best choice for you, you have to calculate the risks and the potential rewards of each decision. The more risks you take, the higher the rewards may be. In Chapter 7, you will learn more about the risks and the rewards that come with starting a business.

Responding to the Various Business Stakeholders

Stakeholders are all the people who stand to gain or lose by the policies and activities of a business. As noted in Figure 1.2, stakeholders include customers, employees, shareholders, suppliers, dealers, bankers, people in the surrounding community (e.g., community interest groups), environmentalists, and elected government leaders. All of these groups are affected by the products, policies, and practices of businesses, and their concerns need to be addressed.

The challenge of the 21st century will be for organizations to balance, as much as possible, the needs of all stakeholders. For example, the need for the business to make profits may be balanced against the needs of employees for sufficient income. The need to stay competitive may call for moving a business overseas, but that might do great harm to the community because many jobs would be lost. It may be legal to move, but would moving be best for everyone? Business leaders must make a decision based on all factors, including the need to make a profit. As you can see, pleasing all stakeholders is not easy and calls for trade-offs that are not always pleasing to one or another stakeholder.

Keep in mind that regardless of temptations, company officials do have a responsibility to their stakeholders. Unfortunately, there are still too many examples of executives who have made decisions that have detrimentally

No occupation in the world is more diverse than entrepreneurship. Opportunities exist for virtually anyone to start and manage a business, from a lawn-mowing service to software training. While Jeff Skoll has founded several companies, you may know him best as eBay's first president. In 2001, he left eBay to focus on philanthropic activities. Through the Skoll Foundation, Jeff supports social entrepreneurs and innovative nonprofit organizations around the world. As for eBay, the company continues to follow the business plan that Jeff created.

revenue
The total amount of money a business takes in during a given period by selling goods and services.

loss
When a business's expenses are more than its revenues.

risk
The chance an entrepreneur takes of losing time and money on a business that may not prove profitable.

stakeholders
All the people who stand to gain or lose by the policies and activities of a business.

FIGURE 1.2

A BUSINESS AND ITS STAKEHOLDERS

Often the needs of a firm's various stakeholders will conflict. For example, paying employees more may cut into shareholders' profits. Balancing such demands is a major role of business managers.

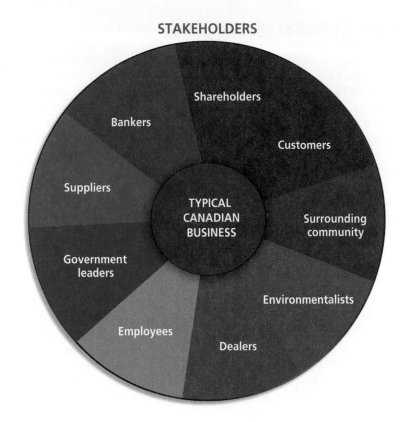

STAKEHOLDERS

Shareholders

Bankers

Customers

Suppliers

TYPICAL CANADIAN BUSINESS

Surrounding community

Government leaders

Environmentalists

Employees

Dealers

impacted their organizations and stakeholders. Examples of such organizations have included Hollinger, Cinar, and Livent.

Such trade-offs are also apparent in the political arena. As will be discussed in Chapter 4, governments make policies that impact many stakeholders. However, budget limitations force governments to make difficult choices, and these decisions often are not popular. Consequently, after years of insufficient funding, any changes in the areas of the environment, health care, and education generate a lot of attention.

As a brief example, let us look at post-secondary education funding. Responding to concerns surrounding escalating tuition fees, in 2004 the Ontario provincial government froze college and university tuitions for two years. The provinces of Manitoba, Quebec, and Newfoundland and Labrador have also capped tuition.[4] This is the opposite of the British Columbia provincial government's decision: in 2002 the government decided to remove its eight-year-long tuition freeze. This freeze had kept post-secondary tuition at the lowest rates in Canada, and its elimination led to cutbacks in services. As you can see, balancing the demands of stakeholders is not limited to for-profit businesses.

Critical Thinking

Imagine that you are thinking of starting a restaurant in your community. Who would be the various stakeholders of your business? What are some of the things you could do to benefit your community other than providing jobs and tax revenue? How could you establish good relationships with your suppliers? With your employees? Do you see any conflict between your desire to be as profitable as possible and your desire to pay people a living wage?

Nonprofit organizations can use business principles to operate effectively. In this ad, advertising is being used to communicate important information to the Canadian public about how Canadian Blood Services would manage the safety and accessibility of the blood supply in light of the emergence of West Nile Virus. Nonprofit organizations need people to handle accounting, finance, human resource management, and other business functions. Would you prefer to work in a for-profit or a nonprofit organization? What do you think would be the key differences?

Using Business Principles in Nonprofit Organizations

Despite their efforts to satisfy all their stakeholders, businesses cannot do everything that is needed to make a community all it can be. **Nonprofit organizations**—such as public schools, religious institutions, charities, and groups devoted to social causes—also make a major contribution to the welfare of society.

You may prefer to work for a nonprofit organization. There are many opportunities in this sector. Canada has 58,000 nonprofit organizations that employ a total of about 900,000 workers—the equivalent of the Canadian oil and gas and mining industries combined.[5] This doesn't mean, however, that you shouldn't study business. If you want to start or work in a nonprofit organization, you'll need to learn business skills such as information management, leadership, marketing, and financial management. Therefore, the knowledge and skills you acquire in this and other business courses will be useful for careers in any organization, including a nonprofit one.

Businesses, nonprofit organizations, and volunteer groups often strive to accomplish the same objectives.[6] All such groups can help feed people, provide them with clothing and housing, educate them on social issues, clean up the environment and keep it clean, and improve the quality of life for all. To accomplish such objectives, however, businesses in Canada must remain competitive with the best businesses in the rest of the world by offering quality goods and services.

nonprofit organization
An organization whose goals do not include making a personal profit for its owners or organizers.

For more information about nonprofit organizations visit the Charity Village Website at www.charityvillage.com. This site is dedicated to supporting Canada's 200,000 charities and nonprofit organizations as well as the stakeholders who support them.

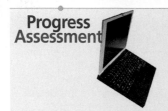

- What is the difference between *revenue* and *profit*?
- What is risk, and how is it related to profit?
- What does the term *stakeholders* mean?

ENTREPRENEURSHIP VERSUS WORKING FOR OTHERS

There are two ways to succeed in business. One way, the way chosen by Meg Whitman, is to rise up through the ranks of large companies like Hasbro or eBay. The advantage of working for others is that somebody else assumes the entrepreneurial risk and provides you with benefits such as paid vacation time and health insurance. Most people choose that option. It is a very good option and can lead to a happy and prosperous life. Businesses need good managers to succeed, and all workers contribute to producing and marketing the goods and services that increase the quality of life and standard of living for others.

The other, more risky path is to start your own business. Many small businesses fail each year; thus, it takes a brave person to start a small business. Furthermore, as an entrepreneur you don't receive any benefits such as paid vacation time and health insurance. You have to provide them for yourself!

Before you take on the challenge of entrepreneurship it makes sense to study the experiences of those who have succeeded to learn the process. Consider the example of Ron Joyce, who in 1963 purchased a Dairy Queen outlet. Two years later, he invested $10,000 to become a franchisee in the first Tim Hortons. (We will discuss franchising in Chapter 6.) By 1967, he became a full partner with Tim Horton. In the early years, both partners worked on expanding the business. When Horton died in 1974, Joyce became the sole owner of the chain. In the following years he continued to develop the business, spending hundreds of hours piloting his plane in search of new franchise opportunities and doing everything from training new store owners to baking donuts. When Joyce sold the chain to Wendy's for US$450 million in 1995, there were more than 1,000 Tim Hortons restaurants. Today, Tim Hortons is Canada's largest national chain in the coffee and fresh baked goods segment, with more than 2,200 stores across Canada and approximately 160 locations in the United States.[7]

What you can learn from successful entrepreneurs like Ron Joyce is that you need to find something that you love to do. Before he became an entrepreneur, Joyce was a police officer. He started to get experience in business with his Dairy Queen outlet, and from there went on to great success with his Tim Hortons restaurants. While there were many challenges along the way, he was willing to put in the long hours needed to be successful. In addition to the original coffee and donut offerings, he continuously added new products to the restaurants in order to meet his customers' needs.

The Spotlight on Small Business box highlights another example of what an entrepreneur can create. Consider if such a challenge would appeal to you.

The Importance of Entrepreneurs to the Creation of Wealth

Have you ever wondered why it is that some countries are relatively wealthy and others are poor? Economists have been studying the issue of wealth creation for many years. They began the process by studying potential sources of wealth to determine which are the most important. Over time, they came

www.robeez.com

Spotlight on Small Business

Small Feet Mean Business at Robeez Footwear Ltd.

When Sandra Wilson was downsized out of her Canadian Airlines job in 1994, she decided that it was the perfect time to turn her idea into a business. This would also allow her to spend more time with her son Robert, the inspiration behind the company's name and designs.

Founded in Richmond, British Columbia, Robeez Footwear Ltd. is a children's shoe manufacturer. Robeez manufactures fun leather shoes for children from newborn up to age four. The biggest selling feature is that the shoes are an easy "slip on but never slip off" design. This is fantastic for tiny feet; the footwear cannot be easily pulled off, which is a common problem with many baby shoes.

Wilson began her business in her basement by making the first 20 pairs of shoes by hand. She took them to the Vancouver Gift Show trade exhibition in 1994, and when she left the show she had 15 new accounts. As the company grew, Wilson was approached to distribute the shoes in the United Kingdom. She turned to Export Development Canada for help in negotiating the distribution deal. Wilson also took advantage of other government programs such as the Program for Export Market Development (PEMD). PEMD allowed Wilson to attend U.S. trade shows and connect with sales professionals interested in representing the company's products.

Robeez has been recognized over the years for its success. The shoes are recommended by medical and childcare experts. The company was chosen as one of Chatelaine magazine's "Top 40 fabulous gift finds" in the December 2002 issue. Robeez was named one of Canada's Fastest Growing Companies by Profit magazine for 2003 (which is no wonder, with revenue growth of 2,309 percent in one year!). In 2003, Robeez generated revenues of $3.1 million.

Today, the company has 200 employees and is the leading manufacturer of soft-soled footwear for its target market in North America. The shoes are distributed in thousands of retail stores in Canada and the United States. The company also has a regional office in the United Kingdom as well as a European Website. Customers appreciate this localized service approach because they can speak to someone in the same time zone, use the same currency, and speak the same lingo. Robeez products are sold in the U.K., Ireland, Japan, Singapore, Germany, France, and Australia.

What do future plans hold for this small business? Robeez is committed to becoming the market leader in Western Europe. And soon, it will have an exciting new product line to launch!

Sources: "Annual Report—Program for Export Market Development 2000/2001" [2002], Ottawa: Department of Foreign Affairs and International Trade. Retrieved May 19, 2004 from http://www.dfait-maeci.gc.ca/pemd/annual_reports/PEMD_ar0001-en.pdf; "Profit 100 Canada's Fastest Growing Companies" [2003], Toronto: PROFITGUIDE.com. Retrieved May 19, 2004 from http://www.profitguide.com/profit100/2003/p100.asp; robeez.com; Interview with Sandra Wilson, May 20, 2004.

up with five factors that seemed to contribute to wealth. They called them **factors of production.** Figure 1.3 describes those five factors. They are:

1. Land (or natural resources).
2. Labour (workers).
3. Capital. (This includes machines, tools, buildings, or whatever else is used in the production of goods. It does *not* include money; money is used to buy factors of production—it is not a factor itself.)
4. Entrepreneurship.
5. Knowledge.

Traditionally, business and economics textbooks have emphasized only four factors of production: land, labour, capital, and entrepreneurship. But management expert and business consultant Peter Drucker says that the most important factor of production in our economy is and will be knowledge. The young workers in the high-tech industries are sometimes called knowledge workers. When high-tech businesses began to fail in the early 2000s, a lot of

factors of production
The resources used to create wealth: land, labour, capital, entrepreneurship, and knowledge.

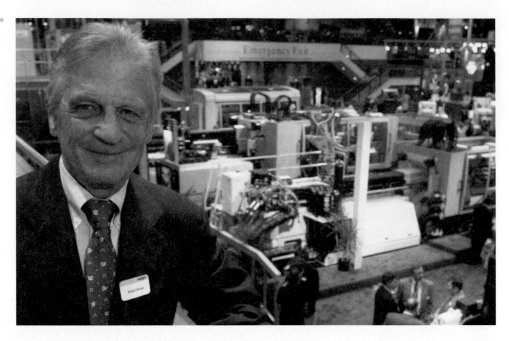

Some of the most successful entrepreneurs are immigrants. Robert Schad (president and CEO of Husky Injection Molding Systems Limited) came from Germany in 1951 with $25 borrowed from an uncle. He founded his company in a Toronto garage in 1953. Today, Husky is the world's largest brand-name supplier of injection moulding equipment for the plastics industry. Schad is shown here at the 2003 National Plastics Exposition in Chicago. Is this an unusual success story, or typical of Canadian entrepreneurship?

knowledge workers had to find new jobs in other parts of the country, but their education and experience made the transition easier.

Such results should motivate today's students to get as much education as possible to prepare themselves for knowledge-oriented jobs and to be prepared to change jobs as the economy demands.[8] Note that information is not the same as knowledge. There is often too much information available and information management is critical. We will study the importance of using technology to manage information in Appendix A.

If you were to analyze rich countries versus poor countries to see what causes the differences in the levels of wealth, you'd have to look at the factors of production in each country. Such analyses have revealed that some relatively poor countries often have plenty of land and natural resources. Russia and China, for example, both have vast areas of land with many resources, but they are not rich countries. In contrast, Japan and Hong Kong are relatively rich countries but are poor in land and other natural resources. Therefore, land isn't the critical element for wealth creation.

Most poor countries have many labourers, so it's not labour that's the primary source of wealth today. Labourers need to find work to make a contribution; that is, they need entrepreneurs to provide jobs for them. Furthermore, capital—machinery and tools—is now becoming available in world

FIGURE 1.3

THE FIVE FACTORS OF PRODUCTION

Land:	Land and other natural resources are used to make homes, cars, and other products.
Labour:	People have always been an important resource in producing goods and services, but many people are now being replaced by technology.
Capital:	Capital includes machines, tools, buildings, and other means of manufacturing.
Entrepreneurship:	All the resources in the world have little value unless entrepreneurs are willing to take the risk of starting businesses to use those resources.
Knowledge:	Information technology has revolutionized business, making it possible to quickly determine wants and needs and to respond with desired products.

Reaching Beyond Our Borders

Freedom and Protective Laws Equal Prosperity

Recent studies have found that the freer a country is, the wealthier its citizens are. Freedom includes freedom from excess taxation, government regulations, and restrictions on trade. The average per capita gross domestic product (GDP)—the total value of all final goods and services produced divided by the number of people in the country—for the freest countries in the early 2000s was over US$21,000. The freest countries are Hong Kong, Singapore, and New Zealand. Canada was considered mostly free and was ranked 18th. For the least free, per capita GDP was under US$3,000. The least free countries include North Korea, Iraq, Libya, Cuba, and Zimbabwe. As a country introduces more freedom, its economy also begins to grow.

The economic and legal environment therefore has much to do with a country's economic prosperity. More freedom equals more prosperity for all. Recently, for example, the Heritage Foundation (a conservative think tank) prepared an index that measures the impact of laws, regulations, and government policies on the economy. This index classifies the governments of Singapore and the United States as among the least restrictive and those of Russia and Cuba as the most restrictive. It may not be a coincidence, then, that Singapore and the United States are relatively wealthy countries and Russia and Cuba are not. Such figures show why businesses must work closely with government to minimize taxes, maximize economic freedom, and establish laws that protect businesspeople.

Sources: www.heritage.org/index/2001/chapters/execsum.html; "Profiles in Prosperity," *World*, June 15, 2002, pp. 70–71; Arch Puddington, "The Resilience of Global Freedom," *Washington Times*, December 27, 2002, p. A21; and Steve Chapman, "Hopeful Signs in a Year That Was," *The Washington Times*, December 29, 2002, p. B1.

markets, so capital isn't the missing ingredient. Capital is not productive without entrepreneurs to put it to use.

Clearly, then, what makes countries rich today is a combination of government policies that support business, entrepreneurship, and the effective use of knowledge. Together, lack of entrepreneurship and the absence of knowledge among workers, along with the lack of freedom, contribute to keeping countries poor. The box called Reaching Beyond Our Borders discusses the importance of freedom to economic development.

Entrepreneurship also makes some provinces and cities in Canada rich while others remain relatively poor. The business environment either encourages or discourages entrepreneurship. In the following section, we'll explore what makes up the business environment and how to build an environment that encourages growth and job creation.

Progress Assessment

- What are some of the advantages of working for others?
- What are the five factors of production?
- Which factor of production is key to wealth? Explain.

THE BUSINESS ENVIRONMENT

The **business environment** consists of the surrounding factors that either help or hinder the development of businesses. Figure 1.4 shows the six elements in the business environment:

1. The legal and regulatory environment.
2. The economic environment.

business environment
The surrounding factors that either help or hinder the development of businesses.

3. The technological environment.
4. The competitive environment.
5. The social environment.
6. The global environment.

Businesses grow and prosper in a healthy environment. The results are job growth and the wealth that makes it possible to have a high quality of life. Companies should be aware of these elements and make it a practice to continuously assess the business environment for changes in trends. These trends could impact the organization's ability to achieve its objectives, steer clear of threats, or take advantage of new opportunities.

The Legal and Regulatory Environment

People are willing to start new businesses if they believe that the risk of losing their money isn't too great. Part of that decision is affected by how governments work with businesses. Governments can do a lot to lessen the risk of starting and running a business through the laws (also known as acts) that are passed by its elected officials. The Constitution Act defines the powers that can be exercised by the different levels of government (i.e., federal, provincial, and municipal). In Chapter 4, we will review some of the responsibilities of these different levels.

FIGURE 1.4

TODAY'S DYNAMIC BUSINESS ENVIRONMENT

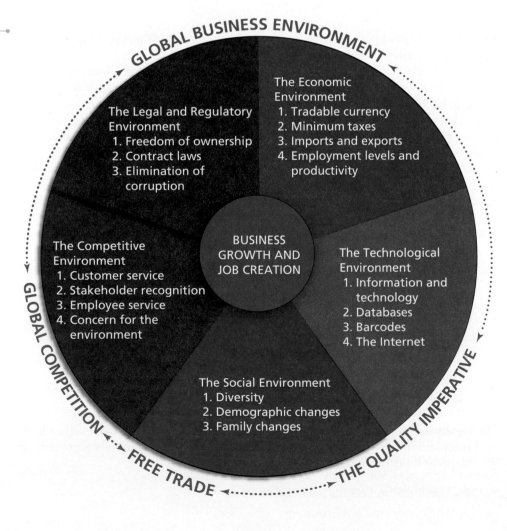

GLOBAL BUSINESS ENVIRONMENT

The Legal and Regulatory Environment
1. Freedom of ownership
2. Contract laws
3. Elimination of corruption

The Economic Environment
1. Tradable currency
2. Minimum taxes
3. Imports and exports
4. Employment levels and productivity

The Competitive Environment
1. Customer service
2. Stakeholder recognition
3. Employee service
4. Concern for the environment

BUSINESS GROWTH AND JOB CREATION

The Technological Environment
1. Information and technology
2. Databases
3. Barcodes
4. The Internet

The Social Environment
1. Diversity
2. Demographic changes
3. Family changes

GLOBAL COMPETITION

FREE TRADE

THE QUALITY IMPERATIVE

An important piece of legislation is the Competition Act. The purpose of the Competition Act is to:

maintain and encourage competition in Canada in order to promote the efficiency and adaptability of the Canadian economy, in order to expand opportunities for Canadian participation in world markets while at the same time recognizing the role of foreign competition in Canada, in order to ensure that small- and medium-sized enterprises have an equitable opportunity to participate in the Canadian economy and in order to provide consumers with competitive prices and product choices.[9]

Other examples of laws include the Canada Small Business Financing Act, the Consumer Packaging and Labelling Act, and the Trade Unions Act. As you can see, these laws are relevant to many businesses.

Each legislation authorizes an agency (such as Industry Canada) to write regulations that interpret the law in more detail and indicate how it will be implemented and enforced. Consequently, **regulations** serve to carry out the purposes of or expand on the general laws.[10] These regulations exist to protect consumers as well as businesses.

regulations
Serve to carry out the purposes of or expand on the general laws passed by elected officials.

Laws Impact Business   Businesses need to be aware of the laws that are in place (or may be passed) that will affect their business. For example, a government can keep taxes and regulations to a minimum, thereby encouraging entrepreneurship and increasing wealth. Entrepreneurs are looking for a high *return on investment* (ROI), including the investment of their time. If the government takes away much of what the business earns through high taxes, ROI may no longer be worth the risk. Provinces and territories that have high taxes and restrictive regulations tend to drive entrepreneurs out, while areas with low taxes and less restrictive regulations attract entrepreneurs.

The government can also lessen the risks of entrepreneurship by passing laws that enable businesspeople to write contracts that are enforceable in court. You can read more about the importance of business law in Canada in Appendix B.

There are many laws in Canada that are intended to minimize corruption, and businesses can flourish when these laws are followed. Nonetheless, corrupt and illegal activities do negatively affect the business community and the economy as a whole. For example, confidence in business has been affected as a result of unacceptable practices at companies like CIBC World Markets, YBM Magnex, RT Capital, and Bre-X. In 2004, the Auditor General released a report on the federal sponsorship program. Implicated in the misuse of public funds were 11 companies that included Via Rail and Canada Post.[11] Such activities are also evident beyond our borders. Companies that have been highly visible in the news for improper business activities have included Parmalat, Enron and Arthur Andersen, and WorldCom.

It is important to note that the effects of business scandals reach beyond our borders. According to the president of the Canadian chapter of Transparency International, Canada's ranking on an international corruption index has fallen due to incidences such as the federal sponsorship scandal, Toronto's municipal computer-leasing

Starting a business in some countries is much harder than in others. In India, for example, a person has to go through an extraordinary and time-consuming bureaucratic process to get permission to start a business—and with no certainty of success. For example, more effort may go into getting something as basic as electricity for that business. Nonetheless, those businesses that do get started can become a major source of wealth and employment. This jewellery business is one small example. Can you imagine the opportunities and wealth that might be created with just a little more freedom in this country of more than a billion people?

Making Ethical Decisions

Ethics Begins With You

Television, movies, and the print media all paint a dismal picture of ethics among businesspeople, government officials, and citizens in general. It is easy to criticize the ethics of people whose names appear in the headlines. It is more difficult to see the moral and ethical misbehaviour of your own social group. Do you find some of the behaviours of your friends morally or ethically questionable?

One of the major trends in business today is that many companies are creating ethics codes to guide their employees' behaviour. We believe that this trend toward improving ethical behaviour is so important that we've made it a major theme of this book. Throughout the text you'll see boxes, like this one, called Making Ethical Decisions. The boxes contain short descriptions of situations that pose ethical dilemmas and ask what you would do to resolve them. The idea is for you to think about the moral and ethical dimensions of every decision you make.

Here is your first ethical dilemma: Soon you will be taking exams in this course. Suppose you didn't prepare for one of the tests as thoroughly as you should have. As luck would have it, on exam day you are sitting in the desk right in front of the instructor, who has just happened to leave the answer key sticking out of her book. The instructor is called out of the room and everyone else is concentrating intently on his or her own work. No one will know if your eyes wander toward the answer key. A good grade on this test will certainly help your average. What is the problem in this situation? What are your alternatives? What are the consequences of each alternative? Which alternative will you choose? Is your choice ethical?

Sources: "What You Can Do to Help America," *Bottom Line Personal*, January 1, 2003, p. 2; and Walter B. Wriston, "A Code of Your Own," *The Wall Street Journal*, January 16, 2003, p. A12.

---

affair, private-sector banking lapses, and the extravagant expense accounts of public servants.[12] While Canada is still perceived to be one of the world's less corrupt nations, it recently ranked 11th among the 133 countries surveyed.

Lapses in ethical behaviour have placed a new emphasis on laws restraining businesspeople from committing unethical or illegal acts. We will explore business ethics in depth in Chapter 5. In the meantime, the Making Ethical Decisions box highlights the importance of individual ethical decision making.

The Economic Environment

The economic environment impacts businesses as well as consumers. For our discussion, the focus will be on businesses. The economic environment looks at income, expenditures, and resources that affect the cost of running a business. Businesses review the results of major economic indicators such as consumer spending, employment levels, and productivity. This analysis will give them a sense of what is happening in the marketplace and what actions they may need to take. Since Chapter 2 is dedicated to how economic issues affect businesses, the discussion here will be very brief.

The movement of a country's currency relative to other currencies also pertains to this environment. Currency movements are especially critical for countries, such as Canada, that generate a great deal of business activity from exports. For example, a lower Canadian dollar value relative to the U.S. dollar makes our exports cheaper and more attractive to the U.S. market as consumers can buy more products with their higher-valued currency.

The government can therefore establish a currency that is tradable in world markets (i.e., you can buy and sell goods and services anywhere in the world using that currency).

One way for governments to actively promote entrepreneurship is to allow private ownership of businesses. In some countries, the government owns most businesses; thus, there's little incentive for people to work hard or create a profit. All around the world today, various countries in which the government formerly owned most businesses are selling those businesses to private individuals to create more wealth. In Chapter 2, we will discuss the different economic systems around the world.

You should soon realize, as we continue with our brief introduction to the other business environments, that the activities occurring in one environment have an impact on the others. In short, all the environments are linked. For example, if a new government regulation decreases business taxes, then the impact will be seen in the economic environment when one considers expenditures. Therefore, as a businessperson you need to scan *all* the environments in order to make good business decisions.

The Technological Environment

Various tools and machines developed throughout history have changed the business environment tremendously. Few technological changes have had a more comprehensive and lasting impact on businesses than the emergence of information technology (IT): computers, modems, cellular phones, and so on. Chief among these developments is the Internet. Although many Internet firms have failed in recent years, the Internet will prove to be a major force in business in the coming years.[13] The Internet is such a major force in business today that we discuss its impact on businesses throughout the text. In addition, we provide Internet exercises at the end of each chapter to give you some hands-on experience with various Internet uses.

technology
Everything from phones and copiers to computers, medical imaging devices, personal digital assistants, and the various software programs that make business processes more efficient and productive.

productivity
The amount of output that is generated given the amount of input.

How Technology Benefits Workers and You   One of the advantages of working for others is that the company often provides the tools and technology to make your job more productive. **Technology** means everything from phones and copiers to computers, medical imaging devices, personal digital assistants, and the various software programs that make business processes more efficient and productive.[14] *Efficiency* means producing items using the least amount of resources. **Productivity** is the amount of output you generate given the amount of input (e.g., hours worked). The more you can produce in any given period of time, the more money you are worth to companies. Tools and technology greatly improve productivity. Such tools vary from hammers and saws to computer-aided design and computer-aided manufacturing machines and artificial intelligence.

Alias is the world's leading innovator of 3D graphics technology. Its Maya software was the core 3D animation software technology used for the *Lord of the Rings* trilogy, produced by Weta Digital. In 2003, Weta Digital won Oscars in the categories of Best Visual Effects and Best Picture, and multiple British Academy of Film and Television Arts (BAFTA) awards for *The Lord of the Rings: The Return of the King.*

Research In Motion Ltd. produces the BlackBerry product line. For more information on how BlackBerry offers a combined phone and e-mail experience, visit its Website at www.blackberry.com.

Technology affects people in all industries. Take Barry Sonnenfeld, for example. He was the director of the movie *Men in Black 2*. He also was involved with films like *The Addams Family* and *Get Shorty*. Sonnenfeld does a lot of his work on the road. Therefore, he carries three cell phones, a Palm VII, a Palm V with wireless service, an IBM Thinkpad, and a pager that he also uses for e-mail. All these devices keep Sonnenfeld in contact with people all over the world and enable him to do other work whenever there is a break in the production process.[15]

The Growth of E-Commerce   One of the major themes of this text is managing change.[16] There are special boxes called Dealing with Change throughout the text that discuss the rapidly changing business environment and the need to adjust to these changes. One of the more important changes of recent years is the growth of e-commerce. There are two major types of e-commerce transactions: business-to-consumer (B2C) and business-to-business (B2B). As important as the Internet has been in the consumer market, it has become even more important in the B2B market, which consists of selling goods and services from one business to another, such as IBM selling consulting services to a local bank. B2B e-commerce is already at least five times as big as B2C e-commerce. While the potential of the B2C e-commerce market is measured in billions, B2B e-commerce is said to be measured in trillions.

The rise of Internet marketing came so fast and furious that it drew hundreds of competitors into the fray. Many of the new Internet companies failed. There is no question that some Internet businesses will continue to grow and prosper, but along the way there will continue to be lots of failures, just as there have been in traditional businesses. For example, Grocery Gateway Inc. was founded in 1998 by a group of entrepreneurs who believed that people had better things to do than grocery shop. One of the few surviving e-grocers, with revenues growing at about 30 percent year over year (expected revenues for 2003 were in the $70-million range), it went into voluntary court receivership in 2004.[17]

Traditional businesses will have to learn how to deal with the new competition from B2B and B2C firms. See the Dealing with Change box for more about how businesses have adapted to e-commerce change. We will be discussing e-commerce throughout the text.

In recent years, many new companies have tried to prosper by combining the time-saving convenience of ordering food and other household products over the Internet with direct delivery. Webvan was one of the first. But Webvan, like many others, failed during the dot-com explosion in 2000–2002. It's not that the Internet does not provide an excellent opportunity to sell things. It does. But the cost of setting up distribution centres and delivery systems and overcoming customer concerns of not being able to see, touch, and examine products has proven too difficult to overcome for business after business. Do you think most customers will eventually change their preference for shopping in stores?

Dealing With Change

Adjusting to the E-commerce Era

One of the more significant changes occurring today is the movement toward doing business on the Internet. Many businesses are finding the new competition overwhelming. That includes, for example, traditional bookstores that now have to compete with eBay and Amazon.ca. Who would have thought that garage sales would be done over the Internet? Or that cars or homes could be sold online? What is this e-commerce revolution and why is it happening now? That is, what are the advantages of e-commerce that other businesses have to accept and incorporate into their long-term strategies?

Businesses are lured to e-commerce by a number of factors, including, but not limited to:

- *Less investment in land, buildings, and equipment.* E-commerce firms can usually sell things for less because they don't have to invest as much in buildings (bricks), and can reach people inexpensively over the Internet (clicks).

- *Low transaction costs.* The automation of customer service lowers costs, which may make it possible for a company to offer products at a lower price.

- *Large purchases per transaction.* Online stores like Amazon.ca often make personalized recommendations to customers that increase their order size.

- *Integration of business processes.* The Internet offers companies the ability to make more information available to customers than ever before. For example, a computer company that tracks each unit through the manufacturing and shipping process can allow customers to see exactly where the order is at any time. This is what overnight package delivery company Federal Express did when it introduced online package tracking.

- *Larger catalogue.* Amazon.ca offers a catalogue of 3 million books on the Internet. Imagine fitting a paper catalogue that size in your mailbox!

- *Flexibility.* Successful Websites are not just glorified mail-order catalogues. The Internet offers companies the ability to configure products and build custom orders, to compare prices between multiple vendors easily, and to search large catalogues quickly.

- *Improved customer interactions.* Online tools allow businesses to interact with customers in ways unheard of before, and at almost instant speeds. For example, customers can receive automatic e-mails to confirm orders and to notify them when orders are shipped.

Despite these many benefits, Internet-based companies have not captured the retail market as expected. Instead, traditional retail stores have adapted to the changing environment and have used the Internet to supplement their traditional stores. The combination of e-commerce with traditional stores is called click-and-brick retailing, for obvious reasons. The top 20 online sellers are names that are quite familiar to most students. They include Dell, Sears, Staples, and Victoria's Secret. Four years after going online, Victoria's Secret sold about a third of its goods on the Internet.

eBay has done quite well as a Web-only firm. We chose Meg Whitman of eBay for the opening profile in this chapter because of her outstanding success in this field.

Sources: "Cornering the Retail Market," *Washington Post,* June 6, 2002, pp. E1, E6; Don Steinberg, "The Ultimate Technology Survival Guide," *SmartBusiness,* February 2002, pp. 37–49; Ruth P. Stevens, "On e*Sale Here," *1 to1 Magazine,* September 2002, pp. 43–46; and Maryanne Murray Buechner, "Cruising the Online Mall," *Time,* April 2003.

Using Technology to Be Responsive to Customers   One of the major themes of this text is that businesses succeed or fail largely because of the way they treat their customers. The businesses that are most responsive to customer wants and needs will succeed, and those that do not respond to customers will not be as successful. One way traditional retailers can respond to the Internet revolution is to use technology to become much more responsive to customers. For example, businesses mark goods with Universal Product Codes (bar codes)—those series of lines and numbers that you see on most consumer packaged goods. Bar codes can be used to tell retailers what product you bought, in what

database
An electronic storage file
where information is kept;
one use of databases is to
store vast amounts of
information about
consumers.

size and colour, and at what price. A scanner at the checkout counter can read that information and put it into a database.

A **database** is an electronic storage file where information is kept. One use of databases is to store vast amounts of information about consumers. For example, a retailer may ask for your name, address, and telephone number so that it can put you on its mailing list. The information you give the retailer is added to the database. Because companies routinely trade database information, many retailers know what you buy and from whom you buy it. Using that information, companies can send you catalogues and other direct mail advertising that offers the kind of products you might want, as indicated by your past purchases. The use of databases enables stores to carry only the merchandise that the local population wants. It also enables stores to carry less inventory, saving them money. We will talk more about how technology helps identify and meet the needs of target markets in Chapters 14 and 15.

The Competitive Environment

Competition among businesses has never been greater than it is today. Some companies have found a competitive edge by focusing on quality. The goal for many companies is zero defects—no mistakes in making the product. Some companies, such as Toyota in Japan, have come close to meeting that standard. However, simply making a high-quality product isn't enough to allow a company to stay competitive in world markets. Companies now have to offer both high-quality products and outstanding service at competitive prices (value). That is why General Motors (GM) is building automobile plants in Argentina, Poland, China, and Thailand. The strategies of combining excellence with low-cost labour and minimizing distribution costs have resulted in larger markets and potential long-term growth for GM. Figure 1.5 shows how competition has changed businesses from the traditional model to a new, world-class model.

Competing by Exceeding Customer Expectations   Manufacturers and service organizations throughout the world have learned that today's customers are very demanding. Not only do they want good quality at low prices, but they want great service as well. In fact, some products in the 21st century will be designed to fascinate and delight customers, exceeding their expectations. Business is becoming customer-driven, not management-driven as in the past. This means that customers' wants and needs must come first.

FIGURE 1.5

**HOW COMPETITION HAS
CHANGED BUSINESS**

TRADITIONAL BUSINESSES	WORLD-CLASS BUSINESSES
Customer satisfaction	Delighting the customer[1]
Customer orientation	Customer and stakeholder orientation[2]
Profit orientation	Profit and social orientation[3]
Reactive ethics	Proactive ethics[4]
Product orientation	Quality and service orientation
Managerial focus	Customer focus

[1] *Delight* is a term from total quality management. *Bewitch* and *fascinate* are alternative terms.

[2] Stakeholders include employees, shareholders, suppliers, dealers, and the community; the goal is to please *all* stakeholders.

[3] A social orientation goes beyond profit to do what is right and good for others.

[4] *Proactive* means doing the right thing before anyone tells you to do it. *Reactive* means responding to criticism after it happens.

Customer-driven organizations include Disney amusement parks (the parks are kept clean and appeal to all ages) and Moto Photo (it does its best to please customers with fast, friendly service). Such companies can successfully compete against Internet firms if they continue to offer better and friendlier service. Successful organizations must now listen more closely to customers to determine their wants and needs, then adjust the firm's products, policies, and practices to meet those demands. We will explore these concepts in more depth in Chapter 14.

Competing with Speed Have you noticed how everyone seems to be in more of a hurry today? Well, the truth is that most people do live at a fast pace, and businesses need to respond or risk losing their business. For example, companies used to say, "Allow six weeks for delivery." Today, many customers want things delivered in two days or less. That's why FedEx and other high-speed delivery firms are doing so well. Most of today's consumers want fast food, fast delivery, fast responses to Internet searches, and so on. Usually, the companies that provide speedy service are those that are winning. Speed isn't everything, however. It has to be accompanied by good quality and reasonable prices, for example. Some consumers may prefer less speed and more helpful service, or less speed and lower prices.

Businesses are demanding fast service from other businesses. The old saying "Time is money" has taken on new importance. The *Harvard Business Review* reports that not since the Industrial Revolution have the stakes of dealing with change been so high. In a marketplace that wants things to happen faster every day, the battle more often than not is going to the swiftest competitor, not necessarily the biggest, strongest, or even the shrewdest. Some small companies have made speedy response the core of their business. That means coming up with new products faster than before and producing those products faster as well. It also means speedy service. We'll explore production and operations management further in Chapter 10.

Competing by Restructuring and Empowerment To meet the needs of customers, firms must give their frontline workers (office clerks, front-desk people at hotels, salespeople, etc.) the responsibility, authority, freedom, training, and equipment they need to respond quickly to customer requests and to make other decisions essential to producing quality goods and providing good service. This is called **empowerment,** and we'll be talking about that process throughout this book. To implement a policy of empowerment, managers must train frontline people to make decisions within certain limits, without the need to consult managers. The new role of supervisors, then, is to support frontline people with training and the technology to do their jobs well, including handling customer complaints quickly and satisfactorily.

empowerment
Giving frontline workers the responsibility, authority, and freedom to respond quickly to customer requests.

In this chapter, we simply want to acknowledge that many businesses must reorganize to make their employees more effective than they are now. Many firms have done so by forming cross-functional teams—that is, teams made up of people from various departments, such as design, production, and marketing. These teams have learned to work without close supervision; thus, they are often called self-managed cross-functional teams.

One aspect of empowerment has been the elimination of managers. Companies that have implemented self-managed teams expect a lot more from their lower-level workers than they did in the past and can therefore do without various levels of managers. Because they have less management oversight, such workers need more education. Increasingly, managers' jobs will be to train, support, coach, and motivate lower-level employees.

Employees with increased responsibility are likely to demand increased compensation based on performance. Often, in larger firms, that may mean giving employees not only higher pay but partial ownership of the firm as well. It will also mean developing entirely new organizational structures to meet the changing needs of customers and employees. We'll discuss such organizational changes and models in Chapter 9.

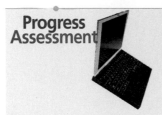

Progress Assessment

- What are four ways the government can foster entreprencurship?
- What is productivity and how does technology enhance it?
- How can companies compete with speed?

The Social Environment

demography
The statistical study of the human population with regard to its size, density, and other characteristics such as age, race, gender, and income.

Demography is the statistical study of the human population with regard to its size, density, and other characteristics such as age, race, gender, and income. In this book, we're particularly interested in the demographic trends that most affect businesses and career choices. The Canadian population is going through major changes that are dramatically affecting how people live, where they live, what they buy, and how they spend their time. Furthermore, tremendous population shifts are leading to new opportunities for some firms and to declining opportunities for others.

The Aging Population   The Canadian population has been aging for several decades. More people are living longer due to better medical knowledge and technology and better health habits, including proper nutrition, more exercise, and a reduction in the number of people who smoke. Figure 1.6 shows past and future population trends over a 40-year period: the youngest age groups have been declining steadily, from 40 percent to 22 percent, while the two oldest age groups are increasing steadily, from 38 to 58 percent.

At the same time, the portion of the population that is very young continues to decrease because of declining birth rates since the mid-1960s. Although the rate is low, the actual number of children being born is still large because

FIGURE 1.6

POPULATION DISTRIBUTION BY AGE GROUP

Percentages for 2001, 2006, and 2011 are projected, and the earlier years are actual percentages. If you compare 1971 and 2011 you will note a pronounced shift to a heavier weighting of older persons and a decline in the proportion of the youngest groups.

YEAR	0–4	5–19	20–34	35–64	65 AND OVER
2011	5%	17%	20%	43%	15%
2006	5	19	20	42	13
2001	6	20	21	41	13
1996	7	20	23	38	12
1991	7	21	26	34	12
1981	7	25	27	31	10
1971	9	31	22	30	8

Source: "Population Distribution by Age Group," adapted from Statistics Canada publication, *Population Projections for Canada, Provinces and Territories, 1993–2016*, Cat. No. 91-520 and from Statistics Canada database http://cansim2.statcan.ca, Matrix 6367, September 2003.

of the *baby-boom echo*. The baby-boom echo (those born in the period from 1980 to 1995) represents the children of the large number of *baby boomers* (those born in the period from 1947 to 1966).[18] Most students are part of this echo generation.

What do such demographics mean for you and for businesses in the future? In his book *Boom Bust & Echo 2000: Profiting from the Demographic Shift in the New Millennium,* economist and demographer David Foot writes that demographics play a pivotal role in the economic and social life of our country. According to Foot, demographics explain about two-thirds of everything—including which products will be in demand in five years.[19]

Think of the goods and services the middle-aged and elderly will need—anything from travel and recreation to medicine, assisted-living facilities, and smaller apartments. Don't forget the baby boomers. More grandparents with more money in their pockets will be buying more gifts for their grandchildren. In Ontario, the baby-boom echo was clearly felt in September 2003, when the double cohort (resulting from the elimination of Grade 13) arrived on college and university campuses. While this dramatic increase in demand for education led to more instructors being hired and more residences being built, there still were larger class sizes and more cramped residence rooms as these institutions tried to meet the demand. It is clear that there should be many opportunities for existing and new businesses to explore in the 21st century.

Managing Diversity   Canada has a strong multicultural population. It has seen a steady increase in immigration since the 1960s; in the 1980s, more than one million immigrants entered Canada. More than half of these were under 30, so many had children. During the 1990s, this number increased to over 1.8 million immigrants. In the 2001 census, more than 18 percent of the population indicated that it was foreign-born. Companies have responded to this diverse customer base by hiring a more diversified workforce to serve them. Today, more than 75 percent of *Fortune* 1000 companies have some sort of diversity initiative. Some, like Kodak, have a chief diversity office (CDO) in the executive suite. In short, companies are taking diversity management seriously.[20]

The management of diverse groups—whether they be different because of race, sex, age, sexual orientation, country of origin, religion, or some other classification—can be difficult. It gets even more difficult as managers go overseas and must respond to all the cultural, political, and social issues that are particular to each country. Nonetheless, companies such as IBM and Ford all believe that they are more successful and more profitable because of their diversity initiatives.

Two-Income Families   Approximately 54 percent of all families in Canada are made up of dual-income earners.[21] Several factors have led to growth in two-income families. The high costs of housing and of maintaining a comfortable lifestyle, the high level of taxes, and the cultural emphasis on "having it all" have made it difficult if not impossible for many households to live on just one income. Furthermore, many women today simply want a career outside the home.

One result of this trend is a host of programs that companies have implemented in response to the demands of busy two-income families. Scotiabank and Procter & Gamble, for example, each offer employees pregnancy benefits, parental leave, and flexible work schedules. Some companies offer referral services that provide counselling to parents in search of child care or elder care.

Many companies are also increasing the number of part-time workers. This enables mothers and fathers to stay home part of the day with children and still earn income. Some companies allow workers to telecommute, which means they work from home and keep in touch with the company through

One of Canada's strengths is its ability to welcome and help prosper people from all over the world. This photo shows a diversity conference. Such conferences often help people with different backgrounds and opinions to be heard and to listen to and learn from others. These interactions also help to clarify and resolve issues among various ethnic groups. What are some of the diversity issues in your community?

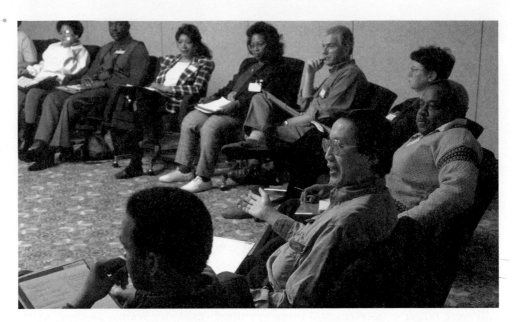

telecommunications (telephone, fax, e-mail, etc.). This lowers the company's cost for office space and also makes it possible for parents to meet the demands of both job and family.

Workplace changes due to the rise of two-income families create many job opportunities in day care, counselling, and other related fields. You'll learn more about what's happening in human resource management in Chapter 12.

Single Parents   The growth of single-parent households (from 8 percent of all families in 1966 to almost 16 percent in 2001) has had a major effect on businesses as well.[22] It is a tremendous task to work full-time and raise a family. Single parents have encouraged businesses to implement programs such as family leave (where workers can take time off to attend to a sick child) and flextime (where workers can come in or leave at selected times). You will be able to read about such programs in more detail in Chapter 12.

The Global Environment

The global environment of business is so important that we show it as surrounding all other environmental influences (refer to Figure 1.4). Two important environmental changes in recent years have been the growth of international competition and the increase of free trade among nations. Japanese manufacturers like Honda, Mitsubishi, and Sony won much of the market for automobiles, videocassette recorders, digital video disk players, television sets, and other products by offering global consumers products of higher quality than those made by domestic manufacturers. This competition hurt many industries, and many jobs were lost. As a result, more businesses have become more competitive.

Today, manufacturers in countries such as China, India, South Korea, and Mexico can produce high-quality goods at low prices because their workers are paid less money than Canadian workers and because they've learned quality concepts from Japanese, German, and U.S. producers. Late in the 1990s, however, Thailand, Malaysia, Hong Kong, Japan, South Korea, and other Asian countries had banking problems that caused a major upheaval in global markets. These problems affected all nations, showing the interdependence of countries around the world today.

Entrepreneurship is an exciting way to make a living, but working for a big company can be equally rewarding. These employees of SAS, a software design firm, are enjoying the company swimming pool—just one of the many employee benefits the company sponsors. Other firms provide indoor tracks, weight rooms, employee cafeterias, and corporate retreats with golf and other facilities. Which would you prefer: the challenge of starting your own business and being your own boss, or working for a larger firm and taking advantage of its employee benefits program?

Better technology, machinery, tools, education, and training enable each worker to be more productive. It is the primary responsibility of businesses to focus on these areas to ensure success. However, the federal government also recognizes that it can play an important role. In 2002, it launched its 10-year innovation strategy (www.innovationstrategy.gc.ca), which "aims to move Canada to the front ranks of the world's most innovative countries." The government plans to do this by moving to build on the investments already made in research and innovation, to make essential research and technological expertise available to firms of all sizes, and to facilitate access to venture capital financing.[23] While the innovation strategy will be discussed in more detail in Chapter 4, one should note that political support also contributes to domestic and global success.

Companies such as Bombardier, Nortel, Magna, and Pratt & Whitney, as well as many smaller companies, are as good as or better than competing organizations anywhere in the world. But some businesses have gone beyond simply competing with organizations in other countries by learning to cooperate with international firms. Cooperation among businesses has the potential to create rapidly growing world markets that can generate prosperity beyond most people's expectations. The challenge is tremendous, but so is the will to achieve. You'll read much more about the importance of trade agreements (such as NAFTA), understanding cultural differences, and global business in general in Chapter 3.

THE EVOLUTION OF CANADIAN BUSINESS

Many managers and workers are losing their jobs in major manufacturing firms. Businesses in Canada have become so productive that, compared to the past, fewer workers are needed in industries that produce goods. **Goods** are tangible products such as computers, food, clothing, cars, and appliances. Due to the increasing impact of technology and global competition, shouldn't we be concerned about the prospect of high unemployment rates and low incomes? Where will the jobs be when you graduate? These important questions prompt us to look briefly at the manufacturing and service sectors.

goods
Tangible products such as computers, food, clothing, cars, and appliances.

Agriculture is an important industry in Canada. The entire process of growing food and getting it to our tables is so smooth that it's easy to take for granted. But behind those well-stocked supermarkets is an army of farmers and distributors who supply our needs. Use of technology has led to increased productivity and made farmers more efficient, resulting in larger farms. This trend has meant less expensive food for us, but a continual reduction in the number of small, family-run farms. Is it still possible for small farms to be successful, and if so, how?

Progress in the Agricultural and Manufacturing Industries

Canada has seen strong economic development since the 1800s. The agricultural industry led the way, providing food for Canadians and people in other parts of the world. Inventions such as the harvester and cotton gin did much to make farming successful, as did ongoing improvements on such equipment. The modern farming industry has become so efficient through the use of technology that the number of farms has dropped. Due to increased competition, many of the farms that existed even 50 years ago have been replaced by some huge farms, some merely large farms, and some small but highly specialized farms. The loss of farm workers over the past century is not a negative sign. It is instead an indication that Canadian agricultural workers are more productive.

Most farmers who lost their jobs went to work in factories. The manufacturing industry, much like agriculture, used technology to become more productive. The consequence, as in farming, was the elimination of many jobs. Again, the loss to society is minimal if the wealth created by increased productivity and efficiency creates new jobs elsewhere. This is exactly what has happened over the past 50 years. Many workers in the industrial sector found jobs in the service sector. Most of those who can't find work today are people who need retraining and education to become qualified for jobs that now exist.

Canada's Manufacturing Industry   The goods-producing sector includes the manufacturing, construction, agriculture, forestry, fishing, and mining industries. Of this sector, manufacturing employs approximately 15 percent of Canada's working population, as noted in Figure 1.7.

Canadian Manufacturers & Exporters is a network that represents many small- and medium-sized manufacturers. Here are some of the network's suggested reasons why this sector is important to Canada:

- Directly, manufacturing accounts for 21 percent of economic activity. But when you consider spin-offs (such as the purchase of products), manufacturers drive 55 percent of the economy;

- Every $1 of manufacturing in Canada generates $3 in total economic activity; and

- Nearly 70 percent of all goods manufactured in Canada are exported, accounting for more than $400 billion of Canada's merchandise exports.[24]

FIGURE 1.7

THE IMPORTANCE OF THE GOODS-PRODUCING AND SERVICES-PRODUCING SECTORS IN CANADA

Canada is a service economy, where the majority of jobs are generated in the services-producing sector. This excerpt from Statistics Canada's Employment by Industry for 2003 also reflects the importance of manufacturing and agriculture to Canadians.

	NUMBER OF EMPLOYED	TOTAL WORKFORCE (%)
Total employed in Canada	15,746,000	100.0
Goods-producing sector	3,986,100	25.3
Agriculture	339,500	2.2
Manufacturing	2,294,000	14.6
Services-producing sector	11,759,900	74.7

Source: "Role of Manufacturing in the Economy," adapted from Statistics Canada CANSIMdatabase http://cansim2.statcan.ca, Tables 379-0017, 379-0020, and 282,0008.

While the manufacturing sector is much smaller today than it was 25 years ago, it is still clearly an integral part of our business economy. We will discuss the manufacturing sector and production in more detail in Chapter 10.

Progress in Service Industries

The service sector is distinct from the goods-producing sector. **Services** are intangible products (i.e., products that cannot be held in your hand) such as education, health care, insurance, recreation, and travel and tourism. In the past, the dominant industries in Canada produced goods such as steel, railroads, and machine tools. Over the last 25 years, the service sector in Canada and around the world has grown dramatically.

> **services**
> Intangible products (i.e., products that can't be held in your hand) such as education, health care, insurance, recreation, and travel and tourism.

The shift in Canada's employment makeup began slowly early in the 20th century, and has accelerated rapidly since the 1950s. Today, the leading firms are in services (such as legal, health, telecommunications, entertainment, financial services, etc.). As noted in Figure 1.7, the services-producing sector employs almost 75 percent of the working population.

There are several reasons why there has been growth in this sector. First, technological improvements have enabled businesses to reduce their payrolls while increasing their output. Since staffing has been downsized by many companies, business has become more complex and specialized companies have relied more heavily on outside services firms. Secondly, as large manufacturing companies seek to become more efficient, they contract out an increasing number of services, creating more opportunities for businesspeople. Other service firms have risen or expanded rapidly to provide traditional services that used to be performed by women at home. Since many women have entered the workforce, there is increased demand for food preparation, child care, and household maintenance, to name just a few.

Keep in mind that service-sector jobs are also impacted by environmental factors. For example, the outbreak of SARS (severe acute respiratory syndrome) first reported in March 2003 impacted the desire of foreigners (and Canadians) to travel throughout our country. Canada's tourism continued to falter when the World Health Organization issued an advisory recommending only essential travel. Among other initiatives, the federal government earmarked $20 million to promote Canada and to assist the recovery of the tourism industry.[25] While many businesses recognized the government's attempt to increase demand for tourism dollars, such initiatives could not fully replace the losses in revenue that were experienced by businesses and workers.

Your Future in Business

Despite the growth in the service sector described above, the service era now seems to be coming to a close as a new era is beginning. We're now in the midst of an information-based global revolution that will alter all sectors of the economy. It's exciting to think about the role you'll play in that revolution. You may be a leader; that is, you may be one of the people who will implement the changes and accept the challenges of world competition based on world quality standards. This book will introduce you to some of the concepts that will make such leadership possible.

Remember that most of the concepts and principles that make businesses more effective and efficient are also applicable to government agencies and nonprofit organizations. This is an introductory business text, so we will focus on business. Business cannot prosper in the future without the cooperation of government and social leaders throughout the world.

> Visit jobfutures.ca to find out what the future's most promising jobs will be—the site provides projections for the next five years by province, territory, and profession.

Critical Thinking

Can you think of any type of service or good not currently on the market that would appeal to the growing number of seniors? Would you be interested in trying to develop that item? Why or why not?

Should Canadians strengthen the manufacturing sector? What can they do? Is there a role for government in this effort?

Have any of the trends discussed in the chapter given you any ideas for a career? Explain. Are you thinking about whether the rest of your education should be broader or more specialized? Should it be both broader and more specialized? Given the globalization of business, should you be acquiring the ability to speak more languages? You will have to think seriously about these options—don't hesitate to consult people whose opinions you respect, both inside and outside your school.

Progress Assessment

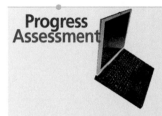

- What are some of the diverse groups of people that managers must manage?
- What are the factors that have led to two-income families?
- What accounts for the growth in service-sector jobs? Why is it so essential for the economy?

Summary

1. Describe the relationship of businesses' profit to risk assumption.

1. A business is any activity that seeks to provide goods and services to others while operating at a profit.
   - ***What are the relationships between risk, profit, and loss?***
   Profit is money a business earns above and beyond the money that it spends for salaries and other expenses. Businesspeople make profits by taking risks. *Risk* is the chance an entrepreneur takes of losing time and money on a business that may not prove profitable. A loss occurs when a business's costs and expenses are more than its revenues.

2. Discuss the groups that are considered stakeholders and indicate which stakeholders are most important to a business.

2. Stakeholders include customers, employees, shareholders, suppliers, dealers, bankers, people in the local community, environmentalists, and elected government leaders.
   - ***Which stakeholders are most important to a business?***
   The goal of business leaders is to try to balance the needs of all stakeholders and still make a profit. Some businesses put the needs of shareholders above the other interests, but most businesses today seek a balance among the needs of the various stakeholders.

3. Explain the importance of entrepreneurship to the wealth of an economy.

3. Entrepreneurs are people who risk time and money to start and manage a business.
   - ***What importance does entrepreneurship hold in the list of the five factors of production?***
   Businesses use five factors of production: land (natural resources), labour (workers), capital (buildings and machinery), entrepreneurship, and knowledge. Of these, the most important are entrepreneurship and knowledge (managed information), because without them land, labour, and capital are not of much use.

4. The business environment consists of the surrounding factors that either help or hinder the development of businesses. The six elements are the legal and regulatory environment, the economic environment, the technological environment, the competitive environment, the social environment, and the global environment.
   - *Explain why the business environment is important to organizations.* Scanning the business environment on a continual basis is important to organizations so that they can take advantage of trends. These trends could impact the organization's ability to achieve its objectives, steer clear of threats, or take advantage of new opportunities.

4. Review the six elements that make up the business environment and explain why the business environment is important to organizations.

5. Competition among businesses has never been greater than it is today.
   - *What are some ways in which businesses meet and beat competition?* Some companies found a competitive edge in the 1980s by focusing on making high-quality products. By the early 1990s, meeting the challenge of making a quality product was not enough to stay competitive in world markets. Companies had to offer quality goods and outstanding service at competitive prices (value). The speed of new product development, production, delivery, and service is also critical. Companies aim to exceed customer expectations. Often that means empowering frontline workers by giving them more training and more responsibility and authority. It also means restructuring the firm to create more teams.

5. Identify various ways in which businesses can meet and beat competition.

6. Canada has evolved from an economy based on manufacturing to one based on services.
   - *Why is manufacturing still a vital industry for Canada?* While the services-producing sector employs almost 75 percent of the working population, the manufacturing industry employs almost 15 percent of workers. Every $1 of manufacturing in Canada generates $3 in total economic activity. Directly, manufacturing accounts for 21 percent of economic activity, but when you consider spin-offs, manufacturers drive 55 percent of the economy.

6. Understand how the service sector has replaced manufacturing as the principal provider of jobs, but why manufacturing remains vital for Canada.

Key Terms

business 4	goods 23	risk 5
business environment 11	loss 5	services 25
database 18	nonprofit organization 7	stakeholders 5
demography 20	productivity 15	technology 15
empowerment 19	profit 4	
entrepreneur 4	regulations 13	
factors of production 9	revenue 5	

Developing Workplace Skills

1. Make a list of nonprofit organizations in your community that might offer you a chance to learn some of the skills you'll need in the job you hope to have when you graduate. How could you make time in your schedule to volunteer or work at one or more of those organizations? Write a letter to a nonprofit organization to inquire about such opportunities.

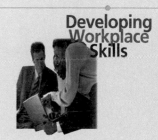

2. In this chapter, Hollinger, Cinar, and Livent were mentioned as examples of companies where some top executives had disregarded their stakeholders. Research why this statement is correct. Present your findings to the class.

3. Use a computer word processing program to write a one-page report on how technology will change society in the next 10 years. Use a computer graphics program to create a chart (or draw a chart by hand) that illustrates the increased use of personal computers in Canadian homes since 1980.

4. Form teams of four or five and discuss the technological and e-commerce revolutions. How many students now shop for goods and services online? What have been their experiences? What other high-tech equipment do they use (e.g., cell phones, pagers, laptop computers, desktop computers, personal digital assistants, portable music players)?

5. This text describes the growth trend in the numbers of businesses in the service sector. Look through your local Yellow Pages or go on the Internet to find and list five businesses that provide services in your area. This text also describes how certain demographic and social changes affect businesses. For each of the local service businesses on your list, describe how social trends might affect it. Include both negative effects and positive effects. Be prepared to explain your answers.

Taking It To The Net

This exercise requires using the Internet. If you do not know how to navigate this powerful computer network, you need to read "Surfing the Internet," on the Online Learning Centre.

Purpose

To gather data about the size of global corporations and the level of profitability of the various global industries.

Exercise

Businesses seek to earn profits by providing goods and services to other businesses and individual consumers. Ever wonder just how much profit the largest companies earn and which companies earn the highest profits? Try to answer the first two questions on the following list before you search for the answers on the Web. Then go to the *Fortune* magazine Website at www.fortune.com. Enter the Global 500 section. You may be surprised by what you find.

1. List the top 10 revenue-producing global corporations. How many small businesses with average revenues of $100,000 a year would it take to match the revenue of the largest global corporation?

2. List the top 10 profit-producing global corporations. How many companies are on both of your lists?

3. How much revenue per employee does the trading industry generate? The tobacco industry? The airline industry? The mail, package, and freight delivery industry?

4. *KNOW YOUR BUSINESS:* Mitsui is one of the highest revenue-producing companies in the world. What industry is the Mitsui company a part of? Where is its home office? What are Mitsui's primary products?

Practising Management Decisions

Case

Canada's 100 Fastest-Growing Companies

Every year, *Profit* magazine publishes a list of Canada's 100 fastest-growing companies. The 2003 issue reported in detail on the 2002 selection. The importance of many of the points we discussed in this chapter was quite evident, especially when one considers the breakdown among the types of companies. Manufacturers are back on top, but retailers rebound. Here is a sector breakdown of some of the top 100:

Business services	25
Software developers	13
IT services	8
Consumer services	6
Distribution	6
Retail	4
Pharmaceutical	5
Publishing	2
Construction	2

While the companies were located across Canada, Ontario and British Columbia represented the majority of these companies:

British Columbia	24
Alberta	15
Ontario	52
Quebec	7
Newfoundland	1
New Brunswick	1

What makes these companies leaders is that they grew rapidly and continue to do so, regardless of what field they are in. It did not matter whether they are high-tech or old-economy companies, manufacturing or service companies. In 2002 these companies created 3,158 jobs, and the expected job growth in fiscal 2003 was 3,333 jobs. Clearly, great teams start with great people. Interesting statistics about the top 100 company presidents include:

1. Average age: 43 years
2. Average hours worked per week: 57
3. Average annual compensation: $285,415
4. Highest level of school completed: 13 completed high school, 7 completed community college, 11 completed some college or university, 45 completed university, and 24 completed post-graduate work.
5. Number of CEOs that have previously founded a business: 48

Keeping employees engaged, challenged, and motivated is the next step. This topic will be discussed later on in this book.

Source: Adapted from www.profitguide.com (retrieved on May 21, 2004).

Decision Questions

1. Which of these data support the information discussed in the chapter? Explain your answer.
2. Can you see how the lines between service and manufacturing companies are getting blurred? Is there a clear distinction between a good and a service?
3. What does all this mean for your career choices? Will you concentrate on high-tech or traditional industries? Do you look for companies that are globally oriented?
4. Visit www.profitguide.com to see the latest information on the Top 100. How much has changed since these results were posted?

Video Case

Toying with Success: The McFarlane Companies

In his school days, Todd McFarlane had dreams of playing major league baseball. Unfortunately, his dream didn't come true. So like most of us, he put his dreams aside and decided that he had to get a job and make a living. But McFarlane did not want to just go to "work" every day; he wanted to do something he enjoyed. As a teen, he liked to draw superheroes. He developed his drawing skill throughout high school and college and began to send out samples of his work, lots of samples. Alas, he got lots of rejections until finally someone offered him a job.

McFarlane's first job was working freelance on obscure comic books for Marvel Comics, the biggest name in the comic book industry. By working relentlessly and turning his high-quality work in on time, McFarlane earned a reputation as a good worker. That reputation earned him the right to work a little on well-known comics like Batman, the Hulk, and Spiderman. He brought Spiderman from relative obscurity to the number-one book with record sales. Over time, he became the highest paid comic book artist at Marvel.

McFarlane began to feel a bit cramped and held back by the way things were done at Marvel. He had many ideas he wanted to try, but was discouraged by the lack of excitement at the company. He decided it was time to quit and start his own comic book business. He was able to persuade several of his best co-workers to come with him.

Many insiders in the comic book industry gave his new company one year at best. McFarlane believed failure was out of the question and he did anything but fail. His first comic, Spawn, sold 1.7 million copies—the rest was history. Today, when it comes to creating comics, producing movies, directing music videos, and running one of the most successful toy companies in the world, McFarlane has done it all. His path to success was similar to other entrepreneurs who learned about their business working for a large company. Chapter 1 shows that the energy and the risk-taking these entrepreneurs apply to the task is what creates jobs and wealth.

Entrepreneurs like McFarlane, however, face many challenges in the business environment: legal and regulatory, economic, technological, competitive, social, and global. For example, the legal system protects his intellectual property and allows him to make contracts that are enforceable. He also takes advantage of the latest in technology to push creativity forward in making toys, movies, and video games. The Internet provides a means to reach the young people who are his key customers. Competitively, McFarlane loves to see competitors turn out shoddy goods because it provides an opportunity for him to make high-quality toys and other products that may cost more, but are well worth the extra few cents. It's impossible to avoid social issues like strikes and global problems like diseases that hold up production. The key is to keep focused and keep business going.

What about his major league dreams? Part of McFarlane's dream started coming true when he bought Mark McGuire's record-breaking 70th home run ball. It cost him a cool $3 million! To his chagrin the record was broken the next year by Barry Bonds. But McFarlane did not give up. Combining it with other McGuire and Sammy Sosa balls he had purchased, he formed the McFarlane Collection and sent it on a tour of every major league stadium. The payoff was good public relations for his firm and the development of a relationship with people in professional sports and management that led to licensing rights to produce major league toys. The $3-million ball may lead to $20 million in profit. Did his dreams come true? He doesn't have a baseball career, but every toy contract with a major league team includes what you might call a signing bonus: the right for McFarlane to hit batting practice in every ballpark that shows his collection. That's not the same as being a player, but McFarlane's not complaining.

Discussion Questions

1. What lessons can you take from Todd McFarlane about how to be a success in life?

2. What dreams do you have, and where could you work where you may be able to fulfill at least a major part of your dream?

3. What skills can you develop working for a larger firm before you go out on your own to become a successful entrepreneur?

4. What are some of the challenges you see in today's dynamic business environment and what are some of the opportunities?

Chapter 2

How Economic Issues Affect Business

Learning Goals

After you have read and studied this chapter, you should be able to

1 Explain what capitalism is and how free markets work.

2 Define supply and demand and explain the relevance of the equilibrium point.

3 Discuss the major differences between socialism and communism.

4 Understand the mixed economy of Canada.

5 Discuss Canada's economic system, including the significance of key economic indicators, productivity, and the business cycle.

Profile

Getting to Know Statistics Canada

Statistics Canada (StatsCan) produces statistics that help Canadians better understand their country. (Many of the Canadian statistics in this textbook were sourced from StatsCan.)

If you wish to find out about Canada's population, resources, economy, government, society, and culture, it is likely that StatsCan can help you. Just visit www.statcan.ca and click on *Canadian Statistics* to find what you are looking for.

When you go to the Website, you will quickly see the latest economic indicators—this chapter introduces you to these concepts, which include the gross domestic product (GDP), the unemployment rate, and the consumer price index (CPI).

Information is not based on just Canada. One can also find data that compares Canada's performance to that of other countries. For example, in 1999 Canada had the third lowest unemployment rate when compared to France, Spain, Sweden, and the United Kingdom.

Providing these statistics is a federal responsibility. As Canada's central statistical agency, StatsCan is legislated to serve this function for the whole country. Consequently, the information it collects is available to the public. This is important as the data provides a solid foundation for informed decisions by businesses, non-profit organizations, government agencies, and consumers like you. If you wish to find newly released information, click on *The Daily*, StatsCan's official release bulletin.

How does StatsCan collect information? A national Census is conducted every five years, and there are about 350 active surveys on virtually all aspects of Canadian life. Data from the most recent Census were collected in spring 2001, when 11.8 million households were asked to fill out the questionnaire. To find these results, you can visit *CANSIM*—Statistics Canada's socio-economic database—and type in key words in the *Search* location, or click on *Census* from the home page.

How can you apply StatsCan information in a business situation? If, for example, you are looking at entering a new market, you can quickly find out the following statistics for the region: population, household sizes, level of unemployment, average income per capita, and more. *Community Profiles* contains additional information on more than 6,000 communities including cities, villages, and Native reserves and settlements. All this, without having to leave your computer!

So the next time you are asked to find socio-economic information, don't forget to visit this site. Much of the information is available free of charge. If not, check with your library—StatsCan data may very well be available as part of the service provided by your school.

Sources: Adapted from Statistics Canada, http://www.statcan.ca; Jill Mahoney, "Census at Risk If U.S. Firm In On It, Critics Say," *The Globe and Mail,* 14 October 2003, sec. A, p. 4; www.statcan.ca, November 1, 2003.

How Economic Conditions Affect Business

If you want to understand the underlying situation and conditions in which Canadian business operates, it is essential that you (1) have some grasp of economics, (2) be aware of the impact of the global environment, and (3) understand the role of the federal and provincial governments in Canada.

The Canadian economy is an integral part of the world economy. Business firms use labour from other countries, export to and import from other countries, buy land in other countries for their facilities, and receive money from foreign investors. To understand events in the Canadian economy, therefore, one has to understand the world economy.

Why is South Korea comparatively wealthy and North Korea suffering economically? Annual income per capita (per person) is US$8,900 in South Korea, but only US$706 in North Korea.[1] Why is China's per capita annual income about $800 while Taiwan's is more than US$15,000? Such questions are part of the subject of economics. In this chapter, we explore the various economic systems of the world and how they either promote or hinder business growth, the creation of wealth, and quality of life.

A major part of business success is due to an economic and social climate that allows businesses to operate freely. Foreign investors like Canada because we have a stable economic and political environment. Investing is risky enough without having to worry about unpredictable governments, massive corruption, and weak laws. Therefore, any change in our economic or political system can have a major influence on businesses.

economics
The study of how society chooses to employ resources to produce goods and services and distribute them for consumption among various competing groups and individuals.

What Is Economics?

Economics is the study of how society chooses to employ resources to produce goods and services and distribute them for consumption among various competing groups and individuals. Remember from Chapter 1 that these resources (land, labour, capital, entrepreneurship, and knowledge) are called *factors of production* ➤**P. 10**◄.

The economic contrast is remarkable. Business in South Korea is booming in Seoul, South Korea (pictured on left). But North Korea, a communist country, is not doing well, as the picture on the right of thousands of workers using old fashioned tools in a work-for-food program shows. South Korea has 110 telephones per 100 residents while North Korea has just 5. The annual income per person in the South is $8,900 versus $706 in the North. North Korea has become a nuclear threat to the world and may soon be exporting nuclear weapons to other countries, largely as a means to raise money. What do you think accounts for the dramatic differences in the economies of these two countries?

Businesses may contribute to an economic system by inventing products that greatly increase available resources. For example, businesses may discover new energy sources, new ways of growing food, and new ways of creating needed goods and services.[2] Ballard Power Systems, a leading developer of fuel cells and fuel cell engines, is doing just this. Among other initiatives, Ballard is working with auto manufacturers to develop the next generation of efficient and clean engines for buses, automobiles, and trucks.[3]

Economists usually work from one or two perspectives: **macroeconomics** looks at the operation of a nation's economy as a whole, and **microeconomics** looks at the behaviour of people and organizations in particular markets. For example, while macroeconomics looks at how many jobs exist in the whole economy, microeconomics examines how many people will be hired in a particular industry or a particular region of the country. Topics discussed in this chapter that are part of macroeconomics include gross domestic product, unemployment rate, and price indexes. Chapter topics that deal with microeconomic issues include pricing and supply and demand.

macroeconomics
The part of economic study that looks at the operation of a nation's economy as a whole.

microeconomics
The part of economic study that looks at the behaviour of people and organizations in particular markets.

Growth Economics and Adam Smith

In 1776, Adam Smith wrote the now-famous book *An Inquiry into the Nations and Causes of the Wealth of Nations*. It was later considered the foundation of the study and understanding of the newly developing capitalist industrial society. Smith was one of the first people to imagine a system for creating wealth and improving the lives of everyone. Smith said that all companies would function best with little government involvement. Under his theory, businesspeople would work primarily for their own prosperity and growth. As people tried to improve their own situation in life, their efforts would serve as an "invisible hand" that would make everything work well in the economy. Thus, the **invisible hand** turns self-directed gain into social and economic benefits for all.

invisible hand
A phrase coined by Adam Smith to describe the process that turns self-directed gain into social and economic benefits for all.

How would this work? Individuals take the risk of investing money to build factories to produce what people want, creating profit for investors and jobs for people. Because more people have jobs and can buy all the new products being produced, their lives would improve. The factory owners make profits that they can reinvest to build new factories to produce more goods and so on. In the end, said Smith, individual producers and buyers make for a prosperous and happy society.

Adam Smith developed a theory of wealth creation more than 200 years ago. His theory relied on entrepreneurs working to improve their lives. To make money, they would provide goods and services, as well as jobs, for others. What countries have adopted the ideas of Adam Smith?

- What is the difference between macroeconomics and microeconomics?
- What does Adam Smith's term *invisible hand* mean? How does the invisible hand create wealth for a country?

Progress Assessment

Although the people of Poland have had some success with capitalism over the past decade or so, they have learned that moving from a communist to a capitalist system is not easy. However, some entrepreneurs flourished from the beginning. Wala Lukaszuk, for example, enjoyed early success with her own salad bar, but she is now experiencing competition from larger businesses. Capitalism does not guarantee success; it only affords the opportunity to try. Typically, communism offers more job security, but provides fewer opportunities. Have you talked with someone familiar with socialism or communism to compare the advantages and disadvantages with capitalism?

capitalism
An economic system in which all or most of the factors of production and distribution are privately owned and operated for profit.

UNDERSTANDING FREE-MARKET CAPITALISM

Basing their ideas on free-market principles, such as those of Adam Smith, businesspeople began to create more wealth than had ever been created before. They hired others to work on their farms and in their factories and nations began to prosper as a result. Businesspeople soon became the wealthiest people in society. While there were great disparities between the wealthy and the poor, there was always the promise of opportunities to become wealthy.

The economic system that has led to wealth creation in much of the world is known as capitalism. **Capitalism** is an economic system in which all or most of the factors of production and distribution (e.g., land, factories, railroads, and stores) are privately owned (not owned by the government) and are operated for profit. In capitalist countries, businesspeople decide what to produce; how much to pay workers; how much to charge for goods and services; where to sell these goods and services; and so on. Capitalism is the popular term used to describe free-market economies.

No country is purely capitalist, however. Often the government gets involved in issues such as determining minimum wages and subsidizing certain sectors, as the federal government does in Canada for the agriculture sector. Today capitalism is the foundation for the economies of Canada, England, Australia, the United States, and most other developed nations. We will discuss Canada's mixed economy in some detail later in this book.

How Free Markets Work

The free market is one in which decisions about what to produce and in what quantities are made by the market—that is, by buyers and sellers negotiating prices for goods and services. Consumers (such as you and me) send signals to tell producers what to make, how many, in what colours, and so on. We do that by choosing to buy (or not to buy) certain goods and services. The Spotlight on Small Business box shares how Songnian Zhou created a product needed by businesses around the world.

Spotlight on Small Business

Small Business's Dynamic Role

www.platform.org

Songnian Zhou, CEO, chairman and co-founder of Platform Computing Corp., based in Markham, Ontario, offers a simple reason for his company's success: it created a software product needed by businesses around the world. As Babe Ruth said, "It ain't bragging if you can do it."

Since it was founded in 1992 to provide Fortune 500 firms with "workload management" systems—software that essentially manages your computer network's complex functions—Platform has had 12 consecutive years of profitability. In 2003, revenues exceeded US$50 million.

An associate professor of computer science at the University of Toronto, Zhou pioneered Platform's LSF (load-sharing facility) software while doing his PhD dissertation in 1987. After developing a prototype that was adopted at Northern Telecom, Zhou and two partners launched Platform commercially. Zhou calls LSF "a suite of systems software for managing workload across heterogeneous computers." Translation: LSF acts as "a virtual manager," ensuring computers on a network carry out their duties in a seamless fashion.

"In a human environment, the manager is not there actually doing the work himself. He's there to coordinate the resources, know who all the people are, and know which skill sets are needed," says Zhou. "It's the same principle for computer systems: our software determines which computers and servers are needed, and then manages all the different application resources across the whole network."

Platform's technology is applicable to a variety of industries and runs on any platform, says Zhou. Available customized or off the shelf, the company exports to many countries but its chief market so far is in the U.S. Customers include Boeing, Shell, and Pacific Data Images (PDI), the California-based animation studio that created *Antz*, the computer-animated box-office hit. PDI used Platform's LSF software to track its myriad computers churning out armies of animated ants. "We made sure that no usable machine would stay idle when there was work to do," says Zhou. "If a machine crashed in the middle of the night, we would recover the job" to run on another computer. *Antz* thus enjoyed faster product development and generated higher profits. Still, Zhou is not resting on his laurels.

Platform invests 30 percent of its profit in R&D. It is constantly developing new products as it operates in a very competitive high-tech field. Platform is a private company with 350 employees in over 20 offices across North America, Asia-Pacific, and Europe. *Antz* aside, staying on top is no picnic.

Adapted from: www.platform.com, May 22, 2004; *Profit,* June 2001, p. 35; David Menzies, *Profit,* June 1999, p. 55; interview with CFO Gordon Booth, June 1, 1999.

Four Seasons Hotels and Resorts is the world's leading operator of luxury hotels and resorts. It manages 62 properties in 29 countries. One of its newest locations is Four Seasons Resort Whistler. This resort offers easy access to the slopes of Whistler Blackcomb (site of the 2010 Olympic Winter Games), a spa, mountainside dining, and wilderness adventures year-round. Listening to the market, Four Seasons offers a growing network of vacation ownership properties and private residences.

How Prices Are Determined

In a free market, prices are not determined by sellers; they are determined by buyers and sellers negotiating in the marketplace. A seller may want to receive $50 for a T-shirt, but the quantity demanded at that price may be quite low. If the seller lowers the price, the quantity demanded is likely to increase. How is a price determined that is acceptable to both buyers and sellers? The answer is found in the microeconomic concepts of supply and demand.

The Economic Concept of Supply

supply
The quantity of products that manufacturers or owners are willing to sell at different prices at a specific time.

Supply refers to the quantity of products that manufacturers or owners are willing to sell at different prices at a specific time. Generally speaking, the amount supplied will increase as the price increases because sellers can make more money with a higher price.

Economists show this relationship between quantity supplied and price on a graph. Figure 2.1 shows a simple supply curve for T-shirts. The price of the shirts in dollars is shown vertically on the left of the graph. The quantity of shirts sellers are willing to supply is shown horizontally at the bottom of the graph. The various points on the curve indicate how many T-shirts sellers would provide at different prices. For example, at a price of $5 a shirt, a T-shirt vendor would provide only 5 T-shirts, but at $50 a shirt the vendor would supply 50 shirts. The supply curve indicates the relationship between the price and the quantity supplied. All things being equal, the higher the price, the more the vendor will be willing to supply.

The Economic Concept of Demand

demand
The quantity of products that people are willing to buy at different prices at a specific time.

Demand refers to the quantity of products that people are willing to buy at different prices at a specific time. Generally speaking, the quantity demanded will increase as the price decreases. Again, the relationship between price and quantity demanded can be shown in a graph. Figure 2.2 shows a simple demand curve for T-shirts. The various points on the graph indicate the quantity demanded at various prices. For example, at a price of $45, the quantity demanded is just 5 shirts; but if the price were $5, the quantity demanded would increase to 35 shirts. The line connecting the dots is called a demand curve. It shows the relationship between quantity demanded and price.

FIGURE 2.1

THE SUPPLY CURVE AT VARIOUS PRICES

The supply curve rises from left to right. Think it through. The higher the price of T-shirts goes (the left margin), the more sellers will be willing to supply.

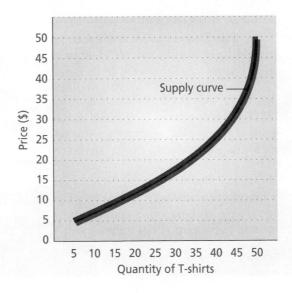

FIGURE 2.2

THE DEMAND CURVE AT VARIOUS PRICES

This is a simple demand curve showing the quantity of T-shirts demanded at different prices. The demand curve falls from left to right. It is easy to understand why. The lower the price of T-shirts, the higher the quantity demanded.

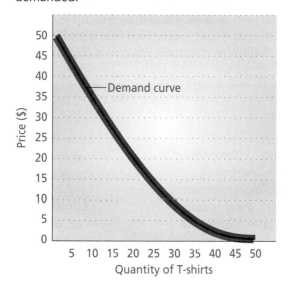

FIGURE 2.3

THE EQUILIBRIUM POINT

The place where quantity demanded and supplied meet is called the equilibrium point. When we put both the supply and demand curves on the same graph, we find that they intersect at a price where the quantity supplied and the quantity demanded are equal. In the long run, the market price will tend toward the equilibrium point.

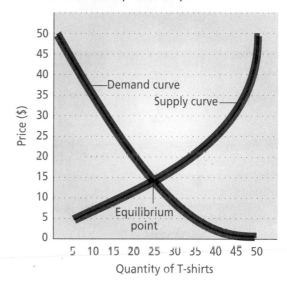

The Equilibrium Point or Market Price

It should be clear to you after reviewing Figures 2.1 and 2.2 that the key factor in determining the quantity supplied and the quantity demanded is *price*. Sellers prefer a high price, and buyers prefer a low price. If you were to lay one of the two graphs on top of the other, the supply curve and the demand curve would cross. At that crossing point, the quantity demanded and the quantity supplied would be equal. Figure 2.3 illustrates that point. At a price of $15, the quantity of T-shirts demanded and the quantity supplied are equal (25 shirts). That crossing point is known as the equilibrium point or the equilibrium price. In the long run, that price would become the market price. **Market price,** then, is determined by supply and demand.

Alexandra Brown, eBay Canada's communications director, explains how the market price is determined at eBay. "Let's say you want to buy something and you're unsure of what to pay, whether it's a used car or a collectible—or even if you want to sell something. You can go on eBay, type in what you're looking for, get listings from around the world, and see what the prices are." Brown added that because the market is being determined by buyers and sellers arriving at a price, it's a good reflection of true values.[4]

Supporters of a free market would argue that, because supply and demand interactions determine prices, there is no need for government involvement or government planning. If surpluses develop (i.e., if quantity supplied exceeds quantity demanded), a signal is sent to sellers to lower the price. If shortages develop (i.e., if quantity supplied is less than quantity demanded), a signal is sent to sellers to increase the price. Eventually, supply will again equal demand if nothing interferes with market forces.

market price
The price determined by supply and demand.

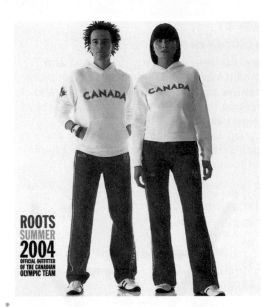

ROOTS
SUMMER
2004
OFFICIAL OUTFITTER
OF THE CANADIAN
OLYMPIC TEAM

For the past six years, Roots has outfitted Canadian Olympic team members. Outfits for the 2004 Olympic Games in Athens carried the distinctive CANADA logo, the '04 maple leaf logo, the Canadian Olympic team crest, and the Roots logo. When considering competition within free markets, under what degree of competition does Roots compete? Can you name other companies whose products compete with Roots?

perfect competition
The market situation in which there are many sellers in a market and no seller is large enough to dictate the price of a product.

monopolistic competition
The market situation in which a large number of sellers produce products that are very similar but that are perceived by buyers as different.

oligopoly
A form of competition in which just a few sellers dominate the market.

monopoly
A market in which there is only one seller for a good or service.

In countries without a free market, there is no such mechanism to reveal to businesses (via price) what to produce and in what amounts, so there are often shortages (not enough products) or surpluses (too many products). In such countries, the government decides what to produce and in what quantity, but the government has no way of knowing what the proper quantities are. Furthermore, when the government interferes in otherwise free markets, such as when it subsidizes farm goods, surpluses and shortages may also develop.

One benefit of the free market is that it allows open competition among companies. Businesses must provide customers with quality products at fair prices with good service; otherwise, they will lose customers to those businesses that do provide such things. We'll discuss the nature of competition next.

Competition within Free Markets

In Chapter 1, you were introduced to the importance of the competitive environment. Economists generally agree that four different degrees of competition exist: (1) perfect competition, (2) monopolistic competition, (3) oligopoly, and (4) monopoly.

Perfect competition exists when there are many sellers in a market and no seller is large enough to dictate the price of a product. Under perfect competition, sellers produce products that appear to be identical. Agricultural products (e.g., apples, corn, potatoes) are often considered to be the closest examples of such products. You should know, however, that there are no true examples of perfect competition. Today, government price supports and drastic reductions in the number of farms make it hard to argue that even farming is an example of perfect competition.

Monopolistic competition exists when a large number of sellers produce products that are very similar but are perceived by buyers as different (e.g., candy, cereal, T-shirts). Under monopolistic competition, product differentiation (the attempt to make buyers think similar products are different in some way) is a key to success. The fast-food industry, in which there are often promotional battles between hamburger places, offers a good example of monopolistic competition.

An **oligopoly** is a form of competition in which just a few sellers dominate a market. Oligopolies exist in industries that produce products such as oil and gas, tobacco, automobiles, aluminum, and aircraft. One reason some industries remain in the hands of a few sellers is that the initial investment required to enter the business is tremendous.

In an oligopoly, prices for products from different companies tend to be close to the same. The reason for this is simple. Intense price competition would lower profits for all the competitors, since a price cut on the part of one producer would most likely be matched by the others. As in monopolistic competition, product differentiation, rather than price, is usually the major factor in market success in a situation of oligopoly.

A **monopoly** occurs when there is only one seller for a good or service, and that one seller controls the total supply of a product and the price. One example is the Canadian Wheat Board (CWB); the Reaching Beyond Our Borders box will introduce you to the CWB. As a result of continuing deregulation, there are fewer examples in Canada of a monopoly. We will discuss deregulation in more detail in Chapter 4.

Reaching Beyond Our Borders   The Canadian Wheat Board

The Canadian Wheat Board (CWB) is the marketing agency for more than 85,000 farmers who grow wheat, durum wheat, and barley in Western Canada. While farmers decide what to produce, the role of the CWB is to sell these grains for the best possible price both within Canada and around the world.

The CWB's value to farmers is based on three pillars:

Single-desk selling—Instead of competing against one another for sales, these farmers sell as one through the CWB and can therefore command a higher return for their grain.

Price pooling—Price pooling means that all CWB sales during an entire crop year (August 1 to July 31) are deposited into pool accounts. This ensures that all farmers delivering the same grade of wheat or barley receive the same return at the end of the crop year regardless of when their grain is sold during the crop year.

Government guarantee—Farmers get a partial payment upon delivery of their grain and the Government of Canada guarantees this payment. The government also guarantees the CWB's borrowings, which are currently about $6 billion.

Sales revenues earned, less marketing costs, are passed back to the farmers. With annual sales revenue between $4 and $6 billion, the CWB is one of Canada's biggest exporters and one of the world's largest grain marketing organizations. Annually, it sells more than 20 million tonnes of wheat and barley to over 70 countries.

There is a perception that Canadian farmers are more subsidized than farmers in other countries. According to information gathered by the Organisation for Economic Co-operation and Development (OECD), Canadian farmers received 17 percent of their income from subsidies. American wheat producers received 49 percent of their income from subsidies, while European Union wheat farmers received 43 percent of their income from subsidies.

Single-desk selling is the mainstay of the CWB. Without it, customers could choose to buy their products from several different competitors. Farmers would be left with an open market where customers could choose to deal with whoever gives them the lowest price, resulting in lower returns for all farmers.

Since 1998, following legislative changes, Western Canadian farmers control their marketing organization through the election of 10 fellow farmers to the board of directors. The 15-member board of directors also includes five directors that are appointed by the federal government. It is up to these directors to oversee the management of the CWB.

Source: www.cwb.ca, May 20, 2004.

Benefits and Limitations of Free Markets

The free market—with its competition and incentives—was a major factor in creating the wealth that industrialized countries now enjoy. Free-market capitalism, more than any other economic system, provides opportunities for poor people to work their way out of poverty.

Yet even as free-market capitalism has brought prosperity, it has brought inequality as well. Business owners and managers make more money and have more wealth than workers. There is much poverty, unemployment, and homelessness. People who are old, disabled, or sick may not be able to support themselves.

Smith assumed that as people became wealthier, they would naturally reach out and help the less fortunate in the community. While this has not always happened, many businesspeople are becoming more concerned about social issues and their obligation to return to society some of what they've earned. In Chapter 1, we shared how Jeff Skoll, through the Skoll Foundation, supports social entrepreneurs and innovative nonprofit organizations around the world. Businessman and philanthropist Michael G. DeGroote donated the largest single cash gift in Canadian history of $105 million to McMaster University in 2003. This gift is intended to support health care research and education at the medical school.[5] It is not only individuals who are contributing, but also organizations. For example, eight of Canada's largest banks donated $103 million to charities in 2003.[6]

Another great danger of free markets is that businesspeople and others may let greed dictate how they act. Recent charges made against some big businesses (e.g., Nortel, Canada Post, Enron) indicate the scope of this danger. We hear more and more examples of businesspeople deceiving the public about their products and others deceiving their shareholders about the value of their stock—all to increase the executives' personal assets.[7]

Clearly, some government rules and regulations are necessary to make sure that all of a business's stakeholders are protected and that people who are unable to work get the basic care they need. To overcome the limitations of capitalism, some countries have adopted an economic system called socialism.

Critical Thinking

Many people say that businesspeople do not do enough for society. Some students choose to work for nonprofit organizations instead of for-profit organizations because they want to help others. However, businesspeople say that they do more to help others than nonprofit groups do because they provide jobs for people rather than giving them charity, which often precludes them from searching for work. Furthermore, they believe that businesses create all the wealth that nonprofit groups distribute. Can you find some middle ground in this debate that would show that both businesspeople and those who work for nonprofit organizations contribute to society and need to work together more closely to help people? Could you use the concepts of Adam Smith to help illustrate your position?

Progress Assessment

- How do businesspeople know what to produce and in what quantity?
- How are prices determined?
- What are some of the limitations of free markets?

UNDERSTANDING SOCIALISM

socialism
An economic system based on the premise that some, if not most, basic businesses should be owned by the government so that profits can be evenly distributed among the people.

Socialism is an economic system based on the premise that some, if not most, basic businesses—such as steel mills, coal mines, and utilities—should be owned by the government so that profits can be evenly distributed among the people. For example, France owns roughly 41 percent of the communications company France Télécom[8] and over 44 percent of the automaker Renault. Entrepreneurs often own and run the smaller businesses, but private businesses and individuals are taxed relatively steeply to pay for social programs.[9] The top personal income tax rate in Canada, for example, is 47 percent, but in more socialist countries, such as Denmark and the Netherlands, the top rate is

60 percent; in Finland the top rate is 57 percent, and in Belgium it is 55 percent.[10] Socialists acknowledge the major benefit of capitalism—wealth creation—but believe that wealth should be more evenly distributed than occurs in free-market capitalism. They believe that the government should be the agency that carries out the distribution.

The Benefits of Socialism

The major benefit of socialism is supposed to be social equality as income is taken from the wealthier people, in the form of taxes, and redistributed to the poorer members of the population through various government programs. Free education, health care, child care, and unemployment insurance are some of the benefits socialist governments distribute to their people (using the money from taxes). Workers in socialist countries usually get longer vacations than workers in capitalist countries. They also tend to work fewer hours per week and have more employee benefits, such as generous sick leave.

The Negative Consequences of Socialism

Socialism may create more equality than capitalism, but it takes away some of businesspeople's incentives to start work early and leave work late. For example, tax rates in some nations once reached 85 percent. Today, doctors, lawyers, business owners, and others who earn a lot of money have very high tax rates (usually over 50 percent). As a consequence, some of them leave socialist countries for more capitalistic countries with lower taxes, such as Canada or the United States.

In the business world, socialism also results in fewer inventions and less innovation because those who come up with new ideas usually don't receive as much reward as they would in a capitalist system. Generally speaking, over the past decade or so, most socialist countries have simply not kept up with more capitalist countries in new inventions, job creation, or wealth creation. It is important, however, not to confuse socialism with communism. We shall explore that system next.

UNDERSTANDING COMMUNISM

The 19th-century German political philosopher Karl Marx saw the wealth created by capitalism, but he also noted the poor working and living conditions

Socialism has been much more successful in some countries than others. The photo on the left of Denmark's modern and clean public transportation system reflects the relative prosperity of that country. Per capita GDP is very high (US$22,800). India (right photo) is not doing nearly as well, but it is beginning to experience economic growth as a result of a move away from agriculture toward more services and industrial firms. What factors could account for this disparity in the economic success of these two socialist countries?

Canada Revenue Agency (CRA) administers the tax laws for the federal government and for most provinces and territories. It also collects the federal taxes. For more information on personal, corporate, and sales taxes, visit its Website at www.cra-arc.gc.ca.

communism
An economic and political system in which the state (the government) makes all economic decisions and owns almost all the major factors of production.

The writings of Karl Marx are diametrically opposed to the capitalist views of writers like Adam Smith and John Maynard Keynes. Visit www.marxist.org to learn more about Marx and his teachings and those who share his views.

of labourers in his time. He decided that workers should take over ownership of businesses and share in the wealth. In 1848 he wrote *The Communist Manifesto*, outlining the process. Marx thus became the father of communism. **Communism** is an economic and political system in which the state (the government) makes almost all economic decisions and owns almost all the major factors of production. Communism impacts personal choices more than socialism does. For example, some communist countries do not allow their citizens to practise certain religions, change jobs, or move to the town of their choice.

One problem with communism is that the government has no way of knowing what to produce because prices don't reflect supply and demand as they do in free markets. The government must guess what the economic needs of the people are. As a result, shortages of many items may develop, including shortages of food and basic clothing. Another problem with communism is that it doesn't inspire businesspeople to work hard, because the government takes most of their earnings. Therefore, although communists once held power in many nations around the world, communism is slowly disappearing as an economic form.

Most communist countries today are now suffering severe economic depression, and some people (for example, in North Korea) are starving.[11] Some parts of the former Soviet Union remain under communist concepts, but the movement there is toward free markets. The trend toward free markets is also appearing in Vietnam and parts of China. The regions in China that are most free have prospered greatly while the rest of the country has grown relatively slowly.

THE TREND TOWARD MIXED ECONOMIES

The nations of the world have largely been divided between those that followed the concepts of capitalism and those that adopted the concepts of communism or socialism.

The experience of the world has been that neither of these systems have resulted in optimum economic conditions. Free-market mechanisms haven't been responsive enough to the needs of the poor, the old, or the disabled. Some people also believe that businesses in free-market economies have not done enough to protect the environment. Over time, voters in free-market countries, such as Canada, have therefore elected officials who have adopted many social and environmental programs such as improved unemployment compensation, and various clean air and water acts. Canada's participation in the Kyoto Protocol—to reduce greenhouse gas emissions—is one such example.

Socialism and communism, for their part, haven't always created enough jobs or wealth to keep economies growing fast enough. As a consequence, communist governments are disappearing and socialist governments have been cutting back on social programs and lowering taxes on businesses and workers. The idea is to generate more business growth and thus generate more revenue.

The trend, then, has been for so-called capitalist countries to move toward more socialism and for so-called socialist countries to move toward more capitalism. We say "so-called" because no country in the world is purely capitalist or purely socialist. All countries have some mix of the two systems. Thus, the long-term global trend is toward a blend of capitalism and socialism. This trend likely will increase with the opening of global markets caused by the Internet. The net effect of capitalist systems moving toward socialism and socialist systems moving toward capitalism is the emergence throughout the world of mixed economies.

Mixed economies exist where some allocation of resources is made by the market and some by the government. Most countries don't have a name for such a system. If the dominant way of allocating resources is by free-market mechanisms, then the leaders of such countries still call their system capitalism. If the dominant way of allocating resources is by the government, then the leaders call their system socialism. Figure 2.4 compares the various economic systems.

mixed economies
Economic systems in which some allocation of resources is made by the market and some by the government.

FIGURE 2.4

COMPARISIONS OF KEY ECONOMIC SYSTEMS

	CAPITALISM	SOCIALISM	COMMUNISM	MIXED ECONOMY
Social and economic goals	Private ownership of land and business. Freedom and the pursuit of happiness. Free trade. Emphasis on freedom and the profit motive for economic growth.	Public ownership of major businesses. Some private ownership of smaller businesses and shops. Government control of education, health care, utilities, mining, transportation, and media. Very high taxation. Emphasis on equality.	Public ownership of all businesses. Government-run education and health care. Emphasis on equality. Many limitations on freedom, including freedom to own businesses, change jobs, buy and sell homes, and to assemble to protest government actions.	Private ownership of land and business with government regulation. Government control of some institutions (e.g., mail). High taxation for the common welfare. Emphasis on a balance between freedom and equality.
Motivation of workers	Much incentive to work efficiently and hard, because profits are retained by owners. Workers are rewarded for high productivity.	Capitalist incentives exist in private businesses. Government control of wages in public institutions limits incentives.	Very little incentive to work hard or to produce quality products.	Incentives are similar to capitalism except in government-owned enterprises, which have few incentives. High marginal taxes can discourage overtime work.
Control over markets	Complete freedom of trade within and among nations. No government control of markets.	Some markets are controlled by the government and some are free. Trade restrictions among nations vary and include some free-trade agreements.	Total government control over markets except for illegal transactions.	Some government control of trade within and among nations (trade protectionism). Government regulation to ensure fair trade within the country.
Choices in the market	A wide variety of products is available. Almost no scarcity or oversupply exists for long because supply and demand control the market.	Variety in the marketplace varies considerably from country to country. Choice is directly related to government involvement in markets.	Very little choice among competing products.	Similar to capitalism, but scarcity and over-supply may be caused by government involvement in the market (e.g., subsidies for farms).

Canada's Mixed Economy

Like most other nations of the world, Canada has a mixed economy. The degree of government involvement in the economy today is a matter of some debate. The government is the largest employer in Canada, which means that the number of workers in the public sector is more than the number in the entire manufacturing sector. There's much debate about the role of government in health care, education, business regulation, and other parts of the economy. The government's perceived goal is to grow the economy while maintaining some measure of social equality. The goal is very hard to attain. Nonetheless, the basic principles of freedom and opportunity should lead to economic growth that is sustainable.

Several features have played a major role in Canada's becoming an independent economic entity with a high percentage of government involvement in the economy. First, we are one of the largest countries in the world geographically, but we have a small population (31.8 million in 2004). We have one of the lowest population densities in the world.

Most important, our neighbour to the south has nine times the population and an economy even greater than that proportion, speaks our language, is very aggressive economically, and is the most powerful country in the world. The United States exerts a very powerful influence on Canada as our largest trading partner. To control our destiny, Canadian governments have passed many laws and regulations to make sure significant economic and cultural institutions, such as banks, insurance companies, and radio and TV stations, remain under Canadian control. (Even powerful countries like the United States and Japan have similar regulations.)

All of these factors led to the Canadian capitalist system taking on many characteristics of a mixed economy. Massive government support was necessary to build our first national rail line, the CPR, in the 1880s. When air transport was beginning in the 1930s no company wanted to risk investing in it in such a large country with only 10 million people spread thinly across the land. So the government set up Air Canada (then called Trans Canada Airlines) to transport mail, people, and freight. There are many such examples of government action to protect the national interest.

In the 1980s many countries, including Canada, began to reduce government involvement in, and regulation of, the economy. This trend toward deregulation was widespread. In Canada, airlines, banks, and the trucking industry have all seen a marked reduction in regulatory control. We will discuss deregulation in Chapter 4.

This trend continues today as many industries—including the telecommunications and insurance industries—continue to lobby the government to relax regulations in order to make them more competitive. There are also many new players entering the Canadian marketplace that are competing with publicly funded (i.e., government-funded) institutions. For example, in 2001, the Alberta government granted the DeVry Institute of Technology, a for-profit, U.S.–based private corporation, the right to grant academic degrees; this decision created the first for-profit university in Canada.[12] In the years to come, we will see more examples of our mixed economy moving toward a purer capitalist system as the private sector will play a greater role in delivering goods and services that have historically been managed by public institutions. The Making Ethical Decisions box reviews some of the negative consequences of cuts in social programs.

This is an interesting time to monitor the relationship between business and government. This is also an interesting time to watch how the Internet affects other such relationships worldwide. The Internet is expected to unite

Making Ethical Decisions

To Cut or Not to Cut?

n this chapter, you have been introduced to Canada's mixed economy. Over the years, the federal government has reduced its involvement and regulation in certain industries. In addition, the federal government and provincial governments embarked on a program of reducing expenditures to avoid increasing their debt load. (We will discuss the national debt in Chapter 4.) To achieve this goal, many civil servants were let go and many programs—such as employment insurance and funds for education, health, welfare, and so on—were reduced, causing more hardship to many people. Many organizations and individuals were strongly opposed to what governments were doing because of the serious adverse effects on so many people of all ages across Canada. Child poverty levels rose, food banks reported a big jump in the number of people applying for food, and pawn shops, dollar stores, and cheque-cashing services began to appear or expand all across Canada. Supporters of the government's actions, as well as governments themselves, argued that there was no choice. If cuts were not made, they said, economic and social conditions would deteriorate further and everyone would be worse off.

What do you think? Did the government go too far? What other alternatives might have produced fewer harsh side effects?

businesses around the world in one electronic mall in which the economic systems of the individual countries involved will be less critical to business success than they ever have been before. The Dealing with Change box explores that development further.

Progress Assessment

- What led to the emergence of socialism?
- What are the benefits and drawbacks of socialism?
- Why do some countries still have a strong communist component to the economy?
- What are the characteristics of a mixed economy?

UNDERSTANDING CANADA'S ECONOMIC SYSTEM

The strength of the economy has a tremendous effect on business. When the economy is strong and growing, most businesses prosper and almost everyone benefits through plentiful jobs, reasonably good wages, and sufficient revenues for the government to provide needed goods and services. When the economy is weak, however, businesses are weakened as well, employment and wages fall, and government revenues decline as a result.

Because business and the economy are so closely linked, business literature is full of terms and concepts. It is virtually impossible to read such business reports with much understanding unless you are familiar with the economic concepts and terms being used. One purpose of this chapter is to help you learn additional economic concepts, terms, and issues—the kinds that you will be seeing daily if you read the business press, as we encourage you to do.

Three major indicators of economic conditions are (1) the gross domestic product (GDP) and the importance of productivity, (2) the unemployment rate,

Dealing With Change

www.woodcam.com

The Internet Integrates World Markets

One of the most important changes of our time in business, especially small business, has been the globalization of markets. In the past, a small business was fairly confined in its market reach. It couldn't afford to advertise nationally, much less globally. Given such constraints, it was possible for the government to regulate businesses closely and for a country to stay isolated from other countries. Today, however, even small businesses have established Websites that allow them to reach global markets quickly and easily.

Woodmere Camera sells rare cameras. The market for such cameras is global, but in the past Woodmere had no way to reach beyond its local clientele. Today, however, Woodmere has established a Website (www.woodcam.com) that provides customers an on-line catalogue and allows them to request information by e-mail and place orders by filling out an electronic order form. ArtSelect LLC (www.artselect.com) sells reproductions of paintings by great artists like Monet and Picasso out of its offices. Each week, Half Price Computer Books (which has been on eBay since 1999) lists 7,000 items for auction on two sites, halfpricecomputer books.com and 99centbookshop.com.

Catalogue retailers are still the masters of selling online. With their established warehouse, shipping, and call-centre facilities, catalogue companies were poised to use the Internet quickly and effectively.

Once traditional retailers learned to get onto the Web to reach other countries, they began bringing the Web into their retail stores. Many stores now have kiosks at which consumers can access the Web and find a wider variety of goods and services than in the store. The question now is not clicks *or* bricks, but rather how best to combine clicks *and* bricks.

People in one country can also work for people in another country—over the Internet. For example, a software developer in India can work for a Quebec company and send his or her programs to the company over the Internet as quickly and efficiently as someone from, say, Alberta could.

Where people live therefore no longer always determines where they work. What has developed because of the Internet is a global market with global workers making global products. Some questions that such changes raise are: To whom shall the small-business worker in India pay income taxes—India, Canada, or both? Who pays worker benefits? When someone is unemployed in India, should he or she be counted in the unemployment figures in Canada? Such questions will be important in an era when workers can live anywhere in the world. The World Wide Web will have a profound effect on all the economies of the world and will likely force countries to adopt similar economic systems or risk becoming social isolates in the world economy. What will that world economic system be? What will the rights of workers be? What union and environmental rules will apply? As you can see, the next few years will present tremendous challenges and opportunities to those who understand economics and business, especially small businesses that have whole new worlds to conquer.

Sources: Jay Krall, "Coming Soon to Stores: Wireless Shopping," *The Wall Street Journal*, July 15, 2002, p. R7; "Kings of E-Commerce," *Business 2.0,* November 2002, p. 38; and Tim Hanrahan, "When Worlds Collide," *The Wall Street Journal*, April 28, 2003, pp. R1–R4; Peter Wilson, "Everybody's one-stop shopping, selling at the eBay," *The Vancouver Sun,"* April 17, 2004.

and (3) the price indexes. When you read business literature, you'll see these terms used again and again. It will greatly increase your understanding if you learn the terms now.

Gross Domestic Product

gross domestic product (GDP)
The total value of goods and services produced in a country in a given year.

Gross domestic product (GDP) is the total value of final goods and services produced in a country in a given year. Either a domestic company or a foreign-owned company may produce the goods and services included in the GDP as long as the companies are located within the country's boundaries. For example, production values from Japanese automaker Toyota's factory in Cambridge, Ontario would be included in the Canadian GDP. Likewise, revenue generated by the Ford car factory in Mexico would be included in Mexico's GDP, even though Ford is a U.S. company.

Almost every discussion about a country's economy is based on GDP. The following table shows how Canada's GDP grew, in annual percentage rates, in the last few decades:[13]

1960s	5.2
1970s	4.3
1980s	3.2
1990s	3.7

We can look at GDP from a dollar perspective as well. In 2002, the total Canadian output was approximately $1.2 trillion, an increase of 4.1 percent from the previous year.[14] What can account for an increase in GDP? This is usually the combination of creating jobs, working longer hours, or working smarter.[15] Working smarter means being more productive through the use of better technology and processes and a more educated and efficient workforce.

The more you produce, the higher the GDP and vice versa. An article in *The Globe and Mail* titled *"Blackout shocks economy in August"* (November 1, 2003) gave one such example. The Ontario blackout led to the largest monthly GDP drop (of 0.7 percent) in more than a decade. Ensuing widespread conservation measures further impacted Ontario's economy, which represents 42 percent of all activity. Workers, such as most of the province's 71,000 federal public servants, were ordered to stay home for six working days to conserve energy.[16]

The economy benefits from a strong GDP. Money that is earned from producing goods and services goes to the employees that produce them in the form of wages. People who own the business generate a return on their investment, and government benefits from tax collection. A strong economy usually leads to a high standard of living for Canadians. The term **standard of living** refers to the amount of goods and services people can buy with the money they have. This includes homes, cars, trips, and the like.

Note that the quality of life is different. **Quality of life** refers to the general well being of a society in terms of political freedom, a clean natural environment, education, health care, safety, free time, and everything else that leads to satisfaction and joy. In your opinion, have too many people in Canada sacrificed their quality of life to have a higher standard of living by working more? Since productivity is central to a country's GDP, we will look at this next.

Productivity in Canada

Productivity is measured by dividing the total output of goods and services of a given period by the total hours of labour required to produce them. A similar calculation is done for countries to compare their rates of productivity. An increase in productivity is achieved by (1) producing a *greater* quantity of a certain quality for a *given* amount of work hours, or (2) producing the *same* quantity with *fewer* work hours.

Labour cost measures the same equation in dollars. The dollar value of outputs is divided by the dollar value of the work hours to arrive at the labour cost per unit. Anything that increases productivity or reduces labour costs makes a business, and a country, more competitive as prices can be lower. The great gains in productivity that have occurred during the last century, especially in the past few decades, are due mainly to the introduction of increasingly efficient machinery, equipment, and processes. The past 15 years in particular saw computers and other technology play a major role in this development.

standard of living
The amount of goods and services people can buy with the money they have.

quality of life
The general well being of a society in terms of political freedom, a clean natural environment, education, health care, safety, free time, and everything else that leads to satisfaction and joy.

productivity
The total output of goods and services in a given period divided by the total hours of labour required to provide them.

Our auto assembly plants are, on average, 10 percent more efficient than those in the United States. According to Jim Stanford, an economist with the Canadian Auto Workers union, this reflects the investment in Canadian plants in recent years and the large number of new robots and equipment. It also reflects a more efficient pattern of labour relations.[17]

Productivity is extremely important to a country as it is a measure of its economic prosperity. Canadian businesses are criticized for not spending enough on research and development, relative to other advanced countries. By not doing so, these businesses will fall behind in the fierce global competitive battle. We will discuss the importance of research and development in Chapter 10.

Of course, technological advances usually lead to people being replaced by machines, often contributing to unemployment. We will now examine this important issue.

The Unemployment Rate

For the past decade, Canada's unemployment rate has ranged from 6.8 to 11.2 percent (see Figure 2.5). This means that officially over 1 million people were constantly being reported as being out of work. The real rate is higher, because Statistics Canada does not include people who have given up looking for jobs, those who are working at part-time or temporary jobs or who stay in

FIGURE 2.5

CANADIAN UNEMPLOYMENT RATE, 1989–2003

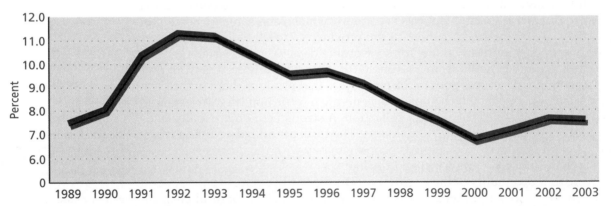

Sources: Statistics Canada, Catalogue No. 85F0018X1E, November 29, 1999; Statistics Canada, CANSIM, tables 282-0002, and 282-0022 and catalogue No. 71F004XCB, September 29, 2003; Statistics Canada, CANSIM table 282-0002, March 29, 2004.

There are several kinds of unemployment:

- *Frictional unemployment* refers to those people who have quit work because they didn't like the job, the boss, or the working conditions and who haven't yet found a new job. It also refers to those people who are entering the labour force for the first time (e.g., new graduates) or are returning to the labour force after significant time away (e.g., parents who raised children). There will always be some frictional unemployment because it takes some time to find a first job or a new job.

- *Structural unemployment* refers to unemployment caused by the restructuring of firms or by a mismatch between the skills (or location) of job seekers and the requirements (or location) of available jobs (e.g., coal miners in an area where mines have been closed).

- *Cyclical unemployment* occurs because of a recession or a similar downturn in the business cycle (the ups and downs of business growth and decline over time). This type of unemployment is the most serious.

- *Seasonal unemployment* occurs where demand for labour varies over the year, as with the harvesting of crops.

or return to school because they cannot find full-time work, and various other categories of people. For example, if you work only one hour per week, you are classified as unemployed.

People are unemployed in Canada for various reasons. Perhaps their employer goes out of business or their company cuts staff. Young persons enter the job market looking for their first job and other employees quit their jobs but have trouble finding new ones. Companies merge and jobs are consolidated or trimmed. Companies transfer their operations to another country, or a branch of a foreign company is closed down. Of course, in a period of economic recession, such as in the early 1980s, 1990s, or in 2000 and 2001, unemployment increases. Different categories of unemployment are discussed in Figure 2.5.

One of the important causes of unemployment in the past decade has been the relentless downsizing by many large corporations. Every few weeks a major company announced layoffs of thousands of employees. These layoffs were driven by intense global competition and technological advances. The former drove the companies to aggressively reduce costs, while the latter enabled them to operate with fewer employees.

An important cause of unemployment is technological advances. When a company acquires a new machine that replaces five existing machines, each tended by one person, then four of the employees may no longer be required. When computer terminals are installed at the desks of senior managers, they may need fewer middle managers and secretaries. They can now access and send information directly. This situation created *technological unemployment*.

Technology can lower costs for companies, making them more competitive and able to expand and hire more people. Although we are now more automated than ever, we also have more people working than ever before. So while people are constantly being displaced by machines, eventually new jobs are created—and somebody has to make and service those new machines.

From the economic point of view, unemployment is a great waste of resources. It means that people who could be producing goods or services are producing nothing—and they may be receiving unemployment benefits or welfare. This reduces GDP. The terrible human cost of continued unemployment—the lack of funds and the demoralization that can destroy individuals and families—must also be considered. Retraining our employable citizens to become more skilled and thus help the country try to become more competitive is a necessity.

Critical Thinking

Would Canada be better off today if we had not introduced modern farm machinery? More people would be employed on the farm if we had not. Would the world be better off in the future if we did not introduce new computers, robots, and machinery? They do take away jobs in the short run. What happened to the farmers who were displaced by machines? What will happen to today's workers who are being replaced by machines?

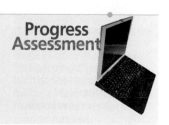

Progress Assessment

- Describe the four different degrees of competition.
- Can you explain the differences between standard of living and quality of life?
- Define four types of unemployment.

The Price Indexes

inflation
A general rise in the prices of goods and services over time.

disinflation
A situation in which price increases are slowing (the inflation rate is declining).

deflation
A situation in which prices are declining.

consumer price index (CPI)
Monthly statistics that measure the pace of inflation or deflation.

industrial product price index (IPPI)
Reflects the prices that producers in Canada receive as goods leave the plant gates to be sold.

raw materials price index (RMPI)
Reflects the prices paid by Canadian manufacturers for key raw materials.

Canadian Economy Online, found at http:// canadianeconomy.gc.ca, is a one-stop guide to the national economy that has information on statistics, federal government facts, and more about economic concepts and events.

The price indexes help to measure the health of the economy by measuring the levels of inflation, disinflation, deflation, and stagflation. **Inflation** refers to a general rise in the prices of goods and services over time. Rapid inflation is scary. If the cost of goods and services goes up by just 7 percent a year, everything would double in cost in just 10 years or so. You can read more about such numbers in the Practising Management Decisions Case on p. 57. Inflation increases the cost of doing business. When a company borrows money, interest costs are higher; employees demand increases to keep up with the rise in the cost of living; suppliers raise their prices and as a result the company is forced to raise its prices. If other countries succeed in keeping their inflation rates down, then Canadian companies will become less competitive in the world market. **Disinflation** describes a condition where price increases are slowing (the inflation rate is declining). **Deflation** means that prices are actually declining.[18] It occurs when countries produce so many goods that people cannot afford to buy them all (too few dollars are chasing too many goods). *Stagflation* occurs when the economy is slowing but prices are going up anyhow.[19]

The **consumer price index (CPI)** consists of monthly statistics that measure the pace of inflation or deflation. Costs of a "basket" of about 600 goods and services for an average family—including housing, food, apparel, medical care, and education—are calculated to see if they are going up or down. For example, Canadians experienced an overall increase of 1.6 percent in the CPI from November 2002 to November 2003. According to StatsCan, some of the contributors were increases in tuition fees, homeowner insurance premiums, and natural gas prices. The CPI is an important figure because some wages and salaries, rents and leases, tax brackets, government benefits, and interest rates are based on it.

The **industrial product price index (IPPI)** reflects the prices that producers in Canada receive as the goods (such as lumber and wood, metal, petroleum, meat, fish, and dairy products) leave the plant gates to be sold.[20] The **raw materials price index (RMPI)** reflects the prices paid by Canadian manufacturers for key raw materials such as crude oil, vegetable products such as wheat and canola, and wood products.[21] These indexes are important as they provide an early warning of possible price increases for consumer products based on the prices businesses pay for these inputs.

Other indicators of the economy's condition include housing starts, retail sales, motor vehicle sales, consumer confidence, and changes in personal income. You can learn more about such indicators by reading business periodicals, listening to business broadcasts on radio and television, and exploring the Internet. As indicated at the beginning of this chapter, StatsCan is also an excellent source of economic information.

Critical Thinking How does the unemployment rate in your area differ from that of other regions in the country? You may want to search the Internet to find out. Do the prices you pay for everyday goods and services seem to be rising or falling?

The Business Cycle

business cycles
The periodic rises and falls that occur in all economies over time.

Many people were caught off guard by the rapid decline of the stock market in 2001–2003. The people most taken by surprise believed that the stock market would continue the rapid rise that occurred during the 1990s. Those people must not have been familiar with the concept of business cycles. **Business cycles** are the periodic rises and falls that occur in economies over time.

Economists look at a number of types of cycles, from seasonal cycles that occur within a year to cycles that occur every 48–60 years.

Economist Joseph Schumpeter identified the four phases of long-term business cycles as boom–recession–depression–recovery:

1. An economic boom is just what it sounds like—business is booming.

2. **Recession** is two or more consecutive quarters of decline in the GDP. In a recession prices fall, people purchase fewer products, and businesses fail. A recession has many negative consequences for an economy: high unemployment, increased business failures, and an overall drop in living standards.

3. A **depression** is a severe recession usually accompanied by deflation. Business cycles rarely go through a depression phase. In fact, while there were many business cycles during the 20th century, there was only one severe depression (1929–1933).

4. A recovery occurs when the economy stabilizes and starts to grow. This eventually leads to an economic boom, starting the cycle all over again.

recession
Two or more consecutive quarters of decline in the GDP.

depression
A severe recession.

The goal of economists is to predict such ups and downs. That is very difficult to do. Business cycles are based on facts, but what those facts describe can be explained only by using theories. Therefore, one cannot say with certainty what will happen next. One can only theorize. But one thing is for sure: The economy and the stock market will rise and fall.

Since dramatic swings up and down in the economy cause all kinds of disruptions to businesses, the government tries to minimize such changes. The government uses fiscal policy and monetary policy to try to keep the economy from slowing too much or growing too rapidly. We will discuss both of these policies in Chapter 4.

- Name three economic indicators and describe how well Canada is doing using each one.
- What's the difference between a recession and a depression?

Progress Assessment

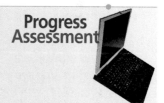

Summary

1. Capitalism is an economic system in which all or most of the means of production and distribution (e.g., land, factories, railroads, and stores) are privately owned and operated for profit.

   1. Explain what capitalism is and how free markets work.

   - *Who decides what to produce under capitalism?*
   In capitalist countries, businesspeople decide what to produce; how much to pay workers; how much to charge for goods and services; whether to produce certain goods in their own countries, import those goods, or have them made in other countries; and so on.

   - *How does the free market work?*
   The free market is one in which decisions about what to produce and in what quantities are made by the market—that is, by buyers and sellers negotiating prices for goods and services. Buyers' decisions in the marketplace tell sellers what to produce and in what quantity. When buyers demand

more goods, the price goes up, signalling suppliers to produce more. The higher the price, the more goods and services suppliers are willing to produce. Price, then, is the mechanism that allows free markets to work.

2. Define supply and demand and explain the relevance of the equilibrium point.	2. Supply refers to the quantity of products that manufacturers or owners are willing to sell at different prices at a specific time. Demand refers to the quantity of products that people are willing to buy at different prices at a specific time. • ***What is the key factor in determining the quantity supplied and the quantity demanded?*** The key factor is price. • ***What is the relevance of the equilibrium point?*** The equilibrium point, also referred to as the equilibrium price, is the point where the quantity demanded is the same as the quantity supplied. In the long run, that price becomes the market price.
3. Discuss the major differences between socialism and communism.	3. Socialism is an economic system based on the premise that some businesses should be owned by the government. • ***What are the advantages and disadvantages of socialism?*** Socialism creates more social equity. Compared to workers in capitalist countries, workers in socialist countries not only receive more education and health care benefits but also work fewer hours, have longer vacations, and receive more benefits in general, such as child care. The major disadvantage of socialism is that it lowers the profits of owners and managers, thus cutting the incentive to start a business or to work hard. Socialist economies tend to have a higher unemployment rate and a slower growth rate than capitalist economies. • ***How does socialism differ from communism?*** Under communism, the government owns almost all major production facilities and dictates what gets produced and by whom. Communism is also more restrictive when it comes to personal freedoms, such as religious freedom. While there are many countries practising socialism, there are only a few (e.g., North Korea) still practising communism.
4. Understand the mixed economy of Canada.	4. A mixed economy is one that is part capitalist and part socialist. That is, some businesses are privately owned, but taxes tend to be high to distribute income more evenly among the population. • ***What countries have mixed economies?*** Canada has a mixed economy, as do most other countries of the world. • ***What does it mean to have a mixed economy?*** A mixed economy has most of the benefits of wealth creation that free markets bring plus the benefits of greater social equality and concern for the environment that socialism offers.
5. Discuss Canada's economic system, including the significance of key economic indicators, productivity, and the business cycle.	5. Three major indicators of economic conditions are (1) the gross domestic product (GDP), (2) the unemployment rate, and (3) the price indexes. • ***What are the key terms used to describe the Canadian economic system?*** Gross domestic product (GDP) is the total value of goods and services produced in a country in a given year. The unemployment rate represents the number of unemployed persons expressed as a percentage of the labour force. The consumer price index (CPI) measures changes in the prices of about 600 goods and services that consumers buy. It contains monthly statistics that measure the pace of inflation (consumer prices going up) or

deflation (consumer prices going down). The industrial product price index (IPPI) and the raw materials price index (RMPI) reflect price changes that are of interest to producers. Productivity is the total volume of goods and services one worker can produce in a given period. Productivity in Canada has increased over the years due to the use of computers and other technologies.

- ***What are the four phases of business cycles?***
In an economic boom, businesses do well. A recession occurs when two or more quarters show declines in the GDP, prices fall, people purchase fewer products, and businesses fail. A depression is a severe recession. Lastly, recovery is when the economy stabilizes and starts to grow.

Key Terms

business cycles 52

capitalism 36

communism 44

consumer price index (CPI) 52

deflation 52

demand 38

depression 53

disinflation 52

economics 34

gross domestic product (GDP) 48

industrial product price index (IPPI) 52

inflation 52

invisible hand 35

macroeconomics 35

market price 39

microeconomics 35

mixed economies 45

monopolistic competition 40

monopoly 40

oligopoly 40

perfect competition 40

productivity 49

quality of life 49

raw materials price index (RMPI) 52

recession 53

socialism 42

standard of living 49

supply 38

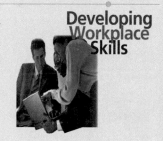

Developing Workplace Skills

1. Show your understanding of the principles of supply and demand by looking at the employment market today. Explain, for example, the high salaries that computer scientists are getting. Also explain why some PhDs aren't getting better pay than computer scientists who only have undergraduate degrees. Why do some librarians make less than some garbage collectors, even though the librarians may have a better education?

2. In teams, review the four degrees of competition. List two products (remember, products are goods or services) that would fall under each category. Next, find a Canadian company that produces or sells these products. Present your findings to the class.

3. This exercise will help you understand socialism from different perspectives. Form three groups. Each group should adopt a different role in a socialist economy: One group will be the business owners, another group will be workers, and another will be government leaders. Within your group discuss and list the advantages and disadvantages to you of lowering taxes on businesses. Then have each group choose a representative to go to the front of the class and debate the tax issue with the representatives from the other groups.

4. Draw a line and mark one end "capitalism" and the other end "communism." Mark where on the line Canada is now. Explain why you marked the spot you chose. Students from other countries may want to do this exercise for their own countries and explain the differences to the class.

5. Break into small groups. In your group discuss how the following changes have affected people's purchasing behaviour and attitudes toward Canada and its economy: September 11, 2001; the war in Iraq in March–April 2003; new illnesses such as SARS; Mad Cow disease; the poultry flu; the growth of the Internet; and the numerous charges against big business as behaving illegally, unethically, and immorally. Have a group member prepare a short summary for the class.

Taking It To The Net

1

Purpose

To familiarize yourself with recent economic indicators that are important to business decision makers.

Exercise

In the chapter-opening vignette, you were introduced to Statistics Canada. Go to the StatsCan Website at www.statcan.ca and answer the following questions as they pertain to Canada.

1. What is the latest indicator for the CPI? What percentage change was there from the previous year? What products reflected an increase in price since last year? What products reflected a decrease in price since last year? What products make up the eight most volatile components?

2. What is the latest indicator for the unemployment rate? How many new full-time jobs were created? How many part-time jobs were created? What sectors created these new jobs? What sectors laid off employees? What province saw the greatest increase in jobs? What province reflects the largest unemployment rate for this past quarter?

3. What is the latest indicator for GDP? What percentage change was there from the previous month? What sectors contributed to an increase in production from the previous month? What is the dollar value of all products that were produced last month?

Taking It To The Net

2

Purpose

To become familiar with forecasting and analyzing tools.

Exercise

1. Analyses of the constantly moving economy are made regularly by various experts and government departments. See if you can find some forecasts, using the keywords *Canadian economic forecasts*, on the current outlook for the Canadian economy by searching Websites such as *The Globe and Mail* (www.theglobeandmail.com), the *National Post* (www.nationalpost.com), and *Canadian Business* magazine (www.canadianbusinesss.com).

2. Visit www.td.com/economics and review the Featured Reports. What are the latest economic forecasts? Is Canada's economic outlook positive? Explain.

3. Can you see, or do any of the articles mention, the possible impact of this information on specific Canadian companies or industries? Perhaps you are considering a career in one of these industries or a job possibility with one of these companies. See if you can find any reports or statements on the Internet from these companies.

Practising Management Decisions

Case

The Rule of 72

No formula is more useful for understanding inflation than the rule of 72. Basically, the rule allows you to quickly compute how long it takes the cost of goods and services to double at various compounded rates of growth. For example, if houses were increasing in cost at 9 percent a year, how long would it take for the price of a home to double? The answer is easy to calculate. Simply divide 72 by the annual increase (9 percent) and get the approximate number of years it takes to double the price (eight years). Of course, the same calculation can be used to predict how high food prices or auto prices will be 10 years from now.

Here's an example of how you can use the rule of 72. If the cost of going to school goes up by 6 percent a year, how much might you have to pay to send your child to school in 24 years (this assumes you will have a child 6 years from now) if school costs are now $10,000 a year?

To find the answer, you divide 72 by 6, which shows that the cost of an education would double in 12 years. It would double twice in 24 years. Your son or daughter can expect to pay $40,000 per year to attend school.

Decision Questions

1. If the cost of a private education is about $20,000 per year now, what will it cost your children per year if costs go up 9 percent a year and your children go to school 16 years from now?
2. If the value of a home doubles in 12 years, what is the annual rate of return? (Hint: Use the rule of 72 in reverse.)
3. If you put $1,000 into a savings account and earned 6 percent per year, how much money would you have in the account after 48 years?

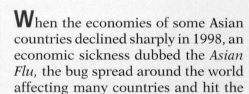

Video Case

Turmoil in the Economy

When the economies of some Asian countries declined sharply in 1998, an economic sickness dubbed the *Asian Flu,* the bug spread around the world affecting many countries and hit the Canadian economy too. Soon, the entire world was hit with a serious recession. A year or two later, other reasons led to another global crisis. This is one of the negative effects of a globalized world of business. It is the economic equivalent of easier and faster plane travel allowing germs to be spread more easily from country to country.

Then things started to pickup a bit, but in 2000 and 2001 there were several serious reverses. First the hi-tech and dot.com bubble burst and their shares collapsed on the stock markets. The final blow was the terrorist attacks in the U.S. on September 11, 2001 which triggered a chain of negative developments in various sectors of the U.S. and Canadian economies.

As a result, the economy in Canada has been on a roller coaster ride the last few years. In 2001 and early 2002 unemployment started to climb as companies continued to lay off employees due to falling demand. Another effect was the weakening value of the Canadian dollar relative to the U.S. dollar. By 2001/02 our dollar was fluctuating in the record low area of 62-63 cents. Both of these developments, as the chapter noted, resulted in an unprecedented number of interest rate reductions by the Bank of Canada in the atempt to boost the economy. The rate reached levels not seen since the 1960s.

What was strange is that, unlike previous recessions, the new, knowledge-based economy was in trouble while the *old* economy was doing well. Because there was no inflation and interest rates were so low consumers were buying cars and homes, the real estate market was booming, and the 2001 Christmas season saw malls packed with customers.

The experts' disagreements about the exact state of the economy and the varying conditions across Canada make it difficult for businesses and governments to make plans for the future.

Discussion Questions

1. As noted in the textbook, the dominant trend in recent times, in the business world, has been favouring unrestricted, free market operations. The current global economic problems have led to a demand for a greater

role for government to limit some of the international free market activities that led to or worsened difficulties in many countries. Discuss the pros and cons of this issue.

2. Imagine you are a CEO of a medium size company in January 2002, located in Alberta and you are aware of the different opinions of business and economic experts about the economy and where it's heading. On January 12 you see a headline in the *Globe and Mail*, "Job losses likely to deepen" followed by a subheading, "Calls mounting for federal action to further stimulate flagging economy." Would you support such a *call?* Or would you feel that it's up to each company to solve their own problems? Would you feel differently if your company was in B.C? Explain your position.

Source: *Venture,* show number 773, "The Coming Storm," February 6, 2001, running time 7:53

Chapter 3

Competing in Global Markets

Learning Goals

After you have read and studied this chapter, you should be able to

1 Discuss the growing importance of the global market and the roles of comparative advantage and absolute advantage in global trade.

2 Explain the importance of importing and exporting, and understand key terms used in global business.

3 Illustrate the strategies used in reaching global markets and explain the role of multinational corporations in global markets.

4 Evaluate the forces that affect trading in global markets.

5 Explain how trade protectionism has contributed to the creation of common markets.

Profile

Getting to Know Li Yifei of MTV Networks China

If asked to think of a company with tremendous influence on the music, style, innovation, and attitude of the teenage and 20-plus population, three letters could come to mind: M-T-V. Imagine bringing MTV's marketing power to China, the most populous nation on earth and a country with not only emerging economic potential but also increasing demand among its teenagers and 20-somethings. Viacom, the owner of MTV, envisions such a future and has entrusted Li Yifei, general manager of MTV Networks China, to make it happen.

It would be an understatement to call Li's job a challenge. Traditional media regulators in China are very conservative and not typically receptive to broadcasting attractive, sometimes scantily clad vee-jays who work for a foreign network. When dealing with her mostly male Chinese business associates, Li has to rein in her usual straightforward, confident business style. As she knows well, Chinese culture expects a woman to be soft and humble when conducting business. What she is doing is obviously working. MTV is now on air in China, even if it is currently limited to four hours of programming a day.

In 2001, Li persuaded CCTV, China's state-owned national TV network, to air the Chinese version of the MTV awards. While the awards did not garner huge ratings, the 7.9-percent rating translated to a viewership of 150 million—more than half the size of the U.S. population. Li promises that future telecasts will attract even larger numbers of viewers. She also has committed herself to gaining more market access for MTV in China by seeking a local partner. She knows it's easier to gain access to markets in China if you have the support of a Chinese partner. To date, Li has cultivated an audience that is growing 40 percent each year, with MTV currently in 60 million Chinese households.

Viacom is counting on Li Yifei's judgment. She brings an interesting background and credentials to the job. A native of Beijing (China's capital city), Li was a national champion in tai chi (a form of martial arts) at 13. A good student, she earned the opportunity to attend the most elite foreign-language university in Beijing. In 1985, at age 21, she left China to go to the United States after receiving a scholarship to attend Baylor University in Waco, Texas. Li earned a master's degree in political science at Baylor and also observed firsthand the differences between the U.S. and Chinese cultures.

After graduation, she was one of 40 students selected for a prestigious internship at the United Nations. There she had the opportunity to produce the television program *U.N. Calling Asia.* After deciding diplomacy was not her career calling, Li became manager of the Beijing office of Burson-Marsteller, a large public relations company. She assisted the firm's clients in business dealings with the Chinese bureaucracy, helped handle complicated paperwork the government required, and assisted with cultural details involved with trade contacts of all kinds. Her work caught the eye of Viacom, and in 1999 she was hired as the general manager of MTV Networks China.

Li Yifei is a vivid example of an emerging global businessperson; that is, a person who speaks different languages, understands cultural events and situations that affect business, and visualizes the vast potential and challenges of global markets in the new millennium. The future of economic growth and the continued economic expansion of developing nations such as China are tied to open markets and global trade. This chapter will explain the opportunities that exist in global markets and the challenges businesspeople must face to succeed globally.

Sources: Jonah Greenberg, "Asia Wants to Rock All Day, All Night in China," Reuters, May 9, 2002; Jennifer Kent, "MTV Exec Tells Baylor U. Students How to Do Business in China," University Wire, April 30, 2002; and "Viacom Invested in China," AsiaInfo Services, May 8, 2002.

THE DYNAMIC GLOBAL MARKET

Have you ever dreamed of travelling to exotic cities like Paris, Tokyo, Rio de Janeiro, or Cairo? In times past, the closest most Canadians ever got to working in such cities was in their dreams. Today, the situation has changed. It's hard to find a major Canadian company that does not cite global expansion as a link to its future growth. A recent study noted that 91 percent of the companies doing business globally believe it's important to send employees on assignments in other countries.

Has the possibility of a career in global business ever crossed your mind? Maybe a few facts will make evaluating such a career more interesting:

- Canada is a market of more than 31 million people, but there are over 6 billion potential customers in the 193 countries that make up the global market. See Figure 3.1 for a map and important statistics about the world's population.

- Every year, the world's population increases by 75 to 80 million people. That's more than 2.5 times the total Canadian population.

- Approximately 75 percent of the world's population lives in developing areas where technology, education, and per capita income still lag considerably behind those of developed (or industrialized) nations such as Canada.[1]

- Combined world trade exceeds $6 trillion each year (a trillion is one million million dollars).

Today, Canadian companies are looking globally to grow their business. Robert Milton, CEO of Air Canada, has indicated that the company's restructuring plan will focus on cutting capacity in the mature domestic market and focus more on international and transborder routes.[2] Phil Lind, vice-chairman of Rogers Communications Inc., has stated that the company would like to make a bigger push into the U.S. market.[3] Two of Canada's leading auto parts makers—Magna International Inc. and Westcast Industries Inc.—are increasing their operations in Japan in the hopes of gaining more business with Honda Motor Co. Ltd., Nissan Motor Co. Ltd., and Toyota Motor Corporation.[4]

Companies also continuously review their global operations to ensure that they are operating at a profit. When this is not the case, plants are closed down.

FIGURE 3.1

WORLD POPULATION BY CONTINENT

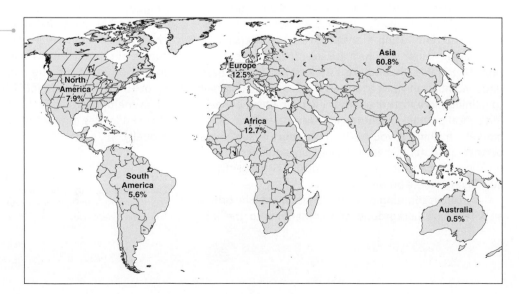

Montreal-based Bombardier Inc. is the world's largest manufacturer of passenger rail equipment and has 50 plants worldwide. It announced plans to close up to six railway equipment facilities to rationalize its capacity in Europe.[5] But note that it is not just Canadian firms that are closing global plants. U.S.–based Levi Strauss & Co. decided to close down its manufacturing operations in Canada and the United States and shift manufacturing to lower-wage nations; it had to "reduce costs and enhance competitiveness" in the market.[6]

Canada is a large exporting nation. **Exporting** is selling products to another country. **Importing** is buying products from another country. Competition in exporting is very intense. Canadian companies face aggressive competition from exporters such as the United States, Japan, China, and the European Union.

exporting
Selling products to another country.

importing
Buying products from another country.

Global trade is big business today and will become increasingly important throughout the 21st century. The purpose of this chapter is to familiarize you with the potential of global business, including its many challenges. The demand for students with training in global business is almost certain to grow as the number of businesses competing in the global market continues to increase. You might even decide that a career in global business is your long-term goal. If you make that choice, prepare yourself to work hard and always be ready for new challenges.

Why Trade with Other Nations?

There are several reasons why countries trade with other countries. First, no country can produce all of the products that its people want and need. Second, even if a country did become self-sufficient, other nations would seek to trade with that country in order to meet the needs of their own people. Third, some nations (e.g., China, Russia) have an abundance of natural resources and a lack of technological know-how, while other countries (e.g., Japan, Taiwan, Switzerland) have sophisticated technology but few natural resources. Trade relations enable each nation to produce what it is most capable of producing and to buy what it needs in a mutually beneficial exchange relationship. This happens through the process of free trade. **Free trade** is the movement of goods and services among nations without political or economic trade barriers. It is often a hotly debated concept. Figure 3.2 offers some of the pros and cons of free trade.

free trade
The movement of goods and services among nations without political or economic obstruction.

FIGURE 3.2

THE PROS AND CONS OF FREE TRADE

PROS	CONS
• The global market contains more than 6 billion potential customers for goods and services.	• Domestic workers (particularly in manufacturing-based jobs) can lose their jobs due to increased imports or production shifts to low-wage global markets.
• Productivity grows when countries produce goods and services in which they have a comparative advantage.	• Workers may be forced to accept pay cuts from employers, who can threaten to move their jobs to lower-cost global markets.
• Global competition and less-costly imports keep prices down, so inflation does not curtail economic growth.	• Moving operations overseas because of intense competitive pressure often means the loss of service jobs and growing numbers of white-collar jobs.
• Free trade inspires innovation for new products and keeps firms competitively challenged.	• Domestic companies can lose their comparative advantage when competitors build advanced production operations in low-wage countries.
• Uninterrupted flow of capital gives countries access to foreign investments, which helps keep interest rates low.	

comparative advantage theory
Theory that states that a country should sell to other countries those products that it produces most effectively and efficiently, and buy from other countries those products that it cannot produce as effectively or efficiently.

The Theories of Comparative and Absolute Advantage

Global trade is the exchange of goods and services across national borders.[7] Exchanges between and among countries involve more than goods and services, however.[8] Countries also exchange art, sports, cultural events, medical advances, space exploration, and labour. **Comparative advantage theory** states that a country should sell to other countries those products that it produces most effectively and efficiently, and buy from other countries those products it cannot produce as effectively or efficiently.

Critical Thinking

Countries like Canada that have a high standard of living ➤**P. 49**◄ are referred to as *industrialized nations;* countries with a low standard of living and quality of life ➤**P. 49**◄ are called *developing countries* (former terms used were *underdeveloped* or *less-developed countries*). What's the reason why developing nations are not fully industrialized? Is it because they lack natural resources? If so, how do you explain the success of industrialized nations like Japan and Singapore, which have few natural resources?

absolute advantage
The advantage that exists when a country has a monopoly on producing a specific product or is able to produce it more efficiently than all other countries.

The theory of comparative advantage dictates that a country should specialize in producing those products it can produce most efficiently and effectively and import those it cannot produce as well or at all. Most Western countries must import rice, as they cannot produce it domestically.

Japan has shown this ability with cars and electronic items. Canada has such an advantage with certain forestry products, aluminum, and various minerals.

In practice, it does not work so neatly. For various reasons, many countries decide to produce certain agricultural, industrial, or consumer products despite a lack of comparative advantage. To facilitate this plan, they restrict imports of competing products from countries that can produce them at lower costs. For example, Japan and South Korea ban all imports of rice. The U.S. makes it difficult to import sugar or cotton and insists that ships carrying cargo between American ports must be U.S.–owned.

Farmers in Europe are subsidized so that their grains can compete with the less expensive ones from countries such as Canada and the U.S. Canada has done the same with cars, textiles, and shoes at different times. The net result of such restraints is that the free movement of goods and services is restricted. We will return to the topic of trade protectionism later in the chapter.

A country has an **absolute advantage** if it has a monopoly on producing a specific product or is able to produce it more efficiently than all other countries. For instance, South Africa once had an absolute advantage in diamond production. Today there are very few instances of absolute advantage in global markets.

GETTING INVOLVED IN GLOBAL TRADE

People interested in finding a job in global business often think of firms like Bombardier, IBM, and Sony, which have large multinational accounts. The real job potential, however, may be with small businesses.

Getting started globally is often a matter of observation, determination, and risk. What does that mean? First, it is important to observe and study global markets. Your library, the Internet, and your fellow classmates are good starting points for doing your research. Second, if you have the opportunity, travelling to different countries is a great way to observe foreign cultures and lifestyles and see if doing business globally appeals to you.

Importing Goods and Services

Figure 3.3 shows that in 2003 Canada imported more than $409 billion worth of goods and services. This was a decrease of almost $14 billion from the previous year. When reviewing import figures, one should consider changes not only

FIGURE 3.3

CANADA'S TRADE 2001–2003, IN MILLIONS OF DOLLARS

	2001	2002	2003	2003 (%)	2001	2002	2003	2003 (%)	2001	2002	2003
	Exports of Goods and Services				*Imports of Goods and Services*				*Goods and Services Balance*		
World	480,404	472,628	457,848		417,908	423,112	409,123		62,496	49,516	48,725
U.S.	387,108	382,101	364,753	79.7	296,400	295,734	279,866	68.4	90,708	86,367	84,887
EU-15	33,886	31,983	33,621	7.3	45,847	46,754	45,966	11.2	−11,961	−14,772	−12,345
Japan	11,929	12,082	11,334	2.5	12,692	13,990	12,579	3.1	−763	−1,908	−1,244
ROW	47,481	46,462	48,140	10.5	62,969	66,634	70,712	17.2	−15,488	−20,171	−22,573
(ROW=Rest of the World)											
	Exports of Goods				*Imports of Goods*				*Goods Balance*		
World	421,519	414,305	401,527		350,632	356,459	341,317		70,887	57,846	60,210
U.S.	352,082	346,991	331,403	82.5	254,953	254,929	239,204	70.1	97,129	92,062	92,199
EU-15	23,872	22,735	24,150	6.0	35,166	36,175	34,898	10.2	−11,294	−13,440	−10,748
Japan	10,228	10,292	9,906	2.5	10,572	11,732	10,659	3.1	−344	−1,441	−753
ROW	35,337	34,287	36,068	9.0	49,941	53,623	56,556	16.6	−14,604	−19,335	−20,488
	Exports of Services				*Imports of Services*				*Services Balance*		
World	58,885	58,323	56,321		67,276	66,653	67,806		−8,391	−8,330	−11,485
U.S.	35,027	35,110	33,351	59.2	41,448	40,805	40,662	60.0	−6,421	−5,695	−7,312
EU-15	10,014	9,246	9,471	16.8	10,681	10,578	11,068	16.3	−667	−1,332	−1,596
Japan	1,701	1,790	1,428	2.5	2,120	2,257	1,919	2.8	−419	−467	−491
ROW	12,143	12,177	12,071	21.4	13,027	13,013	14,157	20.9	−884	−836	−2,086

Source: Department of Foreign Affairs and International Trade—Trade Update March 2004 (Fifth Annual Report on Canada's State of Trade).

Howard Schultz found his "caffeine high" while visiting the neighbourhood coffee and espresso bars in Italy. He returned home and, in 1987, purchased the Starbucks coffee shop in Seattle and built the chain into an international phenomenon. Here, Schultz tips his cup to the newly opened Starbucks in Vienna, Austria, the birthplace of the coffeehouse tradition in 1683. Do you think Vienna represents a good opportunity or a competitive challenge for a newcomer like Starbucks?

in goods, but also in services. Remember, Canada is considered a service economy. Figure 3.4 provides a description and percentage breakdown of the categories of goods (also known as merchandise trade) and services that were imported in 2003. Service imports represented about 16.6 percent of total imports, or nearly one dollar of every six dollars of imports. Commercial services made up the largest portion of the services that were imported. If imports keep decreasing, how might this impact our standard of living and quality of life?

FIGURE 3.4

PERCENTAGE BREAKDOWN
OF CANADIAN IMPORT
AND EXPORT CATEGORIES
FOR 2003

Exporting Goods and Services

You may be surprised at what you can sell in other countries. The fact is, you can sell just about any good or service that is used in Canada to other

MERCHANDISE TRADE		
Categories	**Imports (%)**	**Exports (%)**
Machinery and Equipment		
(incl. industrial and agricultural machinery, aircraft and other transportation equipment, and other)	28.8	22.2
Automotive Products		
(incl. cars, trucks, and parts)	22.4	21.9
Industrial Goods and Materials		
(incl. metal ores, metals and alloys, chemicals, plastics, and fertilizers)	19.1	16.6
Energy Products		
(incl. natural gas, crude petroleum, and petroleum and coal products)	5.7	15.3
Forestry Products		
(incl. lumber and sawmill products and other wood-fabricated materials	0.9	8.6
Agricultural and Fishing Products		
(incl. live animals and meat and meat preparations, other food, feed, beverages, and tobacco)	6.3	7.3
Consumer Goods		
(incl. apparel, footwear, and miscellaneous [such as watches, sporting goods and toys, television and radio sets, and photographic goods])	13.5	4.3
Miscellaneous Adjustment	3.3	4.0

SERVICES TRADE		
Categories	**Imports (%)**	**Exports (%)**
Commercial Services		
(incl. accounting, legal, insurance, financial, architectural, computer, communications and construction services, and royalties and licence fees receipts)	49.5	53.7
Travel		
(incl. business travel and personal travel)	27.9	25.9
Transportation Services		
(incl. air transport services, water transport services, land and other transport services)	21.4	17.8
Government Services		
(incl. international transactions from official representation and military activities)	1.3	2.6

Source: Department of Foreign Affairs and International Trade—Trade Update March 2004 (Fifth Annual Report on Canada's State of Trade).

countries—and often the competition is not nearly as intense for producers in global markets as it is at home. You can, for example, sell snowplows to the Saudi Arabians. They use them to plow sand off their driveways. Tropical Blossom Honey Company was pleasantly surprised to find that Saudis are significant consumers of honey. Why honey? Because the Koran (the Muslim holy book) suggests that it has healing properties.

Figure 3.3 shows that in 2003 Canada had more than $457 billion in exports. Figure 3.4 provides a breakdown of the categories of service exports that overall represented 12.3 percent of total exports. While Canada has a small population, it produces vast quantities of merchandise trade. Thus, we rank very high among nations that export.

Trade with other countries enhances quality of life for Canadians and contributes to our country's economic well-being. Estimates suggest that every $1 billion increase in Canadian exports creates 10,000 jobs in Canada. Overall, foreign trade sustains one out of every four Canadian jobs.[9]

It's important for businesses to be aware of these great opportunities. But don't be misled: Selling in global markets is not by any means easy. Adapting products to specific global markets is potentially profitable but can be very difficult. We shall discuss a number of forces that affect global trading later in this chapter. For now, read how McDonald's attempts to face global challenges in the Reaching Beyond Our Borders box.

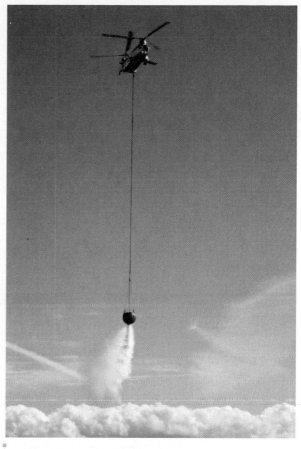

SEI Industries Ltd. of Delta, British Columbia is the inventor of the Bambi Bucket. It is a firefighting system designed like a giant bucket that—with absolute precision—dumps a solid column of water or foam on its target by helicopter. More than 75 percent of SEI's sales are generated by exports worldwide, where some 95 countries now operate the Bambi Bucket.

Measuring Global Trade

In measuring the effectiveness of global trade, nations carefully follow two key indicators: balance of trade and balance of payments. The **balance of trade** is a nation's ratio of exports to imports. A *favourable* balance of trade, or trade surplus, occurs when the value of the country's exports exceeds that of its imports. This is the case for Canada, as shown in Figure 3.3. An *unfavourable* balance of trade, or **trade deficit,** occurs when the value of the country's imports exceeds that of its exports. It is easy to understand why countries prefer to export more than they import. If I sell you $200 worth of goods and buy only $100 worth, I have an extra $100 available to buy other things. However, I'm in an unfavourable position if I buy $200 worth of goods from you and sell you only $100.

The **balance of payments** is the difference between money coming into a country (from exports) and money leaving the country (for imports) plus money flows coming into or leaving a country from other factors such as tourism, foreign aid, military expenditures, and foreign investment. The goal is always to have more money flowing into the country than flowing out of the country; in other words, a *favourable* balance of payments. Conversely, an *unfavourable* balance of payments is when more money is flowing out of a country than coming in.

balance of trade
A nation's ratio of exports to imports.

trade deficit
An unfavourable balance of trade; occurs when the value of a country's imports exceeds that of its exports.

balance of payments
The difference between money coming into a country (from exports) and money leaving the country (for imports) plus money flows from other factors such as tourism, foreign aid, military expenditures, and foreign investment.

Reaching Beyond Our Borders

McDonaldizing the World

The United States changed the landscape of the global market with the tremendous expansion of franchising. Today small, mid-size, and large franchises cover the globe, offering business opportunities in areas from exercise to donuts to education. Still, when the word *franchise* comes to mind, one name dominates all others: McDonald's. "McDonaldization" symbolizes the spread of franchising and the weaving of American pop culture into the world fabric. Whether in South Africa, Mexico, Germany, Brazil, or Hong Kong, no one adapts better and blends the franchise values into the local culture better than McDonald's.

For example, after setting up its first franchises in Hong Kong in 1975, McDonald's altered the breakfast menu after realizing that customers there liked burgers for breakfast, then preferred chicken or fish for the rest of the day. The company also offers unique products such as curry potato pie and red bean sundaes for its Hong Kong customers. In Israel, all meat served in McDonald's restaurants is 100-percent kosher beef. The company also closes its restaurants on the Sabbath and on religious holidays. However, the company also operates nonkosher restaurants for Israelis who don't keep a strict kosher diet and desire to visit McDonald's on the Sabbath and religious holidays. To meet the unique challenge in India and respect the religious sentiments of the population, the company did not introduce beef or pork into the menu.

In Hong Kong, Israel, India, and all other markets in which McDonald's operates, the company continuously listens to customers and adapts to their culture and preferences. The company also must respond to problems and challenges that emerge at its more than 30,000 global restaurants—challenges such as the outbreak of mad cow disease at its restaurants in Europe and Asia. Profits fell by over 14 percent in Japan because of the outbreak of the disease. McDonald's is now funding research for a product that would let it test for the presence of *E. coli* or mad cow disease in its beef. Weak currencies in many countries (e.g., Brazil, Argentina) and government regulations also cause McDonald's global grief. In fact, in Beijing the company was told to remove 30 of its large landmark golden arches in the city because they don't fit with the surrounding architecture. In 2003, the company closed 600 restaurants globally due to poor market conditions.

The first McDonald's restaurant in Canada—and outside of the U.S.—opened in June 1967. Today, there are more than 1,300 McDonald's in Canada. Approximately 65 percent of all McDonald's restaurants are owned and operated by Canadian entrepreneurs. A Canadian milestone occurred in 1988, when, after 12 years of negotiations, George A. Cohon (founder and senior chairman of McDonald's Restaurants of Canada Ltd.) announced an agreement to open 20 McDonald's restaurants in Moscow. In 1990, McDonald's Canada opened Moscow-McDonald's, the first McDonald's restaurant in the Soviet Union, serviced by 27 cash registers and seating 700. This restaurant, in Pushkin Square, is still the largest McDonald's in the world.

Yet, with all its problems and challenges, McDonald's is the leading restaurant in the world, serving over 46 million customers worldwide per day. By using such adaptive strategies in global markets, the company has reaped a large payoff. Today, McDonald's derives more than half of its sales from abroad. Still, the challenge goes on. Some critics even ask whether the golden arches are doomed to fall. It seems the key question is: Can Ronald McDonald make meals all around the globe "happy meals"? Time will tell.

Sources: Carol Matlack and Pallavi Gogoi, "What's This? The French Love McDonald's?" *Business Week,* January 13, 2003, p. 50; and "Big Mac Dips into Giant Loss," *The Mirror* (UK), January 24, 2003, p. 2; www.mcdonalds.ca, May 22, 2004.

Trading in Global Markets: The Canadian Experience

At first glance, Canada's foreign trade statistics are impressive. For a country with fewer than 32 million people, we usually rank within the top ten countries (see Figure 3.5) in volume of world trade. However, if we look carefully at the figures, we see that we are dependent on one country, the United States. Figure 3.3 shows that almost 80 percent of our exports and less than 69 percent of our imports are with the United States. No other modern industrialized country is so dependent on one country for trade and investments.

An even closer look at what we export to the United States shows that the largest category is autos, trucks, and parts, and has been for some time. This is offset by a somewhat smaller amount that we import. All of this stems from the Canada–U.S. Auto Pact signed in the mid-1960s, which was designed to stimulate the auto industry in both countries.

The auto industry is critical to the Canadian economy; in Ontario, one in six jobs is tied to this industry.[10] But today, Canada's assembly industry is shrinking. Plants are being closed and new ones opened in the United States due to lower wages and financial incentives. In response, the Canadian auto industry is aggressively lobbying the government for more assistance. Mark Nantais, president of the Canadian Vehicle Manufacturers' Association, said that governments must move more quickly and forcefully if the Canadian industry is to do better in attracting auto investment and avoid more cuts.[11]

Another traditional major area for Canadian exports is our abundant natural resources across the country, including energy, forestry, agricultural, and fishing products. These products represent approximately 31 percent of our exports (refer to Figure 3.4). Developing countries are continuing to give Canada stiff competition in this area.

What does the future hold? Export Development Canada's chief economist, Stephen Poloz, predicted solid growth (3.9 percent) for exporters in 2004. This is because the world is embarking on its first synchronized expansion—meaning that all major regions are growing at once—since Asia faced a severe economic crisis in 1997.[12]

Trading with China[13]

China is the fastest growing economy in the world and it ranks second in terms of purchasing power. Its trade is expected to total US$1 trillion over the next three years. Canada's Minister of State (New and Emerging Markets) has a mandate to raise Canada's profile in expanding and dynamic markets, like China. Part of this mandate is to brand Canada as a 21st-century economy and as a business partner of choice. To achieve this goal, there are many discussions between these two countries on ways to enhance trade.

FIGURE 3.5

THE WORLD'S LARGEST TRADING COUNTRIES (EXPORTERS OF MERCHANDISE TRADE)

1. United States
2. Germany
3. Japan
4. France
5. China
6. United Kingdom
7. Canada
8. Italy
9. Netherlands
10. Belgium

Source: World Trade Organization, International Trade Statistics (Merchandise Trade) 2003.

Happy Brazilians huddle around the ERJ 170 jet produced by Embraer, the leading exporter in South America's largest country. Embraer hopes its regional jet carrier will surpass those made by Canadian-based Bombardier (the number-one regional aircraft maker in the world), Boeing (U.S.), and Airbus (produced in Europe) as the aircraft of choice in global markets. Over the years, intense competition has led to increased trade disputes among airline manufacturers. For example, several cases involving Bombardier and Embraer have been brought to the World Trade Organization on claims of unfair government subsidies. Exports such as aircraft are critical to a country's effectiveness in global trade. What impact may government support have on the balance of trade?

Canada and China enjoy a well-established relationship. China (not including Hong Kong) is Canada's third largest trading partner, after the U.S. and Japan. China is Canada's fourth largest export market, after the U.S., Japan, and the United Kingdom. In 2002, China replaced Japan as Canada's second largest import supplier. As for Canadian exports, they were around $4.1 billion. But in 2002, Canada ranked just 15th among China's sources of imports and 13th in terms of China's export destinations.

The personal relationships that unite Canada and China are equally important. China and Hong Kong are the leading source of immigrants to Canada, including 33,000 newcomers in 2002 alone. Lastly, more than one million Canadians are of Chinese descent, and Chinese is now the third most spoken language in Canada.

Some Terms and Definitions

foreign direct investment
The buying of permanent property and businesses in foreign nations.

Economists measure a nation's economic strength by comparing several factors. They calculate the amount of money a nation owes to foreign creditors and the value of what foreign creditors own in a particular country, referred to as foreign direct investment. **Foreign direct investment** is the buying of permanent property and businesses in foreign nations. This information is compared to how much money foreign creditors owe to a nation and the value of what a nation owns in other countries. Increasingly, economists and trade analysts have come to agree that a high amount of foreign direct investment in a nation is not necessarily a bad sign. In fact, the amount of foreign direct investment in a country means that other nations perceive that country as a strong economic leader. Figure 3.6 lists the countries with the largest direct foreign investment in Canada.

FIGURE 3.6

FOREIGN DIRECT INVESTMENT POSITIONS AT YEAR-END, 2000–2003

	2000	2001	2002	2003
	Billions of dollars			
Canadian direct investment abroad				
United States	177.9	190.5	197.1	164.9
United Kingdom	35.2	39.8	40.2	40.7
France	4.6	3.8	4.5	11.6
Netherlands	10.5	12.0	11.1	10.7
Japan	5.6	7.0	9.5	9.1
All other countries	122.7	145.8	167.2	162.1
Total	**356.5**	**398.9**	**429.6**	**399.1**
Foreign direct investment in Canada				
United States	193.7	220.2	223.2	228.4
United Kingdom	24.0	26.5	27.6	27.1
France	37.0	31.5	31.3	31.6
Netherlands	15.3	13.7	14.0	15.3
Japan	8.0	7.9	8.9	9.7
All other countries	41.1	41.2	43.9	45.4
Total	**319.1**	**341.0**	**348.9**	**357.5**

Source: Adapted from Statistics Canada, CANSIM database, http://www.statcan.ca/Daily/English/030326/d03026a.htm, Table 376-0038, 376-0051, 376-0053, March 26, 2003.

In supporting free trade, Canada, like other nations, wants to make certain that global trade is conducted fairly.[14] To ensure this level playing field, countries enforce laws to prohibit unfair practices such as dumping.[15] **Dumping** is the practice of selling products in a foreign country at lower prices than those charged in the producing country. Companies sometimes use this tactic to reduce surplus products in foreign markets or to gain a foothold in a new market by offering products for lower prices than domestic competitors do. Dumping benefits foreign firms, as they intentionally charge lower prices to generate more sales. Dumping also benefits purchasers, as they can buy products at a lower price. However, domestic producers do not benefit. Dumping usually leads to a lower share of the market if they do not lower their prices. Lower prices may damage the domestic industry by leading to less revenues and potential job losses. It can take time to prove accusations of dumping, however. There's also evidence that some governments offer financial incentives to certain industries to sell goods in global markets for less than they sell them at home. Dumping promises to remain a difficult trade issue in the 2000s.

Now that you understand some of the basic terms used in global business, we can begin to discuss this topic more deeply. We'll begin by looking at different strategies a business can use to enter global markets. Before doing so, however, let's assess your progress so far.

dumping
Selling products in a foreign country at lower prices than those charged in the producing country.

- How do world population and market statistics support the expansion of Canadian businesses into global markets?
- What is comparative advantage, and what are some examples of this concept in actual global markets?
- How are a nation's balance of trade and balance of payments determined?
- What is dumping?

Progress Assessment

You have read that some 99 percent of the world's population lives outside Canada. Many Canadian companies, especially small businesses, still do not engage in global trade. Why is that? What does this indicate about the potential for increasing Canadian exports? What does it say about career opportunities in global business?

Critical Thinking

STRATEGIES FOR REACHING GLOBAL MARKETS

The many ways in which an organization may participate in global trade include exporting, licensing, franchising, contract manufacturing, creating international joint ventures and strategic alliances, creating foreign subsidiaries, and engaging in foreign direct investment. Each of these strategies provides opportunities for becoming involved in global markets, along with specific commitments and risks. Figure 3.7 places the strategies discussed in the following sections (as well as foreign direct investment, discussed earlier) on a continuum showing the amount of commitment, control, risk, and profit potential associated with each one. Take a few minutes to look over Figure 3.7 before you continue.

| Exporting | Licensing | Franchising | Contract manufacturing | International joint ventures and strategic alliances | Foreign direct investment |

LEAST ← Amount of commitment, control, risk, and profit potential → MOST

FIGURE 3.7

STRATEGIES FOR REACHING GLOBAL MARKETS

Exporting

The simplest way of going international is to export your products. As you will see in the chapters on marketing, many decisions have to be made when a company markets a new product or goes into new markets with existing products. Often the first export sales occur as a result of unsolicited orders received. Regardless of how a company starts exporting, it must develop some goals and strategies for achieving those goals.

Canadian firms may be reluctant to go through the trouble of establishing foreign trading relationships. In such cases, specialists called export-trading companies (or export-management companies) are available to step in and negotiate and establish the trading relationships desired.[16] An export-trading company not only matches buyers and sellers from different countries but also provides needed services (such as dealing with foreign customs offices, documentation requirements, even weights and measures) to ease the process of entering global markets. One such example is Export Development Canada. In Chapter 4 we will illustrate how governments aid exporters. Export-trading companies also help exporters with a key and risky element of doing business globally: getting paid. The Dealing with Change box highlights one of the oldest methods of obtaining payment from global business, with a new technology twist.

Success in exporting often leads to licensing a foreign company to produce the product locally to better serve the local market.

Licensing

licensing
A global strategy in which a firm (the licensor) allows a foreign company (the licensee) to produce its product in exchange for a fee (a royalty).

A firm (the licensor) may decide to compete in a global market by **licensing** the right to manufacture its product or use its trademark to a foreign company (the licensee) for a fee (a royalty). A company with an interest in licensing generally needs to send company representatives to the foreign producer to help set up the production process. The licensor may also assist or work with a licensee in such areas as distribution, promotion, and consulting.

A licensing agreement can be beneficial to a firm in several different ways. Through licensing, an organization can gain additional revenues from a product that it normally would not have generated in its home market. In addition, foreign licensees often must purchase start-up supplies, component materials, and consulting services from the licensing firm. Such agreements have been very profitable for companies like Disney, Coca-Cola, and PepsiCo. These firms often enter foreign markets through licensing agreements that typically extend into

Dealing With Change

Like Money in the Bank

Getting paid is a key concern of exporters when shipping goods to global buyers. Naturally, an exporting firm would like to be paid immediately when goods are shipped. Conversely, importers prefer to know that the exact goods they ordered have in fact been the ones that are shipped (and are in good condition) before they commit payment. In essence, neither side in a transaction wants to take the risk of the other's not following through fully in the agreement. What's an exporter to do? Look to your local bank and the use of a letter of credit.

Letters of credit have been a key part of global trade for centuries. To make a long and sometimes complicated explanation as concise as possible, a letter-of credit transaction works something like this:

1. After signing a contract, an importer requests its bank to issue a letter of credit to pay for the shipment of goods it is buying from an exporter.

2. The importer's bank issues the letter of credit to the exporter's bank; the bank then informs the exporter it has received the letter. The exporter is now assured that it's safe to ship the goods to the foreign buyer.

3. The exporter then signs over title to the goods to its bank and receives a draft from the bank that instructs the importer's bank to send payment for the goods. Acceptance by the importer's bank generally means the exporter will get its money immediately from its bank, and that the bank will take the risk of collecting the money from the importer's bank. Both banks, of course, receive fees for their services.

Again, this is a simplified explanation. If you would like to learn more about letter-of-credit systems, contact a local bank for information.

Also, technology is hard at work to assist would-be exporters in getting their money promptly. The international trade acceptance draft is becoming a faster, less paper-intensive way of ensuring payment for global shipments. Who knows, maybe someday we will bid adieu to the letter of credit.

Sources: Erika Morphy, "Once Again, a Slew of Electronic Products Is Taking Aim at the Venerable Letter of Credit. This Time, They May Finally Prevail," *Global Finance*, May 2001, pp. 36–39; and Russ Banham, "Maiden Voyage," *CFO*, November 2002, pp. 71–76.

---

long-term service contracts. For example, Oriental Land Company and the Hong Kong government have licensing agreements with Walt Disney Company. Oriental Land Company owns and operates Tokyo Disneyland and Tokyo Disney Sea Park under a licensing agreement.[17]

A final advantage of licensing worth noting is that licensors spend little or no money to produce and market their products. These costs come from the licensee's pocket. Therefore, licensees generally work very hard to see that the product they license succeeds in their market.

However, companies that enter into licensing agreements may also experience some problems. One major problem is that often a firm must grant licensing rights to its product for an extended period, maybe 20 years or longer. If a product experiences remarkable growth and success in the foreign market, the bulk of the revenues earned belong to the licensee. Perhaps even more threatening is that a licensing firm is actually selling its expertise in a product area. If a foreign licensee learns the company's technology or product secrets, it may break the agreement and begin to produce a similar product on its own. If legal remedies are not available, the licensing firm may lose its trade secrets, not to mention the agreed-on royalties.

Can Coke really make the world sing in perfect harmony? Let's hope so, especially in trouble spots such as the Middle East. Here Iranians unload the world's best-selling soft drink, enjoyed by billions of customers daily around the globe. Coca-Cola generates approximately 80 percent of its business from global markets primarily through licensing agreements between the company and local bottling companies. What advantages do companies receive from licensing agreements? What are the disadvantages?

熱いにも
ほどがある。

Heat Wave

Domino's Pizza Regular Menu

Domino's Pizza

Been reading too long and need a food break? How about a hot Domino's pizza with squid and sweet mayonnaise? Perhaps a duck gizzard with sprouts pizza will satisfy your craving. Domino's serves pizzas around the world that appeal to different tastes. Franchises like Domino's know the world is a big place and preferences in food, even pizza, can vary considerably. What do franchises have to do to ensure their products are appropriate for global markets they hope to serve?

contract manufacturing
A foreign country's production of private-label goods to which a domestic company then attaches its brand name or trademark; also called *outsourcing*.

Guelph-based Sleeman Breweries is the third-largest brewing company in Canada. For information on its business activities, visit www.sleeman.com.

joint venture
A partnership in which two or more companies (often from different countries) join to undertake a major project or to form a new company.

Franchising

Franchising is an arrangement whereby someone with a good idea for a business sells the rights to use the business name and sell a product or service to others in a given territory. In Canada, there are thousands of franchise units—such as Tim Hortons, Canadian Tire, Molly Maid, and Japan Camera 1 Hour Photo—in many categories of business. Franchising is popular both domestically and internationally and will be discussed in depth in Chapter 6.

Franchisors, however, have to be careful to adapt their good or service in the countries they serve. For example, KFC's first 11 Hong Kong outlets failed within two years. Apparently the chicken was too greasy, and eating with fingers was too messy for the fastidious people of Hong Kong. McDonald's made a similar mistake when entering the Netherlands market. It originally set up operations in the suburbs, as it does in North America, but soon learned that the Dutch mostly live in the cities. Pizza Hut originally approached the global market using a strategy of one-pie-fits-all. The company found out the hard way that Germans like small individual pizzas, not the large pies preferred in North America. Preferences in pizza toppings also differ globally. Japanese customers, for example, enjoy squid and sweet mayonnaise pizza.

Contract Manufacturing

Contract manufacturing involves a foreign company's production of private-label goods to which a domestic company then attaches its own brand name or trademark. The practice is also known as *outsourcing* and it will be discussed in more detail in Chapter 10. For example, Dell Computer contracts with Quanta Computer of Taiwan to make notebook PCs, on which it then puts the Dell brand name. In another example, Sapporo Breweries of Tokyo has contracted Sleeman Breweries to produce the worldwide supply of its 650-mL "Silver Can" product.

Contract manufacturing also enables a company to experiment in a new market without incurring heavy start-up costs such as a manufacturing plant. If the brand name becomes a success, the company has penetrated a new market with relatively low risk. A firm can also use contract manufacturing temporarily to meet an unexpected increase in orders.

International Joint Ventures and Strategic Alliances

A **joint venture** is basically a partnership in which two or more companies (often from different countries) join to undertake a major project or to form a new company. According to Coopers & Lybrand, an international professional services firm, companies that participate in such partnerships grow much faster than their counterpart companies that are not participating. Joint ventures can even be mandated by governments as a condition of doing business in their country. It's often hard to gain entry into a country like China, but agreeing to a joint venture with a Chinese firm can help a company gain such entry. For example, Volkswagen and General Motors entered into joint ventures with Shanghai Automotive Industrial Corporation, China's largest domestic car company, to build cars in China.[18]

Joint ventures are developed for different business reasons as well. Campbell Soup Company formed joint ventures with Japan's Nakano Vinegar Company and Malaysia's Cheong Chan Company to expand its rather low share of the soup market in both countries. Global Engine Alliance, a combination of DaimlerChrysler, Mitsubishi Motors, and Hyundai Motor Company, is a joint venture that will develop aluminum engines that will be used by both Asian manufacturers and DaimlerChrysler's U.S. Chrysler unit.[19]

The benefits of international joint ventures are clear:

Competition has fuelled the growth of joint ventures. Molson USA is a joint venture created by Molson Inc. and the Adolph Coors Company in 2001. Coors is responsible for importing, marketing, selling, and distributing Molson's brands of beer in the United States. Coors paid Molson $65 million for a 49.9-percent interest in the U.S. joint venture. Both companies indicated a desire to merge in 2004. Were they successful?

1. Shared risk.
2. Shared technology.
3. Shared marketing and management expertise.
4. Entry into markets where foreign companies are often not allowed unless their goods are produced locally.
5. Shared knowledge of the local market including local customs, government connections, access to local skilled labour and supplies, and awareness of domestic laws and regulations.

The drawbacks are not so obvious. An important one, however, is that one partner can learn the other's technology and practices, and then go off on its own and use what it has learned. Also, over time, a shared technology may become obsolete or the joint venture may become too large to be as flexible as needed.

Global market potential is also fuelling the growth of strategic alliances. A **strategic alliance** is a long-term partnership between two or more companies established to help each company build competitive market advantages. Such alliances can provide access to markets, capital, and technical expertise.[20] Unlike joint ventures, however, they do not typically involve sharing costs, risks, management, or even profits. Many executives and management consultants predict that few companies in the 21st century will succeed in the global market by going it alone; most will need strategic alliances.[21] Strategic alliances can be flexible, and they can be effective between firms of vastly different sizes.

Two Canadian companies, Research In Motion (RIM) and Consilient Technologies Corporation, have a strategic alliance. One contract involved the New York Fire Department (NYFD). RIM provided its BlackBerry wireless platform and Consilient provided its Mail eXtension (MX) software. The software creates a link between the NYFD's e-mail server and the BlackBerry server, so that NYFD headquarters can communicate securely with its mobile workforce using BlackBerry Wireless Handhelds.[22] For more information about Consilient Technologies, see the Spotlight on Small Business box.

strategic alliance
A long-term partnership between two or more companies established to help each company build competitive market advantages.

Newfoundland's Consilient Technologies Corporation

www.consilient.com

Founded in 2000, Consilient Technologies Corporation was formed by Trevor Adey (President) and Rod White. Consilient specializes in the wireless extension of corporate IT systems using its proprietary technology and products. These products are targeted to businesses that have workers who are away from their primary workplaces (e.g., field service technicians and sales representatives) for extended periods of time. The products enable mobile devices and applications to function similar to those of traditional desktop workstations.

To achieve its goals, Consilient has established strategic alliances with IT solution developers, network carriers, handheld device manufacturers, system integrators, and application developers. These partners include Research In Motion, Sun Microsystems, Bell Mobility, and Telus.

Government agencies provide support to Consilient. One example is the Industrial Research Assistance Program (IRAP), an initiative of the National Research Council of Canada. IRAP works closely with small and medium-sized enterprises to help them increase their competitiveness in the marketplace. Consilient has been identified as one of Canada's Innovation Leaders in the context of Canada's Innovation Strategy. The company won a contract with the New York Fire Department as a result of its participation in a successful Team Canada Atlantic trade mission to New York City in 2002. That same year, it was awarded $1.7 million from the Atlantic Canada Innovation Fund to develop its wireless data mobile technology.

People ask the St. John's entrepreneurs, "Why would you build a software company in Newfoundland?" Adey replies, "It's where I want to live. I don't have to rationalize it." Even so, he does: cheap office costs and, most of all, proximity to Memorial University. A Memorial University graduate himself, Adey believes that "What allows us to build a company in St. John's like this is having a world-class university right here with students who want to stay in Newfoundland and Labrador, but don't think they can." Of the 30 staff, 29 are Newfoundlanders and almost all are under age 30.

What is the company's ultimate goal? According to White, "Microsoft is dominating the desktops and we think the handhelds is still up in the air. We want to dominate the handheld software space." The company has about $1 million in annual sales, even though White says it is still in the "pre-revenue stage." Consilient currently exports 80 percent of its products to the United States. According to Adey, "The Americans have more money to spend, there are more small- to medium-sized companies, and the government is far bigger." As part of its international growth strategy, the company is opening an office in San Francisco later this year and expanding into Australia and Asia Pacific.

Sources: "Consilient technologies corp. awarded $1.7 million from Atlantic Innovation Fund to create state-of-the-art wireless technology" (2 July 2002), Toronto: Canada NewsWire Ltd. Retrieved from the World Wide Web: www.newswire.ca; "Consilient Technologies named a Canadian Innovation Role Model by Allan Rock," (27 September 2002), Ottawa: National Research Council Canada. Retrieved from the World Wide Web: http://www.nrc.cnrc.gc.ca; Gordon Pitts, "Newfoundland duo battle image problem" (25 November 2002), Toronto: globeand mail.com. Retrieved from the World Wide Web: http://www.theglobeandmail.com; "Consilient Technolgogies Corp." (n.d.), Ottawa: Team Canada Atlantic. Retrieved from the World Wide Web: www.teamcanadaatlantic.com; "Look who's talking—and sending data" (2 December 2002), Ottawa: National Research Council Canada. Retrieved from the World Wide Web: http://irap-pari.nrc-cnrc.gc.ca; "NYFD Chooses BlackBerry Wireless Platform and MX Software to Improve Communications" (4 February 2003), Waterloo: Research In Motion. Retrieved from the World Wide Web: http://www.blackberry.com; "Why Trade Matters" (16 June 2003), Ottawa: Department of Foreign Affairs and International Trade. Retrieved from the World Wide Web: www.dfait-maeci.gc.ca; Roy MacGregor, "And not a rubber boot in sight," *The Globe and Mail*, 18 October 2003, sec. A, p. 11; and the company Website at www.consilient.com.

Foreign Direct Investment

foreign subsidiary
A company owned in a foreign country by another company (called the *parent company*).

As you may recall, foreign direct investment is the buying of permanent property and businesses in foreign nations. As the size of a foreign market expands, many firms increase foreign direct investment and establish a foreign subsidiary. A **foreign subsidiary** is a company that is owned in a foreign country by another company (called the *parent company*). Such a subsidiary would operate much like a domestic firm, with production, distribution, promotion, pricing, and other business functions under the control of the foreign subsidiary's management.

The legal requirements of both the country where the parent firm is located (called the *home country*) and the foreign country where the subsidiary is located (called the *host country*) have to be observed. The primary advantage of a subsidiary is that the company maintains complete control over any technology or expertise it may possess. The major shortcoming associated with creating a subsidiary is that the parent company is committing a large amount of funds and technology within foreign boundaries. Should relations with the host country falter, the firm's assets could be taken over by the foreign government. Such a takeover is called *expropriation*.

Canadian subsidiaries of American companies have played a major role in developing the Canadian economy. Recall from Figure 3.6 that U.S. companies alone have invested more than $228 billion in Canada. There are, however, several disadvantages. One is that Canada has been criticized for having a "branch plant economy." This occurs when many subsidiaries are owned by foreign companies and profits are returned to the home country rather than reinvested in Canada. Canadians are concerned that decisions made by the parent company are not primarily based on the needs of Canadians. For example, if a U.S. company decides to reduce its workforce or close a plant, it may more readily do that to a subsidiary than in its home country.

In 1992, Michael Porter, the competition guru from Harvard University Business School, released a report—titled *The Competitive Advantage of Nations*—that was commissioned by the federal government. While more than 10 years old, some of his points still ring true today:

> *One of Canada's competitive problems is the high concentration of foreign-owned firms that perform little sophisticated production or R&D. It matters a lot where a multinational calls home, because a company's home base is where the best jobs exist, where core R&D is undertaken, and where strategic control rests... Home bases are important to an economy because they support high productivity and productivity growth.*[23]

Regardless of these concerns, more countries are welcoming subsidiaries as a way to develop their economies.

Consumer products giant Nestlé is an example of a major firm with many foreign subsidiaries. The Swiss-based company spent billions of dollars acquiring foreign subsidiaries such as Ralston Purina, Chef America (maker of Hot Pockets), and Perrier in France. The company continues to look for opportunities around the globe.[24] Nestlé is also an example of a multinational corporation. A **multinational corporation** is an organization that manufactures and markets products in many different countries; it has multinational stock ownership and multinational management. Multinational corporations are typically extremely large corporations, but not all large firms involved in global business are multinationals. For example, a business could literally be exporting everything it produces, thus deriving 100 percent of its sales and profits globally, and still not be considered a multinational corporation. Only firms that have *manufacturing capacity* or some other physical presence in different nations can truly be called multinational. Examples of Canadian multinationals are BCE, Nortel, Magna, Royal Bank of Canada, and Bombardier.

Becoming involved in global business requires selecting a strategy to enter a market that best fits the goals of the business.[25] As you can see, the different strategies discussed reflect different levels of ownership, financial commitment, and risk that a company can assume. However, this is just the beginning. It's important to be aware of key market forces that affect a business's ability to trade in global markets. After the Progress Assessment, we will discuss these forces.

multinational corporation
An organization that manufactures and markets products in many different countries and has multinational stock ownership and multinational management.

Progress Assessment

- What services are usually provided by an export-trading company?
- What are the advantages to a firm of using licensing as a method of entry in global markets? What are the disadvantages?
- What is the key difference between a joint venture and a strategic alliance?
- What is a multinational corporation?

Can you think of anything more appetizing than a tasty fish head? No? Well, the cheeseburgers and "finger-licking-good" chicken we devour in Canada often get similar reactions in other cultures. Understanding different sociocultural perspectives related to time, change, natural resources, even food can be important in succeeding in global markets. How do you think companies can help employees being assigned to global markets adapt to the different cultures they will encounter and help them avoid culture shock?

FORCES AFFECTING TRADING IN GLOBAL MARKETS

Succeeding in any business takes work and effort, due to the many challenges that exist in all markets. Unfortunately, the hurdles are higher and more complex in global markets than in domestic ones. This is particularly true when dealing with differences in sociocultural forces, economic and financial forces, legal and regulatory forces, and physical and environmental forces. Let's take a look at each of these global market forces to see how they challenge even the most established global businesses.

Sociocultural Forces

Understanding cultural diversity remains one of the true business challenges of the 21st century. The word *culture* refers to the set of values, beliefs, rules, and institutions held by a specific group of people.[26] Primary components of a culture can include social structures, religion, manners and customs, values and attitudes, language, and personal communication. If you hope to get involved in global trade, it's critical to be aware of the cultural differences among nations.

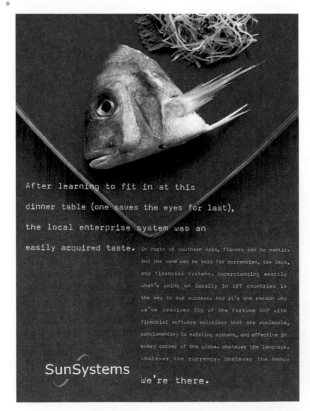

After learning to fit in at this dinner table (one saves the eyes for last), the local enterprise system was an easily acquired taste. In parts of southern Asia, flavors can be exotic. And the same can be said for currencies, tax laws, and financial systems. Understanding exactly what's going on locally in 187 countries is the key to our success. And it's one reason why we've provided 25% of the Fortune 500® with financial software solutions that are scaleable, complementary to existing systems, and effective in every corner of the globe. Whatever the language. Whatever the currency. Whatever the menu.

SunSystems

We're there.

Different nations have very different ways of conducting business. Canadian businesses that wish to compete globally must adapt to those ways. In Canada and the United States, we like to do things quickly. We tend to call each other by our first names and try to get friendly even on the first encounter. In Japan, China, and other countries these actions would be considered surprising and even rude. Canadian negotiators will say no if they mean no, but Japanese negotiators usually say maybe when they mean no.

Religion is an important part of any society's culture and can have a significant impact on business operations. Consider the violent clashes between religious communities in India, Northern Ireland, and the Middle East—clashes that have wounded these areas' economies. Unfortunately, companies at times do not consider the religious implications of business decisions. Both McDonald's and Coca-Cola offended Muslims in Saudi Arabia by putting the Saudi Arabian flag on their packaging. The flag's design contains a passage from the Koran (Islam's sacred scripture), and Muslims feel their holy writ should never be wadded up and thrown away.

Sociocultural differences can also affect important business decisions involving human resource management. In Latin American countries, workers believe that managers are placed in positions of authority to make decisions and be responsible for the well-being of their workers. Consider what happened to one North American manager in Peru who was unaware of this important cultural characteristic. This manager was convinced he could motivate his workers to higher levels of productivity by instituting a more democratic decision-making style than the style already in place. Soon workers began quitting their jobs in droves. When asked why, the Peruvian workers said the new production manager and supervisors did not know their jobs and were asking the workers what to do. All stated they wanted to find new jobs, since obviously this company was doomed because of incompetent managers.

Learning about additional sociocultural perspectives related to time factors, change, competition, natural resources, achievement, and even work itself can be of great assistance in global markets. Today, before managers and their families are sent on a global assignment, firms often give them training on how to adapt to different cultures.

Sociocultural differences affect not only management behaviours but also global marketing strategies. *Global marketing* is the term used to describe selling the same product in essentially the same way everywhere in the world. Some companies—such as Nike, Roots, and Toyota—have developed brand names with widespread global appeal and recognition. However, even these successful global marketers often face difficulties. For example, translating an advertising theme into a different language can be disastrous. To get an idea of the problems companies have faced with translations, take a look at Figure 3.8.

A sound philosophy to adopt in global markets is this: *Never assume that what works in one country will work in another.* Since global marketing works only in limited cases, it's critical that Canadian exporters thoroughly research their objectives before attempting to penetrate global markets. "Think global, act local" is a valuable motto to follow.

Economic and Financial Forces

Economic differences can also make entering global markets more challenging. Surely it's hard for us to imagine buying chewing gum by the stick instead of by the package. Yet this buying behaviour is commonplace in economically depressed nations like Haiti, because customers there have only enough money to buy small quantities. General Foods once squandered millions of dollars in an effort to introduce Japanese consumers to packaged cake mixes. The company failed to note, among other factors, that only three percent of Japanese homes were then equipped with ovens. Factors such as disposable and discretionary income can be critical in evaluating the potential of a market. What might seem like an opportunity of a lifetime may in fact be unreachable due to economic conditions.

- PepsiCo attempted a Chinese translation of "Come Alive, You're in the Pepsi Generation" that read to Chinese customers as "Pepsi Brings Your Ancestors Back from the Dead."
- Coor's Brewing Company put its slogan "Turn It Loose" into Spanish and found it translated as "Suffer from Diarrhea."
- Perdue Chicken used the slogan "It Takes a Strong Man to Make a Chicken Tender," which was interpreted in Spanish as "It Takes an Aroused Man to Make a Chicken Affectionate."
- KFC's patented slogan "finger-lickin' good" was understood in Japanese as "Bite Your Fingers Off."

FIGURE 3.8

OOPS, DID WE SAY THAT?

A global marketing strategy can be very difficult to implement. Look at the problems these well-known companies encountered in global markets.

Global financial markets unfortunately do not have a worldwide currency. Mexicans shop with pesos, South Koreans with won, Japanese with yen, and Canadians with dollars. Globally, the U.S. dollar is considered the world's dominant and most stable form of currency.[27] This doesn't mean, however, that the dollar always retains the same market value or that foreign currency such as the euro may not someday replace or challenge the U.S. dollar's dominance.[28] Since 2002, the euro is the official currency of the European Union (EU). It replaced currencies such as the German deutschmark, the French franc, and the Italian lira. We will discuss the EU and the euro later in this chapter.

The **exchange rate** is the value of one nation's currency relative to the currencies of other countries. Changes in a nation's exchange rates can have important implications in global markets. A *high value of the dollar* means that a dollar would be traded for more foreign currency than normal. The products of foreign producers would be cheaper because it takes fewer dollars to buy them, but the cost of Canadian-produced goods would become more expensive to foreign purchasers because of the dollar's high value. Conversely, a *low value of the dollar* means that a dollar is traded for less foreign currency than normal. Therefore, foreign goods become more expensive because it takes more dollars to buy them, but Canadian goods become cheaper to foreign buyers because it takes less foreign currency to buy Canadian goods.[29] Many Canadian exporters have benefited from such a scenario for years as their products were cheaper for U.S. buyers.

Changes in currency values cause many problems globally. Consider a multinational corporation like Nestlé, which has 479 factories around the world and employs more than 220,000 workers.[30] Costs for labour, raw materials, and machinery can vary considerably as currency values shift. The Canadian dollar's quick rise in 2003 had a negative impact on profits for many exporters. Many of their products were made in Canadian dollars but sold in U.S. dollars. For example, multinational aluminum producer Alcan Inc. indicated that every one-cent (U.S.) rise in the Canadian dollar cut its profits by C$11 million.[31] On the other hand, Calgary-based WestJet Airlines Ltd. has benefited from the rising Canadian dollar. Every one-cent (U.S.) increase in the

exchange rate
The value of one nation's currency relative to the currencies of other countries.

Happy birthday to "Euro"! These Irish misses are dressed as euro coins to celebrate the big day in the history of the European Union (EU). The euro officially became the common currency of 12 of the members of the EU on January 1, 2002, replacing the mark, francs, lira, pesetas, and other former currencies. Do you think the euro will challenge the American dollar for leadership among the world's currencies?

dollar means C$2.1 million per year in pretax profit.[32] According to a company representative, this is because fuel is priced in U.S. dollars, as is a lot of equipment used for maintenance.

Currency valuation problems can be especially harsh on developing economies. Often, the only possibility of trade in many developing nations is through one of the oldest forms of trade: *bartering,* which is the exchange of merchandise for merchandise or service for service with no money involved.[33] **Countertrading** is a complex form of bartering in which several countries may be involved, each trading goods for goods or services for services. It has been estimated that countertrading accounts for more than 20 percent of all global exchanges, especially deals involving developing countries. For example, let's say that a developing country such as Jamaica wants to buy vehicles from Ford Motor Company in exchange for Jamaican bauxite. Ford, however, does not have a need for Jamaican bauxite but does have a need for computer monitors. In a countertrade agreement, Ford may trade vehicles to Jamaica, which then trades bauxite to another country—say, India—which then exchanges computer monitors with Ford. This countertrade is thus beneficial to all three parties. Trading products for products helps businesses avoid some of the financial problems and currency constraints that exist in global markets.

countertrading
A complex form of bartering in which several countries may be involved, each trading goods for goods or services for services.

Legal and Regulatory Forces

In any economy, both the conduct and direction of business are firmly tied to the legal and regulatory environment. In Canada, federal, provincial, and municipal laws and regulations heavily impact business practices. In global markets, no central system of law exists, so several groups of laws and regulations may apply. This makes the task of conducting global business extremely difficult as businesspeople find myriad laws and regulations in global markets that are often inconsistent. Important legal questions related to antitrust rules, labour relations, patents, copyrights, trade practices, taxes, product liability, and other issues are written and interpreted differently country by country.[34]

For example, bribery is not considered legal in Canada. The problem is that this runs contrary to beliefs and practices in many countries where corporate or government bribery not only is acceptable, but also perhaps is the only way to secure a lucrative contract.[35] For a partial list of countries where bribery or other unethical business practices are most common, see Figure 3.9.

To be successful in global markets, it's often important to contact local businesspeople in the host countries and gain their cooperation and sponsorship. Such local contacts can help a company penetrate the market and deal with what can be imposing bureaucratic barriers. Local businesspeople are also familiar with laws and regulations that could have an important impact on a foreign firm's business in their country.

Foreign firms must be aware of the actions of their representatives. In 2003, Canadian multinational Acres International Ltd. lost an appeal against conviction on a charge of bribery.[36] Acres was charged with bribing a top official involved in granting contracts in the $3.3-billion Lesotho Highlands Water Project. Company officials claim they were completely unaware that money paid to their local representative was being used to bribe the official. Acres has been fined $2.8 million. The World Bank has also sanctioned the company; Acres is ineligible to receive any new Bank-financed contracts for three years.[37]

Beyond legal questions are those concerning ethics. The Making Ethical Decisions box gives you an example of one company's dilemma.

FIGURE 3.9

THE MOST CORRUPT COUNTRIES

This partial list is based on the degree of corruption as seen by businesspeople, academics, and risk analysts. Corruption is defined as the misuse of public power for private benefit.

1. Bangladesh
2. Nigeria
3. Haiti
4. Myanmar
   Paraguay
5. Angola
   Azerbaijan
   Cameroon
   Georgia
   Tajikistan

Source: Transparency International, Corruption Perceptions Index 2003.

Making Ethical Decisions

Doing Bad by Trying to Do Good

The CEO of a major pharmaceutical manufacturer decided to set up what she considered to be a generous program to fight the growing AIDS epidemic in developing countries. She decided her company would give its expensive AIDS-related drug for free to government clinics in several of the poor countries. To her surprise, the decision was roundly booed by many humanitarian groups, which complained the company should instead lower the price of the drug so that everyone could afford it rather than give it away to only part of the affected population. The company currently charges regular customers approximately $8 for one pill. Critics claim that the company could lower the price to 40 cents per pill (a few cents over cost) and really help fight the dreaded disease. Puzzled by the reaction, the CEO said, "We are doing more than anyone else and are still criticized. We should work together to fix this problem." What are the CEO's alternatives? What are the consequences of each alternative? What would you do?

Physical and Environmental Forces

Certain physical and environmental forces can also have an important impact on a company's ability to conduct business in global markets. In fact, technological constraints may make it difficult or perhaps impossible to build a large global market. For example, some developing countries have such primitive transportation and storage systems that international distribution is ineffective, if not impossible. This is especially true with regard to food, which is often spoiled by the time it reaches the market in certain countries. Compound this fact with unclean water and the lack of effective sewer systems, and you can sense the intensity of the problem.

Canadian exporters must also be aware that certain technological differences affect the nature of exportable products. For example, houses in most developing countries do not have electrical systems that match those of Canadian homes, in kind or capacity. How would the differences in electricity available (110 versus 220 volts) affect a Canadian appliance manufacturer wishing to export? Also, computer and Internet usage in many developing countries is very spotty or nonexistent. You can see how this would make for a tough business environment in general and would make e-commerce difficult, if not nearly impossible.

TRADE PROTECTIONISM

As we discussed in the previous section, sociocultural, economic and financial, legal and regulatory, and physical and environmental forces are all challenges to trading globally. What is often a much greater barrier to global trade, however, is the political atmosphere between nations. **Trade protectionism** is the use of government regulations to limit the import of goods and services. Advocates of trade protectionism believe it allows domestic producers to survive and grow, producing more jobs. Countries often use protectionist measures to guard against such practices as dumping; many are wary of foreign competition in general. To understand how this political climate affects global business, let's briefly review some global economic history.

Business, economics, and politics have always been closely linked. In the 17th and 18th centuries, businesspeople and governments advocated an economic principle called *mercantilism*. The overriding idea of mercantilism was for

trade protectionism
The use of government regulations to limit the import of goods and services. Advocates of trade protectionism believe that it allows domestic producers to survive and grow, producing more jobs.

a nation to sell more goods to other nations than it bought from them; that is, to have a favourable balance of trade.[38] According to the mercantilists, this condition would result in a flow of money to the country that sold the most globally. This philosophy led governments to assist in this process by charging a **tariff,** basically a tax on imports, thus making imported goods more expensive to buy.

Generally, there are two different kinds of tariffs: protective and revenue. *Protective tariffs* (import taxes) are designed to raise the retail price of imported products so that domestic products will be more competitively priced. These tariffs are meant to save jobs for domestic workers and to keep industries (especially *infant industries,* which consist of new companies in the early stages of growth) from closing down entirely because of foreign competition. *Revenue tariffs* are designed to raise money for the government. Revenue tariffs are also commonly used by developing countries to help infant industries compete in global markets. Today there is still considerable debate about the degree of protectionism a government should practise.

An **import quota** limits the number of products in certain categories that a nation can import. Canada has import quotas on a number of products, including textiles and clothing, agricultural products, steel products, and weapons and munitions.[39] Overall, the goal is to protect companies in order to preserve jobs. An **embargo** is a complete ban on the import or export of a certain product or the stopping of all trade with a particular country. Political disagreements have caused many countries to establish embargoes.

James Thwaits, former president international operations of 3M Co., has said that as much as half of all trade is limited by *nontariff barriers.* In other words, countries have established many strategies that go beyond tariffs to prevent foreign competition. For example, margarine must be sold in cubes in Belgium, closing the market to countries that sell margarine only in tubs.

Other nontariff barriers include safety, health, and labelling standards. The United States has stopped some Canadian goods from entering because it said that the information on the labels was too small. The discovery of a cow in northern Alberta that tested positive for mad cow disease resulted in a ban by importers on Canadian cattle and beef. Although no other cases were discovered, this had a dramatic impact on Canada's $7.5-billion-a-year cattle industry, as it is fuelled by exports.[40]

Sometimes, the intent is clearly to put difficulties in the way of imports. Other times it is not so clear whether the barriers are deliberate or are a normal part of a reasonable set of standards. Of course, when a country is in a protectionist mode, it will exploit these standards or use any excuse to try to reduce imports.

It would be easy for would-be exporters to view the trade barriers discussed above as good reasons to avoid global trade. Overcoming trade constraints, whether they pertain to global (or provincial) markets, is part of the business challenge. In the next sections, we look at organizations and agreements that attempt to eliminate trade barriers and facilitate trade among nations.

The GATT and the WTO

In 1948, government leaders from 23 nations throughout the world formed the **General Agreement on Tariffs and Trade (GATT),** which established an international forum for negotiating mutual reductions in trade restrictions. In short, the countries agreed to negotiate to create monetary and trade agreements that might facilitate the exchange of goods, services, ideas, and cultural programs. On January 1, 1995, the **World Trade Organization (WTO)** assumed the task of supervising the GATT. The WTO, headquartered in Geneva, Switzerland, and comprising 146 member nations, acts as an independent

tariff
A tax imposed on imports.

The Export and Import Controls Bureau is responsible for administering the Export and Import Permits Act. Visit its site at www.dfait-maeci.gc.ca/eicb to find a list of controlled imports and exports. As well, recent issues (such as the softwood lumber dispute with the United States) are presented.

import quota
A limit on the number of products in certain categories that a nation can import.

embargo
A complete ban on the import or export of a certain product.

General Agreement on Tariffs and Trade (GATT)
A 1948 agreement that established an international forum for negotiating mutual reductions in trade restrictions.

World Trade Organization (WTO)
The international organization that replaced the General Agreement on Tariffs and Trade, and was assigned the duty to mediate trade disputes among nations.

Anti-globalization protests in Seattle, Prague, and Genoa (pictured here) have pitted activists against the World Trade Organization (WTO). The demonstrators vented their fears and distrust of globalization being controlled by multinational corporations and international financial entities that have worked to their own benefit and have not addressed the needs of the world's developing countries. What do you believe the role of an organization like the WTO should be in dealing with global trade issues?

entity that oversees key cross-border trade issues and global business practices. It's the world's first attempt at establishing a global mediation centre. Trade issues are expected to be resolved within 12 to 15 months instead of languishing for years, as was the case in the past.

However, before you get the impression that all's well in global trade, it's important to note that the formation of the WTO did not totally eliminate the internal and national laws that impede trade expansion. In September 2003, the Fifth Ministerial Conference took place in Cancun, Mexico—and ended in failure. These negotiations, which include agriculture and non-agricultural market access (NAMA) negotiations, are due to conclude before January 1, 2005. According to the Organisation for Economic Co-operation and Development (OECD), differences arose over the negotiation of four new trade-related issues: investment, competition, trade facilitation, and transparency in government. As well, negotiations toward free trade in agricultural products—where markets are currently receiving more than $200 billion in annual subsidies—encountered opposition.[41] The Sixth Conference will be held in Hong Kong, China. There is much work that needs to be done to reach agreement on these issues.

Progress Assessment

- What are the major hurdles to successful international trade?
- Identify at least two cultural and societal differences that can affect global trade efforts.
- What are the advantages and disadvantages of trade protectionism?
- What is an embargo? Can it be applied for noneconomic reasons?
- What is the relationship between the GATT and the WTO?

International Monetary Fund (IMF)
An international bank that makes short-term loans to countries experiencing problems with their balance of trade.

The IMF and The World Bank

Even before GATT, the **International Monetary Fund (IMF)** was created in 1944. The IMF is an international bank supported by its members that usually makes *short-term* loans to countries experiencing problems with their balance of trade. The IMF's basic objectives are to promote exchange stability, maintain orderly exchange arrangements, avoid competitive currency depreciation, establish a multilateral system of payments, eliminate exchange restrictions, and create standby reserves. The IMF makes *long-term* loans at low interest rates to the world's most destitute nations to help them strengthen their economies. The function of the IMF is very similar to that of the World Bank.

The **World Bank** (the International Bank for Reconstruction and Development), an autonomous United Nations agency, is concerned with developing the infrastructure (roads, schools, hospitals, power plants) in less-developed countries. The World Bank borrows from the more prosperous countries and lends at favourable rates to less developed countries. In recent years, the IMF and the World Bank have forgiven some loans to highly indebted countries, such as Mozambique. In order to qualify for the program, numerous macroeconomic policies (such as inflation and poverty reduction) have to be implemented. These new requirements continue to fulfill the objectives of these lending organizations.

Some countries believed that their economies would be strengthened if they established formal trade agreements with other countries. Some of these agreements involve forming producers' cartels and common markets, to be discussed below.

Producers' Cartels

Producers' cartels are organizations of commodity-producing countries. They are formed to stabilize or increase prices, optimizing overall profits in the long run. The most obvious example today is OPEC (Organization of the Petroleum Exporting Countries). Similar attempts have been made to manage prices for copper, iron ore, bauxite, bananas, tungsten, rubber, and other important commodities. These cartels are all contradictions to unrestricted free trade and letting the market set prices.

Common Markets

One of the issues not resolved by the GATT rounds or at the WTO is whether common markets will create regional alliances at the expense of global expansion. A **common market** (also called a *trading bloc*) is a regional group of countries that have a common external tariff, no internal tariffs, and the coordination of laws to facilitate exchange among member countries. Two such common markets, the European Union (EU) and the North American Free Trade Agreement (NAFTA), are worth looking at briefly.

The EU began in the late 1950s as an alliance of six trading partners (then known as the Common Market and later the European Economic Community). Today the EU is a group of 15 nations that united economically in the early 1990s. The objective was to make Europe, the world's second largest economy (behind the United States)—with almost 20 percent of the world's GDP and representing some 360 million people—an even stronger competitor in global commerce. Europeans see economic integration as the major way to compete for global business. The EU grew to 25 nations by May 2004 (see Figure 3.10) as new members were accepted from the Mediterranean region and Eastern Europe.[42]

The path to European unification, however, was not easy. A significant step was taken on January 1, 1999, when the EU officially launched its joint currency, the euro. The formal transition occurred three years later on January 1, 2002, when the separate currencies of 12 of the EU nations were transformed

The World Trade Organization (www.wto.org) and International Monetary Fund (www.imf.org) Websites provide descriptions of these organizations, their membership, their objectives, and their activities.

World Bank
An autonomous United Nations agency that borrows money from the more prosperous countries and lends it to less-developed countries to develop their infrastructure.

producers' cartels
Organizations of commodity-producing countries that are formed to stabilize or increase prices to optimize overall profits in the long run. (An example is OPEC, the Organization of the Petroleum Exporting Countries.)

common market
A regional group of countries that have a common external tariff, no internal tariffs, and a coordination of laws to facilitate exchange; also called a *trading bloc*. An example is the European Union.

FIGURE 3.10

MEMBERS OF THE EUROPEAN
UNION

EUROPEAN UNION MEMBERS			NEW EU MEMBERS (MAY 2004)	
France	Germany	Italy	Cyprus	Latvia
Belgium	Netherlands	Luxembourg	Czech Republic	Lithuania
Great Britain	Denmark	Greece	Slovak Republic	Malta
Ireland	Portugal	Spain	Estonia	Poland
Austria	Finland	Sweden	Hungary	Slovenia

into a single monetary unit. EU members Great Britian, Sweden, and Denmark elected not to convert to the euro at that time. European businesses expected to save billions each year on currency conversions that had to be made prior to the introduction of the euro.

The EU clearly hopes that having a unified currency will bring its member nations more economic clout, as well as more buying power and greater economic and political stability. Today the EU, with a 2001 population of 377 million people, is the world's largest exporter of products. It accounted for 38.1 percent of the world total in 2001, compared to 13.1 percent for the U.S., and 3.9 percent for Canada.[43]

The Canada–U.S. Free Trade Agreement

An important common market was established between Canada and the United States when the Free Trade Agreement (FTA) came into effect on January 1, 1989. The agreement affected nearly all goods and services traded between Canada and the United States, as well as intercountry investments.

The purpose of the FTA was to phase out most tariffs and other restrictions to free trade between the two countries over a period of 10 years. The FTA made it easier for cross-country investments and buyouts to take place and guaranteed the United States access to our energy resources. The movement of professionals and certain other categories of people across the border was also eased. For various reasons, each side kept certain items outside the FTA. For example, Canada insisted that beer and cultural industries and products be excluded. The United States insisted that shipping be excluded.

One major goal of the Canadian negotiating team was to provide relief from unilateral U.S. trade restrictions. A binational panel would adjudicate on disputes between the two countries. Unfortunately, this has not stopped the United States from continuing what many Canadians feel is harassment of our exporters (three examples are lumber, wheat, and steel). The process requires Canadian exporters to pay heavy legal costs and it draws executives' time away from productive efforts. It also makes foreign companies wary of investing in Canada.

The second aim of the FTA was to expose Canadian companies to greater competition from American companies to force them to become more competitive. This competition was deemed essential for Canada to compete in the tough, globalized business world. The thinking was that, since the world has now become one market, only the best can survive in that fiercely competitive global marketplace. The problem was that the Canadian government gave no aid to help certain industries through what it admitted would be a very difficult transition period, despite promises to do so.

Other countries, such as Japan, Singapore, and Korea, that wanted to raise certain industries to world-class competitiveness, followed a different path.

They gave their companies three years to shape up while protecting them from foreign competition. The governments aided the companies and monitored them closely to see that they were moving forward, and helped to retrain workers whose jobs were disappearing.

The third aim of the FTA was to give better access to the vast American market for Canadian goods and services. This goal was closely related to forcing Canadian companies to become more competitive, since they would have to compete with American companies.

The North American Free Trade Agreement

On January 1, 1993, the **North American Free Trade Agreement (NAFTA)** among Canada, the United States, and Mexico came into effect. This replaced the previous FTA between Canada and the United States. The objectives of NAFTA were to (1) eliminate trade barriers and facilitate cross-border movement of goods and services among the three countries; (2) promote conditions of fair competition in this free-trade area; (3) increase investment opportunities in the territories of the three nations; (4) provide effective protection and enforcement of intellectual property rights (patents, copyrights, etc.) in each nation's territory; and (5) establish a framework for further regional trade cooperation.[44]

North American Free Trade Agreement (NAFTA) Agreement that created a free-trade area among Canada, the United States, and Mexico

NAFTA was driven by the desire of Mexico to have greater access to the U.S. market. Improved access would spur growth, provide more employment for Mexicans, and raise the low standard of living in Mexico. The U.S. government was hoping to create jobs in Mexico and stop the flow of illegal immigrants that were entering its border. Canada was really a minor player in this deal; the Canadian government was concerned that it would be left out or penalized indirectly unless it joined the bloc. Canadians do have something to gain by having freer access to the growing Mexican market, but the country is still a minor customer for Canada. Today, Mexico has replaced Japan as America's second largest trading partner, behind Canada.[45]

Today, the three NAFTA countries have a combined population of 417 million people and a gross domestic product (GDP) of more than $11 trillion.[46] Three-way trade among the countries has more than doubled in the past decade, to more than US$621 billion.[47] According to the agreement, Canada, the United States, and Mexico can lower trade barriers with one another while maintaining independent trade agreements with nonmember countries.

There is continuing concern in Canada, which is even greater in the U.S., that many manufacturing jobs will be lost to Mexico because of NAFTA. Wages and general conditions are much lower in Mexico. This time around (unlike with the FTA), many Canadian businesspeople were opposed because they did not like many of the details. In addition, Mexico has a poor policy on environmental problems, bad working conditions, and a bad record on human rights and political freedom. The country has repeatedly been condemned by many organizations in North America and abroad for serious flaws on all these counts. Others believe that NAFTA will force Mexico to gradually improve these conditions. This has been happening, but at a very slow pace.

The United States, Canada, and Mexico are trying to negotiate a Free Trade Agreement of the Americas (FTAA). Including the countries in Central and South America, this would create a free-trade area of 800 million people and incorporate 34 democratic countries. Advocates say that it could be operational by 2005, but it has encountered several roadblocks. Brazil is resisting Washington's attempt to include investment and competition rules in the negotiations, while the United States is refusing to consider including cuts in agricultural subsidies as part of the talks.[48]

Strong free-trade supporters even suggest that a transatlantic free trade area aligned with the European Union is possible. Some praise such suggestions resoundingly, while other express concern that as the world divides itself into major trading blocs (EU, NAFTA, etc.) poor countries that don't fit into the plans of the common markets will suffer. The issues surrounding common markets and free-trade areas will extend far into the 21st century.

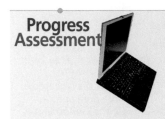

Progress Assessment

- State the objectives of the IMF.
- Why are producers' cartels formed?
- What were the three main purposes of the FTA?
- Name four objectives of NAFTA.

How Does Canada Shape Up as an International Competitor?

For more information on these reports and to see where other countries rank, visit the following Websites: World Economic Forum (www.weforum.org); International Institute for Management Development (www01.imd.ch); and Economist Intelligence Unit (www.eb.eiu.com).

How does Canada rank when compared to other industrialized countries? Canadian businesses have been criticized for years for not being more productive: productivity leads to competitiveness. However, productivity is just one important component. Assessing international competitiveness is complex and open to varying opinions. There are several indexes, and different criteria and weightings are used by the agencies that produce them. You will notice the importance of economic conditions and the role of government when evaluating a country's attractiveness. (These topics are discussed in Chapters 2 and 4.)

For example, the prestigious World Economic Forum (WEF) produces the annual *Global Competitiveness Report*. According to the WEF, one of its indexes—the Growth Competitiveness Index—is based on estimates of each country's ability to grow over the next five to ten years. Thus, economic conditions and institutions (e.g., government and financial markets) are reviewed. The Geneva-based organization blames government policies and red tape as the main reasons why Canada's ranking fell to 16th position in 2003.[49] See Figure 3.11 for a summary of Canada's past rankings.

The International Institute for Management Development (IMD) produces the *World Competitiveness Yearbook*, which ranks the ability of a nation to provide an environment that sustains the competitiveness of enterprises. The ranking considers four criteria: economic performance; government efficiency; business efficiency; and infrastructure. Over the past few years, Canada has consistently ranked in the top five when compared to other countries. Figure 3.11 summarizes Canada's recent rankings.

The Economist Intelligence Unit has developed a global business environment rankings forecast model, which seeks to measure the quality or attractiveness of the business environment. It considers factors such as the political environment; the macroeconomic environment; market opportunities; policy toward private enterprise and competition; policy toward foreign investment; foreign trade and exchange controls; taxes; financing; the labour

	WEF'S *GLOBAL COMPETITIVENESS REPORT* MEASURE: GROWTH COMPETITIVENESS	IMD'S *WORLD COMPETITIVENESS YEARBOOK* MEASURE: OVERALL COUNTRY
YEAR	**INDEX**	**RANKING**
2003	16	3
2002	9	2
2001	3	2
2000	6	2

Sources: *Global Competitiveness Reports* 2003–2004 and 2001–2002; *World Competitiveness Yearbook* 2003.

FIGURE 3.11

CANADA'S GLOBAL COMPETITIVE POSITION, 2000–2003

The World Economic Forum and the International Institute for Management Development produce annual reports that compare the competitiveness of many countries. Notice how Canada's position has changed from 2000 to 2003.

market; and infrastructure. For the years 2004 to 2008, Canada ranked first for future prospects.[50] This is indeed positive news for businesses.

It is clear that there is no one conclusive authority that is able to answer the question of how productive, and therefore how competitive, Canada is. These rankings, however, should give you an idea of how the business environment can change quickly and how challenging it is to be consistently competitive.

Globalization and You

Whether you aspire to be an entrepreneur, a manager, or some other type of business leader, it's becoming increasingly important to think globally as you plan your career. As this chapter points out, global markets offer many opportunities, yet they are laced with significant challenges and complexities. By studying foreign languages, learning about foreign cultures through courses in anthropology and world literature, and taking business courses (including a course in global business), you can develop a global perspective on your future.

As we have emphasized, the potential of global markets does not belong only to the multinational corporations. Small and medium-sized businesses are often better prepared to take the leap into global markets than are large, cumbersome corporations saddled with bureaucracies. It's the ability of small and medium-sized businesses to react quickly to opportunities that gives them an advantage. Don't forget to think about using that advantage. Also don't forget the potential of franchising, which we will examine in more detail in Chapter 6.

Progress Assessment

- Explain what criteria are reviewed by the WEF when ranking countries in the Growth Competitiveness Index.
- Why does Canada's competitiveness differ when it is being ranked by various organizations?

Summary

1. Discuss the growing importance of the global market and the roles of comparative advantage and absolute advantage in global trade.

1. The world market for trade is huge. Some 99 percent of the people in the world live outside Canada. Major Canadian companies routinely cite expansion to global markets as a route to future growth.

   • *Why should nations trade with other nations?*
   (1) No country is self-sufficient, (2) other countries need products that prosperous countries produce, and (3) natural resources and technological skills are not distributed evenly around the world.

   • *What is the theory of comparative advantage?*
   The theory of comparative advantage contends that a country should make and then sell those products it produces most efficiently but buy those it cannot produce as efficiently.

   • *What is absolute advantage?*
   Absolute advantage means that a country has a monopoly on a certain product or can produce the product more efficiently than any other country can. There are few examples of absolute advantage.

2. Explain the importance of importing and exporting, and understand key terms used in global business.

2. Anyone can get involved in world trade through importing and exporting. Businesspeople do not have to work for big multinational corporations.

   • *What kinds of products can be imported and exported?*
   Just about any kind of product can be imported and exported. Companies can sometimes find surprising ways to succeed in either activity. Selling in global markets is not necessarily easy, though.

   • *What terms are important in understanding world trade?*
   Exporting is selling products to other countries. *Importing* is buying products from other countries. The *balance of trade* is the relationship of exports to imports. The *balance of payments* is the balance of trade plus other money flows such as tourism and foreign aid. *Dumping* is selling products for less in a foreign country than in your own country. *Trade protectionism* is the use of government regulations to limit the importation of products. See the Key Terms list on page 91 to be sure you know the other important terms.

3. Illustrate the strategies used in reaching global markets and explain the role of multinational corporations in global markets.

3. A company can participate in world trade in a number of ways.

   • *What are some ways in which a company can get involved in global business?*
   Ways of entering world trade include exporting, licensing, franchising, contract manufacturing, joint ventures and strategic alliances, and direct foreign investment.

   • *How do multinational corporations differ from other companies that participate in global business?*
   Unlike other companies that are involved in exporting or importing, multinational corporations also have manufacturing facilities or some other type of physical presence in different nations.

4. Evaluate the forces that affect trading in global markets.

4. There are many restrictions on foreign trade.

   • *What are some of the forces that can discourage participation in global business?*
   Potential stumbling blocks to world trade include sociocultural forces, economic and financial forces, legal and regulatory forces, and physical and environmental forces.

5. Political differences are often the most difficult hurdles to international trade.

• ***What is trade protectionism?***

Trade protectionism is the use of government regulations to limit the import of goods and services. Advocates believe that it allows domestic producers to survive and grow, producing more jobs. The key tools of protectionism are tariffs, import quotas, and embargoes.

• ***What are some examples of trade organizations that try to eliminate trade barriers and facilitate trade among nations?***

The World Trade Organization (WTO) replaced the General Agreement on Tariffs and Trade (GATT). The purpose of the WTO is to mediate trade disputes among nations. The International Monetary Fund (IMF) is an international bank that makes short-term loans to countries experiencing problems with their balance of trade. The World Bank is a United Nations agency that borrows money from the more prosperous countries and lends it to less-developed countries to develop their infrastructures.

• ***What is a common market? State some examples.***

A common market is a regional group of countries that have a common external tariff, no internal tariff, and a coordination of laws to facilitate exchange. The idea behind a common market is the elimination of trade barriers that existed prior to the creation of this bloc. Examples include the North American Free Trade Agreement (NAFTA) and the European Union (EU).

5. Explain how trade protectionism has contributed to the creation of common markets.

Key Terms

absolute advantage 64
balance of payments 67
balance of trade 67
common market 85
comparative advantage theory 64
contract manufacturing 74
countertrading 81
dumping 71
embargo 83
exchange rate 80
exporting 63

foreign direct investment 70
foreign subsidiary 76
free trade 63
General Agreement on Tariffs and Trade (GATT) 83
import quota 83
importing 63
International Monetary Fund (IMF) 84
joint venture 74
licensing 72

multinational corporation 77
North American Free Trade Agreement (NAFTA) 87
producers' cartels 85
strategic alliance 75
tariff 83
trade deficit 67
trade protectionism 82
World Bank 85
World Trade Organization (WTO) 83

1. Call or visit a business involved with importing foreign goods. Talk with the owner or manager about the problems and joys of being involved in global trade. Compile a list of advantages and disadvantages. Then get together with others in the class and compare notes.

2. Using a computer word-processing program, prepare a short list of the advantages and disadvantages of trade protectionism. Share your ideas with others in the class and debate the following statement: Canada should increase trade protection to save Canadian jobs and companies.

3. The economics of Ontario and British Columbia depend heavily on exports. Ontario relies primarily on trade to the United States and Europe,

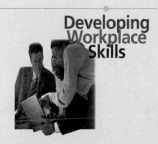

Developing Workplace Skills

while British Columbia relies heavily on trade with Asia. In a group of four, research these statements. Draw up two graphs that break down the exporting countries that trade with each of these provinces. Present your findings to the class.

4. In a group of four, list the top 15 Canadian-based multinationals. When researching, be sure to create a table that will include the following pieces of information: the company names, the year each was created, the number of global employees, the industry or industries in which they operate, annual revenues, and number of countries in which they have offices. Present your findings to the class.

5. Choose a good, service, or idea that you would like to market to a specific country. Identify the benefits of supplying the product to this market. Identify the sociocultural, economic and financial, legal and regulatory, and physical and environmental forces you might encounter. Provide alternatives you can use to address these forces. Form your own joint venture with three classmates to deal with this exercise. Have each member make a list of the strengths and weaknesses he or she would bring to such an assignment. Decide among yourselves whether a joint venture would be worthwhile to achieve your market objectives or whether you each would be better choosing another strategy in entering this market. Explain why your group decided to organize the way it did.

Taking It To The Net 1

Purpose

To discover the role the federal government plays in helping Canadian businesses compete successfully in international trade.

Exercise

The former Department of Foreign Affairs and International Trade has been divided into two separate departments: Foreign Affairs Canada (FAC), and International Trade Canada (ITCan). Visit www.dfait-maeci.gc.ca and answer these questions:

1. What is the mandate for each department?

2. In the Foreign Affairs site, click on the Foreign Policy icon. Read about Canada's agenda abroad by reviewing Canadian International Policy, Canada and Global Organizations, Canada's Relations with Other Countries, and International Development.

3. In the ITCan site, click on Services for Canadian Businesses. Review the links, paying particular attention to Team Canada Inc. What assistance does Team Canada provide?

Taking It To The Net 2

Purpose

To identify those nations with high export potential and those with low export potential (except for basic goods, such as food).

Exercise

Imagine your company is ready to expand its products to foreign countries. Which countries are most likely to buy your products? The potential to export to a specific country is based on a number of factors, including the size of its population and the strength of its GDP.

1. From the population data given on the United Nations Population Information Network Website (www.un.org/popin), prepare a list of the 20 countries with the largest population.

2. Go to the InfoNation section of the UN's Cyber School Bus Website (www.un.org/Pubs/CyberSchoolBus) and find the GDP per person for each of the nations on your population list. Rate each of the nations in your population list for its export potential. Using the GDP per capita and the population size, place each of those nations into the following categories:

   a. High export potential (those nations whose population is one of the 10 largest and whose GDP per capita is greater than $20,000).

   b. Medium-high export potential (those nations whose population is ranked 11 to 21 and whose GDP per capita is greater than $20,000).

   c. Medium export potential (those nations whose population is one of the 10 largest and whose GDP per capita is between $3,000 and $20,000).

   d. Low export potential (those nations whose population is ranked 11 to 21 and whose GDP per capita is less than $3,000).

Practising Management Decisions

Case

To Bribe or Not to Bribe? That Is the Question

Condor Manufacturing has a joint venture with a local company in an African country we shall call Lorino. Condor sent you out to be the general manager for three years to train a Lorinese to take over from you. You are facing certain problems that you do not know how to resolve.

Bribery and kickbacks are normal methods of getting things done in Lorino. This applies to dealings with other companies and with the government. Salaries are very low and bribes are expected to make up the shortfall so that people can survive.

The vice-president of international operations for Condor is not very keen about this way of doing business, especially as it violates the company's ethical code. However, he informs you that these are decisions that you will have to make as the general manager. You have tried to pass the responsibility and it has been passed right back to you.

You have had to bribe people to get certain licences, to get supplies, to have a road repaired, and to get sales contracts signed. You know that other local companies have learned to live with these conditions. Now you are negotiating to buy a piece of land adjacent to the factory because Condor will have to expand in the near future. A substantial bribe is being demanded and you are trying to resist it.

Decision Questions

1. Should you go along with this demand since it is a one-time issue?
2. Should you say nothing and go along with this "normal" way of doing things?
3. Should you try to get a transfer out of Lorino even if you have to cook up some medical or personal reasons?
4. Do you have any other alternatives? What are the likely results of each of these choices?

Video Case

Six Billion Customers and Counting—IBM

When choosing a company to illustrate global business, it's not a bad idea to choose one that has about 315,000 employees around the world. About half are spread among 160 countries or so. The company that fits this global description is IBM.

The company was known as *International Business Machines* long before IBM finally reached its goal of becoming a global powerhouse. (Its first business machine was a scale for weighing meat.) IBM's brand name is now the third most valuable name in the world, after Coke and Microsoft. The brand name alone is said to be worth some $50 billion.

The person responsible for marketing the IBM brand is Lee Green, who is featured in this video. Lee's work includes those funny commercials for which IBM has become well known. IBM tries to maintain a global image by using the same themes in every country where it does business. The ad may change a little to adapt to the culture and the times, but the themes are the same.

A company may reach global markets in various ways, ranging from exporting to foreign direct investment. You can read about each option and the risks and rewards in this chapter. IBM tends to do a great deal of foreign direct investment. That makes it a multinational firm. IBM's annual revenue is greater than many countries' entire GDP.

IBM recognizes that the worldwide population is over 6 billion. As a result, the company has to adapt to a variety of environmental forces: sociocultural, economic, political and legal, and so forth. IBM's global network of employees, research facilities, and offices help create a cohesive company message that reaches customers around the globe. The company mission is to help people in other countries develop their own products by using their own people to develop products specific to their own markets.

IBM clearly has a comparative advantage in producing some goods. It maintains that advantage by changing its product offers over time to match the changing needs of a global economy.

It's interesting to note that IBM works with both small and large businesses and that they recognize that there is a huge potential for small businesses to do more globally, especially using the Internet. IBM's strength is to help businesses of all kinds integrate their operations to become global in scope. The company is trying to "invent the future" not only for itself, but for other companies as well. To do that, it has to maintain its corporate image through advertising and through providing excellent service with every contact, whether that contact is over the Internet, on the phone, or in person.

How could you prepare for a job in global business? You could study a foreign language, sign up for overseas program at your school, or simply make it a matter of researching the topic in as many ways as possible, including talking with those now involved in global business. Lee Green has been in over 100 countries because of his work. If that kind of life sounds glamorous and exciting to you, global business is the thing to study.

Discussion Questions

1. What did you learn from this video that might help you to more effectively pursue a career in global business?
2. From what you have read in this chapter and seen in the video, does it seem that the opportunities in global business are greater in small or large businesses? Why?
3. What impression do you have of multinational firms that have operations in multiple countries? Do they seem to be a major benefit to the world, or are there some negatives that you see? Discuss.

Chapter 4

The Role of Government in Business

Learning Goals

After you have read and studied this chapter, you should be able to

1 Understand the seven categories of government activities that can affect business.

2 Illustrate the historical role of government in the Canadian economy.

3 List some of the major Crown corporations in Canada and indicate their role in the economy.

4 Explain how the federal budget and the national debt are related.

5 Discuss the importance of Canada's Innovation Strategy to the government's plan to improve competitiveness.

Getting to Know Marc Pelland and Maxim Dufour of Woodchuck Skateboards Inc.

www.woodchucklaminates.com
www.premiumskateboards.com
www.averaskateboards.com

A passion for skateboarding paired with business know-how equals a winning combination. Woodchuck Skateboards Inc. is owned by entrepreneurs Marc Pelland and Maxim Dufour. Located in Longueuil, Quebec, Woodchuck is a skateboard manufacturing and distributing business.

Woodchuck was started by Dufour in 1996; Pelland joined in 2000. Dufour explains, "As the company grew, we realized that passion for the sport will get you to a certain level, and then you need the business infrastructure to take that passion and create a vision for business and the organization to support that vision." Today, Woodchuck has 30 employees and annual sales of $3 million. The company sells maple skateboard decks in Canada, Europe, Japan, and Australia. According to Pelland, "We intend to keep growing quite aggressively. We want to be in the top three players in the industry in our market."

Pelland and Dufour have received several awards recognizing their achievements. In 2002, they received the top honour for Quebec in the Business Development Bank of Canada's Young Entrepreneur Awards. This award recognizes the achievements of businesspeople between the ages of 19 and 35. Awards are presented to one company in each province and the three territories. Winners are selected by a panel of judges from the business community who consider such criteria as operating success, innovation, involvement in the new economy, community work, and export performance. For more details on BDC's Young Entrepreneur Awards, go to www.bdc.ca/yea.

Maxim Dufour (left) and Marc Pelland (right).

They were also 2003 finalists in Ernst & Young's Entrepreneur of the Year (EOY) program. The EOY awards honour entrepreneurs who have demonstrated excellence and extraordinary success in areas such as innovation, financial performance, and personal commitment to their businesses and communities.

There are many government agencies mandated to provide support for entrepreneurs. The Business Development Bank of Canada (BDC), a Crown corporation, is one such example. The BDC is a financial institution wholly owned by the Government of Canada. BDC plays a leadership role in recognizing entrepreneurs, as we see in this profile. However, its primary mandate is to deliver financial, investment, and consulting services to Canadian small businesses, with a particular focus on technology and exporting. In this chapter, you will be introduced to the many activities that government provides businesses to help them succeed and compete effectively.

Sources: Sheila McGovern, "Woodchuck Laminates Honored As Canadian Business," *The Gazette,* October 23, 2002. Retrieved from the World Wide Web: http://skateboarddirectory.com/articles/480392_woodchuck_laminates_honoured.html; "Marc Pelland, Maxim Dufour and Marc Mohammed from Woodchuck Inc. win BDC's Young Entrepreneur Award for Quebec," (2002), Montreal: Business Development Bank of Canada. Retrieved from the World Wide Web: http://www.bdc.ca/en/about/mediaroom/news_releases/2002/2002102109.htm; Quebec region finalists named for 10th Anniversary Ernst & Young Entrepreneur of the Year Awards" (July 8, 2003), Toronto: Canada NewsWire. Retrieved from the World Wide Web: http://www.newswire.ca/en/releases/archive/July2003/08/c0465.html.

HOW GOVERNMENT AFFECTS BUSINESS

Government activities that affect business may be divided into seven categories, as shown in Figure 4.1. These include Crown corporations, laws and regulations, taxation and financial policies, financial aid, other expenditures, purchasing policies, and services. Because all of these activities are scattered among different levels of government and many departments, agencies, and corporations that do a variety of things, it is not possible to present this information in such neatly divided categories. However, as you make your way through the rest of the chapter you will be able to see elements of these different aspects of government actions affecting business.

Since the focus of this chapter is on the role of government in business, there will be limited discussion on how business impacts government. It should become obvious as you read through the pages that governments are trying to respond to business needs. This can be anything from creating laws that create a level playing field to providing services that support business initiatives. Reviewing Figure 4.1 will give you a sense of the scope of this relationship.

GOVERNMENT INVOLVEMENT IN THE ECONOMY

As discussed in Chapter 2, the Canadian economic system is often described as a mixed economy—that is, an economic system in which some allocation of resources is made by the market and some by the government. If you look at the Government of Canada section (and equivalent provincial government sections) in the blue pages of a city telephone directory, you will get some idea of the degree of government involvement in our economy today. Every

FIGURE 4.1

GOVERNMENT INVOLVEMENT WITH BUSINESS

Government activities that affect business can be divided into seven categories.

1. **Crown Corporations.** There are hundreds of such companies, and they play an important role in the economy. Crown corporations sometimes compete with regular businesses.
2. **Laws and Regulations.** These cover a wide range, from taxation and consumer protection to environmental controls, working conditions, and labour–management relations.
3. **Taxation and Financial Policies.** All levels of government collect taxes—income taxes, the GST, sales taxes, and property taxes. Taxation is also fine-tuned by government to achieve certain goals or to give effect to certain policies. This is called *fiscal policy*.
4. **Financial Aid.** All levels of government provide a host of direct and indirect aid packages as incentives to achieve certain goals. These packages consist of tax reductions, grants, loans, and loan guarantees.
5. **Other Expenditures.** Governments pay out billions of dollars to the unemployed, to old-age pensioners, to low-income families, to employees injured at work, and to other categories of people. When these recipients spend this money, business benefits.
6. **Purchasing Policies.** Governments are very large purchasers of ordinary supplies, services, and materials to operate the country. Because the federal government is the single largest purchaser in Canada, its policies regarding where to purchase have a major effect on particular businesses and the economy.
7. **Services.** These include a vast array of direct and indirect activities, among them helping specific industries go international, bringing companies to Canada, training and retraining the workforce, and providing a comprehensive statistics service through StatsCan.

country's government is involved in its economy, but the specific ways in which they participate vary a great deal. In Canada, there are particular historical reasons why we developed into a nation in which governments play very important roles.

When Canada was formed as a country in 1867, the federal government was given the power to "regulate trade and commerce." When the western provinces later joined this Confederation, it became clear that it would take special efforts to build a unified Canada. The very small population was scattered across a huge country, and there was no railway to connect it. Trading patterns were in a north to south configuration because, like today, most people lived near the U.S. border.

The United States developed much faster and with a much larger population and a bigger economy—which provided products not available in the provinces, either because they were not made in Canada or because there was no transportation to distribute them.

This led the Canadian governments, starting with our first prime minister, Sir John A. Macdonald, to develop what was called a **National Policy.** The Policy placed high tariffs on imports from the U.S. to protect Canadian manufacturing, which had higher costs. In addition, the government began to grapple with the difficult question of building a costly rail line to the west coast.

National Policy
Government directive that placed high tariffs on imports from the U.S. to protect Canadian manufacturing, which had higher costs.

These two issues set the tone for the continuing and substantial involvement of Canadian governments in developing and maintaining the Canadian economy. As you make your way through the chapter and see their complex activities, you should not be surprised to learn that governments are the largest employers in the country. The federal government and the provinces with the largest populations and levels of economic activity—namely, Ontario, Quebec, British Columbia, and Alberta—have been excellent sources of employment for graduates in the past. Before we go into more detail, let us briefly review how government affects business. You never know—one day you may have a job in one of these areas.

Critical Thinking

The issue of how much government should be involved in the economy has been the subject of much debate in Canada. In the United States, ideology has played a major role in influencing Americans to believe that, in principle, government should "butt out." This thinking ignores the significant role the U.S. government has played and continues to play in the country's economy. In Canada, we are less negative and perhaps more pragmatic: If it works, let's do it. But where do we go from here? Do we need less or more government involvement? Is it a question of the quality of that involvement? Could it be *smarter* rather than just *less*? How can the cost of government involvement decrease?

CROWN CORPORATIONS

In Canada, an important aspect of the role of government is expressed through **Crown corporations,** companies that are owned by the federal or provincial governments. Crown corporations were set up for several reasons. They provided services that were not being provided by businesses, which is how Air Canada came into being in the 1930s. Crown corporations were created to bail out a major industry in trouble, which is how the Canadian National Railway was put together in 1919. Lastly, they provided some special services that could not otherwise be made available, as in the case of Atomic Energy of Canada Ltd. or the Bank of Canada.

Crown corporation
A company that is owned by the federal or provincial government.

VIA Rail Canada Inc. is a Crown corporation that was set up in 1978. It serves some 450 Canadian communities throughout the country. Have you ever taken advantage of the student savings offered by VIA Rail?

Each province also owns a variety of Crown corporations. Typically, a Crown corporation owns the province's electric power company. Some examples are New Brunswick's Power Corporation, SaskPower, and Hydro-Quebec. Ontario owns the Liquor Control Board of Ontario (LCBO). Alberta owns a bank called Alberta Treasury Branches (ATB), originally set up to help farmers in bad times. Two other examples in Alberta and Quebec are discussed next.

The Special Financial Role of Two Provincial Crown Corporations

The Alberta Heritage Savings Trust Fund was established in the 1970s, when the Alberta economy was prospering as a result of the oil boom. The government set aside a part of its oil royalty revenue to start the fund. The Fund's assets now total $12.1 billion.[1] It must operate on a sound financial basis, but, as much as possible, it makes investment decisions that will benefit Alberta.

Quebec has the Caisse de dépôt et placement du Québec, a giant fund that was established to handle the funds collected by the Quebec Pension Plan. With $140.3 billion in assets under management, it is one of the largest pools of funds in North America.[2] This plan was set up parallel to the Canada Pension Plan in 1966. The fund also handles other Quebec government funds, and it is a very powerful investment vehicle that is used to guide economic development in Quebec. Although it too must operate on a sound financial basis, it has a lot of scope to make decisions that will benefit the Quebec economy.

Today: A Smaller Role for Government

Elections in Canada in the 1990s saw federal and provincial governments embark upon a series of measures designed to reduce the role of government in the economy. Over the years, former large corporations like Teleglobe Canada, Air Canada, Canadian National Railway (CNR), and the Post Office were sold. The national system of air traffic control, the management of airports, hundreds of ports and ferries, and other maritime installations were also sold. More recently, the federal government announced its intention to sell its remaining stake (18.75 percent) in Petro-Canada by the end of 2005. This disposal of government assets and companies signalled a minor revolution in Canadian history. The whole process of selling publicly owned corporations is called **privatization.** As well, during this time, industries that had been regulated, such as airlines and trucking, were partially or completely deregulated. This meant that they were no longer subject to certain regulations.

Similar activities were undertaken by provincial governments. Alberta and British Columbia privatized their liquor boards. Ontario sold the toll-road Highway 407 and its share in a land-registry firm. Saskatchewan reduced its interest in giant uranium producer Cameco Corporation. More recently, the British Columbia provincial government sold BC Rail Ltd.

Many previously government-owned corporations, such as the St. Lawrence Seaway, have been privatized in recent years. Privatization and deregulation have been somewhat controversial because these "new" corporations now operate on the profit principle, not necessarily on what is best for consumers. Do you see anything wrong with this?

privatization
The process of governments selling Crown corporations.

Progress Assessment

- What are the seven categories of government involvement with business?
- What are Crown corporations? Why are they created?
- What does privatization refer to? Can you cite any examples?

LAWS AND REGULATIONS

In Chapter 1, you were introduced to the importance of the legal and regulatory environment. These laws and regulations are created by the politicians that, for the most part, have been elected by Canadians. Consequently, the political parties in power can greatly impact the business environment. This is also why it is important to be aware of the beliefs of the different parties. Some think the government should have more say in business, while others think that less government intervention is best.

The power to make laws is based on the British North America Act, 1867. The BNA Act was passed by the British Parliament in 1867. It is the law that created the Canadian Confederation and it sets the legal ground rules for Canada. In 1982, the BNA Act became part of the new Constitution and was renamed the Constitution Act, 1867.

Laws are derived from four sources: the Constitution, precedents established by judges, provincial and federal statutes, and federal and provincial administrative agencies.[3] As a businessperson, you will be impacted by current (and potential) laws and regulations. Appendix B outlines some important elements of business law.

Canada has a legislature in each province and territory to deal with local matters. The Parliament in Ottawa makes laws for all Canadians. The Constitution defines the powers that can be exercised by the federal and provincial governments. In the event of a conflict, federal powers prevail.

Federal Government Responsibilities

The federal government is responsible for issues that affect citizens across Canada. Its primary responsibility is to ensure and support the country's economic performance. Some other responsibilities that may have an impact on business operations include:

- trade regulations (interprovincial and international)
- incorporation of federal companies
- taxation (both direct and indirect)
- the banking and monetary system
- national defence
- unemployment
- immigration
- criminal law
- fisheries

The federal government also oversees such industries as aeronautics, shipping, railways, telecommunications, and atomic energy. Two examples, national security and health care reform, highlight some of these responsibilities.

National Security   Global events impact domestic policies. In the area of transportation, the federal government enacted an air-security charge in response to the 9/11 attacks. This charge applies to all plane tickets in order to pay for enhanced air security. The security fees pay for armed Royal Canadian Mounted Police air marshals on select domestic and international flights, new bomb-detection equipment, and better pre-board screening of passengers.

Health Care Reform   The federal government is trying to reform Canada's health care system. In 2002, former Saskatchewan premier Roy Romanow released his Royal Commission Report outlining sweeping changes. His recommendations included a health council, special programs for homecare, extensive drug coverage, rural health care, more money for high-tech diagnostic care, and the rejection of increased private care within the system. This council would require the cooperation of the provinces and it would monitor spending, set goals for the system, and measure progress in reforming health care. One should know that the national Parliament established nationwide systems of hospital insurance and medical care by making grants to the provinces.[4] While the federal government is responsible for health care, it is still up to the provinces to implement these policies, and their cooperation is critical for success.

www.ic.gc.ca

Industry Canada's corporate information Website provides a wealth of information about the department, its mandate, and the corporate outlook in Canada.

As mentioned in Chapter 1, Industry Canada is a federal agency that administers a variety of laws affecting businesses and consumers. One of the most relevant pieces of legislation is the Competition Act, which aims to make sure that mergers of large corporations will not restrict competition and that fair competition exists among businesses. The Act covers many laws including discriminatory pricing, price fixing, misleading advertising, and the refusal to deal with certain companies. Some of the major consumer protection laws are shown in Figure 4.2.

For example, the clothes you wear have a label showing the country of origin, size, type of fabric, and washing instructions. When you buy 25 litres of gasoline, you can feel confident that you have gotten a true measure because there is a sticker on the equipment showing when it was last inspected. There

Canadian Agricultural Products Standards Act covers a wide range of farm products, such as meat, poultry, eggs, maple syrup, honey, and dairy products.

Consumer Packaging and Labelling Act applies to all products not specifically included in other acts.

Food and Drug Act covers a whole range of regulations pertaining to quality, testing, approval, packaging, and labelling.

Hazardous Products Act covers all hazardous products.

National Trademark and True Labelling Act includes not only labelling, but also accurate advertising.

Textile Labelling Act includes apparel sizing and many other special areas.

Weights and Measures Act applies to all equipment that measures quantities (scales, gas pumps, and so forth).

FIGURE 4.2

SOME MAJOR FEDERAL CONSUMER PROTECTION LAWS

These laws all provide consumers with information and protection, in various ways. There are also provincial consumer protection laws.

are laws that give consumers the right to cancel contracts or return goods within a certain period of time. It is not possible to go through a day and not find an instance where laws have helped you in some way. Appendix B will highlight the importance of business law.

The federal Bureau of Competition Policy and the Competition Tribunal are busy organizations whose work is constantly in the news. One high-profile decision occurred in 1998, when the Bureau recommended against two mergers among four of Canada's largest banks. The minister of finance, who has final say on banking matters, accepted that recommendation. We will discuss this issue in Chapter 18.

Provincial Government Responsibilities

Each province has its own government, while the territories are still governed federally. Issues that affect provincial residents but that do not necessarily affect all Canadians are governed at the provincial level. According to Canadian Constitutional expert Eugene Forsey, "municipal governments—cities, towns, villages, counties, districts, metropolitan regions—are set up by the provincial legislatures, and have such powers as the legislatures see fit to give them."[5]

Provincial governments are responsible for the following areas:

- regulation of provincial trade and commerce
- natural resources within their boundaries
- direct taxation for provincial purposes
- incorporation of provincial companies
- licensing for revenue purposes
- the administration of justice
- health and social services
- municipal affairs
- property law
- labour law
- education

The Honourable Eugene A. Forsey was widely regarded as one of Canada's foremost experts on the country's Constitution. He created *How Canadians Govern Themselves,* a publication that provides useful information on Canada's Constitution, the judicial system, and government powers.

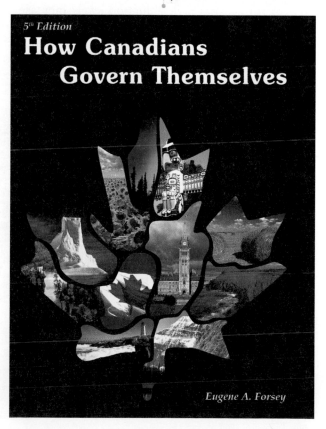
5th Edition
How Canadians Govern Themselves
Eugene A. Forsey

The participation of all provincial governments in federal–provincial, shared-cost arrangements for hospital insurance and medicare has helped ensure nationwide standards of service, despite some differences in their modes of financing and program coverage. In contrast, the retention of a high degree of provincial autonomy in the provision of elementary and secondary school education and the accommodation of religious and linguistic preferences has resulted in a variation in school systems. The following two examples highlight the provincial government's activities.

Education   In Ontario, the provincial government made the decision several years ago to eliminate Grade 13. Consequently, in fall 2003 graduates from both Grade 12 and Grade 13 attended post-secondary institutions. Some concerned parents encouraged their children to apply to schools outside of Ontario: among other things, they were worried that there would not be enough spots in Ontario schools as a result of this "double cohort." As a result of this provincial decision, many out-of-province educational institutions saw an opportunity to increase their enrollment.

No Free Trade between Provinces   The provincial governments have erected walls between the provinces that practically rule out interprovincial government acquisitions. (The municipal governments within a province also follow this procedure.) These protectionist policies favour the companies in each province, but almost eliminate normal free trade and competition. They also create other distortions by insisting, for example, that a beer company must have a plant in a province if it wants to sell beer there, preventing the normal cost savings that could be achieved with fewer but larger plants. Larger-scale production would result in lower costs, called **economies of scale.** This term refers to the situation in which companies can reduce their production costs if they can purchase raw materials in bulk; the average cost of goods goes down as production levels increase. Economies of scale should lead to lower prices for purchasers. Lower costs would make many Canadian companies more competitive on the international scene.

An example that drew a lot of attention years ago was a paving job in the town of Aylmer, Quebec, near the Ontario border. The town bought bricks

economies of scale
The situation in which companies can reduce their production costs if they can purchase raw materials in bulk; the average cost of goods goes down as production levels increase.

Samples of agricultural products such as fruit and vegetables are inspected before they ever make their way onto store shelves. Such inspection is required to ensure the public consumes only safe and healthy produce.

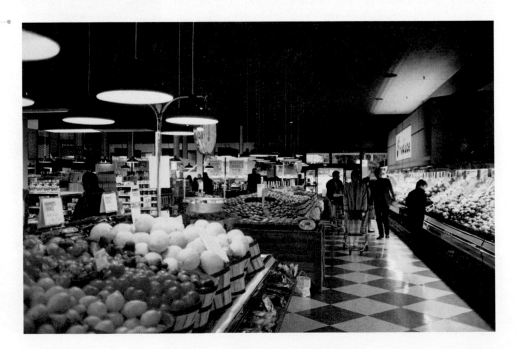

from an Ontario company, but was forced by the provincial government to pull them up and replace them with Quebec bricks. This is an extreme example of a common problem in Canada. It is estimated that there are more than 500 trade barriers between provinces.[6]

Municipal Government Responsibilities

The roughly 4,000 municipal governments in the country provide services such as water supply, sewage and garbage disposal, roads, sidewalks, street lighting, building codes, parks, playgrounds, libraries, and so forth.[7] Municipalities also play a role in consumer protection. For example, they have regulations and laws regarding any establishment that serves food. Inspectors regularly examine the premises of all restaurants for cleanliness. Local newspapers often publish lists of restaurants fined for not maintaining required standards.

There are similar laws about noise, odours, signs, and other activities that may affect a neighbourhood. These are called zoning laws; certain zones are restricted to residences, and others permit only certain quiet businesses to operate.

Zoning requirements also limit the height of buildings and define how far they must be set back from the road. Most Canadian cities require that all highrise buildings have a certain ratio of garage space so that cars have off-street parking places. Parking problems in residential areas due to overflow of vehicles from adjacent businesses have led to parking being limited to residential permit holders on certain streets, so stores and other places of business must offer commercial parking lots for their customers. And, of course, we are all familiar with speed limits set by municipal or provincial authorities.

All businesses must usually obtain a municipal licence to operate so the appropriate department may track them to make sure they are following regulations. Many municipalities also have a business tax and a charge for water consumption.

Progress Assessment

- What are four responsibilities of the federal government? Name two industries that the federal government regulates.
- What are four responsibilities of the provincial government?
- Why are there interprovincial trade barriers?
- Give some examples of how municipalities can impact businesses.

TAXATION AND FINANCIAL POLICIES

Each level of government collects taxes from companies. These taxes allow governments to discharge their legal obligations. Federal and provincial governments rely mostly on the income taxes of individuals (recall our discussion of personal tax rates in Chapter 2) and corporations. Provincial sales taxes are also an important source of revenue for the provinces (only Alberta has no sales tax), while the goods and services tax (GST) brings very substantial monies to the federal government. In some provinces, health care is financed by a tax on the total wages and salaries paid by companies. The main source of income for the municipalities is taxes on property, but there are a variety of other taxes and fees as well.

Stabilizing the Economy through Fiscal Policy

fiscal policy
The federal government's effort to keep the economy stable by increasing or decreasing taxes or government spending.

Fiscal policy refers to the federal government's effort to keep the economy stable by increasing or decreasing taxes or government spending.

The first half of fiscal policy involves taxation. Theoretically, high tax rates tend to slow the economy because they draw money away from the private sector and are remitted to the government. High tax rates may discourage small business ownership because they decrease the profits businesses can make, and this can make the effort less rewarding. It follows, then, that—theoretically—low tax rates would tend to give the economy a boost.[8] The government can use taxation to help move the economy in a desired direction. For example, taxes may be lowered to stimulate the economy when it is weak. Similarly, taxes may be raised when the economy is booming to cool it off and slow down inflation.

Federal and provincial governments constantly use the lever of fiscal policy to stimulate specific geographic and industrial areas. They offer special tax credits to companies that open plants in areas of chronically high unemployment, such as Cape Breton, the Gaspé, or Newfoundland and Labrador. All companies that invest in specific activities considered desirable by the government (such as the technology sector) receive a tax credit that reduces the income tax they have to pay. Unfortunately, many of these programs have been scaled back or eliminated due to budget constraints.

The second half of fiscal policy involves government spending. The government spends money in many areas including social programs, highways, the environment, and so on. If the government spends over and above the amount it gathers in taxes for a specific period of time (namely, a fiscal year), then it has a **deficit.**

deficit
Occurs when a government spends over and above the amount it gathers in taxes for a specific period of time (namely, a fiscal year).

One way to lessen annual deficits is to cut government spending. This is difficult to do. Every year, there is continuous demand by the provinces and territories for increased transfer payments (to be discussed later), the need for funds due to unexpected situations (such as massive forest fires in British Columbia), more pressure from international bodies to increase peacekeeping support, and so on. Some people believe that spending by the government helps the economy grow. Others believe that the money the government spends comes out of the pockets of consumers and businesspeople—especially when taxes have been increased—and this slows growth. What do you think? Let us look at government actions that have been taken over the past decade.

Wiping Out Annual Deficits   For many years, the Canadian government spent more than it received in revenues, and it had to borrow heavily. However, it did not reduce spending when times were good to pay back these loans. In Canada, 25 years of annual deficits, starting in the mid-1970s, have resulted in a huge **national debt.** The national debt is the sum of government debt over time. Today, this debt totals approximately $510.6 billion.[9]

national debt
The sum of government debt over time.

After relentless pressure from business organizations and right-wing political groups, the Canadian government decided in 1996 that the only way out of that recession was to eliminate annual deficits and stop the debt from growing. This plan meant cutting expenses and cash outlays as much as possible, including reducing transfers to the provinces to pay for health care, education, and welfare. The government reduced employment insurance (EI) payments by raising eligibility standards, paying for shorter periods, and paying smaller amounts. The government also laid off thousands of people and reduced pension payments to wealthier senior citizens.

These reductions in spending contributed to Canada's slow recovery from the recession. Increased government borrowing and spending stimulates an

Making Ethical Decisions

Tackling the Deficit

In the late 1990s, the federal government was under strong pressure from the business community to reduce or wipe out the annual deficit in the annual budget. Business was convinced that these constant deficits and the resulting accumulated debt were dragging the Canadian economy down and making Canada uncompetitive with other major countries. To arrive at the surpluses that we have seen to date, the federal government drastically cut its expenditures. This resulted in significant reductions in funding to the provinces for health care, post-secondary education, and other important activities. Combined with other budget-cutting measures that have led to lower and fewer payments to the unemployed, the result has been an increase in poverty levels, especially among children and women.

These facts lead to some ethical questions. How could such severe budget cuts have been avoided? Does the business community bear some responsibility for the increase in poverty in Canada? In other words, was it ethical for business to allow our national debt to grow so large and not challenge the government's annual deficits much earlier? What do you think?

economy, while cuts in spending have the opposite effect—they slow down the economy.

The drastic slashing of government spending in the 1990s was strongly opposed by left-wing political groups and many organizations such as churches, unions, welfare groups, food banks, and other community-centred groups because of the hardship these cuts inflicted on many people. Reduced EI and welfare payments, a reduction in hospital funding, the closing of hospitals, and so on affected many poor and sick people. Cuts to post-secondary education funding resulted in fewer staff members and more students per class, higher fees, increased costs for some services, and a reduction of other services. Food banks across Canada reported a jump in the number of people seeking food. When economic problems become severe, attempts to remedy them can be difficult and painful. Part of the surpluses today are being used to restore some of the funding cuts to health and education. The Making Ethical Decisions box highlights the impact of paying down the national debt.

Over the past six years, the federal government has made debt reduction a priority, consequently raising taxes and cutting programs, as noted earlier. Why is it important to control the debt? Financial security is critical to a country's investment in its people and businesses. A lower debt means that less money will need to go toward paying down the national debt and any outstanding interest. Reducing government spending on interest charges will allow the government to spend more money on social programs or to lower taxes. Lower taxes will stimulate the economy, as companies and individuals will have more disposable income.

With a lower debt, Canada could also be considered a more attractive country to invest in—a healthy and educated workforce is able to work and buy products. In addition, employers like well-funded social programs, as there is less risk that they will be asked to increase employee benefits. A lower debt load also means that in economic slowdowns or if unexpected events occur (such as an outbreak of SARS or mad cow disease) the government may have funds available to alleviate the ensuing pressures. Of course, if the debt is high, there is less money that can be dedicated to social programs and initiatives to assist businesses in becoming more competitive.

surplus
An excess of revenues over expenditures.

Today, the national debt has been reduced by more than $52 billion since the late 1990s. These reductions were the result of surpluses—a **surplus** is an excess of revenues over expenditures. As the debt comes down, the annual interest costs are also reduced. This reduction in the national debt translated into a savings of $3 billion each year on debt interest payments. Looking at this another way, 21 cents of each revenue dollar goes to service the debt. In 1995–96, this number was as high as 37.6 cents of each revenue dollar.[10]

The Federal Budget   During most years in late February, the federal finance minister releases a blueprint for how the government wants to set the country's annual economic agenda. This document, called the **federal budget,** is a comprehensive report that reveals government financial policies for the coming year. It shows how much revenue the government expects to collect, any changes in income and other taxes, and whether a deficit or a surplus is expected. The federal budget answers questions that affect businesses and Canadians, such as: How much money will go to pay down the debt? How much money will go to social programs such as health care? Will there be more money for research and development? and Will taxes go up or down?

federal budget
A comprehensive report that reveals government financial policies for the coming year.

The budget is reviewed carefully by businesses, consumers, and other countries—the information it contains impacts all these stakeholders. It reflects revenues (from taxation) and expenditures (e.g., transfer payments to the provinces) for the past year. In addition, the government will communicate program changes for the future, as well as forecasted growth projections. From this document, stakeholders can get an idea of what issues are important to the government. For example, in the 2003 budget, the government directed $2 billion toward meeting its commitment to reduce greenhouse gas emissions under the Kyoto Accord. Remember that international matters fall under the jurisdiction of the federal government. Other initiatives that were to receive more than $1 billion over the next few years were aimed at foreign aid, children, aboriginals, and health care.[11]

The Department of Finance Canada has the overall responsibility of setting fiscal and financial policies for Canada. Visit www.fin.gc.ca to learn about the budget, economics and fiscal information, financial institutions and markets, international issues, social issues, taxes and tariffs, and transfer payments to the provinces.

Keep in mind that promises made by the federal government in a budget are not necessarily permanent. If a new political party is elected, it can reverse these decisions and announce its own initiatives. This is why the first budget after an election is critical. It clearly communicates to the population whether a new government will support its campaign promises. As well, it sends strong signals to businesses and international markets about the government's priorities.

Provincial governments also release their own budgets. A province's financial stability impacts political decisions and, ultimately, the business environment. For example, when Dalton McGuinty became Premier of Ontario in 2003, he had the province's finances audited. The unforeseen $5.6-billion deficit forced him to reverse his election pledge to keep electricity rates capped. In addition, he made the following decisions to try to eliminate this deficit: increase the general corporate tax rate from 12.5 percent to 14 percent; eliminate a property tax break for seniors; scrap a tax break on private-school tuition; and increase tobacco taxes to meet the national average.[12]

Using Monetary Policy to Keep the Economy Growing

Have you ever wondered who lends the federal government money when it spends more than it collects in taxes? One source is the Bank of Canada. The Bank of Canada is a Crown corporation: its role is to "promote the economic and financial well-being of Canada." The day-to-day administration of monetary policy is the responsibility of the Bank of Canada, in cooperation and in consultation with the federal finance minister.

Monetary policy is the management of the money supply and interest rates. It is controlled by the Bank of Canada. When the economy is booming, the Bank of Canada tends to raise interest rates in an attempt to control inflation. This makes money more expensive to borrow. Businesses thus borrow less, and the economy slows as businesspeople spend less money on everything, including more labour and machinery. The opposite is true when the Bank lowers interest rates. When this happens, businesses tend to borrow more, and the economy improves. Raising and lowering interest rates should therefore help control the business cycles.

monetary policy
The management of the money supply and interest rates.

The Bank of Canada also controls the money supply. A simple explanation is that the more money the Bank of Canada makes available to businesspeople and others, the faster the economy grows. To slow the economy, the Bank of Canada lowers the money supply. You don't need to know all the details to understand that there are two major efforts being made to control the economy: fiscal policy (taxes and spending), and monetary policy (control over interest rates and the money supply).

To learn more about the Bank of Canada, visit www. bankofcanada.ca

- How does the government manage the economy using fiscal policy?
- What is Canada's national debt? Has it been increasing or decreasing over the past six years?
- Explain the purpose of the federal budget.
- What does the term monetary policy mean? What organization is responsible for Canada's monetary policy?

Progress Assessment

FINANCIAL AID

Governments spend huge sums of money on education, health, roads, ports, waterways, airports, and various other services required by businesses and individuals. They also provide direct aid to businesses.

There are many direct and indirect government programs designed to help businesses. We will discuss some examples later in this chapter. Another source, the *Canadian Subsidy Directory*, lists more than 2,600 grants and loans from government departments, foundations, and associations. Governments also intervene on an ad hoc (special, unplanned) basis in important cases. Aid to Saskatchewan and Alberta farmers and Newfoundland and B.C. fishers when their industries faced severe hardships are examples.

Direct Intervention

All levels of government offer a variety of direct assistance programs to businesses, including grants, loans, loan guarantees, consulting advice, information, and other aids that are designed to achieve certain purposes. For example, when this book was being written, Ford Motor Co. of Canada Ltd. was seeking about $200 million from the federal and Ontario governments as part of its $1.1-billion proposal to redevelop its Oakville site.[13] While there were some conditions, to keep and attract new jobs the company appeared to qualify for $100 million in financial aid from the province. Ford was then seeking the balance from the federal government.

Some government aid is designed to help industries or companies that are deemed to be very important—at the cutting edge of technology, providing highly skilled jobs, and oriented toward exports. The federal and Ontario governments and Spar Aerospace Ltd. took a huge gamble developing an all-weather radar satellite that has the potential to start a new multi-billion dollar industry in Canada. Both governments combined bore 51 percent of the cost and have the rights to 51 percent of the data. The U.S. government did likewise for a 15-percent stake. The first results made the space scientists at Spar "whoop for joy" as they saw a clear image of Cape Breton Island produced through rain and in the dark.[14]

Pratt & Whitney Canada Inc., after getting nearly $12 million from the federal and Quebec governments to develop a new aircraft engine (the PW 150 for the de Havilland Dash 8-400 commuter aircraft), was "threatening to move the project outside Canada unless Ottawa [gave] it more." In 1998 the company again warned that it might have to close down. Since this is a $200-million project, both governments agreed to an $11.7-million interest-free loan as part of a $45.7-million program under the Canada-Subsidiary Agreement for Industrial Development.[15]

Major companies often hint or announce outright that they are planning to close a plant that they claim is not efficient enough to be competitive. They often suggest that they will consolidate operations with other plants in Canada or the United States. These announcements naturally result in a flurry of efforts by all affected parties to prevent the closure. Unions, municipalities, and provincial and federal governments all work to save the jobs and economies of the area. There are many examples of such cases in the last decade.

Auto plants, pulp and paper mills, food processing plants, oil refineries, ship-building yards, meat-packing plants, steel mills, and other industries across the country have faced such closures; while in many cases the closures could not have been prevented, some (such as the de Havilland plant north of Toronto) have been saved by such concerted action.

Some of these rescue efforts end in costly failures. For example, in 1999 the federal government announced that it was going to end its long-time financial support of the Cape Breton Development Corp. (Devco), a coal mining operation. After pouring more than a billion dollars into covering deficits, the government decided to close or sell off the mines, as there was no hope of profitable operations.[16] In 2004, the PEI government bought Polar Foods as its bankruptcy put at risk tens of millions of dollars in government investments, and brought into question where Island lobsters would be sold.[17] It was estimated that the government lost close to $27 million when it later sold the company. To assist the approximately 800 unemployed fish plant workers, the government set aside close to $1 million in an aid package. Was it worth it to spend such sums to provide hundreds of jobs in chronically depressed areas? Was it the best way to help the unemployed in areas of high unemployment? These questions are constantly being asked in Canada.

Equalization of Transfer Payments

Canada is a very large country with uneven resources, climate, and geography, which has led to uneven economic development. Ontario and Quebec, with large populations, proximity to the United States, an abundance of all kinds of natural resources, and excellent rail and water transport, were the earliest to develop industrially.

Nova Scotia and New Brunswick began to suffer when wooden ships gave way to metal ships in the last half of the 1800s and their lumber industries declined. The west was sparsely populated until well into the twentieth century. Alberta and British Columbia became strong industrially only in the last 30 years as oil, gas, coal, hydro-electric power and forestry became significant competitive resources for them. Saskatchewan and Manitoba are essentially

www.acoa.ca

A visit to the Website for the Atlantic Canada Opportunities Agency will introduce you to the range of projects it has engaged in as it seeks to facilitate development in its region. Start by selecting the *About Us* button, and then explore its range of activities. See if you can find other Websites for parallel agencies.

tied to the volatile agricultural industry. Newfoundland, which became part of Canada in 1949 and was far behind the average Canadian living standard, has relied mainly on fisheries and pulp and paper. With the collapse of the cod fishery, Newfoundland and Labrador now looks to the development of the offshore Hibernia and other oilfields to become major factors in its economic growth in the 21st century. Nova Scotia is counting on the development of the huge gas fields off Sable Island. The three territories, Yukon, the Northwest Territories, and Nunavut, are all very lightly populated and have difficult climates. The Northwest Territories is rich in diamonds and gas exploration.

Transfer payments are direct payments from governments to other governments or to individuals. Federal transfer payments to individuals include elderly benefits and employment insurance. Such payments provide social security and income support.

Equalization is a federal government program for reducing fiscal disparities among provinces. These payments enable less prosperous provincial governments to provide their residents with public services that are reasonably comparable to those in other provinces, at reasonably comparable levels of taxation. While provinces are free to spend the funds on public services according to their own priorities, these payments are intended to fund medicare, post-secondary education, and smaller programs.

Ottawa distributes more than $10 billion a year in equalization payments to the provinces.[18] This long-standing system of payments (transfers) to poorer provinces, which was financed by wealthier ones (such as Ontario and Alberta), is being gradually reduced. As a result of many complaints, including how the government calculates the transfers of monies from the rich to the poor provinces, Ottawa has promised to re-examine how payments are distributed.

Based on these concerns, the provinces are trying to negotiate with the federal government. However, they don't have the right to demand changes. According to a senior official, "At the end of the day, it's a federal program."

Marketing Boards

In Canada we have a special system of **marketing boards,** which control the supply or pricing of certain agricultural products. Consequently, they often control trade. This supply management is designed to give some stability to an important area of the economy that is normally very volatile. Farmers are subject to conditions that are rather unique and that have a great effect on their business and on our food supply. Weather and disease are major factors in the operation of farms and are beyond the control of the individual farmer. So are unstable prices and changes in supply resulting from uncoordinated decision making by millions of farmers around the world or the exercise of market power by concentrated business organizations.

In the past, farmers have experienced periods of severe drought, flooding, severe cold, and diseases that affect crops, livestock, and poultry. The situation regarding international markets and supply has a serious impact on Canada's grain farmers, since we export much more wheat than we consume domestically. This market fluctuates greatly depending on the supply in other major grain-exporting countries like the United States, Argentina, and Australia. The market also depends on demand from major importers like China and Russia, whose abilities to meet their own requirements are subject to wide variation. Often the Canadian government (like other governments) grants substantial loans with favourable conditions to enable these countries to pay for their imports of our wheat and other agricultural products.

Because we export more than $25 billion of agricultural products annually, the ability to hold our own in international markets has a major impact on the

transfer payments
Direct payments from governments to other governments or to individuals.

marketing boards
Organizations that control the supply or pricing of certain agricultural products in Canada.

The Canadian Wheat Board is one of Canada's largest exporters. It generates annual sales revenues of between $4 and $6 billion. The single largest seller of wheat and barley in the world, it holds more than 20 percent of the international market. This picture was taken at the Mister Donut store in the Mita area of downtown Tokyo. It illustrates a promotion that was held in the 1,300 Mister Donut stores in Japan highlighting the quality of Canadian Western (1CW) red spring wheat.

state of the Canadian economy. When farmers are flourishing, they buy new equipment and consumer goods and their communities feel the effects of ample cash flow. So does the transportation industry. Conversely, when farmers are suffering, all these sectors hurt as well.

To smooth out the effects of these unusual conditions on this sector of our economy, and to ensure a steady supply of food to consumers at reasonable prices, six government agencies have been set up to control wheat and barley, dairy products, and poultry. The Canadian Wheat Board operates in the three Prairie provinces and, as discussed in Chapter 2, is the sole legal exporter of wheat and barley produced in those provinces. The Board is also the sole sales agent domestically for industrial use of these products. The Canadian Dairy Commission controls the output and pricing of milk and other dairy products.

The Canadian Egg Marketing Agency, Chicken Farmers of Canada, Canadian Turkey Marketing Agency, and Canadian Broiler Hatching Egg Marketing Agency consist of representatives from the provinces that produce these items.

All of these bodies, except the Wheat Board, control the amount of production for all the products under their supervision by allocating quotas to each province that produces them. Provincial agencies administer these quotas and set prices for their province. Each agency controls products that are sold only in its province.

Supply Management in Evolution A system to manage the supply of agricultural products can be found in many countries, although not necessarily in the same format as in Canada. Various subsidy and indirect support methods can be found almost everywhere. Supply management of farm products is an effective barrier to their entry into Canada, because imports are also subject to the quota system.

The Canadian system of marketing boards has been under attack by various organizations because it does not permit normal competitive conditions to operate in this field. This, they argue, distorts the whole industry and raises prices to Canadian consumers. Defenders of the system argue that other countries have different systems that have the same effect as our marketing boards but are just less visible. The European Union spends many billions of dollars on subsidies for their farmers. The United States, which often complains about other countries' unreasonable trade barriers, has its own restrictions, such as on peanut and sugar imports. The result is that American consumers pay about 25 percent more than the free market price for sugar.[19]

In Chapter 3 we referred to the World Trade Organization, whose main purpose is to reduce barriers to trade among countries. After lengthy negotiations, Canada agreed in 1994 to a complicated system that replaces the simple restrictive import quota system on these agricultural products. The new system is based on very high tariffs to make it difficult for foreign products to compete with those Canadian agricultural products subject to marketing-board control in Canada. Some people are concerned that this will lead to the end of our long-standing system of marketing boards.

Agricultural economists foresee a very different picture emerging worldwide over the next decade: limited protection for domestic markets, reduced tariffs and other restrictions, and the market having a much greater impact on prices and production. The effect on Canadian farmers, and on the whole agricultural industry in general, will be enormous. The next decade will see everyone trying to cope with the necessary adjustments to the new conditions.

Advances in technology are extremely important to keep a country globally competitive. Since governments do not have unlimited amounts of money to spend, they may have to focus on a few areas. Would it be wise for Canadian governments to concentrate on advanced technology? Should they, in conjunction with business, pick some high-tech industries and give them substantial support? Why might it be a good idea for the government to concentrate on advanced technology? How might the governments, in conjunction with business, pick some high-tech industries and give them substantial support? What would happen to industries in other areas that are in trouble?

OTHER EXPENDITURES: HOW GOVERNMENTS SPEND TAX DOLLARS TO HELP BUSINESS

Governments in Canada help disburse tens of billions of dollars annually in old-age pensions, allowances to low-income families or individuals, employment insurance, welfare, workers' compensation, and various other payments to individuals. As they spend these dollars, large numbers of Canadian companies and their employees benefit. Increasing or lowering the rates or eligibility for these payments results in further fine tuning of the economy. Again, government cutbacks have resulted in the reduction of such payments in recent years.

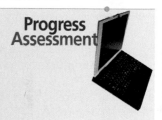

- Give two examples of how government has provided financial aid to businesses.
- What two groups benefit from equalization transfer payments?
- What are marketing boards? Why do some countries disagree with their existence?
- Explain how governments in Canada spend tax dollars to help Canadians.

PURCHASING POLICIES

Most governments are very large purchasers and consumers of goods and services; indeed, in Canada they are the largest buyers. The federal and provincial governments use this enormous purchasing power to favour Canadian companies. The provinces favour these companies in their own territories and have even set up trade barriers between provinces (as discussed earlier). When advanced technology items—civilian or military—must be obtained from foreign companies, our governments usually insist that a certain minimum portion be manufactured in Canada. This enables Canadian companies to acquire advanced technology know-how and to provide employment.

Contracts are awarded most often to help Canadian businesses even if they are sometimes more expensive than bids by non-Canadian companies. This is particularly true in the military acquisitions programs. Whatever can be produced or serviced in Canada—ships, electronics, trucks, artillery, ammunition—is acquired from Canadian companies. These federal and provincial policies are being modified as a result of the general movement to freer trade due to NAFTA. See the Spotlight on Small Business box for an example of a company that depends on government contracts.

Spotlight on Small Business

Uqsiq Communications

Uqsiq Communications, located in Iqaluit, Nunavut, is one of Canada's leading Aboriginal and Northern communications studios. It is the only entirely Inuit–run visual communications and graphic design firm in existence, offering a wide range of services including multimedia, print production and marketing, and consulting services. Uqsiq works in more than 57 different languages and dialects, offering culturally appropriate communication services for northern Canada, government, and Aboriginal markets.

The company was started in 1996 by Kirt Ejesiak and his wife Rannva. Ejesiak is a 1991 graduate from Acadia University with an applied science degree. His wife, from the Faroe Islands in the North Atlantic Ocean, is an architect and designer. When the company was started, Ejesiak noticed that "there were so few businesses owned by Aboriginal people that I wanted to show it could be done, and that we could do things on our own." This was a very difficult process. "I felt like the loneliest person on the planet as there were really no resources when I started."

Up until 1999 the company did not have any government contracts, but with the new government of Nunavut, things changed dramatically. In 1999, the Business Development Bank of Canada presented the 30-year-old Ejesiak with the Young Entrepreneur Award for Nunavut. At that time, Uqsiq's customers were 80 percent Inuit organizations and 19 percent government. Today, its main client is the government.

Ejesiak continues to be involved in government activities. He is a National Selection Committee member for the Broadband for Rural and Northern Development Pilot Program. This committee will review project proposals and make recommendations to the Minister of Industry on which proposals should receive funding for the development and implementation of their business plan. This $105-million program will be available to organizations selected to receive assistance from Industry Canada in deploying broadband or high-capacity Internet to their communities. These organizations represent an estimated 768 First Nations, Northern, and rural communities across Canada.

Sources: "Business Development Bank of Canada honours the achievements of 19 entrepreneurs under the age of 30" (October 19, 1999): Ottawa: Business Development Bank of Canada. Retrieved from the World Wide Web: http://www.bdc.ca/en/about/mediaroom/news_releases/1999/08.htm; Diane Koven, "Uqsiq Communications – Iqaluit-Based Entrepreneur Branches Out" (March 13, 2003), Ottawa: Indian and Northern Affairs Canada. Retrieved from the World Wide Web: http://www.ainc-inac.gc.ca/nr/ecd/ssd/co140_e.html; "Industry Minister Allan Rock Announces National Selection Committee Members for Broadband for Rural and Northern Development Program" (June 16, 2003), Ottawa: Industry Canada. Retrieved from the World Wide Web: http:www.ic.gc.ca/cmb/welcomeic.nsf; www.uqsiq.com.

SERVICES

www.dbic.com
www.cbsc.org

The Doing Business in Canada and Canada Business Service Centres Websites are federal government services, but include information on services provided by provincial governments, other institutional and private organizations, and federal government agencies.

The federal governments have departments that provide services to businesses and consumers. The Dealing With Change box outlines a major initiative to improve access to government services. We will look at two of these important departments: Industry Canada and Foreign Affairs Canada. There are corresponding departments in many of the provinces, especially the four largest and most developed ones (British Columbia, Alberta, Ontario, and Quebec).

Industry Canada

For many years, the federal government has implemented a variety of programs to help small businesses get started. The programs are part of a larger one that involves setting up Canada Business Service Centres in every province and territory. These centres are operated jointly with provincial governments and certain local organizations. Industry Canada publishes brochures, booklets, and guides informing businesspeople of the help available and how and

Dealing With Change

The Government On-Line Initiative

www.gol-ged.gc.ca

The Government On-Line (GOL) initiative was launched to meet the growing service expectations of Canadians and businesses. This initiative should allow interested parties to access information, benefits, and permissions from all levels of government. Information will be available through a secure and integrated access point, using the recipient's choice of Internet, phone, in-person, mail, or fax. By making key information and services available electronically, government can help Canadians to make better decisions, faster and more efficiently.

Canadians are among the world's keenest Internet users. Almost 50 percent of Canadians expect to use the Internet or e-mail as their chief means of interacting with the government in the future. Through the GOL initiative, the goal is to provide online access to the most commonly used federal services by 2005. To accomplish this, in addition to departmental investments, the Government of Canada is spending $880 million over six years (2000–05) to put the most commonly used services online, to develop Websites offering single points of access to related services, and to establish the policies and infrastructure that will protect Internet users' privacy and security.

Every federal department and agency now has a Web presence. For the third year in a row, Accenture (an international consulting firm) has singled out Canada as the world leader in e-government. According to recent statistics, on average more than 1.2 million people visit the Canada site per month: about 190,000 visit the Canadians Gateway, 140,000 visit the Non-Canadians Gateway, and 70,000 visit the Business Gateway.

How can such an initiative help businesses? What if a researcher or a small, not-for-profit organization could, through a single Website, easily learn about all the assistance programs that the government offers? And use the same basic online form to apply for each of these programs? And re-use data from one application to the next? What if it were possible to combine all the information the government has on a specific geographical location in order to provide a comprehensive picture? What if would-be entrepreneurs could register and apply online for the permits and licences they need from all levels of government using one form, with the information submitted automatically routed to the appropriate departments and agencies? These are just a few of the future possibilities for which the GOL initiative is laying the foundation.

Source: "Government On-Line" (June 13, 2003), Ottawa: Treasury Board of Canada Secretariat. Retrieved from the World Wide Web: http://www.tbs-sct.gc.ca/report/gol-ged/2003/gol-ged_e.asp.

---

where to get it. Industry Canada also participates in the production of publications to promote Canadian businesses internationally.

Other programs are designed to encourage businesses to establish themselves or expand in economically depressed areas of the country—populated regions that are industrially underdeveloped, have high unemployment, and lower standards of living. Such regions that were previously mentioned in this chapter include Cape Breton Island of Nova Scotia, the Gaspé region of Quebec, and Newfoundland and Labrador. The programs include help for the tourist industry and for Aboriginal residents of remote areas who want to establish businesses.

Canada's Innovation Strategy[20]   The federal government has developed a strategy to make Canada more competitive by the year 2010. Canada's Innovation Strategy is presented in two papers. Both focus on what Canada must do to ensure innovation in the knowledge society. One paper, *Achieving Excellence: Investing in People, Knowledge and Opportunity,* "recognizes the need to consider knowledge as a strategic national asset. It focuses on how to strengthen our science and research capacity and on how to ensure that this knowledge contributes to building an innovative economy that benefits all Canadians." It examines the role of innovation in the Canadian economy and proposes goals, targets, and federal priorities in four key areas: knowledge performance, skills, the innovation environment, and strengthening communities. Some of the targets to be achieved by 2010 include:

- Rank among the top five countries in the world in terms of research and development (R&D) performance;
- At least double the Government of Canada's current investments in R&D;
- Rank among world leaders in the share of private-sector sales attributable to new innovations;
- Develop at least 10 internationally recognized technology clusters; and
- Significantly improve the innovation performance of communities across Canada.

We discuss the importance of innovation to research and development in Chapter 10.

The second paper, *Knowledge Matters: Skills and Learning for Canadians* "recognizes that a country's greatest resource in the knowledge society is its people. It looks at what (we can do to) strengthen learning in Canada, to develop people's talent, and to provide opportunity for all to contribute to and benefit from the new economy." *Knowledge Matters* calls for a collaborative approach among all sectors of society to ensure Canadians have the tools they need to participate in Canada's workforce. The paper outlines a series of national goals and milestones for children and youth, post-secondary education, the adult labour force, and immigration. Some of the targets for post-secondary education include the following:

- 100 percent of high school graduates have the opportunity to participate in some form of post-secondary education;
- Over the next decade, 50 percent of 25- to 64-year-olds, including an increased proportion of individuals from at-risk groups, have a post-secondary credential (up from the current 39 percent);
- Over the next decade, the number of apprentices completing a certification program doubles (to 37,000); and
- Admission of Masters and PhD students at Canadian universities increases by an average of 5 percent per year through to 2010.

The NRC is located in every province in Canada and it plays a major role in stimulating community-based innovation. Here, NRC researchers and students are pictured collaborating at the NRC Institute for Aerospace Research. Did you know that Canadian aerospace manufacturers stand in third place in worldwide sales?

Many businesses will be able to benefit from programs and support that the government will be implementing to achieve these goals.

The National Research Council   The National Research Council (NRC) is a federal agency that began in 1916. It reports to Parliament through the Ministry of Industry. The NRC plays a significant role in research that helps Canadian industry to remain competitive and innovative. It has been mandated to provide substantial resources to help Canada become one of the world's top five R&D performers by 2010.

This organization of some 4,000 scientists, researchers, and technicians represents Canada's principal science and technology agency. NRC also benefits from the efforts of guest workers, drawn from Canadian and foreign universities, companies, and public- and private-sector organizations. Its Canadian Institute for Scientific and Technical Information (CISTI) has the largest international collection of information on science, technology, and medicine in Canada.

The NRC operates the Industrial Research Assistance Program (IRAP) and 19 specialized institutes in some major industries. These areas of research and industry support are aerospace, biotechnology, engineering and construction, industry support, information and communication stechnologies, and manufacturing.

Department of Foreign Affairs and International Trade

Because exports are particularly important to Canada's economic well-being, the government has a very large and elaborate system to assist companies in their exporting and foreign-investment activities. The federal government and most provincial and all large municipal governments have various ministries, departments, and agencies that provide a variety of such services. These include information, marketing, financial aid, insurance and guarantees, publications, and contacts. All major trading countries provide similar support to their exporters. The Reaching Beyond Our Borders box shows how Cirque de Soleil benefited from provincial support when it was first starting out.

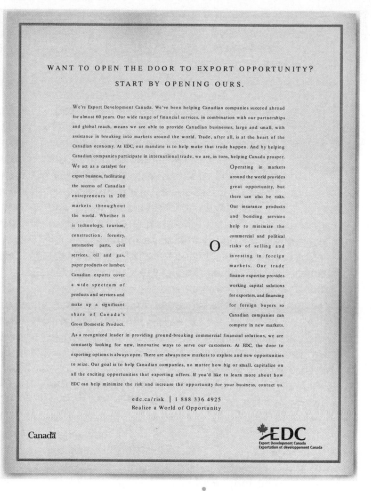

The federal government agency that has the main responsibility for international trade is International Trade Canada (ITCan), formerly part of the Department of Foreign Affairs and International Trade.[21] ITCan is responsible for positioning Canada as a world business leader for the 21st century. It accomplishes this by helping large and small Canadian companies to expand and succeed internationally.

ITCan engages in a variety of activities; a business that is contemplating going international can get almost all the help it needs from this agency. For example, the Trade Commissioner Service provides advice and aid through some 500 trade commissioners around the world in more than 140 cities, in Ottawa, and in trade centres in every province.

See Figure 4.3 for a list of some other government sources that are available to assist Canadian businesses. All of them also provide some support for those that wish to succeed in global markets. We have discussed some of these organizations already in this textbook.

Export Development Canada is a Crown corporation that has helped Canadian businesses grow through exports and international investment since 1944. This advertisement will give you a brief background in what EDC can offer companies wishing to compete in the global market.

- Why do federal and provincial governments tend to favour Canadian companies when contracts are approved?
- How does the NRC contribute to technology advancement in Canada?
- List four organizations that aim to help exporters.

Progress Assessment

Reaching Beyond Our Borders

The Quebec Government and Cirque du Soleil

Having performed for almost 40 million people worldwide, Montreal-based Cirque du Soleil started as a small group of travelling performers and has become a unique entertainment organization. Each show is a theatrical blend of circus arts and street performance, wrapped up in spectacular costumes and fairyland sets and staged to spellbinding music and magical lighting. There are no animals in the show, so all concentration is on the human performers.

Guy Laliberté is the driving force behind the Cirque du Soleil. Born in Quebec City in 1959, Laliberté was an accordion player, stiltwalker, and fire-eater. He recognized and groomed the talents of street entertainers, and in 1982 he organized a street performers' festival in the St. Lawrence Valley town of Baie St. Paul. It was such a success that in 1984 Laliberté and Daniel Gauthier created the Cirque du Soleil.

Initially, bankers declined to financially support the company. As a last resort, they appealed to the Quebec government, which gave the troupe $1.5 million to buy equipment in 1997. They spent all this money on one performance at an arts festival in California, and the critics and fans loved the show.

Today, the mission of the Cirque du Soleil is to *invoke* the imagination, *provoke* the senses, and *evoke* the emotions of people around the world. Creativity is the cornerstone of the organization's identity. Every concept and scenic element is created at the Studio, a training facility established in 1997 in Montreal. Here, more than 1,000 of the 2,500 employees work together to create new shows and costumes. The average age of the employees is 34 years old. More than 25 languages are spoken.

An important element to the success of the Cirque is its global appeal. At the beginning, the life of the show was limited to only summer months. Since it takes 18 months to develop a new show, a much larger audience than Montreal was required to make it a viable operation. The company looked to Japan as a potential market, and with careful research employees were soon able to achieve a similar success there. To extend the show's life even further, attention turned to Europe. Today, the first part of the tour is spent touring North America, the second touring Europe, and the third touring the Asia-Pacific region and Japan.

From the start, the Cirque du Soleil was selling out most performances. While the organization draws approximately 85 percent of its revenues from box-office sales, it also reaps substantial revenues from merchandising, food, and beverage sales. The organization manages the production of its audiovisual works and oversees the marketing of various show soundtracks with BMG Music. Licensing agreements and corporate alliances are formed on a regular basis. The first retail outlet was opened in Walt Disney World in Florida in 1998.

The Cirque du Soleil's mission includes social responsibility to communities all over the world, wherever it operates. As well, it donates money to other parts of the world such as Brazil, Chile, Mexico, Senegal, Ivory Coast, Cameroon, South Africa, and Mongolia. Its focus is on youth at risk, especially street kids. One percent of potential revenues from ticket sales is devoted each year to outreach programs in support of youth in difficulty.

When asked if corporate growth would stifle the risks that have propelled the Cirque du Soleil to such heights, Laliberté has replied no. He says that he keeps the company in private hands, sharing profits with the employees, precisely so they can continue to be creative and take risks. Laliberté approaches business with an entertainment aspect, which is with pleasure and fun. Recognized for his great contribution to Quebec culture, he received the Ordre National du Quebec in 1997, the highest distinction awarded by the Government of Quebec.

So what does the future hold? In 9 years this small organization has become a global success. There are separate shows in Japan, Europe, and North America, with permanent theatres in Orlando and Las Vegas. Guy has indicated that expansion plans call for developing up to a half-dozen entertainment complexes around the world in the next 12 years. Likely starting with London or Las Vegas, each complex could cost from $324 million to $1.3 billion.

Sources: Brian Dunn, "How Quebec's Cirque du Soleil Conquered Europe," *Marketing*, March 4, 1996, p. 5; communications with the marketing department of Cirque du Soleil, August 1999; www.chebucto.ns.ca/Culture/BluenoseJugglers/soleil.html, August 28, 2001; www.cirquedusoleil.com, November 21, 2003.

GOVERNMENT SOURCE	MISSION	WEBSITE
Business Development Bank of Canada (BDC)	BDC plays a leadership role in delivering financial and consulting services to Canadian small business, with a particular focus on technology and exporting.	www.bdc.ca
Export Development Canada (EDC)	EDC provides Canadian exporters with financing, insurance, and bonding services as well as foreign market expertise.	www.edc.ca
Industry Canada—Strategis	Strategis provides online business and consumer information.	www.strategis.gc.ca
National Research Council of Canada (NRC)	NRC helps turn ideas and knowledge into new processes and products. Businesses work with partners from industry, government, and universities.	www.nrc-cnrc.gc.ca
Team Canada Inc.	Team Canada is a network of more than 20 federal departments and agencies working with the provinces, territories, and other partners to help Canadian businesses prepare for the global marketplace. ExportSource is Team Canada's online resource for export information helping businesses succeed in foreign markets.	www.exportsource.ca

FIGURE 4.3

SOME GOVERNMENT SOURCES AVAILABLE TO ASSIST CANADIAN BUSINESSES

ROLE OF THE CANADIAN GOVERNMENT—SOME FINAL THOUGHTS

Some people believe that the best way to protect the Canadian economy is for the federal government to reverse its current direction of privatization. Instead of withdrawing from active direction and participation in the economy, it should develop a long-term industrial policy of leadership and an active role in shaping the future of the economy. An **industrial policy** is a comprehensive coordinated government plan to guide and revitalize the economy. An industrial policy requires close consultation with business and labour to develop a comprehensive program for long-term sustainable industrial development.

Others are opposed in principle to such government involvement. As mentioned earlier in this chapter, the 1980s witnessed a movement toward deregulation, privatization, and less government involvement in Canada and in other countries. To some, these were the right steps for the government to take and it should continue with these activities. One organization that supports less government involvement is the Fraser Institute; you will be asked to investigate some of its opinions in the Developing Workplace Skills portion of this chapter.

Many do agree that the government's Innovation Strategy will establish a strong framework to support Canadian workers and companies both domestically and internationally. It will be interesting to see if five years from now the government has been successful in contributing to Canada's improved global competitiveness with this major initiative.

industrial policy
A comprehensive coordinated government plan to guide and revitalize the economy.

Do you think that Canada's Innovation Strategy will reach all of its targets? Why or why not? What other industrial policy do you think the government should develop to support business and encourage competitiveness?

Critical Thinking

Summary

1. Understand the seven categories of government activities that can affect business.	**1.** The seven categories of government activities are as follows: Crown corporations, laws and regulations, taxation and financial policies, financial aid, other expenditures, purchasing policies, and services. • ***How do governments provide financial aid to businesses?*** All levels of government provide direct and indirect aid packages as incentives to achieve certain goals. These packages can consist of tax reduction, tariffs and quotas on imports, grants, loans, and loan guarantees.
2. Illustrate the historical role of government in the Canadian economy.	**2.** The Canadian government played a key role from the beginning of the country in 1867 in protecting young manufacturing industries and getting the railroad built to the west coast, helping to bind the country together. • ***Why did the government have to do what it did?*** It had the legal power and responsibility. The United States threatened to overwhelm our industry, which was not strong enough by itself to resist or to build the railway.
3. List some of the major Crown corporations in Canada and indicate their role in the economy.	**3.** Crown corporations are one way government did its job. • ***Why were Crown corporations necessary?*** Companies were not willing or able to assume certain responsibilities or fill some needs in the marketplace. The CNR, Air Canada, Hydro-Quebec, and Atomic Energy of Canada Ltd. are some important examples. (The CNR and Air Canada are no longer Crown corporations.)
4. Explain how the federal budget and the national debt are related.	**4.** The national debt is a summary of past government deficits. Each federal budget communicates the financial policies of the government for the upcoming year. The budget highlights expected revenues and expenditures. • ***What is Canada's current national debt?*** Over the past six years, the national debt has been decreasing. Currently, it is $510.6 billion.
5. Discuss the importance of Canada's Innovation Strategy to the government's plan to improve competitiveness.	**5.** The government has developed the Innovation Strategy to make Canada more competitive by the year 2010. This is in answer to lobbying by businesses to provide more support and incentives to be more competitive domestically and globally. • ***What are some targets to be achieved by 2010?*** The government is aiming to rank in the top five countries of the world in terms of R&D. It is also aiming to double the government's investments in R&D, develop at least 10 internationally recognized technology clusters, and increase the number of 25- to 64-year-olds that have a post-secondary credential.

Key Terms

Crown corporation 99	industrial policy 119	privatization 101
deficit 106	marketing boards 111	surplus 108
economies of scale 104	monetery policy 109	transfer payments 111
federal budget 108	national debt 106	
fiscal policy 106	National Policy 99	

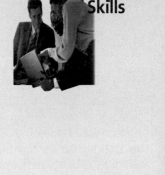

1. Scan your local newspapers, *The Globe and Mail*, the *National Post*, or a Canadian magazine like *Canadian Business* for references to government programs that help Canadian businesses or have assisted a specific company. Bring these articles to class and discuss.

2. Many U.S. states have strong marketing campaigns to attract Canadian businesses. They also offer many incentives (including financial) to lure businesses to move there. Should anything be done about this? Most provincial governments have similar programs to attract foreign companies to their jurisdictions. Check out your provincial government's Website to see what it is doing in this regard. Bring your information to class to discuss this kind of government expenditure.

3. The Fraser Institute is a Canadian think tank that believes in a competitive marketplace, lower taxes, and less regulation. It supports a limited role for government in the marketplace. In a group of four, review some of their research. Some possibilities are economic freedom, fiscal policy, law and markets, regulatory, and trade and globalization. Present your findings to the class. (*Hint:* You can find information on www.fraserinstitute.ca)

4. Although unemployment remains high, especially among young people, businesspeople complain that they cannot find trained employees to fill existing vacancies. Job candidates lack math and science backgrounds and their written English-language skills are weak. (In Quebec there are similar complaints, but the language problems are in French.) Further, too many are high-school dropouts. What can be done about this serious problem? Should business or government be working on it? What exactly should they be doing? Discuss this in a group of three.

Purpose

To become familiar with the financial budget and Canada's fiscal balance.

Exercise

1. Visit the Department of Finance Canada's Website at www.fin.gc.ca. Click on *Budget Info* and answer the following questions.

   a. What was the largest component of the budgetary expenditures for last year's budget as communicated in the most recent budget? How was this different from the previous year's budget?
   b. What was the largest component of the budgetary revenues for last year's budget as communicated in the most recent budget? How was this different from the previous year's budget?
   c. Common revenue sources for provincial (and federal) governments include personal income taxes, corporate income taxes, sales taxes, and payroll taxes. List other provincial revenue sources.
   d. Did Canada experience a deficit or a surplus last year?

2. While still on the Department of Finance Canada site, click on *Transfer Payments to Provinces*. Answer the following questions.

   a. What is the estimated equalization entitlement for next year?
   b. What is the dollar value per resident that the government believes should be used to fund public services?
   c. What provinces are scheduled to receive equalization payments?

Practising Management Decisions

Case

Gambling: A Cash Cow for Provincial Governments

Starting slowly in Quebec in the late 1960s, but catching on quickly across the country, lotteries, casinos, video-lottery terminals (VLTs), and other forms of gambling had become, at the end of the twentieth century, a major source of revenue for many Canadian provincial governments. Quebec went further by heading up a $141-million consortium that built a hotel and casino in Pointe-au-Pic. The hotel is managed by Canadian Pacific Hotels, but the casino is managed by Loto-Québec, the government agency that operates all gambling in the province.

You can get some idea of how large the gambling business has become by looking at the revenues and profits for the Ontario and Quebec governments. For the year ended March 31, 2003, the Ontario Lottery and Gaming Corporation took in $3.6 billion. Loto-Québec has taken in more than $25 billion in its 32 years of operations, with its annual revenues now running more than $3.6 billion. In its 32-year history, Loto-Québec has paid the Quebec government more than $12 billion in the form of profits. Both operations allot millions of dollars to help gamblers whose obsession with gambling has proven destructive to themselves or their families.

Decision Questions

1. Some people and organizations argue that governments should not be in the gambling business, that encouraging gambling is a bad idea. Others argue that private enterprise should run that kind of business and argue further that companies would generate more profit for governments. Governments reply that they want to keep organized crime from controlling gambling so they must own and run such operations. What do you think? Is it okay for governments to be in business? Should they be in the gambling business?

2. Governments seem to believe that gambling is a great way to raise money because we don't seem to mind creating revenue for them by having some fun, and a chance of big winnings, instead of just paying higher taxes. Besides, they argue, nobody is forced to gamble so it's a kind of voluntary tax. How do you feel about that? Do you buy that argument?

3. Some churches and other institutions concerned with personal and family welfare point to the rising number of family and personal breakdowns caused by people becoming gambling addicts. Also, easy access to VLTs is very bad for young persons. Do you agree with either of these concerns? Why? What can be done to improve the situation?

4. Suppose you agree with those who are totally opposed to governments encouraging gambling. Wouldn't taxes have to be raised to replace these revenues? Would you mind paying more taxes? Do you think your parents or family members would mind? Do you have any other suggestions?

Sources: *Montreal Gazette*, June 17, 1999, p. A3, and June 19, 1999, pp. B3, B4; <www.ontariocasino.ca November 19, 2003>; <www.loto-quebec.com November 19, 2003>.

Video Case

Bank of Canada   www.bankofcanada.ca

This chapter reviewed the role of the government as it affects the economy. You will recall that the Bank of Canada was described as a very important institution created by the federal government. Nevertheless, it operates as an independent body with a board appointed by the government. The current Governor of the Bank of Canada is David Dodge.

The Bank has important responsibilities and the way it carries them out has a huge effect on the Canadian economy and on individual businesses. This video shows David Dodge wrestling with the issue of assessing the condition of the economy so that he can take the proper steps to help keep it in good shape. Normally, the Governor of the Bank would base his decisions on information and statistics from various sources.

In the video, the former Minister of Finance comments that it takes too long to get that data. He states that an effective action to counter an economy sliding into a recession requires a quick reaction based on current information and on instinct.

You will see that it is not an easy job but we are fortunate to have David Dodge in charge. He is an economist with many years of experience as Deputy Minister of Finance, and he doesn't lose his cool easily. When necessary, he is decisive and he takes unprecedented actions. During 2001, he lowered interest rates 8 times, to the lowest levels in 40 years, in the attempt to boost a faltering economy.

Discussion Questions

1. In recent decades a strong movement, led by many business organizations, urged the privatization of Crown corporations and less government involvement in the economy. However, the chapter notes that when the economy weakened many voices were heard demanding that the government *do* something. What do you think of this apparent contradiction? Should governments limit their role to crisis intervention?

2. The video mentions the unpopularity of the previous Governor of the Bank of Canada; he raised interest rates to unprecedented levels in his lengthy battle against inflation. His unpopularity resulted from the high unemployment his policy produced.

   The textbook notes that the federal government's more recent policy of reducing the large national debt also led to more unemployment and social hardship. This made it unpopular. Do you think that governments should do what they think is right and not worry about being popular? Why?

3. The textbook examines the wide variety of ways in which the laws, regulations, and actions of all levels of government affect businesses and the economy in Canada. Is there any area where you think that this intervention should be reduced? How would you justify your opinion?

Source: *Venture*, show number 776, "David Dodge," February 27, 2001, running time 7:50.

www.mcgrawhill.ca/college/nickels

Chapter 5

Ethics and Social Responsibility

Learning Goals

After you have read and studied this chapter, you should be able to

1 Explain why legality is only the first step in behaving ethically.

2 Ask the three questions one should answer when faced with a potentially unethical action.

3 Describe management's role in setting ethical standards.

4 Distinguish between compliance-based and integrity-based ethics codes, and list the six steps in setting up a corporate ethics code.

5 Define *corporate social responsibility* and examine corporate responsibility to various stakeholders.

Profile

Getting To Know Sheila Fraser, Auditor General of Canada

The Office of the Auditor General of Canada is an independent organization that provides Parliament with objective and impartial information so that it can effectively hold the government of the day accountable for the way it operates and manages public funds. The Auditor General manages a staff of some 600 employees located in Ottawa and in four regional offices across the country.

The Office has the mandate to examine the spending of most federal government organizations, including most Crown corporations. In addition, the Office audits the governments of the Yukon, the Northwest Territories, Nunavut, and some 15 territorial agencies and corporations.

Canada's current Auditor General is Sheila Fraser. Born in Quebec, she earned a Bachelor of Commerce degree from McGill University. She became a Chartered Accountant in 1974 and an FCA in 1994. Prior to joining the government, Ms. Fraser worked for many years with the accounting firm, Ernst & Young, where she became a partner in 1981. She joined the Office of the Auditor General as Deputy Auditor General, Audit Operations in 1999. Two years later, she became the first woman ever to be appointed as Auditor General of Canada, a position which has a ten-year term.

"The Auditor General plays an important role in our democratic system of government," says Ms. Fraser. "Our audits give information to Parliament, government and Canadians on issues as wide-ranging and varied as national security, pesticide safety, the protection of salmon, the housing of Aboriginal people, and the preservation of heritage."

Here are a few examples of the Auditor General's findings:

- In a 2002 audit, the Office expressed concern about the failure of the Department of Justice to provide Parliament with complete and accurate information about the growing costs of the Canadian Firearms Program. According to the Department, the program, which was originally budgeted to cost about $2 million, after cost recovery from license and registration fees, will cost more than $1 billion by 2005.

- Poor housing on reserves has a negative effect on the health, education, and overall social conditions of First Nations individuals and communities. A 2003 audit of the federal government's support to First Nations housing on reserves found that despite a significant investment of federal funds ($3.8 billion), there continues to be a critical shortage of adequate housing to accommodate a growing on-reserve population. There is still a need for about 8,500 houses on reserves and almost half of the existing houses require renovations. The audit noted that it was vital for Indian and Northern Affairs Canada, the Canada Mortgage and Housing Corporation, and First Nations to agree on their respective roles and responsibilities and to take urgent and coordinated action to alleviate this crisis.

- The government has made a commitment to connect Canadians and provide them with on-line access to services through the Government On-Line initiative. Security and privacy concerns are a key issue in this initiative. A 2002 audit of information technology security revealed that the federal government's systems were not as secure as they needed to be, leaving personal information vulnerable and the systems themselves open to cyber attacks. The audit found that outdated standards used by departments were putting IT systems at risk and that IT security was not being monitored well. In fact, government departments didn't know if their existing level of security was acceptable, nor did they know how to measure future progress.

- In a 2004 audit on national security, the Office noted that the vast majority of the $7.7 billion allocated by the government in response to the terrorist attacks on the United States on September 11, 2001 went to priority areas. Nevertheless, the audit, which was conducted before the government reorganized national security programs on December 12, 2003, found a lack of coordination among security agencies and weaknesses at airports and border crossings that needed to be addressed. Some of the flaws identified were in fundamental elements of routine security systems—such as border watch lists and security clearances of airport workers—that were in place prior to September 2001, and that should have been functioning more effectively at the time of the audit.

In addition to its other audits, the Office of the Auditor General has done work on ethics in the federal government for nearly a decade. Its reports have stressed the need for uncompromising ethical leadership on the part of elected and senior officials, clear responsibility and accountability for decisions, a better integration of values and ethics into the day-to-day operations of government, and a robust and credible mechanism for dealing with cases of wrongdoing.

This chapter introduces you to the importance of ethical behaviour. With the media saturated by stories of high-profile business and government failures, why do we open this chapter on ethics with a profile of Sheila Fraser and the Office of the Auditor General of Canada? Because, by auditing government, the Office plays a key role in promoting good governance and accountability, key to which is a high standard of ethical behaviour. The need for improved governance and better accountability to stakeholders has recently assumed increasing prominence in the private sector as well.

In this chapter, we explore the responsibility of businesses to all of their stakeholders: customers, investors, employees and society. We look at the responsibilities of individuals as well. After all, responsible business behaviour depends on responsible behaviour of each individual in the organization.

Ethics Is More Than Legality

It is not uncommon to hear of instances where businesspeople are involved in unethical behaviour. Canadians were shocked to hear some of the details of the *Auditor General's Report 2004*. In this report, Auditor General Sheila Fraser—the focus of this chapter's opening profile—discussed some of the findings relating to the advertising and sponsorship program run by the federal Public Works Department. As reported by the CBC, Fraser disclosed that "senior government officials running the federal government's advertising and sponsorship contracts in Quebec, as well as five Crown corporations—the RCMP, Via Rail, Canada Post, the Business Development Bank of Canada, and the Old Port of Montreal—wasted money and showed disregard for rules, mishandling millions of dollars since 1995."[1] Nortel, one of the world's largest telecom equipment makers, fired its chief executive officer, chief financial officer, and controller, and said that accounting problems already under investigation by regulators ran deeper than expected; it is expected that a restatement of 2003 net earnings will be cut in half.[2] These are just some examples of scandals that have joined others that have included Livent, Hollinger, Cinar, and CIBC World Markets.

Given the ethical lapses that are so prevalent today, what can be done to restore trust in the free-market system and leaders in general? First, those who have broken the law need to be punished accordingly. Arresting business leaders, putting them in handcuffs, and carting them off to jail may seem harsh, but it is a first step toward showing the public that it is time to get serious about legal and ethical behaviour in business. No one should be above the law: not religious people, not government people, and not businesspeople. New laws making accounting records more transparent (easy to read and understand) and more laws making businesspeople and others more accountable may help. But laws don't make people honest, reliable, or truthful. If laws alone were a big deterrent, there would be much less crime than exists today.

The danger in writing new laws to correct behaviour is that people may begin to think that any behaviour that is within the law is also acceptable. The measure of behaviour, then, becomes, "Is it legal?" A society gets in trouble when it considers ethics and legality to be the same. Ethics and legality are two very different things. Although following the law is an important first step, ethical behaviour requires more than that. Ethics reflects people's proper relations with one another: How should people treat others? What responsibility should they feel for others? Legality is more narrow. It refers to laws we have written to protect ourselves from fraud, theft, and violence. Many immoral and unethical acts fall well within our laws.[3] You can learn more about the fine line between legality and ethics by reading the Making Ethical Decisions box.

Ethical Standards Are Fundamental

We define **ethics** as the standards of moral behaviour; that is, behaviour that is accepted by society as right versus wrong. Many people today have few moral absolutes. Many decide situationally whether it's okay to steal, lie, or drink and drive. They seem to think that what is right is whatever works best for the individual, that each person has to work out for himself or herself the difference

---

ethics
Standards of moral behaviour; that is, behaviour that is accepted by society as right versus wrong.

After an ethics scandal shocked a worldwide audience, Russian skaters Elena Berezhnaya and Anton Sikharulidze had to share the gold medal in the 2002 Winter Olympics pairs event with their Canadian competitors Jamie Sale and David Pelletier. French figure skating judge Marie-Reine Le Gougne admitted she was pressured to inflate the Russian scores. What messages do such actions send to young people watching these competitions?

Making Ethical Decisions

Did Napster Catch the Music Industry Napping?

When 19-year-old Shawn Fanning began writing a new software program, his goal was to create a tool for helping people search for music files on the Internet and to talk to each other about the types of music they liked. When he finished the project and got Napster up on the Web in 1999, it attracted thousands of students looking for an easy way to find tunes. The number of users doubled every five to six weeks. Soon Fanning had the attention of most students—and just about all of the record companies.

What was the attraction? Napster's version of file sharing enabled users to trade music over the Internet—for free. For years, people have been able to use tape recorders to copy music. But until Napster, such copying was usually limited to making one copy at a time to share among friends. Napster's innovation was in allowing an unlimited number of copies to be made and shared with millions of "friends."

The court ordered Napster to close down in 2001. Napster tried to reorganize and reopen as a fee-based business, but it needed more money to do it. German media giant Bertelsmann, which had already invested $85 million in Napster, offered to buy the site outright for $15 million. The deal fell through in September 2002, and Napster filed for bankruptcy and liquidated its few assets. Interestingly, CD-burning software-maker Roxio paid $5 million for the Napster name and technology in May 2003. Roxio will combine Napster with an online music service by Vivendi Universal and Sony Corp., two of the record labels that forced Napster out of business.

Through all of this Napster claimed that it never did anything illegal. Much of the music industry felt otherwise. People were reproducing compact discs and other products for free. To record companies, that's like walking into music stores and stealing CDs. But Napster argued that since no one was selling the music, it wasn't illegal. (Don't get the idea that Napster didn't bring in money simply because it didn't actually sell music.

Bertelsmann didn't invest $85 million in Napster just so cash-poor students could get free music.)

Some Napster supporters said that file sharing was a way of sampling music risk-free and that when they found an artist's work they liked, they actually bought more CDs than they would have bought otherwise. But a recent study indicated that CD purchases plummeted at stores near college campuses (Napster country). A small-business owner in Syracuse, New York, said his business dropped 80 percent in the first six months Napster was out. He said students would check out his bins for new CDs and then go home and download them instead of buying them. He had to close his business.

The debate about file-sharing sites like Napster is really a concern about intellectual property ownership. With Napster, we're talking about music. But the issue includes almost anything in the creative realm: movies, books, art, and so on. Should musicians work without getting paid? Movie producers? Authors? Engineers? If people don't get paid adequately, will they continue to work to produce high-quality music, software, books? Would you work if you didn't get paid fairly?

Technology changes so rapidly that as soon as Napster and the similar sites that had followed it were forced out of business, others took their place. It's more difficult now, but it is still possible to find free music online. Remember, too, that just because something is legal doesn't mean it is ethical. How will you respond to these ethical challenges? Are you willing to pass up the opportunity to get free music if you think that Napster-style file sharing is unethical? If you think that file sharing is ethical, how is this any different from stealing from a corner store?

Sources: Frank Ahrens, "Judge Blocks Napster's Sale to Bertelsmann," *Washington Post*, September 4, 2002, p. E1; "Music Label Sues Napster's Money Backers," *APonline*, April 23, 2003; and "Napster Makes a Comeback, but It's Not Free," *Philadelphia Inquirer*, May 20, 2003, p. B3.

between right and wrong. That is the kind of thinking that has led to the recent scandals in government and business.

This isn't the way it always was. However, in the past decade there has been a rising tide of criticism in Canada (and in other countries) of various business practices that many Canadians find unacceptable.

In a country like Canada, with so many diverse cultures, you might think it is impossible to identify common standards of ethical behaviour. However, among sources from many different times and places—such as the Bible, Aristotle's *Ethics,* William Shakespeare's *King Lear,* the Koran, and the *Analects* of Confucius—you'll find the following basic moral values: integrity, respect for human life, self-control, honesty, courage, and self-sacrifice are right; cheating, cowardice, and cruelty are wrong. Furthermore, all of the world's major religions support a version of the Golden Rule: Do unto others as you would have them do unto you.

Ethics Begins with Each of Us

It is easy to criticize business and political leaders for their moral and ethical shortcomings, but we must be careful in our criticism to note that ethics begins with each of us. Ethical behaviour should be exhibited in our daily lives, not just in a business environment.

Canadians have long had the reputation for leading the world in volunteering, but as fewer Canadians are now helping charitable and non-profit organizations that reputation probably is not deserved today. CBC's *The National* ran a story on February 4, 2002 reviewing volunteering in Canada. The statistics used were based on the 2000 National Survey of Giving, Volunteering and Participating conducted by StatsCan. Between 1997 and 2000, the number of adult Canadian volunteers fell from 31 percent to 27 percent. This translated into a decrease of almost one million volunteers. More than one-third (34 percent) of all volunteer hours were contributed by the 5 percent of volunteers who gave 596 hours or more of their time. The authors of the report observe that Canada "depends heavily upon the contributions of a small core of particularly engaged citizens." In total, volunteering in Canada represented the equivalent of almost 550,000 full-time jobs.[4]

The Fraser Institute's annual Generosity Index measures the propensity to give charitable donations. In 2001, the Institute found that 25.3 percent of Canadian tax filers donated to registered charities. As noted in Figure 5.1, Manitoba, Ontario, and Saskatchewan rank as leaders in both the percentage of tax filers who donate and the percentage of income donated. The three territories rank at the bottom. The Generosity Index has also tracked a drop in the percentage of Canadians who gave to charities between 1995 and 2001. What is interesting is that, like volunteering, the numbers of those who are giving are dropping but those who do give are more generous.[5]

Young people learn from the behaviour of others. When someone tipped off a San Diego State University instructor that one of his classes was getting the answer keys to his quizzes from classes held earlier in the day, he tested the students' honesty by scrambling the questions. A full third of the students simply wrote the answers from the pirated test key. Some of the dishonest students, who subsequently flunked the course, said the instructor should have shared the blame because giving the same test to different classes was "negligent and stupid." Apparently they thought they didn't have a choice but to cheat since the teacher didn't make it impossible for them to do so. What course was it? Business Ethics.[6]

While this example happened in the U.S., it is not to say that such instances do not occur in Canada. Have you seen students cheat on assignments or exams? How did this make you feel? Students use many reasons to rationalize such behaviour, such as "Everyone else is doing it" or "I ran out of time to

Volunteerism in Canada provides information on volunteering. For more results from the 2000 National Survey of Giving, Volunteering and Participating, visit www.volunteer.ca.

The National Hockey League suspended Vancouver Canucks hockey player Todd Bertuzzi (shown here apologizing at a news conference) for the rest of the 2003–04 hockey season (and may extend this suspension for the next season) following his ice-attack on Colorado Avalanche rookie player Steve Moore. Moore was hospitalized due to his injuries and expected to face a long period of recovery. Do you think that Bertuzzi should have received a stiffer penalty? Do hockey fans have any responsibility for encouraging rough behaviour in hockey? What responsibility, if any, does the National Hockey League have in controlling its players?

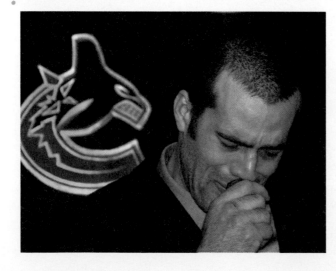

PROVINCE	PERCENT OF RETURNS WITH CHARITABLE DONATIONS (%)	RANK FOR PERCENT OF RETURNS WITH CHARITABLE DONATIONS	PERCENT OF INCOME DONATED (%)	RANK FOR PERCENT OF INCOME DONATED	AVERAGE CHARITABLE DONATION (DOLLARS)	RANK FOR AVERAGE CHARITABLE DONATION
British Columbia	23.7	7	0.68	5	1,165	3
Alberta	25.1	5	0.72	4	1,294	1
Saskatchewan	27.5	3	0.77	2	971	6
Manitoba	28.7	1	0.83	1	1,068	5
Ontario	27.7	2	0.74	3	1,189	2
Quebec	22.6	9	0.30	11	473	13
New Brunswick	23.2	8	0.67	7	964	7
Nova Scotia	23.8	6	0.54	8	808	11
Prince Edward Island	26.5	4	0.67	6	808	10
Newfoundland & Labrador	21.1	10	0.52	9	756	12
Yukon	19.0	11	0.31	10	878	8
Northwest Territories	16.6	12	0.23	12	854	9
Nunavut	11.2	13	0.22	13	1,138	4

Sources: Canada Customs and Revenue Agency; Statistics Canada; calculations by the Fraser Institute.

FIGURE 5.1

THE FRASER INSTITUTE'S ANNUAL GENEROSITY INDEX

prepare but I will do all my own work next time." What do you think of these reasons?

It is always healthy when discussing moral and ethical issues to remember that ethical behaviour begins with you and me. We cannot expect society to become more moral and ethical unless we as individuals commit to becoming more moral and ethical ourselves.

The purpose of the Making Ethical Decisions boxes you see throughout the text is to demonstrate to you that it is important to keep ethics in mind whenever you are making a business decision. The choices are not always easy. Sometimes the obvious solution from an ethical point of view has drawbacks from a personal or professional point of view. For example, imagine that your supervisor at work has asked you to do something you feel is unethical. You have just taken out a mortgage on a new house to make room for your first baby, due in two months. Not carrying out your supervisor's request may get you fired. What would you do? Sometimes there is no desirable alternative. Such situations are called ethical dilemmas because you must choose between equally unsatisfactory alternatives. It can be very difficult to maintain a balance between ethics and other goals such as pleasing stakeholders or advancing in your career. It is helpful to ask yourself the following questions when facing an ethical dilemma:[7]

1. *Is it legal?* Am I violating any law or company policy? Whether you are thinking about having a drink and then driving home, gathering marketing intelligence, designing a product, hiring or firing employees, planning how to get rid of waste, or using a questionable nickname for an employee, it is necessary to think about the legal implications of

Each Wednesday, *The Globe and Mail* newspaper publishes a column titled Workplace Ethics 101. Readers are presented with a dilemma and encouraged to send their answer by fax or e-mail. The following week, the best reply, honourable mentions, and opposing view-points are printed. Visit www.globeand mail.com and search for last week's dilemma and answers. Do you agree with the recommendations?

what you do. This question is the most basic one in behaving ethically in business, but it is only the first.

2. *Is it balanced?* Am I acting fairly? Would I want to be treated this way? Will I win everything at the expense of another party? Win–lose situations often end up as lose–lose situations. There is nothing like a major loss to generate retaliation from the loser. You can see this in the stock market today. Many companies that were merely suspected of wrongdoing have seen their stock drop dramatically. Not every situation can be completely balanced, but it is important to the health of our relationships that we avoid major imbalances over time. An ethical businessperson has a win–win attitude. In other words, such a person tries to make decisions that benefit all parties involved.

3. *How will it make me feel about myself?* Would I feel proud if my family learned of my decision? My friends? Would I be able to discuss the proposed situation or action with my immediate supervisor? The company's clients? How would I feel if my decision were announced on the evening news? Will I have to hide my actions or keep them secret? Has someone warned me not to disclose my actions? Am I feeling unusually nervous? Decisions that go against our sense of right and wrong make us feel bad—they corrode our self-esteem. That is why an ethical businessperson does what is proper as well as what is profitable.

There are no easy solutions to ethical dilemmas. Individuals and companies that develop a strong ethics code and use the three ethics-check questions presented above have a better chance than most of behaving ethically. If you would like to know which style of recognizing and resolving ethical dilemmas you favour, fill out the ethical orientation questionnaire in Figure 5.2.

Critical Thinking

Think of a situation you have been involved in that tested your ethical behaviour. For example, maybe your best friend forgot about a term paper due the next day and asked you if he could copy and hand in a paper you wrote for another instructor last semester. What are your alternatives, and what are the consequences of each one? Would it have been easier to resolve the dilemma if you had asked yourself the three questions listed above? Try answering them now and see if you would have made a different choice.

MANAGING BUSINESSES ETHICALLY AND RESPONSIBLY

Organizational ethics begin at the top. Ethics is caught more than it is taught. That is, people learn their standards and values from observing what others do, not from hearing what they say. This is as true in business as it is at home. The leadership and example of strong top managers can help instill corporate values in employees. The majority of CEOs surveyed recently attributed unethical employee conduct to the "failure of the organization's leadership in establishing ethical standards and culture."[8]

Any trust and cooperation between workers and managers must be based on fairness, honesty, openness, and moral integrity. The same can be said about relationships among businesses and among nations. A business should be managed ethically for many reasons: to maintain a good reputation; to keep

Please answer the following questions.

1. Which is worse?
   A. Hurting someone's feelings by telling the truth.
   B. Telling a lie and protecting someone's feelings.
2. Which is the worse mistake?
   A. To make exceptions too freely.
   B. To apply rules too rigidly.
3. Which is it worse to be?
   A. Unmerciful.
   B. Unfair.
4. Which is worse?
   A. Stealing something valuable from someone for no good reason.
   B. Breaking a promise to a friend for no good reason.
5. Which is it better to be?
   A. Just and fair.
   B. Sympathetic and feeling.

6. Which is worse?
   A. Not helping someone in trouble.
   B. Being unfair to someone by playing favourites.
7. In making a decision you rely more on
   A. Hard facts.
   B. Personal feelings and intuition.
8. Your boss orders you to do something that will hurt someone. If you carry out the order, have you actually done anything wrong?
   A. Yes.
   B. No.
9. Which is more important in determining whether an action is right or wrong?
   A. Whether anyone actually gets hurt.
   B. Whether a rule, law, commandment, or moral principle is broken.

To score: The answers fall in one of two categories, J or C. Count your number of J and C answers using this key:
1. A = J, B = C; 2. A = C, B = J; 3. A = J, B = C; 4. A = C, B = J; 5. A = C, B = J; 6. A = J, B = C; 7. A = C, B = J; 8. A = J, B = C; 9. A = J, B = C

What your score means: The higher your J score, the more you rely on an ethic of *justice*. The higher your C score, the more you prefer an ethic of *care*. Neither style is better than the other, but they are different. Because they appear so different they may seem opposed to one another, but they're actually complementary. In fact, your score probably shows you rely on each style to a greater or lesser degree. (Few people end up with a score of 9 to 0.) The more you can appreciate both approaches, the better you'll be able to resolve ethical dilemmas and to understand and communicate with people who prefer the other style.

An ethic of justice is based on principles like justice, fairness, equality, or authority. People who prefer this style see ethical dilemmas as conflicts of rights that can be solved by the impartial application of some general principle. The advantage of this approach is that it looks at a problem logically and impartially. People with this style try to be objective and fair, hoping to make a decision according to some standard that's higher than any specific individual's interests. The disadvantage of this approach is that people who rely on it might lose sight of the immediate interests of particular individuals. They may unintentionally ride roughshod over the people around them in favour of some abstract ideal or policy. This style is more common in men than women.

An ethic of care is based on a sense of responsibility to reduce actual harm or suffering. People who prefer this style see moral dilemmas as conflicts of duties or responsibilities. They believe that solutions must be tailored to the special details of individual circumstances. They tend to feel constrained by policies that are supposed to be enforced without exception. The advantage of this approach is that it is responsive to immediate suffering and harm. The disadvantage is that, when carried to an extreme, this style can produce decisions that seem not simply subjective, but arbitrary. This style is more common in women than men.

To learn more about these styles and how they might relate to gender, go to www.ethicsandbusiness.org/kg1.htm.

Source: Center for Ethics and Business (www.ethicsandbusiness.org).

FIGURE 5.2

ETHICAL ORIENTATION QUESTIONNAIRE

existing customers; to attract new customers; to avoid lawsuits; to reduce employee turnover; to avoid government intervention (the passage of new laws and regulations controlling business activities); to please customers, employees, and society; and simply to do the right thing.

Some managers think that ethics is a personal matter—that either individuals have ethical principles or they don't.[9] These managers feel that they are not responsible for an individual's misdeeds and that ethics has nothing to do with management. But a growing number of people think that ethics has everything to do with management. Individuals do not usually act alone; they need the implied, if not the direct, cooperation of others to behave unethically in a corporation.

For example, when Sears, Roebuck & Company (parent company of Sears Canada) was besieged with complaints about its automotive services, Sears management introduced new goals and incentives for its auto centre employees. The increased pressure on the Sears employees to meet service quotas caused them to become careless and to exaggerate to customers the need for repairs. Did the managers say directly, "Deceive the customers"? No, but the message was clear anyway. The goals and incentives created an environment in which mistakes did occur and managers did not make efforts to correct the mistakes. Sears settled pending lawsuits by offering coupons to customers who had paid for unnecessary repairs. The estimated cost to Sears was $60 million.[10] Such misbehaviour does not reflect a management philosophy that intends to deceive. It does, however, show an insensitivity or indifference to ethical considerations. In an effort to remedy this insensitivity, Sears replaced 23,000 pages of policies and procedures with a simple booklet called "Freedoms & Obligations," which discusses the company's code of business conduct from a commonsense approach.

Setting Corporate Ethical Standards

Formal corporate ethics codes are popular these days. Eighty percent of the organizations surveyed recently by the U.S. Ethics Resource Center have written codes of ethics. Whether or not a business has a written ethics code seems to be determined by the size of the company. Ninety percent of the organizations with more than 500 employees have written standards.[11] Figure 5.3 offers a sample from one company's code of ethics.

Although ethics codes vary greatly, they can be classified into two major categories: compliance-based and integrity-based. **Compliance-based ethics codes** emphasize preventing unlawful behaviour by increasing control and by penalizing wrongdoers. Compliance-based ethics codes are based on avoiding legal punishment. **Integrity-based ethics codes** define the organization's guiding values, create an environment that supports ethically sound behaviour,

compliance-based ethics codes
Ethical standards that emphasize preventing unlawful behaviour by increasing control and by penalizing wrongdoers.

integrity-based ethics codes
Ethical standards that define the organization's guiding values, create an environment that supports ethically sound behaviour, and stress a shared accountability among employees.

The Canadian Centre for Ethics & Corporate Policy provides links, speeches, articles, and other resources about ethics and corporate policy. Visit its site at ethicscentre.ca for more information.

FIGURE 5.3

OVERVIEW OF JOHNSON & JOHNSON'S CODE OF ETHICS

This is an overview of Johnson & Johnson's code of ethics, what it calls its Credo. To see the company's complete Credo, go to its Website at www.jnj.com/careers/ourcredo.html.

Written in 1943 by long-time Chairman General Robert Wood Johnson, the Johnson & Johnson Credo serves as a conscious plan that represents and encourages a unique set of values. Our Credo sums up the responsibilities we have to the four important groups we serve:

- Our customers—We have a responsibility to provide high-quality products they can trust, offered at a fair price.
- Our employees—We have a responsibility to treat them with respect and dignity, pay them fairly and help them develop and thrive personally and professionally.
- Our communities—We have a responsibility to be good corporate citizens, support good works, encourage better health and protect the environment.
- Our stockholders—We have a responsibility to provide a fair return on their investment.

The deliberate ordering of these groups—customers first, stockholders last—proclaims a bold business philosophy: If we meet our first three responsibilities, the fourth will take care of itself … To ensure our adherence to Credo values, we periodically ask every employee to evaluate the company's performance in living up to them. We believe that by monitoring our actions against the ethical framework of Our Credo, we will best ensure that we make responsible decisions as a company.

FEATURES OF COMPLIANCE-BASED ETHICS CODES		FEATURES OF INTEGRITY-BASED ETHICS CODES	
Ideal:	Conform to outside standards (laws and regulations)	Ideal:	Conform to outside standards (laws and regulations) and chosen internal standards
Objective:	Avoid criminal misconduct	Objective:	Enable responsible employee conduct
Leaders:	Lawyers	Leaders:	Managers with aid of lawyers and others
Methods:	Education, reduced employee discretion, controls, penalties	Methods:	Education, leadership, accountability, decision processes, controls, and penalties

FIGURE 5.4

STRATEGIES FOR ETHICS MANAGEMENT

Integrity-based ethics codes are similar to compliance-based ethics codes in that both have a concern for the law and use penalties as enforcement. Integrity-based ethics codes move beyond legal compliance to create a "do-it-right" climate that emphasizes core values such as honesty, fair play, good service to customers, a commitment to diversity, and involvement in the community. These values are ethically desirable, but not necessarily legally mandatory.

whistleblowers
People who report illegal or unethical behaviour.

and stress a shared accountability among employees. See Figure 5.4 for a comparison of compliance-based and integrity-based ethics codes.

The following six-step process can help improve business ethics:

1. Top management must adopt and unconditionally support an explicit corporate code of conduct.

2. Employees must understand that expectations for ethical behaviour begin at the top and that senior management expects all employees to act accordingly.

3. Managers and others must be trained to consider the ethical implications of all business decisions.

4. An ethics office must be set up. Phone lines to the office should be established so that employees who don't necessarily want to be seen with an ethics officer can inquire about ethical matters anonymously. **Whistleblowers** (people who report illegal or unethical behaviour) must feel protected from retaliation.

5. Outsiders such as suppliers, subcontractors, distributors, and customers must be told about the ethics program. Pressure to put aside ethical considerations often comes from the outside, and it helps employees resist such pressure when everyone knows what the ethical standards are.

6. The ethics code must be enforced. It is important to back any ethics program with timely action if any rules are broken. This is the best way to communicate to all employees that the code is serious.[12]

This last step is perhaps the most critical. No matter how well intended a company's ethics code is, it must be enforced if it is to be taken seriously. By ignoring its written code of ethics, both Enron's board and management sent employees the message that rules could be shelved when inconvenient.[13] Read the Dealing with Change box for more about the Enron case.

Former Olympic champion Myriam Bédard announced that she was asked to leave her job at Via Rail in 2002 after she questioned transactions relating to an advertising company implicated in the government sponsorship scandal. Via Rail chair Jean Pelletier was later fired as a result of comments that he made about Bédard in response to her disclosure. In your opinion, should whistleblower legislation be enacted to protect all workers (not just those in the public sector)? Who should enforce such legislation—government or employers?

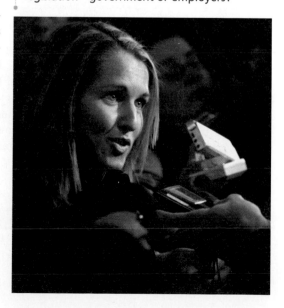

Dealing With Change

Enron: From Ethics Poster Child to Wanted Poster

www.enron.com

Can you think of a company worthy of inclusion in the respected Domini 400 Social Index; the socially minded Calvert Group index; and the socially responsible fund, Pax World Balanced Fund? Would you believe Enron? The managers of these socially responsible investment funds certainly had difficulty believing the company they once rated so highly (Enron was the Pax fund's top holding) was capable of such socially irresponsible behaviour. The case is still under investigation at the time of this writing, but it is alleged (and one executive has confessed) that Enron committed accounting fraud and that the executives sold millions of dollars' worth of stock just before the fraud became public while the company's pension regulations prohibited regular employees from selling their stock. The result was that the executives who bankrupted the company made millions while the employees and other small investors lost millions.

How did the professional managers of Domini, Calvert, and Pax choose such an unethical company? Part of the answer is that Enron's kind of fraud is difficult to detect. The accounting system as it stood was not transparent; that is, it did not require full disclosure. Many people believe that accounting rules need to be changed; others think that dishonest businesses aren't going to reveal their hidden transactions no matter what the disclosure rules are. Socially responsible investing experts believe there are really two areas of special concern: auditors and board members.

Many large accounting firms such as Arthur Andersen, Enron's accounting firm, make more money from consulting with businesses than from auditing them. A conflict of interest arises when an accounting firm audits a company to which it provides consulting services. How can the firm possibly be independent? Arthur Andersen showed that it certainly couldn't be independent—the company was found guilty of shredding Enron documents that could have been evidence in the case. Before the Enron scandal came to light, Pax World would vote against hiring an accounting firm at a holding's annual meeting if the firm made more than 75 percent of its revenues from consulting. It is now considering lowering the acceptable percentage.

Independence of the corporate board is the other major problem. While it is difficult for investors to influence who is on the company's board of directors, experts believe that, at the very least, the board's auditing committee should be managed by a truly independent board member.

There is much more that can be learned from the Enron fiasco—so much that the University of California in Irvine offers a whole course focused on the ethics of Enron. The ex-Enron employee who blew the whistle on the company's scandals was invited to be the star speaker for the course. The class will focus on issues such as what effect incentives have on the management of a company. As the Enron executives go on trial, the students will have ample resources for term papers.

Sources: Laurent Belsie, "Enron's Ex-Role: Model of Ethics," *Christian Science Monitor*, March 4, 2002, p. 20; "Andersen's Bad Experience Yields Sobering Lessons," *USA Today*, April 12, 2002, p. 13A; and "Enron to Become Business Course at California University," Xinhua News Agency, July 9, 2002.

---

worldwidewhistle blowers.com is an informational source on individuals, governments, or businesses that have behaved unethically in the quest for profit or power.

An important factor to the success of enforcing an ethics code is the selection of the ethics officer. The most effective ethics officers set a positive tone, communicate effectively, and relate well with employees at every level of the company. They are equally comfortable serving as counsellors or as investigators. More organizations are recognizing the importance of this role. Associations are also providing support for those in these roles. One such example is EPAC.

The mission of the Ethics Practitioners' Association of Canada (www.epac-apec.ca) is "to enable individuals to work successfully in the field of ethics in organizations by enhancing the quality and availability of ethics advice and services in Canada." This organization includes ethics officers, consultants, educators, and students who are interested in the field of ethics as applied to organizations.

Whistleblowing Legislation[14]   Larry Brown, the Secretary Treasurer for the National Union of Public and General Employees, spoke on November 3, 2003 in Toronto at a conference on whistleblowers. He focused on the need for whistleblowing legislation in Canada. Some of his points were as follows:

- Ontario passed legislation in 1993, but it was never proclaimed.
- New Brunswick and Saskatchewan have some protection in their labour standards laws, but these laws are always hard to enforce in non-union environments.
- The Saskatchewan courts have interpreted the provincial law to require complaints to be made to a lawful authority. Therefore, complaints to senior managers aren't protected.
- The federal government has a whistleblowers' policy for the public service, but even the official in charge of the policy says it's not working and needs to be reinforced.

Neil Shankman has written about a KPMG survey on private corporations' policies on whistleblowers. Almost two-thirds of respondents to the business ethics survey stated that they have a written policy requiring employees to report fraud or misconduct in the workplace. Only 40 percent of respondents reported having formal systems designed to protect whistleblowers from retaliation. One-fifth of respondents lacked any type of protection system.

Clearly, one might suggest that in order for the six steps mentioned earlier to work, there must first be protection in place for the whistleblower. Otherwise, how effective can such a process be? As a result of the sponsorship scandal, the government in 2004 introduced Bill C-25, the Disclosure Protection Act. Known as "whistleblower legislation," the proposed law covers all federal public-sector workers and Crown corporation employees. It is intended to protect people who speak out about problems in the government's bureaucracy. The proposed legislation says that it is "part of the government's broader commitment to ensure transparency, accountability, financial responsibility and ethical conduct." It's the first time public-sector workers have been offered legal protection against punishment for reporting government wrongdoing.

RBC Financial Group is one of Canada's largest corporate donors, with an annual donations budget topping $37 million. The *Corporate Responsibility Report and Public Accountability Statement* is published for all stakeholders including employees, customers, and community partners. This report shares some of the hundreds of initiatives undertaken by RBC's employees around the world to help build stronger communities. To access the report, visit www.rbc.com/community.

The federal government office in charge of protecting whistleblowers is called the Public Service Integrity Office. For more information on its mandate and procedures, visit www.psio-bifp.gc.ca.

Progress Assessment

- When faced with ethical dilemmas, what three questions can you ask yourself that might help you make ethical decisions?
- How are compliance-based ethics codes different from integrity-based ethics codes?
- What are the six steps to follow in establishing an effective ethics program in a business?

CORPORATE SOCIAL RESPONSIBILITY

Corporate social responsibility is the concern businesses have for the welfare of society. It goes well beyond merely being ethical. Just as you and I need to be good citizens, contributing what we can to society, corporations need to be good citizens as well. The social performance of a company has several dimensions:

- **Corporate philanthropy** includes charitable donations to non-profit groups of all kinds. Strategic philanthropy involves companies

corporate social responsibility
A business's concern for the welfare of society as a whole.

corporate philanthropy
Dimension of social responsibility that includes charitable donations.

making long-term commitments to one cause, such as the Tim Horton Children's Foundation. The Children's Foundation was founded by Ron Joyce, co-founder of Tim Hortons, in honour of his friend and deceased partner, Tim Horton. Every year, thousands of children from economically challenged homes participate in one of the six camps.[15]

- **Corporate responsibility** includes everything from hiring minority workers to making safe products, minimizing pollution, using energy wisely, and providing a safe work environment—that is, everything that has to do with acting responsibly within society.

- **Corporate policy** refers to the position a firm takes on social and political issues.

So much news coverage has been devoted to the problems caused by corporations that people tend to get a negative view of the impact that companies have on society. If the news were more balanced, much more could be said about the positive contributions that businesses make.

For example, Microsoft Canada belongs to the *I CAN Program*. The *I Volunteer* element of this program permits employees to volunteer 40 hours during Microsoft work hours.[16] RBC Financial Group (Royal Bank) encourages its employees to volunteer their time through its *Employee Volunteer Grants Program*. Employees who devote a minimum of 40 hours a year to a registered charity are eligible for a $500 grant donated to the organization in their honour. Since 1999, RBC has donated more than $2.5 million on behalf of its employees through this program.[17] In 2002, the company invested more than $27 million with charities in hundreds of communities across Canada.[18]

RBC has received much recognition over the years for its corporate activities. According to Ipsos-Reid's survey of Canada's Most Respected Corporations, for 2003 RBC was voted the most admired and respected corporation in Canada for the second year in a row. Among other areas, it ranked number one in corporate social responsibility.[19] For another example of a company that believes in social responsibility, read the Spotlight on Small Business box.

Two-thirds of the MBA students surveyed by a group called Students for Responsible Business said they would take a lower salary to work for a socially responsible company. But when the same students were asked to define a socially responsible company, things got complicated. It appears that even those who want to be socially responsible can't agree on what it involves.

Corporate Responsibility in the 21st Century

What should be the guiding philosophy for business in the 21st century? For most of the 20th century, there was uncertainty regarding the position top managers should take. The question revolves around the treatment of stakeholders. There are two different views of corporate responsibility to stakeholders:

1. **The strategic approach.** The strategic approach requires that management's primary orientation be toward the economic interests of shareholders. The rationale is this: as owners, shareholders have the right to expect management to work in their best interests; that is, to optimize profits. Furthermore, Adam Smith's notion of the invisible hand suggests that the maximum social gain is realized when managers attend only to their shareholders' interests.

---

corporate responsibility
Dimension of social responsibility that includes everything from hiring minority workers to making safe products.

corporate policy
Dimension of social responsibility that refers to the position a firm takes on social and political issues.

RBC Financial Group is one of Canada's largest corporate donors, with an annual donations budget topping $37 million. The *Corporate Responsibility Report and Public Accountability Statement* is published for all stakeholders including employees, customers, and community partners. This report shares some of the hundreds of initiatives undertaken by RBC's employees around the world to help build stronger communities. To access the report, visit www.rbc.com/community.

www.csrforum.com

See the Corporate Social Responsibility Forum Website for discussions about relevant issues and links to other related sites.

Spotlight on Small Business

Giving Online Through E-Philanthropy: CanadaHelps.org

CanadaHelps.org (CHO) is the only not-for-profit charity portal in Canada. It provides information and ideas about how people can help their communities. CHO finds volunteer opportunities by matching skills and interests. It also processes online donations for any of Canada's 78,000 registered charities without accepting a commission or charging any fees to the donor or the charity. This service is available to all Canadians, living domestically and abroad, in both official languages.

Three university students—Ryan Little, Matthew Choi, and Aaron Pereira—launched CanadaHelps.org in December 2000. They recognized the opportunity e-commerce presented to the voluntary sector to increase efficiency. Since that time, they have contributed an average of 56 hours each week to their program, and have all donated much of their own money toward making their vision become a reality. Together with a diverse group of volunteers, and a committed Board of Advisors and Directors and staff, CHO has gained the support of individuals and organizations in the charitable and corporate sectors. CHO is supported by Hewlett-Packard (Canada) Ltd., Bank of Montreal, CIBC, Scotiabank, RBC Dominion Securities, BCE Emergis Canada, Deloitte & Touche, Canadian Pacific and Nortel Networks, Research In Motion, Steelcase, Navantis, and many others.

"Because of Canadians' increasingly hectic lifestyles, making charitable donations online has clicked in a big way," says Little, Executive Director. "To make things as convenient as possible, CanadaHelps.org has just introduced new features and functionality to the Website to save people more time and keep them more organized." According to a recent poll of CanadaHelps.org online donors, 92 percent said they donate online because of convenience. Forty percent also said efficiency was a key incentive for online donation. The option to print out all tax receipts at one time is a particularly useful function during tax season, when donors are compiling their records.

Not only is donating online convenient and efficient for donors, but charities are benefiting as well. Some organizations raised between 15 and 20 percent of their total contributions online. That growth is encouraging, since the costs of online solicitation are much lower than those associated with traditional methods. Raising funds through the Internet is estimated to cost about 20 percent less than direct mail or telemarketing.

About 800 charities are actively using this site (i.e., signed service agreements), and approximately $2.5 million has been given to charities. By 2003, these numbers are anticipated to increase to 1,500 charities and $3 million in donations. The core annual operating costs of the company are $162,900.

Sources: "Giving just got easier" (2003), St. John's: Community Services Council Newfoundland and Labrador. Retrieved from the World Wide Web: http://www.envision.ca/templates/news.asp?ID=4718; "Volunteers of the Year Awards 2001" [2001?], Toronto: City of Toronto. Retrieved from the World Wide Web: http://www.city.toronto.on.ca/volunteer_awards/winners_2001.htm; and www.canadahelps.org.

For example, IBM's John Akers said that an IBM decision about whether to cease operations in a country would be a business decision: "We are not in business to conduct moral activity; we are not in business to conduct socially responsible action. We are in business to conduct business." The strategic approach encourages managers to consider actions' effects on stakeholders other than owners, but others' interests are secondary. Often those interests are considered only when they would adversely affect profits if ignored.

2. **The pluralist approach.** This approach recognizes the special responsibility of management to optimize profits, but not at the expense of employees, suppliers, and members of the community. This approach recognizes the moral responsibilities of management that apply to all human beings. Managers don't have moral immunity when making managerial decisions. This view says that corporations can maintain their economic viability only when they fulfill their moral responsibilities to society as a whole. When shareholders' interests

compete with those of the community, as they often do, managers must decide, using ethical and moral principles.

The guiding philosophy for the 21st century will be some version of the pluralist approach. Managerial decision making won't be easy, and new ethical guidelines may have to be drawn. But the process toward such guidelines has been started, and a new era of more responsible and responsive management is underway. Maybe it would be easier to understand social responsibility if we looked at the concept through the eyes of the stakeholders to whom businesses are responsible: customers, investors, employees, society in general and the environment.

Responsibility to Customers

One responsibility of business is to satisfy customers by offering them goods and services of real value. A recurring theme of this book is the importance of pleasing customers. This responsibility is not as easy to meet as it seems. Keep in mind that more than half of new businesses fail—perhaps because their owners failed to please their customers. One of the surest ways of failing to please customers is not being totally honest with them. For example, in 1988 a consumer magazine reported that the Suzuki Samurai was likely to roll over if a driver swerved violently in an emergency. When Suzuki executives denied there was a problem, sales plummeted.

In contrast, Daimler-Benz suffered a similar problem in 1997 during a test simulating a swerve around a wayward elk, when its new A-class Baby Benz rolled over. The company quickly admitted a problem, came up with a solution, and committed the money necessary to put that solution into action. In addition, company representatives continued to answer questions in spite of aggressive press coverage. Daimler took out full-page ads that read: "We should like to thank our customers most warmly for their loyalty. You have given us the chance to remedy a mistake." Following the test flip, only 2 percent of the orders for the vehicle were cancelled. The solution cost the company $59 million in 1997 and $118 million each year thereafter. Analysts say those costs probably eliminate any profit on the vehicle. However, the quick resolution of the problem protected the company's reputation, thus allowing its other models to become such hits that Daimler's net earnings remained the same.[20]

The payoff for socially conscious behaviour could result in new business as customers switch from rival companies simply because they admire the company's social efforts—a powerful competitive edge. Consumer behaviour studies show that, all else being equal, a socially conscious company is likely to be viewed more favourably than less socially responsible companies. The important point to remember is that customers prefer to do business with companies they trust and, even more important, do not want to do business with companies they don't trust.

Responsibility to Investors

Economist Milton Friedman made a classic statement when he said that corporate social responsibility means making money for shareholders. Ethical behaviour is good for shareholder wealth. It doesn't subtract from the bottom line; it adds to it.[21] Those cheated by financial wrongdoing are the shareholders themselves. Unethical behaviour may seem to work for the short term, but it guarantees eventual failure.

Some people believe that before you can do good you must do well (i.e., make a lot of money); others believe that by doing good, you can also do well.

For example, Bagel Works, a chain of bagel stores, has a dual-bottom-line approach that focuses on the well-being of the planet as well as profits. Bagel Works has received national recognition for social responsibility. Its mission involves commitments to the environment and to community service. In addition to employing environmentally protective practices such as in-store recycling, composting, using organically grown ingredients, and using nontoxic cleaners, each store includes donations for community causes in its budget. The company donates 10 percent of its pretax profits to charities each year.

Many people believe that it makes financial as well as moral sense to invest in companies that are planning ahead to create a better environment. By choosing to put their money into companies whose goods and services benefit the community and the environment, investors can improve their own financial health while improving society's health.

Michael Jantzi Research Associates Inc. (MJRA), which monitors and reports on the environmental and social performance of Canadian corporations, has developed a Canadian Social Investment Database. The Database contains social and environmental profiles of Canadian companies and income trusts. Institutional investors that incorporate social and environmental criteria—such as corporate governance, environmental performance, ethical business practices, human rights issues, tobacco, and weapons-related production—into their investment decisions use this tool.[22]

A few investors, known as inside traders, have chosen unethical means to improve their own financial health. **Insider trading** involves insiders using private company information to further their own fortunes or those of their family and friends.

A recent case of insider trading involved Andrew Rankin, a former executive with RBC Dominion Securities in the mergers and acquisitions group. He has been charged by the Ontario Securities Commission (OSC) with 10 counts of insider trading and 10 counts of tipping his friend, Daniel Duic. Investigators found that Rankin had alerted Duic to upcoming mergers and acquisitions before they were publicly known. The securities commission alleges that, based on this information, Duic bought and sold investments in 10 companies and saw his investment increase following the release of the merger and acquisition news.[23]

If convicted of these charges under the Ontario Securities Act, Rankin could face a maximum penalty of two years in jail and $1 million in fines for each count, plus three times the profit made from illegal trades.[24] Duic, also charged with 10 counts of insider trading, has reached a settlement with the OSC. First, he will pay $1.9 million (which he made illegally) and $25,000 to the OSC for costs. Second, he will be barred from trading in Ontario and in Ontario-based companies. Finally, he cannot act as a director of a public company.[25]

Companies can misuse information for their own benefit at investors' expense as well. In the case of Nortel, some top executives were fired in April 2004 following an investigation into accounting irregularities. A federal grand jury in Texas has also issued a subpoena for Nortel documents, including financial statements and accounting records. A spokesperson for Nortel said that any results filed after 2000 "should not be relied upon."[26]

Investors were immediately affected by the news: Nortel stock fell 59 cents (or 11 percent), to $4.04. The day's decline

insider trading
An unethical activity in which insiders use private company information to further their own fortunes or those of their family and friends.

In 2003, former Corel Corporation founder Michael Cowpland agreed to pay $575,000 to settle insider trading charges laid against him by the Ontario Securities Commission (OSC). Cowpland said he made "an honest mistake" in 1997 when he sold 2.4 million shares in Corel—worth more than $20 million—four weeks before the company issued an earnings warning. The OSC alleged that Cowpland's private company (MCJC Holdings) sold the shares with knowledge of material facts that were not widely known.

in value in Nortel's shares led to the largest drop (3.5 percent) since September 11, 2001 in Canada's benchmark stock index, the Standard & Poor's/TSX Composite Index. This index (now known as the S&P/TSE Index) will be discussed in Chapter 17. The market decline also caused Canada's dollar to fall to a seven-month low against the U.S. dollar. "Nortel is by far the most traded stock in Canada and the TSX is down much more than other stock markets today," said Carsten Fritsch, a currency strategist at Commerzbank Securities, a unit of Germany's third-biggest bank by assets, in Frankfurt. "Isolated, that has a short-term negative effect on the Canadian dollar."[27]

Responsibility to Employees

Businesses have several responsibilities to employees. First, once a company creates jobs, it has an obligation to see to it that hard work and talent are fairly rewarded. Employees need realistic hope of a better future, which comes only through a chance for upward mobility. People need to see that integrity, hard work, goodwill, ingenuity, and talent pay off. Studies have shown that the factor that most influences a company's effectiveness and financial performance is human resource management. We will discuss human resource management in Chapter 12.

If a company treats employees with respect, they usually will respect the company as well. For example, Fel-Pro, a manufacturer of gaskets and other engine parts, established a summer camp for children of employees. Those who used this company benefit were more productive than they had been before because they felt their children were safe. Employees who made the most of Fel-Pro's corporate social responsibility programs were its highest performers. In addition, the increased benefits reduced employee turnover. It is estimated that replacing employees costs between 150 and 250 percent of their annual salaries; retaining workers is good for business as well as for morale.[28]

When employees feel they've been treated unfairly, they often strike back. Getting even is one of the most powerful incentives for good people to do bad things. Not many disgruntled workers are desperate enough to resort to violence in the workplace, but a great number do relieve their frustrations in more subtle ways, such as blaming mistakes on others, not accepting responsibility for decision making, manipulating budgets and expenses, making commitments they intend to ignore, hoarding resources, doing the minimum needed to get by, and making results look better than they are. The loss of employee commitment, confidence, and trust in the company and its management can be very costly indeed. A recent survey revealed that employee theft more than doubled from 1994 to 2000. Today, employee theft costs companies about five times more than shoplifting does.[29] You will read more about issues that affect employee–management relations in Chapter 12.

Responsibility to Society

One of business's responsibilities to society is to create new wealth. If businesses don't do it, who will? Approximately 900,000 working Canadians receive their salaries from nonprofit organizations that in turn receive their funding from others, who in turn receive their money from business.[30] Foundations,

Crickey, crocodile hunter Steve Irwin is crazy about those crocs! Irwin, the owner and director of the Australia Zoo in Queensland, Australia, is so passionate about animals that he has contributed all of the profits from his successful feature film, *The Crocodile Hunter: Collision Course*, to wildlife preservation programs.

universities, and other nonprofit organizations own billions of shares in publicly held companies. As those stock prices increase, more funds are available to benefit society.

Businesses are also partially responsible for promoting social justice. Business is perhaps the most crucial institution of civil society. For its own well-being, business depends on its employees being active in politics, law, churches and temples, arts, charities, and so on. Rhino Entertainment, a vintage music and video distributor, has a simple mission: "To put out some great stuff, have some fun, make some money, learn from each other, and make a difference wherever we can." Individual staff members are assigned to oversee community and environmental activities. The company has bins for can and paper recycling and for clothing donations spread throughout its offices. Employees receive extra vacation days each year in exchange for 16 hours of community service. They regularly participate in monthly activities at a local youth centre. The company budgets a percentage of its revenues to go to charities that empower groups to help themselves.[31]

Many companies believe that business has a role in building a community that goes well beyond giving back. To them, charity is not enough. Their social contributions include cleaning up the environment, building community toilets, providing computer lessons, caring for the elderly, and supporting children from low-income families. Samsung, a Korean electronics conglomerate, emphasizes volunteer involvement. For example, a busload of Samsung employees and managers are transported each month to a city park, where they spread out to pick up garbage, pull weeds, and plant saplings. Managers even volunteer to help spruce up employee homes. Local employees feel such loyalty to the company that in the height of the 1999 unrest that destroyed many businesses in Indonesia, local employees and their neighbours pulled together to protect Samsung's refrigerator factory there and shielded foreign managers from violence. With the help of relatives in the countryside, the local employees set up a food supply network that helped protect their colleagues from skyrocketing prices for food staples such as rice and palm oil.[32]

The focus of this book is on business; however, one should not forget that government decisions also impact business and society. The Walkerton, Ontario *E. coli* tragedy that killed seven people and made half of the town's 5,000 residents ill due to contaminated water is one such example. After hearing testimony from more than 100 witnesses over nine months, Justice O'Connor concluded that the catastrophe could have been prevented if brothers Stan and Frank Koebel, who ran Walkerton's water system, had properly chlorinated the water and if the Ontario government had heeded warnings about ineffectual testing caused by cuts to the provincial environment ministry.[33] Clearly, the Koebel brothers were responsible for their individual decisions. Unfortunately, the program cutbacks also contributed to this unfortunate tragedy.

Responsibility to the Environment[34]

Businesses are often criticized for their role in destroying the environment. However, we are seeing more examples today of efforts being made to reverse years of neglect. The Sydney Tar Ponds are North America's largest hazardous waste site. More than 80 years of discharges from the steel-producing coke ovens near the harbour have filled Muggah Creek with contaminated sediments. By 1983, Environment Canada had pinpointed the coke ovens as the major source of pollution in the Sydney area. Fishing was banned and the Sydney lobster fishery was closed. Statistics show significantly higher levels

The Resource Recovery Fund Board (RRFB Nova Scotia) is a nonprofit organization whose mission is to ensure that Nova Scotians receive maximum environmental and economic benefits associated with solid waste management. Mandates include funding municipal waste diversion programs and developing education awareness of reduction, reuse, recycling, and composting. RRFB Nova Scotia has developed a guide and poster to assist the restaurant business sector in separating and diverting waste materials from disposal. Do you believe that only nonprofit organizations should be responsible for educating Canadians on how to minimize their impact on the environment?

in causes of death and illness than anywhere else in Canada. The disposal of the toxic waste has been slow. Two decades later, there have been several attempts and more than $100 million spent to clean up this toxic site. In May 2004, the governments of Canada and Nova Scotia committed $400 million to the cleanup. Overseen by the Sydney Tar Ponds Agency, the cleanup will take 10 years.

This is not the only example where government has gotten involved with business. The Great Lakes—Superior, Michigan, Huron, Erie, and Ontario—span more than 1,200 kilometres. The Great Lakes Basin is home to more than one-quarter of Canada's population and more than one-tenth of the U.S. population. Some of the world's largest concentrations of industrial capacity are located in the Great Lakes region. In spite of their large size, the Great Lakes are sensitive to the effects of a wide range of pollutants including runoff of soils and farm chemicals from agricultural lands, waste from cities, and discharges from industrial areas. The Great Lakes Action Plan 2000–05 is a joint effort with government agencies in Canada and the United States. The focus of the Great Lakes Action Plan is to protect the Great Lakes Basin ecosystem. Even though progress has been steady and improvements have been noted, pollution continues to be a major concern.

One hot spot is Sarnia's Chemical Valley. There have been hundreds of spills in the St. Clair River since 1986, with six major ones in the last year alone. Chemical Valley is home to 32 chemical and petroleum companies. They account for about 40 percent of Canada's chemical production and 20 percent of the nation's refineries. Thousands of residents in the area are increasingly concerned about spills, because they draw their drinking water from the river.

Efforts since 1987 were supposed to have reduced the spills into the river virtually to zero. In the Sarnia area, Health Canada statistics show that residents have a higher rate of illnesses ranging from cancer to birth defects. Despite these efforts and the fact that companies have been heavily fined, spills are still occurring. What do you think should be the next step to stop these spills? Is it realistic to expect zero spills?

Businesses are clearly taking more responsibility for helping to make their own environment a better place. Environmental efforts may increase the company's costs, but they also may allow the company to charge higher prices, to increase market share, or both. For example, Ciba Specialty Chemicals, a Swiss textile-dye manufacturer, developed dyes that require less salt than traditional dyes. Since used dye solutions must be treated before they are released into rivers or streams, having less salt and unfixed dye in the solution means having lower water-treatment costs. Patents protect Ciba's low-salt dyes, so the company can charge more for its dyes than other companies can charge for theirs. Ciba's experience illustrates that, just as a new machine enhances labour productivity, lowering environmental costs can add value to a business.

Not all environmental strategies prove to be as financially beneficial to the company as Ciba's, however. For instance, in the early 1990s StarKist

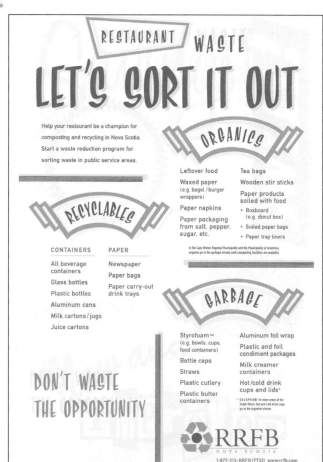

responded to consumer concerns about dolphins dying in the process of tuna fishing because the nets meant to capture tuna also caught dolphins swimming over the yellowfin tuna schools in the eastern Pacific. The company announced that it would sell only tuna from the western Pacific, where the skipjack tuna do not swim underneath dolphins. Unfortunately, the company found that customers were unwilling to pay a premium for the dolphin-safe tuna and that they considered the taste of the skipjack inferior to that of yellowfin tuna. In addition, it turned out that there was no clear environmental gain: In exchange for every dolphin saved by not fishing in the eastern Pacific, thousands of immature tuna and dozens of sharks, turtles, and other marine animals died in the western Pacific fishing process.

Environmental quality is a public good; that is, everyone gets to enjoy it regardless of who pays for it. The trick for companies is to find the right public good that will appeal to their target market. Many corporations are publishing reports that document their net social contribution. To do that, a company must measure its positive social contributions and subtract its negative social impacts. We shall discuss that process next.

Composting decomposes organic materials such as food scraps, leaves and yard trimmings, paper, wood, manures, and the remains of agricultural crops. It is estimated that about 50 percent of the total waste stream could be composted. Composting not only helps to reduce the amount of waste going to landfills, but also produces a valuable soil amendment that can improve the texture and fertility of the soil. Why do you think that not everyone has adopted composting as an important way to recycle?

Social Auditing

It is nice to talk about having organizations become more socially responsible. It is also encouraging to see some efforts made toward creating safer products, cleaning up the environment, designing more honest advertising, and treating women and minorities fairly. But is there any way to measure whether organizations are making social responsibility an integral part of top management's decision making? The answer is yes, and the term that represents that measurement is *social auditing*.

A **social audit** is a systematic evaluation of an organization's progress toward implementing programs that are socially responsible and responsive. One of the major problems of conducting a social audit is establishing procedures for measuring a firm's activities and their effects on society. What should be measured? See Figure 5.5 for an outline of business activities that could be considered socially responsible.

social audit
A systematic evaluation of an organization's progress toward implementing programs that are socially responsible and responsive.

There is some question as to whether positive actions should be added (e.g., charitable donations, pollution control efforts) and then negative effects subtracted (e.g., layoffs, overall pollution levels) to get a net social contribution. Or should just positive actions be recorded? In general, social responsibility is becoming one of the aspects of corporate success that business evaluates, measures, and develops.

FIGURE 5.5

SOCIALLY RESPONSIBLE
BUSINESS ACTIVITIES

- Community-related activities such as participating in local fundraising campaigns, donating executive time to various nonprofit organizations (including local government), and participating in urban planning and development.
- Employee-related activities such as establishing equal opportunity programs, offering flextime and other benefits, promoting job enrichment, ensuring job safety, and conducting employee development programs. (You'll learn more about these activities in Chapters 11 and 12.)
- Political activities such as taking a position on nuclear safety, gun control, pollution control, consumer protection, and other social issues; and working more closely with local, provincial, and federal government officials.
- Support for higher education, the arts, and other nonprofit social agencies.
- Consumer activities such as ensuring product safety, creating truthful advertising, handling complaints promptly, setting fair prices, and conducting extensive consumer education programs.

In addition to the social audits conducted by the companies themselves, there are four types of groups that serve as watchdogs regarding how well companies enforce their ethical and social responsibility policies:[35]

1. *Socially conscious investors* who insist that a company extend its own high standards to all its suppliers.
2. *Environmentalists* who apply pressure by naming names of companies that don't abide by the environmentalists' standards.
3. *Union officials* who hunt down violations and force companies to comply to avoid negative publicity.
4. *Customers* who take their business elsewhere if a company demonstrates unethical or socially irresponsible practices.

What these groups look for constantly changes as the worldview changes. One important thing to remember is that it isn't enough for a company to be right when it comes to ethics and social responsibility. It also has to convince its customers and society that it's right.

INTERNATIONAL ETHICS AND SOCIAL RESPONSIBILITY

Ethical problems and issues of social responsibility are not unique to Canada. Top business and government leaders in Japan were caught in a major "influence-peddling" (read bribery) scheme in Japan. Similar charges have been brought against top officials in South Korea, the People's Republic of China, Italy, Brazil, Pakistan, and Zaire. What is new about the moral and ethical standards by which government leaders are being judged? They are much stricter than in previous years. Top leaders are now being held to a higher standard.

Government leaders are not the only ones being held to higher standards. Many businesses are demanding socially responsible behaviour from their international suppliers by making sure their suppliers do not violate domestic human rights and environmental standards. For example, Sears will not import ➤**X-REF**◄ products made by Chinese prison labour. The clothing manufacturer Phillips–Van Heusen said it would cancel orders from suppliers that violate its ethical, environmental, and human rights code. McDonald's denied rumours that one of its suppliers grazes cattle on cleared rain forest land, but wrote a ban on the practice anyway.

In contrast to companies that demand that their suppliers demonstrate socially responsible behaviour are those that have been criticized for exploiting workers in less developed countries. Nike, the world's largest athletic shoe company, has been accused by human rights and labour groups of treating its workers

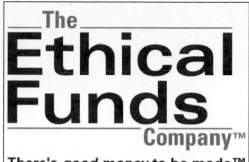

poorly while lavishing millions of dollars on star athletes to endorse its products. An Ernst & Young report on Nike's operations in Asia indicated that thousands of young women laboured more than 10 hours a day, six days a week, in excessive heat, noise, and foul air, for slightly more than $10 a week. The report also found that workers with skin or breathing problems caused by the factory conditions had not been transferred to departments free of chemicals. More than half the workers who dealt with dangerous chemicals did not wear protective masks or gloves.

Nike officials say they are working to improve conditions, but their critics say they are not doing enough quickly enough.[36] While customers still seem to favour brand, price, and quality over their perception of a company's humane treatment and social responsibility, surveys show that the vast majority of respondents would pay an extra few dollars for a garment that had been made in a worker-friendly environment.

The justness of requiring international suppliers to adhere to domestic ethical standards is not as clear-cut as you might think. Is it always ethical for companies to demand compliance with the standards of their own countries? What about countries where child labour is an accepted part of the society and families depend on the children's salaries for survival? What about foreign companies doing business in Canada? Should these companies have to comply with Canadian ethical standards? What about multinational corporations? Since they span different societies, do they not have to conform to any one society's standards? None of these questions are easy to answer, but they give you some idea of the complexity of social responsibility issues in international markets. (See the Reaching Beyond Our Borders box for an example of an ethical culture clash.)

In an effort to identify some form of common global ethic and to fight corruption in global markets, the partners in the Organization of American States signed the Inter-American Convention Against Corruption. A similar anticorruption convention was signed by 29 member states of the Organisation for Economic Co-operation and Development (OECD) and five other states that are home to nearly all of the major multinational corporations. The OECD convention covers only those companies and governments that offer bribes, and not the individuals who accept them. However, such loopholes are expected to be eliminated in the years ahead.[37]

The Kyoto Protocol[38]

The government's international role in supporting ethical behaviour is not limited just to corruption. At the United Nations Earth summit in 2002, Prime Minister Jean Chrétien supported the Kyoto accord on global warming. The Kyoto Protocol is the first global agreement that establishes legally

Ethical Funds is the oldest and most comprehensive family of socially responsible mutual funds in Canada. With approximately $1.5 billion in assets under management, it selects investments based on financial as well as social and environmental criteria. The company does not invest in corporations that derive a significant portion of their income from military weapons, tobacco, or nuclear power. Would you purchase investments that support social consciousness?

The Organization of American States (OAS) includes countries of North, Central and South America, and the Caribbean. Its mission is to strengthen democracy, advance human rights, promote peace and security, expand trade, and tackle problems caused by poverty, drugs, and corruption. Visit its site at www.oas.org for more information.

Reaching Beyond Our Borders

Ethical Culture Clash

Communications and electronics giant Motorola describes itself as dedicated to "uncompromising integrity." Robert W. Galvin, Motorola's board chairman, says that the company's ethical values and standards are an "indispensable foundation" for the company's work, relationships, and business success. Almost half of Motorola's employees are non-American, and more than half of its revenues come from non-American markets. Is it difficult for Motorola employees to adhere to the company's ethical values while at the same time respecting the values of the host countries in which Motorola manufactures and markets its products?

Here's an example of how corporate ethics can clash with cultural ethics. Joe, the oldest son of a poor South American cloth peddler, managed to move to the United States, earn an engineering degree, and get a job with Motorola. After five years, Joe seemed to have bought into the Motorola culture and was happy to have been granted a transfer back to his home country. Joe was told that the company expected him to live there in a safe and presentable home of his choice. To help him afford such a residence, Motorola agreed to reimburse him a maximum of $2,000 a month for the cost of his rent and servants. Each month Joe submitted rental receipts for exactly $2,000. The company later found out that Joe was living in what was, by Western standards, a shack in a dangerous slum area of town. Such a humble home could not have cost more than a couple hundred dollars a month. The company was concerned for Joe's safety as well as for the effect the employee's unseemly residence would have on Motorola's image. The human resource manager was ultimately concerned about Joe's lack of integrity, given that he had submitted false receipts for reimbursement.

Joe was upset with what he considered the company's invasion of his privacy. He argued that he should receive the full $2,000 monthly reimbursement that all of the other Motorola employees received. He explained his choice of housing by saying that he was making sacrifices so he could send the extra money to his family and put his younger siblings through school. This was especially important since his father had died and his family had no one else to depend on but Joe. "Look, my family is poor," Joe said, "so poor that most Westerners wouldn't believe our poverty even if they saw it. This money means the difference between hope and despair for all of us. For me to do anything less for my family would be to defile the honour of my late father. Can't you understand?"

Often it is difficult to understand what others perceive as being ethical. Different situations often turn the clear waters of "rightness" downright muddy. In Joe's case, one could see that Joe was trying to do the honourable thing for his family. One could also argue that Motorola's wish to have its higher-level people live in safe housing is not unreasonable, given the dangerous conditions of the city in which Joe lived. The policy of housing reimbursement supports Motorola's intent to make its employees' stay in the country reasonably comfortable and safe, not to increase their salaries. If Joe worked in Canada, where he would not receive a housing supplement, it would clearly be unethical for him to falsify expense reports in order to receive more money to send to his family. In South America, though, the issue is not so clear.

Sources: R. S. Moorthy, Robert C. Solomon, William J. Ellos, and Richard T. De George, "Friendship or Bribery?" *Across the Board*, January 1999, pp. 43–47; and "Motorola Emphasizes 'People Development in the Information Age' at the Asia Society/Dow Jones Conference in Shanghai, China," news release, May 10, 2000.

binding targets for cutting greenhouse gas emissions believed to upset the Earth's climate and temperature. To date, 98 countries have become parties to the Kyoto Protocol. Canada's target is to decrease gas emissions between 2008 and 2012.

There was much debate domestically regarding participation; some believed that Canada's support would burden businesses with new costs. This was especially true of Alberta, which threatened to go to the Supreme Court of Canada to stop the protocol from being imposed. The province relies heavily on fossil fuels for electricity and its oil sector, the bedrock of its economy, will suffer if industry and automobiles are forced to burn cleaner fuel. (As noted in Chapter 4, natural resources—both air and oil—are considered the jurisdiction of provincial governments. The federal government, however, has the right to sign international treaties and to enact them domestically.) Prime Minister Chrétien, however, felt that, "We cannot wait forever... It's a commitment that the country wants to make in our international obligations." On December 17, 2002, after much debate and compromise, Parliament voted in favour of ratifying the Kyoto Protocol. Now, the focus will be on the implementation phase. The government realizes that it needs to consult with provinces, territories, industry, and other stakeholders in order to make this social responsibility commitment work.

The Climate Change Plan for Canada maps out a comprehensive and detailed approach for reaching Canada's Kyoto target. It is based on clear guidelines: the economy cannot be put at risk; no region will bear an unfair burden; and there must be a favourable climate for investment. Visit www.climatechange. gc.ca for more details.

Progress Assessment

- What is corporate social responsibility, and how does it relate to each of a business's major stakeholders?
- How does the strategic approach differ from the pluralist approach?
- What is a social audit, and what kinds of activities does it monitor?
- What is a major ethical challenge in international business?

Summary

1. Ethics goes beyond obeying laws. It also involves abiding by the moral standards accepted by society.
   - *How is legality different from ethics?*
   Ethics reflects people's proper relation with one another. Legality is more limiting; it refers only to laws written to protect people from fraud, theft, and violence.

   1. Explain why legality is only the first step in behaving ethically.

2. It is often difficult to know when a decision is ethical.
   - *How can we tell if our business decisions are ethical?*
   Our business decisions can be put through an ethics check by asking three questions: (1) Is it legal? (2) Is it balanced? and (3) How will it make me feel?

   2. Ask the three questions one should answer when faced with a potentially unethical action.

3. Some managers think ethics is an individual issue that has nothing to do with management, while others believe ethics has everything to do with management.
   - *What is management's role in setting ethical standards?*
   Managers often set formal ethical standards, but more important are the messages they send through their actions. Management's tolerance or intolerance of ethical misconduct influences employees more than any written ethics codes do.

   3. Describe management's role in setting ethical standards.

4. Ethics codes can be classified as compliance-based or integrity-based.
   - *What's the difference between compliance-based and integrity-based ethics codes?*
   Whereas compliance-based ethics codes are concerned with avoiding legal punishment, integrity-based ethics codes define the organization's guiding

   4. Distinguish between compliance-based and integrity-based ethics codes, and list the six steps in setting up a corporate ethics code.

values, create an environment that supports ethically sound behaviour, and stress a shared accountability among employees.

5. Define *corporate social responsibility* and examine corporate responsibility to various stakeholders.

5. Corporate social responsibility is the concern businesses have for society.
   • ***How do businesses demonstrate corporate responsibility toward stakeholders?***
   Business is responsible to four types of stakeholders: (1) business's responsibility to customers is to satisfy them with goods and services of real value; (2) business is responsible for making money for its investors; (3) business has several responsibilities to employees: to create jobs, to maintain job security, and to see that hard work and talent are fairly rewarded; (4) business has several responsibilities to society: to create new wealth, to promote social justice, and to contribute to making its own environment a better place; and (5) business has the responsibility to minimize its impact on the environment.

   • ***How are a company's social responsibility efforts measured?***
   A corporate social audit measures an organization's progress toward social responsibility. Some people believe that the audit should add together the organization's positive actions and then subtract the negative effects of business to get a net social benefit.

Key Terms

compliance-based ethics
   codes 132
corporate
   philanthropy 135
corporate policy 136

corporate
   responsibility 136
corporate social
   responsibility 135
ethics 126

insider trading 139
integrity-based ethics
   codes 132
social audit 143
whistleblowers 133

Developing Workplace Skills

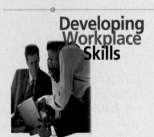

1. What sources have helped shape your personal code of ethics and morality? What influences, if any, have ever pressured you to compromise those standards? Think of an experience you had at work or school that tested your ethical standards. What did you decide to do to resolve your dilemma? Now that time has passed, are you comfortable with the decision you made? If not, what would you do differently?

2. Newspapers and magazines are full of stories about individuals and businesses that are not socially responsible. What about those individuals and organizations that do take social responsibility seriously? We don't normally read or hear about them. Do a little investigative reporting of your own. Identify a public interest group in your community and identify its officers, objectives, sources and amount of financial support, and size and characteristics of membership. List some examples of its recent actions and/or accomplishments. You should be able to choose from environmental groups, animal protection groups, political action committees, and so on. Call your local Chamber of Commerce, the Better Business Bureau, or local government agencies for help. Try using one of the Internet search engines to help you find more information.

3. You are manager of a coffeehouse called the Morning Cup. One of your best employees wants to be promoted to a managerial position; however, the owner is grooming his son for the promotion your employee seeks. The owner's act of nepotism may hurt a valuable employee's chances for

advancement, but complaining may hurt your own chances for promotion. What do you do?

4. You are a salesperson at a clothing store. You walk into the storage room to start ticketing some clothes that came in that morning and you see another co-worker quickly take some pants from a box and put them into her knapsack. Your colleague does not see you enter the room. What do you do? Do you leave and not say anything to your employer? Do you say something to your colleague? Do you tell your employer about this incident? Is your responsibility to your organization, your colleague, or both? What might be the implications of your decision?

5. Contact a local corporation and ask for a copy of its written ethics code. Would you classify its code as compliance-based or integrity-based? Explain.

Taking It To The Net

1

Purpose

To highlight Canada's most respected corporations based on how senior executives view their peers and the organizations they lead.

Exercise

Canada's Most Respected Corporations is an annual survey sponsored by KPMG and is conducted by Ipsos-Reid. Visit www.mostrespected.ca and answer the following questions:

1. How is respect measured by this survey?

2. Are these the right criteria for being most respected? What would you add? What would you delete?

3. Who were the five most admired and respected corporations in the most recent survey?

4. Which corporation was voted number one for innovation? Why was this?

5. Which corporation was voted number one for customer service? Why was this?

6. Which CEO was ranked most respected CEO of the year? Why was this?

7. What were the most admired and respected qualities listed by CEOs?

Taking It To The Net

2

Purpose

To illustrate that ethical behaviour is complex and that even efforts to be socially responsible can create ethical dilemmas.

Exercise

The September 11, 2001 terrorist attacks generated both governmental and charitable assistance of unheard-of magnitude. Gathering the resources was the easy part; deciding how they should be distributed was the unimaginably difficult part. In an effort to distribute relief funds fairly, the U.S. government devised a method of calculating the value of individual lives. Log on to www.usdoj.gov/victimcompensation to calculate yours. For the curious, a single 30-year-old earning $25,000: $470,878. A married 40-year-old earning $225,000 with two children: $3,246,723. Your initial impulse might be to divide the money evenly, but ask yourself the following questions and then decide how you would compensate the families of the September 11 victims if it were up to you:

1. Does the widowed mother of four need more than the widowed father of one? If so, how do you decide how much?

2. Should a family previously living on an income of $25,000 a year receive the same as a family whose breadwinner earned $250,000?

3. The government calculations contain a deduction if the family received insurance benefits. Is it ethical to penalize a family for having the foresight to pay for life insurance policies?

4. The plan provides for pain and suffering. Who suffered more, a widower married 35 years or a widow married six months? How do you place a dollar value on such suffering even if you could determine it? The government decided to pay a flat $250,000. Do you agree that this is the best ethical answer?

Practising Management Decisions

Case

Have a term paper due soon? Dreading the thought of all the work involved? With the advent of the World Wide Web, plagiarism has become as easy as point and click. Some Websites list thousands of term papers on hundreds of topics—and the papers are there to be downloaded 24 hours a day. Boston University developed a plan in which a law student posed as a student wanting to buy a term paper to see how easily it could be done. The student secured papers from eight companies in seven states and paid fees ranging from $45 to $175. The university charged the companies in federal court with wire fraud, mail fraud, racketeering, and violating a Massachusetts law that bans the sale of term papers.

Some Websites are not affected by current laws because they offer the papers for free. The sites are funded by advertisers who buy space on the sites. The owner of one such Website says that the papers on his site are posted there not so that students can plagiarize them, but rather to show the substandard writing skills of many students. You get the idea from the papers on the site that students are rewarded for length. The papers consist of pages and pages of junk, yet many instructors accept them. The owner notes that this says something about the mediocre assignments some professors give year after year. He thinks it is absurd that class assignments can be so vague that a student can go to the Internet, find a generic essay, and receive credit for it. He believes he is doing

Got a Deadline? Click Here

education a favour by forcing professors to give more specific writing assignments and to require extensive endnotes.

If recycling term papers is now so easy, why do professors continue to assign them? While the writing style used for term papers is different from that used in the workplace, writing develops critical thinking skills and the ability to express thoughts and ideas. Tom Rocklin, director of the Center for Teaching at the University of Iowa, puts it this way: "I have sat down with a group of businesspeople, and they say what they are looking for in new hires are skills developed by a traditional liberal arts education. Discussion, reading, and extended writing are a crucial part of that." Yet simply downloading a paper from a Website does nothing to help a student develop these skills.

Decision Questions

1. Would you consider purchasing a paper from a Website and submitting it as your own? Why or why not? Consider that there is now a Website that helps professors check for plagiarism by comparing student papers with millions of online pages using the top 20 search engines. The system even identifies papers composed of bits and pieces of online text. For example, McGill University uses turnitin.com. Does knowing this change your answer to the questions above?

2. Do you agree with the Website owner who said he is improving education by posting certain term papers as the mediocre results of mediocre assignments? Justify your answer.

3. View this issue through the eyes of your professor. The Websites are out there, and your students have access to them. What would you do to discourage your students from committing plagiarism?

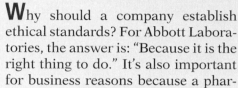

Video Case — Doing Unto Others—Abbott Laboratories

Why should a company establish ethical standards? For Abbott Laboratories, the answer is: "Because it is the right thing to do." It's also important for business reasons because a pharmaceutical company needs to establish trust with all its stakeholders: employees, customers, regulators, shareholders, and so on.

Abbott has been in business for over 100 years. It now employs some 70,000 people around the world and operates in 130 countries. The company makes and distributes pharmaceuticals, medical devices, and nutritional aids. You can imagine the challenge the company faces in meeting the legal, moral, and ethical codes of so many different countries. This is especially true in the pharmaceutical industry because it is involved in numerous issues, like kickbacks, overpricing, and unethical promotions. Only an effort by top management is enough to even begin tackling such major issues.

Abbott has had a compliance-based ethics code for many years. But it's one thing to talk about establishing a strong ethics program and quite another to implement one. That's why the company appointed Charlie Brock as Abbott's chief ethics and compliance officer. Each division has an ethics staff, and Brock is the coordinator over them all. One of Brock's first steps in implementing Abbott's ethics program was to let everyone in the company know what the firm's ethical standards are. But the company did not stop with employees; suppliers, distributors, and customers also needed to know that Abbott has such standards and intends to apply them rigorously. That meant establishing a program based on specific standards that are communicated clearly and are enforced with penalties for noncompliance. Abbott uses the latest technology to train employees in ethical standards. Interactive software presents difficult ethical cases and teaches employees what to do when tough ethical issues arise.

Abbott goes beyond just compliance-based ethics to integrity-based ethics. That is, it has a broad program of "global citizenship" that covers everything from how the company reports information to shareholders to how it treats its employees, to how it manufactures goods, to how it tries to minimize environmental effects. The company has been very generous to many nonprofit groups, but takes special pride in its efforts to conquer AIDS in the world, including developing products to treat and hopefully cure the disease. This effort also means teaching people in developing countries how to test themselves for HIV to prevent spreading AIDS to their children. All told, Abbott will spend over $100 million on such efforts over the next five years. That includes building partnerships with other firms to make a difference in the world.

Abbott is truly a company to be admired for its corporate citizenship and its active involvement in self-regulation. Not only has the company established an ethics office and set clear ethics codes; it vigorously applies those codes. Its community outreach, including a strong commitment to ending the AIDS crisis, sets a model for other companies to benchmark. Most important, the company does it all for the right reason: It is the morally right thing to do!

Discussion Questions

1. Do you think Abbott's ethics program will succeed in creating the trust the company is striving to maintain? Why or why not?

2. Would you be more or less interested in working for a company with such a strong commitment to ethics and community involvement? What does your answer say about the value of such programs?

3. What are some issues involved in manufacturing and selling drugs in countries around the world? How does an ethics code address most of these issues?

4. One way a company like Abbott could make a difference in developing countries might be to sell a treatment for AIDS at or below cost. What would be the long-term consequences of such a decision to the company?

PART 2

Chapter 6

Forms of Business Ownership

Learning Goals

After you have read and studied this chapter, you should be able to

1 Compare the advantages and disadvantages of sole proprietorships.

2 Describe the differences between general and limited partners, and compare the advantages and disadvantages of partnerships.

3 Compare the advantages and disadvantages of corporations.

4 Define what a merger is and give examples of three types of corporate mergers.

5 Outline the advantages and disadvantages of franchises, and discuss the challenges of international franchising.

6 Explain the role of co-operatives.

Getting to Know Yogen Früz

In 1986, brothers Michael and Aaron Serruya, ages 19 and 20, wanted to buy a franchise but no one would take a chance on them—so they started their own frozen yogurt shop, Yogen Früz, in Toronto. One year later, they began franchising with an outlet in London, Ontario. In 1989, their brother Simon joined them. Yogen Früz, headquartered in Markham, Ontario, had a mission to become "the world's largest franchisor of frozen yogurt." In 1994 the company went public and continued to grow and expand. To achieve its mission, the company acquired about a dozen famous companies in the ice cream and dairy industries. In 2000, the company was renamed Cool Brands International Inc. to reflect the variety of frozen dessert brands it now owned and franchised.

CoolBrands International dominates the frozen yogurt market. It operates a family of brands under the names Yogen Früz, I Can't Believe It's Yogurt, Bresler's Premium Ice Cream, Swensen's Ice Cream, Ice Cream Churn, and Golden Swirl. The company also franchises and develops a coffee chain under the name Java Coast Fine Coffees. Due to the merger with Integrated Brands in March 1998, the company also sells pre-packaged frozen dessert products under the Tropicana, Betty Crocker, Yoplait, and Trix trademarks and a variety of other trademarks, pursuant to exclusive long-term licence agreements. With the acquisition of Eskimo Pie Corporation CoolBrands has added the Eskimo Pie brand, and also has long-term licence rights to the Weight Watchers and Welch's brands.

Today, Yogen Früz Worldwide Inc. is the largest international franchisor and licensor of stores serving frozen yogurt desserts. It has more than 5,300 units in over 80 countries. In 2003, it had 805 Canadian franchises, 1,706 U.S. franchises, 2,806 foreign franchises, and 10 company-owned franchises.

To qualify for a franchise, a franchisor must have a net worth of more than $400,000 and cash liquidity of more than $75,000. The total investment is between $150,000 and 200,000. The franchise fee is $25,000, and the ongoing royalty fee is 6 percent.

Yogen Früz has won a number of industry awards. In 2002, *Entrepreneur Magazine* ranked it #5 in the world across all markets, #1 in frozen desserts, and #16 in the fastest-growing franchises. *Profit* magazine has ranked the company 34th on its list of the 100 Fastest Growing Companies in Canada.

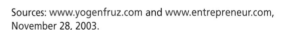

Whether you dream of going into business for yourself, starting a business with a friend, or someday leading a major corporation, it's important to know that each form of business ownership has its advantages and disadvantages. You will learn more about them in this chapter.

Sources: www.yogenfruz.com and www.entrepreneur.com, November 28, 2003.

BASIC FORMS OF BUSINESS OWNERSHIP

sole proprietorship
A business that is owned, and usually managed, by one person.

partnership
A legal form of business with two or more owners.

corporation
A legal entity with authority to act and have liability separate from its owners.

FIGURE 6.1

BUSINESS DISTRIBUTION BY TYPE, NUMBER AND REVENUE

There were almost 3.07 million businesses in Canada at the end of 2003. You may be wondering why there are fewer sole proprietorships than corporations when it is so easy to open a sole proprietorship. To limit their liability, many sole proprietors have chosen to incorporate their businesses. As a result, these businesses are registered as corporations.

Like the Serruya brothers, thousands of people start new businesses in Canada every year. Chances are, you have thought of owning your own business or know someone who has. One key to success in starting a new business is understanding how to get the resources you need. You may have to take on partners or find other ways of obtaining money. To stay in business, you may need help from someone with more expertise than you have in certain areas, or you may need to raise more money to expand. How you form your business can make a tremendous difference in your long-term success. You can form a business in one of several ways. The three major forms of business ownership are (1) sole proprietorships, (2) partnerships, and (3) corporations.

It can be easy to get started in your own business. You can begin a word-processing service out of your home, open a car repair centre, start a restaurant, develop a Website, or go about meeting other wants and needs of your community. A business that is owned, and usually managed, by one person is called a **sole proprietorship.** As noted in Figure 6.1, 30 percent of all registered businesses in Canada fall under this form of ownership.

Many people do not have the money, time, or desire to run a business on their own. They prefer to have someone else or some group of people get together to form the business. When two or more people legally agree to become co-owners of a business, the organization is called a **partnership.**

There are advantages to creating a business that is separate and distinct from the owners. A legal entity with authority to act and have liability separate from its owners is called a **corporation.** There are almost 1.8 million corporations in Canada, and they have the largest share of business revenue by far (see Figure 6.1).

As you will learn in this chapter, each form of business ownership has its advantages and disadvantages. It is important to understand these advantages and disadvantages before attempting to start a business. Keep in mind that just because a business starts in one form of ownership, it doesn't have to stay in that form. Many companies start out in one form, then add (or drop) a partner or two, and eventually may become corporations.

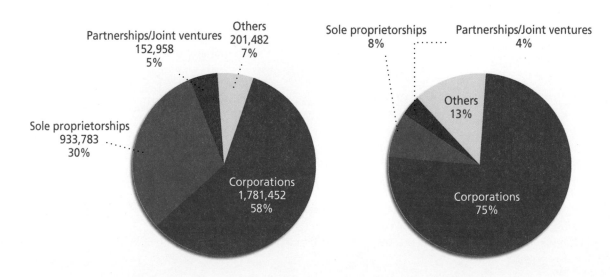

Business Type and Number of Businesses

Partnerships/Joint ventures 152,958 5%
Others 201,482 7%
Sole proprietorships 933,783 30%
Corporations 1,781,452 58%

Revenue Distribution

Sole proprietorships 8%
Partnerships/Joint ventures 4%
Others 13%
Corporations 75%

Another thing that must be looked at before proceeding is the meaning of the term *liability*. Liability is often just another word for *debt*, but it also has a wider and important meaning, as you will see in the following pages. **Liability** for a business includes the responsibility to pay all normal debts and to pay

1. Because of a court order,
2. Because of a law,
3. For performance under a contract, or
4. For damages to a person or property in an accident.

Let's begin our discussion by looking at the most basic form of ownership—the sole proprietorship.

liability
For a business, it includes the responsibility to pay all normal debts and to pay because of a court order or law, for performance under a contract, or payment of damages to a person or property in an accident.

SOLE PROPRIETORSHIPS

Advantages of Sole Proprietorships

Sole proprietorships are the easiest kind of businesses for you to explore in your quest for an interesting career. Every town has sole proprietors you can visit. Talk with some of these businesspeople about the joys and frustrations of being on their own. Most will mention the benefits of being their own boss and setting their own hours. Other advantages they mention may include the following:

1. **Ease of starting and ending the business.** All you have to do to start a sole proprietorship is buy or lease the needed equipment (e.g., a saw, a word processor, a tractor, a lawn mower) and put up some announcements saying you are in business. It is just as easy to get out of business; you simply stop. There is no one to consult or to disagree with about such decisions. You may have to get a permit or licence from the local government, but often that is no problem.

2. **Being your own boss.** Working for others simply does not have the same excitement as working for yourself—at least, that's the way sole proprietors feel. You may make mistakes, but they are your mistakes—and so are the many small victories each day.

3. **Pride of ownership.** People who own and manage their own businesses are rightfully proud of their work. They deserve all the credit for taking the risks and providing needed products.

4. **Leaving a legacy.** Business owners have something to leave behind for future generations.

5. **Retention of company profit.** Other than the joy of being your own boss, there is nothing like the pleasure of knowing that you can earn as much as possible and not have to share that money with anyone else (except the government, in taxes).

6. **No special taxes.** All the profits of a sole proprietorship are taxed as the personal income of the owner, and the owner pays the normal income tax on that money. Another tax advantage for sole proprietors is that they can claim any business losses against other earned income. These losses would decrease the personal taxes they would need to pay.

A small business, such as this ice cream shop, may be set up as a sole proprietorship or a corporation. There are advantages and disadvantages to both forms of ownership.

Making Ethical Decisions

Who Is Liable?

In this chapter you will read about the different legal structures available to individuals who want to operate a business. For example, two people can set up their business as a partnership or as a corporation in which they are the only shareholders. You will learn that each structure has its advantages and disadvantages and that it is possible to go from one format to another one.

Let's look at the partnership Travira Wholesalers, which supplies computer components.

Partners Elvira and Trong have been operating their business for several years. The partners have gotten into a bind and are having difficulty paying their bills. They might have to declare a formal bankruptcy to get out of the mess. However, as they are not a corporation they will still be personally liable for all the unpaid bills of their company, Travira. Trong suggests that they incorporate Travira; that is, form a corporation that takes over all the assets and liabilities of their partnership and continues to operate the business. Then, he explains to Elvira, if the company goes bankrupt they will not be personally liable for the debts of the company because it is now a corporation.

Do you think it is ethical for Elvira and Trong to try to evade their personal liability in this fashion? We will return to this issue at the end of the chapter after you have had time to absorb the material.

Disadvantages of Sole Proprietorships

Not everyone is equipped to own and manage a business. Often it is difficult to save enough money to start a business and keep it going. The costs of inventory, supplies, insurance, advertising, rent, computers, utilities, and so on may be too much to cover alone. There are other disadvantages of owning your own business:

unlimited liability
The responsibility of business owners for all of the debts of the business.

1. **Unlimited liability—the risk of personal losses.** When you work for others, it is their problem if the business is not profitable. When you own your own business, you and the business are considered one. You have **unlimited liability;** that is, any debts or damages incurred by the business are your debts and you must pay them, even if it means selling your home, your car, or whatever else you own. This is a serious risk, and one that requires not only thought but also discussion with a lawyer, an insurance agent, an accountant, and others.[1] For a perspective on the possible legal ramifications of certain ownership types, see the Making Ethical Decisions box.

2. **Limited financial resources.** Funds available to the business are limited to the funds that the one (sole) owner can gather. Since there are serious limits to how much money one person can raise, partnerships and corporations have a greater probability of obtaining the needed financial backing to start a business and keep it going.

3. **Management difficulties.** All businesses need management; that is, someone must keep inventory records, accounting records, tax records, and so forth. Many people who are skilled at selling things or providing a service are not so skilled in keeping records. Sole proprietors often find it difficult to attract good, qualified employees to help run the business because they cannot compete with the salary and fringe benefits offered by larger companies.

4. **Overwhelming time commitment.** Though sole proprietors may say they set their own hours, it's hard to own a business, manage it,

train people, and have time for anything else in life. This is true of any business, but a sole proprietor has no one with whom to share the burden. The owner often must spend long hours working. The owner of a store, for example, may put in 12 hours a day, at least six days a week—almost twice the hours worked by a nonsupervisory employee in a large company. Imagine how this time commitment affects the sole proprietor's family life. Tim DeMello, founder of the successful company Wall Street Games Inc., echoes countless other sole proprietors when he says, "It's not a job, it's not a career, it's a way of life."

5. **Few fringe benefits.** If you are your own boss, you lose the fringe benefits that often come from working for others. You have no paid health insurance, no paid disability insurance, no sick leave, and no vacation pay. These and other benefits may add up to more than one-third of a worker's income.[2]

6. **Limited growth.** Expansion is often slow since a sole proprietorship relies on its owner for most of its creativity, business know-how, and funding.

7. **Limited life span.** If the sole proprietor dies, is incapacitated, or retires, the business no longer exists. The exception is if the business is sold or taken over by the sole proprietor's heirs. This option could have transfer or continuity problems as the direction of the new owner(s) could be different from that of the original sole proprietor.

Don't forget to talk with a few local sole proprietors about the problems they have faced in being on their own. They are likely to have many interesting stories to tell about problems getting loans from the bank, problems with theft, problems simply keeping up with the business, and so on. These problems are also reasons why many sole proprietors choose to find partners to share the load.

> **Critical Thinking**
> Have you ever dreamed of opening your own business? If you did, what kind of business was it? What talents or skills do you have that you could use? Could you start such a business in your own home? How much would it cost to start? Could you begin part-time while you went to school? What satisfaction and profit could you get from owning your own business? What could you lose?

general partnership
A partnership in which all owners share in operating the business and in assuming liability for the business's debts.

limited partnership
A partnership with one or more general partners and one or more limited partners.

general partner
An owner (partner) who has unlimited liability and is active in managing the firm.

limited partner
An owner who invests money in the business but does not have any management responsibility or liability for losses beyond the investment.

limited liability
The responsibility of a business's owners for losses only up to the amount they invest; limited partners and shareholders have limited liability.

PARTNERSHIPS

A partnership is a legal form of business with two or more parties. These parties can be individuals or corporations. Two types of partnerships are general partnerships and limited partnerships. A **general partnership** is a partnership in which all owners share in operating the business and in assuming liability for the business's debts. A **limited partnership** is a partnership with one or more general partners and one or more limited partners. A **general partner** is an owner (partner) who has unlimited liability and is active in managing the firm. Every partnership must have at least one general partner. A **limited partner** is an owner who invests money in the business but does not have any management responsibility or liability for losses beyond the investment. **Limited liability** means that limited partners are not responsible for the debts of the business beyond the amount of their investment—their liability is

Business partners Yves Besner and Isabel Rodriguez founded i4design in 1994. They got their business idea when they were classmates studying technology. i4design now has a staff of 30 and its clients include the Bank of Canada, the Canadian Museum of Civilization, the Supreme Court of Canada, and Nortel. They have won the BDC Young Entrepreneur Award for Quebec. Recently, the company was rated one of the top 100 Canadian IT Professional Services Organizations in Canada on the Branham300 list.

limited to the amount they put into the company; their personal assets are not at risk.

Advantages of Partnerships

There are many advantages to having one or more partners in a business. Often, it is much easier to own and manage a business with one or more partners. Your partner can cover for you when you are sick or go on vacation. Your partner may be skilled at inventory control and accounting, while you do the selling or servicing. A partner can also provide additional money, support, and expertise. Some of the professionals who are enjoying the advantages of partnerships today are doctors, lawyers, dentists, and accountants. Partnerships usually have the following advantages:

1. **More financial resources.**   When two or more people pool their money and credit, it is easier to pay the rent, utilities, and other bills incurred by a business. A limited partnership is specially designed to help raise capital (money). As mentioned earlier, a limited partner invests money in the business but cannot legally have any management responsibility and has limited liability.

2. **Shared management and pooled/complementary skills and knowledge.**   It is simply much easier to manage the day-to-day activities of a business with carefully chosen partners. Partners give each other free time from the business and provide different skills and perspectives. Some people find that the best partner is a spouse. That is why you see so many husband-and-wife teams managing restaurants, service shops, and other businesses.

3. **Longer survival.**   One study that examined 2,000 businesses started since 1960 reported that partnerships were four times as likely to succeed as sole proprietorships. Being watched by a partner can help a businessperson become more disciplined.

4. **Shared risk.**   A partnership shares the risk among the owners. This includes financial risk in starting the business and ongoing risks as the business grows.

5. **No special taxes.**   As with sole proprietorships, all profits of partnerships are taxed as the personal income of the owners, and the owners pay the normal income tax on that money. Similarly, any business losses can be used to decrease earned income from other sources.

Disadvantages of Partnerships

Anytime two people must agree, there is the possibility of conflict and tension. Partnerships have caused splits among families, friends, and marriages. Let's explore the disadvantages of partnerships:

1. **Unlimited liability.**   Each *general* partner is liable for the debts of the firm, no matter who was responsible for causing those debts. You are liable for your partners' mistakes as well as your own. Like sole proprietors, general partners can lose their homes, cars, and everything else they own if the business loses a lawsuit or goes bankrupt.

Spotlight on Small Business

Choose Your Partner

Suppose you need money and want help running your business, and you decide to take on a partner. You know that partnerships are like marriages and that you won't really know the other person until after you live together. How do you choose the right partner? Before you plunge into a partnership, do three things:

1. Talk to people who have been in successful—and unsuccessful—partnerships. Find out what worked and what didn't. Ask them how conflicts were resolved and how decisions were made.

2. Interview your prospective partner very carefully. What skills does the person have? Are they the same as yours, or do they complement your skills? What contacts, resources, or special attributes will the person bring to the business? Do you both feel the same about family members working for the business? Do you share the same vision for the company's future?

3. Evaluate your prospective partner as a decision maker. Ask yourself, "Is this someone with whom I could happily share authority for all major business decisions?"

As in a good marriage, the best way to avoid major conflicts is to begin with an honest communication of what each partner expects to give and get from the partnership.

Sources: Kim T. Gordon, "Partner Power," *Entrepreneur,* August 2001; and Cliff Ennico, "Picking the Right Partner," *Entrepreneur,* April 8, 2002.

---

2. **Division of profits.** Sharing risk means sharing profits, and that can cause conflicts. There is no set system for dividing profits in a partnership, so profits are not always divided evenly. For example, two people form a partnership in which one puts in more money and the other puts in more hours working the business. Each may feel justified in asking for a bigger share of the profits. Imagine the resulting conflicts.

3. **Disagreements among partners.** Disagreements over money are just one example of potential conflict in a partnership. If things are going badly, one partner may blame the other. Who has final authority over employees? Who hires and fires employees? Who works what hours? What if one partner wants to buy expensive equipment for the firm and the other partner disagrees? Potential conflicts are many. Because of such problems, all terms of partnership should be spelled out in writing to protect all parties and to minimize misunderstandings.[3] The Spotlight on Small Business box offers a few tips about choosing a partner.

4. **Difficult to terminate.** Once you have committed yourself to a partnership, it is not easy to get out of it (other than by death, which immediately terminates the partnership). Sure, you can end a partnership just by quitting. However, questions about who gets what and what happens next are

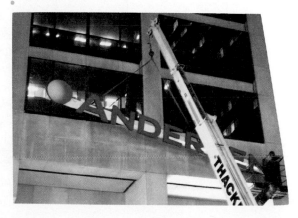

The Andersen name is lowered from its lofty place atop the Center City building in Philadelphia after the company suffered severe losses from its part in the Enron scandal. Since retired Andersen partners' pensions are based on the company's current earnings, retirees' monthly cheques fell as the *current* partners lost business. And if Andersen should stop doing business altogether, the pension cheques to its retirees or their widows stop too. That's a painful lesson on the importance of choosing your partners wisely. Andersen Consulting is now called Accenture.

partnership agreement Legal document that specifies the rights and responsibilities of each partner.

often very difficult to solve when the partnership ends. Surprisingly, law firms often have faulty **partnership agreements** (legal documents that specify the rights and responsibilities of each partner) and find that breaking up is hard to do. How do you get rid of a partner you don't like? It is best to decide such questions up front in the partnership agreement. Figure 6.2 gives you more ideas about what should be included in partnership agreements.

The best way to learn about the advantages and disadvantages of partnerships is to interview several people who have experience with such agreements. They will give you insights and hints on how to avoid problems.

One common fear of owning your own business or having a partner is the fear of losing everything you own if the business loses a lot of money or someone sues the business. Many businesspeople try to avoid this and the other disadvantages of sole proprietorships and partnerships by forming corporations. We discuss this basic form of business ownership in the next section.

FIGURE 6.2

PARTNERSHIP AGREEMENT PROVISIONS

It's not hard to form a partnership, but it's wise for each prospective partner to get the counsel of a lawyer experienced with such agreements. Lawyers' services are usually expensive, so would-be partners should read all about partnerships and reach some basic agreements before calling a lawyer.

For your protection, be sure to put your partnership agreement in writing. The following provisions are usually included in a partnership agreement:

1. The name of the business. All provinces require the firm's name to be registered with the province if the firm's name is different from the name of any of the partners.
2. The names and addresses of all partners.
3. The purpose and nature of the business, the location of the principal offices, and any other locations where business will be conducted.
4. The date the partnership will start and how long it will last. Will it exist for a specific length of time, or will it stop when one of the partners dies or when the partners agree to discontinue?
5. The contributions made by each partner. Will some partners contribute money, while others provide real estate, personal property, expertise, or labour? When are the contributions due?
6. The management responsibilities. Will all partners have equal voices in management, or will there be senior and junior partners?
7. The duties of each partner.
8. The salaries and drawing accounts of each partner.
9. Provision for sharing of profits or losses.
10. Provision for accounting procedures. Who'll keep the accounts? What bookkeeping and accounting methods will be used? Where will the books be kept?
11. The requirements for taking in new partners.
12. Any special restrictions, rights, or duties of any partner.
13. Provision for a retiring partner.
14. Provision for the purchase of a deceased or retiring partner's share of the business.
15. Provision for how grievances will be handled.
16. Provision for how to dissolve the partnership and distribute the assets to the partners.

- Most people who start businesses in Canada are sole proprietors. What are the advantages and disadvantages of sole proprietorships?
- What are some of the advantages of partnerships over sole proprietorships?
- Why would unlimited liability be considered a major drawback to sole proprietorships and general partnerships?
- What is the difference between a limited partner and a general partner?

CORPORATIONS

Although the word *corporation* makes people think of big businesses like Bell Canada, Bank of Montreal, or Irving Oil, it is not necessary to be big to incorporate (start a corporation). Obviously, many corporations are big. However, incorporating may be beneficial for small businesses also.

A corporation is a federally or provincially chartered legal entity with authority to act and have liability separate from its owners. The corporation's owners (called shareholders) are not liable for the debts or any other problems of the corporation beyond the money they invest. Corporate shareholders do not have to worry about losing their houses, cars, and other personal property if the business cannot pay its bills—a very significant benefit. A corporation not only limits the liability of owners, but also enables many people to share in the ownership (and profits) of a business without working there or having other commitments to it. We will discuss the rights of shareholders in Chapter 17.

In Canada, corporations are divided into two classes: public and private. A **public corporation** has the right to issue shares to the public, which means its shares may be listed on a stock exchange. This offers the possibility of raising large amounts of capital and is the reason why all large companies are corporations.

A **private corporation** is not allowed to issue stock (ownership in the company through shares) to the public, so its shares are not listed on a stock exchange, and it is limited to 50 or fewer shareholders. This greatly reduces the costs of incorporating. Most small corporations are in the private category. This is the vehicle employed by individuals or partners who do not anticipate the need for substantial financing, but want to take advantage of limited liability. Private corporations can be very large. Examples include Sun Life Assurance of Canada, Katz Group, and Honda Canada.

One important advantage Canadian-owned private corporations have over public corporations is that the income tax rate on the first $300,000 of business income is charged the lowest federal income tax rate of 12 percent. This is about half of what individuals pay when they are not incorporated and about half of the normal corporate rate. This is another benefit that encourages individuals and partners to incorporate.

Another important advantage for the owner of a private corporation is that he or she can issue shares to

public corporation
Corporation that has the right to issue shares to the public, so its shares may be listed on a stock exchange.

private corporation
Corporation that is not allowed to issue stock to the public, so its shares are not listed on stock exchanges; it is limited to 50 or fewer shareholders.

For a list of Canada's top 300 private companies, visit www.globeinvestor.com/series/top1000.

Burnbrae Farms Ltd. is privately owned and operated by the Hudson family. The company sells eggs and egg products throughout Canada. The Naturegg Omega Pro liquid eggs are a special blend of egg whites, a small amount of yolk, Omega-3 oils, and the antioxidant vitamin E. They contain 80 percent less cholesterol and 50 percent less fat while retaining the taste of shell eggs. This product has captured 5 percent of the egg market in Ontario.

a daughter, a son, or a spouse, making them co-owners of the company. This procedure is not available to a sole proprietor. It is a simple and useful way of recognizing the contribution of these or other family members, or employees, to the company. This procedure may also be a good way for the owner to prepare for retirement by gradually transferring ownership and responsibility to those who will be inheriting the business.

Keep in mind that with any kind of succession planning in private corporations, conflict may arise. In the mid-1990s, brothers Wallace and Harrison McCain of McCain Foods were bitterly divided over who should be picked to lead the company when they were gone. Wallace wanted his son Michael to take over, while Harrison preferred outside management. The fight ultimately wound up in a New Brunswick court, which sided with Harrison. Ousted from the company, Wallace ended up in Toronto, where he took over Maple Leaf Foods with sons Michael and Scott.[4]

There is a formal procedure for forming a corporation that involves applying to the appropriate federal or provincial agency. For small companies this may be done by the founders themselves, thus avoiding the costs of having a legal firm attend to it. The procedure for large or public corporations is much more complex and expensive and definitely requires hiring a legal firm. These costs can easily run into the hundreds of thousands of dollars.

Advantages of Corporations

Most people are prepared to risk what they invest in a business, but are not willing to risk everything to go into business. Yet, for businesses to grow and prosper and create abundance, many people would have to be willing to invest their money in business. The way to solve this problem was to create an artificial being, an entity that exists only in the eyes of the law. That artificial being is called a *corporation*. It has a separate legal identity from the owners—the shareholders—of the company. The corporation files its own tax returns. This entity is a technique for involving people in business without risking their other personal assets. Advantages include:

1. **Limited liability.** A major advantage of corporations is the limited liability of owners. Many corporations in Canada have the letters *Ltd.* after their name. The *Ltd.* stands for "limited liability," probably the most significant advantage of corporations. Remember, limited liability means that the owners of a business are responsible for losses only up to the amount they invest. Corporations can also end with Inc. or Corp.

2. **More money for investment.** To raise money, a corporation can sell ownership stock (through common or preferred shares) to anyone who is interested. This means that thousands of people can own part of major companies like Rogers Communications, TD Canada Trust, Manulife Financial, EnCana Corp., Canadian National Railway Co., and Loblaw Companies, and smaller companies as well. If a company sold 1 million shares for $50 each, it would have $50 million available to build plants, buy materials, hire people, manufacture products, and so on. Such a large amount of money would be difficult to raise any other way.

Corporations can also borrow money from individual investors through issuing bonds. Corporations may also find it easier to obtain loans from financial institutions, since lenders find it easier to place a value on the company when they can review how the shares are trading. Many small or individually owned

Ontario Business Central offers a range of business services that you can perform online, such as Ontario and Canada incorporation, NUANS business name search, and small-business registration. Visit www.ontariobusiness central.ca for more information. If you do not live in Ontario, is a similar service available in your area?

NOVA Chemicals' Joffre manufacturing site lies just east of Red Deer in the heart of Central Alberta's agricultural community. The Joffre site is one of North America's largest petrochemical complexes.

corporations that do not trade actively may not have such opportunities, however. You can read about how corporations raise funds through the sale of shares and bonds in Chapter 17.

3. **Size.** That one word summarizes many of the advantages of some corporations. Because they have the ability to raise large amounts of money to work with, corporations can build modern factories or software development facilities with the latest equipment. They can also hire experts or specialists in all areas of operation. Furthermore, they can buy other corporations in other fields to diversify their risk. (What this means is that a corporation can be involved in many businesses at once so that if one is not doing well, the effect on the total corporation is lessened.) In short, a large corporation with numerous resources can take advantage of opportunities anywhere in the world.

   Remember, however, that corporations do not have to be large to enjoy the benefits of incorporating. Many doctors, lawyers, and individuals, as well as partners in a variety of businesses, have incorporated. Figure 6.3 includes some of the criteria used to measure size in Canada. Figure 6.4 lists some of Canada's largest corporations.

4. **Perpetual life.** Because corporations are separate from those who own them, the death of one or more owners does not terminate the corporation.

5. **Ease of ownership change.** It is easy to change the owners of a corporation. All that is necessary is to sell the stock to someone else.

6. **Ease of drawing talented employees.** Corporations can attract skilled employees by offering such benefits as stock options (the right to purchase shares of the corporation for a fixed price)

CRITERIA	COMPANY	SIZE
Number of employees	George Weston Ltd.	145,000
Assets	Royal Bank of Canada	$403.03 billion
Revenues	General Motors of Canada Ltd.	$36.51 billion
Profits	Caisse de dépôt et placement du Québec	$3.46 billion

Source: FP500, *National Post,* June 2004, pp. 78, 126, and 132.

FIGURE 6.3

SOME CRITERIA USED TO MEASURE SIZE

This figure illustrates some different approaches to measuring size for Canadian companies based on results for 2003. Note that this example is based on publicly available information.

COMPANY	REVENUES ($ BILLIONS)
General Motors of Canada Ltd.	36.51
George Weston Ltd.	29.20
Royal Bank of Canada	24.83
Sun Life Financial Inc.	22.06
Magna International Inc.	21.51
Bombardier Inc.	21.32
Ford Motor Company of Canada Ltd.	20.83
Alcan Inc.	19.09
BCE Inc.	19.06
Imperial Oil Ltd.	17.84

Source: FP500, *National Post,* June 2004, p. 78.

FIGURE 6.4

CANADA'S LARGEST CORPORATIONS IN 2003, BY REVENUE

FIGURE 6.5

HOW OWNERS AFFECT MANAGEMENT

Owners have an influence on how business is managed by electing a Board of Directors. The Board hires the top managers (or fires them). It also sets the pay for top managers. Top managers then select other managers and employees with the help of the human resources department.

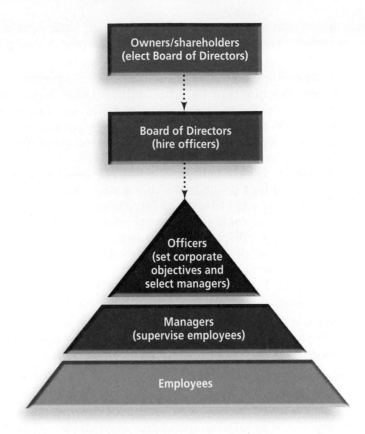

7. **Separation of ownership from management.**   Corporations are able to raise money from many different investors without getting them involved in management. A corporate hierarchy is shown in Figure 6.5.

Disadvantages of Corporations

There are so many sole proprietorships and partnerships in Canada that clearly there must be some disadvantages to incorporating. Otherwise, more people would incorporate their businesses. The following are a few of the disadvantages:

1. **Extensive paperwork.**   The paperwork filed to start a corporation is just the beginning. Tax laws demand that a corporation prove that all its expenses and deductions are legitimate. Corporations must therefore process many forms. A sole proprietor or a partnership may keep rather broad accounting records; a corporation, in contrast, must keep detailed financial records, the minutes of meetings, and more.

2. **Double taxation.**   Corporate income is taxed twice. First the corporation pays tax on income before it can distribute any to shareholders. Then the shareholders pay tax on the income (dividends) they receive from the corporation.

3. **Size.**   Size may be one advantage of corporations, but it can be a disadvantage as well. Large corporations sometimes become too inflexible and too tied down in red tape to respond quickly to market changes.

4. **Difficulty of termination.**   Once a corporation is started, it's relatively hard to end. Legal procedures are costly and more complex than for unincorporated companies.

5. **Possible conflict with shareholders and Board of Directors.** Some conflict may brew if the shareholders elect a board of directors that disagrees with the present management. Since the Board of Directors chooses the company's officers, entrepreneurs could find themselves forced out of the very company they founded. This is what happened to Rod Canion, one of the founders of Compaq Computer.

6. **Initial cost.** Incorporation may cost thousands of dollars and involve expensive lawyers and accountants.

Many people are discouraged by the costs, paperwork, and special taxes corporations must pay. However, many other businesspeople believe the hassles of incorporation outweigh the advantages.[5]

Corporate Governance

Corporate governance refers to the process and policies that determine how an organization interacts with its stakeholders—both internal and external. Rules outline how the organization is to be managed by the board of directors and the officers. Corporate governance is necessary because of the evolution of public ownership. In public corporations, unlike sole proprietorships and partnerships, there is a separation between ownership and management.[6] As a result, the board of directors was created.

> **corporate governance**
> The process and policies that determine how an organization interacts with its stakeholders, both internal and external.

The pyramid in Figure 6.5 shows that the owners/shareholders elect a board of directors. The directors have the responsibility of representing the best interests of the shareholders. The board assumes many of the same responsibilities that would typically rest with the sole proprietors, partners, or owners of a private corporation. On behalf of its shareholders, the directors hire the officers of the corporation and they oversee major policy issues. Board members are often chosen based on their business experience and level of expertise. The owners/shareholders thus have some say in who runs the corporation but they have no control over the daily operation. This is up to the officers and their management team. We will discuss the levels of management in Chapter 8.

In the past, many boards were made up of officers of the company. It was not uncommon to have the chief executive officer hold the chairman of the board position. Given the conflict that can arise, we are seeing changes to the representation of officers on the board. One such example is RBC Financial Group, the top-ranked company in Canada for corporate governance in the 2003 Canada's Most Respected Corporations survey. According to RBC's Website (www.rbc.com/governance), "The strengths of RBC's governance start at the top, with an independent chairman leading a board composed of independent, well-informed directors, who give priority to strategic planning, ensure that standards exist to promote ethical behaviour throughout the organization, and seek continuous improvement in governance practices."

In the wake of corporate scandals, companies and their boards of directors are being scrutinized. Is the board independent from officers? Does the company have a statement of corporate governance practices? To truly represent the shareholders, are directors elected every year? These are just some of the questions that are being addressed by boards across Canada.

Business Regulations

Companies that wish to operate in Canada must follow federal and provincial business laws and regulations. Among other things, this applies to registration, reporting, and general information.

Registration   Governments need to know what businesses are in operation to ensure that a wide range of laws and regulations are being followed. Guaranteeing that the names of businesses are not duplicated is important to avoid confusion. Additionally, governments have to be sure that taxes are being paid. To ensure these and other goals, every company must register its business. This is a simple, routine, and inexpensive procedure.

Companies wanting to incorporate must fill out articles of incorporation and file this with the appropriate provincial/territorial or federal authority. **Articles of incorporation** is a legal authorization from the federal or provincial/territorial government for a company to use the corporate format. The main advantage of being a federally incorporated company is that the company is not restricted in carrying on business throughout Canada. Federal incorporation gives the company name added protection and guarantees its usage across Canada. Depending on the type of business you are considering, you may be required to incorporate federally.

articles of incorporation
A legal authorization from the federal or provincial/territorial government for a company to use the corporate format.

Reporting and Information   Businesses receive many documents from governments during the course of a year. Some are just information about changes in employment insurance, Canada or Quebec Pension Plan, or tax legislation as it affects them or their employees. Then there are various statistics forms that all companies must complete so that governments can compile reports that businesses, individuals, research organizations, and governments need to operate effectively. StatsCan maintains vast databases and creates useful reports from this information.

To find out the details on how one would set up a corporation, visit the Business Start-Up section of the Canada Business Service Centre at bsa.cbsc.org.

All public corporations must file annual reports containing basic data about themselves. An annual report should include the name of the officers, how many shares (to be discussed in Chapter 17) have been issued, and the head office location. Of course, every corporation must also file an annual tax return containing financial statements and pay the necessary taxes during the year.

Other Types of Corporations

When reading about corporations, you may find some confusing terms. A *nonresident corporation* does business in Canada, but has its head office outside Canada. For example, most foreign airlines are nonresident corporations.

Not all corporations are large organizations with hundreds of employees or thousands of shareholders. Individuals can incorporate. A *personal service corporation* is set up by an athlete, entertainer, trucker, doctor, lawyer, or some other high-earning, self-employed person to access some advantages of corporate ownership. Normally, individuals who incorporate do not issue shares to outsiders; therefore, they do not share all of the same advantages and disadvantages of large corporations (such as more money for investment and size). Their major advantage is limited liability and possible tax advantages. Keep in mind that if you are first in business as a sole proprietorship or partnership, the debts the business incurs remain personal liabilities even after they are taken over by a corporation. Legally, it is the status existing *at the time* the debts were incurred that governs, not what happens subsequently.

You can learn about various YMCAs in different Canadian cities by visiting www.ymca.ca.

A *nonprofit corporation* is formed for charitable or socially beneficial purposes. As mentioned in Chapter 1, it is not run for profit. It has many features of business corporations, but it pays no income taxes and it does not issue shares. In short, it does not have owners or shareholders. In some towns, property is tax-exempt if it belongs to a nonprofit organization such as a religious institution, hospital, college, museum, YMCA, or athletic, artistic, or charitable organization.

| | SOLE PROPRIETORSHIP | PARTNERSHIPS | | CORPORATION | |
		GENERAL PARTNERSHIP	LIMITED* PARTNERSHIP	PUBLIC CORPORATION	PRIVATE CORPORATION
Documents needed to start business	None, may need permit or licence	Partnership agreement (oral or written)	Written agreement; must file certificate of limited partnership	Articles of incorporation, bylaws	Articles of incorporation, bylaws; must meet criteria
Ease of termination	Easy to terminate: just pay debts and quit	May be hard to terminate, depending on the partnership agreement	Same as general partnership	Hard and expensive to terminate	Not difficult; pay off debts, sell off assests, withdraw cash, and pay taxes
Length of life	Terminates on the death of owner, sale, or retirement	Terminates on the death or withdrawal of partner	Same as general partnership	Perpetual life	Perpetual life
Transfer of ownership	Business can be sold to qualified buyer	Must have other partner(s)' agreement	Same as general partnership	Easy to change owners; just sell shares	Easy—just sell shares[†]
Financial resources	Limited to owner's capital and loans	Limited to partners' capital and loans	Same as general partnership	More money to start and operate; may sell shares and bonds	Owners' capital and loans; no public share issue allowed
Risk of losses	Unlimited liability	Unlimited liability	Limited liability	Limited liability	Limited liability
Taxes	Taxed as personal income	Taxed as personal income	Same as general partnership	Corporate, double taxation	Same as public corporation
Management responsibilities	Owner manages *all* areas of the business	Partners share management	Can't participate in management	Separate management from ownership	Owners usually manage all areas
Employee benefits	Usually fewer benefits and lower wages	Often fewer benefits and lower wages; promising employee could become a partner	Same as general partnership	Usually better benefits and wages, advancement opportunities	Same as public corporation

* There must be at least one general partner who manages the partnership and has unlimited liability.

† Unless the agreement specifies otherwise.

Figure 6.6 compares different types of organizations. Note that this chapter does not discuss another type of corporation that we reviewed in Chapter 4—you will recall that *Crown corporations* are companies that only the federal or a provincial government can set up.

FIGURE 6.6

COMPARISON OF FORMS OF BUSINESS OWNERSHIP

Progress Assessment

- What are the major advantages and disadvantages of incorporating a business?
- What is the role of owners (shareholders) in the corporate hierarchy?
- If you buy shares in a corporation and someone gets injured by one of the corporation's products, can you be sued? Why or why not? Could you be sued if you were a general partner in a partnership?

CORPORATE EXPANSION: MERGERS AND ACQUISITIONS

merger
The result of two firms forming one company.

acquisition
One company's purchase of the property and obligations of another company.

vertical merger
The joining of two companies involved in different stages of related businesses.

horizontal merger
The joining of two firms in the same industry.

conglomerate merger
The joining of firms in completely unrelated industries.

The last decade saw considerable corporate expansion. It was not uncommon to read of a new merger or acquisition in the news on a weekly basis. What's the difference between mergers and acquisitions? A **merger** is the result of two firms forming one company. It is similar to a marriage joining two individuals as one. An **acquisition** is one company's purchase of the property and obligations of another company. It is more like buying a house than entering a marriage. Most of the new deals involved companies trying to expand within their own fields to save costs, enter new markets, position for international competition, or adapt to changing technologies or regulations.[7] The Dealing with Change box reviews how well some of these newly merged giants have met these goals. Figure 6.7 lists some mergers and acquisitions involving Canadian companies. Most were horizontal mergers.

There are three major types of corporate mergers: vertical, horizontal, and conglomerate. Figure 6.8 illustrates the differences in the three types of mergers. A **vertical merger** is the joining of two firms involved in different stages of related businesses. Think of a merger between a bicycle company and a company that produces bike wheels. Such a merger would ensure a constant supply of wheels needed by the bicycle manufacturer. It could also help ensure quality control of the bicycle company's products. A **horizontal merger** joins two firms in the same industry and allows them to diversify or expand their products. An example of a horizontal merger is the merger of a bicycle company and a tricycle company. The business can now supply a variety of cycling products. A **conglomerate merger** unites firms in completely unrelated industries. The primary purpose of a conglomerate merger is to diversify business operations and investments. The acquisition of a restaurant chain by a bicycle company would be an example of a conglomerate merger.

Rather than merge or sell to another company, some corporations decide to maintain control, or in some cases regain control, of a firm internally. For

FIGURE 6.7

MERGERS AND ACQUISITIONS

This is a list of some mergers and acquisitions in Canada from 2000 to 2003.

YEAR	ACTIVITY
2000	Toronto-Dominion Bank merges with Canada Trust, becoming TD Canada Trust.
	TELUS Corporation acquires Clearnet Communications Inc. to become TELUS Mobility.
2001	Icon Laser Eye Centres Inc. and Lasik Vision Corporation merge, creating the world's largest laser vision correction company.
	Indigo Books & Music Inc. acquires Chapters Inc. to become Canada's largest retail bookstore chain.
2002	Alberta Energy Company Ltd. and Pan Canadian Energy Corporation merge and became EnCana Corporation, one of the world's largest independent oil and gas companies.
	Sun Life Financial Services of Canada merges with Clarica Life Insurance Company.
2003	Great-West Lifeco Inc. acquires Canada Life Financial Corporation to become Canada's biggest insurance firm.
	Canadian National Railway Co. acquires provincially owned BC Rail Ltd.

Dealing With Change

Falling Giants

If history repeats itself, and in this case it appears to be doing so, then approximately two-thirds of the youngest merged giants will fail to meet their goals. The greatest merger mania in history seems to be unravelling before our eyes. These failing corporate giants lost around $2 trillion in market value in 2000 alone. The once high-flying WorldCom filed for bankruptcy. AOL Time Warner executives admitted that combining the two companies hasn't worked out the way they had hoped (Time couldn't even get its AOL e-mail to work right). Manufacturing conglomerate Tyco International used its stock to buy more than 20 companies a year only to end up in trouble in 2001 due to the creative accounting involved in purchasing those companies. Tyco's market cap (the total worth of all of the company's stock) plunged $90 billion in just the first six months of 2002.

Why did CEOs have the urge to merge if so many landmines lay in the way? The booming markets in the mid-1990s convinced many CEOs that they needed to beef up in order to compete and to achieve the double-digit growth Bay Street expected. Deregulation in telecommunications and banking in the U.S. primed the merger pump, and the flow of mergers quickly spread to other industries. The remarkable upward spiral of the stock market gave dot-com entrepreneurs rising stock prices. They used that high-priced stock to buy other companies, which increased their earnings, which raised their stock prices higher, which allowed them to buy more and bigger businesses. Of course, if the CEOs got a big bonus for merger deals no matter what happened to the share price, they were even more eager to merge. Joseph Nacchio, CEO of Qwest Communications, received a $26-million "growth payment" when Qwest bought US West in 1999, and Solomon Trujillo of US West got $15 million for selling. In 2000, Qwest's value was down $20–$30 billion.

Some economists see merger waves in terms of games CEOs play. When one company merges with another, its competitors ask themselves what their next move should be in order to get not the best outcome, but the least bad outcome. Since they fear being left behind, the first deal inspires others. For example, after Daimler bought Chrysler, Ford and GM each bought other carmakers. But which carmakers have remained the most profitable? BMW, Porsche, and Toyota—all of which stayed out of the mania.

Change is constant, of course, so every merger wave is followed by a counterwave. A recent survey revealed that more than a third of the largest international mergers completed in the preceding decade are now being "demerged." For example, luxury goods giant LVMH is selling bits of the empire it accumulated in the 1990s. As of this writing, AOL Time Warner's critics are calling for a breakup.

Sources: Karen Lowery Miller, "The Giants Stumble," *Newsweek,* July 8, 2002, p. 14; Stephanie N. Mehta, "Calling WorldCom's Woes," *Fortune,* July 22, 2002; and Stephanie N. Mehta, "AOL: You Got Mauled!" *Fortune,* August 12, 2002.

example, Steve Stavro, the majority owner and head of a group that invested in the Maple Leaf Gardens Ltd. (owners of the Toronto Maple Leafs hockey team) decided to take the firm private. *Taking a firm private* involves the efforts of a group of shareholders or management to obtain all the firm's stock for themselves. In the Maple Leaf Gardens situation, Stavro's investors group successfully gained total control of the company by buying all of the company's stock. For the first time in 65 years, investors in the open market could no longer purchase stock in the Maple Leafs.[8]

Suppose the employees in an organization feel there is a good possibility they may lose their jobs. Or what if the managers believe that corporate performance could be enhanced if they owned the company? Do either of these groups have an opportunity of taking ownership of the company? Yes—they might attempt a leveraged buyout.

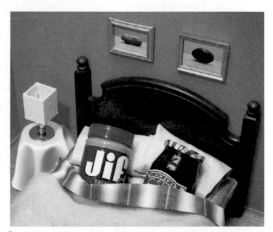

Some may call it a business marriage made in heaven. Smuckers' acquisition of Jif peanut butter from the Procter & Gamble Company united two mainstays, peanut butter and jelly. What's the difference between a merger and an acquisition?

FIGURE 6.8

TYPES OF MERGERS

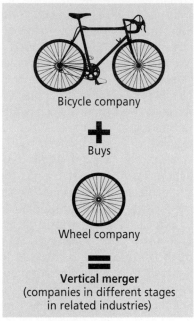

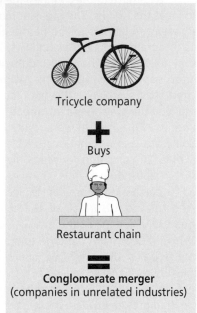

leveraged buyout (LBO)
An attempt by employees, management, or a group of investors to purchase an organization primarily through borrowing.

When Canadian Gerry Schwartz completed his MBA at Harvard University, he became an investment banker in New York City. There, he was part of a team that pioneered new leveraged buyout techniques. He took what he learned on Wall Street and founded his holding company, Onex Corporation, in 1983. Today, Onex Corporation is a highly diversified company with investments in movie exhibitions, auto parts, computer and telecom manufacturing, and healthcare.

franchising
A method of distributing a good or service, or both, to achieve a maximum market impact with a minimum investment.

A **leveraged buyout (LBO)** is an attempt by employees, management, or a group of investors to purchase an organization primarily through borrowing. The funds borrowed are used to buy out the shareholders in the company. The employees, managers, or investors now become the owners of the firm. LBOs have ranged in size from millions to billions of dollars and have involved everything from small family businesses to giant corporations like R. J. Reynolds.

SPECIAL FORMS OF OWNERSHIP

In addition to the three basic forms of business ownership, we shall discuss two special forms of ownership: franchises and cooperatives. Let's look at franchising first.

FRANCHISING[9]

Not everyone wants to start or operate a business as a sole owner. The personality called for is that of a risk taker and innovator. Some people are more cautious or simply want more assurance of success. For them, a very different strategy is available: the opportunity of franchising. Business students often mistakenly identify franchising as an industry. **Franchising** is a *method* of

We are seeing more examples of co-branding. For example, Tim Hortons kiosks can be found in numerous Esso Tiger Express outlets in Canada. As well, there are Tim Hortons/Wendy's combo stores. These combo units have their own separate counter, kitchen, and drive-through, but they share the dining area. Have you seen examples of this in your area?

distributing a good or service, or both, to achieve a maximum market impact with a minimum investment.

Some people develop ideas and build a winning good or service that they attempt to exploit through a franchise agreement. A **franchise agreement** is an arrangement whereby someone with a good idea for a business (the **franchisor**) sells to another (the **franchisee**) the rights to use the business name and sell a product in a given territory. As you might suspect, both franchisors and franchisees have a stake in the success of the **franchise.**

So what looks like a chain of stores—Canadian Tire, Quizno's Sub, Buck or Two—is usually a franchise operation with each unit owned by a different person or company; they are all part of a franchise operation, as explained in the previous paragraph. Sometimes one person or group may own and operate more than one franchise unit. In the following pages you will see the advantages and disadvantages of this type of business operation and ownership and learn what to consider before buying a franchise unit.

The franchise structure of ownership has had an important impact on Canadian business. Franchises employ more than 1.5 million people, and generate annual sales of over $100 billion. According to Richard Cunningham, president of the Canadian Franchise Association, there are about 850 franchisor companies in Canada.[10]

Over 35 percent of restaurant sales and over 45 percent of retail sales are from franchise operations. Of the franchises that opened in Canada within the last five years, 86 percent are still under the same ownership and 97 percent of them were still in business. Figure 6.9 details other interesting facts about franchise operations in Canada.

franchise agreement
An arrangement whereby someone with a good idea for a business sells the rights to use the business name and sell its products in a given territory.

franchisor
A company that develops a product concept and sells others the rights to make and sell the products.

franchisee
A person who buys a franchise.

franchise
The right to use a specific business's name and sell its goods or services in a given territory.

FIGURE 6.9

FRANCHISING IN CANADA

Annual sales	$100 billion
Rate of new franchises	One opens every 2 hours, 365 days a year
Employment	Over 1.5 million people
Total number of units in Canada	75,809
Average franchise fee	$25,000
Average investment by franchisee in Canada	$166,600

Source: CANAM Franchise Development Group, www.canamfranchise.com/Franchising Canada/stats.html, November 26, 2003.
Courtesy of CANAM Franchise Development Group

Cara Operations Limited has a strong presence in the Canadian franchise landscape. With annual system sales in excess of $1.8 billion, Cara is the largest operator of full-service restaurants in Canada. Cara has more than 1,100 outlets, mostly in Canada. It owns Swiss Chalet, Harvey's, Second Cup, Kelsey's Neighbourhood Bar & Grill, Montana's Cookhouse, and, as a franchisee, Outback Steakhouse Restaurants. Cara also owns 74 percent of Milestones Restaurants.[11]

Other Canadian food franchises that you may be familiar with are Tim Hortons, Boston Pizza, Booster Juice, Timothy's World Coffee, Mr. Sub, Crabby Joe's Tap & Grill, and Edo Japan. Keep in mind that there are also non-food franchises, such as Shoppers Drug Mart, Oxford Learning, 1-800-GOT-JUNK?, Home Hardware, and Budget Brake & Muffler.

Three Dog Bakery was started in 1989 by two partners. Their mission was to fresh-bake the world's best dog biscuits and give dog lovers everywhere a healthy, all-natural, *bone-ified* treat for their dog. Today, they have converted their partnership into a corporation and have 27 stores, including 2 in Japan and 2 in Canada. This is a picture of Corby Lee, co-owner of a Three Dog Bakery franchise in Vancouver, with his wife Diane. Their *pâtisserie* for dogs carries cakes, cookies, and all kinds of other treats.

Visit www.canadian franchises.com to find other franchises in Canada.

More than 77,000 employees work in the more than 1,300 McDonald's restaurants in Canada. If you are interested in learning more about franchising opportunities, visit www.mcdonalds.ca/en/careers/franchising_contacts.aspx.

Advantages of Franchises

Franchising has penetrated every aspect of Canadian and global business life by offering goods and products and services that are reliable, convenient, and competitively priced. The worldwide growth of franchising could not have been accomplished by accident. Franchising clearly has some advantages:

1. **Management and marketing assistance.** Compared with someone who starts a business from scratch, a franchisee (the person who buys a franchise) has a much greater chance of succeeding because he or she has an established product (e.g., Wendy's hamburgers, Domino's pizza); help with choosing a location and promotion; and assistance in all phases of operation. It is like having your own store with full-time consultants available when you need them. Franchisors provide intensive training. For example, McDonald's sends all new franchisees to Hamburger University in Oak Brook, Illinois. To be eligible franchisees, applicants are also required to complete 1,600 hours of on-the-job training. Some franchisors are helping their franchisees succeed by helping with local marketing efforts rather than having them depend solely on national advertising. Furthermore, franchisees have a whole network of fellow franchisees who are facing similar problems and can share their experiences. For example, Mail Boxes Etc. provides its franchisees with a software program that helps them build data banks of customer names and addresses. The company also provides one-on-one phone support and quick e-mail access through its help desk. The help desk focuses on personalizing contact with the company's franchisees by immediately addressing their questions and concerns.

2. **Personal ownership.** A franchise operation is still your store, and you enjoy much of the incentives and profit of any sole proprietor. You are still your own boss, although you must follow more rules, regulations, and procedures than you would with your own privately owned store.

3. **Nationally recognized name.** It is one thing to open a gift shop or ice cream store. It is quite another to open a new Hallmark store or a Baskin-Robbins. With an established franchise, you get instant recognition and support from a product group with established customers from around the world.

4. **Financial advice and assistance.** A major problem with small businesses is arranging financing and learning to keep good records.

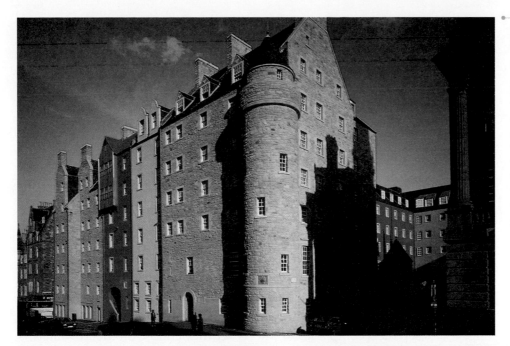

This may look like the set of *Camelot*, but it is actually the Holiday Inn in downtown Edinburgh, Scotland. Holiday Inn franchises try to complement the environment of the areas they serve. What do you think the local reaction would have been if the franchise tried to build the typical North American–style hotel in this area?

Franchisees get valuable assistance and periodic advice from people with expertise in these areas. In fact, some franchisors will even provide financing to potential franchisees they believe will be valuable parts of the franchise system.

5. **Lower failure rate.** Historically, the failure rate for franchises has been lower than that of other business ventures. However, franchising has grown so rapidly that many weak franchises have entered the field, so you need to be careful and invest wisely.

Disadvantages of Franchises

It almost sounds like franchising is too good to be true. There are, however, some potential pitfalls. You must be sure to check out any such arrangement with present franchisees and possibly discuss the idea with an attorney and an accountant. Disadvantages of franchises include the following:

1. **Large start-up costs.** Most franchises will demand a fee just for the rights to the franchise. Fees for franchises can vary considerably. Start up costs for a Kumon Math and Reading Centre include $1,000 for the franchise fee and a minimum investment ranging from $7,500 to $21,000.[12] But if it's Krispy Kreme you're after, you'd better have a lot more dough. An average Krispy Kreme store will cost you approximately US$2 million![13]

2. **Shared profit.** The franchisor often demands either a large share of the profits in addition to the start-up fees or a percentage commission based on sales, not profit. This share demanded by the franchisor is generally referred to as a *royalty*. For example, if a franchisor demands a 10-percent royalty on a franchise's net sales, 10 cents of every dollar collected at the franchise (before taxes and other expenses) must be paid to the franchisor.

3. **Management regulation.** Management "assistance" has a way of becoming managerial orders, directives, and limitations. Franchisees

Canadian Business Franchise magazine is a bi-monthly publication that features articles on franchise advice from bankers, lawyers, and franchise specialists. Visit www.cgb.ca for some advice and to view some profiles on individual franchises.

feeling burdened by the company's rules and regulations may lose the spirit and incentive of being their own boss with their own business. One of the biggest changes in franchising in recent years has been the banding together of franchisees to resolve their grievances with franchisors rather than each fighting their battles alone. For example, franchisees joined forces to sue franchisor Meineke Discount Muffler Shops, Inc. for fraudulently pocketing money they gave the company for advertising. The franchisees won an initial judgment of US$390 million against the company, but the award was overturned on appeal.

4. **Coattail effects.**   What happens to your franchise if fellow franchisees fail? Quite possibly you could be forced out of business even if your particular franchise has been profitable. This is often referred to as a *coattail effect*. The actions of other franchisees clearly have an impact on your future growth and level of profitability. If customers have a negative experience at one franchise location, this may destroy the reputation of other franchisees. Franchisees must also look out for competition from fellow franchisees. For example, TCBY franchisees' love for frozen yogurt melted as the market became flooded with new TCBY stores.

5. **Restrictions on selling.**   Unlike owners of private businesses, who can sell their companies to whomever they choose on their own terms, many franchisees face restrictions in the reselling of their franchises. In order to control the quality of their franchisees, franchisors often insist on approving the new owner, who must meet their standards.

If you are interested, Figure 6.10 gives you some tips on becoming a franchisee.

Home-based Franchises

Home-based businesses offer many obvious advantages, including relief from the stress of commuting, extra time for family activities, and low overhead expenses. But one of the disadvantages of owning a business based at home is the feeling of isolation. Compared to home-based entrepreneurs, home-based franchisees feel less isolated. Experienced franchisors share their knowledge of building a profitable enterprise with franchisees.

For example, when Henry and Paula Feldman decided to quit sales jobs that kept them on the road for weeks, they wanted to find a business to run at home together. The Feldmans started their home-based franchise, Money Mailer, Inc. (a direct mail advertiser), with nothing more than a table and a telephone. Five years later, they owned 15 territories, which they ran from an office full of state-of-the-art equipment. They grossed more than $600,000 during their fifth year. Henry says that the real value of being in a franchise is that the systems are in place: "You don't have to develop them yourself. Just be willing to work hard, listen, and learn. There's no greater magic than that."

E-Commerce in Franchising

We've already talked about how e-commerce is revolutionizing the way we do business. Online business is not limited to those with technical knowledge and the desire to take on the challenge of starting their own business from scratch. Today, Internet users are able to obtain franchises to open online retail stores stocked with merchandise made in all parts of the world. Before you jump online and buy a Web-based franchise, however, make certain that you check out the facts fully. The saying "You get what you pay for" may be old, but it's not old-fashioned.

Since buying a franchise is a major investment, be sure to check out a company's financial strength before you get involved.

CHECKLIST FOR EVALUATING A FRANCHISE

The franchise

Did your lawyer approve the franchise contract you're considering after he or she studied it paragraph by paragraph?

Does the franchise give you an exclusive territory for the length of the franchise?

Under what circumstances can you terminate the franchise contract and at what cost to you?

If you sell your franchise, will you be compensated for your goodwill (the value of your business's reputation and other intangibles)?

If the franchisor sells the company, will your investment be protected?

The franchisor

How many years has the firm offering you a franchise been in operation?

Does it have a reputation for honesty and fair dealing among the local firms holding its franchise?

Has the franchisor shown you any certified figures indicating exact net profits of one or more going firms that you personally checked yourself with the franchisee? Ask for the company's disclosure statement.

Will the firm assist you with

A management training program?
An employee training program?
A public relations program?
Capital?

Credit?
Merchandising ideas?

Will the firm help you find a good location for your new business?

Has the franchisor investigated you carefully enough to assure itself that you can successfully operate one of its franchises at a profit both to itself and to you?

You, the franchisee

How much equity capital will you need to purchase the franchise and operate it until your income equals your expenses?

Does the franchisor offer financing for a portion of the franchising fees? On what terms?

Are you prepared to give up some independence of action to secure the advantages offered by the franchise? Do you have your family's support?

Does the industry appeal to you? Are you ready to spend much or all of the remainder of your business life with this franchisor, offering its product or service to the public?

Your market

Have you conducted any studies to determine whether the good or service that you propose to sell under the franchise has a market in your territory at the prices you'll have to charge?

Will the population in the territory given to you increase, remain static, or decrease over the next five years?

Will demand for the good or service you're considering be greater, about the same, or less five years from now than it is today?

What competition already exists in your territory for the good or service you contemplate selling?

Sources: U.S. Department of Commerce, *Franchise Opportunities Handbook;* and Rhonda Adams, "Franchising Is No Simple Endeavor," Gannett News Services, March 14, 2002.

FIGURE 6.10

BUYING A FRANCHISE

PropertyGuys.com is an example of a franchise that uses e-commerce as an important component of the service it offers. Formed in 1998 in Moncton, New Brunswick, PropertyGuys.com has built on the "For Sale by Owner" (FSBO) Internet concept. Their service is a no-commission, low-cost alternative to pricey real estate commissions. PropertyGuys.com has been used to list homes, land, apartments, commercial buildings, and cottages. According to company literature, what differentiates

Buying a franchise takes time and research. Harness the power of the Internet to find information about specific franchises. A good place to start is by doing the Taking It to the Net exercises at the end of this chapter.

www.entrepreneur. com/Franchise_Zone/ has useful information on franchising including advice on starting an e-business, hot trends, its annual Franchise 500 rankings, and more.

this company from other FSBO sites is its personal touch. A company representative will set up clients, install signage, take photos, and make herself or himself available during the process. Furthermore, it does not rely solely on the Internet to display properties. The packages include a combination of print advertising, direct mail, electronic mail, seller's documentation, For Sale sign, Website listing, and phone answering service.

Many franchisees with existing brick-and-mortar stores are expanding their businesses online. Franchisees that started with a limited territory are now branching out globally. For example, Carole Shutts owns a Rocky Mountain Chocolate Factory franchise. Her Website generates 15 percent of her sales. Other Rocky Mountain franchisees have competing Websites. Right now, Shutts isn't concerned about the competition from her colleagues because she thinks multiple sites will build brand awareness.[14]

Many franchisors prohibit franchisee-sponsored Websites. Conflicts between franchisors and franchisees can erupt if the franchisor then creates its own Website. The franchisees may be concerned that the site will pull sales from their brick-and-mortar locations. Sometimes the franchisors send "reverse royalties" to outlet owners who feel their sales were hurt by the franchisor's Internet sales, but that doesn't always bring about peace. Before buying a franchise, you would be wise to read the small print regarding online sales.

Critical Thinking

Is it fair to say that franchisees have the true entrepreneurial spirit? What do you think of the franchise opportunities of the future? Could you see yourself as a franchisee or franchisor? Which one?

Franchising in International Markets[15]

Based on proximity and language, the United States is by far the most popular target for Canadian-based franchises. In 2003, Montreal-based Alimentation Couche-Tard Inc. paid US$839 million for 2,013 Circle K outlets. With this purchase, Couche-Tard, whose Canadian banners include Mac's, Becker's and Provi-Soir, became the fourth-largest convenience store operator in North America. Beavertails Pastry is another successful franchisor story. First introduced in Ottawa in 1978, there are more than 130 locations in 7 countries. One of the products is a hot pastry treat that resembles—you guessed it—a beaver tail. Expansion opportunities exist in amusement parks, sports venues, tourist destinations, and ski hills.

What makes franchising successful in international markets is what makes it successful domestically: convenience and a predictable level of service. The Reaching Beyond Our Borders box mentions this as one of the reasons for the success of Molly Maid.

CO-OPERATIVES[16]

co-operative
An organization that is owned by members and customers, who pay an annual membership fee and share in any profits.

Some people dislike the notion of having owners, managers, workers, and buyers as separate individuals with separate goals. They envision a world where people cooperate with one another more fully and share the wealth more evenly. These people have formed a different type of organization that reflects their social orientation. This is called a co-operative, or co-op. A **co-operative** is an organization that is owned by members and customers, who pay an annual membership fee and share in any profits (if it is a profit-making organization). Often the members work in the organization a certain number of hours a month as part of their duties.

Reaching Beyond Our Borders — Canadian Franchisor Cleans Up

Molly Maid Inc. set out to provide domestic cleaning services in Mississauga, Ontario in 1979. This organization is built on the fact that families are now busier than ever and need timesaving, convenient services to help manage their responsibilities at home. To date, Molly Maid has performed more than 6 million home cleanings across Canada and over 12 million in the world. This should not be surprising when you scan the business environment. Approximately 75 percent of women between the ages of 18 and 65 are in the workforce today, yet women are still responsible for the majority of the housework. Statistics reveal that working mothers spend as much as five hours each day on household chores. Add an extra nine hours each week if she has one child and an additional two hours for each child beyond that. You can easily see why timesaving services such as residential cleaning will continue to grow.

Research has shown that Molly Maid is practically a household name in Canada. Almost eight out of ten English-speaking Canadians mention Molly Maid first when asked to name a cleaning service. The franchise fee for a new Molly Maid franchise is $14,000. This includes everything needed to start your first team—advertising, administrative forms, and cleaning equipment and supplies. Most franchise owners require a minimum of $7,000 in working capital for vehicle deposits, insurance, and miscellaneous startup expenses.

Today Molly Maid is a $100-million company with more than 500 franchises. It has a presence on three continents and can be found in Canada, the United States, Puerto Rico, Bermuda, the United Kingdom, Portugal, and Japan. Franchise owners have received numerous industry awards. *Success Magazine* ranked Molly Maid 1st in residential cleaning, and 4th in the franchising industry overall in its annual Franchise Gold 200. *Income Opportunities Magazine* ranked Molly Maid 1st in residential cleaning, and 2nd in the franchising industry overall. *Entrepreneur Magazine* has ranked Molly Maid in the top 100 of their Franchise 500 for the past seven years. Since the mid-1990s Molly Maid has experienced double-digit growth, and future predictions call for the same. Way to clean up.

Sources: *Successful* Franchising, April 1996 and Website www.mollymaid.ca, November 20, 2003, "Molly Maid Still Cleaning Up in Canada after 25 years," *Canadian Business Franchise*, March/April 2004, 80–81.

There are 10,000 co-operatives in Canada, engaging 70,000 volunteers and employing 150,000 people. In northern Canada, co-operatives are the most important employer, after government. Co-operatives can be found in many sectors of the economy including the finance, insurance, agri-food and supply, wholesale and retail, housing, health, and service sectors. Are you familiar with any co-operatives?

For example, there are *producer co-ops*. Fishers on both coasts and farmers on the Prairies, in Ontario, and in Quebec each produce their own product, but part of all of their marketing is done through these jointly owned co-ops.

Co-operatives differ from other businesses in several ways:

- **A different purpose.** The primary purpose of co-operatives is to meet the common needs of their members. Most investor-owned businesses have a primary purpose to maximize profit for their shareholders.

- **A different control structure.** Co-operatives use the one-member/one-vote system, not the one-vote-per-share system used by most businesses. This helps the co-operative serve the common need rather than the individual need.

- **A different allocation of profit.** Co-operatives share profits among their member-owners on the basis of how much they use the co-op, not on how many shares they hold. Profits tend to be invested in improving services for the members.

The Canadian Co-operative Association is a national umbrella organization representing co-operatives and credit unions. Visit www.coopcca.com for more information about Canadian co-operatives.

The Co-operative Secretariat was established in 1987 to help the federal government respond more effectively to the concerns and needs of co-operatives. For more information, visit www.agr.gc.ca.

FIGURE 6.11

CANADA'S LARGEST
CO-OPERATIVES IN 2003,
BY ASSETS

FINANCIAL CO-OPERATIVES	ASSETS (US$ BILLIONS)
Desjardins Group†	94.65
Vancouver City Savings C.U.	9.01
Coast Capital Savings C.U.	6.42
Co-operators Group	5.72
NONFINANCIAL CO-OPERATIVES	
Federated Co-operatives	1.45
Cooperative Federée de Que.	0.75
Agropur Co-operative	0.69
United Farmers of Alta. Co-op.	0.35

Source: "The Top 1000: Top Co-ops," July 2004, www.globeinvestor.com/series/top1000/tables/sector/2004/coops.html. Accessed September 12, 2004.

† The Desjardins Group operates 1,753 caisses and service centres in Quebec, New Brunswick, Manitoba, and Ontario. It is a giant co-op with more than 5.5 million members and 38,120 employees.

Mountain Equipment Co-op (MEC) is a collectively owned and democratically controlled retail consumer co-operative. When you purchase your $5.00 lifetime membership, you become part owner and you have a voice in the governance of MEC. Have you heard of MEC? Would you join MEC?

Because co-ops distribute their profits to members as a reduction in members' costs, these profits are not subject to income tax. From time to time various business organizations assert that many co-ops are now more like large businesses and should be taxed. So far this viewpoint does not appear to have extensive support. Figure 6.11 lists some of the largest co-operatives in Canada. Some co-ops are also becoming corporations.

WHICH FORM OF OWNERSHIP IS FOR YOU?

As you can see, you may participate in the business world in a variety of ways. You can start your own sole proprietorship, partnership, corporation, or co-operative—or you can buy a franchise and be part of a larger corporation. There are advantages and disadvantages to each. However, there are risks no matter which form you choose. Before you decide which form is for you, you need to evaluate all of the alternatives carefully.

Progress Assessment

- What are some of the factors to consider before buying a franchise?
- What opportunities are available for starting a global franchise?
- What is a co-operative?

Summary

1. The major forms of business ownership are sole proprietorships, partnerships, and corporations.

   - **What are the advantages and disadvantages of sole proprietorships?**
   The advantages of sole proprietorships include ease of starting and ending, being your own boss, pride of ownership, retention of profits, and no special taxes. The disadvantages include unlimited liability, limited financial resources, difficulty in management, overwhelming time commitment, few fringe benefits, limited growth, and limited life span.

   1. Compare the advantages and disadvantages of sole proprietorships.

2. The three key elements of a general partnership are common ownership, shared profits and losses, and the right to participate in managing the operations of the business.

   - **What are the main differences between general and limited partners?**
   General partners are owners (partners) who have unlimited liability and are active in managing the company. Limited partners are owners (partners) who have limited liability and are not active in the company.

   - **What are the advantages and disadvantages of partnerships?**
   The advantages include more financial resources, shared management and pooled knowledge, and longer survival. The disadvantages include unlimited liability, division of profits, possible disagreements among partners, and difficulty of termination.

   2. Describe the differences between general and limited partners, and compare the advantages and disadvantages of partnerships.

3. A corporation is a legal entity with authority to act and have liability separate from its owners.

   - **What are the advantages and disadvantages of corporations?**
   The advantages include more money for investment, limited liability, size, perpetual life, ease of ownership change, ease of drawing talented employees, and separation of ownership from management. The disadvantages include initial costs, paperwork, size, difficulty of termination, double taxation, and possible conflict with a board of directors.

   - **Why do people incorporate?**
   The most important reason for incorporating is limited liability.

   3. Compare the advantages and disadvantages of corporations.

4. The number of mergers reached a peak at the start of the new millennium.

   - **What is a merger?**
   A merger is the result of two firms forming one company.

   - **Give examples of three types of corporate mergers.**
   A vertical merger is the joining of two companies involved in different stages of related businesses. A horizontal merger is the joining of two firms in the same industry. A conglomerate merger is the joining of firms in completely unrelated industries.

   4. Define what a merger is and give examples of three types of corporate mergers.

5. A person can participate in the entrepreneurial age by buying the rights to market a new product innovation in his or her area.

   - **What are the benefits and drawbacks of being a franchisee?**
   The benefits include a nationally recognized name and reputation, a proven management system, promotional assistance, and the pride of ownership. Drawbacks include high franchise fees, managerial regulation, shared profits, and transfer of adverse effects if other franchisees fail.

   5. Outline the advantages and disadvantages of franchises, and discuss the challenges of international franchising.

• *What is the major challenge to international franchises?*
It may be difficult to transfer an idea or product that worked well in Canada to another culture. It is essential to adapt to the region.

6. Explain the role of co-operatives.

6. People who dislike organizations in which owners, managers, workers, and buyers have separate goals often form co-operatives.

• *What types of co-operatives are found in the economy?*
Co-operatives can be found in many sectors of the economy including the finance, insurance, agri-food and supply, wholesale and retail, housing, health, and service sectors.

• *What is the role of a co-operative?*
Co-operatives are organizations that are owned by members/customers. Some people form co-operatives to give members more economic power than they would have as individuals. Small businesses often form co-operatives to give them more purchasing, marketing, or product development strength.

Key Terms

acquisition   168
articles of
   incorporation   166
conglomerate
   merger   168
co-operative   176
corporate
   governance   165
corporation   154
franchise   171
franchise
   agreement   171

franchisee   171
franchising   170
franchisor   171
general partner   157
general partnership
   157
horizontal merger   168
leveraged buyout
   (LBO)   170
liability   155
limited liability   157

limited partner   157
limited partnership   157
merger   168
partnership   154
partnership
   agreement   160
private corporation   161
public corporation   161
sole proprietorship   154
unlimited liability   156
vertical merger   168

Developing Workplace Skills

1. Research businesses in your area and identify five companies that use each of the following forms of ownership: sole proprietorship, partnership, corporation, and franchise. Arrange interviews with managers from each form of ownership and get their impressions, hints, and warnings. (If you are able to work with a team of fellow students, divide the interviews among team members.) How much does it cost to start? How many hours do they work? What are the specific benefits? Share the results with your class.

2. Have you thought about starting your own business? What opportunities seem attractive? Think of a friend or friends whom you might want for a partner or partners in the business. List all the financial resources and personal skills you will need to launch the business. Then make separate lists of the personal skills and the financial resources that you and your friend(s) might bring to your new venture. How much capital and what personal skills do you need but lack? Develop an action plan to obtain them.

3. Let's assume you want to open one of the following new businesses. What form of business ownership would you choose for each business? Why?

   a. Video game rental store
   b. Wedding planning service

    c. Software development firm
    d. Computer hardware manufacturing company
    e. Online bookstore

4. Find out how much it costs to incorporate a company in your province or territory. Then compare it to the cost of a federal incorporation. Is there a significant difference? Why might you choose not to incorporate federally?

5. Go on the Internet and find information about a business co-operative. Find out how it was formed, who can belong to it, and how it operates. Would you join this co-operative?

Purpose

To explore a change in business ownership.

Exercise

Successful businesses continually change. Methods of change discussed in this chapter include mergers, acquisitions, taking a firm private, and leveraged buyouts. Key in one of these terms on the Internet and find out how this method has changed an organization. How will this change affect the company's stakeholders? What benefits does the change provide? What new challenges does it create?

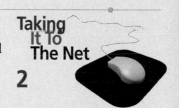

Purpose

To explore current franchising opportunities and to evaluate the strengths and weaknesses of a selected franchise.

Exercise

Go to Be the Boss: The Virtual Franchise Expo (www.betheboss.com).

1. Take the self-test to see if franchising is a good personal choice for you. Find the test by clicking on Franchising, then on Franchising—An Interactive Self-Test under Franchising Basics.

2. Go back to the home page and use the search tool to find a franchise that has the potential of fulfilling your entrepreneurial dreams. Navigate to the profile of the franchise you selected. Explore the franchise's Website if such a link is available. Refer to the questions listed in Figure 6.10 on p. 175 in this chapter and assess the strengths and weaknesses of your selected franchise. (Hint: The Website also contains tips for evaluating a franchise listing.)

3. Did your search give you enough information to answer most of the questions in Figure 6.10? If not, what other information do you need, and where can you obtain it?

Practising Management Decisions

Case
Going Public

George Zegoyan and Amir Gupta face a difficult decision. Their private autoparts manufacturing company has been a great success—too quickly. They cannot keep up with the demand for their product. They must expand their facilities, but have not had the time to accumulate sufficient working capital, nor do they want to acquire long-term debt to finance the expansion. Discussions with their accountants, lawyers, and stockbrokers have confronted them with the necessity of going public to raise the required capital.

They are concerned about maintaining control if they become a public company. They are also worried about the loss of privacy because of the required reporting to various regulatory bodies and to their shareholders. Naturally, they are also pleased that the process will enable them to sell some of their shareholdings to the public and realize a fair profit from their past and expected future successes. They will be able to sell 40 percent of the shares for $500,000, which is 10 times their total investment in the company. It will also let them raise substantial new capital to meet the needs of their current expansion program.

The proposed new structure will allow them to retain 60 percent of the outstanding voting shares, so they will keep control of the company. Nevertheless, they are somewhat uneasy about taking this step, because it will change the whole nature of the company and the informal method of operating they are used to. They are concerned about having "partners" in their operations and profits. They are wondering whether they should remain as they are and try to grow more slowly even if it means giving up profitable orders.

Decision Questions

1. Are George and Amir justified in their concerns? Why?
2. Do they have any other options besides going public? Is the franchise route a viable option? Explain?
3. Do you think they should try to limit their growth to a manageable size to avoid going public, even if it means forgoing profits now? Why?
4. Would you advise them to sell their business now if they can get a good price and then start a new operation? Explain.

Video Case
Making Profits with a Twist—Auntie Anne's Pretzels

Anne Beiler never intended to build a large business. Beiler began selling pizza, snack food, and pretzels at a farmer's market to finance her husband's free counselling centre. Her success encouraged friends and relatives to want to open their own pretzel shops at farmers' markets. Jonas (Beiler's husband) began building booths in the barn, and they soon had 40 locations. What they did not have was a form of business ownership. They explored the idea of a sole proprietorship (because of the ease of starting up and so on) and also considered a partnership or a corporation. (The advantages and disadvantages of each type are covered in this chapter.)

The Beilers contacted a lawyer to look at their business and make a recommendation. They decided franchising was an excellent way to expand. The company now owns 30 of its stores and the rest are franchises. Auntie Anne's currently operates 746 stores and is opening some 40 to 50 additional locations a year.

Franchisees find that franchising is not exactly like being an entrepreneur. They still enjoy the thrill of ownership, but their freedom to do what they please is limited by the franchisor's rules. On the other hand, franchisees have the advantage of marketing assistance. The assurance that franchisors like Auntie Anne's know how to do things right can reduce the franchisee's risk, which means fewer failures.

Unfortunately, franchises have disadvantages as well. One is the cost (sometimes huge) of buying the franchise. Often, however, the franchisor will help with financing to make the purchase easier. Franchising provides some ease of expansion (by using OPM—other people's money), but franchisors have to deal with scores of different owners who have diverse needs. Maintaining consistent quality control when working with so many different people can be a challenge for franchisors.

Auntie Anne's began with a philosophy that stresses customer service, cleanliness, and quality. Establishing good relationships with franchisees solved many potential problems. The company's success, however, has not made Auntie Anne's complacent. The firm works continuously to improve relations with franchisees and has had few problems. In fact, Auntie Anne's focuses so thoroughly on its relationships that the company has had only two cases of litigation with franchisees in 15 years.

Anne Beiler has not forgotten why she went into business in the first place: to help her husband do good in the community. She once considered seeking venture capital investment, but found that venture capitalists didn't share her values. Beiler believes when you give, you get, and then you give some more. She is proud of creating opportunities for women to become franchise owners and proud that a diverse group of people found good jobs in a community-minded company.

Thus far, Auntie Anne's has not done much selling over the Internet, but that may change. Expanding overseas has its challenges as well. Cultural variations are always present. For example, eating on the run is acceptable in North America but frowned on in other countries. People in some countries have never heard of pretzels. Still, with stores in over 13 countries, Auntie Anne's is slowly but surely doing its famous twist around the world.

Discussion Questions

1. What lessons can you take from this case that you could apply in starting or buying your own franchise?
2. What are the advantages of franchising versus incorporating when a company wants to expand?
3. Is it a good idea for a company to have an attitude of "giving to the community" when it starts? What conflicts might arise?
4. How do the advantages and disadvantages of franchising compare to other forms of business?

www.mcgrawhill.ca/college/nickels

Chapter 7

Entrepreneurship and Small Business

Learning Goals

After you have read and studied this chapter, you should be able to

1 Explain why people are willing to become entrepreneurs, and describe the attributes of successful entrepreneurs.

2 Discuss the importance of small business to the Canadian economy.

3 Summarize the major causes of small-business failure.

4 Analyze what it takes to start and run a small business.

5 Outline the advantages and disadvantages small businesses have in entering global markets.

Profile

Getting to Know Chris & Larry's Clodhoppers

When Winnipeg entrepreneurs Chris Emery and Larry Finnson started Krave's Candy Company in 1995, they had no idea of the challenges they would face. They started their company without any business background, let alone a business plan. After scraping up $20,000 from savings, family, and friends, they rented a 700-square-foot industrial space and began to commercialize Emery's grandmother's candy recipe. Their goal was to market the "delicious concoction of vanilla fudge graham wafer clusters with cashews" they called Clodhoppers. The first year, they sold about $60,000 worth—but it would be four more years before they made a profit.

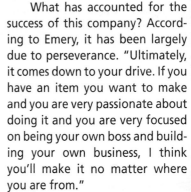

Emery gives his pal Finnson a candy fix

With no insight into marketing, they attended local craft fairs and retailers. They handed out samples in malls and stores in Winnipeg. A local Wal-Mart store agreed to carry their product and before long their product was sold in Wal-Mart Canada. Other retailers soon followed. As a result of an encounter with the president and CEO of Wal-Mart Stores Inc. at a 2000 vendor show in Toronto, they received a contract to test market their candy in 400 U.S. Wal-Mart stores.

Since then, Clodhoppers has been on the shelves of all 2,750-plus Wal-Marts in the United States. During the 2001 holiday season, Wal-Mart alone sold $1 million worth. Today, Clodhoppers can also be found at Bulk Barn, Canada Safeway, Costco (Western Canada), Dairy Queen (in Blizzard form), Goodfare, Giant Tiger, IGA, Loblaws, London Drugs, Overwaitea, Provigo, Save-On-Foods, Shoppers Drug Mart, Sobey's, Zellers, and The Bay. In 2003, deals were signed to put their product on the confectionary shelves of 274 Rogers Video stores and 400 Blockbuster video outlets across Canada.

As sales grew, the entrepreneurs needed to upgrade their equipment and finance their expansion. No matter how strong their sales were, they were always broke. They managed to secure a line of credit from a chartered bank and a $100,000 loan from the Business Development Bank of Canada. In addition, they received venture capital financing and management advice. Changes soon followed. They replaced the fancy boxes with funkier plastic bags adorned with cartoon images of themselves.

They rebranded the candy as Chris & Larry's Clodhoppers. They also developed single-portion bags suitable for convenience stores and gas stations. Today, the company employs 20 people year-round and 35 at peak production times. Kraves Company generated 2002 sales of $7 million, and 2003 projected sales for the Clodhoppers brand alone were $6 million.

What has accounted for the success of this company? According to Emery, it has been largely due to perseverance. "Ultimately, it comes down to your drive. If you have an item you want to make and you are very passionate about doing it and you are very focused on being your own boss and building your own business, I think you'll make it no matter where you are from."

In entering the U.S. market, they relied on advice from mentors, personal contacts in the food products business, and professionals such as customs brokers, freight and logistics specialists, and experts at a nutritional analysis laboratory. "You have to do due diligence, find people that are experienced and ask the right questions or it can cripple you," Finnson says.

What does the future hold for this company? Emery and Finnson are focusing on becoming a top candy brand in Canada. Another target is to sell the company. "We want to build more value before we sell—the longer we hold out, the bigger the price tag," says Finnson. They may eventually succumb to a takeover or they may take the company public.

Stories about people who take risks, like Chris Emery and Larry Finnson, are commonplace in this age of the entrepreneur. As you read about such risk-takers in this chapter, maybe you will be inspired to become a risk-taker yourself!

Sources: Articles retrieved from www.kraves.com: Julie Sloane, "Grandmothered Into Business," *Fortune Small Business*, February 2003; Shanan Sorochynski, "Chris and Larry share experiences," *The Dauphin Herald*, February 18, 2003; Geoff Kirbyson, "City candy firm signs national retail deals," *Winnipeg Free Press*, March 21, 2003; Laurie Nealin, "Growth-focused firms think 'export'," *Winnipeg Free Press*, October 28, 2002; Deirdre McMurdy, "Building future on sweet idea," *Financial Post*, February 11, 2002; and www.kraves.com.

THE AGE OF THE ENTREPRENEUR

A poll of students ready to graduate showed that 56 percent of them were more attracted to starting their own businesses than to joining the corporate ranks.[1] Some people in their 20s and early 30s seem to share the pragmatic view that in this time of downsizing it doesn't make sense to work in a company where your reward can just as easily be a pink slip as a promotion or bonus. Why not get a piece of the action by working in your own company? Schools around the country are responding to this trend by offering more courses on the subject of entrepreneurship. **Entrepreneurship** is accepting the challenge of starting and running a business. Explore this chapter and think about the possibility of entrepreneurship in your future.

entrepreneurship
Accepting the challenge of starting and running a business.

THE JOB-CREATING POWER OF ENTREPRENEURS IN CANADA

Entrepreneurs have played a major role in developing the Canadian economy. Consider just a few of the many entrepreneurs who have created companies that are now household names in Canada:[2]

- In 1922 two brothers—John W. and Alfred J. Billes—with a combined savings of $1,800 bought Hamilton Tire and Garage Ltd. Today, nine out of ten adult Canadians shop at Canadian Tire at least twice a year, and 40 percent of Canadians shop at Canadian Tire every week. Canadian Tire Corporation, Limited is engaged in retail (which includes PartSource and Mark's Work Wearhouse), financial services, and petroleum.

- In 1907 J. W. Sobey started a meat delivery business in Stellarton, Nova Scotia. With a horse-driven meat cart, he purchased and collected livestock from local farmers for resale. The first modern Sobeys supermarket opened in 1947. Today, Sobeys Inc. is one of Canada's two national retail grocery and food distributors. Sobeys owns or franchises more than 1,300 corporate and franchised stores in all 10 provinces under retail banners that include Sobeys, IGA, and Price Chopper.

- Ablan Leon began his career selling clothing from a suitcase door-to-door. When he had enough money, he bought a small building in Welland in 1909 and the A. Leon Company was established. When he died in 1942, the operation of the family business became the responsibility of his children. Today, Leon's Furniture Limited is Canada's largest retailer of home furnishings.

- Kenneth Colin opened Bouctouche, New Brunswick's first garage and service station, in 1924. That same year, he opened a Ford dealership in Saint John and established Irving Oil: he was 25 years old. Today, Irving Oil is a regional energy processing, transporting, and marketing company. It sells a range of finished energy products including gasoline, diesel, home heating fuel, jet fuel, and complementary products.

These stories are all very much the same: one entrepreneur or a couple of entrepreneurs had a good idea and started a business. Each one now employs thousands of people and helps the country prosper.

In 1957 brothers Harrison and Wallace McCain began producing frozen french fries in Florenceville, New Brunswick. Today, nearly one-third of the world's french fries are produced by McCain Foods. The company has operations on six continents, and it employs 20,000 people. Fiscal year 2003 sales totalled $6.4 billion. McCain Foods produces many other products, from juices and drinks and desserts to pizzas, oven-ready entrées, appetizers, and more. Why do you think that company executives moved their product lines beyond just french fries?

WHY PEOPLE TAKE THE ENTREPRENEURIAL CHALLENGE

Taking the challenge of starting a business can be scary and thrilling at the same time. One entrepreneur described it as almost like bungee jumping. You might be scared, but if you watch six other people do it and they survive, you're then able to do it yourself. The following are some of the many reasons why people are willing to take the challenge of starting a business:

- **New idea, process, or product.** Some entrepreneurs are driven by a firm belief, perhaps even an obsession, that they can produce a better product, or a current product at a lower cost, than anybody else. Perhaps they have gotten hold of a new widget or have conceived of an improvement that they are convinced has a large potential market. That's how Travel CUTS started. In 1969, Canadian students established a national travel bureau to provide travel opportunities for students. This was the beginning of the Canadian Universities Travel Service (Travel C.U.T.S.). As Canada's only national student travel bureau, Travel CUTS provides unique student-oriented products to more than 300,000 students each year.[3] Travel CUTS, owned and operated by the Canadian Federation of Students, is the largest travel agency in the world fully owned and operated by a national student organization.

- **Independence.** Some employees who have imagination and confidence in themselves find their jobs too restrictive. They need breathing space and a little elbow room! Perhaps their company does not encourage innovation in their operations, so they make the break. Some corporate managers are tired of big-business life and are quitting to start their own small businesses. They bring with them their managerial expertise and their enthusiasm. Many people cannot conceive of working for someone else. They like doing things their own way without someone standing over them. This type of person gets a great deal of satisfaction out of what he or she achieves.

- **Challenge.** Closely related to the previous factors are the excitement and the challenge of doing something new or difficult. Many people thrive on overcoming challenges. These people welcome the opportunity to run their own business.

- **Family pattern.** Some people grow up in an atmosphere in which family members have started their own businesses, perhaps going back several generations. The talk at the dinner table is often about business matters. This background may predispose young men or women to think along the same lines. Sometimes there is a family business, and the next generation grows up expecting to take its place there in due course.

    For example, the Anne of Green Gables Museum in Prince Edward Island is on a 110-acre property. The property includes the museum, an antique shop, a craft shop with Anne of Green Gables products available, a tearoom, and a variety of activities for families. The Campbell home was built in 1872 by author L. M. Montgomery's uncle and aunt. Montgomery often visited this location, and it has become popular with tourists from around world. The first Campbells settled on the property in 1776 and it is still in the Campbell family after two hundred years.

- **Profit.** It's natural for people to benefit monetarily from their ideas and dedication and to be rewarded for the money they risk and their hard work when they run a business. Yet long after a business has produced substantial profits and amassed personal fortunes for its

Company's Coming, Canada's most popular name in cookbooks, began in the home of Jean Paré in the town of Vermilion, Alberta. Self-employed with a successful catering business at the time, Paré responded to increasing requests for her recipes by publishing her first cookbook in 1981. Since then, more than 100 *Company's Coming* titles have been published, with total sales surpassing 21 million cookbooks. Company's Coming has turned into a three-generation family business: Grant Lovig, Jean Paré's son and co-founder of Company's Coming, oversees business operations; Jean's daughter, Gail Lovig, is responsible for sales; and Jean's granddaughter, Amanda Jean Lovig, handles public relations and communications. These cookbooks are distributed throughout North America and numerous overseas markets. Do you know of any other successful family businesses?

owners, many continue to enjoy the challenge of overcoming the endless problems that every business faces and to enjoy the satisfaction of continued success.

- **Immigrants.** Many immigrants who come to Canada lack educational skills. This, combined with no Canadian job experience and weak language skills, makes it difficult for them to find employment. However, they often have the drive and desire to succeed, and if they can obtain the capital, they can start their own business. We see this in the many immigrants who run convenience stores (called *dépanneurs* in Quebec), as well as other types of businesses, such as importing and manufacturing. Other immigrants arrive with capital, skills, and strong entrepreneurial backgrounds. Vancouver, and B.C. in general have been major beneficiaries of such immigrants from Hong Kong.

What Does It Take to Be an Entrepreneur?

Would you succeed as an entrepreneur? You can learn about the managerial and leadership skills needed to run a firm. However, you may not have the personality to assume the risks, take the initiative, create the vision, and rally others to follow your lead. Those traits are harder to learn or acquire. A list of entrepreneurial attributes you would look for in yourself includes the following:[4]

1. **Self-direction.** You should be a self-starter, with lots of confidence in yourself. You do not hesitate to step into any situation. Doing your own thing should seem like the only way. Furthermore, you are the boss and everything really rests on your shoulders.

2. **Determination.** Closely related to self-direction is the drive you need to see you through all the obstacles and difficulties that you will encounter. You have to keep going when others would give up. This often accompanies the high degree of self-confidence mentioned above.

3. **High energy level.** You must be able to put in long hours every day, six or seven days a week, for the first few years at least. You must be able to work hard, both physically and mentally.

4. **Risk orientation.** Because there is a high risk of failure, you must be able to live with uncertainty. You must accept the fact that all your hard work and money may go down the drain. On a day-to-day basis, you must make decisions that involve varying degrees of risk.

5. **Vision.** Many successful entrepreneurs have some dream or vision they feel impelled to realize. Perhaps it is to make that product better than anyone else can or to provide a new product.

6. **Ability to learn quickly.** Making errors is inevitable. Only those who do nothing make no mistakes. What is important is what you learn from them. Good entrepreneurs are quick to learn such lessons. They adapt and shift gears as required instead of letting pride stand in the way of admitting a mistake.

www.yea.ca

See this Website for more information about the Young Entrepreneurs Association Canada.

It is important to know that most entrepreneurs don't get the ideas for their goods and services from some flash of inspiration. Rather than a flash, the source of innovation is more like a flash*light*. Imagine a search party, walking around in the dark, shining lights, looking around, asking questions, and looking some more. The late Sam Walton used such a flashlight approach. He visited his stores and those of competitors and took notes. He'd see a good idea on Monday, and by Tuesday every Wal-Mart manager in the country knew

FIGURE 7.1

ADVICE FOR POTENTIAL ENTREPRENEURS

- Work for other people first and learn on their money.
- Research your market, but don't take too long to act.
- Start your business when you have a customer. Maybe try your venture as a sideline at first.
- Set specific objectives, but don't set your goals too high. Remember, there's no easy money.
- Plan your objectives within specific time frames.
- Surround yourself with people who are smarter than you—including an accountant and an outside board of directors who are interested in your well-being and who'll give you straight answers.
- Don't be afraid to fail. Former football coach Vince Lombardi summarized the entrepreneurial philosophy when he said, "We didn't lose any games this season, we just ran out of time twice." New entrepreneurs must be ready to run out of time a few times before they succeed.

Sources: Kathleen Lynn, "Entrepreneurs Get Tips on Weathering Recession," *Bergen County (New Jersey) Record*, March 5, 2002, p. l5; and Keith Lowe, "Setting Clear Goals," Entrepreneur.com, August 5, 2002.

about it. He expected his managers to use flashlighting too. Every time they travelled on business, they were expected to come back with at least one idea worth more than the cost of their trip. "That's how most creativity happens," says business author Dale Dauten. "Calling around, asking questions, saying 'What if?' till you get blisters on your tongue."

Keep in mind that necessity isn't always the mother of invention. Entrepreneurs don't always look for what customers need—they look for what they *don't* need as well. Aaron Lapin thought we didn't need the hassles of the touchy process of whipping heavy cream to top our pies. He made millions selling his invention: Reddi Wip. Although we'd rather reach for a can in the refrigerator than whip our own cream, Reddi Wip isn't a necessity. There is also some advice for would-be entrepreneurs in Figure 7.1.

Women Entrepreneurs[5]

A major phenomenon since the late 1970s is the large number of women who have gone into business for themselves. Throughout this book, you will see some examples of such enterprises. StatsCan's Labour Force Survey reports 826,000 self-employed women in Canada, accounting for about one-third of all self-employed people. Over the past 10 years the number of self-employed women has grown by 26 percent, compared with 16-percent growth in male self-employment.

Women owners of small and medium-sized enterprises (SMEs) tend to operate in the wholesale, retail, and professional services industry. One such example is Rachel Arseneau-Ferguson, President of Centre Transmed Center Inc. in Campbellton, New Brunswick. While teaching bilingual medical transcription at a local community college, Rachel started her business after her research revealed that there was no other company in Canada providing bilingual medical transcriptions. Transmed provides bilingual medical transcription and translation for large hospital corporations, private clinics, and doctors' offices throughout central and eastern Canada. Doctors dictate medical reports into a digital voice system to be transcribed for patient files. The company's software can link to any hospital and download voice files with medical reports. Doctors can also punch in codes and dictate reports directly into Transmed's system. "We can do work for anyone, anywhere in the world. It's just a matter of having a phone line."

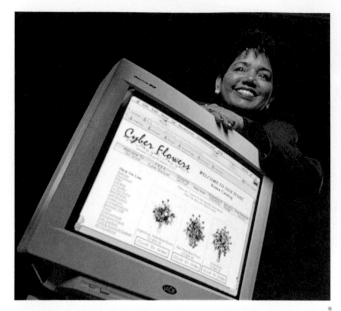

Cellie Gonsalves was a senior executive with a major Canadian corporation when she decided to make a lifestyle change and quit her job. For almost a year, she studied the ways in which technology would build her business and serve customers in new and better ways. Cyberflowers.com went online in November 1998. Today, Gonsalves operates both a flower shop and a thriving online floral site that draws customers from around the world. The number of women starting new businesses and assuming top management roles is also growing each year. What qualities do women have that help them become successful entrepreneurs and managers?

Visit www.profitguide.com/w100/faq.asp for a list of Canada's Top 100 Women Business Owners. This program is open to the women leaders of Canadian-owned private and publicly traded companies headquartered in Canada and with significant operations in Canada. These leaders are ranked on the basis of the gross annual revenues of their companies.

Studies have shown a variety of reasons for this significant emergence of female entrepreneurs:

- **Financial need.** The previous decade saw the average real incomes of Canadian employees drop and unemployment fluctuate (recall Figure 2.5). This has forced many women to support the family budget by starting a business.

- **Lack of promotion opportunities.** Most positions in higher management are still dominated by men. Although the situation is improving, the pace is extremely slow. Many women who are frustrated by this pace take the entrepreneurial route.

- **Women returning to the workforce.** Many women who return to the job market after raising a family find that their skills are outdated. They also encounter subtle age discrimination. These factors encourage many to try self-employment.

- **Family and personal responsibility.** The high rate of divorced women and single mothers in recent years has created a situation in which many women find themselves with children and little or no financial support. Some even refuse such support to be more independent. The development of affordable personal computers and other modern technology has made it possible for women to start businesses based at home.

- **Public awareness of women in business.** As more publicity highlights the fact that growing numbers of women have started their own ventures, the idea catches on and gives others the confidence to try. Often two or more women will team up to form a partnership.

- **Part-time occupations.** Often, women with some particular talent— for example, publicity, writing, designing, making clothes, cooking, organizing, or human relations—are encouraged to develop their hobby or skills on a part-time basis to see how far they can go with it. This procedure has resulted in many notable success stories, some of which are reported in this book.

- **Higher rate of success for women.** Women entrepreneurs seem to have a better success rate than men. Various factors may account for this. Women feel less pressured than men to achieve quick results. They are a little more cautious, so they make fewer mistakes. They also accept advice more readily than men, who may have a macho image of having to know it all. It will be interesting to follow this process to see if women continue to start ventures at the same rate and maintain their remarkable track record.

There are many resources available to help women entrepreneurs to network and to get general support. Some examples include Canadian Women's Business Network (www.cdnbizwomen.com), Women Entrepreneurs of

Canada (www.wec.ca), and Canadian Association of Women Executives & Entrepreneurs (www.cawee.net). Some institutions, such as RBC Royal Bank (www.rbcroyalbank.com/sme/women/) and the BDC (www.bdc.ca/en/i_am/ woman_entrepreneur/default.htm) have information on financing that is targeted to women.

Critical Thinking

Do you know anyone who seems to have the entrepreneurial spirit? What is it about him or her that makes you say that? Are there any similarities between the characteristics demanded of an entrepreneur and those of a professional athlete? Would an athlete be a good prospect for entrepreneurship? Why or why not? Could teamwork be important in an entrepreneurial effort?

Entrepreneurial Teams

An **entrepreneurial team** is a group of experienced people from different areas of business who join together to form a managerial team with the skills needed to develop, make, and market a new product. A team may be better than an individual entrepreneur because team members can combine creative skills with production and marketing skills right from the start. Having a team also can ensure more cooperation and coordination among functions.

One of the exciting companies begun in the 1980s was Compaq Computer. It was started by three senior managers at Texas Instruments: Bill Murto, Jim Harris, and Rod Canion. All three were bitten by the entrepreneurial bug and decided to go out on their own. They debated what industry to enter but finally decided to build a portable personal computer that was compatible with the IBM PC.

The key to Compaq's early success was that the company was built around this "smart team" of experienced managers. The team wanted to combine the discipline of a big company with an environment where people could feel they were participating in a successful venture. The trio of corporate entrepreneurs recruited seasoned managers with similar desires. All the managers worked as a team. For example, the company's treasurer and top engineer contributed to production and marketing decisions. Everyone worked together to conceive, develop, and market products.

Compaq merged with Hewlett-Packard in 2002. Entrepreneurs such as the three from Compaq often turn their companies over to professional managers once the companies reach a certain size. Frequently, such a change is good for the firm because the professionals introduce new ideas and instill new entrepreneurial spirit.

entrepreneurial team
A group of experienced people from different areas of business who join together to form a managerial team with the skills needed to develop, make, and market a new product.

Micropreneurs and Home-based Businesses

Not every person who starts a business has the goal of growing it into a mammoth corporation. Some are interested in simply enjoying a balanced lifestyle while doing the kind of work they want to do. Business writer Michael LeBoeuf calls such business owners **micropreneurs.** While other entrepreneurs are committed to the quest for growth, micropreneurs know they can be happy even if their companies never appear on a list of top-ranked businesses.

Many micropreneurs are owners of home-based businesses. According to the Canadian Home & Micro Business Federation (www.homebiz.ca), there are more than 2.5 million people who work from their home. Micro businesses—defined as those with fewer than five employees—represent 57 percent

micropreneurs
Entrepreneurs willing to accept the risk of starting and managing the type of business that remains small, lets them do the kind of work they want to do, and offers them a balanced lifestyle.

When Maria and Jay Seneses started 1 Cent CDs, their home-based auction business on eBay, they hoped to sell enough CDs to earn a living while spending more time with their young son. They discovered that the same technology that gave them the freedom to run a successful business from home made them feel trapped at work. As Maria says, "At the end of the day you don't get to go home. You're already there and so is the work." What are some other advantages and disadvantages of working at home?

of all employer businesses in Canada, with the majority of home-based businesses in service industries.[6] Micropreneurs include writers, consultants, video producers, architects, bookkeepers, and such. In fact, the development of this textbook involved many home-based business owners. The authors, the developmental editors, the copy editor, and even the text designer operate home-based businesses.

Many home-based businesses are owned by people who are trying to combine career and family. Don't misunderstand and picture home-based workers as female childcare providers; nearly 50 percent are men.[7] In addition to helping business owners balance work and family, other reasons for the growth of home-based businesses include the following:

- Computer technology has levelled the competitive playing field, allowing home-based businesses to look and act as big as their corporate competitors. Approximately 600,000 micropreneurs have access to the Internet.[8] Broadband Internet connections, fax machines, and other technologies are so affordable that setting up a business takes a much smaller initial investment than it used to.

- Corporate downsizing has made workers aware that there is no such thing as job security, leading many to venture out on their own. Meanwhile, the work of the downsized employees still needs to be done and corporations are outsourcing much of the work to smaller companies; that is, they are contracting with small companies to temporarily fill their needs. (We'll talk more about outsourcing in Chapter 10.)

- Social attitudes have changed. Whereas home-based entrepreneurs used to be asked when they were going to get a "real" job, they are now likely to be asked instead for how-to-do-it advice.

Working at home has its challenges, of course. In setting up a home-based business, you could expect the following major challenges:

- **Getting new customers.** Getting the word out can be difficult because you don't have signs or a storefront.

- **Managing time.** Of course, you save time by not commuting, but it takes self-discipline to use that time wisely.

- **Keeping work and family tasks separate.** Often it is difficult to separate work and family tasks. It's great to be able to throw a load of laundry in the washer in the middle of the workday if you need to, but you have to keep such distractions to a minimum. It is also difficult to leave your work at the office if the office is at home. Again, it takes self-discipline to keep work from trickling out of the home office and into the family room.[9]

- **Abiding by city ordinances.** Government ordinances restrict such things as the types of businesses that are allowed in certain parts of the community and how much traffic a home-based business can attract to the neighbourhood.[10]

- **Managing risk.** Home-based entrepreneurs should review their homeowner's insurance policy since not all policies cover business-related claims. Some even void the coverage if there is a business in the home.

Those who wish to get out of an office building and into a home office should focus on finding opportunity instead of accepting security, getting results instead of following routines, earning a profit instead of earning a paycheque, trying new ideas instead of avoiding mistakes, and creating a long-term vision instead of seeking a short-term payoff. Figure 7.2 lists 10 ideas for potentially successful home-based businesses. You can find a wealth of online information about starting a home-based business at www.entrepreneur.com and www.sbinfocanada.about.com.

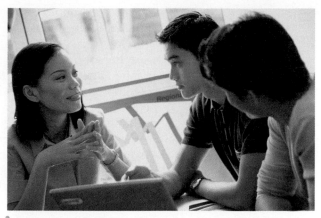

Student Connections is a government and private-sector partnership program that provides small and medium-sized businesses with e-commerce and Internet training. Since 1996, Student Connections has hired and trained postsecondary students and recent graduates as Student Business Advisors. As Advisors, they provide on-site customized training to clients across Canada. Would you consider working in this capacity for a summer job?

Web-based Businesses

The Internet has sprouted a world of small Web-based businesses that sell everything from staplers to refrigerator magnets to wedding dresses. KEH Camera Brokers began as a hobby, grew into a mail-order business, and is now a flourishing Web-based business (www.keh.com). More than 57 percent of the store's sales are made online. Customers have found that the Website is an efficient pipeline for buying and selling cameras. The far reach of the Web was a natural fit for the company. "The Web is a so much better vehicle for our customers [compared with a mail-order catalogue]," store manager Pat Mulherin said. "They want to be able to see our inventory." When KEH's first Web page went active, it was an immediate success. "Within two months it was accounting for 35 percent of our business, then quickly went up." Prior to the Web the small store produced mail-order catalogues listing used cameras for sale. Creating and mailing the catalogues was a slow process; by the time a customer saw a product and tried to order it, another customer could have already purchased it. The KEH Website's

---

Many businesses can be started at home. Listed below are 10 businesses that have low start-up costs, don't require an abundance of administrative tasks, and are in relatively high demand and are easy to sell:

1. Cleaning service.
2. Gift-basket business.
3. Web merchant.
4. Mailing list service.
5. Microfarming (small plots of land for such high-value crops as mushrooms, edible flowers, or sprouts).

6. Tutoring.
7. Résumé service.
8. Web design.
9. Medical claims assistance.
10. Personal coaching.

Look for a business that meets these important criteria: (1) The job is something you truly enjoy doing; (2) you know enough to do the job well or you are willing to spend time learning it while you have another job; and (3) you can identify a market for your product or service.

Source: "Hundreds of Home Based Business Ideas," YourHomeBiz.com, September 2002.

FIGURE 7.2

POTENTIAL HOME-BASED BUSINESSES

listing of available cameras is updated every four hours. A used camera is listed for sale on the Website a few hours after it enters KEH's inventory.[11]

Don't get the idea that a Web-based business is always a fast road to success. It can sometimes be a shortcut to failure. Hundreds of high-flying dot-coms crashed after promising to revolutionize the way we shop. That's the bad news. The good news is that you can learn from someone else's failure and spare yourself some pain. Startupfailures.com serves as a community for those who have tried and failed. The site bills itself as "The place for bouncing back!" It offers job listings, a feature called "Ask the Coach," and a story reminding site visitors that failing doesn't make you a failure, only failing to learn from your mistakes does. If you would like to learn more about the pitfalls of Web-based businesses, the "Lessons Learned" tab on the Startupfailures.com site provides an archive of stories by Internet hopefuls who have been there, done that.

Entrepreneurship within Firms

intrapreneurs
Creative people who work as entrepreneurs within corporations.

Entrepreneurship in a large organization is often reflected in the efforts and achievements of intrapreneurs. **Intrapreneurs** are creative people who work as entrepreneurs within corporations. The idea is to use a company's existing resources—human, financial, and physical—to launch new products and generate new profits. At 3M, which produces a wide array of products from adhesives (Scotch tape) to nonwoven materials for industrial use, managers are expected to devote 15 percent of their time to thinking up new goods or services.[12] You know those bright-coloured Post-it Notes people use to write messages on just about everything? That product was developed by Art Fry, a 3M employee. He needed to mark the pages of a hymnal in a way that wouldn't damage or fall out of the book. He came up with the idea of the self-stick, repositionable paper. The 3M labs soon produced a sample, but distributors thought the product wasn't important and market surveys were inconclusive. Nonetheless, 3M kept sending samples to secretaries of top executives. Eventually, after launching a major sales and marketing program, the orders began pouring in, and Post-it Notes became a big winner. The company continues to update the product; making the notes from recycled paper is just one of the many innovations. Post-it Notes have gone international as well—the notepads sent to Japan are long and narrow to accommodate vertical writing. Now you can even use Post-it Notes electronically—the software program Post-it Software Notes allows you to type messages onto brightly coloured notes and store them on memo boards, embed them in documents, or send them through e-mail.

Hewlett-Packard calls its intrapreneurial approach the Triad Development Process. The idea is to link the design engineer, the manufacturer, and the marketer (the triad) in a cross-functional team from the design phase on. Everything, even the assembly line, shuts down if the Triad team wants to test an innovation.

ENCOURAGING ENTREPRENEURSHIP: WHAT GOVERNMENT CAN DO[13]

The federal and provincial governments provide many services to help entrepreneurs and small businesses to succeed. One way to encourage entrepreneurship was through the creation of the Canada Business Service Centres (CBSCs). The CBSCs provide a wide range of free information on government services, programs, and regulations. This includes assistance in starting a new business or improving an existing one.

The CBSC initiative is a cooperative arrangement among 37 federal business departments, provincial and territorial governments, and, in some cases, private-sector associations, academics, and research communities. Currently, there are 13 CBSCs—one in every province and territory.

There are also specialized programs. For example, the Aboriginal Business Service Network (ABSN) builds on the structure of existing CBSCs located across the country. The ABSN provides Aboriginal entrepreneurs with information and resources to improve their access to capital and to establish or develop their business. The ABSN is one element of the Aboriginal Business Development Initiative.

As mentioned in Chapter 4, the Canadian government is intent on meeting the growing service expectations of businesses. Its Government On-Line (GOL) initiative includes the Small Business Research and Policy Website. This site is designed to encourage small business researchers and policy analysts across Canada to share information on small-business research and policy. It includes an extensive database on research literature on the subject of small business and entrepreneurship, recent reports on small-business financing, small-business statistics, and lists of researchers and policy development offices across Canada. BusinessGateway.ca is another site. It provides a single access point to all the government services and information needed to start, run, and grow a business. It includes information on taxes, regulations, e-business, selling to government, financing, and human resources management. For additional government sources, review the Services section in Chapter 4.

Entrepreneurs and new start-ups can also find assistance from incubators. Incubators were first developed to be centres that offered new businesses low-cost offices with basic business services such as accounting, legal advice, and secretarial help. Since then, the "networked" incubator has emerged with the creation of innovation centres. The networked incubator goes beyond the simple provision of office space and provides entrepreneurs and new companies with access to more services. According to the Canadian Association of Business Incubators (www.cabi.ca), **incubators** today provide hands-on management assistance, education, information, technical and vital business support services, networking resources, financial advice, as well as advice on where to go to seek financial assistance.

The goal of an incubator is not only to ensure the small business survives the start-up period, but also to produce confident, successful graduates who will run a productive business in the future. One example of an incubator that has received worldwide recognition is the Quebec Biotechnology Innovation Centre (QBIC) in Laval. It provides start-ups in the health, environment, agri-food, and forestry sectors with lab space, scientific equipment, and mentoring services. Located in Laval's Biotech City, QBIC is just one organization that fosters entrepreneurship.

According to the National Association of Business Incubators, there are now between 3,500 and 4,500 incubators around the world. In the last two years, the number of private and publicly operated incubators has increased

The Canada Business Service Centres site— www.cbsc.org—contains start-up topics that range from basic steps for starting a business to preparing a business plan, finding new markets, and helping entrepreneurs to export. This information is specific to the province/territory where the business will be located.

incubators
Centres that provide hands-on management assistance, education, information, technical and vital business support services, networking resources, financial advice, as well as advice on where to go to seek financial assistance.

NRC'S Industrial Partnership Facilities (IPFs) go beyond the standard industry services. They offer start-ups access to specialized laboratory space and equipment, regular interaction with NRC researchers, and the opportunity to benefit from a range of NRC technology-transfer initiatives. At many locations, Industrial Technology Advisors from NRC's Industrial Research Assistance Program are on hand to help incubator tenants work through the technical and business challenges of getting an R&D project off the ground. One of NRC's newest IPFs is the NRC Plant Biotechnology Institute in Saskatoon. The facility is strengthening the region's agricultural biotechnology cluster.

Visit www.bdc.ca for more information on the assistance provided by the Business Development Bank of Canada.

from 40 to more than 120 in Canada. To encourage innovation, the federal government has allocated $110 million to support the National Research Council's innovation agenda. One of the initiatives at the NRC is its Industrial Partnership Facilities (IPFs). There are plans to have 12 IPFs across the country by the end of 2003. Similar to incubators, each IPF has a focus on a different technology sector, depending on the specialization of its host institute.

The government can also have a significant effect on entrepreneurship by offering investment tax credits that would give tax breaks to businesses that make the kind of investments that would create jobs. For example, the Biotechnology Development Centre is a tenant in Laval's Biotech City. This Centre is supported by the Canadian and Quebec governments in addition to the City of Laval. These government bodies encourage R&D by granting corporations and individuals tax incentives that foster scientific and technological development. Some of the incentives include the following:

- 30-percent refundable tax credit on capital or rental costs for eligible equipment (up to three years) and
- 75-percent exemption on Quebec corporate tax, tax on capital and employer contributions to the Health Services Fund (up to five years)

While the government provides a great deal of assistance, it is still primarily up to the entrepreneur to make a success of the new business.

Progress Assessment

- Why are people willing to become entrepreneurs?
- What are the advantages of entrepreneurial teams?
- How do micropreneurs differ from other entrepreneurs?
- What are some of the opportunities and risks of Web-based businesses?
- List some services for entrepreneurs provided by the federal government.

GETTING STARTED IN SMALL BUSINESS

Let's suppose you have a great idea for a new business, you have the attributes of an entrepreneur, and you are ready to take the leap into business for yourself. How do you start a business? How much paperwork is involved? That is what the rest of this chapter is about. We will explore small businesses, their role in the economy, and small-business management. It may be easier to identify with a small neighbourhood business than with a giant global firm, yet the principles of management are similar. The management of charities, government agencies, churches, schools, and unions is much the same as the management of small and large businesses. So, as you learn about small-business management, you will make a giant step toward understanding management in general. All organizations demand capital, good ideas, planning, information management, budgets (and financial management in general), accounting, marketing, good employee relations, and good overall managerial know-how. We shall explore these areas as they relate to small businesses and then, later in the book, apply the concepts to large firms, even global organizations.

Small versus Big Business[14]

The Business Registrar of Statistics Canada maintains a count of business establishments. A **business establishment** must have at least one paid employee, have annual sales revenue of $30,000, or be incorporated and have filed a federal corporate income tax return at least once in the previous three years. While there are a little over 2.2 million business establishments in Canada, approximately 1 million of them are employer businesses. An **employer business** meets one of the business establishment criteria and usually maintains a payroll of at least one person, possibly the owner. The rest are classified as "indeterminate." Figure 7.3 breaks down the number of businesses by sector and number of employees.

It would be helpful to define what is meant by the term *small business*. Giant companies like Petro-Canada or Air Canada may look at most companies as small. A **small business** is often defined as a business that is independently owned and operated, is not dominant in its field, and meets certain standards of size in terms of employees or annual revenues.

Many institutions define small business according to their own needs. For example, the Canadian Bankers Association classifies a loan authorization of less than $250,000 as small. Industry Canada often uses a definition based on the number of employees: goods-producing firms are considered small if they have fewer than 100 employees, while services-producing firms with 50 employees or less are considered small. Generally speaking, 50 employees is the upper limit most used when defining a small business based on the number of employees. Medium-sized businesses have 50–499 employees, while large businesses employ more than 500 people. In Figure 7.3, of the over 1 million employer businesses in Canada, 0.3 percent have more than 500 employees. Businesses employing fewer than 50 employees account for the vast majority of all employer businesses.

As you can see, small business is really a big part of the Canadian economy. How big a part? We'll explore that question next.

business establishment
Has at least one paid employee, annual sales revenue of $30,000, or is incorporated and has filed a federal corporate income tax return at least once in the previous three years.

employer business
Meets one of the business establishment criteria and usually maintains a payroll of at least one person, possibly the owner.

small business
A business that is independently owned and operated, is not dominant in its field, and meets certain standards of size in terms of employees or annual revenues.

FIGURE 7.3

NUMBER OF BUSINESS ESTABLISHMENTS BY SECTOR AND FIRM SIZE (NUMBER OF EMPLOYEES), JUNE 2003

Almost 95 percent of Canadian companies are small businesses.

NUMBER OF EMPLOYEES	PERCENTAGE OF EMPLOYER BUSINESSES	NO. OF BUSINESS ESTABLISHMENTS		
		TOTAL	GOODS-PRODUCING SECTOR	SERVICES-PRODUCING SECTOR
Indeterminate[1]		1,181,440	323,786	857,654
Employer Business Total	100.0%	1,047,132	244,942	802,190
Small business (1–49 employees)	94.7%	991,796	229,812	761,984
Medium-sized business (50–499 employees)	5.0%	52,563	14,522	38,041
Large business (500+ employees)	0.3%	2,773	608	2,165
Grand Total		2,228,572	568,728	1,659,844

Note 1: The "indeterminate" category consists of incorporated or unincorporated businesses that do not have a Canada Revenue Agency (CRA) payroll deductions account. The work force of such businesses may consist of contract workers, family members, and/or owners.

"Number of Business Establishments by sector and size (Number of Employees)," adapted from the Statistics Canada Business Registry Survey, June 2004.

Vegetarian living is not only nutritious, it can also be healthy financially. Vicki Slotnick and Jeremy Paige used what they learned in 20 years of vegetarian living to start Organica Foods. By the end of their first year in business, Organica cookies were in 600 7-Eleven stores. How important is it to know your product before starting a business?

Importance of Small Businesses[15]

The small-business sector is a dynamic part of the Canadian economy. Nearly all small businesses are Canadian-owned and managed. This is in contrast to large businesses, of which many are foreign-owned and managed. Small business thus plays a major role in helping to maintain the Canadian identity and Canadian economic independence.

Small businesses also continue to be feeders for future large businesses. As they prosper and develop new goods and services, they are often bought out by large companies, which in turn become more competitive. Alternatively, after small businesses establish a good track record, some of them convert from private to public companies, enabling them to obtain significant financing and become larger companies.

Let's look at some interesting statistics about small business:

- There are almost 2.4 million self-employed persons in Canada.
- While they represent approximately 15 percent of the total labour force, they employ 49 percent of the total private labour force.
- According to the OECD, 43 percent of private-sector GDP can be attributed to businesses that employ fewer than 500 employees.
- During 1994 and 1995, small businesses generated most of the new jobs while large companies were laying off employees. This was not the case in subsequent years until the last quarter of 2001 and the first quarter of 2002. During this period, small firms contributed 145 percent and 104 percent of jobs.

Since most of Canada's jobs are in small businesses, there is a very good chance that you will either work in a small business someday or start one. A quarter of small businesses list "lack of qualified workers" as one of their biggest obstacles to growth.

In addition to providing employment opportunities, small firms believe they offer other advantages that larger companies do not. Owners of small companies report that their greatest advantages over big companies are their more personal customer service and their ability to respond quickly to opportunities.

Bigger is not always better. Picture a hole in the ground. If you fill it with big boulders, there are many empty spaces between them. However, if you fill it with sand, there is no space between the grains. That's how it is in business.

Big businesses don't serve all the needs of the market. There is plenty of room for small companies to make a profit filling those niches.

Wide Diversification

Another significant aspect of small business is the wide diversification of its activities. If you look, you will find small businesses in many sectors:

1. **Service businesses.** You are already familiar with the services provided by car mechanics, dry cleaners, travel agencies, lawncare firms, salons, and other services that cater to you and your family. In your career search, be sure to explore services such as hotels and motels, health clubs, amusement parks, income tax preparation organizations, employment agencies, accounting firms, rental firms of all kinds, management consulting, repair services (for example, computers, VCRs), insurance agencies, real estate firms, stockbrokers, and so on. A major growth area is in computer consulting and the knowledge-based industries generally.

2. **Retail businesses.** You only have to go to a major shopping mall to see the possibilities in retailing. There are stores selling shoes, clothes, hats, skis, housewares, sporting goods, ice cream, groceries, and more. Much more. Watch the trends, and you will see new ideas like fancy popcorn stores and cafés with Internet access areas.

3. **Construction firms.** Drive through any big city and you will see huge cranes towering over major construction sites. Would you enjoy supervising such work? Visit some areas where construction firms are building bridges, roads, homes, schools, buildings, and dams. There is a feeling of power and creativity in such work that excites many observers. How about you? Talk to some of the workers and supervisors and learn about the risks and rewards of small construction firms.

4. **Wholesalers.** Have you ever visited a wholesale food warehouse, jewellery centre, or similar wholesale firm? If not, you are missing an important link in the small-business chain, one with much potential. Wholesale representatives often make more money, have more free time, travel more, and enjoy their work more than similar people in retailing.

5. **Manufacturing.** Of course, manufacturing is still an attractive career for tomorrow's graduates. Surveys show that manufacturers make the most money among small-business owners. There are careers for designers, machinists, mechanics, engineers, supervisors, safety inspectors, and a host of other occupations. Visit some small manufacturers in your area and inquire about such jobs to get some experience before starting your own manufacturing business. The high-tech world of today opens up many opportunities, if you are interested.

There are also thousands of small farmers who enjoy the rural life and the pace of farming. Small farms have been in great trouble for the last few years, but some that specialize in exotic or organic crops do quite well. Similarly, many small mining operations attract college and university students who have a sense of adventure. People who are not sure what career they would like to follow have a busy time ahead. They need to visit service firms, construction firms, farms, mines, retailers, wholesalers, and all other kinds of small and large businesses to see the diversity and excitement available in Canadian business.

Small-Business Success and Failure[16]

You can't be naïve about business practices, or you will go broke. There is some debate about how many new small businesses fail each year. There are many false signals about entries and exits. When small business owners go out of business to start new and different businesses, they may be included in the "failure" category when obviously this is not the case. Similarly, when a business changes its form of ownership from partnership to corporation, it may be counted as a failure. Retirements of sole owners may also be in this category.

Thousands of businesses enter and exit the marketplace throughout the year. In most years, entrants that are one year old account for between 15 and 20 percent of the firms in the economy. Although the chances of business survival may be greater than some used to think, keep in mind that even the most optimistic interpretation of the statistics reflects that for the majority of these firms, life is short. Most new entrants exit shortly after birth and fewer than one in five new firms survive to their tenth birthday. Figure 7.4 lists reasons for small-business failures. Managerial incompetence and inadequate financial planning are two of the biggest reasons for these failures.

Choosing the right type of business is critical. Many of the businesses with the lowest failure rates require advanced training to start—veterinary services, dental practices, medical practices, and so on. While training and degrees may buy security, they do not tend to produce much growth. If you want to be both independent and rich, you need to go after growth. Often high-growth businesses, such as technology firms, are not easy to start and are even more difficult to keep going.

In general, it seems that the easiest businesses to start are the ones that tend to have the least growth and the greatest failure rate (e.g., restaurants).[17] The easiest businesses to keep alive are difficult ones to get started (e.g., manufacturing). And the ones that can make you rich are the ones that are both hard to start and hard to keep going (e.g., automobile assembly). See Figure 7.5 to get an idea of the business situations that are most likely to lead to success.

When you decide to start your own business, you must think carefully about what kind of business you want. You are not likely to find everything you

The *Small Business Quarterly* (http://strategis.ic.gc.ca/epic/internet/insbrp-rppe.nsf/vwGenerated InterE/Home) provides a quick and easy-to-read snapshot of the recent performance of Canada's small-business sector. The SBQ is published by the Small Business Policy Branch of Industry Canada.

FIGURE 7.4

CAUSES OF SMALL-BUSINESS FAILURE

The following are some of the causes of small-business failure:

- Plunging in without first testing the waters on a small scale.
- Underpricing or overpricing goods or services.
- Underestimating how much time it will take to build a market.
- Starting with too little capital.
- Starting with too much capital and being careless in its use.
- Going into business with little or no experience and without first learning something about the industry or market.
- Borrowing money without planning just how and when to pay it back.
- Attempting to do too much business with too little capital.

- Not allowing for setbacks and unexpected expenses.
- Buying too much on credit.
- Extending credit too freely.
- Expanding credit too rapidly.
- Failing to keep complete, accurate records, so that the owners drift into trouble without realizing it.
- Carrying habits of personal extravagance into the business.
- Not understanding business cycles.
- Forgetting about taxes, insurance, and other costs of doing business.
- Mistaking the freedom of being in business for oneself for the liberty to work or not, according to whim.

FIGURE 7.5

SITUATIONS FOR SMALL-BUSINESS SUCCESS

The following factors increase the chances of small business success:

- The customer requires a lot of personal attention, as in a beauty parlour.

- The product is not easily made by mass-production techniques (e.g., custom-tailored clothes or custom auto-body work).

- Sales are not large enough to appeal to a large firm (e.g., a novelty shop).

- A large business sells a franchise operation to local buyers. (Don't forget franchising as an excellent way to enter the world of small business.)

- The owner pays attention to new competitors.

- The business is in a growth industry (e.g., computer services or Web design).

want in one business—easy entry, security, and reward. Choose those characteristics that matter the most to you; accept the absence of the others; plan, plan, plan; and then go for it!

Imagine yourself starting a small business. What kind of business would it be? How much competition is there? What could you do to make your business more attractive than those of competitors? Would you be willing to work 60 to 70 hours a week?

LEARNING ABOUT SMALL-BUSINESS OPERATIONS

Hundreds of would-be entrepreneurs of all ages have asked the same question: "How can I learn to run my own business?" Many of these people had no idea what kind of business they wanted to start; they simply wanted to be in business for themselves. That seems to be a major trend among students today.

There are several ways to get into your first business venture:

1. start your own company
2. buy an existing business
3. buy a franchise unit (see Chapter 6).

Here are some suggestions for learning about small business.

Learn from Others

Your search for small-business knowledge might begin by investigating your local area or school for classes on the subject. There are entrepreneurship programs in postsecondary schools throughout Canada. One of the best things about such courses is that they bring together entrepreneurs from diverse backgrounds. (Many entrepreneurs have started businesses as students—see the Spotlight on Small Business box). An excellent way to learn how to run a small business is to talk to others who have already done it. They will tell you that location is critical. They will caution you not to be undercapitalized; that is, not to start without enough money. They will warn you about the problems of finding and retaining good workers. And, most of all, they will tell you to

Spotlight on Small Business

Riding to Victory

Gérard Vroomen and Phil White founded Cervélo Cycles Inc. in 1995 when, as engineering students at McGill University, they decided to market the new time-trial bikes they were developing. Today, Cervélo is the world's leading maker of time-trial bikes. It is internationally recognized as one of the most innovative bike manufacturers the sport has seen in years. From an original $30,000 investment, the company became profitable by 1997 and has grown to a $10-million business, doubling sales annually.

Why has this small business been successful? According to Vroomen, "Our basic philosophy is that we start by having very strong products. It's much easier to market a good product than a bad one." The results speak for themselves. Cervélo cyclists have ridden to victory in 12 Ironman triathlons, two world time-trial championships, and numerous triathlon, track, and road-racing World Cups.

In 2002 Cervélo entered into a major partnership agreement with Team CSC, a top-ranked international team, to be its exclusive bike supplier. "Having our bikes compete in the Tour de France was a real milestone for us," says White. "It was a goal that we set when we started the company eight years ago." According to Bjarne Riis, Team CSC Manager and the 1996 winner of the Tour de France, "Every little edge I can find for my team can prove to be the deciding factor. That's why we'll be on Cervélo this year." The 2003 Tour de France was the first year that Canadian bikes were racing in the Tour.

The company's growing international reputation got a major boost with its affiliation with Team CSC. "With American Tyler Hamilton as the team leader, Cervélo has been able to increase its visibility in the important U.S. market overnight," says Vroomen. "And with nine other nationalities represented on the team, Cervélo has also been making inroads in Europe, where cycling is one of the most important sports."

Cervélo is an example of a small Toronto-based business that has achieved an excellent reputation in its market. Manufactured in Canada, the United States, and Taiwan, the bikes range in price from $1,600 to $6,000. The bikes are distributed in Canada, the United States, Australia, France, and Western Europe. This year, the company is looking for distributors in the United Kingdom, South Africa, Denmark, and Italy. Exports—primarily to the United States and Europe—account for approximately 80 percent of total sales.

You can see Cervélo in the upcoming IMAX movie *Brainpower*. Team CSC and the 2003 Tour de France are the focus of the film. "We chose the Tour de France to show how the human brain works because behind every great athlete is a great mind," said the film's director, Bayley Silleck. This exposure can only add to Cervélo's visibility and awareness.

Sources: "Canadian Bikes at 2003 Tour de France" (August 11, 2003), Department of Foreign Affairs and International Trade. Retrieved from http://www.dfait-maeci.gc.ca/trade/tna-nac/stories67-en.asp; "Cervelo Apparel—Fit, Function, Fast" (2003), Triathlon Magazine. Retrieved May 27, 2004 from http://www.transitiontimes.com/viewstorylocal.cfm?ID=3577&ett2local=NCEast; "IMAX Focusing on Team CSC, Tour de France" (2003), CSC. Retrieved from http://www.csc.com/features/2003/31.shtml; Sahm Adrangi, "Tiny Toronto firm spins success," *The Globe and Mail*, July 26, 2003, sec. B, p. 1; "Cervelo Cycles seeks international distributors" (May 12, 2004), Bicycle Business. Retrieved from http://www.bikebiz.co.uk/daily-news/article.php?id=4091.

keep good records and hire a good accountant and lawyer before you start. Free advice like this is invaluable.

Get Some Experience

There is no better way to learn small-business management than by becoming an apprentice or working for a successful entrepreneur. Many small-business owners got the idea for their businesses from their prior jobs. An industry standard is: Have three years' experience in a comparable business.

Many new entrepreneurs come from corporate management. They are tired of the big-business life or are being laid off because of corporate downsizing. Such managers bring their managerial expertise and enthusiasm with them.

Making Ethical Decisions

Where to Draw the Line?

You and a co-worker have some ideas about how to make a company like your boss's succeed. You are considering quitting your job and starting your own company that will compete directly with your former employer because you are providing similar services. Can you approach other co-workers about working for your new venture? Will you try to lure your old boss's customers to your own business? What are the legal repercussions of doing this? What are your alternatives? What are the consequences of each alternative? What is the most ethical choice?

By running a small business part-time, during your off hours or on weekends, you can experience the rewards of working for yourself while still enjoying a regular paycheque. This is what John Stanton, founder of the Running Room, did when he first started his company. He kept his full-time job as a vice-president in the grocery sector and he opened the Running Room in a house in Edmonton. At first, he only sold cotton T-shirts and running shoes. Four years later, he was confident that the company had growth potential. He quit his job and concentrated on building the Running Room chain. Today, there are more than 60 locations. Learning a business while working for someone else may also save you money because you are less likely to make "rookie mistakes" when you start your own business. (See the Making Ethical Decisions box, though, for a scenario that raises a number of questions.)

Take Over a Successful Firm

Small-business management takes time, dedication, and determination. Owners work long hours and rarely take vacations. After many years, they may feel stuck in their business. They may think they can't get out because they have too much time and effort invested. Consequently, there are some small-business owners out there eager to get away, at least for a long vacation.

This is where you come in. Find a successful businessperson who owns a small business. Tell him or her that you are eager to learn the business and would like to serve an apprenticeship; that is, a training period. Say that at the end of the training period (one year or so), you would like to help the owner or manager by becoming assistant manager. As assistant manager, you would free the owner to take off weekends and holidays, and to take a long vacation— a good deal for him or her. For another year or so, work very hard to learn all about the business—suppliers, inventory, bookkeeping, customers, promotion, and so on. At the end of two years, make the owner this offer: He or she can retire or work only part-time, and you will take over the business. You can establish a profit-sharing plan for yourself plus a salary. Be generous with yourself; you will earn it if you manage the business. You can even ask for 40 percent or more of the profits.

The owner benefits by keeping ownership in the business and making 60 percent of what he or she earned before—without having to work. You benefit by making 40 percent of the profits of a successful firm. This is an excellent deal for an owner about to retire—he or she is able to keep the firm and a healthy profit flow. It is also a clever and successful way to share in the profits of a successful small business without any personal money investment.

If profit sharing doesn't appeal to the owner, you may want to buy the business outright. How do you determine a fair price for a business? Value is based on (1) what the business owns, (2) what it earns, and (3) what makes it unique. Naturally, your accountant will need to help you determine the business's value.

If your efforts to take over the business through either profit sharing or buying fail, you can quit and start your own business fully trained.

Progress Assessment

- What are the criteria to be considered a business establishment by the Business Registrar of Canada?
- List three factors that increase the chances for small-business success.
- Explain how you can learn to run your own business.

MANAGING A SMALL BUSINESS

The number-one reason for small-business failures is poor management. Keep in mind, though, that the term *poor management* covers a number of faults. It could mean poor planning, poor record keeping, poor inventory control, poor promotion, or poor employee relations. Most likely it would include poor capitalization. To help you succeed as a business owner, in the following sections we explore the functions of business in a small-business setting:

- Planning your business.
- Financing your business.
- Knowing your customers (marketing).
- Managing your employees (human resource development).
- Keeping records (accounting).

Although all of the functions are important in both the start-up and management phases of the business, the first two functions—planning and financing—are the primary concerns when you start your business. The remaining functions are the heart of the actual operations once the business is started.

Begin with Planning

It is amazing how many people are eager to start a small business but have only a vague notion of what they want to do. Eventually, they come up with an idea for a business and begin discussing the idea with professors, friends, and other businesspeople. It is at this stage that the entrepreneur needs a business plan. A **business plan** is a detailed written statement that describes the nature of the business, the target market, the advantages the business will have in relation to competition, and the resources and qualifications of the owner(s). A business plan forces potential owners of small businesses to be quite specific about the goods or services they intend to offer. They must analyze the competition, calculate how much money they need to start, and cover other details of operation. A business plan is also mandatory for talking with bankers or other investors.

If you are looking for bank financing, here are some tips. First, pick a bank that serves businesses the size of yours, have a good accountant prepare a

business plan
A detailed written statement that describes the nature of the business, the target market, the advantages the business will have in relation to competition, and the resources and qualifications of the owner(s).

complete set of financial statements and a personal balance sheet, and make an appointment before going to the bank. Go to the bank with an accountant and all the necessary financial information and demonstrate to the banker that you're a person of good character: civic minded and respected in business and community circles. Finally, ask for all the money you need, be specific, and be prepared to personally guarantee the loan.

Writing a Business Plan

A good business plan takes a long time to write, but you've got to convince your readers in five minutes not to throw the plan away. While there is no such thing as a perfect business plan, prospective entrepreneurs do think out the smallest details. Jerrold Carrington of Inroads Capital Partners advises that one of the most important parts of the business plan is the executive summary. The summary has to catch the reader's interest. Bankers receive many business plans every day. "You better grab me up front," says Carrington. The box on page 207 gives you an outline of a comprehensive business plan.

Sometimes one of the most difficult tasks in undertaking complex projects, such as writing a business plan, is knowing where to start. There are many computer software programs on the market to help you get organized. One highly rated business-plan program is Business Plan Pro. You can find online help with the MiniPlan (www.miniplan.com), a free interactive Web tool that guides you through the business-plan writing process.

Getting the completed business plan into the right hands is almost as important as getting the right information in the plan. Finding the funding requires research. Next, we will discuss some of the many sources of money available to new business ventures. All of them call for a comprehensive business plan. The time and effort you invest before starting a business will pay off many times later. With small businesses, the big payoff is survival.

Getting Money to Fund a Small Business

An entrepreneur has several potential sources of capital for a small business, as listed in Figure 7.6. Half of all small and medium-sized enterprises (SMEs) rely on financial services firms to provide them with business financing. While banks provide 55 percent of this financing, credit unions and caisses populaires, finance companies, insurance companies, and venture capital/investment funds also play a significant role in financing SMEs. Government agencies, such as the Business Development Bank of Canada and Canada Business Service Centres, are also an excellent source of financing. Figure 7.7 outlines some of the financial products available from the BDC.

Investors known as **venture capitalists** may finance your project—for a price. Venture capitalists may ask for a hefty stake (as much as 60 percent) in your company in exchange for the cash to start your business. If the venture capitalist demands too large a stake, you could lose control of the business. Since the burst of the dot-com bubble, venture capitalists have tightened the purse strings on how much they are willing to invest in a business (down from \$5–\$30 million to \$2–\$10 million) and have multiplied the return they expect on their investment if the new company is sold (from the cost of the total investment to three or more times the investment before anyone else gets paid).[18] Therefore, if you're a very small company, you don't have a very good chance getting venture capital. You'd have a better

venture capitalists
Individuals or companies that invest in new businesses in exchange for partial ownership of those businesses.

FIGURE 7.6

SOURCES OF FINANCING FOR SMALL AND MEDIUM-SIZED ENTERPRISES (SMEs)

Many companies use multiple sources of financing. Half of all SMEs rely on financial services firms to provide them with business financing. The following indicates the percentage of owners who said they also use this form of financing.

- supplier credit (39%).
- personal savings (35%).
- personal credit cards (33%).
- retained earnings (31%).
- business credit cards (26%).
- personal lines of credit (21%)
- leasing (16%).
- personal loans (14%).
- loans from friends and relatives (10%).
- government lending agencies (7%).
- angel investment (4%).

Source: Canadian Bankers Association, June 2004.

FIGURE 7.7

FINANCIAL PRODUCTS
AVAILABLE FROM THE
BUSINESS DEVELOPMENT
BANK OF CANADA

Co-Vision: Start-Up Financing Solution—Customized term financing up to $100,000 for new businesses demonstrating long-term viability. If requested, BDC can also provide personalized management support. Co-Vision cannot be used for starting a retail business.

Term Financing Solution—Flexible term financing for a variety of commercially viable projects, including expansion projects, plant overhauls, the purchase of existing businesses and the acquisition of fixed assets. In some cases, financing may be used to reconstitute working capital depleted by capital expenditures or to finance sales growth.

Productivity Plus Financing Solution—Up to $5,000,000 for manufacturers looking to increase their productivity. BDC can offer up to 125% of the cost of new and used equipment; the additional 25% covers incidental costs such as installation, training and working capital.

Innovation Financing Solution—Up to $250,000 in working capital to help innovative businesses position themselves to take advantage of new markets and new technologies available to today's global players.

Tourism Investment Fund—The fund helps finance existing tourism operators, or start-ups in viable destinations. It is designed specifically to finance single season tourism infrastructures or operations that have the potential to expand beyond a single season.

Growth Capital for Aboriginal Business—BDC's specialized business advisors offer support and solutions for Aboriginal entrepreneurs looking to increase their company's growth, be it through financing fixed assets, franchise expenses, or start-up costs. Loan amounts range from $25,000 for start-ups to $100,000 for existing businesses, with flexible repayment methods adapted to the cash flow needs of the business.

Venture Capital—BDC Venture Capital is a major venture capital investor in Canada, active at every stage of a company's development cycle, from start-up through expansion. Its focus is on technology-based businesses with high growth potential that are positioned to become dominant players in their markets.

Subordinate Financing—Subordinate financing mimics debt financing because the borrower has the obligation to repay the loan. Moreover, part of the cost is in the form of a fixed interest coupon (a deductible expense). This type of financing can be used for different types of projects such as acquisitions, management buy-outs, expansions and working capital.

angel investors
Private individuals who invest their own money in potentially hot new companies before they go public.

Azure Dynamics Corporation is a leading developer of hybrid electric powertrains for light- and medium-duty commercial vehicles. Azure Dynamics was created to commercialize technology developed by Vizon SciTec, formerly BC Research Inc., an incubator company formed with private investment money. In late 2000, Azure raised capital from angel investors to advance the technology for commercial sales. This prototype hybrid electric vehicle (HEV), powered by Azure and in partnership with London Taxis International, has been launched in London, England. Among this HEV's technologies is a GPS device that switches the vehicle to clean battery power whenever it enters the central city due to the implementation of a congestion tax. Would you consider buying a car that has this technology?

chance finding an angel investor. **Angel investors** are private individuals who invest their own money in potentially hot new companies before they go public.[19] If your proposed venture does require millions of dollars to start, experts recommend that you talk with at least five investment firms and their clients in order to find the right venture capitalists. As you recall from the chapter profile, Chris Emery and Larry Finnson required venture capital financing to keep their business growing.

For more information on financing, visit the Strategis *Sources of Financing* government Website.

Entrepreneurship and Small Business • CHAPTER 7   207

OUTLINE OF A COMPREHENSIVE BUSINESS PLAN

A good business plan is between 25 and 50 pages long and takes at least six months to write.

Cover letter

Only one thing is certain when you go hunting for money to start a business: You won't be the only hunter out there. You need to make potential funders want to read your business plan instead of the hundreds of others on their desks. Your cover letter should summarize the most attractive points of your project in as few words as possible. Be sure to address the letter to the potential investor by name. "To whom it may concern" or "Dear Sir" is not the best way to win an investor's support.

Section 1—Executive Summary

Begin with a two-page or three-page management summary of the proposed venture. Include a short description of the business, and discuss major goals and objectives.

Section 2—Company Background

Describe company operations to date (if any), potential legal considerations, and areas of risk and opportunity. Summarize the firm's financial condition, and include past and current balance sheets, income and cash-flow statements, and other relevant financial records (you will read about these financial statements in Chapter 16). It is also wise to include a description of insurance coverage. Investors want to be assured that death or other mishaps do not pose major threats to the company.

Section 3—Management Team

Include an organization chart, job descriptions of listed positions, and detailed résumés of the current and proposed executives. A mediocre idea with a proven management team is funded more often than a great idea with an inexperienced team. Managers should have expertise in all disciplines necessary to start and run a business. If not, mention outside consultants who will serve in these roles and describe their qualifications.

Section 4—Financial Plan

Provide five-year projections for income, expenses, and funding sources. Don't assume the business will grow in a straight line. Adjust your planning to allow for funding at various stages of the company's growth. Explain the rationale and assumptions used to determine the estimates. Assumptions should be reasonable and based on industry/historical trends. Make sure all totals add up and are consistent throughout the plan. If necessary, hire a professional accountant or financial analyst to prepare these statements.

Stay clear of excessively ambitious sales projections; rather, offer best-case, expected, and worst-case scenarios. These not only reveal how sensitive the bottom line is to sales fluctuations but also serve as good management guides.

Section 5—Capital Required

Indicate the amount of capital needed to commence or continue operations, and describe how these funds are to be used. Make sure the totals are the same as the ones on the cash-flow statement. This area will receive a great deal of review from potential investors, so it must be clear and concise.

Section 6—Marketing Plan

Don't underestimate the competition. Review industry size, trends, and the target market segment. Discuss strengths and weaknesses of the good or service. The most important things investors want to know are what makes the product more desirable than what's already available and whether the product can be patented. Compare pricing to the competition's. Forecast sales in dollars and units. Outline sales, advertising, promotion, and public relations programs. Make sure the costs agree with those projected in the financial statements.

Section 7—Location Analysis

In retailing and certain other industries, the location of the business is one of the most important factors. Provide a comprehensive demographic analysis of consumers in the area of the proposed business as well as a traffic-pattern analysis and vehicular and pedestrian counts.

Section 8—Manufacturing Plan

Describe minimum plant size, machinery required, production capacity, inventory and inventory-control methods, quality control, plant personnel requirements, and so on. Estimates of product costs should be based on primary research.

Section 9—Appendix

Include all marketing research on the good or service (off-the-shelf reports, article reprints, etc.) and other information about the product concept or market size. Provide a bibliography of all the reference materials you consulted. This section should demonstrate that the proposed company won't be entering a declining industry or market segment.

Canada's Venture Capital & Private Equity Association represents Canada's venture capital and private equity industry. Its mission is to promote the development of the Canadian venture capital industry. For information on its events, resources, and industry statistics, visit www.cvca.ca.

It provides information aimed at helping small and medium-sized businesses, companies, and entrepreneurs in Canada find financing from public- and private-sector sources. You can also find a listing of federal and provincial government assistance programs, tax incentives for small businesses, and a listing of financial providers, including venture capitalists.

Obtaining money from banks, venture capitalists, and government sources can be a challenge for most small businesses. (You will learn more about financing in Chapter 17.) Those who do survive the planning and financing of their new ventures are eager to get their businesses up and running. Your success in running a business depends on many factors. Three important factors for success are knowing your customers, managing your employees, and keeping efficient records; these topics will be discussed next.

Progress Assessment

- A business plan is probably the most important document a small-business owner will ever create. There are nine sections in the business plan outline on page 207. Can you describe at least five of those sections now?

- What are four sources of financing for SMEs?

Knowing Your Customers

market
People with unsatisfied wants and needs who have both the resources and the willingness to buy.

One of the most important elements of small-business success is knowing the market. In business, a **market** consists of people with unsatisfied wants and needs who have both the resources and the willingness to buy. For example, we can confidently state that many of our students have the willingness to take a Caribbean cruise during their spring break. However, few of them have the resources necessary to satisfy this want. Would they be considered a good market for the local travel agency to pursue?

Once you have identified your market and its needs, you must set out to fill those needs. The way to meet your customers' needs is to offer top quality at a fair price with great service. Remember, it isn't enough to get customers—you have to keep them. Everything must be geared to bring the customers the satisfaction they deserve.

One of the greatest advantages that small businesses have over larger ones is the ability to know their customers better and to adapt quickly to their ever-changing needs. You will gain more insights about markets in Chapters 14 and 15. Now let's consider the importance of effectively managing the employees who help you serve your market.

Managing Employees

As a business grows, it becomes impossible for an entrepreneur to oversee every detail, even if he or she is putting in 60 hours per week. This means that hiring, training, and motivating employees is critical.

It is not easy to find good, qualified help when you offer less money, skimpier benefits, and less room for advancement than larger firms do. That is one reason why employee relations is such an important part of small-business management. Employees of small companies are often more satisfied with their jobs than are their counterparts in big business. Why? Quite often they find their jobs more challenging, their ideas more accepted, and their bosses more respectful.

Often entrepreneurs reluctantly face the reality that to keep growing, they must delegate authority to others. Nagging questions such as "Who should be delegated authority?" and "How much control should they have?" create perplexing problems.

This can be a particularly touchy issue in small businesses with long-term employees, and in family businesses. As you might expect, entrepreneurs who have built their companies from scratch often feel compelled to promote employees who have been with them from the start—even when those employees aren't qualified to serve as managers. Common sense probably tells you this could be detrimental to the business.

The same can be true of family-run businesses that are expanding. Attitudes such as "You can't fire family" or you must promote certain workers because "they're family" can hinder growth. Entrepreneurs can best serve themselves and the business if they gradually recruit and groom employees for management positions. By doing this, entrepreneurs can enhance trust and support of the manager among other employees and themselves.

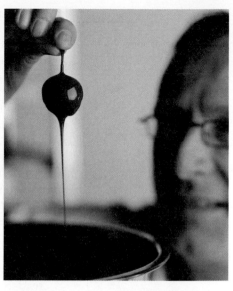

When Heida Thurlow of Chantal Cookware suffered an extended illness, she let her employees handle the work she once had insisted on doing herself. The experience transformed her company from an entrepreneurial company into a managerial one. She says, "Over the long run that makes us stronger than we were." You'll learn more about managing employees in Chapters 11 to 13.

Keeping Records

Small-business owners often say that the most important assistance they received in starting and managing the business involved accounting. A businessperson who sets up an effective accounting system early will save much grief later. Computers simplify record keeping and enable a small-business owner to follow the progress of the business (sales, expenses, profits) on a daily basis. An inexpensive computer system can also help owners with other record-keeping chores, such as inventory control, customer records, and payroll.

A good accountant is invaluable in setting up such systems and showing you how to keep the system operating smoothly. Many business failures are caused by poor accounting practices. A good accountant can help make decisions such as whether to buy or lease equipment and whether to own or rent the building. Help may also be provided for tax planning, financial forecasting, choosing sources of financing, and writing up requests for funds.[20]

Other small-business owners may tell you where to find an accountant experienced in small business. It pays to shop around for advice. You'll learn more about accounting in Chapter 16.

Looking for Help

Small-business owners have learned, sometimes the hard way, that they need outside consulting advice early in the process. This is especially true of legal, tax, and accounting advice but may also be true of marketing, finance, and other areas. Most small and medium-sized firms cannot afford to hire such experts as employees, so they must turn to outside assistance. As a start, ask friends, other entrepreneurs, or family to recommend someone.

A necessary and invaluable aide is a competent, experienced lawyer—one who knows and understands small businesses.[21] Partners have a way of forgetting agreements unless the contract is written by a lawyer and signed.

Chocolaterie Bernard Callebaut Canada was started in 1983 as a manufacturer of what is considered to be the highest-quality line of Canadian-made chocolates and chocolate-related products. Bernard Callebaut arrived from Belgium in 1982 with the idea to produce a quality line of chocolates in North America. His family owned the Callebaut Chocolate Factory in Wieze, Belgium from 1911 until 1980. To maintain quality, Callebaut does not use vegetable oils, animal fats, or artificial additives in its chocolate. Do you know of a business that produces a high-quality product?

Lawyers can help with a variety of matters, including leases, contracts, and protection against liabilities.

Marketing decisions should be made long before a product is produced or a store opened. An inexpensive marketing research study may help you determine where to locate, whom to select as your target market, and what would be an effective strategy for reaching those people. Thus, a marketing consultant with small-business experience can be of great help to you.

Two other invaluable experts are a commercial loan officer and an insurance agent. The commercial account officer can help you design an acceptable business plan and give you valuable financial advice as well as lend you money when you need it.[22] An insurance agent will explain all the risks associated with a small business and how to cover them most efficiently with insurance and other means (e.g., safety devices and sprinkler systems).

Often schools have business professors who will advise small-business owners for a small fee or for free. Some universities have clubs or programs that provide consulting services by master of business administration (MBA) candidates for a nominal fee.

It also is wise to seek the counsel of other small-business owners. Other sources of counsel include local chambers of commerce, the Better Business Bureau, national and local trade associations, (such as the Canadian Federation of Independent Business), the business reference section of your library, and many small-business-related sites on the Internet.

GOING INTERNATIONAL: SMALL-BUSINESS PROSPECTS

As we noted in Chapter 3, the world market is potentially a much larger, much more lucrative market for small businesses than Canada alone. In spite of that potential, most small businesses still do not think internationally, and only a small percentage of small businesses export.

Why are so many companies missing the boat to the huge global markets? Primarily because the voyage involves a few major hurdles: (1) Financing is often difficult to find, (2) many would-be exporters don't know how to get started, (3) potential global businesspeople do not understand the cultural differences of prospective markets, and (4) the bureaucratic paperwork can threaten to bury a small business.

Besides the fact that most of the world's market lies outside of Canada, there are other good reasons for going international. For instance, exporting products can absorb excess inventory, soften downturns in the domestic market, and extend product lives. It can also spice up dull routines.

Small businesses have several advantages over large businesses in international trade:

- Overseas buyers enjoy dealing with individuals rather than with large corporate bureaucracies.
- Small companies can usually begin shipping much faster.
- Small companies provide a wide variety of suppliers.
- Small companies can give more personal service and more undivided attention, because each overseas account is a major source of business to them.

The growth potential of small businesses overseas is phenomenal, and Web-based business applications are helping small businesses cross boundaries like never before. CPI Process Systems Inc., a six-employee import/export

Reaching Beyond Our Borders

Sparkling Success in Cyberspace

www.thaigem.com

Don Kogen went on a backpacking adventure in Asia a decade ago and ended up becoming Thailand's leading Internet entrepreneur at age 26. Kogen was enthralled by the market in Chanthaburi, eastern Thailand, a town where gemstones define the town's way of life. Traders sort sapphires and rubies the way others handle fruits and vegetables. When Kogen first decided to extend his Thai visit, he had to work two jobs to meet his $60-a-month rent. After weeks of begging, he finally talked a local gem trader into paying him a quarter of the already low local wage to cut sapphires into finished jewels. After chipping off too much from a couple of stones, Kogen moved into gem sorting. On his off hours, Kogen learned to speak Thai and sat around the city's market watching traders haggle over stones.

After three years of watching, Kogen decided to try the business himself. He bought low-grade stones from traders who arrived at the market early and then resold them to later-arriving dealers for pennies more. He took out an ad in an American trade magazine and soon had more than 800 mail-order customers in the United States. A new fax machine allowed Kogen to increase orders, reduce delivery times, and save $25,000. He used that money to travel to the gem districts in New York City, Chicago, and San Francisco. Four years later he was earning $250,000.

The business changed dramatically when Kogen began to sell gems over the Internet a month after buying his first PC in 1998. Until the Internet, layers of intermediaries multiplied the price of a gem as much as 1,000 percent from original prices to final retail prices. Kogen's Website, Thaigem.com, cut through all those layers so that stones traded only once from wholesaler to final customer. While 60 percent of his sales are to dealers, 40 percent are to individuals. Thaigem's 2002 revenues were almost $10 million, up from $4.3 million the year before. Online sales accounted for 85 percent of his 2002 revenue.

Kogen sells 200 items a day on eBay and 2,000 a day on Thaigem.com. Kogen isn't the only one selling jewels on the Internet, but he does have certain competitive advantages. He has a worldwide customer base of 68,000 and has earned an excellent reputation (99 percent of his eBay feedback is positive). Another advantage is that the low Thai labour costs are difficult for competitors in more developed countries to beat. "The lesson here is you must know the territory," says Linda Lim, a professor of international business at the University of Michigan. "You'd be surprised how many high-falutin dot-commers ignore this."

Although it's a long way from New York City and Washington, D.C., Chanthaburi suffered a serious blow after the terrorist attacks of September 11, 2001. Since America is the end market for many gemstones, the collapse in consumer confidence in the United States hurt Chanthaburi's businesses. In addition, the halt in travel to the gem markets left many of the skilled stonecutters without work. However, Kogen was able to fight this trend. Although Thaigem did suffer lower sales in September like most other businesses, demand climbed again shortly thereafter, proving to Kogen at least that cyberspace can live up to its potential. Kogen is now hoping to grow even larger by supplying big customers like Wal-Mart and JCPenney. Looks like Thaigem won't lose its lustre anytime soon.

Sources: Robyn Meredith, "From Rocks to Riches," *Forbes*, August 12, 2002, p. 101; and Paul Kangas and Susie Gharib, "Nightly Business Report," *Nightly Business Report*, April 5, 2002

oil-field equipment company, won a contract away from Swiss giant ABB to build a power station in China. CPI won the deal thanks to a strong relationship with small overseas suppliers—a relationship facilitated by frequent e-mail. Dave Hammond, inventor and founder of Wizard Vending, began to push his gum-ball machines into the international market via a Website. In the site's first year, Hammond sold machines in Austria, Belgium, and Germany, and Internet sales accounted for 10 percent of the company's revenues. See the Reaching Beyond Our Borders box for another small business' Internet success story.

Progress Assessment

- Why do many small businesses avoid doing business overseas?
- What are some of the advantages small businesses have over large businesses in selling in global markets?

Summary

1. Explain why people are willing to become entrepreneurs, and describe the attributes of successful entrepreneurs.	**1.** There are many reasons people are willing to take the risks of entrepreneurship. • *What are a few of the reasons people start their own businesses?* Reasons include profit, independence, opportunity, and challenge. • *What are the attributes of successful entrepreneurs?* Successful entrepreneurs are self-directed, self-nurturing, action-oriented, highly energetic, and tolerant of uncertainty.
2. Discuss the importance of small business to the Canadian economy.	**2.** Businesses employing fewer than 50 employees account for almost 95 percent of all employer businesses. • *Why are small businesses important to the Canadian economy?* Small business accounts for almost 43 percent of gross domestic product (GDP). Perhaps more important to tomorrow's graduates, small businesses employ 49 percent of the total private labour force.
3. Summarize the major causes of small-business failure.	**3.** Many people are ready to take the challenge of starting a small business. Unfortunately, more fail than succeed. • *Why do so many small businesses fail?* Many small businesses fail because of managerial incompetence and inadequate financial planning. See Figure 7.4 for a list of causes of small-business failure.
4. Analyze what it takes to start and run a small business.	**4.** Writing a business plan is the first step in organizing a business. See the box on page 207 for what goes into a business plan. • *What sources of funds should someone wanting to start a new business consider investigating?* A new entrepreneur has several sources of capital: personal savings, relatives, banks, finance companies, venture capital organizations, government agencies, and more. • *What are some of the special problems that small-business owners have in dealing with employees?* Small-business owners often have difficulty finding competent employees and grooming employees for management responsibilities. • *Where can budding entrepreneurs find help in starting their businesses?* Help can be found from many sources: accountants, lawyers, marketing researchers, loan officers, insurance agents, the BDC, and even professors.
5. Outline the advantages and disadvantages small businesses have in entering global markets.	**5.** The future growth of some small businesses is in foreign markets. • *What are some advantages small businesses have over large businesses in global markets?*

Foreign buyers enjoy dealing with individuals rather than large corporations because (1) small companies provide a wider variety of suppliers and can ship products more quickly and (2) small companies give more personal service.

- **Why don't more small businesses start trading internationally?**
There are several reasons: (1) financing is often difficult to find, (2) many people don't know how to get started, (3) many do not understand the cultural differences in foreign markets, and (4) the bureaucratic red tape is often overwhelming.

Key Terms

angel investors 206
business
    establishment 197
business plan 204
employer business 197

entrepreneurial
    team 191
entrepreneurship 186
incubators 195
intrapreneurs 194

market 208
micropreneurs 191
small business 197
venture capitalists 205

Developing Workplace Skills

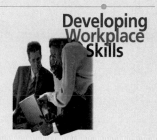

1. Find issues of *Entrepreneur*, *Success*, and *Profit* magazines in the library or on the Internet. Read about the entrepreneurs who are heading today's dynamic new businesses. Write a profile about one entrepreneur.

2. Select a small business that looks attractive as a career possibility for you. Talk to at least one person who manages such a business. Ask how he or she started the business. Ask about financing, personnel problems (hiring, firing, training, scheduling), accounting problems, and other managerial matters. Prepare a summary of your findings, including whether the job was rewarding, interesting, and challenging—and why or why not.

3. Contact a government agency such as Export Development Canada or Business Development Bank of Canada. Write a brief summary of the services that they provide for small businesses. (Hint: Each organization has a Website: www.edc.ca and www.bdc.ca.)

4. Select a small business in your area that has failed. List the factors you think led to its failure. Compile a list of actions the business owners might have taken to keep the company in business.

5. Contact a local bank and make an appointment to speak with a commercial accounts officer. Ask this person what an entrepreneur should consider if she or he is looking for financing. Discuss other sources of financing that might be available to an entrepreneur. Find out what resources this bank has available to assist small-business owners. Bring this information to class and share it with your peers.

Taking It To The Net

Purpose

To assess your potential to succeed as an entrepreneur and to evaluate a sample business plan.

Exercise

1. Go to www.bizmove.com/other/quiz.htm and take the interactive entrepreneurial quiz to find out if you have the qualities to be a successful entrepreneur.

2. If you have entrepreneurial traits and decide you would like to start your own business, you will need to develop a business plan. Go to www.quicken.com/small_business/cch/tools/retailer.rtf and review the business plan for Joe's Redhots. Although Joe's plan does not follow the same format as the business plan outline on page 207, does it contain all of the necessary information listed in the outline? If not, what is missing?

Practising Management Decisions

Case

Starting a Small Business at School

Amanda Harburn, ' a fourth-year student at Mount Royal College, was named the 2004 CIBC Student Entrepreneur of the Year. She was awarded $2,000 for the development and operation of Prestige Dance Academy Inc., a full-service dance studio for children and adults in Calgary. Her business offers a wide range of programs including jazz, ballet, music theatre, hip hop, pre-school, Mom & Me, and private lessons. Amanda was selected from among three finalists who competed in the annual CIBC Student Entrepreneur of the Year Award presented by CIBC and ACE (Advancing Canadian Entrepreneurship Inc.).

One of the judges was the 2003 Student Entrepreneur of the Year, Oliver Towstiak-Davis. In Grade 8, Oliver decided he wanted to make his own spending money while having control over when he would work. Green Meadows Lawn Services is his customer-focused, full-service landscaping company that offers personalized service to its clients. Services range from lawn care to garden design and installation to interlocking brick.

Founded in 1987, ACE is a national, not-for-profit organization. ACE provides and promotes education, training, and instruction to Canadian youth on entrepreneurship and the formation and operation of businesses. ACE entrepreneurship training programs are available to students on 47 university and college campuses across Canada. The CIBC Student Entrepreneur of the Year Award is presented to a full-time Canadian college or university student running his or her own business with at least 51 percent ownership.

Decision Questions

1. What are the advantages and potential problems of starting a business while in school?

2. What kinds of entrepreneurs are operating around your school? Talk to them and learn from their experiences.

3. What opportunities exist for satisfying student needs at your school? Pick one idea, write a business plan, and discuss it in class (unless it is so good you don't want to share it; in that case, good luck).

Source: www.acecanada.ca, May 29, 2004.

Video Case

It's In the Bag: Joe-to-Go

Jerry Andrews was a typical soccer dad: hauling kids to games, bringing snacks, and cheering on the sidelines. One day he volunteered to bring coffee to an early morning game. Later he realized that it wasn't going to be easy getting a dozen cups of hot coffee to the game, especially for Andrews, who was a polio victim since childhood. That night Andrews and his friends talked about the problem of carrying the hot coffee. The idea of a disposable thermos bag came up, and led to a major entrepreneurial idea. Why not call the bag Joe-to-Go? (Joe is a slang term for coffee.) Fortunately, special challenges call for creative solutions and creative solutions are what entrepreneurship is all about. Entrepreneurship has many pitfalls and roadblocks. You have to be passionate and realistic to overcome such barriers. You may have a good idea, but is it marketable? Where will you get the money to start? To be a successful entrepreneur it helps to be self-directed, action-oriented, and highly energetic. You have to be your own cheerleader. You also have to be tolerant of uncertainty since there are no guarantees in entrepreneurship. On the other hand, it is rewarding to work for yourself and to be your own boss. With the right amount of planning, including a good business plan, you just might succeed.

Andrews knew intuitively who his customers were. Still he needed to find help in turning this idea into a viable product. Outside design and production people helped Andrews find just the right product. He also sought advice from accountants, lawyers, marketing researchers, insurance agents, and small-business advisors. Retailers who could reach those customers and tell them about the benefits of a bag that would keep coffee hot were vital. Luckily, his only investor was a salesperson who was eager to find businesses that would promote the Joe-to-Go bags in their stores.

Andrews learned one way to reach coffee retailers was to go to coffee shows where Joe-to-Go samples were displayed prominently. Everyone loved them, but nobody was buying them. Although sales were slow, retailers agreed this was a great product. One company that saw the potential of Joe-to-Go was Dunkin' Donuts. The company saw the potential of selling more coffee to go and felt customers may even buy a few extra donuts to go too.

Other companies soon followed Dunkin' Donuts' lead. Andrews decided to license his product. Therefore, he gets so much a box for every box sold—box after box after box. Companies are free to label the box anything they like. Some call it Joe-to-Go, others add their own name. Dunkin' Donuts, for example, calls it Box of Joe. A major victory for Andrews was getting Starbucks to carry the product. When Andrews would go to a Starbucks that didn't have the product, he would haul one out and show it to them. They would be impressed and orders would pour in.

It took a great deal of patience and persistence to make Joe-to-Go pay off. There's freedom in owning your own business, but little security. Thankfully, there are always new opportunities and new challenges. Being an entrepreneur makes it exciting to get up each morning to see what the day will bring. And that by itself is a kind of success.

Discussion Questions

1. Have you or anyone you know thought of an innovative solution to a problem that could be turned into a successful product like Joe-to-Go? Did it make it to market? If so, what kind of help was needed to move the solution from the idea stage to reality? If it did not make it to market, why not? What could have been done differently to make it a success?

2. Do you have what it takes to become an entrepreneur? Why do you think this?

3. Often people with disabilities have challenges that are not readily apparent to others. What opportunities does that present for new entrepreneurs?

4. Does Jerry Andrews' success make you more interested in becoming an entrepreneur? What are the advantages of working for yourself rather than for someone else?

PART 3

Chapter 8

Management and Leadership

Learning Goals

After you have read and studied this chapter, you should be able to

1 Explain how the changes that are occurring in the business environment are affecting the management function.

2 Describe the four functions of management.

3 Relate the planning process and decision making to the accomplishment of company goals.

4 Describe the organizing function of management.

5 Explain the differences between leaders and managers, and describe the various leadership styles.

6 Summarize the five steps of the control function of management.

Profile

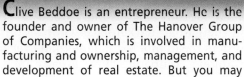

Getting to Know Clive Beddoe of WestJet Airlines Ltd.

Clive Beddoe is an entrepreneur. He is the founder and owner of The Hanover Group of Companies, which is involved in manufacturing and ownership, management, and development of real estate. But you may know him best as being one of the four founders of an organization called WestJet Airlines Ltd.

In 1996, WestJet began by offering low-fare airline travel to western Canada. Six months later, the company was making money. Today, WestJet has routes across Canada and the company accounts for approximately 30 percent of domestic air travel. There are plans to soon add transborder routes. With a focus on having a low cost structure and being as efficient as possible, WestJet has had 28 consecutive quarters of profitability. In 2003, revenue of $680 million generated profits of $60.5 million.

WestJet is a successful company in a tough industry sector. What has contributed to WestJet's success? "In the end it all comes back to one simple thing … the relationship we have with our people," commented Beddoe. "If we have good relations with our employees, then the employees create good relationships with their customers."

Beddoe is the President, CEO, and Executive Chairman of WestJet. Over the years, he has won numerous awards for his leadership. Some examples include Alberta's Most Respected Leader (2004), Top CEO in Canada (2003), Distinguished Business Leader Award (2003), and Outstanding Business Leader of the Year (2002). In 2000, the WestJet founders received the Worldwide Award for Teamwork. While he modestly credits his team and his employees for the success of WestJet, there can be no doubt that it is Beddoe's leadership, creativity, and passion for the business that has impacted the company.

When asked what defines his leadership style, Beddoe stated simply, "I don't know how I lead, I just do what comes naturally to me." Beddoe leads by example. It is not uncommon to see him greet passengers, sell tickets, or even change tires. "Customer service is everything, and part of that is making sure people appreciate it whenever they fly with us," says Beddoe. Employees are encouraged to create a welcoming and fun atmosphere for their "guests." Although low prices lure people to WestJet, it is the company's quirkiness that keeps customers coming back. Despite the stripped-down service (usually no meals, movies, or hot towels), passengers can always count on WestJet's flight attendants for a smile, a corny joke, or even an in-flight toilet paper rolling contest.

In this chapter, you will read about management and the changes occurring in this area. You will also read some examples of how WestJet, under Beddoe's leadership, has become so successful. Like Beddoe, most leaders and managers today are flexible and open to new ideas. They see opportunity and act much faster than they did in the past. They tend to give their workers more responsibility and authority and act more like leaders (visionaries) than hands-on managers who tell people what to do and how to do it.

Sources: Kali Pearson, "10 Trailblazers" (May 2002), PROFIT Magazine. Retrieved from http://www.profitguide.com/magazine/article.jsp?content=926#8; "WestJet CEO Passionate About People" (September 26, 2002), Wilfrid Laurier University. Retrieved from www.wlu.ca/~wwwsbe/sbe2000/images/busleader/Beddoe.PDF; "Clive Beddoe named U of C's 2003 Distinguished Business Leader Award" (January 6, 2003), University of Calgary. Retrieved from http://www.fp.ucalgary.ca/unicomm/news/Jan_03/beddoe.htm; Anthony Davis, "Sky high" (March 2004), PROFIT Guide. Retrieved from http://www.profitguide.com/shared/print.jsp?content= 20040213_171556_4580; Andy Holloway, "All-Star Execs—Top CEO Clive Beddoe" (April 26, 2004), Canadian Business. Retrieved from http://www.canadianbusiness.com/allstars/best_CEO.html; http://www.theglobeandmail.com/servlet/ArticleNews/ TPPrint/LAC/20040508/RWESTJET08/TPBusiness; "What's On Their Minds?" (May 2004), Alberta Venture. Retrieved from http://www.albertaventure.com/articles/archived.cfm?id=3448.

MANAGERIAL CHALLENGES

The need to manage change has become increasingly important in light of today's emphasis on speed in the global marketplace. Global competition is just a click away. National borders mean much less now than ever before, and cooperation and integration among companies have greatly increased. The federal government's innovation strategy (discussed in Chapters 1 and 4) recognizes that organizations must integrate knowledge and innovation if they are to be globally competitive.

The business scandals of the early 2000s put managers under as much scrutiny as they faced at the end of the 19th century, when they were criticized as **robber barons** because of their questionable competitive tactics.[1] Responding to public criticism adds new challenges to already pressure-filled jobs.[2]

Another current source of pressure on managers is the constant change occurring in most industries. For example, Student Express Ltd. of Richmond Hill, Ontario provides student transportation. In 2001, Student Express was struggling to keep up with the volume of calls coming into its charter department, which grew 45 percent in 2000. Employees were stressed out and working too much overtime, and the company was receiving complaints about declining service levels. "There's zero tolerance for error in our industry," says Marnie Walker, president of Student Express. "If a bus is a half-hour late, that's not good enough." To solve this problem, Walker assembled an employee task-force charged with fixing it. It took nine months, but the result was changes in process and technology. Walker quickly noticed a difference in the volume the company could handle, and when it surveyed customers again, "they were delighted."[3] Rapid changes make it more important than ever to have a clear goal that enables the company to stay focused.

As we noted in Chapter 1, the acceleration of technological change has increased the need for a new breed of worker, one who is more educated and more skilled than workers in the past. These new workers (sometimes called knowledge workers) demand more freedom of operation and different managerial styles. The increasing diversity of the workforce is creating additional challenges. Furthermore, because the workforce is becoming increasingly educated and self-directed, many managerial jobs are being eliminated. The corporate term for this is *downsizing* or *rightsizing*, but for the managers, a better term would be *shocking loss of jobs and income*.

The federal government's innovation strategy also recognizes the importance of achieving excellence. The government's initiatives, as outlined in Achieving Excellence and Knowledge Matters, should benefit companies as they continue to adapt to the constantly changing business environment.

robber barons
Capitalists of the 19th century whose wealth came, in part, through dubious, if not criminal acts.

Many of today's workers are called "knowledge workers" because they have the education and skill to compete with companies anywhere in the world. Much of that learning comes from community colleges, universities, and online learning centres of all kinds. What skills will be essential to make you more competitive in tomorrow's job market?

Managers' Roles Are Changing

Managers must practise the art of getting things done through organizational resources (e.g., workers, financial resources, information, and equipment). At one time, managers were called bosses, and their job consisted of telling people what to do and watching over them to be sure they did it. Bosses tended to reprimand those who didn't do things correctly and generally acted stern. Many managers still behave that way. Perhaps you've witnessed such behaviour.

Today, management is becoming more progressive. Many managers are being educated to guide, train, support, motivate, and coach employees rather than to tell them what to do. Managers of high-tech firms realize that workers often know much more about technology than they do. Thus, most modern managers emphasize teamwork and cooperation rather than discipline and order giving.[4] Managers in some high-tech firms and in progressive firms of all kinds tend to be friendly and generally treat employees as partners rather than unruly workers; many even dress more casually than before.

In the past, a worker would expect to work for the same company for many years, maybe even a lifetime. Similarly, companies would hire people and keep them for a long time. Today, many companies don't hesitate to lay off employees, and employees don't hesitate to leave if their needs are not being met. Traditional long-term contracts between management and employees—and the accompanying trust—are often no longer there. This increases the difficulty of the management task because managers must earn the trust of their employees, which includes rewarding them and finding other ways to encourage them to stay in the firm.[5]

In general, management is experiencing a revolution. Managers in the future are likely to be working in teams and to be assuming completely new roles in the firm. We'll discuss these roles and the differences between managers and leaders in detail later in the chapter.

What this means for you and other graduates of tomorrow is that management will demand a new kind of person: a skilled communicator and team player as well as a planner, coordinator, organizer, and supervisor. These trends will be addressed in the next few chapters to help you decide whether management is the kind of career you would like.

Many managers today are working in teams, and this means working *with* employees rather than simply directing them. These teams are likely to be ethnically diverse and include people of varied ages and backgrounds. Since managers will function primarily as trainers, coaches, and motivators of teams, it is expected that members of the team will do year-end evaluations of the manager and vice-versa. How do you think most managers will react to having lower-level employees evaluate *their* effectiveness?

FUNCTIONS OF MANAGEMENT

Well known management consultant Peter Drucker says that managers give direction to their organizations, provide leadership, and decide how to use organizational resources to accomplish goals. Such descriptions give you some idea of what managers do. In addition to those tasks, managers today must deal with conflict resolution, create trust in an atmosphere where trust has been badly shaken, and help create balance between work lives and family lives.[6] Managers must also effectively and efficiently use organizational resources such as buildings, equipment, and supplies. Managers look at the big picture, and their decisions make a major difference in organizations. The following definition of management provides the outline of this chapter: **management** is the process used to accomplish organizational goals through planning, organizing, leading, and controlling people and other organizational resources. (Figure 8.1 summarizes this process.)

Planning includes anticipating trends and determining the best strategies and tactics to achieve organizational goals and objectives. One of those

management
The process used to accomplish organizational goals through planning, organizing, leading, and controlling people and other organizational resources.

planning
A management function that includes anticipating trends and determining the best strategies and tactics to achieve organizational goals and objectives.

FIGURE 8.1

WHAT MANAGERS DO

Some modern managers perform all of these tasks with the full cooperation and participation of workers. Empowering employees means allowing them to participate more fully in decision making.

Planning
- Setting organizational goals.
- Developing strategies to reach those goals.
- Determining resources needed.
- Setting precise standards.

Organizing
- Allocating resources, assigning tasks, and establishing procedures for accomplishing goals.
- Preparing a structure (organization chart) showing lines of authority and responsibility.
- Recruiting, selecting, training, and developing employees.
- Placing employees where they'll be most effective.

Leading
- Guiding and motivating employees to work effectively to accomplish organizational goals and objectives.
- Giving assignments.
- Explaining routines.
- Clarifying policies.
- Providing feedback on performance.

Controlling
- Measuring results against corporate objectives.
- Monitoring performance relative to standards.
- Rewarding outstanding performance.
- Taking corrective action when necessary.

organizing
A management function that includes designing the structure of the organization and creating conditions and systems in which everyone and everything work together to achieve the organization's goals and objectives.

leading
Creating a vision for the organization and guiding, training, coaching, and motivating others to work effectively to achieve the organization's goals and objectives.

controlling
A management function that involves establishing clear standards to determine whether or not an organization is progressing toward its goals and objectives, rewarding people for doing a good job, and taking corrective action if they are not.

objectives is to please customers. The trend today is to have planning teams to help monitor the environment, find business opportunities, and watch for challenges. Planning is a key management function because the other functions depend heavily on having a good plan.

Organizing includes designing the structure of the organization and creating conditions and systems in which everyone and everything work together to achieve the organization's goals and objectives. Many of today's organizations are being designed around the customer. The idea is to design the firm so that everyone is working to please the customer at a profit. Thus, organizations must remain flexible and adaptable because customer needs change, and organizations must either change along with them or risk losing their business. For example, traditional bookstores had to go on the Internet to keep from losing business to Internet booksellers.

Leading means creating a vision for the organization and communicating, guiding, training, coaching, and motivating others to work effectively to achieve the organization's goals and objectives. The trend is to empower ➤P. 19◀ employees, giving them as much freedom as possible to become self-directed and self-motivated. This function was once known as directing; that is, telling employees exactly what to do. In many smaller firms, that is still the role of managers. In most large modern firms, however, managers no longer tell people exactly what to do because knowledge workers and others often know how to do their jobs better than the manager. Nonetheless, leadership is necessary to keep employees focused on the right tasks at the right time along with training, coaching, motivating, and the other leadership tasks. One key to success is for workers to trust the decision-making skills of their boss.[7]

Controlling involves establishing clear standards to determine whether an organization is progressing toward its goals and objectives, rewarding people for doing a good job, and taking corrective action if they are not. Basically, it means measuring whether what actually occurs meets the organization's goals.

The four functions just addressed—planning, organizing, leading, and controlling—are the heart of management, so let's explore them in more detail. The process begins with planning; we'll look at that right after the Progress Assessment.

- What are some of the new challenges facing managers today?
- What's the definition of *management* used in this chapter?
- What are the four functions of management?

Progress Assessment

PLANNING: CREATING A VISION BASED ON VALUES

Planning, the first managerial function, involves setting the organizational vision, goals, and objectives. Executives rate planning as the most valuable tool in their workbench—80 percent of respondents to a managerial survey said they used it.[8] Part of the planning process involves the creation of a vision for the organization. A **vision** is more than a goal; it's an encompassing explanation of why the organization exists and where it's trying to head. A vision gives the organization a sense of purpose and a set of values that, together, unite workers in a common destiny. Managing an organization without first establishing a vision can be counterproductive. It's like motivating everyone in a rowboat to get really excited about going somewhere, but not telling them exactly where. As a result, the boat will just keep changing directions rather than speeding toward an agreed-on goal.

Usually employees work with managers to design a **mission statement,** which is an outline of the organization's fundamental purposes. A meaningful mission statement should address:

Mega Bloks Inc. manufactures and markets fun and educational construction toys. Mega Bloks was founded in 1967 by Vic and Rita Bertrand and it is now under the leadership of their sons, Vic Bertrand Jr. and Marc Bertrand. Mega Bloks' mission statement is to "be the most dynamic and innovative toy company, building quality products that are expandable and universal." The company's goal is to "achieve operational excellence to serve our customer base of parents and children with high-quality toys that encourage creativity and learning." Based on our discussion of mission statements, what is missing from Mega Bloks' statement? Does it really matter?

- The organization's self-concept.
- Company philosophy and goals.
- Long-term survival.
- Customer needs.
- Social responsibility.
- The nature of the company's product.

vision
An encompassing explanation of why the organization exists and where it's trying to head.

mission statement
An outline of the fundamental purposes of an organization.

WestJet's company vision encompasses the many stakeholders that impact its success. WestJet's vision is to "be the leading low-fare airline that: People want to work with … Customers want to fly … and Shareholders want to invest with." The company's mission statement is "to enrich the lives of everyone in WestJet's world by providing safe, friendly, affordable air travel." From what you have read of this company, or experienced, do you think that these statements accurately reflect the company? Figure 8.2 contains Canadian Tire Financial Services' mission statement. How well does this mission statement address all of the issues listed above?

Canadian Tire's vision comes to life through our Team Values:

We are *learners* ... who thrive in a challenging and fast-paced environment.

We are *committed* ... to operate with honesty, integrity and respect.

We are *owners* ... with a passion to continuously improve.

We are *driven* ... to help customers achieve their goals.

We are *accountable* ... to ourselves and each other.

We are *leaders* ... who perform with heart.

The Canadian Tire Way is our foundation and inspiration that will continue to guide our future growth and success.

FIGURE 8.2

CANADIAN TIRE FINANCIAL SERVICES MISSION STATEMENT

goals
The broad, long-term accomplishments an organization wishes to attain.

objectives
Specific, short-term statements detailing how to achieve the organization's goals.

SWOT analysis
A planning tool used to analyze an organization's strengths, weaknesses, opportunities, and threats.

strategic planning
The process of determining the major goals of the organization and the policies and strategies for obtaining and using resources to achieve those goals.

The mission statement becomes the foundation for setting specific goals and selecting and motivating employees. **Goals** are the broad, long-term accomplishments an organization wishes to attain. Goals need to be mutually agreed on by workers and management. Thus, goal setting is often a team process.

Objectives are specific, short-term statements detailing how to achieve the organization's goals. One of your goals for reading this chapter, for example, may be to learn basic concepts of management. An objective you could use to achieve this goal is to answer correctly the chapter's Progress Assessment questions. Objectives must be measurable. For example, you can measure your progress in answering questions by determining what percentage you answer correctly over time.

Planning is a continuous process. It's unlikely that a plan that worked yesterday would be successful in today's market. Most planning follows a pattern. The procedure you would follow in planning your life and career is basically the same as that used by businesses for their plans. Planning answers several fundamental questions for businesses:

1. What is the situation now? What trends are being observed in the business environment? What opportunities exist for meeting customers' needs? What products and customers are most profitable or will be most profitable? Why do people buy (or not buy) our products? Who are our major competitors? What threats are there to our business? These questions are part of what is called the **SWOT analysis.** This is an analysis of an organization's **s**trengths, **w**eaknesses, **o**pportunities, and **t**hreats. The company begins such a process with a general review of the business situation. Then it identifies its internal strengths and weaknesses, *relative to its competitors*. These strengths and weaknesses are for the most part within the control of the organization. Next, a business environment analysis (you were introduced to some elements, such as the legal environment, in Chapter 1) is conducted. Opportunities and threats in the marketplace are identified—and, while they cannot always be controlled, they most definitely impact the organization. Given all of this information gathered in the SWOT analysis, a company can then create an action plan to address the business situation identified. Figure 8.3 lists some of the potential issues companies consider when conducting a SWOT analysis. The Spotlight on Small Business box illustrates some additional examples.

2. Where do we want to go? How much growth do we want? What is our profit goal? What are our social objectives? What are our personal development objectives?

3. How can we get there from here? This is the most important part of planning. It takes four forms: strategic, tactical, operational, and contingency (see Figure 8.4).

Strategic planning determines the major goals of the organization. It provides the foundation for the policies, procedures, and strategies for obtaining and using resources to achieve those goals. In this definition, policies are broad

Potential Internal STRENGTHS
- an acknowledged market leader
- core competencies in key areas
- proven and respected management team

Potential Internal WEAKNESSES
- no clear strategic direction
- weak market image
- subpar profitability

Potential External OPPORTUNITIES
- falling trade barriers in attractive foreign markets
- new government policies (e.g., incentives for R&D, lower taxes, industry deregulation)
- increases in market demand (due to changing buyer needs and tastes, growing incomes)

Potential External THREATS
- recession and changing (negative) economic conditions
- introduction of substitute products (by competitors)
- costly regulatory requirements

FIGURE 8.3

SWOT MATRIX

This matrix identifies potential strengths, weaknesses, opportunities, and threats organizations may consider in a SWOT analysis.

guides to action, and strategies determine the best way to use resources. At the strategic planning stage, the company decides which customers to serve, what goods or services to sell, and the geographic areas in which the firm will compete. Often an opportunity will arise that doesn't fit into the strategy. New customers may emerge and new product ideas may be introduced. But if those customers or products don't fit into the long-term strategy, the company can ignore them to maintain a clear focus. Every firm faces unique challenges that influence what the strategic plans must be. Some firms, for example, need to cut costs, while others need to improve performance, and still others need to increase their profits.

In today's rapidly changing environment, strategic planning is becoming more difficult because changes are occurring so fast that plans—even those set for just months into the future—may soon be obsolete.[9] Therefore, some companies are making shorter-term plans that allow for quick responses to customer needs and requests. The goal is to be flexible and responsive to the market. For example, Yahoo records every click made by every visitor, accumulating some 400 billion pieces of data every day—the equivalent of 800,000 books. Why do Yahoo's managers do it? So they can determine what consumers are interested in and adapt their offerings accordingly.

Tactical planning is the process of developing detailed, short-term statements about what is to be done, who is to do it, and how it is to be done. Tactical planning is normally done by managers or teams of managers at *lower* levels of the organization, whereas strategic planning is done by the *top* managers of the firm (e.g., the president and vice presidents of the organization). Tactical planning, for example, involves setting annual budgets and deciding on other details and activities necessary to meet the strategic objectives. If the strategic plan of a truck manufacturer, for example, is to sell more trucks in northern Canada, the tactical plan might be to fund more research of northern truck drivers' wants and needs, and to plan advertising to reach those people.

tactical planning
The process of developing detailed, short-term statements about what is to be done, who is to do it, and how it is to be done.

Spotlight on Small Business

Taking a SWOT at the Competition

www.alumiplate.com

David Dayton is the CEO of AlumiPlate, a small metal-coating company. As part of the company's annual strategic planning process, Dayton did a SWOT analysis. SWOT, remember, stands for strengths, weaknesses, opportunities, and threats. The analysis gave Dayton a few areas to focus on for the next year. For example, he found that one opportunity for the company was the high barrier to competition; that is, it is not easy to get into the metal-coating business. This could create more opportunities for AlumiPlate as it can take advantage of its strengths in this market without having to worry about additional competitors. Dayton found that the company's proprietary aluminum coating technology was one of its best strengths. Several weaknesses included the company's lack of high-volume production and the heavy demands that were being placed on key personnel.

Some other strengths that CEOs like Dayton might look for include special skills, motivations, technology, or financial capacities. Weaknesses may include lack of capital, shortages of skilled workers, or unproven products. Opportunities are positive circumstances that, if exploited, may boost the company's success. They include things like untapped markets, promising customer relationships, and weak competitors. Threats include both clearly visible threats (such as pending regulations) and potential threats (such as new competitors or changes in consumer tastes). Certainly, the emergence of the Internet has proven to be a threat to those businesses that did not move as quickly as their competitors in tapping this opportunity. This was evident from the sale of automobiles and computers to the sale of insurance and zoo equipment. The chance to go on the Internet and sell products almost anywhere is a real opportunity for some companies that have the structure in place and the resources to compete effectively on this platform.

Sources: Mark Henricks, "Analyze This," *Entrepreneur*, June 1999, pp. 72–75; Steve Glickman, "SWOT Analysis Worthwhile," *London Free Press*, September 28, 2002; "Department of Energy Awards $345,000 to the Eight Northern Indian Pueblos Council Community Reuse Organization," *Regulatory Intelligence Data*, August 28, 2002; and Fred L. Fry, Charles R. Stoner and Richard E. Hattwick, *Business: An Integrative Approach*, 3rd Ed. (Burr Ridge, IL.: McGraw-Hill/Irwin, 2004), pp. 300–301.

FIGURE 8.4

PLANNING FUNCTIONS

Very few firms bother to make contingency plans. If something changes the market, such companies may be slow to respond. Most organizations do strategic, tactical, and operational planning.

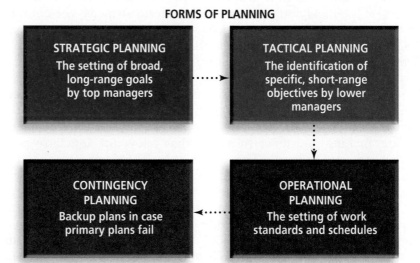

FORMS OF PLANNING

STRATEGIC PLANNING
The setting of broad, long-range goals by top managers

TACTICAL PLANNING
The identification of specific, short-range objectives by lower managers

CONTINGENCY PLANNING
Backup plans in case primary plans fail

OPERATIONAL PLANNING
The setting of work standards and schedules

operational planning
The process of setting work standards and schedules necessary to implement the company's tactical objectives.

Operational planning is the process of setting work standards and schedules necessary to implement the company's tactical objectives. Whereas strategic planning looks at the organization as a whole, operational planning focuses on specific supervisors, department managers, and individual employees. The operational plan is the department manager's tool for daily and weekly operations. An operational plan may include, say, the specific dates for certain truck parts to be completed and the quality specifications those parts must meet. You will read about operations management in more detail in Chapter 10.

Contingency planning is the process of preparing alternative courses of action that may be used if the primary plans don't achieve the organization's objectives. The economic and competitive environments change so rapidly that it's wise to have alternative plans of action ready in anticipation of such changes. For example, if an organization doesn't meet its sales goals by a certain date, the contingency plan may call for more advertising or a cut in prices at that time.

Crisis planning is a part of contingency planning that involves reacting to sudden changes in the environment. For example, the global outbreak of SARS in 2003 forced many health agencies around the world to develop contingency plans to respond to this atypical pneumonia. With more than 800 deaths in 30 countries, this planning was not evident only in government agencies and the health care industry; some companies also saw opportunities for their business.

Morneau Sobeco provides global benefits consulting, administration systems, and outsourcing services. It encourages companies to re-evaluate their thinking regarding contingency planning and the importance of anticipating healthcare related emergencies (HREs). While there was widespread media attention on SARS, other diseases, such as pneumonia and influenza, lead to more deaths annually in Canada. Morneau Sobeco believes that most companies view contingency planning solely as a tool to prevent operational shutdowns. A company should be able to mitigate the potential damage and financial loss resulting from an unforeseen emergency or catastrophe. The benefits of developing an HRE contingency plan are numerous. However, the main goals of such initiatives are ensuring business continuity, reducing risk to employees and their dependents, and maintaining productivity, as well as minimizing the possibility of litigation.[10]

Planning is a key management function because the other management functions depend on having good plans. Instead of creating detailed strategic plans, the leaders of market-based companies (companies that respond quickly to changes in competition or to other environmental changes) set direction. The idea is to stay flexible, listen to customers, and seize opportunities when they come, whether or not those opportunities were expected. The opportunities, however, must fit into the company's overall goals and objectives or the company could lose its focus. Clearly, then, much of management and planning involves decision making.

> **contingency planning**
> The process of preparing alternative courses of action that may be used if the primary plans don't achieve the organization's objectives.

Decision Making: Finding the Best Alternative

All management functions involve some kind of decision making. **Decision making** is choosing among two or more alternatives. It sounds easier here than it is in practice. In fact, decision making is the heart of all the management functions. The rational decision-making model is a series of steps managers often follow to make logical, intelligent, and well-founded decisions. These steps can be thought of as the seven Ds of decision making:

> **decision making**
> Choosing among two or more alternatives.

1. Define the situation.
2. Describe and collect needed information.
3. Develop alternatives.
4. Develop agreement among those involved.
5. Decide which alternative is best.
6. Do what is indicated (begin implementation).
7. Determine whether the decision was a good one and follow up.

problem solving
The process of solving the everyday problems that occur. Problem solving is less formal than decision making and usually calls for quicker action.

brainstorming
Coming up with as many solutions to a problem as possible in a short period of time with no censoring of ideas.

PMI
Listing all the pluses for a solution in one column, all the minuses in another, and the implications in a third column.

The best decisions are based on sound information. Managers often have computer terminals at their desks so that they can easily retrieve internal records and look up external data of all kinds. But all the data in the world can't replace a creative manager who makes brilliant decisions. Decision making is more an art than a science. It's the one skill most needed by managers and leaders in that all the other functions depend on it.

Sometimes decisions have to be made on the spot—with little information available. Managers must make good decisions in all such circumstances. **Problem solving** is the process of solving the everyday problems that occur. It is less formal than the decision-making process and usually calls for quicker action. Problem solving teams are made up of two or more workers who are given an assignment to solve a specific problem (e.g., Why are customers not using our service policies?). Problem solving techniques that companies use include **brainstorming** (i.e., coming up with as many solutions as possible in a short period of time with no censoring of ideas)[11] and **PMI** (i.e., listing all the **p**luses for a solution in one column, all the **m**inuses in another, and the **i**mplications in a third column). For more on these and other tools, see the list of problem-solving analytical techniques on the Mind Tools Website at www.psywww.com/mtsite/page2.html.

Progress Assessment

- What's the difference between goals and objectives?
- What does a company analyze when it does a SWOT analysis?
- What's the difference between strategic, tactical, and operational planning?
- What are the seven Ds in decision making?

ORGANIZING: CREATING A UNIFIED SYSTEM

After managers have planned a course of action, they must organize the firm to accomplish their goals.[12] Operationally, organizing means allocating resources (such as funds for various departments), assigning tasks, and establishing procedures for accomplishing the organizational objectives. When organizing, a manager develops a structure or framework that relates all workers, tasks, and resources to each other. That framework is called the organization structure. In Chapter 9 we will look at several structure examples and will review some of the challenges in developing an organization structure.

organization chart
A visual device that shows the relationship and divides the organization's work; it shows who is accountable for the completion of specific work and who reports to whom.

Most organizations draw a chart showing these relationships. This tool is called an **organization chart.** An organization chart is a visual device that shows the relationships among people and divides the organization's work; it shows who is accountable for the completion of specific work and who reports to whom. Figure 8.5 shows a simple one. Each rectangle indicates a position (and usually who holds this position) within the organization. The chart plots who reports to whom (as indicated by the lines) and who is responsible for each task. For example, in Figure 8.5, Manager A is the production manager, and this middle manager reports directly to the president. Reporting directly to the production manager are three first-line supervisors; three employees report directly to each of these first-line supervisors. The corporate hierarchy illustrated on the organization chart includes top, middle, and first-line managers. The problems involved in developing an organization structure will be discussed later in the text. For now, it's important to know that the corporate hierarchy usually includes three levels of management (see Figure 8.6).

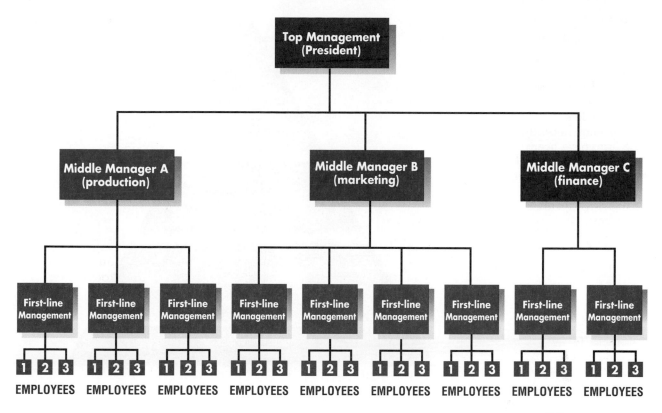

Top management (the highest level of management) consists of the president and other key company executives who develop strategic plans. Terms you're likely to see often are chief executive officer (CEO), chief operating officer (COO), chief financial officer (CFO), and chief information officer (CIO), or (in some companies) chief knowledge officer (CKO). The CEO is often the president of the firm and is responsible for all top-level decisions in the firm. CEOs are responsible for introducing change into an organization. The COO is responsible for putting those changes into effect. His or her tasks include structuring work, controlling operations, and rewarding people to ensure that everyone strives to carry out the leader's vision. The CFO is responsible for obtaining funds, planning budgets, collecting funds, and so on. The CIO or CKO is responsible for getting the right information to other managers so they can make correct decisions.

Middle management includes general managers, division managers, and branch and plant managers who are responsible for tactical planning and controlling. Many firms have eliminated some middle managers through downsizing because fewer are needed when employees work in self-managed teams (discussed later in this chapter).

Supervisory management includes those who are directly responsible for supervising workers and evaluating their daily performance; they're often known as first-line managers (or supervisors) because they're the first level above workers.

Tasks and Skills at Different Levels of Management

Few people are trained to be good managers. Usually a person learns how to be a skilled accountant or sales representative or production-line worker, and then—because of his or her skill—is selected to be a manager. The tendency is for such managers to become deeply involved in showing others how to do

---

FIGURE 8.5

TRADITIONAL ORGANIZATION CHART

This is a rather standard chart with middle managers for major functions and supervisors reporting to these managers.

top management
Highest level of management, consisting of the president and other key company executives who develop strategic plans.

middle management
The level of management that includes general managers, division managers, and branch and plant managers who are responsible for tactical planning and controlling.

supervisory management
Managers who are directly responsible for supervising workers and evaluating their daily performance.

FIGURE 8.6

LEVELS OF MANAGEMENT

This figure shows the three levels of management. In many firms, there are several levels of middle management. Recently, some firms have been eliminating middle-level managers because fewer are needed to oversee self-managed teams of employees.

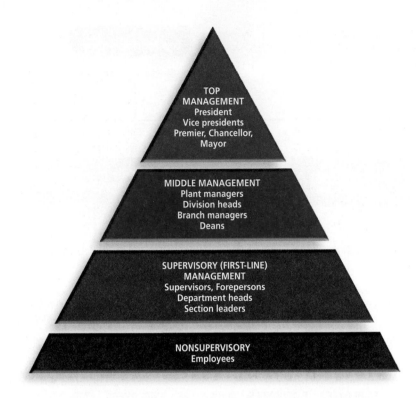

TOP MANAGEMENT
President
Vice presidents
Premier, Chancellor, Mayor

MIDDLE MANAGEMENT
Plant managers
Division heads
Branch managers
Deans

SUPERVISORY (FIRST-LINE) MANAGEMENT
Supervisors, Forepersons
Department heads
Section leaders

NONSUPERVISORY
Employees

things, helping them, supervising them, and generally being very active in the operating task.

The further up the managerial ladder a person moves, the less important his or her original job skills become. At the top of the ladder, the need is for people who are visionaries, planners, organizers, coordinators, communicators, morale builders, and motivators. As Figure 8.7 illustrates, a manager must have three categories of skills:

technical skills
Skills that involve the ability to perform tasks in a specific discipline or department.

human relations skills
Skills that involve communication and motivation; they enable managers to work through and with people.

conceptual skills
Skills that involve the ability to picture the organization as a whole and the relationship among its various parts.

1. **Technical skills** involve the ability to perform tasks in a specific discipline (such as selling a product or developing software) or department (such as marketing or information systems).

2. **Human relations skills** involve communication and motivation; they enable managers to work through and with people. Such skills also include those associated with leadership, coaching, morale building, delegating, training and development, and help and supportiveness.

3. **Conceptual skills** involve the ability to picture the organization as a whole and the relationships among its various parts. Conceptual skills are needed in planning, organizing, controlling, systems development, problem analysis, decision making, coordinating, and delegating.

Looking at Figure 8.7, you'll notice that first-line managers need to be skilled in all three areas. Most of their time is spent on technical and human relations tasks (assisting operating personnel, giving directions, etc.). First-line managers spend little time on conceptual tasks. Top managers, in contrast, need to use few technical skills. Instead, almost all of their time is devoted to human relations and conceptual tasks. A person who is competent at a low level of management may not be competent at higher levels, and vice versa. The skills needed are different at each level of management.

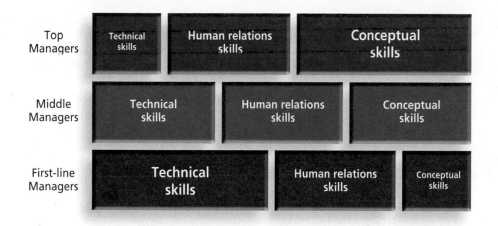

Top Managers	Technical skills	Human relations skills	Conceptual skills
Middle Managers	Technical skills	Human relations skills	Conceptual skills
First-line Managers	Technical skills	Human relations skills	Conceptual skills

FIGURE 8.7

SKILLS NEEDED AT VARIOUS LEVELS OF MANAGEMENT

All managers need human relation skills. At the top, managers need strong conceptual skills and rely less on technical skills. First-line managers need strong technical skills and rely less on conceptual skills. Middle managers need to have a balance between technical and conceptual skills.

The Trend toward Self-Managed Teams

One trend in Canada, especially in larger firms, is toward placing workers on cross-functional teams composed of people from various departments of the firm, such as marketing, finance, and human resources. Many of these teams are self-managed. This means that more planning, organizing, and controlling are being delegated to lower-level managers. What does this trend mean for managers and leaders in the 21st century? It means developing and training employees to assume greater responsibility in planning, teamwork, and problem solving.

Teamwork usually aids communication, improves cooperation, reduces internal competition, and maximizes the talents of all employees on a project. Companies use cross-functional teams to explore ways to make their companies operate faster and become more responsive to customers and other stakeholders, such as suppliers and the community. For example, Canada Post smoothly executed the delivery of more than 70,000 copies of *Harry Potter and the Order of the Phoenix* across Canada on its first day of release to customers who had pre-ordered the book on Amazon.ca and Chapters.indigo.ca.[13] "This success was the result of cross-functional teams including delivery, operations, network, customer engineering, and commercial sales planning and working together for months in advance," says Tom Charlton, senior vice-president of operations.[14] You'll read more about such teams in Chapter 9.

Texas Instruments is a technology firm that makes extensive use of self-managed teams in its plant in Malaysia. What kinds of issues might emerge as companies try to form self-managed teams in other countries?

The Stakeholder-Oriented Organization

A dominating question of the past 20 years or so has been how to best organize a firm to respond to the needs of customers and other stakeholders. Remember, stakeholders ➤P. 5◄ include anyone who's affected by the organization and its policies and products. That includes employees, customers, suppliers, dealers, environmental groups, and the surrounding communities. The consensus seems to be that smaller organizations are more responsive than larger organizations. Therefore, many large firms are being restructured into smaller, more customer-focused units.

The point is that companies are no longer organizing to make it easy for managers to have control. Instead, they're organizing so that customers

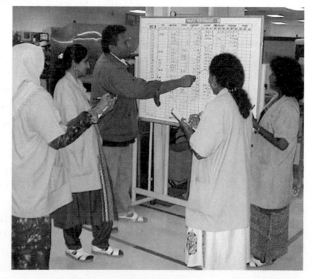

have the greatest influence. The change to a customer orientation is being aided by technology ➤**P. 15**◀. For example, establishing a dialogue with customers on the Internet enables some firms to work closely with customers and respond quickly to their wants and needs.[15] For instance, in 1998 WestJet invested in systems to give customers the option to book flights via the Web. This innovation has been successful for several reasons. First of all, the company generated cost savings. It costs $2 when a customer buys direct online, compared with as much as $20 when a travel agent books the flight. Secondly, WestJet encourages online sales by offering Air Miles and $6 off any roundtrip fare purchased over the Web, which helps explain why 69 percent of WestJet bookings are now made online.[16]

There's no way an organization can provide high-quality goods and services to customers unless suppliers provide world-class parts and materials with which to work. Thus, managers have to establish close relationships with suppliers.[17] To make the entire system work, similar relationships have to be established with those organizations that sell directly to consumers—namely retailers.

In the past, the goal of the organization function in the firm was to clearly specify who does what within the firm. Today, the organizational task is much more complex because firms are forming partnerships, joint ventures, and other arrangements that make it necessary to organize the whole system; that is, several firms working together, often across national boundaries.[18] One organization working alone is often not as effective as many organizations working together. Creating a unified system out of multiple organizations will be one of the greatest management challenges of the 21st century.[19] We'll discuss this issue in more depth in Chapter 9.

Staffing: Getting and Keeping the Right People

staffing
A management function that includes hiring, motivating, and retaining the best people available to accomplish the company's objectives.

Staffing involves recruiting, hiring, motivating, and retaining the best people available to accomplish the company's objectives. Recruiting good employees has always been an important part of organizational success. Today, however, it is critical, especially in the Internet and high-tech areas. At most high-tech companies, like Research In Motion and Corel, the primary capital equipment is brainpower. One day the company may be selling books (Amazon.com) and suddenly an employee comes up with the idea of selling music or having auctions online or whatever. Any of these opportunities may prove profitable in the long run. The opportunities seem almost limitless. Thus the firms with the most innovative and creative workers can go from start-up to major competitor with leading companies in just a year or two.

John Featherstone, employment director at Sun Microsystems, says that his company hires about 6,000 people a year, and competition among companies for the best new hires is incredibly intense. To win, Sun has developed an online recruiting program. The company pays bonuses of $1,500 to current employees who provide good leads for new workers. Sun's Website is easy to use and has an employment button that puts employment data a mouse click away.

Once they are hired, good people must be retained. Many people are not willing to work at companies unless they are treated well and get fair pay. Employees may leave to find companies that offer them a better balance between work and home. Staffing is becoming a greater part of each manager's assignment, and all managers need to cooperate with human resource management to win and keep good workers. At WestJet, employees are eligible for the company's profit-sharing plan (approximately $15 million was paid to employees in 2003) and the employee share purchase plan. For the share purchase plan,

WestJet matches every dollar an employee invests in company stock, to a maximum of 20 percent of the employee's annual salary.[20] Clive Beddoe explains that a less generous formula would not give employees a genuine opportunity to own a significant piece of the company. "It has to be lucrative enough to turn all our employees into partners ... We want them to think like owners, think like shareholders and then drive the company to success."[21]

Staffing is such an important subject that we cannot cover it fully in this chapter. It is enough for now to understand that staffing is becoming more and more important as companies search for skilled and talented workers.[22] All of Chapter 12 will be devoted to human resource issues, including staffing. All managers must also become more aware of diversity, another human resource area, because of today's diverse workforce. We'll explore that important topic next.

Managing Diversity

Managing diversity means building systems and a climate that unite different people in a common pursuit without undermining their individual strengths. Diversity includes but also goes beyond differences in race, gender, ethnicity, sexual orientation, abilities, and religious affiliation.

If people are to work on teams, they have to learn to work together with people who have different personalities, different priorities, and different lifestyles. In the past, firms tended to look for people much like those who were already working at the firm. Today, such recruiting would probably be illegal, and it certainly would be less than optimal.

Managing and working with a diverse group of people often causes difficulties in a firm. For example, young people don't always understand the traditional values and the work ethic of older workers. Nonetheless, research has shown that heterogeneous (mixed) groups are often more productive than homogeneous (similar) groups in the workplace. Men and women, young and old, and all other mixes of people not only can learn to work together but also can do so successfully. Furthermore, it is often quite profitable to have employees who match the diversity of customers so that the company as a whole can understand cultural differences and match them effectively.[23] Managers must learn how to work with people from many different cultures, and many will also be asked to work in foreign countries. The more you can do now to learn other languages and work with diverse cultural groups, the better off you'll be when you become a manager.

managing diversity
Building systems and a climate that unite different people in a common pursuit without undermining their individual strengths.

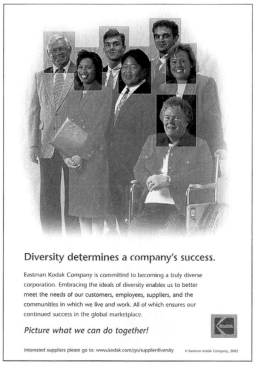

Diversity determines a company's success.

Eastman Kodak Company is committed to becoming a truly diverse corporation. Embracing the ideals of diversity enables us to better meet the needs of our customers, employees, suppliers, and the communities in which we live and work. All of which ensures our continued success in the global marketplace.

Picture what we can do together!

Interested suppliers please go to: www.kodak.com/go/supplierdiversity   © Eastman Kodak Company, 2002

Kodak says in this ad that "Diversity determines a company's success." Diversity helps the company to adapt to the needs of its customers, suppliers, employees, and the community. From your perspective, what advantages and disadvantages do you see in such diversity programs?

LEADING: PROVIDING CONTINUOUS VISION AND VALUES

In business literature there's a trend toward separating the notion of management from that of leadership. One person might be a good manager but not a good leader. Another might be a good leader without being a good manager. One difference between managers and leaders is that managers strive to produce order and stability, whereas leaders embrace and manage change. Leadership is creating a vision for others to follow, establishing corporate values and

Canada's Top 40 Under 40 is a national program to celebrate the leaders of today and tomorrow. As well, it honours Canadians who have reached a significant level of success before the age of 40. Winners have demonstrated qualities such as vision and leadership, innovation and achievement, impact, and community involvement and contribution. For a list of winners, visit www.top40award-canada.org.

ethics, and transforming the way the organization does business in order to improve its effectiveness and efficiency. Good leaders motivate workers and create the environment for workers to motivate themselves. *Management is the carrying out of the leadership's vision*. Can you see how Clive Beddoe (the subject of this chapter's opening profile) might be considered more of a leader than a manager?

Now and in the future, all organizations will need leaders who can supply the vision as well as the moral and ethical foundation for growth. You don't have to be a manager to be a leader. All employees can lead. That is, any employee can contribute to producing order and stability and can motivate others to work well. All employees can also add to a company's ethical environment and report ethical lapses when they occur.

Organizations will need workers and managers who share a vision and know how to get things done cooperatively. The workplace is changing from an environment in which a few dictate the rules to others to an environment in which all employees work together to accomplish common goals. Furthermore, managers must lead by doing, not just by saying.

In summary, leaders must:

- **Communicate a vision and rally others around that vision.** In doing so, the leader should be openly sensitive to the concerns of followers, give them responsibility, and win their trust.

- **Establish corporate values.** These values include a concern for employees, for customers, for the environment, and for the quality of the company's products. When companies set their business goals today, they're defining the values of the company as well.

- **Promote corporate ethics.** Ethics ➤P. 126◄ include an unfailing demand for honesty and an insistence that everyone in the company gets treated fairly. That's why we stress ethical decision making throughout this text.

- **Embrace change.** A leader's most important job may be to transform the way the company does business so that it's more effective (does things better) and efficient (uses fewer resources to accomplish the same objectives).

The area of leader compensation has been receiving increasing media attention. Today, there is much debate around the importance of CEOs and their large salaries. Donald Johnston, Secretary General of the OECD, said investor skepticism now runs deep because of headline-making scandals such as Enron and WorldCom. McGill professor Henry Mintzberg has been vocal on his disagreement with the increasing CEO compensation packages. In his view, many CEOs focus solely on the short-term increase in the share value of the company and their bonuses. "Find me a chief executive who refuses those bonuses, who takes the long-term view and says his team will share the spoils of their mandate in 10 years time, and I'll show you a leader," he said.[24]

Over the past 10 years, there has been an increasing trend in compensation packages. These packages have been justified as necessary to attract and keep good leaders. Do you agree that top executives should receive such lucrative packages in today's environment?

As you think about leadership, keep in mind, too, that it is now a global issue. The Reaching Beyond Our Borders box explores the importance of learning about managing businesses in global markets.

Henry Mintzberg of McGill University is one of the world's authorities on management. He has written extensively on organizational structure and strategy.

Reaching Beyond Our Borders

Learning About Managing Businesses in Volatile Global Markets

Business schools are seeing a change these days. As students read about countries that make up the former Soviet Union going to a market economy and eastern Europeans opening their doors to western businesses, they're demanding to know more about global business management. Many young people know they'll be involved in international business even if they never leave Canada. They also know that Canadian companies are looking to business schools for managers who know how to work in the new global context.

How are business schools responding to this student demand? Many are revamping their existing curriculums by integrating international examples into basic courses. This reduces the need for specifically international courses. The idea is to bring international dimensions into the mainstream.

Still, some students demand more. They feel that global enterprise is too important to be mixed in with other courses, and they want courses that are entirely international. Many business schools offer semester exchange programs with business schools in other countries. Professors are encouraged to participate in international research to gain teaching experience overseas. Students are encouraged—and in some cases required—to study foreign languages. Students have caught the international fever and have passed the sense of urgency on to their colleges and universities.

Businesses, too, are changing the way they educate employees. Rather than send them for a traditional MBA, firms are teaching their managers how to work in teams, how to use the latest technology, and how to operate in a global economy. It's possible, if not likely, that the entire nature of business education will change over the next decade. Much more information will be available and accessible via computers and computer networks. More courses will be customized to fit the needs of individual firms. Many senior managers are expressing dissatisfaction with the MBA program at most Canadian universities, and some newer dynamic companies are not keen on hiring MBAs. Complaints vary, but it would seem that what companies are seeking are more flexible employees who are tuned in to a fast-moving, fast-changing, volatile global market—employees who can "think on their feet." In any case, the future of management promises to be exciting, and so does the future of management education.

Sources: Brian O'Reilly, "How Execs Learn Now," *Business Week*, April 5, 1993, pp. 52–58; Brian O'Reilly, "Reengineering the MBA," *Fortune*, January 24, 1994, pp. 38–47; © 2001 Time Inc. All rights reserved; Harvey Schacter, "Programmed for Obsolescence?" *Canadian Business*, June 25/July 9, 1999, pp. 49–51.

The Importance of Middle Managers to Leadership[25]

The Conference Board of Canada released a report in 2003 on the changing role of middle managers. "A decade ago, senior managers viewed middle managers poorly—they thought middle managers blocked change and prevented the transfer of authority to front-line employees," researcher Carolyn Farquhar said. "A fundamental shift has occurred, and middle managers are now considered an essential link to making change throughout the organization and a training ground for executives of the future."

Carolyn Clark, vice-president of human resources for Fairmont Hotels & Resorts Inc., said that a growing body of research shows "people don't quit their companies, they quit their managers. Therefore, leadership quality is of critical importance at all levels of the company."

Dofasco Inc. has also elevated the role of middle managers as key players "in repositioning the company for a new group of leaders." According to the report, the greatest challenge facing Dofasco is its aging workforce. Most of the executive team will be gone in the next five to seven years, and over the next decade up to one-third of the workforce will turn over. Middle management will help to ensure that Dofasco's unique culture is retained, even with the influx of a large number of new employees.

The Conference Board of Canada report notes that not all organizations recognize the importance of middle managers. However, there are more examples seen today than in the past. This is indeed positive news for those middle managers who survived the downsizing of the past five years and were left with heavy workloads. According to the report, opportunities for middle managers to do challenging and rewarding work are increasing. "In just a few years, middle managers have moved from traditional roles of planning, monitoring, and controlling, to assuming additional roles relating to strategy and process."

Leadership Styles

Nothing has challenged researchers in the area of management more than the search for the "best" leadership traits, behaviours, or styles. Thousands of studies have been made just to find leadership traits; that is, characteristics that make leaders different from other people. Intuitively, you would conclude about the same thing that researchers have found: Leadership traits are hard to pin down. In fact, results of most studies on leadership have been neither statistically significant nor reliable. Some leaders are well groomed and tactful, while others are unkempt and abrasive—yet the latter may be just as effective as the former.

Just as there's no one set of traits that can describe a leader, there's also no one style of leadership that works best in all situations. Even so, we can look at a few of the most commonly recognized leadership styles and see how they may be effective (see Figure 8.8):

1. **Autocratic leadership** involves making managerial decisions without consulting others. Such a style is effective in emergencies and when absolute followership is needed—for example, when fighting fires. Autocratic leadership is also effective sometimes with new, relatively unskilled workers who need clear direction and guidance.

autocratic leadership
Leadership style that involves making managerial decisions without consulting others.

FIGURE 8.8

VARIOUS LEADERSHIP STYLES

Source: Reprinted by permission of the *Harvard Business Review*. An exhibit from "How to Choose a Leadership Pattern" by Robert Tannenbaum and Warren Schmidt (May/June 1973). Copyright © 1973 by the President and Fellows of Harvard College, all rights reserved.

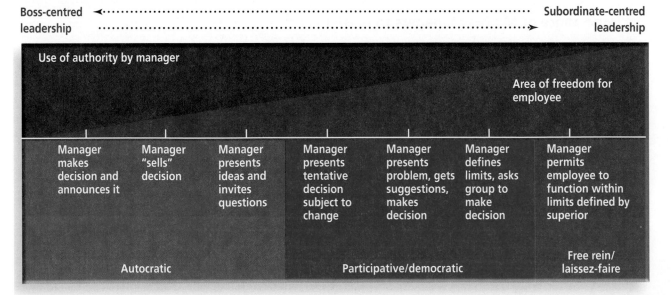

Dealing With Change

John Chambers Uses Participative Management at Cisco

Few managers have faced more perils of the stock market than John Chambers of Cisco Systems. Not too long ago, people considered John Chambers to be the number-one business leader in the United States. He's the CEO of Cisco Systems. Despite the stock market's ups and downs, Cisco keeps chugging along. Its fiscal-year revenues in 2002 were $4.8 billion, up from $4.3 billion in 2001. Cisco's stock could make a big comeback if and when the stock market turns upward again.

What does Cisco do? Cisco changes so quickly that one cannot easily define everything that it does. Put simply, it is involved in computer networking—providing the equipment that ties computers together into complex, integrated systems. It is a leading company of the Internet age. More than 75 percent of all Net traffic travels over products from Cisco.

One way Chambers ensures that Cisco remains an Internet leader is by acquiring other companies that develop improved technology. Cisco has bought not just dozens of companies but dozens of companies *per year.* All together, it has bought 55 companies for a combined total of over $20 billion. In the fiscal fourth quarter of 2002, Cisco bought both Hammerhead Networks, Inc., and Navaro Networks, Inc.

Acquiring businesses is a good way of acquiring better technology. It is also a clever way to acquire top engineering talent. Competition for Internet engineers is intense; buying another company and retaining its top engineers is one way Chambers succeeds in building a superior staff.

Getting talented people through an acquisition is one thing; keeping them is another. Chambers is a good manager in that respect as well. Howard Charney, a Cisco senior vice president, could be a CEO in some other company, but he stays at Cisco, he says, because of Chambers: "John treats us like peers ... He asks our advice. He gives us power and resources, then sets the sales targets incredibly high, which keeps us challenged." A true leader, Chambers has a participative managerial style that brings out the best in people.

The keys to Chambers's success at managing change include providing the best products by acquiring the best companies, retaining the best employees by motivating and compensating them well (and seeking their input using a participative managerial style), and focusing relentlessly on customer needs. Chambers says of Cisco, "Everything we do here is based on four principles: our customers' success, the quality of our team, our own aggressive use of information technology, and all of that applied to our overall strategy."

Source: "The Top 25 Managers to Watch," *Business Week,* January 8, 2001, p. 77.

2. **Participative (democratic) leadership** consists of managers and employees working together to make decisions. Research has found that employee participation in decisions may not always increase effectiveness, but it usually increases job satisfaction. Many progressive organizations are highly successful at using a democratic style of leadership that values traits such as flexibility, good listening skills, and empathy.

> At meetings in such firms, employees discuss management issues and resolve those issues together in a democratic manner. That is, everyone has some opportunity to contribute to decisions. Many firms have placed meeting rooms throughout the company and allow all employees the right to request a meeting. The Dealing with Change box explores this managerial style at Cisco.

participative (democratic) leadership
Leadership style that consists of managers and employees working together to make decisions.

3. **Free-rein (laissez-faire) leadership** involves managers setting objectives and employees being relatively free to do whatever it takes to accomplish those objectives. In certain organizations, where managers deal with doctors, engineers, or other professionals, often the most successful leadership style is free rein. The traits needed by managers in such organizations include warmth, friendliness, and understanding. More and more firms are adopting this style of leadership with at least some of their employees.

free-rein (laissez-faire) leadership
Leadership style that involves managers setting objectives and employees being relatively free to do whatever it takes to accomplish those objectives.

Individual leaders rarely fit neatly into just one of these categories. Researchers illustrate leadership as a continuum with varying amounts of employee participation, ranging from purely boss-centred leadership to subordinate-centred leadership.

Which leadership style is best? Research tells us that successful leadership depends largely on what the goals and values of the firm are, who's being led, and in what situations. It also supports the notion that any leadership style, ranging from autocratic to free-rein, may be successful depending on the people and the situation. In fact, a manager may use a variety of leadership styles, depending on a given situation. A manager may be autocratic but friendly with a new trainee; democratic with an experienced employee who has many good ideas that can only be fostered by a flexible manager who's a good listener; and free-rein with a trusted, long-term supervisor who probably knows more about operations than the manager does.

There's no such thing as a leadership trait that is effective in all situations, or a leadership style that always works best. A truly successful leader has the ability to use the leadership style most appropriate to the situation and the employees involved (see Figure 8.9).

Empowering Workers

Historically, many leaders gave explicit instructions to workers, telling them what to do to meet the goals and objectives of the organization. The term for such a process is *directing*. In traditional organizations, directing involves giving assignments, explaining routines, clarifying policies, and providing feedback on performance. Many organizations still follow this model, especially in firms like fast-food restaurants and small retail establishments where the employees don't have the skill and experience needed to work on their own, at least at first.

Progressive leaders, such as those in many high-tech firms and Internet companies, are less likely than traditional leaders to give specific instructions to employees. Rather, they're more likely to empower employees to make decisions on their own. Empowerment ►P. 19◄ means giving employees the authority (the right to make a decision without consulting the manager) and responsibility (the requirement to accept the consequences of one's actions) to respond quickly to customer requests. Managers are often reluctant to give up the power they have to make such decisions; thus, empowerment is often resisted. In those firms that are able to implement the concept, the manager's role is becoming less that of a boss and director and more that of a coach, assistant, counsellor, or team member. **Enabling** is the term used to describe giving workers the education and tools they need to make decisions. Clearly, enabling is the key to the success of empowerment. Without the right education, training, coaching, and tools, workers cannot assume the responsibilities and decision-making roles that make empowerment work. At WestJet, employees are encouraged through regular training sessions to resolve issues with WestJet customers. "From handing out flight credits to sending out for hamburgers to feed stranded passengers, they take care of things up front," says Don Bell, WestJet's senior vice-president and co-COO. "That kind of commitment comes from hiring the right people, aligning their interests to the company, and hooking the success of the business to their pocketbooks."[26]

enabling
Giving workers the education and tools they need to make decisions.

Managing Knowledge

There's an old saying that still holds true today: "Knowledge is power." Empowering employees means giving them knowledge—that is, getting them the information they need to do the best job they can. Finding the right

THE 12 RULES OF LEADERSHIP	THE SEVEN DON'TS OF LEADERSHIP

1. *Set a good example*. Your subordinates will take their cue from you. If your work habits are good, theirs are likely to be too.

2. *Give your people a set of objectives and a sense of direction*. Good people seldom like to work aimlessly from day to day. They want to know not only what they're doing but why.

3. *Keep your people informed of new developments of the company and how they'll affect them*. Let people know where they stand with you. Let your close assistants in on your plans at an early stage. Let people know as early as possible of any changes that will affect them. Let them know of changes that won't affect them but about which they may be worrying.

4. *Ask your people for advice*. Let them know that they have a say in your decisions whenever possible. Make them feel a problem is their problem too. Encourage individual thinking.

5. *Let your people know that you support them*. There's no greater morale killer than a boss who resents a subordinate's ambition.

6. *Don't give orders*. Suggest, direct, and request.

7. *Emphasize skills, not rules*. Judge results, not methods. Give a person a job to do and let him or her do it. Let an employee improve his or her own job methods.

8. *Give credit where credit is due*. Appreciation for a job well done is the most appreciated of fringe benefits.

9. *Praise in public*. This is where it will do the most good.

10. *Criticize in private*.

11. *Criticize constructively*. Concentrate on correction, not blame. Allow a person to retain his or her dignity. Suggest specific steps to prevent recurrence of the mistake. Forgive and encourage desired results.

12. *Make it known that you welcome new ideas*. No idea is too small for a hearing or too wild for consideration. Make it easy for them to communicate their ideas to you. Follow through on their ideas.

On the other hand, these items can cancel any constructive image you might try to establish.

1. *Trying to be liked rather than respected*. Don't accept favors from your subordinates. Don't do special favors in trying to be liked. Don't try for popular decisions. Don't be soft about discipline. Have a sense of humor. Don't give up.

2. *Failing to ask subordinates for their advice and help*.

3. *Failing to develop a sense of responsibility* in subordinates. Allow freedom of expression. Give each person a chance to learn his or her superior's job. When you give responsibility, give authority too. Hold subordinates accountable for results.

4. *Emphasizing rules rather than skill*.

5. *Failing to keep criticism constructive*. When something goes wrong, do you tend to assume who's at fault? Do you do your best to get all the facts first? Do you control your temper? Do you praise before you criticize? Do you listen to the other side of the story?

6. *Not paying attention to employee gripes and complaints*. Make it easy for them to come to you. Get rid of red tape. Explain the grievance machinery. Help a person voice his or her complaint. Always grant a hearing. Practice patience. Ask a complainant what he or she wants to do. Don't render a hasty or biased judgment. Get all the facts. Let the complainant know what your decision is. Double-check your results. Be concerned.

7. *Failing to keep people informed*.

Sources: "To Become an Effective Executive: Develop Leadership and Other Skills," *Marketing News*, April 1984, p. 1; and Brian Biro, *Beyond Success*. (New York: Berkley, 2001).

FIGURE 8.9

RULES OF LEADERSHIP

information, keeping the information in a readily accessible place, and making the information known to everyone in the firm together constitutes **knowledge management**.[27] For example, Canadian Tire is the first major Canadian retailer to use an Internet-based eLearning program. eLearning is an online training and education program that delivers product knowledge and skills training on everything from plumbing to paint mixing. The program is credited with improved customer and employee satisfaction levels. According to Janice Wismer, vice-president of human resources, "People say the lessons have increased their confidence that they're happier working here because the company is committing to their growth and development."[28] This is good news for store sales.

knowledge management
Finding the right information, keeping the information in a readily accessible place, and making the information known to everyone in the firm.

"WILSON, WHAT EXACTLY IS A KNOWLEDGE WORKER AND DO WE HAVE ANY ON THE STAFF?"

New management concepts come and go over time. One that is important at this time is knowledge management and the idea of knowledge workers. This cartoon suggests that management is not always aware of the latest techniques and how they are applied. What exactly is "knowledge management?" Does it seem like a passing fad or do you think it will be an important part of management for a long time?

The first step to developing a knowledge management system is determining what knowledge is most important. Do you want to know more about your customers? Do you want to know more about competitors? What kind of information would make the company more effective or more efficient or more responsive to the marketplace? Once you have decided what you need to know, you set out to find answers to those questions.

Knowledge management tries to keep people from reinventing the wheel—that is, duplicating the work of gathering information—every time a decision needs to be made. A company really progresses when each person in the firm asks continually, "What do I still not know?" and "Whom should I be asking?" It's as important to know what's not working as what is working. Employees and managers now have e-mail, fax machines, intranets, and other means of keeping in touch with each other, with customers, and with other stakeholders. The key to success is learning how to process that information effectively and turn it into knowledge that everyone can use to improve processes and procedures. That is one way to enable workers to be more effective. We'll discuss information technology and knowledge management in much more detail later in the text.

Critical Thinking

Is the democratic management style the most appropriate in all situations? Why or why not? Can you see a manager getting frustrated when he or she can't control others? Can someone who's trained to give orders (e.g., a military sergeant) be retrained to be a democratic manager? What problems may emerge? What kind of manager would you be? Do you have evidence to show that?

Progress Assessment

- What are some characteristics of leadership today that make leaders different from traditional managers?

- Explain the differences between autocratic and democratic leadership styles.

- Describe empowerment and explain to which of the four management functions it is related.

- What is the first step in developing a knowledge management system?

Controlling: Making Sure It Works

The control function involves measuring performance relative to the planned objectives and standards, rewarding people for work well done, and then taking corrective action when necessary. Thus, the control process (see Figure 8.10) is the heart of the management system because it provides the feedback that enables managers and workers to adjust to any deviations from plans and

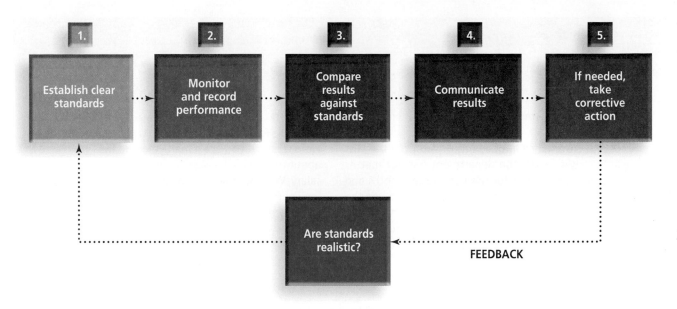

FIGURE 8.10

THE CONTROL PROCESS

The whole control process is based on clear standards. Without such standards, the other steps are difficult, if not impossible. With clear standards, performance measurement is relatively easy and the proper action can be taken.

to changes in the environment that have affected performance. Controlling consists of five steps:

1. Establishing clear performance standards. This ties the planning function to the control function. Without clear standards, control is impossible.
2. Monitoring and recording actual performance (results).
3. Comparing results against plans and standards.
4. Communicating results and deviations to the employees involved.
5. Taking corrective action when needed and providing positive feedback for work well done.

This control process is ongoing *throughout* the year. Continuous monitoring ensures that if corrective action is required, there is enough time to implement changes. When corrective action is necessary, the decision-making process is a useful tool to apply (recall the seven Ds of decision making). Simply, managers are encouraged to review the situation and, based on collected information, develop alternatives with their staff and implement the best alternative. The focus is to meet the standards that were initially established during the planning stage or the standards that have since been modified. This process is also ongoing. It may take several attempts before standards are successfully met.

The control system's weakest link tends to be the setting of standards. To measure results against standards, the standards must be specific, attainable, and measurable.[29] Vague goals and standards such as "better quality," "more efficiency," and "improved performance" aren't sufficient because they don't describe what you're trying to achieve. For example, let's say you're a runner and you say you want to improve your distance. When you started your improvement plan last year, you ran 2 kilometres a day. Now you run 2.1 kilometres a day. Did you meet your goal? Well, you did increase your distance, but certainly not by very much. A more appropriate goal statement would be: To increase running distance from 2 kilometres a day to 4 kilometres a day by January 1. It's important to have a time period established for when specific

Making Ethical Decisions

To Tell or Not to Tell?

You are an ambitious, hard-working, younger manager. Your department head is an older, experienced manager whose performance has been inconsistent in the past two years. The department has not met its monthly target for the past three months and unless the results improve rapidly, his job may be on the line. By chance, you come across some information that your department head does not have and you know it would help him improve the department's performance

significantly. Despite your youth you have had excellent evaluations on your job performance and you think you would have a good chance of replacing your boss if he were let go. If you are a man, imagine that your wife is about to give birth—you could certainly use a boost in salary. What should you do? If you are a woman, imagine your husband has just lost his job. Would you give the information to your superior or keep quiet? Would your answer be different if you did not have a partner and were single? Explain.

goals are to be met. Here are examples of goals and standards that meet these criteria:

- Cut the number of finished-product rejects from 10 per 1,000 to 5 per 1,000 by March 31, 2005.
- Increase the number of times managers praise employees from 3 per week to 12 per week by the end of the quarter.
- Increase sales of product X from $10,000 per month to $12,000 per month by July 31.

One way to make control systems work is to establish clear procedures for monitoring performance. Accounting and finance are often the foundations for control systems because they provide the numbers management needs to evaluate progress. We shall explore both accounting and finance in detail later in the text. Before you move to the next section, review the Making Ethical Decisions box, which is based on the importance of meeting targets.

A New Criterion for Measurement: Customer Satisfaction

The criterion for measuring success in a customer-oriented firm is customer satisfaction. This includes satisfaction of both external and internal customers. **External customers** include dealers, who buy products to sell to others, and ultimate customers (also known as end users) such as you and me, who buy products for their own personal use. **Internal customers** are individuals and units within the firm that receive services from other individuals or units. For example, the field salespeople are the internal customers of the marketing research people who prepare research reports for them. One goal today is to go beyond simply satisfying customers to "delighting" them with unexpectedly good products.

Other criteria of organizational effectiveness may include the firm's contribution to society and its environmental responsibility in the area surrounding the business.[30] The traditional measures of success are usually financial; that is, success is defined in terms of profits or return on investment. Certainly these measures are still important, but they're not the whole purpose of the firm. The purpose of the firm today is to please employees, customers, and other stakeholders. Thus, measurements of success must take all these groups

external customers
Dealers, who buy products to sell to others, and ultimate customers (or end users), who buy products for their own personal use.

internal customers
Individuals and units within the firm that receive services from other individuals or units.

into account. Firms have to ask questions such as these: Do we have good relations with our employees, our suppliers, our dealers, our community leaders, the local media, our shareholders, and our bankers? What more could we do to please these groups? Are the corporate needs (such as making a profit) being met as well?

The Corporate Scorecard

A broad measurement tool that has grown in popularity in the last few years is the corporate scorecard. In addition to measuring customer satisfaction, the corporate scorecard measures financial progress, return on investment, and all else that needs to be managed for the firm to reach its final destination— profits. One scorecard, for example, might simultaneously follow customer service (Is it getting better or worse?) and product defects (Are there fewer or more?). Some companies use software that enables everyone in the firm to see the results of the corporate scorecard and work together to improve them. Some companies, like Shell Oil, use strictly financial measures of success. Others, like Motorola, use a more balanced approach. That is, they measure both financial progress and other, softer issues, such as employee and customer satisfaction. Most companies would do better by having a balanced approach that measures both financial growth and employee and customer satisfaction.

Management will be discussed in more detail in the next few chapters. Let's pause now, review, and do some exercises. Management is doing, not just reading.

What kind of management are you best suited for. human resource, marketing, finance, accounting, production, or what? Why do you feel this area is most appropriate? Would you like to work for a large firm or a small business? Private or public? In an office or out in the field? Would you like being a manager? If you aren't sure, read the following chapters and see what's involved.

Critical Thinking

- What are the five steps in the control process?
- What's the difference between internal and external customers?
- Why might a company use a corporate scorecard?

Progress Assessment

Summary

1. Many managers are changing their approach to corporate management.
   - ***What reasons can you give to account for these changes in management?***
   Businesspeople are being challenged to be more ethical and to make their accounting practices more visible to investors and the general public. Change is now happening faster than ever, and global competition is just a click away. Managing change is an important element of success,

1. Explain how the changes that are occurring in the business environment are affecting the management function.

particularly in light of today's emphasis on speed in the global market-place. National borders mean much less now than ever before, and cooperation and integration among companies have greatly increased. Within companies, knowledge workers are demanding managerial styles that allow for freedom, and the workforce is becoming increasingly diverse, educated, and self-directed.

• *How are managers' roles changing?*

Managers are being educated to guide, train, support, and teach employees rather than tell them what to do.

2. Describe the four functions of management.

2. Managers perform a variety of functions.

• *What are the four primary functions of management?*

The four primary functions are (1) planning, (2) organizing, (3) leading, and (4) controlling.

• *Describe each of the four functions.*

Planning includes anticipating trends and determining the best strategies and tactics to achieve organizational goals and objectives. Organizing includes designing the structure of the organization and creating conditions and systems in which everyone and everything works together to achieve the organization's goals and objectives. Leading involves creating a vision for the organization and guiding, training, coaching, and motivating others to work effectively to achieve the organization's goals and objectives. Controlling involves establishing clear standards to determine whether or not an organization is progressing toward its goals and objectives, rewarding people for doing a good job, and taking corrective action if they are not.

3. Relate the planning process and decision making to the accomplishment of company goals.

3. The planning function involves the process of setting objectives to meet the organizational goals. Goals are broad, long-term achievements that organizations aim to accomplish.

• *What are the four types of planning, and how are they related to the organization's goals and objectives?*

Strategic planning is broad, long-range planning that outlines the goals of the organization. Tactical planning is specific, short-term planning that lists organizational objectives. Operational planning is part of tactical planning and involves setting specific timetables and standards. Contingency planning involves developing an alternative set of plans in case the first set doesn't work out.

• *What are the steps involved in decision making?*

The seven Ds of decision making are (1) define the situation, (2) describe and collect needed information, (3) develop alternatives, (4) develop agreement among those involved, (5) decide which alternative is best, (6) do what is indicated (begin implementation), and (7) determine whether the decision was a good one and follow up.

4. Describe the organizing function of management.

4. Organizing means allocating resources (such as funds for various departments), assigning tasks, and establishing procedures for accomplishing the organizational objectives.

• *What are the three levels of management in the corporate hierarchy?*

The three levels of management are (1) top management (highest level consisting of the president and other key company executives who develop strategic plans); (2) middle management (general managers, division managers, and plant managers who are responsible for tactical planning and controlling); and (3) supervisory management (first-line managers/supervisors who evaluate workers' daily performance).

- *What skills do managers need?*

Managers must have three categories of skills: (1) technical skills (ability to perform specific tasks such as selling products or developing software), (2) human relations skills (ability to communicate and motivate), and (3) conceptual skills (ability to see organizations as a whole and how all the parts fit together). Managers at different levels need different skills.

5. Executives today must be more than just managers; they must be leaders as well.

5. Explain the differences between leaders and managers, and describe the various leadership styles.

- *What's the difference between a manager and a leader?*

A manager plans, organizes, and controls functions within an organization. A leader has vision and inspires others to grasp that vision, establishes corporate values, emphasizes corporate ethics, and doesn't fear change.

- *Which leadership style is best?*

Figure 8.8 shows a continuum of leadership styles ranging from boss-centred to subordinate-centred leadership. The best (most effective) leadership style depends on the people being led and the situation.

- *What does empowerment mean?*

Empowerment means giving employees the authority and responsibility to respond quickly to customer requests. Enabling is the term used to describe giving workers the education and tools they need to assume their new decision-making powers. Knowledge management is another way of enabling workers to do the best job they can.

6. The control function of management involves measuring employee performance against objectives and standards, rewarding people for a job well done, and taking corrective action if necessary.

6. Summarize the five steps of the control function of management.

- *What are the five steps of the control function?*

Controlling incorporates (1) setting clear standards, (2) monitoring and recording performance, (3) comparing performance with plans and standards, (4) communicating results and deviations to employees, and (5) providing positive feedback for a job well done and taking corrective action if necessary.

- *What qualities must standards possess to be used to measure performance results?*

Standards must be specific, attainable, and measurable.

Key Terms

autocratic leadership 234

brainstorming 226

conceptual skills 228

contingency planning 225

controlling 220

decision making 225

enabling 236

external customers 240

free-rein (laissez-faire) leadership 235

goals 222

human relations skills 228

internal customers 240

knowledge management 237

leading 220

management 219

managing diversity 231

middle management 227

mission statement 221

objectives 222

operational planning 224

organization chart 226

organizing 220

participative (democratic) leadership 235

planning 219

PMI 226

problem solving 226

robber barons 218

staffing 230

strategic planning 222

supervisory management 227

SWOT analysis 222

tactical planning 223

technical skills 228

top management 227

vision 221

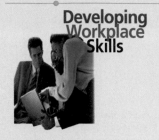

Developing Workplace Skills

1. Allocate some time to do some career planning by doing a SWOT analysis of your present situation. What does the marketplace for your chosen career(s) look like today? What skills do you have that will make you a winner in that type of career? What weaknesses might you target to improve? What are the threats to that career choice? What are the opportunites? Prepare a two-minute presentation to the class.

2. Bring several decks of cards to class and have the class break up into teams of four or so members. Each team should then elect a leader. Each leader should be assigned a leadership style: autocratic, participative, or free-rein. Have each team try to build a house of cards by stacking them on top of each other. The team with the highest house wins. Each team member should then report his or her experience under that style of leadership.

3. In class, discuss the advantages and disadvantages of becoming a manager. Does the size of the business make a difference? What are the advantages of a career in a profit-seeking business versus a career in a nonprofit organization?

4. Review Figure 8.8 and discuss managers you have known, worked for, or read about who have practised each style. Students from other countries may have interesting experiences to add. Which managerial style did you like best? Why? Which were most effective? Why?

5. Because of the illegal and unethical behaviour of a few managers, managers in general are under suspicion for being greedy and dishonest. Discuss the fairness of such charges, given the thousands of honest and ethical managers. What could be done to improve the opinion of managers among the students in your class?

Taking It To The Net

1

Purpose

To discover some of Canada's leaders and find out what makes them great leaders.

Exercise

There are many national awards given out each year recognizing Canadian business leaders. Go on the Web and see if you can find some of these leaders. Two sites you may wish to visit are www.canadianbusiness.com/allstars/ and www.top40award-canada.org.

1. What are some common characteristics that you found in these leaders?

2. Analyze the criteria used to choose these leaders. Are these measures reflective of the theory discussed in this chapter?

3. What other criteria do you suggest should be included?

4. Visit www.robmagazine.com and review the best-paid executives in Canada. Did you find some of Canada's top leaders on this list? Is salary reflective of a great leader? Explain.

Purpose

To perform a simple SWOT analysis.

Taking It To The Net 2

Exercise

Go to www.marketingteacher.com/Lessons/lesson_swot.htm. Click on [Exercise] at the bottom of the page and complete the SWOT analysis for the Highly Brill Leisure Center.

1. What are the company's strengths and weaknesses? What are the opportunities and threats in the business environment?

2. Analyze the company's weaknesses. How do you think the company's strengths might be used to overcome some of its weaknesses?

3. Analyze the opportunities and threats. What additional opportunities can you suggest? What additional threats can you identify?

Practising Management Decisions

Case

Leading in a Leaderless Company

In a *Business Week* issue devoted to the future of business, writer John Byrne speculated about the future of leadership. He said that the 21st century would be unfriendly to leaders who try to run their companies by the sheer force of will. He said that success would come instead to companies that are "leaderless"— or companies whose leadership is so widely shared that they resemble ant colonies or bee-hives. In a world that is becoming more dependent on brain-power, having teams at the top will make more sense than having a single top manager. The Internet enables companies to act more like beehives because information can be shared horizontally rather than sent up to the top manager's office and then back down again. Decisions can be made instantly by the best people equipped to make them.

In the past, uniform thinking from the top could cripple an organization. Today, however, team leadership is ideally suited for the new reality of fast-changing markets. Urgent projects often require the coordinated contribution of many talented people working together. Such thinking does not happen at the top of the organization; it takes place down among the workers.

In the future, therefore, managers are more likely to be chosen for their team experience and their ability to delegate rather than make all key decisions themselves. Companies in the future, it is said, will be led by people who understand that in business, as in nature, no one person can be really in control.

Decision Questions

1. What would you look for on a résumé that would indicate that a candidate for work was a self-motivated team player? Are you that type? How do you know?

2. Given your experience with managers in the past, what problems do you see some managers having with letting employees decide for themselves the best way to do things and giving them the power to obtain needed equipment?

3. What would happen if all the businesses in your area had their employees mix with customers to hear their comments and complaints? Would that be a good or bad thing? Why?

4. What are the various ways you can think of for companies to pay bonuses to team members? One way is to divide the money equally. What are other ways? Which would you prefer as a team member?

Sources: John A. Byrne, "The Global Corporation Becomes a Leaderless Corporation," *Business Week*, August 30, 1999, pp. 88–90, and Etienne C. Wenger and William M. Synder, "Communities of Practice: The Organizational Frontier," *Harvard Business Review*, January–February 2000, pp. 139–145.

Video Case

The Trouble with Teams

It's a lovely ideal—democracy in the workplace. In the 1980s business gurus told businesses that they needed to embrace teamwork. The authoritarian structure was no longer effective, but with teamwork businesses would be more successful.

Today, these same gurus are changing their minds. While teams were once actively promoted, individual leaders are now being promoted as the key to success. One of the several companies spotlighted in this video is ESG Canada. Five equal partners produce a sound monitoring system used in underground mines. While the product is a big success, teamwork takes so much time and effort that the partners are considering a change.

The concept of teamwork was first embraced by the auto industry. Automakers were losing market share to the Japanese imports. Many felt that the key to Japanese automakers' success was teamwork. Unlike American workers, Japanese workers did not work in traditional assembly lines. They worked in teams and were given a voice and encouraged to make productivity suggestions.

This concept quickly spread into the auto sector, into other manufacturing sectors, and then into other industries. While many firms have tried to embrace teamwork, it has not led to the success that many expected. Today, while teamwork can provide many benefits, it is still not completely understood what conditions need to be in place for teams to be successful and under what conditions teams can derail.

Discussion Questions

1. What are some of the benefits of teamwork? What are some of the challenges of teamwork?
2. Is there proof that teams improve a company's performance in the long run?
3. Why have automakers not used teams to the extent expected?
4. What impact does our society have on the potential success of teams?

Source: *Venture*, show number 703, "The Trouble with Teams," November 10, 1998, running time 6:16.

Chapter 9

Adapting Organizations to Today's Markets

Learning Goals

After you have read and studied this chapter, you should be able to

1. Explain the historical organizational theories of Fayol and Weber.

2. Discuss the various issues involved in structuring organizations.

3. Describe and differentiate the various organizational models.

4. List the concepts involved in interfirm cooperation and coordination.

5. Discuss the tools that are available to assist organizations in adapting to change.

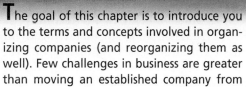

Getting to Know Heather Reisman of Indigo Books & Music Inc.

The goal of this chapter is to introduce you to the terms and concepts involved in organizing companies (and reorganizing them as well). Few challenges in business are greater than moving an established company from the slow-moving, management-oriented style of the past to the fast-moving, team-oriented, Internet-based, and customer-based firms that most of today's markets demand.

No one understands the fast-paced business environment better than Heather Reisman, founder and CEO of Indigo Books & Music Inc., Canada's largest book retailer. Indigo operates bookstores in all provinces under the names Indigo Books Music & More, Chapters, The World's Biggest Book Store, and Coles. Indigo also operates www.chapters.indigo.ca, an online retailer of books, gifts, videos, and DVDs.

Reisman has over 25 years of business experience. For the first 16 years of her career, she was Managing Director of Paradigm Consulting, the strategy and change management firm she co-founded in 1979. Paradigm was the world's first strategic change consultancy and it pioneered many organizational change strategies in use today. Reisman left Paradigm to become president of Cott Corporation. During her tenure, Cott grew from a regional bottler to the world's largest retailer-branded beverage supplier.

Reisman created Indigo Books & Music in 1996. Launching Indigo was the culmination and integration of a lifelong passion for books and music, and an entire career focused on understanding and building new age organizations. By 2000, the chain had expanded to 14 locations across Canada. Indigo was the first book retail chain to add music, gifts, and licensed cafés to its store locations.

Indigo's closest competitor was Chapters. In 1996, Chapters Inc. opened its two first book superstores and from there it grew to become the largest book retailer in Canada, operating bookstores in all provinces. In November 2000, Trilogy Retail Enterprises L.P. (co-owned by Reisman and her husband Gerry Schwartz) announced its intent to purchase a controlling interest in Chapters.

"We are truly excited by the prospects of this merger," Reisman said in an interview. "It makes great sense. It allows us to take advantage of a broader base of expertise, substantial cost savings, synergies and efficiencies, all of which will have a positive impact on our customers, shareholders, and suppliers." In August 2001, Chapters and Indigo legally merged under the corporate name Indigo Books & Music Inc.

Since merging Indigo and Chapters, Reisman has been involved in creating the infrastructure necessary to position Indigo for sustained high performance. In 2003, Indigo's consolidated revenues were $779.2 million and net profit for the year was $1.4 million. "We are extremely pleased to have turned the profitability corner and are now committed to making Indigo an industry-leading performer," said Reisman.

To this end, Indigo will be increasing its sales of gifts and accessories while depending on books for a smaller proportion of its business as it revamps its stores. According to Reisman, books will remain Indigo's core product as it repositions itself as a "book lover's cultural department store." The 87 Indigo and Chapters superstores will increase "quite meaningfully" their sales of books, music, DVDs, and other products such as cards and jewellery. "We imagine over the next three or four years that books, which are now 80 or 85 percent of our offering, will evolve to be approximately 60 percent of our offering, although the selection will still be as meaningful," Reisman said. The company plans to transform its 167 Coles mall locations, which account for 21 percent of sales, into IndigoLite stores, adding gifts and paper products to their inventories. Indigo is also forming partnerships with experts in health, business, religion, and other fields who will advise the bookseller and customers on the best resources for their needs.

Sources: "Chapters, Indigo unveil merger details (June 13, 2001), CBC News. Retrieved from http://www.cbc.ca/stories/2001/06/13/business/chapters_010611; www.chapters.indigo.ca, June 4, 2004; and Nancy Carr, "Indigo sees itself as purveyor of lifestyle," Toronto Star, September 15, 2004. Retrieved from http://www.thestar.com/NASApp/cs/ContentServer?pagename=thestar/Layout/Article_Type1&call_pageid=971358637177&c=Article&cid=1095199811221.

BUILDING AN ORGANIZATION FROM THE BOTTOM UP

Management, as you learned in Chapter 8, begins with planning. Let's say, for example, that you and two of your friends plan to start a lawn-mowing business. One of the first steps is to organize your business. Organizing, or structuring, begins with determining what work needs to be done (mowing, edging, trimming, etc.) and then dividing up tasks among the three of you; this is called a *division of labour*. One of you, for example, might have a special talent for trimming bushes, while another is better at mowing. Dividing tasks into smaller jobs is called *job specialization*. The success of a firm often depends on management's ability to identify each worker's strengths and assign the right tasks to the right person. Often a job can be done quickly and well when each person specializes.

If your business is successful, you will probably hire more workers. You might then organize them into teams or departments to do the various tasks. One team, for example, might mow the lawn while another team uses blowers to clean up the leaves and cut grass. If you are really successful over time, you might hire an accountant to keep records for you, various people to do your marketing (e.g., advertising), and repair people to keep the equipment in good shape. You can see how your business might evolve into a company with several departments: production (mowing the lawns and everything related to that), marketing, accounting, and repair. The process of setting up individual departments to do specialized tasks is called *departmentalization*. Finally, you would need to assign authority and responsibility to people so that you could control the whole process. If something went wrong in the accounting department, for example, you would know who was responsible.

Structuring an organization, then, consists of devising a division of labour (sometimes resulting in specialization); setting up teams or departments to do specific tasks (e.g., production and accounting); and assigning responsibility and authority to people. Part of the process would include allocating resources (such as funds for various departments), assigning specific tasks, and establishing procedures for accomplishing the organizational objectives. Right from the start, you have to make some ethical decisions about how you will treat your workers (see the Making Ethical Decisions box). Finally, as you learned in Chapter 8, you may develop an organization chart ➤P. 226◄ that shows relationships among people: It shows who is accountable for the completion of specific work and who reports to whom.

The Changing Organization

Never before in the history of business has so much change been introduced so quickly—sometimes too quickly.[1] As you learned in earlier chapters, much of that is due to the dynamic business environment, including more global competition and faster technological change. Equally important to many businesses is the change in customer expectations.[2] Consumers today expect high-quality goods and fast, friendly service—at a reasonable cost. Managing change, then, has become a critical managerial function. That sometimes includes changing the whole organizational structure. Many organizations in the past were designed more to facilitate management than to please the customer. Companies designed many rules and regulations to give managers control over employees.

We shall explore in brief the history of organizational design so that you can see what the foundations are. Then we shall explore the newest forms of organization, forms that are being designed to better serve today's customer. Though often dramatic and disruptive, such changes keep companies competitive in today's dynamic business environment.

Imagine that you have begun a successful lawn-mowing service in your neighbourhood. You have talked to your neighbours and established several long-term agreements to mow lawns, trim hedges, and do other yardwork as necessary. It occurs to you that this could be a great long-term career for you. You would have to sign up more customers, hire people to help, and buy the appropriate equipment to do the work. That equipment might include lawn mowers of different sizes, gas-powered blowers for removing leaves, a shredder to get rid of tree branches, and more. You may even buy a machine to spray liquid fertilizer on the lawns.

To get some input on what is needed, you observe other lawn-mowing services in the area. Several seem to hire untrained workers, many of them from other countries. The companies pay the workers minimum wage or slightly more. Most obviously, however, the owners often provide no safety equipment. Workers don't have ear protection against the loud mowers and blowers. Most don't wear goggles when operating the shredder. Very few workers wear masks when spraying potentially harmful fertilizers.

You are aware that there are many hazards connected with yardwork. You also know that safety gear can be expensive and that workers often prefer to work without such protection. You are interested in making as much money as possible, but you also are somewhat concerned about the safety and welfare of your workers. Furthermore, you are aware of the noise pollution caused by blowers and other equipment and would like to keep noise levels down, but quiet equipment is expensive.

Clearly, most other lawn services don't seem too concerned about safety and the environment. On the one hand, you know that the corporate culture you create as you begin your service will last for a long time. If you emphasize safety and environmental concern from the start, your workers will adopt your values. On the other hand, you can see the potential for making faster profits by ignoring as many safety rules as you can and by paying as little attention as you can to the environment. What are the consequences of each choice? Which would you choose?

The Historical Development of Organizational Design

To understand what is happening in organizations today, it is best to begin with a firm foundation of organizational principles. Many principles of traditional organizational design are still relevant today. However, some have lost importance and others may no longer apply at all—and organizational leaders need to understand which principles are still important and which are not.

Until the 20th century, most businesses were rather small, the processes for producing goods were relatively simple, and organizing workers was fairly easy. Organizing workers is still not too hard in most small firms, such as a lawn-mowing service or a small shop that produces custom-made boats. Not until the 1900s and the introduction of *mass production* (efficiently producing large quantities of goods) did business production processes and organization become complex. Usually, the bigger the plant, the more efficient production became.

Business growth led to economies of scale. Recall from Chapter 4 that this term refers to the fact that companies can reduce their production costs if they can purchase raw materials in bulk; the average cost of goods goes down as production levels increase. The cost of building a car, for example, got much cheaper when the automobile companies went to mass production. You may have noticed the same benefits of mass production with houses and computers.

During the era of mass production, organization theorists emerged. In France, Henri Fayol published his book *Administration industrielle et générale* in 1919. Sociologist Max Weber (pronounced "Vay-ber") was writing about organization theory in Germany about the same time Fayol was writing his books in France. Note that it was less than 60 years ago that organization theory became popular in North America.

Fayol's Principles of Organization   Fayol introduced such principles as the following:

- **Unity of command.**   Each worker is to report to one, and only one, boss. The benefits of this principle are obvious. What happens if two different bosses give you two different assignments? Which one should you follow? Reporting to only one manager prevents such confusion.
- **Hierarchy of authority.**   All workers should know to whom they should report. Managers should have the right to give orders and expect others to follow.
- **Division of labour.**   Functions are to be divided into areas of specialization such as production, marketing, and finance. This principle, as you will read later, is now being questioned or modified.
- **Subordination of individual interests to the general interest.**   Workers are to think of themselves as a coordinated team. The goals of the team are more important than the goals of individual workers.
- **Authority.**   Managers have the right to give orders and the power to enforce obedience. Authority and responsibility are related: Whenever authority is exercised, responsibility arises. This principle is also being modified as managers are beginning to empower employees.
- **Degree of centralization.**   The amount of decision-making power vested in top management should vary by circumstances. In a small organization, it's possible to centralize all decision-making power in the top manager. In a larger organization, however, some decision-making power should be delegated to lower-level managers and employees on both major and minor issues.
- **Clear communication channels.**   All workers should be able to reach others in the firm quickly and easily.
- **Order.**   Materials and people should be placed and maintained in the proper location.
- **Equity.**   A manager should treat employees and peers with respect and justice.
- **Esprit de corps.**   A spirit of pride and loyalty should be created among people in the firm.

Management courses throughout the world taught these principles for years, and they became synonymous with the concept of management. Organizations were designed so that no person had more than one boss, lines of authority were clear, and everyone knew to whom they were to report. Naturally, these principles tended to be written down as rules, policies, and regulations as organizations grew larger. That process of rule making often led to rather rigid organizations that didn't always respond quickly to consumer requests.

Max Weber and Organizational Theory   Max Weber's book *The Theory of Social and Economic Organizations*, like Fayol's, also appeared in North America in the late 1940s. It was Weber who promoted the pyramid-shaped organization structure that became so popular in large firms. Weber put great trust in managers and felt that the firm would do well if employees simply did what they were told. The less decision making employees had to do, the better. Clearly, this is a reasonable way to operate if you're dealing with relatively uneducated and untrained workers. Often, such workers were the only ones available at the time Weber was writing; most employees did not have the kind of educational background and technical skills that today's workers generally have.

Weber's principles of organization were similar to Fayol's. In addition, Weber emphasized:

- Job descriptions.
- Written rules, decision guidelines, and detailed records.
- Consistent procedures, regulations, and policies.
- Staffing and promotion based on qualifications.

When you go to a store and the clerk says, "I'm sorry I can't do that, it's against company policy," you can blame Max Weber and his theories. At one time, less-educated workers were best managed, it was believed, by having them follow many strict rules and regulations monitored by managers or supervisors. Are there industries or businesses today where you think it would be desirable or necessary to continue to use such controls?

Weber believed that large organizations demanded clearly established rules and guidelines that were to be followed precisely. In other words, he was in favour of bureaucracy (to be discussed in the next section). Although his principles made a great deal of sense at the time, the practice of establishing rules and procedures sometimes became so rigid in some companies that it became counterproductive.[3] However, some organizations today still thrive on Weber's theories. United Parcel Service (UPS), for example, still has written rules and decision guidelines that enable the firm to deliver packages quickly because employees don't have to pause to make decisions. The procedures to follow are clearly spelled out for them.

Turning Principles into Organizational Design

Following the concepts of theorists like Fayol and Weber, managers in the latter part of the 1900s began designing organizations so that managers could control workers. Most organizations are still organized that way, with everything set up in a hierarchy. A **hierarchy** is a system in which one person is at the top of the organization and there is a ranked or sequential ordering from the top down of managers and others who are responsible to that person. Since one person can't keep track of thousands of workers, the top manager needs many lower-level managers to help. The **chain of command** is the line of authority that moves from the top of the hierarchy to the lowest level. (Review Figure 8.5 for a traditional organization structure.)

Some organizations have a dozen or more layers of management between the chief executive officer (CEO) and the lowest-level employees. If employees want to introduce work changes, they ask a supervisor (the first level of management), who asks his or her manager, who asks a manager at the next level up, and so on. Eventually a decision is made and passed down from manager to manager until it reaches the employees. Such decisions can take weeks or months to be made. Max Weber used the word *bureaucrat* to describe a middle manager whose function was to implement top management's orders. Thus, **bureaucracy** came to be the term used for an organization with many layers of managers who set rules and regulations and oversee all decisions. It is such

hierarchy
A system in which one person is at the top of the organization and there is a ranked or sequential ordering from the top down of managers who are responsible to that person.

chain of command
The line of authority that moves from the top of a hierarchy to the lowest level.

bureaucracy
An organization with many layers of managers who set rules and regulations and oversee all decisions.

How we look at every Five Star retailer.

Now there's a process that puts dealers under the microscope so you don't have to. Five Star. With audits and customer satisfaction scores determining initial certification as well as annual recertification, it basically redefines the way cars and trucks are sold and serviced. With exacting standards that scrutinize what each retailer does and how they can do it better, only our very best make the grade. Take a closer look at a Five Star Certified Chrysler, Plymouth, Jeep, or Dodge retailer. For the one nearest you, call 1-800-677-5-STAR or visit us on the Web at www.fivestar.com. We're sure you'll really like what you see—but only where you see the Five Star sign.   **Five Star. It's Better. We'll Prove It.**

Jeep is a registered trademark of DaimlerChrysler.

Casual conversations with people who have bought cars often reveal that the most irritating thing about car dealers, other than pushy salespeople, is poor service. What can an auto manufacturer do to assure customers of the finest service through its dealers? The answer for DaimlerChrysler is to use annual audits and customer satisfaction surveys to establish standards for quality service and to monitor dealer performance and achievement. DaimlerChrysler is convinced that a Five Star Certified dealer will ultimately win the loyalty of customers and generate increased profit. If you were a dealer what would your perspective be on this initiative by DaimlerChrysler?

bureaucracy that forces employees to say to customers, "I will have to get back to you. I can't make that decision."

When employees have to ask their managers for permission to make a change, the process may take so long that customers become annoyed. Such consumer discontent may happen either in a small organization such as a flower shop or in a major organization such as an automobile dealership or a large construction firm. The employee has to find the manager, get permission to make the requested change, come back to the customer, explain what the management decision was, and so on. Has this happened to you in a department store or some other organization? Since many customers want efficient service—and they want it now—slow service is simply not acceptable in many of today's competitive firms.[4]

To make customers happier, some companies are reorganizing to give employees power to make more decisions on their own. Rather than always having to follow strict rules and regulations, they are encouraged to please the customer no matter what. As you read in Chapter 8, giving employees such authority and responsibility to make decisions and please customers is called empowerment ►**P. 19**◄ Remember that empowerment works only when employees are given the proper training and resources to respond.

It is important to note that well-run bureaucratic organizations can be extremely effective in certain contexts—little innovation in the marketplace, consistency in demand, low-skilled workers, and a lot of time to weigh the consequences of decisions. Many firms today do not operate under these conditions; therefore, there is a need to reorganize.

Progress Assessment

- What do the terms *division of labour* and *specialization* mean?
- What are the principles of management outlined by Fayol?
- What did Weber add to the principles of Fayol?

Critical Thinking

Now that you have learned some of the basic principles of organization, pause and think of where you have already applied such concepts yourself or have been involved with an organization that did. Did you find that a division of labour was necessary and helpful? Were you assigned specific tasks or were you left on your own to decide what to do? Were promotions based strictly on qualifications, as Weber suggested? What other factors may have been considered? What problems seem to emerge when an organization gets larger?

ISSUES INVOLVED IN STRUCTURING ORGANIZATIONS

What decisions are involved in structuring an organization? Since the turn of the century, many business leaders believed that there was one best way to structure an organization. However, this is changing. A starting point is the mission, goals, and objectives of the organization. These directives will impact the firm's structure, as employees must be organized so that they can achieve results. Structuring begins with this stage but must include other criteria.

Henry Mintzberg supports the current view that there is no single structure that will lead to success for all organizations. "Structure should reflect the organization's situation—for example, its age, size, type of production system, and the extent to which its environment is complex and dynamic. As well, a firm's design decisions (such as span of control, centralization versus decentralization, and matrix structures) need to be chosen so they can work within the chosen structure and design."[5] (These design decisions will be discussed in this chapter.)

C. K. Prahalad and Gary Hamel believe that businesses need to organize around their core competencies. **Core competencies** are those functions that the organization can do as well as or better than any other organization in the world. For example, Nike is great at designing and marketing athletic shoes. Those are its core competencies. It outsources the manufacturing of those shoes, however, to other companies that can make shoes better and less expensively than Nike itself can. Similarly, Dell is best at marketing computers and outsources most other functions, including manufacturing and distribution.[6]

By their nature, many organizational structures today are slow and unwieldy. One Canadian management consultant reported that research shows 85 to 95 percent of service, quality, or productivity problems stem from the organization's structure and processes ... Ask the question: "For whose convenience are systems designed?" Too often they serve accountants, technocrats, or management. Get the cart behind the horse. Your systems should serve your customers or those producing, delivering, or supporting your products.[7]

That is why current trends are toward smaller, more flexible structures that let companies react more quickly to today's fast-changing, technologically competitive business climate. They also unleash employees' initiative and enable them to participate in decision making.

When designing responsive organizations, firms have had to deal with several organizational issues: (1) centralization versus decentralization, (2) span of control, (3) tall versus flat organization structures, and (4) departmentalization.

core competencies
Those functions that an organization can do as well as or better than any other organization in the world.

Centralization versus Decentralization of Authority

Imagine for a minute that you're a top manager for a retail company such as Roots. Your temptation may be to preserve control over all your stores in order to maintain a uniform image and merchandise. You've noticed that such control works well for McDonald's; why not Roots? The degree to which an organization allows managers at the lower levels of the managerial hierarchy to make decisions determines the degree of decentralization that an organization practises.

Centralized authority occurs when decision-making authority is maintained at the top level of management at the company's headquarters. **Decentralized authority** occurs when decision-making authority is delegated to lower-level managers and employees who are more familiar with local conditions than headquarters' management could be. Figure 9.1 lists some advantages and disadvantages of centralized versus decentralized authority.

centralized authority
An organization structure in which decision-making authority is maintained at the top level of management at the company's headquarters.

decentralized authority
An organization structure in which decision-making authority is delegated to lower-level managers more familiar with local conditions than headquarters management could be.

FIGURE 9.1

ADVANTAGES AND
DISADVANTAGES OF
CENTRALIZED VERSUS
DECENTRALIZED
MANAGEMENT

ADVANTAGES	DISADVANTAGES
Centralized	
• Greater top-management control	• Less responsiveness to customers
• More efficiency	• Less empowerment
• Simpler distribution system	• Interorganizational conflict
• Stronger brand/corporate image	• Lower morale away from headquarters
Decentralized	
• Better adaptation to customer wants	• Less efficiency
• More empowerment of workers	• Complex distribution system
• Faster decision making	• Less top-management control
• Higher morale	• Weakened corporate image

Roots customers in Kelowna, for example, are likely to demand clothing styles different from those demanded in Charlottetown or Lethbridge. It makes sense, therefore, to give store managers in various cities the authority to buy, price, and promote merchandise appropriate for each area. Such a delegation of authority is an example of decentralized management.

In contrast, McDonald's feels that purchasing, promotion, and other such decisions are best handled centrally. There's usually little need for each McDonald's restaurant to carry different food products. McDonald's would therefore lean toward centralized authority. However, today's rapidly changing markets, added to global differences in consumer tastes, tend to favour more decentralization and thus more delegation of authority, even at McDonald's. Its restaurants in England offer tea, those in France offer a Croque McDo (a hot ham-and-cheese sandwich), those in Japan offer rice, and so on.[8] Rosenbluth International is a service organization in the travel industry. It too has decentralized so that its separate units can offer the kinds of services demanded in each region while still getting needed resources from corporate headquarters. The Reaching Beyond Our Borders box describes how Ford Motor Company used the Internet to decentralize decision making.

Choosing the Appropriate Span of Control

span of control
The optimum number of subordinates a manager supervises or should supervise.

Span of control refers to the optimum number of subordinates a manager supervises or should supervise. There are many factors to consider when determining span of control. At lower levels, where work is standardized, it's possible to implement a wide span of control (15 to 40 workers). For example, one supervisor can be responsible for 20 or more workers who are assembling computers or cleaning up movie theatres. However, the number gradually narrows at higher levels of the organization because work is less standardized and there's more need for face-to-face communication. Variables in span of control include the following:

- **Capabilities of the manager.** The more experienced and capable a manager is, the broader the span of control can be. (A large number of workers can report to that manager.)
- **Capabilities of the subordinates.** The more the subordinates need supervision, the narrower the span of control should be. Employee turnover at fast-food restaurants, for example, is often so high that

Reaching Beyond Our Borders

The Internet Assists with Decision Making

Nothing has done more to the organizations throughout the world than the emergence of the Internet. The Internet is a ready-made marketplace that consists of $1 trillion worth of computer power, network connections, and databases stuffed with information about individual consumers and groups. What's more amazing is that it's available to anyone with a personal computer, a modem, and an Internet connector—and it's open 24 hours a day, seven days a week. This may sound wonderful to you, but it is a tremendous challenge to traditional organizations organized in traditional ways. They simply cannot respond quickly enough to marketplace changes or reach global markets as quickly and efficiently as new companies can—companies designed to take advantage of the Internet. But what are they to do? How do they reorganize to match such competition?

The CEO of Ford Motor Company says that traditional companies have to become more nimble and more closely attuned to consumers. One source at Ford says, "You've got to break down the business into the smallest possible units to give the employees in them authority and accountability." (Throughout this text, we call that empowerment.) In the past, Ford centralized worldwide responsibility for functions such as product development, purchasing, design, and manufacturing. The new model decentralizes such decisions so that managers in Canada, Europe, and South America can readily adapt to consumers in those markets.

Did you know that Ford now owns Volvo? And Mazda? And Jaguar? And Land Rover? Did you also know that, to appeal to environmentalists, Ford has developed a car that runs on fuel cells? At first, fuel-cell cars will go to fleet customers (people who buy Fords in volume), but they will be available to the public soon as well. You can see how the company is trying to make cars that will appeal to almost everyone everywhere.

How does a company keep in touch with such widespread manufacturing and customer bases? By using the Internet. You can read more about Ford's new developments on its Website (www.ford.com).

Sources: Kathleen Kerwin and Jack Ewing, "Nasser: Ford Be Nimble," *Business Week*, September 27, 1999, pp. 42–43; "Ambitious Ford Aims High as It Sets Targets," *Birmingham Post*, January 12, 2001, p. 22; and John D. Wolpert, "Breaking Out of the Innovation Box," *Harvard Business Review*, August 2002, pp. 77–83.

---

managers must constantly be training new people and thus need a narrow span of control.

- **Geographical closeness.** The more concentrated the work area is, the broader the span of control can be.

- **Functional similarity.** The more similar the functions are, the broader the span of control can be.

- **Need for coordination.** The greater the need for coordination, the narrower the span of control might be.

- **Planning demands.** The more involved the plan, the narrower the span of control might be.

- **Functional complexity.** The more complex the functions are, the narrower the span of control might be.

Other factors to consider include the professionalism of superiors and subordinates and the number of new problems that occur in a day.

In business, the span of control varies widely. The number of people reporting to a company president may range from 1 to 80 or more. The trend is to expand the span of control as organizations reduce the number of middle managers and hire more educated and talented lower-level employees. That is all included in the idea of empowerment. It's possible to increase the span of control as employees become more professional, as information technology makes it possible for managers to handle more information, and as employees take on more responsibility for self-management. More companies could expand the span of control if they trained their employees better and were willing to trust them more.

Tall versus Flat Organization Structures

tall organization structure
An organization structure in which the pyramidal organization chart would be quite tall because of the various levels of management.

In the early 20th century, organizations grew bigger and bigger, adding layer after layer of management until they came to have what are called tall organization structures. A **tall organization structure** is one in which the pyramidal organization chart would be quite tall because of the various levels of management. Some organizations had as many as 14 levels, and the span of control was small (that is, there were few people reporting to each manager). You can imagine how a message would be distorted as it moved up the organization from manager to manager and then back down. When viewing such a tall organization, you saw a huge complex of managers, management assistants, secretaries, assistant secretaries, supervisors, trainers, and so on. The cost of keeping all these managers and support people was quite high. The paperwork they generated was enormous, and the inefficiencies in communication and decision making often became intolerable.

flat organization structure
An organization structure that has few layers of management and a broad span of control.

The result was the movement toward flatter organizations. A **flat organization structure** is one that has few layers of management (see Figure 9.2) and a broad span of control (that is, there are many people reporting to each manager). Such structures can be highly responsive to customer demands because authority and responsibility for making decisions may be given to lower-level

FIGURE 9.2

NARROW VERSUS WIDE SPAN OF CONTROL

This figure describes two ways to structure an organization with the same number of employees. The tall structure with a narrow span of control has two managers who supervise four employees each. Changing to a flat surface with a wide span of control, the company could eliminate two managers and perhaps replace them with one or two employees, but the top manager would have to supervise 10 people instead of two.

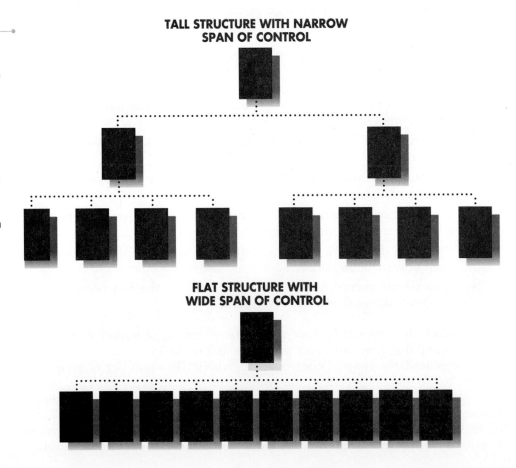

TALL STRUCTURE WITH NARROW SPAN OF CONTROL

FLAT STRUCTURE WITH WIDE SPAN OF CONTROL

ADVANTAGES	DISADVANTAGES
Narrow	
• More control by top management	• Less empowerment
• More chances for advancement	• Higher costs
• Greater specialization	• Delayed decision making
• Closer supervision	• Less responsiveness to customers
Wide	
• Reduced costs	• Fewer chances for advancement
• More responsiveness to customers	• Overworked managers
• Faster decision making	• Loss of control
• More empowerment	• Less management expertise

FIGURE 9.3

ADVANTAGES AND DISADVANTAGES OF A NARROW VERSUS A WIDE SPAN OF CONTROL

employees and managers can be spared from certain day-to-day tasks. In a bookstore that has a flat organization structure, employees may have the authority to arrange shelves by category, process special orders for customers, and so on. In many ways, large organizations were trying to match the friendliness of small firms, whose workers often knew the customers by name. The flatter organizations became, the larger the span of control became for most managers, and many managers lost their jobs. Figure 9.3 lists some advantages and disadvantages of a narrow versus a wide span of control.

Advantages and Disadvantages of Departmentalization

Departmentalization is the dividing of organizational functions (design, marketing, etc.) into separate units. The traditional way to departmentalize organizations is by function. Functional structure is the grouping of workers into departments based on similar skills, expertise, or resource use. A company might have, for example, a production department, a human resources department, and a finance department. Departmentalization by function enables employees to specialize and work together efficiently. It may also save costs. Other advantages include the following:

departmentalization
The dividing of organizational functions into separate units.

1. Employees can develop skills in depth and can progress within a department as they master those skills.

2. The company can achieve economies of scale in that it can centralize all the resources it needs and locate various experts in that area.

3. There's good coordination within the function, and top management can easily direct and control various departments' activities.

As for disadvantages of departmentalization by function,

1. There may be a lack of communication among the different departments. For example, production may be so isolated from marketing that the people making the product do not get the proper feedback from customers.

2. Individual employees may begin to identify with their department and its goals rather than with the goals of the organization as a whole. For example, the purchasing department may find a good value somewhere and buy a huge volume of goods that have to be stored at a high cost to

the firm. Such a deal may make the purchasing department look good, but it hurts the overall profitability of the firm.

3. The company's response to external changes may be slow.

4. People may not be trained to take different managerial responsibilities; rather, they tend to become narrow specialists.

5. People in the same department tend to think alike (engage in group-think) and may need input from outside the department to become more creative.

Alternative Ways to Departmentalize   Functional separation isn't always the most responsive form of organization. So what are the alternatives? Figure 9.4 shows five ways a firm can departmentalize. One form of departmentalization is by product. A book publisher might have a trade book department (books sold to the general public), a textbook department, and a technical book department. Customers for each type of book are different, so separate development and marketing processes must be created for each product. Such product-focused departmentalization usually results in good customer relations.

It makes more sense in some organizations to departmentalize by customer group. A pharmaceutical company, for example, might have one department that focuses on the consumer market, another that calls on hospitals (the institutional market), and another that targets doctors. You can see how the customer groups might benefit from having specialists satisfying their needs.

Some firms group their units by geographic location because customers vary so greatly by region. Japan, Europe, and Korea may involve separate departments. Again, the benefits are the same. Geographic locations may also be on a smaller scale; for example, by province (e.g., Manitoba) or by city (e.g., Regina).

The decision about which way to departmentalize depends greatly on the nature of the product and the customers served. A few firms find that it's most efficient to separate activities by process. For example, a firm that makes leather coats may have one department cut the leather, another dye it, and a third sew the coat together. Such specialization enables employees to do a better job because they can focus on a few critical skills.

Some firms use a combination of departmentalization techniques; they would be called hybrid forms. For example, a company could departmentalize simultaneously among the different layers by function, by geography, and by customers.

The development of the Internet and intranets has created whole new opportunities for reaching customers. Not only can you sell to customers directly over both channels, but you can also interact with them, ask them questions, and provide them with any information they may want. Companies must now

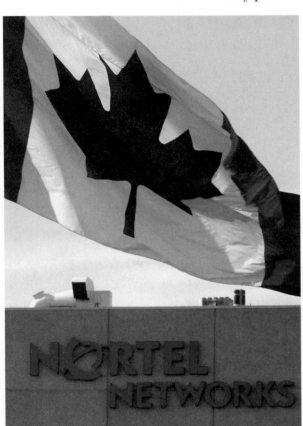

Nortel Networks keeps changing its organizational structure. In the 1980s, Nortel was mainly a telecommunications equipment provider organized into three geographic businesses—Canada, United States, and World Trade—each with its own marketing and manufacturing to serve the telephone monopolies. As Nortel globalized and telephone monopolies deregulated, the company reorganized around three product groups and four geographically based subsidiaries. Unfortunately, this structure was confusing and increased conflict between geographical and product heads. Today, Nortel is mainly structured around three client groups—service provider, enterprise, and small/medium business—as well as three geographical groups.

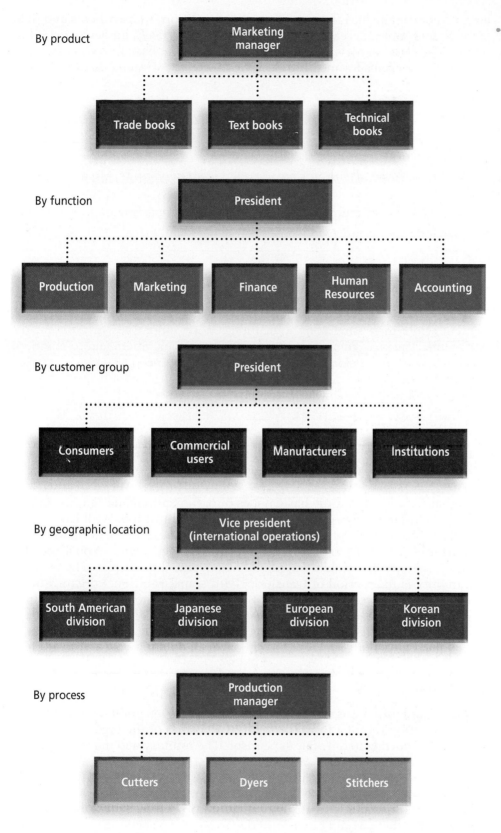

By product

Marketing manager

Trade books | Text books | Technical books

By function

President

Production | Marketing | Finance | Human Resources | Accounting

By customer group

President

Consumers | Commercial users | Manufacturers | Institutions

By geographic location

Vice president (international operations)

South American division | Japanese division | European division | Korean division

By process

Production manager

Cutters | Dyers | Stitchers

FIGURE 9.4

WAYS TO DEPARTMENTALIZE

A computer company may want to departmentalize by geographic location, a manufacturer by function, a pharmaceutical company by customer group, a leather manufacturer by process, and a publisher lby product. In each case the structure must fit the firm's goals.

learn to coordinate the efforts made by their traditional departments and their technology people to create a friendly, easy-to-use process for accessing information and buying goods and services.[9] The firms that have implemented such coordinated systems for meeting customer needs are winning market share.

Progress Assessment

- What is bureaucracy? What challenges do bureaucratic organizations face in a time of rapid change?
- Why are organizations becoming flatter?
- What are some reasons for having a small span of control in an organization?
- What are the advantages and disadvantages of departmentalization?
- What are the various ways a firm can departmentalize?

Critical Thinking

Businesses are now trying to redesign their structures to optimize skill development while increasing communication among employees in different departments. The goal, remember, is to better serve customers and to win their loyalty. What kind of skills and attributes might you need to prepare yourself to work in such an organization? What can you do to increase your personal ability to feel comfortable with change in your work setting?

ORGANIZATION MODELS

Now that we've explored the basic issues of organizational design, we can explore in depth the various ways to structure an organization. We'll look at four models: (1) line organizations, (2) line-and-staff organizations, (3) matrix-style organizations, and (4) cross-functional self-managed teams. You'll see that some of these models violate traditional management principles. The business community is in a period of transition, with some traditional organizational models giving way to new structures. Such transitions not only can be painful but also can be fraught with problems and errors. It will be easier for you to understand the issues involved after you have learned the basics of organizational modelling.

Line Organizations

line organization
An organization that has direct two-way lines of responsibility, authority, and communication running from the top to the bottom of the organization, with all people reporting to only one supervisor.

A **line organization** has direct two-way lines of responsibility, authority, and communication running from the top to the bottom of the organization, with all people reporting to only one supervisor. The military and many small businesses are organized this way. For example, Mario's Pizza Parlour has a general manager and a shift manager. All the general employees report to the shift manager, and he or she reports to the general manager or owner. A line organization does not have any specialists who provide managerial support. For example, there would be no legal department, no accounting department, no personnel department, and no information technology (IT) department. Such organizations follow all of Fayol's traditional management rules. Line managers can issue orders, enforce discipline, and adjust the organization as conditions change.

In large businesses, a line organization may have the disadvantages of being too inflexible, of having few specialists or experts to advise people along the line, of having lines of communication that are too long, and of being unable to handle the complex decisions involved in an organization with thousands of sometimes unrelated products and literally tonnes of paperwork. Such organizations usually turn to a line-and-staff form of organization.

Line-and-Staff Organizations

To minimize the disadvantages of simple line organizations, many organizations today have both line and staff personnel. A couple of definitions will help. **Line personnel** are part of the chain of command that is responsible for achieving organizational goals. Included are production workers, distribution people, and marketing personnel. **Staff personnel** advise and assist line personnel in meeting their goals (e.g., marketing research, legal advising, information technology, ethics advising, and human resource management). See Figure 9.5 for a diagram of a line-and-staff organization. One important difference between line and staff personnel is authority. Line personnel have formal authority to make policy decisions. Staff personnel have the authority to *advise* the line personnel and make suggestions that might influence those decisions, but they can't make policy changes themselves. The line manager may choose to seek or to ignore the advice from staff personnel.

Many organizations have benefited from the expert advice of staff assistants in areas such as safety, legal issues, quality control, database management, motivation, and investing. Staff positions strengthen the line positions and are not inferior or lower-paid. Having people in staff positions is like having well-paid consultants on the organization's payroll.

line personnel
Employees who are part of the chain of command that is responsible for achieving organizational goals.

staff personnel
Employees who advise and assist line personnel in meeting their goals.

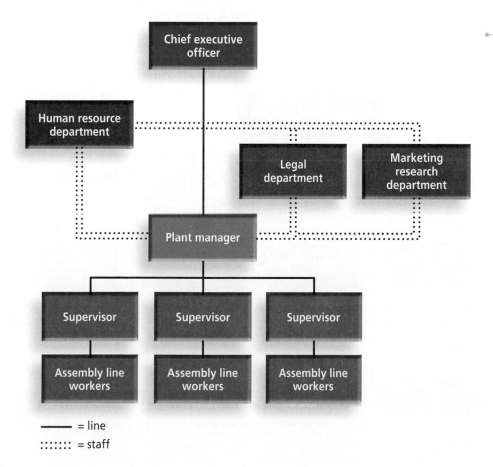

FIGURE 9.5

A SAMPLE LINE-AND-STAFF ORGANIZATION

Matrix-Style Organizations

Both line and line-and-staff organization structures suffer from a certain inflexibility. Both allow for established lines of authority and communication, and both work well in organizations with a relatively unchanging environment and slow product development, such as firms selling consumer products like toasters and refrigerators. In such firms, clear lines of authority and relatively fixed organization structures are assets that ensure efficient operations.

Today's economic scene, however, is dominated by high-growth industries (e.g., telecommunications, nanotechnology, robotics, biotechnology, and aerospace) unlike anything seen in the past. In such industries, competition is stiff and the life cycle of new ideas is short. Emphasis is on product development, creativity, special projects, rapid communication, and interdepartmental teamwork. The economic, technological, and competitive environments are rapidly changing.

From those changes grew the popularity of the matrix organization. In a **matrix organization,** specialists from different parts of the organization are brought together to work on specific projects but still remain part of a line-and-staff structure. (See Figure 9.6 for a diagram of a matrix organization.) In other words, a project manager can borrow people from different departments to help design and market new product ideas.

Matrix organization structures are now used in banking, management consulting firms, accounting firms, ad agencies, and school systems. Advantages of a matrix organization structure include the following:

- It gives flexibility to managers in assigning people to projects.
- It encourages interorganizational cooperation and teamwork.
- It can result in creative solutions to problems such as those associated with product development.
- It provides for efficient use of organizational resources.

matrix organization
An organization in which specialists from different parts of the organization are brought together to work on specific projects but still remain part of a line-and-staff structure.

FIGURE 9.6

A MATRIX ORGANIZATION

In a matrix organization, project managers are in charge of teams made up of members of several departments. In this case, project manager 2 supervises employees A, B, C, and D. These employees are accountable not only to project manager 2 but also to the head of their individual departments. For example, employee B, a market researcher, reports to project manager 2 *and* to the vice president of marketing.

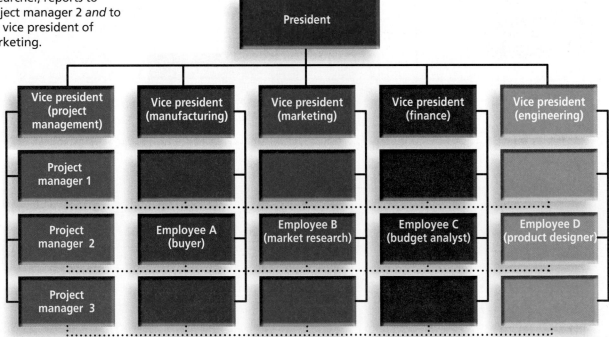

Although it works well in some organizations, the matrix style doesn't work well in others. As for disadvantages,

- It's costly and complex.
- It can cause confusion among employees as to where their loyalty belongs—to the project manager or to their department.
- It requires good interpersonal skills and cooperative employees and managers; communication problems can emerge.
- It may be only a temporary solution to a long-term problem.

If it seems to you that matrix organizations violate some traditional managerial principles, you're right. Normally a person can't work effectively for two bosses. Who has the real authority? Which directive has the first priority: the one from the project manager or the one from the employee's immediate supervisor? In reality, however, the system functions more effectively than you might imagine. To develop a new product, a project manager may be given temporary authority to "borrow" line personnel from production, marketing, and other line functions.[10] Together, the employees work to complete the project and then return to their regular positions. Thus, no one really reports to more than one manager at a time. The effectiveness of matrix organizations in high-tech firms has led to the adoption of similar concepts in many firms, including such traditional firms as Rubbermaid. During the past decade, Rubbermaid turned out an average of one new product every day using the team concept from matrix management.

cross-functional self-managed teams
Groups of employees from different departments who work together on a long-term basis.

A potential problem with matrix management, however, is that the project teams are not permanent. They are formed to solve a problem or develop a new product, and then they break up. There is little chance for cross-functional learning because experts from each function are together for such little time.

Rubbermaid creates new products quickly, sometimes as fast as one a day. This photo shows one of their new products that organizes sports equipment, reducing household clutter. Cross-functional teams at Rubbermaid help create new products and get them to market quickly. What do you see as some of the advantages and potential challenges of working with people from various departments on new-product development?

Cross-Functional Self-Managed Teams

An answer to the disadvantage of the temporary teams created by matrix management is to establish long-lived teams and to empower them to work closely with suppliers, customers, and others to quickly and efficiently bring out new, high-quality products while giving great service. **Cross-functional self-managed teams** are groups of employees from different departments who work together on a long-term basis (as opposed to the temporary teams established in matrix-style organizations). Usually the teams are empowered to make decisions on their own without having to seek the approval of management. That's why the teams are called self-managed. The barriers between design, engineering, marketing, distribution, and other functions fall when interdepartmental teams are created.

Mike DiGiovanni thought he had a great idea. He wanted General Motors to buy the rights to the Hummer, a military vehicle, with the idea of creating a smaller, friendlier version—the H2. He wanted a team made up of veterans who knew what they were doing. He also wanted people who wanted to be on the team, not people who were next in line for a job. Hummer became a top-selling vehicle for GM. How important do you think a committed team leader and team members are to the success of such an operation?

Sometimes the teams are interfirm. Hummer, for example, has become one of the hottest divisions at General Motors (GM). A cross-functional team from GM designs, engineers, and markets Hummers, but AM General manufactures the vehicles in a plant built with a loan from GM.[11]

For empowerment and cross-functional self-managed teams to work effectively, the organization has to change. Moving from a manager-driven to an employee-driven or team-driven company isn't easy. Managers often resist giving up their authority over workers, while workers often resist the responsibility that comes with self-management. Nonetheless, many of the world's leading organizations are moving in that direction. They're trying to develop an organizational design that best serves the needs of all stakeholders ➤**P. 5**◄—employees, customers, shareholders, and the community.

Shell Canada has organized its entire workforce in its plant in Brockville, Ontario, into self-managing teams. This $75-million lubricants factory employs only 75 people, of whom 15 are senior managers (called coordinators) or purely administrative staff. There are 60 team operators. All of these employees are expected to manage everything themselves as individuals or team members. "The teams are responsible for discipline, cost control (including absenteeism), and arranging their own vacation and training schedules."[12]

Figure 9.7 lists the advantages and disadvantages of these four types of organizations.

Going Beyond Organizational Boundaries Cross-functional teams work best when the voice of the customer is brought into organizations. Customer input is especially valuable to product development teams. Suppliers and distributors should be included on the team as well. A cross-functional team that includes customers, suppliers, and distributors goes beyond organizational boundaries.

Some firms' suppliers and distributors are in other countries. Thus, cross-functional teams may share market information across national boundaries. The government may encourage the networking of teams, and government coordinators may assist such projects. In that case, cross-functional teams break the barriers between government and business. The use of cross-functional teams is only one way in which businesses have changed to interact with other companies. In the next section of this chapter we look at other ways that organizations manage their various interactions.

Progress Assessment

- What is the difference between line and staff personnel?
- What management principle does a matrix-style organization challenge?
- What may hinder the development of cross-functional teams?

	ADVANTAGES	DISADVANTAGES
Line	• Clearly defined responsibility and authority • Easy to understand • One supervisor for each person	• Too inflexible • Few specialists to advise • Long lines of communication • Unable to handle complex questions quickly
Line and staff	• Expert advice from staff to line personnel • Establishes lines of authority • Encourages co-operation and better communication at all levels	• Potential overstaffing • Potential overanalyzing • Lines of communication can get blurred • Staff frustrations because of lack of authority
Matrix	• Flexible • Encourages cooperation among departments • Can produce creative solutions to problems • Allows organization to take on new projects without adding to the organizational structure • Provides for more efficient use of organizational resources	• Costly and complex • Can confuse employees • Requires good interpersonal skills and cooperative managers and employees • Difficult to evaluate employees and to set up reward systems
Cross-functional, self-managed teams	• Greatly increases interdepartmental coordination and cooperation • Quicker response to customers and market conditions • Increased employee motivation and morale	• Some confusion over responsibility and authority • Perceived loss of control by management • Difficult to evaluate employees and to set up reward systems • Requires self-motivated and highly trained workers

FIGURE 9.7

TYPES OF ORGANIZATIONS

Each form of organization has its advantages and disadvantages.

MANAGAING THE INTERACTIONS AMONG FIRMS

Whether it involves customers, suppliers and distributors, or the government, **networking** is using communications technology and other means to link organizations and allow them to work together on common objectives. Organizations are so closely linked by the Internet that each can find out what the others are doing in real time. **Real time** simply means the present moment or the actual time in which something takes place. Internet data is available in real time because it is sent instantly to various organizational partners as it is developed or collected. The net effect is a rather new concept called transparency. **Transparency** occurs when a company is so open to other companies working with it that the once-solid barriers between them become see-through and electronic information is shared as if the companies were one. Because of this integration, two companies can now work as closely together as two departments once did in traditional firms.

Can you see the implications for organizational design? Most organizations are no longer self-sufficient or self-contained. Rather, many modern organizations are part of a vast network of global businesses that work closely together. An organization chart showing what people do within any one organization is simply not complete, because the organization is part of a much larger system of firms. A modern organization chart would show people in different organizations and indicate how they are networked. This is a relatively new concept, however, so few such charts are yet available.

The organization structures tend to be flexible and changing. That is, one company may work with a design expert from a different company in Italy for

networking
Using communications technology and other means to link organizations and allow them to work together on common objectives.

real time
The present moment or the actual time in which something takes place; data sent over the Internet to various organizational partners as they are developed or collected are said to be available in real time.

transparency
A concept that describes a company being so open to other companies working with it that the once-solid barriers between them become see-through and electronic information is shared as if the companies were one.

FIGURE 9.8

A VIRTUAL CORPORATION

A virtual corporation has no permanent ties to the firms that do its production, distribution, legal, and other work. Such firms are very flexible and can adapt to changes in the market quickly.

virtual corporation
A temporary networked organization made up of replaceable firms that join and leave as needed.

benchmarking
Comparing an organization's practices, processes, and products against the world's best.

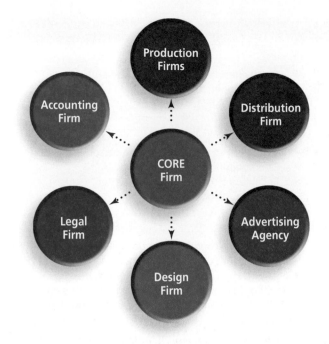

Knowledge is increasing and technology is developing so fast that companies can only maintain a leading edge by benchmarking everything they do against the best in all industries. That's how K2 was able to find the best materials and processes for making its skis. Think of how you could apply this concept in your own life. Who might you study to learn the best way to prepare for classes and exams?

a year and then not need that person anymore. Another expert from another company in another country may be hired next time for another project. Such a temporary networked organization, made up of replaceable firms that join and leave as needed, is called a **virtual corporation** (see Figure 9.8). This may sound confusing because it is so different from traditional organization structure, and in fact, traditional managers do often have trouble adapting to the speed of change and the impermanence of relationships that have come about in the age of networking. We discuss adaptation to change in the final section of this chapter; first, though, we describe how organizations are using benchmarking and outsourcing to manage their interactions with other firms.

Benchmarking and Outsourcing

Traditionally, organizations have tried to do all functions themselves. That is, each organization had a separate department for accounting, finance, marketing, production, and so on. Today's organizations are looking to other organizations to help them in areas where they are not able to generate world-class quality.[13] **Benchmarking** (also referred to as best practices) involves comparing an organization's practices, processes, and products against the world's best. For example, K2 is a company that makes skis, snowboards, in-line skates, and related products. It studied the compact-disc industry and learned to use ultraviolet inks to print graphics on skis. It went to the aerospace industry to get Piezo technology to reduce vibration in its snowboards (the aerospace industry uses the technology for wings on planes). And, finally, it learned from the cable-TV industry how to braid layers of fibreglass and carbon, and adapted that knowledge to make skis.

Benchmarking is also used in a more directly competitive way. For example, Zellers may compare itself to Wal-Mart to see what, if anything, Wal-Mart does better. Zellers would then try to improve its practices or processes to become even better than Wal-Mart. Sam Walton used to do competitive benchmarking regularly. He would visit the stores of competitors and see what, if anything, the competitor was doing better. When he found something better—say, a pricing program—he would come back to Wal-Mart and make the appropriate changes.

Benchmarking has become a significant activity in Canada. Governments and large and small companies are all involved in procedures to discover and apply the best practices available. Industry Canada and StatsCan have accumulated extensive statistics on the use of benchmarking in a variety of industries. Some examples are breweries, flour mixing and cereal production, electronic computing, paperboard manufacturing, musical instruments, and the recording industry.

If an organization can't do as well as the best in any particular area, such as shipping, it often will try to outsource the function to an organization that *is* the best (e.g., FedEx).[14] **Outsourcing** is assigning various functions, such as accounting, production, security, maintenance, and legal work, to outside organizations.[15] Some functions, such as information management and marketing, may be too important to assign to outside firms.[16] In that case, the organization should benchmark on the best firms and restructure its departments to try to be equally good.

outsourcing
Assigning various functions, such as accounting, production, security, maintenance, and legal work, to outside organizations.

A recent article titled *"Offshore Outsourcing Seen Reshaping the Tech Sector"* highlights this growing trend. The article states the following points:

> Increasing global competition to decrease prices has led technology players to find low-cost partners or contract out work, according to Ramalinga Raju, chairman of Satyam Computer Services Ltd, a tech provider based in India. "Competition is something you cannot wish away. More often than not, off-shore delivery has meant an offset in costs." Potential savings are dramatic. In Canada, the average computer programmer with two to three years' experience earns between $33,000 and $65,000 annually. In comparison, programmers in India earn between $8,000 and $13,000 annually. Canadian partners include document management software maker Hummingbird Ltd. of Toronto and business intelligence software provider Cognos Inc. of Ottawa.
>
> In addition to lower costs, outsourcing frees up financial resources for better use, reports ATI Technologies Inc. of Markham, Ontario. All of the company's graphics chips are made for it by low-cost manufacturers in Taiwan, allowing the company to invest more heavily in research and development.[17]

ADAPTING TO CHANGE

Once you have structured an organization, you must be prepared to adapt that structure to changes in the market. That is not always easy to do. Over a number of years, it is easy for an organization to become stuck in its ways. Employees have a tendency to say, "That's the way we've always done things. If it isn't broken, don't fix it." Managers also get stuck in their ways. Managers may say that they have 20 years' experience when the truth is that they've had one year's experience 20 times. Introducing change into an organization is thus one of the hardest challenges facing any manager.[18] Several companies have been cited in the business literature as having difficulty reinventing themselves in response to changes in the competitive environment. They include Polaroid and Eaton's.[19] New cameras (digital) and new kinds of film brought about the downfall of Polaroid, which filed for bankruptcy and was later sold. Eaton's was unable to manage the competition from other retailers, and filed for bankruptcy. New managers at these firms face tremendous hurdles as they try to revive them.

Celestica Inc. is a global leader in electronics manufacturing services (EMS), with operations in Asia, Europe, and the Americas. In response to demands for lower prices, approximately 70 percent of Celestica's production is now in lower-cost geographies around the world, such as Asia, Mexico, and the Czech Republic. Would you be more or less likely to invest in a Canadian company like Celestica that outsources most of its production? Do you believe that Canadian companies have a responsibility to keep jobs in Canada? Why or why not?

Mergers and acquisitions pose special challenges in adapting to change. That's why so many mergers of big corporations fail and why so many people were watching the merger of Indigo and Chapters (discussed in this chapter's opening profile) with such interest.

Restructuring for Empowerment

restructuring
Redesigning an organization so that it can more effectively and efficiently serve its customers.

To implement the empowerment of employees, firms often must reorganize dramatically. Sometimes that may mean restructuring the firm to make front-line workers the most important people in the organization. **Restructuring** is redesigning an organization so that it can more effectively and efficiently serve its customers. Until recently, front-desk people in hotels, clerks in department stores, and tellers in banks hadn't been considered the key personnel. Instead, managers were considered the key people, and they were responsible for directing the work of the frontline people. The organization chart in a typical firm looked something like the traditional organization pyramid shown in Figure 9.9.

inverted organization
An organization that has contact people at the top and the chief executive officer at the bottom of the organization chart.

A few service-oriented organizations have turned the traditional organization structure upside down. An **inverted organization** has contact people at the top and the chief executive officer at the bottom. There are few layers of management, and the manager's job is to assist and support frontline people, not boss them around. Figure 9.9 illustrates the difference between an inverted and a traditional organizational structure.

A good example of an inverted organization is NovaCare, a provider of rehabilitation care. At its top are some 5,000 physical, occupational, and speech therapists. The rest of the organization is structured to serve those therapists. Managers consider the therapists to be their bosses, and the manager's job is to support the therapists by arranging contacts with nursing homes, handling accounting and credit activities, and providing training.

Companies based on this organization structure support frontline personnel with internal and external databases, advanced communication systems, and professional assistance. Naturally, this means that frontline people have to be better educated, better trained, and better paid than in the past. It takes a lot of trust for top managers to implement such a system—but when they do, the payoff in customer satisfaction and in profits is often well worth the effort. In the past, managers controlled information—and that gave them power. In

FIGURE 9.9

COMPARISON OF AN INVERTED ORGANIZATION STRUCTURE AND A TRADITIONAL ORGANIZATION STRUCTURE

Traditional Organization   Inverted Organization

more progressive organizations, everyone shares information, often through an elaborate database system.

It's not easy to move from an organization dominated by managers to one that relies heavily on self-managed teams. How you restructure an organization depends on the status of the present system. If the system already has a customer focus, but isn't working well, a total quality management approach may work.

Total quality management (TQM) is the practice of striving for maximum customer satisfaction by ensuring quality from all departments. TQM calls for *continual improvement of present processes*. Processes are sets of activities strung together for a reason, such as the process for handling a customer's order. The process may consist of getting the order in the mail, opening it, sending it to someone to fill, putting the order into a package, and sending it out. In Chapter 10 we will review the importance of quality control in production management.

Continuous improvement (CI) means constantly improving the way the organization does things so that customer needs can be satisfied. Many of the companies spotlighted in this book practise it. Meat-packer Schneider Foods of Kitchener, Ontario, attributes its success in overcoming difficult adjustments to market changes to CI.[20]

It's possible, in an organization with few layers of management and a customer focus, that new computer software and employee training could lead to a team-oriented approach with few problems. In bureaucratic organizations with many layers of management, however, TQM is not useful. Continual improvement doesn't work when the whole process is being done incorrectly. When an organization needs dramatic changes, only reengineering will do.

The Restructuring Process

Reengineering is the fundamental rethinking and radical redesign of organizational processes to achieve dramatic improvements in critical measures of performance. Note the words *radical redesign* and *dramatic improvements*. At IBM's credit organization, for example, the procedure for handling a customer's request for credit once went through a five-step process that took an average of six days. By completely reengineering the customer-request process, IBM cut its credit request processing time from six days to four hours! In reengineering, narrow, task-oriented jobs become multidimensional. Employees who once did as they were told now make decisions on their own. Functional departments lose their reason for being. Managers stop acting like supervisors and instead behave like coaches. Workers focus more on the customers' needs and less on their bosses' needs. Attitudes and values change in response to new incentives. Practically every aspect of the organization is transformed, often beyond recognition.

Can you see how reengineering is often necessary to change a firm from a managerial orientation to one based on cross-functional self-managed teams? Reengineering may also be necessary to adapt an organization to fit into a virtual network. Remember, reengineering involves *radical* redesign and *dramatic*

total quality management (TQM)
Striving for maximum customer satisfaction by ensuring quality from all departments.

continuous improvement (CI)
Constantly improving the way the organization does things so that customer needs can be better satisfied.

reengineering
The fundamental rethinking and radical redesign of organizational processes to achieve dramatic improvements in critical measures of performance.

G.A.P Adventures is an adventure travel company that offers small group travel and eco tours throughout the world. The company's mission statement is to satisfy every customer, every time, through outstanding, personalized service. G.A.P is focused on continuous improvement— employees constantly strive to improve the quality and effectiveness of the company's offerings. Can you think of an example of a company where continuous improvement is not a focus?

improvements. Not all organizations need such dramatic change. In fact, because of the complexity of the process, many reengineering efforts fail. In firms where reengineering is not feasible, restructuring may do. As discussed earlier in this chapter, restructuring involves making relatively minor changes to an organization in response to a changing environment. For example, a firm might add an Internet marketing component to the marketing department. That is a restructuring move, but it is not drastic enough to be called reengineering.

Creating a Change-Oriented Organizational Culture

Any organizational change is bound to cause some stress and resistance among members of the firm. Firms adapt best when they have a change-oriented culture. **Organizational (or corporate) culture** may be defined as widely shared values within an organization that provide unity and cooperation to achieve common goals. It's obvious from visiting any McDonald's restaurant that effort has been made to maintain a culture that emphasizes quality, service, cleanliness, and value. Each restaurant has the same feel, the same look, the same atmosphere. In short, each has a similar organizational culture.

An organizational culture can also be negative. Have you ever been in an organization where you feel that no one cares about service or quality? The clerks may seem uniformly glum, indifferent, and testy. The mood seems to pervade the atmosphere so that patrons become unhappy or upset. It may be hard to believe that an organization, especially a profit-making one, can be run so badly and still survive. Are there examples in your area?

Mintzberg notes that culture impacts the way employees are chosen, developed, nurtured, interrelated, and rewarded. The kinds of people attracted to an organization and the way they can most effectively deal with problems and each other are largely a function of the culture a place builds—and the practices and systems that support it.[21]

The very best organizations have cultures that emphasize service to others, especially customers.[22] The atmosphere is one of friendly, concerned, caring people who enjoy working together to provide a good product at a reasonable price. Those companies that have such cultures have less need for close supervision of employees, not to mention policy manuals; organization charts; and formal rules, procedures, and controls. The key to a productive culture is mutual trust. You get such trust by giving it.[23] The very best companies stress high moral and ethical values such as honesty, reliability, fairness, environmental protection, and social involvement. The Spotlight on Small Business box looks at how one small organization successfully implemented a customer-oriented culture.

Thus far, we've been talking as if organizational matters were mostly controllable by management. The fact is that the formal organization structure is just one element of the total organizational system. In the creation of organizational culture, the informal organization is of equal or even greater importance. Let's explore this notion next.

The Informal Organization

All organizations have two organizational systems. One is the **formal organization,** which is the structure that details lines of responsibility, authority, and position. It's the structure shown on organization charts. The other is the **informal organization,** which is the system of relationships that develop spontaneously as employees meet and form power centres. It consists of the various cliques, relationships, and lines of authority that develop outside the formal organization. It's the human side of the organization that doesn't show on any organization chart.

No organization can operate effectively without both types of organization. The formal system is often too slow and bureaucratic to enable the organization to adapt quickly. However, the formal organization does provide helpful guides and lines of authority to follow in routine situations.

The informal organization is often too unstructured and emotional to allow careful, reasoned decision making on critical matters. It's extremely effective, however, in generating creative solutions to short-term problems and providing a feeling of camaraderie and teamwork among employees.

In any organization, it's wise to learn quickly who the important people are in the informal organization. Typically, there are formal rules and procedures to follow for getting certain supplies or equipment, but those procedures may take days. Who in the organization knows how to obtain supplies immediately without following the normal procedures? Which administrative assistants should you see if you want your work given first priority? These are the questions to answer to work effectively in many organizations.

The informal organization's nerve centre is the *grapevine* (the system through which unofficial information flows between and among managers and employees). The key people in the grapevine usually have considerable influence in the organization.

In the old "us-versus-them" system of organizations, where managers and employees were often at odds, the informal system often hindered effective management. In the new, more open organizations, where managers and employees work together to set objectives and design procedures, the informal organization can be an invaluable managerial asset that often promotes harmony among workers and establishes the corporate culture. That's a major advantage, for example, of self-managed teams.

As effective as the informal organization may be in creating group cooperation, it can still be equally powerful in resisting management directives. Employees may form unions, go on strike together, and generally disrupt operations.[24] Learning to create the right corporate culture and to work within the informal organization is a key to managerial success.

Richard Tait (left) calls himself the grand poo-bah for Cranium, producer of the highly successful board game of that name. Whit Alexander, who does product development and manufacturing, is called the chief noodler. Their criteria for decision making are clever, high quality, innovative, friendly, and fun (CHIFF). What kind of leadership style and company culture might you expect in a company that is so casual?

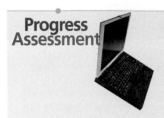

Progress Assessment

- What is an inverted organization?
- How is continuous improvement different from reengineering?
- Why do organizations outsource functions?
- What is organizational culture?

Summary

1. Explain the historical organizational theories of Fayol and Weber.

1. Until the 20th century, most businesses were rather small, the processes of producing goods were rather simple, and organizing workers was fairly easy. Not until the 1900s and the introduction of mass production did businesses become complex. During this era, business theorists emerged.

   • ***What concepts did Fayol and Weber contribute?***

   Fayol introduced principles such as unity of command, hierarchy of authority, division of labour, subordination of individual interests to the general interest, authority, clear communication channels, order, and equity. Weber added principles of bureaucracy such as job descriptions, written rules and decision guidelines, consistent procedures, and staffing and promotions based on qualifications.

2. Discuss the various issues involved in structuring organizations.

2. Issues involved in structuring and restructuring organizations include (1) centralization versus decentralization, (2) span of control, (3) tall versus flat organization structures, and (4) departmentalization.

   • ***What are the basics of each?***

   The problem with tall organizations is that they slow communications. The trend is to eliminate managers and flatten organizations. The span of control becomes larger as employees become self-directed. Departments are often being replaced or supplemented by matrix organizations and cross-functional teams. Use of cross-functional teams results in decentralization of authority.

   • ***How do inverted organizations fit into these concepts?***

   An inverted organization usually results from a major reengineering effort because the changes are dramatic in that employees are placed at the top of the hierarchy and are given much training and support, while managers are at the bottom and are there to train and assist employees.

3. Describe and differentiate the various organizational models.

3. Organizational design is the coordinating of workers so that they can best accomplish the firm's goals. New forms of organization are emerging that enable firms to be more responsive to customers.

   • ***What are the traditional forms of organization and their advantages?***

   The two traditional forms of organization explored in the text are (1) line organizations and (2) line-and-staff organizations. A line organization has the advantages of having clearly defined responsibility and authority, being easy to understand, and providing one supervisor for each person. Most organizations have benefited from the expert advice of staff assistants in areas such as safety, quality control, computer technology, ethics counselling, human resource management, and investing.

   • ***What are the new forms of organization?***

   Matrix organizations and cross-functional self-managed teams.

• *How do they differ?*

Matrix organizations involve *temporary* assignments (projects) that give flexibility to managers in assigning people to projects and encourage interorganizational cooperation and teamwork. Cross-functional self-managed teams are *long term* and have all the benefits of the matrix style.

4. Networking is using communications technology and other means to link organizations and allow them to work together on common objectives.

4. List the concepts involved in interfirm cooperation and coordination.

• *What is a virtual corporation?*

A virtual corporation is a networked organization made up of replaceable firms that join the network and leave it as needed.

• *What's the difference between restructuring and reengineering?*

It's basically a matter of degree. Restructuring is making needed changes in the firm so that it can more effectively and efficiently serve its customers. For example, a firm may add more computers or change how it processes orders. Reengineering is the fundamental rethinking and radical redesign of organizational processes to achieve dramatic improvements in critical measures of performance.

• *Why do firms outsource some of their functions?*

Some firms are very good at one function: for example, marketing. Competitive benchmarking tells them that they are not as good as some companies at production or distribution. The company may then outsource those functions to companies that can perform those functions more effectively and efficiently. The functions left are called the firm's core competencies.

5. Restructuring, organizational culture, and informal organizations can help businesses adapt to change. Restructuring involves redesigning an organization so that it can more effectively and efficiently serve its customers. Organizational culture refers to widely shared values within an organization that provide coherence and cooperation to achieve common goals.

5. Discuss the tools that are available to assist organizations in adapting to change.

• *How can organizational culture and the informal organization hinder or assist organizational change?*

The very best organizations have cultures that emphasize service to others, especially customers. The atmosphere is one of friendly, concerned, caring people who enjoy working together to provide a good product at a reasonable price. Companies with such cultures have less need than other companies for close supervision of employees; policy manuals; organization charts; and formal rules, procedures, and controls. This opens the way for self-managed teams.

Key Terms

benchmarking 268
bureaucracy 253
centralized authority 255
chain of command 253
continuous improvement (CI) 271
core competencies 255
cross-functional self-managed teams 265
decentralized authority 255
departmentalization 259

flat organization structure 258
formal organization 272
hierarchy 253
informal organization 272
inverted organization 270
line organization 262
line personnel 263
matrix organization 264
networking 267
organizational (or corporate) culture 272

outsourcing 269
real time 267
reengineering 271
restructuring 270
span of control 256
staff personnel 263
tall organization structure 258
total quality management (TQM) 271
transparency 267
virtual corporation 268

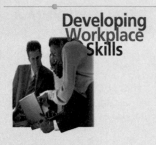

Developing Workplace Skills

1. There is no better way to understand the effects of having many layers of management on communication accuracy than to play the game of Message Relay. Choose seven or more members of the class and have them leave the classroom. Then choose one person to read the following paragraph and another student to listen. Call in one of the students from outside and have the "listener" tell him or her what information was in the paragraph. Then bring in another student and have the new listener repeat the information to him or her. Continue the process with all those who left the room. Do not allow anyone in the class to offer corrections as each listener becomes the storyteller in turn. In this way, all the students can hear how the facts become distorted over time. The distortions and mistakes are often quite humorous, but they are not so funny in organizations such as Ford, which once had 22 layers of management.

   Here's the paragraph:

   Dealers in the Maritimes have received over 130 complaints about steering on the new Commander and Roadhandler models of our minivans. Apparently, the front suspension system is weak and the ball joints are wearing too fast. This causes slippage in the linkage and results in oversteering. Mr. Berenstein has been notified, but so far only 213 out of 4,300 dealers have received repair kits.

2. Describe some informal groups within an organization with which you are familiar (at school, at work, etc.). What have you noticed about how those groups help or hinder progress in the organization?

3. Imagine you are working for Kitchen Magic, an appliance manufacturer that produces, among other things, dishwashers for the home. Imagine further that a competitor introduces a new dishwasher that uses sound waves to clean dishes. The result is a dishwasher that cleans even the worst burnt-on food and sterilizes the dishes and silverware as well. You need to develop a similar offering fast, or your company will lose the market. Write an e-mail to management outlining the problem and explaining your rationale for recommending use of a cross-functional team to respond quickly.

4. Divide the class into teams of five. Imagine that your firm has been asked to join a virtual network. You are a producer of athletic shoes. What might you do to minimize the potential problems of being involved with a virtual corporation? Begin by defining a virtual corporation and listing the potential problems. Also, list the benefits of being part of such a system.

5. Imagine that your organization is changing to be more responsive to stakeholders. As a result, your job is changing. What would you do if you were faced with the following decisions?

   • The call centre you are working for has been moved to another province. Your job is secure. Will you go?

   • As a result of reengineering, your job has been thoroughly redesigned and you need to use skills that you do not possess and are not comfortable with. What do you do?

   • You were a technical customer support consultant for the company and have been asked to expand your role to selling goods to customers. What would you do to become comfortable with your new role?

Taking It To The Net

Purpose

To describe Ford Motor Company's formal and informal organizational structures.

Exercise

When you think of how Ford Motor Company is organized, you may think of it in terms of its brands (Mazda, Mercury, Lincoln, Aston Martin, Jaguar, Land Rover, Volvo) or its businesses (Automotive Operations, Ford Financial, Hertz). However, the company serves all of its brands and businesses through what it calls hiring organizations. Learn more about it by going to www.mycareer.ford.com/OurCompany.asp.

1. How are Ford's hiring organizations organized?

2. Click on the link of one of the hiring organizations. What types of positions does this function provide? What are the preferred qualifications of the candidates Ford would like to find to fill these positions?

3. Describe Ford's unique hiring process. If you've applied for jobs before, how does Ford's hiring process differ from what you've experienced? What could this process tell you about Ford's organizational culture? How does the process help Ford find employees who will fit into its culture?

Practising Management Decisions

Case

IBM Is Both an Outsourcer and a Major Outsource for Others

Few companies are better known for their manufacturing expertise than IBM. Nonetheless, even IBM has to adapt to the dynamic marketplace of today. In the area of personal computers, for example, IBM was unable to match the prices or speed of delivery of mail-order firms such as Dell Computer. Dell built machines after receiving orders for them and then rushed the computers to customers. IBM, in contrast, made machines ahead of time and hoped that the orders would match its inventory.

To compete against firms like Dell, IBM had to custom-make computers for its business customers, but IBM was not particularly suited to do such work. However, IBM did work with several distributors that were also having problems. The distributors were trying to custom-make IBM machines but were forced to carry a heavy inventory of parts and materials to do so. Distributors were also tearing IBM computers apart and putting them back together with other computer companies' parts to produce custom-made computers.

IBM decided to allow its distributors to store parts and materials and then custom-make computers to customer demand. In other words, IBM outsourced about 60 percent of its commercial PC business. Distributors such as Inacom

Corporation became profitable, and IBM was able to offer custom-made PCs competitive in price with those of Dell and other direct-mail companies.

More recently, IBM has begun selling its technology—tiny disk drives, speedy new chips, and more—to its former competitors! For some of these new partners, IBM will design their new products and let them explore its labs. In short, IBM is doing a bit of reverse outsourcing in that it is offering itself as a research and product development company ready to work with others. Thus, IBM will sell networking chips to Cisco Systems and not compete with that company anymore. And it will likewise sell disk drives to EMC. IBM benchmarked its final products against these companies and saw that it was not winning. The winning strategy, it decided, was to join them and become an even better team. IBM's long-range strategy is to move away from hardware toward software development. It acquired PricewaterhouseCoopers to put more emphasis on services rather than hardware.

Decision Questions

1. What does it say about today's competitive environment when leading companies such as

IBM give up competing and decide to work with competitors instead?

2. What effects will outsourcing have on trade relationships among countries?

3. If more Canadian companies unite their technologies, what will that do to competitors in other countries? Should foreign companies do more uniting with Canadian companies themselves? What about Canadian companies uniting with foreign companies?

4. How much influence will the Internet have on world trade and outsourcing among countries? What does the Internet provide that wasn't available before?

Sources: Michael Useem and Joseph Harder, "Leading Laterally in Company Outsourcing," *Sloan Management Review*, Winter 2000, pp. 25–36; Daniel Eisenberg, "There's a New Way to Think @ Big Blue," *Time*, January 20, 2003, pp. 49–53; and Alison Overholt, "In the Hot Seat," *Fast Company*, January 2003, p. 46.

Video Case

One Smooth Stone

David slew Goliath with one smooth stone, and thus was born the name of the company One Smooth Stone (OSS). It's an unusual name for an unusually interesting company. The company is in the business of providing materials for big corporate events: sales meetings, client meetings, and product presentations. Most people in the industry have attended many such meetings, so to keep them entertained is a major challenge. And that's where OSS comes in: It uses project teams to come up with original and captivating presentations for its customers.

You read about the history of organizational design in this chapter. You learned, for example, about Fayol and his principles of organization. The first principle is unity of command (every worker is to report to one, and only one, boss). Other principles include order, equity, and esprit de corps. This video shows that OSS is one company that understands the importance of esprit de corps. It is a fun and interesting place to work, and turnover is very low. The company does not follow many of Weber's principles dealing with written rules and consistent procedures. Quite the contrary: OSS is structured to be flexible and responsive to its clients. There are no set rules, and the company is certainly not consistent with its projects. Everything is custom made to the needs of each client.

OSS uses a flat organization structure. There are a few project managers, who have workers under them, but they don't look over the employees' shoulders telling them what to do or how to do it. That means there is decentralized authority. Whereas many companies are structured by department—design, engineering, marketing, finance, accounting, and so forth—OSS is structured using project teams. Each team is structured to meet the needs of an individual client. For example, the company will go out and hire people with specific skills as they are needed. The term for this is *outsourcing*,

and OSS outsources many of its tasks to freelance professionals. Together, they work as self-managed teams. The focus of the team is on client needs. There are some staff workers to help with personnel, legal, and other such services.

The company is not keen on making strategic plans because its environment changes so rapidly that such plans are obsolete as soon as they are made. So the company does what is calls "strategic improvising." Although OSS sounds less structured and more informal than most companies, it still focuses on total quality and it practices continuous improvement.

In addition, the company is particularly concerned about its corporate culture. It has three values: smart, fast, and kind. It works smart, responds quickly, and is always kind to others, including its own workers. Because of its culture and responsiveness, the company has been able to capture big accounts like Motorola, Sun Microsystems, and International Truck and Engine.

The long-run success of the firm, however, is based on its project management teams. They carefully listen to what clients are trying to accomplish and then come up with solutions to their problems. You can see the creativity in this video. Clearly, OSS has been able to impress the Goliaths of big business with its presentations.

Discussion Questions

1. What have you learned from this video about the use of teams as an organizational tool versus the traditional line or line-and-staff forms of organization?

2. Does working at OSS look like more or less fun than working for a company with a more traditional approach to organizational structure and operations? Why?

3. From what you saw in the video, what do you think the core competencies of the company might be?

www.mcgrawhill.ca/college/nickels

Chapter 10

Producing World-Class Goods and Services

Learning Goals

After you have read and studied this chapter, you should be able to

1 Define operations management and explain what types of firms use it.

2 Describe the operations management planning issues involved in both the manufacturing and service sectors, including facility location, facility layout, and quality control.

3 Discuss the problem of measuring productivity in the service sector, and tell how new technology is leading to productivity gains in service companies.

4 Explain manufacturing processes, MRP, and ERP.

5 Describe the seven new manufacturing techniques that have improved the productivity of companies: just-in-time inventory control, Internet purchasing, flexible manufacturing, lean manufacturing, mass customization, competing in time, and computer-aided design and manufacturing.

Profile

Getting to Know Frank Stronach of Magna International Inc.

Frank Stronach is the founder and chairman of Magna International Inc., one of the world's largest and most diversified suppliers of automotive components, systems, and modules. Magna designs and engineers a complete range of exterior and interior vehicle systems for its customers, the world's major carmakers. Magna also provides complete vehicle assembly and engineering. In 2003, revenues were US$15.3 billion. As of June 2004, Magna employed approximately 77,000 people in 215 manufacturing divisions and 48 product development and engineering centres throughout North and South America, Mexico, Europe, and Asia. Let us look at how all of this started.

Austrian-born Stronach left school at 14 to apprentice as a tool and die maker. Driven by a desire to travel the world, he arrived in Montreal in 1954 and travelled by bus to Kitchener, Ontario, where he landed a job as a dishwasher in a local hospital. After saving enough money, he moved to Toronto to look for work in his toolmaking trade.

In 1957 he formed a tool and die company, Multimatic Investments Limited, which subsequently expanded into the production of automotive components. In 1969, Multimatic Investments Limited merged with the Magna Electronics Corporation Limited, with Stronach as one of the controlling shareholders. In 1973, Magna Electronics Corporation Limited was transformed into Magna International Inc.

The entrepreneurial culture at Magna is based on Stronach's management philosophy, which is known as Fair Enterprise. An annual percentage of profits are shared between employees, management, and investors, making every employee a shareholder in the company. Stronach believes every employee should own a part of the company. This philosophy has also benefited Stronach—in 2003, he made $53.5 million.

Stronach coordinates global strategies for Magna in regard to technology, marketing, product development, and key management. Stronach and other managers are taking operations management beyond the control of one plant to the control of multiple plants in multiple locations, often in multiple countries. In this chapter, you will learn some basics about production and operations management. You will then be better prepared to understand the dramatic changes taking places in this area.

Sources: Mel James, "Frank Stronach Fair Enterprise Founder" (n.d.), Industry Canada. Retrieved from http://collections.ic.gc.ca/heirloom_series/volume5/338-339.htm; "Frank Stronach, Magna chairman, pulls in $52M in compensation for 2003" (March 31, 2004), CANOE Money. Retrieved from http://money.canoe.ca/News/Sectors/Industrials/Magna/2004/03/31/403550-cp.html; Steve Erwin, "Frank Stronach defends Magna against 'smearing attack' over his $53.5M in pay" (May 6, 2004), CANOE Money. Retrieved from http://money.canoe.ca/News/Other/2004/05/06/449594-cp.html; www.magna.com, June 6, 2004; and www.magna.com, September 17, 2004.

CANADA TODAY

Canada is a large industrial country with many major industries. We are one of the largest producers in the world of forest products, with plants in nearly all provinces turning out a vast array of wood, furniture, and paper products. There are giant aluminum mills in Quebec and B.C.; auto and automotive plants in Ontario and Quebec; aircraft plants in Ontario, Quebec, and Manitoba. Oil, natural gas, and coal are produced in Alberta, Saskatchewan, Newfoundland and Labrador, Nova Scotia, and B.C. and processed there or in other provinces; a vast array of metals and minerals come from all parts of Canada. These are only some of the thousands of components, products, and natural resources produced or processed in Canada.

Canada is now facing some serious challenges to its ability to remain a modern, competitive, industrial country. Today's business climate is characterized by constant and restless change and dislocation, as ever newer technologies and increasing global competition force companies to respond quickly to these challenges. Many factors account for our difficulties in the world's competitive race. Among them are inadequate improvement in productivity and unrelenting competition from the United States, Japan, Germany, and more recently from India, China, and other Southeast Asian countries; inadequate education and retraining programs for our workforce; our "branch plant economy," whereby many subsidiaries are owned by foreign parent companies and profits are mostly returned to these foreign-based companies rather then invested in Canada; and not enough money spent on research and development.

Despite these challenges, Canada still ranks fairly well in world competitiveness, as discussed in Chapter 3. However, one cannot expect this to continue as other countries are becoming stronger and more competitive. In response, the federal government's innovation strategy will, among other areas, focus on research and development as a way to improve our competitiveness. Let us look at research and development next.

Research and Development

research and development (R&D)
Work directed toward the innovation, introduction, and improvement of products and processes.

According to the Canadian Oxford Dictionary, **research and development (R&D)** is defined as work directed toward the innovation, introduction, and improvement of products and processes. When evaluating why some companies are more competitive than others, the terms technology and innovation often come up. What do these terms mean?

The Centre for Canadian Studies at Mount Allison University, in co-operation with the Canadian Heritage Canadian Studies Programme, produces the *About Canada* series. Innovation in Canada is the focus of one of these documents.

innovation
A new product or process that can be purchased.

> Technology is know-how, knowing how to make and use the tools for the job. It's the combination of technology with markets that creates innovation and gives a competitive edge. An **innovation** is a new product or process that can be purchased. Put another way, an idea may lead to an invention, but it cannot be called an innovation until it is commercialized. When technological know-how is developed, sold, distributed, and used, then it becomes an innovation.[1]

In the Survey of Innovation conducted in 1999 by StatsCan, respondents indicated that the three most important objectives of innovation are to improve product quality, to increase production capacity, and to extend product range.

| RANK | | COMPANY | R&D EXPENDITURES | | | REVENUE FY2002 $000 | R&D RATIO | INDUSTRY |
2002	2001		FY2002 $000	FY2001 $000	% CHANGE 2001–2002		R&D AS % OF REVENUE**	
1	1	Nortel Networks Corporation*	$3,501,992	$4,992,042	–29.8	$16,583,424	21.1	Comm/telecom equipment
2	4	Magna International Inc.*	$574,766	$359,229	60.0	$20,369,658	2.8	Automotive
3	3	Pratt & Whitney Canada Corp.(fs)	$428,000	$440,000	–2.7	$2,390,000	17.9	Aerospace
4	2	JDS Uniphase Corporation*	$400,138	$504,624	–20.7	$1,724,613	23.2	Comm/telecom equipment
5	7	IBM Canada Ltd.(fs)(e)	$315,300	$250,000	26.1	$5,275,000	6.0	Software and computer services
6	119	Bell Canada††	$300,000	$285,000	5.3	$14,403,000	2.1	Telecommunications services
7	6	ATI Technologies Inc.*	$286,361	$255,436	12.1	$1,604,512	17.8	Computer equipment
8	16	Bombardier Inc.	$233,500	$123,400	89.2	$21,633,800	1.1	Aerospace
9	5	Ericsson Canada Inc.(fs)	$201,000	$270,000	–25.6	$482,000	41.7	Comm/telecom equipment
10	8	Alcan Inc.*	$180,596	$209,034	–13.6	$19,692,816	0.9	Mining and metals

R&D Expenditures: We have attempted, wherever possible, to provide gross R&D expenditures before deduction of investment tax credits or government grants. FY2001 R&D expenditure figures may have been adjusted, as more accurate information became available. Canadian-owned company results include worldwide R&D expenditures; foreign subsidiaries include R&D expenditures for Canadian operations.
Revenue: We have attempted, wherever possible, to provide revenue figures net of interest and investment income.

* = converted to CDN$ at average 2002 = $1.5704, 2001 = 1.5484 (Bank of Canada)　　** = $1 million or more of revenue
fs = foreign subsidiary　　nd = not disclosed　　e = RE$EARCH Infosource Inc. estimate　　†† = Bell Canada has revised its reporting for FY2002, FY2001 number has been adjusted accordingly

© Research Infosource Inc. 2003

FIGURE 10.1

CANADA'S TOP CORPORATE R&D SPENDERS, 2003

Since that time, the Science, Innovation, and Electronic Information Division (SIEID) of StatsCan has piloted more surveys that focus on the importance of innovation. In a more recent Working Paper titled "Starting the New Century: Technological Change in the Canadian Private Sector, 2000–2002," the importance of innovation to economic growth and development is reviewed. As a synopsis, "It is through innovation that new products are introduced in the market, new production processes are developed and introduced, and organizational changes are made. Through the adoption of newer, more advanced technologies and practices, industries can increase their production capabilities, improve their productivity, and expand their lines of new goods and services."[2]

Figure 10.1 outlines Canada's top 10 corporate R&D spenders in 2002. As you may note, three of these organizations are part of the communications/telecommunications equipment industry. This is not surprising, given the growth potential in the global market. A review of the corporate R&D spenders reflected that 24 companies spent more than $100 million in 2002. Such expenditures clearly show that these companies understand that R&D is a critical component in ensuring their growth and competitiveness both domestically and internationally.

Research Infosource publishes an in-depth report on Canadian R&D trends. To view the most recent report, which includes the top 100 R&D spending firms, visit its Website at www.researchinfo source.com/top100. shtml.

CANADA'S EVOLVING MANUFACTURING AND SERVICES BASE

During the 1970s and 1980s, foreign manufacturers captured huge chunks of the North American market for basic products such as steel, cement, machinery,

Each year companies discover new ways of automating that eliminate the need for human labour. This photo shows a new, automated apparatus known as a Flipper. It can pour a dozen pancakes and flip them when needed on one griddle while, at the same time, flipping burgers on another grill. Are Harvey's or any other restaurants in your area already using equipment like this?

and farm equipment using the latest in production techniques. That competition forced companies to greatly alter their production techniques and managerial styles. Many firms are now as good as or better than competitors anywhere in the world. What have manufacturers done to regain a competitive edge? They've emphasized the following:

- Focusing on customers.
- Maintaining close relationships with suppliers and other companies to satisfy customer needs.
- Practising continuous improvement.
- Focusing on quality.
- Saving on costs through site selection.
- Relying on the Internet to unite companies.
- Adopting new manufacturing techniques such as enterprise resource planning, computer-integrated manufacturing, flexible manufacturing, and lean manufacturing.

As you may recall from Chapter 1, manufacturing employs approximately 15 percent of Canada's working population.[3] Manufacturing not only is important in employing Canadians, but also is critical to our economy as manufacturers perform 75 percent of private-sector R&D in Canada. Manufacturers have been increasing their utilization of advanced production technologies at an average annual rate of more than 20 percent over the last several years.[4]

We will discuss the developments noted above in detail in this chapter. You'll see that operations management has become a challenging and vital element of Canadian business. The growth of Canada's manufacturing base will likely remain a major business issue in the near future. There will be debates about the merits of moving production facilities to foreign countries. Serious questions will be raised about replacing workers with robots and other machinery. Major political decisions will be made regarding protection of Canadian manufacturers through quotas and other restrictions on free trade. Regardless of how these issues are decided, however, there will be many opportunities along the way.

The service sector will also continue to get attention as it becomes a larger and larger part of the overall economy. Service productivity is a real issue, as is the blending of service and manufacturing through the Internet. Since many of tomorrow's graduates will likely find jobs in the service sector, it is important to understand the latest operations management concepts for this sector.

production
The creation of finished goods and services using the factors of production: land, labour, capital, entrepreneurship, and knowledge.

From Production to Operations Management

Production is the creation of goods ➤P. 23◀ and services ➤P. 25◀ using the factors of production ➤P. 10◀: land, labour, capital, entrepreneurship ➤P. 186◀, and knowledge. Production has historically been associated with manufacturing, but the nature of business has changed significantly in the last 20 years or so. The service sector, including Internet services, has grown dramatically, and the manufacturing sector has not grown much at all. As stated in Chapter 1, Canada now has what is called a service economy—that is, one dominated by the service sector. This can be a benefit to future graduates because many of the top-paying jobs are in legal services; medical services; entertainment; broadcasting; and business services such as accounting, finance, and management consulting.

Production management has been the term used to describe all the activities managers do to help their firms create goods. To reflect the change in importance from manufacturing to services, the term *production* often has been replaced by *operations* to reflect both goods and services production. **Operations management,** then, is a specialized area in management that converts or transforms resources (including human resources) into goods and services. It includes inventory management, quality control, production scheduling, follow-up services, and more. In an automobile plant, operations management transforms raw materials, human resources, parts, supplies, paints, tools, and other resources into automobiles. It does this through the processes of fabrication and assembly. In a school, operations management takes inputs—such as information, professors, supplies, buildings, offices, and computer systems—and creates services that transform students into educated people. It does this through a process called education.

Some organizations—such as factories, farms, and mines—produce mostly goods. Others—such as hospitals, schools, and government agencies—produce mostly services. Still others produce a combination of goods and services. For example, an automobile manufacturer not only makes cars but also provides services such as repairs, financing, and insurance. And at Harvey's you get goods such as hamburgers and fries, but you also get services such as order taking, order filling, and cleanup.

production management
The term used to describe all the activities managers do to help their firms create goods.

operations management
A specialized area in management that converts or transforms resources (including human resources) into goods and services.

Bombardier Inc. is a leading manufacturer of transportation solutions, from regional aircraft and business jets to rail transportation equipment. Bombardier does not just manufacture goods—it also provides services. One example is its operations and maintenance (O&M) organization. O&M provides a complete range of services for any rapid transit, light rail, monorail, or peoplemover system. What other companies can you think of that manufacture goods *and* provide services?

Manufacturers Turn to a Customer Orientation and Services for Profit

Many manufacturers have spent an enormous amount of money on productivity and quality initiatives. Companies that have prospered and grown—General Electric and Dell, to name just a couple—have all taken a similar road to success. They've expanded operations management out of the factory and moved it closer to the customer, providing services such as custom manufacturing, fast delivery, credit, installation, and repair.[5]

Another example of the growing importance of services is in the area of corporate computing. The average company spends only one-fifth of its annual personal computer budget on purchasing hardware. The rest (80 percent) goes to technical support, administration, and other maintenance activities. Because of this, IBM has shifted from its dependence on selling computer hardware to becoming a major supplier of computer services, software, and technology components.[6] It recently bought PricewaterhouseCoopers's tech consulting affiliate to increase its presence in the service sector. General Electric is doing the same; it generates more than $5 billion a year in worldwide revenues from Internet transactions.[7]

Companies such as Celestica and Ford have outsourced ➤P. 269◀ much of their production processes and are focusing more on building customer relationships and building brand images.[8] As you can see, operations management has become much more focused on services because that's where the growth and profits are.

Progress Assessment

- What are some challenges that Canada is facing in its ability to remain a competitive country?
- How is innovation related to research and development?
- Explain the difference between production management and operations management.

OPERATIONS MANAGEMENT PLANNING

Operations management planning in the service sector involves many of the same issues as operations management planning in the manufacturing sector. Overlapping issues include facility location, facility layout, and quality control. The resources used may be different, but the management issues are similar. Companies today are making strategic decisions when establishing, operating, and closing facilities.

Facility Location

facility location
The process of selecting a geographic location for a company's operations.

Facility location is the process of selecting a geographic location for a company's operations. In keeping with the need to focus on customers, one strategy in facility location is to find a site that makes it easy for consumers to access the company's service and to maintain a dialogue about their needs. For example, Hewlett-Packard (Canada) Company opened a new computer manufacturing facility in Toronto in a bid to speed new machines to Canadian business customers as fast as archrival Dell Incorporated. In doing so, HP became the only major computer vendor active in Canada to actually assemble machines here.[9] Flower shops and banks are putting facilities in supermarkets so that their products are more accessible than they are in free-standing facilities. You can find a Second Cup inside some Home Depot stores. There are even Tim Hortons outlets in some gas stations now. Customers can order and pay for their meals at the pumps and by the time they are finished filling their tanks, go to the window to pick up their food orders. Of course, the ultimate in convenience is never having to leave home at all to get services. That's why there is so much interest in Internet banking, Internet car shopping, Internet education, and so on.[10] For brick-and-mortar businesses (e.g., retail stores) to beat such competition, they have to choose good locations and offer outstanding service to those who do come. Study the location of service-sector businesses—such as hotels, banks, athletic clubs, and supermarkets—and you will see that the most successful ones are conveniently located.

Facility Location for Manufacturers   A major issue of the recent past has been the shift of manufacturing organizations from one city or province to another in Canada, or to other foreign sites. Such shifts sometimes result in pockets of unemployment in some geographic areas and lead to tremendous economic growth in others that benefit from these shifts.

Why would companies spend millions of dollars to move their facilities from one location to another? Issues that influence site selection include labour costs; availability of resources, such as labour; access to transportation that can reduce time to market; proximity to suppliers; proximity to customers; low crime rates; quality of life for employees; cost of living; and the ability to train or retrain the local workforce.

One of the most common reasons for a business move is the availability of inexpensive labour or the right kind of skilled labour. Even though labour cost is becoming a smaller percentage of total cost in some highly automated industries, the low cost of labour remains a key reason many producers move their plants. For example, low-cost labour is one reason why some firms are moving to Malaysia, Mexico, and other countries with low wage rates.

Some of these firms have been charged with providing substandard working conditions and/or exploiting children in the countries where they have set up factories. Others, such as Grupo Moraira (Grupo M), a real estate construction and sales company in the Dominican Republic, are being used as role models for global manufacturing. Grupo M provides its employees with higher pay relative to local businesses, transportation to and from work, daycare centres, discounted food, and health clinics. Its operations are so efficient that it can compete in world markets and provide world-class services to its employees.[11]

Inexpensive resources are another major reason for moving production facilities. Companies usually need water, electricity, wood, coal, and other basic resources. By moving to areas where natural resources are inexpensive and plentiful, firms can significantly lower costs—not only the cost of buying such resources but also the cost of shipping finished products. Often the most important resource is people, so companies tend to cluster where smart and talented people are. Witness the Ottawa area, also known as Silicon Valley North.

The Canadian Auto Workers (CAW) has an ongoing auto policy campaign. In 1999, Canada ranked as the fourth largest auto producer in the world. Today, according to the CAW, Canada is ranked just seventh. Thousands of jobs have been lost to other countries where wages are cheaper. Besides cheaper labour, what other factors may influence companies to relocate?

Making Ethical Decisions

Stay or Leave?

www.ethicsweb.ca/resources

Suppose that the hypothetical company ChildrenWear Industries has long been the economic foundation for its hometown. Most of the area's small businesses and schools support ChildrenWear, either by supplying the materials needed for production or by training its employees. ChildrenWear learned that if it moved its production facilities to Asia, it could increase its profits by half. Closing operations in the company's hometown would cause many of the town's other businesses to fail and schools to close, leaving a great percentage of the town unemployed, with no options for reemployment there. As a top manager at ChildrenWear, you must help decide whether the plant should be moved and, if so, when to tell the employees about the move. The law says that you must tell them at least 60 days before closing. What alternatives do you have? What are the consequences of each? Which will you choose?

Reducing time-to-market is another decision-making factor. As manufacturers attempt to compete globally, they need sites that allow products to move through the system quickly, at the lowest costs, so that they can be delivered rapidly to customers.[12] Access to various modes of transportation (i.e., highways, rail lines, airports, water, and the like) is thus critical. Information technology (IT) is also important to quicken response time, so many firms are seeking countries with the most advanced information systems.

Another way to work closely with suppliers to satisfy your customers' needs is to locate your production facilities near supplier facilities. That cuts the cost of distribution and makes communication easier.

Many businesses are building factories in foreign countries to get closer to their international customers. That's a major reason why the U.S. automaker General Motors builds cars in Windsor and Japanese automaker Toyota builds cars in Cambridge. When firms select foreign sites, they consider whether they are near airports, waterways, and highways so that raw materials and finished goods can be moved quickly and easily.

Businesses also study the quality of life for workers and managers. Quality-of-life questions include these: Are there good schools nearby? Is the weather nice? Is the crime rate low? Does the local community welcome new businesses? Do the chief executive and other key managers want to live there? Sometimes a region with a high quality of life is also an expensive one, which complicates the decision. In short, facility location has become a critical issue in operations management. The Making Ethical Decisions box explores one of the major ethical issues involved.

Canada's Auto Industry[13]   The auto industry is critical to Canada's manufacturing economy. According to the Canadian Vehicle Manufacturers' Association, Canada is the sixth largest vehicle producer in the world. The industry is the biggest contributor to manufacturing GDP. It is also the largest manufacturing employer, employing one out of every seven Canadians. The industry comprises more than 20 assembly plants, 554 parts manufacturers, 3,600 dealerships, and many other related industries.

It is no wonder that this industry is Canada's largest, both domestically and in exports (recall the value of these exports from Chapter 3). As well, it should be of no surprise that this industry has also faced increased competition from international players. In recent years, several plants have closed, eliminating thousands of jobs. Other plant expansion projects have gone south of the border.

To potential investors, Canada offers cost advantages with free health care and a low currency. However, southern U.S. states such as Alabama, Georgia, and Mississippi are luring billions of dollars worth of auto industry assembly plants with more attractive incentives, including land and training. These incentives are also starting to be offered to parts makers. To respond to the decreasing trend in new auto investments, a joint industry–government council was established. A major goal of the Canadian Automotive Partnership Council (CAPC) is to improve the future of the assembly industry. The Council has been proposing tax cuts, less red tape, investment in research, and improved transportation routes, especially at border crossings. Time will tell if this will contribute to improving the industry's health.

Taking Operations Management to the Internet   Many of today's rapidly growing companies do very little production themselves. Instead, they outsource
➤ P. 269 ◀ engineering, design, manufacturing, and other tasks to other companies that specialize in those functions.[14] Furthermore, companies are creating whole new relationships with suppliers over the Internet, so that operations management is becoming an interfirm process in which companies work together to design, produce, and ship products to customers. Coordination among companies today can be as close as coordination among departments in a single firm was in the past.

Many of the major manufacturing companies (e.g., Microsoft) are developing new Internet-focused strategies that will enable them and others to compete more effectively in the future. These changes are having a dramatic effect on operations managers as they adjust from a one-firm system to an interfirm environment and from a relatively stable environment to one that is constantly changing and evolving. This linking of firms is called supply chain management. We will briefly introduce you to this concept later in the chapter.

Facility Location in the Future   New developments in information technology (computers, modems, e-mail, voice mail, teleconferencing, etc.) are giving firms and employees more flexibility than ever before in choosing locations while staying in the competitive mainstream.[15] As we noted in Chapter 1, telecommuting (working from home via computer and modem) is a major trend in business. Companies that no longer need to locate near sources of labour will be able to move to areas where land is less expensive and the quality of life may be nicer. The Reaching Beyond Our Borders box discusses living in Hawaii and doing business throughout the world.

One big incentive to locate or relocate in a particular city or province is the tax situation and degree of government support. Those with lower taxes, like Alberta, may be more attractive to companies. Some provinces and local governments have higher taxes than others, yet many engage in fierce competition by giving tax reductions and other support, such as zoning changes and financial aid, so that businesses will locate there.

Facility Layout

Facility layout is the physical arrangement of resources (including people) in the production process. The idea is to have offices, machines, storage areas, and other items in the best possible position to enable workers to produce goods and provide services for customers. Facility layout depends greatly on the processes that are to be performed. For services, the layout is usually

facility layout
The physical arrangement of resources (including people) in the production process.

Reaching Beyond Our Borders

www.origin.to

Why Not Live in Hawaii and Do Business Globally?

With Internet technology, you can work almost anywhere and telecommute. Chelsea Hill, for example, moved to the Hawaiian island of Maui to start a Web-based business called Origin—The Language Agency. Her company has offices in Victoria, Seattle, and Bristol, England. Her workers consist of freelance translators from all over the world. One of Maui's new entrepreneurs says, "When you are as physically isolated as we are on this island, you become aware of the importance of connectivity—not just broadband, but with fellow professionals."

In 1988, Hawaii passed an important telecommunications act that provided for enough funding for infrastructure upgrades and made the islands a great place for Pacific Rim telecom investors. Another act offers incentives for high-tech small businesses to relocate their research and development operations in Hawaii. Hawaii is now one of the three most networked states in the U.S. If you can operate a business from anywhere, why not in a beautiful paradise like Hawaii?

Sources: Kevin Voight, "For 'Extreme Telecomuters,' Remote Work Means Really Remote," *The Wall Street Journal,* January 31, 2001, p. B1; and Allison Overholt, "Want to Web the Surf?," *Fast Company,* September 2002, p. 42.

The Igus manufacturing plant in Cologne, Germany, can shrink or expand in a flash. Its flexible design keeps it competitive in a fast-changing market. Because the layout of the plant changes so often, some employees use scooters in order to more efficiently provide needed skills, supplies, and services to multiple workstations. A fast-changing plant needs a fast-moving employee base to achieve maximum productivity.

designed to help the consumer find and buy things.[16] More and more, that means helping consumers find and buy things on the Internet.[17] Some stores have added kiosks that enable customers to search for goods on the Internet and then place orders in the store. The store also handles returns and other customer-contact functions. In short, services are becoming more and more customer-oriented in how they design their stores and their Internet services. Some service-oriented organizations, such as hospitals, use layouts that improve the efficiency of the production process, just as manufacturers do.

For manufacturing plants, facilities layout has become critical because the possible cost savings are enormous. A Delphi Automotive Systems plant makes catalytic converters for 40 different automobile manufacturers. Catalytic converters are stainless-steel pollution strainers in automobile exhaust systems. Delphi has a history that goes back almost 100 years. Its facility layout was typical of older plants—an assembly line that made all of the converters. The plant floor is now organized around modular, portable customer-focused work cells. Product delivery once took 21 days, but with today's more modern layout, delivery takes less than a week. The plant was redesigned to reduce cost, to increase productivity ➤P. 15◀, to simplify the process, and to speed things up. Compared to the old plant, the new plant uses only half of the space, 2 percent of its powered conveyor system, and 230 fewer processes. Productivity increased by more than 25 percent, and the plant is now more profitable.[18]

Many companies like Delphi are moving from an *assembly line layout,* in which workers do only a few tasks at a time, to a *modular layout,* in which teams of workers combine to produce more complex units of the final product. For example, there may have been a dozen or more workstations on an assembly line to complete an automobile engine in the past, but all of that work may be done in one module today. A *process layout* is one in which similar equipment and functions are grouped together. The order in which the product visits a function depends on the design of the item. This allows for flexibility. When working on a major project, such as a bridge or an airplane, companies use a *fixed-position layout* that allows workers to congregate around the product to be completed. Figure 10.2 illustrates typical layout designs.

Quality Control

Quality is consistently producing what the customer wants while reducing errors before and after delivery to the customer. Before, quality control was often done by a quality control department at the end of the production line. Products were completed *and then tested.* This resulted in several problems:

What happens when you combine the zeal of technical innovators with the six sigma discipline of a large company like General Electric? You get a medical breakthrough. Janet Burki and her 280-person operations team developed the world's fastest CT scanner. It works 10 times faster than other systems and produces clear 3-D images of the beating heart. Can you see how efforts to build in quality lead to better (and faster) products?

1. There was a need to inspect other people's work. This took extra people and resources.

2. If an error was found, someone would have to correct the mistake or scrap the product. This, of course, was costly.

3. If the customer found the mistake, he or she might be dissatisfied and might even buy from someone else thereafter.

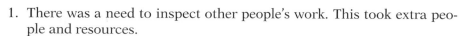

Such problems led to the realization that quality is not an outcome; it is a never-ending process of continually improving what a company produces. Therefore, quality control should be part of the operations management planning process rather than simply an end-of-the-line inspection.

Companies have turned to the use of modern quality control standards, such as six sigma. **Six sigma quality** (just 3.4 defects per million opportunities) detects potential problems to prevent their occurrence. **Statistical quality control (SQC)** is the process some managers use to continually monitor all phases of the production process to ensure that quality is being built into the product from the beginning. **Statistical process control (SPC)** is the process of taking statistical samples of product components at each stage of the production process and plotting those results on a graph.[19] Any variances from quality standards are recognized and can be corrected if beyond the set standards. Making sure products meet standards all along the production process eliminates or minimizes the need for having a quality control inspection at the end. Any mistakes would have been caught much earlier in the process. SQC and SPC thus save companies much time and many dollars. The idea is to find potential errors *before* they happen.

quality
Consistently producing what the customer wants while reducing errors before and after delivery to the customer.

six sigma quality
A quality measure that allows only 3.4 defects per million events.

statistical quality control (SQC)
The process some managers use to continually monitor all phases of the production process to ensure that quality is being built into the product from the beginning.

statistical process control (SPC)
The process of taking statistical samples of product components at each stage of the production process and plotting those results on a graph. Any variances from quality standards are recognized and can be corrected if beyond the set standards.

A. ASSEMBLY-LINE LAYOUT
Used for repetitive tasks.

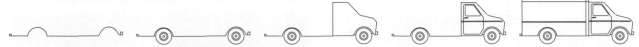

B. PROCESS LAYOUT
Frequently used in operations that serve different customers' different needs.

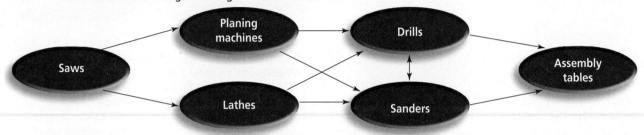

C. MODULAR LAYOUT
Can accommodate changes in design or customer demand.

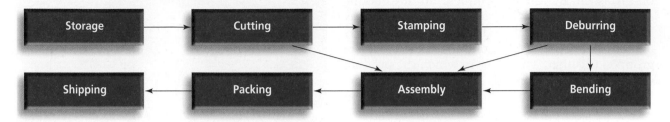

D. FIXED POSITION LAYOUT
A major feature of planning is scheduling work operations.

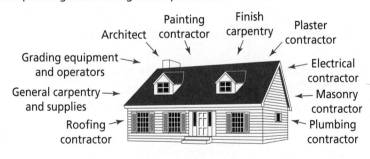

FIGURE 10.2

TYPICAL LAYOUT DESIGNS

Quality, as you can see, has become a major issue in operations management. The following are examples of how quality is being introduced into service and manufacturing firms:

- Holiday Inn authorized its hotel staff to do almost anything to satisfy an unhappy customer, from handing out gift certificates to eliminating charges for certain services. Empowerment ➤P. 19◄ gives managers and employees the authority to waive charges for the night's stay if the customer is still unhappy.

- Motorola set a goal of attaining six sigma quality. The Spotlight on Small Business box discusses how small businesses are also using this standard.

Spotlight on Small Business

Meeting the Six Sigma Standard

www.sixsigmasystems.com

Six sigma is a quality measure that allows only 3.4 defects per million opportunities. It is one thing for Dofasco or Celestica to reach for such standards, but what about a small company like Dolan Industries? Dolan is a 41-person manufacturer of fasteners. It spent a few years trying to meet ISO 9000 standards, which are comparable to six sigma.

Once the company was able to achieve six sigma quality itself, it turned to its suppliers and demanded six sigma quality from them as well. It had to do that because its customers were demanding that level of quality. The benefits include increases in product performance and, more important, happy customers—and profit growth.

Here is how six sigma works: If you can make it to the level of one sigma, two out of three products will meet specifications. If you can reach the two sigma level, then more than 95 percent of products will qualify. But when you meet six sigma quality, as we've said, you have only 3.4 defects in a million (which means that 99.99966 percent of your products will qualify). The bottom line is that small businesses are being held to a higher standard, one that reaches near perfection. Service organizations are also adopting six sigma standards.

Sources: Mark Henricks, "Is It Greek to You?" *Entrepreneur,* July 1999, pp. 65–67; and Thomas Pyzdek, "Six Sigma: Needs Standardization," *Quality Digest,* March 2001, p. 20; Michael Arndt, "Quality Isn't Just for Widgets," *Business Week,* July 22, 2002, pp. 72–73; and Kennedy Smith, "Six Sigma for the Service Sector," *Quality Digest,* May 2003, pp. 23–28.

- In the past, Xerox found 97 defects for every 100 copiers coming off the assembly line. Now it finds only 12.

Dozens of other manufacturers and service organizations could be discussed here, but you get the idea: The customer is ultimately the one who determines what the standard for quality should be. Businesses are getting serious about providing top customer service, and many are already doing it. Service organizations are finding it difficult to provide outstanding service every time because the process is so labour intensive. Physical goods (e.g., a gold ring) can be designed and manufactured to near perfection. However, it is hard to reach such perfection when designing and providing a service experience such as a dance on a cruise ship or a cab drive through Vancouver.

Quality Function Deployment   Six sigma and other quality standards are designed to eliminate mistakes. **Quality function deployment (QFD)** is a process of linking the needs of end users (customers) to design, development, engineering, manufacturing, and service functions. The goal is to go beyond not making mistakes to maximizing customer satisfaction. One way to do that is to identify customers' spoken and *unspoken* needs and to meet as many of those needs as possible by constantly improving. QFD is a subject worth researching—see the second Taking It to the Net exercise at the end of this chapter. The Dealing with Change box explores how quality is changing today.

quality function deployment (QFD)
A process of linking the needs of end users (customers) to design, development, engineering, manufacturing, and service functions.

Quality Award: The Canada Awards for Excellence[20]   The National Quality Institute (NQI) is a not-for-profit organization that provides strategic focus and direction for Canadian organizations to achieve excellence. Created in 1992, NQI assists both public and private organizations to increase productivity, heighten the level of organizational excellence, and develop healthy workplaces.

Dealing With Change

Why Is Service Still So Bad?

Are you happy with the service you receive at retail stores, from auto repair facilities, and from businesses and other organizations? One of the improvements that managers need to make, and make quickly, is the betterment of consumer relations. It is one thing to talk about quality function deployment, six sigma quality, and all that in a class; it is quite another thing to find quality in the real world—especially at the consumer level (you and I shopping at the mall).

Quality Digest has been addressing that issue. One article was called "Why Is Quality Still So Bad?" and the other was called "Mining the TQM Mother Load." TQM stands for total quality management and is a traditional quality approach. Both articles place the blame for poor quality squarely on management. The first article says, "The blame lies not with the humble quality manager, but entirely, and I do mean entirely, with senior management. With very few exceptions, today's CEOs, presidents, and the like just don't give quality as much attention as they should." The article went on to say that all the statistical measures in the world won't help if the company doesn't focus on service to the customer as well.

The second article has a different perspective. It says that quality begins with the managers themselves. They must put quality into their duties: allocating resources, selecting leaders, developing processes, setting priorities, and the like. If these responsibilities are not fulfilled, any total quality effort is likely to fail. Joseph M. Juran, a quality expert, says that 80 to 85 percent of all problems are caused by management. Some 62 percent of those problems could be controlled by first- and second-level managers. But those managers are not always involved in top-level meetings and don't always see the big picture. In short, the change needed in corporations today is for top managers to get serious about quality and then give first- and second-level managers the information and the tools necessary to implement quality initiatives. Will we see such changes soon? Let's go to the mall and find out.

Sources: Scott Madison Paton, "Grading Quality: Why Is Quality Still So Bad?" *Quality Digest,* April 2002, p. 4; and H. James Harrington, "Mining the TQM Mother Load," *Quality Digest,* April 2002, p. 12.

The Canada Awards for Excellence are presented annually to private, public, and not-for-profit organizations that have displayed outstanding performance in the areas of quality and healthy workplace. Since 1984, the award has honoured more than 200 Canadian organizations, including Dofasco Inc., Research In Motion Ltd., British Columbia Transplant Society, and Delta Hotels. More recently, Statistics Canada, Envision Financial (Canada's third largest credit union), and the College of Physicians & Surgeons of Nova Scotia have been honoured. For more information, visit www.nqi.ca.

ISO 9000
The common name given to quality management and assurance standards.

ISO 9000 and ISO 14000 Standards The International Organization for Standardization (ISO) is a worldwide federation of national standards bodies from more than 140 countries that set the global measures for the quality of individual products. ISO is a nongovernmental organization established in 1947 to promote the development of world standards to facilitate the international exchange of goods and services. **ISO 9000** is the common name given to quality management and assurance standards. The latest standards, called ISO 19011:2002, were published in 2002.[21] The new standards require that a company must determine what customer needs are, including regulatory and legal requirements. The company must also make communication arrangements to handle issues such as complaints. Other standards involve process control, product testing, storage, and delivery.[22]

Prior to the establishment of the ISO standards, there were no international standards of quality against which to measure companies. It is important to know that ISO did not start as a quality certification, the way many people think. In the beginning, it simply meant that your process was under control. In short, it looked to see that companies were consistently producing the same products each time. There is a difference between consistency (flawed products every time) and quality (products free from defects).

What makes ISO 9000 so important is that the European Union (EU), the group of European countries that have established free-trade agreements, is demanding that companies that want to do business with the EU be certified by ISO standards. Some major Canadian companies are also demanding that suppliers meet such standards. There are several accreditation agencies in Europe and in North America whose function is to certify that a company meets the standards for all phases of its operations, from product development through production and testing to installation.

ISO 14000 is a collection of the best practices for managing an organization's impact on the environment. It does not prescribe a performance level. ISO 14000 is an environmental management system (EMS). The requirements for certification include having an environmental policy, having specific improvement targets, conducting audits of environmental programs, and maintaining top management review of the processes. Certification in both ISO 9000 and ISO 14000 would show that a firm has a world-class management system in both quality and environmental standards. In the past, firms assigned employees separately to meet both standards. Today, ISO 9000 and 14000 standards have been blended so that an organization can work on both at once.

ZENON Environmental Inc. has its ISO 9001 designation. ZENON is a global leader in the manufacturing and marketing of membrane technologies for drinking water treatment, wastewater treatment, and water reuse applications. This membrane technology forms an absolute barrier to impurities. ZENON has had hundreds of successful installations around the world, including this wastewater treatment plant in Brescia, Italy. Why is ISO accreditation so important to Canadian companies such as ZENON?

ISO 14000
A collection of the best practices for managing an organization's impact on the environment.

Outsourcing   The previous chapter noted that many companies now try to divide their production between *core competencies*, work *they* do best in-house, and *outsourcing*, letting outside companies service them by doing what *they* are experts at. The result sought is the best-quality products at the lowest possible costs.

Outsourcing goods and services has become a hot practice in North America. Software development, call-centre, and back-office jobs have been moving to developing countries for some time. The range of jobs now shifting to these countries includes accounting, financial analysis, medicine, architecture, aircraft maintenance, law, film production, and other banking activities.[23] Some examples of outsourcing include the following:

- In 2003, Nortel announced that it was expanding its product R&D work in India through increased outsourcing. Over the past five years, Nortel has spent more than $300 million in India due to lower labour costs and a reputation for high-quality work.[24]

- By the end of 2003, Celestica plans to have 70 percent of its manufacturing capacity outsourced in low-cost geographies such as central Europe and China. According to Celestica's CEO, "The firm's customers are demanding cheaper ways to make and assemble their products, prompting the company to shift production to plants where labour and material costs are less expensive ... If you don't respond to it, then someone else will."[25]

Keep in mind that Canadian companies are also benefiting from other countries' outsourcing. For example, Procter & Gamble's bar soap for North America is now manufactured by Newmarket-based Trillium Health Care Products. This contract makes Trillium—already the leader in making private-label soap for retailers—the second- or third-largest bar soap maker on the continent.[26] In another example, BMW signed a contract with Magna to assemble BMW's X3 sport-utility vehicle. Beginning in 2004, this contract will generate US$1 billion in annual revenues for Magna, and it will strengthen its growing presence in complete vehicle assembly.[27]

There can be instances, however, when jobs do not need to be lost to foreign locations. When the Bank of Montreal (BMO) outsourced its human resources processing services to California-based Exult Inc., it negotiated an unusual condition: Take our business, take our people. As part of this $75-million a year contract for the next 10 years, more than 100 former BMO employees now work for Exult in the same office tower. Exult sees this as an excellent opportunity to expand its business in Canada, and these new employees have a mandate to bring in more Canadian clients.[28] Unfortunately, examples such as this are not the norm.

supply chain management
The process of managing the movement of raw materials, parts, works in process, finished goods, and related information through all the organizations involved in the supply chain; managing the return of such goods, if necessary; and recycling materials when appropriate.

supply chain
The sequence of linked activities that must be performed by various organizations to move goods from the sources of raw materials to ultimate consumers.

Supply Chain Management   Some companies have been successful in attracting more customers due to their supply chain management efficiencies. **Supply chain management** may involve three parts. First, it is the process of managing the movement of raw materials, parts, works in progress, finished goods, and related information through all the organizations involved in the **supply chain.** Managing the return of such goods, if necessary, may be another function of supply management. Thirdly, recycling materials, when appropriate, can also be a function of supply chain management.

The application of supply chain management is evident in different industries and among many firms. Two examples are as follows:

- Canadian National Railway (CN) purchased supply chain management planning software from i2 Technologies to manage its intermodal business. CN has 10,000 freight cars and 7,000 containers that it owns, along with equipment belonging to shippers and other railways. While implementing this software is still a work in progress, CN expects to increase the level of speed and reliability of hauling containers and truck trailers from ports and major cities across North America.[29]

- Only Canada's Armed Forces surpasses the Cirque du Soleil in terms of the level of supply chain and logistics planning required to deploy large amounts of equipment, supplies, and people all over the world. According to Mr. Migneron, director of international headquarters operations, "we use computers for a lot of what we do." The planning and logistics work for each performance begins 12 to 18 months before the first act enters the tent.[30]

OPERATIONS MANAGEMENT IN THE SERVICE SECTOR

Operations management in the service industry is all about creating a good experience for those who use the service. For example, in a Four Seasons hotel, operations management includes restaurants that offer the finest in service, elevators that run smoothly, and a front desk that processes people quickly.

It may include placing fresh-cut flowers in the lobbies and dishes of fruit in every room. More important, it may mean spending thousands of dollars to provide training in quality management for every new employee.

Operations management in luxury hotels is changing with today's new executives. As customers in hotels, executives are likely to want in-room Internet access and a help centre with toll-free telephone service. Also, when an executive has to give a speech or presentation, he or she needs video equipment and a whole host of computer hardware and other aids. Foreign visitors would like multilingual customer-support services. Hotel shops need to carry more than souvenirs, newspapers, and some drugstore and food items to serve today's high-tech travellers. The shops may also carry laptop computer supplies, electrical adapters, and the like. Operations management is responsible for locating and providing such amenities to make customers happy.

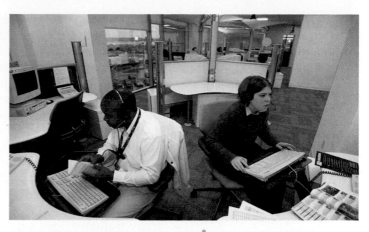

British Airways customer service representatives are monitored by software that tracks productivity in sales and customer-complaint resolution. The system also tracks the amount of time spent on things like breaks and personal phone calls. Incentive dollars are associated with effective work. What would be your response to having your work so closely monitored? Would it make a difference if your pay were increased as a result?

In short, delighting customers by anticipating their needs has become the quality standard for luxury hotels, as it has for most other service businesses. But knowing customer needs and satisfying them are two different things. That's why operations management is so important: It is the implementation phase of management.

Measuring Quality in the Service Sector

There's strong evidence that productivity in the service sector is rising, but productivity measures don't capture improvements in *quality*. In an example from health care, positron emission tomography (PET) scans are much better than X-rays, but the quality difference is not reported in productivity figures. The traditional way to measure productivity ➤**P. 15**◄ involves tracking inputs (worker-hours) compared to outputs (dollars). Notice that there is no measure for quality improvement. When new information systems are developed to measure the quality improvement of goods and services—including the speed of their delivery and customer satisfaction—productivity in the service sector will go up dramatically.

Using computers is one way the service sector is improving productivity, but not the only way. Think about labour-intensive businesses like hospitals and fast-food restaurants, where automation plays a big role in controlling costs and improving service. Today at Burger King, for example, customers fill their own drink cups from pop machines, which allows workers to concentrate on preparing the food. And, because the people working at the drive-up window now wear headsets instead of using stationary mikes, they aren't glued to one spot anymore and can do four or five tasks while taking an order.

Most of us have been exposed to similar productivity gains in banking. For example, people in most cities no longer have to wait in long lines for tellers to help them deposit and withdraw money. Instead, they use automated teller machines (ATMs), which usually involve little or no waiting and are available 24 hours a day.

Another service that was once annoyingly slow was grocery-store checkout. The system of marking goods with universal product codes (UPC) enables computerized checkout and allows cashiers to be much more productive than before. Now many stores are setting up automated systems that enable customers to go through the checkout process on their own. Some grocery chains, such as Longo's, are implementing Internet services that allow customers to place orders online and receive home delivery. The potential for productivity gains in this area are enormous.

In short, operations management has led to tremendous productivity increases in the service sector but still has a long way to go. Also, service workers are losing jobs to machines just as manufacturing workers did. The secret to obtaining and holding a good job is to acquire appropriate education and training. Such education and training must go on for a lifetime to keep up with the rapid changes that are happening in all areas of business. That message can't be repeated too frequently.

Services Go Interactive

The service industry has always taken advantage of new technology to increase customer satisfaction. Jet travel enabled Purolator to deliver goods overnight. Cable TV led to pay-per-view services. And now interactive computer networks are revolutionizing services. Interactive services are already available from banks, stockbrokers, travel agents, and information providers of all kinds. More individuals may soon be able to participate directly in community and national decision making via telephone, cable, and computer networks.

You can now buy a greater variety of books and CDs on the Internet than you can in most retail stores. You can also search for and buy new and used automobiles and new and used computers. As computers and modems get faster, the Internet may take over more of traditional retailing. Regardless of what is being sold, however, the success of service organizations in the future will depend greatly on establishing a dialogue with consumers so that the operations managers can help their organizations adapt to consumer demands faster and more efficiently. Such information systems have been developed and should prove highly useful.

Progress Assessment

- Can you name and define three functions that are common to operations management in both the service and manufacturing sectors?
- What are the major criteria for facility location?
- What is involved in implementing each of the following: six sigma, SQC, SPC, QFD, ISO 9000, and ISO 14000?

OPERATIONS MANAGEMENT IN THE MANUFACTURING SECTOR

Common sense and some experience have already taught you much of what you need to know about production processes. You know what it takes to write a term paper or prepare a dinner. You need money to buy the materials, you need a place to work, and you need to be organized to get the task done. The same is true of the production process in industry. It uses basic inputs to produce outputs (see Figure 10.3). Production adds value, or utility, to materials or processes. **Form utility** is the value added by the creation of finished goods and services, such as the value added by taking silicon and making computer chips or putting services together to create a vacation package. Form utility can exist at the retail level as well. For example, a butcher can produce a specific cut of beef from a whole cow or a baker can make a specific type of cake out of basic ingredients.

form utility
The value added by the creation of finished goods and services.

FIGURE 10.3

THE PRODUCTION PROCESS

The production process consists of taking the factors of production (land, etc.) and using those inputs to produce goods, services, and ideas. Planning, routing, scheduling, and the other activities are the means to accomplish the objective—output.

To be competitive, manufacturers must keep the costs of inputs down. That is, the costs of workers, machinery, and so on must be kept as low as possible. Similarly, the amount of output must be relatively high. The question today is: How does a producer keep costs low and still increase output? This question will dominate thinking in the manufacturing and service sectors for years to come. In the next few sections, we explore manufacturing processes and the latest technology being used to cut costs.

Manufacturing Processes

There are several different processes manufacturers use to produce goods. Andrew S. Grove, chairman of computer chip manufacturer Intel, uses a great analogy to explain production:

> To understand the principles of production, imagine that you're a chef ... and that your task is to serve a breakfast consisting of a three-minute soft-boiled egg, buttered toast, and coffee. Your job is to prepare and deliver the three items simultaneously, each of them fresh and hot.

Grove goes on to say that the task here encompasses the three basic requirements of production: (1) to build and deliver products in response to the demands of the customer at a scheduled delivery time, (2) to provide an acceptable quality level, and (3) to provide everything at the lowest possible cost.

Using the breakfast example, it's easy to understand two manufacturing terms: process and assembly. **Process manufacturing** physically or chemically changes materials. For example, boiling physically changes the egg. (Similarly, process manufacturing turns sand into glass or computer chips.) The **assembly process** puts together components (eggs, toast, and coffee) to make a product (breakfast). Cars are made through an assembly process that puts together the frame, engine, and other parts.

In addition, production processes are either continuous or intermittent. A **continuous process** is one in which long production runs turn out finished goods over time. As the chef in our diner, you could have a conveyor belt that lowers eggs into boiling water for three minutes and then lifts them out on a continuous basis. A three-minute egg would be available whenever you wanted one. (A chemical plant, for example, is run on a continuous process.)

It usually makes more sense when responding to specific customer orders to use an **intermittent process.** This is an operation where the production run is short (one or two eggs) and the machines are changed frequently to make different products (like the oven in a bakery or the toaster in the diner). Manufacturers of custom-designed furniture would use an intermittent process.

Today, most new manufacturers use intermittent processes. Computers, robots, and flexible manufacturing processes allow firms to turn out custom-made goods almost as fast as mass-produced goods were once turned out. We'll discuss how they do that in detail later in the chapter. For now, let's look at some of the newer techniques being used to make the production process more efficient.

process manufacturing
That part of the production process that physically or chemically changes materials.

assembly process
That part of the production process that puts together components.

continuous process
A production process in which long production runs turn out finished goods over time.

intermittent process
A production process in which the production run is short and the machines are changed frequently to make different products.

MATERIALS REQUIREMENT PLANNING

materials requirement planning (MRP)
A computer-based production management system that uses sales forecasts to make sure that needed parts and materials are available at the right time and place.

Materials requirement planning (MRP) is a computer-based operations management system that uses sales forecasts to make sure that needed parts and materials are available at the right time and place. In our diner, for example, we could feed the sales forecast into the computer, which would specify how many eggs and how much coffee to order and then print out the proper scheduling and routing sequence. The same can be done with the seats and other parts of an automobile.

MRP is now considered old; it was most popular with companies that made products with a lot of different parts. MRP quickly led to MRP II, an advanced version of MRP that allowed plants to include all the resources involved in the efficient making of a product, including projected sales, personnel, plant capacity, and distribution limitations. MRP II was called manufacturing resource (not materials requirement) planning because the planning involved more than just material requirements.

enterprise resource planning (ERP)
A computer application that enables multiple firms to manage all of their operations (finance, requirements planning, human resources, and order fulfillment) on the basis of a single, integrated set of corporate data.

The newest version of MRP is **enterprise resource planning (ERP).** ERP is a computer application that enables *multiple* firms to manage all of their operations (finance, requirements planning, human resources, and order fulfillment) on the basis of a single, integrated set of corporate data (see Figure 10.4). The result is shorter time between orders and payment, less staff to do ordering and order processing, reduced inventories, and better customer service for all the firms involved. By entering customer and sales information in an ERP system, a manufacturer can generate the next period's demand forecast, which in turn generates orders for raw materials, production scheduling, and financial projections.

ERP software enables the monitoring of quality and customer satisfaction as it is happening. ERP systems are going global now that the Internet is powerful enough to handle the data flows. At the plant level, dynamic performance monitoring enables plant operators to monitor the use of power, chemicals, and other resources and to make needed adjustments. In short, flows to, through, and from plants have become automated.

Some firms are providing a service called sequential delivery. These firms are suppliers that provide components in an order sequenced to their customers' production process. For example, Ford's seat supplier loads seats onto a truck such that, when off-loaded, the seats are in perfect sequence for the type of vehicle coming down the assembly line.

While ERP can be an effective tool, it also can have its problems. The Royal Canadian Mint was having difficulties extracting and manipulating data. Departments were operated independently, and because it took so long to produce reports for analysis employees did not trust the reliability of the information once it was in their hands. "Anyone who has used an ERP system

FIGURE 10.4

ENTERPRISE RESOURCE PLANNING

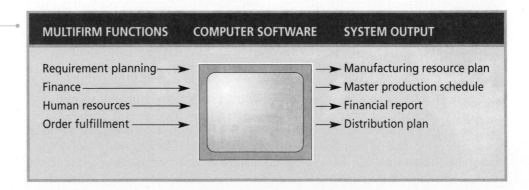

knows that reporting can be problematic," says Azfar Ali Khan, director of operations and systems at the Mint's sales and marketing departments. "They're wonderful transactional engines, but getting the richness of the data in front of the people in a context they can understand is particularly challenging."[31]

Information technology (IT) has had a major influence on the whole production process, from purchasing to final delivery. Many IT advances have been add-ons to ERP. To solve its difficulties, the Mint turned to Cognos (www.cognos.com) for its enterprise solution. Cognos' Analytic Applications solution made it possible for users to access data right to the day, as well as to create new reporting opportunities. The Mint's self-service, Web-enabled, enterprise-wide solution has enabled it to act quickly and thereby improve customer service. According to Ali, "Buying a prepackaged solution and customizing it to our own unique business requirements has saved us a lot of time and a lot of money."[32]

- Can you explain the production process?
- Can you define and differentiate the following: process manufacturing, assembly process, continuous process, and intermittent process?
- What is the difference between materials resource planning (MRP) and enterprise resource planning (ERP)?

Progress Assessment

MODERN PRODUCTION TECHNIQUES

The ultimate goal of manufacturing and process management is to provide high-quality goods and services instantaneously in response to customer demand. As we have stressed throughout this book, traditional organizations were simply not designed to be so responsive to the customer. Rather, they were designed to make goods efficiently (inexpensively). The whole idea of *mass production* was to make a large number of a limited variety of products at very low cost.

Over the years, low cost often came at the expense of quality and flexibility. Furthermore, suppliers didn't always deliver when they said they would, so manufacturers had to carry large inventories of raw materials and components. Such inefficiencies made companies less competitive than foreign competitors that were using more advanced production techniques.

As a result of global competition, largely from Japan and Germany, companies today must make a wide variety of high-quality, custom designed products at very low cost. Clearly, something had to change on the production floor to make that possible. Seven major developments have radically changed the production process. They are: (1) just-in-time inventory control, (2) Internet purchasing, (3) flexible manufacturing, (4) lean manufacturing, (5) mass customization, (6) competing in time, and (7) computer-aided design and manufacturing.

Just-in-Time Inventory Control

One major cost of production is holding parts, motors, and other items in storage for later use. Storage not only subjects such items to obsolescence, pilferage, and damage but also requires construction and maintenance of costly warehouses. To cut such costs, the Japanese implemented a concept called **just-in-time (JIT) inventory control.** JIT systems keep a minimum of inventory on the premises and parts, supplies, and other needs are delivered just in time to go on the assembly

just-in-time (JIT) inventory control
A production process in which a minimum of inventory is kept on the premises and parts, supplies, and other needs are delivered just in time to go on the assembly line.

There is no question that reduced supplier costs should lead to more profit, but how, exactly, does one go about cutting these costs? One answer, as this ad suggests, is to use SAS supplier intelligence software. By using this type of software, companies can identify opportunities to cut spending, minimize risk, and maximize profit. Can you see how such software could be part of enterprise resource planning (ERP)?

line. There is a scarcity of land in Japan, so minimizing the area needed for storage is a major issue. There is much more land available in Canada. Nonetheless, some manufacturers have adopted JIT and are quite happy with the results. To work effectively, however, the process requires excellent coordination with carefully selected suppliers. Sometimes the supplier builds new facilities close to the main producer to minimize distribution time.

A lot of planning and logistics effort is focused on ensuring the successful implementation of JIT. However, this system is still vulnerable to environmental factors, especially when suppliers are farther away. Shipments may be delayed due to poor weather, worker strikes, and events such as the power outage in Ontario in the summer of 2003. This was particularly evident after the September 11, 2001 terrorist attacks. Border delays were so long that auto manufacturers had to temporarily stop their assembly lines because parts did not arrive on time. With more than $1.3 billion worth of goods crossing the Canada–U.S. border each day, the efficient flow of products and people is vital to Canada's economy.[33] Any delays require that companies adjust their JIT schedules. Today, the longer delays at borders due to increased traffic and security measures have forced companies to do just that. Other limitations are that JIT works best with standard products, demand needs to be high and stable to justify the cost and savings, and suppliers need to be extremely reliable.

Here's how it works: A manufacturer sets a production schedule using ERP or one of the other systems just described (e.g., MRP), and then determines what parts and supplies will be needed. It informs suppliers electronically of what it will need. The suppliers must deliver the goods just in time to go on the assembly line. Naturally, this calls for more effort (and more costs) on the suppliers' part. The manufacturer maintains efficiency by linking electronically to the suppliers so that the suppliers become more like departments in the firm than separate businesses.

ERP and JIT systems make sure the right materials are at the right place at the right time at the cheapest cost to meet both customer and production needs. That's the first step in modern production innovation. Part of that process is rethinking the purchasing process. We shall explore that issue next.

Internet Purchasing

purchasing
The function in a firm that searches for quality material resources, finds the best suppliers, and negotiates the best price for goods and services.

Purchasing is the function in a firm that searches for quality material resources, finds the best suppliers, and negotiates the best price for quality goods and services. In the past, manufacturers tended to deal with many different suppliers with the idea that, if one supplier or another couldn't deliver, materials would be available from someone else. Today, however, manufacturers are relying more heavily on one or two suppliers because the firms share so much information that they don't want to have too many suppliers knowing their business. The Hudson's Bay Company is shifting to single merchandise buyers for a growing number of departments at its Bay, Zellers, and Home Outfitters chains. This move is designed to help improve product selection and save money through less duplication and larger purchase orders.[34] The relationship between suppliers and manufacturers is thus much closer than ever before.

The Internet has transformed the purchasing function in recent years. For example, a business looking for supplies can contact an Internet-based purchasing service and find the best supplies at the best price. Similarly, a company wishing to sell supplies can use the Internet to find all the companies looking for such supplies. The cost of purchasing items has thus been reduced tremendously. Through sites like aeroxchange.com, airline carriers such as Air Canada are achieving "average per unit savings of about 25 percent" according to Harry Hall, the airline's director of supply chain management. Mark Williams, president and CEO of Skyservice Airlines, has "seen savings of 30 to 40 percent for smaller airlines." There are a number of reasons why buying online saves airlines money. First there is efficiency, whereby searching for parts online buyers can access the full range of potential suppliers and get the best price. Before, buyers would go to their list of suppliers but did not know if they were getting the best price. Second, buyers can take advantage of volume discounts because their purchases are being added to those of other airlines. Third, airline downtime can be decreased by finding necessary parts faster and cheaper. All this can equal a lot of savings. As Wade Staddon, Air Canada's e-procurement manager, says, "Eventually, we expect to save $11 to $14 million a year."[35]

Flexible Manufacturing

Flexible manufacturing involves designing machines to do multiple tasks so that they can produce a variety of products. Flexible manufacturing is one reason that Japanese and German manufacturers of automobiles in North America are so profitable.[36] Such sites allow automakers to shift production based on market demand; the assembly line can be adjusted for different models using the same equipment, whereas an older factory requires retooling to avoid being rendered redundant if its product fails to sell.[37]

> **flexible manufacturing**
> Designing machines to do multiple tasks so that they can produce a variety of products.

Flexible manufacturing not only leads to improved productivity, but also may result in cost savings. As a result of its new flexible manufacturing, DaimlerChrysler AG's North American unit was successful in saving $500 million in the fastest product launch in company history. In Windsor, the 2001 minivan models were built, tested, and launched on the same assembly line as the 2000 models. According to Gary Henson, the unit's manufacturing chief, these savings resulted from reducing plant downtime by 80 percent as the company avoided 65 days of lost time during the changeover. It is estimated that the new flexible manufacturing will help save more than $3 billion through 2004 product launches by decreasing plant downtime.[38]

With flexible manufacturing, turnaround times can vary from a few hours to a few weeks, depending on the system's complexity.[39] Allen-Bradley (part of Rockwell Automation), a maker of industrial automation controls, uses flexible manufacturing to build motor starters. Orders come in daily, and within 24 hours the company's 26 machines and robots manufacture, test, and package the starters—which are untouched by human hands. Allen-Bradley's machines are so flexible that a special order, even a single item, can be included in the assembly without slowing down the process.

Lean Manufacturing

Lean manufacturing is the production of goods using less of everything compared to mass production: less human effort, less manufacturing space,

> **lean manufacturing**
> The production of goods using less of everything compared to mass production.

less investment in tools, and less engineering time to develop a new product. A company becomes lean by continuously increasing its capacity to produce high-quality goods while decreasing its need for resources.

General Motors (GM) also uses lean manufacturing. To make the Saturn automobile, for example, GM abandoned its assembly-line production process. The fundamental purpose of restructuring was to dramatically cut the number of worker-hours needed to build a car. GM made numerous changes, the most dramatic of which was to switch to modular construction. GM suppliers pre-assemble most of the auto parts into a few large components called modules. Workers are no longer positioned along kilometres of assembly line. Instead, they're grouped at various workstations, where they put the modules together. Rather than do a few set tasks, workers perform a whole cluster of tasks. Trolleys carry the partly completed car from station to station. Compared to the assembly line, modular assembly takes up less space and calls for fewer workers—both money-saving factors.

Finally, GM greatly expanded its use of robots in the manufacturing process. A *robot* is a computer-controlled machine capable of performing many tasks requiring the use of materials and tools. Robots, for example, spray-paint cars and do welding. Robots usually are fast, efficient, and accurate. Robots and other machines perform routine, repetitive jobs quickly, efficiently, and accurately. This provides opportunities for workers to be more creative.

Critical Thinking

People are being replaced by robots and other machines. On the one hand, that is one way companies compete with cheap labour from other countries. No labour at all is less expensive than cheap labour. On the other hand, automation eliminates many jobs. Are you concerned that automation may increase unemployment or underemployment in Canada and around the world?

Mass Customization

mass customization
Tailoring products to meet the needs of individual customers.

To customize means to make a unique good or provide a specific service to an individual. Although it once may have seemed impossible, **mass customization,** which means tailoring products to meet the needs of a large number of individual customers, is now practised widely. The National Bicycle Industrial Company in Japan, for example, makes 18 bicycle models in more than 2 million combinations, with each combination designed to fit the needs of a specific customer. The customer chooses the model, size, colour, and design. The retailer takes various measurements from the buyer and faxes the data to the factory, where robots handle the bulk of the assembly. Thus, flexible manufacturing, as described above, is one of the factors that makes mass customization possible. Given the exact needs of a customer, flexible machines can produce a customized good as fast as mass-produced goods were once made.

More and more manufacturers are learning to customize their products. For example, some companies produce custom-made books with a child's name inserted in key places, and custom-made greeting cards have appeared on the market. The Custom Foot stores use infrared scanners to precisely measure each foot so that shoes can be crafted to fit perfectly. You can also buy custom-made sneakers and even M&Ms. Motorola's Pager Division has 30 million possible permutations of pagers.

Mass customization is coming to services as well. Health clubs now offer unique fitness programs for individuals, travel agencies provide vacation packages that vary according to individual choices, and some schools allow students to design their own majors. Actually, it is much easier to custom-design service programs than it is to custom-make goods, because there is no fixed tangible good that has to be adapted. Each customer can specify what he or she wants, within the limits of the service organization—limits that seem to be ever widening.[40]

Competing in Time

Competing in time means being as fast as or faster than competitors in responding to consumer wants and needs and getting goods and services to them. Speedy response is essential to competing at all in a global marketplace.[41] Ford Motor Company estimates that, to match the best, it must be 25 percent faster than it is now in creating new products. Using the latest in technology, Ford should have no problem meeting that goal. The following section explores dramatic changes that are increasing the speed of production processes and otherwise maintaining companies' competitive strength in manufacturing. Such changes as computer-aided design and manufacturing enable firms to compete in time and in efficiency.

Computer-Aided Design and Manufacturing

The one development in the recent past that appears to have changed production techniques and strategies more than any other has been the integration of computers into the design and manufacturing of products. The first thing computers did was help in the design of products; this is called **computer-aided design (CAD).** The latest CAD systems allow designers to work in three dimensions. The next step was to involve computers directly in the production process; this is called **computer-aided manufacturing (CAM).**

CAD/CAM (the use of both computer-aided design and computer-aided manufacturing) made it possible to custom-design products to meet the needs of small markets with very little increase in cost. A manufacturer programs the computer to make a simple design change, and that change can be incorporated directly into the production line.

CAD and CAM are invading the clothing industry. A computer program establishes a pattern and cuts the cloth automatically. Today, a person's dimensions can be programmed into the machines to create custom-cut clothing at little additional cost. In food service, CAM is used to make cookies in fresh-baked cookie shops. On-site, small-scale, semiautomated, sensor-controlled baking makes consistent quality easy to achieve.

CAD has doubled productivity in many firms. But it's one thing to design a product and quite another to set the specifications to make a machine do the work. The problem in the past was that CAD machines couldn't talk to CAM machines directly. Recently, however, software programs have been designed to unite CAD with CAM: the result is **computer-integrated manufacturing (CIM).** The new software is expensive, but it cuts as much as 80 percent of the time needed to program machines to make parts.

competing in time
Being as fast as or faster than competitors in responding to consumer wants and needs and getting goods and services to them.

computer-aided design (CAD)
The use of computers in the design of products.

computer-aided manufacturing (CAM)
The use of computers in the manufacturing of products.

computer-integrated manufacturing (CIM).
The uniting of computer-aided design with computer-aided manufacturing.

This photo shows computer-aided design (CAD) in operation. When linked with computer-aided manufacturing (CAM), these software systems can greatly improve the design and production process. What advantages might this technology offer to smaller manufacturing companies? What types of industries would benefit most from CAD/CAM?

Critical Thinking

Computer-integrated manufacturing (CIM) has begun to revolutionize the production process. Now everything from cookies to cars can be designed and manufactured much more cheaply than before. Furthermore, customized changes can be made with very little increase in cost. What will such changes mean for the clothing industry, the shoe industry, and other fashion-related industries? What will they mean for other consumer and industrial goods industries? How will you benefit as a consumer?

CONTROL PROCEDURES: GANTT CHARTS

An important function of an operations manager is to be sure that products are manufactured and delivered on time, on budget, and to specifications. The question is: How can one be sure that all of the assembly processes will go smoothly and end up completed by the required time? One popular technique used by manufacturers for measuring production progress is a Gantt chart. A **Gantt chart** (named for its developer, Henry L. Gantt) is a bar graph that clearly shows what projects are being worked on and how much has been completed at any given time. Figure 10.5 shows a Gantt chart for a doll manufacturer. The chart shows that the dolls' heads and bodies should be completed before the clothing is sewn. It also shows that at the end of week 3, the dolls' bodies are ready, but the heads are about half a week behind. All of this calculation was once done by hand. Now the computer has taken over. Using a Gantt-like computer program, a manager can trace the production process minute by minute to determine which tasks are on time and which are behind so that adjustments can be made to allow the company to stay on schedule.

PREPARING FOR THE FUTURE

Canada is a major industrial country, and it is likely to become even stronger. This means that there are tremendous opportunities for careers in operations management. Today relatively few graduates have majored in production and

Gantt chart
Bar graph showing production managers what projects are being worked on and what stage they are in at any given time.

To create great-looking Gantt charts quickly and easily, visit the SmartDraw site at www.smartdraw.com/resources/ for free software, symbols, and templates.

FIGURE 10.5

GANTT CHART FOR A DOLL MANUFACTURER

A Gantt chart enables a production manager to see at a glance when projects are scheduled to be completed and what the status now is. For example, the dolls' heads and bodies should be completed before the clothing is sewn, but they could be a little late as long as everything is ready for assembly in week 6. This chart shows that at the end of week 3, the dolls' bodies are ready, but the heads are about half a week behind.

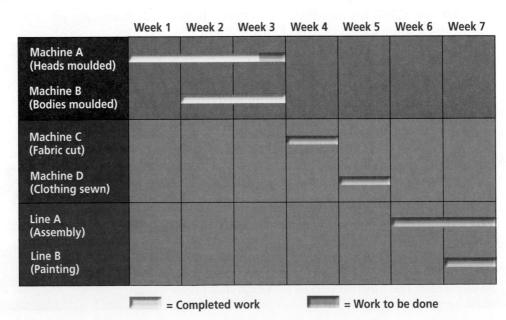

operations management, inventory management, and other areas involving manufacturing and operations management in the service sector. That means more opportunities for those students who can see the future trends and have the skills to own or work in tomorrow's highly automated, efficient factories, mines, service facilities, and other production locations.

Progress Assessment

- What is just-in-time inventory control?
- How does flexible manufacturing differ from lean manufacturing?
- What are CAD, CAM, and CIM?
- How could you use a Gantt chart to keep track of production?

Summary

1. Operations management is a specialized area in management that converts or transforms resources (including human resources) into goods and services.
   - *What kind of firms use operations managers?*
   Firms in both the manufacturing and service sectors use operations managers.

   1. Define operations management and explain what types of firms use it.

2. Functions involved in both the manufacturing and service sectors include facility location, facility layout, and quality control.
   - *What is facility location and how does it differ from facility layout?*
   Facility location is the process of selecting a geographic location for a company's operations. Facility layout is the physical arrangement of resources (including people) to produce goods and services effectively and efficiently.

   - *Why is facility location so important, and what criteria are used to evaluate different sites?*
   The very survival of manufacturing depends on its ability to remain competitive, and that means either making inputs less costly (reducing costs of labour and land) or increasing outputs from present inputs (increasing productivity). Labour costs and land costs are two major criteria for selecting the right sites. Other criteria include whether (1) resources are plentiful and inexpensive, (2) skilled workers are available or are trainable, (3) taxes are low and the local government offers support, (4) energy and water are available, (5) transportation costs are low, and (6) the quality of life and quality of education are high.

   - *What are the latest quality control concepts?*
   Six sigma quality (just 3.4 defects per million products) detects potential problems before they occur. Statistical quality control (SQC) is the process some managers use to continually monitor all processes in the production process to ensure that quality is being built into the product from the beginning. Statistical process control (SPC) is the process of taking statistical samples of product components at each stage of the production process and plotting those results on a graph. Any variances from quality standards are recognized and can be corrected. Quality function deployment (QFD) is a process of linking the needs of end users

   2. Describe the operations management planning issues involved in both the manufacturing and service sectors, including facility location, facility layout, and quality control.

(customers) to design, development, engineering, manufacturing, and service functions. The goal is to go beyond not making mistakes to maximizing customer satisfaction.

- *What quality standards do firms use in Canada?*

International standards Canadian firms strive to meet include ISO 9001:2000 (ISO 9000) and ISO 14000. The first is a European standard for quality and the second is a collection of the best practices for managing an organization's impact on the environment.

3. Discuss the problem of measuring productivity in the service sector, and tell how new technology is leading to productivity gains in service companies.

3. There's strong evidence that productivity in the service sector is rising, but this is difficult to measure.

- *Why is productivity so hard to measure?*

The traditional way to measure productivity involves tracking inputs (worker-hours) compared to outputs (dollars). Quality improvements are not weighed. New information systems must be developed to measure the quality of goods and services, the speed of their delivery, and customer satisfaction.

- *How is technology creating productivity gains in service organizations?*

Computers have been a great help to service employees, allowing them to perform their tasks faster and more accurately. ATMs make banking faster and easier; automated checkout machines enable grocery clerks (and customers) to process items faster. In short, operations management has led to tremendous productivity increases in the service sector but still has a long way to go.

4. Explain manufacturing processes, MRP, and ERP.

4. There are several different processes manufacturers use to produce goods.

- *What is process manufacturing, and how does it differ from assembly processes?*

Process manufacturing physically or chemically changes materials. Assembly processes put together components.

- *Are there other production processes?*

Production processes are either continuous or intermittent. A continuous process is one in which long production runs turn out finished goods over time. An intermittent process is an operation where the production run is short and the machines are changed frequently to produce different products.

- *What relationship does enterprise resource planning (ERP) have with the production process?*

ERP is a computer application that enables multiple firms to manage all of their operations (finance, requirements planning, human resources, and order fulfillment) on the basis of a single, integrated set of corporate data. The result is shorter time between orders and payment, less staff to do ordering and order processing, reduced inventories, and better customer service for all the firms involved. It is an advanced form of MRP.

5. Describe the seven new manufacturing techniques that have improved the productivity of companies: just-in-time inventory control, Internet purchasing, flexible manufacturing, lean manufacturing, mass customization, competing in time, and computer-aided design and manufacturing.

5. Companies are using seven new production techniques to become more profitable: (1) just-in-time inventory control, (2) Internet purchasing, (3) flexible manufacturing, (4) lean manufacturing, (5) mass customization, (6) competing in time, and (7) computer-aided design and manufacturing.

- *What is just-in-time (JIT) inventory control?*

JIT involves having suppliers deliver parts and materials just in time to go on the assembly line so they don't have to be stored in warehouses.

- *How have purchasing agreements changed?*

Purchasing agreements now involve fewer suppliers who supply quality goods and services at better prices in return for getting the business. Many new Internet companies have emerged to help both buyers and sellers complete the exchange process more efficiently.

- *What is flexible manufacturing?*

Flexible manufacturing involves designing machines to produce a variety of products.

- *What is lean manufacturing?*

Lean manufacturing is the production of goods using less of everything compared to mass production: less human effort, less manufacturing space, less investment in tools, and less engineering time to develop a new product.

- *What is mass customization?*

Mass customization means making custom-designed goods and services for a large number of individual customers. Flexible manufacturing makes mass customization possible. Given the exact needs of a customer, flexible machines can produce a customized good as fast as mass-produced goods were once made.

- *How does competing in time fit into the process?*

Getting your product to market before your competitors is essential today, particularly in the electronics industry. Thus, competing in time is critical. Computer-aided design and manufacturing enable firms to compete in time and in efficiency.

- *How do CAD/CAM systems work?*

Design changes made in computer-aided design (CAD) are instantly incorporated into the computer-aided manufacturing (CAM) process. The linking of the two systems—CAD and CAM—is called computer-integrated manufacturing (CIM).

Key Terms

assembly process 299
competing in time 305
computer-aided design (CAD) 305
computer-aided manufacturing (CAM) 305
computer-integrated manufacturing (CIM) 305
continuous process 299
enterprise resource planning (ERP) 300
facility layout 289
facility location 286
flexible manufacturing 303
form utility 298

Gantt chart 306
innovation 282
intermittent process 299
ISO 9000 294
ISO 14000 295
just-in-time (JIT) inventory control 301
lean manufacturing 303
mass customization 304
materials requirement planning (MRP) 300
operations management 285
process manufacturing 299
production 284
production management 285

purchasing 302
quality 291
quality function deployment (QFD) 293
research and development (R&D) 282
six sigma quality 291
statistical process control (SPC) 291
statistical quality control (SQC) 291
supply chain 296
supply chain management 296

Developing Workplace Skills

1. Choosing the right location for a manufacturing plant or a service organization is often critical to its success. Form small groups and have each group member pick one manufacturing plant or one service organization in town and list at least three reasons why its location helps or hinders its success. If its location is not ideal, where would be a better one?

2. In teams of four or five, discuss the need for better operations management at airports and with the airlines in general. Have the team develop a three-page report listing (*a*) problems team members have encountered in travelling by air and (*b*) suggestions for improving operations so such problems won't occur in the future.

3. Discuss some of the advantages and disadvantages of producing goods overseas using inexpensive labour. Summarize the moral and ethical issues of this practice.

4. Think of any production facility (e.g., sandwich shop or woodworking facility) or service centre (e.g., library, copy room) at your school and redesign the layout (make a pencil drawing placing people and materials) so that the facility could more effectively serve its customers and so that the workers would be more effective and efficient.

5. Think about some of the experiences you have had with service organizations recently (e.g., the admissions office at your school), and select one incident in which you had to wait for an unreasonable length of time to get what you wanted. Tell what happens when customers are inconvenienced, and explain how management could make the operation more efficient and customer-oriented.

Taking It To The Net 1

Purpose

To illustrate production processes.

Exercise

Take a virtual tour of the Hershey Foods Corporation's chocolate factory by going to www.hersheys.com/tour/index.shtml. If you have a high-speed Internet connection, you can choose the video tour. If not, the picture tour is a faster choice.

1. Does Hershey use process manufacturing or the assembly process? Is the production of Hershey's chocolate an example of an intermittent or continuous production process? Justify your answers.

2. What location factors might go into the selection of a manufacturing site for Hershey's chocolate?

Taking It To The Net 2

Purpose

To learn more about the links between quality function deployment (QFD) and other quality concepts.

Exercise

Go to the Quality Function Deployment Institute Website at www.qfdi.org and click on "What is QFD?" Then click on "Frequently Asked Questions about QFD."

1. How does QFD differ from other quality initiatives?

2. Who are the founders of QFD?

3. What are "expected quality" and "exciting quality"?

Practising Management Decisions

Case

Why Big Companies Fail to Innovate

Matthew Kiernan, based in Unionville, Ontario, is a management consultant whose views command attention. He has a PhD degree in strategic management from the University of London and was a senior partner with an international consulting firm, KPMG Peat Marwick. Subsequently he founded his own firm, Innovest Group International, with a staff operating out of Geneva, London, and Toronto. He was also a director of the Business Council for Sustainable Development based in Geneva.

His book *Get Innovative or Get Dead* took aim at big corporations for their poor record on innovation. Any five-year-old could tell you that companies must innovate to survive, he said, so what's the problem? According to Kiernan, it's one thing to understand something in your head but quite another thing to really feel it in your gut. This is further complicated by the difficulty of getting a big company to shift gears, to turn its culture around so that innovation becomes the norm rather than the special effort.

Kiernan called for a company to develop a style and atmosphere that favours individual risk taking, the intrapreneurial approach discussed in Chapter 7. That means that if a team tries something that doesn't work, you don't shoot them down. Encouraging innovation, which inevitably involves taking risks with the unknown, means accepting the fact that it may take two or three attempts before something useful is developed. Further, it requires "creative thinking to see the potential" in something new or untested.

The 3M company is often used as a great example of a company that encourages creativity. Its policy dictates that 30 percent of annual sales come from products less than four years old. But 3M wasn't always that progressive. When the now legendary Post-it Notes were first developed by an employee, he had a hard time getting the company to see the potential in his idea. This ultimately triggered a major change in the company's policy.

Kiernan pointed out that most companies give lip service to the necessity of innovation but do not act in a credible way as far as their employees are concerned. If you mean business you must take that "bright guy out of the basement, [the one] everybody knows is a genius, but whose last two enterprise efforts came to grief, and visibly promote him."

Decision Questions

1. Do large companies find it difficult to innovate because they resist change? Is it because they are big or because they are afraid of the unknown? Why is that?

2. Do smaller companies do better at innovation because they are not so risk-averse? Is that because most of them are private companies and not accountable to outside stakeholders?

3. Can you see any connection between innovation and continuous improvement? Does CI require innovation?

4. If you were a vice-president in charge of production at a big corporation, how would you encourage innovation?

Video Case

Reality On Request—Digital Domain

As Chairman and CEO of Digital Domain, Scott Ross runs one of the largest digital production studios in the world. His studio won an Academy Award for doing the simulation of the sinking of the *Titanic* in the movie with the same name. It also created the digital waves that wiped out the horsemen in *Lord of the Rings*.

Operations management is unique at Digital Domain because no two projects are ever the same. One day they may be making a digital cow (*O Brother, Where Art Thou*), on another a digital spaceship (*Apollo 13*), and on still another digital waves (*Titanic*). Digital is both a production and service provider. How so? In addition to producing digital scenes for movies, the company advises movie producers as to what is possible to do digitally. Still, certain activities, such as facility location and facility layout, are common to both service organizations and production firms.

Since many movies are made in Los Angeles, it's important for Digital Domain to be close to the city. Actors are often chosen from that area, as are workers and specialists at Digital. The company's most important resource, however, is its workers. Thus, facilities layout is designed to make the job of workers easier, yet efficient. For example, there's a combination conference room and cafeteria. Given the company's passion for *quality*, everything is designed to be clean and logical. Facility layout assists workers in developing the highest-quality product possible given time and money constraints.

Materials requirement planning (MRP) is a computer-based operations management system that uses sales forecasts to make needed parts and materials available at the right time and place. Since Digital's primary resource is people, the company lists 54 key disciplines in its database, so it's easy to find the right person for the right job. For example, a project may come up on Wednesday that demands having resources available the next Monday. People have to be contacted and hired *just in time* to keep the project on time and within budget.

The company does much of its purchasing on the Internet. It also uses *flexible manufacturing*. To keep costs down, Digital also uses *lean manufacturing*, the production of goods using less of everything: less human effort, less manufacturing space, less investment in tools, and less engineering time for a given project. To keep costs down the company does a lot of pre-visualizing—simulating projects to determine the best way to proceed.

Of course, *mass customization* is basically what Digital Domain is all about: creating new and different scenes that can't be duplicated. However, once the company learns to create artificial waves or some other image, it is easier to duplicate a similar image next time. Since film is very expensive, many ideas are created using pen and pencil first. From such "primitive" tools, the company goes on to use *computer-aided design*.

Making movies is expensive. Everything needs to be done as planned. Scott Ross knows it's show *business*, and the accent is on business, and making a profit. For this reason, Digital uses computerized Gantt charts to follow goods in process. Getting things done right and on time is the hallmark at Digital Domain.

Discussion Questions

1. Do you have an appreciation for operations management now that you've seen how exciting such a job can be at a company like Digital Domain?
2. Mass customization is critical in the production of movies and special effects. As a consumer, what benefits do you see in being able to buy custom-made shoes, clothes, automobiles, and more?
3. What lessons did you learn from this video that you could apply at any job you might get?
4. This video points out that certain workers are very focused on quality and that there comes a time when you have to stop improving things because time has a cost. Have you had to make a trade-off between perfection and "good enough"? What were the consequences?

PART 4

Chapter 11

Motivating Employees

Learning Goals

After you have read and studied this chapter, you should be able to

1 Relate the significance of Taylor's scientific management and the Hawthorne studies to management.

2 Identify the levels of Maslow's hierarchy of needs, and relate their importance to employee motivation.

3 Distinguish between the motivators and hygiene factors identified by Herzberg.

4 Explain how job enrichment affects employee motivation and performance.

5 Differentiate between Theory X and Theory Y.

6 Describe the key principles of goal-setting, expectancy, reinforcement, and equity theories.

7 Explain how open communication builds teamwork, and describe how managers are likely to motivate teams in the future.

Getting to Know David Wexler of Alias

With an honours Bachelor of Arts degree from York University, David Wexler started his business career with one of the biggest companies in the world, Procter & Gamble. Five years at Digital Equipment Corporation as Director of Operations for Eastern Canada gave him more experience at handling a tremendous scale of responsibility. He experienced corporate life at a small software start-up, VARNET, where he was vice president of operations. Today, Wexler is the vice president of global human resources at Alias®.

Alias is the world's leading innovator of 3D graphics technology. The company develops award-winning software, support, custom development, and training solutions for the film, video, game development, interactive media, industrial design, and visualization markets. Among the company's many awards, Alias has been acknowledged as one of Canada's top 100 employers.

How does a company get on this list? The best employers do more than issue paycheques. They improve life in the workplace and in the surrounding community. The organizations selected are the best in their class and they get there because they want not only to woo the best employees but to keep them as well.

"As much as I love the business we're in, I love the people who work in this business even more," says Wexler. "The company is full of people who are very creative, very bright, very turned on by doing great work and very ethical and honest. Everyone says that people are a company's strength," he continues. "I believe that people *are* the company, so you can't pay lip service to employee development, ethics, or compensation. At Alias, the senior management has the courage, vision, and ethics to make that a reality."

According to Wexler, "What differentiates the good companies from the great ones is the ability to unleash that talent. It comes down to making an employee feel comfortable enough to use all of his/her skills. And that's what we're trying to do here. On top of employing first-rate talent, we're also conscious of providing our staff with a unique working environment, one that encourages personalities of all types to shine. Perks include a rooftop terrace with BBQ overlooking the city, free dinner to employees who work late, a time-off leave program (with pay), regular celebrations, a pool table and Playstations, and a parking lottery, to name just a few. We've created a work and social atmosphere that is second to none."

Thousands of books and articles have been written about how to motivate a workforce. Not surprisingly, there are many conflicting points of view. Peter Drucker, probably the most respected management theorist in the world, believes that the majority of workers today are knowledge workers. Therefore, to motivate them, employees need autonomy and continual innovation and learning, which should be built into the job.

In this chapter, you will be introduced to some motivation theories. Motivated workers are critical as they contribute to the success of an organization. As you read through this chapter, consider situations where you have been involved. Did you witness some of the theories being applied? Looking back, could some of these situations have been handled differently to better motivate the audience?

Alias is a registered trademark of Alias Systems Corp. in the United States and/or other countries.

Sources: Harvey Schachter, "Drucker's Take on Management This Century," *The Globe and Mail*, May 26, 1999, p. M1; Katherine Macklem, "Top 100 Employers," October 20, 2003, *Macleans*. Retrieved from http://www.macleans.ca/webspecials/article.jsp?content=20031020_67488_67488#; and "Alias Recognized as One of Canada's Top 100 Employers," October 22, 2003, Alias Systems. Retrieved from http://www.alias.com/eng/press/press_releases/20031022_alias_top_100_employers.shtml.

THE IMPORTANCE OF MOTIVATION

The importance of workforce satisfaction cannot be overstated. Happy workers lead to happy customers, and happy customers lead to successful businesses.[1] On the opposite side, unhappy workers are likely to leave the company, and when this happens, the company usually loses out. Losing a valuable, highly skilled employee could cost more than $100,000 for such things as exit interviews, severance pay, the process of hiring a replacement worker, and lost productivity while the new employee is learning the job. The "soft" costs are even greater: loss of intellectual capital, decreased morale, increased employee stress, and a negative reputation.[2] Motivating the right people to join and remain with the organization is a key function of managers.

People are willing to work, and work hard, if they feel that their work makes a difference and is appreciated. People are motivated by a variety of things, such as recognition, accomplishment, and status.[3] An **intrinsic reward** is the personal satisfaction you feel when you perform well and complete goals. The belief that your work makes a significant contribution to the organization or society is a form of intrinsic reward. An **extrinsic reward** is something given to you by someone else as recognition for good work. Such things as pay increases, praise, and promotions are examples of extrinsic rewards. Although ultimately motivation—the drive to satisfy a need—comes from within an individual, there are ways to stimulate people that bring out their natural drive to do a good job.[4]

As an example, Canadian Tire Financial Services (CTFS) has awarded more than 50 *Customers for Life* awards to its employees. Initiated in 1997, the award is a way to recognize and reward employees who have demonstrated superior customer service. Candidates are nominated based on outstanding conduct witnessed by fellow employees or customer feedback. The CFL award criteria include direct customer contact, positive customer perception of experience, and an experience that meets World Class Customer Service Standards and upholds CTFS's Values and Mission Statement.

The purpose of this chapter is to help you understand the concepts, theories, and practice of motivation. The most important person to motivate, of course, is yourself. One way to do that is to find the right job in the right organization—one that enables you to reach your goals in life.[5] The whole

intrinsic reward
The good feeling you have when you have done a job well.

extrinsic reward
Something given to you by someone else as recognition for good work; extrinsic rewards include pay increases, praise, and promotions.

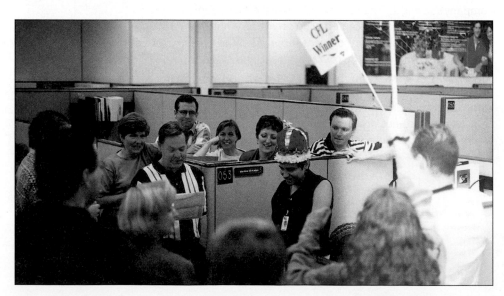

Employees never know when they will receive a *Customers for Life* award. Each award presentation is preceded by a procession that includes the CFL committee and flag-waving. Here, Canadian Tire Financial Services President Tom Gauld reads why Martine McKenny went above and beyond the requirements of her job. CFL award recipients receive a plaque, a day off—and they get to keep the crown! All stories are framed on the CFL wall. Can you think of examples of extrinsic rewards that you have witnessed?

purpose of this book is to help you in that search and to teach you how to succeed once you get there. One secret of success is to recognize that everyone else is on a similar search. Naturally, some are more committed than others. The job of a leader is to find that commitment, encourage it, and focus it on some common goal.

This chapter begins with a look at some of the traditional theories of motivation. You will learn about the Hawthorne studies because they created a new interest in worker satisfaction and motivation. Then you'll look at some assumptions about employees that come from the traditional theorists. You will see the names of these theorists over and over in business literature and courses: Taylor, Mayo, Maslow, Herzberg, and McGregor. Finally, you will learn the modern applications of motivation theories and the managerial procedures for implementing them.

Frederick Taylor: The Father of Scientific Management

Several books in the 19th century presented management principles, but not until the early 20th century did there appear any significant works with lasting implications. One of the most well-known, *The Principles of Scientific Management,* was written by American efficiency engineer Frederick Taylor and published in 1911. This book earned Taylor the title "father of scientific management." Taylor's goal was to increase worker productivity in order to benefit both the firm and the worker. The way to improve productivity ➤**P. 15**◀, Taylor thought, was to scientifically study the most efficient ways to do things, determine the one "best way" to perform each task, and then teach people those methods. This became known as **scientific management.** Three elements were basic to Taylor's approach: time, methods, and rules of work. His most important tools were observation and the stopwatch. It's Taylor's thinking that is behind today's measures of how many burgers McDonald's expects its flippers to flip and how many callers the phone companies expect operators to assist.

scientific management
Studying workers to find the most efficient ways of doing things and then teaching people those techniques.

A classic Taylor story involves his study of men shovelling rice, coal, and iron ore with the same type of shovel. Taylor felt that different materials called for different shovels. He proceeded to invent a wide variety of sizes and shapes of shovels and, with stopwatch in hand, measured output over time in what were called **time-motion studies**—studies of the tasks performed to complete a job and the time needed to do each task. Sure enough, an average person could shovel more (in fact, from 25 to 35 tons more per day) using the most efficient motions and the proper shovel. This finding led to time-motion studies of virtually every factory job. As the most efficient ways of doing things were determined, efficiency became the standard for setting goals.

time-motion studies
Studies, begun by Frederick Taylor, of which tasks must be performed to complete a job and the time needed to do each task.

Taylor's scientific management became the dominant strategy for improving productivity in the early 1900s. Hundreds of time-motion specialists developed standards in plants throughout the country. One follower of Taylor was Henry L. Gantt (see Chapter 10 for a discussion of Gantt charts). Engineers Frank and Lillian Gilbreth used Taylor's ideas in a three-year study of bricklaying. They developed the **principle of motion economy,** which showed that every job could be broken down into a series of elementary motions. They then analyzed each motion to make it more efficient.

principle of motion economy
Theory developed by Frank and Lillian Gilbreth that every job can be broken down into a series of elementary motions.

Scientific management viewed people largely as machines that needed to be properly programmed. There was little concern for the psychological or human aspects of work. Taylor felt simply that workers would perform at a high level of effectiveness (that is, be motivated) if they received high enough pay.

Some of Taylor's ideas are still being implemented. Some companies still place more emphasis on conformity to work rules than on creativity, flexibility, and responsiveness. For example, UPS tells drivers how fast to walk

(90 centimetres per second), how many packages to pick up and deliver a day (average of 400), and how to hold their keys (teeth up, third finger). Drivers even wear "ring scanners," electronic devices on their index fingers wired to a small computer on their wrists that shoot a pattern of photons at a bar code on a package to let a customer using the Internet know exactly where his or her package is at any given moment.

The benefits of relying on workers to come up with solutions to productivity problems have long been recognized, as we shall discover next.

Elton Mayo and the Hawthorne Studies

One of the studies that grew out of Frederick Taylor's research was conducted at the Western Electric Company's Hawthorne plant in Cicero, Illinois. The study began in 1927 and ended six years later. Let's see why it was one of the major studies in management literature.

Elton Mayo and his colleagues from Harvard University came to the Hawthorne plant to test the degree of lighting associated with optimum productivity. In this respect, theirs was a traditional scientific management study; the idea was to keep records of the workers' productivity under different levels of illumination. But the initial experiments revealed what seemed to be a problem: The productivity of the experimental group compared to that of other workers doing the same job went up regardless of whether the lighting was bright or dim. This was true even when the lighting was reduced to about the level of moonlight. These results confused and frustrated the researchers, who had expected productivity to fall as the lighting was dimmed.

A second series of experiments was conducted. In these, a separate test room was set up where temperature, humidity, and other environmental factors could be manipulated. In the series of 13 experimental periods, productivity went up each time; in fact, it increased by 50 percent overall. When the experimenters repeated the original condition (expecting productivity to fall to original levels), productivity increased yet again. The experiments were considered a total failure at this point. No matter what the experimenters did, productivity went up. What was causing the increase?

In the end, Mayo guessed that some human or psychological factor was involved. He and his colleagues then interviewed the workers, asking them about their feelings and attitudes toward the experiment. The researchers' findings began a profound change in management thinking that has had repercussions up to the present. Here is what they concluded:

- The workers in the test room thought of themselves as a social group. The atmosphere was informal, they could talk freely, and they interacted regularly with their supervisors and the experimenters. They felt special and worked hard to stay in the group. This motivated them.
- The workers were involved in the planning of the experiments. For example, they rejected one kind of pay schedule and recommended another, which was used. The workers felt that their ideas were respected and that they were involved in managerial decision making. This, too, motivated them.

Elton Mayo and his research team forever changed managers' fixed assumptions about what motivates employees. Mayo and his team gave birth to the concept of human-based motivation after conducting studies at the Western Electric Hawthorne plant (pictured here). Before the studies at Hawthorne, workers were often programmed to behave like human robots.

- No matter what the physical conditions were, the workers enjoyed the atmosphere of their special room and the additional pay they got for more productivity. Job satisfaction increased dramatically.

Researchers now use the term **Hawthorne effect** to refer to the tendency for people to behave differently when they know they're being studied. The Hawthorne study's results encouraged researchers to study human motivation and the managerial styles that lead to more productivity. The emphasis of research shifted away from Taylor's scientific management and toward Mayo's new human-based management.

Mayo's findings led to completely new assumptions about employees. One of those assumptions, of course, was that pay was not the only motivator. In fact, money was found to be a relatively ineffective motivator. That change in assumptions led to many theories about the human side of motivation. One of the best-known motivation theorists was Abraham Maslow, whose work we discuss next.

Hawthorne effect
The tendency for people to behave differently when they know they are being studied.

MOTIVATION AND MASLOW'S HIERARCHY OF NEEDS

Psychologist Abraham Maslow believed that to understand motivation at work, one must understand human motivation in general. It seemed to him that motivation arises from need. That is, people are motivated to satisfy unmet needs; needs that have been satisfied no longer provide motivation. He thought that needs could be placed on a hierarchy of importance.

Figure 11.1 shows **Maslow's hierarchy of needs,** whose levels are as follows:

Physiological needs: basic survival needs, such as the need for food, water, and shelter.

Safety needs: the need to feel secure at work and at home.

Social needs: the need to feel loved, accepted, and part of the group.

Esteem needs: the need for recognition and acknowledgement from others, as well as self-respect and a sense of status or importance.

Self-actualization needs: the need to develop to one's fullest potential.

Maslow's hierarchy of needs
Theory of motivation that places different types of human needs in order of importance, from basic physiological needs to safety, social, and esteem needs to self-actualization needs.

FIGURE 11.1

MASLOW'S HIERACHY OF NEEDS

Maslow's hierarchy of needs is based on the idea that motivation comes from need. If a need is met, it's no longer a motivator, so a higher-level need becomes the motivator. Higher-level needs demand the support of lower-level needs. This chart shows the various levels of need.

Self-actualization needs

Esteem needs

Social needs

Safety needs

Physiological needs

When one need is satisfied, another, higher-level need emerges and motivates the person to do something to satisfy it. The satisfied need is no longer a motivator. For example, if you just ate a full-course dinner, hunger would not (at least for several hours) be a motivator, and your attention may turn to your surroundings (safety needs) or family (social needs). Of course, lower-level needs (e.g., thirst) may emerge at any time they are not met and take your attention away from higher-level needs such as the need for recognition or status.

Most of the world's workers struggle all day simply to meet the basic physiological and safety needs. In developed countries, such needs no longer dominate, and workers seek to satisfy growth needs (social, esteem, and self-actualization).

To compete successfully, firms must create a work environment that motivates the best and the brightest workers. That means establishing a work environment that includes goals such as social contribution, honesty, reliability, service, quality, dependability, and unity.

Critical Thinking   Your job right now is to finish reading this chapter. How strongly would you be motivated to do that if you were sweating in a 40°C room? Imagine now that your roommate has turned on the air-conditioning. Now that you are more comfortable, are you more likely to read? Look at Maslow's hierarchy of needs to see what need would be motivating you at both times. Can you see how helpful Maslow's theory is in understanding motivation by applying it to your own life?

Progress Assessment

- What are the similarities and differences between Taylor's time-motion studies and Mayo's Hawthorne studies?
- How did Mayo's findings influence scientific management?
- Can you draw a diagram of Maslow's hierarchy of needs? Label and describe the parts.

HERZBERG'S MOTIVATING FACTORS

Another direction in managerial theory is to explore what managers can do with the job itself to motivate employees (a modern-day look at Taylor's research). In other words, some theorists ask: Of all the factors controllable by managers, which are most effective in generating an enthusiastic work effort?

The most discussed study in this area was conducted in the mid-1960s by psychologist Frederick Herzberg. He asked workers to rank various job-related factors in order of importance relative to motivation. The question was: What creates enthusiasm for workers and makes them work to full potential? The results showed that the most important motivating factors were the following:

1. Sense of achievement.
2. Earned recognition.
3. Interest in the work itself.
4. Opportunity for growth.
5. Opportunity for advancement.
6. Importance of responsibility.

7. Peer and group relationships.
8. Pay.
9. Supervisor's fairness.
10. Company policies and rules.

11. Status.
12. Job security.
13. Supervisor's friendliness.
14. Working conditions.

Herzberg noted that the factors receiving the most votes were all clustered around job content. Workers like to feel that they contribute to the company (sense of achievement was number 1). They want to earn recognition (number 2) and feel their jobs are important (number 6). They want responsibility (which is why learning is so important) and want recognition for that responsibility by having a chance for growth and advancement. Of course, workers also want the job to be interesting.

Herzberg noted further that factors having to do with the job environment were not considered motivators by workers. It was interesting to find that one of those factors was pay. Workers felt that the absence of good pay, job security, friendly supervisors, and the like could cause dissatisfaction, but the presence of those factors did not motivate them to work harder; they just provided satisfaction and contentment in the work situation.

The conclusions of Herzberg's study were that certain factors, called **motivators,** did cause employees to be productive and gave them a great deal of satisfaction. These factors mostly had to do with job content. Herzberg called other elements of the job **hygiene factors** (or maintenance factors). These had to do mostly with the job environment and could cause dissatisfaction if missing but would not necessarily motivate employees if increased. See Figure 11.2 for a list of both motivators and hygiene factors.

Considering Herzberg's motivating factors, we come up with the following conclusion: The best way to motivate employees is to make the job interesting, help them achieve their objectives, and recognize that achievement through advancement and added responsibility.

motivators
In Herzberg's theory of motivating factors, job factors that cause employees to be productive and that give them satisfaction

hygiene factors
In Herzberg's theory of motivating factors, job factors that can cause dissatisfaction if missing but that do not necessarily motivate employees if increased.

Applying Herzberg's Theories

In 2002, BC Biomedical Laboratories, British Columbia's largest community lab, was identified as *Report On Business* magazine's best company to work for in Canada. Why? You might think that its employees would point to the staff profit-sharing plan and a health program that gives each employee a $250 disbursement each year, in addition to their regular benefits. Or perhaps they

MOTIVATORS	HYGIENE (MAINTENANCE) FACTORS
(These factors can be used to motivate workers.)	(These factors can cause dissatisfaction, but changing them will have little motivational effect.)
Work itself	Company policy and administration
Achievement	Supervision
Recognition	Working conditions
Responsibility	Interpersonal relations (co-workers)
Growth and advancement	Salary, status, and job security

FIGURE 11.2

HERZBERG'S MOTIVATORS AND HYGIENE FACTORS

There's some controversy over Herzberg's results. For example, sales managers often use money as a motivator. Recent studies have shown that money can be a motivator if used as part of a recognition program.

Herzberg believed that motivational factors such as recognition increase worker performance. Managers of Wal-Mart obviously agree with his theory. Here, a Wal-Mart employee receives an award for high productivity. How do you think Herzberg's motivational factors encourage workers to a higher level of performance on the job?

would cite the flexibility in shifts and scheduling where the company offers part-time casual work, flex hours, and job sharing. Or the annual barbecues, picnics, and Christmas parties for employees and their families. Debbie Miotto, a medical laboratory technologist, says what makes her happy is that "I can pick up the phone and talk to my CEO, no problem. I'm taking a computer course and I just called him up to help me with my project."[6]

Melissa Sturgeon is an assistant team leader at Flight Centre. She says she loves her job because "There's faith in me. I can make judgment calls without getting everything approved by five people."[7]

Improved working conditions (such as better wages or increased security) are taken for granted after workers get used to them. This is what Herzberg meant by hygiene (or maintenance) factors: their absence causes dissatisfaction, but their presence (maintenance) does not motivate. The best motivator for some employees is a simple and sincere "Thanks, I really appreciate what you're doing."[8]

Many surveys conducted to test Herzberg's theories have supported his finding that the number-one motivator is not money but a sense of achievement and recognition for a job well done.[9] A recent survey that includes responses from 100 executives with Canada's 1,000 largest companies reinforces this point. "Employees are most productive when they feel their contributions are valued and their feedback is welcomed by management," said Max Messmer, chairman of Accountemps and author of *Motivating Employees For Dummies*. "The reverse is also true—an unsupportive atmosphere can lead to reduced performance levels and higher turnover for businesses."[10]

If you're skeptical about this, think about the limitations of money as a motivating force. Most organizations review an employee's performance only once a year and allocate raises at that time. To inspire and motivate employees to perform at their highest level of capability, managers must recognize their achievements and progress more than once a year.

Look back at Herzberg's list of motivating factors and identify the ones that tend to motivate you. Rank them in order of importance to you. Keep these factors in mind as you consider jobs and careers. What motivators do your job opportunities offer to you? Are they the ones you consider important? Evaluating your job offers in terms of what's really important to you will help you make a wise career choice.

A review of Figure 11.3 shows that there is a good deal of similarity in Maslow's hierarchy of needs and Herzberg's theory of factors.

JOB ENRICHMENT

job enrichment
A motivational strategy that emphasizes motivating the worker through the job itself.

Both Maslow's and Herzberg's theories have been extended by job enrichment theory. **Job enrichment** is a motivational strategy that emphasizes motivating the worker through the job itself. Work is assigned to individuals so that they have the opportunity to complete an identifiable task from beginning to end. They are held responsible for successful completion of the task. The motivational effect of job enrichment can come from the opportunities for personal achievement, challenge, and recognition. Go back and review Maslow's and Herzberg's work to see how job enrichment grew out of those theories.

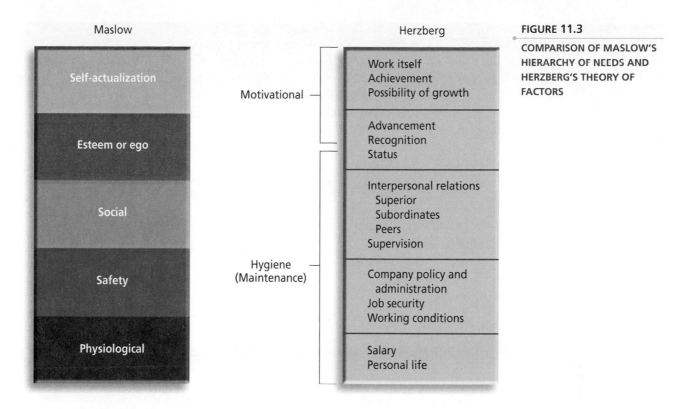

FIGURE 11.3

COMPARISON OF MASLOW'S HIERARCHY OF NEEDS AND HERZBERG'S THEORY OF FACTORS

Those who advocate job enrichment believe five characteristics of work to be important in affecting individual motivation and performance:

1. **Skill variety.**   The extent to which a job demands different skills.
2. **Task identity.**   The degree to which the job requires doing a task with a visible outcome from beginning to end.
3. **Task significance.**   The degree to which the job has a substantial impact on the lives or work of others in the company.
4. **Autonomy.**   The degree of freedom, independence, and discretion in scheduling work and determining procedures.
5. **Feedback.**   The amount of direct and clear information that is received about job performance.

Variety, identity, and significance contribute to the meaningfulness of the job. Autonomy gives people a feeling of responsibility, and feedback contributes to a feeling of achievement and recognition.

Job enrichment is what makes work fun. The word *fun* can be misleading. We're not talking about having parties all the time. For example, Roger Sant, founder and chairman of the global electricity company AES, says that what makes working at AES fun is that people are fully engaged: "They have total responsibility for decisions. They are accountable for results. What they do every day matters to the company, and it matters to the communities we operate in. We do celebrate a lot—because lots of great things are happening. We just did a billion-dollar deal, for instance, and that called for a party. But it's what happens before the celebrations that's really fun."[11]

Job enrichment is based on Herzberg's higher motivators such as responsibility, achievement, and recognition. It stands in contrast to *job simplification,* which produces task efficiency by breaking down a job into simple steps and assigning people to each of those steps.

Spotlight on Small Business

Motivating Employees in a Small Business

When you run a small business, every dollar counts. When you waste the intelligence, energy, or skills of your employees, it's like throwing money out the window, according to Rhonda Abrams, author of *Wear Clean Underwear: Business Wisdom from Mom*. Abrams says the surest way to get the best value from your employees is to treat them with respect: "When you allow your employees to think about how to solve problems, not just carry out specific tasks, you can unleash an amazing amount of creativity and energy. To do so, however, they'll need information, patience, and a sense they won't be 'punished' if they make an honest mistake."

To help your employees be more productive, Abrams recommends that you:

- Train your employees to do a wide variety of tasks. In a small business, employees have to pitch in on many jobs, so instead of teaching them specific tasks, you need to teach them about the whole business and encourage problem solving.

- Communicate frequently. Tom Pace of Pace/Butler Corporation holds 15-minute motivation sessions each morning. Employees compliment each other for recent behaviours, both minor and major. Then each person shares something they've done well. Pace says, "These meetings raise individual self-esteem and set the tone for the rest of the day."

- Empower your employees to make decisions. Let them use their brains, not just their backs.

- Be innovative with rewards and compensation. Look at long-term rewards such as profit-sharing and short-term rewards that involve personal or family life. Most importantly, always be equitable with salaries to create a work environment that fosters fairness.

- Be an employer of choice. Make your business environment an attractive one by giving employees high-profile projects that will help them grow professionally.

- Get feedback from employees, even those who leave. Conduct exit interviews to find out why people are leaving and what measures you can take to encourage them to stay.

- Acknowledge their contributions. The least productive thing you can say is "I don't need to thank employees; I pay them." We all need to be thanked and recognized.

It's difficult for a small company to match the financial benefits of large corporations, so it's even more important for small-business owners to make every employee feel valued, included, and respected. As your employees grow, your business is more likely to grow.

Sources: Rhonda Abrams, "How Small Business Has Grown and Changed," *Arizona Republic*, January 30, 2001, p. D2; and Neal St. Anthony, "Doing Right by Its Employees Pays Off for Reell," *Minneapolis Star Tribune*, January 24, 2003, p. 1D; "Employee Loyalty in Your Small Business: How to Retain It," September 16, 2003, Business Development Bank of Canada. Retrieved from http://www.bdc.ca/en/about/events_publications/profits/2002-22-02/13.htm?iNoC=1.

---

job enlargement
A job enrichment strategy that involves combining a series of tasks into one challenging and interesting assignment.

job rotation
A job enrichment strategy that involves moving employees from one job to another.

Another type of job enrichment used for motivation is **job enlargement,** which combines a series of tasks into one challenging and interesting assignment. For example, Maytag, the home appliance manufacturer, redesigned the production process of its washing machines so that employees could assemble an entire water pump instead of just one part. **Job rotation** also makes work more interesting and motivating by moving employees from one job to another. One problem with job rotation, of course, is having to train employees to do several different operations. However, the resulting increase in employee motivation and the value of having flexible, cross-trained employees offsets the additional costs.

Job enrichment is one way to ensure that workers enjoy responsibility and a sense of accomplishment. The Spotlight on Small Business box offers advice on using job enrichment strategies in small businesses.

McGregor's Theory X and Theory Y

The way managers go about motivating people at work depends greatly on their attitudes toward workers. Management theorist Douglas McGregor observed that managers' attitudes generally fall into one of two entirely different sets of managerial assumptions, which he called Theory X and Theory Y.

Theory X

The assumptions of Theory X management are as follows:

- The average person dislikes work and will avoid it if possible.
- Because of this dislike, workers must be forced, controlled, directed, or threatened with punishment to make them put forth the effort to achieve the organization's goals.
- The average worker prefers to be directed, wishes to avoid responsibility, has relatively little ambition, and wants security.
- Primary motivators are fear and money.

The natural consequence of such attitudes, beliefs, and assumptions is a manager who is very "busy" and who watches people closely, telling them what to do and how to do it. Motivation is more likely to take the form of punishment for bad work rather than reward for good work. Theory X managers give workers little responsibility, authority, or flexibility. With his scientific management, Taylor and other theorists who preceded him would have agreed with Theory X. That is why management literature focused on time-motion studies that calculated the one best way to perform a task and the optimum time to be devoted to a task. It was assumed that workers needed to be trained and carefully watched to see that they conformed to the standards.

Theory X management still dominates some organizations. Many managers and entrepreneurs ➤P. 4◀ still suspect that employees cannot be fully trusted and need to be closely supervised. No doubt you have seen such managers in action. How did this make you feel? Were these managers' assumptions accurate regarding the workers' attitudes?

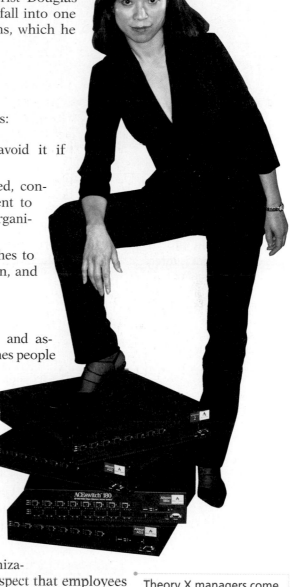

Theory X managers come in all sizes and shapes; like Selina Lo of Alteon Websystems, for example. She may not fit the typical Theory X stereotype, but on the job she is a tough and exacting Theory X manager with an in-your-face style that has earned her a reputation as one of the toughest managers in the industry. Would you prefer to work for a Theory X manager or a Theory Y manager?

Theory Y

Theory Y makes entirely different assumptions about people:

- Most people like work; it is as natural as play or rest.
- Most people naturally work toward goals to which they are committed.
- The depth of a person's commitment to goals depends on the perceived rewards for achieving them.

Pat Croce, owner of the NBA's Philadelphia 76ers, lives by Theory Y management, making him a winner with his players, workers, and fans. His mission statement is three simple words: quality, profit, and fun. The words obviously ring clear since the team's value has increased by 70 percent since his involvement.

- Under certain conditions, most people not only accept but also seek responsibility.
- People are capable of using a relatively high degree of imagination, creativity, and cleverness to solve problems.
- In industry, the average person's intellectual potential is only partially realized.
- People are motivated by a variety of rewards. Each worker is stimulated by a reward unique to that worker (time off, money, recognition, etc.).

Rather than emphasize authority, direction, and close supervision, Theory Y emphasizes a relaxed managerial atmosphere in which workers are free to set objectives, be creative, be flexible, and go beyond the goals set by management. A key technique in meeting these objectives is empowerment ➤P. 19◄. Empowerment gives employees the ability to make decisions and the tools to implement the decisions they make. For empowerment to be a real motivator, management should follow these three steps:

1. Find out what people think the problems in the organization are.
2. Let them design the solutions.
3. Get out of the way and let them put those solutions into action.

Often employees complain that although they're asked to become involved in company decision making, their managers fail to actually empower them to make decisions. Have you ever worked in such an atmosphere? How did that make you feel?

The trend in many businesses is toward Theory Y management. One reason for this trend is that many service industries are finding Theory Y helpful in dealing with on-the-spot problems. Dan Kaplan of Hertz Rental Corporation would attest to this. He empowers his employees in the field to think and work as entrepreneurs. Leona Ackerly of Mini Maid, Inc., agrees: "If our employees look at our managers as partners, a real team effort is built." See Figure 11.4 for a comparative summary of Theories X and Y.

FIGURE 11.4

A COMPARISON OF THEORIES X AND Y

THEORY X	THEORY Y
1. Employees dislike work and will try to avoid it.	1. Employees view work as a natural part of life.
2. Employees prefer to be controlled and directed.	2. Employees prefer limited control and direction.
3. Employees seek security, not responsibility.	3. Employees will seek responsibility under proper work conditions.
4. Employees must be intimidated by managers to perform.	4. Employees perform better in work environments that are nonintimidating.
5. Employees are motivated by financial rewards.	5. Employees are motivated by many different needs.

GOAL-SETTING THEORY

Goal-setting theory is based on the idea that setting ambitious but attainable goals can motivate workers and improve performance if the goals are accepted, accompanied by feedback, and facilitated by organizational conditions. All members of an organization should have some basic agreement about the overall goals of the organization and the specific objectives to be met by each department and individual.

It follows, then, that there should be a system to involve everyone in the organization in goal setting and implementation. Notice that goal-setting potentially improves employee performance in two ways: (1) by stretching the intensity and persistence of effort, and (2) by giving employees clearer role perceptions so that their effort is channeled toward behaviours that will improve work performance.[12]

At Montreal-based The Messaging Architects Inc., CEO Pierre Chamberland believes that employees need to be involved in setting company goals. "It's total disclosure, and it works to build a culture of ownership within the organization," says Chamberland. With a clearer understanding of how business works employees can participate, whether it's asking questions or setting targets. "They are more motivated to achieve targets because they set their own," says Chamberland.[13]

> **goal-setting theory**
> The idea that setting ambitious but attainable goals can motivate workers and improve performance if the goals are accepted, accompanied by feedback, and facilitated by organizational conditions.

MEETING EMPLOYEE EXPECTATIONS: EXPECTANCY THEORY

According to Victor Vroom's **expectancy theory,** employee expectations can affect an individual's motivation. Therefore, the amount of effort employees exert on a specific task depends on their expectations of the outcome.[14] Vroom contends that employees ask three questions before committing maximum effort to a task: (1) Can I accomplish the task? (2) If I do accomplish it, what's my reward? (3) Is the reward worth the effort? (See Figure 11.5.)

Think of the effort you might exert in your class under the following conditions: Your instructor says that to earn an A in the course you must achieve an average of 90 percent on coursework plus jump two metres high. Would you exert maximum effort toward earning an A if you knew you could not possibly jump two metres high? Or what if your instructor said any student can earn an A in the course but you know that this instructor has not awarded an A in 25 years of teaching? If the reward of an A seems unattainable, would you exert significant effort in the course? Better yet, let's say that you read in the newspaper that businesses actually prefer hiring C-minus students to hiring

> **expectancy theory**
> Victor Vroom's theory that the amount of effort employees exert on a specific task depends on their expectations of the outcome.

FIGURE 11.5

EXPECTANCY THEORY

The amount of effort employees exert on a task depends on their expectations of the outcome.

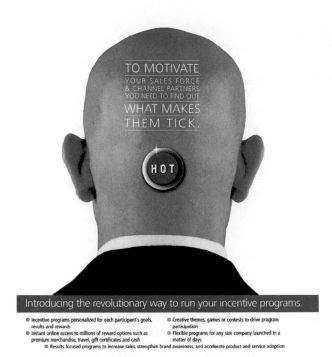

Victor Vroom believed employees can be motivated if they feel enhanced job performance leads to valued rewards. Identifying what rewards are important to employees is not an easy task. Companydna helps managers find out what makes their employees tick and then personalizes incentive programs to ensure employees receive the rewards they value and expect. What incentives would motivate you to improve your job performance?

A-plus students. Does the reward of an A seem worth it? Now think of the same types of situations that may occur on the job.

Expectancy theory does note that expectation varies from individual to individual. Employees therefore establish their own views in terms of task difficulty and the value of the reward. Researchers David Nadler and Edward Lawler modified Vroom's theory and suggested that managers follow five steps to improve employee performance:

1. Determine what rewards are valued by employees.
2. Determine each employee's desired performance standard.
3. Ensure that performance standards are attainable.
4. Guarantee rewards tied to performance.
5. Be certain that rewards are considered adequate.[15]

REINFORCING EMPLOYEE PERFORMANCE: REINFORCEMENT THEORY

reinforcement theory
Theory that positive and negative reinforcers motivate a person to behave in certain ways.

Reinforcement theory is based on the idea that positive and negative reinforcers motivate a person to behave in certain ways. In other words, motivation is the result of the carrot-and-stick approach (reward and punishment). Individuals act to receive rewards and avoid punishment. Positive reinforcements are rewards such as praise, recognition, or a pay raise. Negative reinforcement includes reprimands, reduced pay, and layoff or firing. A manager might also try to stop undesirable behaviour by not responding to it. This is called *extinction*, because the hope is that the unwanted behaviour will eventually become extinct.[16] Figure 11.6 illustrates how a manager can use reinforcement theory to motivate workers.

TREATING EMPLOYEES FAIRLY: EQUITY THEORY

equity theory
The idea that employees try to maintain equity between inputs and outputs compared to others in similar positions.

Equity theory deals with the questions "If I do a good job, will it be worth it?" and "What's fair?" It has to do with perceptions of fairness and how those perceptions affect employees' willingness to perform. The basic principle is that employees try to maintain equity between inputs and outputs compared to others in similar positions. Equity comparisons are made from the information that is available through personal relationships, professional organizations, and so on.

When workers do perceive inequity, they will try to reestablish equitable exchanges in a number of ways. For example, suppose you compare the grade you earned on a term paper with your classmates' grades. If you think you received a lower grade compared to the students who put out the same effort as you, you will probably react in one of two ways: (1) by reducing your effort on

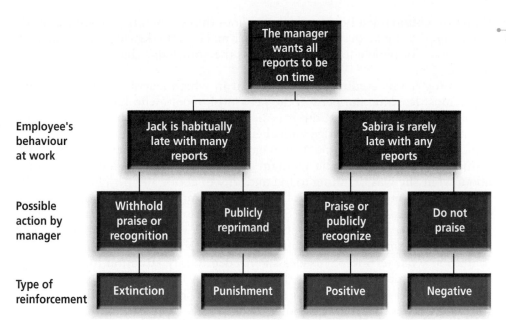

FIGURE 11.6

REINFORCEMENT THEORY

A manager can use both positive and negative reinforcement to motivate employee behaviour.

future class projects or (2) by rationalizing. The latter may include saying, "Grades are overvalued anyway!" If you think your paper received a higher grade than comparable papers, you will probably (1) increase your effort to justify the higher reward in the future or (2) rationalize by saying, "I'm worth it!" In the workplace, inequity may lead to lower productivity ➤P. 15◀, reduced quality ➤P. 291◀, increased absenteeism, and voluntary resignation.

Remember that equity judgments are based on perceptions and are therefore subject to errors in perception. When workers overestimate their own contributions—as happens often—they are going to feel that any rewards given out for performance are inequitable. Sometimes organizations try to deal with this by keeping employee salaries secret, but secrecy may make things worse; employees are likely to overestimate the salaries of others in addition to overestimating their own contribution. In general, the best remedy is clear and frequent communication. Managers must communicate as clearly as possible both the results they expect and the outcomes that will occur when those results are achieved or when they are not.

- Briefly describe the managerial attitudes behind Theories X and Y.
- Relate job enrichment to Herzberg's motivating factors.
- Evaluate expectancy theory. Can you think of situations in which expectancy theory could apply to your efforts or lack of effort?
- Explain the principles of equity theory.

Progress Assessment

BUILDING TEAMWORK THROUGH OPEN COMMUNICATION

Companies with highly motivated workforces usually have several things in common. Among the most important factors are open communication systems and self-managed teams. Open communication helps both top managers and team members understand the objectives and work together to achieve them.

Communication must flow freely throughout the organization when teams are empowered to make decisions—they can't make these decisions in a vacuum. It is crucial for people to be able to access the knowledge they need when they need it.

Having teams creates an environment in which learning can happen because most learning happens at the peer level—peers who have an interest in helping each other along. Empowerment ➤P. 19◀ works when people volunteer to share their knowledge with their colleagues. For example, when Flora Zhou, a business development manager at global power company AES, was putting together a bid to the Vietnam government, she sent a detailed e-mail about what she was planning to bid and why to about 300 people within AES. She asked for and received lots of advice and comments. Most people thought her proposal was fine, but Sarah Slusser, a group manager in Central America, sent Zhou a three-page response that contained a wealth of information about a similar situation she had encountered with a plant in the Yucatan. Slusser told Zhou what technology issues she needed to pay attention to. A few days later, Zhou made the bid. It was the lowest bid by two-tenths of a percent. Did Slusser tell Zhou the exact dollar to bid? No, but she and many others, including plant leaders and board members, gave her the best information and judgments they had to help her make her decision. They shared everything they knew with her.

Teamwork does not happen by itself. The whole organization must be structured to make it easy for managers and employees to talk to one another. Procedures for encouraging open communication include the following:[17]

- **Create an organizational culture that rewards listening.** Top managers must create places to talk, and they must show employees that talking with superiors counts—by providing feedback, adopting employee suggestions, and rewarding upward communication—even if the discussion is negative. Employees must feel free to say anything they deem appropriate. Jerry Stead, chairman of technology provider Ingram Micro, has his own 24-hour toll-free phone line to take calls from employees. Yes, he really answers it. He says: "If we are doing something right, I love to hear about it. If there's something we should be doing differently, I want to know that too." Stead has also given his home number to all 13,000 Ingram Micro employees.

- **Train supervisors and managers to listen.**   Most people receive no training in how to listen, either in school or anywhere else, so organizations must do such training themselves or hire someone to do it.

- **Remove barriers to open communication.**   Having separate offices, parking areas, bathrooms, and dining rooms for managers and workers only sets up barriers in an organization. Other barriers are different dress codes and different ways of addressing one another (e.g., calling workers by their first names and managers by their last). Removing such barriers may require imagination and willingness on the part of managers to give up their special privileges.

- **Actively undertake efforts to facilitate communication.** Large lunch tables at which all organization members eat, conference rooms, organizational picnics, organizational athletic teams, and other such efforts all allow managers to mix with each other and with workers.

Let's see how one organization addresses the challenge of open communication in teams.

Does seeing this sleek Mustang convertible make you want to put down your text and head for the road? At Ford Motor Company, the 400-member "Team Mustang" was empowered to create a car that does just that. The work team, suppliers, the company, and consumers worked together to make the Mustang a winner in a very competitive market.

Applying Open Communication in Self-Managed Teams

Kenneth Kohrs, vice-president of car product development at Ford Motor Company, says that an inside group known as "Team Mustang" sets the guidelines for how production teams should be formed. Given the challenge to create a car that would make people dust off their old "Mustang Sally" records and dance into the showrooms, the 400-member team was also given the freedom to make decisions without waiting for approval from headquarters or other departments. The team moved everyone from various departments into cramped offices under one roof of an old warehouse. Drafting experts sat next to accountants, engineers next to stylists. Budgetary walls that divided departments were knocked down as department managers were persuaded to surrender some control over their subordinates.

When the resulting Mustang convertible displayed shaking problems, suppliers were called in and the team worked around the clock to solve the problem. The engineers were so motivated to complete the program on schedule and under budget that they worked late into the night and slept on the floors of the warehouse when necessary. The senior Ford executives were tempted to overrule the program, but they stuck with their promise not to meddle. The team solved the shaking problem and still came in under budget and a couple of months early. The new car was a big hit in the marketplace, and sales soared.[18]

To implement such teams, managers at most companies must reinvent work. This means respecting workers, providing interesting work, rewarding good work, developing workers' skills, allowing autonomy, and decentralizing authority. In the process of reinventing work, it is essential that managers behave ethically toward all employees. The Making Ethical Decisions box illustrates a problem managers may face when filling temporary positions.

MOTIVATION IN THE FUTURE

What can you learn from all the theories and companies discussed in this chapter? You should have learned that people can be motivated to improve

Making Ethical Decisions

Motivating Temporary Employees

Say that you work as a manager for the hypothetical Highbrow's, a rather prestigious department store. Each year, in order to handle the large number of holiday shoppers, you must hire temporary employees. Because of store policy and budget constraints, all temporaries must be discharged on January 10. As you interview prospective employees, however, you give the impression that the store will hire at least two new full-time retail salespeople for the coming year. You hope that this will serve to motivate the temporary workers and even foster some competition among them. You also instruct your permanent salespeople to reinforce the falsehood that good work during the holiday season is the path to full-time employment. Is this an ethical way to try to motivate your employees? What are the dangers of using a tactic such as this?

Ninety percent of CAE Inc.'s annual revenues are derived from worldwide exports. CAE is a leading provider of integrated training solutions and advanced simulation and controls technologies to civil aviation, military, and marine customers. The next-generation CAE Sim XXI™ full-flight simulator, noted here, represents the latest in simulation technology. CAE made the Canada's Top 100 Employers list in 2004. What motivates the company's employees? Notable perks include a huge on-site training centre, banking, dry cleaning, and a subsidized cafeteria. Would these benefits motivate you?

productivity and quality of work if managers know which technique to use and when. You should now be aware that:

- The growth and competitiveness of industry and business in general depend on a motivated, productive workforce. As mentioned in previous chapters, to sustain competitive advantage in the global marketplace a company's workforce must be engaged in continual improvement and innovation. Only motivated employees can achieve improvement and innovation as normal methods of operations.

- Motivation is largely internal, generated by workers themselves; giving employees the freedom to be creative and rewarding achievement when it occurs will release their energy.

- The first step in any motivational program is to establish open communication among workers and managers so that the feeling generated is one of cooperation and teamwork. A family-type atmosphere should prevail.

Today's customers expect high-quality, customized goods ➤ P. 23 ◄ and services ➤ P. 25 ◄. This means that employees must provide extensive personal service and pay close attention to details. Employees will have to work smart as well as hard. No amount of supervision can force an employee to smile or to go the extra step to help a customer. Managers need to know how to motivate their employees to meet customer needs.

Tomorrow's managers will not be able to use any one formula for all employees. Rather, they will have to get to know each worker personally and tailor the motivational effort to the individual. As you have learned in this chapter, different employees respond to different managerial and motivational styles. This is further complicated by the increase in global

Reaching Beyond Our Borders

Global Teamwork

The global economy has altered the world landscape by bringing goods and services to every corner of the earth and helping many people in less developed countries improve their quality of life. Business globalization has also resulted in the creation of global work teams, a rather formidable task.

Even though the concept of teamwork is nothing new, building a harmonious global work team is a new task and can be complicated. Global companies must recognize differing attitudes and competencies in the team's cultural mix and the technological capabilities among team members. For example, a global work team needs to determine whether the culture of its members is high-context or low-context. In a high-context team culture, members build personal relationships and develop group trust before focusing on tasks. In the low-context culture, members often view relationship building as a waste of time that diverts attention from the task. Koreans, Thais, and Saudis (high-context cultures), for example, often view North American team members as insincere due to their need for data and quick decision making.

When Digital Equipment Corporation (now a part of Hewlett-Packard) decided to consolidate its operations at six manufacturing sites, the company recognized the need to form multicultural work teams. Realizing the challenge it faced, Digital hired an internal organization-development specialist to train the team in relationship building, foreign languages, and valuing differences. All team members from outside the United States were assigned American partners and invited to spend time with their families. Digital also flew the flags of each employee's native country at all its manufacturing sites. As communication within the teams increased, the company reduced the time of new-product handoffs from three years to just six months.

Understanding the motivational forces in global organizations and building effective global teams is still new territory for most companies. Developing group leaders who are culturally astute, flexible, and able to deal with ambiguity is a challenge businesses must face in the 21st century.

business and the fact that managers now work with employees from a variety of cultural backgrounds. Different cultures experience motivational approaches differently; therefore, the manager of the future will have to study and understand these cultural factors in designing a reward system. The Reaching Beyond Our Borders box describes how Digital Equipment Corporation dealt with these cultural issues within global teams.

Cultural differences are not restricted to groups of people from various countries. Such differences also exist between generations raised in the same country. Canadian demographer David Foot has studied the importance of demographic groups on business. He has categorized groups as follows: the baby boomers (those born between 1947 and 1966), Generation X—a subgroup of the baby boomers (those born between 1961 and 1966), the baby bust (those born between 1967 and 1979), the baby-boom echo (those born between 1980 and 1995), and the millennium busters (those born between 1996 and 2010).[19]

Note that in your general reading you may encounter different categories of generations, depending on the source. For example, U.S. demographers often define generations as follows: baby boomers (those born between 1946 and 1964); Generation X (those born between 1965 and 1980), and Generation Y (those born between 1981 and 1994). For this discussion, we will use the Canadian demographic groups coined by David Foot.

Back to generational differences, members in each generation are linked through shared life experiences in their formative years—usually the first 10 years of life. The beliefs you gather as a child affect how you view risk and challenge, authority, technology, relationships, and economics. If you are in a management position, they can affect even whom you hire, fire, or promote.

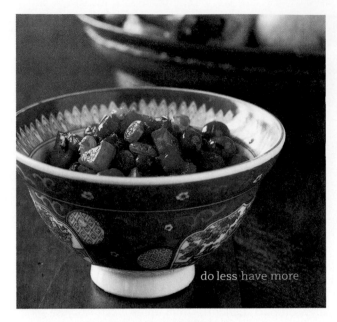

REALSIMPLE.
the magazine for a simpler life, home, body and soul

There's no magic formula to successfully motivating every worker. Each generation of employees has different attitudes about what's important to them in seeking a balance between a successful career and happy private life. *Real Simple* is a new magazine that appeals to people yearning for more simplicity in life. What's most important to you in your career and home life?

Some generalities apply to these different groups. Baby boomers were raised in families that experienced unprecedented economic prosperity, parents with secure jobs, and optimism about the future. On the other hand, baby busters were raised in dual-career families with parents who focused on work. As children, they attended daycare or became latchkey kids. Their parents' successive layoffs added to their insecurity about a lifelong job.

How do these generational differences affect motivation in the workplace? For the boomer managers, it means that they will need to be flexible with their baby bust employees or they will lose them. For baby bust employees, it means that they will need to use their enthusiasm for change and streamlining to their advantage. Although many baby busters are unwilling to pay the same price for success that their parents and grandparents did, concern about undue stress and long work hours does not mean they lack ambition. Baby busters' desire for security typically equals that of older workers, but there is a big difference in their approach to achieving it. Rather than focusing on job security, baby busters tend to focus on career security. As they look for opportunities to expand their skills and grow professionally, they are willing to change jobs to do it.[20]

Many baby busters are now or soon will be managers themselves and responsible for motivating other employees. What type of management will this generation provide? In general, they will be well equipped to motivate people. They understand that there is more to life than work, and they think a big part of motivating people is letting them know you recognize that fact. As a result, these managers may tend to focus more on results than on hours in the workplace. They will be flexible and good at collaboration and consensus building. They tend to think in broader terms than their predecessors because, through the media, they have been exposed to a lot of problems around the world. They may tend to have a great impact on their team members because they will likely give the people working for them the goals and the parameters of the project and then leave them alone to do their work.

Perhaps their best asset might be their ability to give their employees feedback, especially positive feedback. One reason they may be better at providing feedback is that they expect more of it themselves. One new employee remarked that he was frustrated because he hadn't received feedback from his boss since he was hired—two weeks earlier. In short, managers will need to realize that young workers demand performance reviews and other forms of feedback more than once or twice a year.

In every generational shift, the old generation says the same thing about the new generation: They break the rules. The generation that lived through the Great Depression and the Second World War said it of the baby boomers. Now boomers look at baby busters and say, "Why are they breaking the rules?" And you can be sure the baby busters will look at the next group and say, "What's wrong with these kids?" In fact, those that are part of the baby-boom echo are entering the professional workforce now. As a group, they tend to share a number of common characteristics: They are considered impatient, skeptical, blunt and expressive, image driven, and inexperienced. Like any generation, what may make this newer generation difficult to deal with on the job is also what could make it uniquely skilled. For example, a number of talents and tendencies dominate this group: They are adaptable, tech savvy, able to grasp new concepts, practised at multitasking, efficient, and tolerant. Perhaps the most surprising attribute many share is a sense of commitment. What do you think are the most effective strategies managers can use to motivate these workers?

One thing in business is likely to remain constant, though: Motivation will come from the job itself rather than from external punishments or rewards. Managers will need to give workers what they need to do a good job: the right tools, the right information, and the right amount of cooperation.

Motivation doesn't have to be difficult. It begins with acknowledging a job well done. You can simply tell those who do such a job that you appreciate them—especially if you make this statement in front of others. After all, as we said earlier in this chapter, the best motivator is frequently a sincere "Thanks, I really appreciate what you're doing."

Progress Assessment

- What are several steps firms can take to increase internal communications and thus motivation?
- What problems may emerge when trying to implement participative management?
- Why is it important today to adjust motivational styles to individual employees? Are there any general principles of motivation that today's managers should follow?

Summary

1. Human efficiency engineer Frederick Taylor was one of the first people to study management. He did time-motion studies to learn the most efficient way of doing a job and then trained workers in those procedures.
   - *What led to management theories that stress human factors of motivation?*
   The greatest impact on motivation theory was generated by the Hawthorne studies in the late 1920s and early 1930s. In these studies, Elton Mayo found that human factors such as feelings of involvement and participation led to greater productivity gains than did physical changes in the workplace.

   1. Relate the significance of Taylor's scientific management and the Hawthorne studies to management.

2. Abraham Maslow studied basic human motivation and found that motivation was based on needs; he said that a person with an unfilled need would be motivated to satisfy it and that a satisfied need no longer served as motivation.
   - *What were the various levels of need identified by Maslow?*
   Starting at the bottom of Maslow's hierarchy of needs and going to the top, the levels of need are physiological, safety, social, esteem, and self-actualization.

   2. Identify the levels of Maslow's hierarchy of needs, and relate their importance to employee motivation.

• *Can managers use Maslow's theory?*
Yes, they can recognize what unmet needs a person has and design work so that it satisfies those needs.

3. Distinguish between the motivators and hygiene factors identified by Herzberg.

3. Frederick Herzberg found that some factors are motivators and others are hygiene (or maintenance) factors; hygiene factors cause job dissatisfaction if missing but are not motivators if present.
• *What are the factors called motivators?*
The work itself, achievement, recognition, responsibility, growth, and advancement are motivators.
• *What are hygiene (maintenance) factors?*
Factors that do not motivate but must be present for employee satisfaction, such as company policies, supervision, working conditions, interpersonal relations, and salary are examples of hygiene factors.

4. Explain how job enrichment affects employee motivation and performance.

4. Job enrichment describes efforts to make jobs more interesting.
• *What characteristics of work affect motivation and performance?*
The job characteristics that influence motivation are skill variety, task identity, task significance, autonomy, and feedback.
• *Name two forms of job enrichment that increase motivation.*
Job enrichment strategies include job enlargement and job rotation.

5. Differentiate between Theory X and Theory Y.

5. Douglas McGregor held that managers will have one of two opposing attitudes toward employees. They are called Theory X and Theory Y.
• *What is Theory X?*
Theory X assumes that the average person dislikes work and will avoid it if possible. Therefore, people must be forced, controlled, and threatened with punishment to accomplish organizational goals.
• *What is Theory Y?*
Theory Y assumes that people like working and will accept responsibility for achieving goals if rewarded for doing so.

6. Describe the key principles of goal-setting, expectancy, reinforcement, and equity theories.

6. Goal-setting theory is based on the notion that setting ambitious but attainable goals will lead to high levels of motivation and performance if the goals are accepted, accompanied by feedback, and facilitated by organizational conditions.
• *What are the key elements involved in expectancy theory?*
Expectancy theory centres on three questions employees often ask about performance on the job: (1) Can I accomplish the task? (2) If I do accomplish it, what's my reward? and (3) Is the reward worth the effort?
• *What are the variables in reinforcement theory?*
Positive reinforcers are rewards like praise, recognition, or raises that a worker might strive to receive after performing well. Negative reinforcers are punishments such as reprimands, pay cuts, or firing that a worker might be expected to try to avoid.
• *According to equity theory, employees try to maintain equity between inputs and outputs compared to other employees in similar positions. What happens when employees perceive that their rewards are not equitable?*
If employees perceive that they are underrewarded, they will either reduce their effort or rationalize that it isn't important. If they perceive that they are overrewarded, they will either increase their effort to justify the higher reward in the future or rationalize by saying, "I'm worth it!" Inequity leads to lower productivity, reduced quality, increased absenteeism, and voluntary resignation.

7. Companies with highly motivated workforces often have open communication systems and self-managed teams.
   - *Why is open communication so important in building effective self-managed teams?*

   Open communication helps both top managers and team members understand the objectives and work together to achieve them. Teams establish an environment in which learning can happen because most learning happens at the peer level.

   - *How are baby bust managers likely to be different from their baby-boomer predecessors?*

   Baby boomers are willing to work long hours to build their careers and often expect their subordinates to do likewise. Baby busters strive for a more balanced lifestyle and are likely to focus on results rather than on how many hours their teams work. Baby busters are better than previous generations at working in teams and providing frequent feedback. They are not bound by traditions that may constrain those who have been with an organization for a long time. Baby busters are willing to try new approaches to solving problems.

7. Explain how open communication builds teamwork, and describe how managers are likely to motivate teams in the future.

Key Terms

equity theory 328
expectancy theory 327
extrinsic reward 316
goal-setting theory 327
Hawthorne effect 319
hygiene factors 321
intrinsic reward 316
job enlargement 324

job enrichment 322
job rotation 324
Maslow's hierarchy of needs 319
motivators 321
principle of motion economy 317

reinforcement theory 328
scientific management 317
time-motion studies 317

Developing Workplace Skills

1. Talk with several of your friends about the subject of motivation. What motivates them to work hard or not work hard on projects in teams? How important is self-motivation to them?

2. Look over Maslow's hierarchy of needs and try to determine where you are right now on the hierarchy. What needs of yours are not being met? How could a company go about meeting those needs and thus motivate you to work better and harder?

3. One of the most recent managerial ideas is to let employees work in self-managed teams. There is no reason why such teams could not be formed in schools as well as businesses. Discuss the benefits and drawbacks of dividing your class into self-managed teams for the purposes of studying, creating reports, and so forth.

4. Think of all the groups with which you have been associated over the years—sports groups, friendship groups, and so on—and try to recall how the leaders of those groups motivated the group to action. What motivational tools were used and to what effect?

5. Herzberg concluded that pay was not a motivator. If you were paid to get better grades, would you be motivated to study harder? In your

employment experiences, have you ever worked harder to obtain a raise or as a result of receiving a large raise? Do you agree with Herzberg?

Taking It To The Net

1

Purpose

To assess your personality type using the Keirsey Character Sorter and to evaluate how well the description of your personality type fits you.

Exercise

Sometimes understanding differences in employees' personalities helps managers understand how to motivate them. Find out about your personality by going to the Keirsey Temperament Sorter Website (www.keirsey.com) and answer the 36-item Keirsey Character Sorter questionnaire or the 70-item Keirsey Temperament Sorter questionnaire. Each test identifies four temperament types: Guardian, Artisan, Idealist, and Rational. (Disclaimer: The Keirsey tests, like all other personality tests, are only preliminary and rough indicators of personality.)

1. After you identify your personality, read the corresponding personality portrait. How well or how poorly does the identified personality type fit?

2. Sometimes a personality test does not accurately identify your personality, but it may give you a place to start looking for a portrait that fits. After you have read the portraits on the Keirsey Website, ask a good friend or relative which one best describes you.

3. Based on this information, how do you think a manager can best motivate you?

Taking It To The Net

2

Purpose

To analyze why employees of the Container Store agree with *Fortune* magazine that their employer is an excellent company to work for.

Exercise

Employees at the Container Store sell boxes and garbage cans for a living. Find out why *Fortune* magazine has rated it at or near the top of its "100 Best Companies to Work For" list for four straight years. Go to the company's Website (www.containerstore.com) and click on "About Us."

1. What are the Container Store's foundation principles?

2. Give an example of how the Container Store's employees are empowered to please their customers.

3. The national average annual turnover rate for salespeople is 73.6 percent. The Container Store's turnover rate is a mere 28 percent. Many of its employees took pay cuts to join the company. Identify at least five ways the company motivates its employees and explain why they are extremely motivated.

Practising Management Decisions

Case

The Workplace: Does It Help or Hinder Motivation?

A useful article in the Report on Business section of *The Globe and Mail* started with the provocative question: "Does the atmosphere inside your company resemble Calcutta in the summer or France's Fontainebleau forest in the spring?" This question was put to prestigious international business executives in luxurious Davos, Switzerland.

The speaker was Sumantra Ghoshal, an internationally recognized author, professor, and authority on management issues. His weighty audience was attending the annual World Economic Forum, which is probably the most important annual meeting of senior government and business leaders in the world. He was obviously trying to alert them to what he feels is a major problem confronting companies in today's highly competitive global economy.

Ghoshal noted that if you want high performance from your employees, look first at the atmosphere in your company before you start thinking about "changing each individual employee." Before you set out to teach old dogs new tricks, you better change the "smell of the place." It is his belief that most firms create a "stifling atmosphere in which employees feel constrained, controlled, and forced to comply with a rigid contract that governs their behaviour."

Ghoshal's equally famous colleague and co-author, Christopher Bartlett of Harvard University, noted that now that "information, knowledge, and expertise" have become just as important as capital was in the past, emphasis has shifted from the corporation to the individual. This means that whereas earlier managers had to fit into the corporation and become organization people, now the corporation must become flexible and find ways to fit the individual manager.

Decision Questions

1. Do you find it surprising that senior executives have to be reminded of these things? Why are they not already aware of this issue, since it has been actively discussed in business schools and business periodicals for some years?
2. Why are companies so slow to adapt to new conditions? Don't they want a better-motivated workforce?
3. Is it possible that corporations' concentration on downsizing in recent years has blinded them to the changed needs of their remaining employees and managers?
4. What is your own experience in jobs you have had? Did you find the atmosphere conducive to employee motivation?

Source: Madeleine Drohan, "Your Workplace: Hole or Haven?" *Globe and Mail*, *Report on Business*, February 7, 1996, p. B9. Reprinted with permission from *The Globe and Mail*.

Video Case

Working for the Best: The Container Store

Looking for a company where motivational techniques are effectively applied? Look no further than the Container Store.

What's the secret to hiring highly motivated people who feel their company is the country's best? First, you need good products. Employees are motivated when they know that the products they sell are helpful to consumers and top quality. Second, you have to empower workers to do what they can to exceed customer expectations, even if that means having them go out in the parking lot to give a customer a driving lesson.

One of the cornerstones at the Container Store is: Hire Great People. Management believes that one great person is worth three good people. They cite famed home-run hitter Babe Ruth, who hit 56 home runs in one year; the second-best home-run hitter hit only 13. A great player may be worth more than four times what a good player is worth. The challenge is to find and keep great workers. The Container Store often does that by hiring part-time people and then motivating the best of them to stay.

Workers must be taught to provide astonishing levels of customer service. One such case is the worker who loaned her car to a stranded customer. How do you encourage such outstanding service? Management at the Container Store knows motivational principles. They know, for example, that Frederick Taylor looked at workers as if they were machines to be programmed, and that such a style is no longer effective in most organizations. They also know that Elton Mayo introduced a more human-based form of motivation.

It's clear that the store uses Maslow's needs hierarchy. Wages paid are above the industry standard, meeting the physiological needs of workers. Safety needs are met by tolerating mistakes and urging employees to do what's necessary to please customers. Employees also feel secure because the store emphasizes proper values, including integrity, honesty, and open communications. Good employees are recognized for their contribution and the social atmosphere is one of "family." It's clear the Container Store used McGregor's Theory Y concepts.

Herzberg claims that a good job environment is not a motivator; it is considered a hygiene factor (i.e., it doesn't motivate workers if it is present, but causes dissatisfaction if missing). Container Store employees place a high importance on the job environment, including the quality of their co-workers. This implies that people like to work with others who are equally motivated and responsible. This also fits into Maslow's level of social needs.

The Container Store focuses on job enrichment. Employees are trained to do a variety of jobs that help prepare them to become managers when openings are available. The store uses daily coaching so employees can understand and implement management by objectives. The store also uses open communication to stress that good work will be rewarded. That includes peer-to-peer communication where everyone helps everyone else to do the best job possible.

In short, the Container Store uses a humanistic approach coupled with empowerment, strong values, cross training, and open communication to motivate employees to the point where they will continue to be one of the best companies to work for.

Discussion Questions

1. What have you learned from this video that could be used by any firm seeking a motivated workforce that loves working for the business?
2. There is some debate whether or not money is a motivator. If you were offered twice as much pay, would you or could you work twice as hard?
3. What has motivated you to do a great job and what has discouraged you from doing your best?
4. What can you do to increase your self-motivation? Does it always help working with self-motivated people who do quality work?

Chapter 12

Human Resource Management: Finding and Keeping the Best Employees

Learning Goals

After you have read and studied this chapter, you should be able to

1 Explain the importance of human resource management as a strategic contributor to organizational success, and summarize the five steps in human resource planning.

2 Describe methods that companies use to recruit new employees, and explain some of the issues that make recruitment challenging.

3 Outline the five steps in selecting employees.

4 Illustrate the use of various types of employee training and development methods.

5 Trace the six steps in appraising employee performance.

6 Summarize the objectives of employee compensation programs, and describe various pay systems and employee benefits.

7 Describe the ways employees can move through a company: promotion, reassignment, termination, and retirement.

Profile

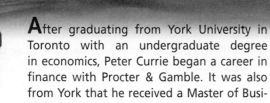

Getting to Know Peter Currie of RBC Financial Group

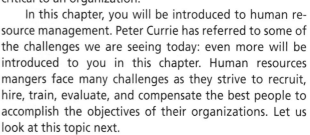

After graduating from York University in Toronto with an undergraduate degree in economics, Peter Currie began a career in finance with Procter & Gamble. It was also from York that he received a Master of Business Administration degree in 1978. He joined Northern Telecom in 1979 as assistant controller. In 1985, he was appointed group controller for the firm's major operating unit in the U.S. Two years later, he returned to Toronto to become vice-president, finance of the Canadian operating parent company. Following two years with North American Life Assurance Company, where he was executive vice-president and chief financial officer (CFO) from 1992 to 1994, Currie returned to Northern Telecom as senior vice-president and CFO.

Currie joined Royal Bank in 1997 and was the vice-chairman and CFO of RBC Financial Group (the brand name for Royal Bank of Canada and its subsidiaries). As a member of RBC Financial Group's management committee, he was one of nine executives responsible for setting the group's overall strategic direction.

By now you may be asking yourself why we are profiling a CFO, when this chapter's focus is human resource management (HRM). The reason is that Currie's approach to people management earned him the title of Canada's CFO of the Year for 2003 from PricewaterhouseCoopers.

Currie believes that, contrary to popular opinion, it is not hard to convince a CEO or a CFO to invest in human capital. He says that when suggestions are turned down it is often not because the programs are not valuable, but because HR people have portrayed themselves as employee advocates as opposed to businesspeople. It is therefore critical that a solid business case be made for any initiatives.

Investments in human capital are just that—investments. Companies should consider where they want to be in five years and start taking the steps to get there.

This is where HRM has a huge impact, because it is about development and retention and skills enrichment within an organization. HRM clearly holds a strategic role in these areas.

In consideration of some current trends, Currie has spoken about the aging workforce. It doesn't worry him—he is more concerned about bridging the gap between different generations. "It will be a challenge to find ways to let baby boomers disengage gradually as this will require very flexible attitudes in companies."

Another current trend is outsourcing. Currie says that outsourcing HR is a poor idea. "If you are going to outsource something like recruiting, how silly is that? Your recruiting is probably one of the most important things you do as a company." However, he does not see any problems with outsourcing tasks such as payroll and benefits administration. "To me, that is not outsourcing. That is just deciding who can most effectively handle your administrative activities." In his opinion, a company should not outsource HR, IT, internal audit, and core accounting functions, which are critical to an organization.

In this chapter, you will be introduced to human resource management. Peter Currie has referred to some of the challenges we are seeing today; even more will be introduced to you in this chapter. Human resources mangers face many challenges as they strive to recruit, hire, train, evaluate, and compensate the best people to accomplish the objectives of their organizations. Let us look at this topic next.

Sources: "Canada's CFO of the Year for 2003 Peter Currie, RBC Financial Group," June 13, 2003, PricewaterhouseCoopers. Retrieved from http://www.pwcglobal.com/ca/eng/about/main/sponsorships/cfoaward-currie.html; David Brown, "Viewing HR from the CFO's seat," *Canadian HR Reporter*, October 20, 2003, 2–3; and www.rbc.com, September 27, 2004.

THE HUMAN RESOURCE FUNCTION

human resource management (HRM)
The process of determining human resource needs and then recruiting, selecting, developing, motivating, evaluating, compensating, and scheduling employees to achieve organizational goals.

This chapter will discuss various aspects of human resource management. **Human resource management** (HRM) is the process of determining human resource needs and then recruiting, selecting, developing, motivating, evaluating, compensating, and scheduling employees to achieve organizational goals (see Figure 12.1). Let's explore some of the trends in human resource management.

Trends and Issues in HRM

Like many other aspects of Canadian business mentioned in other chapters, HRM has been greatly affected by technology and global competition. Both of these factors have forced Canadian companies to downsize their workforces. While technological developments are having an enormous effect on people and jobs in businesses, it is worthwhile to consider what one person said: "One machine can do the work of 50 men [but] no machine can do the work of one extraordinary man."[1] (We can assume that the speaker was referring to women as well.)

The nature of work and management has changed enormously. For example, other employees work at home and go to company premises only occasionally. Employees participate more in decision making through teamwork, and there is a greater emphasis on quality and customer satisfaction. Better-trained and better-educated employees are now required to work in a more high-tech global business climate. This is only a short list of some of the major

FIGURE 12.1

HUMAN RESOURCE MANAGEMENT

As this figure shows, human resource management is more than hiring and firing personnel. All activities are designed to achieve organizational goals within the laws that affect human resource management. (Note that human resource management includes motivation, as discussed in Chapter 11, and union relations, as discussed in Chapter 13.)

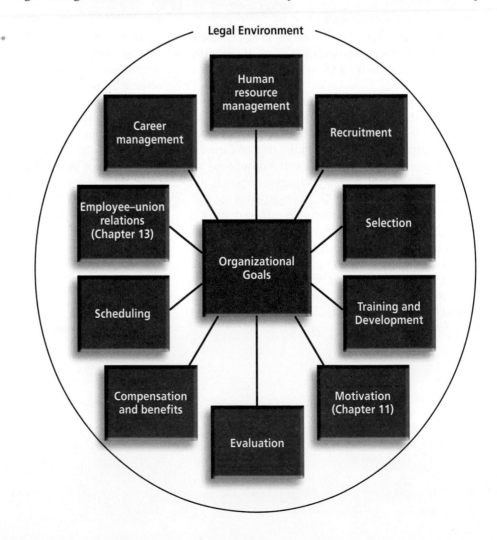

Legal Environment

Human resource management

Career management

Recruitment

Employee–union relations (Chapter 13)

Selection

Organizational Goals

Scheduling

Training and Development

Compensation and benefits

Evaluation

Motivation (Chapter 11)

issues that are increasing the importance of, and causing a revolution in, HRM operations.

Importance of HRM

One reason why human resource management is receiving increased attention now is the major shift from traditional manufacturing industries to service industries and high-tech manufacturing organizations that require more technical job skills. Companies now have fewer employees, but the ones who remain require more education and skills. A major problem today is retraining workers for new, more challenging jobs.

BC Telephone has set up an education centre in Burnaby, B.C., to provide proper training for its employees. The National Bank of Canada has set up a banking school by teaming up with the Institute of Canadian Bankers and Université de Québec.[2] These are but two examples of how companies are moving to ensure a properly trained workforce. Here are some other examples:

- Canada Mortgage and Housing Corp., a Crown corporation, has numerous training programs and job exchanges. Temporary vacancies are often filled by people from other departments wanting to enrich their own experience. Each year, CMHC hires 10 university graduates under a two-year training program that exposes them to 10 or 12 departments.

- Allen-Bradley Canada Ltd. manufactures industrial automation equipment. It has more than a thousand employees in three plants in Ontario and emphasizes training. At its Cambridge plant it employs seven full-time and three part-time instructors. The other locations have four full-time instructors. New marketing employees go through a three-month training and orientation program. All new employees attend a two-week business course.[3]

- The Bank of Montreal spent $40 million setting up an Institute for Learning for its employees. The aim of the director of the complex, Dr. James Rush, is to ensure continuing opportunities for the bank's employees to learn and to be creative.[4]

Some people have called employees the ultimate resource, and when you think about it, nothing could be truer. People develop the ideas that eventually become the products that satisfy consumers' wants and needs. Take away their creative minds, and leading firms such as Bombardier, DuPont, and Scotiabank would be nothing. The problem is that human resources have always been relatively plentiful, so there was little need to nurture and develop them. If you needed qualified people, you simply went out and hired them. If they didn't work out, you fired them and found others. But *qualified* labour is scarcer today, and that makes recruiting more difficult.

Historically, most firms assigned the job of recruiting, selecting, training, evaluating, compensating, motivating, and, yes, firing people to the various functional departments. For years, the personnel department was more or less responsible for clerical functions such as screening applications, keeping records, processing the payroll, and finding people when necessary.

Today, the job of human resource management has taken on an entirely new role in the firm.[5] Figure 12.2 reflects research results produced by DBM, an HR consulting firm. In the survey, HR people believe that the changing workforce means increased pressure to provide strategic input and less time and energy spent on HR administration.[6]

The Canadian Council of Human Resources Associations (CCHRA) is the result of the collaborative efforts of 10 provincial and specialist Human Resource Associations that currently represent the interests of more than 18,000 professionals across Canada. Visit www.cchra-ccarh.ca/en3/members_association.asp to find the association for your area.

FIGURE 12.2

HUMAN RESOURCES AND THE WORKFORCE IN 10 YEARS

500 Canadian human resources professionals were asked what role and skill level their HR department currently has and what role they expect to play in 2013.

Source: *Canadian HR Reporter*, October 20, 2003, p. 1.

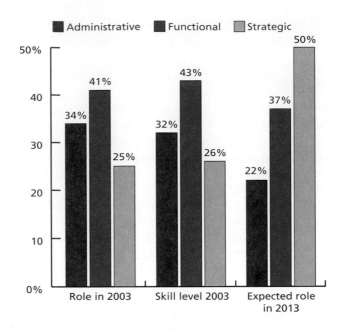

Canadian HR Reporter (www.hrreporter.com) is the national journal of human resource management. Its site has information on benefits, compensation, employment law, healthy workplace, HR strategies, HR technology, industrial relations, payroll, pensions, recruitment and staffing, and training and development.

This survey reinforces what David Weiss, a partner of GSWconsultants, communicated in his best-selling book *Higher Performance HR: Leveraging Human Resources for Competitive Advantage*. He states that as companies are beginning to shed outdated processes and unprofitable lines of business, HR is in danger of extinction if it continues to rely solely on recruiting, employee relations, and compensation and training. In his book, Weiss examines how HR should instead streamline its core responsibilities and align its efforts with the company's vision ➤**P. 221**◄ and customer needs. This alignment will allow HR to take advantage of unique qualifications that will enable it to provide strategic value to the company and the company's customers.[7]

In the future HR may become the most critical function, in that it will be responsible for dealing with all aspects of a firm's most critical resource—people. In fact, the human resource function has become so important that it is no longer the function of just one department; it is a function of all managers. Most human resource functions are shared between the professional human resource manager and the other managers. What are some of the challenges in the human resource area that managers face? We'll outline a few of those challenges next.

The Human Resource Challenge

The changes in the business environment that have had the most dramatic impact on the workings of the free enterprise system are the changes in the labour force. The ability of businesses to compete in international markets depends on new ideas, new products, and new levels of productivity ➤**P. 15**◄—in other words, on people with good ideas. The following are some of the challenges and opportunities being encountered in the human resource area:

- Shortages in people trained to work in the growth areas of the future, such as computers, biotechnology, robotics, and the sciences.[8]
- The growing number of skilled and unskilled workers from declining industries, such as steel, automobiles, and garment making, who are

unemployed or underemployed and who need retraining. Underemployed workers are those who have more skills or knowledge than their current jobs require.[9]

- The challenge of creating an environment where workplace diversity is respected. The Canadian Charter of Rights and Freedoms allows and encourages Canadians to maintain their mother tongue, traditions, and culture. The Human Rights legislation has reinforced this by protecting employees from discrimination, bias, prejudice, and harassment. However, some Canadian workers still experience harassment, as witnessed by certain ethnic groups after September 11, 2001, or after the SARS scare in 2003.

- The increased need for college- and university-educated/trained workers. According to Canada's innovation strategy, about 70 percent of all new jobs created by 2004 are expected to require some form of postsecondary education, and only six percent of new jobs will be held by those who have not finished high school.[10]

- The reality of retirement accounting for an expected one million job openings over the next five years. Sales and service, business, finance, and administration will account for more than 45 percent of all retirements.[11]

- A shift in the age composition of the workforce, due to aging baby boomers. A wide range of occupations—from doctors and nurses to teachers, plumbers, and electricians—will be facing worker shortfalls by 2011, when almost one-fifth of Canadian baby boomers will be at least 61 years of age.[12] The Dealing with Change box discusses the new human resource challenges faced by an aging workforce.

- A complex set of laws and regulations involving hiring, safety, unionization, and equal pay that require organizations to go beyond a profit orientation and be more fair and socially conscious.[13]

- An increasing number of both single-parent and two-income families, resulting in rising demand for day care, job sharing, maternity leave, and special career advancement programs for women.[14]

- A shift in employee attitudes toward work. Leisure time has become a much higher priority, as have concepts such as flextime and a shorter workweek.[15]

- Continued downsizing that is taking a toll on employee morale as well as increasing the demand for temporary workers.[16]

- A challenge from overseas labour pools whose members are available for lower wages and subject to many fewer laws and regulations. This results in many jobs being shifted overseas.[17]

- An increased demand for benefits tailored to the individual.[18]

- A growing concern over such issues as health care, elder care, childcare, equal opportunities for people with disabilities, and special attention given to employment equity programs.[19]

- A decreased sense of employee loyalty resulting in increased employee turnover and increased costs of replacing lost workers.[20]

Given all of these issues, and others that are sure to develop, you can see why human resource management has taken a more central position in management thinking than ever before. Let's see what is involved.

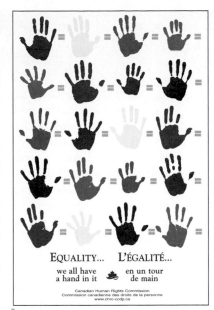

Visit the Canadian Human Rights Commission Website at www.chrc-ccdp.ca for information relevant to employees and employers.

Dealing With Change

Who Will Replace the Greying Workers?

Wine connoisseurs believe that most great wines get better with age. Unfortunately, the economies of industrialized countries cannot make the same claim. By 2050, the average age of the world's population is expected to rise from 26 to 36. In Spain the average will be 55. This aging of the population presents huge economic implications. Who will do the work in geriatric societies? Who will support the increasing number of pensioners? What will happen to economic growth with a declining labour force? Nations such as Japan, Russia, and Brazil will have huge numbers of retirees; in Europe only two working-age people will be supporting each European over 65 instead of the four who support each retiree today.

Canada has similar problems but has faced this challenge differently than European and Asian countries. For the past two decades Canada has been importing workers to increase the labour force. Few countries other than Canada have the administrative capabilities or the desire to absorb many foreigners annually. These workers supply important technical and scientific talent, start new companies, and help hold down prices by filling low-wage jobs. Even with this influx of foreign workers, Canada is still expected to experience labour shortages by 2011.

Labour unions view immigrant recruitment with mixed emotions. Many labour leaders feel that the growing numbers of immigrants entering the country will fuel future union growth. Some labour leaders also support the immigration of skilled workers to staff growth industries that don't have an adequate supply of qualified workers in Canada. However, labour decries the loss of union jobs to low-paid immigrants in many service industries and the shift of manufacturing jobs to areas with growing numbers of immigrants.

Sources: Moon Ihlwan, Pete Engardio, and Aaron Burnstein, "The Coming Battle for Immigrants," *Business Week,* August 26, 2002, pp. 138–39; and "Groups Urge Overhaul of Immigration," AP Online, March 11, 2002; and "Census Forecasts Shortages within a Decade," February 11, 2003, Canada.com News. Retrieved from http://www.canada.com/national/features/census/story.html?id={3A2C6DEC-8AC1-47F...

Critical Thinking

Given the complex situations you'd be addressing, does human resource management seem like a career area that interests you? What have been your experiences in dealing with people who work in human resource management?

DETERMINING YOUR HUMAN RESOURCE NEEDS

All management, including human resource management, begins with planning. Five steps are involved in the human resource planning process:

job analysis
A study of what is done by employees who hold various job titles.

job description
A summary of the objectives of a job, the type of work to be done, the responsibilities and duties, the working conditions, and the relationship of the job to other functions.

job specifications
A written summary of the minimum qualifications required of workers to do a particular job.

1. **Preparing a human resource inventory of the organization's employees.** This inventory should include ages, names, education, capabilities, training, specialized skills, and other information pertinent to the specific organization (e.g., languages spoken). Such information reveals whether or not the labour force is technically up-to-date, thoroughly trained, and so forth.

2. **Preparing a job analysis.** A **job analysis** is a study of what is done by employees who hold various job titles. Such analyses are necessary in order to recruit and train employees with the necessary skills to do the job. The results of job analysis are two written statements: job descriptions and job specifications. A **job description** specifies the objectives of the job, the type of work to be done, the responsibilities and duties, the working conditions, and the relationship of the job to other functions. **Job specifications** are a written

summary of the minimum qualifications (education, skills, etc.) required of workers to do a particular job. In short, job descriptions are statements about the job, whereas job specifications are statements about the person who does the job. See Figure 12.3 for hypothetical examples of a job description and job specifications.

3. **Assessing future human resource demand.** Because technology changes rapidly, training programs must be started long before the need is apparent. Human resource managers who are proactive—that is, who anticipate the organization's requirements identified in the forecasting process—make sure that trained people are available when needed.

4. **Assessing future supply.** The labour force is constantly shifting: getting older, becoming more technically oriented, attracting more women, and so forth. There are likely to be increased shortages of some workers in the future (e.g., computer and robotic repair workers) and an oversupply of others (e.g., assembly line workers).

5. **Establishing a strategic plan.** The plan must address recruiting, selecting, training and developing, appraising, compensating, and scheduling the labour force. Because the previous four steps lead up to this one, this chapter will focus on these elements of the strategic human resource plan.

Finding skilled workers to fill jobs is always a difficult task. However, finding unskilled workers can be just as challenging. Take restaurateur Lorrie Ambrose. Her dining room had long lines of hungry customers, but it did not have an adequate number of workers to get the food to the diners and the dishes off the tables. Ambrose was eventually forced to put the restaurant up for sale. What can the new owners do to ensure a steady supply of dedicated workers?

JOB ANALYSIS

Observe current sales representatives doing the job.
Discuss job with sales managers.
Have current sales reps keep a diary of their activities.

JOB DESCRIPTION	JOB SPECIFICATIONS
Primary objective is to sell company's products to stores in Territory Z. Duties include servicing accounts and maintaining positive relationships with clients. Responsibilities include <ul><li>Introducing the new products to store managers in the area.</li><li>Helping the store managers estimate the volume to order.</li><li>Negotiating prime shelf space.</li><li>Explaining sales promotion activities to store managers.</li><li>Stocking and maintaining shelves in stores that wish such service.</li></ul>	Characteristics of the person qualifying for this job include <ul><li>Two years' sales experience.</li><li>Positive attitude.</li><li>Well-groomed appearance.</li><li>Good communication skills.</li><li>High-school diploma and two years of postsecondary credit.</li></ul>

FIGURE 12.3

JOB ANALYSIS

A job analysis yields two important statements: job descriptions and job specifications. Here you have a job description and job specifications for a sales representative.

RECRUITING EMPLOYEES FROM A DIVERSE POPULATION

recruitment
The set of activities used to obtain a sufficient number of the right people at the right time.

Recruitment is the set of activities used to obtain a sufficient number of the right people at the right time. Its purpose is to select those who best meet the needs of the organization. One would think that, with a continuous flow of new people into the workforce, recruiting would be easy. On the contrary, recruiting has become very difficult, for several reasons:

- Some organizations have policies that demand promotions from within, operate under union regulations, or offer low wages, which makes recruiting and keeping employees difficult or subject to outside influence and restrictions.

- Legal restrictions, such as the Charter of Rights and Freedoms, make it necessary to consider the proper mix of women, minorities, people with disabilities, and other qualified individuals.

- The emphasis on corporate culture, teamwork, and participative management makes it important to hire people who not only are skilled but also fit in with the culture and leadership style of the organization.[21]

- Sometimes people with the necessary skills are not available; in this case, workers must be hired and then trained internally.[22]

Because recruiting is a difficult chore that involves finding, hiring, and training people who are an appropriate technical and social fit, human resource managers turn to many sources for assistance (see Figure 12.4). These sources are classified as either internal or external. Internal sources include employees who are already within the firm (and may be transferred or promoted) and employees who can recommend others to hire. Using internal sources is less expensive than recruiting outside the company. The greatest advantage of hiring from within is that it helps maintain employee morale. It isn't always possible to find qualified workers within the company, however,

Workopolis is updated daily and it posts thousands of job opportunities in Canada weekly.

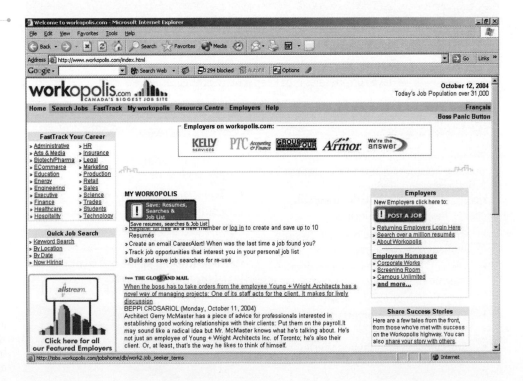

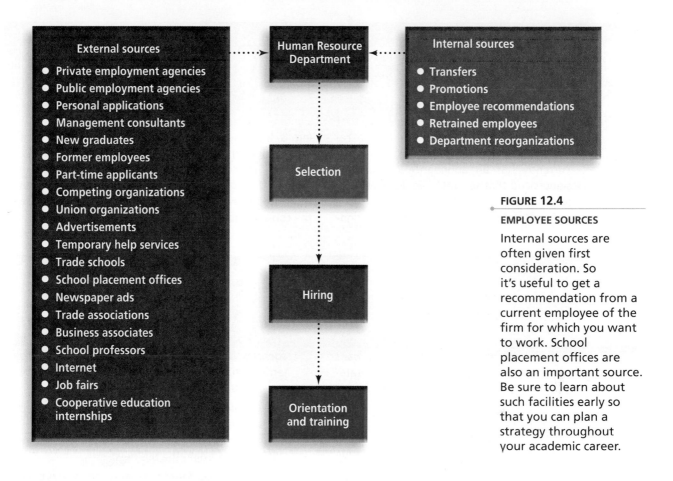

FIGURE 12.4

EMPLOYEE SOURCES

Internal sources are often given first consideration. So it's useful to get a recommendation from a current employee of the firm for which you want to work. School placement offices are also an important source. Be sure to learn about such facilities early so that you can plan a strategy throughout your academic career.

so human resource managers must use external recruitment sources such as advertisements, public and private employment agencies, school placement offices, management consultants, professional organizations, referrals, and walk-in applications. While most external sources are straightforward, some may involve difficult decisions; the Making Ethical Decisions box presents questions about recruiting employees from competitors.

Recruiting qualified workers may be particularly difficult for small businesses ➤**P. 197**◄ that don't have enough staff members to serve as internal sources and may not be able to offer the sort of competitive compensation that attracts external sources. The Spotlight on Small Business box outlines some ways in which small businesses can address their recruiting needs. Newer tools for recruiting employees include Internet services such as Workopolis.com and Monster.ca (see the first Taking It to the Net exercise at the end of this chapter).

SELECTING EMPLOYEES WHO WILL BE PRODUCTIVE

Selection is the process of gathering information and deciding who should be hired, under legal guidelines, for the best interests of the individual and the organization. Selecting and training employees have become extremely expensive processes in some firms. Think of what's involved: interview time, medical exams in some instances, training costs, unproductive time spent learning the job, moving expenses, and so on. It's easy to see how selection expenses can amount to more than $130,000 for a top-level manager.

selection
The process of gathering information and deciding who should be hired, under legal guidelines, for the best interests of the individual and the organization.

Making Ethical Decisions

Recruiting Employees from Competitors

As the human resources director for Technocrat, Inc., it is your job to recruit the best employees. Your most recent human resource inventory indicated that Technocrat currently has an abundance of qualified designers and that several lower-level workers will soon be eligible for promotions to designer positions as well. In spite of the surplus of qualified designers within the firm, you are considering recruiting a designer who is now with a major competitor. Your thinking is that the new employee will be a source of information about the competition's new products. What are your ethical considerations in this case? Will you lure the employee away from the competition even though you have no need for a designer? What will be the consequences of your decision?

Spotlight on Small Business

Competing for Qualified Workers

It's difficult for small-business owners to find qualified employees. Small businesses want top talent but often can't afford corporate-level benefits or expensive recruiters to hunt down the best people. Despite the hurdles, small-business management consultants say there are many ways to lure desirable workers:

- *Post job openings on the Internet.* Running a 60-day job posting on an online service like Monster.ca will cost $495. Running a job posting (where information must fit within a four-inch by two-inch box) in the Careers section of *The Globe and Mail* newspaper for three days will cost $2,256.

- *Let your staff help select hires.* The more staff people involved in the interview process, the better chance you have to find out who has the personality and skills to fit in.

- *Create a dynamic workplace to attract local, energetic applicants.* Sometimes word of mouth is the most effective recruiting tool.

- *Test-drive an employee.* Hiring temporary workers can allow you to test candidates for a few months before deciding whether to make an offer or not.

- *Hire your customer.* Loyal customers sometimes make the smartest employees.

- *Check community groups and local government agencies.* Don't forget to check out provincial and territory–run employment agencies. New programs may turn up excellent candidates you can train.

- *Lure candidates with a policy of promotions and raises.* Most employees want to know that they can move up in the company. Give employees an incentive for learning the business.

- *Outsource fringe benefit management to a professional employer organization (PEO).* PEOs may be able to offer lower insurance rates for benefit programs because of greater economies of scale. While this may not bring a small business's benefits program all the way up to the level of those offered by most large companies, it may help close the gap and therefore help attract qualified workers.

Sources: Susan T. Port, "Staff Leasing Firms Help Small Businesses Compete," *Palm Beach Post*, January 27, 2001, p. 2D; Brian S. Klass, John McClendon, and Thomas W. Gainey, "Trust and the Role of Professional Employer Organizations: Managing HR in Small and Medium Enterprises," *Journal of Managerial Issues*, April 1, 2002, p. 31; "Improving Worker Coverage and Benefits," Government Accounting Office report, April 9, 2002; and http://recruiter.monster.ca/login.asp?redirect=http%3A%2F%2Frecruiter%2Emonster%2Eca%2Findex%2Easp, June 9, 2004; and *The Globe and Mail* (1-800-387-9012), June 9, 2004.

It can even cost one and a half times the employee's annual salary to recruit, process, and train an entry-level worker.[23] Thus, the selection process is an important element of any human resource program. A typical selection process would involve five steps:

1. **Obtaining complete application forms.** Once this was a simple procedure with few complications. Today, however, legal guidelines

limit the kinds of questions that may appear on an application form. Nonetheless, such forms help the employer discover the applicant's educational background, past work experience, career objectives, and other qualifications directly related to the requirements of the job. Large employers like Blockbuster make the application process more effective and efficient by using an artificial intelligence program called Smart Assessment, developed by application-service provider Unicru. An applicant sits down at a computer and spends a half hour answering questions about job experience, time available to work, and personality. Ten minutes later, a report is e-mailed to a hiring manager. The reports tell the manager whether to interview the applicant or not. If an interview is recommended, the report even suggests questions the manager can ask to find the best-fitting position for the applicant. Blockbuster says Unicru's system helped the company cut the hiring process from two weeks to three days and has reduced the employee turnover rate by 30 percent.[24]

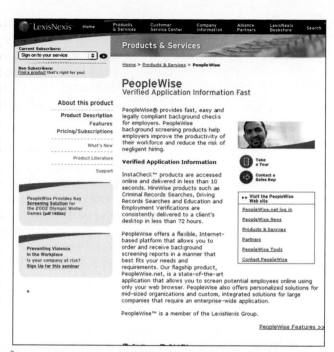

Unfortunately, businesses have learned that hiring the wrong person to fill a job costs valuable time and money. Today, companies like PeopleWise reduce the risk of making a bad choice by offering a flexible means to screen potential employees online. PeopleWise provides carefully screened background checks of potential employees to see who best fits the needs of a company.

2. **Conducting initial and follow-up interviews.** A staff member from the human resource department often screens applicants in a first interview. If the interviewer considers the applicant a potential employee, the manager who will supervise the new employee interviews the applicant as well. It's important that managers prepare adequately for the interview to avoid selection decisions they may regret.[25] Certain mistakes, such as asking an interviewee about his or her family, no matter how innocent the intention, could later be used as evidence if that applicant files discrimination charges.[26]

3. **Giving employment tests.** Organizations use tests to measure basic competencies in specific job skills (e.g., welding, word processing) and to help evaluate applicants' personalities and interests.[27] In using employment tests, it's important that they be directly related to the job. Many companies test potential employees in assessment centres, where applicants perform actual tasks of the real job. Such testing is likely to make the selection process more efficient and will generally satisfy legal requirements.

4. **Conducting background investigations.** Most organizations now investigate a candidate's work record, school record, credit history, and references more carefully than they have in the past.[28] It is simply too costly to hire, train, and motivate people only to lose them and have to start the process over. Background checks help an employer identify which candidates are most likely to succeed in a given position. Websites such as PeopleWise allow prospective employers not only to conduct speedy background checks of criminal records, driving records, and credit histories but also to verify work experience and professional and educational credentials.

5. **Establishing trial (probationary) periods.**   Often, an organization will hire an employee conditionally. This enables the person to prove his or her worth on the job. After a specified probationary period (perhaps three months or a year), the firm may either permanently hire or discharge that employee on the basis of evaluations from supervisors. Although such systems make it easier to fire inefficient or problem employees, they do not eliminate the high cost of turnover.

The selection process is often long and difficult, but it is worth the effort to select new employees carefully because of the high costs of replacing workers. The process helps ensure that new employees meet the requirements in all relevant areas, including communication skills, education, technical skills, experience, personality, and health. Finally, where a company has a collective labour agreement—a union contract with its employees—the selection process must also follow the provisions of that agreement. This is discussed in more detail in the next chapter.

Hiring Contingent Workers

contingent workers
Workers who do not have regular, full-time employment.

When more workers are needed in a company, human resource managers may want to consider finding creative staffing alternatives rather than simply hiring new full-time employees. A company with varying needs for employees—from hour to hour, day to day, week to week, and season to season—may find it cost-effective to hire contingent workers. **Contingent workers** are defined as workers who do not have regular, full-time employment. Such workers include part-time workers (anyone who works fewer than 30 hours per week), temporary workers (workers paid by temporary employment agencies), seasonal workers, independent contractors, interns, and co-op students.

A varying need for employees is the most common reason for hiring contingent workers. Companies may also look to hire contingent workers when full-time employees are on some type of leave (such as maternity leave), when there is a peak demand for labour, or when quick service to customers is a priority. Companies in areas where qualified contingent workers are available, and in which the jobs require minimum training, are most likely to consider alternative staffing options.

Contingent workers receive few benefits; they are rarely offered health insurance, vacation time, or private pensions. They also tend to earn less than permanent workers do. On the positive side, some of those on temporary assignments may eventually be offered full-time positions. Managers see using temporary workers as a way of weeding out poor workers and finding good hires.

Many people find that temporary work offers them a lot more flexibility than permanent employment. For example, student Daniel Butrym found that the transition from student to temp worker was not difficult. Butrym says, "You come back in town. You don't have to interview. You don't have to waste a lot of time looking for a job. The first time you walk into [the temporary staffing] office, they meet you, sit you down and they find out your skills. Once you're in their computer, they have all your stats, they know what you can do and you're done. [Later] I can call from school, say 'I'm going to be home for spring break, I need some money.'" As soon as Butrym calls, he's put into the system for work assignments.

Butrym is not alone. Andy Williams of Randstad North America, the staffing services giant, welcomes students. "A lot of the students are computer-literate, and they are familiar with many of the popular software programs that the companies use. And, they are quick to get up to speed on [any] proprietary software an employer might use … Every customer is different. Some assignments come for one day. Some assignments are for weeks or for the whole summer," Williams says.[29]

In an era of downsizing and rapid change, some contingent workers have even found that temping can be more secure than full-time employment.[30]

TRAINING AND DEVELOPING EMPLOYEES FOR OPTIMUM PERFORMANCE

Because employees need to learn how to work with new equipment—such as word processors, computers, and robots—companies are finding that they must offer training programs that often are quite sophisticated.

Training and development include all attempts to improve productivity by increasing an employee's ability to perform. Training focuses on short-term skills, whereas development focuses on long-term abilities. But both training and development programs include three steps: (1) assessing the needs of the organization and the skills of the employees to determine training needs; (2) designing training activities to meet the identified needs; and (3) evaluating the effectiveness of the training.[31] Some common training and development activities are employee orientation, on-the-job training, apprenticeship programs, off-the-job training, online training, vestibule training, and job simulation.

- **Employee orientation** is the activity that initiates new employees to the organization; to fellow employees; to their immediate supervisors; and to the policies, practices, values, and objectives of the firm. Orientation programs include everything from informal talks to formal activities that last a day or more; they may involve such activities as scheduled visits to various departments and required reading of handbooks.[32] For example, all new Canadian Tire Financial Services (CTFS) employees attend Canadian Tire University, Niagara campus. According to vice-president of human resources Sharon Patterson, during their orientation employees learn about

training and development
All attempts to improve productivity by increasing an employee's ability to perform. Training focuses on short-term skills, whereas development focuses on long-term abilities.

employee orientation
The activity that introduces new employees to the organization; to fellow employees; to their immediate supervisors; and to the policies, practices, values, and objectives of the firm.

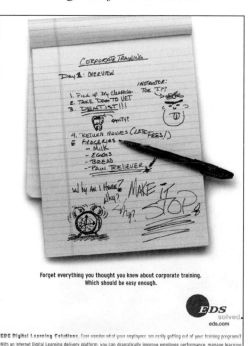

Forget everything you thought you knew about corporate training. Which should be easy enough.

How can companies make sure that their employees are getting the most out of the training they provide? Many companies use electronic delivery systems such as those developed by EDS Digital Learning Systems. EDS helps companies monitor what employees have learned through online training and provides additional help when it is needed. Do you prefer traditional classroom-type instruction or online training? Why?

the company. They are introduced to the differences between the Canadian Tire Corporation divisions, and what CTFS does. This includes CTFS's structure, vision, purpose, and team values. (Recall CTFS's mission statement from Figure 8.2.)

on-the-job training
Training in which the employee immediately begins his or her tasks and learns by doing, or watches others for a while and then imitates them, all right at the workplace.

- **On-the-job training** is the most fundamental type of training. The employee being trained on the job immediately begins his or her tasks and learns by doing, or watches others for a while and then imitates them, right at the workplace. Salespeople, for example, are often trained by watching experienced salespeople perform. Naturally, this can be either quite effective or disastrous, depending on the skills and habits of the person being watched. On-the-job training is obviously the easiest kind of training to implement when the job is relatively simple (such as clerking in a store) or repetitive (such as collecting refuse, cleaning carpets, or mowing lawns). More demanding or intricate jobs require a more intense training effort. Intranets and other new forms of technology are leading to cost-effective on-the-job training programs available 24 hours a day, all year long. Computer systems can monitor workers' input and give them instructions if they become confused about what to do next. Such an intranet ▶P. 593◀ system helped furniture maker Steelcase not only reduce its number of training courseware developers from 20 to 5 but also totally eliminate its $30,000 training materials printing budget. The Web allows greater flexibility, but the company believes its greatest advantage is the ability to make changes and updates in real time.[33]

apprentice programs
Training programs involving a period during which a learner works alongside an experienced employee to master the skills and procedures of a craft.

- **Apprentice programs** involve a period during which a learner works alongside an experienced employee to master the skills and procedures of a craft. Some apprenticeship programs also involve classroom training. Many skilled crafts, such as bricklaying and plumbing, require a new worker to serve as an apprentice for several years. Trade unions often require new workers to serve apprenticeships to ensure excellence among their members as well as to limit entry to the union. Workers who successfully complete an apprenticeship earn the classification of *journeyman*. In the future, there are likely to be more but shorter apprenticeship programs to prepare people for skilled jobs in changing industries. For example, auto repair will require more intense training as new automobile models include advanced computers and other electronic devices.[34]

off-the-job training
Training that occurs away from the workplace and consists of internal or external programs to develop any of a variety of skills or to foster personal development.

online training
Training programs in which employees "attend" classes via the Internet.

- **Off-the-job training** occurs away from the workplace and consists of internal or external programs to develop any of a variety of skills or to foster personal development. Training is becoming more sophisticated as jobs become more sophisticated. Furthermore, training is expanding to include education (through the PhD level) and personal development—subjects may include time management, stress management, health and wellness, physical education, nutrition, and even art and languages.

These apprentice welders are learning their craft from a skilled professional. Practical hands-on experience is usually combined with classroom training.

- **Online training** offers an example of how technology is improving the efficiency of many off-the-job training programs. In such training, employees "attend" classes via the Internet. Many colleges and universities now offer a wide variety of Internet courses.[35] Such programs are sometimes called *distance learning* because the students are separated by distance from the instructor or content source.

- **Vestibule training** (near-the-job training) is done in classrooms where employees are taught on equipment similar to that used on the job. Such classrooms enable employees to learn proper methods and safety procedures before assuming a specific job assignment in an organization. Computer and robotics training is often completed in a vestibule classroom.

- **Job simulation** is the use of equipment that duplicates job conditions and tasks so that trainees can learn skills before attempting them on the job. Job simulation differs from vestibule training in that the simulation attempts to duplicate the *exact* combination of conditions that occur on the job. This is the kind of training given to astronauts, airline pilots, army tank operators, ship captains, and others who must learn difficult procedures off the job.

No, this is not an NBA tryout. Employees of overnight delivery giant FedEx are playing blindfolded basketball, a bonding exercise intended to build trust among workers and managers. FedEx spends six times more than the average company on training, but enjoys a remarkably low four-percent employee turnover rate. Would a commitment to training similar to FedEx help other companies retain employees? Why?

vestibule training
Training done in schools where employees are taught on equipment similar to that used on the job.

job simulation
The use of equipment that duplicates job conditions and tasks so that trainees can learn skills before attempting them on the job.

For example, imagine that a very large crude carrier (VLCC) takes 9.6 kilometres to stop when running at 15 knots. By reversing the engines, you can cut the stopping distance to 3.2 kilometres. At any of the half-dozen training institutions in Canada, trainees learn how to pilot such ships on a simulator that resembles a giant video game. You can imagine piloting a ship that is as long as the C.N. Tower is high through a narrow passage with boats all around you. Any accident can cause serious environmental damage. You don't want to learn such skills on the job in a trial-and-error fashion!

Management Development

Managers need special training. To be good communicators, they especially need to learn listening skills and empathy. They also need time management, planning, and human relations skills.

Management development, then, is the process of training and educating employees to become good managers and then monitoring the progress of their managerial skills over time. Management development programs have sprung up everywhere, especially at colleges, universities, and private management development firms. Managers participate in role-playing exercises, solve various management cases, attend films and lectures, and so on. In some organizations, managers are paid to take university-level courses through to the doctoral level.

management development
The process of training and educating employees to become good managers and then monitoring the progress of their managerial skills over time.

Management development is increasingly being used as a tool to accomplish business objectives. For example, Ford Motor Company is teaching executives how to be more responsive to customers. Most management training programs also include several of the following:

- **On-the-job coaching.** This means that a senior manager will assist a lower-level manager by teaching him or her needed skills and generally providing direction, advice, and helpful feedback.[36]

The dictionary says a mentor is a wise and trusted counsellor or teacher. In business, a mentor can be a whole lot more. Mentors not only counsel and teach lower-level employees, but also often introduce them to the right people within an organization who can help the employees advance. Firms like Lockheed Martin (shown here) have a formal system of assigning mentors to employees who show strong potential. What types of guidance can mentors offer lower-level employees?

- **Understudy positions.** Job titles such as *undersecretary* and *assistant* are part of a relatively successful way of developing managers. Selected employees work as assistants to higher-level managers and participate in planning and other managerial functions until they are ready to assume such positions themselves.

- **Job rotation.**   So that they can learn about different functions of the organization, managers are often given assignments in a variety of departments. Through job rotation, top managers gain the broad picture of the organization necessary to their success.

- **Off-the-job courses and training.**   Managers periodically go to schools or seminars for a week or more to hone their technical and human relations skills. Such courses expose them to the latest concepts and create a sense of camaraderie as the managers live, eat, and work together in a school-type atmosphere. Case sudies and simulation exercises of all kinds are often part of such training. Many companies offer tuition reimbursement for such courses as an employee benefit. Other companies, such as canadian Tire Corporation, have their own "school" for managers. At Canadian Tire University, managers and potential franchise owners attend courses to develop their skills.

Networking

networking
The process of establishing and maintaining contacts with key managers in one's own organization and other organizations and using those contacts to weave strong relationships that serve as informal development systems.

mentor
An experienced employee who supervises, coaches, and guides lower-level employees by introducing them to the right people and generally being their organizational sponsor.

performance appraisal
An evaluation in which the performance level of employees is measured against established standards to make decisions about promotions, compensation, additional training, or firing.

Networking is the process of establishing and maintaining contacts with key managers in one's own organization and in other organizations and using those contacts to weave strong relationships that serve as informal development systems. Of equal or greater importance to potential managers is a **mentor,** a corporate manager who supervises, coaches, and guides selected lower-level employees by introducing them to the right people and generally being their organizational sponsor. In reality, an informal type of mentoring goes on in most organizations on a regular basis as older employees assist younger workers. However, many organizations, such as Intel, use a formal system of assigning mentors to employees considered to have strong potential.[37]

It's also important to remember that networking and mentoring can go beyond the business environment. For example, school is a perfect place to begin networking. Associations you nurture with professors, with local businesspeople through internships, and especially with your classmates might provide you with a valuable network you can turn to for the rest of your career.

APPRASING EMPLOYEE PERFORMANCE TO GET OPTIMUM RESULTS

Managers must be able to determine whether or not their workers are doing an effective and efficient job, with a minimum of errors and disruptions. They do so by using performance appraisals. A **performance appraisal** is an evaluation in which the performance level of employees is measured against established standards to make decisions about promotions, compensation, additional training, or firing. Performance appraisals consist of these six steps:

1. **Establishing performance standards.** This is a crucial step. Standards must be understandable, subject to measurement, and reasonable. They must be accepted by both the manager and subordinates.

2. **Communicating those standards.** Often managers assume that employees know what is expected of them, but such assumptions are dangerous at best. Employees must be told clearly and precisely what the standards and expectations are and how they are to be met.

3. **Evaluating performance.** If the first two steps are done correctly, performance evaluation is relatively easy. It is a matter of evaluating the employee's behaviour to see if it matches standards.

4. **Discussing results with employees.** Most people will make mistakes and fail to meet expectations at first. It takes time to learn a new job and do it well. Discussing an employee's successes and areas that need improvement can provide managers with an opportunity to be understanding and helpful and to guide the employee to better performance. Additionally, the performance appraisal can be a good source of employee suggestions on how a particular task could be better performed.

5. **Taking corrective action.** As an appropriate part of the performance appraisal, a manager can take corrective action or provide corrective feedback to help the employee perform his or her job better. Remember, the key word is *performance*. The primary purpose of conducting this type of appraisal is to improve employee performance if possible.

6. **Using the results to make decisions.** Decisions about promotions, compensation, additional training, or firing are all based on performance evaluations. An effective performance appraisal system is a way of satisfying certain legal conditions concerning such decisions.

Effective management means getting results through top performance by employees. That is what performance appraisals are for—at all levels of the organization. Even top-level managers benefit from performance reviews made by their subordinates. The latest form of performance appraisal is called the 360-degree review because it calls for feedback from all directions in the organization. Instead of an appraisal based solely on the employee's and the supervisor's perceptions, opinions are gathered from those under, above, and on the same level as the worker. The goal is to get an accurate, comprehensive idea of the worker's abilities.[38]

At Canadian Tire Financial Services, 360-degree evaluations are voluntary. This is a customized online tool for Canadian Tire employees. As Sharon Patterson explains, feedback is anonymously provided on character and the competencies of the person being evaluated. While most companies stop at the coaching session that is built at the end of this process, CTFS's model goes one step further. There is a workshop that allows the person being evaluated to "walk through" the feedback and see where to build his or her own competencies and where he or she can develop as a leader. This allows the feedback to be more effective.

Figure 12.5 illustrates how managers can make performance appraisals more meaningful.

FIGURE 12.5

CONDUCTING EFFECTIVE
APPRAISALS AND REVIEWS

1. **DON'T** attack the employee personally. Critically evaluate his or her work.

2. **DO** allow sufficient time, without distractions, for appraisal. (Take the phone off the hook or close the office door.)

3. **DON'T** make the employee feel uncomfortable or uneasy. *Never* conduct an appraisal where other employees are present (such as on the shop floor).

4. **DO** include the employee in the process as much as possible. (Let the employee prepare a self-improvement program.)

5. **DON'T** wait until the appraisal to address problems with the employee's work that have been developing for some time.

6. **DO** end the appraisal with positive suggestions for employee improvement.

Progress Assessment

• Can you name and describe four training techniques?

• What is the primary purpose of a performance appraisal?

• What are the six steps in a performance appraisal?

• Why do employers and employees find the appraisal process so difficult?

COMPENSATING EMPLOYEES: ATTRACTING AND KEEPING THE BEST

Companies don't just compete for customers; they also compete for employees. Compensation is one of the main marketing tools companies use to attract qualified employees, and it is one of the largest operating costs for many organizations. The long-term success of a firm—perhaps even its survival—may depend on how well it can control employee costs and optimize employee efficiency. For example, service organizations such as hospitals, airlines, and banks have recently struggled with managing high employee costs. This is not unusual since these firms are considered labour intensive; that is, their primary cost of operations is the cost of labour. Manufacturing firms in the auto, airline, and steel industries have asked employees to take reductions in wages to make the firms more competitive (as was seen, for example, during the restructuring of Air Canada). Many employees have agreed, even union employees who have traditionally resisted such cuts. They know that not to do so is to risk going out of business and losing their jobs forever. In other words, the competitive environment is such that compensation and benefit packages are being given special attention. In fact, some experts believe that determining how best to pay people has replaced downsizing as today's greatest human resources challenge.

A carefully managed compensation and benefits program can accomplish several objectives:

• Attracting the kinds of people needed by the organization, and in sufficient numbers.

• Providing employees with the incentive to work efficiently and productively.

• Keeping valued employees from leaving and going to competitors, or starting competing firms.

- Maintaining a competitive position in the marketplace by paying competitively and by keeping costs low through high productivity from a satisfied workforce.
- Providing employees with some sense of financial security through insurance and retirement benefits.

Compensation for Women

For many years, statistics have supported that on average Canadian women earn less than men. In 2002, female employees earned 82 cents for every dollar earned by men, which was virtually unchanged from the year before.[39] There are many historical reasons for this large wage gap. The traditional women's jobs—teachers, nurses, and secretaries—have tended to pay poorly. As more women obtain university degrees, the salary differential in professional and executive categories should continue to decrease. But there has also been evidence of outright salary discrimination in other types of jobs.

The WorkRights Website (www. workrights.ca) contains information that will help employees work toward better rights, better protection, and better wages and benefits.

There are now laws banning such discrimination. At the federal level, the Canadian Human Rights Act makes it a discriminatory practice to pay men and women differently for performing work of equal value. Canada's 13 provincial and territorial jurisdictions provide for some type of equal pay in their human rights legislation although it may refer only generally to job discrimination rather than specifically to equity in wages.[40]

For some organizations, this legislation has been difficult to implement. First, how do you define equal (or comparable) value? For example, which job has more value, that of a nurse or that of a trash collector? As well, officials cite budget cutbacks and the huge costs of making up for past inequitable compensation to female employees as the reasons for delaying the implementation of this legislation.

The federal government has set up a task force to review section 11 of the Canadian Human Rights Act, which deals with this topic. The task force hopes to make recommendations as necessary and appropriate to clarify the way in which pay equity should be implemented in a modern society.[41]

Pay Systems

How an organization chooses to pay its employees can have a dramatic effect on motivation (as discussed in Chapter 11) and productivity. Managers want to find a system that compensates employees fairly. Figure 12.6 outlines some of the most common pay systems.

Many companies still use the pay system devised by Edward Hay for General Foods. Known as the Hay system, this compensation plan is based on job tiers, each of which has a strict pay range. In some firms, you're guaranteed a raise after 13 weeks if you're still working for the company. Conflict can arise when an employee who is performing well earns less than an employee who is not performing well simply because the latter has worked for the company longer.

John Whitney, author of *The Trust Factor*, believes that companies should begin with some base pay and give all employees the same percentage merit raise. Doing so, he says, sends out the message that everyone in the company is important. Fairness remains the issue. What do you think is the fairest pay system?

Compensating Teams

Thus far we've talked about compensating individuals. What about teams? Since you want your teams to be more than simply a group of individuals, would you compensate them as you would individuals? If you can't answer that

FIGURE 12.6

PAY SYSTEMS

Some of the different pay systems are as follows:

- **Salary:** Fixed compensation computed on weekly, biweekly, or monthly pay periods (e.g., $1,500 per month or $400 per week). Salaried employees do not receive additional pay for any extra hours worked.

- **Hourly wage or daywork:** Wage based on number of hours or days worked, used for most blue-collar and clerical workers. Often employees must punch a time clock when they arrive at work and when they leave. Hourly wages vary greatly. This does not include benefits such as retirement systems, which may add 30 percent or more to the total package.

- **Piecework system:** Wage based on the number of items produced rather than by the hour or day. This type of system creates powerful incentives to work efficiently and productively.

- **Commission plans:** Pay based on some percentage of sales. Often used to compensate salespeople, commission plans resemble piecework systems.

- **Bonus plans:** Extra pay for accomplishing or surpassing certain objectives. There are two types of bonuses: monetary and cashless. Money is always a welcome bonus. Cashless rewards include written thank-you notes, appreciation notes sent to the employee's family, movie tickets, flowers, time off, gift certificates, shopping sprees, and other types of recognition.

- **Profit-sharing plans:** Share of the company's profits over and above normal pay. Companies set goals with the input from employees ahead of time. Bonuses are based on progress in meeting the goals.

- **Cost-of-living allowances (COLAs):** Annual increases in wages based on increases in the consumer price index, usually found in union contracts.

- **Stock options:** Right to purchase stock in the company at a specific price over a specific period of time. Often this gives employees the right to buy stock cheaply despite huge increases in the price of the stock in the marketplace. For example, Rob Gordon started out at Home Depot 10 years ago as an assistant manager. Today, at 39, he's a general manager—and a millionaire due to the growth of Home Depot's stock price. With his stock options, Gordon was able to buy stock worth $63.75 a share for as little as $15 a share. Once a perk given only to top-ranking executives, stock options in the past few years began being offered to lower-level employees. Such options plans are often offered by the high-tech, pharmaceutical, and financial services sectors to attract and retain skilled workers.

question immediately, you are not alone. While most managers believe in using teams, fewer are sure about how to pay them.[42] This suggests that team-based pay programs are not as effective or as fully developed as managers would hope. Measuring and rewarding individual performance on teams while at the same time rewarding team performance can be tricky. Nonetheless, it can be done. Football players are rewarded as a team when they go to the play-offs and to the Super Bowl, but they are paid individually as well. Companies are now experimenting with and developing similar incentive systems.

Jay Schuster, co-author of an ongoing study of team pay, found that when pay is based strictly on individual performance, it erodes team cohesiveness and makes it less likely that the team will meet its goals as a collaborative effort. Schuster recommends basing pay on team performance.[43] Skill-based pay and profit-sharing are the two most common compensation methods for teams.

Skill-based pay is related to the growth of both the individual and the team. Base pay is raised when team members learn and apply new skills. For example, Eastman Chemical Company rewards its teams' proficiency in technical, social, and business knowledge skills. A cross-functional compensation policy team defines the skills. The drawbacks of the skill-based pay system are twofold: the system is complex, and it is difficult to correlate skill acquisition and bottom-line gains.[44]

In most gain sharing systems, bonuses are based on improvements over a previous performance baseline. For example, Behlen Manufacturing, a diversified maker of agricultural and industrial products, calculates its bonuses by dividing quality pounds of product by worker-hours. *Quality* means no defects; any defects are subtracted from the total. Workers can receive a monthly gain-sharing bonus of up to $1 an hour when their teams meet productivity goals.

It is important to reward individual team players also. Outstanding team players—those who go beyond what is required and make an outstanding individual contribution to the firm—should be separately recognized for their additional contribution. Recognition can include cashless as well as cash rewards. A good way to avoid alienating recipients who feel team participation is uneven is to let the team decide which members get what type of individual award. After all, if you really support the team process, you need to give teams freedom to reward themselves.

Employee Benefits

Employee benefits include sick-leave pay, vacation pay, pension plans, health plans, and other benefits that provide additional compensation to employees. They may be divided into three categories. One group derives from federal or provincial legislation (which varies somewhat from province to province) and requires compulsory deductions from employees' paycheques, employer contributions, or both. These include the Canada/Quebec Pension Plan, employment insurance, health care, and workers' compensation. You have probably seen some of these deductions from your pay. The second group consists of legally required benefits, including vacation pay, holiday pay, time and a half or double time for overtime, and unpaid maternity leave with job protection.

The third category includes all other benefits and stems from voluntary employer programs or from employer–union contracts. Some are paid by the employer alone and others are jointly paid by employer and employee. Among the most common are bonuses, company pension plans, group insurance, sick leave, termination pay, and paid rest periods.

The list of benefits is long and has become quite significant—benefits account for more than one-third of total labour costs, compared with 15 percent half a century ago.[45] Often, labour negotiations are more likely to concern employee benefits than wage rates. They are no longer at the fringe of negotiations.

Employee benefits can also include everything from paid vacations to group insurance plans, recreation facilities, company cars, country club memberships, daycare services, and executive dining rooms. Managing the benefits package is a major HRM issue. Employees want packages to include dental care, legal counselling, maternity leave, and more.

From about 51,000 candidates, the editors of the 2004 edition of *Canada's Top 100 Employers* selected companies based on criteria ranging from vacations to

employee benefits
Benefits such as sick-leave pay, vacation pay, pension plans, and health plans that represent additional compensation to employees beyond base wages.

The Globe and Mail calls *Canada's Top 100 Employers* "an instant bible for human resources managers and job-seekers." Published by Mediacorp Canada Inc. and featured in *Maclean's* magazine each year, *Canada's Top 100 Employers* (www.Canadas Top100.com) is an annual competition to determine which employers lead their industries in providing the best benefits and working conditions. Would you consider reviewing this resource if you were looking for a job? Would it impact which companies you would target?

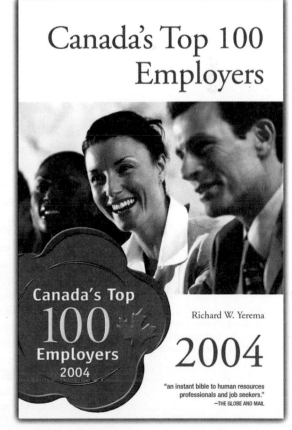

Canada's Top 100 Employers
Richard W. Yerema
2004
"an instant bible to human resources professionals and job seekers." —THE GLOBE AND MAIL

Is vacation time the primary benefit you look for in a job? Well, better check the want ads in Naples or Palermo, Italy. As this illustration shows, Italians take an average of 42 days of vacation per year, while the average Canadian worker receives 26 days—and many don't even take all of the vacation time they are entitled to.

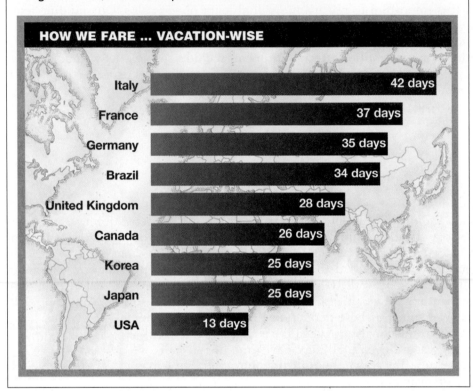

Less Rest Assured
Is your downtime too far down?

Here is how we rank, according to the World Trade Organization, when compared with other countries.

HOW WE FARE ... VACATION-WISE

Italy	42 days
France	37 days
Germany	35 days
Brazil	34 days
United Kingdom	28 days
Canada	26 days
Korea	25 days
Japan	25 days
USA	13 days

cafeteria-style benefits
Benefit plans that allow employees to choose which benefits they want up to a certain dollar amount.

philanthropy. Calgary-based Suncor Energy Inc. offers its employees 17 annual personal days off, giving them the equivalent of six weeks' vacation. Adacel Inc., based in Brossard, Quebec, offers its employees four vacation weeks in the first year with opportunities to advance in its global offices. Fredericton, N.B.–based Neill and Gunter Ltd. offers job opportunities across Canada and the United States. Top performers can win access to the company's chalet in Maine. Vancouver City Savings Credit Union offers transit subsidies and discounted car loans for hybrid-fuel vehicles. SAS Institute (Canada) Inc.'s top salespeople can win paid vacations and use of a Porsche. Employees are also eligible for four days off annually to volunteer in the community. As you can see, there are a variety of employee benefits that companies can consider.

To counter these growing demands, more than half of all large firms offer **cafeteria-style benefits** plans, from which employees can choose the benefits they want, up to a certain dollar amount. Choice is the key to these flexible plans. At one time, most employees' needs were similar. Today, employees are more varied and more demanding. Some employees may need childcare benefits, whereas others may need relatively large pension benefits. Rather than giving all employees identical benefits, managers can equitably and cost-effectively meet employees' individual needs by allowing employees some choice.[46]

Reaching Beyond Our Borders

Managing a Global Workforce

Many companies send employees to different countries. How do human resource personnel manage employees in, say, an office in Spain, a service centre in Brazil, or a new plant in Korea? How do they cope with hiring employees from other countries for a company's headquarters in Canada? Human resource people who manage a global workforce begin by understanding the customs, laws, and local business needs of every country in which the organization operates.

Varying cultural and legal standards can affect a variety of human resource functions:

- *Compensation.* Salaries must be converted to and from foreign currencies. Often employees with international assignments receive special allowances for relocation, children's education, housing, travel, or other business-related expenses.

- *Health and pension standards.* Human resource managers must consider the different social contexts for benefits in other countries. For example, in the Netherlands the government provides retirement income and health care.

- *Paid time off.* Cultural differences can be quite apparent when it comes to paid time off. Employees in other countries may enjoy more vacation time than those in Canada. For example, four weeks of paid vacation is the standard of many European employers. But other countries do not

have the short-term and long-term absence policies we have in Canada. They do not have sick leave, personal leave, or family and medical leave. Global companies need a standard definition of what time off is.

- *Taxation.* Different countries have varying taxation rules, and the payroll department is an important player in managing immigration information.

- *Communication.* When employees leave to work in another country they often feel a disconnection from their home country. Wise companies use their intranet and the Internet to help these faraway employees keep in direct contact. Several companies use these tools for posting both job vacancies and notices to help returning employees find positions back in Canada.

Human resource policies will be influenced more and more by conditions and practices in other countries and cultures. Human resource managers will need to move away from the assumed dominance and/or superiority of Canadian business practices and sensitize themselves and their organizations to the cultural and business practices of other nations.

Sources: "Employee Benefits and Ownership Part 1," United Press International, March 16, 2002; and "Employee Benefits and Ownership, Part 2," United Press International, March 17, 2002.

Managing the benefits package will continue to be a major human resource issue in the future. The cost of administering benefits programs has become so great that a number of companies outsource ➤**P. 269**◀ this function—that is, they hire outside companies to run their employee benefits plans. IBM, for example, decided to spin off its human resources and benefits operation into a separate company, Workforce Solutions, which provides customized services to each of IBM's independent units. The new company saves IBM $45 million each year. Workforce Solutions now handles benefits for other organizations such as the National Geographic Society. In addition to saving them money, outsourcing fringe benefits administration helps companies avoid the growing complexity and technical requirements of the plans.

Managing benefits can be especially complicated when employees are located in other countries. The Reaching Beyond Our Borders box above discusses the human resource challenges faced by global businesses. To put it simply, benefits are as important to wage negotiations and recruitment now as is salary. In the future, benefits may become even more important than salary.

SCHEDULING EMPLOYEES TO MEET ORGANIZATIONAL AND EMPLOYEE NEEDS

By now, you are quite familiar with the trends occurring in the workforce that result in managers' and workers' demands regarding companies' flexibility and responsiveness. From these trends have emerged several new or renewed ideas such as flextime, in-home employment, and job sharing.[47] Let's see how these innovations affect the management of human resources.

Flextime Plans

flextime plan
Work schedule that gives employees some freedom to choose when to work, as long as they work the required number of hours.

core time
In a flextime plan, the period when all employees are expected to be at their job stations.

compressed workweek
Work schedule that allows an employee to work a full number of hours per week but in fewer days.

FIGURE 12.7

A FLEXTIME CHART

At this company, employees can start work anytime between 6:30 and 9:30 AM. They take a half hour for lunch anytime between 11:00 AM and 1:30 PM, and can leave between 3:00 and 6:30 PM. Everyone works an eight-hour day. The blue arrows show a typical employee's flextime day.

Almost 60 percent of Canadian employers offer flexible work hours as an option to employees.[48] A **flextime plan** gives employees some freedom to choose when to work, as long as they work the required number of hours. The most popular plans allow employees to come to work between 7:00 and 9:00 AM and leave between 4:00 and 6:00 PM. Usually, flextime plans will incorporate what is called core time. **Core time** refers to the period when all employees are expected to be at their job stations. For example, an organization may designate core time as between 9:30 and 11:00 AM and between 2:00 and 3:00 PM. During these hours all employees are required to be at work (see Figure 12.7). Flextime plans, like job-sharing plans, are designed to allow employees to adjust to the demands of the times; two-income families find them especially helpful. The federal government has experimented extensively with flextime and found it to be a boost to employee productivity ➤P. 15◀ and morale.[49]

There are some real disadvantages to flextime as well. Flextime is certainly not for all organizations. For example, it cannot be offered in assembly line processes, where everyone must be at work at the same time. It also is not effective for shift work.

Another disadvantage to flextime is that managers often have to work longer days in order to assist and supervise employees. Some organizations operate from 6:00 AM to 6:00 PM under flextime—a long day for supervisors. Flextime also makes communication more difficult; certain employees may not be there when others need to talk to them. Furthermore, if not carefully supervised, some employees could abuse the system, and that could cause resentment among others. You can imagine how you'd feel if half the workforce left at 3:00 PM on Friday and you had to work until 6:00 PM.

Another popular option used in approximately 24 percent of companies is a **compressed workweek.** That means that an employee works a full number of hours in less than the standard number of days. For example, an employee may work four 10-hour days and then enjoy a long weekend instead

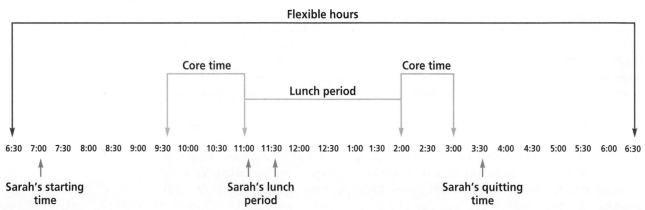

Flexible hours

Core time   Core time

Lunch period

6:30 7:00 7:30 8:00 8:30 9:00 9:30 10:00 10:30 11:00 11:30 12:00 12:30 1:00 1:30 2:00 2:30 3:00 3:30 4:00 4:30 5:00 5:30 6:00 6:30

Sarah's starting time

Sarah's lunch period

Sarah's quitting time

of working five 8-hour days with a traditional weekend. There are the obvious advantages of working only four days and having three days off, but some employees get tired working such long hours, and productivity could decline. Many employees find such a system of great benefit, however, and are quite enthusiastic about it.

Although many companies offer flexible schedules, few employees take advantage of them.[50] Most workers report that they resist using the programs because they fear it will hurt their careers. Managers signal (directly or indirectly) that employees who change their hours are not serious about their careers.

Home-based and Other Mobile Work

Telecommuting, also known as telework, has grown tremendously in recent years. Home-based workers can choose their own hours, interrupt work for child care and other tasks, and take time out for various personal reasons. Working at home isn't for everyone, however. Recall from Chapter 7 that to be successful, a home-based worker must have the discipline to stay focused on the work and not be easily distracted.[51]

According to the Canadian Telework Association (www.ivc.ca), the following are just some reasons why there is increasing company support for telework:

- *More information workers.* With Canada's high per-capita ratio of government, high-tech, and information workers, a large number of Canadian employees are ready, willing, and able to telework;

- *Increased computer ownership.* A 2002 Ipsos-Reid survey shows that more than two-thirds of Canadian households own a computer, making Canada one of the most wired nations in the world. Daily improvements in security and technology make it easier and easier to work from home;

- *Faster Internet speeds (bandwidth).* A 2003 study places Canada third in the world in broadband use, after South Korea and Hong Kong;

- *Reduced Internet access costs.* Canada and Australia share the world's cheapest Internet access—just one reason why we use the Internet so much;

- *Increased population density.* Geographically, Canada is the world's second largest country. Telework presents a good alternative to travelling long distances; and

- *Comparative cost of relocation.* Relocations are expensive. Statistics Canada estimates that it costs companies an average of $42,000 to relocate the average homeowner to another city. Telework can help reduce the need for relocations.[52]

Telecommuting can be a cost saver for employers.[53] For example, IBM used to have a surplus of office space, maintaining more offices than there were employees. Now the company has cut back on the number of offices, with employees telecommuting, "hotelling" (being assigned to a desk through a reservations system), and "hot-desking" (sharing a desk with other employees at different times).[54] When Accenture,

Mobile workers create virtual offices that allow them to work from places other than the traditional office. They can use laptops, cellphones, pagers, fax machines, and network services to conduct business wherever it is convenient.

a technology and management consulting company, built its new head-quarters, it added only 250 seats for 700 workers. By doing away with the concept of one seat per employee, Accenture spent half of what it would have for more conventional offices. When employees enter the Accenture office, they check a computer to find out where they've been assigned for the day. Depending on how much space they need, they might be in a cubicle, a small office, or a conference room. If they just need to make a quick phone call or check their e-mail, there are club chairs, phones, and Internet connections. Or they can hang out in the company's Internet café, which features a fireplace, a TV, a snack bar, and an outside terrace with Internet access at each table.[55]

The list of organizations that use telework is growing every day and includes Alberta Red Cross, Bell Canada, Pfizer Canada Inc., Sony Music Canada, Trimark, and Xerox Canada. While telework is not for everyone, for every job, or for every organization, even if it applies only to a small percentage of employees and new hires it represents a significant tool in the ability to attract and retain employees.[56] That's true even if they know they can telework only a day or two per week, which is the norm.[57]

Job-sharing Plans

job sharing
An arrangement whereby two part-time employees share one full-time job.

Job sharing is an arrangement whereby two part-time employees share one full-time job. The concept has received great attention as more and more women with small children have entered the labour force. Job sharing enables parents to work only during the hours their children are in school. It has also proved beneficial to others with special needs, such as students and older people who want to work part-time before fully retiring. The benefits include:

- Employment opportunities for those who cannot or prefer not to work full-time.
- A high level of enthusiasm and productivity.
- Reduced absenteeism and tardiness.
- Ability to schedule people into peak demand periods (e.g., banks on payday) when part-time people are available.
- Retention of experienced employees who might have left otherwise.

However, as you might suspect, disadvantages include having to hire, train, motivate, and supervise twice as many people and to prorate some fringe benefits. Nonetheless, most firms that were at first reluctant to try job sharing are finding that the benefits outweigh the disadvantages.

Critical Thinking   How can compensation be used to motivate employees?

Progress Assessment
- Can you name and describe five alternative compensation techniques?
- What advantages do compensation plans such as profit sharing offer an organization?
- What are the benefits and challenges of flextime? Telecommuting? Job sharing?

MOVING EMPLOYEES UP, OVER, AND OUT

Employees don't always stay in the position they were initially hired to fill. They may excel and move up the corporate ladder or fail and move out the front door. In addition to being moved through promotion and termination, employees can be moved by reassignment and retirement. Of course, employees often choose to move themselves by quitting and going to another company.

Promoting and Reassigning Employees

Many companies find that promotion from within the company improves employee morale. Promotions are also cost-effective in that the promoted employees are already familiar with the corporate culture and procedures and do not need to spend valuable time on basic orientation.

Due to the prevalence of flatter corporate structures, there are fewer levels for employees to reach now than there were in the past. Therefore, it is more common today for workers to move *over* to a new position than to move *up* to one. Such transfers allow employees to develop and display new skills and to learn more about the company overall. This is one way of motivating experienced employees to remain in a company with few *upward* advancement opportunities.

Terminating Employees

As we discussed in previous chapters, downsizing and restructuring, increasing customer demands for greater value, and the relentless pressure of global competition and shifts in technology have human resource managers struggling to manage layoffs and firings.

In the case of layoffs, older employees are often offered early retirement packages (to be discussed soon). Companies may counsel other laid-off employees to enable them to better cope with the loss of their jobs and to help them find new jobs. Some set up in-house outplacement facilities so that employees can get counselling on how to obtain a new job. For senior managers, companies usually pay for private-agency career counselling.

The threat of job losses has introduced a strong feeling of insecurity into the Canadian workforce. Insecurity undermines motivation, so HRM must deal with this new issue. Keeping employees fully informed and having a clear policy on termination pay helps to remove some insecurity. It is important to note that most Canadian jurisdictions require that larger companies give three to six months' notice before large layoffs.

Even companies that regain financial strength, however, are hesitant to re-hire new full-time employees. Why? One reason is that the cost of terminating employees is prohibitively high. Termination usually involves special costs such as terminal pay or penalties, which may be determined by contract for executives, or by union contracts or government regulations. When large companies announce a substantial downsizing, you will usually see reference to a special cost charge for the current year that can easily run into many tens of millions of dollars. The cost of firing comes from lost training costs as well as damages and legal fees paid in wrongful-discharge suits. Figure 12.8 outlines advice on how to minimize the chance of wrongful-discharge lawsuits.

To save money, many companies are either using temporary employees or outsourcing ➤P. 269◀ certain functions. As mentioned in the chapter-opening profile, companies need to carefully consider which functions they wish to outsource.

FIGURE 12.8

HOW TO AVOID WRONGFUL-DISCHARGE LAWSUITS

Consultants offer this advice to minimize the chance of a lawsuit for wrongful discharge:

- Prepare before hiring by requiring recruits to sign a statement that retains management's freedom to terminate at will.
- Don't make unintentional promises by using such terms as *permanent employment.*
- Document reasons before firing and make sure you have an unquestionable business reason for the firing.
- Fire the worst first and be consistent in discipline.
- Buy out bad risk by offering severance pay in exchange for a signed release from any claims.
- Be sure to give employees the true reasons they are being fired. If you do not, you cannot reveal it to a recruiter asking for a reference without risking a defamation lawsuit.
- Disclose the reasons for an employee's dismissal to that person's potential new employers. For example, if you fired an employee for dangerous behaviour and you withhold that information from your references, you can be sued if the employee commits a violent act at his or her next job.

Sources: "In Economics Old and New, Treatment of Workers Is Paramount," *Washington Post,* February 11, 2001, p. L1; and www.us/aw.com.

Retiring Employees

In addition to layoffs, another tool used to downsize companies is to offer early retirement benefits to entice older (and more expensive) workers to retire. Such benefits usually involve financial incentives such as one-time cash payments, known in some companies as *golden handshakes.* The advantage of offering early retirement benefits over laying off employees is that early retirement offers increase the morale of the surviving employees. Retiring senior workers also increases promotion opportunities for younger employees.

Losing Employees

In spite of a company's efforts to retain talented workers by offering flexible schedules, competitive salaries, and attractive fringe benefits, some employees will choose to pursue opportunities elsewhere. Learning about their reasons for leaving can be invaluable in preventing the loss of other good people in the future.[58] One way to learn the real reasons employees leave is to have a third party (not the employee's direct manager) conduct an exit interview.

turnover rate
A measure of the percentage of employees that leave a firm each year.

One tool that human resources specialists can consult is their turnover rate. The **turnover rate** measures the percentage of employees that leave the firm each year. The most reliable way to use turnover rates is to compare an organization against itself over time, says Ken Strom, senior consultant specializing in strategic rewards at the Toronto office of Watson Wyatt Worldwide.[59] That said, some turnover rates, as listed in Figure 12.9, can be used as a rough benchmark.

LAWS AFFECTING HUMAN RESOURCE MANAGEMENT

Legislation has made hiring, promotion, firing, and managing employee relations in general very complex and subject to many legal complications and challenges. Since Canada is a confederation of provinces and territories, jurisdiction over many aspects of our lives is divided between the federal and provincial governments. As noted in Chapter 4, the federal government legislates on national issues such as employment insurance. However, the provinces have jurisdiction over most provincial matters. This includes employment standards in areas such as minimum wage, hours of work, overtime, statutory holidays, parental leave, employment of people under 18, and discrimination in the workplace. For example, Ontario's general minimum wage was increased from $6.85 per hour to $7.15 per hour on February 1, 2004. Further increases will follow on an annual basis, bringing the minimum wage to $8 per hour by February 2007.[60]

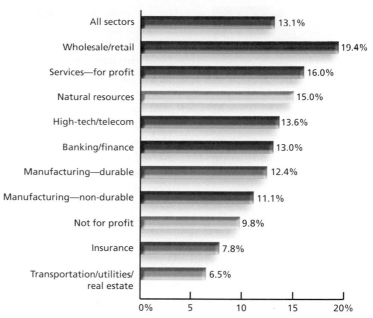

FIGURE 12.9

CANADIAN TURNOVER RATES

Source: *Canadian HR Reporter*, October 20, 2003.

But it's a little more complicated than that. The federal government also has jurisdiction over certain types of businesses that are deemed to be of a national nature. Banks, insurance companies, airlines, railways, shipping companies, telephone, radio, TV, cable companies, and others are subject to federal law, as are all federal employees. Fewer than 10 percent of all Canadian employees are subject to federal legislation. However, the Canadian Charter of Rights and Freedoms, which is part of the Constitution, overrides all other laws. For example, the federal government had to amend the Unemployment Insurance Act because the Supreme Court had ruled that the Act went against the Charter in denying coverage to employees over age 64.

What all this means is that there are literally hundreds of laws and regulations, federal and provincial, that apply to all aspects of HRM. Furthermore, they are constantly being revised because of social pressure or rulings by human rights commissions or courts. One of the most regulated areas involves discrimination.

Laws in all jurisdictions in Canada make it illegal to discriminate against employees because of age, sex, nationality, ethnicity, religion, marital status, disability, and sexual orientation. Some other forms of human rights discrimination are banned in some provinces, while not in others. For example, one's political beliefs or association are not considered grounds for discrimination in Alberta, New Brunswick, Northwest Territories, Nunavut, Ontario, and Saskatchewan. Source of income is considered a ground for discrimination in only Alberta, Manitoba, Nunavut, Prince Edward Island, and Yukon Territory.

Employment Equity

A well-known 1980s case of discrimination highlights a major problem and how it was solved. A group of women accused the CNR of not hiring them because they was women. The CNR, like many other companies, did not hire women for jobs that were thought to be traditional men's jobs, those for which heavy physical labour was required. In this case, the jobs involved maintenance and repairs of the tracks. The Canadian Human Rights Commission ruled in favour of the women. The CNR appealed and the courts ruled against it all the way to the Supreme Court of Canada.

Nobody has a shelf life.

In Ontario, an ad campaign features posters of older people with stickers on their foreheads that read *Best Before*—like the date tags on perishable groceries. There are different posters for employment, transportation, health care, and housing. The campaign not only combats ageism, but also empowers those experiencing this discrimination to recognize what ageism is and how to respond. Do you think that seniors, employers, educators, service providers and the general public will respond favourably to such ads?

employment equity
Employment activities designed to "right past wrongs" by increasing opportunities for minorities and women.

reverse discrimination
The unfairness unprotected groups (say whites or males) may perceive when protected groups receive preference in hiring and promotion.

The purpose of the Employment Equity Act is to ensure that federally regulated employers provide equal employment opportunities for women, Aboriginal peoples, persons with disabilities, and members of visible minorities. **Employment equity** (known as affirmative action in the United States) refers to employment activities designed to "right past wrongs" by increasing opportunities for minorities and women. This means that in the CNR example, CNR had to develop a plan that would result in more women than men being hired for such jobs until the balance was more even. The result is that when a man and a woman are equally qualified, the woman must be given preference. This would occur for a period of time until the balance of male and female workers was adjusted more equally.

Interpretation of the employment equity law eventually led employers to actively recruit and give preference to women and minority-group members. As you might expect, interpretation of the law was often controversial and enforcement was difficult. Questions persist about the legality of employment equity and the effect the program could have in creating a sort of reverse discrimination in the workplace.

Reverse discrimination refers to the unfairness unprotected groups (say whites or males) may perceive when protected groups receive preference in hiring and promotion. Charges of reverse discrimination have occurred when companies have been perceived as unfairly giving preference to women or minority group members in hiring and promoting. The Canadian Charter of Rights and Freedoms specifically allows for employment equity as a method to overcome long-standing discrimination against specific groups. Therefore, the courts accept it as being nondiscriminatory in the legal sense. Be aware that this continues to be a controversial issue today.

Laws That Protect the Disabled

Legislation protects people with disabilities. Businesses cannot discriminate against people on the basis of any physical or mental disability. Employers are required to give disabled applicants the same consideration for employment as people without disabilities. It also requires that businesses make "reasonable accommodations" for people with disabilities. Accommodation may include modifying equipment or widening doorways, putting up barriers to isolate people readily distracted by noise, reassigning workers to new tasks, and making changes in supervisors' management styles.[61] Reasonable accommodations are not always expensive. For about $6 per month, a company can rent a headset phone that allows someone with cerebral palsy to talk on the phone and write at the same time. Equal opportunity for people with disabilities promises to be a continuing issue into the next decade.

Laws That Protect Older Employees[62]

Employees are guaranteed protection against age discrimination in the workplace. Courts have ruled against firms in unlawful-discharge suits where age appeared to be the major factor in dismissal.

This topic of older employees is expected to gain more attention in the years to come as labour shortages are forecast due to aging baby boomers. While there is no law in Canada that requires retirement at 65, many workplaces mandate it at that age. The issue of changing the mandatory retirement age is now being considered by the federal government. The federal government's 160,000 public servants are currently forced to leave their jobs at age 65. Six of Canada's ten provinces (British Columbia, New Brunswick, Newfoundland and Labrador, Nova Scotia, Ontario, and Saskatchewan) also have a mandatory retirement age. A change to the mandatory retirement age—as is being considered by the Ontario government—would provide opportunities for companies to retain workers who wish to work past age 65.

Most provinces protect over-65 workers in their labour or human rights legislation, except for British Columbia, Newfoundland and Labrador, Ontario, and Saskatchewan.

Effects of Legislation

Clearly, laws and regulations affect all areas of HRM. It should be apparent that a career in HRM offers a challenge to anyone willing to put forth the effort. In summary:

- Employers must know and act in accordance with the legal rights of their employees or risk costly court cases.

- Legislation affects all areas of HRM, from hiring and training to compensating, promoting, retiring, laying off, or firing employees.

- Managers must be sensitive not only to legal requirements, but also to union contracts and social standards and expectations, which can be even more demanding.

- Court cases have made it clear that it is sometimes legal to go beyond providing equal rights for minorities and women to provide special employment (employment equity) and training to correct past discrimination.

- New court cases and legislation change HRM almost daily. The only way to keep current is to read business literature and become familiar with the issues.

For more information on employment standards, human rights legislation, and occupational health and safety legislation in Canadian jurisdictions, visit the Developing Human Resources in the Voluntary Sector Website at www.hrvs.ca.

Progress Assessment

- Can you name the three areas of HRM responsibility affected by government legislation?
- Explain what employment equity is and give one example.
- Why should HRM be concerned about legislation or court rulings when terminating employees?

Summary

1. Human resource management is the process of evaluating human resource needs, finding people to fill those needs, and getting the best work from each employee by providing the right incentives and job environment, all with the goal of meeting organizational objectives. Like all other types of management, human resource management begins with planning.

   - **What are the steps in human resource planning?**
   The five steps are (1) preparing a human resource inventory of the organization's employees; (2) preparing a job analysis; (3) assessing future demand; (4) assessing future supply; and (5) establishing a strategic plan for recruiting, hiring, educating, appraising, compensating, and scheduling employees.

1. Explain the importance of human resource management as a strategic contributor to organizational success, and summarize the five steps in human resource planning.

2. Describe methods that companies use to recruit new employees, and explain some of the issues that make recruitment challenging.

2. Recruitment is the set of activities used to obtain a sufficient number of the right people at the right time to select those who best meet the needs of the organization.

• *What methods do human resource managers use to recruit new employees?*

Recruiting sources are classified as either internal or external. Internal sources include hiring from within the firm (transfers, promotions, etc.) and employees who recommend others to hire. External recruitment sources include advertisements, public and private employment agencies, school placement offices, management consultants, professional organizations, referrals, walk-in applications, and the Internet.

• *Why has recruitment become more difficult?*

Legal restrictions complicate hiring and firing practices. Finding suitable employees can also be made more difficult if companies are considered unattractive workplaces.

3. Outline the five steps in selecting employees.

3. Selection is the process of gathering and interpreting information to decide which applicants should be hired.

• *What are the five steps in the selection process?*

The steps are (1) obtaining complete application forms; (2) conducting initial and follow-up interviews; (3) giving employment tests; (4) conducting background investigations; and (5) establishing a trial period of employment.

4. Illustrate the use of various types of employee training and development methods.

4. Employee training and development include all attempts to improve employee performance by increasing an employee's ability to perform through learning.

• *What are some of the activities used for training?*

After assessing the needs of the organization and the skills of the employees, training programs are designed that may include the following activities: employee orientation, on-the-job training, apprenticeship programs, off-the-job training, online training, vestibule training, and job simulation. The effectiveness of the training is evaluated at the conclusion of the activities.

• *What methods are used to develop managerial skills?*

Management development methods include on-the-job coaching, understudy positions, job rotation, and off-the-job courses and training.

• *How does networking fit in this process?*

Networking is the process of establishing contacts with key managers within and outside the organization to get additional development assistance.

5. Trace the six steps in appraising employee performance.

5. A performance appraisal is an evaluation of the performance level of employees against established standards to make decisions about promotions, compensation, additional training, or firing.

• *How is performance evaluated?*

The steps are (1) establish performance standards; (2) communicate those standards; (3) evaluate performance; (4) discuss results; (5) take corrective action when needed; and (6) use the results for decisions about promotions, compensation, additional training, or firing.

6. Employee compensation is one of the largest operating costs for many organizations.

   • *What kind of compensation systems are used?*
   They include salary systems, hourly wages, piecework, commission plans, bonus plans, profit-sharing plans, and stock options.

   • *What types of compensation systems are appropriate for teams?*
   The most common are gains-sharing and skill-based compensation programs. It is also important to reward outstanding individual performance within teams.

   • *What are employee benefits?*
   Employee benefits include such items as sick leave, vacation pay, pension plans, and health plans that provide additional compensation to employees beyond basc wages. Many firms offer cafeteria-style fringe benefits plans, in which employees can choose the benefits they want, up to a certain dollar amount.

6. Summarize the objectives of employee compensation programs, and describe various pay systems and employee benefits.

7. Employees often move from their original positions in a company.

   • *How can employees move within a company?*
   Employees can be moved up (promotion), over (reassignment), or out (termination or retirement) of a company. Employees can also choose to leave a company to pursue opportunities elsewhere.

7. Describe the ways employees can move through a company: promotion, reassignment, termination, and retirement.

Key Terms

apprentice programs 356

cafeteria-style benefits 364

compressed workweek 366

contingent workers 354

core time 366

employee benefits 363

employee orientation 355

employment equity 372

flextime plan 366

human resource management (HRM) 344

job analysis 348

job description 348

job sharing 368

job simulation 357

job specifications 348

management development 357

mentor 358

networking 358

off-the-job training 356

online training 356

on-the-job training 356

performance appraisal 358

recruitment 350

reverse discrimination 372

selection 351

training and development 355

turnover rate 370

vestibule training 357

Developing Workplace Skills

1. Look in the classified ads in your local newspaper or on the Internet and find at least two positions that you might like to have when you graduate. List the qualifications specified in each of the ads. Identify methods the companies might use to determine how well applicants meet each of those qualifications.

2. Read several current business periodicals to find information on the latest court rulings involving pay equity, employment equity, unjustified firing, discrimination, and other human resource issues. Compose a summary of your findings. What seems to be the trend? What will this mean for tomorrow's graduates?

3. Recall the various training programs you have experienced. Think of both on-the-job and off-the-job training sessions. What is your evaluation of such programs? Write a brief critique of each. How would you improve them? Share your ideas with the class.

4. Consider these occupations: car salesperson, computer software developer, teacher, and assembly worker. Identify the method of compensation you think is appropriate for determining the wages for each of these workers. Explain your answer.

5. Imagine that you are the human resources manager at your company. You get a call from a company doing a reference check for a former employee. This former employee is being considered for a position. During the call, you are asked to provide information on the employee's medical history and his marital status. You have recently reviewed changes to the privacy laws for your province/territory through the Office of the Privacy Commissioner of Canada (www.privcom.gc.ca/information/comms_e.asp). What do you tell this person on the phone?

Taking It To The Net 1

Purpose

To use job-search Websites to identify employment opportunities and to compare the services offered by several recruiting-related sites.

Exercise

There are many recruiting-related sites on the Internet. Some examples are

a. canadiancareers.com

b. monster.ca

c. workopolis.com

d. plusjobs.ca

e. cooljobscanada.com

The Government of Canada has created several sites that provide information on jobs, workers, training, and careers. One site is the Department of Human Resources and Skills Development (www.hrdc-drhc.gc.ca/hrsd/home); a second is Job Futures (www.jobfutures.ca).

1. Access these job information sites and examine what they contain. Do you find any important differences?

2. Do you see any positions that might interest you if you were graduating this term?

Taking It To The Net 2

Purpose

The purpose of this exercise is twofold. From a manager's perspective, the purpose is to illustrate the types of questions managers typically ask during interviews. From an applicant's perspective, the purpose is to practise answering such questions in a safe environment.

Exercise

Go to Monster Interview Centre at http://interview.monster.ca. Answer the sample interview questions in the Virtual Interview section. This interactive section gives you the opportunity to test your answers so that when you do go on an actual interview you are less likely to fumble for an answer.

Practising Management Decisions

Case
Dual Career Planning

Carey Moler is a 32-year-old account executive for a communications company. She is married to Mitchell Moler, a lawyer. Carey and Mitchell did not make any definite plans about how to juggle their careers and family life until Carey reached age 30. Then they decided to have a baby, and career planning took on a whole new dimension. A company named Catalyst talked to 815 dual-career couples and found that most of them, like the Molers, had not made any long-range career decisions regarding family lifestyle.

From the business perspective, such dual-career families create real concerns. There are problems with relocation, with child care, and so on that affect recruiting, productivity, morale, and promotion policies.

For a couple such as the Molers, having both career and family responsibilities is exhausting. But that is just one problem. If Carey is moving up in her firm, what happens if Mitchell gets a terrific job offer a thousand kilometres away? What if Carey gets such an offer? Who is going to care for the baby? What happens if the baby becomes ill? How do they plan their vacations when there are three schedules to balance? Who will do the housework?

Dual careers require careful planning and discussion, and those plans need to be reviewed over time. A couple who decide at age 22 to do certain things may change their minds at 30. Whether or not to have children, where to locate, how to manage the household—all such issues and more can become major problems if not carefully planned.

The same is true for corporations. They too must plan for dual-career families. They must give attention to job sharing, flextime, parental leave policies, transfer policies, nepotism rules (i.e., rules about hiring family members), and more.

Decision Questions

1. What are some of the issues you can see developing because of dual-career families? How is this affecting children in such families?
2. What kind of corporate policies need changing to adapt to these new realities?
3. What are the advantages of dual careers? Disadvantages? What can newlywed couples do to minimize the problems of dual careers? How can a couple achieve the advantages?

Video Case

SAS

Jeff Chambers is vice-president of human resources at SAS, the world's largest privately owned software company. At such a company, employees are the most important asset because the company can't produce any software or provide any service without good, quality people. Part of Jeff's job is to find and keep such employees. Finding people who want to work at SAS isn't difficult; there are about 93,000 applicants for 500 jobs. The challenge is to screen those people to find those who fit in best.

The company assesses future labour requirements, prepares job analyses to see what various jobs entail, and then tries to find employees within the firm to meet those future needs. If they are not available, the company must search outside the firm to find the best people. Its strategic plan calls for interviewing, testing, and evaluating prospects. Spending more time in the hiring process means spending less time later trying to replace workers who were not a good fit in the firm.

In the future, there will be a great demand for skilled workers; thus, employee retention is critical at SAS. Evidence of how successfully the company retains people is the fact that turnover each year is about 4 percent, way below the industry average. One way to keep employees is to promote from within, and that means training people to move up within the organization. Such training includes in-house classes, online training, internships, and apprenticeships. Of course, managers get management training to keep them up to date and more qualified for promotion.

Keeping employees means more than providing them with a satisfying job and a good chance for promotion. It also means providing employee benefits that employees want and need. That includes health care, day care, and an in-house recreation centre. Medical insurance carries over to retired workers as well. SAS tries to accommodate the needs of individual workers as much as possible. If someone needs to take off early, he or she can. Employees can work from home (telecommuting) if they prefer. The company also has job sharing and flextime.

At a company like SAS, performance evaluations are very important. That's why the company doesn't use a simple form like so many others do. Instead, the company works closely with each employee to make sure the person understands the goals of the firm and how she or he fits into those goals.

SAS has a great relationship with its customers. The company spends 25 percent of its bottom line on research and development (R&D). Its quality products result in customer retention rates in the 98-percent range. The company treats its employees with the same care that it treats its customers. Because employees are so happy and turnover is so low, the company has more funds to invest in R&D and more happy customers. All this leads to more business and therefore the need to hire even more people.

Discussion Questions

1. What skills appear to be most important to getting hired at SAS: technical skills, people skills, team-building skills, or some combination? Which skills would you expect prospective workers to lack the most?

2. After watching this video, do you think that being a human resource manager at a high-tech firm would be an interesting and challenging job? Why or why not?

3. Is there more to human resource management than you first believed? What are some duties you hadn't previously anticipated for this position?

www.mcgrawhill.ca/college/nickels

Chapter 13

Understanding Employee–Management Issues and Relations

Profile

Getting to Know Buzz Hargrove of the Canadian Auto Workers

When one thinks of employee–management relations, the name Buzz Hargrove often comes to mind. He is regularly in the news supporting labour-relations issues, lobbying the government for improved worker benefits, and defending the rights of Canadians to unionize. Hargrove has a reputation for being an outspoken and action-oriented leader who is not afraid to go on strike if necessary.

Hargrove is the National President of the Canadian Auto Workers (CAW). Since his acclamation in 1992, he has been re-elected every three years. A Windsor Local 444 auto worker, he held several elected local positions before joining the union's staff in 1975. In 1978, he became the assistant to Bob White and was involved in leading the separation of the Canadian region from the UAW (United Auto Workers). In 1985, the CAW was formed.

Today, the CAW is the largest private-sector union in Canada. It represents workers in sectors that have been particularly challenged due to globalization and government cutbacks. The auto and health care sectors are two such examples. Consequently, it should be no surprise that the CAW is often in the news trying to protect its members, renegotiate better contracts, and educate the public on the relevant issues.

Hargrove has extensive bargaining experience and a commitment to economic, social, and political issues affecting workers and their families both in Canada and internationally. In recognition of his contribution to society, Brock University honoured him with a Doctorate of Laws degree at its convocation ceremonies in 1998. As well, Hargrove received an honorary doctorate from the University of Windsor in 2003 and from Wilfrid Laurier University in 1994.

Hargrove believes that the attack on workers' rights, especially trade union rights, by right-wing governments at both the federal and provincial levels across the country is one of the big issues facing unions today. He believes that these levels of government have worked to establish an environment where private-sector employers feel comfortable attacking the past gains of their unions.

In his experience, union–management relations are no different today than they were when he started 37 years ago as a union representative in the plant. While the companies are more sophisticated, so are the unions. The challenge in distributing the wealth that is produced is the same today as it has been in the past. How does he see the future of such relations? He has said that, "As long as government continues to undermine unions in the legislation and employers keep demanding concessions on past gains, the trade union movement will continue to fight back on behalf of our members, their families and our communities across the country."

Managers in both profit-seeking and nonprofit organizations address labour-relations challenges every day. This chapter discusses some of these employee–management relations and issues. You will be introduced to a brief history of trade unions in Canada. The union movement has been particularly challenged over the past decade due to the ever-changing business environment. In an attempt to be more competitive, companies have been demanding more from their employees. In exchange, unions have also been demanding better wages and benefits from these employers. While the relationship is constantly changing, proactive leaders must work toward solving such issues.

Sources: www.caw.ca, June 16, 2004; and e-mail interview with Buzz Hargrove, June 16, 2004.

The Canadian Auto Workers (CAW) has negotiated with companies such as General Motors to ensure that clauses related to job security and job retraining are included in their contract.

EMPLOYEE–MANAGEMENT ISSUES

The relationship between management (representing owners or shareholders) and employees has never been very smooth. Management has the responsibility of producing a profit through maximum productivity ▶P. 15◀. Managers have to make hard decisions that often do not win them popularity contests. Labour (the collective term for non-management workers) is interested in fair and competent management, human dignity, decent working conditions, a reasonable share in the wealth that its work generates, and assurance that the conditions of the contract and government labour laws will not be ignored.

Like other managerial challenges, employee–management issues must be worked out through open discussion, goodwill, and compromise. How management and labour adapt to the changing business environment will determine our economic and political well-being in the years ahead. In order to make a reasoned decision, it is important to know both sides of an issue.

Canadian companies have been trying to compete more effectively under the demands of technology and world competitiveness. While coping with a changing economy, management has been laying off employees, automating operations, and demanding more flexibility in how it uses its remaining workforce. Management must do what its strongest competitors are doing: adopt the most advanced technological methods, simplify and thin out organizational structure, and increase productivity.

Over the years, these pressures on companies have led to numerous layoffs, plant closings, and the loss of hundreds of thousands of manufacturing jobs. Skilled employees with 15, 20, or 25 years of experience have found themselves without a job. In the 1990s, many companies announced that they were closing, laying people off, or moving all or part of their operations to other lower-wage countries such as Mexico, Asia, or the United States. The loss of these jobs was primarily the reason why unions were so opposed to the North American Free Trade Agreement (NAFTA). As more traditional labour-intensive jobs are lost due to technology and competition from lower-wage countries, the issues of job security and retraining for the new information-age jobs have become key concerns for unions and the people they represent.

The Need for Trade Unions

union
An employee organization that has the main goal of representing members in employee–management bargaining over job-related issues.

Any discussion of employee–management relations in Canada should begin with a discussion of unions. A **union** (known as trade union in British English or a labor union in U.S. English)[1] is an employee organization that has the main goal of representing members in employee–management bargaining over job-related issues. Workers originally formed unions to protect themselves from intolerable work conditions and unfair treatment. They also united to secure some say in the operations of their jobs. As the number of union members grew, workers gained more negotiating power with managers and more political power as well. Historically, employees turned to unions for assistance in gaining specific workplace rights and benefits. Trade unions were largely responsible for the establishment of minimum-wage laws, overtime rules, workers' compensation, severance pay, child-labour laws, job safety regulations, and more.

Recently, however, union strength has waned. Throughout the 1990s and early 2000s, unions failed to regain the power they once had and membership continued to decline.[2] Business observers suggest that global competition, shifts from manufacturing to service and high-tech industries, growth in part-time work, and changes in management philosophies are some of the reasons for labour's decline. Some analysts also contend the decline is related to labour's success in seeing the issues it championed become law.

While many labour analysts forecast that unions will regain strength in the 21st century, others insist that unions have seen their brightest days.[3] Still, few doubt that the role and position of unions in the workplace will continue to arouse emotions and opinions that contrast considerably. Let's briefly look at trade unions and then analyze other key issues affecting employee–management relations in the 21st century.

UNIONS FROM DIFFERENT PERSPECTIVES

Are trade unions essential in the Canadian economy today? This question is certain to evoke emotional responses from various participants in the workplace. An electrician carrying a picket sign in Sudbury might elaborate on the dangers to our free society if employers continue to try to bust, or break apart, authorized unions.[4] Small manufacturers would likely embrace a different perspective and complain about having to operate under union wage and benefit obligations in an increasingly global economy.

Most historians generally agree that today's unions are an outgrowth of the economic transition caused by the Industrial Revolution of the 19th and early 20th centuries. Workers who once toiled in the fields, dependent on the mercies of nature for survival, suddenly became dependent on the continuous roll of the factory presses and assembly lines for their living. Breaking away from an agricultural economy to form an industrial economy was quite difficult. Over time, workers learned that strength through unity (unions) could lead to improved job conditions, better wages, and job security.

Critics of organized labour maintain that few of the inhuman conditions that once dominated Canadian industry still exist in the workplace. Many of the gains won by unions, such as working conditions and hours of work, are now protected by laws. They charge that organized labour has in fact become a large industrial entity in itself and that the real issue of protecting workers has become secondary. Critics also maintain that the current legal system and changing management philosophies minimize the chances that the sweatshops (workplaces with unsatisfactory and often unsafe or oppressive labour conditions) of the late 19th and early 20th centuries will reappear.[5] Unfortunately, sweatshops are present in other countries, and many workers around the world are struggling to

The manufacture of Nike footwear is left to offshore contractors who employ 500,000 workers in countries like China, Indonesia, and Vietnam. The minimum wage in Indonesia is US$2.46 a day. The Nike Campaign has become an international movement demanding that Nike accept truly independent monitoring of working conditions at all its contract factories. Campaign supporters believe that Nike should also ensure that its workers are paid a living wage and their right to organize and bargain collectively is recognized and respected.

gain the right to join unions.[6] A short discussion of the history of trade unions will cast a better light on the issues involved.

HISTORY AND THE ROLE OF TRADE UNIONS IN CANADA

A long, rocky road has been travelled in Canada to arrive at the current stage of relatively civilized relationships between owners and managers of businesses and their employees. A complex and often bitter series of events over the last century and a half has involved workers, owners and managers, and governments in a long process of evolution that has transformed the rights and obligations of all the parties. This evolution was occurring not only in Canada but also in England, the United States, and other countries experiencing the Industrial Revolution.

The Beginning of Trade Unionism

craft union
An organization of skilled specialists in a particular craft or trade

The presence of formal labour organizations in Canada dates back to the 1800s. Early unions on the wharves of Halifax, St. John's, and Quebec during the War of 1812 existed to profit from labour scarcity. Others, such as the Montreal shoemakers or the Toronto printers of the 1830s, were craft unions. A **craft union** is an organization of skilled specialists in a particular craft or trade.[7] These unions were formed to address fundamental work issues of pay, hours, conditions, and job security—many of the same issues that dominate labour negotiations today. By forming a union, these skilled workers hoped to protect their craft and status from being undermined.

Many of the early labour organizations were local or regional in membership. Also, most were established to achieve some short-range goal (e.g., a pay increase) and disbanded after attaining a specific objective. This situation changed dramatically in the late 19th century with the expansion of the Industrial Revolution.[8]

The Rise of Industrial Capitalism

The 19th century witnessed the emergence of modern industrial capitalism. The system of producing the necessities of society in small, home-based workplaces gave way to production in large factories driven by steam and later electricity. Enormous productivity increases were gained through mass production and job specialization. However, this brought problems for workers in terms of productivity expectations, hours of work, wages, and unemployment.

Workers were faced with the reality that production was vital. Anyone who failed to produce lost his or her job. People had to go to work even if they were ill or had family problems. Accidents were frequent and injured workers were simply thrown out and replaced by others. Over time, the increased emphasis on production led firms to expand the hours of work. The length of the average workweek in 1900 was 60 hours, but an 80-hour workweek was not uncommon.[9] Wages were low and the use of child labour was widespread. For example, small boys worked long hours in mines, in areas that were inaccessible to adults, for a few cents an hour. Minimum-wage laws and unemployment benefits were non-existent, which meant that periods of unemployment were hard on families who earned subsistence wages. As you can sense, these were not short-term issues that would easily go away. The workplace was ripe for the emergence of labour organizations.

The struggle for more humane working conditions and wages was not an easy one, because before 1872 it was illegal to attempt to form a union in

Canada. The pioneers in the early struggles were treated as common criminals. They were arrested, beaten, and often shot. In 1919, for example, two protesting strikers were shot and killed by police during the Winnipeg General Strike. This was followed by 428 strikes across the country.[10]

As the years progressed, more unions were formed and more employees joined them. Other union types were created—such as industrial unions—to represent certain workers. An **industrial union** is one that consists of unskilled and semi-skilled workers in mass-production industries such as automobile manufacturing and mining.[11]

Long after it was no longer illegal, the idea of workers forming unions to protect their interests was still regarded with suspicion by employers and governments in Canada. Democratic rights for all was still a weak concept, and the idea of people getting together to fight for their rights was not accepted as it is today. The union movement was greatly influenced by immigrants from Europe (especially Britain), who brought with them the ideas and experiences of a more advanced and often more radical background. The growing union movement in the United States also influenced Canada. Many Canadian unions started as locals of American unions, and this relationship persists today. As democracy gradually gained strength, the union movement grew with it. Its participation, in turn, helped democracy sink deeper, wider roots in Canada.

industrial union
Consists of unskilled and semi-skilled workers in mass-production industries such as automobile manufacturing and mining.

THE STRUCTURE AND SIZE OF TRADE UNIONS IN CANADA[12]

The organization structure of unions in Canada is quite complex. The most basic unit is the union local. One local usually represents one school, government office, or a specific factory or office of a company. However, that local can also cover several small companies or other work units. A local is part of a larger structure, namely a national or international body. For example, a local of the Ford plant in Windsor, Ontario is part of the Canadian Auto Workers (CAW) union, which is a national body. A local of the Stelco plant in Hamilton is part of the United Steel Workers (USW) union, which is an international (Canada and U.S.) body based in the United States.

In turn, both the CAW and the USW are part of a central labour organization called the Canadian Labour Congress (CLC), which will be discussed soon. The USW is also affiliated with another central body, the AFL-CIO, which is based in the United States. The American Federation of Labour–Congress of Industrial Organizations (AFL-CIO) was a merger of these two separate organizations in 1955. Today, the AFL-CIO includes affiliations with 66 national and international labour organizations and has 13 million members.[13]

Other union locals are part of a union that is affiliated with a different central body called the Canadian Federation of Labour (CFL). Some of these are also affiliated with the AFL-CIO and some are not. In addition, some Canadian locals are part of international unions that are affiliated only with the AFL-CIO central body. There are also provincial and some regional bodies to which various unions belong. These are usually unions that are part of the CLC, the AFL-CIO, or both.

There are also unions that are not connected to any of the central bodies mentioned. For example, the Confédération des Syndicats Nationaux/Confederation of National Trade Unions (CSN/CNTU) is a federation of mostly Quebec-based unions. This is also the case for the Centrale des Syndicats du Québec (CSQ).

Approximately 67.7 percent of all union members belong to a national union, 27.3 percent belong to an international union, and the rest belong directly to chartered unions and independent local organizations.[14]

Before we discuss the general level of unionization in Canada, let us briefly look at three major organizations that are often in the news.

FIGURE 13.1

UNION MEMBERSHIP BY CONGRESS AFFILIATION, 2003

This figure shows how union membership is distributed by type of affiliation to central labour federations.

CONGRESS AFFILIATION	MEMBERSHIP	%
CLC	3,031,705	72.6
CLC only	1,917,855	45.9
AFL-CIO/CLC	1,113,850	26.7
CSN	279,150	6.7
CSQ	123,030	2.9
CSD	61,430	1.5
CCU	8,510	0.2
AFL-CIO only	27,830	0.7
Unaffiliated International	1,500	0.0
Unaffiliated National	490,670	11.7
Independent Local	154,630	3.7
Total	4,178,455	100.0

Source: Directory of Labour Organizations in Canada, Union Membership in Canada, 2003.

The Canadian Labour Congress[15]

The Canadian Labour Congress (CLC) is the national voice of the labour movement. As noted in Figure 13.1, the majority of national and international unions in Canada belong to the Congress. The CLC includes 12 provincial and territorial federations and 137 district labour councils. While it represents 2.5 million unionized workers, it also speaks on behalf of those who don't belong to a union and need to be represented. The belief is that if the Congress will not fight for those who are not represented, then no one else will do so.

To find out more information about the CLC and CUPE, visit their sites at www.clc-ctc.ca and www.cupe.ca

The CLC promotes decent wages and working conditions and improved health and safety laws. It lobbies the government for fair taxes and strong social programs, including childcare, medicare, and pensions. It lobbies for and develops job training and job creation programs. Members work for social equality and to end racism and discrimination. The Congress attempts to increase solidarity between workers in Canada and other countries.

The Canadian Union of Public Employees[16]

Formed in 1963, the Canadian Union of Public Employees (CUPE) is Canada's largest union, with more than half a million members. CUPE's structure encompasses more than 2,200 locals, 12 divisions, and numerous councils and committees. More than 600 staff provide services from 66 offices across the country.

The union represents workers in health care, education, municipalities, libraries, universities, social services, public utilities, transportation, emergency services, and airlines. CUPE members are service providers, white-collar workers, technicians, labourers, skilled tradespeople, and professionals. More than half are women, and about one-third work part time.

The Canadian Auto Workers[17]

The Canadian Auto Workers (CAW) was founded in 1985 after the Canadian members of the U.S.–based United Auto Workers (UAW) decided to form their own Canadian-controlled union. Today, the CAW is the largest private-sector union in Canada, representing 260,000 workers in a wide range of industries. The CAW is the largest union in the following sectors: auto assembly, auto parts manufacturing, aerospace, shipbuilding, fisheries, and railway transportation. It also has a major presence in the airline, mining, electrical products, retail, health care, and hospitality sectors.

Members are organized into 282 local unions and more than 1,600 bargaining units. Women represent nearly 30 percent of the total membership. Every year, the CAW negotiates more than 500 collective agreements and organizes an average of more than 4,000 new members.

Size of Trade Unions in Canada

Union density measures the percentage of workers who belong to unions. According to Human Resources Development Canada, unions represented more than four million workers—which equated to 30.4 percent of all non-agricultural paid workers—in 2003. To contrast, when unions were most powerful, they represented 41.8 percent of workers in 1984. As noted in Figure 13.2, union density has been slightly declining since 1996.

Unionization rates are much higher in the public sector than in the private sector. Consequently, it should not be surprising that the rate of unionization is high in public administration (69.2 percent) and utilities (67.9 percent), and very low in trade (13.0 percent). Newfoundland and Labrador has the highest rate of unionization, while Alberta is the least unionized province. There is now little difference between the rates of unionization among men and women. It has been more challenging to unionize younger workers than it has been for older workers. Figure 13.3 summarizes union membership and coverage by selected characteristics.

YEAR	UNION MEMBERSHIP (MILLIONS)	UNION MEMBERSHIP (PERCENTAGE)
1993	4.07	36.0
1994	4.08	36.1
1995	4.00	34.7
1996	4.00	34.3
1997	4.07	34.5
1998	3.94	32.7
1999	4.01	32.6
2000	4.06	31.9
2001	4.11	31.3
2002	4.17	31.1
2003	4.18	30.4

Source: Directory of Labour Organizations in Canada, Workplace Information Directorate, Labour Program, Human Resources Development Canada, Union Membership in Canada, 2003.

FIGURE 13.2

UNION MEMBERSHIP IN CANADA, 1993–2003

union density
A measure of the percentage of workers who belong to unions.

FIGURE 13.3

UNION MEMBERSHIP AND COVERAGE BY SELECTED CHARACTERISTICS, 2004.

		Provinces		Selected Industry	
Total	30.5%	Newfoundland and Labrador	39.4%	Manufacturing	30.5%
Men	30.3%			Construction	31.4%
Women	30.6%	Prince Edward Island	30.8%	Transportation	41.0%
Public sector	72.3%			Utilities	67.9%
Private sector	17.8%	Nova Scotia	27.7%	Trade	13.0%
		New Brunswick	28.4%	Accommodation and food	6.9%
Age		Quebec	37.6%		
15–24	13.4%	Ontario	27.0%	Finance, insurance, real estate and leasing	8.7%
25–44	29.9%	Manitoba	35.1%		
45–54	41.3%	Saskatchewan	34.8%	Education	69.0%
55 and over	36.1%	Alberta	22.1%	Health care and social assistance	53.6%
Full time	32.0%	British Columbia	32.9%		
Part time	23.6%			Public administration	69.2%

Source: Adapted from Statistics Canada, Perspectives on Labour & Income, August 2004, Vol. 5, No. 8, Catalogue No. 75-001-XIE, Fact-Sheet on Unionization p. 4.

Progress Assessment

- Why were unions originally formed?
- List three reasons why union membership has been decreasing.
- Describe the structure of unions. Why would a local union affiliate itself with the CLC?

LABOUR LEGISLATION

The growth and influence of organized labour in Canada have depended primarily on two major factors: the law and public opinion.

As with other movements for greater fairness and equity in our society—such as women's right to vote, equal rights for minorities and women, and protection for children—when support for employees' rights became widespread in Canada, laws were passed to enforce them. Today we have laws establishing minimum wage, paid minimum holidays and vacation, maximum hours, overtime pay, health and safety conditions, workers' compensation, employment insurance, the Canada/Quebec Pension Plan, and a host of other rights. It is strange to realize that at one time or another these were all on the agenda of unions and were opposed by employers and governments for many years. They often denounced these demands as radical notions.

The effect of unions goes far beyond their numbers. Companies that want to keep unions out often provide compensation, benefits, and working conditions that match or exceed those found in union plants or offices. Thus, the levels established by unions spill over to non-union companies. Michelin Tire plants in Nova Scotia and Dofasco in Ontario are good examples. Read the Spotlight on Small Business box for a look at small-business sector unionization.

As indicated in Chapter 4, the federal government has control over specified fields of activity that are national in nature. In Chapter 12, it was mentioned that such activities apply to approximately 10 percent of Canadian workers. They work for banks, railways, airlines, telephone and cable systems, and radio and broadcasting companies. The federal government also has jurisdiction over many First Nation activities. So federal legislation applies to unions and labour–management relations in these businesses as well as to all federal Crown corporations and federal civil servants.

The major legislation that governs labour–management relations for these employees is the Canada Labour Code. Provincial or territorial laws apply to the other 90 percent of the Canadian workforce. The Canada Labour Code is administered by Human Resources Development Canada. It is also responsible for the Employment Equity Act as well as other legislation on wages and working conditions.

Labour Relations Boards[18]

labour relations board (LRB)
A quasi-judicial body consisting of representatives from government, labour, and business. It functions more informally than a court but has the full authority of the law.

A **labour relations board (LRB)** is a quasi-judicial body consisting of representatives from government, labour, and business. It functions more informally than a court but it has the full authority of the law. The federal and provincial governments have their own boards that oversee their specific legislation.

For example, the federal government has created the Canada Industrial Relations Board (CIRB). Its mandate is to contribute to and promote effective industrial relations in any work, undertaking, or business that falls within the authority of the Parliament of Canada. Its jurisdiction covers some

Spotlight on Small Business

www.ufcw.org

Unionizing in a Challenging Sector

Unions are rare in the small-business sector. According to research conducted by CIBC, only six percent of small companies are unionized. As you read on, you will see why in some sectors creating a union is particularly challenging.

The very first Tim Hortons franchise store opened in Hamilton, Ontario in 1964. Today, the chain has more than 2,200 outlets across Canada, and a handful of them are unionized. One location is the first Tim Hortons franchise in Quebec, where about 40 employees received union accreditation with Local 500R of the United Food and Commercial Workers on August 14, 2003. UFCW spokesperson Martin Church said workers were looking for better working conditions and to have seniority respected.

The majority of the 40 workers are women between the ages of 20 and 45 years of age. A spokesperson for the Quebec Federation of Labour stated that the approval was granted quickly due to a recent reform of the Quebec Labour Code.

The organizing victory is a breakthrough of sorts for the workers. Organizing restaurants is difficult. Unions often cite the high turnover among young workers as the main reason why there are few successful union drives. For example, about 75 percent of workers in Quebec's restaurant sector are under 20 years of age, according to Tony Filato, secretary-treasurer of UFCW 500R. They're not paid very well, and they don't stay in one place too long. Consequently, organizing them is extremely challenging.

Sources: "Small Business Stats Facts," May 12, 2003, GDSourcing. Retrieved from www.gdsourcing.com/newsletter/newsletter404.htm; "First Union at a Tim Hortons in Quebec gets Labour Relations Board Approval," August 14, 2003, Foodservice News. Retrieved from www.foodservice.com/news_homepage_expandtitle_fromhome.cfm?passid=7238; "Do Workers Looking for Unions Need a BUB?" September 3, 2003, MFS. Retrieved from http://www.ufcw.net/articles/docs/2003-09-03_do_workers_need_a_bub.html; and www.timhortons.com, June 14, 2004.

700,000 employees. The CIRB plays an active role in helping parties resolve their disputes through mediation ➤P. 394◄ and alternative dispute resolution approaches. It also undertakes a wide range of industrial relations activities, including the following:

- certifying trade unions;
- investigating complaints of unfair labour practices;
- issuing cease and desist orders in cases of unlawful strikes and lockouts; and
- rendering decisions on jurisdictional issues.

Similar provincial codes and labour relations boards operate in each province for those areas under their jurisdiction. The laws, regulations, and procedures vary from province to province.

To find out more information about federal legislation, provincial offices of the ministry of labour, and provincial labour relations boards, visit www.cirb-ccri.gc.ca/related/index_e.html.

The Collective Bargaining Process

The Labour Relations Board oversees **collective bargaining,** the process by which a union represents employees in relations with their employer. During this process, union and management representatives form a labour–management agreement, or contract for workers. Collective bargaining includes how unions are selected, the period prior to a vote, certification, ongoing contract negotiations, and behaviour while a contract is in force and during a breakdown in negotiations for a renewal of contract. The whole bargaining process and the important certification procedure are shown in detail in Figure 13.4. It is illegal for employers to fire employees for union activities.

collective bargaining
The process whereby union and management representatives form a labour–management agreement, or contract, for workers.

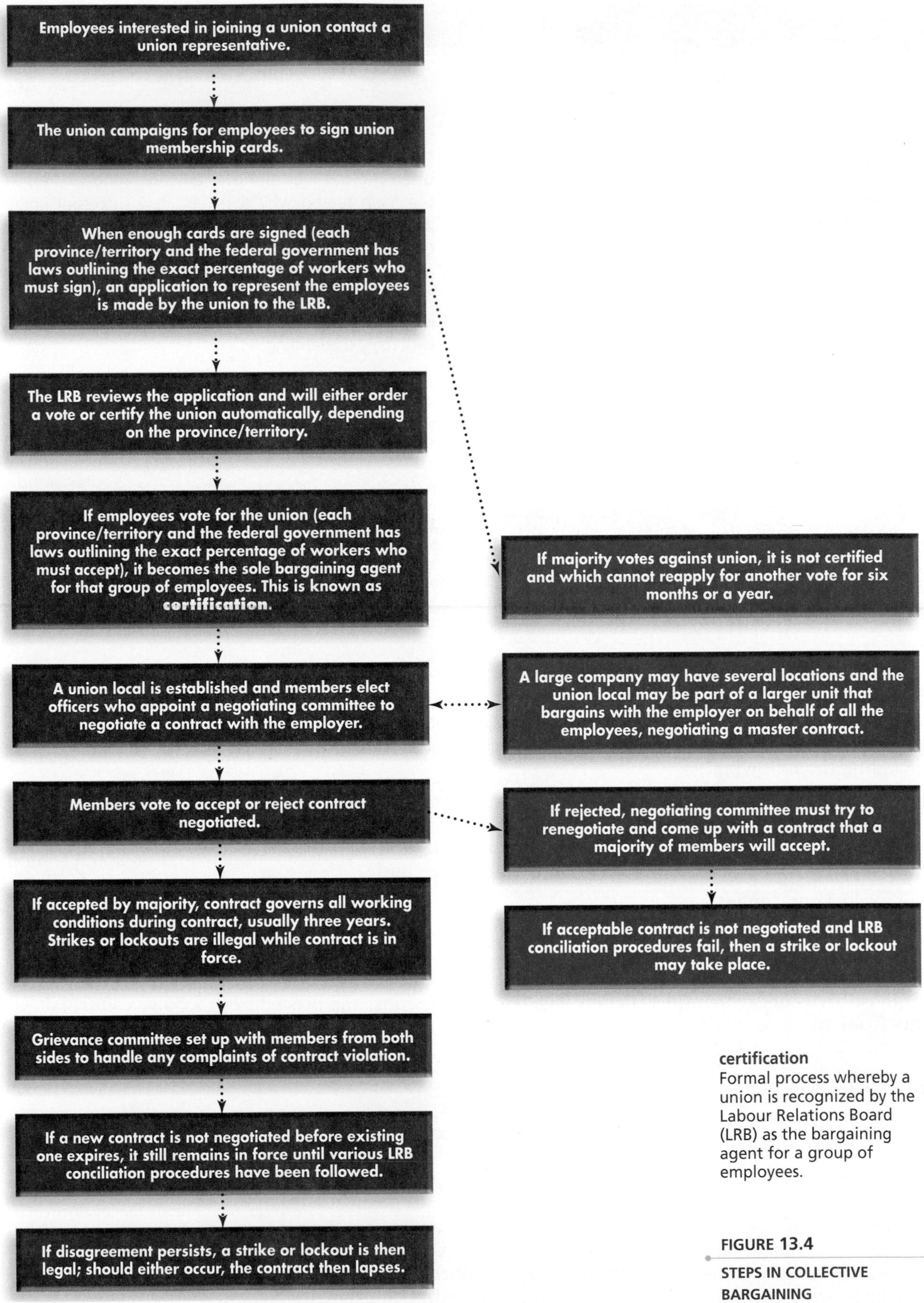

Employees interested in joining a union contact a union representative.

The union campaigns for employees to sign union membership cards.

When enough cards are signed (each province/territory and the federal government has laws outlining the exact percentage of workers who must sign), an application to represent the employees is made by the union to the LRB.

The LRB reviews the application and will either order a vote or certify the union automatically, depending on the province/territory.

If employees vote for the union (each province/territory and the federal government has laws outlining the exact percentage of workers who must accept), it becomes the sole bargaining agent for that group of employees. This is known as **certification**.

If majority votes against union, it is not certified and which cannot reapply for another vote for six months or a year.

A union local is established and members elect officers who appoint a negotiating committee to negotiate a contract with the employer.

A large company may have several locations and the union local may be part of a larger unit that bargains with the employer on behalf of all the employees, negotiating a master contract.

Members vote to accept or reject contract negotiated.

If rejected, negotiating committee must try to renegotiate and come up with a contract that a majority of members will accept.

If accepted by majority, contract governs all working conditions during contract, usually three years. Strikes or lockouts are illegal while contract is in force.

If acceptable contract is not negotiated and LRB conciliation procedures fail, then a strike or lockout may take place.

Grievance committee set up with members from both sides to handle any complaints of contract violation.

If a new contract is not negotiated before existing one expires, it still remains in force until various LRB conciliation procedures have been followed.

If disagreement persists, a strike or lockout is then legal; should either occur, the contract then lapses.

certification
Formal process whereby a union is recognized by the Labour Relations Board (LRB) as the bargaining agent for a group of employees.

FIGURE 13.4

STEPS IN COLLECTIVE BARGAINING

As you can see, the process is quite regulated and controlled, so that employers and employees as well as unions have to follow a strict procedure to ensure that everybody is playing by the rules. The procedure is democratic, and, as in any election, the minority has to accept the majority's decision. The actual contract is quite complex, covering a wide range of topics. We will look at some of the major ones shortly.

Objectives of Organized Labour

The objectives of unions frequently change because of shifts in social and economic trends. For example, in the 1970s the primary objective of unions was to obtain additional pay and benefits for their members. Throughout the 1980s, objectives shifted toward issues related to job security and union recognition. In the 1990s and early 2000s, unions again focused on job security, but the issue of global competition and its effects often took centre stage. As mentioned earlier, unions were a major opponent of NAFTA, passed by Parliament in 1994: they feared that their members would lose their jobs to low-wage workers in other countries. Today, we are seeing increasing emphasis on skills-upgrading as the basis of job security. In some industries, union jobs have been declining due to outsourcing. Unions recognize that they must work closely with management if jobs are going to be kept within our borders. Having a skilled and productive workforce is one major way to do this.

The **negotiated labour–management agreement,** more informally referred to as the labour contract, sets the tone and clarifies the terms and conditions under which management and organized labour will function over a specific period. Negotiations cover a wide range of topics and can often take a long time. Figure 13.5 provides a list of topics commonly negotiated by labour and management during contract talks.

Trade unions generally insist that contracts contain a union security clause. A **union security clause** stipulates that employees who reap benefits from a union must either officially join or at least pay dues to the union. There are basically four types of clauses:

negotiated labour–management agreement (labour contract)
Agreement that sets the tone and clarifies the terms under which management and labour agree to function over a period of time.

union security clause
Provision in a negotiated labour–management agreement that stipulates that employees who benefit from a union must either officially join or at least pay dues to the union.

FIGURE 13.5

ISSUES IN A NEGOTIATED LABOUR–MANAGEMENT AGREEMENT

Labour and management often meet to discuss and clarify the terms that specify employees' functions within the company. The topics listed in this figure are typically discussed during these meetings.

1. Management rights
2. Union recognition
3. Union security clause
4. Strikes and lockouts
5. Union activities and responsibilities
   a. Dues checkoff
   b. Union notices
   c. Shop stewards on the floor
6. Wages
   a. Wage structure
   b. Shift differentials
   c. Wage incentives
   d. Bonuses
   e. Piecework conditions
   f. Tiered wage structures
7. Hours of work and time-off policies
   a. Regular hours of work
   b. Holidays
   c. Vacation policies
   d. Overtime regulations
   e. Leaves of absence
   f. Break periods
   g. Flextime
   h. Mealtime allotments
8. Job rights and seniority principles
   a. Seniority regulations
   b. Transfer policies and bumping
   c. Promotions
   d. Layoffs and recall procedures
   e. Job bidding and posting
9. Discharge and discipline
   a. Suspension
   b. Conditions for discharge
10. Grievance procedures
    a. Arbitration agreement
    b. Mediation procedures
11. Employee benefits, health, and welfare

closed shop
A workplace in which all new hires must already be union members.

union shop
A workplace in which the employer is free to hire anybody, but the recruit must then join the union within a short period, perhaps a month.

agency shop (Rand formula)
A workplace in which a new employee is not required to join the union but must pay union dues. This historic formula was devised by Justice Rand.

open shop
A workplace in which employees are free to join or not join the union and to pay or not pay union dues.

check-off clause
A contract clause requiring the employer to deduct union dues from employees' pay and remit them to a union.

1. The one favoured by unions is called a **closed shop,** which means that all new hires must be union members. In effect, hiring is done through the union. Unemployed members of the union register for employment or show up daily at a union hiring hall.

2. One step down is a union shop. In a **union shop,** the employer is free to hire anybody but the recruit must then join the union within a short period, perhaps a month.

3. One of the most common conditions is an **agency shop,** which is based on the **Rand formula.** The new employee is not required to join the union but must pay union dues. This historic formula was devised by Supreme Court Justice Rand in 1946 when he arbitrated a major case involving Ford of Canada Ltd. The argument for this requirement is that all employees who benefit from a contract signed by the union should help to pay for the costs of maintaining that union—its officers, union expenses, negotiating committee, shop stewards, and so forth.

4. The hiring condition least popular with unions and the one favoured by employers is the **open shop,** where employees are free to join or not join the union and to pay or not pay union dues.

Regardless of which hiring condition prevails, the contract usually contains a **check-off clause** requiring the employer to deduct union dues from employees and pay and remit them to the union (except for nonmembers in case 4). It would obviously be a lot harder to collect union dues individually.

Success of Trade Unions

How successful have trade unions been in negotiating improved wages and benefits for their members? Figure 13.6 summarizes some of the advantages of

FIGURE 13.6

ADVANTAGES OF JOINING A UNION

AVERAGE HOURLY EARNINGS	UNION MEMBERS	NON-UNION MEMBERS	UNION ADVANTAGE
All employees	$19.46	$15.31	$4.15 per hour
Full-time employees	$19.86	$16.58	$3.28 per hour
Part-time employees	$16.81	$10.20	$6.61 per hour

BENEFITS	UNION MEMBERS	NON-UNION MEMBERS	UNION MEMBERS WIN BIG IN EVERY BENEFIT
Employees covered by pension/group RRSP	83%	33%	Union
Sick leave	77%	45%	Union
Supplemental health care plan	84%	45%	Union
Paid vacation leave entitlement	84%	65%	Union
Paid vacation 4 weeks or more	60%	30%	Union
Dental care plan coverage	77%	45%	Union

Source: www.caw.ca, September 28, 2004 (based on Statistics Canada 2001 data).

joining a union. This figure supports that higher average hourly wages and benefits are indeed one of the major benefits of joining a union.

In the future, the focus of union negotiations will most likely shift as issues such as child and elder care, worker retraining, two-tiered wage plans, outsourcing ➤ **P. 269** ◄, employee empowerment ➤ **P. 19** ◄, and even integrity and honesty testing further challenge union members' rights in the workplace. Unions also intend to carefully monitor immigration policies and global agreements to see that Canadian jobs are not lost.[19]

Trade unions play a key workplace role in countries other than Canada as well. In Europe organized labour is a major force throughout the continent. The Reaching Beyond Our Borders box discusses a formidable challenge the European Union faces with its unions as it works toward the goals of regional unity and a single currency, the euro.

Critical Thinking

You have seen how the nature of work is changing. Companies are downsizing and modernizing, so fewer workers are to be found in large workplaces. More and more people are working out of their homes. What adjustments do you think unions will have to make to accommodate these new developments? What signs are there that they are making such changes? Will the nature of unions change? Do you foresee fast-food chains becoming more unionized?

Resolving Labour–Management Disputes

The rights of labour and management are outlined in the negotiated labour–management agreement. Upon acceptance by both sides, the agreement becomes a guide to work relations between union members and managers. However, signing the agreement doesn't necessarily end the employee–management negotiations. There are sometimes differences concerning interpretations of the labour–management agreement. For example, managers may interpret a certain clause in the agreement to mean that they are free to select who works overtime. Union members may interpret the same clause to mean that managers must select employees for overtime on the basis of employee seniority. If controversies such as this cannot be resolved between the two parties, employees may file a grievance. A **grievance** is a formal protest by an individual employee or a union when they believe a particular management decision breaches the union contract.

Companies in which relations between management and union are poor or deteriorating usually have a big backlog of unresolved grievances. This is not good for the morale of the employees and, if allowed to continue for any length of time, will ultimately result in lower productivity. Where relations are good, there are few grievances and those that arise are quickly settled.

Overtime rules, promotions, layoffs, transfers, job assignments, and so forth are generally sources of employee grievances. Handling such grievances demands a good deal of contact between union officials and managers. Grievances, however, do not imply that the company has broken the law or the labour agreement. In fact, the vast majority of grievances are negotiated and resolved by **shop stewards** (union officials who work permanently in an organization that represent employee interests in a daily basis) and supervisory-level managers. However, if a grievance is not settled at this level, formal grievance procedures will begin.

grievance
A formal protest by an individual employee or a union when they believe a particular management decision breaches the union contract.

shop stewards
Union officials who work permanently in an organization and represent employee interests on a daily basis.

Reaching Beyond Our Borders

The Euro Strikes Out with the Unions

On January 1, 2002, cash registers rang out across Europe officially launching the euro, the new joint currency of 12 member nations of the European Union (EU). Businesses boasted that they would save billions on the currency conversions that had to be made prior to the euro. Other supporters cheered the euro as an economic elixir that would improve European competitiveness and provide an economic edge in the global economy. Well, the cheering has stopped, at least among many of the trade unions in the EU.

The euro lays bare comparative wage costs across Europe. Trade unions (and some economists) believe this will inevitably lead to greater competition among workers in the EU. The problem is that the hourly wage rate varies greatly among the member countries of the EU. Wages in France are about 25 percent below those in Germany but 30 percent above those in Spain. Ireland has labour costs double those of Portugal but one-third lower than those of the Netherlands. It's these wage differences that cause unions to fear that competitive pressures will encourage companies to go from country to country to test how far down they can get wages. Trade unions in high-wage countries such as Germany, the Netherlands, and Belgium view the presence of a single currency as a threat to their members.

IG Metall, a powerful German trade union with 2.8 million members, insists that German manufacturing jobs are already migrating to Portugal, where workers work longer hours and are paid less than one-third of what German workers earn. Reiner Hoffman, director of the European Trade Union Institute in Brussels, argues, "Trade unions do not want to fall into a trap in which we compete with each other in Europe to undercut wages. This is what the euro could force us to do."

For the first time in European history, there have been discussions of transnational collective bargaining to reach common salary and benefits among union members. However, even the most strident labour leaders admit that common salary and benefit policies would be difficult to implement across national borders. Plus, low-wage nations are less than eager for such talks because they hope that their low wages will help attract new businesses and new jobs.

Christoph Schmidt, a professor at the University of Heidelberg and specialist on European wage statistics, believes that wage competition will get even stronger. Still, the unions are firm in their resolve and promise to fight on toward common salaries that would protect current high-wage workers and press countries to compete for new business on the basis that their workers are productive rather than cheap.

Sources: Laura D'andrea Tyson, "Why Europe Is Even More Sluggish Than the U.S.," *Business Week,* January 13, 2003, p. 26; John Schmid, "Euro Weakens Union's Iron Grip on Germany," *International Herald Tribune*, March 25, 2002; Portugal's Labor Cost Lowest in the EU," Xinhua News Agency, March 6, 2003; Michael Heise Heise, "Europe Misses the Point," *Newsweek International,* January 27, 2003, p. 39.

Figure 13.7 indicates all the steps, specified by the contract for a plant, in the processing of a grievance. Typically there are five or six levels in this procedure. If the grievance cannot be settled at one level it moves up to the next level. The final step is an outside arbitrator or arbitration board (arbitration will be discussed after mediation). But in practice this is quite rare. Many complaints are settled informally and never put in writing.

Mediation

bargaining zone
Range of options between the initial and final offer that each party will consider before negotiations dissolve or reach an impasse.

mediation
The use of a third party, called a mediator, who encourages both sides in a dispute to continue negotiating and often makes suggestions for resolving the dispute.

During the negotiation process, there is generally what's called a **bargaining zone,** which is a range of options between the initial and final offer that each party will consider before negotiations dissolve or reach an impasse. If labour–management negotiators aren't able to agree on alternatives within this bargaining zone, meditation may be necessary. **Mediation** is the use of a third party, called a mediator, who encourages both sides in a dispute to consider negotiating and often makes suggestions for resolving the dispute. However,

	MANAGEMENT	UNION
Stage 1	First-level supervisor	Shop steward
Stage 2	Second-level supervisor	Chief steward
Stage 3	Plant manager	Chief grievance officer
Stage 4	Director of industrial relations	National or international union official
Stage 5	CEO or president	President of union or central labour body
Stage 6	Dispute goes to arbitration (quite rare)	

FIGURE 13.7

STAGES IN PROCESSING GRIEVANCES

The representatives from each side are listed with the stages.

arbitration
The process of resolving all disputes, not only grievances, through an outside, impartial third party. The decision is binding.

it's important to remember that mediators evaluate facts in the dispute and then make suggestions, not decisions. Elected officials (current and past), attorneys, and professors are often called on to serve as mediators in labour disputes.

Mediators must possess certain important qualities to undertake such a difficult task. After all, they are attempting to bring together parties that are far apart or that may be hardly talking to each other. They obviously must be well respected, have excellent negotiating skills, and be patient and determined. It is a high-pressure job involving long sessions and sometimes around-the-clock meetings.

The Federal Mediation and Conciliation service provides federal mediators when requested by both sides in a dispute. For example, two mediators were appointed in the dispute between Telus Communications Inc. and the Telecommunications Workers Union in January 2004. The collective agreement between both parties, covering 10,000 communications employees, expired December 31, 2000.[20]

Arbitration

A more extreme approach used to resolve conflict is arbitration. **Arbitration** is the process of resolving all disputes, not only grievances, through an outside, impartial third party. The arbitrator renders a decision that is binding on both disputing parties. The arbitrator may be a single person or a panel of arbitrators that is acceptable to both sides. The arbitrator decides in favour of one of the parties.

Arbitration may be *voluntary*: both sides decide to submit their case to an arbitrator. Or it may be *compulsory*: imposed by the government or by Parliament or a provincial legislature. Compulsory arbitration usually occurs in a major or prolonged strike with serious consequences for the public. Usually, nongrievance arbitration (say, for contract disputes) is voluntary and grievance arbitration is compulsory.

It should be noted that both arbitration and mediation can be difficult, long, and costly procedures, especially when both sides are locked into rigid positions. That is why negotiators from both sides usually try to settle their differences before resorting to these steps.

Sometimes, negotiators fail to reach an agreement and want to "snap each other's heads off." If that happens, it often makes sense to enlist the services of an arbitrator to resolve the impasse. An arbitrator must be acceptable to both sides and the decision reached is binding. What type person would make a good arbitrator?

Progress Assessment

- How do labour relations boards regulate labour–management relations?
- In the collective bargaining process, what happens after certification?
- What is the difference between arbitration and mediation?

TACTICS USED IN LABOUR–MANAGEMENT CONFLICTS

Because the media give a lot of attention to strikes, you might get the impression that this is the usual pattern of negotiations. But in reality, only a small fraction of contract negotiations between unions and management end in such bitter altercations. Let us examine what happens when an agreement is not reached. What tactics and strategies are available to each side?

Usually, the union is demanding some improvement in benefits, working conditions, job security, or pay increases. The employer usually offers less or very little or sometimes nothing. The union must take actions to try to force the employer to meet its demands. These actions may include such tactics as work-to-rule (working to the exact letter of the agreement), slowdowns, refusal to work overtime, and booking off sick. A favourite negotiating tactic of the police is to refuse to hand out tickets, thus reducing the flow of income to provincial or municipal governments that are unwilling to budge from their bargaining position.

If labour and management reach an impasse in collective bargaining and negotiations break down, either side or both sides may use specific tactics to enhance their position and perhaps sway public opinion. The primary tactics used by organized labour are the strike and the boycott. Unions might also use pickets and work slowdowns to get desired changes. Management, for its part, may implement lockouts, injunctions, and even strikebreakers. The following sections look briefly at each of these contrasting tactics.

Union Tactics

The strike has historically been the most potent tactic unions use to achieve their objectives in labour disputes. A **strike** is when workers collectively refuse to go to work. Strikes can attract public attention to a labour dispute and at times cause operations in a company to slow down or totally cease.

If union leaders feel that there is strong support among the members, they will call for a strike vote, which is a secret ballot authorizing the union leadership to call a strike. If the union gets a strong mandate—say, more than 80 percent in favour of a strike—they use this as a lever to convince management to accept their demands without actually going on strike. If management does not agree to union demands, the union will have to strike. Of course, if the secret ballot vote results in a slim majority (say, 55 percent) of employees approving a strike, union leaders will be hesitant to call a strike.

Before a strike can be called, all legal requirements must be met. In most jurisdictions in Canada, the union must first ask the government (through the Ministry of Labour) to appoint a conciliator. A conciliator has a certain amount of time to try to bring the parties together and to

strike
A union strategy in which workers refuse to go to work; the purpose is to further workers' objectives after an impasse in collective bargaining.

Bell Canada employees demonstrate in front of the Yellow Pages offices to further their contract demands. During a strike action, employees do not receive wages or a salary.

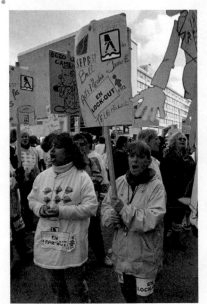

agree on a collective agreement. If the conciliator fails, the union is then in a legal position to strike. The employer is also free to declare a lockout (to be discussed later.)

Besides refusing to work, striking workers usually *picket* the place (or places) of employment. This means that they walk around the outside of the entrance to the organization carrying signs and talking with the public and the media about issues in the labour dispute. The aim of these picketers is to publicize the strike. While some picketers may try to discourage or prevent people, vehicles, materials, and products from going in and out of the location, it is important to note that picket obstruction is illegal. They usually allow management personnel through, after a delay. Unions also use picketing as an informational tool before going on strike. The purpose is to alert the public to an issue that is stirring labour's unrest even though no strike has been voted.

Unions also use boycotts as a means to obtain their objectives in a labour dispute. A **primary boycott** is when organized labour encourages both its members and the general public not to buy the products of a firm involved in a labour dispute. A **secondary boycott** is an attempt by labour to convince others to stop doing business with a firm that is the subject of a primary boycott. For example, a union can initiate a secondary boycott against a supermarket chain because the chain carries goods produced by a company that is the target of a primary boycott.

As a member of the Screen Actors Guild, Rob Schneider encouraged the public to boycott Procter & Gamble products when the company used nonunion workers in its commercials in place of striking members of the Screen Actors Guild. Boycotts or strikes are often used by unions if they fail to reach an agreement under collective bargaining. Why do unions and management typically work hard to prevent strikes?

Other Tactics

Union tactics include rotating strikes—on and off or alternating among different plants or cities—rather than a full-fledged strike in which all employees are off the job for the duration. With rotating strikes, employees still get some pay, which would not be the case in an all-out strike. Many unions build up a strike fund from union dues and use it to give their members strike pay, but that's usually a fraction of their normal wages. Sometimes, in important or long-lasting strikes, other unions will give moral or financial aid.

Management may announce layoffs or a shortened workweek and blame it on declining business. It may say the company is having trouble competing due to high labour costs. It may even adopt the lockout tactic (to be discussed below) when it seems less costly to close down and cease paying wages than to put up with slowdowns, rotating strikes, or work-to-rule union tactics, all of which can be very disruptive. This tactic may force the union to reduce its demands if individual members cannot do without an income for very long or if there is a weak strike-vote majority.

Remember that arbitration and mediation are always available to the parties in dispute. They may take advantage of these procedures before, during, or after a strike or lockout.

primary boycott
When a union encourages both its members and the general public not to buy the products of a firm involved in a labour dispute.

secondary boycott
An attempt by labour to convince others to stop doing business with a firm that is the subject of a primary boycott.

Battles for Public Support

In major cases where the public is affected—the postal service, nurses, doctors, teachers, transportation, telecommunication, and civil servants at all levels—each side plays a propaganda game to win the public to its side. It can be difficult for those not directly involved to really sort out the issues. Sometimes management, if it thinks the public is on its side and the union is perhaps not well organized or lacks strong support, will provoke the union into an unsuccessful strike, weakening the union's bargaining position.

Management Tactics

lockout
An attempt by management to put pressure on unions by temporarily closing the business.

Like labour, management also uses specific tactics to achieve its workplace goals. A **lockout** is an attempt by managers to put pressure on union workers by temporarily closing the business. If workers are not working, they are not paid. Clearly a strike is a weapon of last resort for unions, when all else fails. Similarly, management is reluctant to lock out its employees and call a halt to operations. No products, no profits.

Some lockouts have received a lot of attention. The lockout of National Basketball Association (NBA) players by the owners in June 1998 is one example. After six months of on-and-off negotiations, there was still no settlement in this bitter dispute. In December, the board of governors and the commissioner of basketball threatened to cancel the remaining season if no settlement was in place by January 7, 1999.[21] The dispute was finally resolved in February 1999 with everybody agreeing to a shortened season so that the playoffs could commence on time. We can see how important the public's attitude is in such conflicts by looking at the slogans the league used. Prior to the lockout the well-known NBA slogan was "I love the game." To win back public support after the lockout, the slogan became "I STILL love this game." The Dealing With Change box highlights another example of a lockout.

Sometimes, a company may try to bring in replacement workers (known as *scabs* by the union). These replacement workers (also called strikebreakers) are workers who are hired to do the jobs of striking employees until the labour dispute is resolved. This often leads to violence. Picketers mass in large numbers to block buses carrying these strikebreakers, threats are uttered, articles are thrown, vehicles may be attacked, and so on.

Some Canadian jurisdictions have legislation banning the use of replacement workers when a legal strike is in progress. Quebec has had such legislation in place since 1977, and British Columbia since 1993. Ontario brought in replacement-worker legislation in 1993, but it was repealed in 1995. Federally, this legislation has been in place since 1999. Quite often, management employees may continue to work and try to do some of the tasks formerly done by the striking workforce. Be sure to read the Making Ethical Decisions box dealing with this issue for further insight.

injunction
A court order directing someone to do something or to refrain from doing something.

If management's tactics are not successful, it may ask for police protection for the vehicles or ask the courts for an injunction. An **injunction** is a court order directing someone to do something or to refrain from doing something. Management has sought injunctions to order striking workers back to work, limit the number of pickets that can be used during a strike, or otherwise deal with actions that could be detrimental to the public welfare. Injunctions are not as commonly granted now as they used to be in the past.

There are restrictions on the right to strike of various levels of civil servants and quasi-government employees such as hospital workers and electric and telephone utility workers. The provinces and the federal government forbid some employees under their jurisdiction from striking. In other cases, certain minimum levels of service must be provided. For example, when the federal civil service went out on strike in the fall of 1991, employees of the customs service, prison guards, meat inspectors, airport firefighters, and certain other employees were not allowed to strike. When employees of the public bus system in Montreal went on strike in 1990, the provincial Essential Services Council decided what minimum level of services had to be provided during the strike. The same thing happened when Quebec nurses went on strike in 1999. In nearly all provinces, firefighters and police officers are not allowed to strike.

www.ilwu.org

Dealing With Change

Sitting on the Docks

Nobody wants to lose his or her job to new technology. More than 400 jobs were threatened in the fall of 2002 when shipping managers on the U.S. West Coast wanted to upgrade container-tracking technology with scanners and other computer-aided devices. Until then, containers being moved onboard ships and on docks were tracked by longshore clerks who manually entered information into the shippers' databases. With their members' jobs at risk, the dockworkers union went into action—or, as the managers saw it, the union went into *inaction*. Shipping managers accused the dockworkers of intentionally slowing work down to a crawl and thus interrupting the flow of goods into the United States. The union denied the claims, saying that they simply told their workers to work at a safer speed since five dockworkers died in work-related accidents earlier in the year.

The management initiated a lockout of all dockworkers in response to the work slowdown. Shipping on the West Coast came to a complete halt. With billions of dollars' worth of perishable goods rotting on ships and countless other goods unable to be delivered to shore, the U.S. economy was in danger of losing $1–$2 billion a day. The critical Christmas shopping season was about to begin with literal boatloads of merchandise stranded at sea rather than stocking store shelves. The Bush administration considered this economic loss a risk to national security and therefore invoked the Taft-Hartley Act. Dockworkers were ordered back to work, and both sides were ordered back to the bargaining table under the Taft-Hartley Act's 80-day cooling-off period.

After the 12-day lockout and months of collective bargaining, the International Longshore and Warehouse Union ratified a new six-year contract. The agreement allows shippers to use the new technology. Although 400 jobs will be eliminated, the affected workers will be retrained for other positions rather than being let go. The union maintains control over the remaining positions as well as any new ones created via the technology. While salary increases were not a major issue, the agreement raised salaries approximately 12 percent, making the average dockworker's salary around $90,000 a year. Pension benefits increased 60 percent, and employers are required to absorb the total bill for the skyrocketing health care costs they had hoped to have the workers help cover.

"I think both sides, in very general terms, got what they wanted to get," said William Gould, former chair of the National Labor Relations Board. "The unions got job security and enhanced income for those who are contemplating retirement, and the employers got technological innovation." And since dockworkers unloaded enough products to stock the nation's stores in time for the holiday shopping season, most shoppers got what they wanted for Christmas.

Sources: Paul Nyhan, "Dockworkers Vote to Ratify Contract by 89% Margin," *Seattle Post-Intelligencer,* January 23, 2003; David Bacon, "Dockworkers' Contract Postpones Crucial Jurisdiction Questions," *Labor Notes,* February 2003; and "West Coast Dockworkers Vote on Contract," Reuters Business, January 6, 2003.

www.ethicsweb.ca/resources

Making Ethical Decisions

Crossing the Line or Double-Crossing?

Assume you read over the weekend that More-4-Less, a local grocery chain in your town, is seeking workers to replace members of the Commercial Food Workers Union who are currently on strike against the company. Some of the students at your school are employed at More-4-Less and are supporting the strike, as are several people employed by the company in your neighbourhood. More-4-Less argues that its management has made a fair offer to the union and

that the demands of the workers are clearly excessive and could ruin the company. More-4-Less is offering an attractive wage rate and flexible schedules to workers willing to cross the picket line and come to work during the strike. As a student, you could certainly use the job and the extra money for tuition and expenses. What would you do? What will be the consequences of your decision? Is your choice ethical? What are the ethical dilemmas faced by unions? Give some examples. How do these differ from those faced by management?

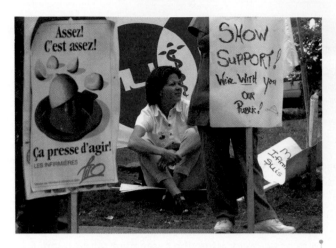

This nurse is taking a break as her colleagues walk the picket line during an illegal strike staged in 1999 by Quebec nurses.

Legislating Strikers Back to Work

Governments have the power to end a particular strike by passing specific legislation to that effect. Provincial and federal governments have done this from time to time to end strikes by teachers, nurses, postal workers, bus drivers, and others. Governments pass back-to-work legislation when they believe they have enough support among the population for such action because of serious hardship to businesses or individuals. For example, the British Columbia government passed legislation in 2001 forcing an end to a four-month strike by 3,500 members of the Vancouver-area public transit authority. The Quebec and Saskatchewan governments did the same when the nurses went on strike in 2001. This also occurred in Nova Scotia.

Back-to-work legislation is a denial of the legal right to strike, so it is to a certain extent a restriction of the democratic rights of individuals. Consequently, there is often much controversy about such legislation. It is rarely used to deal with strikes against private businesses. If union members remain on strike after they have been legislated back to work they are engaging in an illegal strike and are subject to punishment, as are all lawbreakers. In the case of the Quebec nurses the union had to pay substantial fines.

HOW ETHICAL ARE UNIONS?

An oft-heard opinion is that unions are too powerful in Canada. This opinion is demonstrated by the inconvenience caused by strikes that disrupt public services from time to time. We also hear charges that some union leaders are more interested in building and protecting their little empires than in protecting their members' interests. Added to this list of criticisms is the charge of a lack of democracy in union operations and even some cases of corruption. It is important to maintain a proper perspective when considering these and other charges against unions. An overall assessment is difficult in this complex situation.

We should remember that occasionally businesses are accused of illegally trying to fix prices. They are also charged with polluting the environment or breaking environmental laws. Companies that provide food or pharmaceutical products are sometimes accused of playing with people's health. Some of these companies are found guilty of the charges. Obviously this does not mean that all managements should be condemned. Similarly, we should exercise caution when evaluating corruption or careerism in unions. We should not forget unions' significant achievements of improving the living standards and working conditions of millions of Canadians.

The Future of Unions and Labour–Management Relations

Many new labour–management issues have emerged that affect trade unions and management relations. Increased global competition, advancing technology, and the changing nature of work have threatened or altered the jobs of many workers. To save jobs, many unions have granted concessions, or

givebacks, to management. In such acts, union members give back previous gains from labour negotiations. For example, the CAW Local 2002 agreed to $150 million in payroll savings over each of the next six years in order to give Air Canada the funding relief it needed to complete its restructuring.[22] The Air Canada flight attendants, members of CUPE's Airline Division, also agreed to concessions that will save the airline $1.1 billion a year for six years.[23]

To grow, unions will have to include more white-collar, female, and foreign-born workers than they have traditionally included. The AFL-CIO, for example, plans to specifically target membership campaigns to women in relatively low-paying fields, such as health care and garment sewing. Other union efforts are focused on organizing contingent workers ➤**P. 354**◀ like freelancers, temporary employees, telecommuters, and high-tech consultants. It's safe to assume that the role of unions in the 21st century is likely to be quite different from their role in the past. Union leaders and members are aware that firms must remain competitive with foreign firms. Organized labour knows it must do its best to maintain competitiveness. In the future, unions and management will face compromises and confrontations. In many ways, trade unions have already taken on a new role in assisting management in training workers, redesigning jobs, and assimilating the 21st-century workforce; that is, unions are helping recruit and train foreign workers, unskilled workers, and others who need special help in adapting to the job requirements of the new economy. Business has witnessed such cooperation already at companies like Saturn, where the union has taken a leadership role with management in making things happen.

Unions, undoubtedly, will also face confrontations and disagreements with management in the first decade of the 2000s. Organized labour, for example, helped lead the charge for corporate governance reform after the corporate scandals involving Enron, WorldCom, and other companies in the early 2000s.

The rewards unions can expect for cooperating with management include improved job security, profit sharing, and sometimes increased wages. Management for its part can expect a productive, dedicated workforce to handle the challenges of growing competition. How organized labour and management handle these major challenges may well define the future for trade unions.

givebacks
Concessions made by union members to management; gains from labour negotiations are given back to management to help employers remain competitive and thereby save jobs.

- Why do the objectives of unions change over time?
- What are the major tactics used by unions and by management to assert their power in contract negotiations?
- What kinds of workers are joining unions today, and why are they joining?

Progress Assessment

CURRENT EMPLOYEE–MANAGEMENT TOPICS

This is an interesting time in the history of employee–management relations. Organizations are involved in outsourcing ➤**P. 269**◀, technology change, and global expansion. In Chapter 12, you were introduced to some changes that employers are implementing in the workplace to try to attract and retain valued employees in such a competitive environment. Some examples included flexible work schedules and cafeteria-style benefits packages. Government initiatives, such as employment equity, were also discussed.

I'm a fighter...
...for an active life
...for work that works for me
...for human rights and everyone's right to a decent life

Carol McShagne, frontline worker, union and human rights activist.

Disability doesn't stop me. Discrimination can.

Canadian Labour Congress
Congrès du travail du Canada   CLC Disability Rights Working Group

Unions are increasingly negotiating disability rights clauses in their collective agreements. Is there such a clause in your place of employment?

The government has eliminated some social benefits to workers. For example, employment insurance eligibility requirements are stricter today than they were 10 years ago. In other instances, the government is taking a more active role in mandating what benefits and assurances businesses must provide to workers. The extension of maternity-leave benefits from six months to one year in 2001 and the implementation of a new compassionate care program in 2004 are just two such instances.

It is important to note that *all* employees are protected under the Employment Standards Act. Recall that this Act covers issues such as minimum wage, holiday pay, and so on. In a non-union environment, if an employer violates the Act it is up to the employee to file a complaint. An employee may seek advice and assistance from an officer of the Ministry of Labour in the province where he or she works. The employee can also contact the Canadian Human Rights Commission or a Human Resources Development Canada office, where he or she can talk to a federal government labour affairs officer.[24]

Union supporters point out that a labour contract would further protect workers, as the union would represent the employee if there were a breach of the Act or the labour contract. If an employee is not part of a trade union, there is no legal contract with the employer.[25]

Employees today are raising questions about fairness and workplace benefits. They are looking increasingly at company policies as they apply to workplace discrimination (e.g., wages and sexual orientation), sexual harassment, and mandatory testing (e.g., HIV, alcohol, and drug-testing). Three other areas that are increasingly in the news are executive compensation, childcare, and elder care. Let us briefly look at each of these areas.

Executive Compensation

Workplace.ca is a gateway to Canadian management and workplace resources. It provides tools to create and use successful management and human resource strategies.

When considering the year 2003, one need look no further than the total direct compensation (base salary plus annual bonus plus long-term incentive) received by some of Canada's top executives. Is it out of line for Frank Stronach, chair of Magna Corporation, to make $52.14 million in total direct compensation? Or for Richard Harrington, president and CEO of Thomson Corp., to receive a base salary of $1.93 million? Or for J. R. Shaw, executive chair of Shaw Communications, to receive an annual bonus of $6.33 million?

Employees can visit www.workrights.ca to find out about work issues and salary comparisons. Other topics include finding a job, getting paid, health and safety, human rights, losing a job, and making a complaint.

In Chapter 2, we explained that the free-market system is built on incentives that allow top executives to make such large amounts—or more. Today, however, the government, boards of directors, shareholders, unions, and employees are challenging this principle and arguing that executive compensation has gotten out of line.

In the past, an executive's compensation and bonuses were generally determined by the firm's profitability or an increase in its stock price. The assumption in using such incentives is that the CEO will improve the performance of the company and raise the price of the firm's stock. Today, most executives receive stock options (the ability to buy company stock at a set price at a later date) as part of their compensation. Many believe that a problem arises when executives are compensated with stock options and the shareholders or employees are not—or worse, when executives sell their stock at a high price and then the stock collapses, leaving shareholders in the lurch.[26]

For example, Robert Milton, CEO of Air Canada, was offered a compensation package providing some $21 million worth of shares, to be paid over four years, by Victor Li of Trinity.[27] This transaction never occurred, as Trinity's offer to purchase Air Canada expired. However, the damage was done: many Air Canada employees were outraged to hear of this retention bonus. They were angry given the concessions they had made due to Air Canada's bankruptcy-protection status. Subsequent contract negotiations for further employee concessions were delayed due to this anger and mistrust.

In a different example, in Nortel's fiscal year 2000, then-CEO John Roth took home $71 million in total compensation. Most of this included stock-option gains that he realized when he sold his shares. In the same year, Nortel placed last in *Report On Business* magazine's list of most profitable companies, posting a $3-billion loss.[28] Roth has been criticized for exercising options worth $135 million before the company's downward spiral.[29] You can imagine the anger of shareholders. How about those thousands of employees who lost their jobs as the company tried to restructure itself back to profitability?

These examples are not rare. In 2003 and the first two months of 2004, Power Financial Corp. CEO Robert Gratton cashed out 5.28 million stock options for a gain of $215 million; at Biovail Corp., CEO Eugene Melnyk made a total of $226 million on his stock options in 2000–2002 combined.[30]

What's even more confusing is that a CEO whose poor performance forced him or her to resign can still walk away with lofty compensation. For example, CEO Richard McGinn of Lucent Technologies was rewarded with $12.5 million for getting fired.[31] Many CEOs have also walked away with fat retainers, consulting contracts, and lavish perks when they retired.

Noted management consultant Peter Drucker has criticized executive pay levels since the mid-1980s, when he suggested that CEOs should not earn more than 20 times the salary of the company's lowest-paid employee. Many companies have clearly ignored this advice. Various figures for the United States have pegged the average CEO pay at anywhere from 300 to 500 times the level of the average hourly worker's pay in 2002.[32]

As global competition intensifies, looking at what executives in other countries earn provides another point of view. In Japan, CEOs do not generally receive stock options. American CEOs typically earn two to three times as much as executives in Canada and Europe. It is worth noting that European companies often have workers who sit on the board of directors according to a process called co-determination. Since boards set executive pay, this could be a reason why the imbalance between starting pay and top pay is less for European executives than for their U.S. counterparts.[33]

According to Ken Hugessen, a consultant on executive compensation and related government consultant of Mercer Human Resource Consulting in Toronto, "pay has been grossly out of line with shareholder experience. Shareholders have complained to directors, who are becoming more responsive to shareholders." Historically, says Hugessen, executive pay levels were decided by management with a "thin veneer" of involvement from the board's compensation committee. As a result of corporate scandals, there is now a spotlight on CEOs setting their own pay, and compensation committees are now taking charge.[34]

The Report on Business publishes *Canada's Power Book,* a guide to corporate performance in Canada. To find out the pay of Canada's top executives, visit www.globeinvestor. com/series/top1000/ and click on Best Paid Executives.

Today the CEO of a major corporation makes 411 times what the average hourly worker earns. This bounty does not include additional job perks that would make a Roman emperor feel neglected. Pay consultant Graef Crystal places a large part of the blame on boards of directors that routinely act as rubber stamps for CEOs. What do you think would be a fair system of compensation for CEOs? Should workers have input?

In a study by Mercer, directors' pay is also revealed to be increasing. Greater responsibility and heavier workloads have caused many Canadian companies to offer higher retainers and fees. The average annual retainer paid to directors in 2003 was $32,663.[35] Stock options are declining in popularity for both executives and directors, as many see them as distancing management's interests from shareholders.[36]

It's important to recognize, however, that many executives are responsible for multibillion-dollar corporations and work 70-plus hours a week. Many can show that their decisions turned around potential problems into success and rewards for employees and shareholders. Clearly, there is no easy answer to the question of what is fair compensation for executives, but it's a safe bet that many changes are likely to take place in the 2000s.

Childcare

Childcare became an increasingly important workplace issue in the 1990s and promises to remain a workplace concern in the 21st century. Questions involving responsibilities for childcare subsidies, childcare programs, and even parental leave are topics that promise to be debated in the private and public sectors of the economy. Many workers strongly question workplace benefits for parents, and argue that single workers and single-income families should not subsidize childcare for dual-income families. Although men are increasingly shouldering childcare responsibility, most of the responsibility still falls on women. This often leads to greater stress and absenteeism in the workplace. Employers are increasingly concerned as businesses lose millions annually in lost productivity. Employee childcare also raises the controversial workplace question of who should pay for childcare services.

The number of companies that offer childcare as an employee benefit is growing. *Working Mother* magazine highlighted companies such as Colgate-Palmolive, IBM, and General Mills as being particularly sympathetic to working mothers.[37] Other large firms that offer extensive childcare programs include Johnson & Johnson, American Express, and Campbell Soup. A few companies even provide emergency childcare services for employees whose children are ill or whose regular childcare arrangements are disrupted.

As the number of single-parent and two-income households continues to grow in the 21st century, childcare is certain to remain a hotly debated employee–management issue. However, a new workplace storm is brewing over an issue employees and managers have not faced in times past: elder care. Let's look at this next.

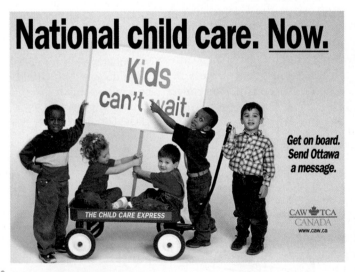

The CAW is lobbying the government for a national childcare program. Some companies already recognize the need to adjust to the changing demands of the workforce by offering employees access to on-site childcare centres.

Elder Care

The workforce in Canada is aging. While baby boomers will not have to concern themselves with finding childcare for their children, they will confront another problem: how to care for older parents and other relatives. In the future, more workers are expected to be involved in the time-consuming and stressful task of caring for an aging relative. Current estimates suggest that companies are seeing reduced productivity, and increased absenteeism and turnover from employees who are responsible for aging relatives.[38] Denise Talbot-White, a gerontology specialist for MetLife Mature Market Institute, suggests that elder care is the childcare of the new millennium.

Employees with elder care responsibilities need information on medical, legal, and insurance issues, as well as the full support of their supervisors and company. This issue may require some employees to move to flextime, telecommuting, part-time employment, or job sharing.[39] Some firms have reacted to the effect of elder care on their workforce. At Boeing and AT&T, employees are offered elder care programs that include telephone hotlines workers can call to seek help or counselling for older relatives. Unfortunately, few companies (large, medium, or small) now provide any type of elder care programs or benefits. "What often puts elder care on the agenda," according to Anne Martin-Matthews, a professor of family studies at the University of Guelph, who did a survey on this issue, "is when a (senior) executive … has a mother who breaks her hip." That's when the company's traditional evaluation of what a good employee is begins to be questioned.[40]

Andrew Scharlach, a professor of aging at the University of California–Berkeley, expects costs to companies to rise even higher as more and more experienced and high-ranking employees become involved in caring for older parents and other relatives. His arguments make sense. Since the jobs older workers hold are often more critical to a company than those held by younger workers (who are most affected by childcare problems), many businesses will see the cost of elder care skyrocket. Already some firms note that transfer and promotion decisions are especially difficult for employees whose elderly parents need ongoing care. Whereas managers might have said that the first one in the office in the morning and the last to leave at night is the best employee, they are now being encouraged to focus on output rather than time spent at the office. So an employee (often a woman) who works fewer hours because of elder care (or childcare) responsibilities is not automatically rated below best. What is accomplished, rather than when it is done, becomes more important in progressive companies.

You and Unions

Do you think that unions are still necessary? We are fortunate to be living in a democratic country where free and private enterprise is the vital feature of our capitalist economic system. We believe that all citizens have the right to do what they can, within legal and ethical limits, to better themselves. Improving your financial situation is an admired goal, and those who do so are usually seen as good examples.

If you select the entrepreneurial route, you will try to build a successful company by providing a necessary service or product in a manner that your customers appreciate. If you are successful, you will ultimately accumulate profits and personal wealth and financial security for yourself and your family. One of the costs of doing business that you will be keeping an eye on is wages, salaries, and benefits paid to employees. Will you want a well-trained, smart workforce capable of keeping up with the rapid pace of technological advances, or will you want your employees to work "cheap"? Will you consider unions nothing but a hindrance?

Suppose you do not see yourself as an entrepreneur and instead go the employee route. Imagine yourself 10 years down the road: you have a partner and two children and are now a computer specialist working for a large company in a nonmanagerial role. Will you seek the best salary you can possibly get? How about working hours? Your partner also works and you need flexible arrangements to be able to spend time with your children and deliver them to school and various other activities. How about overtime demands on the job that cut into time with your children? Will you have adequate, affordable childcare?

Can you and your co-workers arrange these and a host of other issues—bonuses, sick leave, termination pay, pensions, retraining, holidays, and more—on a personal basis? Or are you better off with an organization—a union—to represent all of you in making proper contractual arrangements with your employer so that your rights and obligations as well as the employer's are clearly spelled out?

What about all the workers who are less skilled than you are? Some are illiterate and others did not graduate from high school. Hundreds of thousands of employees have lost their jobs in the past decade through no fault of their own. Do they need a strong union to protect their interests? Hopefully this chapter has given you an understanding of the importance of employee–management issues.

In summary, firms that have healthy employee–management relations have a better chance to prosper than those that don't. As managers, taking a proactive approach is the best way to ensure workable employee–management environments. The proactive manager anticipates potential problems and works toward resolving those issues before they get out of hand—a good lesson to remember.

Progress Assessment

- What is the relationship between injunctions and picketing?
- When is back-to-work legislation used?
- What are some issues related to childcare and elder care? How are companies addressing these issues?

Critical Thinking

Top executives' high pay creates tremendous incentives for lower-level executives to work hard to get those jobs. Their high pay also creates resentment among workers, some shareholders, and some members of the general public. What's your position on the proper level of top-executive compensation? Is there a way to make the pay equitable?

How do you justify the fact that many sports and entertainment stars make millions of dollars? Should top executives take a cut in pay when these people don't? What's the difference between the two groups?

Summary

1. Organized labour in Canada dates back to the 1800s. Early unions on the wharves of Halifax, St. John's, and Quebec existed during the War of 1812 to profit from labour scarcity. Craft unions represented shoemakers and printers. Many of the early labour organizations were local or regional in nature.

   • **Describe some of the main objectives of labour and whether they were achieved.**
   Unions hoped to improve workers' poor conditions and wages by forming unions that would fight for workers' rights. All this has largely been achieved and many early demands are now entrenched in law.

   • **Describe some of the unions in existence today.**
   The Canadian Union of Public Employees (CUPE) and the Canadian Auto Workers (CAW) are two of the largest unions in Canada. They represent workers from different sectors in the economy. Many unions in Canada are national in nature. Many belong to international organizations. The Canadian Labour Congress, representing 2.5 million unionized workers, is the national voice of the labour movement in Canada.

2. Much labour legislation has been passed by federal and provincial governments.

   • **What is the major piece of legislation?**
   The Canada Labour Code outlines labour legislation as it applies to federal government employees. Federal government employees represent approximately 10 percent of all workers in Canada. Each provincial jurisdiction in Canada has its own labour legislation and employment standards that apply to workers within those borders.

3. The objectives of trade unions shift in response to changes in social and economic trends.

   • **What topics typically appear in labour–management agreements?**
   See Figure 13.5 on page 391.

4. Collective bargaining is the process by which a union represents employees in relations with their employer.

   • **What is included in collective bargaining?**
   Collective bargaining includes how unions are selected, the period prior to a vote, certification, ongoing contract negotiations, and behaviour while a contract is in force.

   • **What are the steps in the collective bargaining process?**
   Refer to Figure 13.4 for the steps in the collective bargaining process.

5. If negotiations between labour and management break down, either or both sides may use certain tactics to enhance their position or sway public opinion.

   • **What are the tactics used by unions and management in conflicts?**
   Unions can use strikes, boycotts, and picketing. Management can use injunctions and lockouts.

   • **What will unions have to do to cope with declining membership?**
   In order to grow, unions will have to adapt to an increasingly white-collar, female, and culturally diverse workforce. To help keep businesses

1. Trace the history of organized labour in Canada.

2. Discuss the major legislation affecting trade unions.

3. Outline the objectives of trade unions.

4. Understand the collective bargaining process.

5. Describe the tactics used by labour and management during conflicts, and discuss the role of unions in the future.

competitive in international markets, unions must soften their historical "us-versus-them" attitude and build a new "we" attitude with management.

6. Explain some of today's employee–management issues.

6. Some employee–management issues are executive compensation, childcare, and elder care.

- ***What is a fair wage for managers?***
The market and the businesses in it set managers' salaries. What is fair is open to debate.

- ***How are some companies addressing the childcare issue?***
Responsive companies are providing childcare on the premises, discounts with childcare chains, vouchers to be used at the employee's chosen care centre, and referral services.

- ***What is elder care, and what problems do companies face with regard to this growing problem?***
Workers with older parents or other relatives often need to find some way to care for them. It's becoming a problem that will perhaps outpace the need for childcare. Workers who need to care for dependent parents are generally more experienced and vital to the mission of the organization than younger workers are. The cost to business is very large and growing.

Key Terms

agency shop (Rand formula) 392
arbitration 395
bargaining zone 394
certification 390
check-off clause 392
closed shop 392
collective bargaining 389
craft union 384
givebacks 401

grievance 393
industrial union 385
injunction 398
Labour Relations Board (LRB) 388
lockout 398
mediation 394
negotiated labour–management agreement (labour contract) 391

open shop 392
primary boycott 397
secondary boycott 397
shop steward 393
strike 396
union 382
union density 387
union security clause 391
union shop 392

Developing Workplace Skills

1. Debate the following statement with several classmates: "Unions are dinosaurs that have outlived their usefulness in today's business world." Consider such questions as these: Do unions serve a key purpose in some industries? Do unions make Canada less competitive in global markets? To get a better feeling for the other side's point of view, take the opposite side of this issue from the one you normally would. Include information from outside sources to substantiate your position.

2. Debate the following in class: Business executives receive a total compensation package that is far beyond their value. Take the opposite side of the issue from your normal stance to get a better feel for the other point of view.

3. Find the latest information on federal and provincial legislation related to childcare, parental leave, and elder care benefits for employees. In what direction are the trends pointing? What will be the cost to businesses for these new initiatives? Do you favour such advancements in workplace legislation? Why or why not?

4. At the time that this textbook was being written in September 2004, the collective agreement between the National Hockey League Players' Association and the owners expired. The players were locked out and fans were left wondering if there would be a hockey season at all. What were the issues involved? Where did each side stand? How and when was this lockout resolved? What new terms were negotiated? How do you think that this lockout could have been avoided, if at all? Share your research with your class.

5. Do businesses and government agencies have a duty to provide additional benefits to employees beyond fair pay and good working conditions? Does providing benefits such as childcare and elder care to some employees discriminate against those who do not require such assistance? Propose a benefits system that you consider fair and workable for both employees and employers.

Taking It To The Net

1

Purpose

To understand why workers choose to join unions and how unions have made differences in certain industries.

Exercise

Visit the CAW Website at www.caw.ca. Navigate through the site and find information regarding why workers join unions and what the benefits have been.

1. What are some reasons why people join unions?

2. The CAW site presents the union's perspective on labour issues. Choose one of these issues and find other sources that support management's perspective on the issue. You may wish to consider The Fraser Institute (www.fraserinstitute.ca) as one resource.

Taking It To The Net

2

Purpose

To understand some of the issues that are being promoted by the Canadian Labour Congress (CLC).

Exercise

Visit the CLC site at www.clc-ctc.ca. Navigate through the site and find information on issues that are currently being promoted by this organization.

1. What is the mandate of the Social and Economic Policy Department?

2. What are some of the social and economic policy issues being promoted by the CLC?

3. Pick an issue and present it to your classmates.

Practising Management Decisions

Plant Closings, Unions, and Concessions

The last decade has been challenging for hundreds of thousands of Canadian employees, especially in the manufacturing area. Plants and offices have laid off thousands of people or closed because of bankruptcy, consolidation, or transfer of operations to other lower-wage countries. In some cases, management advised unions that the only way that they could avoid closing would be substantial concessions in wages and other changes in existing contracts.

For example, in 2004 Air Canada completed its contract renegotiations as part of its restructuring conditions. According to a company spokesperson, "The labour cost realignments in addition to the restructuring of supplier contracts and aircraft leases effectively reduce Air Canada's operating costs by approximately $2 billion. With lower operating costs and our continued focus on bringing online new technology to further automate and simplify our customers' travel experience, we have successfully transitioned to a new business model that will allow us to compete effectively and profitably in the new market reality."

Tentative agreements were reached with all the unions representing Air Canada employees: the International Association of Machinists and Aerospace Workers (IAMAW), the Air Canada Pilots Association (ACPA), the Canadian Airline Dispatchers Association (CALDA), the Canadian Union of Public Employees (CUPE), and the Canadian Auto Workers (CAW). Tentative agreements were also reached with all unions representing Air Canada Jazz employees: the Airline Pilots Association (ALPA), CALDA, CAW, and Teamsters Canada. Air Canada management and non-unionized staff also contributed to the $200-million cost savings.

Keep in mind that non-unionized employees also saw tens of thousands of job eliminated. At Nortel alone, more than 65,000 jobs were eliminated as the company restructured to try to regain profitability; this was from a global peak of 100,000 employees. No employees are safe as companies try to become more competitive and efficient in the marketplace.

Union leaders and their members are in a quandary when faced with such decisions. Sometimes they think management is bluffing. Sometimes they are reluctant to give up contract conditions they fought long and hard for. Accepting wage cuts or benefit reductions when the cost of living continues to rise is not easy. Agreeing to staff reductions to save other jobs is also a tough decision. Unions worry about where these concessions will end. Will there be another round of layoffs or even worse in a few months?

These examples highlight some of the dilemmas facing unions. The business environment demands that companies become more efficient and productive. However, this will not happen unless there is mutual respect between management and labour. What is clear, as noted in the chapter profile, is that the trade movement will continue to fight on behalf of workers to ensure that their rights are protected.

Decision Questions

1. What would you recommend to union workers whose employer is threatening to close down unless they agree to wage or other concessions?
2. Is there some alternative to cutting wages or closing down? What is it?
3. Union workers often feel that the company is bluffing when it threatens to close. How can such doubts be settled so that more open negotiations can take place?
4. Laws have been passed that require plants with more than a certain number of employees to give up to six months' notice of intention to close. Do you think that such legislation helps businesses to show employees that they are serious about closing a plant and thus get concessions from labour? Are such tactics ethical? Do these laws have any effect on investment decisions?

Sources: Jan Wong, "Gone: The Last Days of Nortel," October 25, 2002, Natural Convergence. Retrieved from http://www.naturalconvergence.com/making_waves/press_coverage/last-daynn.html; and "Air Canada Reaches Tentative Agreement with CAW and Achieves Overall Cost Realignment Target; Deutsche Bank and GECAS Conditions Satisfied," May 20, 2003, Air Canada. Retrieved from http://micro.newswire.ca/release.cgi?rkey=1205206254&view=13213-0&Start=0.

Video Case

Overworked and Underpaid: Nurses Strike Back

Across Canada, nurses went on illegal strikes. They risked their seniority and their jobs to make up for frozen or cut salaries from the 1990s. While they provided essential services, hospitals were closed and only emergency surgeries were performed. Patients were sent home and some patients were flown out of the province for service.

Nurses across Canada have complained about being underpaid and overworked in overcrowded hospitals. Nurses were angry because 10 years ago a nursing shortage had been identified. Despite this, the federal and provincial governments cut back the amount of funding for health care, resulting in bed closures and staff layoffs. They were told to work harder and with fewer nurses, providing the same service to the same number of people.

Now, things have improved economically. Shortages are getting worse, and when nurses ask for changes they are told they need to make more sacrifices. As a result, nurses have walked off the job and gone on strike. Even after the provincial government imposed heavy fines and ordered them back, nurses still remained on strike in Quebec.

It is not just the nurses. Across Canada, other workers went on strike. Picket lines sprung up for Bell telephone operators, Air Canada pilots, and teachers in Ontario. There was an angry mood across Canada, as labour demanded that employers improve their contract terms.

Discussion Questions

1. Why did Canada see an increase in strikes across different sectors?
2. The nurses went on an illegal strike. What measures can a government take to force federal or provincial employees back to work?
3. Should employees who provide essential services, such as nurses and police officers, be allowed to go on strike? Explain.
4. How does the economy suffer if workers go on strike?

PART 5

Chapter 14

Marketing: Building Customer and Stakeholder Relationships

Learning Goals

After you have read and studied this chapter, you should be able to

1 Define marketing and describe the four Ps of marketing.

2 Describe the marketing research process, and explain how marketers use environmental scanning to learn about the changing marketing environment.

3 Explain how marketers meet the needs of the consumer market through market segmentation, relationship marketing, and the study of consumer behaviour.

4 List ways in which the business-to-business market differs from the consumer market.

5 Draw the product life cycle, describe each of its stages, and outline marketing strategies at each stage.

6 Show how the marketing concept has been adapted to fit today's modern markets to include stakeholder marketing and customer relationship management (CRM).

Profile

Getting to Know Christine Magee of Sleep Country Canada Inc.

"Sleep Country Canada! Why Buy A Mattress Anywhere Else?" is the jingle for Sleep Country Canada, repeated in all of its television and radio commercials across Canada. Its spokesperson—Christine Magee—has become synonymous with mattresses. As Magee explains, "The goal was to create a brand name and associate the name Christine Magee with it." This has been reinforced in each of the company's stores, with Magee's image being featured along with stories about her and the business.

Highly specialized in sleep products, Sleep Country Canada was started in 1994 by three partners: Christine Magee (President), Stephen Gunn, and Gordon Lownds. Today, there are 89 stores in three provinces: British Columbia, Alberta, and Ontario.

A graduate from the University of Western Ontario with an honours degree in business, Magee spent 12 years in commercial and corporate banking. During that time, she was involved in the areas of commercial, corporate, and merchant lending, including leverage and management buyouts. Previous to that, she worked in the retail sector, managing a women's apparel store, where she gained valuable merchandising and retail experience.

While employed in the banking industry, Magee decided to enter the mattress business, despite its negative image. "Opportunity often exists where you least expect it, and I recognized that. We came to the conclusion that the retail business for mattresses and box springs wasn't being done well and could be done better. It had always been dominated by department stores that really didn't specialize." Magee validated the idea for Sleep Country Canada by visiting a company based in Seattle that was providing the level of service Sleep Country Canada was designed to provide. Along with her two partners, she bought the trademark name and infamous jingle, and borrowed a few marketing tools from the U.S. store. In 1994, the partners moved to Vancouver and opened their first store. At this time, the Sleep Country TV and radio ads were produced. Today, the company operates in seven regions with eight distribution centres and 92 stores. Part of the company's advertising power is repetition: the ads are everywhere and they are played over and over again.

While the marketing program has contributed to its success, it is the firm's mission of complete dedication to customer service that has given it a competitive edge. The mission is to exceed customer expectations when they purchase a new sleep set. This is the firm's opportunity to earn the trust of their customers. Customer assurances of value and service are provided by offering a comprehensive assortment of quality sleep products, guarantees, and free services—in attractive, convenient retail stores staffed by a knowledgeable, helpful, and friendly salesforce. A dedicated team of customer-service and delivery associates support all these efforts. Company ads feature testimonials from satisfied customers. They are talking about the service, not the product. They say such things as, "They came to deliver my mattress just when they said they would" and "I was so impressed when I saw the men putting on those little booties before they walked into my house."

As part of the commitment that Sleep Country Canada has to its customers, there is also a commitment to the community. Part of its service is the Donated Bed Program, where Sleep Country Canada provides free removal of old mattresses. These old mattresses are then made available to charitable organizations to assist those in need. Sleep Country Canada is also a supporter of many community charities including Covenant House, Massey Centre, Starlight Children's Foundation, the United Way, and Youth Without Shelter.

In this chapter you will be introduced to the importance of marketing. Like Sleep Country Canada, businesses must conduct an environmental scan to discover opportunities and threats in their industry. Customers demand a four-P marketing mix that will meet their expectations. With a greater customer relationship management (CRM), focus today, marketers need to also reach their customers wherever they may be.

Sources: www.ryerson.ca/baar/news/past/winter99_presidents_note.htm; www.uwo.ca/alumni/gazette/winter99/magee.htm; www.ryerson.ca/CESAR/NightViews/May%20June%2001.htm; sbinfocanada.about.com/library/weekly/aa120200a.htm; and www.sleepcountry.ca, September 26, 2004.

WHAT IS MARKETING?

marketing
The process of determining customer needs and wants and then developing goods and services that meet or exceed these expectations.

Marketing is the process of determining customer needs and wants and then developing goods and services ➤PP. 23, 25◀ that meet or exceed these expectations. Needs are not created by marketers but in fact are basic to all humans and exist at some level. For example, all humans need water, food, and security. (Recall Maslow's hierarchy of needs in Chapter 11.) If you are hungry, you *need* food; however, do you *want* pasta, a hamburger and fries, or a plate of vegetables to sustain your body? If you choose a hamburger, do you want a Harvey's burger, a McDonald's burger, or a Lick's burger? The successful marketer will be able to influence this want by producing a burger that you recognize and believe will meet your need, available at a reasonable price and in a location near you.

The main term in marketing is *market*. Recall that a market is defined as a group of people with unsatisfied wants and needs, who have the resources and the willingness to buy products. A market is, therefore, created as a result of this demand for goods and services. Thus, if there are people who want a high-fibre, low-sugar cereal—like Fiberrific—and if these people are willing to buy this cereal, can afford the price, and make the final decision to buy the cereal, then there is a market for this product. Later in this chapter we will review the marketing research process that will outline a process to help marketers answer questions such as "Is there a demand for my product?"

The Evolution of Marketing

The evolution of marketing involved four eras: (1) production, (2) sales, (3) marketing concept, and (4) customer relationship.

The Production Era   From the time the first European settlers arrived in Canada until the start of the 1900s, the general philosophy of business was to produce as much as possible. Given the limited production capabilities and the vast demand for products in those days, such a *production orientation* was both logical and profitable as demand exceeded supply. Manufacturers focused on production, as most goods were bought as soon as they became available. The important marketing needs were for distribution and storage.

The Sales Era   By the 1920s, businesses had developed mass-production techniques (e.g., automobile assembly lines) and production capacity often exceeded the immediate market demand ➤P. 38◀. Therefore, the business philosophy turned from an emphasis on production to an emphasis on selling. Most companies emphasized selling and advertising in an effort to persuade consumers to buy existing products; few offered service after the sale.

The Marketing Concept Era   After the Second World War ended in 1945, there was a tremendous demand for goods and services among the returning veterans and soldiers who were starting new careers and beginning families. Those postwar years launched the baby boom (a sudden increase in the birthrate) and a boom in consumer spending. Competition for the consumer's dollar was fierce. Businesses recognized the need to be responsive to consumers if they wanted to get their business, and a philosophy emerged in the 1950s called the marketing concept.

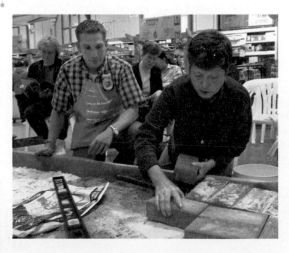

Home Depot's research discovered that women wanted to learn more about home maintenance and repair, including, as this photo shows, learning about such things as how to install bricks for a walkway. The concept of "find a need and fill it" has led Home Depot to begin offering classes for women called "Do It Herself Night." Are there other stores in your area that could increase revenues by being more responsive to the needs of women?

The **marketing concept** had three parts:

1. **A customer orientation.**   Find out what consumers want and provide it for them. (Note the emphasis on consumers rather than on sales.)
2. **A service orientation.**   Make sure everyone in the organization has the same objective—customer satisfaction. This should be a total and integrated organizational effort.
3. **A profit orientation.**   Focus on those goods and services that will earn the most profit and enable the organization to survive and expand to serve more consumer wants and needs.

It took a while for businesses to implement the marketing concept. That process went slowly during the 1960s and 70s. During the 1980s, businesses began to apply the marketing concept more aggressively than they had done over the preceding 30 years. That led to the focus on customer relationship management (CRM) that has become so important today. We shall explore that concept next.

The Customer Relationship Era   In the 1990s, managers extended the marketing concept by adopting the concept of customer relationship management. **Customer relationship management (CRM)** is the process of learning as much as possible about customers and doing everything you can to satisfy them—or even exceed their expectations—with goods and services over time.[1] The idea is to enhance customer satisfaction and stimulate long-term customer loyalty. For example, most airlines offer frequent-flier programs that reward loyal customers with free flights. We shall explore CRM in more depth later in the chapter.

Nonprofit Organizations Prosper from Marketing

Even though the marketing concept emphasizes a profit orientation, marketing is a critical part of all organizations, whether for-profit or nonprofit. Charities use marketing to raise funds (e.g., world hunger) or to obtain other resources.[2] For example, Canadian Blood Services uses promotion to encourage people to donate blood when local or national supplies run low. Greenpeace uses marketing to promote ecologically safe technologies.

Provinces use marketing to attract new businesses and tourists. Some provinces, for example, have competed to get automobile companies from other countries to locate plants in their area. Schools use marketing to attract new students. Other organizations, such as arts groups, unions, and social groups, also use marketing.[3]

The Importance of Ethics

Marketers today recognize that their behaviour and products impact not only their consumers, but also society in general. By focusing on all three elements—the needs of consumers, the firm's goals, and the interests of society—an organization is adopting a broader *societal marketing orientation.* There is much pressure on businesses to become involved in programs designed to train the disadvantaged, improve the community, reduce the

---

marketing concept
A three-part business philosophy: (1) a customer orientation, (2) a service orientation, and (3) a profit orientation.

customer relationship management (CRM)
The process of learning as much as possible about customers and doing everything you can to satisfy them—or even exceed their expectations—with goods and services over time.

City Harvest is a nonprofit organization that gathers food for distribution to the poor. This ad features Harrison Ford as a spokesperson for the cause. How would you rate the marketing efforts of the nonprofit organizations in your area? Are they better or worse than marketing efforts for profit-seeking businesses?

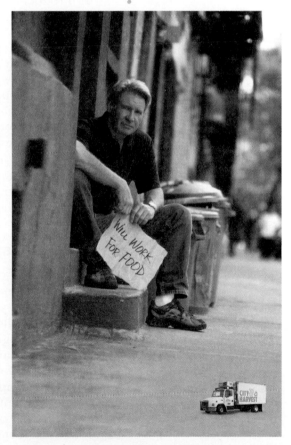

use of energy and pollution emissions, involve employees in community projects, and generally respond to the broader needs of society.

An example is the Johnson & Johnson (J&J) recall of its Tylenol product in 1982. Eleven people died from swallowing cyanide-laced capsules, and although the firm believed that the pills had been altered in only a few stores, not in the factory, J&J quickly recalled its entire product. The recall cost the company $240 million in earnings, but in the long run the company's swift recall of Tylenol strengthened consumer confidence and loyalty.[4]

There was more. J&J immediately stopped advertising the product and made television announcements advising the public of the problem, it established a hotline, and it offered a refund to those who had purchased capsules. Finally, J&J quickly redesigned the package to make it more tamper-resistant.[5]

Critical Thinking

Which of your needs are not being met by businesses and/or nonprofit organizations in your area? Are there enough people with similar needs to attract an organization that would meet those needs? How would you find out?

THE MARKETING MIX

Pleasing customers has become a priority for marketers. Much of what marketing people do has been conveniently divided into four factors, called the four Ps, to make them easy to remember and implement. They are

1. Product
2. Price
3. Place
4. Promotion

Managing the controllable parts of the marketing process, then, involves (1) designing a want-satisfying *product*, (2) setting a *price* for the product, (3) placing the product in a *place* where people will buy it, and (4) *promoting* the product. These four factors are called the **marketing mix** because they are blended together in a marketing program. A marketing manager designs a marketing program that effectively combines the ingredients of the marketing mix (see Figure 14.1). The Dealing with Change box discusses how the automobile industry is adjusting to the market using the four Ps.

marketing mix
The ingredients that go into a marketing program: product, price, place, and promotion.

Applying the Marketing Process

The four Ps are a convenient way to remember the basics of marketing, but they don't include everything that goes into the marketing process. One of the best ways for you to understand the entire marketing process is to take a product and follow the process that led to its development and sale (see Figure 14.2). Imagine that you and your friends don't have time to eat big breakfasts. You want something for breakfast that's fast, nutritious, and good tasting. Some of your friends eat a cereal made with 100 percent natural oats and honey, but you and others are not happy with this product. In fact, you know that the Centre for Science in the Public Interest placed this cereal at the top of its list of "10 Foods You Should Never Eat!" because of its high sugar and fat content. Furthermore, you've read in a magazine that the cereal industry has been slow to innovate. You sense opportunity. Finding such

Dealing With Change

Applying the Four Ps

You can see the four Ps of marketing in action if you closely follow changes that are occurring in the automobile industry. New products are being designed to meet market niches. There are, for example, sports cars designed to compete with the Porsche Boxster and appeal to successful young executives, and sport-utility vehicles (SUVs) for nearly every taste. Pickup trucks have features like four-wheel drive, grocery-bag hooks, and centre armrests that double as laptop workstations.

Never before have there been more choices in cars—for small personal cars to large vans to "green" cars that run on a combination of gas and battery power. And in those cars is every conceivable convenience from phones to CD players, cup holders, and global positioning systems. Automobile companies truly seem to be listening to customers and trying to meet their needs. This is the *product* part of the four Ps.

When it comes to *pricing*, there is a whole new revolution going on in this industry. On the Web, sites such as Cars4u.com, Usedcarscanada.com, and Autobytel.com provide product and price information and dealer referrals. Customers can thus determine the best price before going to a dealership. To eliminate one of the most annoying parts of buying a car, some dealers are offering no-haggle pricing.

Getting cars to a *place* that is convenient for customers is also being done by auto Websites. Autobytel.com and Usedcarscanada.com help customers find the dealer closest to them that will offer the best price for the automobile they choose. Ford and General Motors (GM) are experimenting with Websites and factory-owned stores. GM's service, called BuyPower, gives consumers access to every vehicle on participating dealers' lots as well as independent data about competing models.

Promotion for new and used cars is also changing. Dealers are trying low-pressure sales tactics because they know that customers are now armed with much more information than in the past. More and more power is being shifted to consumers. They can go on the Internet; learn about various cars and their features, including safety features; pick which features they want; get the best price available; and order the car—all without leaving their homes. In such an atmosphere the marketing task shifts from helping the seller sell to helping the buyer buy. Internet sellers make every effort to help buyers find the car that best meets their needs and minimize the hassle involved in getting that car.

In the future, the real difference among dealers may be in postpurchase (after-sale) service. Those dealers who treat customers best through relationship marketing (discussed later in this chapter) may develop loyalty that can't be matched in any other way. Such relationships are built through service contracts, guarantees, reminder cards telling customers when to come in for various services, parties with customers, and more.

Sources: Bob Thompson, "If Profit Is the Point, Loyalty Is the Key," *Business Week* (advertisement), July 3, 2000, pp. 67 ff.; Amy Tsao, "Online Retailing Finds Its Legs," *Business Week*, December 20, 2002; and Amy Tsao, "Harley: A Good Time for a Ride?" *Business Week Online*, Spring 2003; and Kathleen Kerwin, "Hybrids: How Detroit Can Gun the Engines," *Business Week*, February 17, 2003, p. 80.

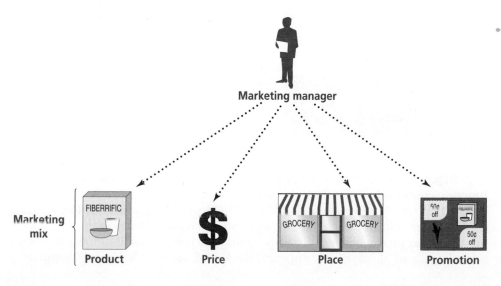

Marketing manager

Marketing mix

Product   **Price**   **Place**   **Promotion**

FIGURE 14.1

MARKETING MANAGERS AND THE MARKETING MIX

Marketing managers must choose how to implement the four Ps of the marketing mix: product, price, place, and promotion. The goals are to please customers and make a profit.

FIGURE 14.2

**THE MARKETING PROCESS
WITH THE FOUR Ps**

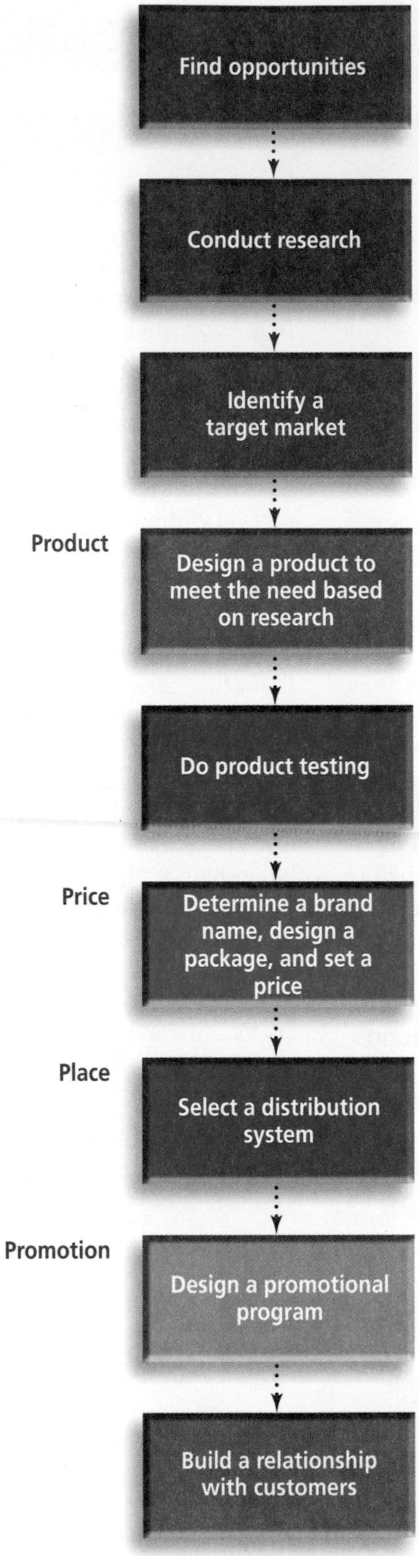

Find opportunities

Conduct research

Identify a
target market

Product

Design a product to
meet the need based
on research

Do product testing

Price

Determine a brand
name, design a
package, and set a
price

Place

Select a distribution
system

Promotion

Design a promotional
program

Build a relationship
with customers

product
Any physical good, service,
or idea that satisfies a want
or need.

test marketing
The process of testing
products among potential
users.

brand name
A word, letter, or group
of words or letters that
differentiates one seller's
goods and services.

opportunities is a great first step toward becoming a successful marketer.

You ask around among your acquaintances and find that a huge demand exists for a good-tasting breakfast cereal that's nutritious, high in fibre, and low in sugar. This fact leads you to conduct a more extensive marketing research study to determine whether there's a large enough market for such a cereal. Your research supports your assumption: there is a large market for a high-fibre cereal. You have completed one of the first steps in marketing: researching consumer wants and needs and finding a need for a product that's either not yet available or could be greatly improved. We shall discuss marketing research in detail later in the chapter.

Designing a Product to Meet Needs

Once you have researched consumer needs and found a target market (to be discussed later) for your product, the four Ps of marketing begin. You start by developing a product. A **product** is any physical good, service, or idea that satisfies a want or need plus anything that would enhance the product in the eyes of consumers, such as the brand. In this case, your proposed product is a health-enhancing multigrain cereal made with an artificial sweetener. It's a good idea at this point to do *concept testing*. That is, you develop an accurate description of your product and ask people, in person or online, whether the concept (the idea of the cereal) appeals to them. If it does, you might go to a manufacturer that has the equipment and skills to design such a cereal, and begin making prototypes. *Prototypes* are samples of the product that you take to consumers to test their reactions. The process of testing products among potential users is called **test marketing.**

If consumers like the product and agree they would buy it, you may turn the production process over to an existing manufacturer or you may decide to produce the cereal yourself. *Outsourcing* ➤**P. 269**◀, remember, is the term used to describe the allocation of production and other functions to outside firms. The idea is to retain only those functions that you can do most efficiently and outsource the rest. The Reaching Beyond Our Borders box discusses the resources available to help you reach global markets.

Once the product meets taste and quality expectations, you have to design a package and think of an appropriate brand name.[6] A **brand name** is a

Reaching Beyond Our Borders

Problems and Solutions

Now that Internet companies are selling globally, they have to abide by all the rules of all the countries they are in—and that is not easy. For example, Lands' End got into trouble in Germany by promoting its guarantee on goods purchased. Such guarantees are not legal in Germany. Germany's reasoning is that the cost of offering a guarantee is hidden in a higher sales price. Anyhow, small companies advertising on the Internet must be careful to not break any laws of the countries they reach. The cost of fighting such laws is too high for a small firm. Lands' End may have the money, but most small firms do not. Many companies are now having second thoughts about selling goods and services globally on the Internet. One of the problems that occurs regularly is learning how to ship goods across national boundaries.

How does a firm adapt to the demands of a global market? The answer is that companies have emerged to provide third-party services to help other companies reach and serve foreign customers. Such services include marketing support, e-commerce development, and transportation.

At first, only large companies such as UPS World Wide Logistics provided third-party services to global marketers. But lately smaller companies have emerged to offer more specialized services, such as Website development and follow-up services after the sale. Selling in China, for example, has never been easy for firms. But East-West Equipment and Technology, Inc., now operates as a development and trade management company with offices in Beijing and Wuhan. The company was originally set up to sell secondhand equipment to Chinese buyers. It turned out that Chinese buyers didn't have enough information as they tried to choose from thousands of pieces of used equipment. So East-West began providing guidance and detailed information to Chinese buyers. It now does the same for buyers who need information about Chinese business practices.

Firms once found it difficult to set up distribution networks in Mexico. Now GATX Corporation has a logistics subsidiary in Mexico that helps firms reach Mexican consumers. The company also operates in Chile. Many more companies could be cited that provide services to firms wishing to sell internationally. The Internet may provide access to global markets, but there still is the problem of transporting goods. Transportation and logistics services in general (e.g., warehousing) are available in most countries to help finalize the sale.

Sources: "Globalization: Lessons Learned," *Business Week*, November 6, 2000, p. 228; Robert Selwitz, "The Logistics of Geography," *Global Business*, February 2000, pp. 48–56; Krivda, "E-Supply Chain," *Fortune* (advertisement), June 21, 2000, pp. 341 ff.; Keith H. Hammonds, "The New Face of Global Competition," *Fast Company*, February 2003, pp. 91–97; and Sarah Mc Bride, "Kia's Audacious Sorento Plan," *The Wall Street Journal*, April 8, 2003, p. A12.

---

word, letter, or group of words or letters that differentiates one seller's goods and services from those of competitors. Cereal brand names, for example, include Cheerios, Frosted Flakes, and Raisin Bran. Let's say that you name your cereal Fiberrific to emphasize the high fibre content and terrific taste.

Setting an Appropriate Price

After you have developed the product or designed the service you want to offer consumers, you have to set an appropriate price.[7] That price depends on a number of factors. For example, in the cereal business, the price should probably be close to what other cereal makers charge since most cereals are priced competitively. You also have to consider the costs involved in producing, distributing, and

Cereal makers have long used discount coupons as a central part of their ongoing strategies to build and promote their brands. Part of their thinking is that if the discount induces you to try a particular cereal you will become a repeat customer. Would you be inclined to use this strategy to launch a new cereal like Fiberrific? Why?

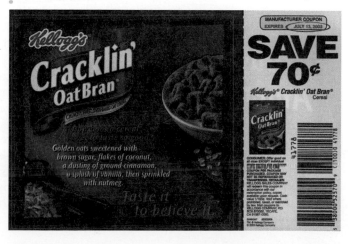

promoting the product. You might price the product higher than other cereals to create an image of quality.

Getting the Product to the Right Place

Once the product is manufactured, you have to choose how to get it to the consumer. Remember, *place* is the third P in the marketing mix. You may want to sell the cereal directly to supermarkets or health-food stores, or you may want to sell it through organizations that specialize in distributing food products. Such organizations, called *intermediaries*, are in the middle of a series of organizations that distribute goods from producers to consumers. (The more traditional word for such companies is *middlemen*.)[8] Getting the product to consumers when and where they want it is critical to market success.

Developing an Effective Promotional Strategy

promotion
All the techniques sellers use to motivate customers to buy their products.

The last of the four Ps of marketing is promotion. **Promotion** consists of all the techniques sellers use to motivate customers to buy their products. They include advertising; personal selling; public relations; and various sales promotion efforts, such as coupons, and samples. We will discuss the four Ps in some detail in Chapter 15.

This last step in the marketing process often includes relationship building with customers. That includes responding to suggestions consumers may make to improve the product or its marketing. Postpurchase, or after-sale, service may include exchanging goods that weren't satisfactory and making other adjustments to ensure consumer satisfaction, including recycling. Marketing is an ongoing process. To remain competitive, companies must continually adapt to changes in the market and to changes in consumer wants and needs.

Progress Assessment

- Define marketing.
- What are the three parts of the marketing concept?
- How does the marketing concept drive both for-profit and nonprofit organizations?
- What are the four Ps of the marketing mix?

PROVIDING MARKETERS WITH INFORMATION

marketing research
The analysis of markets to determine opportunities and challenges, and to find the information needed to make good decisions.

Every step in the marketing process depends on information that is used to make the right decisions. **Marketing research** is the analysis of markets to determine opportunities and challenges, and to find the information needed to make good decisions.

Marketing research helps determine what customers have purchased in the past and what situational changes have occurred to alter not only what consumers want now but also what they're likely to want in the future. In addition, marketers conduct research on business trends, the ecological impact of their decisions, international trends, and more. Businesses need information in order to compete effectively, and marketing research is the activity that gathers that information. Note, too, that in addition to listening to customers, marketing researchers should pay attention to what employees, shareholders, dealers, consumer advocates, media representatives, and other stakeholders ➤P. 5◄ have to say.

The Marketing Research Process

A simplified marketing research process consists of four key steps:

1. Defining the question (problem or opportunity) and determining the present situation;
2. Collecting data;
3. Analyzing the research data; and
4. Choosing the best solution and implementing it.

The following sections look at each of these steps.

Defining the Question and Determining the Present Situation   Marketing researchers should be given the freedom to help discover what the present situation is, what the problems or opportunities are, what the alternatives are, what information is needed, and how to go about gathering and analyzing data.

Collecting Data   Obtaining usable information is vital to the marketing research process. Research can become quite expensive, so some trade-off must often be made between the need for information and the cost of obtaining that information. Normally the least expensive method is to gather information that has already been compiled by others and published in journals and books or made available online. Such existing data are called **secondary data** since you aren't the first one to gather them. Figure 14.3 lists the principal sources of secondary marketing research information. Despite its name, secondary data should be gathered first to avoid incurring unnecessary expense.

Often, secondary data do not provide all the necessary information. These data were collected for other purposes and may be out of date, incomplete, or not applicable to your specific question. When additional in-depth data are needed, marketers must do their own research. This new information is called **primary data.** Primary data are facts and figures that you have gathered yourself.

One primary research technique is *observation*. This occurs when trained people observe and record the actions of potential buyers. For example, companies have followed customers into supermarkets to record their purchasing behaviours for products such as meat, bread, and laundry detergent. These marketers may observe that consumers do not bend to look at products, that they compare prices, and that they touch the product to see how heavy it is. This method may provide insight into behaviours that consumers do not even know they exhibit when shopping.

A more formal way to gather primary data is to develop a list of questions and to conduct a *survey* (also known as a questionnaire). Telephone surveys, mail surveys, and online surveys are the most common forms. Often confidential, you can use the information to understand behaviours, perceptions, preferences, and opinions. While the information gathered is useful, there are some disadvantages to this method. Not everyone who is approached may be willing to answer your questions, respondents may not be truthful, and, for written surveys, not everyone can read and write. To increase the response and accuracy rate, marketers use personal interviews.

Personal interviews are a face-to-face opportunity to ask consumers prepared questions. While it is easy for consumers to throw out a mail survey or ignore an online survey, marketers may be more successful with this method. While this research method can be more expensive than surveys, the interviewer has the opportunity to observe reactions and to dig a little deeper with the questions if the respondent wishes to add more information. As with

secondary data
Information that has already been compiled by others and published in journals and books or made available online.

primary data
Data that you gather yourself (not from secondary sources such as books and magazines).

FIGURE 14.3

SOURCES OF SELECTED PRIMARY AND SECONDARY INFORMATION

For a list of local and national Canadian newspapers, visit www.world-newspapers.com/canada.html. On this site, you will also find some news sites.

focus group
A small group of people who meet under the direction of a discussion leader to communicate their opinions about an organization, its products, or other issues.

Using two-way mirrors, observers are able to watch participants in a focus group without disturbing them. Focus groups help companies learn about the benefits and features consumers seek in various products and what they like and don't like. What would you have said had you participated in a focus group about this text and this class?

PRIMARY SOURCES	
Observation	Personal interview
Survey/questionnaire	Focus group

SECONDARY SOURCES

Government Publications
Annual Retail Trade
Canadian Economic Observer
Family Expenditure Guide
Market Research Handbook
Statistics Canada Catalogue

Newspapers
Toronto Star
The Globe and Mail
The National Post
Local newspapers (e.g., *Calgary Herald* and *Halifax Daily News*)

Internal Sources
Company records
Financial statements
Prior research reports

Indexes and Directories
Business Periodical Index
Canadian Business Index
Canadian Statistics Index
Scott's Directories
Standards Periodical Directory

Trade Sources
A.C. Nielsen
Conference Board of Canada

Compusearch
Dun & Bradstreet
Direct Marketing Association
Retail Council of Canada

General Internet Sites
Strategis: Industry Canada's Website— www.strategis.gc.ca
Statistics Canada's Website— www.statcan.ca
To find a business or person— canada411.ca
Track market news, industries, annual reports, etc.— ca.finance.yahoo.com

Periodicals
Adweek
Canadian Business
Journal of Marketing
Maclean's
Marketing Magazine

Databases
ABI/Inform
CANSIM (Statistics Canada)
Canadian Business and Current Affairs (CBCA)
LexisNexis Academic

surveys and interviews, this method is useful to understand behaviours, perceptions, preferences, and opinions.

Focus groups are another method of gathering primary data. A *focus group* is a small group of people (usually 8 to 14 individuals) who meet under the direction of a discussion leader. These respondents are asked to communicate their opinions about an organization, its products, or other issues.

Analyzing the Research Data The data collected in the research process must be turned into useful information.[9] Careful, honest interpretation of the data collected can help

Making Ethical Decisions

Are We Too Star Struck?

Many producers use brand association to sell their products—often to young people. Brand association is the linking of a brand to other favourable images. They use famous people, like Michael Jordan, in their ads to attract the attention of the audience. This is true for many products. An ethical question raised by such ads is: "What if the star in the ad doesn't really use the product?" If young people are lured into trying soft drinks, fast food, overly revealing clothes, and the like because they see their idols on TV or in the movies using them, who is responsible for the harm that may be caused? The producer? The TV show? The network? The person in the ad? Have you been persuaded to buy such products because of celebrity endorsements? Was your experience a positive one? Do you have any feeling of responsibility for your buying behaviour? What are the ethical choices?

a company find useful alternatives to specific marketing challenges. For example, by doing primary research, Fresh Italy, a small Italian pizzeria, found that its pizza's taste was rated superior compared to the larger pizza chains. However, the company's sales lagged behind the competition. Secondary research on the industry revealed that free delivery (which Fresh Italy did not offer) was more important to customers than taste. Fresh Italy now delivers—and it has increased its market share.

Choosing the Best Solution and Implementing It   After collecting and analyzing data, market researchers determine alternative strategies and make recommendations as to which strategy may be best and why. This final step in a research effort involves following up on the actions taken to see if the results were as expected. If not, the company can take corrective action and conduct new studies in the ongoing attempt to provide consumer satisfaction at the lowest cost. You can see, then, that marketing research is a continuous process of responding to changes in the marketplace and changes in consumer preferences.

Company Websites have vastly improved the marketing research process in both domestic and global markets. Businesses can now continuously interact with their customers as they strive to improve goods and services. The information exchanged can be useful in determining what customers want. Keeping customer information in a database ▶P. 18◀ enables a company to improve its product offerings over time and to design promotions that are geared exactly to meet the needs of specific groups of consumers.

In today's customer-driven market, ethics ▶P. 126◀ is also important in every aspect of marketing. Companies should therefore do what's right as well as what's profitable. This step could add greatly to the social benefits of marketing decisions. See the Making Ethical Decisions box for such an example.

The Personal Information Protection and Electronic Documents Act[10]   The Personal Information Protection and Electronic Documents Act (PIPEDA) is Canada's new private-sector privacy law. PIPEDA sets ground rules for how organizations may collect, use, or disclose information about you in the course of commercial activities. The law also gives you the right to see and ask for corrections to information an organization may have collected about you. If you think an organization covered by the Act is not living up to its responsibilities under the law, you have the right to lodge an official complaint.

To find out more about privacy legislation, visit the Office of the Privacy Commissioner of Canada's Website at www.privcom.gc.ca/index_e.asp.

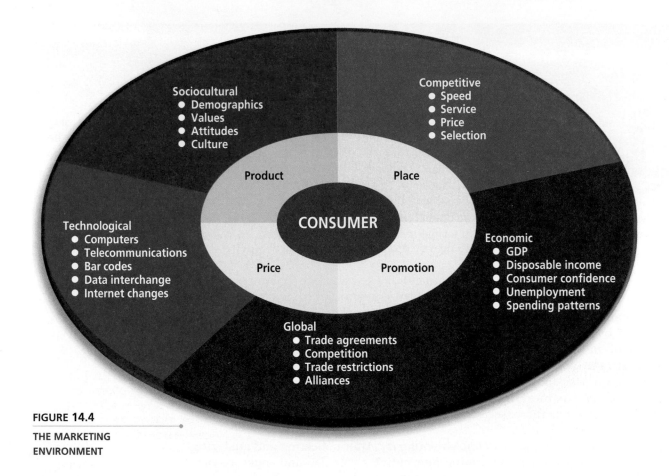

FIGURE 14.4

THE MARKETING
ENVIRONMENT

The Marketing Environment

environmental scanning
The process of identifying
the factors that can affect
marketing success.

Marketing managers must be aware of the surrounding environment when
making marketing mix decisions. **Environmental scanning** is the process of
identifying the factors that can affect marketing success. As you can see in
Figure 14.4, those factors include global, technological, sociocultural, competitive, and economic influences. We discussed these factors in some detail
in Chapter 1, but it is helpful to review them from a strictly marketing
perspective as well.

Global Factors   The most dramatic global change is probably the growth of the
Internet. Now businesses can reach many of the consumers in the world relatively easily and carry on a dialogue with them about the goods and services
they want. This globalization of marketing puts more pressure on those whose
responsibility is to deliver products. Many marketers outsource that function
to companies like Purolator, which has a solid reputation for delivering goods
quickly.

Technological Factors   The most important technological changes also involve
the Internet and the growth of consumer databases. Using consumer databases, companies can develop products and services that closely match the
needs of consumers. As you read in Chapter 10, it is now possible to produce
customized goods and services for about the same price as mass-produced
goods. Thus, flexible manufacturing and mass customization ➤P. 304◀ are
also major influences on marketers.

Sociocultural Factors   There are a number of social trends that marketers must monitor to maintain their close relationship with customers. Population growth and changing demographics are examples of social trends that can have an effect on sales.

The fastest-growing segment of the Canadian population is the baby boomers. By 2031, one in every four Canadians will be 65 years or older.[11] As this segment ages, there will be growing demand for recreation, travel, continuing education, health care, and nursing homes. As well, opportunities exist for firms that target Canada's 2.4 million "tweens" (ages 9 to 14).[12] According to a study conducted by YTV, these children of the baby boomers control $1.8 billion in spending, with most of their money spent on candy, clothes, shoes, and music.[13]

Competitive Factors   Of course, marketers must pay attention to the dynamic competitive environment. Many brick-and-mortar companies must be aware of new competition from the Internet, including those that sell automobiles, insurance, music videos, and clothes.[14] In the book business, Indigo is competing with Amazon.ca's huge selection of books at good prices.[15] Now that consumers can literally search the world for the best buys through the Internet, marketers must adjust their pricing policies accordingly. Similarly, they have to adjust to competitors who can deliver products quickly or provide excellent service.

Economic Factors   Marketers must pay close attention to the economic environment. As we began the new millennium, Canada was experiencing unparalleled growth and customers were eager to buy expensive automobiles, watches, and vacations. But as the economy slowed, marketers had to adapt by offering products that were less expensive and more tailored to consumers with modest incomes.[16] Marketers in countries such as Indonesia had already gone through such an economic fall and are now recovering. You can see, therefore, that environmental scanning is critical to a company's success during rapidly changing economic times.

Liquidation World has been successful when the economy has been strong or weak. As explains, Dale Gillespie, CEO, "when times are good, customers have more to spend, and manufacturers get rid of excess inventory more willingly. When times are tough, cash-strapped shoppers beat down the door in search of low prices. As more and more businesses are boarded up, Liquidation World is there to snatch up their inventories at rock-bottom prices."[17]

TLN Television (Telelatino Network Inc.) was launched in the fall of 1984. TLN is Canada's only national Italian and Hispanic broadcaster, reaching almost 3.5 million households across Canada. It is carried by all of the major Canadian cable systems and on both of Canada's satellite systems. Are you aware of any other ethnic segments that are targeted by television channels?

What marketing environment changes are occurring in your community? What business environment changes are most likely to change your career prospects in the future? How can you learn more about those changes? What might you do to prepare for them?

Critical Thinking

Two Different Markets: Consumer and Business-to-Business (B2B)

Marketers must know as much as possible about the market they wish to serve. Recall that a market consists of people with unsatisfied wants and needs who have both the resources and the willingness to buy.

There are two major markets in business: the consumer market and the business-to-business market. The **consumer market** consists of all the individuals or households that want goods and services for personal consumption or use and have the resources to buy them. The **business-to-business (B2B) market** consists of all the individuals and organizations that want goods and services to use in producing other goods and services or to sell, rent, or supply goods to others. Oil-drilling bits, cash registers, display cases, office desks, public accounting audits, and corporate legal advice are examples of B2B goods and services. Traditionally, they have been known as industrial goods and services because they are used in industry.

The important thing to remember is that the buyer's reason for buying—that is, the end use of the product—determines whether a product is considered a consumer product or a B2B product. For example, a box of Fiberrific cereal bought for a family's breakfast is considered a consumer product. However, if The Golden Griddle purchased the same box of Fiberrific to sell to its breakfast customers, the cereal would then be considered a B2B product. The following sections will outline in more detail consumer and B2B markets.

consumer market
All the individuals or households that want goods and services for personal consumption or use.

business-to-business (B2B) market
All the individuals and organizations that want goods and services to use in producing other goods and services or to sell, rent, or supply goods to others.

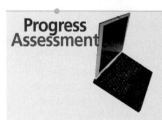

Progress Assessment

- What are the four steps in the marketing research process?
- What is environmental scanning?
- Can you define the terms *consumer market* and *business-to-business market*?

THE CONSUMER MARKET

The total potential consumer market consists of the more than 6 billion people in global markets. Because consumer groups differ greatly in age, education level, income, and taste, a business usually can't fill the needs of every group. Therefore, it must first decide which groups to serve and then develop products specially tailored to their needs.

Take Air Canada, for example, as a company that targets consumers (as well as the B2B market). Air Canada is just one company that has studied the market, broken it down into categories, and then developed products for separate groups of purchasers. On October 22, 2002, Air Canada's executive vice-president of corporate development and strategy, M. Calvin Rovinescu, spoke at the Calgary Chamber of Commerce about how the company was segmenting its markets, among other strategies, to become more competitive. According to Rovinescu, "We believe that there is no longer such a thing as a premium traveller or a discount traveller but rather a premium product and a discount product. Consumers choose different products at different times for different reasons."

For example, the full-service *Air Canada* provided a full-fare product with two classes of services and served customers on medium- to long-haul routes. *Air Canada Jetz* was a jet charter service offering a premium business service for corporate groups, sports teams, or rock bands. *Jazz* was Air Canada's regional airline, created when all five regional airlines were combined. *Air Canada Tango* was Air Canada's low-fare, no-frills brand. *Zip*, which operated short-haul routes within Western Canada, was Air Canada's second discount airline and was targeted to those who wanted low-fare, high-value air service.[18]

The importance of continuously scanning the business environment and making necessary changes cannot be overstressed. Less than two years after Rovinescu's speech, Air Canada was being restructured. Its two discount brands, Air Canada Tango and Zip Air Inc., were dropped.[19] Tango has been criticized as a flop by some airline analysts, but Air Canada spokesperson Laura Cooke insisted that both it and Zip proved to be "effective transition vehicles" for Air Canada as it lowered its operating costs.[20]

The process of dividing the total market into several groups whose members have similar characteristics is called **market segmentation.** Selecting which groups (market segments) an organization can serve profitably is called **target marketing.** For example, a shoe store may choose to sell only women's shoes, only children's shoes (e.g., Kiddie Kobbler), or only athletic shoes. The issue is finding the right target market (the segment that would be most profitable to serve) for the new venture.

Segmenting the Consumer Market

There are several ways a firm can segment the consumer market (see Figure 14.5). For example, rather than trying to sell Fiberrific throughout Canada, you might try to focus on just one or two regions of the country where you might be most successful. Dividing the market by geographic area (cities, counties, provinces, etc.) is called **geographic segmentation.**

Alternatively, you could aim Fiberrific's promotions toward people aged 25 to 45 who have some university training and have above-average incomes. Automobiles such as Lexus are often targeted to this audience. Segmentation by age, income, and education level are ways of **demographic segmentation.** Also included are religion, ethnic origin, and profession. This is the most used segmentation variable, but not necessarily the best.

You may want Fiberrific ads to portray a group's lifestyle. To do that, you could study the group's lifestyle, values, attitudes, and interests. This segmentation strategy is called **psychographic segmentation.** For example, if you decide to target teenagers, you would do an in-depth study of their values and interests. Such research reveals which TV shows they watch and which actors they like the best. That information could then be used to develop advertisements for those TV shows using those stars. PepsiCo did such a segmentation study for its Mountain Dew brand. The resulting promotion dealt with teenagers living life to the limit.

What Fiberrific benefits might you talk about? Should you emphasize high fibre, low sugar, price, nutritional benefits, or what? **Behavioural segmentation** divides the market based on behaviour with or toward a product.[21] You can determine which benefits are preferred by consumers and promote the product based on these benefits. You may choose to separate the market by product

market segmentation
The process of dividing the total market into groups whose members have similar characteristics.

target marketing
Marketing directed toward those groups (market segments) an organization decides it can serve profitably.

geographic segmentation
Dividing the market by geographic area.

demographic segmentation
Dividing the market by age, income, and education level.

psychographic segmentation
Dividing the market using the group's values, attitudes, and interests.

behavioural segmentation
Dividing the market based on behaviour with or toward a product.

Pepsi's latest effort at market segmentation and targeting is illustrated in its new products, which include Pepsi Blue, lemon-lime Sierra Mist, and Mountain Dew Code Red. Pepsi wants to build on its foundation of Pepsi and Mountain Dew to appeal to smaller market segments. Will one or more of these new flavours appeal to you? What, if any, factors might keep Pepsi or Coke from developing many additional brands of pop?

FIGURE 14.5

MARKET SEGMENTATION

This table shows some of the methods marketers use to divide the market. The aim of segmentation is to break the market into smaller units.

MAIN DIMENSION	SAMPLE VARIABLES	POSSIBLE SEGMENTS
City or Country Size		
	Region	British Columbia, Prairies, Nunavut, Eastern Quebec, Sydney, St. John's
	City or Country Size	under 5,000; 5,000–20,000; 20,001–50,000; 50,001–100,000; 100,001–250,000; 250,001–500,000; 500,001–1,000,000; 1,000,000+
	Density	urban; suburban; rural
Demographic Segmentation		
	Gender	male; female
	Marital Status	single; married; widowed; divorced
	Age	0–5; 6–11; 12–17; 18–24; 25–34; 35–49; 50–64; 65+
	Education Attainment	some education; high-school graduation certificate; trades certificate or diploma; college certificate or diploma; university certificate or diploma below bachelor level; bachelor's degree; university certificate or diploma above bachelor level; medical degree; master's degree; earned doctorate
	Ethnic Origin	Canadian; English; French; Scottish; Irish; German; Italian; Chinese; Ukrainian; North American; Indian; Dutch; Polish; East Indian; Jewish; Russian; American; Jamaican; Vietnamese; other
	Occupation	professional; technical; clerical; sales supervisor; farmer; homemaker; self-employed; student; unemployed; retired; other
	Religion	Catholic; Protestant; Christian Orthodox; other Christian; Muslim; Jewish; Buddhist; Hindu; Sikh; Eastern religions; other; no affiliation
Psychographic Segmentation		
	Personality	gregarious; compulsive; extroverted; aggressive; ambitious
	Social Class	lower lowers; upper lowers; working class; middle class; upper middles; lower uppers; upper uppers
Behavioural Segmentation		
	Benefits Sought	quality; service; low price; luxury; safety; status
	Usage Rate	light user; medium user; heavy user
	User Status	non-user; ex-user; prospect; first-time user; regular user
	Loyalty Status	none; medium; strong

usage. For example, you could determine who the big cereal eaters are. Children certainly eat a good deal of cereal, but so do adults.

In summary, the best segmentation strategy is to use all these bases to come up with a target market (or more) that is sizeable, reachable, and profitable. On the one hand, that may mean not segmenting the market at all and instead going after the total market (everyone). On the other hand, it may mean going after smaller and smaller segments. We'll discuss that strategy next.

Reaching Smaller Market Segments

Niche marketing is the process of finding small but profitable market segments and designing or finding products for them. Just how small such a segment can be is illustrated by Fridgedoor.com. This company sells refrigerator magnets on the Internet. It keeps some 1,500 different magnets in stock and sells as many as 400 a week.

One-to-one (individual) marketing means developing a unique mix of goods and services for *each individual customer*. Travel agencies often develop such packages, including airline reservations, hotel reservations, rental cars, restaurants, and admission to museums and other attractions for individual customers. This is relatively easy to do in B2B markets, where each customer may buy in huge volume. One-to-one marketing is now becoming possible in consumer-goods markets as well. Dell provides a unique computer system for each customer. Automakers are starting to customize cars as well.

One-to-one marketing means designing a separate product for each individual customer. An example is Kool Calendars. Using Xerox technology, the company can take pictures that you give them and make a customized calendar from those pictures. It is easier to customize services because you only have to find what a customer wants and then adapt the service accordingly. For example, it is relatively easy to customize a workout schedule at a health club. What other services could be customized to each individual?

Moving toward Relationship Marketing

In the world of mass production following the Industrial Revolution, marketers responded by practising mass marketing. **Mass marketing** means developing products and promotions to please large groups of people. That is, there is little segmentation. The mass marketer tries to sell products to as many people as possible. That means using mass media, such as TV, radio, and newspapers. Although mass marketing led many firms to success, marketing managers often got so caught up with their products and competition that they became less responsive to the market.

In his famous article titled "Marketing Myopia," Theodore Levitt speaks of the pitfalls that some industries have encountered because they defined themselves too narrowly. In his opinion, the railroads were in trouble because they let others take customers away from them because they assumed themselves to be in the railroad business rather than in the transportation business. At the onset of television, had Hollywood been customer-oriented (providing entertainment) rather than product-oriented (making movies), it too would not have gone through a drastic reorganization.[22]

Relationship marketing tends to lead away from mass production and toward custom-made goods and services. The goal is to keep individual customers over time by offering them new products that exactly meet their requirements. The latest in technology enables sellers to work with individual buyers to determine their wants and needs and to develop goods and

niche marketing
The process of finding small but profitable market segments and designing or finding products for them.

one-to-one (individual) marketing
Developing a unique mix of goods and services for each individual customer.

mass marketing
Developing products and promotions to please large groups of people.

relationship marketing
Marketing strategy with the goal of keeping individual customers over time by offering them products that exactly meet their requirements.

services specifically designed for them (e.g., hand-tailored shirts and unique vacations). One-way messages in mass media give way to a personal dialogue among participants. Relationship marketing combined with enterprise resource planning (ERP) ➤P. 300◄ links firms in a smooth customer-oriented system.[23] The following are just a couple of examples of relationship marketing:

- Airlines, rental car companies, and hotels have frequent-user programs through which loyal customers can earn special services and rewards. For example, a traveller can earn bonus "miles" good for free flights on an airline through a loyalty program such as Aeroplan. Founded in 1984, Aeroplan has six million members.[24] A customer can also earn benefits at a car rental agency (that includes no stopping at the rental desk—just pick up a car and go) and special services at a hotel, including faster check-in and check-out procedures, flowers in the room, free breakfasts, and free use of exercise rooms.

- The Hard Rock Cafe used customer relationship management software to launch a loyalty program, personalize its marketing campaigns, and provide the contact centre with more customer information. The result was that response times to customer inquiries were cut from a week to 24 hours.[25]

Relationship marketing is more concerned with retaining old customers than with creating new ones. Special deals, fantastic service, loyalty programs (e.g., frequent-flier programs), and the like are just the beginning. By maintaining current databases, companies can custom-make products for individuals. Levi-Strauss, for example, tried to recapture lost market share by permitting some stores to sell custom-made Levi's for about $10 more than mass-produced Levi's. Through an agreement with Levi's, once the store has your measurements, you can be assured of a perfect fit every time (as long as you don't gain or lose weight) at a reasonable price. The Spotlight on Small Business box shows how a small business can compete with larger firms by using relationship marketing.

Relationship marketing depends greatly on understanding consumers and responding quickly to their wants and needs. Therefore, knowing how consumers make decisions is important to marketers. An understanding of the consumer decision-making process helps marketers adapt their strategies in reaching customers and developing lasting relationships.

Critical Thinking

Retailers such as Hudson's Bay Company (HBC Rewards) and Canadian Tire (Canadian Tire money) offer loyalty programs. Are you encouraged to visit these retailers more often as a result of such programs? Do you buy more products as a result of such programs? Many retailers also offer incentives to use their credit cards. For example, you may get 10 percent off your purchase if you open an HBC credit card account. Points that you accumulate on your Canadian Tire Options MasterCard can be redeemed on Canadian Tire merchandise, auto parts, or auto labour. Do you feel that companies are trying to bribe you to support their business, or do you think that these are good business practices? Explain.

Spotlight on Small Business

Relationship Marketing of Bicycles

Putting into practice old marketing techniques has enabled small retailers to compete with the giants such as Wal-Mart and Sears. Zane's Cycles is a good example. Chris Zane, the owner, began the shop when he was still a teenager. Early on, he learned that to keep customers a store has to offer outstanding service and more. The principle behind such service is a concept now called customer relationship management (CRM). Long before such a concept emerged, however, small stores knew that the secret to long-term success against giant competitors is to give superior service.

Most large stores focus on making the sale; they give follow-up service little thought. The goal is to make the transaction, and that is the end of it; thus, such an approach is called *transactional marketing.*

With CRM, in contrast, the goal is to keep a customer for life. Zane's Cycles attracts customers by setting competitive prices (and providing free coffee). Chris Zane keeps customers by giving them free lifetime service on their bicycles. He also sells helmets to young people at cost to encourage safety.

Zane keeps a database on customers so that he knows what they need and when they will need it.

For example, if he sells a bicycle with a child's seat, he knows that soon the customer who purchased that bike may be buying a regular bicycle for the child—and he can send out an appropriate brochure at just the right time. Zane encourages people to give him their names, addresses, and other such information by offering to make exchanges without receipts for those people whose transaction information is in the database.

Zane also establishes close community relationships by providing scholarships for local students. Because of Zane's competitive prices, great service, and community involvement, his customers recommend his shop to others. No large store can compete with Zane's in the areas of friendly service and personal attention to each customer. That is what the new style of marketing is all about.

Sources: Rekha Balu, "Listen Up," *Fast Company,* May 2000, pp. 304–14; Ross Atkin, "Getting Past the Schwinn Mentality," *Christian Science Monitor,* August 8, 2000, p. 16; Donna Fenn, "A Bigger Wheel," *Inc.,* November 2000, pp. 78–88; www.zanes.com, 2003; and Jennifer Monahan, "Why Customers Buy Is More Important than What They Buy," *1 to 1 Magazine,* May/June 2003, pp. 52–53.

The Consumer Decision-Making Process

A major part of the marketing discipline is called consumer behaviour. Figure 14.6 shows the consumer decision-making process and some of the outside factors that influence it. The five steps in the process are often studied in courses on consumer behaviour. Problem recognition may occur, say, when your washing machine breaks down. This leads to an information search—you look for ads about washing machines and read brochures about them. You may even consult a secondary data source like *Consumer Reports* or other information sources. And, most likely, you will seek advice from other people who have purchased washing machines. After compiling all this information, you evaluate alternatives and make a purchase decision. But the process does not end here. After the purchase, you may first ask the people you spoke to previously how their machines perform and then do other comparisons. Marketing researchers investigate consumer thought processes and behaviour at each stage to determine the best way to facilitate marketing exchanges.

Consumer behaviour researchers also study the various influences that impact on consumer behaviour. Figure 14.6 shows several such influences that affect consumer buying: marketing mix variables (the four Ps); psychological influences, such as perception and attitudes; situational influences,

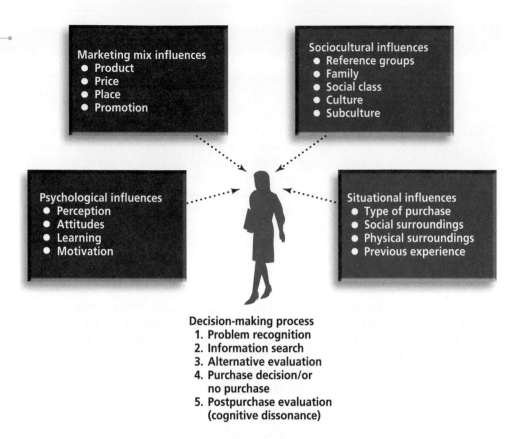

Marketing mix influences
- Product
- Price
- Place
- Promotion

Sociocultural influences
- Reference groups
- Family
- Social class
- Culture
- Subculture

Psychological influences
- Perception
- Attitudes
- Learning
- Motivation

Situational influences
- Type of purchase
- Social surroundings
- Physical surroundings
- Previous experience

Decision-making process
1. Problem recognition
2. Information search
3. Alternative evaluation
4. Purchase decision/or no purchase
5. Postpurchase evaluation (cognitive dissonance)

such as the type of purchase and the physical surroundings; and sociocultural influences, such as reference groups and culture. Other factors important in the consumer decision-making process whose technical definitions may be unfamiliar to you include the following:

- **Learning** involves changes in an individual's behaviour resulting from previous experiences and information. For example, if you've tried a particular brand of shampoo and you don't like it, you may never buy it again.

- **Reference group** is the group that an individual uses as a reference point in the formation of his or her beliefs, attitudes, values, or behaviours. For example, a student who carries a briefcase instead of a backpack may see businesspeople as his or her reference group.

- **Culture** is the set of values, attitudes, and ways of doing things that are transmitted from one generation to another in a given society. "National identity is a very important issue for Canadians, and we look endlessly for qualities that make us distinct [from Americans] … If they're brash risk-takers, then we're solid, reliable, and decent. Canadians are more class-aware, law-abiding, and group-oriented.[26]

- **Subculture** is the set of values, attitudes, and ways of doing things that results from belonging to a certain ethnic group, religious group, or other group with which one closely identifies (e.g., teenagers). The subculture is one small part of the larger culture. Your subculture may prefer rap and hip-hop music, while your parents' subculture may prefer light jazz.

- **Cognitive dissonance** is a type of psychological conflict that can occur after a purchase. Consumers who make a major purchase like a car may have doubts about whether they got the best product at the best price. Marketers must therefore reassure such consumers after the sale that they made a good decision.

Consumer behaviour courses are a long-standing part of a marketing curriculum. Today, schools are expanding their offerings in marketing to include courses in business-to-business marketing. The following section will give you some insight into that growing and important area.

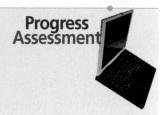

- Can you name and describe four ways to segment the consumer market?
- What is niche marketing and how does it differ from one-to-one marketing?
- List the six steps in the decision-making process.

Progress Assessment

THE BUSINESS-TO-BUSINESS MARKET

B2B marketers include manufacturers; intermediaries such as retailers; institutions (e.g., hospitals, schools, and charities); and the government. The B2B market is larger than the consumer market because items are often sold and resold several times in the B2B process before they are sold to the final consumer. The marketing strategies often differ from consumer marketing because business buyers have their own decision-making process. Several factors make B2B marketing different; some of the more important are as follows:

1. The number of customers in the B2B market is relatively few; that is, there are just a few construction firms or mining operations compared to the more than 31 million potential customers in the Canadian consumer market.

2. The size of business customers is relatively large; that is, a few large organizations account for most of the employment and production of various goods and services. Nonetheless, there are many small to medium-sized firms in Canada that together make an attractive market.

3. B2B markets tend to be geographically concentrated (for example, diamonds tend to be concentrated in Canada's territories). Consequently, marketing efforts may be concentrated on a particular geographic area and distribution problems can be minimized by locating warehouses near industrial centres.

4. Business buyers are generally thought to be more rational (as opposed to emotional) than ultimate consumers in their selection of goods and services; they use specifications and often more carefully weigh the total product offer, including quality, price, and service.

5. B2B sales tend to be direct. Manufacturers sell products, such as tires, directly to auto manufacturers but tend to use intermediaries, such as wholesalers and retailers, to sell to ultimate consumers.

6. There is much more emphasis on personal selling in B2B markets than in consumer markets. Whereas consumer promotions are based more on advertising, B2B sales are based on personal selling. That is because there are fewer customers who demand more personal service, and the quantities being purchased justify the expense of a salesforce.

BUSINESS-TO-BUSINESS MARKET		CONSUMER MARKET
Market structure	Relatively few potential customers Larger purchases Geographically concentrated	Many potential customers Smaller purchases Geographically dispersed
Products	Require technical, complex products Frequently require customization Frequently require technical advice, delivery, and after-sale service	Require less technical products Sometimes require customization Sometimes require technical advice, delivery, and after-sale service
Buying procedures	Buyers are trained Negotiate details of most purchases Follow objective standards Formal process involving specific employees Closer relationships between marketers and buyers Often buy from multiple sources	No special training Accept standard terms for most purchases Use personal judgment Informal process involving household members Impersonal relationships between marketers and consumers Rarely buy from multiple sources

FIGURE 14.7

COMPARING BUSINESS-TO-BUSINESS AND CONSUMER BUYING BEHAVIOUR

Figure 14.7 shows some of the differences between buying behaviour in the B2B market compared to the consumer market.

Critical Thinking

When businesses buy goods and services from other businesses, they usually buy in large volume. Salespeople in the business-to-business area usually are paid on a commission basis; that is, they earn a certain percentage of each sale they make. Can you see why B2B sales *may* be a more financially rewarding career area than consumer sales? Industrial companies sell goods such as steel, lumber, computers, engines, parts, and supplies. Where would you find the names of such companies?

THE PRODUCT LIFE CYCLE

product life cycle
A theoretical model of what happens to sales and profits for a product class over time.

Once a product has been developed and tested, it is placed on the market. Products often go through a life cycle consisting of four stages: introduction, growth, maturity, and decline. This is called the product life cycle (see Figure 14.8). The **product life cycle** is a theoretical model of what happens to sales and profits for a product class (e.g., all dishwasher soaps) over time. However, not all products follow the life cycle, and particular brands may act differently. For example, while frozen foods as a generic class may go through the entire cycle, one brand may never get beyond the introduction stage. Also, some products become classics and never experience much of a decline. Others may be withdrawn from the market altogether. Nonetheless, the product life cycle may provide some basis for anticipating future market developments and for planning marketing strategies. Some products, such as microwave ovens, stay in the introductory stage for years. Other products, such as fad clothing, may go through the entire cycle in a few months.

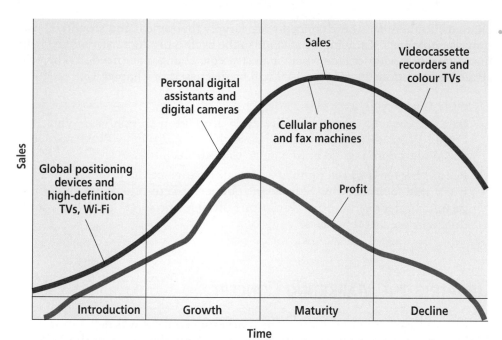

FIGURE 14.8

SALES AND PROFITS DURING THE PRODUCT LIFE CYCLE

Note that profit levels start to fall *before* sales reach their peak. This is due to increasing price competition. When profits and sales start to decline, it's time to come out with a new product or to remodel the old one to maintain interest and profits.

	MARKETING MIX ELEMENTS			
LIFE CYCLE STAGE	**PRODUCT**	**PRICE**	**PLACE**	**PROMOTION**
Introduction	Offer market-tested product; keep mix small	Go after innovators with high introductory price (skimming strategy) or use penetration pricing	Use wholesalers, selective distribution	Dealer promotion and heavy investment in primary demand advertising and sales promotion to get stores to carry the product and consumers to try it
Growth	Improve product; keep product mix limited	Adjust price to meet competition	Increase distribution	Heavy competitive advertising
Maturity	Differentiate product to satisfy different market segments	Further reduce price	Take over wholesaling function and intensify distribution	Emphasize brand name as well as product benefits and differences
Decline	Cut product mix; develop new-product ideas	Consider price increase	Consolidate distribution; drop some outlets	Reduce advertising to only loyal customers

FIGURE 14.9

SAMPLE STRATEGIES FOLLOWED DURING THE PRODUCT LIFE CYCLE

The Importance of the Product Life Cycle

The importance of the product life cycle to marketers is this: Different stages in the product life cycle call for different marketing strategies. The table in Figure 14.9 outlines the marketing mix decisions that might be made. As you go through the table, you'll see that each stage calls for multiple marketing mix changes. Remember, these concepts are largely theoretical and should be used only as guidelines. Knowing what stage in the cycle a product has reached helps marketing managers decide when such strategic changes are needed. The price strategies mentioned in Figure 14.9 will be discussed in Chapter 15.

Critical Thinking

- In what stage of the product life cycle are laptop computers? What does Figure 14.9 indicate firms should do at that stage? What will the next stage be? What might you do at that stage to optimize profits?

- Peanut butter is in the maturity or decline stage of the product life cycle. Does that explain why Skippy introduced a reduced-fat version of its peanut butter? What other variations on older products have been introduced in the last few years?

UPDATING THE MARKETING CONCEPT

As we noted earlier in the chapter, the marketing concept was developed in the 1950s to meet the consumer needs of the time. Now that we're in the 21st century, marketers have to readjust their strategies to meet the needs of modern consumers. That means each of the elements of the marketing concept—a consumer orientation, a service orientation, and a profit orientation—all have to be updated. Let's explore each of those changes next.

Unfortunately, what makes this cartoon so humorous is its reflection of what consumers perceive as everyday reality. Companies often will promise delivery of a product on a certain day, but not at a precise time, or even whether it will be morning or afternoon, forcing customers to wait. Have you had such an experience? What was your reaction?

A serviceman will be there sometime between 8am tomorrow & next spring. Please have someone home during that time.

From Providing Customer Satisfaction to Exceeding Expectations

Marketing's goal in the past was to provide customer satisfaction. Today, the goal of some six sigma quality firms is to exceed customer expectations by providing goods and services that exactly meet their requirements. One objective of a company's marketing effort, therefore, is to make sure that the response to customer wants and needs is so fast and courteous that customers are truly surprised and pleased by the experience.

You don't have to look far to see that most organizations haven't yet reached the goal of meeting, much less exceeding, customer expectations. Retail stores, government agencies, and other organizations may still irritate customers as often as they please them. Nonetheless, global competition is forcing organizations to adopt quality concepts, which means, above all, adapting organizations to customers.

Businesses have learned that employees won't provide first-class goods and services to customers unless they receive first-class treatment themselves. Marketers must therefore work with others in the firm, such as human resource personnel, to help make sure that employees are pleased. In some firms, such as IBM, employees are called *internal customers* to show the need to treat them well—like customers.

Benchmarking and Uniting Organizations

As we explained in Chapter 9, determining whether organizations are providing world-class service and quality is done through competitive benchmarking ➤P. 268◄. That means that companies compare their processes and products with those of the best companies in the world to learn how to improve them. Xerox Corporation, for example, has benchmarked its functions against corporate leaders such as American Express (for billing) and Ford (for manufacturing floor layout).

Manufacturers, unfortunately, cannot always exceed customer expectations on their own. They have to have the cooperation of suppliers to assure customers that they are getting the finest parts. They have to have close relationships with dealers to make sure that the dealers are providing fast, friendly service. We shall discuss the close relationships among marketing intermediaries in Chapter 15.

Maintaining a Profit Orientation

Marketing managers must make sure that everyone in the organization understands that the purpose behind pleasing customers and uniting organizations is to ensure a profit ➤P. 4◄ for the firm. Using that profit, the organization can then satisfy other stakeholders ➤P. 5◄ of the firm such as shareholders, environmentalists, and the local community.

It has been estimated that reducing by 5 percent the number of customers who defect—that is, who switch from buying your products to buying another company's—can increase profit by as much as 85 percent (though this figure varies by industry). Some of that profit comes from increased purchases and some from referrals. Thus, customer relationship management is becoming an intimate part of any organization seeking to maximize profits.

> **stakeholder marketing**
> Establishing and maintaining mutually beneficial exchange relationships over time with all the stakeholders of the organization.

ESTABLISHING RELATIONSHIPS WITH ALL STAKEHOLDERS

The traditional marketing concept emphasized giving *customers* what they want. Modern marketing goes further by recognizing the need to please other stakeholders as well. If you go too far in giving customers what they want, the organization may lose money and hurt other stakeholders, such as investors. Likewise, you could please customers but harm the environment, thus harming relationships with the larger community. Balancing the wants and needs of all the firm's stakeholders is a much bigger challenge than marketing has attempted in the past.

Stakeholder marketing, then, is establishing and maintaining mutually beneficial exchange relationships over time with all the stakeholders of the organization. Organizations that adopt stakeholder marketing take the community's needs into mind when designing and marketing products. For example, many companies have responded to the environmental movement by introducing green products into the marketplace. A *green product* is one whose production, use, and disposal

"Green marketing" is involved with products that are ecologically safe, clean, and in the case of the "Think" bike, cheap. What could be better ecologically than travelling to work or school on a bicycle rather than in a SUV? This bike, designed by Ford, lets you do that. It will go as fast as 28 km/h and when needed to climb hills or to travel longer distances you can switch to its battery power. What hesitation might you have in using such a bike for short errands or travel to school?

don't damage the environment.[27] For example, Patagonia sells many items of outdoor clothing made from organically grown cotton; that means less use of fertilizers to pollute the soil. Patagonia also pledges 1 percent of sales or 10 percent of pretax profit, whichever is greater, to local preservation efforts.

Customer Relationship Management (CRM) Goes High Tech

In marketing, the 80/20 rule says that 80 percent of your business is likely to come from just 20 percent of your customers. That's why some companies, like banks, have found it more profitable to discourage some unprofitable customers and put more focus on profitable ones—giving them better, more personal service. Also, it is far more expensive to get a new customer than to strengthen a relationship with an existing one. That is what CRM is all about.

One reason why CRM is so popular today is that many companies are competing to provide computer software to make the process more effective. These companies have made CRM an all-encompassing business strategy, and a "customer-centric" philosophy of doing business.[28]

Your Prospects in Marketing

There is a wider variety of careers in marketing than in most business disciplines. Therefore, if you were to major in marketing, an array of career options would be available to you. You could become a manager in a retail store. You could do marketing research or get involved in product management. You could go into selling, advertising, sales promotion, or public relations. You could get involved in transportation, storage, or international distribution. You could design interactive Websites to implement CRM. These are just a few of the possibilities. As you read the following marketing chapter, consider whether a marketing career would interest you.

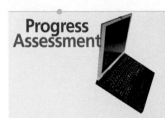

Progress Assessment

- What are four key factors that make industrial markets different from consumer markets?
- Can you draw a product life cycle and label its parts?
- What is stakeholder marketing?

Summary

1. Define marketing and describe the four Ps of marketing.

1. Marketing is the process of determining customer wants and needs and then providing customers with goods and services that meet or exceed these expectations. The marketing mix consists of the four Ps of marketing: product, price, place, and promotion.

   - *How do marketers implement the four Ps?*
   The idea is to design a *product* that people want, *price* it competitively, *place* it in a location where consumers can find it easily, and *promote* it so that consumers know it exists.

2. Describe the marketing research process, and explain how marketers use environmental scanning to learn about the changing marketing environment.

2. Marketing research is the analysis of markets to determine opportunities and challenges and to find the information needed to make good decisions.

- ***What are the steps to follow when conducting marketing research?***
(1) Define the question and determine the present situation, (2) collect data, (3) analyze the research data, and (4) choose the best solution and implement it.

- ***What is environmental scanning?***
Environmental scanning is the process of identifying the factors that can affect marketing success. Marketers pay attention to all the environmental factors that create opportunities and threats.

- ***What are some of the more important environmental trends in marketing?***
The most important global and technological change is probably the growth of the Internet. An important technological change is the growth of consumer databases. Using consumer databases, companies can develop products and services that closely match the needs of consumers. There are a number of social trends that marketers must monitor to maintain their close relationship with customers—population growth and shifts, for example. Of course, marketers must also monitor the dynamic competitive environment and pay attention to the economic environment.

3. The process of dividing the total market into several groups whose members have similar characteristics is called market segmentation.

   - ***What are some of the ways marketers segment the consumer market?***
   Geographic segmentation means dividing the market into different regions. Segmentation by age, income, and education level are ways of *demographic segmentation*. We could study a group's values, attitudes, and interests; this segmentation strategy is called *psychographic segmentation*. Determining which benefits customers prefer and using those benefits to promote a product is called *benefit segmentation*. The best segmentation strategy is to use all the variables to come up with a consumer profile (a target market) that's sizable, reachable, and profitable.

   - ***What is the difference between mass marketing and relationship marketing?***
   Mass marketing means developing products and promotions to please large groups of people. Relationship marketing tends to lead away from mass production and toward custom-made goods and services. Its goal is to keep individual customers over time by offering them goods or services that meet their needs.

   - ***What are some of the factors that influence the consumer decision-making process?***
   See Figure 14.6 for some of the major influences on consumer decision making. Some other factors in the process are learning, reference group, culture, subculture, and cognitive dissonance.

4. The B2B market consists of manufacturers, intermediaries such as retailers, institutions (e.g., hospitals, schools, and charities), and the government.

   - ***What makes the business-to-business market different from the consumer market?***
   The number of customers in the B2B market is relatively small, and the size of business customers is relatively large. B2B markets tend to be geographically concentrated, and industrial buyers generally are more rational than ultimate consumers in their selection of goods and services. B2B sales tend to be direct, and there is much more emphasis on personal selling in B2B markets than in consumer markets.

3. Explain how marketers meet the needs of the consumer market through market segmentation, relationship marketing, and the study of consumer behaviour.

4. List ways in which the business-to-business market differs from the consumer market.

5. Draw the product life cycle, describe each of its stages, and describe marketing strategies at each level.

5. Once a product is placed on the market, marketing strategy varies as the product class goes through various stages of acceptance called the product life cycle.

• *What are the theoretical stages of the product life cycle?*
They are introduction, growth, maturity, and decline.

• *How do marketing strategies theoretically change at the various stages?*
See Figure 14.9 for sample strategies followed during the product life cycle.

6. Show how the marketing concept has been adapted to fit today's modern markets to include stakeholder marketing and customer relationship management (CRM).

6. Marketing is becoming more customer-oriented as it tries to exceed customer expectations. Companies are counting on their suppliers, dealers, and others to help provide world-class service to customers. And profit is being maintained by focusing on present customers rather than finding new customers all the time.

• *What is stakeholder marketing and customer relationship marketing (CRM)?*
Stakeholder marketing is establishing and maintaining mutually beneficial exchange relationships over time with all the stakeholders of the organization. Organizations that adopt stakeholder marketing take the community's needs into mind when designing and marketing products. Customer relationship management (CRM) is learning as much as possible about customers and doing everything you can to satisfy them with products over time.

Key Terms

behavioural segmentation 427
brand name 418
business-to-business (B2B) market 426
consumer market 426
customer relationship management (CRM) 415
demographic segmentation 427
environmental scanning 424
focus group 422

geographic segmentation 427
market segmentation 427
marketing 414
marketing concept 415
marketing mix 416
marketing research 420
mass marketing 429
niche marketing 429
one-to-one (individual) marketing 429
primary data 421

product 418
product life cycle 434
promotion 420
psychographic segmentation 427
relationship marketing 429
secondary data 421
stakeholder marketing 437
target marketing 427
test marketing 418

Developing Workplace Skills

1. Think of an effective marketing mix for one of the following products: a new electric car, an easy-to-use digital camera, or a car wash for your neighbourhood. Be prepared to discuss your ideas in class.

2. Working in teams of five, think of a product that your friends want but cannot get on or near campus. You might ask your friends at other schools what's available there. What kind of product would fill that need? Discuss your results in class and how you might go about marketing that new product.

3. Relationship marketing efforts include frequent-flier deals at airlines, special discounts for members at certain supermarkets (e.g., A&P), and

Websites that remember your name and what you've purchased in the past and recommend new products that you may like (e.g., Amazon.ca). Evaluate any one of these programs. (If you have no personal experience with them, look up such programs on the Internet.) What might they do to increase your satisfaction and loyalty? Be prepared to discuss these programs in class.

4. Working in teams of four or five, list as many brand names of cars as you can. Merge your list with the lists from other groups. Then try to identify the "target market" for each brand. Do they all seem to be after the same market, or are there different brands for different markets? What are the separate appeals?

5. A "smoke shop" near the University of Toronto campus sells bongs and other items related to the use of marijuana. It also sells markers that young people sniff to get a high. People question the ethics of selling such items near campus. Others question the sale of guns, cigarettes, liquor, condoms, and pornography anywhere. Should marketers be allowed to sell anything they want? If not, what do you think the limits should be and why? Write a one-page defence of your position.

Taking It To The Net 1

Purpose

To understand some aspects of the Canadian population.

Exercise

Visit the Statistics Canada Website at www.statcan.ca and click on Canadian Statistics.

1. Under The People, visit the Population link. Answer these questions.

   a. What are the top three non-official languages spoken by Canadians?

   b. When viewing the population that is 15 years and over, what is the highest degree, certificate, or diploma that has been achieved by the largest portion of Canadians?

   c. What degree, certificate, or diploma has been attained by the fewest number of Canadians?

2. Under The People, visit Families, Households, and Housing. Answer these questions.

   a. Under Marital Status, Marriage, and Divorce, what percentage of males and females are single? What percentage of males and females are married?

   b. Under Families, what is the number and average size of families in Canada?

   c. Under Income, what is the average total income for a non-elderly, male earner? What is it for a non-elderly, female earner?

Taking It To The Net 2

Purpose

To demonstrate how the Internet can be used to enhance relationship marketing.

Exercise

Nike wants to help its customers add soul to their soles and express their individuality by customizing their own shoes. See for yourself at www.nike.com. Click on NIKEiD and build a shoe that fits your style.

1. What if you're in the middle of your shoe design and have questions about what to do next? Where can you go for help?

2. How does Nike's Website help the company strengthen its relationships with its stakeholders? Give examples to support your answer.

3. How do the elements of the Website reflect Nike's target market?

4. Does Nike invite comments from visitors to its Website? If so, how does this affect its attempt to build positive relationships with its customers?

Practising Management Decisions

Case
Applying Customer-Oriented Marketing Concepts at Thermos

Thermos is the company made famous by its Thermos bottles and lunch boxes. Thermos also manufactures cookout grills. Its competitors include Sunbeam and Weber. To become a world-class competitor, Thermos completely reinvented the way it conducted its marketing operations. By reviewing what Thermos did, you can see how new marketing concepts affect organizations.

First, Thermos modified its corporate culture. It had become a bureaucratic firm organized by function: design, engineering, manufacturing, marketing, and so on. That organizational structure was replaced by flexible, cross-functional, self-managed teams. The idea was to focus on a customer group—for example, buyers of outdoor grills—and build a product development team to create a product for that market.

The product development team for grills consisted of six middle managers from various disciplines, including engineering, manufacturing, finance, and marketing. They called themselves the Lifestyle Team because their job was to study grill users to see how they lived and what they were looking for in an outdoor grill. To get a fresh perspective, the company hired Fitch, Inc., an outside consulting firm, to help with design and marketing research. Team leadership was rotated based on needs of the moment. For example, the marketing person took the lead in doing field research, but the R&D person took over when technical developments became the issue.

The team's first step was to analyze the market. Together, they spent about a month on the road talking with people, videotaping, barbecues, conducting focus groups, and learning what people wanted in an outdoor grill. The company found that people wanted a nice-looking grill that didn't pollute the air and was easy to use. It also had to be safe enough for apartment dwellers, which meant it had to be electric.

As the research results came in, engineering began playing with ways to improve electric grills. Manufacturing kept in touch to make sure that any new ideas could be produced economically. Design people were already building models of the new product. R&D people relied heavily on Thermos's strengths. Thermos's core strength was the vacuum technology it had developed to keep hot things hot and cold things cold in Thermos bottles. Drawing on that strength, the engineers developed a domed lid that contained the heat inside the grill.

Once a prototype was developed, the company showed the model to potential customers, who suggested several changes. Employees also took sample grills home and tried to find weaknesses. Using the input from potential customers and employees, the company used continuous improvement to manufacture what became a world-class outdoor grill.

No product can become a success without communicating with the market. The team took the grill on the road, showing it at trade shows and in retail stores. The product was such a success that Thermos is now using self-managed, customer-oriented teams to develop all its product lines.

Decision Questions

1. How could the growth of self-managed cross-functional teams affect marketing departments in other companies? Do you believe that would be a good change or not? Why?

2. How can Thermos now build a closer relationship with its customers using the Internet?

3. What other products might Thermos develop that would appeal to the same market segment that uses outdoor grills?

Video Case

LifeMates

Dating in the 21st century can be challenging. Outsourcing the problem is one solution. Some singles are turning to dating services to find a suitable partner. Dating services used to have a stigma attached to them, but they are becoming more socially acceptable. For a fee and an interview, a dating service promises that you will meet a person with the characteristics that you want in a partner.

LifeMates says that it is the largest relationship company. With almost 800 pre-approved matches per week, the company is on track for 40,000 pre-approved matches in the year. Located in ten cities, it has signed 17,000 members in Canada. There are plans to open in the United States.

During the interview, clients are encouraged to reveal aspects of their personal life and discuss their past relationships. Clients need to bring in two pieces of identification, of which one is a credit card. The price is discussed during the interview and it depends on the package chosen by the client.

Dating service consultants are hired based on their empathy, people skills, and ability to sell. While consultants are trained to follow a script, as you will see in this video, sometimes they do not completely follow it. Some clients have complained about their experiences with dating services and actions have commenced against LifeMates and other dating services in Alberta and Ontario.

Discussion Questions

1. How do you see the four Ps of marketing applied to dating services?
2. What are some variables that are used by dating services to segment the consumer market?
3. How are purchasers protected by the legal system from unethical companies?
4. Would you consider using a dating service? Why or why not?

Source: *Marketplace*, July 24, 2002.

Chapter 15

Managing the Marketing Mix: Product, Price, Place, and Promotion

After you have read and studied this chapter, you should be able to

1 Explain the concept of a total product offer.

2 Describe the various kinds of consumer products.

3 Explain various pricing objectives and strategies.

4 Explain why nonpricing strategies are growing in importance.

5 Explain the concept of marketing channels and the value of marketing intermediaries.

6 Explain the various kinds of nonstore retailing.

7 Define promotion and list the four traditional tools that make up the promotion mix.

8 Explain the importance of various forms of sales promotion.

Profile

Getting to Know Erica Van Kamp of Mattel Canada Inc.

When Erica Van Kamp graduated with a bachelor of science degree in biology in 1992, little did she know that she would one day be working with toys. Her marketing career began as an assistant brand manager at Good Humor-Breyers in 1997. Over the next two years, she launched seven new products. During this time, she also issued monthly market research reports and managed budgets for advertising, research, public relations, and consumer and trade promotions. In marketing, as in other functional areas of business, teamwork is a part of most positions. Working with the company's advertising agency, Van Kamp was involved in developing creative television commercials. In another group effort, Van Kamp led a packaging optimizing team. These initiatives led to improved product placement and increased store inventory levels.

Building on this experience, Van Kamp started at Mattel Canada in June 1999 as the product manager on the Barbie Brand. Mattel, Inc. is the parent company of Mattel Canada. Mattel, Inc. is the worldwide leader in the design, manufacture, and marketing of toys and family products. This includes Barbie, the most popular fashion doll ever introduced. The Mattel family of toys and games comprises such best-selling brands as Hot Wheels, Matchbox, American Girl, and Fisher-Price, which also includes Little People, Rescue Heroes, and Power Wheels. In addition, there is a wide array of entertainment-inspired toy lines. Mattel employs more than 25,000 people in 36 countries and sells products in more than 150 countries throughout the world.

The year 2000 proved to be an exciting one in Van Kamp's career. Not only did she complete her part-time MBA, but she also received several promotions. Early in 2000, Van Kamp was promoted to senior product manager on the Barbie brand, where she was responsible for the $100-million-plus brand (with seven sub-brands). In September 2000, a promotion to marketing manager followed. In this role, Van Kamp was responsible for the $150-million-plus category, which included seven brands and seven sub-brands. Today, Van Kamp is the director of sales, where she oversees all account activity for Toys"R"Us Canada for Mattel, in addition to her co-lead role for the Boys Brand business unit.

What is a typical day like in this position? Given the highly competitive nature of this business, Van Kamp reviews sales data and looks at trends and forecasts. She meets with her team of five employees to discuss the status of the business and to resolve any issues that need facilitation. Based on all of this information, she touches base with the vice-president of sales to exchange any updates. She also communicates with key retailers to see what is happening with consumers. In her management role, she spends time on long-term strategy planning, where she checks the business progress toward key scorecards and measures. In addition to all of this, there are meetings and lots of e-mails.

In the future, Van Kamp will focus on growing her sales skill and will continue to work in a capacity where she can leverage both the strong sales and marketing experiences that she has had. When asked what advice she would give to students that are interested in a career in marketing, Van Kamp responded that there are so many facets to marketing, she encourages students to expose themselves to as much as possible. In her words, "Keep your eyes open—almost everything you touch during the course of the day has passed by a marketing professional!"

Sources: Interview with Erica Van Kamp, June 21, 2004; and www.mattel.com, June 24, 2004.

PRODUCT DEVELOPMENT AND THE TOTAL PRODUCT OFFER

value
Good quality at a fair price. When consumers calculate the value of a product, they look at the benefits and then subtract the cost to see if the benefits exceed the costs.

International competition today is so strong that Canadian businesses could lose some part of the market to foreign producers if they are not careful. The only way to prevent such losses is to design and promote better products, meaning products that are perceived to have the best **value**—good quality at a fair price. When consumers calculate the value of a product, they look at the benefits and then subtract the cost to see if the benefits exceed the costs. As we'll see in this chapter, whether a consumer perceives a product as the best value depends on many factors, including the benefits they seek and the service they receive.[1] To satisfy consumers, marketers must learn to listen better than they do now and to adapt constantly to changing market demands.[2] Managers must also constantly adapt to price challenges from competitors.[3]

Learning to manage change, especially new-product changes, is critical for tomorrow's managers. That is why Dell Computer is adding printers, storage, and handhelds.[4] An important part of the impression consumers get about products is the price.[5] This chapter will therefore explore the four key parts of the marketing mix: product, price, place (also known as distribution), and promotion.

Adapting products to new competition and new markets is an ongoing necessity. An organization can't do a one-time survey of consumer wants and needs, design a group of products to meet those needs, put them in the stores, and then just relax. It must constantly monitor changing consumer wants and needs, and adapt products, and policies, accordingly. The Reaching Beyond Our Borders box explores how some companies are responding to potential customers that make less than $2 a day.

Product development, then, is a key activity in any modern business, anywhere in the world. There's a lot more to new-product development than merely introducing goods ➤**P. 23**◀ and services ➤**P. 25**◀, however. What marketers do to create excitement for those products is as important as the products themselves.

How would you like a beer or glass of wine with your Big Mac? You can get both at this McDonald's in Paris. Also, notice how this McDonald's restaurant in Paris fits into the architectural scheme of the city. In Europe, McDonald's frequently adapts its menus and interior restaurant designs to fit the tastes and cultural demands of each country.

Reaching Beyond Our Borders

Designing Products for the Poor

When designing products for the world market, it is easy to forget that more than 2 billion people in this world make $2 a day or less. They are not necessarily interested in the latest PalmPilot or DVD player. However, in some countries, people are buying cell phones and renting them out to their neighbours. The owners make a few cents a call and everyone in the village is able to communicate better with others. To sell in such villages, other companies must learn to make and sell products that are meant to be shared. That often means helping buyers finance the product and teaching them how to begin a business as a renter of goods.

Unilever, the Anglo-Dutch consumer-goods giant, has taken a lead in developing products for people in less developed countries. The idea was to develop small packages with low prices, thus making it possible for people with very little money to have access to products they want. In India, for example, Unilever sells single-use packages of Sunsilk shampoo for as little as 2 cents. It also has a deodorant stick that sells for 16 cents. The deodorant is a big hit in the Philippines, Bolivia, Peru, and India. There is also a nickel-sized package of Vaseline and a small tube of Close Up toothpaste that sells for 8 cents.

Poor people often cannot afford eyeglasses. Scojo Vision now sells glasses in El Salvador, India, Haiti, and Guatemala for $2 a pair. Scojo is training entrepreneurs in those countries to use eye charts so they can prescribe the right correction (there are three different ones). London's Freeplay Energy Group is making radios for countries in which electricity doesn't exist and batteries are too expensive—the radios are powered by cranking a handle.

Microlending firms are giving entrepreneurs loans of $100 to $300 or so to start their own businesses. With a little capital, these entrepreneurs are able to generate money to send their children to school and to buy food and other necessities. They can also buy a few "luxury" goods like soap and deodorant, if the price is right. Doing business globally means learning to adapt to the wants and needs of everyone, and that includes the wants and needs of the very poor. As they learn to become entrepreneurs themselves, they will have the resources to buy other products and someday to trade globally themselves.

Sources: Manjeet Kripalani and Pete Engardio, "Small Is Profitable," *Business Week*, August 26, 2002, pp. 112–14; Pete Engardio, Declan Walsh, and Manjeet Kripalani, "Global Poverty," *Business Week*, October 14, 2002, pp. 108–18; and Chris Prystay, "Companies Market to India's Have-Littles," *The Wall Street Journal*, June 5, 2003, pp. B1 and B12.

FIGURE 15.1

POTENTIAL COMPONENTS OF A TOTAL PRODUCT OFFER

Price	Brand name	Convenience	Package
Store surroundings	Service	Internet access	Buyer's past experience
Guarantee	Speed of delivery	Image created by advertising	Reputation of producer

Developing a Total Product Offer

From a strategic marketing viewpoint, a total product offer is more than just the physical good or service. A **total product offer** (also called a *value package*) consists of everything that consumers evaluate when deciding whether to buy something. Thus, the basic good or service may be a washing machine, an insurance policy, or a beer, but the total product offer also may consist of the value enhancers that appear in Figure 15.1.

When people buy a product, they may evaluate and compare total product offers on all these dimensions. Note that some of the attributes are tangible (the product itself and its package), whereas others are intangible (the reputation of the producer and the image created by advertising). A successful marketer must begin to think like a consumer and evaluate the total product offer as a collection of impressions created by all the factors listed in Figure 15.1. It is wise to talk with consumers to see which features and benefits are most important to them; that is, which value enhancers to include in the final offerings.

total product offer
Everything that consumers evaluate when deciding whether to buy something; also called a value package.

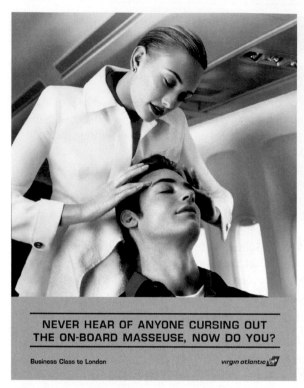

NEVER HEAR OF ANYONE CURSING OUT THE ON-BOARD MASSEUSE, NOW DO YOU?

Business Class to London   virgin atlantic

What is included in a total product offer? For Virgin Atlantic, in a certain class of service, it may even include a massage. What other services would you enjoy on a long airline flight? What services can you think of that would successfully differentiate the value packages of Virgin Atlantic's competitors—while offering comparable pricing?

Let's go back and look at the highly nutritious, high-fibre, low-sugar breakfast cereal Fiberrific, which we introduced in Chapter 14. The total product offer as perceived by the consumer is much more than the cereal itself. Anything that enhances a consumer's perceptions about the cereal's benefits and value may determine whether that consumer purchases the cereal. The price certainly is an important part of the perception of product value.

A high price may indicate exceptional quality. The store surroundings also are important. If the cereal is being sold in an exclusive health-food store, it takes on many characteristics of the store (e.g., healthy and upscale). A guarantee of satisfaction can increase the product's value in the mind of consumers, as can a well-known brand name.[6] Advertising can create an attractive image, and word of mouth can enhance the reputation. Thus, the Fiberrific total product offer is more than a cereal; it's an entire bundle of impressions.

Different consumers may want different total product offers, so the company may develop a variety of offerings. For example, auto companies sometimes offer customers a choice between zero-percent financing and a rebate of thousands of dollars. Of course, the autos themselves may have features such as automatic fold-down seats, cup holders, global positioning systems, VCRs, and more—lots more.

Critical Thinking

What value enhancers affected your choice of the school you attend? Did you consider size, location, price, reputation, library services, sports, placement, and selection of courses offered? What factors were most important? Why?

Product Lines and the Product Mix

product line
A group of products that are physically similar or are intended for a similar market.

product mix
The combination of product lines offered by a manufacturer.

Companies usually don't sell just one product. Rather, they sell several different but complementary products. Figure 15.2 shows product lines for Procter & Gamble (P&G). A **product line** is a group of products that are physically similar or are intended for a similar market. They usually face similar competition. P&G's product lines include shampoos and toothpastes. In one product line, there may be several competing brands. Thus, P&G has many brands in its laundry detergent product line, including Cheer, Tide, and Ivory Snow. All of P&G's product lines make up its **product mix,** which is the combination of product lines offered by a manufacturer.

Service providers have product lines and product mixes as well. For example, financial services firms such as banks may offer a variety of services. A bank's product mix may include savings products (such as chequing

PRODUCT LINES	BRANDS
Laundry detergents	Bold, Cheer, Dash, Dreft, Era, Gain, Ivory Snow, Liquid Bold-3, Liquid Cheer, Liquid Tide, Oxydol, Solo, Tide
Dishwashing detergents	Cascade, Dawn, Ivory Liquid, Joy, Liquid Cascade
Shampoos	Head & Shoulders, Ivory, Lilt, Pert-Plus, Prell
Toothpastes	Crest, Denquel, Gleem
Disposable diapers	Luvs, Pampers

FIGURE 15.2

SOME OF PROCTER & GAMBLE'S PRODUCT LINES

Most large companies make more than one product. Here we see various products and brands Procter & Gamble makes. Note how physically similar the products are. Why would one company sell so many laundry detergents?

accounts and term deposits), credit products (including loans, mortgages, and credit cards), and a variety of other services (such as safety deposit boxes).

Companies must decide what mix is best. The mix may include both goods and services to ensure that all of the customer's needs are being met. As well, a diversified mix would minimize the risks associated with focusing all of a firm's resources on only one target market.

PRODUCT DIFFERENTIATION

Product differentiation is the creation of real or perceived product differences. Actual product differences are sometimes quite small, so marketers must use a creative mix of pricing, advertising, and packaging (value enhancers) to create a unique, attractive image. Various bottled water companies, for example, have successfully attempted product differentiation. The companies made their bottled waters so attractive through pricing and promotion that now restaurant customers often order water by brand name instead of other popular cola drinks.

product differentiation
The creation of real or perceived product differences.

There's no reason why you couldn't create an attractive image for your product, Fiberrific. With a high price and creative advertising, it could become the Perrier or Evian of cereals. But different products call for different marketing strategies.

Small businesses ▶**P. 197**◀ can often win market share with creative product differentiation. For example, yearbook photographer Charlie Clark competes with other yearbook photographers by offering multiple clothing changes, backgrounds, and poses along with special allowances, discounts, and guarantees. He has been so successful that companies use him as a speaker at photography conventions. This is just one more example of how small businesses may have the advantage of being more flexible than big businesses in adapting to customer wants and needs and giving them attractive product differences.

Marketing Different Classes of Consumer Products

Several attempts have been made to classify consumer products. One classification, based on consumer purchasing behaviour, has four general categories—convenience, shopping, specialty, and unsought.

1. **Convenience products** are those goods and services that the consumer wants to purchase frequently and with a minimum of effort (e.g., candy, gum, milk, snacks, gas, banking services). Location, brand

convenience products
Goods and services that the consumer wants to purchase frequently and with a minimum of effort.

awareness, and image are important for marketers of convenience products. The Internet has taken convenience to a whole new level, especially for service companies, such as real estate firms.

shopping products
Goods and services that the consumer buys only after comparing value, quality, price, and style from a variety of sellers.

2. **Shopping products** are goods and services that the consumer buys only after comparing value, quality, price, and style from a variety of sellers. Shopping products are sold largely through shopping centres where consumers can make comparisons. Because many consumers carefully compare such products, marketers can emphasize price differences, quality differences, or some combination of the two. Examples include clothes, shoes, appliances, and auto repair.

specialty products
Consumer goods and services with unique characteristics and brand identity. Because these products are perceived as having no reasonable substitute, the consumer puts forth a special effort to purchase them.

3. **Specialty products** are consumer goods and services with unique characteristics and brand identity. Because these products are perceived as having no reasonable substitute, the consumer puts forth a special effort to purchase them. Examples include fine watches, fur coats, and expensive cigars, as well as services provided by medical specialists or business consultants. These products are often marketed through specialty magazines.

unsought products
Goods and services that consumers are unaware of, haven't necessarily thought of buying, or find that they need to solve an unexpected problem.

4. **Unsought products** are goods and services that consumers are unaware of, haven't necessarily thought of buying, or find that they need to solve an unexpected problem. Some examples of unsought products are emergency car-towing services, burial services, and insurance.

The marketing task varies depending on the category of product; that is, convenience goods are marketed differently from specialty goods, and so forth. The best way to promote convenience goods is to make them readily available and to create the proper image. Some combination of price, quality, and service is the best appeal for shopping goods. Specialty goods rely on reaching special market segments through advertising. Unsought goods such as life insurance often rely on personal selling; car towing relies heavily on Yellow Pages advertising.

Whether a good or service falls into a particular class depends on the individual consumer. A shopping good for one consumer (e.g., coffee) could be a specialty good for another consumer (e.g., flavoured gourmet coffee). Some people shop around to compare different dry cleaners, so dry cleaning is a shopping service for them. Others go to the closest store, making it a convenience service. Therefore, marketers must carefully monitor their customer base to determine how consumers perceive their products. Can you see how Fiberrific could be either a convenience good or a shopping good?

industrial goods
Products used in the production of other products. Sometimes called business goods or B2B goods.

The Jill Stuart brand jeans on the left and the Diesel Fanker's on the right sell for over $140. The price for the Mavi brand jeans in the middle is closer to $50. Regular old denim pants are often sold as convenience goods; that is, you can even buy them from a vending machine. Do you think that designer jeans, like these, are shopping goods or specialty goods? Does it depend on the wealth of the shopper?

Marketing Industrial Goods and Services

Industrial goods (sometimes called business goods or B2B goods) are products used in the production of other products. They are sold in the business-to-business (B2B) market ►P. 427◄. Some products can be classified as both consumer goods and industrial goods. For example, personal computers could be sold to consumer markets or B2B markets. As a consumer good, the computer might be sold through electronics stores like Future Shop or through computer magazines. Most of the promotional task would go to advertising. As an industrial good, personal computers are more likely to be sold by salespeople or on the Internet. Advertising would be less of a factor in the promotion strategy. You can see that classifying goods by user category helps determine the proper marketing mix strategy.

Progress Assessment

- What value enhancers may be included in a total product offer?
- What's the difference between a product line and a product mix?
- Name the four classes of consumer products, and give examples of each.

PACKAGING CHANGES THE PRODUCT

It's surprising how important packaging can be in evaluating the total product offer. Companies have used packaging to change and improve their basic product. Thus, we have squeezable ketchup bottles that stand upside down on their caps for easier pouring; square paint cans with screw tops and integrated handles; toothpaste pumps; packaged dinners that can be cooked in a microwave oven; and so forth.[7] In each case, the package changed the product in the minds of consumers and opened large markets.

Packaging can also help make a product more attractive to retailers. For example, the Universal Product Codes (UPCs) on many packages help stores control inventory; the UPC is the combination of a bar code (those familiar black and white lines) and a preset number that gives the retailer information about the product (price, size, colour, etc.). In short, packaging changes the product by changing its visibility, usefulness, or attractiveness.

The Growing Importance of Packaging

Today, packaging carries more of the promotional burden than in the past. Many products that were once sold by salespersons are now being sold in self-service outlets, and the package has been given more sales responsibility. The package must perform the following functions:

1. Protect the goods inside, stand up under handling and storage, be tamperproof, deter theft, and yet be easy to open and use.
2. Attract the buyer's attention.
3. Describe the contents and give information about the contents.
4. Explain the benefits of the good inside.
5. Provide information on warranties, warnings, and other consumer matters.
6. Give some indication of price, value, and uses.

Packaging of services also has been getting more attention recently. For example, Virgin Airlines includes door-to-door limousine service and in-flight massages in its total package. Financial institutions are offering everything from financial advice to help in purchasing insurance, stocks, bonds, mutual

The Quebec Winter Carnival is the world's biggest snow carnival. For 17 days, the Bonhomme Carnaval greets visitors and plays a central role in the events. More than 1 million participants a year visit this event. The Carnival generates direct economic returns of $28 million a year.

brand
A name, symbol, or design (or combination thereof) that identifies the goods or services of one seller or group of sellers and distinguishes them from the goods and services of competitors.

trademark
A brand that has been given exclusive legal protection for both the brand name and the pictorial design.

brand equity
The combination of factors—such as awareness, loyalty, perceived quality, images, and emotions—that people associate with a given brand name.

brand loyalty
The degree to which customers are satisfied, like the brand, and are committed to further purchase.

funds, and more. When combining goods or services into one package, it's important not to include so much that the price gets too high. It's best to work with customers to develop value enhancers that meet their individual needs.

BRANDING AND BRAND EQUITY

Closely related to packaging is branding. A **brand** is a name, symbol, or design (or combination thereof) that identifies the goods or services of one seller or group of sellers and distinguishes them from the goods and services of competitors. The word *brand* is sufficiently comprehensive to include practically all means of identification of a product. Brand names ▶P. 419◀ you may be familiar with include Air Canada, Roots, and President's Choice. Such brand names give products a distinction that tends to make them attractive to consumers.

A **trademark** is a brand that has been given exclusive legal protection for both the brand name and the pictorial design. Trademarks such as McDonald's golden arches are widely recognized. Trademarks need to be protected from other companies that may want to trade on the trademark holder's reputation and image. Companies often sue other companies for too-closely matching brand names. McDonald's might sue to prevent a company from selling, say, McDonnel hamburgers. Another example is the Bonhomme Carnaval, Quebec's winter carnival mascot. In 2001, Pierre de Nos wrote a police thriller and his cover featured a murderous Bonhomme Carnaval pointing a pistol. A character in the novel smuggled drugs across the Canada–U.S. border inside the Bonhomme's snowman costume.[8] The cover was withdrawn after Carnaval organizers threatened a court injunction. They felt that this family-oriented event could be tainted by any suggestion of a giant snowman attacking visitors.

For the buyer, a brand name assures quality, reduces search time, and adds prestige to purchases. For the seller, brand names facilitate new-product introductions, help promotional efforts, add to repeat purchases, and differentiate products so that prices can be set higher.

Generating Brand Equity and Loyalty

A major goal of marketers in the future will be to reestablish the notion of brand equity. **Brand equity** is the combination of factors—such as awareness, loyalty, perceived quality, images, and emotions—that people associate with a given brand name. In the past companies tried to boost their short-term performance by offering coupons and price discounts to move goods quickly. This eroded consumers' commitment to brand names. Now companies realize the value of brand equity and are trying to measure the earning power of strong brand names.

The core of brand equity is brand loyalty. **Brand loyalty** is the degree to which customers are satisfied, like the brand, and are committed to further purchases.[9] A loyal group of customers represents substantial value to a firm, and that value can be calculated.

Brand awareness refers to how quickly or easily a given brand name comes to mind when a product category is mentioned. Advertising helps build strong brand awareness. Established brands, such as Coca-Cola and Pepsi, are usually the highest in brand awareness. Event sponsorship (e.g., Rogers AT&T Cup tennis tournament) helps improve brand awareness.

brand awareness
How quickly or easily a given brand name comes to mind when a product category is mentioned.

Perceived quality is an important part of brand equity. A product that's perceived as having better quality than its competitors can be priced accordingly. The key to creating a perception of quality is to identify what consumers look for in a high-quality product and then to use that information in every message the company sends out. Factors influencing the perception of quality include price, appearance, and reputation.

Brand Management

A **brand manager** (known as a product manager in some firms) has direct responsibility for one brand or one product line. This responsibility includes all the elements of the marketing mix. Thus, the brand manager might be thought of as president of a one-product firm. Imagine being the brand manager for Fiberrific. You'd be responsible for everything having to do with that one brand. One reason why many large consumer-product companies created the position of brand manager is to have greater control over new-product development and product promotion. Some companies have brand-management teams to bolster the overall effort.

brand manager
A manager who has direct responsibility for one brand or one product line; called a product manager in some firms.

Progress Assessment

- What six functions does packaging now perform?
- What's the difference between a brand name and a trademark?
- What are the key components of brand equity?
- Explain the role of brand managers.

COMPETITIVE PRICING

Pricing is the only element of the four Ps that generates revenue. It is one of the most difficult of the four Ps for a manager to control. That is important because price is a critical ingredient in consumer evaluations of the product. In this section, we'll explore price both as an ingredient of the total product offer and as a strategic marketing tool.

Pricing Objectives

A firm may have several objectives in mind when setting a pricing strategy. When pricing Fiberrific, we may want to promote the product's image. If we price it high and use the right promotion, maybe we can make it the Evian of cereals, as we discussed earlier. We also might price it high to achieve a certain profit objective or return on investment. We could also price Fiberrific lower than its competitors because we want poor people and older people to be able to afford this nutritious cereal. That is, we could have some social or ethical goal in mind. Low pricing may also discourage competition because the profit potential is less in this case. A low price may also help us capture a larger share of the market. The point is that a firm may have several pricing objectives over time, and it must formulate these objectives clearly before developing an overall pricing strategy. Popular objectives include the following:

1. **Achieving a target return on investment or profit.** Ultimately, the goal of marketing is to make a profit ➤P. 4◀ by providing goods and services to others. Naturally, one long-run pricing objective of almost all firms is to optimize profit.[10]

2. **Building traffic.** Supermarkets often advertise certain products at or below cost to attract people to the store. These products are called *loss leaders*. The long-run objective is to make profits by following the short-run objective of building a customer base. Yahoo once provided an auction service for free in competition with eBay. Why give such a service away free? To increase advertising revenue on the Yahoo site and attract more people to Yahoo's other services.

3. **Achieving greater market share.** The North American auto industry is in a fierce international battle to capture and hold market share. One way to capture a larger part of the market is to offer low finance rates (e.g., zero-percent financing), low lease rates, or rebates. Recently, many auto companies used such discounts, but the result was a large loss in profits.[11] Computer companies offered free digital cameras and printers, rebates, and daily sweepstakes to capture business from Dell. Dell responded by offering buyers the chance to win $50,000. Such counterattacks have enabled Dell to maintain and even grow its market share.

4. **Creating an image.** Certain watches, perfumes, and other socially visible products are priced high to give them an image of exclusivity and status.

5. **Furthering social objectives.** A firm may want to price a product low so that people with little money can afford the product. The government often gets involved in pricing farm products so that everyone can get basic needs such as milk at a low price.

Note that a firm may have short-run objectives that differ greatly from its long-run objectives. Both should be understood at the beginning and put into the strategic marketing plan. Pricing objectives should be influenced by other marketing decisions regarding product design, packaging, branding, distribution, and promotion. All of these marketing decisions are interrelated.

People believe intuitively that the price charged for a product must bear some relation to the cost of producing the product. In fact, we'd generally agree that prices are usually set somewhere above cost. But as we'll see, prices and cost aren't always related. In fact, there are three major approaches to pricing strategy: cost-based, demand-based (target costing), and competition-based.

Cost-based Pricing

Producers often use cost as a primary basis for setting price. They develop elaborate cost accounting systems to measure production costs (including materials, labour, and overhead), add in some margin of profit, and come up with a price. The question is whether the price will be satisfactory to the market as well. In the long run, the market—not the producer—determines what the price will be. Pricing should take into account costs, but it should also include the expected costs of product updates, the objectives for each product, and competitor prices.

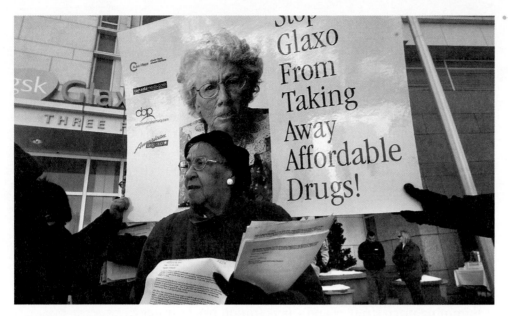

Product development is often a very expensive process, especially when it comes to making prescription drugs for specific illnesses. Without the incentive to make substantial profits, some drug companies say they can't afford the costs of research and development. That was a major issue in this protest of GlaxoSmithKline's decision not to sell drugs to Canadian pharmacies and wholesalers that, in turn, resold them to American consumers at much cheaper prices. Why would companies such as GlaxoSmithKline sell their products at different prices in different countries?

Demand-based Pricing

An opposing strategy to cost-based pricing is one called target costing. **Target costing** is demand based. It means designing a product so that it satisfies customers and meets the profit margins desired by the firm. Target costing makes the final price an input to the product development process, not an outcome of it. You estimate the selling price people would be willing to pay for a product and subtract the desired profit margin. The result is the target cost of production. Japanese companies such as Isuzu Motors, Komatsu Limited, and Sony all have used target costing.

target costing
Designing a product so that it satisfies customers and meets the profit margins desired by the firm.

Competition-based Pricing

Competition-based pricing is a strategy based on what all the other competitors are doing. The price can be at, above, or below competitors' prices. Pricing depends on customer loyalty, perceived differences, and the competitive climate. **Price leadership** is the procedure by which one or more dominant firms set the pricing practices that all competitors in an industry follow. You may have noticed this practice among oil and cigarette companies.

competition-based pricing
A pricing strategy based on what all the other competitors are doing. The price can be set at, above, or below competitors' prices.

price leadership
The procedure by which one or more dominant firms set the pricing practices that all competitors in an industry follow.

Break-even Analysis

Before you go into the business of producing Fiberrific cereal, it may be wise to determine how many boxes of cereal you'd have to sell before making a profit. You'd then determine whether you could reach such a sales goal. **Break-even analysis** is the process used to determine profitability at various levels of sales. The break-even point is the point where revenues from sales equal all costs. The formula for calculating the break-even point is as follows:

break-even analysis
The process used to determine profitability at various levels of sales.

$$\text{Break-even point (BEP)} = \frac{\text{Total fixed cost (FC)}}{\text{Price of one unit (P)} - \text{Variable cost (VC) of one unit}}$$

total fixed costs
All the expenses that remain the same no matter how many products are made or sold.

Total fixed costs are all the expenses that remain the same no matter how many products are made or sold. Among the expenses that make up fixed costs are the amount paid to own or rent a factory or warehouse and the amount

variable costs
Costs that change according to the level of production.

paid for business insurance. **Variable costs** change according to the level of production. Included are the expenses for the materials used in making products and the direct costs of labour used in making those goods. For producing Fiberrific cereal, let's say you have a fixed cost of $200,000 (for mortgage interest, real estate taxes, equipment, and so on). Your variable cost (e.g., labour and materials) per box of cereal is $2. If you sold the cereal for $4 a box, the break-even point would be 100,000 boxes. In other words, you wouldn't make any money selling cereal unless you sold more than 100,000 boxes of it:

$$\text{BEP} = \frac{\text{FC}}{\text{P} - \text{VC}} = \frac{\$200,000}{\$4.00 - \$2.00} = \frac{\$200,000}{\$2.00} = 100,000 \text{ boxes}$$

Pricing Strategies for New Products

Imagine a firm has just developed a new line of products, such as high-definition television (HDTV) sets. The firm has to decide how to price these sets at the introductory stage of the product life cycle ➤**P. 434◄**. Two strategies are a skimming price strategy and a penetration price strategy.

skimming price strategy
A strategy in which a new product is priced high to make optimum profit while there's little competition.

A **skimming price strategy** is one in which a new product is priced high to make optimum profit while there's little competition. With such a strategy, marketers can try to quickly recover R&D costs. A skimming price strategy also sends a message that the product is a quality product and, therefore, a high price is warranted. Such a strategy would be successful when there are few competitors, there is prestige attached to product ownership, and there are enough consumers who are willing and able to pay the high price to justify production and profit goals. When marketers have exhausted the market demand at this initial price, then they will lower the price to make the product price more attractive to new consumers.

As time goes on (and as more competitors enter the market as a result of the profit potential), marketers will continue to decrease the price. This is what happened when high-priced HDTVs were introduced in the 1990s. We have also seen prices decrease for microwave ovens, computers, and DVD players.

penetration price strategy
A strategy in which the product is priced low to attract many customers and discourage competitors.

A **penetration price strategy** is one in which the product is priced low to attract many customers and discourage competitors. A low initial price would attract more customers and would enable the firm to penetrate or capture a large market share quickly. It would also be a barrier to competitors that couldn't match the low price, as there would be little incentive for customers to switch. Such a strategy would be successful if consumers are price-sensitive and enough people purchase the product for the firm to 1) get a large market share and 2) take advantage of economies of scale ➤**P. 104◄**. Finally, the low price must deter competitors from entering the market with their own product versions.

The Japanese successfully used a penetration strategy with videocassette recorders. No American firms could compete with the low prices offered by the Japanese manufacturers and they quickly gained a large share of the market. One strong drawback of a penetration strategy is that it is difficult for manufacturers to raise prices once consumers have become used to the low price. Therefore, it is critical that production and pricing work well together.

Other Pricing Strategies

everyday low pricing (EDLP)
Setting prices lower than competitors and then not having any special sales.

There are several pricing strategies used by retailers. One is called **everyday low pricing (EDLP).** That's the pricing strategy used by Home Depot and Zellers. Such stores set prices lower than competitors and usually do not have many special sales. The idea is to have consumers come to those stores whenever they want a bargain rather than waiting until there is a sale, as they do for most department stores.

Department stores and other retailers most often use a **high–low pricing strategy.** The idea is to have regular prices that are higher than those at stores using EDLP but also to have many special sales in which the prices are lower than those of competitors. The problem with such pricing is that it teaches consumers to wait for sales, thus cutting into profits. As the Internet grows in popularity, you may see fewer stores with a high–low strategy because consumers will be able to find better prices on the Internet and begin buying more and more from online retailers.

Some retailers use price as a major determinant of the goods they carry. For example, there are stores that promote goods that sell for only $1 or only $10. Outlet stores sell brand-name goods at discount prices. Other stores, called discount stores, sell "seconds," or damaged goods. Consumers must take care to carefully examine such goods to be sure the flaws are not too major.

Bundling means grouping two or more products together and pricing them as a unit. For example, a store might price washers and dryers as a unit. Jiffy Lube offers an oil change and lube, and then checks your car's fluid levels and air pressure and bundles them all into one price. **Psychological pricing** means pricing goods and services at price points that make the product appear less expensive than it is. For example, a house might be priced at $299,000 with the idea that it sounds like a lot less than $300,000.

How Market Forces Affect Pricing

Ultimately, price is determined by supply ➤P. 38◄ and demand ➤P. 38◄ in the marketplace, as described in Chapter 2. For example, if you charge $3 for Fiberrific and nobody buys your cereal at that price, you'll have to lower the price until you reach a point that's acceptable to customers and to you. The price that results from the interaction of buyers and sellers in the marketplace is called the *market price.*

Recognizing the fact that different consumers may be willing to pay different prices, marketers sometimes price on the basis of consumer demand rather than cost or some other calculation. That's called *demand-oriented pricing* and it's reflected by movie theatres with low rates for children and by drugstores with discounts for senior citizens.

Marketers are facing a new pricing problem: Customers can now compare prices of many goods and services on the Internet. For example, you may want to check out deals on sites such as Travelocity.ca, Hotels.ca, or cars4you.com. Priceline.ca introduced consumers to a "demand collection system," in which buyers post the prices they are willing to pay and invite sellers to either accept or decline the price. Consumers can get great prices on airlines, hotels, and other products by naming the price they are willing to pay. You

high–low pricing strategy
Set prices that are higher than EDLP stores, but have many special sales where the prices are lower than competitors.

bundling
Grouping two or more products together and pricing them as a unit.

psychological pricing
Pricing goods and services at price points that make the product appear less expensive than it is.

With hundreds of digital cameras to compare, you'll definitely find one that clicks.
If you're into digital photos or video, finding the right camera is no longer a shot in the dark. That's because PriceGrabber.com provides the fastest, most convenient way to locate and research the best products and prices online. Simply choose your criteria, click, and within moments you're comparing cameras by brand, features, popularity and price. While you're at it, get the lowdown on products and merchants from buyers just like you. Bottom line? Whether you're shopping for cameras, computers, TVs, or thousands of other popular items, PriceGrabber provides all the information you need to make the best buying decisions.

• Computers • Software • **Electronics** • Video Games • Movies • Music • Books • Toys • Office Products

PriceGrabber.com
Comparison Shopping Beyond Compare™

How much of an impact do you think comparison shopping on the Internet is having on the pricing practices of marketers? PriceGrabber.com enables people to comparison shop quickly and easily for an increasingly wide range of products. From your perspective, how important are product descriptions and follow-up service to such sales, or is price the major determinant?

can also buy used goods online. Have you or any of your friends bought or sold anything on eBay or Amazon.ca? Clearly, price competition is going to heat up as consumers have more access to price information from all around the world.[12] As a result, nonprice competition is likely to increase.

NONPRICE COMPETITION

In spite of the emphasis placed on price in microeconomic theory, marketers often compete on product attributes other than price. You may have noted that price differences are small with products such as gasoline, men's haircuts, candy bars, and even major products such as compact cars. Typically, you will not see price used as a major promotional appeal on television. Instead, marketers tend to stress product images and consumer benefits such as comfort, style, convenience, and durability.

Many small organizations promote the services that accompany basic products rather than price in order to compete with bigger firms. The idea is that good service will enhance a relatively homogeneous product. Danny O'Neill, for example, is a small wholesaler who sells gourmet coffee to upscale restaurants. He has to watch competitors' prices and see what services they offer so that he can charge the premium prices he wants. To charge high prices, he has to offer superior service. Larger companies often do the same thing. For example, some airlines stress friendliness, promptness, abundant flights, good meals, and other such services. High-priced hotels stress "no surprises," cable TV, business services, health clubs, and other extras.[13]

Nonprice Strategies

Often marketers emphasize nonprice differences because prices are so easy to match. However, few competitors can match the image of a friendly, responsive, consumer-oriented company. The following are some other strategies for avoiding price wars:

1. **Add value.** Some drugstores with elderly customers add value by offering home delivery. Training videos add value to any product that's difficult to use. Lawn-mower manufacturer Toro gives "lawn parties" during which it teaches customers lawn care strategies.

2. **Educate consumers.** Home Depot teaches its customers how to use the equipment it sells and how to build decks and other do-it-yourself projects.

3. **Establish relationships.** Customers will pay extra for goods and services when they have a friendly relationship with the seller. Today many auto dealers, like Saturn, send out cards reminding people when service is needed. They may also have picnics and other special events for customers. Airlines, credit card providers, supermarkets, hotels, and car rental agencies have frequent-buyer clubs that offer all kinds of fringe benefits to frequent users. The services aren't always less expensive, but they offer more value.

Progress Assessment

- Can you list two short-term and two long-term pricing objectives? Can the two be compatible?
- What's wrong with using a cost-based pricing strategy?
- Can you calculate a product's break-even point if producing it costs $10,000 and revenue from the sale is $20.00?

THE IMPORTANCE OF CHANNELS OF DISTRIBUTION

There are thousands of marketing intermediaries whose job it is to help move goods from the raw-material state to producers and then on to consumers. **Marketing intermediaries** are organizations that assist in moving goods and services from producers to business and consumer users. They're called intermediaries because they're in the middle of a whole series of organizations that join together to help distribute goods from producers to consumers. A **channel of distribution** consists of a whole set of marketing intermediaries, such as agents, brokers, wholesalers, and retailers, who join together to transport and store goods in their path (or channel) from producers to consumers. **Agents/brokers** are marketing intermediaries who bring buyers and sellers together and assist in negotiating an exchange, but don't take title to the goods—that is, at no point do they own the goods. A **wholesaler** is a marketing intermediary that sells to other organizations, such as retailers, manufacturers, and institutions (e.g., hospitals). They are part of the business-to-business (B2B) ▶**P. 427**◀ system. A **retailer** is an organization that sells to ultimate consumers (that is, people like you and me) who buy for their own use.

Channels of distribution ensure communication flows and the flow of money and title to goods. They also help ensure that the right quantity and assortment of goods will be available when and where needed. Figure 15.3 pictures selected channels of distribution for both consumer and industrial (or B2B) goods.

marketing intermediaries
Organizations that assist in moving goods and services from producers to industrial and consumer users.

channel of distribution
A whole set of marketing intermediaries, such as wholesalers and retailers, that join together to transport and store goods in their path (or channel) from producers to consumers.

agents/brokers
Marketing intermediaries who bring buyers and sellers together and assist in negotiating an exchange but don't take title to the goods.

wholesaler
A marketing intermediary that sells to other organizations.

retailer
An organization that sells to ultimate consumers.

FIGURE 15.3

SELECTED CHANNELS OF DISTRIBUTION FOR INDUSTRIAL AND CONSUMER GOODS AND SERVICES

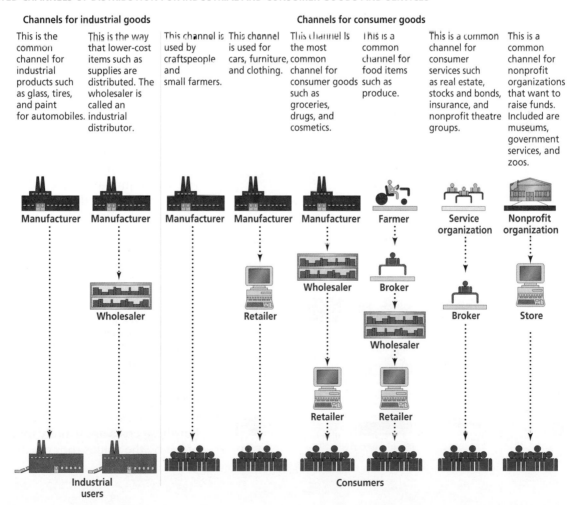

Channels for industrial goods

This is the common channel for industrial products such as glass, tires, and paint for automobiles.

This is the way that lower-cost items such as supplies are distributed. The wholesaler is called an industrial distributor.

Channels for consumer goods

This channel is used by craftspeople and small farmers.

This channel is used for cars, furniture, and clothing.

This channel is the most common channel for consumer goods such as groceries, drugs, and cosmetics.

This is a common channel for food items such as produce.

This is a common channel for consumer services such as real estate, stocks and bonds, insurance, and nonprofit theatre groups.

This is a common channel for nonprofit organizations that want to raise funds. Included are museums, government services, and zoos.

Why Marketing Needs Intermediaries

Manufacturers don't always need marketing intermediaries to sell their goods to consumer and business buyers. Figure 15.3 shows that some manufacturers sell directly to buyers. So why have marketing intermediaries at all? The answer is that intermediaries perform certain marketing tasks—such as transporting, storing, selling, advertising, and relationship building—faster and cheaper than most manufacturers could. A simple analogy is this: You could deliver packages in person to people anywhere in the world, but usually you don't. Why not? Because it's usually cheaper and faster to have them delivered by Canada Post or a private firm such as Purolator.

Similarly, you could sell your home by yourself, or buy stock directly from other people, but you probably wouldn't do so. Why? Again, because there are specialists (agents and brokers) who make the process more efficient and easier than it would be otherwise. Agents and brokers are marketing intermediaries. They facilitate the exchange process.

How Intermediaries Create Exchange Efficiency

The benefits of using marketing intermediaries can be illustrated rather easily. Suppose that five manufacturers of various food products each tried to sell directly to five retailers. The number of exchange relationships that would have to be established is 5 times 5, or 25. But picture what happens when a wholesaler enters the system. The five manufacturers would contact one wholesaler to establish five exchange relationships. The wholesaler would have to establish contact with the five retailers. That would also mean five exchange relationships. Note that the number of exchanges is reduced from 25 to only 10 by the addition of a wholesaler. Figure 15.4 shows this process.

Some economists have said that intermediaries add costs (anywhere up to 75 cents for every 25 cents in manufacturing costs), and need to be eliminated. Marketers say that intermediaries add value and that the value greatly exceeds the cost. While this debate is ongoing, there are three basic points about intermediaries that you should know:

FIGURE 15.4

HOW INTERMEDIARIES CREATE EXCHANGE EFFICIENCY

This figure shows that adding a wholesaler to the channel of distribution cuts the number of contacts from 25 to 10. This improves the efficiency of distribution.

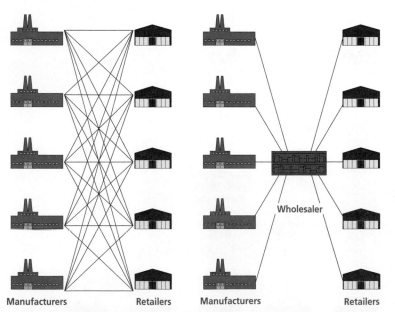

Manufacturers   Retailers   Manufacturers   Wholesaler   Retailers

- Marketing intermediaries can be eliminated, but their activities can't; that is, you can eliminate some wholesalers and retailers, but then consumers or someone else would have to perform the retailer's tasks, including transporting and storing goods, finding suppliers, and establishing communication with suppliers.[14]

- Intermediary organizations have survived in the past because they have performed marketing functions faster and cheaper than others could. To maintain their competitive position in the channel, intermediaries must adopt the latest in technology.[15]

- Intermediaries add costs to products, but these costs are usually more than offset by the values they create.

Which intermediary do you think is most important and why? If intermediaries were eliminated, would financial returns to the producers go up or down? Why?

THE UTILITIES CREATED BY INTERMEDIARIES

Utility is the value or want-satisfying ability that is added to goods or services when the products are made more useful and accessible to consumers. Six utilities are added: Form, time, place, information, possession, and service utility. Although some utilities are performed by producers, most are performed by marketing intermediaries.

Form utility is performed mostly by producers that take raw materials and change their form so that they become more useful products ➤**P. 419**◀. Thus, a Tim Hortons staff member who makes coffee just the way you want it is creating form utility. *Time utility* is created when products are available *when* they are needed (e.g., coffee was ready) and *place utility* looks after having these products available *where* people want them (e.g., a Tim Hortons around the corner).

Information utility opens two-way flows of information between marketing participants. For example, Joseph can't decide what personal computer to buy. He speaks with several retailers about the benefits and features of several models. He also reviews several ads, as well as some brochures that he brought home. This is not considered a two-way flow of information, yet still provides information utility.

Possession utility is doing whatever is necessary to transfer ownership from one party to another, including providing credit, delivery, installation, guarantees, and follow-up service. Possession utility also makes it possible for consumers to use goods through renting or leasing. In his discussion with the salespeople, Joseph discovers that there is a special loan promotion and he would not have to make a payment for one year.

Lastly, marketers add *service utility* by providing fast, friendly service during and after the sale and by teaching consumers how to best use products over time. Both the computer manufacturer and the retailer where Joseph bought his computer continue to offer help whenever he needs it. He also gets software updates for a small fee to keep his computer up-to-date. Service utility is rapidly becoming the most important utility for many retailers because without it they could lose business to direct marketing (e.g., marketing by catalogue or on the Internet). The Dealing With Change box illustrates how technology such as the Internet has helped change the way intermediaries create utility.

utility
An economic term that refers to the value or want-satisfying ability that's added to goods or services by organizations when the products are made more useful or accessible to consumers than before.

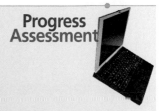

- What is a channel of distribution, and what intermediaries are involved?
- Why do we need intermediaries?
- Can you give examples of the utilities created by intermediaries and how intermediaries perform them?

Dealing With Change

How Technology Helped Change the Way Intermediaries Create Utility

Technology such as the Internet has changed the way intermediaries create utility. For example, imagine how intermediaries can use the Internet to create form utility by making specialized product offerings for business buyers. Business owners can go to a Website such as MadeToOrder.com to order customized items (e.g., mugs, key chains, rulers, calendars, shirts) printed with their business's logo on them. The value provided by the intermediary doesn't change; just the means.

Time utility takes on a whole new dimension when you add the Internet to the process. You can buy insurance, put money in the bank, pay your bills, and look for the best car deal online—24/7, which means you can do such things any time you want.

How can the Internet add place utility? Sometimes it is easier to order items without having to go anywhere. Sure, stores are sometimes conveniently placed, but sometimes they are not. What if you live way out in the country? There may not be any stores nearby. Place utility is also provided by companies that deliver goods right to your home. Some companies even make the Web available to shoppers by placing Internet kiosks in their stores. After searching the Net, customers can order items right at the store's counter.

Another issue that emerges when selling goods and services online is payment (possession utility). How can sellers be sure that buyers will pay for what they order? The online auction company eBay bought PayPal to solve that problem. PayPal acts as an online broker that allows people to move money from one person's bank or credit card account into another. PayPal and other financial institutions have emerged to help marketers provide credit and to manage payments; thus, they too can be considered as intermediaries that help in the exchange process.

Perhaps one of the most widely acclaimed benefits of the Internet is the service utility business Websites offer. Take, for example, WeddingChannel.com. This company helps people with the complex task of planning a wedding. Multiple vendors are recommended for things like flowers, caterers, wedding gowns, event venues, printers, travel providers, and more. Through Wedding Channel a couple can establish a Website that acts as a registry. Once the couple is married, the Website directs them to another site having to do with beginning married life. Note that intermediaries have not disappeared; they have merely taken on new tasks, sometimes in new places. What Websites have you used to get information about products and places?

Sources: Heather Green and Robert D. Hof, "Lessons of the Cyber Survivors," *Business Week*, April 22, 2002, p. 42; and Timothy J. Mullaney, Heather Green, Michael Arndt, Robert D. Hof, and Linda Himelstein, "The E-Biz Surprise," *Business Week*, May 12, 2003, pp. 60–68.

RETAIL INTERMEDIARIES

Perhaps the most useful marketing intermediaries, as far as you're concerned, are retailers. They're the ones who bring goods and services to your neighbourhood and make them available day and night. Next time you go to the supermarket to buy groceries, stop for a minute and look at the tremendous variety of products in the store. Think of how many marketing exchanges were involved to bring you the 18,000 or more items that you see. Some products (e.g., spices) may have been imported from halfway around the world. Other products have been processed and frozen so that you can eat them out of season (e.g., corn and green beans).

Retailing is important to the Canadian economy. Retailers sold a total of $316 billion worth of goods and services in 2003.[16] There are approximately 242,872 retail trade establishments and this number does not include the retail Websites on the Internet.[17] Retail organizations employ more than 1.5 million Canadians[18] and they are major employers of marketing graduates.

Figure 15.5 lists, describes, and gives examples of various kinds of retailers. Have you shopped in each kind of store? What seems to be the advantage of each?

TYPE	DESCRIPTION	EXAMPLE
Department store	Sells a wide variety of products (clothes, furniture, housewares) in separate departments	The Bay, Sears
Discount store	Sells many different products at prices generally below those of department stores	Zellers, Wal-Mart
Supermarket	Sells mostly food with other nonfood products such as detergent and paper products	Ultramart, Sobeys, Provigo
Warehouse club	Sells food and general merchandise in facilities that are usually larger than supermarkets and offer discount prices; membership may be required	Costco, Sam's Club
Convenience store	Sells food and other often-needed items at convenient locations; may stay open all night	Mac's, Becker's, Couche-Tard
Category killer	Sells a huge variety of one type of product to dominate that category of goods	Indigo Books & Music, Sleep Country Canada, Staples
Outlet store	Sells general merchandise directly from the manufacturer at a discount; items may be discontinued or have flaws ("seconds")	Nike, Rockport, Liz Claiborne
Specialty store	Sells a wide selection of goods in one category	Jewellery stores, shoe stores, bicycle shops
Supercentre	Sells food and general merchandise at discount prices; no membership required	Loblaws (some locations)

FIGURE 15.5

TYPES OF RETAIL STORES

There are five major ways in which retailers compete for the consumer's dollar: price, service, location, selection, and entertainment. Since consumers are constantly comparing retailers on price, service, and variety, it is important for retailers to use benchmarking to compare themselves against the best in the field to make sure that their practices and procedures are the most advanced.

Retail Distribution Strategy

A major decision marketers must make is selecting the right retailers to sell their products. Different products call for different retail distribution strategies.

Intensive distribution puts products into as many retail outlets as possible, including vending machines. Products that need intensive distribution include convenience goods such as candy, cigarettes, gum, and popular magazines.

Selective distribution is the use of only a preferred group of the available retailers in an area. Such selection helps to assure producers of quality sales and service. Manufacturers of shopping goods (appliances, furniture, and clothing) usually use selective distribution.

Exclusive distribution is the use of only one retail outlet in a given geographic area. The retailer has exclusive rights to sell the product and is therefore likely to carry a large inventory, give exceptional service, and pay more attention to this brand than to others. Auto manufacturers usually use exclusive distribution, as do producers of specialty goods such as skydiving equipment or fly-fishing products.

intensive distribution
Distribution that puts products into as many retail outlets as possible.

selective distribution
Distribution that sends products to only a preferred group of retailers in an area.

exclusive distribution
Distribution that sends products to only one retail outlet in a given geographic area.

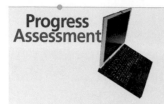

- What are some of the ways in which retailers compete?
- What kinds of products would call for each of the different distribution strategies: intensive, selective, exclusive?

NONSTORE RETAILING

electronic retailing
Selling goods and services to ultimate customers (e.g., you and me) over the Internet.

telemarketing
The sale of goods and services by telephone.

Nonstore retailing categories include electronic retailing; telemarketing; vending machines, kiosks, and carts; direct selling; and direct marketing. Small business can use nonstore retailing to open up new channels of distribution for their products.

Electronic Retailing

Electronic retailing consists of selling products to ultimate consumers (e.g., you and me) over the Internet. But getting customers is only half the battle. The other half is delivering the goods, providing helpful service, and keeping your customers. When electronic retailers fail to have sufficient inventory or fail to deliver goods on time (especially during busy periods), customers give up and go back to brick-and-mortar stores.

Most Internet retailers now offer e-mail confirmation. But sometimes electronic retailers are not so good at handling complaints, taking back goods that customers don't like, and providing personal help. Some Websites are trying to improve customer service by adding help buttons that lead customers to almost instant assistance from a real person.

Old brick-and-mortar stores are rapidly going online also. The result, sometimes called a brick-and-click store, allows customers to choose which shopping technique suits them best.

Telemarketing

Telemarketing is the sale of products by telephone. Some 80,000 companies use telemarketing today to supplement or replace in-store selling and to complement online selling. Many send a catalogue to consumers and let them order by calling a toll-free number. As we noted, many electronic retailers provide a help feature online that serves the same function.

You won't believe what you can buy from vending machines these days. This photo, for example, shows a vending machine that sells fish bait, including live worms. What are some of the limitations you perceive for vending machines? Can you see a day when those limitations are overcome and you can buy almost anything small enough to fit into a machine? Can you think of a product that should be, but isn't yet, offered in vending machines?

Vending Machines, Kiosks, and Carts

A vending machine dispenses convenience goods when consumers deposit sufficient money in the machine. Vending machines carry the benefit of location—they're found in airports, schools, service stations, and other areas where people want convenience items.

Carts and kiosks have lower overhead costs than stores do; therefore, they can offer lower prices on items such as T-shirts and umbrellas. You often see vending carts outside stores on the sidewalk or along walkways in malls; mall owners love them because they're colourful and create a marketplace atmosphere. Kiosk workers often dispense coupons and provide all kinds of helpful information to consumers, who tend to enjoy the interaction.

Direct Selling

Direct selling involves selling to consumers in their homes or where they work. Major users of this category include cosmetics producers (Avon) and vacuum cleaner manufacturers (Electrolux). Trying to emulate the success of those companies, other businesses are now venturing into direct selling. Lingerie, artwork, and plants are just a few of the goods now sold at "house parties" sponsored by sellers.

Because so many women work outside the home, companies that use direct selling are sponsoring parties at workplaces or in the evenings and on weekends. Some companies, such as those in encyclopedia sales, have dropped most of their direct selling efforts in favour of Internet selling.

direct selling
Selling to consumers in their homes or where they work.

Direct Marketing

Direct marketing includes any activity that directly links manufacturers or intermediaries with the ultimate consumer. Thus, direct retail marketing includes direct mail, catalogue sales, and telemarketing as well as online marketing. Popular consumer catalogue companies that use direct marketing include Lee Valley and Victoria's Secret. Direct marketing has created tremendous competition in some high-tech areas as well. For example, direct sales by Dell Computers, Gateway 2000, and other computer manufacturers have led IBM and Hewlett-Packard to use price-cutting tactics to meet the competition. Hewlett-Packard also decided to go online to compete more directly and to offer its own custom-designed computers.

Direct marketing has become popular because shopping from home or work is more convenient for consumers than going to stores. People can "shop" in catalogues and freestanding advertising supplements in the newspaper and then buy by phone, mail, or computer. Online selling is expected to provide increasing competition for retail stores in the near future.

direct marketing
Any activity that directly links manufacturers or intermediaries with the ultimate consumer.

BUILDING COOPERATION IN CHANNEL SYSTEMS

One way that traditional retailers can stay competitive with online retailers is to make the whole system so efficient that online retailers can't beat them out on cost—given the need for customers to pay for delivery. That means that manufacturers, wholesalers, and retailers (members of the channel of distribution) must work closely together to form a unified system. How can manufacturers get wholesalers and retailers to cooperate in such a system? One way is to somehow link the firms together in a formal relationship. Four systems have emerged to tie firms together: corporate systems, contractual systems, administered systems, and supply chains. Since we discussed supply chains in Chapter 10, we will introduce you to the other three systems next.

Corporate Distribution Systems

A **corporate distribution system** is one in which all of the organizations in the channel of distribution are owned by one firm. If the manufacturer owns the retail firm, clearly it can maintain a great deal of control over its operations.

corporate distribution system
A distribution system in which all of the organizations in the channel of distribution are owned by one firm.

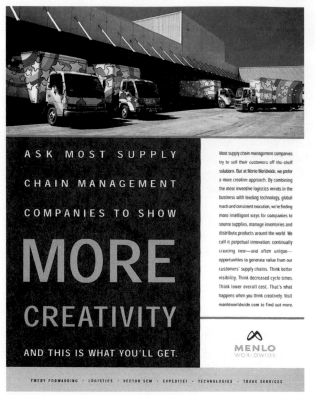

ASK MOST SUPPLY
CHAIN MANAGEMENT
COMPANIES TO SHOW
MORE
CREATIVITY
AND THIS IS WHAT YOU'LL GET.

Most supply chain management companies try to sell their customers off-the-shelf solutions. But at Menlo Worldwide, we prefer a more creative approach. By combining the most inventive logistics minds in the business with leading technology, global reach and consistent execution, we're finding more intelligent ways for companies to source supplies, manage inventories and distribute products around the world. We call it perpetual innovation: continually creating new—and often unique—opportunities to generate value from our customers' supply chains. Think better visibility. Think decreased cycle times. Think lower overall cost. That's what happens when you think creatively. Visit menloworldwide.com to find out more.

MENLO
WORLDWIDE

EMERY FORWARDING · LOGISTICS · VECTOR SCM · EXPEDITE! · TECHNOLOGIES · TRADE SERVICES

Supply chain management (SCM) ties companies together in a unified system designed to generate efficiencies that are hard for other firms to compete against. But creating an effective SCM system is easier said than done. That's where companies like Menlo come in. They provide a full-service outlet where you can find ways of cutting costs and providing better service at the same time. Do you see any disadvantages to working with companies like Menlo?

contractual distribution system
A distribution system in which members are bound to cooperate through contractual agreements.

administered distribution system
A distribution system in which producers manage all of the marketing functions at the retail level.

Sherwin-Williams, for example, owns its own retail stores and thus coordinates everything: display, pricing, promotion, inventory control, and so on.

Contractual Distribution Systems

If a manufacturer can't buy retail stores, it can try to get retailers to sign a contract to cooperate. A **contractual distribution system** is one in which members are bound to cooperate through contractual agreements. There are three forms of contractual systems:

1. **Franchise systems** such as M&M Meat Shops, Pizza Pizza, and Edo Japan. The franchisee ▶P. 170◀ agrees to all of the rules, regulations, and procedures established by the franchisor. This results in the consistent quality and level of service you find in most franchised organizations.
2. **Wholesaler-sponsored chains** such as Home Hardware and IGA food stores. Each store signs an agreement to use the same name, participate in chain promotions, and cooperate as a unified system of stores, even though each store is independently owned and managed.
3. **Retail cooperatives** such as Mountain Equipment Co-op (MEC). This arrangement is much like a wholesaler-sponsored chain except that it is initiated by the retailers. The same degree of cooperation exists, however, and the stores remain independent. Normally in such a system, retailers agree to focus their purchases on one wholesaler, but cooperative retailers could also purchase a wholesale organization to ensure better service.

Administered Distribution Systems

If you were a producer, what would you do if you couldn't get retailers to sign an agreement to cooperate? One thing you could do is to manage all the marketing functions yourself, including display, inventory control, pricing, and promotion. A system in which producers manage all of the marketing functions at the retail level is called an **administered distribution system.** Kraft does that for its cheeses; Scott does it for its seed and other lawn care products. Retailers cooperate with producers in such systems because they get a great deal of free help. All the retailer has to do is ring up the sale.

CHOOSING THE RIGHT DISTRIBUTION MODE

A primary concern of supply-chain managers is selecting a transportation mode that will minimize costs and ensure a certain level of service. (*Modes,* in

MODE	COST	SPEED	ON-TIME DEPENDABILITY	FLEXIBILITY HANDLING PRODUCTS	FREQUENCY OF SHIPMENTS	REACH
Railroad	Medium	Slow	Medium	High	Low	High
Trucks	High	Fast	High	Medium	High	Most
Pipeline	Low	Medium	Highest	Lowest	Highest	Lowest
Ships (water)	Lowest	Slowest	Lowest	Highest	Lowest	Low
Airplane	Highest	Fastest	Low	Low	Medium	Medium

FIGURE 15.6

COMPARING TRANSPORTATION MODES

Combining trucks with railroads lowers cost and increases the number of locations reached. The same is true when combining trucks with ships. Combining trucks with airlines speeds goods long distances and gets them to almost any location.

the language of distribution, are the various means used to transport goods, such as by truck, train, plane, ship, and pipeline.) Generally speaking, the faster the mode of transportation, the higher the cost. Today supply chains involve more than simply moving products from place to place; they involve all kinds of activities such as processing orders and taking inventory of products. In other words, logistics systems involve whatever it takes to see that the right products are sent to the right place quickly and efficiently.

The job of the supply-chain manager is to find the most efficient combination of these forms of transportation. Figure 15.6 shows the advantages and disadvantages of each mode.

Progress Assessment

- Describe the systems that have evolved to tie together members of the channel of distribution.
- Which transportation mode is fastest, which is cheapest, and which is most flexible?

PROMOTION AND THE PROMOTION MIX

The fourth and final element of the marketing mix is promotion. Recall from Chapter 14 that *promotion* consists of all the techniques sellers use to motivate customers to buy their products. Marketers use many different tools to promote their goods and services. Traditionally, as shown in Figure 15.7, those tools included advertising, personal selling, public relations, and sales promotion. The combination of promotional tools an organization uses is called its **promotion mix.** The product ➤P. 419◄ is shown in the middle of the figure to illustrate the fact that the product itself can be a promotional tool (e.g., through giving away free samples). We'll discuss all of the promotional tools later in this chapter.

FIGURE 15.7

THE TRADITIONAL PROMOTION MIX

Advertising

Personal selling

Product

Public relations

Sales promotion

promotion mix
The combination of promotional tools an organization uses.

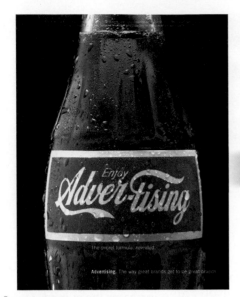

Advertising, as this advertisement suggests, is the way brands get to be great brands. How much has the advertising for Coke influenced your choice of Coke over Pepsi? Or did the Pepsi ads win you over? Or don't you drink either? Are you aware of any influence advertising has had on items that you have purchased? Which items?

integrated marketing communication (IMC)
A technique that combines all the promotional tools into one comprehensive and unified promotional strategy.

advertising
Paid, nonpersonal communication through various media by organizations and individuals who are in some way identified in the advertising message.

Integrated marketing communication (IMC) combines all the promotional tools into one comprehensive and unified promotional strategy. The idea is to use all the promotional tools and company resources to create a positive brand image and to meet the strategic marketing and promotional goals of the firm.[19]

As we discuss each of the promotional tools, we will explore the changes that are occurring in those areas. We begin the exploration of promotional tools by looking at advertising.

ADVERTISING: PERSUASIVE COMMUNICATION

Advertising is paid, nonpersonal communication through various media by organizations and individuals who are in some way identified in the advertising message. Figure 15.8 lists various categories of advertising. The Spotlight on Small Business box discusses the benefits of testimonials in advertising.

The public benefits from advertising expenditures. First, ads are informative. Newspaper advertising is full of information about products, prices, features, and more. So is direct mail advertising. Advertising not only informs us about products but also provides us with free TV, community newspapers, and radio programs: The money advertisers spend for commercial time pays for the production costs. Advertising also covers the major costs of producing newspapers and magazines. When we buy a magazine, we pay mostly for mailing or promotional costs. Figure 15.9 discusses the advantages and disadvantages of various advertising media to the advertiser.

Marketers must choose which media can best be used to reach the audience they desire.

Different kinds of advertising are used by various organizations to reach different market targets. Major categories include the following:

- *Retail advertising*—advertising to consumers by various retail stores such as supermarkets and shoe stores.
- *Trade advertising*—advertising to wholesalers and retailers by manufacturers to encourage them to carry their products.
- *Business-to-business advertising*—advertising from manufacturers to other manufacturers. A firm selling motors to auto companies would use business-to-business advertising.
- *Institutional advertising*—advertising designed to create an attractive image for an organization rather than for a product. "Beautiful British Columbia" and "Ontario—Yours To Discover" are examples of provincial government campaigns that create an attractive image.
- *Product advertising*—advertising for a good or service to create interest among consumer and industrial buyers.
- *Advocacy advertising*—advertising that supports a particular view of an issue (e.g., an ad supporting responsible drinking or protecting the environment). Such advertising is also known as cause advertising.
- *Comparison advertising*—advertising that compares competitive products. For example, an ad that compares two different cold care products' speed and benefits is a comparative ad.
- *Interactive advertising*—customer-oriented communication that enables customers to choose the information they receive, such as interactive video catalogues that let customers select which items to view.
- *Online advertising*—advertising messages that appear on computers as people visit different Websites.

FIGURE 15.8

MAJOR CATEGORIES OF ADVERTISING

MEDIUM	ADVANTAGES	DISADVANTAGES
Newspapers	Good coverage of local markets; ads can be placed quickly; high consumer acceptance; ads can be clipped and saved.	Ads compete with other features in paper; poor colour; ads get thrown away with paper (short life span).
Television	Uses sight, sound, and motion; reaches all audiences; high attention with no competition from other material.	High cost; short exposure time; takes time to prepare ads.
Radio	Low cost; can target specific audiences; very flexible; good for local marketing.	People may not listen to ad; depends on one sense (hearing); short exposure time; audience can't keep ad.
Magazines	Can target specific audiences; good use of colour; long life of ad; ads can be clipped and saved.	Inflexible; ads often must be placed weeks before publication; cost is relatively high.
Outdoor	High visibility and repeat exposures; low cost; local market focus.	Limited message; low selectivity of audience.
Direct mail	Best for targeting specific markets; very flexible; ad can be saved.	High cost; consumers may reject ad as junk mail; must conform to post office regulations.
Yellow Pages advertising	Great coverage of local markets; widely used by consumers; available at point of purchase.	Competition with other ads; cost may be too high for very small businesses.
Internet	Inexpensive global coverage; available at any time; interactive.	Relatively low readership.

FIGURE 15.9

ADVANTAGES AND DISADVANTAGES OF VARIOUS ADVERTISING MEDIA

The most effective media are often very expensive. The inexpensive media may not reach your market. The goal is to use the medium that can reach your desired market most efficiently.

Advertising and Promotion on the Internet

Advertising on the Internet is a relatively new phenomenon in marketing.[20] Despite the fact that most people tend to ignore Internet ads, companies continue to use them because they hope to tap into the huge potential that on-line marketing offers. Ultimately, the goal is to get customers and potential customers to a Website where they can learn more about the company and its products—and vice versa.

The Internet is changing the whole approach to working with customers. Note that we said "working with" rather than "promoting to." The current trend is to build relationships with customers over time.[21] That means carefully listening to what consumers want, tracking their purchases, providing them with better service, and giving them access to more information.

Global Advertising

Harvard professor Theodore Levitt believes that companies should develop a product and promotional strategy that can be implemented worldwide. Certainly global advertising would save companies money in research and design. However, other experts think that promotions targeted at specific countries or regions may be much more successful than global promotions since each country or region has its own culture, language, and buying habits.

The evidence supports the theory that promotional efforts specifically designed for individual countries often work best. For example, commercials for Camay soap that showed men complimenting women on their appearance were jarring in cultures where men don't express themselves that way. A different campaign is needed in such countries.

Well-known companies have encountered problems in global marketing. People in Canada may have difficulty with Krapp toilet paper from Sweden. Clairol introduced its curling iron, the Mist Stick, to the German market, not

Spotlight on Small Business

Using Testimonials to Build Business

Carol Boucher of Valley Forge, Pennsylvania, has a small company called Bridal Event that gives bridal shows. There is a lot of competition for audiences among such shows, and Boucher wanted her company to stand out from the others. She went to an advertising consultant who recommended the following:

1. Top your ads with an attention-capturing headline like "I DO."

2. Put in a series of testimonials from attendees at previous shows. (For example, start with a statement such as "I DO prefer the Bridal Event because ..." and then list the positive things people have said.)

3. Remember that satisfied customers provide your best ad copy.

Some small companies pay their previous customers to recommend new customers. For example, they may give a previous customers $5 for every new customer who comes to the show because of their recommendation.

Small businesses find that an important part of promotion is getting local papers to print stories about them. One way a bridal company can get such free publicity is to take a picture of several brides and grooms and write interesting stories about how each couple met and why they went to a bridal show. Other stories could feature new wedding gowns, fun things to do at wedding receptions, or unusual flower arrangements. The latest thing is to fax the stories to the various papers or to make a short video and mail it to them. If the stories are interesting enough, the local paper will print them as news.

According to *American Demographics,* 83 percent of consumers in the market for a particular product ask for information from those they know already own the product. Gathering testimonials makes the whole process easier because potential customers can see what others are saying without having to search out for themselves someone who can speak about the product. How impressed are you with testimonials from your friends and others?

realizing that *Mist* in German can mean "manure." As you can see, getting the words right in international advertising is tricky and critical. So is understanding the culture.

Even in Canada we have regional differences that are important enough to constitute separate market segments. Each province has its own history and culture. The large metropolitan areas like Toronto, Montreal, Vancouver, and Edmonton are different from the rest of the provinces in which they are located. All require their own promotions and advertising.

In short, much advertising today is moving from globalism (one ad for everyone in the world) to regionalism (specific ads for each country or for specific groups within a country). In the future, marketers will prepare more custom-designed promotions to reach smaller audiences—audiences as small as one person.

Critical Thinking

Now that there is a greater possibility of interactive communications between companies and potential customers, do you think the importance of traditional advertising will grow or decline? What will be the effect, if any, on the price we consumers must pay for newspapers and magazines?

PERSONAL SELLING: PROVIDING PERSONAL ATTENTION

personal selling
The face-to-face presentation and promotion of goods and services.

Personal selling is the face-to-face presentation and promotion of goods ►P. 23◄ and services ►P. 25◄. It also involves the search for new prospects and follow-up service after the sale. Effective selling isn't simply a matter of persuading others to buy. In fact, it's more accurately described today as helping others satisfy their wants and needs.

Given that perspective, you can see why salespeople are starting to use the Internet, portable computers, paging devices, fax machines, and other technology. They can use this technology to help customers search the Net, design custom-made products, look over prices, and generally do everything it takes to complete the order. The benefit of personal selling is that there is a person there to help you complete a transaction. The salesperson is there to listen to your needs, help you reach a solution, and do all that is possible to make accomplishing that solution smoother and easier.

It is costly to provide customers with personal attention, especially since some companies are replacing salespeople with Internet services and information. Therefore, those companies that retain salespeople must train them to be especially effective, efficient, and helpful.

Get-Real-Dolls Inc. is a successful producer of sports-action dolls. The owners, shown here, say the trick isn't making the dolls, it is getting companies like Toys "R" Us to carry them. And that requires sending out experienced salespeople who know how to promote and persuade the stores' buyers to offer the dolls for sale in their stores. Jana Machin and Julz Chavez understood this because both had experience selling for larger manufacturers before starting Get-Real-Dolls.

The Business-to-Consumer (B2C) Sales Process

Most sales to consumers take place in retail stores, where the role of the salesperson differs somewhat. It is important to understand as much as possible about the type of people who shop at a given store. One thing for sure, though, is that a salesperson needs to focus on the customer and refrain from talking to fellow salespeople—or, worse, talking on the phone to friends—when customers are around.

The first formal step in the B2C sales process, then, is the approach. Too many salespeople begin with a line like "May I help you?" That is not a good opening because the answer too often is "No." A better approach is "What may I help you with?" or, simply, "How are you today?" The idea is to show the customer that you are there to help and that you are friendly and knowledgeable. Also, you need to discover what the customer wants.

According to what the customer tells you, you then make a presentation. You show customers how the products you have meet their needs. You answer questions that help them choose the products that are right for them. The more you learn about the customers' specific wants, the better you are able to help them choose the right product or products to meet those wants.

As in B2B selling, it is important to make a trial close. "Would you like me to

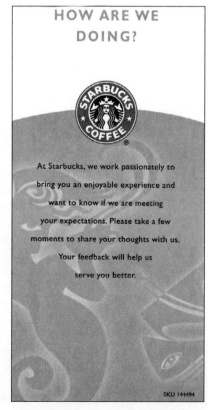

Marketers try hard to please you, but they don't always know what you're thinking: what you do and don't like about what they are doing. You can help marketers to be more responsive to your preferences by filling out customer inquiry forms like this one from Starbucks. A minute of your time may make a significant difference in the service you get next time. Do you have friends who complain about poor products but are unwilling to provide businesses with feedback?

FIGURE 15.10

STEPS IN THE BUSINESS-
TO-CONSUMER (B2C) SELLING
PROCESS

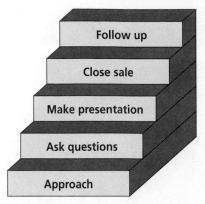

put that on hold?" or "Will you be paying for that with your store credit card?" are two such efforts. A store salesperson walks a fine line between being helpful and being pushy. Selling is an art, and a salesperson must learn just how far to go. Often individual buyers need some time alone to think about the purchase. The salesperson must respect that need and give them time and space, but still be clearly available when needed.

After-sale follow-up is an important but often neglected step in B2C sales.[22] If the product is to be delivered, the salesperson should follow up to be sure it is delivered on time. The same is true if the product has to be installed. There is often a chance to sell more merchandise when a salesperson follows up on a sale. Figure 15.10 shows the whole B2C selling process.

Critical Thinking

What kind of products do you think you would enjoy selling? Think of the customers for that product. Can you imagine yourself going through the selling process with them? Which steps would be hardest? Which would be easiest? Can you picture yourself going through most of the sales process on the phone (telemarketing)?

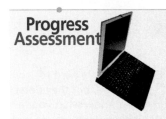

Progress Assessment

• What are the four traditional elements of the promotion mix?
• What are the five steps in the B2C selling process?

Public Relations: Building Relationships

public relations (PR)
The management function that evaluates public attitudes, changes policies and procedures in response to the public's requests, and executes a program of action and information to earn public understanding and acceptance.

Public relations (PR) is defined as the management function that evaluates public attitudes, changes policies and procedures in response to the public's requests, and executes a program of action and information to earn public understanding and acceptance.

Public relations demands a dialogue with customers so that information can be exchanged over time and trust can be developed through responsiveness.[23] Customers today often complain that it is hard to find someone to talk to in a firm. They may spend literally hours on the phone going through automated choices, waiting, and not being satisfied. In desperation, they often call the PR department. In the past, the PR department sent such callers off to someone else in a long and futile chase for someone to handle the problem. Today, however, PR is taking a much more active role in listening to consumers and working with them to handle problems.[24] That means that PR must establish good relationships with production and service people so they can find answers to customer questions quickly.

It is the responsibility of the PR department to maintain close ties with the media, community leaders, government officials, and other corporate stakeholders ➤ **P. 5** ◀. The idea is to establish and maintain a dialogue with all stakeholders so that the company can respond to inquiries, complaints, and suggestions quickly.[25]

What kinds of problems can emerge if a firm doesn't communicate with environmentalists, the news media, and the local community? In your area have you seen examples of firms that aren't responsive to the community? What have been the consequences?

Critical Thinking

Publicity: The Talking Arm of PR

Publicity is the talking arm of public relations. **Publicity** is any information about an individual, product, or organization that's distributed to the public through the media and that's not paid for, or controlled by, the seller. You might prepare a publicity release describing Fiberrific and the research findings supporting its benefits and send it to the various media. Much skill is involved in writing such releases so that the media will want to publish them. You may need to write different stories for different media. If the stories are published, release of the news about Fiberrific will reach many potential consumers (and investors, distributors, and dealers), and you may be on your way to becoming a wealthy marketer. Review the Making Ethical Decisions box for a dilemma that you might face as a marketer.

Publicity works only if the media find the material interesting or newsworthy. The idea, then, is to write publicity that meets those criteria. Besides being free, publicity has several further advantages over other promotional tools, such as advertising. For example, publicity may reach people who wouldn't read an ad. It may appear on the front page of a newspaper or in some other prominent position, or be given air time on a television news show. Perhaps the greatest advantage of publicity is its believability. When a newspaper or magazine publishes a story as news, the reader treats that story as news—and news is more believable than advertising. That's why Gardenburger and other companies that sell soybean products have been so intent on sending out publicity releases about their health benefits.

There are several disadvantages to publicity as well. For example, marketers have no control over how, when, or if the media will use the story. The media aren't obligated to use a publicity release, and most are thrown away. Furthermore, the story may be altered so that it's not so positive. There's good publicity (IBM comes out with a new supercomputer) and bad publicity (Firestone tires cause accidents). Also, once a story has run, it's not likely to be repeated. Advertising, in contrast, can be repeated as often as needed. One way to see that publicity is handled well by the media is to establish a friendly relationship with media representatives, being open with them when they seek information. Then, when you want their support, they're more likely to cooperate.

publicity
Any information about an individual, product, or organization that's distributed to the public through the media and that's not paid for or controlled by the seller.

Few new products are able to get the publicity that Dean Kamen received with his motorized scooter, the Segway. Even the President of the United States tried it—and fell! Kamen is shown here demonstrating the Segway the day it was introduced. How important is early and widespread consumer awareness to new products like the Segway?

Making Ethical Decisions

Is the Ad as Honest as the Product?

You are producing a high-fibre, nutritious cereal called Fiberrific and are having a modest degree of success. Research shows that your number of customers, or market segment, is growing but is still a relatively small percentage of breakfast cereal buyers. Generally, Fiberrific appeals mostly to health-conscious people in age groups from 25 to 60. You are trying to broaden the appeal of your cereal to the under 25 and over-60 age groups. You know that Fiberrific is a tasty and healthy product that is good for customers' health. Joan, one of your managers, suggests that you should stretch the truth a bit in your advertising and publicity material so that it will attract more consumers in the age groups you are targeting. After all, your product can't hurt anybody and is actually good for them.

Joan's idea is to develop two ads, each with two segments. The first segment of one ad would show a young woman on a tennis court holding a racquet and talking across the net to a young man. She is complaining that she seems to tire easily. The next segment would show the same two people, with the woman looking lively and saying that she tried this new breakfast cereal, Fiberrific, for two weeks and feels so energized, like a new person. A similar ad would be used to show two senior citizens walking uphill and talking. The first segment would have the man wondering why he tires so easily and the second one would show the same scene, with one man now a little ahead of the other, looking lively and stating that he is amazed at the improvement in his energy and endurance after eating Fiberrific for only two weeks. Would you go along with Joan's suggestion? What is your decision based on? Explain.

Progress Assessment

- What are the three steps involved in setting up a public relations program?
- What are the advantages and disadvantages of publicity versus advertising?

SALES PROMOTION: GETTING A GOOD DEAL

sales promotion
The promotional tool that stimulates consumer purchasing and dealer interest by means of short-term activities.

Sales promotion is the promotional tool that stimulates consumer purchasing and dealer interest by means of short-term activities. Sales promotion programs are designed to supplement personal selling, advertising, and public relations efforts by creating enthusiasm for the overall promotional program. See Figure 15.11 for a list of sales promotion techniques.

Sales promotion can take place both internally (within the company) and externally (outside the company). Often it's just as important to generate employee enthusiasm about a product as it is to attract potential customers. The most important internal sales promotion efforts are directed at salespeople and other customer-contact people, such as complaint handlers and clerks. Internal sales promotion efforts include (1) sales training; (2) the development of sales aids such as flip charts, portable audiovisual displays, and videotapes; and (3) participation in trade shows where salespeople can get leads. Other employees who deal with the public may also be given special training to improve their awareness of the company's offerings and make them an integral part of the total promotional effort.

After generating enthusiasm internally, it's important to get distributors and dealers involved so that they too are eager to help promote the product.

FIGURE **15.11**

BUSINESS-TO-BUSINESS AND CONSUMER SALES PROMOTION TECHNIQUES

BUSINESS-TO-BUSINESS

Trade shows	Catalogues
Portfolios for salespeople	Conventions
Deals (price reductions)	Event Sponsorship

CONSUMER SALES

Coupons	Bonuses (buy one, get one free)
Cents-off promotions	Catalogues
Sampling	Demonstrations
Premiums	Special events
Sweepstakes	Lotteries
Contests	In-store displays

Trade shows are an important sales promotion tool because they allow marketing intermediaries to see products from many different sellers and make comparisons among them. Today, virtual trade shows—trade shows on the Internet—enable buyers to see many products without leaving the office. Furthermore, the information is available 24/7.

After the company's employees and intermediaries have been motivated with sales promotion efforts, the next step is to promote to final consumers using samples, coupons, displays, and so on. Sales promotion is an ongoing effort to maintain enthusiasm, so different strategies must be used over time to keep the ideas fresh.

sampling
A promotional tool in which a company lets consumers have a small sample of a product for no charge.

Sampling Is a Powerful Sales Promotion Tool

One popular sales promotion tool is **sampling**—letting consumers have a small sample of the product for no charge. Because many consumers won't buy a new product unless they've had a chance to see it or try it, grocery stores often have people standing in the aisles handing out small portions of food and beverage products. Sampling is a quick, effective way of demonstrating a product's superiority at the time when consumers are making a purchase decision.

How New Technologies Are Affecting Promotion

As people purchase goods and services on the Internet, companies keep track of those purchases and gather other facts and figures about those consumers. Over time, companies learn who buys what, when, and how often. They can then use that information to design catalogues and brochures specifically to meet the wants and needs of individual consumers as demonstrated by their actual purchasing behaviour. So, for example, a flower company may send you a postcard first reminding

This International Manufacturing Trade Show in Chicago featured 4,000 booths, giving buyers for other businesses thousands of new products to explore and purchase. Can you see why trade shows in many industries are an efficient and necessary way to stay abreast of the latest developments, your competitors, and consumer reactions and needs?

Abuse or mistreat your customers and you and your business may be the one who ultimately gets burned. Thanks to a number of Websites like Complaints.com, consumers now have an option to get even, and get even they do. Have you ever consulted one of these sites before buying from or doing business with an unfamiliar company?

you that your partner's birthday is coming up soon and that you bought a particular flower arrangement last time, and then recommending a new arrangement this time. Because so much information about consumers is now available, companies are tending to use the traditional promotional tools (e.g., advertising) less than before and are putting more money into direct mail and other forms of direct marketing.

New technology offers consumers a continuous connection to the Internet and enables marketers to send video files and other data to them faster than ever before. Using such connections, marketers can interact with consumers in real time. That means that you can talk with a salesperson online and chat with other consumers about their experiences with products. You can also search the Net for the best price and find any product information you may want in almost any form you want—text, sound, video, or whatever.

Such technology gives a great deal of power to consumers like you. You no longer have to rely on advertising or other promotions to learn about products. You can search the Net on your own and find as much information as you want, when you want it. If the information is not posted, you can request it and get it immediately. Thus, promotion has become much more interactive than ever before.

MANAGING THE PROMOTION MIX: PUTTING IT ALL TOGETHER

Each target group calls for a separate promotion mix. For example, large, homogeneous groups of consumers (i.e., groups whose members share specific similar traits) are usually most efficiently reached through advertising. Large organizations are best reached through personal selling. To motivate people to buy now rather than later, sales promotion efforts such as sampling, coupons, discounts, special displays, and so on may be used. Publicity adds support to the other efforts and can create a good impression among all consumers.

Promotional Strategies

There are two key ways to facilitate the movement of products from producers to consumers. The first is called a push strategy. In a **push strategy,** the producer uses all the promotional tools to convince wholesalers and retailers to stock and sell merchandise. If the push strategy works, consumers will then walk into a store, see the product, and buy it. The idea is to push the product through the distribution system to the stores.

In a **pull strategy,** heavy advertising and sales promotion efforts are directed toward consumers so that they'll request the products from retailers. If the pull strategy works, consumers will go to the store and order the products.

push strategy
Promotional strategy in which the producer uses all the promotional tools to convince wholesalers and retailers to stock and sell merchandise.

pull strategy
Promotional strategy in which heavy advertising and sales promotion efforts are directed toward consumers so that they'll request the products from retailers.

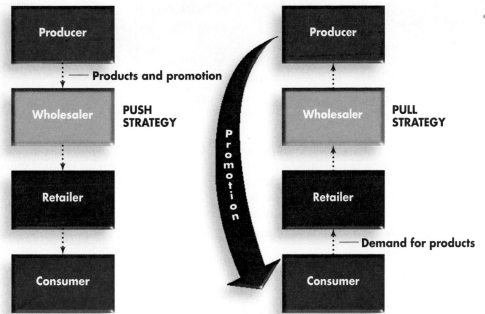

FIGURE 15.12

PUSH AND PULL STRATEGY

Seeing the demand for the products, the store owner will then order them from the wholesaler. The wholesaler, in turn, will order them from the producer. Products are thus pulled down through the distribution system. When movie producers keep advertising new films on TV, they use a pull strategy, hoping that viewers will ask for those movies at movie theatres. See Figure 15.12 for a visual explanation of both of these strategies.

Of course, a company could use both push and pull strategies at the same time in a major promotional effort. The latest in pull and push strategies are being conducted on the Internet, with companies sending messages to both consumers and businesses.

How much of your buying behaviour has moved from stores to the Internet? If you don't actually buy things on the Internet, do you use it to compare goods and prices? Do you or your friends take advantage of the low prices on used goods from eBay? Do you see yourself turning to the Internet over time for an increasing number of purchases? Why or why not?

Critical Thinking

- What are the sales promotion techniques used to reach consumers? What promotion techniques are used to reach businesses?
- Describe how to implement a push strategy and a pull strategy.

Progress Assessment

Summary

1. Explain the concept of a total product offer.

1. A total product offer consists of everything that consumers evaluate when deciding whether to buy something.

   • *What's included in a total product offer?*
   A total product offer includes price, brand name, satisfaction in use, and more.

   • *What's the difference between a product line and a product mix?*
   A product line is a group of physically similar products with similar competitors. A product line of gum may include bubble gum and sugarless gum. A product mix is a company's combination of product lines. A manufacturer may offer lines of gum, candy bars, chewing tobacco, and so on.

   • *How do marketers create product differentiation for their goods and services?*
   Marketers use a mix of pricing, advertising, and packaging to make their products seem unique and attractive.

2. Describe the various kinds of consumer products.

2. Consumer products are sold to ultimate consumers like you and me and not to businesses.

   • *What are the four classifications of consumer products and how are they marketed?*
   There are convenience goods and services (requiring minimum shopping effort), shopping goods and services (for which people go searching and compare price and quality), specialty goods and services (which consumers go out of their way to get, and often demand specific brands), and unsought goods and services (which consumers did not intend to buy when they entered the store). Convenience products are best promoted by location, shopping products by some price/quality appeal, and specialty products by specialty magazines and interactive Websites.

   • *What are industrial goods, and how are they marketed differently from consumer goods?*
   Industrial goods are products sold in the business-to-business market (B2B), and are used in the production of other products. They're sold largely through salespeople and rely less on advertising.

3. Explain various pricing objectives and strategies

3. Pricing is one of the four Ps of marketing.

   • *What are pricing objectives?*
   Objectives include achieving a target profit, building traffic, increasing market share, creating an image, and meeting social goals.

   • *What's the break-even point?*
   At the break-even point, total cost equals total revenue. Sales beyond that point are profitable. The break-even point = Total fixed costs divided by (Price of one unit − Variable cost of one unit).

   • *What strategies can marketers use to determine a new product's price?*
   A *skimming price strategy* is one in which the product is priced high to make optimum profit while there's little competition, whereas a *penetration strategy* is one in which a product is priced low to attract more customers and discourage competitors.

4. Explain why nonpricing strategies are growing in importance.

4. In spite of emphasis placed on price in microeconomic theory, marketers often compete on product attributes rather than price.

• *Why do companies use nonprice strategies?*

Pricing is one of the easiest marketing strategies to copy. Therefore, often it is not a good long-run competitive tool. Instead, marketers may compete using nonprice strategies that are less easy to copy including offering great service, educating consumers, and establishing long-term relationships with customers.

5. A channel of distribution consists of a whole set of marketing intermediaries, such as agents, brokers, wholesalers, and retailers, who join together to transport and store goods in their path (or channel) from producers to consumers.

• *How do marketing intermediaries add value?*

Intermediaries perform certain marketing tasks—such as transporting, storing, selling, advertising, and relationship building—faster and cheaper than most manufacturers could. Channels of distribution ensure communication flows and the flow of money and title to goods. They also help ensure that the right quantity and assortment of goods will be available when and where needed.

• *What are the principles behind the use of such intermediaries?*

Marketing intermediaries can be eliminated, but their activities can't. Intermediary organizations have survived in the past because they have performed marketing functions faster and cheaper than others could. Intermediaries add costs to products, but these costs are usually more than offset by the value they create.

5. Explain the concept of marketing channels and the value of marketing intermediaries.

6. Nonstore retailing is retailing done outside a store.

• *What are some forms of nonstore retailing?*

Nonstore retailing includes online marketing; telemarketing (marketing by phone); vending machines, kiosks, and carts (marketing by putting products in convenient locations, such as in the halls of shopping centres); direct selling (marketing by approaching consumers in their homes or places of work); and direct marketing (direct mail and catalogue sales). Online marketing is also a form of direct marketing.

6. Explain the various kinds of nonstore retailing.

7. Promotion is an effort by marketers to inform and remind people in the target market about products and to persuade them to participate in an exchange.

• *What are the four traditional promotional tools that make up the promotional mix?*

The four traditional promotional tools are advertising, personal selling, public relations, and sales promotion. The product itself can be a promotional tool: that's why it is shown in the middle of Figure 15.7.

7. Define promotion and list the four traditional tools that make up the promotion mix.

8. Sales promotion motivates people to buy now instead of later.

• *How are sales promotion activities used both within and outside the organization?*

Internal sales promotion efforts are directed at salespeople and other customer-contact people to keep them enthusiastic about the company. Internal sales promotion activities include sales training, sales aids, audiovisual displays, and trade shows. External sales promotion (promotion to consumers) involves using samples, coupons, cents-off deals, displays, store demonstrators, premiums, and other such incentives.

8. Explain the importance of various forms of sales promotion.

Key Terms

administered distribution systems 466
advertising 468
agents/brokers 459
brand 452
brand awareness 453
brand equity 452
brand loyalty 452
brand manager 453
break-even analysis 455
bundling 457
channel of distribution 459
competition-based pricing 455
contractual distribution system 466
convenience products 449
corporate distribution system 465
direct marketing 465
direct selling 465
electronic retailing 464

everyday low pricing (EDLP) 456
exclusive distribution 463
high-low pricing strategy 457
industrial goods 450
integrated marketing communication (IMC) 468
intensive distribution 463
marketing intermediaries 459
penetration price strategy 456
personal selling 470
price leadership 455
product differentiation 449
product line 448
product mix 448
promotion mix 467
psychological pricing 457

public relations (PR) 472
publicity 473
pull strategy 476
push strategy 476
retailer 459
sales promotion 474
sampling 475
selective distribution 463
shopping products 450
skimming price strategy 456
specialty products 450
target costing 455
telemarketing 464
total fixed costs 455
total product offer 447
trademark 452
unsought products 450
utility 461
value 446
variable costs 456
wholesaler 459

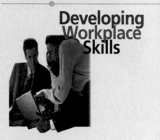

Developing Workplace Skills

1. Many students have worked in retailing, and some want to continue such careers after their studies; however, few students consider similar jobs in wholesaling. Discuss in class the differences between retailing and whole-saling and why retailing may have more appeal. Since there are fewer students seeking jobs in wholesaling, do you think such jobs may be easier to get? Explain.

2. How important is price to you when buying the following products: shoes, milk, computers, haircuts, and auto rentals? What nonprice factors are more important, if even, in making these choices? How much time does it take to evaluate factors other than price when making such purchases?

3. Imagine that you are involved in a money-raising activity for your school. You decide to sell large pizzas for $12 each. You buy a used pizza oven for $12,000. That is the only fixed cost. The variable cost per unit is $6.00. Calculate the break-even point and decide whether or not you should go ahead with the project. That is, do you think you could sell enough pizzas to make a sizable profit?

4. In small groups, discuss whether or not you are purchasing more products using catalogues and/or the Internet and why. Do you look up information on the Internet before buying products? How helpful are such searches? Present your findings to the class.

5. In small groups, make a list of five products (goods and services) that most students own or use and then discuss which promotional techniques

prompt you to buy these goods and services: advertising, personal selling, public relations, and sales promotion. Which tool seems to be most effective for your group? Why do you suppose that is?

Taking It To The Net

1

Purpose

To determine the appropriate pricing strategy for specific products.

Exercise

Go to www.marketingteacher.com/Lessons/lesson_pricing.htm and review the various types of pricing strategies.

1. Click on the Exercise button at the top of the page and place the products listed in the appropriate cells of the grid provided.

2. Click on the Answer button at the top of the page to check your work. If you do not agree with the answers, scroll down the screen for an explanation.

Taking It To The Net

2

Purpose

To learn about online sales promotion efforts.

Exercise

Many marketers put coupons in magazines and newspapers. Some place tear-coupons in supermarket and other store displays. The latest in couponing is Internet placement. To find such sites, go to www.couponmountain.com and click on various links to explore what is available. Sometimes the best deal is to pay nothing at all. To check out free offers on the Internet, go to www.yesfree.com and explore what is available there.

1. Are you willing to register at these sites to get free coupons faxed to you? Why or why not?

2. What could these Websites do to become more user-friendly for you and your friends?

3. Have you become more price conscious now that Websites give so much competitive information about price and coupons? Is that a good thing for marketers or not?

Practising Management Decisions

Case
Multilevel Marketing

Multilevel marketing often doesn't get the respect it deserves in marketing literature When multilevel marketing companies succeed their growth is often unbelievable. At least six multilevel marketing companies have reached the $500 million level in sales.

Multilevel marketing companies work like this: The founders begin by recruiting a few good people to go out and find managers to sell their products and to recruit other supervisors. These supervisors then recruit additional salespeople.

Let's say that 20 people recruit 6 people each. That means 120 salespeople. Those people then recruit 6 people each, and you have 720 salespeople. If in turn those people all recruit 6 people, you then have almost 5,000 salespeople. All supervisors earn commissions on what they sell as well as on what everyone under them sells. When you get thousands of salespeople selling for you, commissions can be quite large. One company promotes the fact that 1 percent from 100 salespeople is as good as

100 percent from one successful salesperson. Companies often add new products or expand to other countries to keep a continuous growth pattern.

Distribution under multilevel marketing is relatively easy. Often the salespeople will carry inventory in their own homes and deliver products as ordered. Many companies also offer direct shipping to customers using delivery firms, such as Purolator.

Marketers cannot ignore the success of this sales and distribution strategy. Nu Skin (a seller of health and beauty products) alone will soon have $1 billion in sales. Looking for more growth, the company started a new division, Interior Design Nutrition, to make and sell vitamins and weight-control products. Amway, perhaps one of the most well-known multilevel marketers, has chosen the international route for growth; recently, its sales of home and personal care products increased by over $1 billion in one year.

Decision Questions

1. Amway and others have been successful in Japan. To what other countries could you lead such companies so that you could become a top earner?
2. What will happen as multilevel marketing distributors begin selling and recruiting others using the latest in technology such as the Internet?
3. Why do you suppose multilevel marketing hasn't received the same acceptance as other retail innovations such as catalogue sales? What could the companies do to improve their image?
4. If multilevel marketing works so well for beauty and health care products, why not use the same concept to sell other products?

Video Case

Buzz Marketing

Advertising is everywhere. With buzz marketing, you do not normally know that you are being pitched an ad. The running shoe giant Adidas is looking for an extra push to its advertising campaign. Enter Matthew George, a product seeder. He is looking for someone who will wear the shoes he is promoting. The objective is simple: sway others to buy the company's shoes.

Here is how buzz marketing works. Find a trend-setter, someone cool who stands out from the crowd. Give this person a free product, turning him or her into a walking ad. Marketers hope that this will get others talking about the product, spreading the word, creating a buzz. Thus, buzz marketing.

Critics say that buzz marketing is a controversial approach that may influence you and your buying habits without you even knowing it. The mass audience is becoming increasingly difficult to reach, and marketers believe that buzz marketing works in tandem with mass marketing.

Discussion Questions

1. How is buzz marketing different from other advertising campaigns?
2. According to a recent study, how important is word of mouth to sales? Is word of mouth important in your buying decisions? Does its relevance vary with the type of purchase?
3. Who is Adidas trying to reach with its current campaign? Why is this target market so difficult to reach?
4. Do you think that buzz marketing is ethical? Explain.

Source: *Marketplace*, June 19, 2003.

PART 6

Chapter 16

Understanding Accounting and Financial Information

Learning Goals

After you have read and studied this chapter, you should be able to

1 Describe the importance of accounting and financial information.

2 Define and explain the different areas of the accounting profession.

3 Distinguish between accounting and bookkeeping, list the steps in the accounting cycle, and explain how computers are used in accounting.

4 Explain how the three major financial statements differ.

5 Describe the role of amortization, LIFO, and FIFO in reporting financial information.

6 Explain the importance of ratio analysis in reporting financial information.

Profile

Getting to Know Marilyn Viger of the B.C./Yukon Region of Citizenship and Immigration Canada

Marilyn Viger grew up on a farm on Washademoak Lake in Coles Island, New Brunswick, near Fredericton. While studying for her CGA (certified general accountant) designation, she worked in the finance department of Canada Post. She then moved to Revenue Canada (now Canada Revenue Agency). She credits her CGA studies with getting her in the door at the tax department. "I was in second or third year at that point," she says, adding that all the courses were relevant to her job.

Viger stayed with Revenue Canada for almost 25 years, where after several moves, she ended up in Vancouver. There, she worked as assistant director of the Verification & Enforcement Division at the Vancouver Tax Services Office prior to her move to Citizenship and Immigration Canada (CIC). Previous to that, she worked as regional director of tax programs for the assistant commissioner for the B.C./Yukon Region, and, at the national level in Ottawa, as the director of Federal and Provincial Affairs. "It's been almost like a kaleidoscope over the years with the Revenue Agency. It is a large organization and very multi-dimensional," Viger says. "I opened myself up to opportunities that provided a chance to learn. I've been active in moving around in everything from field audit, to the public relations side, to the more technical, legislative analysis, to internal audit, to management in every different dimension you could think of—all of this primarily because I like to learn."

As director general of the B.C./Yukon Region of CIC, Viger's mandate is to both facilitate entry and control access to Canada. She oversees the operations of approximately 500 staff in offices across B.C. and Yukon. These operations include six major land border points, four marine ports, eight inland offices, and three international airports. The mandate welcomes hundreds of thousands of new immigrants, refugees, temporary workers, foreign students, and tourists, while also refusing entry or removing those who are here illegally. "We have a challenge here," she says. "It's a huge region, with a daunting coastline that includes the Queen Charlotte and the Gulf Islands, to name a few."

Viger sees many similarities between her work at Revenue Canada and that at CIC. Similar management dimensions exist in both departments: an enforcement dimension, a client-service dimension, finance and administration and human resources challenges, for example. "Program-wise, you're thinking in the same vein at a management level, except the mandates are very different. The tax world—money, tax returns—is quite different from the people, the humanitarian and the security aspects that all come bundled in a job like this," she says. "This one is very much linked to the security as well as the economic agenda for Canada right now. It's a very different dynamic because of its emphasis on security and the movement of people, as opposed to the movement of money."

Controlling costs, managing cash flows, understanding profit margins and taxes, and reporting finances accurately are keys to survival for both profit-seeking and nonprofit organizations. This chapter will indroduce you to the accounting fundamentals and financial information critical to business success. As you read in this profile, a background in accounting can provide the foundation to be successful in a variety of careers. The chapter also briefly explores the financial ratios that are essential in measuring business performance.

Source: Alison Arnot, "Mountainous Mandate," May 28, 2004, *CGA Magazine*. Retrieved from www.cga-canada.org/eng/designation/profiles/marilyn_viger.htm.

THE IMPORTANCE OF ACCOUNTING AND FINANCIAL INFORMATION

In Chapter 8, we learned that the four functions of management include planning, organizing, leading, and controlling. Accounting supports the controlling function and it is designed to assist decision makers—both external and internal. It is imperative that the integrity of management information generated by the accounting system be assured. Small and sometimes large businesses falter or even fail because they do not follow good financial procedures. Financial information is the heartbeat of competitive businesses. Accounting keeps the heartbeat stable.

Accounting is different from marketing, management, and human resource management in that most of us have limited understanding of accounting principles. As consumers, we have all had some experience with marketing. As workers or students, we have observed and are familiar with many management concepts. But accounting? What is it? Is it difficult to learn? What do accountants do? Is the work interesting? Is this a career path you may wish to pursue?

You have to know something about accounting if you want to succeed in business. You also have to understand the relationship of bookkeeping to accounting and how accounts are kept. It's almost impossible to run a business without being able to read, understand, and analyze accounting reports and financial statements.

Accounting reports and financial statements reveal as much about a business's health as pulse rate and blood pressure readings tell us about a person's health. The purpose of this chapter is to introduce you to the process of obtaining needed financial information using basic accounting principles. By the end of this chapter, you should have a good idea of what accounting is, how it works, and why it is important. You should also know some accounting terms and understand the purpose of accounting statements. It's important to understand how accounting statements are constructed, but it's even more important to know what they mean to the business. A few hours invested in learning this material will pay off handsomely as you become more involved in business or investing, or simply in understanding what's going on in the world of business and finance.

What Is Accounting?

accounting
The recording, classifying, summarizing, and interpreting of financial events and transactions to provide management and other interested parties the information they need to make good decisions.

Financial information is primarily based on information generated from accounting. **Accounting** is the recording, classifying, summarizing, and interpreting of financial events and transactions to provide management and other interested parties the information they need to make good decisions. Financial transactions can include such specifics as buying and selling goods ➤P. 23◄ and services ➤P. 25◄, acquiring insurance, paying employees, and using supplies. Once the business's transactions have been recorded, they are usually classified into groups that have common characteristics. For example, all purchases are grouped together, as are all sales transactions. The method used to record and summarize accounting data into reports is called an accounting system (see Figure 16.1).

One purpose of accounting is to help managers evaluate the financial condition and the operating performance of the firm so that they can make well-informed decisions. Another major purpose is to report financial information to people outside the firm such as owners, creditors, suppliers, employees, investors, and the government (for tax purposes). In basic terms, accounting is

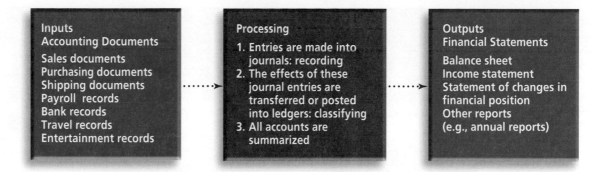

the measurement and reporting of financial information to various users (inside and outside the organization) regarding the economic activities of the firm (see Figure 16.2). Accounting work is divided into several major areas. Let's look at those areas next.

AREAS OF ACCOUNTING

Accounting has been called the language of business. Without closer scrutiny, you may think that accounting is only for profit-seeking firms. Nothing could be further from the truth; remember the chapter opening profile of Marilyn Viger from Citizenship and Immigration Canada. It is also the language used to report financial information about nonprofit organizations such as churches, schools, hospitals, and government agencies. The accounting profession is divided into five key working areas: managerial and financial accounting, auditing, tax accounting, and governmental and not-for-profit accounting. All five areas are important, and all create career opportunities for students who are willing to put forth the effort to study accounting.

Managerial Accounting

Managerial accounting is used to provide information and analyses to managers within the organization to assist them in decision making. Managerial accounting is concerned with measuring and reporting costs of production, marketing, and other functions; preparing budgets (planning); checking whether or not units are staying within their budgets (controlling); and designing strategies to minimize taxes (tax accounting).

FIGURE 16.1

THE ACCOUNTING SYSTEM

The inputs to an accounting system include bank records and other documents. The data are recorded, classified, and summarized. They're then put into summary financial statements such as the income statement and balance sheet.

managerial accounting
Accounting used to provide information and analyses to managers within the organization to assist them in decision making.

USERS	TYPE OF REPORT
Government taxing authorities (e.g., Canada Revenue Agency)	Tax returns
Government regulatory agencies	Required reports
People interested in the organization's income and financial position (e.g., owners, creditors, financial analysts, suppliers)	Financial statements found in annual reports (e.g., income statement, balance sheet, statement of changes in financial position)
Managers of the firm	Financial statements and various internally distributed financial reports

FIGURE 16.2

USERS OF ACCOUNTING INFORMATION AND THE REQUIRED REPORTS

Many types of organizations use accounting information to make business decisions. The reports needed vary according to the information each user requires. An accountant must prepare the appropriate forms.

Assembling a marine diesel engine involves many tools, parts, raw materials, and other components. Keeping these costs at a minimum and setting realistic production schedules is critical to industry survival. Management accountants team with managers from production, marketing, and other areas to ensure company competitiveness.

Simple analysis of corporate figures can disclose important information. For example, a slight month-to-month increase in payroll costs may not appear significant. But multiply that increase by 12 months and the increase in costs can be important. Monitoring profit margins, unit sales, travel expenses, cash flow, inventory turnover, and other such data is critical to the success of a firm. Management decision making is based on such data.

Some of the questions that managerial accounting reports are designed to answer include:

- What goods and services are selling the most and what promotional tools are working best?
- How quickly is the firm selling what it buys?
- How much profit is the firm making?
- What are the firm's major expenses? What are the total costs?
- How much money does the firm make on the owners' investment in the business?
- How much tax is the firm paying, and how can it minimize that amount?
- Will the firm have enough cash to pay its bills? If not, has it made arrangements to borrow that money?

In all cases, results are compared with plans to see if the results are achieving the targets set for the month, for the quarter, and for the year. When they do not, management must figure out how performance can be improved. Results are also compared with those of the particular industry to see that they are in line with, or better than, the results in competing firms. Finally, trends that the results may reveal are carefully examined to ensure that good trends are continued and unfavourable ones reversed. This prevents negative activities from continuing unnoticed until they create serious problems. You can see how important such information is. That is why accounting is a good subject to learn.

Financial Accounting

Financial accounting differs from managerial accounting in that the information and analyses it generates are for people outside the organization. The information goes to owners and prospective owners, creditors and lenders, employee unions, customers, suppliers, government agencies, and the general public. These external users are interested in the organization's profits, its ability to pay its bills, and other important financial information. Much of the information derived from financial accounting is contained in the company's **annual report,** a yearly statement of the financial condition, progress, and expectations of an organization. Various quarterly (every three months) reports keep the users more current. These reports are required by law for the shareholders of all public corporations. As pressure builds from stakeholders, companies are pouring more information than ever into their annual reports.[1]

Financial accounting reports provide the information that allows readers to answer questions such as:

- Has the company's income been satisfactory? Should we invest in this company?
- Should we lend money to this company? Will it be able to pay it back?
- Are our costs getting out of control?
- Is the company financially strong enough to stay in business to honour product warranties?
- Should we sell to this company? Will it be able to pay its bills?

We hope you are getting the idea that accounting is critical to business and to anyone who wants to understand business. You may want to know more about accounting firms, the people who prepare these reports, and how you can be sure that they know what they are doing. Accounting data can be compiled by accountants who work for the firm or by independent accounting firms.

Accounting Designations

A prestigious professional accounting designation is that of chartered accountant. A **chartered accountant (CA)** is an accountant who has met the examination, education, and experience requirements of the Canadian Institute of Chartered Accountants (CICA). All provincial institutes together have organized the CICA, which sets the accounting and auditing standards across Canada. Such a structure is also the case for CMA Canada and CGA-Canada, which will soon be introduced.

One of the responsibilities of the CICA is to prepare the Uniform Evaluation—the UFE—which is administered every year over a three-day period in many cities across Canada. This testing is rigorous in order to ensure that only qualified candidates will earn the CA designation. Those who successfully pass the UFE are granted their CA designation by a provincial Institute of Chartered Accountants (L'Ordre des comptables agréés in Quebec) that supervises the training, education, and practice of chartered accountants in that province. There are chartered accountants or their equivalents in all industrialized countries.

If you are a business major, it is almost certain you will be required to take a course in managerial accounting. You may even elect to pursue a career as a certified management accountant A **certified management accountant (CMA)** is a professional accountant who has met certain educational and

You can find important financial information about Canadian companies (such as Bell Canada Enterprises) in their annual reports. Corporations spend millions of dollars on these yearly updates, which contain a wealth of accounting information. Did you know that *The Globe and Mail* has a free annual report service?

financial accounting
Accounting information and analyses prepared for people outside the organization.

annual report
A yearly statement of the financial condition, progress, and expectations of an organization.

chartered accountant (CA)
An accountant who has met the examination, education, and experience requirements of the Canadian Institute of Chartered Accountants.

certified management accountant (CMA)
An accountant who has met the examination, education, and experience requirements of the Society of Management Accountants of Canada.

experience requirements, passed a qualifying exam in the field, and been certified by the Society of Management Accountants of Canada (CMA Canada). With growing emphasis on global competition, company rightsizing, outsourcing, and organizational cost-cutting, managerial accounting may be one of the most important areas you study in your school career.

At the time of this writing, a proposed CA and CMA merger was being evaluated. If approved by both the CICA and CMA Canada, the new organization would be one of the largest professional bodies in the world, effective January 2005. The designation for members of the new profession would be CA—Chartered Accountant. The three principal areas of practice would be management, audit and assurance, and tax.[2]

The Certified General Accountants Association of Canada (CGA-Canada) also trains and certifies accountants. **Certified general accountants (CGAs)** are those who have met the examination, education, and experience requirements of CGA-Canada. Marilyn Viger, the focus of this chapter's Profile, is a CGA. CGAs offer expertise in taxation, finance, information technology, and strategic business management.[3]

Accountants work in all areas of business. Many financial accountants are CAs, whereas managerial accountants generally choose to get a CMA designation. Many CGAs are employed by different levels of government, while others are in public practice.

certified general accountant (CGA)
An accountant who has met the examination, education, and experience requirements of the Certified General Accountants Association of Canada.

private accountants
Accountants who work for a single firm, government agency, or nonprofit organization.

public accountant
An accountant who provides his or her accounting services to individuals or businesses on a fee basis.

Chartered Accountants of Canada represents a membership of approximately 68,000 CAs and 8,000 students. The CICA conducts research into current business issues and sets accounting and auditing standards for business, nonprofit organizations, and governments.

Private and Public Accountants

It's critical for firms to keep accurate financial information. Because of this, many organizations employ **private accountants,** who work for a single firm, government agency, or nonprofit organization ➤P. 7◄. However, not all organizations want or need a full-time accountant. Therefore, they hire independent public accounting firms.

An accountant who provides his or her services to individuals or businesses on a fee basis is called a **public accountant.** Through independent firms, public accountants can provide a variety of services including accounting, auditing (to be discussed in another section), and other professional advice. Professional services can include designing an accounting system for a firm, helping select the correct computer and software to run the system, analyzing the financial strength of an organization, and providing consulting services.[4] Large accounting and auditing firms operate internationally to serve large transnational companies.

It is vital for the accounting profession to assure users of financial information that the information provided is accurate. Accountants must follow a set of *generally accepted accounting principles (GAAP).*[5] If financial reports are prepared in accordance with GAAP, users can expect that the information is reported according to standards agreed upon by accounting professionals.[6] We will discuss GAAP later on in this chapter.

In the early 2000s, the accounting profession suffered through perhaps the darkest period in its history.[7] Accounting scandals involving high-profile

www.forensisgroup.com

Dealing With Change

Elementary, Mr. Auditor, Elementary!

Having problems with an audit that's gone awry? Think there's some hidden debt buried in a far corner of your company's books? Who are you going to call? Ghostbusters? No, it's time to call the accounting industry's version of Sherlock Holmes: the forensic accountant.

According to ex-RCMP chief Norman Inkster, President of the Inkster Group, forensic accounting is the gathering of accounting information for presentation as evidence in a court of law. "In today's burgeoning global village, time and distance are no longer relevant," he said, "and even language and cultural differences do not count as before. Greater complexity now marks many business deals and with it comes more possibilities for wrongdoing."

Forensic accountants have a somewhat sexy job in the normally quiet world of accounting. Forensic accountant Bill Kauppila sums it up well: "Our job is coming up with the story behind the story." Many companies found out the hard way that even the slightest whiff of accounting irregularities can be detrimental to the firm's health. Unfortunately, the pressure to meet earnings expectations caused some companies to play fast and loose with their financial reporting. Enter the accounting supersleuths.

Stealthily uncovering paper trails left behind by company rogues starts the detailed forensic work. Mining computer hard drives, financial papers, and bank records in a search for a smoking gun consumes the attention of the forensic accountant. However, forensic accountants also see part of their job as behavioural, meaning they get out and listen to employees who have concerns about supervisors encouraging them to "cook the books" or "hide some costs." Larry Crumbley, editor of the *Journal of Forensic Accounting*, compares looking for accounting fraud through forensic analysis to taking a metal detector to a garbage dump to find rare coins: "You're going to find a lot of junk out there." As pressures mount on companies to provide accurate financial information, we can expect forensic accountants to stay busy.

If you are interested in this career, according to Inkster a forensic accountant needs the following skills: a CA designation; knowledge of the business; an enquiring mind; puzzle-solving ability; writing skills; and the ability to tell the story in court.

Sources: Bill Cramer, "Fraud Squad," *CFO*, April 2003, pp. 36–44; Stan Lomax, "Cooking the Books," *Business and Economics Review*, April–June 2003, pp. 3–8; William Poe, "Forensic Accounting," *St. Louis Commerce*, March 2002, pp. 44–45; and Edward Iwata, "Accounting Detectives in Demand," *USA Today*, February 28, 2003, p. 3B; and "Challenges in the Global Village," Fall 1997, The University of Waterloo. Retrieved from www.accounting.uwaterloo.ca/accnews/fall97/forensic.htm.

companies such as Enron, WorldCom, and Tyco raised public suspicions and led to the downfall of one of the big five accounting firms: Arthur Andersen.[8] Andersen was convicted of obstruction of justice in 2002 for its actions in the Enron case.[9] More recently, Nortel and Biorail were investigated for their accounting practices. It's important for the accounting profession to ensure that the accountants they employ are as professional as doctors or lawyers. Today, scrutiny of the accounting industry is more intense than ever.[10] The Dealing with Change box offers an example of just how intense this scrutiny has become and what some companies are doing about it.

Auditing

The job of reviewing and evaluating the records used to prepare a company's financial statements is referred to as **auditing.** Accountants within the organization often perform internal audits to ensure that proper accounting procedures and financial reporting are being carried out within the company.[11] Public accountants also conduct independent audits of accounting and related records. Financial auditors today not only examine the financial health of an organization but also look into operational efficiencies and effectiveness.[12]

The most important function and income generator for public accounting firms is performing independent audits (examinations) of the books and

auditing
The job of reviewing and evaluating the records used to prepare a company's financial statements.

independent audit
An evaluation and unbiased opinion about the accuracy of a company's financial statements.

financial statements of companies. An **independent audit** is an evaluation and unbiased opinion about the accuracy of a company's financial statements. All stakeholders, including the public, governments, financial institutions, and shareholders (owners) are interested in the results of these audits. This audit is required by law for all public corporations in Canada. A firm's annual report often includes a written opinion by an auditor that is important to read for useful information.[13]

After accounting scandals such as the ones mentioned earlier, the legitimacy of allowing a company to do both auditing and consulting work for the same firm was questioned.[14] Many felt that the resultant conflict of interest could affect the quality of the audit. As a result, most firms now hire two separate organizations; one for consulting and another for auditing.

Tax Accounting

Taxes are the price we pay for roads, parks, schools, police protection, the military, and other functions provided by government. Federal and provincial governments require submission of tax returns that must be filed at specific times and in a precise format. A *tax accountant* is trained in tax law and is responsible for preparing tax returns or developing tax strategies. Since governments often change tax policies according to specific needs or objectives, the job of the tax accountant is certainly challenging. Also, as the burden of taxes grows in the economy, the role of the tax accountant becomes increasingly important to the organization or entrepreneur.

Governmental and Not-for-Profit Accounting

Government and not-for-profit accounting involves working for organizations whose purpose is not generating a profit but serving ratepayers, taxpayers, and others according to a duly approved budget. The different levels of government require an accounting system that satisfies the needs of their information users. The primary users of government accounting information are citizens, special interest groups, legislative bodies, and creditors. These users want to ensure that government is fulfilling its obligations and making the proper use of taxpayers' money. For example, as noted in the Chapter 5 profile, Canada's Auditor-General, Sheila Fraser, is a CA. Her office regularly audits the federal government.

Not-for-profit organizations also require accounting professionals. In fact, not-for-profit organizations have a growing need for trained accountants since contributors to nonprofits want to see exactly how and where the funds they contribute are being spent. Charities (like the Canadian Cancer Society and the United Way of Canada), universities and colleges, hospitals, and labour unions all hire accountants to show how the funds they raise are being spent.

As you can see, managerial and financial accounting, auditing, tax accounting, and governmental and not-for-profit accounting each require specific training and skill. Yet some people are confused about the difference between an accountant and a bookkeeper. We'll clarify that difference right after the Progress Assessment.

Progress Assessment

- Could you define accounting to a friend so that he or she would clearly understand what's involved?
- Can you explain the difference between managerial and financial accounting?
- Describe the three accounting designations.
- What's the difference between a private accountant and a public accountant?

ACCOUNTING VERSUS BOOKKEEPING

Bookkeeping involves the recording of business transactions. Bookkeeping is an important part of financial reporting, but accounting goes far beyond the mere recording of financial information. Accountants classify and summarize financial data provided by bookkeepers, and then interpret the data and report the information to management. They also suggest strategies for improving the financial condition and progress of the firm. Accountants are especially important in financial analysis and income tax preparation.

If you were a bookkeeper, the first task you would perform is to divide all of the firm's transactions into meaningful categories such as sales documents, purchasing receipts, and shipping documents. The bookkeeper's challenge is to keep the information organized and manageable. Therefore, bookkeepers must begin by recording financial data from the original transaction documents (sales slips and so forth) into record books called journals. A **journal** is the record book or computer program where accounting data are first entered. It's interesting that the word *journal* comes from the French word *jour*, which means "day." A journal is where the day's transactions are kept.

DAVE CARPENTER. HARVARD BUSINESS REVIEW, JULY 2002

" I'LL TELL YOU HARRIS, THEY DON'T MAKE ACCOUNTANTS LIKE THEY USED TO. THOSE I HAD IN THE 1990'S NEVER BROUGHT ME FIGURES LIKE THESE."

The integrity of a firm's financial statements is vital. Accounting irregularities that occurred at firms like Livent, Nortel, and Parmalat made the companies look stronger than they actually were. Accountants are now committed to regaining the trust and respect their profession enjoyed in the past. What part should the government play in overseeing the accounting industry?

Double-Entry Bookkeeping

It is quite possible when recording financial transactions that you could make a mistake. For example, you could easily write or enter $10.98 as $10.89. For that reason, bookkeepers record all their transactions in two places. They can then check one list of transactions against the other to make sure that they add up to the same amount. If they don't equal the same amount, the bookkeeper knows that he or she made a mistake. The practice of writing every transaction in two places is called **double-entry bookkeeping.** In double-entry bookkeeping, two entries—one in the journal and one in the ledgers (discussed next)—are required for each company transaction. First, let us look at an example of double-entry bookkeeping. As the name implies, two entries are made for each transaction in the journal: a debit and a credit. For example, when a noncash sale is made on credit for $100, the accounts receivable account is debited for $100 and the sales account is credited with $100. When the customer pays for the sale, the cash account is debited and the accounts receivable account is credited.

To see how this system works, let's suppose a business wanted to determine how much it paid for office supplies in the first quarter of the year. Without a specific bookkeeping tool, that would be difficult even with accurate accounting journals. Therefore, bookkeepers make use of a set of books with pages labelled *office supplies, cash,* and so on. The entries in the journal are transferred, or posted, to these pages, making information about various accounts available quickly and easily.

A **ledger,** then, is a specialized accounting book or computer program in which information from accounting journals is recorded into specific categories and posted so that managers can find all the information about a single account in one place. Today, computerized accounting programs post

bookkeeping
The recording of business transactions.

journal
The record book or computer program where accounting data are first entered.

double-entry bookkeeping
The concept of writing every business transaction in two places.

ledger
A specialized accounting book or computer program in which information from accounting journals is accumulated into specific categories and posted so that managers can find all the information about one account in the same place.

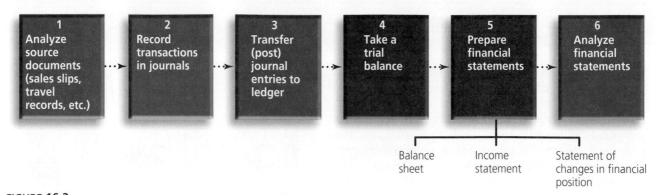

FIGURE 16.3

STEPS IN THE ACCOUNTING CYCLE

information from journals into ledgers daily or instantaneously. This way the financial information is readily available whenever the organization needs it.

The Six-Step Accounting Cycle

accounting cycle
A six-step procedure that results in the preparation and analysis of the two major financial statements: the balance sheet and the income statement.

trial balance
A summary of all the data in the account ledgers to show whether the figures are correct and balanced.

The **accounting cycle** is a six-step procedure that results in the preparation and analysis of the major financial statements (see Figure 16.3). The accounting cycle generally involves the work of both the bookkeeper and the accountant. The first three steps are continual: (1) analyzing and categorizing documents, (2) putting the information into journals, and (3) posting that information into ledgers. The fourth step involves preparing a trial balance. A **trial balance** is a summary of all the financial data in the account ledgers to check whether the figures are correct and balanced. If the information in the account ledgers is not accurate, it must be corrected before the firm's financial statements are prepared. The fifth step, then, is to prepare the financial statements, including a balance sheet, income statement, and statement of changes in financial position. The sixth step occurs when the accountant analyzes the financial statements and evaluates the financial condition of the firm. Computers and accounting software have simplified this process considerably.[15]

The Impact of Computers on Accounting

Financial information and transactions may be recorded by hand or by computer. Computers greatly simplify the mechanical tasks involved in accounting, enabling managers and other interested users to get financial reports exactly when and how they want them. Also, as a business grows, the number of accounts a firm must keep and the reports that need to be generated expand in scope. Because computers can rapidly handle large amounts of financial information, accountants are freed up to do more important tasks such as financial analysis. Computerized accounting programs have been especially helpful to small-business owners, who often lack the strong accounting support within their companies that larger firms enjoy.

Accounting software packages include programs that handle tasks involving general ledgers, sales processing, accounts receivable, purchase orders, accounts payable, cash flow analysis, and inventory control.[16] Tax returns and tax planning can also be performed using tax accounting programs.[17] Many of the latest accounting packages, such as Simply Accounting, Quicken, and QuickTax, address the specific needs of small businesses, which are often significantly different from the needs of a major corporation. Large public accounting firms often assist in developing accounting programs for their biggest clients.

Using computers to record and analyze data and to print out financial reports allows managers to obtain up-to-the-minute financial information for the business. It's now possible, thanks to computers, to have continuous auditing, which helps managers prevent cash flow problems and other financial difficulties by allowing them to spot trouble earlier than ever before. Today's software programs allow even novices to do sophisticated financial analyses within days.[18]

It's important to remember, though, that no computer yet has been programmed to make good financial decisions by itself. Granted, a computer is a wonderful tool for businesspeople to use. Yet business owners should understand exactly what computer system and which programs are best suited for their particular needs. That's one reason why it's suggested that before entrepreneurs get started in a small business ►**P. 197**◄, they should hire or consult with an accountant to identify the particular needs of their proposed firm. Then, a specific accounting system can be developed that works with the pre-designed accounting software that's been chosen. Today's accounting packages offer ease of use, customization, and efficient interactions with the Internet.

Computers help ease the monotony of bookkeeping and accounting work. Still, the work of an accountant requires training and very specific competencies. It's interesting that beginning business students sometimes assume that opportunities in accounting are rather narrow in scope. Nothing could be further from the truth. Accountants not only provide financial information to the firm but also are vital in interpreting and analyzing that information. After the Progress Assessment, we will look at the balance sheet, income statement, and statement of changes in financial position—and the important information each provides.

Progress Assessment

- Can you explain the difference between accounting and bookkeeping?
- What's the difference between an accounting journal and a ledger?
- Why does a bookkeeper prepare a trial balance?
- What key advantages do computers provide businesses in maintaining and compiling accounting information?

Critical Thinking

In business, hundreds of documents are received or created every day, so you can appreciate the valuable role an accountant plays. Can you see why most businesses have to hire people to do this work? Would it be worth the owners' time to do all the paperwork? Can you understand why most accountants find it easier to do this work on a computer?

UNDERSTANDING KEY FINANCIAL STATEMENTS

A **financial statement** is a summary of all the transactions that have occurred over a particular period. Financial statements indicate a firm's financial health and stability. That's why shareholders (the owners of the firm), bondholders and banks (people and institutions that lend money to the firm), labour unions, employees, and the Canada Revenue Agency are all interested in a firm's

financial statement
A summary of all the transactions that have occurred over a particular period.

financial statements. The following are the key financial statements of a business:

1. The *balance sheet,* which reports the firm's financial position at the end of that period.
2. The *income statement,* which summarizes revenues, cost of goods, and expenses (including taxes), for a specific period of time and highlights the total profit or loss the firm experienced during that period.
3. The *statement of changes in financial position,* which provides a summary of money coming into and going out of the firm that tracks a company's cash receipts and cash payments.

The differences among the financial statements can be summarized this way: The balance sheet details what the company owns and owes on a certain day; the income statement shows what a firm sells its products for and what its selling costs are over a specific period; and the statement of changes in financial position highlights the difference between cash coming in and cash going out of a business. To fully understand important financial information, you must be able to understand the purpose of an organization's financial statements. We'll explain each statement in more detail next.

The Fundamental Accounting Equation

Imagine that you don't owe anybody money. That is, you don't have any liabilities (debts). In this case, your assets (cash and so forth) are equal to what you *own* (equity). However, if you borrow some money from a friend, you have incurred a liability. Your assets are now equal to what you *owe* plus what you own. Translated into business terms, Assets = Liabilities + Owners' equity.

In accounting, this equation must always be balanced. For example, suppose you have $50,000 in cash and decide to use that money to open a small coffee shop. Your business has assets of $50,000 and no debts. The accounting equation would be:

$$\text{Assets} = \text{Liabilities} + \text{Owners' equity}$$
$$\$50,000 = \$0 \qquad + \$50,000$$

You have $50,000 cash and $50,000 owners' equity (the amount of your investment in the business—sometimes referred to as net worth). However, before opening the business, you borrow $30,000 from a local bank; the equation now changes. You have $30,000 of additional cash, but you also have a debt (liability) of $30,000. Remember, with each business transaction there is a recording of two transactions. (Recall the discussion of double-entry bookkeeping earlier in this chapter.)

Your financial position within the business has changed. The equation is still balanced but is changed to reflect the transaction:

$$\text{Assets} = \text{Liabilities} + \text{Owners' equity}$$
$$\$80,000 = \$30,000 \quad + \$50,000$$

fundamental accounting equation
Assets = liabilities + owners' equity; this is the basis for the balance sheet.

This formula is called the **fundamental accounting equation** and is the basis for the balance sheet. As Figure 16.4 (a sample balance sheet for Fiberrific, the hypothetical cereal company we introduced in Chapter 14) highlights, on the balance sheet you list assets in a separate column from liabilities and owners' (or shareholders') equity. The assets are equal to or are balanced with the liabilities and owners' (or shareholders') equity. It's that simple. What's often

FIBERRIFIC
Balance Sheet
December 31, 2005

Assets

① Current assets

Cash	$ 15,000	
Accounts receivable	200,000	
Notes receivable	50,000	
Inventory	335,000	
Total current assets		$600,000

② Capital assets

Land		$40,000	
Building and improvements	$200,000		
Less: Accumulated amortization	− 90,000		
		110,000	
Equipment and vehicles	$120,000		
Less: Accumulated amortization	− 80,000		
		40,000	
Furniture and fixtures	$26,000		
Less: Accumulated amortization	− 10,000		
		16,000	
Total fixed assets			206,000

③ Intangible assets

Goodwill	$20,000	
Total intangible assets		20,000
Total assets		$826,000

Liabilities and Owners' or Shareholders' Equity
Liabilities

④ Current liabilities

Accounts payable	$40,000	
Notes payable (due June 2006)	8,000	
Accrued taxes	150,000	
Accrued salaries	90,000	
Total current liabilities		$288,000

⑤ Long-term liabilities

Notes payable (due Mar. 2009)	$ 35,000	
Bonds payable (due Dec. 2014)	290,000	
Total long-term liabilities		325,000
Total liabilities		$613,000

⑥ Shareholders' equity

Common stock (1,000,000 shares)	$100,000	
Retained earnings	113,000	
Total shareholders' equity		213,000
Total liabilities & shareholders' equity		$826,000

FIGURE 16.4

SAMPLE FIBERRIFIC BALANCE SHEET

① Current assets: Items that can be converted to cash within one year.

② Capital assets: Items such as land, buildings, and equipment that are relatively permanent.

③ Intangible assets: Items of value such as patents and copyrights that don't have a physical form.

④ Current liabilities: Payments that are due in one year or less.

⑤ Long-term liabilities: Payments not due for one year or longer.

⑥ Shareholders' equity: The value of what shareholders own in a firm (also called owners' equity).

complicated is determining what is included in the asset account and what is included in the liabilities and owners' equity accounts. It's critical that businesspeople understand the important financial information on the balance sheet, so let's take a closer look.

The Balance Sheet

balance sheet
The financial statement that reports a firm's financial condition at a specific time.

A **balance sheet** is the financial statement that reports a firm's financial condition at a specific time. It's composed of three major accounts: assets, liabilities, and owners' equity. It gets its name because it shows a *balance* between two figures: the company's assets on the one hand, and its liabilities plus owners' equity on the other. (These terms will be defined fully in the next sections.) Note that the income statement reports on changes *over a period* and the balance sheet reports conditions *at the end of that period*.

The following analogy will help explain the idea behind the balance sheet. Let's say that you want to know what your financial condition is at a given time. Maybe you want to buy a new house or car and therefore need to calculate your available resources. One of the best measuring sticks is your balance sheet. First, you would add up everything you own—cash, property, money owed you, and so forth (assets). Subtract from that the money you owe others—credit card debt, IOUs, current car loan, and so forth (liabilities)—and you have a figure that tells you your net worth (equity). This is fundamentally what companies do in preparing a balance sheet. In that preparation, it's important they follow clearly established accounting procedures.[19] The fundamental accounting equation is what sets those procedures.

Assets

assets
Economic resources (things of value) owned by a firm.

Assets are economic resources (things of value) owned by a firm. Assets include productive, tangible items (e.g., equipment, buildings, land, furniture, fixtures, and motor vehicles) that help generate income, as well as intangibles with value (e.g., patents, trademarks, copyrights, or goodwill).[20] Think, for example, of the value of brand names ▶**P. 419**◀ such as Roots, Air Canada, and Canadian Tire. Intangibles such as brand names can be among the firm's most valuable assets. Goodwill is the value that can be attributed to factors such as reputation, location, and superior products.[21] It is included on the balance sheet when a firm acquiring another firm pays more than the value of that firm's tangible assets.[22] Not all companies, however, list intangible assets on their balance sheets.

liquidity
How fast an asset can be converted into cash.

Assets are listed on the firm's balance sheet according to their liquidity. **Liquidity** refers to how fast an asset can be converted into cash. For example, an account receivable is an amount of money owed to the firm that it expects to be paid within one year. Accounts receivable are considered liquid assets. Land, however, is difficult to turn into cash quickly because it takes much time and paperwork to sell land; thus, land is a long-term asset (an asset expected to last more than one year) and not considered liquid. Thus, assets are divided into three categories according to how quickly they can be turned into cash:

current assets
Items that can or will be converted into cash within one year.

capital assets
Assets that are relatively permanent, such as land, buildings, and equipment.

intangible assets
Long-term assets (e.g., patents, trademarks, copyrights) that have no real physical form but do have value.

1. **Current assets** are items that can or will be converted into cash within one year. Current assets include cash, accounts receivable, and inventory.
2. **Capital assets** are items that are relatively permanent goods, such as land and buildings, acquired to produce products for a business. They are not bought to be sold but to generate revenue. (These assets are also referred to as fixed assets or property, plant, and equipment.)
3. **Intangible assets** are long-term assets that have no real physical form but do have value. Patents, trademarks, copyrights, and goodwill are examples of intangible assets.

You can see why one of the key words in accounting is *assets*. Take a few minutes to go through the list, visualizing the assets. Notice that they are things of value.

The valuation of assets can be a complex matter beyond the scope of this book. All assets are normally recorded at the cost of acquisition. When you look at a balance sheet, you see assets listed at their original cost. The real values are often different from their *book values*. In other words, the market value—what would be realized if the asset were sold—is normally different from the value as shown on the books.

The long, steady period of inflation we have witnessed since the 1960s has resulted in most book values being substantially below market value. For example, a building purchased in 1960 for $1 million could have a market value of perhaps 30 times that amount today. Nevertheless, it remains on the books at original cost. This asset, and therefore total assets, are grossly understated.

Obviously, this is not a satisfactory state of affairs. The accounting profession and other interested parties have been struggling with alternatives for many years. It's a problem awaiting a creative solution that will not cause more problems than it solves. Perhaps you will take up the challenge and come up with the answer.

Liabilities and Owners' Equity Accounts

Another important accounting term is liabilities. **Liabilities** are what the business owes to others (debts). *Current liabilities* are debts due in one year or less; *long-term liabilities* are debts not due for one year or longer. The following are common liability accounts recorded on a balance sheet (refer to Figure 16.4):

liabilities
What the business owes to others (debts).

1. **Accounts payable** are current liabilities involving money owed to others for merchandise or services purchased on credit but not yet paid. If you have a bill you haven't paid, you have an account payable.
2. **Accrued expenses payable** are expenses the firm owes but that have not been billed by the end of the month, when financial statements are prepared (e.g., utilities bills, credit card statements).
3. **Bonds payable.**   Long-term loans to the business.
4. **Notes payable.**   Usually shorter-term loans from banks.
5. **Taxes payable.**   Sales taxes and GST collected, and income tax payable.

As the fundamental accounting equation highlighted earlier, the value of things you own (assets) minus the amount of money you owe others (liabilities) is called *equity*. The value of what shareholders own in a firm (minus liabilities) is called *shareholders' equity* (or *stockholders' equity*). Because shareholders are the owners of a firm, shareholders' equity can also be called owners' equity.

The **owners' equity** in a company consists of all that the owners have invested in the company *plus* all the profits that have accumulated since the business commenced but that have not yet been paid out to them. This figure *always* equals the book value of the assets minus the liabilities of the company.

owners' equity
The amount of the business that belongs to the owners minus any liabilities owed by the business.

In a partnership, owners' equity is called *partners' equity* or *capital*. In a sole proprietorship, it is called owner's or *proprietor's equity* or capital. In a corporation, it is called *shareholders' equity* and is shown in two separate accounts. The amount the owners (shareholders) invest is shown in one account, called *common stock*; the accumulated profit that remains after dividends have been paid to shareholders is shown in an account called *retained earnings*. We will discuss dividends in Chapter 17. Take a few moments to review Figure 16.4 and see what facts you can determine about Fiberrific from its balance sheet.

Progress Assessment

- What's the formula for the balance sheet? What do we call this formula?
- What does it mean to list various assets by liquidity?
- What goes into the account called liabilities?
- What is owners' equity and how is it determined?

The Income Statement

The financial statement that shows a firm's bottom line—that is, its profit after costs, expenses, and taxes—is the **income statement** (also called the profit and loss statement). The income statement summarizes all of the resources (called revenue) that have come into the firm from operating activities, money resources that were used up, expenses incurred in doing business, and what resources were left after all costs and expenses, including taxes, were paid. The resources (revenue) left over are referred to as **net income or net loss** (see Figure 16.5).

income statement
The financial statement that shows a firm's profit after costs, expenses, and taxes; it summarizes all of the resources that have come into the firm (revenue), all the resources that have left the firm, and the resulting net income.

net income or net loss
Revenue left over after all costs and expenses, including taxes, are paid.

The income statement reports the firm's financial operations over a particular period of time, usually a year, a quarter of a year, or a month.[23] It's the financial statement that reveals whether the business is actually earning a profit or losing money. The formula used to prepare an income statement is as follows:

Beginning inventory + Purchases − Ending inventory = Cost of goods sold

Revenue − Cost of goods sold = Gross profit (or gross margin)

Gross profit − Operating expenses = Net income before taxes

Net income before taxes − Taxes = Net income (or loss)

The income statement includes valuable financial information for shareholders, lenders, investors (or potential investors), and employees. Because of the importance of this financial report, let's take a moment to look at the income statement and learn what each step means. Before we start, however, take a quick look at how the income statement is arranged according to generally accepted accounting principles (GAAP):

Revenue
− Cost of goods sold
_____

Gross profit (gross margin)
− Operating expenses
_____

Net income before taxes
− Taxes
_____

Net income or loss

Revenue

revenue
The value of what is received for goods sold, services rendered, and other financial sources.

Revenue is the value of what is received for goods sold, services rendered, and other financial sources. Note that there is a difference between revenue and sales. Most revenue (money coming into the firm) comes from sales, but there could be other sources of revenue, such as rents received, money paid to the

FIGURE 16.5

SAMPLE FIBERRIFIC INCOME STATEMENT

FIBERRIFIC
Income Statement
For the Year Ended December 31, 2005

① Revenues

Gross sales		$720,000
Less: Sales returns and allowances	$12,000	
Sales discounts	8,000	−20,000
Net sales		$700,000

② Cost of goods sold

Beginning inventory, Jan. 1		$200,000
Merchandise purchases	$400,000	
Freight	40,000	
Net purchases		440,000
Cost of goods available for sale	$640,000	
Less ending inventory, Dec. 31		−230,000
Cost of goods sold		−410,000

③ Gross profit $290,000

④ Operating expenses

Selling expenses

Salaries for salespeople	$90,000	
Advertising	18,000	
Supplies	2,000	
Total selling expenses		$110,000

General expenses

Office salaries	$67,000	
Amortization	1,500	
Insurance	1,500	
Rent	28,000	
Light, heat, and power	12,000	
Miscellaneous	2,000	
		112,000

Total operating expenses	222,000
Net income before taxes	$68,000
Less: Income tax expense	19,000
⑤ Net income after taxes	$49,000

① Revenues: Value of what's received from goods sold, services rendered, and other financial sources.

② Cost of goods sold: Cost of merchandise sold or cost of raw materials or parts used for producing items for resale.

③ Gross profit: How much the firm earned by buying or selling merchandise.

④ Operating expenses: Cost incurred in operating a business.

⑤ Net income after taxes: Profit or loss over a specific period after subtracting all costs and expenses including taxes.

firm for use of its patents, and interest earned, that's included in reporting revenue. Be careful not to confuse the terms *revenue* and *sales,* or to use them as if they were synonymous. Also, a quick glance at the income statement shows you that *gross sales* are the total of all sales the firm completed. *Net sales* are gross sales minus returns, discounts, and allowances.

Cost of Goods Sold (Cost of Goods Manufactured)

The **cost of goods sold** (or **cost of goods manufactured**) is a measure of the cost of merchandise sold or cost of raw materials and supplies used for producing items for resale. It's common sense to calculate how much a business

cost of goods sold (or cost of goods manufactured)
A measure of the cost of merchandise sold or cost of raw materials and supplies used for producing items for resale.

earned by selling merchandise over the period being evaluated, compared to how much it spent to buy the merchandise. The cost of goods sold includes the purchase price plus any freight charges paid to transport goods plus any costs associated with storing the goods. In other words, all the costs of buying and keeping merchandise for sale are included in the cost of goods sold. It's critical that companies accurately report and manage this important income statement item.

gross profit (gross margin)
How much a firm earned by buying (or making) and selling merchandise.

When you subtract the cost of goods sold from net sales, you get what is called gross profit or gross margin. **Gross profit (gross margin)** is how much a firm earned by buying (or making) and selling merchandise. In a service firm, it's possible there may be no cost of goods sold; therefore, net revenue could equal gross profit. In either case (selling goods or services), the gross profit doesn't tell you everything you need to know about the financial performance of the firm. The financial evaluation of an income statement also includes determining the *net* profit or loss a firm experienced. To get that, you must subtract the business's expenses.

Operating Expenses and Net Profit or Loss

operating expenses
Costs involved in operating a business, such as rent, utilities, and salaries.

In the process of selling goods or services, a business experiences certain expenses. **Operating expenses** are the costs involved in operating a business. Obvious operating expenses include rent, salaries, supplies, utilities, insurance, research, and even amortization of equipment. (We will look at amortization a little later.) Expenses can generally be classified into two categories: selling and general expenses. *Selling expenses* are expenses related to the marketing and distribution of the firm's goods or services (such as salaries for salespeople, advertising, and supplies.) *General expenses* are administrative expenses of the firm (such as office salaries, amortization, insurance, and rent). Accountants are trained to help you record all applicable expenses and find other relevant expenses you need to deduct.

After all expenses are deducted, the firm's net income before taxes is determined (refer to Figure 16.5). After allocating for taxes, we get to what's called the *bottom line*, which is the net income (or perhaps net loss) the firm incurred from revenue minus sales returns, costs, expenses, and taxes.[24] It answers the question "How much did the business earn or lose in the reporting period?" Net income can also be referred to as net earnings or net profit.

The retained earnings account is the link between the income statement and the balance sheet. The net income shown at the bottom of the income statement is transferred to the retained earnings account each year.

The terms associated with the balance sheet and income statement may seem a bit confusing to you at this point, but you actually use similar accounting concepts all the time. For example, you know the importance of keeping track of costs and expenses when you prepare your own budget. If your expenses (e.g., rent and utilities) exceed your revenues (how much you earn), you are in trouble. If you need more money (revenue), you may need to sell some of the things you own to meet your expenses. The same is true in business. Companies need to keep track of how much money is earned and spent, how much cash they have on hand, and so on. The only difference is that companies tend to have more complex problems and a good deal more information to record than you as an individual do.

Users of financial statements are very interested in handling the flow of cash into and the flow of cash out of a business. Cash flow problems can plague both businesses and individuals. Keep this fact in mind as we look at the statement of changes in financial position in the next section.

The Statement of Changes in Financial Position

The **statement of changes in financial position** (also known as the statement of cash flows) reports cash receipts and disbursements related to the three major activities of a firm:

- **Operations** cash transactions associated with running the business.
- **Investments** cash used in or provided by the firm's investment activities.
- **Financing** cash raised from the issuance of new debt or equity capital or cash used to pay business expenses, past debts, or company dividends. We will discuss these terms in Chapter 17.

Accountants analyze all of the cash changes that have occurred from operating, investing, and financing, and determine the firm's net cash position. The statement of changes in financial position also gives the firm some insight into how to handle cash better so that no cash flow problems (e.g., having no cash on hand) occur.[25]

Figure 16.6 shows a statement of changes in financial position, again using the example of Fiberrific. As you can see, this financial statement answers such questions as: How much cash came into the business from current operations? That is, how much cash came into the firm from buying and selling

statement of changes in financial position
Financial statement that reports cash receipts and disbursements related to a firm's three major activities: operations, investments, and financing.

FIBERRIFIC
Statement of Changes in Financial Position
For the Year Ended December 31, 2005

① Cash flows from operating activities

Cash received from customers	$150,000	
Cash paid to suppliers and employees	(90,000)	
Interest paid	(5,000)	
Income tax paid	(4,500)	
Interest and dividends received	1,500	
Net cash provided by operating activities		$52,000

② Cash flows from investing activities

Proceeds from sale of plant assets	$4,000	
Payments for purchase of equipment	(10,000)	
Net cash provided by investing activities		(6,000)

③ Cash flows from financing activities

Proceeds from issuance of short-term debt	$3,000	
Payment of long-term debt	(7,000)	
Payment of dividends	(15,000)	
Net cash inflow from financing activities		(19,000)
Net change in cash and equivalents		$27,000
Cash balance (beginning of year)		(2,000)
Cash balance (end of year)		$25,000

FIGURE 16.6

SAMPLE FIBERRIFIC STATEMENT OF CHANGES IN FINANCIAL POSITION

① Cash receipts from sales, commissions, fees, interest, and dividends. Cash payments for salaries, inventories, operating expenses, interest, and taxes.

② Includes cash flows that are generated through a company's purchase or sale of long term operational assets, investments in other companies, and its lending activities.

③ Cash inflows and outflows associated with the company's own equity transactions or its borrowing activities.

Making Ethical Decisions

On the Accounting Hot Seat

You are the only accountant employed by a small manufacturing firm. You are in charge of keeping the books for the company, which has been suffering from an economic downturn that shows no signs of lightening up in the near future.

You know that your employer is going to ask the bank for an additional loan so the company can continue to pay its bills. Unfortunately, the financial statements for the year will not show good results, and your best guess is that the bank will not approve a loan increase on the basis of the financial information you will present.

Your boss approaches you in early January before you have closed the books for the preceding year and suggests that perhaps the statements can be "improved" by treating the sales that were made at the beginning of January as if they were made in December. He also asks you to do a number of other things that will cover up the trail so that the auditors will not discover the padding of the year's sales.

You know that these results go against the professional rules, and you argue with your boss. Your boss tells you that, if the company does not get the additional bank loan, there's a very good chance the business will close. That means you and everyone else in the firm will be out of a job. You believe your boss is probably right and you know that with the current economic downturn finding a job will be tough for you and almost impossible for others in the company. What are your alternatives? What are the likely consequences of each alternative? How will jobs be impacted? What will you do?

goods and services? Was cash used to buy stocks, bonds, or other investments? Were some investments sold that brought in cash? How much money came into the firm from issuing stock?

These and other financial transactions are analyzed to see their effect on the cash position of the firm. Understanding cash flow can mean the success or failure of any business. We will analyze cash flow a bit more in depth in the next section. But first, consider the above and then read the Making Ethical Decisions box to see how accountants can sometimes face some tough ethical challenges in reporting the flow of funds into a business.

The Importance of Cash Flow Analysis

Understanding cash flow is an important part of financial reporting. If not properly managed, cash flow problems can cause a business much concern.[26] Cash flow analysis is really rather simple to comprehend. Let's say you borrow $100 from a friend to buy a used bike and agree to pay your friend back at the end of the week. In turn, you sell the bike for $150 to someone else, who also agrees to pay you in a week. Unfortunately, at the end of the week the person who bought the bike from you does not have the money as promised. This person says that he will have to pay you next month. Meanwhile, your friend wants the $100 you agreed to pay her by the end of the week! What seemed like a great opportunity to make an easy $50 profit is a real cause for concern. Right now, you owe $100 and have no cash. What do you do when your friend shows up at the end of the week and demands to be paid? If you were a business, this might cause you to default on the loan and possibly go bankrupt, even though you had the potential for profits.[27]

It is very possible that a business can increase sales and profits, and still suffer greatly from cash flow problems. **Cash flow** is simply the difference between cash coming in and cash going out of a business. A common mistake among start-ups is to focus on the product and not the running of the business, explained Blair Davidson, KPMG partner in the Financial Advisory Services

cash flow
The difference between cash coming in and cash going out of a business.

Group, at a recent York Technology Association and Canadian Technology Network breakfast speech. "Business can be viewed as a triangle of operations: making, selling and scorekeeping. If you devote yourself only to production and neglect the other sides, the imbalance will show up in the bottom line and shake the confidence of potential investors in the future," he said.[28]

Cash flow is a constant challenge for businesses of all sizes. Consider how critical this is for seasonal businesses (such as ski resorts) in which the flow of cash into the business is sporadic. Sometimes, very large companies are forced to sell off one or more of their profitable subsidiaries to raise cash because of a recession or other unexpected development. This is the problem that caused the huge Olympia & York Developments to go bankrupt in 1992. Sometimes, a company can nearly be destroyed by cash flow problems. This was evident when Air Canada had to restructure its operations under the Companies' Creditors Arrangement Act (CCAA) in 2003. To improve its cash flow, General Electric's corporate finance division granted Air Canada more than $1 billion in financing.[29]

What often happens to a business is that, in order to meet the demands of customers, the business buys more and more goods on credit (no cash is involved). Similarly, more and more goods are sold on credit (no cash is involved). This goes on until the firm uses up all the credit it has with its lenders. When the firm requests more money from its bank to pay a crucial bill, the bank refuses the loan because the credit limit has been reached. All other credit sources refuse funds as well. The company desperately needs funds to pay its bills, or it could be forced into bankruptcy. Unfortunately, all too often, the company does go into bankruptcy because there was no cash available when it was most needed.

Cash flow analysis also points out clearly that a business' relationship with its banker(s) is critical. Maintaining a working relationship with a bank is a path to preventing cash flow problems that often develop. See the Spotlight on Small Business box for more details. The value that accountants provide to businesses in dealing with cash flow is also critical. Accountants can advise the firm whether it needs cash and, if so, how much. They can also offer advice on how a company is managing its cash position, and provide key insights into how, when, and where finance managers can get the money a firm needs. The statement of changes in financial position is a good barometer of measuring the cash position within a firm.

APPLYING ACCOUNTING KNOWLEDGE IN BUSINESS

If accounting consisted of nothing more than repetitive functions of gathering and recording transactions and preparing financial statements, the tasks could be assigned solely to computers. In fact, most medium and large firms as well as growing numbers of small businesses have done just that. The Internet has initiated a new way of managing a firm's finances: online accounting. But the truth is that *how* you record and report financial data is also critically important.

Generally Accepted Accounting Principles

Business transactions require certain guidelines that help accountants make proper and consistent decisions. These guidelines are called *generally accepted accounting principles (GAAP).* They are published in the handbook of the Canadian Institute of Chartered Accountants, along with many other important guidelines. This handbook is the ultimate authority of the accounting

Keep Your Banker Happy with a Steady Flow of Information

As you learned in Chapter 7, positive or negative relations with your banker can often be predictors of success or failure for a small business. Entrepreneurs learn fast that keeping their banker happy can pay off, particularly if the company finds itself in a financial crunch. How do you keep your bank happy? One answer is with accounting information. Few entrepreneurs realize that financial ratios are important numbers to bankers and often form the basis of the decisions bankers make concerning financing requests.

Financial ratios not only can help the entrepreneur manage his or her business more efficiently, but they also can make your banker a more reliable business partner. Bankers see ratios as useful measurements for comparing a company's financial position to that of competing companies. Also, bankers see ratios as an effective guide for evaluating the firm's performance compared to industry standards or trends that are occurring in the market. What are some of the more important ratios at which the banker looks closely?

Bankers believe that a firm's ability to repay bank loans and make timely interest payments is important for evaluating financial requests. Liquidity ratios such as the current ratio (current assets divided by current liabilities) are important in determining the firm's short-term financial strength. Is it best for a firm to always maintain a high current ratio? Not necessarily! If a company has too high a current ratio, bankers may feel it is making poor use of resources. If your current ratio is falling, you must be prepared to explain why this is happening. Staying on top of the situation may mean receiving continued financial support from your bank. Keeping track of inventory and the debt position of the firm will also impress your banker. Low inventory turnover could suggest to bankers that trouble is ahead. Excess inventory can boost interest rates and possibly lower profits. Ratios such as inventory turnover can offer valuable insights into how to prevent these problems and keep the bank on your side. Debt is a potential source of worry for both the businessperson and the bank. Therefore, debt to equity and total debt to total assets are ratios of major concern.

What should small business managers do to build a working relationship with their bankers? Working closely with their accountant, they should prepare and regularly update a report binder that contains key financial ratios as well as cash-flow forecasts and projections. The entrepreneurs should discuss with the banker what ratios are most relevant to their businesses and then keep track of them on a regular basis. With such diligence, you not only build a good working relationship with your banker, but you also build a relationship with an informed partner.

profession. Bankers, financial analysts, and others also refer to it. From time to time (and after much discussion) it is updated or modified.

There are about a dozen important accounting principles. Every audited set of financial statements includes a series of notes explaining how these principles have been applied, as well as a report by the auditors that GAAP have been used. This makes it possible for financial statements to be compared from one year to the next as well as from one company to another. As noted in the Reaching Beyond Our Borders box, accountants all over the world are working to harmonize GAAP.

Amortization

Take a look at Figure 16.4 again. Note that Fiberrific lists accumulated amortization on its property, plant, and equipment. What exactly does this mean, and how does it affect the company's financial position?

amortization
The systematic write-off of the cost of a tangible asset over its estimated useful life.

Amortization is the systematic write-off of the cost of a tangible asset over its estimated useful life. (*Depreciation* is the term used in the U.S. to describe amortization.) Have you ever heard the comment that a new car depreciates in market value as soon as you drive it off the dealer's lot? The same principle

www.ifac.org

Reaching Beyond Our Borders

Accounting Problems When Going International

As you have made your way through this book, you have read of examples of Canadian companies that have developed important ties beyond our borders. As part of the globalization of business, Canadian companies look to joint ventures and alliances with other companies in the Pacific Rim, Europe, Mexico, and elsewhere. For example, McDonald's Canada Ltd. formed a joint venture with a Russian agency to operate the largest McDonald's unit in the world, in Moscow. Sometimes Canadian businesses buy out other companies, or merge with others.

One problem that often arises is how to determine the real value of the foreign company. The starting point is an examination of its financial statements. Have they been prepared on the basis of the same generally accepted accounting principles (GAAP) that are applied in Canada and the foreign company's country? Often there are major differences that make it difficult to determine the real value of the company. Obviously, this is very important, especially if you are trying to establish how much you should offer to buy the company or you want to be sure that the assets being contributed to a joint venture have the value your partner claims.

Accounting bodies all over the world have been working for many years toward establishing a common set of GAAP through organizations like the International Federation of Accountants (IFAC). It is a major task that is slowly being achieved. In response to accounting scandals, IFAC has also developed a compliance program to provide clear benchmarks to current and potential member organizations. The primary focus is on providing guidelines to improve and encourage high-quality performance by accountants worldwide.

holds true for equipment and other specific assets, such as machinery and equipment. Companies are permitted to recapture the cost of these assets over time using amortization as an operating expense of the business.[30]

Subject to certain technical accounting rules (set by GAAP and the Canada Revenue Agency) that are beyond the scope of this chapter, a firm may use one of several different techniques for calculating amortization. The key thing to understand right now is that different amortization techniques could result in a different net income for the firm. Accountants are able to offer financial advice and recommend ways of legally handling questions regarding amortization, as well as other accounts such as inventory, where different valuation methods can affect a firm's financial performance. Let's look briefly at how accountants can value inventory.

The valuation of a firm's inventory presents another interesting accounting application. Inventories are a key part of many companies' financial statements and are important in determining a firm's cost of goods sold (or manufactured) on the income statement. Look again at Fiberrific's income statement in Figure 16.5. When a firm sells merchandise from its inventory, it can calculate the cost of that item in different ways. In financial reporting, it doesn't matter when a particular item was actually placed in a firm's inventory, but it does matter how an accountant records the cost of the item when it was sold. Sound a bit confusing? Look at the example below.

Let's say that a bookstore buys textbooks for resale. It buys 100 copies of a particular textbook in July 2005 at a cost of $50 a copy. When classes begin in September, the bookstore sells 50 copies of the text to students for $60 each. The 50 copies not sold are placed in the bookstore's inventory for next term. In late December the bookstore orders 50 additional copies of the same text to sell for the coming term. Unfortunately, the price of the book to the bookstore has increased to $60 a copy due to inflation and other costs. The bookstore now has 100 copies of the same textbook from different purchase cycles in its inventory (same book, but different costs to the bookstore). If the bookstore sells

FIGURE 16.7

ACCOUNTING USING LIFO
VERSUS FIFO INVENTORY
VALUATION

	FIFO	LIFO
Revenue	$70	$70
Cost of goods sold	50	60
Income before taxes	20	10
Taxes of 40%	8	4
Net income	12	6

first in, first out (FIFO)
An accounting method
for calculating cost of
inventory; it assumes that
the first goods to come in
are the first to go out.

last in, first out (LIFO)
An accounting method
for calculating cost of
inventory; it assumes that
the last goods to come in
are the first to go out.

50 copies of the book to students for a price of $70 at the beginning of the new term in January, what's the bookstore's cost of the book for accounting purposes? It depends.

The books are identical but the accounting treatment would be different. If the bookstore uses a method called **first in, first out (FIFO),** the cost of goods sold (cost of 50 textbooks sold) would be $50 each, because the textbook that was bought first cost $50. The bookstore, however, could use another method, called **last in, first out (LIFO).** Using LIFO, the bookstore's last purchase of the textbooks that cost $60 each would be the cost of each of the 50 textbooks sold. If the book sells for $70, you can see how the difference in accounting methods affects the bookstore's net income. FIFO would report $10 more of net income (per book) before taxes than LIFO would (see Figure 16.7).

What's important to understand about amortization and inventory valuation is that generally accepted accounting principles (GAAP) can permit an accountant to use different methods of amortizing a firm's long-term assets and valuing a firm's inventory. That's why companies provide readers of their financial statements complete information concerning their financial operations.[31]

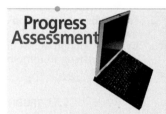

Progress Assessment

- What's the formula for the income statement?
- What's the difference between revenue and income on the income statement?
- What is the connection between the income statement and the balance sheet?
- Why is the statement of changes in financial position important in evaluating a firm's operations?
- What's the difference between LIFO and FIFO inventory valuation? How could the use of these methods change financial results?

ANALYZING FINANCIAL STATEMENTS: RATIO ANALYSIS

ratio analysis
The assessment of a
firm's financial condition
and performance through
calculations and interpretations of financial ratios
developed from the firm's
financial statements.

Accurate financial information from the firm's financial statements forms the basis of the financial analysis performed by accountants inside and outside the firm. **Ratio analysis** is the assessment of a firm's financial condition and performance through calculations and interpretation of financial ratios developed from the firm's financial statements. Financial ratios are especially useful in analyzing the actual performance of the company compared to its financial objectives and compared to other firms within its industry. At first glance, ratio analysis may seem complicated. The fact is most of us already use ratios quite often. For example, in basketball, the number of shots made from the foul line is expressed by a ratio: shots made to shots attempted. A player who shoots 85 percent from the foul line is considered an outstanding foul shooter, and suggestions are to not foul him or her in a close game.

Whether ratios measure an athlete's performance or the financial health of a business, they provide a good deal of valuable information. Financial ratios provide key insights into how a firm compares to other firms in its industry in the important areas of liquidity (speed of changing assets into cash), debt (leverage), profitability, and business activity. Understanding and interpreting business ratios is a key to sound financial analysis. Let's look briefly at four key types of ratios businesses use to measure financial performance.

Liquidity Ratios

As explained earlier, the word *liquidity* refers to how fast an asset can be converted to cash. Liquidity ratios measure a company's ability to turn assets into cash to pay its short-term debts (liabilities that must be repaid within one year). These short-term debts are of particular importance to creditors of the firm, who expect to be paid on time.[32] Two key liquidity ratios are the current ratio and the acid-test ratio.

The *current ratio* is the ratio of a firm's current assets to its current liabilities. This information can be found on the firm's balance sheet. Look back at Figure 16.4, which details Fiberrific's balance sheet. Fiberrific lists current assets of $600,000 and current liabilities of $288,000. The firm therefore has a current ratio of 2.08, which means Fiberrific has $2.08 of current assets for every $1 of current liabilities. See below:

$$\text{Current ratio} = \frac{\text{Current assets}}{\text{Current liabilities}} = \frac{\$600,000}{\$288,000} = 2.08$$

An obvious question to ask is "How well positioned financially is Fiberrific for the short term (less than one year)?" It depends! Usually a company with a current ratio of 2 or better is considered a safe risk for granting short-term credit since it appears to be performing in line with market expectations. However, it's important to compare Fiberrific's current ratio to that of competing firms in its industry. It's also important for the firm to compare its current ratio with the same ratio from the previous year to note any significant changes.

Faucets, faucets, and more faucets. Home Depot stores stock more than 36,000 items that cover 130,000 square feet of floor space. Maintaining such an enormous inventory is no small task. What financial ratios would help Home Depot make sure it is managing its inventory efficiently?

Another key liquidity ratio, called the *acid-test* or *quick ratio*, measures the cash, marketable securities (such as stocks and bonds), and receivables of a firm, compared to its current liabilities:

$$\text{Acid test ratio} = \frac{\text{Cash} + \text{Accounts receivable} + \text{Marketable securities}}{\text{Current liabilities}}$$

$$= \frac{\$265,000}{\$288,000} = .92$$

This ratio is particularly important to firms with difficulty converting inventory into quick cash. It helps answer such questions as the following: What if sales drop off and we can't sell our inventory? Can we still pay our short-term debt? Though ratios vary among industries, an acid-test ratio of between 0.50 and 1.0 is usually considered satisfactory, but a ratio under 1.0 could also be a hint of some cash flow problems. Therefore, Fiberrific's acid-test ratio of .92 could raise concerns that perhaps the firm may not meet its short-term debt and may therefore have to go to a high-cost lender for financial assistance.

Leverage (Debt) Ratios

Leverage (debt) ratios measure the degree to which a firm relies on borrowed funds in its operations. A firm that takes on too much debt could experience problems repaying lenders or meeting promises made to shareholders. The *debt to owners' equity ratio* measures the degree to which the company is financed by borrowed funds that must be repaid. Again, we can use Figure 16.4 to measure Fiberrific's level of debt:

$$\text{Debt to owners' equity} = \frac{\text{Total liabilities}}{\text{Owners' equity}} = \frac{\$613,000}{\$213,000} = 287\%$$

A ratio above 1 (above 100 percent) shows that a firm has more debt than equity. With a ratio of 287 percent, Fiberrific has a rather high degree of debt compared to its equity, which implies that the firm may be perceived as quite risky to lenders and investors. However, it's always important to compare a firm's debt ratios to those of other firms in its industry because debt financing is more acceptable in some industries than it is in others.[33] Comparisons with past debt ratios can also identify trends that may be occurring within the firm or industry.

Profitability (Performance) Ratios

Profitability (performance) ratios measure how effectively a firm is using its various resources to achieve profits. Management's performance is often measured by the firm's profitability ratios. Three of the more important ratios used are earnings per share, return on sales, and return on equity.

Companies report their quarterly earnings per share in two ways: basic and diluted. The *basic earnings per share (basic EPS) ratio* helps determine the amount of profit earned by a company for each share of outstanding common stock. The *diluted earnings per share (diluted EPS) ratio* measures the amount of profit earned by a company for each share of outstanding common stock, but this ratio also takes into consideration stock options, warrants, preferred stock, and convertible debt securities, which can be converted into common stock. For simplicity's sake, we will compute only the basic earnings per share (EPS).

EPS is a very important ratio for a company because earnings help stimulate growth in the firm and pay for such things as shareholders' dividends. Continued earnings growth is well received by both investors and lenders. The basic EPS ratio calculated for Fiberrific is as follows:

$$\text{Basic earnings per share} = \frac{\text{Net income after taxes}}{\text{Number of common stock shares outstanding}}$$

$$= \frac{\$49,000}{1,000,000} = \$.049 \text{ per share}$$

Another reliable indicator of performance is obtained by using a ratio that measures the return on sales. Firms use this ratio to see if they are doing as well as the companies they compete against in generating income from the sales they achieve. *Return on sales* is calculated by comparing a company's net income to its total sales: Fiberrific's return on sales is 7 percent, a figure that must be measured against competing firms in its industry to judge its performance:

$$\text{Return on sales} = \frac{\text{Net income}}{\text{Net sales}} = \frac{\$49,000}{\$700,000} = 7\% \text{ (return on sales)}$$

Risk is a market variable that concerns investors. The higher the risk involved in an industry, the higher the return investors expect on their investment. Therefore, the level of risk involved in an industry and the return on investment of competing firms is important in comparing the firm's performance. *Return on equity* measures how much was earned for each dollar invested by owners. It's calculated by comparing a company's net income to its total owners' equity. Fiberrific's return on equity looks reasonably sound:

$$\text{Return on equity} = \frac{\text{Net income}}{\text{Total owners' equity}} = \frac{\$49,000}{\$213,000} = 23\% \text{ return on equity}$$

It's important to remember that profits help companies like Fiberrific grow. Therefore, these and other profitability ratios are considered vital measurements of company growth and management performance.

Activity Ratios

Converting the firm's resources to profits is a key function of management. Activity ratios measure the effectiveness of a firm's management in using the assets that are available.

The *inventory turnover ratio* measures the speed of inventory moving through the firm and its conversion into sales. Inventory sitting by idly in a business costs money. Think of the fixed cost of storing inventory in a warehouse as opposed to the revenue available when companies sell (turn over) inventory. The more efficiently a firm manages its inventory, the higher the return. The inventory turnover ratio for Fiberrific is measured as follows:

$$\text{Inventory turnover} = \frac{\text{Cost of goods sold}}{\text{Average inventory}} = \frac{\$410,000}{\$215,000} = 1.9 \text{ times}$$

Note that the average inventory is calculated by adding the beginning and ending inventories and dividing by two.

BALANCE SHEET ACCOUNTS		
ASSETS	OWNERS' LIABILITIES	SHAREHOLDERS' EQUITY
Cash	Accounts payable	Capital stock
Accounts receivable	Notes payable	Retained earnings
Inventory	Bonds payable	Common stock
Investments	Notes payable	
Equipment	Taxes payable	
Land		
Buildings		
Motor vehicles		
Goodwill		

INCOME STATEMENT ACCOUNTS			
REVENUES	COST OF GOODS SOLD	EXPENSES	
Sales revenue	Cost of buying goods	Wages	Interest
Rental revenue	Cost of storing goods	Rent	Donations
Commissions revenue		Repairs	Licences
Royalty revenue		Travel	Fees
		Insurance	Supplies
		Utilities	Advertising
		Entertainment	Taxes
		Storage	Research

FIGURE 16.8

ACCOUNTS IN THE BALANCE SHEET AND INCOME STATEMENT

A lower-than-average inventory turnover ratio in an industry often indicates obsolete merchandise on hand or poor buying practices. A higher than average ratio may signal lost sales because of inadequate stock. An acceptable turnover ratio is generally determined industry by industry. Fiberrific's inventory turnover of 1.9 times would need to be measured with its main competitors to estimate its efficiency in managing its inventory. Managers need to be aware of proper inventory control and expected inventory turnover to ensure proper performance. Have you ever worked as a food server in a restaurant? How many times did your employer expect you to turn over a table (keep changing customers at the table) in an evening? The more times a table turns, the higher the return to the owner.

Accountants and other finance professionals use several other specific ratios, in addition to the ones we have discussed, to learn more about a firm's financial condition. The key purpose here is to acquaint you with what financial ratios are, the relationship they have with the firm's financial statements, and how businesspeople—including investors, creditors, lenders, and managers—use them. If you can't recall where the accounting information used in ratio analysis comes from, see Figure 16.8 for a quick reference. It's also important for you to keep in mind that financial analysis begins where the accounting statements end.

We hope that you can see from this chapter that there is more to accounting than meets the eye. It can be fascinating and is critical to the firm's operations. It's worth saying one more time that, as the language of business, accounting is a worthwhile language to learn.

Progress Assessment

- How do financial ratios benefit stakeholders?
- What are the four main categories of financial ratios?

Summary

1. Financial information is critical to the growth and development of an organization. Accounting provides the information necessary to measure a firm's financial condition.

   1. Describe the importance of accounting and financial information.

   • **What is accounting?**
   Accounting is the recording, classifying, summarizing, and interpreting of financial events and transactions that affect an organization. The methods used to record and summarize accounting data into reports are called an accounting system.

2. The accounting profession covers five major areas: managerial accounting, financial accounting, auditing, tax accounting, and governmental and not-for-profit accounting.

   2. Define and explain the different areas of the accounting profession.

   • **How does managerial accounting differ from financial accounting?**
   Managerial accounting provides information and analyses to managers within the firm to assist them in decision making. Financial accounting provides information and analyses to external users of data such as creditors and lenders.

   • **What is the job of an auditor?**
   Auditors review and evaluate the standards used to prepare a company's financial statements. An independent audit is conducted by a public accountant and is an evaluation and unbiased opinion about the accuracy of company financial statements.

   • **What is the difference between a private accountant and a public accountant?**
   A public accountant provides services for a fee to a variety of companies, whereas a private accountant works for a single company. Private and public accountants do essentially the same things with the exception of independent audits. Private accountants do perform internal audits, but only public accountants supply independent audits.

3. Many people confuse bookkeeping and accounting.

   3. Distinguish between accounting and bookkeeping, list the steps in the accounting cycle, and explain how computers are used in accounting.

   • **What is the difference between bookkeeping and accounting?**
   Bookkeeping is part of accounting and includes the mechanical part of recording data. Accounting also includes classifying, summarizing, interpreting, and reporting data to management.

   • **What are journals and ledgers?**
   Journals are original-entry accounting documents. This means that they are the first place transactions are recorded. Summaries of journal entries are recorded (posted) into ledgers. Ledgers are specialized accounting books that arrange the transactions by homogeneous groups (accounts).

   • **What are the six steps of the accounting cycle?**
   The six steps of the accounting cycle are (1) analyzing documents; (2) recording information into journals; (3) posting that information into ledgers; (4) developing a trial balance; (5) preparing financial statements (the balance sheet, income statement and statement of changes in financial position); and (6) analyzing financial statements.

   • **How can computers help accountants?**
   Computers can record and analyze data and provide financial reports. Software is available that can continuously analyze and test accounting

systems to be sure they are functioning correctly. Computers can help decision making by providing appropriate information, but they cannot make good financial decisions independently. Accounting applications and creativity are still human traits.

4. Explain how the three major financial statements differ.

4. Financial statements are a critical part of the firm's financial position.

- ***What is a balance sheet?***

A balance sheet reports the financial position of a firm on a particular day. The fundamental accounting equation used to prepare the balance sheet is Assets = Liabilities + Owners' equity.

- ***What are the major accounts of the balance sheet?***

Assets are economic resources owned by the firm, such as buildings and machinery. Liabilities are amounts owed by the firm to others (e.g., creditors, bondholders). Owners' equity is the value of the things the firm owns (assets) minus any liabilities; thus, owners' equity equals assets minus liabilities.

- ***What is an income statement?***

An income statement reports revenues, costs, and expenses for a specific period of time (e.g., for the year ended December 31, 2005). The formula is Revenue − Cost of goods sold = Gross margin; Gross margin − Operating expenses = Net income before taxes; and Net income before taxes − Taxes = Net income (or net loss). Note that the income statement is sometimes called the profit and loss statement.

- ***What is a statement of changes in financial position?***

Cash flow is the difference between cash receipts (money coming in) and cash disbursements (money going out). The statement of changes in financial position reports cash receipts and disbursements related to the firm's major activities: operations, investments, and financing.

5. Describe the role of amortization, LIFO, and FIFO in reporting financial information.

5. Applying accounting knowledge makes the reporting and analysis of data a challenging occupation. Amortization is a key account that accountants evaluate. Two accounting techniques for valuing inventory are known as LIFO and FIFO.

- ***What is amortization?***

Amortization is the systematic writing off of the value of a tangible asset over its estimated useful life. Amortization must be noted on both the balance sheet and the income statement.

- ***What are LIFO and FIFO?***

LIFO and FIFO are methods of valuing inventory. FIFO means first in, first out; LIFO means last in, first out. The method an accountant uses to value inventory, FIFO or LIFO, can affect its net income.

6. Explain the importance of ratio analysis in reporting financial information.

6. Financial ratios are a key part of analyzing financial information.

- ***What are the four key categories of ratios?***

There are four key categories of ratios: liquidity ratios, leverage (debt) ratios, profitability (performance) ratios, and activity ratios.

- ***What is the major value of ratio analysis to the firm?***

Ratio analysis provides the firm with information about its financial position in key areas compared to similar firms in its industry and its past performance. This information is then compared to that of similar-sized firms in the same industry, as well as to the firm's past ratio performance.

Key Terms

accounting 486	current assets 498	liquidity 498
accounting cycle 494	double-entry bookkeeping 493	managerial accounting 487
amortization 506	financial accounting 489	net income or net loss 500
annual report 489	financial statement 495	
assets 498	first in, first out (FIFO) 508	operating expenses 502
auditing 491		owners' equity 499
balance sheet 498	fundamental accounting equation 496	private accountants 490
bookkeeping 493		public accountant 490
capital assets 498	gross profit (gross margin) 502	ratio analysis 508
cash flow 504		revenue 500
certified general accountant (CGA) 490	income statement 500	statement of changes in financial position 503
certified management accountant (CMA) 489	independent audit 492	trial balance 494
	intangible assets 498	
chartered accountant (CA) 489	journal 493	
	last in, first out (LIFO) 508	
cost of goods sold (or cost of goods manufactured) 501	ledger 493	
	liabilities 499	

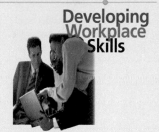

Developing Workplace Skills

1. Visit, telephone, or e-mail a professional accountant from a local company in your area, or talk with one in your school's business department. Ask what challenges, changes, and opportunities he or she foresees in the accounting profession in the next five years. List the forecasts on a sheet of paper and then compare them with the information in this chapter.

2. Obtain the most recent annual report for a company of your choice. *The Globe and Mail* has a free annual reports service; call to order a report at 1-888-301-0506. Many companies post their annual reports on their Web-sites. Hints: Look over the company's financial statements and see if they coincide with the information in this chapter. Read the opinion of the auditing firm (usually at the end of the report). Write down important conclusions the auditors have made about the company's financial statements.

3. Take a sheet of paper. On every fourth line, write one of the following headings: assets, liabilities, owners' equity, expenses, and revenues. Then list as many items as you can for each business classification under each heading. When you are finished, look up the lists in the text and add to your own. Keep the lists for your notes. As you complete the lists, create a mental picture of each account so that you can understand the concepts behind accounts and accounting.

4. Place yourself in the role of a small-business consultant. One of your clients, Be Pretty Fashions, is considering opening two new stores. The problem is that the business often experiences cash flow problems due to continuous style changes that occur in the fashion industry. Prepare a formal draft memo to Be Pretty Fashions explaining the problems a firm experiences when it encounters the cash flow problems that typically occur with such growth. Think of a business option Be Pretty Fashions could try to avoid cash flow problems.

5. Write your own explanation of how small businesses get into trouble with cash flow by expanding too rapidly. Think of several ways a business could expand rapidly and still avoid such problems. Discuss your thoughts with the class.

Taking It To The Net 1

Purpose

To research careers in accounting.

Exercise

Go to the Websites of the three large professional accounting organizations in Canada:

    a. Chartered Accountants of Canada (www.cica.ca)

    b. Society of Management Accountants of Canada (www.cma-canada.org)

    c. Certified General Accountants Association of Canada (www.cga-canada.org).

Browse through the sites and find information concerning the requirements to become a CA, CMA, and a CGA.

1. What are the requirements of each program?

2. Which program is of most interest to you? Why?

3. Was the merger between CAs and CMAs approved? If no, why not? If yes, what were the resulting changes?

Taking It To The Net 2

Purpose

To calculate and analyze current ratios and quick (acid-test) ratios.

Exercise

Thingamajigs and Things, a small gift shop, has total assets of $45,000 (including inventory valued at $30,000) and $9,000 in liabilities. WannaBees, a specialty clothing store, has total assets of $150,000 (including inventory valued at $125,000) and $85,000 in liabilities. Both businesses have applied for loans. Use the calculators on the Bankrate.com Website to answer the following questions:

1. Calculate the current ratio for each company. Comparing the ratios, which company is more likely to get the loan? Why?

2. The quick (acid-test) ratio is considered an even more reliable measure of a business's ability to repay loans than the current ratio. Because inventory is often difficult to liquidate, the value of the inventory is subtracted from the total current assets. Calculate the quick ratio for each business. Do you think either business will get the loan? Why?

Practising Management Decisions

Case

Getting Through the Hard Times at Hard Rock

In the mid-1990s, the theme-dining business seemed like a path lined with gold. With regularity, celebrity stargazers, enthusiastic press from around the globe, and hungry customers gathered at the openings of theme restaurants like Planet Hollywood and Motown Cafe. Unfortunately, the situation changed. In the late 1990s and early 2000s, Planet Hollywood filed for bankruptcy protection and Motown Cafe closed units across the country. Consumer boredom, a slowing economy, and a saturated market were blamed.

The changing "eatertainment" market raised eyebrows at the granddaddy of theme restaurants, the Hard Rock Cafe (HRC). HRC knew that its market position was shaky due to increased competition and shifting consumer attitudes. The company also felt growing financial pressures and speculated that a change in financial management might be needed. HRC had operated with a traditional, competent accounting department that made sure the company paid its bills, had money left at the end of the day, and could state how much it was earning. The problem was that HRC lacked the ability to analyze its financial information fully and use it to improve operations. To address these concerns, the company recruited a new chief financial officer (CFO) and dedicated itself to changing the financial reporting and information structure at the company.

Hard Rock Cafe believed that it had a tremendous undervalued asset—a premium global brand. The company dedicated itself to protecting and expanding that asset. However, it was evident that, without revenue, brand loyalty doesn't matter. Hard Rock's CFO was astonished to find that HRC sold $180 million a year in merchandise (primarily its well known T-shirts) in addition to food, yet could not explain exactly how these individual items contributed to the firm's profit. It was then the company realized that Hard Rock Cafe's accounting and financial management had to change.

To start things off, the company piloted a food and beverage management system to track usage and item profitability. This system included information such as daily and seasonal buying patterns, profitability of one menu versus another, average weekly guest counts per restaurant, and specific cost of sales and profit margins per item. The company then shifted the responsibility of the firms's accountants. Instead of being responsible for profit-and-loss statements for a certain number of restaurants, company accountants now were responsible for one major financial category only, such as cost of goods sold, for all the company's operations. The objective was to compile companywide information for sound financial decision making.

Hard Rock Cafe also broke down the barriers that existed between the finance and accounting departments and operations, merchandising, and marketing. Today, financial information is shared directly with managers who can execute the recommendations at the restaurant level. Still, the company realized this was not going to be a quick fix but rather an ongoing challenge. Last year, 27 million people visited a Hard Rock Cafe at the company's 103 locations. Even so, competitors such as Rainforest Cafe promise to make the fight for eatertainment customers an interesting one.

Decision Questions

1. Why is it important for Hard Rock Cafe to know how different products contribute financially to overall company profits?
2. Do you think hard Rock Cafe's focus on improved financial reporting helped its company planning capabilities? How?
3. Would a company like Hard Rock Cafe be most likely to use a FIFO or a LIFO form of inventory valuation? Why?

Sources: Larry Bleiberg. "Cafe Quest Has Retiree on a Roll," *Dallas Morning News*, March 15, 2000, p. 12G: "Rank Is Belting on Another Good Year," *Birmingham (UK) Post*, March 1, 2003, p. 15; and Jon Griffin, "Rank Is Backing a Winner," *Evening Mail (UK)*, February 28, 2003, p. 26.

Video Case

Talking the Language of Business: AON

Joe Prochaska, senior vice-president and comptroller at AON, is familiar with all the names used to describe accountants: bean-counters, pencil-pushers, number-crunchers, to name just a few. Like most accountants, he ignores these unflattering titles because he knows one simple fact: You can't understand business unless you understand accounting, because accounting is the language of business. Whether you operate your own small business from your home or work for a multinational corporation like AON, an understanding of accounting will help you in whatever business career you choose. Prochaska's company is the largest insurance broker in the world, with over 550 offices in 130 countries. If the name AON is not familiar to you, it's because AON actually does most of its business in reinsurance: It sells insurance to insurance companies.

You learned in this chapter that accounting is the process of recording, categorizing, and interpreting financial transactions. You also learned there are several types of accountants. *Managerial accountants* interpret financial data for internal use in a company. *Financial accountants* provide accounting information for persons outside the firm, such as potential investors and the owners themselves. *Auditors* are like financial detectives; they come in and check the accounting records to make sure that the records are accurate and follow all the rules of accounting. *Tax accountants* prepare tax statements and make sure the firm fully complies with tax rules while minimizing the taxes it must pay.

It's important that accountants follow standard procedures so that financial information is similar company by company. The Financial Accounting Standards Board (FASB) created generally accepted accounting principles (GAAP) for this reason.

The six-step accounting cycle leads to the preparation of the firm's key financial statements: the balance sheet, income statement, and statement of cash flows. In his role as comptroller at AON, Joe Prochaska is responsible for seeing this process is done correctly. However, the real challenge comes when Prochaska and his staff are called on to analyze what the financial statements mean to AON in terms of how well the firm is doing financially and what improvements it can make to perform even better.

Financial information is crucial to AON as it is to all firms. Being in the reinsurance business, AON helps insurance companies estimate their "catastrophic exposure." In other words, if a disaster hits, will insurance companies be able to cover the losses suffered by policyholders? The financial data collected will tell the firms, for example, whether they need to raise premiums and, if so, by how much.

Without question, accounting is critical to the long-term success of any organization. Furthermore, it is challenging and interesting work. Most important, accounting is something that everyone needs to understand to comprehend the "language of business."

Discussion Questions

1. If you prepared a balance sheet and income statement for your own finances as the chapter suggested, what did you learn and how could you improve your financial condition in the future?
2. Why is the government concerned with accounting practices? Does the government seem to be less or more involved with accounting procedures in recent years? Why?
3. What group or groups are interested in a company's financial statements? Why would people be interested in compiling financial ratios for a firm?

Chapter 17

Financial Management

Learning Goals

After you have read and studied this chapter, you should be able to

1 Describe the importance of finance and financial management to an organization, and explain the responsibilities of financial managers.

2 Outline the financial planning process, and explain the three key budgets in the financial plan.

3 Explain the major reasons why firms need operating funds, and identify various types of financing that can be used to obtain these funds.

4 Identify and describe different sources of short-term financing.

5 Identify and describe different sources of long-term financing.

Profile

Getting to Know Randy Casstevens, CFO of Krispy Kreme Doughnuts

Krispy Kreme Doughnuts, Inc. was founded in 1937 in Winston-Salem, North Carolina. Krispy Kreme is a leading branded specialty retailer of premium quality doughnuts. It has more than 365 stores in the United States, Canada, Australia, the United Kingdom, and Mexico.

The job of measuring the financial implications of expansion belongs to the company's chief financial officer (CFO) Randy Casstevens. Today the line of people trying to buy a Krispy Kreme franchise seems as long as the lines waiting to buy hot doughnuts in the stores. When Casstevens analyzed company revenue he found that Krispy Kreme has higher profit margins than other fast-food businesses. In fact, Krispy Kreme's cash flow margins tend toward the mid–20 percent range, compared to 10 to 15 percent for competitors. Casstevens learned that the average Krispy Kreme generates cash—big cash—from the first day a store opens. After a 12-month honeymoon period, the average Krispy Kreme takes in yearly revenues of approximately US$2.4 million, compared to a typical McDonald's (US$1.5 million), Dunkin' Donuts (US$744,000), and Cinnabon (US$408,000).

Casstevens considered two questions: How far and how fast should the company expand in the next five years? Should the company expand opportunities for franchisees to get in on the dough (pun intended), or is it best for the company to open only company-owned stores? Casstevens recommended that Krispy Kreme not attempt to be the next Starbucks by opening large numbers of company-owned stores. He also suggested that the company continue its franchising efforts with a few key changes for prospective new franchisees. One, they will have a partner: Krispy Kreme Doughnuts, Inc. Two, the company will push for megafranchisees who will commit to opening at least 10 stores in a given region.

KremeKo Inc. was the first international franchisee of the company. KremeKo is the private Canadian company that has exclusive rights to develop the Krispy Kreme brand in all provinces, except British Columbia. Krispy Kreme owns 40 percent of KremeKo's common shares. The first store was opened in Canada two and a half years ago, and today there are 18 stores. KremeKo invests $2.4 million in each start-up operation, a high sum because most stores are in newly constructed buildings on land averaging 1 to 1.25 acres in size and equipment is specially designed, according to Roly Morris, president and CEO of KremeKo. Morris does not view Tim Hortons as a competitor because doughnuts account for only 10–15 percent of that chain's sales while they represent 93 percent of Krispy Kreme's. Morris plans to expand to 40 stores in the next few years, concentrating on areas where the population is at least 400,000.

Krispy Kreme found its niche by massive giveaways ("sample, sample, sample") and customer service, Morris said. A dissatisfied customer is given a "recovery coupon" for a dozen doughnuts. As of May, stores now open 12 minutes before and 12 minutes after the posted hours, if a customer is around. Morris admits the novelty of Krispy Kreme wears off soon after the hoopla surrounding store openings. That's one reason why Krispy Kreme is now sold in two major supermarkets, Wal-Mart, Petro-Canada convenience stores, and at Famous Players movie theatres in Toronto.

Krispy Kreme became a public company in 2000. The funds obtained from this initial public offering (IPO) helped the company increase its cash position and reduce corporate debt. Risk, complexity, and uncertainty clearly define the role of financial management, especially in fast-growing companies such as Krispy Kreme. Add to these challenges fluctuations in interest rates, expectations of investors and lenders, budgeting, and managing funds, and the job of the financial manager takes on even more intensity. In this chapter, you'll explore the role of finance in business and learn about the tools financial managers use to seek financial stability and future growth.

Sources: Janice Arnold, "The Secrets of Selling Doughnuts Revealed by Krispy Kreme Head," *The Canadian Jewish News,* July 1, 2004. Retrieved from www.cjnews.com/viewarticle.asp?id=3791; Courtesy of the *Canadian Jewish News*; Ronald Fink, "The Fear of All Sums," *CFO,* August 2002, pp. 34–42; Carlye Adler, "Would You Pay $2 Million for This Franchise?" *Fortune Small Business,* May 1, 2002, pp. 36–41; and "Smithsonian to Celebrate Krispy Kreme—A Hole Lot of History," *Washington Times,* March 19, 2002.

THE ROLE OF FINANCE AND FINANCIAL MANAGERS

finance
The function in a business that acquires funds for the firm and manages those funds within the firm.

financial management
The job of managing a firm's resources so it can meet its goals and objectives.

financial managers
Managers who make recommendations to top executives regarding strategies for improving the financial strength of a firm.

Finance is the function in a business that acquires funds for the firm and manages those funds within the firm. Finance activities include preparing budgets; doing cash flow analysis; and planning for the expenditure of funds on such assets as plant, equipment, and machinery. **Financial management** is the job of managing a firm's resources so it can meet its goals and objectives. Without a carefully calculated financial plan, the firm has little chance for survival, regardless of its product or marketing effectiveness.

Financial managers examine the financial data prepared by accountants and make recommendations to top executives regarding strategies for improving the health (financial strength) of the firm. They can make sound financial decisions only if they understand accounting information. Figure 17.1 highlights a financial manager's tasks. As you can see, some responsibilities are to obtain money and then control the use of that money effectively.

As you may remember from Chapter 7, financing a small business ➤P. 197◀ is a difficult but essential function if a firm expects to survive those important first five years. The following are three of the most common ways for a firm to fail financially: (1) undercapitalization (lacking funds to start and run the business), (2) poor control over cash flow, and (3) inadequate expense control. Therefore, the need for careful financial management goes well beyond the first five years and remains a challenge that a business, large or small, must face throughout its existence.

The Importance of Understanding Finance

Consider the financial problems encountered by a small organization called Parsley Patch. Two friends, Elizabeth Bertani and Pat Sherwood, started the company on what can best be described as a shoestring budget. It began when Bertani prepared salt-free seasonings for her husband, who was on a no-salt diet. Her friend Sherwood thought the seasonings were good enough to sell. Bertani agreed, and Parsley Patch Inc., was born.

The business began with an investment of $5,000, which was rapidly eaten up for a logo and a label design. Bertani and Sherwood quickly learned the

FIGURE 17.1

WHAT FINANCIAL
MANAGERS DO

importance of capital in getting a business going. Eventually, the two women personally invested more than $100,000 to keep the business from experiencing severe undercapitalization.

The partners believed that gourmet shops would be an ideal distribution point for their product. Everything started well, and hundreds of gourmet shops adopted the product line. But when sales failed to meet expectations, the women decided that the health-food market offered more potential than gourmet shops, because salt-free seasonings were a natural for people with restricted diets. The choice was a good one. Sales soared and approached $30,000 a month. Still, the company earned no profits.

Bertani and Sherwood were not trained in monitoring cash flow ►P. 514◄ or in controlling expenses. In fact, they had been told not to worry about costs, and they hadn't. They eventually hired a chartered accountant (CA) and an experienced financial manager, who taught them how to compute the costs of the various blends they produced and how to control their expenses. The financial specialists also offered insight into how to control cash coming in and out of the company (cash flow). Soon Parsley Patch earned a comfortable margin on operations that ran close to $1 million a year. Luckily, the owners were able to turn things around before it was too late.

If Bertani and Sherwood had understood finance before starting their business, they may have been able to avoid the problems they encountered. The key word here is *understood*. You do not have to pursue finance as a career to understand finance. Financial understanding is important to anyone who wants to start a small business, invest in stocks and bonds (to be discussed later in this chapter), or plan a retirement fund. In short, finance and accounting are two areas everyone involved in business needs to study. Since accounting was discussed in Chapter 16, let's look at what financial management is all about.

WHAT IS FINANCIAL MANAGEMENT?

Financial managers are responsible for seeing that the company pays its bills. Finance functions such as buying merchandise on credit (accounts payable) and collecting payment from customers (accounts receivable) are responsibilities of financial managers. Therefore, financial managers are responsible for paying the company's bills at the appropriate time and for collecting overdue payments to make sure that the company does not lose too much money to bad debts (people or firms that don't pay their bills). While these functions are critical to all types of businesses, they are particularly critical to small and medium-sized businesses, which typically have smaller cash or credit cushions than large corporations.

It's vital that financial managers in any business stay abreast of changes or opportunities in finance and prepare to adjust to them. For example, tax payments represent an outflow of cash from the business. Therefore, financial managers have become increasingly involved in tax management. In keeping with changes in the law, financial managers carefully analyze the tax implications of various managerial decisions in an attempt to minimize the taxes paid by the business.[1] It's critical that businesses of all sizes concern themselves with managing taxes.

Usually a member of the firm's finance department, the internal auditor, checks on the journals, ledgers, and financial statements prepared by the accounting department to make sure that all transactions have been treated in accordance with generally accepted accounting principles (GAAP).[2] If such audits were not done, accounting statements would be less reliable. Therefore, it is important that internal auditors be objective and critical of any improprieties or deficiencies they might note in their evaluation.[3] Regular, thoroughly conducted internal audits offer the firm assistance in the important role of financial planning, which we'll look at next.

FINANCIAL PLANNING

Financial planning involves analyzing short-term and long-term money flows to and from the firm. The overall objective of financial planning is to optimize the firm's profitability and make the best use of its money. It involves three steps: (1) forecasting both short-term and long-term financial needs, (2) developing budgets to meet those needs, and (3) establishing financial control to see how well the company is doing what it set out to do (see Figure 17.2). Let's look at each step and the role these steps play in improving the financial health of an organization.

Forecasting Financial Needs

short-term forecast
Forecast that predicts revenues, costs, and expenses for a period of one year or less.

cash flow forecast
Forecast that predicts the cash inflows and outflows in future periods, usually months or quarters.

Forecasting is an important part of any firm's financial plan. A **short-term forecast** predicts revenues, costs, and expenses for a period of one year or less. This forecast is the foundation for most other financial plans, so its accuracy is critical. Part of the short-term forecast may be in the form of a **cash flow forecast**, which predicts the cash inflows and outflows in future periods, usually months or quarters. The inflows and outflows of cash recorded in the cash flow forecast are based on expected sales revenues and on various costs and expenses incurred and when they'll come due. The company's sales

FIGURE 17.2

FINANCIAL PLANNING

Note the close link between financial planning and budgeting.

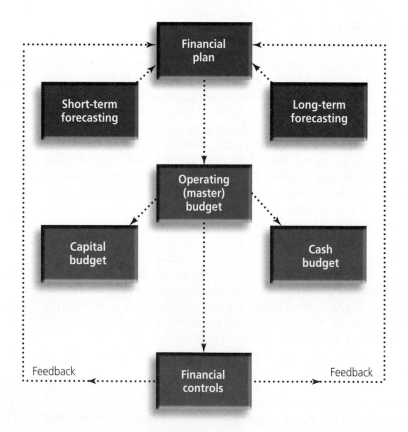

forecast estimates the firm's projected sales for a particular period. A business often uses its past financial statements as a basis for projecting expected sales and various costs and expenses.

A **long-term forecast** predicts revenues, costs, and expenses for a period longer than 1 year, and sometimes as far as 5 or 10 years into the future. This forecast plays a crucial part in the company's long-term strategic plan. Remember, a firm's strategic plan asks questions such as these: What business are we in? Should we be in it five years from now? How much money should we invest in technology and new plant and equipment over the next decade? Will there be cash available to meet long-term obligations?

The long-term financial forecast gives top management, as well as operations managers, some sense of the income or profit potential possible with different strategic plans. Additionally, long-term projections assist financial managers with the preparation of company budgets.

long-term forecast
Forecast that predicts revenues, costs, and expenses for a period longer than 1 year, and sometimes as far as 5 or 10 years into the future.

Working with the Budget Process

The budgeting process depends on the accuracy of the firm's financial statements. Put simply, a budget is a financial plan. Specifically, a **budget** sets forth management's expectations for revenues and, on the basis of those expectations, allocates the use of specific resources throughout the firm. The key financial statements—the balance sheet, income statement, and statement of changes in financial position—form the basis for the budgeting process. Financial information from the firm's past is what's used as the basis to project future financial needs. A budget becomes the primary guide for the firm's financial operations and financial needs.

Most firms compile yearly budgets from short-term and long-term financial forecasts. It's important that these financial forecasts be as accurate as possible. Therefore, businesses use cost and revenue information derived from past financial statements as the basis for forecasting company budgets.[4] Budgeting is clearly tied to forecasting. There are usually several types of budgets established in a firm's financial plan:

- A capital budget.
- A cash budget.
- An operating (master) budget.

A **capital budget** highlights a firm's spending plans for major asset purchases that often require large sums of money. The capital budget primarily concerns itself with the purchase of such assets as property, buildings, and equipment.

A **cash budget** estimates a firm's projected cash inflows and outflows that the firm can use to plan for any cash shortages or surpluses during a given period (e.g., monthly). Cash budgets are important guidelines that assist managers in anticipating borrowing, debt repayment, operating expenses, and short-term investments. A sample cash budget for our continuing example company, Fiberrific, is provided in Figure 17.3.

budget
A financial plan that sets forth management's expectations, and, on the basis of those expectations, allocates the use of specific resources throughout the firm.

capital budget
A budget that highlights a firm's spending plans for major asset purchases that often require large sums of money.

cash budget
A budget that estimates a firm's projected cash inflows and outflows that the firm can use to plan for any cash shortages or surpluses during a given period.

Special processing equipment turns an average potato into the chips and fries we consume. The firm's capital budget is the financial tool that controls business spending for expensive assets such as this processing equipment. Such major assets are referred to as capital assets or property, plant, and equipment. What items are in your school's capital budget?

FIGURE 17.3

A SAMPLE CASH BUDGET FOR FIBERRIFIC, INC.

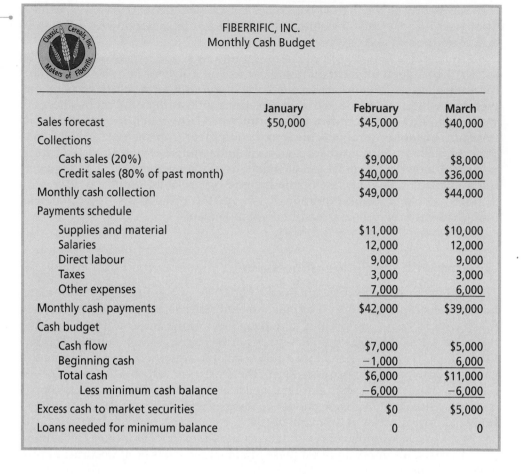

FIBERRIFIC, INC.
Monthly Cash Budget

	January	February	March
Sales forecast	$50,000	$45,000	$40,000
Collections			
Cash sales (20%)		$9,000	$8,000
Credit sales (80% of past month)		$40,000	$36,000
Monthly cash collection		$49,000	$44,000
Payments schedule			
Supplies and material		$11,000	$10,000
Salaries		12,000	12,000
Direct labour		9,000	9,000
Taxes		3,000	3,000
Other expenses		7,000	6,000
Monthly cash payments		$42,000	$39,000
Cash budget			
Cash flow		$7,000	$5,000
Beginning cash		−1,000	6,000
Total cash		$6,000	$11,000
Less minimum cash balance		−6,000	−6,000
Excess cash to market securities		$0	$5,000
Loans needed for minimum balance		0	0

operating (master) budget
The budget that ties together all of a firm's other budgets; it is the projection of dollar allocations to various costs and expenses needed to run or operate the business, given projected revenues.

The **operating (master) budget** ties together all the firm's other budgets and summarizes the business's proposed financial activities. It can be defined more formally as the projection of dollar allocations to various costs and expenses needed to run or operate a business, given projected revenues. How much the firm will spend on supplies, travel, rent, advertising, research, salaries, and so forth is determined in the operating (master) budget. The operating budget is generally the most detailed and most used budget that a firm prepares.

Once a company has forecast its short-term and long-term financial needs and established budgets to show how funds will be allocated, the final step in financial planning is to establish financial controls. We will discuss this topic in a moment; but first, the Spotlight on Small Business box challenges you to develop a monthly budget.

Critical Thinking

Budgets are designed to keep decision makers informed on progress against company plans. An important theme of this book is the need for managers to be flexible so that they can adapt quickly to rapidly changing conditions. This often means modifying previous plans. Do you see any conflict between budgets and such flexibility? How do managers stay within the confines of budgets when they must shift gears to accommodate a rapidly changing world? Which forecasts are more affected by these problems, short-term or long-term? Why?

Spotlight on Small Business

You, Incorporated, Monthly Budget

Let's develop a monthly budget for You, Inc. Be honest and think of everything that needs to be included for an accurate monthly budget for You!

	Expected	Actual	Difference
Monthly income:			
Wages (net pay after taxes)	___	___	___
Savings account withdrawal	___	___	___
Family support	___	___	___
Other sources	___	___	___
Total monthly income	___	___	___
Monthly expenses:			
Fixed expenses			
Rent or mortgage	___	___	___
Car payment	___	___	___
Life insurance	___	___	___
Tuition or fees	___	___	___
Other fixed expenses	___	___	___
Subtotal of fixed expenses	___	___	___
Variable expenses			
Food	___	___	___
Clothing	___	___	___
Entertainment	___	___	___
Transportation	___	___	___
Phone	___	___	___
Utilities	___	___	___
Publications	___	___	___
Internet connection	___	___	___
Cable television	___	___	___
Other expenses	___	___	___
Subtotal of variable expenses	___	___	___
Total expenses	___	___	___
Total income − Total expenses = Cash on hand/(Cash deficit)	___	___	___

Establishing Financial Controls

Financial control is a process in which a firm periodically compares its actual revenues, costs, and expenses with its budget. Most companies hold at least monthly financial reviews as a way to ensure financial control. Such control procedures help managers identify variances to the financial plan and allow them to take corrective action if necessary. Financial controls also provide feedback to help reveal which accounts, which departments, and which people are varying from the financial plans. Finance managers can judge if such variances may or may not be justified. In either case, managers can make some financial adjustments to the plan when needed. The Making Ethical Decisions

financial control
A process in which a firm periodically compares its actual revenues, costs, and expenses with its projected ones.

box details a situation a manager can face related to financial control. After the Progress Assessment, we shall explore specific reasons why firms need to have funds readily available.

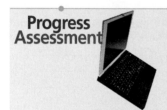

Progress Assessment

- Name three finance functions important to the firm's overall operations and performance.
- What are the three primary financial problems that cause firms to fail?
- In what ways do short-term and long-term financial forecasts differ?
- What is the organization's purpose in preparing budgets? Can you identify three different types of budgets?

THE NEED FOR OPERATING FUNDS

In business, the need for operating funds never seems to cease. That's why sound financial management is essential to all businesses. Like our personal financial needs, the capital needs of a business change over time. For example, as a small business grows, its financial requirements shift considerably. (Remember the example of Parsley Patch.) The same is true with large corporations such as Bell Canada, Vincor International, and McCain Foods. As they venture into new product areas or markets, their capital needs increase. Different firms need funds available for different reasons. However, in virtually all organizations there are certain operational needs for which funds must be available. Key areas include:

- Managing day-by-day needs of the business.
- Controlling credit operations.
- Acquiring needed inventory.
- Making capital expenditures.

Let's look at the financial needs that affect both the smallest and the largest of businesses.

Managing Day-by-Day Needs of the Business

If workers expect to be paid on Friday, they don't want to have to wait until Monday for their paycheques. If tax payments are due on the 15th of the month, the government expects the money on time. If the interest payment on a business loan is due on the 30th, the lender doesn't mean the 1st of the next month. As you can see, funds have to be available to meet the daily operational costs of the business.

The challenge of sound financial management is to see that funds are available to meet these daily cash needs without compromising the firm's investment potential. Money has what is called a time value. In other words, if someone offered to give you $200 today or $200 one year from today, you would benefit by taking the $200 today. Why? It's very simple. You could start collecting interest or invest the $200 you receive today, and over a year's time your money would grow. The same thing is true in business; the interest gained on the firm's investments is important in maximizing the profit the company will gain. That's why financial managers encourage keeping a firm's cash expenditures to a minimum.[5] By doing this, the firm can free up funds for investment in interest-bearing accounts. It's also not unusual for finance managers to suggest that a company pay its bills as late as possible (unless a cash discount is available) but try to collect what's owed to it as fast as possible. This way, they maximize the investment potential of the firm's funds. Efficient cash management is particularly important to small firms in conducting their daily operations because their access to capital is generally much more limited than that of larger businesses.[6]

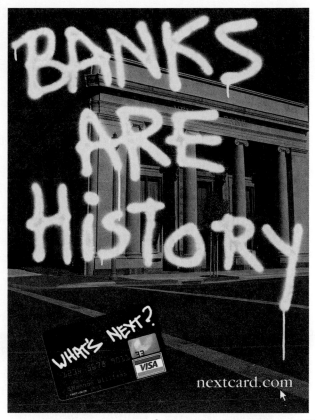

Collecting accounts receivable from some customers can be time-consuming and costly. Accepting credit cards like Visa, MasterCard, or American Express simplifies transactions, guarantees payment, and provides convenience for both customers and businesses. For what sort of purchases do you regularly use a credit card?

Controlling Credit Operations

Financial managers know that making credit available helps keep current customers happy and attracts new customers. In today's highly competitive business environment, many businesses would have trouble surviving without making credit available to customers.

The major problem with selling on credit is that as much as 25 percent or more of the business's assets could be tied up in its credit accounts (accounts receivable). This means that the firm needs to use some of its available funds to pay for the goods or services already sold to customers who bought on credit. Financial managers in such firms must develop efficient collection procedures. For example, businesses often provide cash or quantity discounts to buyers who pay their accounts by a certain time. Also, finance managers carefully scrutinize old and new credit customers to see if they have a favourable history of meeting their credit obligations on time.[7] In essence, the firm's credit policy reflects its financial position and its desire to expand into new markets.

One way to decrease the time, and therefore expense, involved in collecting accounts receivable is to accept bank credit cards such as MasterCard or Visa.[8] This is convenient for both the customer and the business. The banks that issue such credit cards have already established the customer's creditworthiness, which reduces the business's risk. Businesses must pay a fee to accept credit cards, but the fees are generally not excessive compared to the benefits the cards provide. In fact, credit card rates are dropping as competition in the industry intensifies.[9]

Acquiring Inventory

As we noted earlier in the text, effective marketing implies a clear customer orientation. This focus on the customer means that high-quality service and availability of goods are vital if a business expects to prosper in today's markets.[10] Therefore, to satisfy customers, businesses must maintain inventories that often involve a sizable expenditure of funds. Although it's true that firms expect to recapture their investment in inventory through sales to customers, a carefully constructed inventory policy assists in managing the firm's available funds and maximizing profitability.

Innovations such as just-in-time inventory help reduce the amount of funds a firm must tie up in inventory. Also, by carefully evaluating its inventory turnover ratio (discussed in Chapter 16) a firm can better control its outflow of cash for inventory. It's important for a business of any size to understand that a poorly managed inventory system can seriously impact cash flow and drain its finances dry.

Making Capital Expenditures

capital expenditures
Major investments in either tangible long-term assets such as land, buildings, and equipment or intangible assets such as patents, trademarks, and copyrights.

Capital expenditures are major investments in either tangible long-term assets such as land, buildings, and equipment, or intangible assets such as patents, trademarks, and copyrights. In many organizations the purchase of major assets—such as land for future expansion, manufacturing plants to increase production capabilities, research to develop new-product ideas, and equipment to maintain or exceed current levels of output—is essential. As you can imagine, these expenditures often require a huge portion of the organization's funds.

For example, business expansion into new markets can cost large sums of money with no guarantee that the expansion will be commercially successful. Therefore, it's critical that companies weigh all the possible options before committing what may be a large portion of their available resources.[11] For this reason, financial managers and analysts evaluate the appropriateness of such purchases or expenditures. Consider the situation in which a firm needs to expand its production capabilities due to increases in demand. One option is to buy land and build a new plant. Another option would be to purchase an existing plant or consider renting. Can you think of financial and accounting considerations that would come into play in this decision?

Obviously, the need for operating funds raises several questions in any firm: How does the firm obtain funds to finance operations and other business necessities? Will specific funds be needed by the firm in the long term or short term? How much will it cost to obtain these needed funds? Will these funds come from internal or external sources? Let's address these questions next.

Sources of Funds

Earlier in the chapter, you learned that finance is the function in a business that is responsible for acquiring and managing funds within the firm. Determining the amount of money needed for various periods and finding out the most appropriate sources from which to obtain these funds are fundamental

FIGURE 17.4

SOURCES OF SHORT-TERM AND LONG-TERM FINANCING

SHORT-TERM FINANCING	LONG-TERM FINANCING
Trade credit	**A. DEBT FINANCING**
Promissory notes	Lending institutions (e.g., loan)
Family and friends	Selling bonds
Financial institutions (e.g., line of credit)	
Short-term loans	**B. EQUITY FINANCING**
Factoring	Retained earnings
Commercial paper	Venture capital
	Selling stock

steps in sound financial management. **Short-term financing** refers to funds borrowed that will be repaid within one year. In contrast, **long-term financing** refers to funds borrowed for major purchases that will be repaid over a specific period longer than one year.

We shall explore different sources of short- and long-term financing fully in the next sections. But first it's important to know that businesses can use different methods of raising money. A firm can seek to raise needed capital through borrowing money (debt), selling ownership (equity), or earning profits (retained earnings). **Debt financing** refers to funds raised through various forms of borrowing that must be repaid. Firms can borrow either short-term funds, due to be repaid within one year, or long-term funds, due over a period longer than one year. **Equity financing** is money raised from within the firm (from operations) or through the sale of ownership in the firm (e.g., the sale of stock). Figure 17.4 summarizes the sources that can be used to acquire these needed short- and long-term funds. Let us look at these examples next.

short-term financing
Borrowed capital that will be repaid within one year.

long-term financing
Borrowed capital that will be repaid over a specific period longer than one year.

debt financing
Funds raised through various forms of borrowing that must be repaid.

equity financing
Funds raised from operations within the firm or through the sale of ownership in the firm.

- Why are accounts receivable a financial concern to the firm?
- What's the primary reason an organization spends a good deal of its available funds on inventory and capital expenditures?
- What's the difference between debt and equity financing?

Progress Assessment

OBTAINING SHORT-TERM FINANCING

The bulk of a finance manager's job does not involve obtaining long-term funds. In fact, in small businesses, long-term financing is often out of the question. Instead, the day-to-day operation of the firm calls for the careful management of short-term financial needs. Firms need to borrow short-term funds for purchasing additional inventory or for meeting bills that come due unexpectedly. Also, as we do in our personal lives, a business sometimes needs to obtain short-term funds when the firm's cash reserves are low. This is particularly true, again, of small businesses. Let's look at the major forms of short-term financing and what's meant by secured and unsecured financing with regard to different ways of obtaining needed funds.

Trade Credit

The most widely used source of short-term funding, trade credit (an account payable), is the least expensive and most convenient form of short-term financing. **Trade credit** is the practice of buying goods ➤P. 23◄ or services ➤P. 25◄ now and paying for them later. For example, when a firm buys merchandise, it receives an invoice (a bill) much like the one you receive when you buy something with a credit card.

It is common for business invoices to contain terms such as *2/10, net 30*. This means that the buyer can take a 2-percent discount for paying the invoice within 10 days. The total bill is due (net) in 30 days if the purchaser does not take advantage of the discount. Finance managers need to pay close attention to such discounts because they create opportunities to reduce the cost of financing. Think about it for a moment: If the discount offered to the customer is 2/10, net 30, the customer will pay 2 percent more for waiting an extra 20 days to pay the invoice.

Some uninformed businesspeople feel that 2 percent is insignificant, so they pay their bills after the discount period. In the course of a year, however, 2 percent for 20 days adds up to a 36-percent interest rate (because there are eighteen 20-day periods in the year). If the firm is capable of paying within 10 days, it is needlessly (and significantly) increasing its cost of financing by not doing so.

Promissory Notes

Some suppliers hesitate to give trade credit to organizations with a poor credit rating, no credit history, or a history of slow payment. In such cases, the supplier may insist that the customer sign a promissory note as a condition for obtaining credit. A **promissory note** is a written contract with a promise to pay a supplier a specific sum of money at a definite time. Promissory notes can be sold by the supplier to a bank at a discount (the amount of the note less a fee for the bank's services in collecting the amount due).

Family and Friends

Many small firms obtain short-term funds by borrowing money from family and friends. Because such funds are needed for periods of less than a year, friends or relatives are sometimes willing to help. Such loans can create problems, however, if the firm does not understand cash flow. As we discussed earlier, the firm may suddenly find itself having several bills coming due at the same time with no sources of funds to pay them. It is better, therefore, not to borrow from friends or relatives; instead, go to a commercial bank that fully understands the business's risk and can help analyze your firm's future financial needs.

If an entrepreneur does, however, decide to ask family or friends for financial assistance, it's important that both parties (1) agree on specific loan terms, (2) put the agreement in writing, and (3) arrange for repayment in the same way they would for a bank loan. Such actions help keep family relationships and friendships intact.

Commercial Banks and Other Financial Institutions

Banks are highly sensitive to risk and are often reluctant to lend money to small businesses. Nonetheless, a promising and well-organized venture may be able to get a bank loan. If it is able to get such a loan, a small or medium-sized business should have the person in charge of the finance function keep in close touch with the bank. It's also wise to see a banker periodically (as often as once a month) and send the banker all the firm's financial statements so that the bank continues to supply funds when needed.

If you try to imagine the different types of businesspeople who go to banks for a loan, you'll get a better idea of the role of financial management. Picture, for example, a farmer going to the bank to borrow funds for seed, fertilizer, equipment, and other needs. The farmer may buy such supplies in the spring and pay for them after the fall harvest. Now picture a local toy store buying merchandise for holiday-season sales. The store may borrow the money for such purchases in the summer and pay it back after the holidays. Restaurants may borrow funds at the beginning of the month and pay by the end of the month. Can you see that how much a business borrows and for how long depends often on the kind of business it is and how quickly the merchandise purchased with a bank loan can be resold or used to generate funds?

Hopefully, you can also imagine how important it is for specialists in a company's finance and accounting departments to do a cash flow forecast. Unfortunately, small-business owners generally lack the luxury of such specialists and must monitor cash flow themselves. By anticipating times when many bills will come due, a business can begin early to seek funds or sell other assets to prepare for the crunch. This is why it's important for a businessperson to keep friendly and close relations with his or her banker.[12] An experienced banker may spot cash flow problems early or be more willing to lend money in a crisis if a businessperson has established a strong, friendly relationship built on openness, trust, and sound management practices. It's important to remember that your banker wants you to succeed almost as much as you do.

Different Forms of Short-Term Loans

Banks and other financial institutions offer different types of loans to customers. A **secured loan** is a loan that's backed by something valuable, such as property. The item of value is called *collateral*. If the borrower fails to pay the loan, the lender may take possession of the collateral. For example, an automobile loan is a secured loan. If the borrower fails to pay the loan, the lender will repossess the car. Collateral takes some of the risk out of lending money.

Accounts receivable are assets that are often used by businesses as collateral for a loan; the process is called *pledging*. Some percentage of the value of accounts receivables pledged (usually about 75 percent) is advanced to the borrowing firm. As customers pay off their accounts, the funds received are forwarded to the lender in repayment of the funds that were advanced.[13] Inventory such as raw materials (e.g., coal, steel) is also often used as collateral or security for a business loan. Other assets that can be used as collateral include buildings, machinery, and company-owned stocks and bonds (to be discussed soon).

The most difficult kind of loan to get from a bank or other financial institution is an unsecured loan. An **unsecured loan** doesn't require a borrower to offer the lending institution any collateral to obtain the loan. It's basically a

'Tis the season to shop. Ever wonder how retailers get the money to buy all of the items available during the holiday season? Department stores and other large retailers make extensive use of commercial banks and other lenders to borrow the money needed to buy merchandise to stock their shelves.

The Canadian Bankers Association (CBA) is the main representative body for banks in Canada. Visit its Website at www.cba.ca to find useful information about small-business services, bank services, and quick facts about this sector.

secured loan
A loan backed by something valuable, such as property.

unsecured loan
A loan that's not backed by any specific assets.

loan that's not backed by any assets. Normally, a lender will give unsecured loans only to highly regarded customers (e.g., long-standing customers or customers considered financially stable).

If a business develops a good relationship with a bank, the bank may open a line of credit for the firm. A **line of credit** is a given amount of unsecured funds a bank will lend to a business. In other words, a line of credit is not guaranteed to a business. The primary purpose of a line of credit is to speed the borrowing process so that a firm does not have to go through the process of applying for a new loan every time it needs funds. The funds are generally available as long as the credit limit set by the bank is not exceeded. As businesses mature and become more financially secure, the amount of credit often is increased. Some firms will even apply for a **revolving credit agreement,** which is a line of credit that's guaranteed. However, banks usually charge a fee for guaranteeing such an agreement. Both lines of credit and revolving credit agreements are particularly good sources of funds for unexpected cash needs.

If a business is unable to secure a short-term loan from a bank, a financial manager may obtain short-term funds from **commercial finance companies.** These non-deposit-type organizations (often called nonbanks) make short-term loans to borrowers who offer tangible assets (e.g., property, plant, and equipment) as collateral. Since commercial finance companies accept higher degrees of risk than commercial banks, they usually charge higher interest rates than banks. Commercial finance companies often make loans to individuals and businesses (e.g., General Electric lent money to Air Canada as the airline restructured its business) that cannot get funds elsewhere.

Factoring

One relatively expensive source of short-term funds for a firm is **factoring,** which is the process of selling accounts receivable for cash. Here's how it works: Let's say that a firm sells many of its products on credit to consumers and other businesses, creating a number of accounts receivable. Some of the buyers may be slow in paying their bills, causing the firm to have a large amount of money due to it. A factor is a market intermediary (usually a financial institution like a commercial bank or commercial finance company) that agrees to buy the accounts receivable from the firm, at a discount, for cash. The factor then collects and keeps the money that was owed the firm when it collects the accounts receivable. How much this costs the firm depends on the discount rate the factor requires. The discount rate, in turn, depends on the age of the accounts receivable, the nature of the business, and the condition of the economy.

Even though factoring can be an expensive way of raising cash, it is popular among small businesses. It's important for you to note that factoring is not a loan; factoring is the sale of an asset (accounts receivable). And while it's true that discount rates charged by factors are usually higher than loan rates charged by banks or commercial finance companies, remember that many small businesses cannot qualify for a loan. Also, a company can reduce the cost of factoring if it agrees to reimburse the factor for slow-paying accounts, and it can reduce them even further if it assumes the risk of those people who don't pay at all.

Factoring is very common in the clothing and furniture business and is also popular in financing growing numbers of global trade ventures. Read the Reaching Beyond Our Borders box to see why firms often turn to export factoring as a means of financing global trade.

line of credit
A given amount of unsecured funds a bank will lend to a business.

revolving credit agreement
A line of credit that is guaranteed by the bank.

commercial finance companies
Organizations that make short-term loans to borrowers who offer tangible assets as collateral.

factoring
The process of selling accounts receivable for cash.

Commercial Paper

Sometimes a large corporation needs funds for just a few months and wants to get lower rates of interest than those charged by banks. One strategy is to sell commercial paper. **Commercial paper** consists of unsecured promissory notes, in amounts of $100,000 and up, that mature (come due) in 365 days (366 days in a leap year) or less. Commercial paper states a fixed amount of money the business agrees to repay to the lender (investor) on a specific date. The interest rate for commercial paper is stated in the agreement.

Because it is unsecured, only financially stable firms (mainly large corporations with excellent credit reputations) are able to sell commercial paper.[14] For these companies it's a way to get short-term funds quickly and for less than the interest charged by commercial banks. Since most commercial paper matures in 30 to 90 days, it's also an investment opportunity for buyers who can afford to put up cash for short periods to earn some interest on their money.

commercial paper
Unsecured promissory notes of $100,000 and up that mature (come due) in 365 days or less.

- What does the term *2/10, net 30* mean?
- What's the difference between trade credit and a line of credit at a bank?
- What's the difference between a secured loan and an unsecured loan?
- What is factoring? What are some of the considerations involved in establishing a discount rate in factoring?

Progress Assessment

OBTAINING LONG-TERM FINANCING

Forecasting helps the firm to develop a financial plan. This plan specifies the amount of funding the firm will need over various time periods and the most appropriate sources for obtaining those funds. In setting long-term financing objectives, financial managers generally ask three major questions:

1. What are the organization's long-term goals and objectives?
2. What are the financial requirements needed to achieve these long-term goals and objectives?
3. What sources of long-term capital are available, and which will best fit our needs?

In business, long-term capital is used to buy capital assets such as plant and equipment, to develop new products, and to finance expansion of the organization. In major corporations, decisions involving long-term financing normally involve the board of directors and top management, as well as finance and accounting managers. Take pharmaceutical producer Merck, for example. A seven-member chairperson's staff at Merck makes senior policy decisions involving factors such as long-term financing at the company. Merck spends more than $3 billion a year researching new products.[15] The actual development of a new innovative medicine can sometimes take 10 years or more and cost $800 million in company funds before the product is ever introduced in the market.

It's easy to see why long-term financing decisions involve high-level managers at Merck. In small and medium-sized businesses, it's inevitable that the owners are always actively involved in analyzing long-term financing opportunities that affect their company.

As we noted earlier in the chapter, long-term funding comes from two major types of financing, debt financing or equity financing. Let's look at these two important sources of long-term financing next.

Debt Financing

The first type of long-term funding involves borrowing money. If a company uses debt financing, it has a legal obligation to repay the amount borrowed. All businesses must keep in mind this legal requirement. Firms can borrow funds by either getting a loan from a lending institution or by issuing bonds to interested investors.

Debt Financing by Borrowing Money from Lending Institutions   Firms that establish and develop rapport with a bank, insurance company, pension fund, commercial finance company, or other financial institution often are able to secure a long-term loan. Long-term loans are usually repaid within 3 to 7 years but may extend to 15 or 20 years. For such loans, a business must sign what is called a term-loan agreement. A **term-loan agreement** is a promissory note that requires the borrower to repay the loan in specified instalments (e.g., monthly or yearly). A major advantage of a business using this type of financing is that the interest paid on the long-term debt is tax deductible.

Because they involve larger amounts of funding, long-term loans are often more expensive to the firm than short-term loans are. Also, since the repayment period could be as long as 20 years, lenders are not assured that their capital will be repaid in full. Therefore, most long-term loans require collateral, which may be in the form of real estate, machinery, equipment, stock, or other

term-loan agreement
A promissory note that requires the borrower to repay the loan in specified instalments.

items of value. Lenders will also often require certain restrictions on a firm's operations to force it to act responsibly in its business practices. The interest rate for long-term loans is based on the adequacy of collateral, the firm's credit rating, and the general level of market interest rates. The greater the risk a lender takes in making a loan, the higher the rate of interest a lender requires. This principle is known as the **risk/return trade-off.**

Debt Financing by Issuing Bonds　If an organization is unable to obtain its long-term financing needs by getting a loan from a lending institution, it may try to issue bonds. A **bond** is a corporate certificate indicating that a person has lent money to a firm. A company that issues a bond has a legal obligation to make regular interest payments to investors and to repay the entire bond principal amount at a prescribed time, called the maturity date.

Bonds can be issued by different levels of government, government agencies, corporations, and foreign governments and corporations. Maybe your community is building a new stadium or cultural centre that requires selling municipal bonds. **Institutional investors** are large organizations—such as pension funds, mutual funds, insurance companies, and banks—that invest their own funds or the funds of others. Potential investors (individuals and institutions) measure the risk involved in purchasing a bond against the return (interest) the bond promises to pay and the company's ability to repay the bond when promised.

Interest is paid to the holder of the bond until the principal amount is due. Thus, in this context, **interest** is the payment the issuer of the bond makes to the bondholders for use of the borrowed money. The interest rate paid on a bond may also be called the bond's *coupon rate*. This term dates back to when bonds were issued as bearer bonds and the holder, or bearer, was considered the owner. The company issuing the bond kept no accounts of transfers in ownership, and the interest on the bond was obtained by clipping coupons attached to the bond and sending them to the issuing company for payment. Today bonds are registered to particular owners, and changes in ownership are recorded electronically.

The interest rate paid on a bond varies according to factors such as the state of the economy, the reputation of the company issuing the bond, and the going interest rate for government bonds or bonds of similar companies. Once an interest rate is set for a corporate bond issue (except in the case of what's called a floating-rate bond), it cannot be changed.

Bonds of all types are evaluated (rated) in terms of their risk to investors by independent rating firms such as Dominion Bond Rating Service (www.dbrs.com) and Canadian Bond Rating Services (www.cbrs.com). Bond ratings can range from high-quality to bonds considered junk (which we discuss later in this chapter). Naturally, the higher the risk associated with the bond issue, the higher the interest rate the organization must offer investors. Investors should not assume high levels of risk if they don't feel the potential return is worth it.

Bonds are issued with a *denomination*, which is the amount of debt represented by one bond. (Bonds are almost always issued in multiples of $1,000.) The *principal* is the face value of a bond. The issuing company is legally bound to repay the bond principal to the bondholder in full on the **maturity date.** For example, if Fiberrific issues a $1,000 bond with an interest rate of 5 percent and a maturity date of 2025, the company is agreeing to pay a bondholder a total of $50 in interest each year until a specified date in 2025, when the full $1,000 must be repaid. Though bond interest is quoted for an entire year, it is usually paid in two instalments (semi-annually). Maturity dates for bonds can vary. For example, firms such as Disney and Coca-Cola have issued bonds with 50-year maturity dates.

risk/return trade-off
The principle that the greater the risk a lender takes in making a loan, the higher the interest rate required.

bond
A corporate certificate indicating that a person has lent money to a firm.

institutional investors
Large organizations—such as pension funds, mutual funds, insurance companies, and banks—that invest their own funds or the funds of others.

interest
The payment the issuer of the bond makes to the bondholders for use of the borrowed money.

You may own investments like Canada Savings Bonds. For more information on these bonds, visit www.csb.gc.ca.

maturity date
The exact date the issuer of a bond must pay the principal to the bondholder.

Advantages and Disadvantages of Issuing Bonds   Bonds offer several long-term financing advantages to an organization. The decision to issue bonds is often based on advantages such as the following:

- Bondholders are creditors, not owners, of the firm and seldom have a vote on corporate matters; thus, management maintains control over the firm's operations.
- Interest paid on bonds is tax deductible to the firm issuing the bond.
- Bonds are a temporary source of funding for a firm. They're eventually repaid and the debt obligation is eliminated.
- Bonds can be repaid before the maturity date if they contain a call provision. Some may also be converted to common shares.

But bonds also have their drawbacks:

- Bonds increase debt (long-term liabilities) and may adversely affect the market's perception of the firm.
- Paying interest on bonds is a legal obligation. If interest is not paid, bondholders can take legal action to force payment.
- The face value (denomination) of bonds must be repaid on the maturity date. Without careful planning, this repayment can cause cash flow problems when the bonds come due.

debenture bonds
Bonds that are unsecured (i.e., not backed by any collateral such as equipment).

Different Classes of Bonds   Corporations can issue two different classes of corporate bonds. The first class is *unsecured bonds*, which are not backed by any collateral (such as equipment). These bonds are usually referred to as **debenture bonds.** Generally, only well-respected firms with excellent credit ratings can issue debenture bonds, since the only security the bondholder has is the reputation and credit history of the company.

The second class of bonds is *secured bonds*, which are backed by some tangible asset (collateral) that is pledged to the bondholder if bond interest isn't paid or the principal isn't paid back when promised. For example, a mortgage bond is a bond secured by company assets such as land and buildings. In issuing bonds, a company can choose to include different features in the various bond issues. Let's look at some possible special bond features.

sinking fund
A reserve account in which the issuer of a bond periodically retires some part of the bond principal prior to maturity so that enough capital will be accumulated by the maturity date to pay off the bond.

Special Bond Features   By now you should understand that bonds are issued with an interest rate, are unsecured or secured by some type of collateral, and must be repaid at their maturity date. This repayment requirement often leads companies to establish a reserve account called a **sinking fund,** whose primary purpose is to ensure that enough money will be available to repay bondholders on the bond's maturity date. Firms issuing sinking-fund bonds periodically retire (set aside) some part of the bond principal prior to maturity so that enough capital will be accumulated by the maturity date to pay off the bond. Sinking funds can be attractive to issuing firms and potential investors for several reasons:

- They provide for an orderly retirement (repayment) of a bond issue.
- They reduce the risk the bond will not be repaid.
- The market price of the bond is supported because the risk of the firm's not repaying the principal on the maturity date is reduced.

Another special feature that can be included in a bond issue is a call provision. A *callable bond* permits the bond issuer to pay off the bond's principal (i.e., call the bond) prior to its maturity date. Call provisions must be included when a bond is issued, and bondholders should be aware of whether a bond is callable. Callable bonds give companies some discretion in their long-term forecasting. For example, suppose Fiberrific issued $50 million in 20-year bonds in 2005 with an interest rate of 10 percent. The yearly interest expense would be $5 million ($50 million times 10 percent). If market conditions change in 2010, and bonds issued of the same quality are only paying 7 percent, Fiberrific would be paying 3 percent, or $1.5 million ($50 million times 3 percent), in excess interest yearly. Obviously, Fiberrific could benefit if it could call in (pay off) the old bonds and issue new bonds at the lower interest rate. If a company calls a bond before maturity, investors in the bond are often paid a price above the bond's face value.

Another feature sometimes included in bonds is convertibility. A *convertible bond* is a bond that can be converted into common shares in the issuing company.[16] This feature is often an incentive for an investor to buy a bond. Why, you may ask, would bond investors want to convert their investment to shares? That's easy. If the value of the firm's common shares grows sizably over time, bondholders can compare the value of continued bond interest with the possible sizable profit they could gain by converting to a specified number of common shares. When we discuss common shares in the next section, this advantage will become more evident to you.

Progress Assessment

- What are the major forms of debt financing available to a firm?
- What role do bond rating services play in the bond market?
- What does it mean when a firm states that it is issuing a 9-percent debenture bond due in 2025?
- What are advantages and disadvantages of bonds?
- Why do companies like callable bonds? Why might investors dislike them?
- Why are convertible bonds attractive to investors?

Equity Financing

If a firm cannot obtain a long-term loan from a lending institution, or if it is unable to sell bonds to investors, it may look for long-term funding from equity financing. Equity financing comes from the owners of the firm. Therefore, equity financing involves using earnings that have been retained by the company to reinvest in the business (retained earnings). A business can also seek equity financing by selling ownership in the firm to venture capitalists. Or, it involves selling ownership in the firm in the form of shares. Figure 17.5 compares debt and equity financing options.

Equity Financing by Selling Stock   Regardless of whether a firm can obtain debt financing, there usually comes a time when it needs additional funds. One way to obtain such funds is to sell stock to private investors. **Stocks** represent ownership in a company. Both common and preferred shares (to be discussed soon) form the company's *capital stock*, also known as *equity* capital.[17]

The purchasers of stock become owners in the organization. The number of shares of stock that will be available for purchase is generally decided by the organization's board of directors. The first time a corporation offers to sell new stock to the general public is called an **initial public offering (IPO).**

stocks
Shares of ownership in a company.

initial public offering (IPO)
The first public offering of a corporation's stock.

FIGURE 17.5

DIFFERENCES BETWEEN DEBT
AND EQUITY FINANCING

| CONDITIONS | TYPE OF FINANCING | |
	DEBT	EQUITY
Management influence	There's usually none unless special conditions have been agreed on.	Common shareholders have voting rights.
Repayment	Debt has a maturity date. Principal must be repaid.	Stock has no maturity date. The company is never required to repay equity.
Yearly obligations	Payment of interest is a contractual obligation.	The firm isn't legally liable to pay dividends.
Tax benefits	Interest is tax deductible.	Dividends are paid from after-tax income and aren't deductible.

Equity Financing from Retained Earnings   Have you ever heard a business-person say that he or she reinvests the firm's profits right back into the business? You probably remember from Chapter 16 that the profits the company keeps and reinvests in the firm are called retained earnings. Retained earnings often are a major source of long-term funds. This is especially true for small businesses, which have fewer financing alternatives, such as selling bonds or stock, than large businesses do. However, large corporations also depend on retained earnings for needed long-term funding. In fact, retained earnings are usually the most favoured source of meeting long-term capital needs since a company that uses them saves interest payments, dividends (payments for investing in stock), and any possible underwriting fees for issuing bonds or stock. Also, if a firm uses retained earnings, there is no new ownership created in the firm, as occurs with selling stock.

The major problem with relying on retained earnings as a source of funding is that many organizations do not have sufficient retained earnings on hand to finance extensive capital improvements or business expansion. If you think about it for a moment, it makes sense. What if you wanted to buy an expensive personal asset such as a new car? The ideal way to purchase the car would be to go to your personal savings account and take out the necessary cash. No hassle! No interest! Unfortunately, few people have such large amounts of cash available. Most businesses are no different. Even though they would like to finance long-term needs from operations, few have the resources on hand to accomplish this.

Equity Financing from Venture Capital   The hardest time for a business to raise money is when it is just starting or moving into early stages of expansion. A start-up business typically has few assets and no market track record, so the chances of borrowing significant amounts of money from a bank are slim. Recall from Chapter 7 that venture capitalists are a potential source of funds. **Venture capital** is money that is invested in new or emerging companies that are perceived as having great profit potential. Venture capital firms are a possible source of start-up capital for new companies or companies moving into expanding stages of business.

An entrepreneur or finance manager must remember that venture capitalists invest in a company in return for part ownership of the business. Venture capitalists concede that they expect higher-than-average returns and competent management performance for their investment. Therefore, a start-up company has to be careful when choosing a venture capital firm.

venture capital
Money that is invested in new or emerging companies that are perceived as having great profit potential.

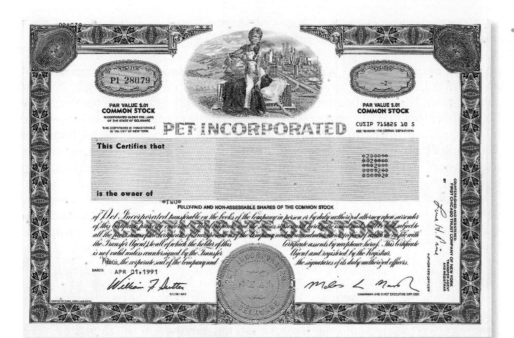

A **stock certificate** is evidence of stock ownership that specifies the name of the company, the number of shares it represents, and the type of stock being issued (see Figure 17.6). Today stock certificates are generally held electronically for the owners of the stock. Certificates sometimes indicate a stock's *par value*, which is a dollar amount assigned to each share of stock by the corporation's charter. Since par values do not reflect the market value of the stock, most companies issue "no-par" stock. **Dividends** are part of a firm's profits that may be distributed to shareholders as either cash payments or additional shares of stock. Dividends are declared by a corporation's board of directors and are generally paid quarterly. Although it's a legal obligation for companies that issue bonds to pay interest, companies that issue stock are not required to pay dividends.[18]

stock certificate
Evidence of stock ownership that specifies the name of the company, the number of shares it represents, and the type of stock being issued.

dividends
Part of a firm's profits that may be distributed to shareholders as either cash payments or additional shares of stock.

Advantages and Disadvantages of Issuing Stock   The following are some advantages to the firm of issuing stock:

- As owners of the business, shareholders never have to be repaid.
- There's no legal obligation to pay dividends to shareholders; therefore, income (retained earnings) can be reinvested in the firm for future financing needs.
- Selling stock can improve the condition of a firm's balance sheet since issuing stock creates no debt. (A corporation may also buy back its stock to improve its balance sheet and make the company appear stronger financially.)

Disadvantages of issuing stock include the following:

- As owners, shareholders (usually only common shareholders) have the right to vote for the company's board of directors. Typically one vote is granted for each share of stock. Hence, the direction and control of the firm can be altered by the sale of additional shares of stock.
- Dividends are paid out of profit after taxes and thus are not tax deductible.[19]
- Management's decisions can be affected by the need to keep stockholders happy.

Companies can issue two classes of shares: common and preferred. Let's see how these two forms of equity financing differ.

common shares
The most basic form of ownership in a firm; it confers voting rights and the right to share in the firm's profits through dividends, if offered by the firm's board of directors.

Issuing Common Shares   **Common shares** are the most basic form of ownership in a firm. In fact, if a company issues only one type of stock, it must be common. Holders of common stock have the right (1) to vote for company board directors and important issues affecting the company, and (2) to share in the firm's profits through dividends, if approved by the firm's board of directors. Having voting rights in a corporation allows common shareholders to influence corporate policy since the elected board chooses the firm's top management and makes major policy decisions. Common shareholders also have what is called a *preemptive right*, which is the first right to purchase any new common shares the firm decides to issue. This right allows common shareholders to maintain a proportional share of ownership in the company.

Critical Thinking

Considering the disadvantages and advantages of different forms of raising funds, which method would you adopt if you had to make that decision in your company? How would your decision be affected in a high-interest year? If your company was doing well, what would you do for short-term financing? For long-term financing? How would you justify your choices?

preferred shares
Stock that gives its owners preference in the payment of dividends and an earlier claim on assets than common shareholders if the company is forced out of business and its assets sold.

Issuing Preferred Shares   Owners of **preferred shares** enjoy a preference (hence the term *preferred*) in the payment of dividends; they also have a prior claim on company assets if the firm is forced out of business and its assets sold. Normally, however, preferred shares do not include voting rights in the firm. Preferred shares are frequently referred to as a hybrid investment because they have characteristics of both bonds and stocks. To illustrate this, consider the treatment of preferred share dividends.

Preferred share dividends differ from common share dividends in several ways. Preferred shares are generally issued with a par value that becomes the base for the dividend the firm is willing to pay. For example, if a preferred share's par value is $100 a share and its dividend rate is 4 percent, the firm is committing to a $4 dividend for each share of preferred stock the investor owns (4 percent of $100 = $4). An owner of 100 shares of this preferred stock is promised a fixed yearly dividend of $400. In addition, the preferred shareholder is also assured that this dividend must be paid in full before any common share dividends can be distributed.[20]

Preferred shares are therefore quite similar to bonds; both have a face (or par) value and both have a fixed rate of return. Also, like bonds, rating services rate preferred shares according to risk. So how do bonds and preferred shares differ? Remember that companies are legally bound to pay bond interest and to repay the face value (denomination) of the bond on its maturity date. In contrast, even though preferred share dividends are generally fixed, they do not legally have to be paid; also shares (preferred or common) never have to be repurchased. Though both bonds and stock can increase in market value, the price of stock generally increases at a higher percentage than bonds. Of course, the market value of both could also go down. Figure 17.7 compares features of bonds and stock.

Special Features of Preferred Shares   Preferred shares can have special features that do not apply to common shares. For example, like bonds, preferred shares can be callable. This means that preferred shareholders could be required to sell back their shares to the corporation. Preferred shares can also be convertible to common shares.[21] Another important feature of preferred

	BONDS	COMMON SHARE	PREFERRED SHARE
Interest or Dividends			
Must be paid	Yes	No	No
Pays a fixed rate	Yes	Yes	No
Deductible from payor's income tax	Yes	No	No
Canadian payee is taxed		(if payor company is Canadian)	
at reduced rate	No	Yes	Yes
Stock or bond			
Has voting rights	No	Not normally	Yes
May be traded on the stock exchange	Yes	Yes	Yes
Can be held indefinitely	No	Usually	Yes
Is convertible to common shares	Maybe	Maybe	Not applicable

FIGURE 17.7

COMPARISON OF BONDS AND STOCK OF PUBLIC COMPANIES

The different features help both the issuer and the investor decide which vehicle is right for each of them at a particular time.

PREFERRED SHARE FEATURE	DESCRIPTION
Convertible	The shares may be exchanged after a stated number of years for common shares at a preset rate, at the option of the shareholder.
Cumulative	If the dividend is not paid in full in any year, the balance is carried forward (accumulates). The cumulative unpaid balance must be paid before any dividends are paid to common shareholders.
Callable	The company that issued the shares has the right after a stated number of years to call them back by repaying the shareholders their original investment.*
Redeemable	After a stated number of years, the investor may return the stock and ask for repayment of his or her investment.*

*If the shares are also cumulative, all dividend arrears must be paid as well.

FIGURE 17.8

OPTIONAL FEATURES AVAILABLE WITH PREFERRED SHARES

Each feature holds some attraction for the potential investor.

shares is that they can often be cumulative. That is, if one or more dividends are not paid when promised, the missed dividends will be accumulated and paid later to a cumulative preferred shareholder. This means that all dividends, including any back dividends, must be paid in full before any common share dividends can be distributed. Figure 17.8 lists some optional features of preferred shares.

- What are the major forms of equity financing available to a firm?
- Name at least two advantages and two disadvantages of issuing stock as a form of equity financing.
- What are the major differences between common shares and preferred shares?
- In what ways are preferred shares similar to bonds? How are they different?

Progress Assessment

Summary

1. Describe the importance of finance and financial management to an organization, and explain the responsibilities of financial managers.

1. Finance comprises those functions in a business responsible for acquiring funds for the firm, managing funds within the firm (e.g., preparing budgets and doing cash flow analysis), and planning for the expenditure of funds on various assets.

   - *What are the most common ways firms fail financially?*
   The most common financial problems are (1) undercapitalization, (2) poor control over cash flow, and (3) inadequate expense control.

   - *What do financial managers do?*
   Financial managers plan, budget, control funds, obtain funds, collect funds, audit, manage taxes, and advise top management on financial matters.

2. Outline the financial planning process, and explain the three key budgets in the financial plan.

2. Financial planning involves forecasting short- and long-term needs, budgeting, and establishing financial controls.

   - *What are the three budgets of finance?*
   The capital budget is the spending plan for expensive assets, such as property, plant, and equipment. The cash budget is the projected cash balance at the end of a given period. The operating (master) budget summarizes the information in the other two budgets; it projects dollar allocations to various costs and expenses given various revenues.

3. Explain the major reasons why firms need operating funds, and identify various types of financing that can be used to obtain these funds.

3. During the course of a business' life, its financial needs shift considerably.

   - *What are the major financial needs for firms?*
   Businesses have financial needs in four major areas: (1) managing day-by-day needs of the business, (2) controlling credit operations, (3) acquiring needed inventory, and (4) making capital expenditures.

   - *What's the difference between short-term and long-term financing?*
   Short-term financing refers to funds that will be repaid in less than one year, whereas long-term financing refers to funds that will be repaid over a specific time period of more than one year.

   - *What's the difference between debt financing and equity financing?*
   Debt financing refers to funds raised by borrowing (going into debt), whereas equity financing is raised from within the firm (through retained earnings) or by selling ownership in the company to venture capitalists or by issuing shares to other investors.

4. Identify and describe different sources of short-term financing.

4. Sources of short-term financing include trade credit, promissory notes, family and friends, commercial banks and other financial institutions, factoring, and commercial paper.

   - *Why should businesses use trade credit?*
   Trade credit is the least expensive and most convenient form of short-term financing. Businesses can buy goods today and pay for them sometime in the future.

   - *What's a line of credit?*
   It is an agreement by a bank to lend a specified amount of money to the business at any time. A revolving credit agreement is a line of credit that guarantees a loan will be available—for a fee.

   - *What's the difference between a secured loan and an unsecured loan?*
   An unsecured loan has no collateral backing it. Secured loans have collateral backed by assets such as accounts receivable, inventory, or other property of value.

- *Is factoring a form of secured loan?*

No, factoring means selling accounts receivable at a discounted rate to a factor (an intermediary that pays cash for those accounts).

- *What's commercial paper?*

Commercial paper is a corporation's unsecured promissory note maturing in 365 days or less.

5. One of the important functions of a finance manager is to obtain long-term financing.

5. Identify and describe different sources of long-term financing.

- *What are the major sources of long-term financing?*

Debt financing involves the sale of bonds and long-term loans from banks and other financial institutions. Equity financing is obtained through the sale of company stock, from the firm's retained earnings, or from venture capital firms.

- *What are the two major forms of long-term financing?*

Debt financing comes from two sources: selling bonds and borrowing from individuals, banks, and other financial institutions. Bonds can be secured by some form of collateral or can be unsecured. The same is true of loans.

Key Terms

bond 537
budget 525
capital budget 525
capital expenditures 530
cash budget 525
cash flow forecast 524
commercial finance companies 534
commercial paper 535
common shares 542
debenture bonds 538
debt financing 531
dividends 541
equity financing 531
factoring 534
finance 522

financial control 527
financial management 522
financial managers 522
initial public offering (IPO) 539
institutional investors 537
interest 537
line of credit 534
long-term financing 531
long-term forecast 525
maturity date 537
operating (master) budget 526
preferred shares 542
promissory note 532

revolving credit agreement 534
risk/return trade-off 537
secured loan 533
short-term financing 531
short-term forecast 524
sinking fund 538
stock certificate 541
stocks 539
term-loan agreement 536
trade credit 532
unsecured loan 533
venture capital 540

Developing Workplace Skills

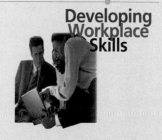

1. Obtain annual reports from three major corporations. Read the information provided by each company and review each balance sheet. How much have the companies borrowed? (Look under liabilities.) Which one is in the best financial condition? Why?

2. Visit a local bank lending officer. Ask what the current interest rate is and what rate small businesses pay for short- and long-term loans. Ask for blank forms that borrowers use to apply for loans. Share these forms with your class, and explain the types of information they ask for.

3. Use information from the Canadian and Dominion Bond Rating Services to find their evaluation of the bonds of three large Canadian companies. Ask the librarian what similar references are available. Report what you find to the class.

4. Many businesses try to raise funds through initial public offerings (IPOs). Go to the library and obtain recent financial publications like *The Globe and Mail* or the *National Post,* or visit securities dealers' Websites such as bmonesbittburns.com and tdwaterhouse.ca. Find two IPOs that have been offered during the past six months. Track the performance of each IPO from its introduction to its present price.

5. Analyze the risks and opportunities of investing today in bonds and stock. Assume your great-aunt Hildi just left you $10,000. Since you and your parents have already saved enough money to cover your education bills, you decide to invest the money so that you can start your own business after you graduate. How will you invest your money? Why? Name specific investments.

Taking It To The Net

1

Purpose

To research the current lending practices between banks and small businesses.

Exercises

1. Check out the Website of the Canadian Bankers Association at www.cba.ca to see if you can find information on the trend of lending to small businesses. What was the rate of refusal of loans to small businesses during the last few years? Is the refusal rate rising, declining, or unchanged?

2. Look through the Website of the Business Development Bank of Canada (BDC) at www.bdc.ca to see how helpful it is. If you were starting a small business, would the information lead you to apply for a loan with the BDC? Is there anything you were looking for that you could not find? Is there much information for those wanting to start an Internet-based company?

Practising Management Decisions

Case

Making Dreams Come True

Carlos Galendez had big dreams but very little money. He had worked more than 10 years washing dishes and then as a cook for two major restaurants. Finally, his dream to save enough money to start his own Mexican restaurant came true. Galendez opened his restaurant, Casa de Carlos, with a guaranteed loan. His old family recipes and appealing Hispanic decor helped the business gain immediate success. He repaid his small-business loan within 14 months and immediately opened a second location and then a third. Casa de Carlos became one of the largest Mexican restaurant chains in the area.

Galendez decided the company needed to go public to help finance expansion. He believed that continued growth was beneficial to the company, and that offering ownership was the way to bring in loyal investors. Nevertheless, he wanted to make certain his family maintained a controlling interest in the firm's stock. Therefore, in its initial public offering (IPO), Casa de Carlos offered to sell only 40 percent of the company's available shares to investors. The Galendez family kept control of the remaining 60 percent.

As the public's craving for Mexican food grew, so did the fortunes of Casa de Carlos, Inc.

By early 2001, the company enjoyed the enviable position of being light on debt and heavy on cash. But the firm's debt position changed dramatically when it bought out Captain Ahab's Seafood Restaurants and, two years later, expanded into full-service wholesale distribution of seafood products with the purchase of Ancient Mariner Wholesalers.

The firm's debt increased, but the price of its stock was up and all its business operations were booming.

Then tragedy struck the firm when Carlos Galendez died suddenly from a heart attack. His oldest child, Maria, was selected to take control as chief executive officer. Maria Galendez had learned the business from her father, who had taught her to keep an eye out for opportunities that seemed fiscally responsible. Even so, the fortunes of the firm began to shift. Two major competitors were taking market share from Casa de Carlos, and the seafood venture began to flounder (pun intended). Also, consumer shifts

in eating habits and the slight recession in 2002 encouraged consumers to spend less, causing the company some severe cash flow problems. It was up to Maria Galendez as CEO to decide how to get the funds the firm needed for improvements and other expenses. Unfortunately, several local banks wouldn't expand the firm's credit line, so she considered the possibility of a bond or stock offering to raise capital for the business. Her decision could be crucial to the future of the firm.

Decision Questions

1. What advantages do bonds offer a company such as Casa de Carlos? What disadvantages do bonds impose?
2. What would be the advantages and disadvantages of the company's offering new stock to investors?
3. Are any other options available to Maria Galendez?
4. What choice would you make and why?

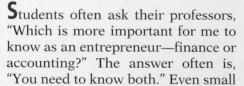
Video Case

Financial Management

Students often ask their professors, "Which is more important for me to know as an entrepreneur—finance or accounting?" The answer often is, "You need to know both." Even small businesses need careful financial planning, but there is a difference between small and large businesses when it comes to major financial decisions. For example, a small business doesn't get involved in commercial paper. It is issued when a big company has millions of dollars it wants to invest immediately.

It helps when the financial manager understands fully what information is needed by top management. Naturally, the most important goal is to stay in business. The most common reasons why businesses fail are undercapitalization (not starting with enough money to carry the business through its growth period), poor cash flow (not having enough cash on hand to pay bills), and inadequate expense control (spending more than the company makes). We learned in Chapter 16 about cash flow. Chapter 17 looks at money management (like budgeting), which will help prevent cash flow problems.

Big business and small business have many financial similarities. They both budget, they both pay taxes, and they both audit their books. The major difference is scale. A small business is not going to lose $5 billion, as a large business might do. Regardless of size, a business should ask for a budget request from all departments. The capital budget is used for major purchases, like buying a building or truck. The cash budget controls cash flow. The operating budget provides the "big picture"—how much profit a business can expect to make and what to do with the money.

Both small and large businesses sometimes need short-term financing. Sources include trade credit, promissory notes, family and friends, commercial bank loans, factoring, and commercial paper. Trade credit is the most commonly used short-term financing. When a business gets a bill, it will usually have terms such as 2/10, net 30, which means that the bill must be paid within 30 days, but a 2-percent discount can be earned by paying within 10 days. Since the difference is 20 days and there are 18 20-day periods in a year, a business may save about 36 percent by paying within 10 days—a sizable discount. On the other hand, customers don't always pay on time. If a business pays its bills early but its customers pay late, it may run into cash flow problems.

Friends and family are often sources of emergency funds, but businesses must pay them back like any other creditor. Similarly, business owners can borrow from their own savings, but that is dangerous and may ruin their credit rating if they are late or default on payments, which is hard to rebuild. Businesses would like to fund most projects out of retained earnings, but there often isn't enough money there to fund larger projects.

When it comes to longer-term financing, companies may issue stock or bonds, but that is more likely to take place in larger firms. Smaller firms often have to turn to commercial banks or other sources for funds. Because the risk is so high, even commercial banks may turn a small business down. You have to have a good credit rating to get a loan. But if you had a good credit rating, you probably would not need a loan. As the video says, "It's a Catch 22 situation." Those who need funds have trouble getting them and those who don't need funds can get them more easily.

The moral of the story is this: All businesspeople need to understand accounting and finance. It is not enough to have a good idea and run out and start making and marketing a product. You need money to make things and to market things. Where do you get that money? How do you budget it? Where should you invest funds? Where should you turn for emergency funds? These are the kinds of questions any businessperson needs to ask, and those schooled in finance can readily answer them.

Discussion Questions

1. What insights did you get from this video about the importance of finance to both small and large firms?
2. Which sources of funds are most available to a small business? What additional sources may large businesses tap? Why?
3. Does the management of money look more or less complicated now that you have seen the video? What are some of the trickier concepts?

www.mcgrawhill.ca/college/nickels

Chapter 18

The Financial Services Industry in Canada

Learning Goals

After you have read and studied this chapter, you should be able to

1 Describe the importance of the financial services industry in Canada.

2 Explain what money is and how its value is determined.

3 Discuss the role that banks play in providing services.

4 List the five key criteria when selecting investment options.

5 Explain the opportunities in mutual funds as investments and the benefits of diversifying investments.

Profile

Getting to Know Thomas Gauld of Canadian Tire Financial Services

Though he spent much of his career in consumer and sporting goods, Thomas Gauld is now president of one of Canada's most progressive financial institutions—Canadian Tire Financial Services (CTFS) Limited. CTFS originated in 1961 as Midland Shoppers Credit Limited, a small financial services company offering third-party credit processing for local retailers. During the 1960s, the Canadian Tire Associate Stores became clients. In 1968, Midland became a subsidiary of Canadian Tire Corporation and was renamed Canadian Tire Acceptance Limited (CTAL).

In the decades that followed, CTAL continued to provide credit processing. In 1995, it became the first non–deposit taking financial institution worldwide to launch a MasterCard. In 2000, it expanded the Canadian Tire "Money" loyalty program by launching Canadian Tire "Money" on the card. Now, people could accumulate points by using their MasterCard anywhere in the world and redeem their points in any Canadian Tire store on merchandise, auto parts, or auto labour. In 2002, CTAL's name was changed to Canadian Tire Financial Services Limited to better reflect the company's stronger and broader position within the financial services industry. In July 2003, Canadian Tire Bank, a wholly owned subsidiary of CTFS, began operations.

As the financial services arm of Canadian Tire Corporation, Ltd., CTFS is primarily engaged in financing and managing the Options MasterCard. CTFS also markets a variety of insurance and warranty products to more than four million of Canadian Tire's customers. In addition, it operates Canadian Tire Auto Club, Canadian Tire's emergency roadside service.

So how did Gauld end up at the helm of CTFS? When he graduated from the University of Windsor with a bachelor of arts in geography, he combined his love of travel with a business career by assuming a role with Unilever in South Africa. In the years that followed, he held general management positions with General Foods, Bristol Myers in Canada and in the U.S.A., and SmithKline

Beecham in Canada and South America. After serving as vice-president of marketing at SmithKline Beecham, he made the transition to the sporting goods industry: he became the president of Spalding Sports Canada Ltd. for three years, and later assumed the role of managing director of Spalding Sports in Europe. In 1993, he joined CTFS as vice-president of marketing. Three years later, he became the president of CTFS.

Gauld serves on the board of directors for Canadian Tire Bank and MasterCard Canada. He believes strongly in CTFS's mission statement (noted in Figure 8.2) that supports community involvement. As a result, he serves on the board of trustees of Brock University and on the Board of Governors at Niagara College. In the past, he has served on the board of the Shaw Festival Theatre.

Since becoming president Gauld has led a major restructuring of the business—today, 99 percent of the business is focused on marketing to Canadian Tire customers, with a strategy of adding value through its products. Under his leadership, CTFS generated $116.2 million in earnings in fiscal year 2003. Over the past three years, the company has doubled its size and earnings, with fewer employees—now approximately 1,500—than it had three years ago and 9 percent more customers.

Gauld believes that it is his responsibility to create an environment where regular people do extraordinary things. The employees are motivated to do well as they clearly understand the company's mission statement and their role in making it happen. In the future, Gauld sees CTFS continuing to grow its business through providing world-class customer service to Canadian Tire customers. Since one out of four Canadian households already has a relationship with CTFS, Gauld believes that there are many opportunities to offer new services to loyal customers. A line of credit and term loans are currently being tested as the company considers other financial services products.

Sources: "Canadian Tire Bank Receives Approval to Commence Operations," Decision-Plus M.C. Inc. June 27, 2003. Retrieved from www.decisionplus.com/fr/fintools/stock_news.asp?Market=TSE&Symbol=CTR&NewsID=20030627/142500; www.ctsf.com, June 8, 2004; and interview with Thomas Gauld, June 10, 2004.

The Financial Services Industry in Canada

Money, banking, investing, insurance, financing, financial planning—every day across the country, consumers, businesses, and governments depend on the products provided by financial institutions.[1] According to the Financial Consumer Agency of Canada, the financial services sector plays an important role in the Canadian economy as it:[2]

- employs more than half a million Canadians;
- supports approximately half a million other jobs indirectly through purchases of supplies, equipment, and services;
- provides a yearly payroll of more than $22 billion;
- exports nearly $50 billion worth of services annually;
- represents 5 percent of Canada's GDP, exceeded only by the manufacturing sector;
- yields more than $9 billion in tax revenue to all levels of government;
- ranks 5th worldwide in terms of international competitiveness; and
- is widely recognized as one of the safest and healthiest in the world.

Until the middle of the 1980s, the financial services industry in Canada was termed a "four-pillar system." These four pillars were banks, trust companies, insurance companies, and securities dealers. Regulation ➤P. 13◀ was designed to foster competition within each pillar, but not among them. When the government permitted commercial banks to acquire securities firms in 1987, this segregation of functions began to erode.

Since that time, changes in regulations have eliminated many of the old barriers that prohibited financial institutions from competing in each other's business. Today, it is increasingly difficult to distinguish firms by type of function as this industry has become highly competitive. For example, a life insurance company can now own a bank, and vice versa. As a result of Bill C-8 (in force since October 2001), important changes were made to federal financial institutions legislation and how the financial services industry is regulated. Among other changes, ownership and organization rules for banks were loosened. Consequently, we see nontraditional financial services providers—such as Canadian Tire Financial Services (mentioned in the chapter-opening profile)—taking advantage of changes in the regulatory environment to offer new products and build on their customer base.

Participants in the Financial Services Industry

credit unions
Non-profit, member-owned financial cooperatives that offer a full variety of banking services to their members.

trust company
A financial institution that can administer estates, pension plans, and agency contracts, in addition to other activities conducted by banks.

nonbanks
Financial organizations that accept no deposits but offer many services provided by regular banks.

Canada's financial services industry consists of traditional banks (also called commercial banks), credit unions, caisses populaires, and trust companies. **Credit unions** are non-profit, member-owned financial cooperatives that offer a full variety of banking services to their members. Caisses populaires, a form of credit unions, are located predominantly in Quebec. You will learn more about credit unions and caisses populaires near the end of this chapter when you complete the Taking It to the Net exercise. A **trust company** is a financial institution that conducts activities like a bank. However, because of its fiduciary role, a trust company can administer estates, pension plans, and agency contracts, which banks cannot do. As a result of changes in legislation, we have seen instances of banks acquiring trust companies, such as Scotiabank's acquisition of Montreal Trust and National Trust.

There are also a variety of other institutions that traditionally have been called nonbanks. **Nonbanks** are financial organizations that accept no deposits but offer many services provided by regular banks. Examples include pension funds, insurance companies, commercial finance companies, consumer finance companies, and brokerage houses. We will discuss brokerage houses below.

Pension funds are amounts of money put aside by corporations, nonprofit organizations, or unions to cover part of the financial needs of their members when they retire. Contributions to pension funds are made either by employees, by employers, or by both employees and employers.

Life insurance companies provide financial protection for policyholders, who periodically pay premiums. In addition, insurers invest the funds they receive from policyholders in a variety of vehicles, including corporate and government bonds. In recent years, more insurance companies have begun to provide long-term financing for real estate development projects.

Commercial and consumer finance companies offer short-term loans to businesses or individuals who either cannot meet the credit requirements of regular banks or have exceeded their credit limit and need more funds. Typically, these finance companies' interest rates are higher than those of regular banks. The primary customers of these companies are new businesses and individuals with no credit history. One should be careful when borrowing from such institutions, because the interest rates can be quite high. Corporate financial systems established at major corporations such as General Electric, Sears, General Motors, and American Express offer considerable financial services to customers.

In the past, they were often called nonbanks because they did not accept deposits but offered many of the services provided by regular banks. As competition among these organizations and banks has increased, the dividing line between banks and nonbanks has become less and less apparent. Today, many of these nonbanks offer select banking products, including taking deposits, making loans, and issuing credit cards.[3] Review Figure 18.1 to get an idea of the range of suppliers of financial services in Canada.

Since all of these financial institutions have one thing in common—money—we will discuss the importance of money to the economy. This will be followed by an introduction to three main players in the overall financial services industry: the banking industry, the securities industry, and the mutual fund industry. But first, let us briefly review how this industry is regulated.

pension funds
Amounts of money put aside by corporations, nonprofit organizations, or unions to cover part of the financial needs of their members when they retire.

How the Financial Services Industry Is Regulated[4]

Because of its important role in the economy, the financial industry is one of the most regulated sectors in the country. Regulation is designed to ensure the integrity, safety, and soundness of financial institutions and markets. Legislative, self-regulatory, and other initiatives help minimize crises and company failures. In addition, they protect investors, depositors, and policyholders.

In Canada, there is no single body that regulates the entire industry. It's a responsibility shared among different organizations and levels of government. To start with, financial institutions may be regulated at either the federal or the provincial level, or jointly. For example, banks are federally regulated. Securities dealers, credit unions, and caisses populaires are provincially regulated. Insurance, trust and loan companies, and cooperative credit associations may be federally and/or provincially regulated, depending on the jurisdiction under which the company is incorporated or registered.

FIGURE 18.1

THE CANADIAN FINANCIAL SERVICES INDUSTRY

- Canada's six largest domestic banks
- 13 smaller domestic banks
- 30 foreign bank subsidiaries
- 23 branches of foreign banks (19 full-service branches and four lending branches)
- 25 trust companies
- Over 100 life insurance companies
- Over 1,300 credit unions and caisses populaires
- Over 150 investment dealers
- 55 mutual fund companies
- 69 pension fund managers
- Over 4,000 independent financial, deposit, and mortgage brokers
- 6,550 financing firms with assets of at least $5 million

Source: "Competition in the Canadian Financial Sector," Canadian Bankers Association, July 2004.

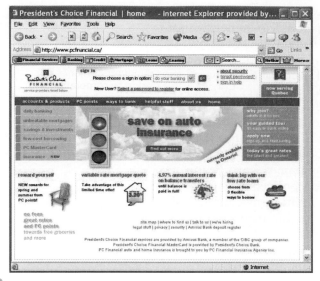

Who would have thought 10 years ago that a grocer would own a bank? President's Choice Financial services, complete with the President's Choice Financial MasterCard and the PC Points rewards program, offers unique financial services designed by Loblaw Companies Limited. The President's Choice Financial MasterCard is provided by President's Choice Bank, while banking services are provided by Amicus Bank, a member of the CIBC group of companies. Do you prefer to bank with a traditional full-service bank such as TD Canada Trust or Scotiabank? Are programs such as no-fee banking and points reward programs incentives to switch your banking?

For institutions under federal responsibility, the Department of Finance is charged with overseeing their overall powers—in other words, what they can and cannot do. The Department of Finance relies on three federal agencies to supervise the ongoing operations of these institutions and their compliance with legislation:

- The **Office of the Superintendent of Financial Institutions** (www.osfi-bsif.gc.ca) monitors the day-to-day operations of institutions with respect to their financial soundness.
- Overseeing the deposit insurance system is the **Canada Deposit Insurance Corporation** (www.cdic.ca), protecting deposits that Canadians have in their federal financial institutions. CDIC will be discussed below.
- The **Financial Consumer Agency of Canada** (www.fcac-acfc.gc.ca) monitors financial institutions to ensure they comply with federal consumer protection measures, which range from disclosure requirements to complaint-handling procedures.

For institutions under provincial jurisdiction, the province(s) in which a company is incorporated or registered is (are) responsible for regulating the company's overall powers. As at the federal level, provinces are supported by agencies and organizations that supervise the ongoing operations of these institutions.

The Canada Deposit Insurance Corporation[5]   The Canada Deposit Insurance Corporation (CDIC) is a federal Crown corporation that was created in 1967 to provide deposit insurance and contribute to the stability of Canada's financial system. CDIC insures eligible deposits at member institutions (e.g., banks and trust companies) against these institutions' failure or collapse. CDIC guarantees deposits up to $60,000 (principal and interest) in each member institution. It is funded primarily by premiums paid by banks and trust companies that belong to this program.

Keep in mind that CDIC does not cover all types of deposits. For example, foreign currency accounts, term deposits with a maturity of greater than five years, and investments in mortgages, stocks, and mutual funds are not covered.

To date, CDIC has provided protection to depositors in 43 member institution failures. As of April 2003, CDIC had insured some $363 billion in deposits.

Progress Assessment

- What components of the financial services industry were known as the four pillars?
- Describe some changes to the industry as a result of Bill C-8.
- Contrast credit unions and caisses populaires.
- List some nonbank competitors.
- Describe the responsibilities of three federal agencies that oversee financial institutions.
- What deposits are not secured by CDIC?

WHY MONEY IS IMPORTANT

The Canadian economy depends heavily on money: its availability and its value relative to other currencies. Economic growth and the creation of jobs depend on money. Money is so important to the economy that many institutions have evolved to manage money and to make it available to you when you need it. Today you can easily get cash from an automated teller machine (ATM) almost anywhere in the world, but in many places cash isn't the only means of payment you can use. Most organizations will accept a cheque, credit card, and debit card for purchases.[6] Behind the scenes of this free flow of money is a complex system of banking that makes it possible for you to do all these things.

The complexity of the banking system has increased as the electronic flow of money from country to country has become as free as that from province to territory. Each day, more than $1.5 trillion is exchanged in the world's currency markets. Therefore, what happens to any major country's economy has an effect on the Canadian economy and vice versa. Clearly, there's more to money and its role in the economies of the world than meets the eye. There's no way to understand the economy without understanding global money exchanges and the various institutions involved in the creation and management of money.

What Is Money?

Money is anything that people generally accept as payment for goods and services. In the past, objects as diverse as salt, feathers, stones, rare shells, tea, and horses have been used as money. In fact, until the 1880s, cowrie shells were one of the world's most abundant currencies. **Barter** is the trading of goods and services for other goods and services directly; though barter may sound like something from the past, many people have discovered the benefits of bartering online. Others still barter goods and services the old-fashioned way—face-to-face. For example, in Siberia two eggs have been used to buy one admission to a movie, and customers of Ukraine's Chernobyl nuclear plant have paid in sausages and milk. Some of the trade in Russia over recent years has been done in barter.

The problem is that eggs and milk are difficult to carry around. People need some object that's portable, divisible, durable, and stable so that they can trade goods and services without carrying the actual goods around with them. One answer to that problem over the years was to create coins made of silver or gold. Coins met all the standards of a useful form of money:

- **Portability.** Coins are a lot easier to take to market than are pigs or other heavy products.

- **Divisibility.** Different-sized coins could be made to represent different values. Because silver is now too expensive, today's coins are made of other metals, but the accepted values remain.

- **Stability.** When everybody agrees on the value of coins, the value of money is relatively stable.

money
Anything that people generally accept as payment for goods and services.

barter
The trading of goods and services for other goods and services directly.

Some of the security features on the $100 note include a holographic stripe, watermark, see-through number, and windowed thread. In addition, there is raised print, fine-line printing, fluorescence, and a tactile feature. Do you check your notes for security features?

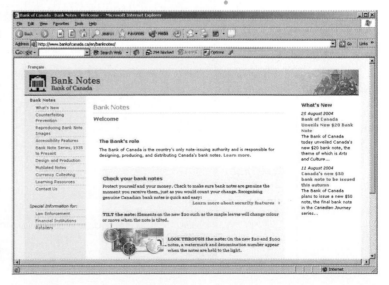

- **Durability.**   Coins last for thousands of years, even when they've sunk to the bottom of the ocean, as you've seen when divers find old Roman coins in sunken ships.
- **Uniqueness.**   It's hard to counterfeit, or copy, elaborately designed and minted coins. But with the latest colour copiers, people are able to duplicate the look of paper money relatively easily. Thus, the government has had to go to extra lengths to make sure real dollars are readily identifiable. That's why some denominations have raised print or raised ink, watermarks, and fine-line patterns.[7]

When coins and paper money become units of value, they simplify exchanges. Most countries have their own coins and paper money, and they're all about equally portable, divisible, and durable. However, they're not always equally stable. For example, the value of money in Russia is so uncertain and so unstable that other countries won't accept Russian money (rubles) in international trade.

Electronic cash (e-cash) is the latest form of money.[8] In addition to being able to make online bill payments using software programs such as Quicken or Microsoft Money, you can e-mail e-cash to anyone using Websites such as PayPal.com. Recipients get an e-mail message telling them they have several choices for how they can receive the money: automatic deposit (the money will be sent to their bank), e-dollars for spending online, or a traditional cheque in the mail.

What Is the Money Supply?

money supply
The amount of money the Bank of Canada makes available for people to buy goods and services.

The **money supply** is the amount of money the Bank of Canada (introduced in Chapter 4) makes available for people to buy goods and services. The money supply can be measured in a number of different ways. Some of these different measures, called monetary aggregates, are described in Figure 18.2.

M1 represents money that can be accessed quickly and easily. M2, M2+, and M2++ are even broader measures of the money supply. Before we consider how the Bank of Canada controls the money supply, let us first consider why the money supply needs to be controlled and its impact on the global exchange of money.

FIGURE 18.2

MEASURES OF MONEY—
CANADA'S MONEY SUPPLY

MEASURES OF MONEY (MONETARY AGGREGATES)	DEFINITION OF THE MONETARY AGGREGATES
M1	The currency (bank notes and coins) in circulation plus personal chequing accounts and current accounts at banks.
M2	Includes personal savings accounts and other chequing accounts, term deposits, and non-personal deposits requiring notice before withdrawal.
M2+	Includes all deposits at non-bank deposit-taking institutions, money-market mutual funds, and individual annuities at life insurance companies.
M2++	Includes all types of mutual funds and Canada Savings Bonds.

Source: "Canada's Money Supply," Bank of Canada, February 29, 2004. www.bankofcanada.ca/en/backgrounders/bg-m2.htm.

Why Does the Money Supply Need to Be Controlled?

Imagine what would happen if governments or nongovernmental organizations were to generate twice as much money as exists now. There would be twice as much money available, but there would be the same amount of goods and services. What would happen to prices in that case? Think about the answer for a minute. (Hint: Remember the laws of supply ➤P. 38◄ and demand ➤P. 38◄ from Chapter 2.) The answer is that prices would go up because more people would try to buy goods and services with their money and would bid up the price to get what they wanted. This is called inflation ➤P. 52◄. That is why some people define inflation as "too much money chasing too few goods."

Now think about the opposite: What would happen if the Bank of Canada took some of the money out of the economy? What would happen to prices? Prices would go down because there would be an oversupply of goods and services compared to the money available to buy them; this is called deflation.[9] If too much money is taken out of the economy, a recession ➤P. 53◄ might occur. That is, people would lose jobs and the economy would stop growing.

Now we come to a second question about the money supply: Why does the money supply need to be controlled? The money supply needs to be controlled because doing so allows us to manage the prices of goods and services somewhat. And controlling the money supply affects employment and economic growth or decline.

The Global Exchange of Money

A *falling dollar value* means that the amount of goods and services you can buy with a dollar decreases.[10] A *rising dollar value* means that the amount of goods and services you can buy with a dollar goes up.

What makes the dollar weak (falling dollar value) or strong (rising dollar value) is the position of the Canadian economy relative to other economies. When the economy is strong, the demand for dollars is high, and the value of the dollar rises. When the economy is perceived as weakening, however, the demand for dollars declines, and the value of the dollar falls. The value of the dollar thus depends on a strong economy. Clearly, control over the money supply is important. In the following section, we'll discuss briefly how the money supply is controlled.

Control of the Money Supply[11]

You already know that money plays a huge role in the economy. Therefore, it's important to have an organization that controls the money supply to try to keep the economy from growing too quickly or too slowly. Theoretically, with proper monetary policy ➤P. 109◄ you can keep the economy growing without causing inflation. The organization in charge of monetary policy is the Bank of Canada.

The Bank of Canada monitors the money supply. Indicators such as M1 provide useful information about changes that are occurring in the economy. The availability of money and credit must expand over time, and the Bank of Canada is responsible for ensuring that the rate at which more money is introduced into the economy is consistent with long-term stable growth.

The bank's economic research indicates that the growth of M1 provides useful information on the future level of production in the economy. The growth of the broader monetary aggregates is a good leading indicator of the rate of inflation.

The objective of the Bank of Canada's monetary policy is to support a level of spending by Canadians that is consistent with the Bank's goal of price stability. This is defined as keeping inflation within the inflation-control target range [of 1 to 3 percent]. By influencing the rate at which the supply of money and credit is growing, total spending on goods and services in the economy can be stabilized.

The Bank of Canada manages the rate of money growth indirectly through the influence it exercises over short-term interest rates. When these rates change, they carry other interest rates—such as those paid by consumers for loans from commercial banks—along with them. When interest rates rise, consumers and businesses are apt to hold less money, to borrow less, and to pay back existing loans. The result is a slowing in the growth of M1 and the other broader monetary aggregates.[12]

The Bank of Canada has an influence on very short-term interest rates through changes in its Target for the Overnight Rate. The Target for the Overnight Rate is the main tool used by the Bank of Canada to conduct monetary policy. It tells major financial institutions the average interest rate the Bank of Canada wants to see in the marketplace where they lend each other money for one day, or "overnight." When the Bank changes the Target for the Overnight Rate, this change usually affects other interest rates charged by commercial banks. The **prime rate** is the interest rate banks charge their most creditworthy customers.

When the Bank changes the Target for the Overnight Rate, this sends a clear signal about the direction in which it wants short-term interest rates to go. These changes usually lead to moves in the prime rate at commercial banks. The prime rate serves as a benchmark for many of their loans. These changes can also indirectly affect mortgage rates, and the interest paid to consumers on bank accounts, term deposits, and other savings.

When interest rates go down, people and businesses are encouraged to borrow and spend more, boosting the economy. But if the economy grows too fast, it can lead to inflation. The Bank may then raise interest rates to slow down borrowing and spending, putting a brake on inflation.

In choosing a Target for the Overnight Rate, the Bank of Canada picks a level that it feels will keep future inflation low, stable and predictable. Keeping inflation low and stable helps provide a good climate for sustainable economic growth, investment and job creation.[13]

prime rate
The interest rate banks charge their most creditworthy customers.

The monetary policy formulated by the Bank of Canada contributes to solid economic performance and rising living standards for Canadians by keeping inflation low, stable, and predictable. To find out in more detail how the Bank of Canada tries to do this, visit its site at www.bankofcanada.ca.

Progress Assessment

- What are the characteristics of useful money?
- What is the money supply and why is it important?
- What are the various ways the Bank of Canada controls the money supply?

THE BANKING INDUSTRY

Following legislative changes in 1992, banks were allowed to own insurance, trust, and securities subsidiaries. Today most of Canada's large banks have subsidiaries in these areas. As major players in Canada's financial industry,

FIGURE 18.3

CANADA'S SIX LARGEST BANKS

BANK NAME	TOTAL ASSETS	TOTAL LOANS	NET INCOME FOR FISCAL YEAR ENDED OCTOBER 31, 2003
	($ MILLIONS)		
RBC Financial Group	403,185	206,683	3,005
Scotiabank	285,892	170,967	2,477
CIBC	277,147	153,764	2,063
TD Bank Financial Group	273,532	135,533	1,076
BMO Financial Group	256,494	140,585	1,825
National Bank of Canada	82,423	42,336	624
Total 6 Banks	1,578,673	849,867	11,070

Source: "Data of Canada's Six Largest Banks," Canadian Bankers Association, n.d.

the banks serve millions of customers. They include individuals, small- and medium-sized businesses, large corporations, governments, institutional investors, and non-profit organizations. The major banks offer a full range of banking, investment, and financial services. They have extensive nationwide distribution networks and also are active in the United States, Latin America, the Caribbean, Asia, and other parts of the world. Close to half of their earnings are generated outside of Canada.

Figure 18.3 outlines Canada's six largest banks. Strong players in the Canadian economy, Canada's banks are also extremely profitable. These financial results have garnered criticism by some who believe that the banks are taking advantage of customers by charging high service charges. The reality is that bank revenues are increasingly being generated from international activities. As well, banks distribute a good portion of their net income to their shareholders. Most Canadians own bank shares, whether they know it or not; bank shares form a large part of many major mutual funds (to be discussed later in this chapter) and pension funds.[14] In 2003, Canada's banks distributed $4.7 billion worth of dividends to their shareholders, which represented 25 percent of the banks' net earnings.[15]

As indicated in Chapter 4, some of the major banks have been trying to merge for several years. They believe that if they were permitted to merge, they would be able to take advantage of economies of scale ▶P. 104◀ and be more efficient. They argue that they are not big players globally (see Figure 18.4), and that they are increasingly being forced to look outside Canada for more opportunities due to the laws and regulations that control their domestic activities. Shareholders continue to demand good returns, and the banks are under more pressure to continue to deliver, year after year. This is an issue that will not go away in the years to come.

FIGURE 18.4

WORLDWIDE BANK RANKINGS, 2003

RANK	BANK	ASSETS (CAD$ BILLIONS)
1	Mizuho Financial Group	1,667
50	Royal Bank of Canada	390
61	Scotiabank	274
62	CIBC	267
63	Toronto-Dominion Bank	262
66	Bank of Montreal	246
123	Desjardins Group	95
142	National Bank of Canada	78

Source: "Bank Rankings," Canadian Bankers Association, July 2004.

Commercial Banks

commercial bank
A profit-seeking organization that receives deposits from individuals and corporations in the form of chequing and savings accounts and then uses some of these funds to make loans.

A **commercial bank** is a profit-seeking organization that receives deposits from individuals and corporations in the form of chequing and savings accounts and then uses some of these funds to make loans. Commercial banks have two types of customers: depositors and borrowers (those who take out loans). A commercial bank is equally responsible to both types of customers. Commercial banks try to make a profit by efficiently using the funds depositors give them. In essence, a commercial bank uses customer deposits as inputs (on which it pays interest) and invests that money in interest-bearing loans to other customers (mostly businesses). Commercial banks make a profit if the revenue generated by loans exceeds the interest paid to depositors plus all other operating expenses.

The Canadian Bankers Association has a series of free publications on a variety of financial topics. Some examples are Getting Started in Small Business, Small Business Financing, Getting Value for Your Service Fees, Investing Your Dollars, Managing Your Money, and Planning for Retirement. For more details, visit www.cba.ca.

Some Services Provided by Banks

Individuals and corporations that deposit money in a chequing account have the privilege of writing personal cheques to pay for almost any purchase or transaction. Typically, banks impose a service charge for cheque-writing privileges or demand a minimum deposit. Banks might also charge a small handling fee for each cheque written. For business depositors, the amount of the service charge depends on the average daily balance in the chequing account, the number of cheques written, and the firm's credit rating and credit history.

In addition to chequing accounts, commercial banks offer a variety of savings account options. As for the chequing accounts, each individual needs to evaluate the different features of each account as they differ from institution to institution.

A *term deposit* (also known as a guaranteed investment certificate or a certificate of deposit) is a savings account that earns interest to be delivered at the end of the specified period. The depositor agrees not to withdraw any of the funds in the account until the end of the specified term (e.g., one year). The longer the term deposit is to be held by the bank, the higher the interest rate for the depositor.

Banks also offer a variety of other products. Some examples of credit products for creditworthy customers include credit cards, lines of credit, loans, mortgages, and overdraft protection on chequing accounts. Additional products are access to automated

Making Ethical Decisions

To Tell the Teller or Not?

You have been banking at the same bank for some time, but the tellers at the bank keep changing, so it is difficult to establish a relationship with any one teller. You do not like using the automated teller machine because the bank has decided to charge for each transaction. Therefore, you are working with a teller and withdrawing $300 for some expenses you expect to incur. The teller counts out your money and says: "OK, here's your $300." Before you leave the bank, you count the money once more. You notice that the teller has given you $350 by mistake. You return to the teller and say, "I think you have made a mistake in giving me this money." She replies indignantly, "I don't think so. I counted the money in front of you."

You are upset by her quick denial of a mistake and her attitude. You have to decide whether or not to give her back the overpayment of $50. What are your alternatives? What would you do? Is that the ethical thing to do?

---

teller machines (ATMs), life insurance coverage on credit products, brokerage services, financial counselling, telephone and Internet bill payment options, safe-deposit boxes, registered retirement accounts, and traveller's cheques. Visit a local bank branch to find out the details for all of these types of products. It is up to each individual to compare the different features on each type of account or service as they vary from institution to institution. Features and rates are competitive. The Making Ethical Decisions box highlights a human error that can easily be made.

ATMs give customers the convenience of 24-hour banking at a variety of outlets such as supermarkets, department stores, and drugstores in addition to the bank's regular branches. Depositors can—almost anywhere in the world—transfer funds, make deposits, and get cash at their own discretion with the use of a computer-coded personalized plastic access card. Beyond all that, today's ATMs are doing even more. New ATMs can dispense maps and directions, phone cards, and postage stamps. They can sell tickets to movies, concerts, sporting events, and so on. They can even show movie trailers, news tickers, and video ads. Some can take orders for flowers and DVDs, and download music and games.[16] The convenience chain 7-Eleven is testing machines that cash cheques and send wire transfers.[17] What next?

Services to Borrowers In addition to other financial services firms and government agencies (such as the Business Development Bank of Canada), banks offer a variety of services to individuals and corporations in need of a loan. Generally, loans are given on the basis of the recipient's creditworthiness. Banks want to manage their funds effectively and are supposed to screen loan applicants carefully to ensure that the loan plus interest will be paid back on time. Small businesses often search out banks that cater to their needs. The Spotlight on Small Business box highlights some reasons why small business loan requests are denied.

Creditworthiness is based in part on your credit history. To request a free copy of your credit history, contact Equifax Canada (www.equifax.ca) or TransUnion Canada (www.tuc.ca).

Many consumers, especially first time credit card owners, are unable to properly manage them and often end up with severely damaged credit ratings—or worse, in bankruptcy. That's why it may be a good idea for you to pass up the free T-shirt or other offer made by credit card companies.

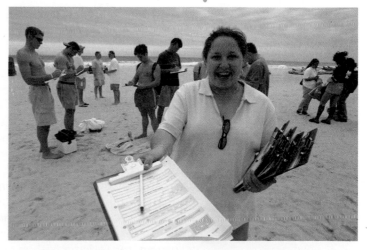

Spotlight on Small Business

When the Bank Says No

Throughout this text, we have stressed the importance of establishing a strong relationship with a banker. Bankers are there to assist small business owners and to provide advice on how their business can grow. But what happens when an entrepreneur walks into the bank with a brilliant business idea and a detailed plan—and comes out empty-handed? Sometimes, even the best-prepared borrowers get turned down. Here are some of the more common reasons.

1. **Your bank already does a lot of business with other companies in your industry.** "The banks calculate what their exposure is to any particular industry segment," says Russell Garrard, senior manager of commercial banking with the National Bank. "For example, if the bank is heavily weighted in the auto sector, it may be less inclined to do a deal in that sector. It's just good business practice not to have all your eggs in one basket."

2. **Your management team just doesn't inspire the banker's confidence.** "You may have a good idea, but a bad management team," says Garrard. "From experience we know that the strong managers tend to survive downturns in the economy, recessions, etc., but the bad ones don't."

3. **Timing.** "You could have a great business idea, but it just so happens that it's the wrong time for it,"

says Rick Leask, senior business advisor with CIBC. "Interest rates may be on the way up, or the price of real estate may be rising, and you won't be able to run your business."

4. **The economy.** You could have a great product, but the bank may feel that the economy is headed towards a downturn in which your customers won't be able to afford your products.

5. **Chemistry.** Maybe one of your jokes rubbed a banker the wrong way. Maybe you're the ninth caller of the day and he's just tired. You and your banker are both human, and sometimes relationships just don't happen. If either you or your banker don't feel comfortable with each other, you know what to do: find another banker.

In the banking world, nothing is black and white. Every deal is looked at individually, and decisions are sometimes made based on factors completely beyond your control. If you've put your best foot forward and things don't work out, never hesitate to step right up and knock on another bank's door. A "no" from one banker doesn't mean that another lender won't decide to take you on. Persistence and confidence are an entrepreneur's best tools.

Source: Jack Kazmierski, "When the Bank Says "No" (2001)," PROFITguide.com. Retrieved from www.profitguide.com/maximize/article.jsp?content=664.

Managing Your Personal Finances

A major reason for studying business is that it prepares you for finding and keeping a good job. You already know that one of the secrets to finding a well-paying job is to have a good education. With your earnings, you can take vacations, raise a family, make investments, buy the products you want, and give generously to others.

Money management, however, is not easy. You have to earn the money in the first place. Then you have to learn how to save money; spend money wisely; and insure yourself against any financial and health risks. While these topics are important from a personal perspective, they are outside the scope of this chapter. However, given their importance, you can visit the Online Learning Centre for an introduction into managing your personal finances. Starting with the six steps of learning to control your assets, we discuss ways to build a financial asset base, explain how to buy the appropriate insurance, and outline a strategy for retiring with enough money to last a lifetime.

The Internet and Global Banking

www.ml.com

The Canadian market for banking services is relatively mature; therefore, the growth markets of the future will be overseas. Few firms understand the potential of international banking better than Merrill Lynch, a leader in brokering and in financing corporations.

To expand overseas, Merrill Lynch bought the British brokerage Smith New Court; Spain's Iversiones; and stakes in brokerages in India, Thailand, South Africa, Indonesia, and Italy. It is also expanding to Latin America and recently acquired Australia's McIntosh Securities. In all, it is present in over 40 countries. As a consequence, about 30 percent of Merrill Lynch's revenues now come from overseas. Merrill Lynch is using the same concepts it developed domestically to develop globally. In fact, it was one of the biggest losers during the Asian banking crisis.

Jeff Bahrenburg, global investment strategist at Merrill Lynch, says, "The Internet hastens the speed of financial flows and the pace at which the world is getting smaller." Andrew W. Lo, an economist at MIT, adds, "The most significant effect of the Internet on finance is that it will greatly facilitate the efficient matching of borrowers and investors in the global economy." To give you some idea of the dollar amount involved, consider this: In 1980, the world's stock of equities, bonds, and cash totaled some $11 trillion; by 2000 these financial figures were at $78 trillion.

Other leading investment firms, insurance companies, and banks are going global as well. Names like RBC Financial Group and Scotiabank are becoming familiar all over the world. Citigroup estimates that total personal loans in Western Europe, which now amount to about $450 billion, could one day rival those in the United States, at about $750 billion. That is an attractive situation for brokers and other financial institutions from all nations. It also means that there will be opportunities for tomorrow's graduates in finance to work anywhere in the world.

Sources: Daniel Fairlamb and Stanley Reed, "Uber Bank," *Business Week,* March 20, 2000, pp. 52–53; "The Global Giants," *The Wall Street Journal,* October 14, 2002, pp. R10, R11; Stephanie Miles, "What's a Check?" *The Wall Street Journal,* October 21, 2002, p. R5; and Erik Portanger and Paul Beckett, "Banks Vie for Europe's Consumers," *The Wall Street Journal,* Feburary 24, 2003, pp. C1, C5.

Electronic Banking on the Internet

Not only have banking, insurance, and brokerage services been combined in one company, but they are also available online. All of Canada's top banks allow customers access to their accounts online, and all have bill-paying capacity. Thus, you are now able to do all of your financial transactions from home, using your telephone or your computer. That includes banking transactions such as transferring funds from one account to another (e.g., savings to chequing), paying your bills, and finding out how much is in your various accounts.[18] In some instances, you can apply for a loan online and get a response almost immediately. The company can check your financial records and give you a reply while you wait. Buying and selling stocks, and bonds ▶**P. 547**◀ is equally easy. (See the Dealing with Change box for a discussion of the Internet and global banking.)

New Internet banks (e.g., ING) have been created that offer online banking only; they do not have physical branches. Such banks can offer high interest rates and low fees because they do not have the costs of physical overhead that traditional banks have. While many consumers are pleased with the savings and convenience, not all are entirely happy with the service they receive from Internet banks. Why are they dissatisfied? First of all, they are nervous about security. People fear putting their financial information into cyberspace, where others may see it. Despite all the assurances of privacy, people are still concerned. Furthermore, some people want to be able to talk to a knowledgeable person when they have banking problems. They miss the service, the one-on-one help, and the security of local banks.

Because of these issues, the future seems to be with organizations like TD Bank Financial Group and BMO Financial Group, which are traditional banks that offer both online services and brick-and-mortar facilities.[19] Combined online and brick-and-mortar banks not only offer online services of all kinds but also have automated teller machines (ATMs), places to go to deposit and get funds, and real people to talk to in person.

Progress Assessment

- Why are some banks interested in merging?
- List some services provided by commercial banks.
- What are some benefits of electronic banking to users?

THE CANADIAN SECURITIES INDUSTRY[20]

securities dealer
A firm that trades securities for its clients and offers investment services.

The Investment Dealers Association of Canada (IDA) is the national self-regulatory organization and representative of the securities industry. The Association regulates the business activities and conduct of investment dealers. For more information, visit www.ida.ca.

A **securities dealer** (also known as an investment dealer or brokerage house) is a firm that trades securities for its clients and offers investment services. Such firms also assist companies in raising all forms of capital for new and expanding businesses. As a result, this industry allows investors to trade in open capital markets. In 2003, there were 207 firms that employed more than 37,000 people. Since 1987, when federally regulated financial institutions were permitted to own securities firms, most of Canada's large, full-service securities firms have been bank-owned. Some examples are noted in Figure 18.5.

More Canadians are turning to the securities industry to ensure their financial security. The past decade has seen extraordinary growth in the number of individuals participating in Canadian capital markets. Roughly one-half of all working Canadians are directly and indirectly invested in the equities market. In the ten years to 2003, investors' holdings of shares have more than doubled to more than $660 billion. Ten years ago, 20 percent of the average investor's financial assets (bank accounts, registered retirement savings plans, pension, insurance, etc.) were stocks. Today, this ratio has grown to 27 percent.

FIGURE 18.5

CANADA'S BANK-OWNED SECURITIES FIRMS

FIRM	MAJORITY OWNER
BMO Nesbitt Burns	Bank of Montreal
CIBC World Markets	Canadian Imperial Bank of Commerce
National Bank Financial	National Bank
RBC Dominion Securities	Royal Bank of Canada
Scotia Capital	The Bank of Nova Scotia
TD Securities	The Toronto-Dominion Bank

Source: "The Canadian Securities Industry: The Canadian Financial System," June 2000 (September 5, 2003), Department of Finance Canada, September 5, 2003. Retrieved from http://www.fin.gc.ca/toce/2000/cansec_e.html.

Securities Regulations[21]

As mentioned earlier in the textbook, one of the reasons why private corporations become public corporations is to raise capital in order to expand their existing operations. In recent times, companies such as SEAMARK Asset Management Ltd., Sleep Country Canada, and The Brick became publicly traded companies following the successful completion of their first IPO.

Companies seeking public financing must issue a prospectus. A **prospectus** is a condensed version of economic and financial information that a company must make available to investors before they purchase the security. The prospectus must be approved by the securities commission in the province where the public funding is being sought. The **securities commission** is a government agency that administers provincial securities legislation.[22] For example, the mandate of the Ontario Securities Commission is to "protect investors from unfair improper and fraudulent practices, foster fair and efficient capital markets and maintain public and investor confidence in the integrity of those markets."

Canada's ten provinces and three territories are responsible for the securities regulations within their respective borders. The Canadian Securities Administrators (CSA) is a forum for these securities regulators to coordinate and harmonize regulation of the Canadian capital markets. The CSA brings provincial and territorial securities regulators together. The focus of these meetings is to share ideas, work at designing policies and regulations that are consistent across the country, and ensure the smooth operation of Canada's securities industry. By collaborating on rules, regulations, and other programs, the CSA helps avoid duplication of work and streamlines the regulatory process for companies seeking to raise investment capital and others working in the investment industry.

At the time that this chapter was written, Canada's regulatory framework was being evaluated. A steering committee made up of ministers from six provinces agreed in the summer of 2003 to try to fix Canada's patchwork regulatory system. In 2004, this steering committee recommended a national securities regulator. Quebec, Alberta, and British Columbia were opposed to giving up their control over securities regulations. The federal Minister of Finance continued to encourage a solution that would address the problems of a costly, cumbersome regulatory framework. Today, have there been any changes to this framework? Have the provinces maintained their control over the activities within their borders, or has a national body been created to oversee all securities activities?

prospectus
A condensed version of economic and financial information that a company must make available to investors before they purchase a security.

securities commission
A government agency that administers provincial securities legislation.

To find out more about individual CSA members, CSA news, and investor information, visit www.csa-acvm.ca.

THE FUNCTION OF SECURITIES MARKETS

A **stock exchange** is an organization whose members can buy and sell (exchange) securities for companies and investors. A *security* is a transferable certificate of ownership of an investment product such as a stock or bond.[23] The Toronto Stock Exchange and the Montreal Exchange are just two examples of securities markets in Canada. These institutions serve two major functions: First, they assist businesses in finding long-term funding to finance capital needs, such as beginning operations, expanding their businesses, or buying major goods and services. Second, they provide private investors a place to buy and sell securities (investments), such as stocks, bonds, and mutual funds (to be discussed later in this chapter) that can help them build their financial future.

Securities markets are divided into primary and secondary markets. *Primary markets* handle the sale of new securities. This is an important point

stock exchange
An organization whose members can buy and sell (exchange) securities for companies and investors.

TSX Group Inc. operates Canada's two national stock exchanges, the Toronto Stock Exchange and the TSX Venture Exchange. For more information about these exchanges, visit www.tse.com.

In the past ten years, there have been more than 2,200 IPOs issued in Canada, valued at more than $33 billion. To find Canadian IPO information, visit http://ipo. investcom.com.

stockbroker
A registered representative who works as a market intermediary to buy and sell securities for clients.

to understand. Corporations make money on the sale of their securities only once—when they are first sold on the primary market through an IPO.[24] After that, the *secondary market* handles the trading of securities between investors, with the proceeds of a sale going to the investor selling the stock, not to the corporation whose stocks are sold. For example, if you, the maker of Fiberrific cereal, offer 2 million shares of stock in your company at $15 a share, you would raise $30 million at this initial offering. However, if Shareholder Jones sells 100 shares of her Fiberrific stock to Investor Smith, Fiberrific collects nothing from this transaction. Smith bought the stock from Jones, not from Fiberrific. However, it's possible for companies like Fiberrific to offer additional shares to raise additional capital.

The importance of long-term funding to businesses can't be overemphasized. Unfortunately, many new companies start without sufficient capital, and many established firms fail to do adequate long-term financial planning. If given a choice, businesses normally prefer to meet long-term financial needs by using retained earnings or by borrowing from a lending institution (bank, pension fund, insurance company). However, if such types of long-term funding are not available, a company may be able to raise funds by issuing corporate bonds (debt) or selling stock (ownership). Recall from Chapter 17 that issuing corporate bonds is a form of debt financing and selling stock in the corporation is a form of equity financing. These forms of debt or equity financing are not available to all companies, especially small businesses. However, many firms use such financing options to meet long-term financial needs.

How to Invest in Securities

Investing in bonds, stocks, or other securities is not very difficult. First, you decide what bond or stock you want to buy. After that, it's necessary to find a registered representative authorized to trade stocks and bonds who can call a member of the stock exchange to execute your order. A **stockbroker** is a registered representative who works as a market intermediary to buy and sell securities for clients. Stockbrokers place an order with a stock exchange member, who goes to the place at the exchange where the bond or stock is traded and negotiates a price. After the transaction is completed, the trade is reported to your broker, who notifies you to confirm your purchase. Large brokerage firms like RBC Capital Markets and BMO Nesbitt Burns maintain automated order systems that allow their brokers to enter your order the instant you make it. Seconds later, the order can be confirmed. Online brokers (discussed next), such as Scotia McLeod Direct Investing, can also confirm investor trades in a matter of seconds.[25]

The same procedure is followed if you wish to sell stocks or bonds. Brokers historically held on to stock or bond certificates for investors to ensure safekeeping and to allow investors to sell their securities easily and quickly. Today brokers keep most records of bond or stock ownership electronically, and transactions are almost instantaneous.

The Toronto Stock Exchange and the TSX Venture Exchange are not the only fish in the stock exchange sea. Exchanges like the London Exchange (pictured here) are located throughout the world, even in former communist-bloc countries like Poland and Hungary. If you think a foreign company is destined to be the next Magna, Nortel, or Bombardier, call a broker and get in on the opportunity.

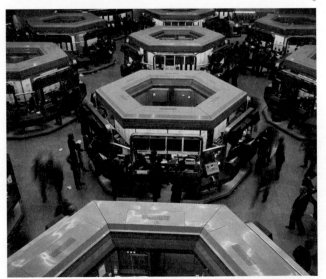

A broker can be a valuable source of information about what stocks or bonds would best meet your financial objectives. It's important, however, that you learn about and follow stocks and bonds on your own, because investment analysts' advice may not always meet your specific expectations and needs.[26]

Progress Assessment

- Describe the Canadian securities industry. Why are more Canadians turning to this industry?
- What is the role of the Canadian Securities Administrators?
- What is the primary purpose of a stock exchange? Can you name a stock exchange in Canada?

Investing Online

As we have stressed throughout this book, technology has affected virtually every aspect of business, and trading in investment securities is no exception. Investors can use online trading services to buy and sell stocks and bonds in place of using traditional brokerage services.[27] BMO Investorline (www. bmoinvestorline.com), TD Waterhouse (www.tdwaterhouse.ca), and E*Trade Canada (www.etrade.ca) are a few of the leading providers of Web-based stock trading services. The commissions charged by these trading services are far less than those of regular stockbrokers. Trades that used to cost hundreds of dollars with full-service brokerage firms may cost as low as $5 each on the Web.

Today, customers interested in online trading services are primarily investors willing to do their own research and make their own investment decisions without the assistance of a broker. The leading online services, however, do provide important market information such as company financial data, price histories of a stock, and consensus analysts' reports. Often the level of information services provided by online brokers depends on the size of your account and level of trading. Online brokers are also exploring other financial services alternatives. For example, online broker E*Trade has recast itself as a financial services supermarket. The company offers banking services, chequing accounts, mortgages, car loans, credit cards, and insurance.[28]

Whether you decide to trade stocks and bonds using an online broker or decide to invest through a traditional stockbroker, it is important to remember that investing means committing (and risking) your money with the expectation of making a profit.[29] As the market downturn in the early 2000s highlighted, investing is certainly a risky business. Therefore, the first step in any investment program is to analyze such factors as desired income, cash requirements, growth prospects, level of risk, and hedging against inflation. You are never too young or too old to get involved in investments, so let's look at some alternatives and questions you should consider before investing.

The Canadian Securities Institute offers a variety of courses for those interested in a career in financial services or in learning about their own investments. For more information, visit www.csi.ca

SEDAR is a central database containing public records of all companies publicly traded on the Canadian markets. To view a company's recent news releases or financial statements, visit the SEDAR Website at www.sedar.com.

Choosing the Right Investment Strategy

As you might suspect, investment objectives change over the course of a person's life. Key investment decisions often centre on personal objectives such as growth and income. For example, a young person can afford more high-risk investment options (such as stocks) than a person nearing retirement. Often young investors are looking for significant growth in the value of their

Crystal Hanlan started with Home Depot as a cashier several years ago. She began buying shares in the company as part of an employee ownership plan and is now worth over a million dollars. There are over a million other employees who got to be millionaires the same way. Are you getting the idea that it is a good idea to participate in such ownership programs and to put the maximum you can into such accounts?

investments over time. Therefore, if stocks go into a tail-spin and decrease in value, the younger person has time to wait for stocks to rise again. An older person, perhaps on a fixed income, doesn't have the luxury of waiting, and might be prone to invest in bonds that offer a steady return as a protection against inflation. To an elderly investor, additional income is probably more important than potential growth.

What's inherent in any investment strategy is the risk/return trade-off ➤ P. 547◄. Investors must evaluate investment strategies related to growth, income, inflation protection, or liquidity. For example, should you consider stocks or bonds? Do you want common or preferred shares? Do you want corporate-issued or government-issued bonds? These are tough questions whose answers vary investor by investor. That's why it's important for investors to consider five key criteria when selecting investment options:

1. **Investment risk**—the chance that an investment will be worth less at some future time than it's worth now.
2. **Yield**—the expected rate of return on an investment, such as interest or dividends, usually over a period of one year.
3. **Duration**—the length of time your money is committed to an investment.
4. **Liquidity**—how quickly you can get back your invested funds if you want them or need them.
5. **Tax consequences**—how the investment will affect your tax situation.

Since new investors are not generally well versed in the world of investing or in choosing proper investment strategies, an investment planner or a short course in investments can be very useful. Setting investment objectives such as growth or income should clearly set the tone for your investment strategy.

Bonds, stocks, and mutual funds all offer opportunities for investors to enhance their financial future. We will look first at the potential of bonds as an investment, then move on to stocks and mutual funds.

INVESTING IN BONDS

For investors who desire low risk and guaranteed income, government bonds are a secure investment because these bonds have the financial backing and full faith and credit of the government. Corporate bonds are a bit more risky and challenging.

One question often bothers first-time corporate bond investors. It is "If I purchase a corporate bond, do I have to hold it until the maturity date?" The answer is no, you do not have to hold a bond until maturity. Bonds are bought and sold daily on major securities exchanges. However, if you decide to sell your bond to another investor before its maturity date, you are not guaranteed to get the face value of the bond (usually $1,000). For example, if your bond does not have features (high interest rate, early maturity, etc.) that make it attractive to other investors, you may be forced to sell your bond at a *discount;* that is, a price less than the bond's face value. But if your bond is highly valued by other investors, you may be able to sell it at a *premium;* that is, a price above its face value. Bond prices generally fluctuate inversely with current market interest rates. *As interest rates go up, bond prices fall, and vice versa.* Thus, like all investments, bonds have a degree of risk.

Investors will invest in a bond that is considered risky only if the potential return to them is high enough. It's important to remember that investors have many investment options besides bonds. One such option is to buy stock.

INVESTING IN STOCKS

Buying stock makes the investor an owner of the firm. Stocks provide investors an opportunity to participate in the success of emerging or expanding companies. As owners, however, stockholders can also lose money if a company does not do well or the overall stock market is declining. The early 2000s were proof of that. Again, it's up to investors to choose the investment that best fits their overall investment objectives.

According to investment analysts, the market price (and growth potential) of a common share depends heavily on the overall performance of the corporation in meeting its business objectives. If a company reaches its stated objectives, there are great opportunities for capital gains. **Capital gains** are the positive difference between the price at which you bought a stock and what you sell it for. For example, a $1,000 investment made in Microsoft when its stock was first offered to the public would be worth more than $1 million today. Stocks can be subject to a high degree of risk, however. Drops in the stock market such as the ones in 1987, 1997, and 2000–2002 certainly caught investors' attention.

> **capital gains**
> The positive difference between the purchase price of a stock and its sale price.

Stock investors are often called bulls or bears depending on their perceptions of the market. *Bulls* are investors who believe that stock prices are going to rise, so they buy stock in anticipation of the increase. When overall stock prices are rising, the market is called a bull market. *Bears* are investors who expect stock prices to decline. Bears sell their stocks in anticipation of falling prices. When the prices of stocks decline steadily, the market is called a bear market.[30]

As we discussed previously, setting investment objectives such as growth, income, inflation protection, or cash can set the tone for your investment strategy. Investors may select several different investment opportunities in stock depending on their strategy. *Growth stocks,* for example, are stocks of corporations (often technology, biotechnology, or Internet-related firms) whose earnings are expected to grow at a rate faster than other stocks in the market. While often considered very risky, such stocks offer investors the potential for high returns. Another option is *income stocks.* These are stocks that offer investors a rather high dividend yield on their investment. Public utilities are often considered good income stocks that will generally keep pace with inflation.

> What goes up can also go down. Investing in stock is always a risky venture, as investors found out in the bear market (declining stock prices) of 2000–2002. It's important to set an investment strategy and continuously monitor how your strategy is progressing. What type of investment option (bonds, stocks, mutual funds) is most appealing to you?

The stock of high-quality companies such as Petro-Canada and Canadian National (CN) are referred to as *blue-chip stocks.* These stocks pay regular dividends and generally experience consistent growth in the company's stock price. Investors can even invest in a type of stock called a penny stock. *Penny stocks* are stocks that sell for less than $2 (some analysts say less than $5).[31] Such stocks frequently represent ownership in firms, such as mining or oil exploration companies, that compete in high-risk industries. Suffice it to say, penny stocks are considered very risky investments.

"YOU CAN COME BACK IN. IT'S JUST A CORRECTION."

It's also interesting to note that investors who buy stock have more options for placing an order than investors buying and selling bonds. Stock investors, for example, can place a *market order,* which tells a broker to buy or to sell a stock immediately at the best price available. This type of order can be processed quickly, and the trade price can be given to the investor almost instantaneously. A *limit order* tells the broker to buy or to sell a particular stock at a specific price, if that price becomes available. Let's say, for example, that a stock is selling for $40 a share; you believe that the price will go up eventually but that it might drop a little before it goes higher. You could place a limit order at $36. The broker will buy the stock for you at $36 if the stock drops to that price. If the stock never falls to $36, the broker will not purchase it. See Figure 18.6 for a summary of some transactions. Which investments generated a capital gain (excluding any commissions) of more than $.50 per share based on the closing price from the previous day?

Stock Indexes

Stock indexes measure the trend of different stock exchanges. Every country with a stock exchange has such indexes. In Canada, there are several thousand companies listed and the prices of their shares fluctuate constantly. Some may be rising over a certain period and others may be falling. Various indexes have been developed to give interested parties useful information about significant trends.

In Canada, a commonly analyzed index is the S&P/TSE Composite Index. There is no requirement for the index to hold a certain number of companies. The number of stocks that make up the index will vary over time and will be included in the index if they qualify (based on size and liquidity) after quarterly reviews.[32] In the United States, the Dow Jones Industrial Average (the Dow, as it is commonly called) is the major index. The Dow represents the average cost of 30 selected industrial stocks. Like the S&P/TSE Composite Index, new stocks are substituted on the Dow when it's deemed appropriate. Likewise, it is also used as an indicator of the direction of the stock market (up or down) over time.

Staying abreast of what is happening in the market will help you decide what investments seem most appropriate to your needs and objectives. However, it's important to remember two key investment realities: (1) your personal financial objectives will change over time, and (2) markets can be volatile.

Buying on Margin

buying on margin
Purchasing securities by borrowing some of the cost from the broker.

Buying on margin means you purchase securities by borrowing some of the cost from your broker, who holds them as collateral security until you pay the balance due. In effect, the broker lends you the money and charges you interest. Provincial regulatory agencies, such as the Ontario Securities Commission, control all aspects of this industry, including what minimum percentage of the purchase price must be paid in cash. For example, if the current rate is 50 percent for shares and 10 percent for bonds, you would have to invest a minimum of $4 to buy an $8 share (plus commissions to the broker), and $97 for a bond selling for $970.

Buying on margin is risky. If the stock or bond drops in price, you will get a *margin call* from your broker. This means that you will have to make a payment to your broker to maintain the margin of collateral protection that the broker is obligated to observe. In this case, the loan cannot exceed 50 percent of the stock value, or 90 percent of the bond value.

| 365-day | | | | | | | | | Vol. | | P/E |
High	Low	Stock	Sym	Div	High	Low	Close	Chg	(100s)	Yield	ratio
2.00	0.65	M8 Entert	MEE.A		0.65	0.65	0.65	−0.28	55		54.2
9.40	7.80	MCAP Inc	MKP	0.78	8.95	8.76	8.95	−0.05	5	8.7	7.8
12.30	**8.65**	♣ **MCM**	**MUH.A**	**1.20**	**10.25**	**9.40**	**10.25**	**+0.75**	**16**	**11.7**	**3.2**
16.75	15.20	♣ MCM	MUH.PR.A	.867	16.00	16.00	16.00		20	5.4	
22.25	12.77	MDC Part	MDZ.A		15.75	15.65	15.67	−0.08	197		
23.31	17.95	MDS Inc	MDS	0.10	19.00	18.85	18.99	+0.01	1776	0.5	
12.00	5.12	MDSI Mo	MMD		5.95	5.75	5.75	−0.20	47		
41.00	23.89	MI Develp	MIM.A	.473	31.40	30.30	30.45	−0.05	69	1.6	
27.35	20.75	MacDonld	MDA		26.49	26.10	26.15	−0.25	605		20.9
3.95	2.25	Magellan	MAL		3.15	3.06	3.14	+0.04	1482		
0.12	0.04	Magella	MAL.RT		.065	.055	.055	+.005	12759		
9.40	5.00	Magna En	MEC.A		7.97	7.72	7.77	−0.06	265		5.0
115.79	90.67	Magna	MG.A	1.996	99.50	97.93	98.41	+0.07	911	2.0	13.1
26.94	25.04	Magn	MG.PR.A	2.157	25.44	25.31	25.44	+0.04	34	8.5	
5.95	3.00	♣ Mainstre	MEQ		5.60	5.60	5.60	−0.09	30		
11.25	5.25	♣ Major Dril	MDl		7.20	6.85	7.00	+0.10	303		25.9
46.99	42.12	Manitoba	MBT.B	2.60	42.27	42.20	42.27		92	6.2	
53.98	39.38	Manitoba	MBT	2.60	42.30	42.18	42.30	+0.05	3671	6.2	11.2
55.00	37.70	Manulife Fi	MFC	1.04	54.71	54.16	54.30	−0.20	8862	1.9	15.0
26.45	23.30	Manuli	MFC.PR.A	1.025	25.39	25.26	25.35	+0.09	36	4.0	
13.99	9.80	Maple Leaf	MFI	0.16	12.89	12.40	12.75	−0.13	364	1.2	21.2
28.50	25.17	♣ Mariti	MMF.PR.C	1.525	27.13	27.13	27.13	+0.07	7	5.6	
25.85	23.75	♣ Marit	MMF.PR.A	.675	25.21	25.20	25.20	−0.15	7	2.7	
26.99	25.26	♣ Marit	MMF.PR.B	1.525	25.60	25.40	25.40	−0.20	30	6.0	
6.25	3.60	Marsulex	MLX		5.55	5.55	5.55	+0.15	1038		50.5
8.38	5.36	Martinrea	MRE		5.55	5.45	5.55	+0.10	160		21.4
38.49	27.40	Masonite	MHM		33.69	32.75	33.10	+0.10	718		10.8
4.74	2.05	♣ Matrikon	MTK		3.25	3.20	3.21	+0.05	199		40.1
40.03	19.60	Maverick	MAV		40.03	39.21	40.03	+1.85	33		
3.70	2.30	Mavrix Fun	MVX		2.59	2.55	2.59	−0.06	30		
38.25	32.75	McGrw-Hil	MHR	0.72	33.75	34.99	34.75		z 16	2.1	13.3
13.00	8.00	Mediagrif	MDF		9.95	9.70	9.70		20		19.4
2.85	0.97	Medicure	MPH		1.28	1.20	1.24	−0.01	552		
3.24	1.68	Medisys Hlt	MHG		3.00	2.85	3.00	+0.05	290		25.0
26.49	19.11	Mega Bloks	MB		19.70	19.56	19.65	+0.05	137		13.9
20.50	12.11	MeridinGl	MNG		17.35	16.86	16.87	−0.49	2122		32.2
85.64	62.72	Merrill Lyn	MIC	0.85	67.75	67.21	67.55	+0.65	13	1.3	11.0
9.60	1.61	Metallic Vn	MVG		1.76	1.73	1.75		550		
2.95	1.07	♣ Metallica	MR		1.49	1.37	1.40	−0.05	521		
1.24	0.21	♣ Metallica	MR.WT		0.34	0.33		0.33	1217		
18.44	12.40	♣ Methanx	MX	0.42	17.80	17.58	17.75	+0.26	4865	2.4	
22.75	17.22	♣ Metro	MRU.A	0.34	18.41	18.20	18.41	+0.12	1083	1.9	11.0
1.10	0.56	Microbix Bi	MBX		1.10	1.01	1.02	+0.02	304		
32.90	11.00	Microcll	MT.B		31.36	31.36	31.36	+0.36	1		
12.86	0.91	Microcll	MT.WT.B		10.75	10.60	10.60	+0.03	14		
1.28	0.45	♣ Micrologix	MBI		0.90	0.82	0.85	+0.03	440		
8.25	5.25	Midnight Oi	MOG		6.65	6.60	6.65		118	44.3	
1.55	0.36	Milagro Enr	MIG		0.42	.405	.405	+.005	290		
13.87	7.75	♣ Minefindr	MFL		8.84	8.54	8.61	−0.19	784		
3.74	1.11	Miramar	MAE		1.32	1.28	1.31	+0.01	2259		

FIGURE 18.6

DAILY STOCK TRANSACTIONS

This is a small segment of the list of stocks traded on the Toronto Stock Exchange (September 2, 2004), as reported the following day in *The Globe and Mail*.

Here is an explanation of what the column headings mean:

A & B: highest and lowest price in the last year

C: abbreviated name of the company

D: the symbol used to identify the company for trading purposes

E: annual dividend per share

F, G, & H: highest, lowest, and closing price for *that day*

I: change in closing price from the previous day

J: number of shares traded that day in hundreds (e.g., first line is 5,500 shares)

K: *yield* refers to the estimated percent income your investment would yield if you bought at closing price and kept the stock for a year. It is the ratio of annual dividend to closing price. There is no yield for those companies that show no dividend paid.

L: *P/E ratio* refers to ratio of closing price to estimated earnings per share (which is not shown but is known). Where no ratio is shown it means either that the company is not making any profits or that no estimate of earnings is available.

Progress Assessment

- What is the key advantage to online investing? What do investors need to remember if they decide to do their investing online?
- What is a stock split? Why do companies sometimes split their stock?
- What is meant by buying on margin?

---

stock splits
An action by a company that gives shareholders two or more shares of stock for each one they own.

mutual fund
An organization that buys stocks and bonds and then sells shares in those securities to the public.

AIC Limited is Canada's largest privately held mutual fund company. Michael Lee-Chin, the chairman and CEO of AIC, acquired the company in 1987. Since that time, the company has grown from $1 million to more than $12 billion in assets under management. Over the past three years, AIC's charitable giving has surpassed one percent of its pre-tax domestic profits. As a result, AIC has joined Imagine, Canada's national program to promote public and corporate giving, volunteering, and support for the community. Are you more likely to invest in a Canadian-owned mutual investment company or a foreign-owned one?

Stock Splits

Companies and brokers prefer to have stock purchases conducted in *round lots;* that is, purchases of 100 shares at a time. However, investors often buy stock in *odd lots,* or purchases of fewer than 100 shares at a time. The problem is that many investors cannot afford to buy 100 shares of a stock in companies that may be selling for perhaps as high as $100 per share. Such high prices often induce companies to declare **stock splits;** that is, they issue two or more shares for every share of stock that's currently outstanding. For example, if Fiberrific stock were selling for $100 a share, Fiberrific could declare a two-for-one stock split. Investors who owned one share of Fiberrific would now own two shares; each share, however, would now be worth only $50 (one-half as much as before the split). As you can see, there is no change in the firm's ownership structure and no change in the investment's value after the stock split.[33] Investors, however, generally approve of stock splits because often the demand for the stock at $50 per share may be greater than the demand at $100 per share. Thus, the $50 stock price may go up in the near future.

INVESTING IN MUTUAL FUNDS

A **mutual fund** is a fund that buys a variety of securities and then sells units of ownership in the fund to the public. A mutual fund company, then, uses its capital to invest in other companies. Funds are created to meet specific criteria and goals. Mutual fund managers are experts who pick what they consider to be the best securities.

Investors can buy shares of the mutual funds and thus take part in the ownership of many different companies that they may not have been able to afford to invest in individually. Thus, for a normally small fee, mutual funds provide professional investment management and help investors diversify. The three main categories of fees for mutual funds are management fees (to pay for the management of the fund), sales fees (to pay for buying and selling the fund units), and special fees (for specific administrative costs).[34]

In Canada, mutual fund companies fall under the jurisdiction of the provincial securities commissions. Some examples of companies that manage mutual fund assets include Investors Group, AIM Funds Management, Mackenzie Financial, and TD Asset Management. According to the Investment Funds Institute of Canada, total assets under administration were $468.1 billion in August 2004.[35]

FIGURE 18.7

COMPARING INVESTMENTS

Investment	Degree of risk	Expected income	Possible growth (capital gain)
Bonds	Low	Secure	Little
Preferred shares	Medium	Steady	Little
Common shares	High	Variable	Good
Mutual funds	Medium	Variable	Good

The Mutual Fund Fee Impact Calculator will help you understand how fees and other expenses can affect your mutual fund investments. You can also use it to compare different funds. To review this tool, visit www.investored.ca/en/interactive/mffcalculator/calculator.htm.

Buying shares in a mutual fund is probably the best way for a small or beginning investor to get started. Funds available range in purpose from very conservative funds (that invest only in government securities or secure corporate bonds) to others that specialize in emerging high-tech firms, Internet companies, foreign companies, precious metals, and other investments with greater risk. These are balanced funds that invest in a combination of conservative securities and equities. Some mutual funds even invest exclusively in socially responsible companies.[36]

With mutual funds, investors benefit from diversification. **Diversification** involves buying several different investment alternatives to spread the risk of investing. Consequently, a mutual fund investor is not 100-percent invested in only one company. So, if one company's shares decrease, hopefully there will be increases in the value of other companies' shares. This is also applicable if a mutual fund holds bonds. See the Reaching Beyond Our Borders box for information on one company's investments include global companies.

diversification
Buying several different investment alternatives to spread the risk of investing.

One key advantage of mutual funds is that you can buy some funds directly and save any fees or commissions. The Internet has made access in and out of mutual funds easier than ever. A true no-load fund is one that charges no commission to investors to either buy or sell its shares. A load fund would charge a commission to investors to buy shares in the fund or would charge a commission when investors sell shares in the fund. It's important to check the costs involved in a mutual fund, such as fees and charges imposed in the managing of a fund, because these can differ significantly. It's also important to check the long-term performance record of the fund's management.[37] Some funds, called *open-end funds,* will accept the investments of any interested investors. *Closed-end* funds offer a specific number of shares for investment; once a closed-end fund reaches its target number, no new investors can buy into the fund.

Most financial advisers put mutual funds high on the list of recommended investments for small or beginning investors. Figure 18.7 evaluates bonds, stocks, and mutual funds according to risk, income, and possible investment growth (capital gain).

- What is a mutual fund and what is the role of mutual fund managers?
- How do mutual funds benefit small investors?
- Describe the degree of risk, expected income, and possible growth one can expect with mutual funds.

Progress Assessment

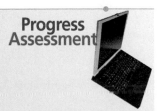

Reaching Beyond Our Borders

AIC Limited and Mutual Fund Investments

At AIC Limited, the framework for rational wealth creation is based on four components. The first is a *philosophy* of how wealth is created. Secondly, *principles* guide investment decisions. *Practices* measure and evaluate businesses for investment, and the *people*—the investment professionals—provide the dedication, knowledge, and expertise to produce consistent investment decisions.

According to Jonathan Wellum, chief investment officer and portfolio manager at AIC, "Our goal is to create long-term wealth for our clients by utilizing a disciplined buy-and-hold investment philosophy. Our essential principles are that we buy businesses, not stocks. We understand thoroughly the businesses we invest in and we measure long-term success, not short-term stock price movements."

These principles guide the company to invest in businesses that are understood completely; have honest and competent management; possess long-term competitive advantages; operate in industries with strong, long-term economic fundamentals; and can be purchased at attractive prices. Consequently, the average AIC Canadian equity fund holds fewer than 20 businesses. This is far different from the average Canadian equity funds, which hold the stocks of more than 225 businesses.

When considering the third component, practices, each business is evaluated on ten vital measures. Some criteria when considering companies include strong brand equity in the business, high returns on equity, a strong balance sheet, and breadth of products and clients. Excellent businesses have strong industry fundamentals such as above-average growth, consistent growth, and growing demand for products sold by the business.

Among other investments, AIC offers 18 mutual funds. Almost all of these funds have some component of foreign investment. By investing in countries other than Canada, an investor can have a diversified portfolio and not be completely dependent on what happens within our borders. Take the AIC Global Diversified Fund, as of May 31, 2004. Top holdings included Aventis S.A., Novartis AG, Nestlé S.A., Pernod Richard S.A., Molson Inc., and Berkshire Hathaway Inc. Investments by geographic area were as follows: the United Kingdom (20.6%), France (17.0%), Switzerland (13.2%), Canada (11.2%), the United States (10.9%), the Far East (4.8%), and Sweden (4.6%). The difference was in cash and other assets.

Ensuring strong investor returns depends on a sound research foundation. Since company shares within the fund will typically be held anywhere from three to five years (recall the buy and hold investment philosophy), AIC's Portfolio Management Team monitors daily news releases. Research analysts refer to the company's extensive database and ensure that a thorough analysis leads to understanding what is happening in each industry. Quarterly, earnings results are evaluated to make certain that investments continue to meet AIC's stringent principles and practices. If there is a material event, such as an acquisition, then a detailed evaluation will occur. Each company that is represented in a fund is visited by an AIC representative on a yearly basis. This may be through a personal visit or discussions with company representatives at conferences. Just because many investments are beyond our borders, it does not mean that they are not constantly evaluated.

"From conception to regulatory approval to execution, a new fund will take approximately six months," says Wellum. Continuously scanning the business environment and listening to their customers has led to plans to create a new fund in the months ahead. Such a move would offer a more complete product line to investors.

Sources: Interview with Jonathan Wellum, June 16, 2004; and www.aic.com.

INVESTING CHALLENGES IN THE 21ST-CENTURY MARKET

In dealing with the stock market, what goes up can also go down. Furthermore, it's a safe bet to presume that 21st-century markets will undergo changes and experience events that will only heighten their risk.

Investor confidence and trust in corporations and the stock market also eroded in the early 2000s. Investor trust that the real value of companies was fairly reflected in company financial statements was shattered by disclosures of financial fraud at companies such as Nortel, Corel, and Livent.[38]

Investment analysts also came under fire as information revealed that they often provided wildly optimistic evaluations about companies they knew were not worth their current prices.

Traditional brokers are changing the way they do business due to challenges from online brokers, which are attracting more and more investors. These challenges and changes, along with the growing influence and activity of institutional investors, promise to make securities markets exciting but not always stable places to be in the 21st century.

The basic lessons to keep in mind are the importance of diversifying your investments and understanding the risks of investing. Taking a long-term perspective is also a wise idea. The 1990s saw the market reach unparalleled heights only to collapse into a deep bear market in 2000–2002. Advertisements by brokerage firms in print and on television could make you think that investing in the market is guaranteed money in the bank. Don't be fooled, and don't be driven by greed. It's critical for you to know that there's no such thing as easy money or a sure thing. Investing is a challenging and interesting field that's always changing. If you carefully research companies and industries, keep up with the news, and make use of investment resources—such as newspapers, magazines, newsletters, the Internet, and TV programs—the payoff can be highly rewarding.

Summary

1. Figure 18.1 briefly lists the variety of financial organizations that comprise this industry.

   - **Why is this industry important to Canada?**

   The financial services industry employs more than one million Canadians, directly or indirectly. Its activities represent 5 percent of Canada's GDP. On a yearly basis, more than $9 billion in tax revenue to all levels of government is generated. Nearly $50 billion worth of services are exported annually. Because of its important role in the economy, the financial industry is one of the most regulated sectors in the country. Regulation is designed to ensure the integrity, safety, and soundness of financial institutions and markets.

   1. Describe the importance of the financial services industry in Canada.

2. Money is anything that people generally accept as payment for goods and services.

   - **How is the value of money determined?**

   The value of money depends on the money supply; that is, how much money is available to buy goods and services. Too much money in circulation causes inflation. Too little money causes deflation, recession, and unemployment.

   2. Explain what money is and how its value is determined.

3. As major players in Canada's financial industry, banks serve millions of customers.

   - **Who benefits from the services offered by banks?**

   Bank customers include individuals, small- and medium-sized businesses, large corporations, governments, institutional investors, and non-profit organizations. The major banks offer a full range of banking, investment, and financial services.

   3. Discuss the role that banks play in providing services.

4. List the five key criteria when selecting investment options.

4. The risk/return tradeoff is inherent in any investment strategy.

   • *What are the key criteria when selecting investment options?*
   Five key criteria are investment risk (the chance that an investment will be worth less at some future time than it's worth now); yield (the expected rate of return on an investment over a period of time); duration (the length of time your investment is committed to an investment); liquidity (how quickly you can get your money back if you need it); and tax consequences (how the investment will affect your tax situation).

5. Explain the opportunities in mutual funds as investments and the benefits of diversifying investments.

5. Diversification means buying several different types of investments (e.g., government bonds, preferred shares, common shares, etc.) with different degrees of risk. The purpose is to reduce the overall risk an investor would assume by investing in just one type of security.

   • *How can mutual funds help individuals diversify their investments?*
   A mutual fund is a fund that buys a variety of securities and then sells units of ownership in the fund to the public. Individuals who buy shares in a mutual fund are able to invest in many different companies they could not afford to invest in otherwise.

Key Terms

barter 555
buying on margin 570
capital gains 569
commercial bank 560
credit unions 552
diversification 573
money 555
money supply 556

mutual fund 572
nonbanks 552
pension funds 553
prime rate 558
prospectus 565
securities
  commission 565
securities dealer 564

stockbroker 566
stock exchange 565
stock splits 572
trust company 552

Developing Workplace Skills

1. In a small group discuss the following: What services do you use from banks? Does anyone use Internet banking? What seem to be the pluses and minuses of such online banking? Use this opportunity to compare the rates and services of various local banks.

2. Poll the class to see who uses banks and who uses a credit union or caisse populaire. (See the Taking It To The Net exercise for a background on credit unions and caisses populaires.) Have class members compare the services at each (interest rates given on accounts, the services available, and the loan rates). If anyone uses an online service, see how those rates compare. If no one uses a credit union or online bank, discuss the reasons.

3. Break up into small groups and discuss when and where you use cheques versus credit cards and cash. Do you often write cheques for small amounts? Would you stop doing that if you calculated how much it costs to process such cheques? Discuss your findings with others in the class.

4. Write a one-page paper on the role of the World Bank and the International Monetary Fund in providing loans to countries. Is it important for Canadian citizens to lend money to people in other countries through such organizations? Why or why not? Be prepared to debate the value of these organizations in class.

Purpose

To learn more about credit unions and caisses populaires in Canada.

Exercise

Credit Union Central is the national trade association and central finance facility for credit unions in Canada. Visit its Website at www.cucentral.ca and answer these questions.

1. How many credit unions and affiliated caisses populaires are there in Canada? What are their combined assets? How many members do they serve?

2. What is the credit union difference? Why might one prefer to conduct financial services transactions with a credit union instead of a commercial bank?

3. How are credit unions regulated?

4. If a credit union is not part of CDIC, how are deposits insured?

Purpose

To learn about services that are available to help consumers make educated decisions.

Exercise

Visit the Resource Centre at the Financial Consumer Agency of Canada, found at www.fcac-acfc.gc.ca/eng/consumers/resource. Answer the following questions.

1. What information must you receive when you open up a bank account?

2. Using the interactive tool Credit Card Costs Calculator, which credit card will cost you the least in interest and fees over a year, based on how you use your card?

3. What are some suggestions for protecting yourself against debit card fraud?

4. Using the Financial Services Charges Calculator, see if you can save on service fees when looking at different financial institutions.

5. If you have a complaint or problem with a federally regulated financial institution, what are the steps that you need to follow?

Practising Management Decisions

Case

Becoming Financially Secure

Mike and Priscilla Thomas are a married couple with two incomes and no children. Their cars are both paid for. They've saved enough money to buy a new house without selling their old one. (Real estate is typically a sound investment.) They're renting out their town house for added income. They hope to buy more rental property to use as an income producer so that they can both retire at age 50!

Priscilla runs a company called Cost Reduction Services and Associates. It advises small firms on ways to cut overhead expenses. The couple also owned a window-washing business when they were in college. Priscilla loves being in business for herself because, she says, "when you own your own business, you can work hard and you get paid for your hard work." Mike is a pharmaceutical salesperson.

How did the Thomases get the money to start their own businesses and buy a couple of homes? They committed themselves from the beginning of their marriage to live on Mike's income and to save Priscilla's income. Furthermore, they decided to live frugally. The goal of early retirement was their incentive. They "lived like college kids" for five years, cutting out coupons and saving every cent they could. They don't often go out to eat, and they rent movies for their VCR instead of going to the movie theatre.

Mike puts the maximum amount into his company's pension plan. It's invested in a very aggressive growth fund: half Canadian stocks and half international stocks. Now that the couple is financially secure, they're planning to have children.

Discussion Questions

1. When considering investment risk, where would you rank real estate relative to stocks, bonds, and mutual funds?
2. How can a financial services firm help a person develop a budget in order to achieve one's goals?
3. Do you agree with how Mike has allocated his pension plan contributions? Explain.
4. Can you see why money management is one of the keys to both entrepreneurship and personal financial security?

Source: *Marketplace*, July 31, 2002.

Video Case

ATMs

Many of us depend on bank machines for ready cash. You may also have noticed that many of these machines have changed in appearance. This video looks at a trend that may be coming to an ATM near you. This trend will cost you more money when you withdraw funds from your financial institution.

White-label machines are privately held cash machines with generic labels. They may be owned by financial institutions or by other private companies. They provide limited services; you cannot deposit money, transfer money, or pay bills. All they do is allow you to withdraw money.

Users are charged a surcharge (from $1 to $2) every time they withdraw money from a white-label machine. These machines are located in convenient locations such as variety stores and airports. Maybe you have seen one or used one.

Discussion Questions

1. Why are white-label machines attractive to financial institutions?
2. What surcharge do you pay if you use another institution's bank machine to withdraw your money? How is this surcharge divided among the financial institutions?
3. Do you think that it is good business for financial institutions to replace some of their branded machines with white-label machines? Explain.
4. Have you used a white-label machine? Seeing this video, are you less likely to use them in the future? Explain.

Appendix A

Using Technology to Manage Information

THE ROLE OF INFORMATION TECHNOLOGY

Throughout this text, we have emphasized the need for managing information flows among businesses and their employees, businesses and their suppliers, businesses and their customers, and so on. Since businesses are in a constant state of change, those managers who try to rely on old ways of doing things will simply not be able to compete with those who have the latest in technology and know how to use it.

Until the late 1980s, business technology was just an addition to the existing way of doing business. Keeping up-to-date was a matter of using new technology on old methods. But things started to change as the 1990s approached. Businesses shifted to using new technology on new methods. Business technology then became known as **information technology (IT),** and its role became to change business.

Obviously, the role of the information technology staff has changed as the technology itself has evolved. The chief information officer (CIO) has moved out of the back room and into the boardroom. Today the role of the CIO is to help the business use technology to communicate better with others while offering better service and lower costs.[1]

information technology (IT)
Technology that helps companies change business by allowing them to use new methods.

How Information Technology Changes Business

Time and place have always been at the centre of business. Customers had to go to the business during certain hours to satisfy their needs. We went to the store to buy clothes. We went to the bank to arrange for a loan. Businesses decided when and where we did business with them. Today, IT allows businesses to deliver goods ➤P. 23◀ and services ➤P. 25◀ whenever and wherever it is convenient for the customer. Thus, you can order clothes from The Shopping Channel, arrange a home mortgage loan by phone or computer, or buy a car on the Internet at any time you choose.

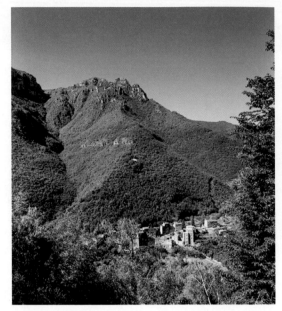

Thirteenth-century Italian village Colletta di Castelbianco found a new lease on life when an architect gave it a new design and high-speed Internet connectivity. The village is now a haven for mobile knowledge workers who want to live in medieval Italy but remain connected to the rest of the world. Do you think such "televillages" could become a model for future communities?

virtualization
Accessibility through technology that allows business to be conducted independent of location.

FIGURE A.1

HOW INFORMATION TECHNOLOGY IS CHANGING BUSINESS

This table shows a few ways that information technology is changing businesses, their employees, suppliers, and customers.

As IT breaks time and location barriers, it creates organizations and services that are independent of location. For example, the Toronto Stock Exchange and the TSX Venture Exchange are electronic stock exchanges without trading floors. Buyers and sellers make trades by computer.

Being independent of location brings work to people instead of people to work. With IT, data and information can flow thousands of kilometres in a second, allowing businesses to conduct work around the globe continuously. We are moving toward what is called **virtualization,** which is accessibility through technology that allows business to be conducted independent of location. For example, you can carry a virtual office in your pocket or purse. Such tools as cellular phones, pagers, laptop computers, and personal digital assistants allow you to access people and information as if you were in an actual office. Likewise, people who otherwise would not have met are forming virtual communities through computer networks.[2]

The way people do business drastically changes when companies increase their technological capabilities. Electronic communications can provide substantial time savings whether you work in an office, at home, or on the road. E-mail ends the tedious games of telephone tag and is far faster than paper-based correspondence.[3] Instant messaging (IM), best known as the preferred way for millions of teenagers to communicate with each other, is now a favourite business real-time communication tool.

Internet and intranet communication using shared documents and other methods allow contributors to work on a common document without time-consuming meetings. See Figure A.1 for other examples of how information technology changes business.

Organization	Technology is breaking down corporate barriers, allowing functional departments or product groups (even factory workers) to share critical information instantly.
Operations	Technology shrinks cycle times, reduces defects, and cuts waste. Service companies use technology to streamline ordering and communication with suppliers and customers.
Staffing	Technology eliminates layers of management and cuts the number of employees. Companies use computers and telecommunication equipment to create "virtual offices" with employees in various locations.
New products	Information technology cuts development cycles by feeding customer and marketing comments to product development teams quickly so that they can revive products and target specific customers.
Customer relations	Customer service representatives can solve customers' problems instantly by using companywide databases to complete tasks from changing addresses to adjusting bills. Information gathered from customer service interactions can further strengthen customer relationships.
New markets	Since it is no longer necessary for customers to walk down the street to get to stores, online businesses can attract customers to whom they wouldn't otherwise have access.

Moving from Information Technology toward Knowledge Technology

In the mid-1990s, yet another change occurred in the terminology of business technology as we started moving away from information technology and toward knowledge technology (KT). Knowledge is information charged with enough intelligence to make it relevant and useful. KT adds a layer of intelligence to filter appropriate information and deliver it when it is needed.

KT changes the traditional flow of information; instead of an individual going to the database ▶**P. 18**◀, the data comes to the individual.[4] For example, using KT business training software, AT&T can put a new employee at a workstation and then let the system take over to do everything from laying out a checklist of the tasks required on a shift to answering questions and offering insights that once would have taken up a supervisor's time.

KT "thinks" about the facts according to an individual's needs, reducing the time that person must spend finding and getting information. Businesspeople who use KT can focus on what's important: deciding about how to react to problems and opportunities.

The New Economy, in which technology is the key to growth, is based on brains, not brawn. The businesses that build flexible information infrastructures will have a significant competitive advantage. Constant changes in technology interact with each other to create more change. Maintaining the flexibility to successfully integrate these changes is crucial to business survival. History is filled with stories of once-mighty companies that couldn't keep up with the challenge of change: Packard Bell and RCA once dominated their industries but failed to compete effectively and have lost market share. They had size and money, but not flexibility. Knowledge sharing is at the heart of keeping pace with change.

In times past, businesspeople faced the problem of finding useful information; today, the problem is dealing with infoglut, which can confuse issues rather than clarify them. How can you judge the usefulness of the information you access?

MANAGING INFORMATION

Even before the use of computers, managers had to sift through mountains of information to find what they needed to help them make decisions. Today, businesspeople are deluged with information from voice mail, the Internet, fax machines, e-mail, and instant messaging. Businesspeople refer to this information overload as *infoglut*. Too much information can confuse issues rather than clarify them. How can managers keep from getting buried in the infoglut? Stepping back to gain perspective is the key to managing the flood of information.

The most important step toward gaining perspective is to identify the four or five key goals you wish to reach. Eliminating the information that is not related to those top priorities can reduce the amount of information flowing into your office by half. For example, as we were gathering information to include in this appendix, we collected more than 500 journal articles. Feeling the pressure of information overload, we identified the goals we wanted the appendix to accomplish and eliminated all the articles that didn't address those goals. As we further refined our goals, the huge stack of paper gradually dropped to a manageable size.

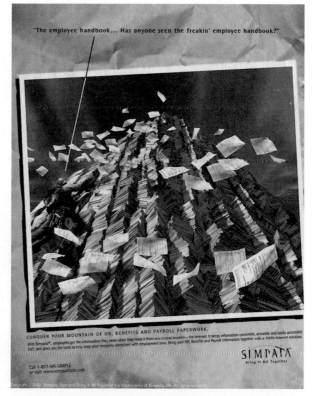

"The employee handbook... Has anyone seen the freakin' employee handbook?"

CONQUER YOUR MOUNTAIN OF HR, BENEFITS AND PAYROLL PAPERWORK.

SIMPATA
Bring It All Together

Call 1-877-HR-SIMPLE
or visit www.nomountain.com

Obviously, not all of the information that ends up on your desk will be useful. The usefulness of management information depends on four characteristics:

1. **Quality.**   Quality means that the information is accurate, valid, and reliable.

2. **Completeness.**   There must be enough information to allow you to make a decision but not so much as to confuse the issue. Today, as we have noted, the problem is often too much information rather than too little.

3. **Timeliness.**   Information must reach managers quickly. If a customer has a complaint, that complaint should be handled instantly if possible and certainly within no more than one day.

4. **Relevance.**   Different managers have different information needs. Again, the problem today is that information systems often make too much data available. Managers must learn which questions to ask to get the answers they need.

The important thing to remember when facing information overload is to relax. Set goals for yourself, and do the best you can. Remember, just because there is a public library doesn't mean you should feel guilty about not reading every book in it. And so it is with information.

Storing and Mining Data

It doesn't matter how interesting your information is if nobody's paying attention or can't get to the information they need when they need it. Storing, sorting, and getting useful information to the right people at the right time are the goals in managing information. How do businesses organize a data glut into useful information? The answer for many companies is a data warehouse. A *data warehouse* stores data on a single subject over a specific period of time.[5]

The whole purpose of a data warehouse is to get data out. *Data mining* is looking for hidden patterns in a data warehouse. Data mining software discovers previously unknown relationships among the data. Wal-Mart is an expert user of data mining. The retail giant has massive data warehouses that track sales on a minute-by-minute basis that can reveal regional and local sales trends. Using this information, Wal-Mart customizes each store's offerings on the basis of local demand, keeping it and its suppliers informed about how each of the 70,000 products in the stores is selling.[6]

The success of data mining depends on a number of factors, but perhaps the most important is access to data to mine in the first place. Frequently, organizations have a multitude of data storage systems that run on incompatible platforms. The divergent systems must be integrated in some way before the data can be connected.

Can a small firm look like an industry giant without spending giant sums of money? Bob Shallenberger of Rug World Oriental Rugs believed his company could. He needed contacts in the industry until he found a software program that specifically fit his firm's needs, for just a few thousand dollars.

THE ROAD TO KNOWLEDGE: THE INTERNET, INTRANETS, EXTRANETS, AND VIRTUAL PRIVATE NETWORKS

To manage knowledge, a company needs to learn how to share information throughout the organization and to implement systems for creating new knowledge. This

Neon HOT NOW signs signal us that Krispy Kreme's finest are ready. Store managers can't see the firm's sign at head office, but the firm's Web portal keeps store managers in direct contact with headquarters. Forecasting, ordering, and inventory are all done online.

need is leading to new technologies that support the exchange of information among staff, suppliers, and customers. Who wins and who loses in the new economy will be decided by who harnesses the technology that provides the pipeline of two-way interaction and information flow between individuals and organizations. At the heart of this technology are the Internet, intranets, extranets, and virtual private networks.

You already know that the Internet is a network of computer networks. Internet users can point and click their way from site to site with complete freedom. But what if you don't want just anybody to have access to your Website? You might create an intranet.

An **intranet** is a companywide network, closed to public access, that uses Internet-type technology. To prevent unauthorized outsiders (particularly the competition) from accessing their sites, companies can construct a firewall between themselves and the outside world to protect corporate information from unauthorized users. A firewall can consist of hardware, software, or both.[7] Firewalls allow only authorized users to access the intranet. Some companies use intranets to publish information for employees only, such as phone lists and employee policy manuals. These companies do not enjoy as high a return on their investment as other companies that create interactive intranet applications. Such applications include allowing employees to update their addresses or submit company forms such as supply requisitions, timesheets, or payroll forms online. These applications save money or generate revenue increases because they eliminate paper handling and enable decision making.

Many businesses choose to open their intranets to other, selected companies through the use of extranets. An **extranet** is a semiprivate network that uses Internet technology and allows more than one company to access the same information or allows people on different servers to collaborate.[8] One of the most common uses of extranets is to extend an intranet to outside customers. Extranets change the way we do business. No longer are the advantages of electronic data interchange (EDI) available only to the large companies that can afford such a system. Now almost all companies can use extranets to share data and process orders, specifications, invoices, and payments.

intranet
A companywide network, closed to public access, that uses Internet-type technology.

extranet
A semiprivate network that uses Internet technology and allows more than one company to access the same information or allows people on different servers to collaborate.

Notice that we described an extranet as a semiprivate network. This means that outsiders cannot access the network easily; but, since an extranet does use public lines, knowledgeable hackers (people who break into computer systems for illegal purposes such as transferring funds from someone's bank account to their own without authorization) can gain unauthorized access. Most companies want a network that is as private and secure as possible. One way to increase the probability of total privacy is to use dedicated lines (lines reserved solely for the network). There are two problems with this method: (1) It's expensive, and (2) it limits use to computers directly linked to those lines. What if your company needs to link securely with another firm or individual for just a short time? Installing dedicated lines between companies in this case would be too expensive and time-consuming. Virtual private networks are a solution.

virtual private network (VPN)
A private data network that creates secure connections, or "tunnels," over regular Internet lines.

A **virtual private network (VPN)** is a private data network that creates secure connections, or "tunnels," over regular Internet lines.[9] The idea of the VPN is to give the company the same capabilities at much lower cost by using shared public resources rather than private ones. This means that companies no longer need their own leased lines for wide-area communication but can instead use public lines securely. Just as phone companies provide secure shared resources for voice messages, VPNs provide the same secure sharing of public resources for data. This allows for on-demand networking: An authorized user can join the network for any desired function at any time, for any length of time, while keeping the corporate network secure.

The Front Door: Enterprise Portals

How do users log on to an organization's network? Frequently, through an enterprise portal that centralizes information and transactions. Portals serve as entry points to a variety of resources, such as e-mail, financial records, schedules, and employment and benefits files. Portals are more than simply Web pages with links. They identify users and allow them access to areas of the intranet according to their roles: customers, suppliers, employees, and so on. They make information available in one place so that users don't have to deal with a dozen different Web interfaces. The challenge to the CIO is to integrate resources, information, reports, and so on—all of which may be in a variety of places—so that they appear seamless to the user.[10]

Broadband Technology

As traffic on the Internet increases, the slower the connection becomes. New technologies unlock many of the traffic jams on the information superhighway. For example, **broadband technology** offers users a continuous connection to the Internet and allows them to send and receive mammoth files that include voice, video, and data much faster than ever before. The more bandwidth, the bigger the pipe for data to flow through—and the bigger the pipe, the faster the flow. Whether the broadband connection is by cable modem, digital subscriber lines (DSL), satellite, or fixed wireless, the impact is much the same. With broadband, data can reach you more than 50 times faster than with a dial-up connection using a 56k modem (the kind that came with most computers in the late 1990s and early 2000s).[11]

broadband technology
Technology that offers users a continuous connection to the Internet and allows them to send and receive mammoth files that include voice, video, and data much faster than ever before.

Even with broadband technology, the traffic on the information superhighway has become so intense that early Net settlers—scientists and other scholars—have found themselves being squeezed off the crowded Internet and thus unable to access, transmit, and manipulate complex mathematical models, data sets, and other digital elements of their craft. Their answer? Create another Internet, reserved for research purposes only.

The new system, **Internet2,** runs more than 22,000 times faster than today's public infrastructure and supports heavy-duty applications such as videoconferencing, collaborative research, distance education, digital libraries, and full-body simulations known as teleimmersion. A key element of Internet2 is a network called *very-high-speed backbone network service* (vBNS), which was set up in 1995 as a way to link government supercomputer centres and a select group of universities. The power of Internet2 makes it possible for a remote medical specialist to assist in a medical operation over the Internet without having to contend with deterioration of the connection as, say, home users check sports scores.[12]

Although Internet2 became available to only a few select organizations in late 1997, by 2002 there were more than 200 member universities.[13] Whereas the public Internet divides bandwidth equally among users (if there are 100 users, they each get to use 1 percent of the available bandwidth), Internet2 is more capitalistic. Users who are willing to pay more can use more bandwidth.

Cynics say that soon Internet2 itself will be overrun by networked undergrads engaged in song swapping and other resource-hogging pursuits. But the designers of Internet2 are thinking ahead. Not only do they expect Internet history to repeat itself, but they are counting on it. They are planning to filter the Internet2 technology out to the wider Internet community in such a way that there is plenty of room on the road for all of us—at a price, of course.

THE ENABLING TECHNOLOGY: HARDWARE

Rather than add potentially outdated facts to your information overload, we offer you a simple overview of the current computer technology.

Hardware includes computers, pagers, cellular phones, printers, scanners, fax machines, personal digital assistants (PDAs), and so on. The mobile worker can find travel-size versions of computers, printers, and fax machines that are almost as powerful and feature-laden as their big brothers. All-in-one devices that address the entire range of your communications needs are also available. For example, there are handheld units that include a wireless phone, fax and e-mail capabilities, Web browsers, and a personal information manager (PIM).

Cutting the Cord: Wireless Information Appliances

Some experts think we have entered the post-PC era—that is, they believe we are moving away from a PC-dominant environment and toward an array of Internet appliance options. Internet appliances are designed to connect people to the Internet and to e-mail.[14] They include equipment like PDAs (e.g., Blackberry and PalmPilot), smart phones, two-way paging devices, and in-dash computers for cars.[15]

The standardization of wireless networking has set the common PC free as well. No longer chained to their desks, laptop computer users find it liberating to have the mobility and flexibility to work on the Internet or company network anywhere they can tap into a wireless network. Wireless networks use a technology called Wi-Fi, from the term *wireless fidelity*. (Techies call Wi-Fi by its official name, 802.11, but Wi-Fi will do just fine for us.)[16] Wireless local-area networks in hotel rooms and airport lounges allow users with laptops outfitted

There's the right tool for every job. Bigger isn't always better. The first step in choosing the right information technology tool is to identify what it is you want to accomplish and then go from there. For example, there is no need to invest in a screaming, state-of-the-art computer if you plan to use it only for simple word processing.

Internet2
The new Internet system that links government supercomputer centres and a select group of universities; it runs more than 22,000 times faster than today's public infrastructure and supports heavy-duty applications.

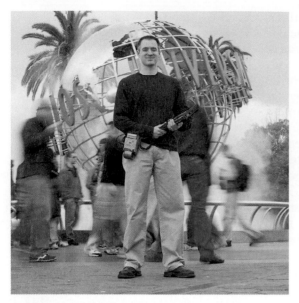

network computing system (client/server computing) Computer systems that allow personal computers (clients) to obtain needed information from huge databases in a central computer (the server).

with wireless modems to connect to the Web and download at 50 times the speed of typical dial-up connections.

Computer Networks

Perhaps the most dynamic change in business technology in recent years has been the move away from mainframe computers that serve as the centre of information processing and toward network systems that allow many users to access information at the same time. In an older system, the mainframe performed all the tasks and sent the results to a "dumb" terminal that could not perform those tasks itself. In a **network computing system** (also called **client/server computing**), personal computers (clients) can obtain needed information from huge databases in a central computer (the server). Networks connect people to people and people to data; they allow companies the following benefits:

- **Saving time and money.** SynOptics Communications found that electronic delivery of mail and files increased the speed of project development by 25 percent.

- **Providing easy links across functional boundaries.** With networks, it's easy to find someone who can offer insightful solutions to a problem. The most common questions on computer bulletin boards begin, "Does anyone know . . . ?" Usually, someone does.

- **Allowing employees to see complete information.** In traditional organizations, information is summarized so many times that it often loses its meaning. For example, a sales representative's two-page summary may be cut to a paragraph in the district manager's report and then to a few numbers on a chart in the regional manager's report. Networks, in contrast, catch raw information.

Networks have their drawbacks as well. Maintaining a fleet of finicky desktop PCs can be expensive. Studies show that the cost of maintaining one corporate Windows desktop computer can run up to $10,000 a year.[17] The cost of the computer itself is just the down payment. Computing costs go up with productivity losses as you upgrade and troubleshoot equipment and train employees to use it. By the time you've recouped your costs, it's time for another upgrade. A large part of PC support costs comes from adding software that causes conflicts or disables other software on the system. Making upgrades to two or three PCs in a small home office is annoying; making them to dozens or hundreds of PCs in a corporation is daunting. Using networks requires so many organizational changes and incurs such high support and upgrade costs that some companies that tried networking PCs are now looking at other options.

One option is a hybrid of mainframe and network computing. In this model, applications and data reside on a server, which handles all of the processing needs for all the client machines on the networks. The client machines look like the PCs that most people use, but they lack the processing power to handle applications on their own. Called *thin-client networks*, these new networks may resemble the ill-tempered dumb terminals of the 1980s, but the execution is much better. Users can still use the Windows applications that they had been using. In a thin-client network, software changes and upgrades need to be made only on the server, so the cost of ownership can be reduced by 20 percent.

Another option is to rent software and hardware access by way of the Internet as needed instead of trying to maintain your own network. Back in the Web boom, companies called application service providers (ASPs) ran software at data centres and rented access to these functions to customers who didn't want to buy expensive servers and software. Most ASPs went out of business because CIOs were slow to hand over their critical data to companies with no track record or little experience in their specific industries. But the fall of little ASPs didn't stop the flow of outsourcing ▶P. 269◀ IT functions to big service providers like IBM. IBM offers pay-as-you-go computing, even hourly rentals, involving all types of IT, from server access to supply-chain-management ▶P. 296◀ software.[18]

SOFTWARE

Computer software provides the instructions that enable you to tell the computer what to do. Although many people looking to buy a computer think first of the equipment, it is important to find the right software before finding the right hardware. The type of software you want dictates the kind of equipment you need.

Some programs are easier to use than others. Some are more sophisticated and can perform more functions than others. A businessperson must decide what functions he or she wants the computer system to perform and then choose the appropriate software. That choice will help determine what brand of computer to buy, how much power it should have, and what other peripherals it needs.

Although most software is distributed commercially through suppliers like retail stores or electronic retailers, there is some software, called **shareware,** that is copyrighted but distributed to potential customers free of charge. The users are asked to send a specified fee to the developer if the program meets their needs and they decide to use it. The shareware concept has become very popular and has dramatically reduced the price of software. **Public domain software (freeware)** is software that is free for the taking. The quality of shareware and freeware varies greatly. To help you have an idea of the quality of such programs, find a Website that rates shareware and freeware programs. For example, Sharewarejunkies.com lists the programs downloaded most often, editors' picks, and links to downloadable programs.

Businesspeople most frequently use software for (1) writing (word processors), (2) manipulating numbers (spreadsheets), (3) filing and retrieving data (databases), (4) presenting information visually (graphics), (5) communicating (e-mail and instant messaging), and (6) accounting. Today's software can perform many functions in one kind of program known as integrated software or a software suite. Another class of software program, called groupware, is used on networks. See Figure A.2 for a description of this software.

shareware
Software that is copyrighted but distributed to potential customers free of charge.

public domain software (freeware)
Software that is free for the taking.

EFFECTS OF INFORMATION TECHNOLOGY ON MANAGEMENT

The increase of information technology has affected management greatly and will continue to do so. Three major issues arising out of the growing reliance on information technology are human resource changes, security threats, and privacy concerns.

Word processing programs	With word processors, standardized letters can be personalized quickly, documents can be updated by changing only the outdated text and leaving the rest intact, and contract forms can be revised to meet the stipulations of specific customers. The most popular word processing programs include Corel WordPerfect, Microsoft Word, and Lotus WordPro.
Desktop publishing (DTP) software	DTP combines word processing with graphics capabilities that can produce designs that once could be done only by powerful page-layout design programs. Popular DTP programs include Microsoft Publisher, Adobe PageMaker Plus, and Corel Print Office.
Spreadsheet programs	A spreadsheet program is simply the electronic equivalent of an accountant's worksheet plus such features as mathematical function libraries, statistical data analysis, and charts. Using the computer's speedy calculations, managers have their questions answered almost as fast as they can ask them. Some of the most popular spreadsheet programs are Lotus 1-2-3, Quattro Pro, and Excel.
Database programs	A database program allows users to work with information that is normally kept in lists: names and addresses, schedules, inventories, and so forth. Using database programs, you can create reports that contain exactly the information you want in the form you want it to appear in. Leading database programs include Q&A, Access, Approach, Paradox, PFS: Professional File, PC-File, R base, and FileMaker Pro for Apple computers.
Personal information managers (PIMs)	PIMs or contact managers are specialized database programs that allow users to track communication with their business contacts. Such programs keep track of everything—every person, every phone call, every e-mail message, every appointment. Popular PIMs include Goldmine, Lotus Organizer, ACT, and ECCO Pro.
Graphics and presentation programs	Computer graphics programs can use data from spreadsheets to visually summarize information by drawing bar graphs, pie charts, line charts, and more. Inserting sound clips, video clips, clip art, and animation can turn a dull presentation into an enlightening one. Some popular graphics programs are Illustrator and Freehand for Macintosh computers, Microsoft PowerPoint, Harvard Graphics, Lotus Freelance Graphics, Active Presenter, and Corel Draw.
Communications programs	Communications software enables a computer to exchange files with other computers, retrieve information from databases, and send and receive electronic mail. Such programs include Microsoft Outlook, ProComm Plus, Eudora, and Telik.
Message centre software	Message centre software is more powerful than traditional communications packages. This new generation of programs has teamed up with fax/voice modems to provide an efficient way of making certain that phone calls, e-mail, and faxes are received, sorted, and delivered on time, no matter where you are. Such programs include Communicate, Message Centre, and WinFax Pro.
Accounting and finance programs	Accounting software helps users record financial transactions and generate financial reports. Some programs include online banking features that allow users to pay bills through the computer. Others include "financial advisers" that offer users advice on a variety of financial issues. Popular accounting and finance programs include Peachtree Complete Accounting, Simply Accounting, Quicken, and QuickBooks Pro.
Integrated programs	Integrated software packages (also called suites) offer two or more applications in one package. This allows you to share information across applications easily. Such packages include word processing, database management, spreadsheet, graphics, and communications. Suites include Microsoft Office, Lotus SmartSuite, and Corel WordPerfect Suite.
Groupware	Groupware is software that allows people to work collaboratively and share ideas. It runs on a network and allows people in different areas to work on the same project at the same time. Groupware programs include Lotus Notes, Frontier's Intranet Genie, MetaInfo Sendmail, and Radnet Web Share.

FIGURE A.2

TYPES OF POPULAR
COMPUTER SOFTWARE

Human Resource Issues

By now, you may have little doubt that computers are increasingly capable of providing us with the information and knowledge we need to do our daily tasks. The less creative the tasks, the more likely they will be managed by computers. For example, many telemarketing workers today have their work structured by computer-driven scripts. That process can apply to the work lives of customer service representatives, stockbrokers, and even managers. Technology makes the work process more efficient as it replaces many bureaucratic functions. Computers often eliminate middle management functions and thus flatten organization structures.

One of the major challenges technology creates for human resource managers is the need to recruit employees who know how to use the new technology or train those who already work in the company. Often companies hire consultants instead of internal staff to address these concerns. Outsourcing technical training allows companies to concentrate on their core businesses.

Perhaps the most revolutionary effect of computers and the increased use of the Internet and intranets is that of telecommuting. Mobile employees using computers linked to the company's network can transmit their work to the office, and back, from anywhere as easily as (and sometimes more easily than) they can walk into the boss's office.

Naturally, such work decreases travel time and overall costs, and often increases productivity. Telecommuting helps companies save money by allowing them to retain valuable employees during long pregnancy leaves or to tempt experienced employees out of retirement. Companies can also enjoy savings in commercial property costs, since having fewer employees in the office means a company can get by with smaller, and therefore less expensive, offices than before.

Studies show that telecommuting is most successful among people who are self-starters, who don't have home distractions, and whose work doesn't require face-to-face interaction with co-workers. Even as telecommuting has grown in popularity, however, some telecommuters report that a consistent diet of long-distance work gives them a dislocated feeling of being left out of the office loop. Some feel a loss of the increased energy people can get through social interaction. In addition to the isolation issue is the intrusion that work brings into what is normally a personal setting. Often people working from home don't know when to turn the work off. Some companies are pulling away from viewing telecommuting as an either–or proposition: either at home or at the office. Such companies are using telecommuting as a part-time alternative. In fact, industry now defines telecommuting as working at home a minimum of two days a week.

Electronic communication can never replace human communication for creating enthusiasm and esprit de corps. Efficiency and productivity can become so important to a firm that people are treated like robots. In the long run, such treatment decreases efficiency and productivity. Computers are a tool, not a total replacement for managers or workers, and creativity is still a human trait. Computers should aid creativity by giving people more freedom and more time. Often they do, but unfortunately many Canadians take the results of their productivity gains not in leisure (as do the Europeans), but in increased consumption, making them have to work even harder to pay for it all.

Security Issues

One current problem with computers that is likely to persist in the future is that they are susceptible to hackers.

Computer security is more complicated today than ever before. When information was processed in a mainframe environment, the single data centre was easier to control because there was limited access to it. Today, however, computers are accessible not only in all areas within the company but also in all areas of other companies with which the firm does business.

An ongoing security issue involves the spread of computer viruses over the Internet. A **virus** is a piece of programming code inserted into other programming to cause some unexpected and, for the victim, usually undesirable event. Viruses are spread by downloading infected programming over the Internet or by sharing an infected diskette. Often the source of the file you downloaded is unaware of the virus. The virus lies dormant until circumstances cause its code to be executed by the computer. Some viruses are playful ("Kilroy was here!"), but some can be quite harmful, erasing data or causing your hard drive to crash. There are programs, such as Norton's AntiVirus, that "inoculate" your computer so that it doesn't catch a known virus. But because new viruses are being developed constantly, antivirus programs may have only limited success. Therefore, you should keep your antivirus protection program up-to-date and, more important, practise "safe computing" by not downloading files from unknown sources and by using your antivirus program to scan diskettes before transferring files from them.

Existing laws do not address the problems of today's direct, real-time communication. As more and more people merge onto the information superhighway, the number of legal issues will likely increase. Today, copyright and pornography laws are crashing into the virtual world. Other legal questions—such as those involving intellectual property and contract disputes, online sexual and racial harassment, and the use of electronic communication to promote crooked sales schemes—are being raised as millions of people log on to the Internet.

virus
A piece of programming code inserted into other programming to cause some unexpected and, for the victim, usually undesirable event.

The Internet can add to worker productivity. Unfortunately, not all Internet activity is work-related. Workers often trade stocks, play games, or download music on the job. Companies such as N2H2 serve as virtual office tattle-tales as they manage and report employee Internet usage to managers. Do companies like N2H2 violate the privacy of workers on the job?

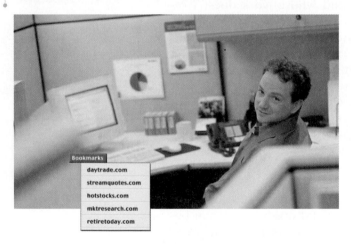

Some of your employees do so well with their day trading
that they only work part of the time.

Not all Internet activity at the office is work-related. Your company's productivity, bandwidth and legal liability are impacted when employees trade stocks or shop online, play video games, or download music or pornography. That's where N2H2 comes in. We manage, filter and report Internet content usage through proprietary interactive solutions that combine the latest technology and human review. In fact, with 12 million users, no one manages more Internet activity than we do. N2H2: Delivering the Web you want. To see how we can help your company, visit n2h2.com/enterprise1

Internet Usage Management | Monitoring | Reporting | Filtering

Privacy Issues

The increasing use of technology creates major concerns about privacy. For example, e-mail is no more private than a postcard. You don't need to be the target of a criminal investigation to have your e-mail snooped as more and more companies scan employee e-mail regularly and legally. Just as employers can log and listen to employees' telephone conversations, they can track e-mail in a search for trade secrets, non–work-related traffic, harassing messages, and conflicts of interest. Also, most e-mail travels over the Internet in unencrypted plain text. Any hacker with a desire to read your thoughts can trap and read your messages. This also applies to customers' and suppliers' data. Some e-mail systems, such as Lotus Notes, can encrypt messages so that you can keep corporate messages private. If you use browser-based e-mail, you can obtain a certificate that has an encryption key from a company such as VeriSign; the cost is about $10 a year. Of course, legitimate users who want to decrypt your mail need to get an unlocking key.

The Internet presents increasing threats to your privacy, as more and more personal information is stored in computers and people are able to access that data, legally or illegally. The Internet allows Web surfers to access all sorts of information about you. For example, some Websites allow people to search for vehicle ownership from a licence number or to find individuals' real estate property records. One key question in the debate over protecting our privacy is "Isn't this personal information already public anyway?" While it is, the difference is that the Net makes obtaining personal information too easy.

Average PC users are concerned that Websites have gotten downright nosy. In fact, many Web servers track users' movements online. Web surfers seem willing to swap personal details for free access to online information. This personal information can be shared with others without your permission. Websites often send **cookies** to your computer that stay on your hard drive. These are pieces of information, such as registration data or user preferences, sent by a Website over the Internet to a web browser that the browser is expected to save and send back to the server whenever the user returns to that Website. These little tidbits often simply contain your name and a password that the Website recognizes the next time you visit the site so that you don't have to re-enter the same information every time you visit. Other cookies track your movements around the Web and then blend that information with a database so that a company can tailor the ads you receive accordingly. Do you mind someone watching over your shoulder while you're on the Web?

cookies
Pieces of information, such as registration data or user preferences, sent by a Website over the Internet to a Web browser that the browser software is expected to save and send back to the server whenever the user returns to that Website.

Stability Issues

Although technology can provide significant increases in productivity and efficiency, instability in technology also has a significant impact on business. For example, candy maker Hershey discovered the Halloween trick was on it when the company couldn't get its treats to the stores on time. Failure of its new $115 million computer system disrupted shipments, and retailers were forced to order Halloween treats from other companies. Consequently, Hershey suffered a 12-percent decrease in sales that quarter. The list of computer glitches that have caused delays, outages, garbled data, and general snafus could go on and on.

What's to blame? Experts say it is a combination of computer error; human error; malfunctioning software; and an overly complex marriage of software, hardware, and networking equipment. Some systems are launched too quickly to be bug-proof, and some executives are too naive to challenge computer specialists. Industry consultant Howard Rubin says, "This stuff is becoming more critical to big business, yet some of it is built like Lego sets and Tinker Toys. It's not built for rigorous engineering, and people aren't properly trained to use it. As things get more complex, we'll be prone to more errors."[19]

www.mcgrawhill.ca/college/nickels

Key Terms

broadband
  technology 584
cookies 591
extranet 583
information
  technology (IT) 579
Internet2 585

intranet 583
network computing
  system (client/server
  computing) 586
public domain software
  (freeware) 587
shareware 587

virtual private
  network (VPN) 584
virtualization 580
virus 590

Appendix B

Working within the Legal Environment of Business*

THE NEED FOR LAWS

Imagine a society without laws. Just think, no speed limits to control how fast we drive, no age restrictions on the consumption of alcoholic beverages, no limitations on who can practise medicine—a society in which people are free to do whatever they choose, with no interference. Obviously, the more we consider this possibility, the more unrealistic we realize it is. Laws are an essential part of a civilized nation. Over time, though, the depth and scope of the body of laws must change to reflect the needs and changes in society. In the Canadian system of government, which uses the English model, there are three branches of government. Each has a role in the legal system, though sometimes the lines get blurred. The primary function of the *legislative branch* (comprised of the Parliament of Canada, the legislatures of the provinces, and the municipal councils) is to *make* the laws. The *executive branch* (e.g., government departments, administrative boards, and police departments) *administers* the laws, putting them into practice. The *judicial branch* (i.e., the courts) *interprets* and applies the laws when there is a dispute.

The Canadian court system has both federal and provincial courts, with jurisdiction that parallels the constitutional division of power between the central and provincial governments. The courts hear cases involving both criminal and civil law. *Criminal law* defines crimes, establishes punishments, and regulates the investigation and prosecution of people accused of committing crimes. *Civil law* involves legal proceedings that do not involve criminal acts; it includes laws regulating marriage, payment for personal injury, and so on. There are also appeal courts that hear appeals of decisions made at the initial trial, brought by the losing party in the case. Appeal courts can review and overturn decisions made by the trial court.

The law also governs the activities and operations of business in general. In fact, businesspeople often complain that the government is stepping in more and more to govern the behaviour of business. Thus, we have laws and

* Written by Ray Klapstein, Dalhousie University.

regulations regarding sexual harassment on the job, hiring and firing practices, leave for family emergencies, environmental protection, safety, and more. As you may suspect, businesspeople prefer to set their own standards of behaviour. However, the business community has not been perceived as implementing acceptable practices fast enough. To hasten the process, governments have expanded their control and enforcement procedures. In this appendix we will look at some of the laws and regulations now in place and how they affect business.

Business law refers to rules, statutes, codes, and regulations ➤P. 13◄ that are established to provide a legal framework within which business may be conducted and that are enforceable by court action. A businessperson should be familiar with laws regarding product liability, sales, contracts, fair competition, consumer protection, taxes, and bankruptcy. Let's start at the beginning and discuss the foundations of the law. It's hard to understand the law unless you know what the law is.

business law
Rules, statutes, codes, and regulations that are established to provide a legal framework within which business may be conducted and that are enforceable by court action.

STATUTORY AND COMMON LAW

There are two major kinds of law: statutory law and common law. Both are important for businesspeople.

Statutory law includes the laws that are made by the Parliament of Canada and the provincial legislatures, international treaties, and regulations and bylaws—in short, written law. You can read the statutes that make up this body of law, but they are often written in language whose meaning must be determined in court. That's one reason why there are so many lawyers in Canada! **Common law** is the body of law that comes from decisions handed down by judges. Common law is often referred to as *unwritten law* because it does not appear in any legislative enactment, treaty, or other such document. Under common law principles, what judges have decided in previous cases is very important to today's cases. Such decisions are called **precedents,** and they guide judges in the handling of new cases. Common law evolves through decisions made in trial courts, appellate courts, and special courts. Lower courts (trial courts) must abide by the precedents set by higher courts (appeal courts) such as the Supreme Court of Canada. In law classes, therefore, students study case after case to learn about common law as well as statutory law.

The Canadian legal system is complicated by the fact that federal law and provincial (including municipal) law in nine provinces operate under the English common law system. Provincial law in the Province of Quebec, though, operates under the French **civil law** system. The difference lies in that under the common law system courts actually *make* law through their decisions, while under the civil law system courts are restricted to *interpreting* the law that is provided by the provincial civil code.

statutory law
Federal and provincial legislative enactments, treaties of the federal government, and bylaws/ordinances—in short, written law.

common law
The body of law that comes from decisions handed down by judges; also referred to as *unwritten law.*

precedent
Decisions judges have made in earlier cases that guide the handling of new cases.

civil law
Legal proceedings that do not involve criminal acts.

Administrative Agencies

Different organizations within the government issue many rules, regulations, and orders. **Administrative agencies** are federal or provincial institutions and other government organizations created by Parliament or provincial legislatures with delegated power to pass rules and regulations within their mandated area of authority. Legislative bodies can not only create administrative agencies but also dissolve them. Some administrative agencies hold quasi-legislative, quasi-executive, and quasi-judicial powers. This means an agency is allowed to pass rules and regulations within its area of authority, conduct

administrative agencies
Federal or state institutions and other government organizations created by Parliament or provincial legislatures with delegated power to pass rules and regulations within their mandated area of authority.

investigations in cases of suspected rule violations, and hold hearings when it feels the rules and regulations have been violated.

Administrative agencies actually issue more rulings affecting business and settle more disputes than courts do. There are administrative agencies at the federal, provincial, and local levels of government. For example, these include:

1. **At the federal level:** The CRTC (i.e., Canadian Radio-television and Telecommunications Commission) regulates the use of the airwaves, OSFI (i.e., the Office of the Superintendent of Financial Institutions) regulates the operation of banks and other financial institutions, and the Commissioner of Competition is responsible for investigating complaints that the Competition Act has been violated.

2. **At the provincial level:** Public utility commissions and boards regulate prices for services like electricity, licensing boards set the qualifications required for practising trades and professions (e.g., the practice of medicine or law), and labour relations boards ➤P. 388◄ oversee the certification of unions.

3. **At the local level:** Zoning boards and planning commissions control land use and development, and there are school boards and police commissions.

TORT LAW

tort
A wrongful act that causes injury to another person's body, property, or reputation.

The tort system is an example of common law at work. A **tort** is a wrongful act that causes injury to another person's body, property, or reputation. This area of law comes within provincial jurisdiction, so legislation dealing with the topic comes from the provincial legislatures.

Although torts often are not criminal acts, victims can be awarded compensation. This is especially true if the conduct that caused harm is considered *intentional*. An intentional tort is a wilful act that results in injury. On the other hand, **negligence** is behaviour that causes unintentional harm or injury. Decisions involving negligence can often lead to huge judgments against businesses. In a highly publicized U.S. case, McDonald's lost a lawsuit to a person severely burned by its hot coffee. The jury felt the company failed to provide an adequate warning on the cup. Product liability is another example of tort law that's often very controversial. This is especially true regarding torts related to business actions. Let's look briefly at this issue.

negligence
In tort law, behaviour that does not meet the standard of care required and causes unintentional harm or injury.

Product Liability

Few issues in business law raise as much debate as product liability. Critics believe product liability laws have gone too far and deter product development. Others feel these laws should be expanded to include products such as software and fast food. **Product liability,** covered under tort law, holds businesses liable for harm that results from the production, design, sale, or use of products they market. At one time the legal standard for measuring product liability was whether a producer knowingly placed a hazardous product on the market. Today, many provinces have extended product liability to the level of **strict product liability.** Legally, this means *without regard to fault*. Thus, a company could be held liable for damages caused by placing a defective product on the market even if the company did not know of the defect at the time of sale. In such cases, the company is required to compensate the injured party financially. The rule of strict liability has caused

product liability
Part of tort law that holds businesses liable for harm that results from the production, design, sale, or use of products they market.

strict product liability
Legal responsibility for harm or injury caused by a product regardless of fault.

serious problems for businesses. For example, companies that produced lead-based paint in the past could be subject to expensive legal liabilities even though lead paint has not been sold for many years. The manufacturers of chemicals and drugs are also often susceptible to lawsuits under strict product liability. A producer may place a drug or chemical on the market that everyone agrees is safe. Years later, a side effect or other health problem could emerge. Under the doctrine of strict liability, the manufacturer could still be held liable. Businesses and insurance companies have called for legal relief from huge losses awarded in strict product liability suits. They have lobbied to set limits on the amounts of damages for which they are liable should their products harm consumers.

Intellectual Property: Patents, Copyrights, and Trademarks

Many people, perhaps including you, have invented products that are assumed to have commercial value. The question that obviously surfaces is what to do next. One step may be to apply for a patent. A **patent** gives inventors exclusive rights to their inventions for 20 years from the date they file their patent application. The Canadian Intellectual Property Office (http://cipo.gc.ca) receives the application and grants the patent. In addition to filing forms, the inventor must make sure the product is truly unique. Most inventors rely on lawyers who specialize in the field to manage the filing process.

patent
A document that gives inventors exclusive rights to their inventions for 20 years.

Patent owners have the right to sell or license the use of a patent to others. Foreign companies are also eligible to file for Canadian patents. Recent changes in the Patent Act and an international patent cooperation treaty permit any inventor who applies within 12 months of filing in his or her own country to obtain a uniform filing date in all participating countries.

The penalties for violating a patent can be very severe, but the defense of patent rights is solely the job of the patent holder. In a rather famous U.S. case (where the law regarding patents is much the same as in Canada), the camera and film company Polaroid was able to force Kodak to recall all of its instant cameras because Polaroid had several patents that Kodak violated. Kodak lost millions of dollars, and Polaroid maintained market leadership in instant cameras for many years. The possible remedies for patent infringement include money damages, injunctions prohibiting further infringements, and an accounting for all profits gained from the infringement.

Just as a patent protects an inventor's right to a product or process, a **copyright** protects a creator's rights to materials such as books, articles, photos, paintings, and cartoons. Copyright is protected by the Copyright Act, a federal statute. The protection of a copyright extends for the life of the original author plus 50 years after his or her death. Registration of the copyright is not required, but provides the benefit of public notice of its existence and provides proof of the copyright holder's ownership of the work.

copyright
A document that protects a creator's rights to materials such as books, articles, photos, and cartoons.

Recall from Chapter 15 that a trademark is a brand that has been given legal protection for both the brand name ▶P. 418◀ and the pictorial design. Trademarks generally belong to the owner forever, as long as they are properly registered and renewed every 15 years. Some well-known trademarks include the Pillsbury Doughboy, the Disney Company's Mickey Mouse, the Nike swoosh, and the golden arches of McDonald's. Like a patent, a trademark is protected from infringement. Companies fight hard to protect trademarks, especially in global markets where pirating can be extensive. Like patents, there are specific requirements imposed by the Trade-marks Act, the most difficult one being that the trademark must be "distinctive."

The fourth type of intellectual property protected by federal legislation in Canada is an **industrial design.** Industrial designs differ from things that can be copyrighted by the fact that they are produced by an industrial process.

industrial design
Visible feature(s) of a finished product that identify it and are protected by the law (e.g., its shape or ornamentation).

For example, fine china dinnerware would be a product that would fall into this category. As with the other types of intellectual property, the design of the subject matter must be original.

THE SALE OF GOODS

Each of Canada's provinces has a statute called the Sale of Goods Act. With limited exceptions (i.e., contracts where the price is below the minimum set by the individual province's Act), this Act applies to all contracts for the sale of goods. A sale contract is different from others in that there must be a transfer of ownership of goods in return for money consideration. Except in Ontario and British Columbia, a contract for the sale of goods must be written. There are exceptions, though. For example, where part of the goods have actually been received by the buyer, there has been partial payment of the price, or an "earnest" has been given to demonstrate sincerity. The Sale of Goods Act establishes the rules and requirements associated with the deal, establishing the respective rights and obligations of the parties of the contract.

Warranties

A warranty guarantees that the product sold will be acceptable for the purpose for which the buyer intends to use it. There are two types of warranties. **Express warranties** are specific representations by the seller that buyers rely on regarding the goods they purchase. The warranty you receive in the box with a clock, toaster, or DVD player is the express warranty. It spells out the seller's warranty agreement. **Implied warranties** are legally imposed on the seller. It is implied, for example, that the product will conform to the customary standards of the trade or industry in which it competes. For example, it's expected that a toaster will toast your bread to your desired degree (light, medium, dark) or that food bought for consumption off an establishment's premises is fit to eat.

Warranties offered by sellers can be either full or limited. A full warranty requires a seller to replace or repair a product at no charge if the product is defective, whereas a limited warranty typically limits the defects or mechanical problems that are covered. Many of the rights of buyers, including the acceptance and rejection of goods, are spelled out in the Sale of Goods Act, so both buyers and sellers should be familiar with its provisions.

express warranties
Specific representations by the seller that buyers rely on regarding the goods they purchase.

implied warranties
Guarantees legally imposed on the seller.

NEGOTIABLE INSTRUMENTS

Negotiable instruments are forms of commercial paper, and come in three types: promissory notes, cheques, and bills of exchange. A promissory note ▶P. 532◀ is a written contract with a promise to pay a sum of money in the future. A cheque is an instruction to a bank to make a payment. A bill (or draft) is an order to make a payment. They are regulated by the federal Bills of Exchange Act. All three types are transferable among businesses and individuals and represent a promise to pay a specified amount. They must be (1) written and signed by the maker or drawer, (2) payable on demand or at a certain time, (3) payable to the bearer (the person holding the instrument) or to a specific order, and (4) contain an unconditional promise to pay a specified amount of money. Negotiable instruments are transferred (negotiated for payment) when the payee signs the back. The payee's signature is referred to as an *endorsement*.

negotiable instruments
Forms of commercial paper (such as cheques) that are transferable among businesses and individuals and represent a promise to pay a specified amount.

CONTRACT LAW

If I offer to sell you my bike for $35 and later change my mind, can you force me to sell the bike, saying we had a contract? If I lose $120 to you in a poker game, can you sue in court to get your money? If I agree to sing at your wedding for free and back out at the last minute, can you claim I violated a contract? These are the kinds of questions that contract law answers.

A **contract** is a legally enforceable agreement between two or more parties. **Contract law** specifies what constitutes a legally enforceable agreement. Basically, a contract is legally binding if the following conditions are met:

1. **An offer is made.** An offer to do something or sell something can be oral or written. If I agree to sell you my bike for $35, I have made an offer. That offer is not legally binding, however, until other conditions are met.

2. **There is a voluntary acceptance of the offer.** Both parties to a contract must voluntarily agree on the terms. If I used duress in getting you to agree to buy my bike, the contract would not be legal. Duress occurs if there is coercion through force or threat of force. You couldn't use duress to get me to sell my bike, either. Even if we both agree, though, the contract is still not legally binding without the next four conditions.

3. **Both parties give consideration.** **Consideration** means something of value, and there must be a flow of consideration in both directions. If I agree to sell you my bike for $35, the bike and the $35 are consideration, and we have a legally binding contract. If I agree to sing at your wedding and you do not give me anything in return (consideration), we have no contract.

4. **Both parties are competent.** A person under the influence of alcohol or drugs, or a person of unsound mind (e.g., one who has been legally declared incompetent), cannot be held to a contract. In many cases, a minor may not be held to a contract either. For example, if a 15-year-old agrees to pay $10,000 for a car, the seller will not be able to enforce the contract due to the buyer's lack of competence.

5. **The contract must be legal.** A contract to do something illegal cannot be enforced. For example, a contract for the sale of illegal drugs or stolen merchandise would be unenforceable since both types of sales are violations of criminal law.

6. **The contract is in proper form.** Provincial legislation in each province requries that an agreement for the sale of goods for more than a fixed amount (e.g., $200) must be in writing. Contracts that cannot be fulfilled within one year and contracts regarding real property (land and everything attached to it) must be in writing as well.

Breach of Contract

Breach of contract occurs when one party fails to follow the terms of a contract. Both parties may voluntarily agree to end a contract. While in force, however, if one person violates the contract, the following remedies may be available.

1. **Specific performance.** The person who violated the contract may be required to live up to the agreement if money damages would not be adequate. For example, if I legally offered to sell you a rare painting, I would have to actually sell you that painting.

---

contract
A legally enforceable agreement between two or more parties.

contract law
Set of laws that specify what constitutes a legally enforceable agreement.

consideration
Something of value; consideration is one of the requirements of a legal contract.

breach of contract
When one party fails to follow the terms of a contract.

damages
The monetary settlement awarded to a person who is injured by a breach of contract.

2. **Payment of damages.**   The term **damages** refers to the monetary settlement awarded by the court to a person who is injured by a breach of contract. If I fail to live up to a contract, you can sue me for damages, usually the amount you would lose from my nonperformance. If we had a legally binding contract for me to sing at your wedding, for example, and I failed to come, you could sue me for the cost of hiring a new singer.

3. **Discharge of obligation.**   If I fail to live up to my end of a contract, you could agree to drop the matter. Generally you would not have to live up to your end of the agreement either.

Lawyers would not be paid so handsomely if the law were as simple as implied in these rules of contracts. In fact, it is always best to have a contract in writing even if not required under law. The offer and consideration in a contract should be clearly specified, and the contract should be signed and dated. A contract does not have to be complicated as long as it has these elements: it is in writing, mutual consideration is specified, and there is a clear offer and agreement.

LAWS TO PROMOTE FAIR AND COMPETITIVE PRACTICES

One objective of legislators is to pass laws that the judiciary will enforce to ensure a competitive atmosphere among businesses and promote fair business practices. In Canada, the Competition Bureau and other government agencies serve as watchdogs to ensure that competition among sellers flows freely and that new competitors have open access to the market. The scope of the governments' approach on this is broad and extensive.

There was, however, a time when big businesses were able to drive smaller competitors out of business with little resistance. The following discussion shows how government responded to these troubling situations in the past and how businesses must deal with new challenges facing them today.

The changing nature of business from manufacturing to knowledge technology has called for new levels of regulation on the part of federal agencies.

For example, Microsoft's competitive practices have been the focus of intense investigation in countries around the globe. One of the major accusations against the computer software giant was that it hindered competition by refusing to sell the Windows operating system to computer manufacturers unless they agree to sell Windows-based computers exclusively. This gives computer manufacturers a difficult choice: buy only Windows or don't buy Windows at all! Given that many consumers wanted Windows, the computer companies had little choice but to agree.

LAWS TO PROTECT CONSUMERS

consumerism
A social movement that seeks to increase and strengthen the rights and powers of buyers in relation to sellers.

Consumerism is a social movement that seeks to increase and strengthen the rights and powers of buyers in relation to sellers. Although consumerism is not a new movement, it has taken on new vigour and direction in the early 2000s because of the corporate scandals and greed involving companies such as Enron and WorldCom. Consumers have been particularly critical of government for its lack of oversight and action in the securities markets.

The protection of consumers has only recently come into vogue as a suitable topic for legislation. In earlier times, legislators deemed it appropriate to leave this to the common law, supplemented by the provisions of the Sale of

Goods Act. The modern phenomenon of concentration of economic power in large manufacturing and distributing companies and in financial institutions has dramatically eroded the relative bargaining power of the consumer. The technical sophistication of modern products makes it impossible for consumers to detect product defects in advance. Price, quality, and safety have become matters that are often not negotiable: the consumer's choice is to accept or not accept the product, as is. Because of the inequality of bargaining power held by consumers in comparison to large retailers, manufacturers, and financial institutions, legislators have deemed it appropriate to intervene, readjusting the balance by protecting the consumer. The topics that have received the most attention are product performance and business practices.

Product Performance

The Parliament of Canada has enacted several major statutes dealing with consumer safety and product performance. The Consumer Packaging and Labelling Act establishes requirements for disclosing ingredients and quantities, and includes provision for some standardization of package sizes. The Textile Labelling Act requires disclosure of the fabrics and fibres in wearing apparel, together with recommended cleaning procedures. The Weights and Measures Act establishes a uniform system for weighing and measuring goods sold to consumers. The Food and Drugs Act provides for inspection and regulation of food and drugs, requires purity and sanitary storage, and restricts the distribution of potentially harmful substances. The Hazardous Products Act establishes a list of dangerous products that it is illegal to manufacture, and regulations governing the manufacture, packaging, and distribution of other products that can be harmful. The Motor Vehicle Safety Act and the Aeronautics Act establish national standards, specifying safety features that must be provided in motor vehicles and aircraft.

This federal legislation is supplemented by provincial legislation in all provinces. Some provinces have been much more active in this regard than others. In most, this legislation appears in a provincial consumer protection Act, but provisions designed to protect consumers appear in other Acts as well.

Business Practices

With respect to door-to-door sales, most provinces have legislation permitting the consumer to rescind a purchase contract within a specified "cooling off" period. All provinces also have registration and licensing requirements for door-to-door sellers and collection agencies, designed to prevent the use of harassment and pressure. Most also provide that a consumer who receives unsolicited goods through the mail is not liable to pay for them, or even to return them. Most provinces have also established statutory warranties with regard to contracts for the purchase and sale of consumer durables, voiding attempts to negate the warranties implied by the Sale of Goods Act.

Misleading Advertising

One of the major topics addressed by the Competition Act, mentioned earlier in this appendix, is misleading advertising. False or misleading representations about the characteristics of a product are prohibited. These include statements, warranties, and guarantees about the performance, efficacy, or length of life of a product that are not based upon adequate or proper testing, and by placing the onus on anyone making such representations to prove that they are based on testing. Misleading representations about the "ordinary" price of a product are also prohibited, as is the advertising of products for sale at a "bargain" price when the advertiser does not have reasonable quantities available for sale.

Most provinces supplement the federal legislation in this area, in much the same way as they do with regard to product performance requirements. The Ontario Business Practices Act, for example, prohibits false representations about product performance.

TAX LAWS

Mention the word *taxes* and most people frown. That's because taxes affect almost every individual and business in the country. Taxes are how the government (federal, provincial, and local) raises money. Traditionally, taxes have been used primarily as a source of funding for government operations and programs. They have also been used as a method of encouraging or discouraging taxpayers from doing something. For example, if the government wishes to reduce the use of certain classes of products (cigarettes, liquor, etc.), it passes what are referred to as *sin taxes*. The additional cost of the product from increased taxes perhaps discourages additional consumption. In other situations, the government may encourage businesses to hire new employees or purchase new equipment by offering a tax credit. A tax credit is an amount that can be deducted from a tax bill.

Taxes are levied from a variety of sources. Income (personal and business), sales, and property are the major bases of tax revenue. The federal government receives its largest share of taxes from income. Provinces and local communities often make extensive use of sales taxes and taxes on real property. School districts are often largely dependent on real property taxes. The tax policies of provinces and cities are taken into consideration when businesses seek to locate operations. Tax policies also affect personal decisions such as retirement. A key tax issue sure to reappear in the 21st century involves Internet taxation, especially taxing Internet transactions (e-commerce). The European Union has already decided to levy certain Internet taxes. Expect this issue to be debated fiercely in the years ahead.

BANKRUPTCY AND INSOLVENCY

bankruptcy
The legal process by which a person, business, or government entity unable to meet financial obligations is relieved of those obligations by a court that divides any assets among creditors, allowing creditors to get at least part of their money and freeing the debtor to begin anew.

voluntary bankruptcy
Legal procedures initiated by a debtor.

involuntary bankruptcy
Bankruptcy procedures filed by a debtor's creditors.

The **bankruptcy** process recognizes that a debtor can reach a point where he or she will never be able to meet all obligations to creditors. The process is designed to minimize the negative impact of this situation for both debtor and creditor. The Bankruptcy and Insolvency Act, a federal statute, establishes a uniform national system for dealing with the problem. It is designed to achieve a reasonable and fair distribution of the debtor's assets among creditors, and to release the honest debtor in this position from ongoing obligations that cannot possibly be met, allowing him or her to resume business activity without them.

The provinces continue to have jurisdiction over an individual's financial affairs until he or she becomes insolvent or bankrupt. Once a person becomes bankrupt, the central government has jurisdiction to enact laws governing the rights and obligations of bankrupts and their creditors.

Bankruptcy can be either voluntary or involuntary. In **voluntary bankruptcy** cases the debtor applies for bankruptcy, whereas in **involuntary bankruptcy** cases the creditors start legal procedures against the debtor. Most bankruptcies today are voluntary because creditors usually want to wait in hopes that they will be paid all of the money due them rather than settle for only part of it.

The Bankruptcy and Insolvency Act establishes the scheme of distribution to be followed by the trustee in settling the claims of a bankrupt person's creditors. There are three basic categories of creditors for these purposes.

The highest priority is given to *secured creditors*, who have a direct claim against a specified asset of the debtor. When a debtor goes through bankruptcy proceedings, secured creditors are entitled to the entire proceeds realized on the sale of the asset in which they hold security, up to the secured amount owed to them by the debtor.

The second class of creditors is *preferred creditors*, and they have priority over general or unsecured creditors. This category includes trustees and lawyers involved in the process, unpaid employees of the bankrupt individual, and unpaid taxes.

The third group is the *unsecured creditors*, who do not have a direct claim against any asset and are not given preferred treatment by the Act. Unsecured claims include amounts owed to secured or preferred creditors that are in excess of the amount secured or preferred. All unsecured claims are treated equally by the Act, with each entitled to receive the same amount per dollar owed from the trustee in settlement of the amount claimed.

The bankrupt's contractual obligations to his or her creditors are discharged once he or she has complied fully with the terms of the arrangement that has been made by the trustee and accepted by the court. Payment of the established proportion of unsecured obligations, rather than payment in full, is sufficient to discharge all obligations. However, the discharge of a bankrupt is not automatic; it is a matter within the court's discretion. Whether a discharge is granted depends on matters like whether the person is a first-time bankrupt. Also, a discharge doesn't cover absolutely all obligations. Some obligations continue anyway. These include fines, child support payments, and amounts gained through fraud.

The Companies' Creditors Arrangement Act

The Companies' Creditors Arrangement Act (CCAA) is a federal statute that provides a second option in the commercial context for insolvent debtors to avoid bankruptcy proceedings. It makes provision for the restructuring of business debt when a company is unable to meet its financial obligations. The CCAA enables a company to submit a proposal to its creditors for an arrangement without bankruptcy proceedings. It permits a company to remain in business even though insolvent, and protects it from proceedings by creditors who might wish to force it into bankruptcy. The benefit to creditors is orderly conduct of the debtor's affairs, by maintaining the status quo while the debtor attempts to gain its creditors' approval of the plan and, if the plan is approved, payment by its terms. The attempts to financially restructure Air Canada and Stelco in the early years of this decade have been made under the CCAA.

The CCAA and the Bankruptcy and Insolvency Act work in concert with each other. The Bankruptcy and Insolvency Act expressly provides that it does not affect the operation of the CCAA, and allows the court to order continuation of a proposal made under the Bankruptcy and Insolvency Act under the CCAA.

DEREGULATION

Canada now has laws and regulations covering almost every aspect of business. In recent years public concern that there are *too* many laws and regulations,

deregulation
Government withdrawal of certain laws and regulations that seem to hinder competition.

and that these laws and regulations cost the public too much money, has developed. Thus began the movement toward deregulation. **Deregulation** means that the government withdraws certain laws and regulations that seem to hinder competition. Perhaps the most publicized examples of deregulation were those in the airlines and telecommunications industries. Government used to severely restrict airlines with regard to where they could land and fly. When such restrictions were lifted, the airlines began competing for different routes and charging lower prices. This has provided a clear benefit to consumers, but puts tremendous pressure on the airlines to be competitive. Airlines such as WestJet have taken advantage of the opportunities, while Air Canada has had difficulty adapting. Similar deregulation in telecommunications has given consumers a flood of options in the telephone service market.

It seems some regulation of business is necessary to ensure fair and honest dealings with the public. Still, businesses have adapted to the laws and regulations, and have done much toward producing safer, more effective products. However, corporate scandals since the turn of the century have soured what appeared to be better dialogue and cooperation between business and government. Many in government and society called for even more government regulation and control of business operations to protect investors and workers. With global competition increasing and small and medium-sized businesses striving to capture selected markets, business and government need to continue to work together to create a competitive environment that is fair and open. If businesses do not want additional regulation, they must accept their responsibilities to all their stakeholders.

Key Terms

administrative agencies 593
bankruptcy 600
breach of contract 597
business law 593
civil law 593
common law 593
consideration 597
consumerism 598
contract 597
contract law 597

copyright 595
damages 598
deregulation 602
express warranties 596
implied warranties 596
industrial design 595
involuntary bankruptcy 600
negligence 594

negotiable instruments 596
patent 595
precedent 593
product liability 594
statutory law 593
strict product liability 594
tort 594
voluntary bankruptcy 600

References

Chapter 1

1. "Riders on the Storm," *Forbes,* March 18, 2002, p. 101; and "100 Wealthiest People in Canada," [n.d.], *Canadian Business,* Retrieved from http://www.canadianbusiness.com/rich100.
2. "Did You Know That?" *Bottom Line Personal,* January 1, 2003, p. 7.
3. "My Big Fat Greek Wedding," *Fortune,* December 30, 2002, p. 174.
4. Caroline Alphonso. "University students get degree of relief," *The Globe and Mail,* September 3, 2004, p. A5.
5. Immen Wallace. "Non-profits hurt by lack of benefits," *The Globe and Mail,* October 15, 2003, p. C1.
6. Shahrzad Elghanayan, "Loan Ranger," *Worth,* January/February 2003, p. 46.
7. A. Mlynek, "Live and Let Learn," *Canadian Business,* July 2, 2003. Retrieved May 14, 2004 from http://canadianbusiness75.com/profile15.htm; and "The History of Tim Hortons," [n.d.], Oakville: The TDL Group Ltd., Retrieved May 17, 2004 from http://www.timhortons.com.
8. Brook Manville and Josiah Ober, "Beyond Empowerment," *Harvard Business Review,* January 2003, pp. 48–53.
9. "Sources of Canadian Law," April 24, 2003, Canada: Department of Justice Canada. Retrieved from http://canada.justice.gc.ca/en/dept/pub/just/CSJ_page7.html.
10. "Competition Act (1985, c. C34)," August 8, 2003, Canada: Department of Justice Canada. Retrieved from http://laws.gc.ca/en/C-34/34446.html.
11. "Indepth: Sponsorship Scandal—Who's who: Companies," February 17, 2004, Toronto: CBC News. Retrieved from http://www.cbc.ca/news/background/groupaction/sponsorshipprogram.html.
12. E. Oziewicz, "Scandals lower Canada's corruption-scale ranking," *The Globe and Mail,* October 8, 2003. Retrieved from http://www.theglobeandmail.com/servlet/ArticleNews/TPPrint/LAC/20031008/UCORRM/TPNational.
13. Mark Athitakis, "How to Make Money on the Net," *Business2.0,* May 2003, pp. 83–84.
14. David Kirkpatrick, "Stupid-Journal Alert: Why HBR's View of Tech Is Dangerous," *Fortune,* June 9, 2003, p. 190.
15. Brad Wieners, "Escape from L.A.," *Business 2.0,* July 2002, p. 63.
16. Robert J. Samuelson, "The Spirit of America," *Newsweek,* January 13, 2003, p. 47.
17. Marina Strauss, "Longo to acquire Grocery Gateway, *The Globe and Mail,* August 25, 2004, p. B6.
18. David Foot with Daniel Stoffman, *Boom Bust & Echo 2000* (Toronto: Macfarlane Walter & Ross, 1998), 24–31.
19. Ibid.
20. "Immigrant population by place of birth and period of immigration," May 13, 2003, Ottawa: Statistics Canada. Retrieved from www.statscan.ca/english/Pgdb/demo25.htm; "Proportion of foreign-born population, provinces and territories," May 12, 2003, Ottawa: Statistics Canada. Retrieved from www.statscan.ca/english/Pgdb/demo46a.htm.
21. John Conway, *Canadian Family in Crisis,* 5th ed. (Toronto: James Lorimer & Co. Ltd., 2003), 260.
22. Ibid., 261.
23. "Canada's Innovation Strategy," April 16, 2004, Ottawa: Government of Canada. Retrieved from http://www.innovationstrategy.gc.ca/gol/innovation/interface.nsf/engdocBasic/3.html.
24. "Employment by industry and sex," September 29, 2003, Ottawa: Statistics Canada. Retrieved from www.statscan.ca/english/Pgdb/labour10bb.htm.
25. "Allan Rock and the Canadian Tourism Commission to Dedicate $20 Million to Promoting Canadian Tourism," May 10, 2003, Ottawa: Industry Canada. Retrieved from http://www.ic.gc.ca/cmb/.

Chapter 2

1. Moon Ihlwan and Brian Bremmer, "The Other Korean Crisis," *Business Week,* January 20, 2003, pp. 44–52.
2. Justin Gillis, "Old Laws, New Fish," *Washington Post,* January 15, 2003, p. E1.
3. "Transportation," 2004, Burnaby: Ballard Power Systems. Retrieved May 22, 2004 from http://www.ballard.com/tC.asp?pgid=44.
4. Peter Wilson, "Everybody's one-stop shopping, selling at the eBay," *The Vancouver Sun,* April 17, 2004, p. A10.
5. "McMaster University receives Canada's largest cash gift," December 17, 2003, Hamilton: McMaster University. Retrieved from http://www.newswire.ca/en/releases/archive/December 2003/17/c3727.html.
6. Bank Revenues and Earnings (Profits)," June 2004, Toronto: Canadian Bankers Association. Retrieved from www.cbc.ca/en/ViewDocument.asp?fl=6651=111&H=docid=420.
7. Geoffrey Colvin, "Shareholders Are No Fools—Anymore," *Fortune,* July 7, 2003, p. 42.
8. Astrid Wendlandtland and Alison Tudor, "Government to sell part of France Telecom stake," *The Globe and Mail,* September 3, 2004, sec. B.
9. Jack Anderson, "Companies Hate Misery," *Fortune,* June 23, 2003, p. 58.
10. Figures are from the year 2000.
11. Moon Ihlwan and Brian Bremmer, "The Other Korean Crisis," *Business Week,* January 20, 2003, pp. 44–52.
12. "Council Condemns DeVry's Status," *CAUT Bulletin,* June 2001, p. A8.
13. Daily Archives, Statistics Canada, www.statcan.ca, May 1999.
14. "Gross domestic product, expenditure-based," September 16, 2003, Ottawa: Statistics Canada. Retrieved from www.statscan.ca/english/Pgdb/econ04.htm.
15. Bruce Little, "Standard of living tied to job growth, productivity gains," *The Globe and Mail,* June 9, 2003, p. B3.
16. Marian Stinson, "Blackout shocks economy in August," *The Globe and Mail,* November 1, 2003, p. B1.
17. Art Chamberlain, "Is productivity all it's cracked up to be?" *The Globe and Mail,* September 17, 2003, p. C6.
18. "Deflation Warning," *Washington Times,* January 9, 2003, p. A16.
19. Neil Weinberg, "Hot Commodities," *Forbes,* January 20, 2003, pp. 97–99.

20. "Industrial product and raw materials price indexes," April 30, 2003, Ottawa: Statistics Canada. Retrieved from www.statscan.ca/Daily/English/030430/d030430b.htm.
21. Ibid.

Chapter 3

1. Erin Kelly, "Sanders Going to China to Battle Trade Imbalance," Gannett News Service, January 8, 2003.
2. Keith McArthur, "Air Canada future lies abroad, Milton says," *The Globe and Mail*, October 29, 2003, p. B1.
3. Simon Tuck, "Rogers eyes U.S. market for growth," *The Globe and Mail*, October 8, 2003, p. B18.
4. Greg Keenan, "As Big Three lost ground, auto parts firms expand in Japan," *The Globe and Mail*, October 24, 2003, p. B4.
5. Patrick White, "Bombardier to shut European plants," *The Globe and Mail*, October 8, 2003, p. B12.
6. Shirley Won, "Levi's to shut three remaining plants in Canada," *The Globe and Mail*, September 26, 2003, p. B1.
7. Pete Engardio, Aaron Bernstein, and Manjeet Kripalani, "The New Global Job Shift," *Business Week*, February 3, 2003, p. 50.
8. Ibid.
9. "Why Trade Matters," September 15, 2003, Ottawa: Department of Foreign Affairs and International Trade. Retrieved from http://www.dfait-maeci.gc.catna-nac/text-en.asp.
10. Greg Keenan, "Ontario Liberals urged to give Ford aid," *The Globe and Mail*, October 8, 2003, p. B1.
11. Simon Tuck, "Auto industry says taxes, federal neglect taking toll," *The Globe and Mail*, October 22, 2003, p. B3.
12. Bruce Little, "Solid growth forecast for exports," *The Globe and Mail*, October 28, 2003, p. B3.
13. Information in this section is from the following sources: "Why Trade Matters: Trade and the Canadian Economy—New and Emerging Markets—Canadian Companies in China, February 19, 2004, Ottawa: Department of Foreign Affairs and International Trade. Retrieved from http://www.dfait-maeci.gc.ca/tna-nac/stories88-en.asp; Geoffrey York, "PM wants greater slice of Chinese import trade," *The Globe and Mail*, October 23 2003, p. B3; "Why Trade Matters: Canada and China: Diversifying Relations," October 27, 2003, Ottawa: Department of Foreign Affairs and International Trade. Retrieved from http://www.dfait-maeci.gc.ca/tna-nac/stories-en.asp.
14. Paul Magnusson, "A U.S. Trade Ploy That Is Starting to Boomerang," *Business Week*, July 29, 2002, pp. 64–65.
15. Naomi Koppel, "Fifteen Countries Call for Tightening of Anti-Dumping Rules in World Trade Organization," AP Worldstream, February 5, 2003.
16. Courtney Fingar, "The ABCs of EMCs," *Global Business*, May 2002, pp. 51–56.
17. Marc Gunther, "Has Eisner Lost the Disney Magic?" *Fortune*, January 7, 2002, pp. 64–69.
18. "Business: The Great Leap Forward; Cars in China," *The Economist*, February 1, 2003, p. 62.
19. "Daimler, Mitsubishi, Hyundai Ink Car Engine Pact," Reuters, May 4, 2002.
20. Ron Ameln, "Strategic Alliances as a Growth Strategy," *St.Louis Small Business Monthly*, July 2002, p. 36.
nic38767_notes.qxd 11/7/03 1:40 PM Page N-1
21. Eric Krell, "The Alliance Advantage," *Business Finance*, July 2002, pp. 16–23.
22. "NYFD Chooses BlackBerry Wireless Platform and MX Software to Improve Communications," February 4, 2003, Waterloo: Research In Motion. Retrieved November 2, 2003 from http://www.blackberry.com/news/press/pr-04_02_2003.shtml.
23. Michael Porter, *The Competitive Advantage of Nations*.
24. Matthew Fordahl, "Häagen-Dazs Scoops Up Dreyer's in Cool Deal for Shareholders," Associated Press, June 18, 2002, Business Edition.
25. "India: Losing Sheen for U.S. Multinationals," United Press International, January 27, 2003.
26. Geert Hofstede, *Culture and Organizations: Software of the Mind* (New York: McGraw-Hill, 1997), pp. 3–19.
27. Anne Tergesen, "Bucking a Weaker Buck," *Business Week*, June 3, 2002, p. 88.
28. Daniel Bases, "Dollar Hits 3-Year Low Versus the Euro," Reuters Business, January 20, 2003.
29. Steve H. Hanke, "The Strong Dollar Charade," *Forbes*, February 3, 2003, p. 122.
30. www.nestle.com.
31. Richard Bloom, "Dollar's quick rise pinches profits," *The Globe and Mail*, p. B1.
32. Ibid.
33. Matt Krantz, "Regulators Look Closely at Bartering," *USA Today*, May 21, 2002, p. 35.
34. Alan O. Sykes, "New Directions in Law and Economics," *American Economist*, April 1, 2002, p. 10.
35. Takure Yhangazha, "AIPPA Fosters Corrupt Environment," Africa News Service, January 23, 2003.
36. Karen MacGregor, "Acres loses appeal on bribery charge in Lesotho," *The Globe and Mail*, August 18, 2003, p. B3.
37. "World Bank Sanctions Acres International Ltd.," July 23, 2004, Washington: The World Bank Group. Retrieved from web.worldbank.org.
38. Alma Olaechea, "Globalization Is Best for All," University Wire, February 13, 2002.
39. "About the Export and Import Controls Bureau (EICB) Controlled Goods," February 21, 2003. Ottawa: Department of Foreign Affairs and International Trade. Retrieved from http://www.dfait-maeci.gc.ca/eicb/eicbintro-en.asp.
40. "Livestock estimates," August 19, 2003. Ottawa: Statistics Canada. Retrieved from http://www.statcan.ca/Daily/English/030819/d030819b.htm.
41. "Cancun trade talk breakdown: what now?" [n.d.], Organisation for Economic Co-operation and Development. Retrieved November 4, 2003 from http://www.oecd.org/document/52/0,2340,en_2649_201185_9060788_1_1_1_1,00.html.
42. George Melloan, "Europe Builds an Edifice, but Will It Stand?" *The Wall Street Journal*, December 17, 2002, p. A17; and "Enlargement: EU Finalizes Accession Treaty for Candidate Countries," *European Report*, February 8, 2003.
43. "Trade and Investment Relations," May 20, 2003. Ottawa: Government of Canada. Retrieved from http://www.dfait-maeci.gc.ca/canadaeuropa/canada-eu-b2-en.asp.
44. John Cavanagh, Sarah Anderson, Jaime Serra, and J. Enrique Espinosa, "Happily Ever NAFTA," *Foreign Policy*, September 1, 2002, p. 58.
45. "Trade & Investment Relations," May 20, 2003, Ottawa: Government of Canada. Retrieved from http://www.dfait-maeci.gc.ca/canadaeuropa/canada-eu-b2-en.asp.
46. John Cavanagh, et al., "Happily Ever NAFTA."
47. Ibid.
48. Ibid.
49. Heather Scoffield, "Economic ranking puts Canada 16," *The Globe and Mail*, October 30, 2003, p. A4.
50. "Assessing the general business environment" [n.d.], New York: Economic Intelligence Unit Ltd. Retrieved from http://www.eb.eiu.com/site_infoasp?info_name=eeb_business_methodology.

Chapter 4

1. "Heritage Fund FAQs," August 30, 2004, Edmonton: Alberta Revenue. Retrieved from http://www.revenue.gov.ab.ca/business/ahstf/faqs.html#value.

2. "The Caisse de depot et placement du Quebec announces the addition of a new investor to the Capital Infragaz Limited Partnership: The Solidarity Fund of QFL," July 23, 2004, Montreal: Caisse de depot et placement du Quebec. Retrieved from http://www.lacaisse.com/LaCaisse/CommuniquePresse/en/HTML/2009_en_aspx.

3. "Sources of Canadian Law," April 24, 2003, Ottawa: Department of Justice Canada. Retrieved from http://canada.justice.gc.ca/en/dept/pub/just/CSJ_page7.html.

4. Eugene A. Forsey, *How Canadians Govern Themselves.* 5th ed. Ottawa: Library of Parliament, 2003, p. 22.

5. Ibid., p. 48.

6. Joe Bryan, "DelegatesWill Week Way to Untangle Barriers to Interprovincial Trade," *Montreal Gazette,* February 1, 1992, p. B1.

7. Forsey, p. 48.

8. Alan Reynolds, "Improvements . . . and Horror Replays," *Washington Times,* January 12, 2003, p. B8.

9. "Welcome to the Canadian Economy Online—Federal Debt," November 13, 2003, Ottawa: Government of Canada. Retrieved from http://canadianeconomy.gc.ca.

10. "Presentation by the Honourable John Manley, P.C., M.P. to the House of Commons Standing Committee on Finance," November 3, 2003, Ottawa: Department of Finance Canada. Retrieved from http://www.fin.gc.ca/ec2003/speeche.html; Sandra Cordon, "Strong Growth Forecast," *Montreal Gazette,* May 20, 1999, p. A1; and "Sheltered from the Global Storm," *ScotiaPlus,* Spring/Summer 1999, p. 5.

11. Keith McArthur, "The five big winners," *The Globe and Mail,* February 19, 2003, p. A11.

12. Gloria Galloway, "Deficit drives McGuinty to end power rate freeze," *The Globe and Mail,* October 31, 2003, P. A1.

13. Greg Keenan, "Ontario indicates commitment to provide financial aid to Ford," September 8, 2004, CTV.ca. Retrieved from http://ctv.workopolis.com/servlet/Content/fasttrack/20040908/RFORD08?section=Finance.

14. Oliver Bertin, "Spar's Radarstat Succeeds in Sending Clear Image," *The Globe and Mail, ROB,* December 15, 1995, p. B9.

15. Barrie McKenna, "$200-Million Aerospace Project Threatened," *The Globe and Mail, ROB,* January 19, 1996, p. B1.

16. CBC News, January 27, 1999.

17. "Ocean Choice buys Polar Foods," March 24, 2004, Toronto: PEI.CBC.CA. Retrieved from http://pei.cbc.ca/regional/servlet/View?filename=pe_oceanbuys20040324.

18. Heather Scoffield, "Provinces chide Ottawa on revenue distribution," *The Globe and Mail,* September 11, 2003, p. B2.

19. "US Agricultural Policy Facing Radical Changes," *The Globe and Mail, ROB,* September 11, 1995, p. B10.

20. "National Summit on Innovation and Learning," June 4, 2004, Ottawa: Government of Canada. Retrieved from http://innovation.gc.ca/gol/innovation/interface.nsf/VSSGBasic/in04289e.htm.

21. "International Trade Canada," May 20, 2004, Ottawa: International Trade Canada. Retrieved from http://www.itcan-cican.gc.ca/menu-en.asp.

Chapter 5

1. Auditor General's Report 2004, February 11, 2004, Ottawa: CBC News. Retrieved from http://www.cbc.ca/news/background/auditorgeneral/report2004.html.

2. "Nortel accounting problems cast pall over sector," April 28, 2004. Retrieved from http://finance.lycos.com/qc/news/story.aspx?symbols=NASDAQ:CIEN&story=200404282148_RTR_N28360472.

3. Pallavi Guniganti, "Ethics' Place in Education," *University Wire,* April 16, 2002.

4. Daniel Schwartz, "Volunteering in Numbers," February 2002, Toronto: CBC News. Retrieved from http://www.cbc.ca/news/bigpicture/volunteer/volunteering.html; "Trends in volunteerism" [n.d.], Ottawa: Volunteerism in Canada. Retrieved from http://www.volunteer.ca/volcan/eng/volincan/trendsinvol.php?display=2,0,9.

5. Sylvia LeRoy, Todd Gabel, and Niels Veldhius, "Comparing Charitable Giving in Canada & the United States: Canada's Generosity Gap, December 2003. Vancouver: The Fraser Institute. Retrieved from http://www.fraserinstitute.ca/shared/readmore.asp?sNav=nr&id=574.

6. Jamie Reno, "Need Someone in Creative Accounting?" *Newsweek,* May 17, 1999.

7. Kenneth Blanchard and Norman Vincent Peale, *The Power of Ethical Management* (New York: William Morrow, 1996).

8. "Small Business Owners Doing Little to Promote Ethics," Ascribe Newswire, June 25, 2002.

9. Peter Worthington, "Ethics: Either You Have Them or You Don't," *Edmonton Sun,* June 1, 2002, p. 11.

10. John McCormick, "The Sorry Side of Sears," *Newsweek,* February 22, 1999, pp. 36–39.

11. Ethics Resource Center, 2000 National Business Ethics Survey (www.ethics.org/2000survey.html).

12. Craig Savoye, "Workers Say Honesty Is Best Company Policy," *Christian Science Monitor,* June 15, 2000, p. 3; and Andrea Kay, "Tread Carefully Before Becoming a Whistleblower," Gannett News Service, February 21, 2002.

13. Matthew Murray and Anna Ossipova, "Code Could Have Done Enron Some Good," *St. Petersburg Times,* February 26, 2002; and "Shameful Antics of Some Give the Business Calling a Bad Rap," *Tampa Tribune,* January 3, 2003, p. 12.

14. Larry Brown, "The case for whistleblowing legislation in Canada," November 3, 2003, Nepean: National Union of Public and General Employees. Retrieved from http://www.nupge.ca/news_2003/n06no03a.htm; "Whistleblower legislation Bill C-25, Disclosure Protection," April 28, 2004, Ottawa: CBC News Online. Retrieved from http://www.cbc.ca/news/background/whistleblower/.

15. The Tim Hortons Children's Foundation [n.d.]. Oakville: Tim Hortons. Retrieved from http://www.timhortons.com.

16. "Empower Employees to be active in their communities" [n.d.], Redmond: Microsoft Corporation. Retrieved from http://www.microsoft.com/canada/ican/communityfocus/employees.aspx.

17. "Donations," 2004, Toronto: RBC Financial Group. Retrieved from http://www.rbc.com/community/donations/.

18. Ibid.

19. "CEOs say RBC Financial Group (Royal Bank) most respected corporation," 2003, Toronto: KPMG LLP. Retrieved from http://www.mostrespected.ca.

20. Anita Lienhart, "She Drove, He Drove Mercedes C320," Gannett News Service, January 9, 2001; Menke-Gluckert, "Baby Benz Faces the Moose," *Europe,* February 2, 1998, pp. 40–44; and Earle Eldridge, "Luxury Sales Up: 'Move Up' Market Strong," *Edmonton Sun,* June 21, 2002, p. DR16.

21. "Charity Is Good Business," AAP General News, June 28, 2002.

22. "About MJRA," 2004, Toronto: Michael Jantzi Research Associates Inc. Retrieved from http://www.mjra-jsi.com.

23. "Former RBC Dominion Securities exec faces insider trading charges," February 5, 2004, Ottawa: CBC News Online.

Retrieved from http://www.cbc.ca/stories/2004/02/04/rankin040204.

24. Nancy Carr, "Daniel Duic to pay $1.9M, stop trading in Ont., testify at Rankin trial: OSC," March 3, 2004, Canoe Money. Retrieved from http://money.canoe.ca/News/Other/2004/03/03/369029-cp.html

25. Ibid.

26. Jeffrey Hodgson, "Canadian Regulator Sees Trade Ban for Nortel Execs," May 3, 2004, Toronto: Globeinvestor.com. Retrieved from http://www.globeinvestor.com/servlet/ArticleNews/story/ROC/20040503/2004-05-03T224716Z_01_N03688119_RTRIDST_0_BUSINESS-NORTEL-COL; "Nortel fires CEO, finance execs," April 29, 2004, Detroit: Detroit Free Press. Retrieved from http://www.freep.com/money/business/nortel29_20040429.htm.

27. Ibid.

28. Teresa M. McAleavy, "How Big Companies Lose Millions When Their Good Workers Defect," The Record, May 31, 2002.

29. David D. Perlmutter, "Business Ethics Should Be Part of the Bottom Line," Newsday, July 9, 2002, p. A27.

30. Wallace Immen, "Non-profits hurt by lack of benefits," The Globe and Mail, October 15, 2003, p. C1.

31. www.rhino.com/about/support.html.

32. James Graff, "Business/World Economic Forum: Giving Some of It Back," Time International, February 15, 1999, p. 40; and "Samsung Thrives on People, Technology, Future," KoreaTimes, January 30, 2000.

33. Colin Perkel, "Harris apologizes for government's role in tragedy," January 18. 2002, Canoe C-Health. Retrieved from http://www.canoe.ca/EcoliTragedy/020118_report-cp.html.

34. "Tar ponds in Sydney, Nova Scotia," 2002, PageWise Inc. Retrieved from http://tntn.essortment.com/tarpondssydney_rhxq.htm; "Sydney Nova Scotia Tar Ponds Move Closer to Cleanup" [n.d.], Ellicott. Retrieved from htttp://www.dredge.com/casestudies/enviro8.htm; "Our Site Overview," 2004, Province of Nova Scotia: Sydney Tar Ponds Agency. Retrieved from http://www.gov.ns.ca/stpa; "The Great Lakes Atlas," 2003, United States Environmental Protection Agency. Retrieved from www.epa.gov/glnpo/atlas; Pat Currie, "All's not well in this valley," April 3, 2004, Lake Ontario Waterkeeper. Retrieved from http://www.waterkeeper.ca/lok; Chris Sebastian, "Canada getting tough on spills," May 12, 2004, Times Herald. Retrieved from http:www.thetimesherald.com/news/stories/20040512/localnews/403633.html.

35. By Russ Wiles, "Shareholder Resolutions Boom: Social Responsibility a Top Concern," Arizona Republic, June 10, 2002, p. D1; Laurent Belsie, "Tough Times Test Firms' Lofty Standards," Christian Science Monitor, January 28, 2002, p. 20; and Susan Scherreik, "Following Your Conscience Is Just a Few Clicks Away," Business Week, May 13, 2002, p. 116.

36. "Nike, Adidas Under Fire for Low Wages," United Press International, March 8, 2002;"Vietnam Labour Body Defends Nike After Court Ruling," Reuters, May 3, 2002;"Nike and Adidas 'Have Failed to Stop Sweatshop Abuses,'" Independent, March 8, 2002, p. 17; and Don Cronin, "Nike, Adidas Do Better but Lag, Study Says," USA Today, March 8, 2002.

37. "Social Responsibility: Commission Presents Ideas for Special Forum," European Report, June 29, 2002.

38. "Taking Action on Climate Change," April 8, 2003, Ottawa: Department of Foreign Affairs and International Trade. Retrieved from http://dfait-maeci.gc.ca/department/focus/kyotoprotocol-en.asp; Seven Chase, "Chretien aims for green legacy," The Globe and Mail, September 3, 2002, p. A1; and John Ibbitson, "Alberta can't beat Ottawa in battle of Kyoto," The Globe and Mail, September 3, 2002, p. A1.

Chapter 6

1. Yvette Armendariz, "Sole Ownership a Mixed Bag," Arizona Republic, July 1, 2002, p. D3.

2. Jerome R. Stockfish, "Profiting from Benefits," Tampa Tribune, July 1, 2002, p. 10.

3. Simone Kaplan, "The Right Fit," CIO, December 1, 2001.

4. "McCain business empire has deep roots," March 19, 2004, Canadian Broadcasting Corporation. Retrieved from http://www.cbc.ca/stories/2004/03/19/mccainbiz_040319.

5. Paul Edwards and Sarah Edwards, "Should You INC or Not?" Entrepreneur, June 2002.

6. "The Basics of Corporate Governance," February 28, 2003, Investopedia.com. Retrieved from Corporate Governance.

7. David M. Schweiger, "Merge Right," Business & Economic Review, April–June 2002.

8. Rob Longley, "Bucks and Pucks: So, Who Calls the Shots at Maple Leaf Sports and Entertainment Ltd?." London Free Press, July 15, 2002, p. B6.

9. "Franchising in Canada," 2002, Vancouver: CANAM Franchise Development Group. Retrieved from http://www.franchise.com; Anne Evans, "25 successful Canadian franchises for 2004," Canadian Business Franchise, March/April 2004, p. 54.

10. Richard Cunningham, President, Canadian Franchise Association, telephone interview by Rita Cossa, January 5, 2004.

11. "Company Overview" and "Divisions," 2001, Toronto: Cara Operations Limited. Retrieved from http://www.cara.com.

12. "Franchise Listings," Canadian Business Franchise, March/April 2004, 90.

13. Carlye Adler, "Would You Pay $2 Million for This Franchise?" Fortune Small Business, May 1, 2002.

14. Dan Morse, "Individual Outlet Owners Set Up E-Commerce Sites," The Wall Street Journal, March 28, 2000.

15. "Canadian Franchisors Looking South," Canadian Business Franchise, March/April 2004, p. 22; "Beavertails Pastry," 2004, World Franchising. Retrieved from http://www.worldfranchising.com/profiles/BeaverTail.htm.

16. "About Co-Operatives" [n.d.], Ottawa: Canadian Co-Operative Association. Retrieved from http://www.coopscanada.coop/aboutcca/; "Co-operative Development Initiative General Information" [n.d.], Ottawa: Government of Canada. Retrieved from http://www.agr.gc.ca/policy/coop/information_e.phtml.

Chapter 7

1. Ellen McCarthy, "Entrepreneurial Students More Grounded; As Dot-Com Dreams Fade, Business Basics Come to Fore," Washington Post, March 19, 2002, p. E5.

2. Retrieved May 27, 2004 from the following company Websites: www.leons.ca/history/default.asp; www2.canadiantire.ca/CTenglish/h_ourstory.html; www.sobeys.ca; http://www.leons.ca/history/default.asp; and http://www.irvingoilco.com/aboutus.htm.

3. "Travel Cuts," [n.d.], The Alberta College of Art & Design Students' Association. Retrieved from www.acadsa.ca/cfstravel.html.

4. Samuel Fromartz, "Newbiz: Entrepreneurs Not Braking for Economic Slowdown," Reuters Business Report, March 20, 2002; Kathy Wagstaff, "Pointers Offered for Small Businesses," Atlanta Journal and Constitution, May 30, 2002, p. J3.

5. "Key Small Business Statistics—April 2004," April 26, 2004, Ottawa: Industry Canada. Retrieved from http://strategis.ic.gc.ca/epic/internet/insbrp-rppe.nsf/en/rd00760e.html; "Rachel Arseneau-Ferguson" [n.d.], Royal

Bank of Canada. Retrieved from http://www.royalbank.com/sme/women/profiles/pro_rachel_arseneau_ferguson.html.

6. "Key Small Business Statistics—April 2004," April 26, 2004, Ottawa: Industry Canada. Retrieved from http://strategis.ic.qc.ca/epic/internet/insbrp-rppe.nsf/en/rd00760e.html.

7. "US Census Bureau: 9.3 Million People Worked at Home in 1997, Census Bureau Reports," M2 PressWIRE, January 17, 2002.

8. "We Work for Home-Based and Micro Business Owners Like You," [n.d.], British Columbia: The Canadian Home & Micro Business Foundation. Retrieved from the www.homebiz.ca/Advocacy/communityhome.html.

9. "A Home Office Works," *Washington Times*, January 16, 2002.

10. Karen E. Spaede, "Know the Law: Understanding Zoning and Other Restrictions Before You Start Your Business Will Save You Big Headaches (and Money) Later," Entrepreneur.com, February 18, 2002.

11. Bill Husted, "Dot-Com Success: Camera Dealer Develops a Niche," *Atlanta Journal and Constitution*, September 1, 2002, p. Q1.

12. Jerry Useem, "[3M] [General Electric]? Jim McNerney Thinks He Can Turn 3M from a Good Company into a Great One—With a Little Help from His Former Employer, General Electric," *Fortune*, August 12, 2002, p. 127.

13. "Canada Business Service Centres," August 1, 2003, Ottawa: Government of Canada. Retrieved from http://www.cbsc.org/english/aboutus.cfm; Arthur J. Carty, "Incubation in Canada: Moving to the Next Level," January 22, 2003. Ottawa: National Research Council Canada. Retrieved from http://www.nrc-cnrc.gc.ca/newsroom/speeches/incubation03_e.html; Jean-Pierre Trudel, "Laval's Biotech City adds two new biotech development centres to its complex," *LifeSciencesWorld*, September 26, 2003. Retrieved from http://www.biotecfind.com/pages/articles_eg/laval/laval.htm; and "Small Business Research and Policy," October 14, 2003, Ottawa: Industry Canada. Retrieved from http://strategis.ic.gc.ca/epic/internet/insbrp-rppe.nsf/vwGeneratedInterE/Home.

14. "Key Small Business Statistics—April 2004," April 26, 2004, Ottawa: Industry Canada. Retrieved from http://strategis.ic.gc.ca/epic/internet/insbrp-rppe.nsf/en/rd00760e.html

15. Ibid.

16. Ibid; John Baldwin, "Failing Concerns: Business Bankruptcy in Canada," April 1, 1998, Ottawa: Statistics Canada. Retrieved from http://statcan.ca/english/IPS/Data/61-525-XIE.htm.

17. Nathan Vardi, "No Free Lunch," *Forbes*, February 3, 2003, pp. 70–71.

18. Linda Himelstein, "Entrepreneurs: VCs Turn the Screws," *Business Week*, May 27, 2002, p. 82.

19. Janet Forgrieve, "Boulder Company Offers 'Angels' Tips, Would-Be Invertors in Startups Get Advice on Making Choices," *Denver Rocky Mountain News*, July 26, 2002, p. 4B; and David Nicklaus, "Angel Investors Won't Take Many Flying Leaps Today," *St. Louis Post-Dispatch*, April 3, 2002, p. C1.

20. Keith Lowe, "Why You Need an Accountant," Entreprenuer.com, June 3, 2002.

21. Keith Lowe, "Developing a Solid Relationship with Your Attorney," Entrepreneur.com, May 6, 2002.

22. Keith Lowe, "Keep Your Banker Informed," Entrepreneur.com, April 1, 2002.

Chapter 8

1. Walter B. Wriston, "A Code of Our Own," *The Wall Street Journal*, January 16, 2003, p. A12.

2. "A Bullet Partially Dodged," *The Wall Street Journal*, July 31, 2002, p. A14.

3. "Problem Solved—Top 100 Business Women Owners," (2004), PROFITguide.com. Retrieved from http://www.profitguide.com/w100/2003/article.asp?ID=1274&page=2.

4. Deborah Ancona, Henrik Bresman, and Katrin Kaeufer, "The Comparative Advantage of X-Teams," *Sloan Management Review*, Spring 2002, pp. 33–39.

5. Jack Otter, "Memo to Imperial CEOs: Party's Over," *SmartMoney*, September 2002, pp. 32–35.

6. W. Chan Kim, "Fair Process: Managing in the Knowledge Economy," *Harvard Business Review*, January 2003, pp. 127–36.

7. Ibid.

8. Darrell Rigby, "Don't Get Hammered by Management Fads," *The Wall Street Journal*, May 21, 2001, p. A22.

9. Sarah Kaplan and Eric D. Beinhocker, "The Real Value of Strategic Planning," *Sloan Management Review*, Winter 2003, pp. 71–76.

10. "The New Contingency Plan—Health-Related Emergencies," May 27, 2003, Toronto: Morneau Sobeco. Retrieved from http://www.morneausobeco.com/PDF/SARS Communiqué_E.pdf.

11. Robert Barker, "The Art of Brainstorming," *Business Week*, August 26, 2002, pp. 168–69.

12. Michael Goold and Andrew Campbell, "Do You Have a Well-Designed Organization?" *Harvard Business Review*, March 2002, pp. 117–24.

13. "Canada Post Delivered the Magic to Amazon.ca and chapters.indigo.ca Customers," June 23, 2003, Canada Post. Retrieved from http://www.canadapost.ca/business/corporate/about/newsroom/pr/archive-e.asp?prid=922.

14. Ibid.

15. Don Steinberg, "The Ultimate Technology Survival Guide," *SmartBusiness*, February 2002, pp. 37–49.

16. Anthony Davis, "Sky high," March 2004, PROFIT Guide. Retrieved from http://www.profitguide.com/shared/print.jsp?content=20040213_171556_4580.

17. Laura Rock Kopczak and M. Eric Johnson, "The Supply-Chain Management Effect," *Sloan Management Review*, Spring 2003, pp. 27–34.

18. Kathleen M. Eisenhardt, "Has Strategy Changed?" *Sloan Management Review*, Winter 2002, pp. 88–91.

19. Lauren Keller Johnson, "The Organizational Identity Trap," *Sloan Management Review*, Summer 2002, p. 11.

20. Davis, "Sky high," March 2004, From .

21. Ibid.

22. Bob Weinstein, "What We Can Learn About Leadership from Sam Walton," *Washington Times*, February 25, 2002, p. E2.

23. Elizabeth Wasserman, "A Race for Profits," *mbajungle.com*, March / April 2003, pp. 40–41.

24. Bertrand Marotte, "Management guru assails excessive CEO salaries," *The Globe and Mail*, May 8, 2003, p. B7.

25. Virginia Galt, "Anything but middling," *The Globe and Mail*, April 11, 2003, p. C1.

26. Davis, "Sky high," March 2004, From .

27. H. James Harrington, "Knowledge Management Takes Us from Chance to Choice," *Quality Digest*, April 2003, pp. 14–16.

28. Laura Bogomolny, "Most Innovative Exec/Canadian Tire—Janice Wismer," 2004, *Canadian Business*. Retrieved from http://www.canadianbusiness.com/allstars/best_innovative_exec.html.

29. Ibid.

30. Joy Riggs, "Empowering Workers by Setting Goals," *Nation's Business*, January 1995, p. 6.

31. Lori Ioannou, "Corporate America's Social Conscience," *Fortune*, May 26, 2003, pp. S1–S10.

Chapter 9

1. Linda Teschler, "Is Your Company up to Speed?," *Fast Company,* June 2003, pp. 81–111.
2. Scott M. Paton, "Customer Satisfaction vs. Customer Service," *Quality Digest,* May 2003, p. 4.
3. Brook Manville and Josiah Ober, "Beyond Empowerment: Building a Company of Citizens," *Harvard Business Review,* January 2003, p. 139.
4. Jon E. Hilsenrath, "Retailers Score Points in Keeping Consumers Happy," *The Wall Street Journal,* February 19, 2002, p. A2.
5. Henry Mintzberg and James Brian Quinn. *The Strategy Process: Concepts and Contexts.* (New Jersey: Prentice Hall Inc., 1992).
6. Pip Coburn, "China's Magic Number," *Red Herring,* February 2003, p. 67.
7. Jim Clemmer, "How to Make Empowerment Work," *The Globe and Mail,* classroom edition, April 1993, p. 17.
8. Carol Matlack and Pallavi Gogoi, "What's This? The French Love McDonald's?" *Business Week,* January 13, 2003, p. 50.
9. Mark Athitakis, "How to Make Money on the Net," *Business 2.0,* May 2003, pp. 83–90.
10. Fara Warner, "Microsoft Eats the Dog Food," *Fast Company,* September 2002, pp. 46–48.
11. Fara Warner, "GM Goes Off-Road," *Fast Company,* February 2003, pp. 40–42.
12. Bruce Little, "How to Make a Small Smart Factory," *The Globe and Mail, ROB,* February 2, 1993, p. B24.
13. Michael F. Corbett, "An Inside Look at Outsourcing," *Fortune,* June 9, 2003, pp. 51–56.
14. Pete Engardio, Aaron Bernstein, and Manjeet Kriplani, "Is Your Job Next?," *Business Week,* February 3, 2003, pp. 50–60.
15. Darlene Superville, "Washington Increasingly Outsources Work," *Washington Times,* February 8, 2003, pp. C8 & C9.
16. Paul Craig Roberts, "Lethal Outsourcing," *Washington Times,* February 27, 2003, p. A19.
17. Keith Damsell, "Offshore outsourcing seen reshaping the tech sector," *The Globe and Mail,* November 3, 2003, sec. B.
18. Paul J. Kampas, "Shifting Cultural Gears," *Sloan Management Review,* Winter 2003, pp. 41–48.
19. Lauren Keller Johnson, "The Organizational Identity Trap," *Sloan Management Review,* Summer 2002, p. 11.
20. D.B. Scott, "Lean Machine," *Globe and Mail, ROB,* November 1992, p. 90.
21. Henry Mintzberg and James Brian Quinn. *The Strategy Process: Concepts and Contexts.* (New Jersey: Prentice Hall Inc., 1992).
22. Mary Kwak, "The True Value of a Lost Customer," *Sloan Management Review,* Winter 2003, p. 9.
23. Walter R. Wreston, "A Code of Our Own," *The Wall Street Journal,* June 16, 2003, p. A12.
24. "Will CEO Pain Lead to Labor Gains?" *Business Week,* September 16, 2002, p. 6.]

Chapter 10

1. "Innovation in Canada" [n.d.], Sackville: Centre for Canadian Studies at Mount Allison University. Retrieved from http://www.mta.ca/faculty/arts/canadian_studies/english/about/innovation/.
2. "Starting the new century: technological change in the Canadian private sector, 2000–2002," January 19, 2004, Ottawa: Statistics Canada. Retrieved from http://www.statcan.ca/english/IPS/Data/88F0006XIE2004001.htm.

3. "Employment by industry and sex," March 11, 2004, Ottawa: Statistics Canada. Retrieved from www.statcan.ca/english/Pgdb/labor10a.htm.
4. "Manufacturing Facts" [n.d.], Ottawa: Canadian Manufacturers & Exporters. Retrieved from http://www.cme-mec.ca/manufac.asp?s=ss1&1=EN&div=undefined.
5. Kathryn Jones, "The Dell Way," *Business 2.0,* February 2003, pp. 61–66.
6. Spencer E. Ante, "The New Blue," *Business Week,* March 17, 2003, pp. 80–88.
7. Daniel Eisenberg, "There's a New Way to Think @ Big Blue," *Time,* January 20, 2003, pp. 49–53.
8. Pete Engardio, Aaron Bernstein, and Manjeet Kripalani, "Is Your Job Next?" *Business Week,* February 3, 2003, pp. 50–60.
9. David Atkin, "HP Toronto Plant Aimed at Dell," *The Globe and Mail,* November 14, 2003, B1.
10. Timothy J. Mullaney, "What's Glowing Online Now?" *Business Week,* September 2, 2002, pp. 94–95.
11. Mary Ellen Mark, "The New Fabric of Success," *Fast Company,* June 2000, pp. 252–70.
12. Laura Rock Kopzak and M. Eric Johnson, "The Supply-Chain Management Effect," *Sloan Management Review,* Spring 2003, pp. 27–34.
13. Greg Keenan, "Auto investments bypass Canada," *The Globe and Mail,* August 2, 2003, p. B4; Simon Tuck, "Ottawa, Ontario rev up interest in auto industry," *The Globe and Mail,* April 21, 2003, p. B1; and Greg Keenan, "Parts makers follow auto firms to southern U.S.," *The Globe and Mail,* November 2, 2002, p. B2.
14. Michael F. Corbett, "An Inside Look at Outsourcing," *Fortune,* June 9, 2003, pp. S1–S6.
15. May Wong, "Anytime, Anyplace: Telework Flourishing," *Washington Times,* June 21, 2002, p. A2.
16. Paul Keegan, "The Architect of Happy Customers," *Business 2.0,* August 2002, pp. 85–87.
17. Mary Set-Du Vall, "From the Pot to the Kettle," *Houston Chronicle,* March 9, 2003, pp. D4 and D7.
18. David Dorsey, "Change Factory," *Fast Company,* June 2000, pp. 209–24.
19. "SPC Software," *Quality Digest,* January 2003, p. 165.
20. "More about NQI" and "Canada Awards for Excellence" [n.d.]. Toronto: National Quality Institute. Retrieved from http://www.nqi.ca.
21. Russell T. Westcott, "Overlooked and Underutilized," *Quality Digest,* July 2003, pp. 49–52.
22. Russell Y. Thornton, "Going Green: A Step-by-Step Guide to ISO 14001 Compliance," *Quality Digest,* March 2003, pp. 31–34.
23. David Crane, "We've got to use our brains more than our brawn," *The Toronto Star,* p. D2.
24. Ibid
25. Showwei Chu, "Celestica shifting production," *The Globe and Mail,* February 11, 2003, p. B7.
26. Gordon Pitts, "Small producer cleans up making soap," *The Globe and Mail,* July 28, 2003, p. B1.
27. Greg Keenan, "Magna sees $1-billion boost in BMW contract," *The Globe and Mail,* November 1, 2001, p. B1.
28. Virginia Galt, "Take our business, take our people: BMO," *The Globe and Mail,* May 19, 2003, p. B1.
29. "Grocery chain in drive to improve," *National Post,* October 31, 2001, p. JV3.
30. "The Juggling act behind the Cirque," *National Post,* October 31, 2001, p. JV4.
31. "Royal Canadian Mint," September 2003, Cognos. Retrieved from http://www.cognos.com/products/applications/success.html.

32. Ibid.
33. Isabel Teotonio, "Keep borders open for trade, industry warns, *Toronto Star,* October 27, 2001, p. A13.
34. Marina Strauss, "HBC set to revamp purchase system," *The Globe and Mail,* July 21, 2003, p. B1.
35. James Careless, "Airlines going on-line with 'virtual marketplace'," *The Globe and Mail,* July 31, 2003, p. B8.
36. Daren Fonda, "Why the Most Profitable Cars Made in the U.S.A. are Japanese and German," *Time,* June 2003, A9–A13.
37. Steve Erwin, "Flexing muscle: Canada's auto sector seeks more manufacturing flexibility," September 13, 2004, *CANOE Money.* Retrieved from http://money.canoe.ca/News/Other/2004/09/13/628065-cp.html.
38. "Chrysler hails record retooling," *Toronto Star,* August 26, 2000.
39. Erwin, "Flexing muscle."
40. Faith Keenan, Stanley Holmes, Jay Greene, and Roger O. Crockett, "A Mass Market of One," *Business Week,* December 2, 2002, pp. 68–72.
41. "Is Your Company Up to Speed?," *Fast Company,* June 2003, pp. 81–86.

Chapter 11

1. Vicky Uhland, "Cooking Up a Rare Approach: Springs Consultants Help Restaurant Hire, Keep Good Employees," *Denver Rocky Mountain News,* January 4, 2002, p. 8B; Donna Rosato, "Service Training Gets Emphasis," *USA Today,* September 17, 2002, p. 7E; and Jamie Herzlich, "Hospitality Lessons for Hospital Staff," *Newsday,* February 8, 2003, p. A44.
2. Teresa M. Mcaleavy, "How Big Companies Lose Millions When Their Good Workers Defect," *The Bergen County (New Jersey) Record,* May 31, 2002, p. B1.
3. "Workforce: Challenges Keep Staff from Curse of Boredom," *Birmingham Post,* May 30, 2002, p. 26; Bruce Rosenstein, "Experts: Leaders Can Motivate If They Exude the Right Vibes," *USA Today,* March 25, 2002, p. 9B; and Karen Howe, "What Makes an Employee Tick?" *Toronto Sun,* January 4, 2003, p. 35.
4. "The 'Motivation' Myth? Part 1," Africa News Service, July 15, 2002; Sherri Cruz, "Gearworks Strives to Be a Motivating Place to Work," *Minneapolis Star Tribune,* May 22, 2002, p. 2D; and Michelle Conlin, "The Workplace: Productivity: The Big Squeeze on Workers," *Business Week,* May 13, 2002, p. 96.
5. Ellen Goldhar, "Working the Right Job," *London Free Press,* May 27, 2002, p. 6.
6. Steve Brearton and John Daly, "The fifty best companies to work for in Canada—BC Biomedical," December 27, 2002, *Report on Business Magazine.* Retrieved from http://www.workopolis.com/servlet/Content/robmag/20021227/RO150BCBIO?gateway=#URL_gateway.
7. Steve Brearton and John Daly, "The fifty best companies to work for in Canada—Flight Centre," December 27, 2002, *Report on Business Magazine.* Retrieved from http://www.workopolis.com/servlet/Content/printerfriendly/20021227/RO150FLIGHT.
8. J. C. Conklin, "High Praise Often Produces Whale of a Job: Management Technique Emphasizes Importance of Encouraging Words," *Dallas Morning News,* February 26, 2002, p. 2D; and Kerry Hannon, "A Little Praise Goes Long Way Toward Success," *USA Today,* January 6, 2003, p. 6B.
9. "Personal Satisfaction More Important Than Money: Survey," AAP General News (Australia), January 11, 2002; and John A. Byrne, "How to Lead Now," *Fast Company,* August 2003, pp. 62–70.

10. "Getting along with your boss?" March 12, 2003, *Career Connection.* Retrieved from http://www.canoe.ca/CareerConnectionNews/031203_flash2.html.
11. "Organizing for Empowerment: An Interview with AES's Roger Sant and Dennis Bakke," *Harvard Business Review,* January 1, 1999, p. 110.
12. Steven L. McShane, *Canadian Organizational Behaviour,* 4th ed. (Toronto: McGraw-Hill Ryerson Limited, 2001), p. 78.
13. Deena Waisberg, "Simple steps to super growth: Open the books," 2003, *Profit.* Retrieved from www.profitguide.com/profit100/2003/article.asp?ID=1265.
14. Jamie Talan, "A Neuron Link to Motivation, Reward," *Newsday,* June 10, 2002, p. D3; and U.S. General Accounting Office, "Actions and Plans to Build a Results-Oriented Culture," www.gao.gov, January 17, 2003.
15. David Nadler and Edward Lawler, "Motivation—a Diagnostic Approach," in *Perspectives on Behavior in Organizations.* (New York: McGraw-Hill, 1977).
16. Conklin, "High Praise." ed. Richard Hackman, Edward Lawler, and Lyman Porter.
17. Donde P. Ashmos and Maria L. Nathan, "Team Sense-Making: A Mental Model for Navigating Uncharted Territories," *Journal of Managerial Issues,* July 1, 2002, p. 198; Minda Zetlin, "Pulse of the Organization," *Computerworld,* June 3, 2002, p. 40;"Teckchek: Skills Assessment Tool Launched for Project Managers; Online Adaptive Skills Assessment Application Developed for IT Project Teams," M2 PressWIRE, June 25, 2002; Keith L. Alexander, "Cultivating a Culture; and Companies See Strong Link Between Worker Attitudes, Profits," *Washington Post,* April 21, 2002, p. H1.
18. Tom Incantalupo, "Road Test/Mustang Cobra: An Iconic, Affordable, Muscular Car," *Newsday,* September 19, 2002, p. D9; and Tom Incantalupo, "Ford's Lightly Pumped-Up Version of Its Muscle Car," *Newsday,* January 23, 2003, p. D5.
19. David K. Foot, *Boom Bust & Echo 2000* (Toronto: Macfarlane Walter & Ross, 1998), pp. 24–31.
20. Ellen Goldhar, "How to Manage Gen X Workers," *London Free Press,* August 19, 2002, p. 7; Ellen Goldhar, "Gen-Xers Require Whole New Management Style," *Toronto Sun,* August 14, 2002, p. C8; Lisi de Bourbon, "Business Watercooler Stories," AP Online, January 22, 2002; "Overtime: When Generations Collide," United Press International, May 21, 2002; Andrea Sachs, Generation Hex? A New Book Identifies Four Age Groups Warring at Work," *Time,* March 11, 2002, p. Y22; and Toddi Gutner, "Businessweek Investor: A Balancing Act for Gen X Women," *Business Week,* January 21, 2002, p. 82.

Chapter 12

1. M. Kesterson (quoting Elbert Hubbard), "Social Studies," *The Globe and Mail,* August 2, 2001, p. A14.
2. Campbell Clark, "National Sets Up Banking School," *Montreal Gazette,* February 7, 1996, p. D8.
3. E. Innes, J. Lyons, and J. Harris, *The Financial Post 100 Best Companies to Work for in Canada* (Toronto: HarperCollins, 1990).
4. Salem Alaton, "The Learning Organization," *The Globe and Mail, ROB,* December 19, 1995, p. B24.
5. Steve Bates, "Facing the Future," *HR Magazine,* July 2002.
6. David Brown, "HR and the workforce 10 years from now," *Canadian HR Reporter,* October 20, 2003, p. 2.
7. Susan Carr and Lydia Morris Brown, "People Perfect", [n.d.], Business of Management. Retrieved from http://learning.indiatimes.com/bm/features/books/book2.htm.
8. "Survey Sees Demand Returning for Information-Tech Workers," AP Worldstream, May 6, 2002; Victor Godinez,

"IT Job Market: Set for a Thaw?" *Dallas Morning News,* May 26, 2002, p. 7L; and Eve Epstein, "Mastering the Moment," *InfoWorld,* June 3, 2002.

9. Jim Abrams, "Senate Trade Bill to Go Well Beyond President's Request for Trading Authority," AP Worldstream, April 3, 2002; and Jim Abrams, "Senate Democrats Unveil Trade Plan," AP Online, May 1, 2002.

10. "Executive Summary—Knowledge Matters—Skills and Learning for Canadians—Canada's Innovation Strategy," March 18, 2004, Government of Canada. Retrieved from www11.sdc.gc.ca/s1-ca/doc/summary.shtml.

11. Ibid

12. "Census Forecasts Shortages within a Decade," February 11, 2003, Canada.com News. Retrieved from http://www.canada.com/national/features/census/story.html?id={3A2C6DEC-8AC1-47F.

13. Stephen Barr, "EEOC Weighs Changes in Bias Complaint Procedures," *Washington Post,* June 13, 2002, p. B2.

14. Paul Glader, "Day Care Becomes a Growth Industry; Big Companies Move into Prince William," *Washington Post,* June 30, 2002, p. C1; and Rebecca R. Kahlenberg, "When Stay-at-Home Moms Want a Second Job," *Washington Post,* February 7, 2002, p. C10.

15. Sarah Godinez, "Success Story," *Dallas Morning News,* June 2, 2002, p. 22.

16. Michelle Conlin, "The Workplace: Productivity: The Big Squeeze on Workers," *Business Week,* May 13, 2002, p. 96.

17. Mike Allen and Juliet Eilperin, "Health Care Debate Prompts Standoff on Trade Legislation; Senate Democrats Back Subsidies for Displaced Workers," *Washington Post,* May 2, 2002, p. A2; and Paul Magnusson, "Washington Outlook: Fast Track May Be Just a Horse Trade Away," *Business Week,* April 22, 2002, p. 47.

18. Jerome R. Stockfisch, "Profiting from Benefits," *Tampa Tribune,* July 1, 2002, p. 10; and Stephen Barr, "House Panel to Sample Opinion on Cafeteria-Style Benefits," *Washington Post,* May 21, 2002, p. B2.

19. David Stires, "The Coming Crash in Health Care," *Fortune,* October 14, 2002, p. 205; Katherine Yung, "Child Care Slips on Corporate Agenda: Some Firms Easing Burden, but Most Working Parents on Their Own," *Dallas Morning News,* February 3, 2002, p. 1A; Pamela Yip, "Caring Concerns: Struggles to Help Elderly Can Put Kin in Financial Need," *Dallas Morning News,* August 26, 2002, p. 1D; Steny H. Hoyer, "Not Exactly What We Intended, Justice O'Connor," *Washington Post,* January 20, 2002, p. B1; and "Excellence and Diversity," *St. Louis Post-Dispatch,* May 20, 2002, p. B6.

20. Andrea Kay, "How to Encourage Loyalty at Work," Gannett News Service, August 1, 2002.

21. Mark Albright, "Matching Up the Stripes: Some Retailers Apply Personality Testing to Find 'Corporate Fit,' " *Edmonton Sun,* March 30, 2002, p. 56.

22. "Prepares Youths for Careers in Automotive Technology; Ford Supports Training Centers," *Washington Times,* June 21, 2002.

23. "Log On to the Virtual Reality of Top-Flight Job Opportunities," *Birmingham Post,* February 6, 2001, p. 23; and Monty Phan, "Businesses Keep Tabs on Talent Via Alumni Sites," *Newsday,* November 25, 2001, p. C9.

24. Alison Overholt, "True or False: You're Hiring the Right People," *Fast Company,* February 2002, p. 110.

25. "Jobs: How to Survive 'Killer Questions,' " *Evening Telegraph,* March 14, 2002, p. 45.

26. Keith L. Alexander, "Cultivating a Culture; Companies See Strong Link Between Worker Attitudes, Profits," *Washington Post,* April 21, 2002, p. H1.

27. Steve Bates, "Personality Counts," *HR Magazine,* February 2002.

28. Gillian Flynn, "A Legal Examination of Testing," *Workforce,* June 2002, pp. 92–94.

29. Maria Mallory White, "Student Gives Temp Work 'A' Experience, Pay Found Rewarding," *Atlanta Journal and Constitution,* July 14, 2002, p. R1.

30. Barbara A. Wiens-Tuers and Elizabeth T. Hill, "How Did We Get Here from There? Movement into Temporary Employment," *Journal of Economic Issues,* June 1, 2002, p. 303; Clecia Thompson, "When Workers Opt for Impermanence," *The Bergen County (New Jersey) Record,* July 19, 2002, p. B1; and Stephen Barr, "Looking for a More Permanent Solution to Extended Use of Temporary Workers," *Washington Post,* April 5, 2002, p. B2.

31. Julekha Dash, "The ROI of Training," *Computerworld,* March 18, 2002, p. 58.

32. Sharlene Massie, "Training Key for Success," *Calgary Sun,* May 19, 2002, p. CC3.

33. Brian Sullivan, "Steelcase Streamlines SAP Training," *Computerworld,* September 2, 2002, p. 26.

34. "Apprenticeship Program Wins Federal Approval," *Sound & Video Contractor,* February 1, 2002.

35. Judy A. Serwatka, "Improving Student Performance in Distance Learning Courses," *Technological Horizons in Education,* April 1, 2002, p. 46; Lucinda Kimsel, "Distance Learning Gives U. Hawaii Students More Options," University Wire, September 4, 2002; Colleen Brandao and Julie Young, "Teaching Online: Harnessing Technology's Power at Florida Virtual School," *Technological Horizons in Education,* May 1, 2002, p. 37; Karen Paulson, "FIPSE: Thirty Years of Learning Anytime and Anywhere," *Change,* September 1, 2002, p. 36; and Adrienne Moore, "Merits of Web, TV Classes Stir Debate," University Wire, April 3, 2002.

36. "'The Coaching Manager': New Business Book by Babson College Professors Helps Managers Develop Top Talent," Ascribe Newswire, June 17, 2002; and Andrea C. Poe, "Establish Positive Mentoring Relationships," *HR Magazine,* February 2002.

37. Fara Warner, "Inside Intel's Mentoring Movement," *Fast Company,* March 15, 2002, p. 116.

38. John Kirkpatrick, "Talent Too Often Goes Unrecognized at Firms: Evaluation Systems May Not Identify the Quiet Hidden Stars," *Dallas Morning News,* April 30, 2002, p. 2D; and Bruce Pfau and Ira Kay, "Does 360-Degree Feedback Negatively Affect Company Performance?" *HR Magazine,* June 2002.

39. Statistics Canada, "Compensation for Women," *Labour Force Historical Review, 2002,* 71F0004XCB (Mills Library Data Text CA1 BS71 F0004).

40. "Human Rights—Pay Equity" [n.d.], Burnaby: WorkRights. Retrieved from http://www.workrights.ca/Human+Rights/Pay+Equity.htm.

41. "Pay Equity Review," September 9, 2003, Ottawa: Government of Canada. Retrieved from http://www.payequityreview.gc.ca/index-e.html.

42. Donde P. Ashmos and Maria L. Nathan, "Team Sense-Making: A Mental Model for Navigating Uncharted Territories," *Journal of Managerial Issues,* July 1, 2002, p. 198.

43. Perry Pascarella, "Compensating Teams," *Across the Board,* February 1997, pp. 16–23.

44. Stephanie Sandoval, "City Implements New Pay Plan for Dispatchers: Rather Than Length of Service, Raises Will Be Based on Skill Levels," *Dallas Morning News,* October 12, 2001, p. 4Y.

45. Virginia Galt, "Benefits Coverage on the Rise," *The Globe and Mail,* May 22, 2003, p. B5.

46. Jennifer Hutchins, "How to Make the Right Voluntary Benefit Choices," *Workforce,* March 2002, pp. 42–48.

47. Suzanne Koudsi, "You Want More but Your Company Doesn't Have It: Suzanne Koudsi Finds Out How to Get a Raise When the Well Has Run Dry," *Fortune,* April 29, 2002, p. 177; "Analysis: The Future of Work," United Press International, June 27, 2002; James P. Burton, Thomas W. Lee, and Brooks C. Holtom, "The Influence of Motivation to Attend, Ability to Attend, and Organizational Commitment on Different Types of Absence," *Journal of Managerial Issues,* July 1, 2002, p. 181; and Brian Tumulty, "Many Working Moms Lack Flexibility in Workplace," Gannett News Service, May 10, 2002.

48. Virginia Galt, "More Firms Offering Flextime Option," *The Globe and Mail,* August 11, 2003, p B1.

49. "Pentagon Policy-Makers Battle with Waning Morale," *Washington Times,* August 12, 2002.

50. Matt Moore, "Business Watercooler Stories," AP Online, September 3, 2002.

51. Amy Martinez, "New Technology Helps Some Avoid the Office," *Palm Beach Post,* May 24, 2002, p. 13A; "A Home Office Works," *Washington Times,* January 6, 2002.

52. "Canadian Telework Scene," [n.d.], Canadian Telework Association. Retrieved from http://www.ivc.ca/part12.html.

53. Owen S. Good, "Commuters Get Perks Employers Aim to Soften Impact of Traffic with Pools, Odd Shifts, Working at Home," *Denver Rocky Mountain News,* April 8, 2002, p. 22A; "Telecommuters Could Solve Traffic Problems," *Toronto Star,* August 31, 2002.

54. Mark Harrington, "Stand By for IBM's 'Office of the Future': At Big Blue, Adjustable Space, Electronic Sensors, No Cubicle Walls," *Newsday,* March 31, 2002, p. D7.

55. Vicky Uhland, "Accenture Workers Have No Office to Call Their Own," *Denver Rocky Mountain News,* January 12, 2002, p. 5C.

56. "Canadian Telework Scene," [n.d.], Canadian Telework Association. Retrieved from http://www.ivc.ca/part12.html.

57. Ibid.

58. Victor Godinez, "Positive Exit Interview Can Pay Dividends Later Staying Rational and Cordial Is Key When Facing Job Loss, Outplacement Expert Says," *Dallas Morning News,* February 10, 2002, pp. 11L; and Anne Fisher, "Break All the Rules: after Polling Thousands of Companies, Gallup Created a New Approach to Managing That Has Helped It and Many Others Grow," *Fortune Small Business,* September 1, 2002, p. 52.

59. Uyen Vu, "What's our turnover rate?", *Canadian HR Reporter,* October 20, 2003, p. 5.

60. "Ontario's minimum wage increase," December 1, 2003. Toronto: Ontario Ministry of Labour. Retrieved from http://www.gov.on.ca/lab/english/news/2003/03-65f.html.

61. Sacha Cohen, "High-Tech Tools Lower Barriers for Disabled," *HR Magazine,* October 2002.

62. Virginia Galt, "Valued workers could stay after 65," *The Globe and Mail,* May 2, 2003, p. C1; and Alexander Panetta, "Martin wants debate on retirement age," December 19, 2003, Canoe. Retrieved from http://cnews.canoe.ca/CNEWS/Canada/2003/12/19/pf-292358.html.

Chapter 13

1. "Labor union" (1 February 2004), [place of creation unknown]: Wikipedia. Retrieved from http://en.wikipedia.org/wiki/Labor_union.

2. Leigh Strope, "Union Membership in U.S. Hits New Low," AP Online, February 26, 2003.

3. Aaron Bernstein, "Labor: Palace Coup at the AFL-CIO," *Business Week,* March 17, 2003, p. 78.

4. Stephanie Armour, "Wal Mart Takes Hit on Worker Treatment," *USA Today,* February 10, 2003, p. 1B.

5. Diana Fu, "Sweatshops Provoke More Than a Moral Outcry," University Wire, January 29, 2003.

6. Nicholas Stein, "No Way Out: Competition to Make Products for Western Companies Has Revived an Old Form of Abuse—Debt Bondage," *Fortune,* January 20, 2003, p. 102.

7. Liz Fedor, "Union Leader Forsees Consolidated Airline Industry," *Minneapolis Star Tribune,* January 19, 2003, p. 1D.

8. Andrew Curry, "Why We Work," *U.S. News & World Report,* February 24, 2003, p. 49.

9. Marlon Manuel, "Warped Speed: Where Has All the Time Gone?" *Atlanta Journal and Constitution,* May 12, 2002, p. A1.

10. "Labour Unions," March 19, 2004, Statistics Canada. Retrieved from http://142.206.72.67/02/02e/02e_011_e.htm.

11. Leigh Strope, "12 Unions Join to Boost Political Power," AP Online, February 4, 2003.

12. Directory of Labour Organizations in Canada, Human Resources and Development Canada, 1998.

13. www.aflcio.com.

14. "Union Membership in Canada—2003," [n.d.], Ottawa: Human Resources Development Canada. Retrieved from http://labour.hrdc-drhc.gc.ca/pdf/pdf_e/UnionMembership2003_eng.pdf.

15. "About the Canadian Labour Congress," [n.d.], Ottawa: Canadian Labour Congress. Retrieved from http://www.clc-ctc.ca/web/menu/english/en_index.htm.

16. "About Our Union," [n.d.], Ottawa: The Canadian Union of Public Employees. Retrieved from http://www.cupe.ca/www/AboutOurUnion/.

17. "Membership Profile—The CAW: A Dynamic Union," [n.d.], Ottawa: Canadian Auto Workers. Retrieved from http://www.caw.ca/whoweare/ourmembers/profile_index.asp.

18. "The Board's Role," October 23, 2003, Ottawa: Canada Industrial Relations Board. Retrieved from http://www.cirb-ccri.gc.ca/about/role_e.html.

19. Wendy Zellner, "Hiring Illegals: The Risk Grows," *Business Week,* May 13, 2002, p. 94.

20. "Federal Labour Minister Appoints Mediators in Telus Dispute," January 15, 2004, Ottawa: Government of Canada. Retrieved from http://www.hrdc-drhc.gc.ca/common/news/labour/040115.shtml.

21. Yahoo Internet site, www.dailynews.yahoo.com, December 31, 1998.

22. "CAW Reaches Pension Funding Agreement with Air Canada," February 19, 2004. Ottawa: Canadian Auto Workers. Retrieved from http://www.caw.ca/news/newsnow/news.asp?art10=369.

23. Allan Swift, "Storm gathers over sky-high compensation for top Air Canada executives," November 16, 2003, Toronto: Canoe. Retrieved from http://money.canoe.ca/News/Sectors/Consumer/AirCanada/2003/11/16/pdf-259744.html.

24. "Labour laws and human rights," [n.d.], CIC Canada. Retrieved from www.cic.gc.ca/english/newcomer/welcome/wel-10e.html.

25. "What the Employer Will Tell You," [n.d.], CAW. Retrieved from www.caw.ca/jointhecaw/organizinglaws/canada/fact3.asp.

26. Joann Muller, Kathleen Kerwin, and David Welch, "Autos: A New Industry," *Business Week,* July 15, 2002, pp. 98–108.

27. Swift, "Storm gathers over sky-high compensation for top Air Canada executives."

28. Jim Stanford, "New Economy, Same Old Pink Slip," July 3, 2001, Canadian Auto Workers. Retrieved from www.caw.ca/news/factsfromthefringe/issue39.asp.

29. Elizabeth Raymer, "Executive compensation under scrutiny," April 1, 2003, *The Globe and Mail.* Retrieved from www.globeinvestor.com/servlet/ArticleNews/print/GAM/20030401/CGPAYY.

30. Janet McFarland, "How much is too much? And have we reached the maximum acceptable limit for CEO pay?" April 30, 2004, The Globe and Mail. Retrieved from www.globeinvestor.com/servlet/ArticleNews/story/GAM/20040430/RLEVEL30+janet+mcfarland+how+much+is+too+much103F&hl=en.

31. Joann S. Lublin, "As Their Companies Crumbled, Some CEOs Got Big Money Payouts," *The Wall Street Journal,* February 26, 2002, p. B1.

32. McFarland, "How much is too much?"

33. Meg Richards, "Troubled Companies Wrestle with Issue of CEO Pay," AP Worldstream, February 11, 2003.

34. Elizabeth Raymer, "Executive compensation under scrutiny," April 1, 2003, *The Globe and Mail.* Retrieved from www.globeinvestor.com/servlet/ArticleNews/story/GAM/20030401/CGPAVY.

35. Janet McFarland, "Flat fees for directors seen as way of the future," May 18, 2004, *The Globe and Mail.* Retrieved from http://www.theglobeandmail.com/servlet/story/RTGAM.20040430.wxcompside-20430/BNPrint/Front.

36. Raymer, "Executive compensation under scrutiny."

37. Ann Merrill, "General Mills Lauded for Aid to Working Mothers," *Minneapolis Star Tribune,* September 24, 2002, p. 1D.

38. Laura Koss-Feder, "Providing for Parents the 'Sandwich Generation' Looks for New Solutions," *Time,* March 17, 2003, p. G8.

39. Stephen Barr, "Elder Care Becoming Major Issue for Many Workers," *Washington Post,* August 20, 2002, p. B2.

40. Gayle McDonald, "Who's Minding the Parents?" *Globe and Mail, ROB,* January 30, 1996, p. B12.

Chapter 14

1. Jerry Bowles, "Customers for Life," *Forbes,* June 9, 2003, pp. 119 ff.

2. Danna Harman, "Aid Workers Seek to Break Hunger Cycle," *Washington Times,* January 30, 2003, p. A14.

3. Jacqueline Trescott, "Nonprofit Arts Groups Say They Generate $134 Billion Annually," *Washington Post,* June 11, 2002, p. C4.

4. Philip Kotler, et al. Principles of Marketing, 4th Cdn ed. (Scarborough: Prentice Hall Canada Inc. 1999), p. 20.

5. Rich Kish and Mary Ann Platt, "Product Recall and Crisis Management," p. 4, http://www.foodquality.com/prorcal.html., accessed August 14, 2001.

6. Larry Yu, "The Global-Brand Advantage," *Sloan Management Review,* Spring 2003, p. 13.

7. Charles Fishman, "Which Price Is Right?," *Fast Company,* March 2003, pp. 92–102.

8. Scott McMurray, "Return of the Middleman," *Business 2.0,* March 2003, pp. 52–54.

9. Gary Loveman, "Diamonds in the Data Mine," *Harvard Business Review,* May 2003, pp. 109–113.

10. "The Personal Information Protection and Electronic Documents Act," May 10, 2004, The Privacy Commissioner of Canada. Retrieved from http://www.privcom.gc.ca/legislation/02_06_01_e.asp.

11. Lynda Hurst, "How the boomers will go bust," *Toronto Star,* September 23, 2000, p. A20.

12. Shawna Steinberg, "Have Allowance Will Transform Economy" *Canadian Business,* May 13, 1998, p. 60.

13. Paul Brent, "2.5 million 'tweens' pack financial power in their pockets," *Financial Post,* November 17, 2000.

14. Michael Totty, "The Masses Have Arrived," *The Wall Street Journal,* January 27, 2003, p. R8.

15. Jonathan Krim and Dina ElBoghdady, "Amazon Posts Profit for Second Time," *Washington Post,* January 24, 2003, pp. E1, E3.

16. Gregory L. White and Joseph B. White, "Luxury Lite," *The Wall Street Journal,* February 7, 2003, pp. W1, W7.

17. Raizel Robin, "Your pain his gain," *Canadian Business,* March 19, 2001, p. 38.

18. "About Air Canada—Investor Relations," October 22, 2002, Air Canada. Retrieved from www.aircanada.ca/about-us/investor/021022_calgary.html.

19. John Partridge, "No more Zip?" June 3, 2004, *The Globe and Mail.* Retrieved from www.globeinvestor.com/servlet/ArticleNews/story/RTGAM/20040603/wxaircanada0603.

20. Ibid.

21. Eric Berkowitz et al., *Marketing,* 4th Canadian Edition. (Toronto: McGraw Hill Ryerson, 2000). p. 261.

22. Theodore Levitt, "Marketing Myopia (with Retrospective Commentary)," *Harvard Business Review,* September–October 1975, p. 29.

23. Bill Millar, "ERP Meets CRM . . . and Neither Blinks," *1 to 1 Magazine,* January/February 2002, p. 42.

24. "Facts and Figures," [n.d.], Aeroplan. Retrieved from http://infoaeroplan.com/en/mediacentre/facts.php.

25. Jo Bennett, "Hard Rock Cafe Pumps Up the Volume on CRM," *1to1 Magazine,* March 2002, p. 5.

26. Cheryl Krivda and Michael Krivda, "The Book of ROI," (advertisement), *Business 2.0,* June 2002, pp. S24–S26.

27. Stanley J. Shapiro, et al. *Basic Marketing: A Global Managerial Approach.* 10th Canadian ed. (Toronto: McGraw Hill Ryerson, 2002), p. 86; and Seymour Lipset, *Continental Divide: The Values and Institutions of the United States and Canada* (New York: Routledge, 1990).

28. Marc Gunther, "Tree Huggers, Soy Lovers, and Profits," *Fortune,* June 23, 2003, pp. 98–104.

Chapter 15

1. Kate Macarthur, "McDonald's Tests Ads That Focus on Service," *Advertising Age,* January 6, 2003, p. 3.

2. Mohanbir Sawhney, Emanuela Prandelli, and Gianmario Verona, "The Power of Innomediation," *Sloan Management Review,* Winter 2003, pp. 77–82.

3. Joann Muller, "Outpsyching the Car Buyer," *Forbes,* February 17, 2003, p. 52.

4. Andrew Park, Faith Keenan, and Cliff Edwards, "Whose Lunch Will Dell Eat Next?" *Business Week,* August 12, 2002, pp. 66–67.

5. Mila D'Antonio, "Targeted Mailings Help BFS Migrate Customers into Higher Spending Brackets," *1to1,* January/February 2003, p. 11.

6. Douglas B. Holt, "What Becomes an Icon Most?" *Harvard Business Review,* March 2003, pp. 43–49.

7. "Dutch Boy Twist & Pour Delivery System," *Business Week,* July 7, 2003, p. 72.

8. Ingrid Peritz, "Publisher ices Bonhomme 'murderer' book cover," *Globe and Mail,* July 11, 2001, p. A2.

9. Andy Serwer, "The Hole Story," *Fortune,* July 7, 2003, pp. 52–62.

10. Faith Keenan, "The Price Is Really Right," *Business Week,* March 31, 2003, pp. 62–67.

11. Dan McGinn, "Low Riders," *bajungle.com,* March/April 2003, pp. 16–18.

12. Charles Fishman, "Which Price Is Right?" *Fast Company,* March 2003, pp. 92–102.

13. Keith L. Alexander, "Hotels Try Personal Touch to Lure Guests," *Washington Post,* November 20, 2002, p. E1.
14. Scott McMurray, "Return of the Middleman," *Business 2.0,* March 2003, pp. 53–54.
15. Mila D'Antonio, "Supply Chain Management Becomes Larger Priority," *1to1 Magazine,* April 2003, p. 46.
16. "Retail trade," February 26, 2004, Ottawa: Statistics Canada. Retrieved from http://www.statcan.ca/Daily/English/040226/d040226b.htm.
17. "Establishments by industry," July 24, 2001, Ottawa: Statistics Canada. Retrieved from http://www.statcan.ca/english/Pgdb/econ18.htm.
18. Eric N. Berkowitz et al., *Marketing,* 5th Canadian ed. (Toronto: McGraw-Hill Ryerson, 2003), p. 444.
19. Jack Neff, "Ad Buyers: 'Show Us the GRPs,' " *Advertising Age,* March 3, 2003, p. S14.
20. Scott Hays, "Online Media Slowly Discovers Its Fair Share," *Advertising Age,* January 13, 2003, p. M1.
21. James C. Anderson and James A. Narus, "Selectively Pursuing More of your Customer's Business," *Sloan Management Review,* Spring 2003, pp. 42–49.
22. Marji McClure, "A Perfect Fit," *1to1 Magazine,* January/February 2003, pp. 23–27.
23. Claire Atkinson, "Edelman at 50," *Advertising Age,* September 23, 2002, pp. C2–C10.
24. Claire Atkinson, "Comstock Took the PR Path to Reach Top Destination at GE," *Advertising Age,* April 14, 2003, p. 40.
25. Clark S. Judge, "PR Lessons from the Pentagon," *The Wall Street Journal,* April 1, 2003 p. B2.

Chapter 16

1. Mike McNamee, "Finance: Annual Reports: Still Not Enough Candor," *Business Week,* March 24, 2003, p. 74.
2. "Highlights—Proposed CA and CMA Merger," May 11, 2004, Chartered Accountants of Canada. Retrieved from www.cica.ca/index.cfm/ci_id/21464/la_id/1.html.
3. "Become a CGA," [n.d.], CGA-Canada. Retrieved from www.cga-canada.org/eng/designation/cga-become.htm.
4. Michael Connor, "Accountants Group Sees Continued Role," Reuters Business, March 20, 2003.
5. David Henry, "The Business Week 50: Investing for Growth: Cleaning Up the Numbers," *Business Week,* March 25, 2003, p. 126.
6. David Henry and Robert Berner, "Finance: Accounting: Ouch! Real Numbers," *Business Week,* March 24, 2003, p. 72.
7. Greg Farrell, "CPAs Look for an Ad Agency to Rebuild Images," *USA Today,* February 26, 2003, p. 2B.
8. Paul Craig Roberts, "Unintended Consequences of Earlier Reforms Bit Market Hard," *Washington Times,* March 16, 2003.
9. Kristen Hays, "Andersen OKs $40 Million for Enron Claims," AP Online, August 27, 2002.
10. "SEC Acts to Keep Companies Honest/Bar Those That Don't Follow New Audit Rules," *Newsday,* April 1, 2003, p. A53.
11. Stacy A. Teicher, "Job of 'Policing' Companies May Fall More to Auditors," *Christian Science Monitor,* March 31, 2003, p. 18.
12. Carrie Johnson Washington, "Corporate Audit Panels to Gain Power; SEC Passes New Rules," *Washington Post,* April 2, 2003, p. E2.
13. Matt Krantz, "More Annual Reports Delayed," *USA Today,* April 2, 2003, p. 1B; and Mike McNamee, "Finance: Annual Reports: Still Not Enough Candor," *Business Week,* March 24, 2003, p. 74.

14. Jackie Spinner, "Ease Up on Accounting Curbs, Pitt Says," *Washington Post,* March 21, 2002, p. E1.
15. Jeffrey Battersby, "QuickBooks Pro 5.0," *MacWorld,* April 1, 2003, p. 34.
16. Ibid.
17. Larry Blasko, "Feds Push Tax-Preparation Software," AP Online, January 27, 2003.
18. Timothy J. Mullaney, "Information Technology: Software: The Wizard of Intuit," *Business Week,* October 28, 2002, p. 60.
19. Robert Barker, "A Cloud Clears for a Gene Mapper," *Business Week,* March 3, 2003, p. 134.
20. Samuel Greengard, "Get a Grip on Assets," *Business Finance,* January 2002, pp. 39–42.
21. Anne Tergesen, "The Fine Print: How Much Is the Goodwill Worth?" *Business Week,* September 16, 2002, p. 83.
22. Ann Harrington, "Honey, I Shrunk the Profits: Accounting Made a Bad Year Look a Whole Lot Worse," *Fortune,* April 14, 2003, pp. 197–99.
23. "Fortune 5 Hundred Notes," *Fortune,* April 14, 2003, p. F-22.
24. Elizabeth MacDonald, "The Ebitda Folly," *Forbes,* March 17, 2003, p. 165.
25. Michael Sivy, "Stocks for a Muddled Market," *Money,* April 1, 2003, p. 67.
26. Deepa Babington, "Cash Flow Numbers Scarce Despite Scandals," Reuters Business, October 27, 2002.
27. Gary Anthes, "Net Present Value," *Computerworld,* February 17, 2003, p. 30.
28. "Warning! How to tell if you are having cash flow problems before it's too late," [n.d.], Visa Canada. Retrieved from www.visa.ca/smallbusiness/article.cfm?cat=3&subcat=95&articleID=101.
29. Jason Kirby, "Mr. Moneybags," March 15, 2004, *Canadian Business Magazine.* Retrieved from www.canadianbusiness.com/columns/article.jsp?content=20040315_59015_59015.
30. Leonard Wiener, "Gimme a Break," *U.S. News & World Report,* March 10, 2003, p. 40; and Elizabeth MacDonald, "The EBITDA Folly," *Forbes,* March 17, 2003, p. 165.
31. Mike McNamee, "Annual Reports: Still Not Enough Candor," *Business Week,* March 24, 2003, p. 74.
32. Lewis Braham, "Stocks: Weighting the Balance Sheet," *Business Week,* April 1, 2002, p. 84.
33. Dee Depass, "Moody's Downgrades St. Paul Company's Debt," *Minneapolis Star Tribune,* April 4, 2003, p. 3D.

Chapter 17

1. Nanette Byrnes and Louis Lavelle, "The Corporate Tax Game," *Business Week,* March 31, 2003, pp. 78–83.
2. Stacy A. Teicher, "Job of Policing Companies May Fall More to Insiders," *Christian Science Monitor,* March 31, 2003, p. 18.
3. Carrie Johnson Washington, "Corporate Audit Panels to Gain Power: SEC Passes New Rules," *Washington Post,* April 2, 2003, p. E2.
4. Mara Der Hovanesian, "Cash: Burn, Baby, Burn," *Business Week,* April 28, 2003, pp. 82–83.
5. Anne Tergesen, "Cash-Flow Hocus-Pocus," *Business Week,* July 16, 2002, pp. 130–32.
6. Paul Katzeff, "Manage Accounts Receivable Upfront before There's a Problem," *Investors Business Daily,* January 27, 2003, p. A4.
7. Krissah Williams Washington, "How Stores Play Their Cards: They'll Give Discounts and Awards to Get Interest and Bigger Sales," *Washington Post,* February 2, 2003, p. H5.
8. Linda Stern, "Credit Card Issuers Offer Some Good Deals," Reuters Business, March 1, 2003.

9.   David Skrobot, "Customer Service A-to-Z," *Ward's Dealer Business,* January 1, 2003, p. 35.

10. Lisa McLaughlin, "New Brew on the Block," *Time,* January 20, 2003, p. 143.

11. Courtney McGrath, "Bankers You Can Love," *Kiplinger's,* April 2003, pp. 46–48.

12. Janice Revell, "How Debt Triggers Can Sink a Stock," *Fortune,* March 18, 2002, pp. 147–51.

13. John M. Berry, "Low Interest Rates Are Allowing Corporations to Boost Profit," *Washington Post,* April 19, 2003, p. D12.

14. Toni Clarke and Jed Stelzer, "Merck Profit Rises on Higher Drug Sales," Reuters Business, April 21, 2003.

15. Jeff Ostrowski, "Proposal Would Cut Flood of Delistings," *Palm Beach Post,* February 6, 2003, p. 4D.

16. *The Canadian Securities Course 1993* (Toronto: The Canadian Securities Institute, 1992), p. 63.

17. Justin Fox, "Show Us the Money," *Fortune,* February 3, 2003, pp. 76–78.

18. Walter Updegrave, "Dividend Mania, What the Bush Dividend Plan Would Really Mean for You," *Money,* March 1, 2003, pp. 69–74.

19. "The Preferred Route to Income Preferred Stocks Offer the Most Sumptuous Dividend Payments Around," *Money,* March 1, 2003, p. 54B.

20. Michael Barbaro, "Primus Agrees to Sell Convertible Preferred Stock," *Washington Post,* January 1, 2003, p. E5.

Chapter 18

1.   "About the Financial Services Sector," May 28, 2003. Financial Consumer Agency of Canada. Retrieved from www.fcac-acfc.gc.ca/eng/financialservices/default.asp.

2.   "About the Financial Services Sector—Facts & Figures," May 28, 2003, Financial Consumer Agency of Canada. Retrieved from www.fcac-acfc.gc.ca/eng/financialservices/facts.asp.

3.   "Competition in the Canadian Financial Services Sector," May 2004, Canadian Bankers Association. Retrieved from http://www.cba.ca/en/content/stats/fastfacts/040528_Competitionffact.pdf.

4.   "How the industry is regulated," May 29, 2003, Financial Consumer Agency of Canada. Retrieved from http://www.fcac-acfc.gc.ca/eng/financialservices/picture.asp.

5.   "Homepage," January 29, 2004, Ottawa: The Canada Deposit Insurance Corporation. Retrieved from http://www.cdic.ca/?id=100.

6.   Evan I. Schwartz, "How You'll Pay," *Technology Review,* January 2003, pp. 50–56.

7.   "Counterfeit Detection," [n.d.], Ottawa: Bank of Canada. Retrieved from www.bankofcanada.ca/en/banknotes/counterfeit/security/index100b.html.

8.   Catherine Siskos, "Cash in a Flash," *Kiplinger's,* October 2002, pp. 30–31.

9.   "Deflation Warning," *Washington Times,* May 14, 2003, p. A20.

10. Patrick Barta and Michelle Higgins, "Dollar's Fall Could End Many Bargains," *The Wall Street Journal,* January 9, 2003, pp. D1, D4.

11. "Canada's Money Supply," January 2000. Ottawa: Bank of Canada. Retrieved from http://www.bankofcanada.ca/en/backgrounders/bg-m2.htm; "Target for the Overnight Rate," July 2001. Ottawa: Bank of Canada. Retrieved from http://www.bankofcanada.ca/en/backgrounders/bg-p9.htm.

12. "Canada's Money Supply," January 2000, Ottawa: Bank of Canada. Retrieved from http://www.bankofcanada.ca/en/backgrounders/bg-m2.htm.

13. "Target for the Overnight Rate," July 2001, Ottawa: Bank of Canada. Retrieved from http://www.bankofcanada.ca/en/backgrounders/bg-p9.htm.

14. "Bank Earnings," April 2003, Toronto: Canadian Bankers Association. Retrieved from http://www.cba.ca/en/ViewDocument.asp?fl=6&sl=111&tl=&docid=420.

15. "Bank Revenues and Earnings (Profits)" (July 2004), Canadian Bankers Association. Retrieved from http://www.cba.ca/en/ViewDocument.asp?fl=6&sl=111&tl=&docid=420.

16. Julie Rawe, "A Mini-Mall in Your ATM," *Time,* April 8, 2002, p. 61.

17. Michelle Higgins, "ATMs to Go Far Beyond Cash," *The Wall Street Journal,* June 6, 2002, pp. D1, D2.

18. Stephanie Miles, "What's a Check?" *The Wall Street Journal,* October 21, 2002, p. R5.

19. Pallavi Gogoi, "The Hot News in Banking: Bricks and Mortar," *Business Week,* April 21, 2003, pp. 83–84.

20. "Financial Consumer Agency of Canada Glossary—Investment Dealer Definition," February 26, 2004, Financial Consumer Agency of Canada. Retrieved from http://www.fcac-acfc.gc.ca/eng/glossary.asp; "Canadian Securities Industry Profile," [2004], Investment Dealers Association of Canada. Retrieved from http://www.ida.ca/IndIssues/IndProfile_en.asp; and "The Canadian Securities Industry—The Canadian Financial System—June 2000," September 5, 2003, Department of Finance Canada. Retrieved from http://www.fin.gc.ca/toce/2000/cansec_e.html.

21. Bertrand Marotte, "Regulator assails plan for national stock watchdog," *The Globe and Mail,* January 22, 2004, p. B6; Karen Howlett and Heather Scoffield, "Consensus elusive over regulator," *The Globe and Mail,* January 20, 2004, p. B6; "What is the CSA?" and "Who are the Canadian Securities Administrators?" June 2001: Canadian Securities Administrators. Retrieved from http://www.csa-acvm.ca/html_CSA/about_who_are_csa.html and http://www.csa-acvm.ca/html_CSA/about.html.

22. "Financial Consumer Agency of Canada Glossary—Securities Commission Definition," February 26, 2004, Financial Consumer Agency of Canada. Retrieved from http://www.fcac-acfc.gc.ca/eng/glossary.asp.

23. "Financial Consumer Agency of Canada Glossary—Security Definition," February 26, 2004, Financial Consumer Agency of Canada. Retrieved from http://www.fcac-acfc.gc.ca/eng/glossary.asp.

24. "The Case for Going Private: Corporate Ownership," *The Economist,* January 25, 2003, p. 67.

25. www.etrade.com.

26. Ben White and Kathleen Day, "SEC Approves Wall Street Settlement; Conflict of Interest Targeted," *Washington Post,* April 29, 2003, p. A1.

27. Mara Der Hovanesian, "The Market's Closed—Wake Up," *Business Week,* March 3, 2003, p. 132.

28. Louise Lee, "Finance: Brokerages: Did E-Trade Just Trade Up?" *Business Week,* February 10, 2003, p. 68.

29. Ben White, "A Crisis of Trust on Wall Street," *Washington Post,* May 4, 2003, p. F1.

30. Eric Troseth, "Finding a Rally in Bearish Times," *Christian Science Monitor,* May 5, 2003, p. 14.

31. Jyoti Thottam, "Are Penny Stocks Worth a Look?" *Time,* August 12, 2002, p. 46.

32. "Hillsdale Hedge Funds Prepared for May 1st S+P/TSE Composite Index Changes," February 2002, Toronto: Hillsdale Investment Management. Retrieved from www.hillsdaleinv.com/research/pdf/tse_change.pdf.

33. Matt Krantz, "Microsoft Stock Splits into 10 Billion Shares," *USA Today,* February 19, 2003, p. 1B.

34. "Canada's Mutual Fund Industry—March 2002," March 8, 2004, Department of Finance Canada. Retrieved from http://www.fin.gc.ca/toce/2002/cmfi_e.html.

35. "Industry Statistics," June 15, 2004, The Investment Funds Institute of Canada. Retrieved from http://www.ific.ca/eng/home/index.asp.
36. Martha Graybow, "Do Good Mutual Funds Gain in Rough Market?" Reuters Business, February 9, 2003.
37. John Rekenthaler, "When Mutual Funds Die, Companies Bury Their Mistakes, Distorting Returns," *Money,* April 2003, pp. 49–53.
38. Kathleen Day and Carrie Johnson Washington, "New Strength at the SEC's Helm; Donaldson Surprises Consumer Advocates," *Washington Post,* May 7, 2003, p. E1.

Appendix A

1. Alan Goldstein, "Techies Are Seeing, Being Seen: As Computing Has Changed, So Has Former Basement Dwellers' Role," *Dallas Morning News,* March 20, 2002, p. 1D; Kathleen Melymuka, "35 Years of IT Leadership: The Evolution of the IT Leader," *Computerworld,* September 30, 2002, p. 28; John J. Ciulla, "Step Up and Lead, *CIO,* June 15, 2002, pp. 48–50; and Jean Consilvio, "Q&A: A CIO's First Year on the Job," *Computerworld,* February 10, 2003, p. 46.
2. Laura Koss-Feder, "Providing for Parents, the 'Sandwich Generation' Looks for New Solutions," *Time,* March 17, 2003, p. G8.
3. Megan Santosus, "The Doctor Is In—Always," *CIO,* June 15, 2002, pp. 16–18; and Daniel J. Horgan, "You've Got Conversation," *CIO,* October 15, 2002, p. 38.
4. Jim Kerstetter, "The Web at Your Service," *Business Week e.biz,* March 18, 2002.
5. Lynn Greiner, "The House That Data Built," *Computing Canada,* August 9, 2002, p. 12; Tommy Peterson, "Data Scrubbing," *Computerworld,* February 10, 2003, p. 32; and Robert L. Scheier, "How Will You Automate Your Enterprise?" *Computerworld,* January 6, 2003, p. 18.
6. Bill Saporito, "Can Wal-Mart Get Any Bigger?" *Time,* January 13, 2003, p. 38; and Jerry Useem, "One Nation under Wal-Mart," *Fortune,* March 3, 2003, p. 64.
7. Lea Goldman, "A Fortune in Firewalls," *Forbes,* March 18, 2002, p. 102; and Wayne Rash and P. J. Connolly, "Zone Labs Simplifies Personal-Firewall Management," *InfoWorld,* February 10, 2003.
8. Steve Alexander, "How Will You Build Business on the Web?" *Computerworld,* January 6, 2003, p. 21; and "Attenda Has Appetite for IT Contract," M2 PressWIRE, February 19, 2003.
9. James Cope, "Outsourcing VPNS: Privacy for Hire," *Computerworld,* February 11, 2002, p. 36; and "IP Virtual Private Networks Increasingly Outsourced," *Europemedia,* February 4, 2003.
10. Steve Burrell, "The New Digital Campus," *Technological Horizons in Education,* September 1, 2002, p. 20; Luisa Kroll,

"R-E-S-P-E-C-T," *Forbes,* July 22, 2002, p. 184; Samuel Greengard, "Get the Most Out of Your HR or Enterprise Portal," *Workforce,* April 2002, p. 38; and "Sun ONE Portal Virtualizes Manufacturing Processes, Supplier Management and Collaboration," M2 PressWIRE, March 5, 2003.
11. Alex Salkever, "Ready to Supercharge Your Surfing," *Business Week Online,* September 17, 2002; Anick Jesdanun, "Will Speedy Connections Improve Life?" AP Online, March 11, 2002; and Toby Weber, "Premium Fuel for Wireless," *Wireless Review,* March 1, 2003.
12. Joe Licavoli, "High Speed Internet2 on the Move in the Cal State System," University Wire, February 27, 2002; "World's First Long-Distance Super HD Transmission over IP Network," *TV Meets the Web,* October 30, 2002; Stephanie DeMoor, "Louisiana State U. Acquires Videoconferencing Technology," University Wire, July 16, 2002; "Brain Images from Patients with Schizophrenia Will Be Shared in First Nationwide Imaging Network," Ascribe Newswire, October 29, 2002; and Mark Hall, "Internet2 and You," *Computerworld,* January 20, 2003, p. 32.
13. Peter Shinkle, "Internet2 Attracts Research Centers, Universities," *St. Louis Post-Dispatch,* April 17, 2002, p. E1; and "Sun Microsystems Laboratories Contributes XACML Security Standard Implementation to Open Source Project," M2 PressWIRE, February 19, 2003.
14. Jim Krane, "For Las Vegas Gadget Show, Technology Boom Never Went Bust," *AP Worldstream,* January 7, 2003.
15. Harry Wessel, "Efficiency in Hand," *Bergen County (New Jersey) Record,* March 10, 2003, p. L5; Carlos A. Soto, "2002's Top Products Hint at Future; Bigger, Smaller, Safer, Faster, Cheaper, Friendlier, Better," *Washington Post,* January 9, 2003, p. E7; and Jefferson Graham, "Hello, Tech Designers? This Stuff Is Too Small," *USA Today,* March 4, 2003, p. 1D.
16. "Mobility, Flexibility, and Security," M2 PressWIRE, May 8, 2002; Amey Stone, "How Wi-Fi Can Remake the Workplace," *Business Week Online,* April 1, 2002; and Kevin Fitchard, "Carriers, Vendors Warm Up to Wi-Fi," *Telephony,* January 27, 2003.
17. Barry Kipnis, "Technology 2001: A Glimpse to the Future," *National Real Estate Investor,* January 1, 2001.
18. Alex Salkever, "Dev Mukherjee: IT Service, à la Carte," *Business Week Online,* October 1, 2002; and Thomas Hoffman, "All or Nothing," *Computerworld,* March 10, 2003, p. 42.
19. Jane Black, "Faceless Snoopers Have the Upper Hand," *Business Week,* June 5, 2002; and Don Oldenburg, "Identity Theft: It Pays to Be Diligent," *Washington Post,* January 7, 2003, p. C9.
20. Strauss, "When Computers Fail," *USA Today,* December 7, 1999, p. A2; Fara Warner, "Microsoft Eats the Dog Food," *Fast Company,* September 2002, pp. 46–48; "Computer Kills 8,500," *The Mirror,* January 10, 2003, p. 19.

Glossary

Absolute advantage (p. 64) The advantage that exists when a country has a monopoly on producing a specific product or is able to produce it more efficiently than all other countries.

Accounting (p. 486) The recording, classifying, summarizing, and interpreting of financial events and transactions to provide management and other interested parties the information they need to make good decisions.

Accounting cycle (p. 494) A six-step procedure that results in the preparation and analysis of the two major financial statements: the balance sheet and the income statement.

Acquisition (p. 168) One company's purchase of the property and obligations of another company.

Administered distribution system (p. 466) A distribution system in which producers manage all of the marketing functions at the retail level.

Administrative agencies (p. 593) Federal or state institutions and other government organizations created by Parliament or provincial legislatures with delegated power to pass rules and regulations within their mandated area of authority.

Advertising (p. 468) Paid, nonpersonal communication through various media by organizations and individuals who are in some way identified in the advertising message.

Agency shop (Rand formula) (p. 392) A workplace in which a new employee is not required to join the union but must pay union dues. This historic formula was devised by Justice Rand.

Agents/brokers (p. 459) Marketing intermediaries who bring buyers and sellers together and assist in negotiating an exchange but don't take title to the goods.

Amortization (p. 506) The systematic write-off of the cost of a tangible asset over its estimated useful life.

Angel investors (p. 206) Private individuals who invest their own money in potentially hot new companies before they go public.

Annual report (p. 489) A yearly statement of the financial condition, progress, and expectations of an organization.

Apprentice programs (p. 356) Training programs involving a period during which a learner works alongside an experienced employee to master the skills and procedures of a craft.

Arbitration (p. 395) The process of resolving all disputes, not only grievances, through an outside, impartial third party. The decision is binding.

Articles of incorporation (p. 166) A legal authorization from the federal or provincial/territorial government for a company to use the corporate format.

Assembly process (p. 299) That part of the production process that puts together components.

Assets (p. 498) Economic resources (things of value) owned by a firm.

Auditing (p. 491) The job of reviewing and evaluating the records used to prepare a company's financial statements.

Autocratic leadership (p. 234) Leadership style that involves making managerial decisions without consulting others.

Balance of payments (p. 67) The difference between money coming into a country (from exports) and money leaving the country (for imports) plus money flows from other factors such as tourism, foreign aid, military expenditures, and foreign investment.

Balance of trade (p. 67) A nation's ratio of exports to imports.

Balance sheet (p. 498) The financial statement that reports a firm's financial condition at a specific time.

Bankruptcy (p. 600) The legal process by which a person, business, or government entity unable to meet financial obligations is relieved of those obligations by a court that divides any assets among creditors, allowing creditors to get at least part of their money and freeing the debtor to begin anew.

Bargaining zone (p. 394)   Range of options between the initial and final offer that each party will consider before negotiations dissolve or reach an impasse.

Barter (p. 555)   The trading of goods and services for other goods and services directly.

Behavioural segmentation (p. 427)   Dividing the market based on behaviour with or toward a product.

Benchmarking (p. 268)   Comparing an organization's practices, processes, and products against the world's best.

Bookkeeping (p. 493)   The recording of business transactions.

Bond (p. 537)   A corporate certificate indicating that a person has lent money to a firm.

Brainstorming (p. 226)   Coming up with as many solutions to a problem as possible in a short period of time with no censoring of ideas.

Brand (p. 452)   A name, symbol, or design (or combination thereof) that identifies the goods or services of one seller or group of sellers and distinguishes them from the goods and services of competitors.

Brand awareness (p. 453)   How quickly or easily a given brand name comes to mind when a product category is mentioned.

Brand equity (p. 452)   The combination of factors—such as awareness, loyalty, perceived quality, images, and emotions—that people associate with a given brand name.

Brand loyalty (p. 452)   The degree to which customers are satisfied, like the brand, and are committed to further purchase.

Brand manager (p. 453)   A manager who has direct responsibility for one brand or one product line; called a product manager in some firms.

Brand name (p. 418)   A word, letter, or group of words or letters that differentiates one seller's goods and services.

Breach of contract (p. 597)   When one party fails to follow the terms of a contract.

Break-even analysis (p. 455)   The process used to determine profitability at various levels of sales.

Broadband technology (p. 584)   Technology that offers users a continuous connection to the Internet and allows them to send and receive mammoth files that include voice, video, and data much faster than ever before.

Budget (p. 525)   A financial plan that sets forth management's expectations, and, on the basis of those expectations, allocates the use of specific resources throughout the firm.

Bundling (p. 457)   Grouping two or more products together and pricing them as a unit.

Bureaucracy (p. 253)   An organization with many layers of managers who set rules and regulations and oversee all decisions.

Business (p. 4)   Any activity that seeks to provide goods and services to others while operating at a profit.

Business cycles (p. 52)   The periodic rises and falls that occur in all economies over time.

Business environment (p. 11)   The surrounding factors that either help or hinder the development of businesses.

Business establishment (p. 197)   Has at least one paid employee, annual sales revenue of $30,000, or is incorporated and has filed a federal corporate income tax return at least once in the previous three years.

Business law (p. 593)   Rules, statutes, codes, and regulations that are established to provide a legal framework within which business may be conducted and that are enforceable by court action.

Business plan (p. 204)   A detailed written statement that describes the nature of the business, the target market, the advantages the business will have in relation to competition, and the resources and qualifications of the owner(s).

Business-to-business (B2B) market (p. 426)   All the individuals and organizations that want goods and services to use in producing other goods and services or to sell, rent, or supply goods to others.

Buying on margin (p. 570)   Purchasing securities by borrowing some of the cost from the broker.

Cafeteria-style benefits (p. 364)   Benefit plans that allow employees to choose which benefits they want up to a certain dollar amount.

Capital assets (p. 498)   Assets that are relatively permanent, such as land, buildings, and equipment.

Capital budget (p. 525)   A budget that highlights a firm's spending plans for major asset purchases that often require large sums of money.

Capital expenditures (p. 530)   Major investments in either tangible long-term assets such as land, buildings, and equipment or intangible assets such as patents, trademarks, and copyrights.

Capital gains (p. 569)   The positive difference between the purchase price of a stock and its sale price.

Capitalism (p. 36)   An economic system in which all or most of the factors of production and distribution are privately owned and operated for profit.

Cash budget (p. 525)   A budget that estimates a firm's projected cash inflows and outflows that the firm can use to plan for any cash shortages or surpluses during a given period.

Cash flow (p. 504)   The difference between cash coming in and cash going out of a business.

Cash flow forecast (p. 524)   Forecast that predicts the cash inflows and outflows in future periods, usually months or quarters.

Centralized authority (p. 255)   An organization structure in which decision-making authority is maintained at the top level of management at the company's headquarters.

Certification (p. 390)   Formal process whereby a union is recognized by the Labour Relations Board (LRB) as the bargaining agent for a group of employees.

Certified general accountant (CGA) (p. 490)   An accountant who has met the examination, education, and experience requirements of the Certified General Accountants Association of Canada.

Certified management accountant (CMA) (p. 489)   An accountant who has met the examination, education, and experience requirements of the Society of Management Accountants of Canada.

Chain of command (p. 253)   The line of authority that moves from the top of a hierarchy to the lowest level.

Channel of distribution (p. 459)   A whole set of marketing intermediaries, such as wholesalers and retailers, that join together to transport and store goods in their path (or channel) from producers to consumers.

Chartered Accountant (CA) (p. 489)   An Accountant who has met the examination, education, and experience requirements of the Canadian Institute of Chartered Accountants.

Check-off clause (p. 392)   A contract clause requiring the employer to deduct union dues from employees' pay and remit them to a union.

Civil law (p. 593)   Legal proceedings that do not involve criminal acts.

Closed shop (p. 392)   A workplace in which all new hires must already be union members.

Collective bargaining (p. 389)   The process whereby union and management representatives form a labour–management agreement, or contract, for workers.

Commercial bank (p. 560)   A profit-seeking organization that receives deposits from individuals and corporations in the form of chequing and savings accounts and then uses some of these funds to make loans.

Commercial finance companies (p. 534)   Organizations that make short-term loans to borrowers who offer tangible assets as collateral.

Commercial paper (p. 535)   Unsecured promissory notes of $100,000 and up that mature (come due) in 365 days or less.

Common market (p. 85)   A regional group of countries that have a common external tariff, no internal tariffs, and a coordination of laws to facilitate exchange; also called a *trading bloc*. An example is the European Union.

Common law (p. 593)   The body of law that comes from decisions handed down by judges; also referred to as *unwritten law*.

Common shares (p. 542)   The most basic form of ownership in a firm; it confers voting rights and the right to share in the firm's profits through dividends, if offered by the firm's board of directors.

Communism (p. 44)   An economic and political system in which the state (the government) makes all economic decisions and owns almost all the major factors of production.

Comparative advantage theory (p. 64)   Theory that states that a country should sell to other countries those products that it produces most effectively and efficiently, and buy from other countries those products that it cannot produce as effectively or efficiently.

Competing in time (p. 305) Being as fast as or faster than competitors in responding to consumer wants and needs and getting goods and services to them.

Competition-based pricing (p. 455) A pricing strategy based on what all the other competitors are doing. The price can be set at, above, or below competitors' prices.

Compliance-based ethics codes (p. 132) Ethical standards that emphasize preventing unlawful behaviour by increasing control and by penalizing wrongdoers.

Compressed workweek (p. 366) Work schedule that allows an employee to work a full number of hours per week but in fewer days.

Computer-aided design (CAD) (p. 305) The use of computers in the design of products.

Computer-aided manufacturing (CAM) (p. 305) The use of computers in the manufacturing of products.

Computer-integrated manufacturing (CIM) (p. 305) The uniting of computer-aided design with computer-aided manufacturing.

Conceptual skills (p. 228) Skills that involve the ability to picture the organization as a whole and the relationship among its various parts.

Conglomerate merger (p. 168) The joining of firms in completely unrelated industries.

Consideration (p. 597) Something of value; consideration is one of the requirements of a legal contract.

Consumer market (p. 426) All the individuals or households that want goods and services for personal consumption or use.

Consumer price index (CPI) (p. 52) Monthly statistics that measure the pace of inflation or deflation.

Consumerism (p. 598) A social movement that seeks to increase and strengthen the rights and powers of buyers in relation to sellers.

Contingency planning (p. 225) The process of preparing alternative courses of action that may be used if the primary plans don't achieve the organization's objectives.

Contingent workers (p. 354) Workers who do not have regular, full-time employment.

Continuous improvement (CI) (p. 271) Constantly improving the way the organization does things so that customer needs can be better satisfied.

Continuous process (p. 299) A production process in which long production runs turn out finished goods over time.

Contract (p. 597) A legally enforceable agreement between two or more parties.

Contract law (p. 597) Set of laws that specify what constitutes a legally enforceable agreement.

Contract manufacturing (p. 74) A foreign country's production of private-label goods to which a domestic company then attaches its brand name or trademark; also called *outsourcing*.

Contractual distribution system (p. 466) A distribution system in which members are bound to co-operate through contractual agreements.

Controlling (p. 220) A management function that involves establishing clear standards to determine whether or not an organization is progressing toward its goals and objectives, rewarding people for doing a good job, and taking corrective action if they are not.

Convenience products (p. 449) Goods and services that the consumer wants to purchase frequently and with a minimum of effort.

Cookies (p. 591) Pieces of information, such as registration data or user preferences, sent by a Website over the Internet to a Web browser that the browser software is expected to save and send back to the server whenever the user returns to that Website.

Co-operative (p. 176) An organization that is owned by members and customers, who pay an annual membership fee and share in any profits.

Copyright (p. 595) A document that protects a creator's rights to materials such as books, articles, photos, and cartoons.

Core competencies (p. 255) Those functions that an organization can do as well as or better than any other organization in the world.

Core time (p. 366) In a flextime plan, the period when all employees are expected to be at their job stations.

Corporate distribution system (p. 465) A distribution system in which all of the organizations in the channel of distribution are owned by one firm.

Corporate governance (p. 165)   The process and policies that determine how an organization interacts with its stakeholders, both internal and external.

Corporate philanthropy (p. 135)   Dimension of social responsibility that includes charitable donations.

Corporate policy (p. 136)   Dimension of social responsibility that refers to the position a firm takes on social and political issues.

Corporate responsibility (p. 136)   Dimension of social responsibility that includes everything from hiring minority workers to making safe products.

Corporate social responsibility (p. 135)   A business's concern for the welfare of society as a whole.

Corporation (p. 154)   A legal entity with authority to act and have liability separate from its owners.

Cost of goods sold (or cost of goods manufactured) (p. 501)   A measure of the cost of merchandise sold or cost of raw materials and supplies used for producing items for resale.

Countertrading (p. 81)   A complex form of bartering in which several countries may be involved, each trading goods for goods or services for services.

Craft union (p. 384)   An organization of skilled specialists in a particular craft or trade.

Credit unions (p. 552)   Non-profit, member-owned financial cooperatives that offer a full variety of banking services to their members.

Cross-functional self-managed teams (p. 265)   Groups of employees from different departments who work together on a long-term basis.

Crown corporation (p. 99)   A company that is owned by the federal or provincial government.

Current assets (p. 498)   Items that can or will be converted into cash within one year.

Customer relationship management (CRM) (p. 415)   The process of learning as much as possible about customers and doing everything you can to satisfy them—or even exceed their expectations—with goods and services over time.

Damages (p. 598)   The monetary settlement awarded to a person who is injured by a breach of contract.

Database (p. 18)   An electronic storage file where information is kept; one use of databases is to store vast amounts of information about consumers.

Debenture bonds (p. 538)   Bonds that are unsecured (i.e., not backed by any collateral such as equipment).

Debt financing (p. 531)   Funds raised through various forms of borrowing that must be repaid.

Decentralized authority (p. 255)   An organization structure in which decision-making authority is delegated to lower-level managers more familiar with local conditions than headquarters management could be.

Decision making (p. 225)   Choosing among two or more alternatives.

Deficit (p. 106)   Occurs when a government spends over and above the amount it gathers in taxes for a specific period of time (namely, a fiscal year).

Deflation (p. 52)   A situation in which prices are declining.

Demand (p. 38)   The quantity of products that people are willing to buy at different prices at a specific time.

Demographic segmentation (p. 427)   Dividing the market by age, income, and education level.

Demography (p. 20)   The statistical study of the human population with regard to its size, density, and other characteristics such as age, race, gender, and income.

Departmentalization (p. 259)   The dividing of organizational functions into separate units.

Depression (p. 53)   A severe recession.

Deregulation (p. 602)   Government withdrawal of certain laws and regulations that seem to hinder competition.

Direct marketing (p. 465)   Any activity that directly links manufacturers or intermediaries with the ultimate consumer.

Direct selling (p. 465)   Selling to consumers in their homes or where they work.

Disinflation (p. 52)   A situation in which price increases are slowing (the inflation rate is declining).

Diversification (p. 573)   Buying several different investment alternatives to spread the risk of investing.

Dividends (p. 541)   Part of a firm's profits that may be distributed to shareholders as either cash payments or additional shares of stock.

Double-entry bookkeeping (p. 493)   The concept of writing every business transaction in two places.

Dumping (p. 71)   Selling products in a foreign country at lower prices than those charged in the producing country.

Economics (p. 34)   The study of how society chooses to employ resources to produce goods and services and distribute them for consumption among various competing groups and individuals.

Economies of scale (p. 104)   The situation in which companies can reduce their production costs if they can purchase raw materials in bulk; the average cost of goods goes down as production levels increase.

Electronic retailing (p. 464)   Selling goods and services to ultimate customers (e.g., you and me) over the Internet.

Embargo (p. 83)   A complete ban on the import or export of a certain product.

Employee benefits (p. 363)   Benefits such as sick-leave pay, vacation pay, pension plans, and health plans that represent additional compensation to employees beyond base wages.

Employee orientation (p. 355)   The activity that introduces new employees to the organization; to fellow employees; to their immediate supervisors; and to the policies, practices, values, and objectives of the firm.

Employer business (p. 197)   Meets one of the business establishment criteria and usually maintains a payroll of at least one person, possibly the owner.

Employment equity (p. 372)   Employment activities designed to "right past wrongs" by increasing opportunities for minorities and women.

Empowerment (p. 19)   Giving frontline workers the responsibility, authority, and freedom to respond quickly to customer requests.

Enabling (p. 236)   Giving workers the education and tools they need to make decisions.

Enterprise resource planning (ERP) (p. 300)   A computer application that enables multiple firms to manage all of their operations (finance, requirements planning, human resources, and order

fulfillment) on the basis of a single, integrated set of corporate data.

Entrepreneur (p. 4)   A person who risks time and money to start and manage a business.

Entrepreneurial team (p. 191)   A group of experienced people from different areas of business who join together to form a managerial team with the skills needed to develop, make, and market a new product.

Entrepreneurship (p. 186)   Accepting the challenge of starting and running a business.

Environmental scanning (p. 424)   The process of identifying the factors that can affect marketing success.

Equity financing (p. 531)   Funds raised from operations within the firm or through the sale of ownership in the firm.

Equity theory (p. 328)   The idea that employees try to maintain equity between inputs and outputs compared to others in similar positions.

Ethics (p. 126)   Standards of moral behaviour; that is, behaviour that is accepted by society as right versus wrong.

Everyday low pricing (EDLP) (p. 456)   Setting prices lower than competitors and then not having any special sales.

Exchange rate (p. 80)   The value of one nation's currency relative to the currencies of other countries.

Exclusive distribution (p. 463)   Distribution that sends products to only one retail outlet in a given geographic area.

Expectancy theory (p. 327)   Victor Vroom's theory that the amount of effort employees exert on a specific task depends on their expectations of the outcome.

Exporting (p. 63)   Selling products to another country.

Express warranties (p. 596)   Specific representations by the seller that buyers rely on regarding the goods they purchase.

External customers (p. 240)   Dealers, who buy products to sell to others, and ultimate customers (or end users), who buy products for their own personal use.

Extranet (p. 583)   A semiprivate network that uses Internet technology and allows more than one company to access the same information or allows people on different servers to collaborate.

Extrinsic reward (p. 316)   Something given to you by someone else as recognition for good work; extrinsic rewards include pay increases, praise, and promotions.

Facility layout (p. 289)   The physical arrangement of resources (including people) in the production process.

Facility location (p. 286)   The process of selecting a geographic location for a company's operations.

Factoring (p. 534)   The process of selling accounts receivable for cash.

Factors of production (p. 9)   The resources used to create wealth: land, labour, capital, entrepreneurship, and knowledge.

Federal budget (p. 108)   A comprehensive report that reveals government financial policies for the coming year.

Finance (p. 522)   The function in a business that acquires funds for the firm and manages those funds within the firm.

Financial accounting (p. 489)   Accounting information and analyses prepared for people outside the organization.

Financial control (p. 527)   A process in which a firm periodically compares its actual revenues, costs, and expenses with its projected ones.

Financial management (p. 522)   The job of managing a firm's resources so it can meet its goals and objectives.

Financial managers (p. 522)   Managers who make recommendations to top executives regarding strategies for improving the financial strength of a firm.

Financial statement (p. 495)   A summary of all the transactions that have occurred over a particular period.

First in, first out (FIFO) (p. 508)   An accounting method for calculating cost of inventory; it assumes that the first goods to come in are the first to go out.

Fiscal policy (p. 106)   The federal government's effort to keep the economy stable by increasing or decreasing taxes or government spending.

Flat organization structure (p. 258)   An organization structure that has few layers of management and a broad span of control.

Flexible manufacturing (p. 303)   Designing machines to do multiple tasks so that they can produce a variety of products.

Flextime plan (p. 366)   Work schedule that gives employees some freedom to choose when to work, as long as they work the required number of hours.

Focus group (p. 422)   A small group of people who meet under the direction of a discussion leader to communicate their opinions about an organization, its products, or other issues.

Foreign direct investment (p. 70)   The buying of permanent property and businesses in foreign nations.

Foreign subsidiary (p. 76)   A company owned in a foreign country by another company (called the *parent company*).

Form utility (p. 298)   The value added by the creation of finished goods and services.

Formal organization (p. 272)   The structure that details lines of responsibility, authority, and position; that is, the structure shown on organization charts.

Franchise (p. 171)   The right to use a specific business's name and sell its goods or services in a given territory.

Franchise agreement (p. 171)   An arrangement whereby someone with a good idea for a business sells the rights to use the business name and sell its products in a given territory.

Franchisee (p. 171)   A person who buys a franchise.

Franchising (p. 170)   A method of distributing a good or service, or both, to achieve a maximum market impact with a minimum investment.

Franchisor (p. 171)   A company that develops a product concept and sells others the rights to make and sell the products.

Free trade (p. 63)   The movement of goods and services among nations without political or economic obstruction.

Free-rein (laissez-faire) leadership (p. 235)   Leadership style that involves managers setting objectives and employees being relatively free to do whatever it takes to accomplish those objectives.

Fundamental accounting equation (p. 496) Assets = liabilities + owners' equity; this is the basis for the balance sheet.

Gantt chart (p. 306) Bar graph showing production managers what projects are being worked on and what stage they are in at any given time.

General Agreement on Tariffs and Trade (GATT) (p. 83) A 1948 agreement that established an international forum for negotiating mutual reductions in trade restrictions.

General partner (p. 157) An owner (partner) who has unlimited liability and is active in managing the firm.

General partnership (p. 157) A partnership in which all owners share in operating the business and in assuming liability for the business's debts.

Geographic segmentation (p. 427) Dividing the market by geographic area.

Givebacks (p. 401) Concessions made by union members to management; gains from labour negotiations are given back to management to help employers remain competitive and thereby save jobs.

Goals (p. 222) The broad, long-term accomplishments an organization wishes to attain.

Goal-setting theory (p. 327) The idea that setting ambitious but attainable goals can motivate workers and improve performance if the goals are accepted, accompanied by feedback, and facilitated by organizational conditions.

Goods (p. 23) Tangible products such as computers, food, clothing, cars, and appliances.

Grievance (p. 393) A formal protest by an individual employee or a union when they believe a particular management decision breaches the union contract.

Gross domestic product (GDP) (p. 48) The total value of goods and services produced in a country in a given year.

Gross profit (gross margin) (p. 502) How much a firm earned by buying (or making) and selling merchandise.

Hawthorne effect (p. 319) The tendency for people to behave differently when they know they are being studied.

Hierarchy (p. 253) A system in which one person is at the top of the organization and there is a ranked or sequential ordering from the top down of managers who are responsible to that person.

High–low pricing strategy (p. 457) Set prices that are higher than EDLP stores, but have many special sales where the prices are lower than competitors.

Horizontal merger (p. 168) The joining of two firms in the same industry.

Human relations skills (p. 228) Skills that involve communication and motivation; they enable managers to work through and with people.

Human resource management (HRM) (p. 344) The process of determining human resource needs and then recruiting, selecting, developing, motivating, evaluating, compensating, and scheduling employees to achieve organizational goals.

Hygiene factors (p. 321) In Herzberg's theory of motivating factors, job factors that can cause dissatisfaction if missing but that do not necessarily motivate employees if increased.

Implied warranties (p. 596) Guarantees legally imposed on the seller.

Import quota (p. 83) A limit on the number of products in certain categories that a nation can import.

Importing (p. 63) Buying products from another country.

Income statement (p. 500) The financial statement that shows a firm's profit after costs, expenses, and taxes; it summarizes all of the resources that have come into the firm (revenue), all the resources that have left the firm, and the resulting net income.

Incubators (p. 195) Centres that provide hands-on management assistance, education, information, technical and vital business support services, networking resources, financial advice, as well as advice on where to go to seek financial assistance.

Independent audit (p. 492) An evaluation and unbiased opinion about the accuracy of a company's financial statements.

Industrial design (p. 595) Visible feature(s) of a finished product that identify it and are protected by the law (e.g., its shape or ornamentation).

Industrial goods (p. 450) Products used in the production of other products. Sometimes called business goods or B2B goods.

Industrial policy (p. 119) A comprehensive coordinated government plan to guide and revitalize the economy.

Industrial product price index (IPPI) (p. 52) Reflects the prices that producers in Canada receive as goods leave the plant gates to be sold.

Industrial union (p. 385) Consists of unskilled and semi-skilled workers in mass-production industries such as automobile manufacturing and mining.

Inflation (p. 52) A general rise in the prices of goods and services over time.

Informal organization (p. 272) The system of relationships and lines of authority that develops spontaneously as employees meet and form power centres; that is, the human side of the organization that does not appear on any organization chart.

Information technology (IT) (p. 579) Technology that helps companies change business by allowing them to use new methods.

Initial public offering (IPO) (p. 539) The first public offering of a corporation's stock.

Injunction (p. 398) A court order directing someone to do something or to refrain from doing something.

Innovation (p. 282) A new product or process that can be purchased.

Insider trading (p. 139) An unethical activity in which insiders use private company information to further their own fortunes or those of their family and friends.

Institutional investors (p. 537) Large organizations—such as pension funds, mutual funds, insurance companies, and banks—that invest their own funds or the funds of others.

Intangible assets (p. 498) Long-term assets (e.g., patents, trademarks, copyrights) that have no real physical form but do have value.

Integrated marketing communication (IMC) (p. 468) A technique that combines all the promotional tools into one comprehensive and unified promotional strategy.

Integrity-based ethics codes (p. 132) Ethical standards that define the organization's guiding values, create an environment that supports ethically sound behaviour, and stress a shared accountability among employees.

Intensive distribution (p. 463) Distribution that puts products into as many retail outlets as possible.

Interest (p. 537) The payment the issuer of the bond makes to the bondholders for use of the borrowed money.

Intermittent process (p. 299) A production process in which the production run is short and the machines are changed frequently to make different products.

Internal customers (p. 240) Individuals and units within the firm that receive services from other individuals or units.

International Monetary Fund (IMF) (p. 84) An international bank that makes short-term loans to countries experiencing problems with their balance of trade.

Internet2 (p. 585) The new Internet system that links government supercomputer centres and a select group of universities; it runs more than 22,000 times faster than today's public infrastructure and supports heavy-duty applications.

Intranet (p. 583) A companywide network, closed to public access, that uses Internet-type technology.

Intrapreneurs (p. 194) Creative people who work as entrepreneurs within corporations.

Intrinsic reward (p. 316) The good feeling you have when you have done a job well.

Inverted organization (p. 270) An organization that has contact people at the top and the chief executive officer at the bottom of the organization chart.

Invisible hand (p. 35) A phrase coined by Adam Smith to describe the process that turns self-directed gain into social and economic benefits for all.

Involuntary bankruptcy (p. 600) Bankruptcy procedures filed by a debtor's creditors.

ISO 9000 (p. 294) The common name given to quality management and assurance standards.

ISO 14000 (p. 295) A collection of the best practices for managing an organization's impact on the environment.

Job analysis (p. 348) A study of what is done by employees who hold various job titles.

Job description (p. 348) A summary of the objectives of a job, the type of work to be done, the responsibilities and duties, the working conditions, and the relationship of the job to other functions.

Job enlargement (p. 324) A job enrichment strategy that involves combining a series of tasks into one challenging and interesting assignment.

Job enrichment (p. 322) A motivational strategy that emphasizes motivating the worker through the job itself.

Job rotation (p. 324) A job enrichment strategy that involves moving employees from one job to another.

Job sharing (p. 368) An arrangement whereby two part-time employees share one full-time job.

Job simulation (p. 357) The use of equipment that duplicates job conditions and tasks so that trainees can learn skills before attempting them on the job.

Job specifications (p. 348) A written summary of the minimum qualifications required of workers to do a particular job.

Joint venture (p. 74) A partnership in which two or more companies (often from different countries) join to undertake a major project or to form a new company.

Journal (p. 493) The record book or computer program where accounting data are first entered.

Just-in-time (JIT) inventory control (p. 301) A production process in which a minimum of inventory is kept on the premises and parts, supplies, and other needs are delivered just in time to go on the assembly line.

Knowledge management (p. 237) Finding the right information, keeping the information in a readily accessible place, and making the information known to everyone in the firm.

Labour Relations Board (LRB) (p. 388) A quasi-judicial body consisting of representatives from government, labour, and business. It functions more informally than a court but has the full authority of the law.

Last in, first out (LIFO) (p. 508) An accounting method for calculating cost of inventory; it assumes that the last goods to come in are the first to go out.

Leading (p. 220) Creating a vision for the organization and guiding, training, coaching, and motivating others to work effectively to achieve the organization's goals and objectives.

Lean manufacturing (p. 303) The production of goods using less of everything compared to mass production.

Ledger (p. 493) A specialized accounting book or computer program in which information from accounting journals is accumulated into specific categories and posted so that managers can find all the information about one account in the same place.

Leveraged buyout (LBO) (p. 170) An attempt by employees, management, or a group of investors to purchase an organization primarily through borrowing.

Liabilities (p. 499) What the business owes to others (debts).

Liability (p. 155) For a business, it includes the responsibility to pay all normal debts and to pay because of a court order or law, for performance under a contract, or payment of damages to a person or property in an accident.

Licensing (p. 72) A global strategy in which a firm (the licensor) allows a foreign company (the licensee) to produce its product in exchange for a fee (a royalty).

Limited liability (p. 157) The responsibility of a business's owners for losses only up to the amount they invest; limited partners and shareholders have limited liability.

Limited partner (p. 157) An owner who invests money in the business but does not have any management responsibility or liability for losses beyond the investment.

Limited partnership (p. 157) A partnership with one or more general partners and one or more limited partners.

Line of credit (p. 534) A given amount of unsecured funds a bank will lend to a business.

Line organization (p. 262) An organization that has direct two-way lines of responsibility, authority, and communication running from the top to the bottom of the organization, with all people reporting to only one supervisor.

Line personnel (p. 263) Employees who are part of the chain of command that is responsible for achieving organizational goals.

Liquidity (p. 498)   How fast an asset can be converted into cash.

Lockout (p. 398)   An attempt by management to put pressure on unions by temporarily closing the business.

Long-term financing (p. 531)   Borrowed capital that will be repaid over a specific period longer than one year.

Long-term forecast (p. 525)   Forecast that predicts revenues, costs, and expenses for a period longer than 1 year, and sometimes as far as 5 or 10 years into the future.

Loss (p. 5)   When a business's expenses are more than its revenues.

Macroeconomics (p. 35)   The part of economic study that looks at the operation of a nation's economy as a whole.

Management (p. 219)   The process used to accomplish organizational goals through planning, organizing, leading, and controlling people and other organizational resources.

Management development (p. 357)   The process of training and educating employees to become good managers and then monitoring the progress of their managerial skills over time.

Managerial accounting (p. 487)   Accounting used to provide information and analyses to managers within the organization to assist them in decision making.

Managing diversity (p. 231)   Building systems and a climate that unite different people in a common pursuit without undermining their individual strengths.

Market (p. 208)   People with unsatisfied wants and needs who have both the resources and the willingness to buy.

Market price (p. 39)   The price determined by supply and demand.

Market segmentation (p. 427)   The process of dividing the total market into groups whose members have similar characteristics.

Marketing (p. 414)   The process of determining customer needs and wants and then developing goods and services that meet or exceed these expectations.

Marketing boards (p. 111)   Organizations that control the supply or pricing of certain agricultural products in Canada.

Marketing concept (p. 415)   A three-part business philosophy: (1) a customer orientation, (2) a service orientation, and (3) a profit orientation.

Marketing intermediaries (p. 459)   Organizations that assist in moving goods and services from producers to industrial and consumer users.

Marketing mix (p. 416)   The ingredients that go into a marketing program: product, price, place, and promotion.

Marketing research (p. 420)   The analysis of markets to determine opportunities and challenges, and to find the information needed to make good decisions.

Maslow's hierarchy of needs (p. 319)   Theory of motivation that places different types of human needs in order of importance, from basic physiological needs to safety, social, and esteem needs to self-actualization needs.

Mass customization (p. 304)   Tailoring products to meet the needs of individual customers.

Mass marketing (p. 429)   Developing products and promotions to please large groups of people.

Materials requirement planning (MRP) (p. 300)   A computer-based production management system that uses sales forecasts to make sure that needed parts and materials are available at the right time and place.

Matrix organization (p. 264)   An organization in which specialists from different parts of the organization are brought together to work on specific projects but still remain part of a line-and-staff structure.

Maturity date (p. 537)   The exact date the issuer of a bond must pay the principal to the bondholder.

Mediation (p. 394)   The use of a third party, called a mediator, who encourages both sides in a dispute to continue negotiating and often makes suggestions for resolving the dispute.

Mentor (p. 358)   An experienced employee who supervises, coaches, and guides lower-level employees by introducing them to the right people and generally being their organizational sponsor.

Merger (p. 168)   The result of two firms forming one company.

Microeconomics (p. 35) The part of economic study that looks at the behaviour of people and organizations in particular markets.

Micropreneurs (p. 191) Entrepreneurs willing to accept the risk of starting and managing the type of business that remains small, lets them do the kind of work they want to do, and offers them a balanced lifestyle.

Middle management (p. 227) The level of management that includes general managers, division managers, and branch and plant managers who are responsible for tactical planning and controlling.

Mission statement (p. 221) An outline of the fundamental purposes of an organization.

Mixed economies (p. 45) Economic systems in which some allocation of resources is made by the market and some by the government.

Monetary policy (p. 109) The management of the money supply and interest rates.

Money (p. 555) Anything that people generally accept as payment for goods and services.

Money supply (p. 556) The amount of money the Bank of Canada makes available for people to buy goods and services.

Monopolistic competition (p. 40) The market situation in which a large number of sellers produce products that are very similar but that are perceived by buyers as different.

Monopoly (p. 40) A market in which there is only one seller for a product or service.

Motivators (p. 321) In Herzberg's theory of motivating factors, job factors that cause employees to be productive and that give them satisfaction.

Multinational corporation (p. 77) An organization that manufactures and markets products in many different countries and has multinational stock ownership and multinational management.

Mutual fund (p. 572) An organization that buys stocks and bonds and then sells shares in those securities to the public.

National debt (p. 106) The sum of government debt over time.

National Policy (p. 99) Government directive that placed high tariffs on imports from the U.S. to protect Canadian manufacturing, which had higher costs.

Negligence (p. 594) In tort law, behaviour that does not meet the standard of care required and causes unintentional harm or injury.

Negotiated labour–management agreement (labour contract) (p. 391) Agreement that sets the tone and clarifies the terms under which management and labour agree to function over a period of time.

Negotiable instruments (p. 596) Forms of commercial paper (such as cheques) that are transferable among businesses and individuals and represent a promise to pay a specified amount.

Net income or net loss (p. 500) Revenue left over after all costs and expenses, including taxes, are paid.

Network computing system (client/server computing) (p. 586) Computer systems that allow personal computers (clients) to obtain needed information from huge databases in a central computer (the server).

Networking (p. 267) The process of establishing and maintaining contacts with key managers in one's own organization and other organizations and using those contacts to weave strong relationships that serve as informal development systems.

Networking (p. 358) Using communications technology and other means to link organizations and allow them to work together on common objectives.

Niche marketing (p. 429) The process of finding small but profitable market segments and designing or finding products for them.

Nonbanks (p. 552) Financial organizations that accept no deposits but offer many services provided by regular banks.

Nonprofit organization (p. 7) An organization whose goals do not include making a personal profit for its owners or organizers.

North American Free Trade Agreement (NAFTA) (p. 87) Agreement that created a free-trade area among Canada, the United States, and Mexico.

Objectives (p. 222) Specific, short-term statements detailing how to achieve the organization's goals.

Off-the-job training (p. 356) Training that occurs away from the workplace and consists of internal or external programs to develop any of a variety of skills or to foster personal development.

Oligopoly (p. 40)   A form of competition in which just a few sellers dominate the market.

One-to-one (individual) marketing (p. 429)   Developing a unique mix of goods and services for each individual customer.

Online training (p. 356)   Training programs in which employees "attend" classes via the Internet.

On-the-job training (p. 356)   Training in which the employee immediately begins his or her tasks and learns by doing, or watches others for a while and then imitates them, all right at the workplace.

Open shop (p. 392)   A workplace in which employees are free to join or not join the union and to pay or not pay union dues.

Operating (master) budget (p. 526)   The budget that ties together all of a firm's other budgets; it is the projection of dollar allocations to various costs and expenses needed to run or operate the business, given projected revenues.

Operating expenses (p. 502)   Costs involved in operating a business, such as rent, utilities, and salaries.

Operational planning (p. 224)   The process of setting work standards and schedules necessary to implement the company's tactical objectives.

Operations management (p. 285)   A specialized area in management that converts or transforms resources (including human resources) into goods and services.

Organization chart (p. 226)   A visual device that shows the relationship and divides the organization's work; it shows who is accountable for the completion of specific work and who reports to whom.

Organizational (or corporate) culture (p. 272)   Widely shared values within an organization that provide coherence and cooperation to achieve common goals.

Organizing (p. 220)   A management function that includes designing the structure of the organization and creating conditions and systems in which everyone and everything work together to achieve the organization's goals and objectives.

Outsourcing (p. 269)   Assigning various functions, such as accounting, production, security, maintenance, and legal work, to outside organizations.

Owners' equity (p. 499)   The amount of the business that belongs to the owners minus any liabilities owed by the business.

Participative (democratic) leadership (p. 235)   Leadership style that consists of managers and employees working together to make decisions.

Partnership (p. 154)   A legal form of business with two or more owners.

Partnership agreement (p. 160)   Legal document that specifies the rights and responsibilities of each partner.

Patent (p. 595)   A document that gives inventors exclusive rights to their inventions for 20 years.

Penetration price strategy (p. 456)   A strategy in which the product is priced low to attract many customers and discourage competitors.

Pension funds (p. 553)   Amounts of money put aside by corporations, nonprofit organizations, or unions to cover part of the financial needs of their members when they retire.

Perfect competition (p. 40)   The market situation in which there are many sellers in a market and no seller is large enough to dictate the price of a product.

Performance appraisal (p. 358)   An evaluation in which the performance level of employees is measured against established standards to make decisions about promotions, compensation, additional training, or firing.

Personal selling (p. 470)   The face-to-face presentation and promotion of goods and services.

Planning (p. 219)   A management function that includes anticipating trends and determining the best strategies and tactics to achieve organizational goals and objectives.

PMI (p. 226)   Listing all the pluses for a solution in one column, all the minuses in another, and the implications in a third column.

Precedent (p. 593)   Decisions judges have made in earlier cases that guide the handling of new cases.

Preferred shares (p. 542)   Stock that gives its owners preference in the payment of dividends and an earlier claim on assets than common shareholders if the company is forced out of business and its assets sold.

Price leadership (p. 455) The procedure by which one or more dominant firms set the pricing practices that all competitors in an industry follow.

Primary boycott (p. 397) When a union encourages both its members and the general public not to buy the products of a firm involved in a labour dispute.

Primary data (p. 421) Data that you gather yourself (not from secondary sources such as books and magazines).

Prime rate (p. 558) The interest rate banks charge their most creditworthy customers.

Principle of motion economy (p. 317) Theory developed by Frank and Lillian Gilbreth that every job can be broken down into a series of elementary motions.

Private accountant (p. 490) Accountants who work for a single firm, government agency, or nonprofit organization.

Private corporation (p. 161) Corporation that is not allowed to issue stock to the public, so its shares are not listed on stock exchanges; it is limited to 50 or fewer shareholders.

Privatization (p. 101) The process of governments selling Crown corporations.

Problem solving (p. 226) The process of solving the everyday problems that occur. Problem solving is less formal than decision making and usually calls for quicker action.

Process manufacturing (p. 299) That part of the production process that physically or chemically changes materials.

Producers' cartels (p. 85) Organizations of commodity-producing countries that are formed to stabilize or increase prices to optimize overall profits in the long run. (An example is OPEC, the Organization of Petroleum Exporting Countries.)

Product (p. 418) Any physical good, service, or idea that satisfies a want or need.

Product differentiation (p. 449) The creation of real or perceived product differences.

Product liability (p. 594) Part of tort law that holds businesses liable for harm that results from the production, design, sale, or use of products they market.

Product life cycle (p. 434) A theoretical model of what happens to sales and profits for a product class over time.

Product line (p. 448) A group of products that are physically similar or are intended for a similar market.

Product mix (p. 448) The combination of product lines offered by a manufacturer.

Production (p. 284) The creation of finished goods and services using the factors of production: land, labour, capital, entrepreneurship, and knowledge.

Production management (p. 285) The term used to describe all the activities managers do to help their firms create goods.

Productivity (p. 15) The amount of output that is generated given the amount of input.

Productivity (p. 49) The total output of goods and services in a given period divided by the total hours of labour required to provide them.

Profit (p. 4) The amount a business earns above and beyond what it spends for salaries and other expenses.

Promissory note (p. 532) A written contract with a promise to pay.

Promotion (p. 420) All the techniques sellers use to motivate customers to buy their products.

Promotion mix (p. 467) The combination of promotional tools an organization uses.

Prospectus (p. 565) A condensed version of economic and financial information that a company must make available to investors before they purchase a security.

Psychographic segmentation (p. 427) Dividing the market using the group's values, attitudes, and interests.

Psychological pricing (p. 457) Pricing goods and services at price points that make the product appear less expensive than it is.

Public accountant (p. 490) An accountant who provides his or her accounting services to individuals or businesses on a fee basis.

Public corporation (p. 161) Corporation that has the right to issue shares to the public, so its shares may be listed on a stock exchange.

Public domain software (freeware) (p. 587) Software that is free for the taking.

Public relations (PR) (p. 472) The management function that evaluates public attitudes, changes policies and procedures in response to the public's requests, and executes a program of action and information to earn public understanding and acceptance.

Publicity (p. 473) Any information about an individual, product, or organization that's distributed to the public through the media and that's not paid for or controlled by the seller.

Pull strategy (p. 476) Promotional strategy in which heavy advertising and sales promotion efforts are directed toward consumers so that they'll request the products from retailers.

Purchasing (p. 302) The function in a firm that searches for quality material resources, finds the best suppliers, and negotiates the best price for goods and services.

Push strategy (p. 476) Promotional strategy in which the producer uses all the promotional tools to convince wholesalers and retailers to stock and sell merchandise.

Quality (p. 291) Consistently producing what the customer wants while reducing errors before and after delivery to the customer.

Quality function deployment (QFD) (p. 293) A process of linking the needs of end users (customers) to design, development, engineering, manufacturing, and service functions.

Quality of life (p. 49) The general well being of a society in terms of political freedom, a clean natural environment, education, health care, safety, free time, and everything else that leads to satisfaction and joy.

Ratio analysis (p. 508) The assessment of a firm's financial condition and performance through calculations and interpretations of financial ratios developed from the firm's financial statements.

Raw materials price index (RMPI) (p. 52) Reflects the prices paid by Canadian manufacturers for key raw materials.

Real time (p. 267) The present moment or the actual time in which some thing takes place; data sent over the internet to various organizational partners as they are developed or collected are said to be available in real time.

Recession (p. 53) Two or more consecutive quarters of decline in the GDP.

Recruitment (p. 350) The set of activities used to obtain a sufficient number of the right people at the right time.

Reengineering (p. 271) The fundamental rethinking and radical redesign of organizational processes to achieve dramatic improvements in critical measures of performance.

Regulations (p. 13) Serve to carry out the purposes of or expand on the general laws passed by elected officials.

Reinforcement theory (p. 328) Theory that positive and negative reinforcers motivate a person to behave in certain ways.

Relationship marketing (p. 429) Marketing strategy with the goal of keeping individual customers over time by offering them products that exactly meet their requirements.

Research and development (R&D) (p. 282) Work directed toward the innovation, introduction, and improvement of products and processes.

Restructuring (p. 270) Redesigning an organization so that it can more effectively and efficiently serve its customers.

Retailer (p. 459) An organization that sells to ultimate consumers.

Revenue (p. 5) The total amount of money a business takes in during a given period by selling goods and services.

Revenue (p. 500) The value of what is received for goods sold, services rendered, and other financial sources.

Reverse discrimination (p. 372) The unfairness unprotected groups (say whites or males) may perceive when protected groups receive preference in hiring and promotion.

Revolving credit agreement (p. 534) A line of credit that is guaranteed by the bank.

Risk (p. 5) The chance an entrepreneur takes of losing time and money on a business that may not prove profitable.

Risk/return trade-off (p. 537) The principle that the greater the risk a lender takes in making a loan, the higher the interest rate required.

Robber barons (p. 218) Capitalists of the 19th century whose wealth came, in part, through dubious, if not criminal acts.

Sales promotion (p. 474)   The promotional tool that stimulates consumer purchasing and dealer interest by means of short-term activities.

Sampling (p. 475)   A promotional tool in which a company lets consumers have a small sample of a product for no charge.

Scientific management (p. 317)   Studying workers to find the most efficient ways of doing things and then teaching people those techniques.

Secondary boycott (p. 397)   An attempt by labour to convince others to stop doing business with a firm that is the subject of a primary boycott.

Secondary data (p. 421)   Information that has already been compiled by others and published in journals and books or made available online.

Secured loan (p. 533)   A loan backed by something valuable, such as property.

Securities commission (p. 565)   A government agency that administers provincial securities legislation.

Securities dealer (p. 564)   A firm that trades securities for its clients and offers investment services.

Selection (p. 351)   The process of gathering information and deciding who should be hired, under legal guidelines, for the best interests of the individual and the organization.

Selective distribution (p. 463)   Distribution that sends products to only a preferred group of retailers in an area.

Services (p. 25)   Intangible products (i.e., products that can't be held in your hand) such as education, health care, insurance, recreation, and travel and tourism.

Shareware (p. 587)   Software that is copyrighted but distributed to potential customers free of charge.

Shop stewards (p. 393)   Union officials who work permanently in an organization and represent employee interests on a daily basis.

Shopping products (p. 450)   Goods and services that the consumer buys only after comparing value, quality, price, and style from a variety of sellers.

Short-term financing (p. 531)   Borrowed capital that will be repaid within one year.

Short-term forecast (p. 524)   Forecast that predicts revenues, costs, and expenses for a period of one year or less.

Sinking fund (p. 538)   A reserve account in which the issuer of a bond periodically retires some part of the bond principal prior to maturity so that enough capital will be accumulated by the maturity date to pay off the bond.

Six sigma quality (p. 291)   A quality measure that allows only 3.4 defects per million events.

Skimming price strategy (p. 456)   A strategy in which a new product is priced high to make optimum profit while there's little competition.

Small business (p. 197)   A business that is independently owned and operated, is not dominant in its field, and meets certain standards of size in terms of employees or annual revenues.

Social audit (p. 143)   A systematic evaluation of an organization's progress toward implementing programs that are socially responsible and responsive.

Socialism (p. 42)   An economic system based on the premise that some, if not most, basic businesses should be owned by the government so that profits can be evenly distributed among the people.

Sole proprietorship (p. 154)   A business that is owned, and usually managed, by one person.

Span of control (p. 256)   The optimum number of subordinates a manager supervises or should supervise.

Specialty products (p. 450)   Consumer goods and services with unique characteristics and brand identity. Because these products are perceived as having no reasonable substitute, the consumer puts forth a special effort to purchase them.

Staff personnel (p. 263)   Employees who advise and assist line personnel in meeting their goals.

Staffing (p. 230)   A management function that includes hiring, motivating, and retaining the best people available to accomplish the company's objectives.

Stakeholder marketing (p. 437)   Establishing and maintaining mutually beneficial exchange relationships over time with all the stakeholders of the organization.

Stakeholders (p. 5)   All the people who stand to gain or lose by the policies and activities of a business.

Standard of living (p. 49)   The amount of goods and services people can buy with the money they have.

Statement of changes in financial position (p. 503) Financial statement that reports cash receipts and disbursements related to a firm's three major activities: operations, investments, and financing.

Statistical process control (SPC) (p. 291) The process of taking statistical samples of product components at each stage of the production process and plotting those results on a graph. Any variances from quality standards are recognized and can be corrected if beyond the set standards.

Statistical quality control (SQC) (p. 291) The process some managers use to continually monitor all phases of the production process to ensure that quality is being built into the product from the beginning.

Statutory law (p. 593) Federal and provincial legislative enactments, treaties of the federal government, and bylaws/ordinances—in short, written law.

Stock certificate (p. 541) Evidence of stock ownership that specifies the name of the company, the number of shares it represents, and the type of stock being issued.

Stock exchange (p. 565) An organization whose members can buy and sell (exchange) securities for companies and investors.

Stocks (p. 539) Shares of ownership in a company.

Stock splits (p. 572) An action by a company that gives shareholders two or more shares of stock for each one they own.

Stockbroker (p. 566) A registered representative who works as a market intermediary to buy and sell securities for clients.

Strategic alliance (p. 75) A long-term partnership between two or more companies established to help each company build competitive market advantages.

Strategic planning (p. 222) The process of determining the major goals of the organization and the policies and strategies for obtaining and using resources to achieve those goals.

Strict product liability (p. 594) Legal responsibility for harm or injury caused by a product regardless of fault.

Strike (p. 396) A union strategy in which workers refuse to go to work; the purpose is to further workers' objectives after an impasse in collective bargaining.

Supervisory management (p. 227) Managers who are directly responsible for supervising workers and evaluating their daily performance.

Supply (p. 38) The quantity of products that manufacturers or owners are willing to sell at different prices at a specific time.

Supply chain (p. 296) The sequence of linked activities that must be performed by various organizations to move goods from the sources of raw materials to ultimate consumers.

Supply chain management (p. 296) The process of managing the movement of raw materials, parts, works in process, finished goods, and related information through all the organizations involved in the supply chain; managing the return of such goods, if necessary; and recycling materials when appropriate.

Surplus (p. 108) An excess of revenues over expenditures.

SWOT analysis (p. 222) A planning tool used to analyze an organization's strengths, weaknesses, opportunities, and threats.

Tactical planning (p. 223) The process of developing detailed, short-term statements about what is to be done, who is to do it, and how it is to be done.

Tall organization structure (p. 258) An organization structure in which the pyramidal organization chart would be quite tall because of the various levels of management.

Target costing (p. 455) Designing a product so that it satisfies customers and meets the profit margins desired by the firm.

Target marketing (p. 427) Marketing directed toward those groups (market segments) an organization decides it can serve profitably.

Tariff (p. 83) A tax imposed on imports.

Technical skills (p. 228) Skills that involve the ability to perform tasks in a specific discipline or department.

Technology (p. 15) Everything from phones and copiers to computers, medical imaging devices, personal digital assistants, and the various software programs that make business processes more efficient and productive.

Telemarketing (p. 464) The sale of goods and services by telephone.

Term-loan agreement (p. 536) A promissory note that requires the borrower to repay the loan in specified installments.

Test marketing (p. 418) The process of testing products among potential users.

Time-motion studies (p. 317) Studies, begun by Frederick Taylor, of which tasks must be performed to complete a job and the time needed to do each task.

Top management (p. 227) Highest level of management, consisting of the president and other key company executives who develop strategic plans.

Tort (p. 594) A wrongful act that causes injury to another person's body, property, or reputation.

Total fixed costs (p. 455) All the expenses that remain the same no matter how many products are made or sold.

Total product offer (p. 447) Everything that consumers evaluate when deciding whether to buy something; also called a value package.

Total quality management (TQM) (p. 271) Striving for maximum customer satisfaction by ensuring quality from all departments.

Trade credit (p. 532) The practice of buying goods and services now and paying for them later.

Trade deficit (p. 67) An unfavourable balance of trade; occurs when the value of a country's imports exceeds that of its exports.

Trade protectionism (p. 82) The use of government regulations to limit the import of goods and services. Advocates of trade protectionism believe that it allows domestic producers to survive and grow, producing more jobs.

Trademark (p. 452) A brand that has been given exclusive legal protection for both the brand name and the pictorial design.

Training and development (p. 355) All attempts to improve productivity by increasing an employee's ability to perform. Training focuses on short-term skills, whereas development focuses on long-term abilities.

Transfer payments (p. 111) Direct payments from governments to other governments or to individuals.

Transparency (p. 267) A concept that describes a company being so open to other companies working with it that the once-solid barriers between them become see-through and electronic information is shared as if the companies were one.

Trial balance (p. 494) A summary of all the data in the account ledgers to show whether the figures are correct and balanced.

Trust company (p. 552) A financial institution that can administer estates, pension plans, and agency contracts, in addition to other activities conducted by banks.

Turnover rate (p. 370) A measure of the percentage of employees that leave a firm each year.

Union (p. 382) An employee organization that has the main goal of representing members in employee–management bargaining over job-related issues.

Union density (p. 387) A measure of the percentage of workers who belong to unions.

Union security clause (p. 391) Provision in a negotiated labour–management agreement that stipulates that employees who benefit from a union must either officially join or at least pay dues to the union.

Union shop (p. 392) A workplace in which the employer is free to hire anybody, but the recruit must then join the union within a short period, perhaps a month.

Unlimited liability (p. 156) The responsibility of business owners for all of the debts of the business.

Unsecured loan (p. 533) A loan that's not backed by any specific assets.

Unsought products (p. 450) Goods and services that consumers are unaware of, haven't necessarily thought of buying, or find that they need to solve an unexpected problem.

Utility (p. 461) An economic term that refers to the value or want-satisfying ability that's added to goods or services by organizations when the products are made more useful or accessible to consumers than before.

Value (p. 446) Good quality at a fair price. When consumers calculate the value of a product, they look at the benefits and then subtract the cost to see if the benefits exceed the costs.

Variable costs (p. 456) Costs that change according to the level of production.

GLOSSARY

Venture capital (p. 540) Money that is invested in new or emerging companies that are perceived as having great profit potential.

Venture capitalists (p. 205) Individuals or companies that invest in new businesses in exchange for partial ownership of those businesses.

Vertical merger (p. 168) The joining of two companies involved in different stages of related businesses.

Vestibule training (p. 357) Training done in schools where employees are taught on equipment similar to that used on the job.

Virtual corporation (p. 268) A temporary networked organization made up of replaceable firms that join and leave as needed.

Virtual private network (VPN) (p. 584) A private data network that creates secure connections, or "tunnels," over regular internet lines.

Virtualization (p. 580) Accessibility through technology that allows business to be conducted independent of location.

Virus (p. 590) A piece of programming code inserted into other programming to cause some unexpected and, for the victim, usually undesirable event.

Vision (p. 221) An encompassing explanation of why the organization exists and where it's trying to head.

Voluntary bankruptcy (p. 600) Legal procedures initiated by a debtor.

Whistleblowers (p. 133) People who report illegal or unethical behaviour.

Wholesaler (p. 459) A marketing intermediary that sells to other organizations.

World Bank (p. 85) An autonomous United Nations agency that borrows money from the more prosperous countries and lends it to less-developed countries to develop their infrastructure.

World Trade Organization (WTO) (p. 83) The international organization that replaced the General Agreement on Tariffs and Trade, and was assigned the duty to mediate trade disputes among nations.

Photo Credits

Chapter 15

p. 446 Ray Reiss Photography; p. 448 © Virgin Atlantic Airways; p. 451 Bonnie Weller/Inquirer Staff Photographer; p. 452 Canadian Press CP Photography by Jacques Boissinot; p. 458 Eric Mencher/Inquirer Staff Photographer; p. 461 PriceGrabber.com, LLC; p. 470 Elizabeth Robertson/Inquirer Suburban Staff; p. 474 © 2003 Menlo Worldwide, LLC; p. 477 Reprinted with permission of the AAF; p. 481 Peter Ross; p. 482 Courtesy of Burrston House; p. 484 AP Wide World Photos; p. 487 Courtesy of Complaints.com

Chapter 16

p. 495 Ron Sangha; p. 498 Michael Rosenfeld/Getty Images; p. 500 Reproduced with permission of the Canadian Institute of Chartered Accountants; p. 502 Reprinted with permission from BCE Inc.; p. 503 Dave Carpenter; p. 520 Courtesy of Home Depot

Chapter 17

p. 521 Courtesy of Krispy Kreme; p. 525 Jeff Greenberg/PhotoEdit; p. 529 Courtesy of nextcard.com; p. 533 Vic Bider/PhotoEdit

Chapter 18

p. 551 Courtesy Canadian Tire Financial Services; p. 554 Courtesy Loblaw Companies; p. 556 © Bank of Canada—used with permission; p. 560 Reprinted with permission of the Canadian Bankers Association; p. 561 Courtesy of Citi-Card; p. 566 Christian Lagereek/Getty Images; p. 568 AP WideWorld Photo; p. 569 Mick Stevens; p. 572 Photo printed with permission from AIC Limited

Appendix A

p. 580 Brian Dobin; p. 581 Christoph Rehben/SI International; p. 582 Kate Swan; p. 583 © Ofer Wolberger; p. 585 Courtesy of Veritas; p. 586 Amanda Marsalis; p. 590 Courtesy of N2H2/Photo by Greg Sweeny

Organization Index

Subject Index

URL Index